An Introduction to Social Psychology

SIXTH EDITION

BPS Textbooks in Psychology

BPS Wiley presents a comprehensive and authoritative series covering everything a student needs in order to complete an undergraduate degree in psychology. Refreshingly written to consider more than North American research, this series is the first to give a truly international perspective. Written by the very best names in the field, the series offers an extensive range of titles from introductory level through to final year optional modules, and every text fully complies with the BPS syllabus in the topic. No other series bears the BPS seal of approval!

Each book is supported by a companion website, featuring additional resource materials for both instructors and students, designed to encourage critical thinking and providing for all your course lecturing and testing needs.

For other titles in this series, please go to **http://psychsource.bps.org.uk**.

An Introduction to Social Psychology

SIXTH EDITION

EDITED BY

MILES HEWSTONE
WOLFGANG STROEBE
KLAUS JONAS

The British
Psychological Society

WILEY

Registered office

John Wiley & Sons Ltd, The Atrium, Southern Gate, Chichester, West Sussex, PO19 8SQ, United Kingdom.

For details of our global editorial offices, for customer services and for information about how to apply for permission to reuse the copyright material in this book, please see our website at www.wiley.com.

Library of Congress Cataloging-in-Publication Data

An introduction to social psychology / edited by Miles Hewstone, Wolfgang Stroebe, Klaus Jonas. – Sixth edition.
    pages cm
   Includes bibliographical references and index.
   ISBN 978-1-118-82353-8 (pbk.)
    1. Social psychology. 2. Social psychology–Europe. I. Hewstone, Miles.   II. Stroebe, Wolfgang.   III. Jonas, Klaus.
 Wolfgang.   III. Jonas, Klaus.
   HM1033.I59 2015
   302–dc23

                                                    2015003375

ISBN 9781118823538 (pbk)
ISBN 9781118959879 (ebk)
ISBN 9781118959855 (ebk)

A catalogue record for this book is available from the British Library.

Set in 11/12.5 pt Dante MT by MPS Limited, Chennai, India
Printed and bound in Italy by Printer Trento Srl.

The British Psychological Society's free Research Digest e-mail service rounds up the latest research and relates it to your syllabus in a user-friendly way. To subscribe, go to www.researchdigest.org.uk or send a blank e-mail to subscribe-rd@lists.bps.org.uk.

To

The memory of Audrey Cole Hewstone (1929–2010)

Lisa and Emma Stroebe

Jessie and Julie Jonas and Alexandra

Brief Contents

Notes on Contributors   xix

Preface to Sixth Edition   xxi

Guided Tour   xxiii

Accompanying Online Resources for Instructors and Students   xxvii

Chapter 1   **Introducing Social Psychology**   1
             Wolfgang Stroebe, Miles Hewstone and Klaus Jonas

Chapter 2   **Research Methods in Social Psychology**   25
             Antony S. R. Manstead and Andrew G. Livingstone

Chapter 3   **Social Perception and Attribution**   55
             Brian Parkinson

Chapter 4   **Social Cognition**   93
             Louise Pendry

Chapter 5   **The Self**   123
             Carolyn C. Morf and Sander L. Koole

Chapter 6   **Attitudes**   171
             Geoffrey Haddock and Gregory R. Maio

Chapter 7   **Strategies of Attitude and Behaviour Change**   201
             Wolfgang Stroebe

Chapter 8   **Social Influence**   233
             Miles Hewstone and Robin Martin

Chapter 9   **Aggression**   273
             Barbara Krahé

Chapter 10   **Prosocial Behaviour**   309
             Mark Levine and Rachel Manning

Chapter 11   **Attraction and Close Relationships**   347
             Johan C. Karremans and Catrin Finkenauer

Chapter 12   Group Dynamics   379
Bernard A. Nijstad and Daan van Knippenberg

Chapter 13   Group Performance and Leadership   407
Stefan Schulz-Hardt and Felix C. Brodbeck

Chapter 14   Prejudice and Intergroup Relations   439
Russell Spears and Nicole Tausch

Chapter 15   Cultural Social Psychology   489
Peter B. Smith

References   527
Glossary   597
Name Index   609
Subject Index   627

Contents

Notes on Contributors — xix

Preface to Sixth Edition — xxi

Guided Tour — xxiii

Accompanying Online Resources for Instructors and Students — xxvii

Chapter 1   **Introducing Social Psychology** — 1
Wolfgang Stroebe, Miles Hewstone and Klaus Jonas

INTRODUCTION — 3
  Some classic studies — 3
A DEFINITION OF SOCIAL PSYCHOLOGY — 6
  The core characteristics of social psychology — 6
THE UNIQUE PERSPECTIVE OF SOCIAL PSYCHOLOGY — 7
  The study of the individual and the social — 7
A BRIEF HISTORY OF SOCIAL PSYCHOLOGY — 10
  The beginning — 10
  The early years — 13
  The years of expansion — 14
  The crisis years — 17
  Overcoming the crisis — 19
SOCIAL PSYCHOLOGY IN EUROPE — 19
SOCIAL PSYCHOLOGY TODAY — 21
Chapter Summary — 23
Suggestions for Further Reading — 24

Chapter 2   **Research Methods in Social Psychology** — 25
Antony S. R. Manstead and Andrew G. Livingstone

INTRODUCTION — 27
  Summary — 28
RESEARCH STRATEGIES — 30
  Experiments and quasi-experiments — 30
  Survey research — 33
  Qualitative approaches — 34
  Summary — 36
A CLOSER LOOK AT EXPERIMENTATION IN SOCIAL PSYCHOLOGY — 36
  Features of the social psychological experiment — 36
  Experimental designs — 38
  Threats to validity in experimental research — 41
  Social psychological experiments on the Internet — 43
  Problems with experimentation — 45
  Summary — 46

DATA COLLECTION METHODS — 47

Observational methods — 47

Self-report methods — 48

Implicit and physiological methods — 49

Choosing a mcthod — 50

Social neuroscience — 51

Summary — 51

Chapter Summary — 51

Suggestions for Further Reading — 52

Chapter 3   **Social Perception and Attribution** — **55**

Brian Parkinson

INTRODUCTION — 57

SOCIAL PERCEPTION — 57

Summary — 61

ATTRIBUTION THEORY — 61

Correspondent inference theory — 62

Covariation theory — 64

Access to covariation information — 66

Knowledge, expectation and covariation — 67

Learning about causation using covariation and causal power — 68

Attributions and achievement — 69

Attribution and depression — 70

Misattribution of arousal — 73

Attributional biases — 76

Explaining intentional behaviour — 85

The naïve scientist metaphor — 86

Attributions as discourse — 88

Summary — 88

SOCIAL PERCEPTION AND SOCIAL REALITY — 88

AUTOMATIC AND CONTROLLED SOCIAL PERCEPTION — 90

Chapter Summary — 90

Suggestions for Further Reading — 91

Chapter 4   **Social Cognition** — **93**

Louise Pendry

INTRODUCTION — 95

JUMPING TO CONCLUSIONS OR WORKING THINGS OUT SLOWLY — 95

THE AUTOMATIC PILOT WITHIN — 96

What makes a process automatic? — 96

The pervasive nature of social categorization — 97

Schemas: the next step in the process? — 100

Making judgements when you don't have all the data: cognitive heuristics — 101

Why do we fall prey to judgemental heuristics? — 104

Schema activation and behaviour — 105

Summary — 108

GOING THE EXTRA MILE: REGAINING COGNITIVE CONTROL — 108

Stereotype? What stereotype? How goals can stop the stereotype being activated in the first place — 108

Quashing the effects of stereotype activation once it has occurred — 110

Summary — 120

Chapter Summary — 121

Suggestions for Further Reading — 122

Chapter 5	**The Self**	**123**
	Carolyn C. Morf and Sander L. Koole	
	INTRODUCTION	125
	WHERE SELF-KNOWLEDGE COMES FROM	126
	Through our own observation: personal sources	126
	Through the help of others: social sources	129
	Experiencing a coherent self: autobiographical memories and the self as narrative	131
	Summary	132
	THE ORGANIZATIONAL FUNCTION OF THE SELF: THE SELF AS MENTAL REPRESENTATION	133
	The nature of the self-concept	133
	The nature of self-esteem	136
	Cultural and gender influences on self-knowledge	140
	The neural underpinnings of self-knowledge	143
	Summary	145
	THE MOTIVATIONAL FUNCTIONS OF THE SELF	145
	Know thyself: the self-assessment motive	146
	Bigger, better, faster, stronger: the self-enhancement motive	146
	The puzzle of low self-regard: self-verification	153
	Why do we self-enhance?	154
	The pros and cons of pursuing self-esteem	156
	Summary	157
	THE REGULATORY FUNCTIONS OF THE SELF: THE SELF IN CONTROL	157
	Self-awareness theory	159
	Self-regulation theory	160
	The consequences of self-regulation	164
	Escaping the self	165
	Autonomous self-regulation as a resource	166
	Summary	166
	SELF STABILITY AND CHANGE	167
	Chapter Summary	168
	Suggestions for Further Reading	169
Chapter 6	**Attitudes**	**171**
	Geoffrey Haddock and Gregory R. Maio	
	INTRODUCTION	173
	WHAT IS AN ATTITUDE?	173
	Summary	174
	THE CONTENT OF ATTITUDES	174
	The cognitive component of attitudes	174
	The affective component of attitudes	175
	The behavioural component of attitudes	176
	How related are the components of attitudes?	177
	Summary	179
	THE STRUCTURE OF ATTITUDES	179
	Summary	180
	WHY DO WE HOLD ATTITUDES?	181
	Object appraisal	182
	Utilitarian versus value-expressive attitudes	182
	Summary	184
	LINKING ATTITUDE CONTENT, STRUCTURE AND FUNCTION	184
	Content, structure, function and attitude strength	184
	Summary	185

THE MEASUREMENT OF ATTITUDES 185

Explicit measures of attitudes 186

Issues relevant to the explicit measurement of attitudes 187

Implicit measures of attitudes 187

Are attitude measures reliable and valid? 189

Summary 190

DO ATTITUDES PREDICT BEHAVIOUR? 191

When do attitudes predict behaviour? 191

Do explicit and implicit measures of attitude predict different types of behaviour? 193

Models of attitude–behaviour relations 195

Summary 199

Chapter Summary 199

Suggestions for Further Reading 199

Chapter 7   **Strategies of Attitude and Behaviour Change**   **201**

Wolfgang Stroebe

INTRODUCTION 203

PERSUASION 203

Theories of systematic processing 203

Summary 207

A dual-process theory of persuasion 207

Summary 216

Changing implicit attitudes 216

Summary 217

Advertising as applied persuasion 217

Summary 224

INCENTIVE-INDUCED ATTITUDE CHANGE 224

Counterattitudinal behaviour and attitude change 225

Some paradoxical effects of incentives and sanctions 228

Further limitations of the effectiveness of incentive-induced change 229

Summary 229

Chapter Summary 230

Suggestions for Further Reading 230

Chapter 8   **Social Influence**   **233**

Miles Hewstone and Robin Martin

INTRODUCTION 235

INCIDENTAL SOCIAL INFLUENCE 235

Social facilitation 235

The impact of social norms 237

Summary 241

WHY DOES SOCIAL INFLUENCE OCCUR? 241

Summary 245

DELIBERATE SOCIAL INFLUENCE 245

Inducing compliance 245

The influence of numerical majorities and minorities 247

Group decision making 258

Obedience to authority 264

Summary 270

Chapter Summary 270

Suggestions for Further Reading 271

Chapter 9   **Aggression**   **273**
Barbara Krahé

INTRODUCTION   275
DEFINITION AND MEASUREMENT OF AGGRESSIVE BEHAVIOUR   275
   Observation of aggressive behaviour   277
   Obtaining reports of aggressive behaviour   277
   Summary   279
THEORIES OF AGGRESSION   279
   Biological approaches   280
   Psychological approaches   281
   Summary   286
PERSONAL AND SITUATIONAL VARIABLES AFFECTING AGGRESSIVE
     BEHAVIOUR   286
   Individual differences in aggressive behaviour   287
   Situational influences on aggressive behaviour   288
   Summary   294
AGGRESSION AS A SOCIAL PROBLEM   294
   Intimate partner violence   294
   Sexual aggression   297
   Bullying in school and the workplace   298
   Intergroup violence   300
   Summary   304
PSYCHOLOGICAL PREVENTION AND INTERVENTION   304
   Catharsis   304
   Punishment   305
   De-escalation through eliciting incompatible responses   305
   Summary   306
Chapter Summary   307
Suggestions for Further Reading   308

Chapter 10   **Prosocial Behaviour**   **309**
Mark Levine and Rachel Manning

INTRODUCTION   311
PROSOCIAL BEHAVIOUR, HELPING AND ALTRUISM   312
   Definitions   312
   The altruism–egoism debate   313
   Prosocial behaviours   316
   Summary   317
WHY PEOPLE DON'T HELP   317
   A decision-making model of bystander behaviour   319
   Summary   323
WHY PEOPLE DO HELP   323
   The costs and rewards of helping   323
   Groups, identity and prosocial behaviour   325
   Helping outgroups   326
   Social identity and the bystander effect   328
   Social identity, emotion and bystander intervention   329
   Summary   329
ISSUES IN RESEARCHING PROSOCIAL BEHAVIOUR   330
   Violence and helping   330
   Gender and helping   331

Long-term, sustained helping behaviours   332
Summary   336
EVOLUTION, GENES AND HELPING   336
When helping is not self-interested   338
Summary   339
THE SOCIAL NEUROSCIENCE OF HELPING   339
Summary   340
HELPING IN THE REAL WORLD   340
Selfish vs. altruistic behaviour in life-threatening emergencies   341
Summary   344
Chapter Summary   344
Suggestions for Further Reading   345

Chapter 11   Attraction and Close Relationships   347
Johan C. Karremans and Catrin Finkenauer

INTRODUCTION   349
THE IMPORTANCE OF RELATIONSHIPS   349
Relationships and psychological well-being   349
Relationships and physical well-being   350
The role of social support   350
The immediate effects of social exclusion   351
The need to belong   352
Attachment   353
Summary   356
INTERPERSONAL ATTRACTION   356
The benefits of physical attractiveness   356
What is beautiful is good   356
The features that determine physical attractiveness   357
Contextual influences on physical attractiveness   359
Psychological attraction   360
Proximity   360
Familiarity   362
Similarity   363
Underestimating the power of the situation   364
Summary   364
ROMANTIC RELATIONSHIPS   364
Love   365
Relationship satisfaction and stability   365
Thoughts and behaviours that enhance relationship functioning   367
Summary   371
GENERAL RELATIONSHIP PROCESSES   371
Types of relationships   371
Disclosure   372
Perceived partner responsiveness   374
Relationship ending   376
Summary   376
Chapter Summary   377
Suggestions for Further Reading   378

Chapter 12   **Group Dynamics**   **379**
Bernard A. Nijstad and Daan van Knippenberg

INTRODUCTION   381
THE PHENOMENOLOGY OF GROUPS   381
  Defining groups   381
  Why groups?   381
  Types of groups, entitativity and group functions   382
  Summary   384
INDIVIDUALS IN GROUPS: THE INDIVIDUAL LEVEL OF ANALYSIS   386
  Joining a group and group socialization: becoming a full member   387
  Being in a group: maintenance and role negotiation   389
  Leaving a group: divergence and exit   390
  Summary   392
GROUP DEVELOPMENT AND STRUCTURE: THE GROUP LEVEL OF ANALYSIS   392
  Group development   392
  On being similar: norms, shared cognition and cohesion   394
  On being different: status and roles   398
  Summary   401
GROUPS IN THEIR ENVIRONMENT: THE INTERGROUP LEVEL OF ANALYSIS   401
  The intergroup context and the salience of group membership   401
  The intergroup context, group perceptions and social influence   403
  Summary   404
Chapter Summary   404
Suggestions for Further Reading   405

Chapter 13   **Group Performance and Leadership**   **407**
Stefan Schulz-Hardt and Felix C. Brodbeck

INTRODUCTION   409
SOME CORE CONCEPTS: ACTUAL GROUP PERFORMANCE, GROUP POTENTIAL
    AND TASK TYPE   409
  Actual and potential group performance   409
  Basic types of group tasks and their implications for group potential   410
  Summary   411
PROCESS LOSSES VERSUS PROCESS GAINS IN GROUP PERFORMANCE   411
  Types of process losses and process gains   411
  Summary   418
GROUP PERFORMANCE MANAGEMENT   418
  Three basic principles of group performance management   418
  Summary   425
LEADERSHIP   426
  Approaches to the study of leadership   426
  Summary   433
LEADERSHIP IN GROUPS   433
  Group and task design   434
  Group synchronization   434
  Group development and learning   435
  Summary   436
Chapter Summary   436
Suggestions for Further Reading   437

Chapter 14   **Prejudice and Intergroup Relations**   **439**
Russell Spears and Nicole Tausch

INTRODUCTION   441
PERSONALITY APPROACHES TO PREJUDICE   443
   The authoritarian personality   *443*
   Prejudice and a desire for social dominance   *444*
   Authoritarianism and social dominance orientation as ideologies   *445*
   Summary   *448*
THE COGNITIVE APPROACH TO PREJUDICE   449
   Outgroup homogeneity, stereotyping and prejudice   *449*
   Illusory correlation: a cognitive account of prejudiced stereotype formation   *450*
   Developments and integrations   *451*
   Summary   *453*
GROUP APPROACHES TO PREJUDICE   453
   Intragroup processes, ingroup bias and prejudice   *453*
   Intergroup explanations of prejudice and discrimination   *454*
   The individual's relation to the group: group identification and its components   *458*
   Elaborating the intergroup level   *461*
   Integrative intergroup theories   *466*
   Can emotions help to explain the variety and intensity of prejudice?   *468*
   Summary   *471*
PSYCHOLOGICAL INTERVENTIONS TO REDUCE PREJUDICE AND IMPROVE
   INTERGROUP RELATIONS   472
   The 'contact hypothesis'   *472*
   Varying levels of categorization   *476*
   Psychological processes involved in intergroup contact and prejudice reduction   *480*
   Other prejudice-reduction techniques   *482*
   The wider implications of prejudice reduction   *483*
   Summary   *485*
Chapter Summary   486
Suggestions for Further Reading   486

Chapter 15   **Cultural Social Psychology**   **489**
Peter B. Smith

INTRODUCTION   491
CULTURE AND CULTURAL DIFFERENCES   491
   Defining culture   *492*
   Nations as cultures   *493*
   Measuring culture   *494*
   Overcoming methodological challenges   *496*
   Summary   *499*
CULTURE AND COGNITION   500
   Summary   *503*
CULTURE AND SELF-CONSTRUAL   503
   Cross-cultural variation in self-enhancement   *504*
   Self-construal as an explanation of cultural differences   *506*
   Self-construal over time   *507*
   Summary   *508*

INTERPERSONAL RELATIONS   509
   Prosocial behaviour with strangers   *509*
   Intimate relationships   *509*
   Summary   *510*
GROUP PROCESSES   511
   Summary   *513*
INTERGROUP RELATIONS   515
   Group honour   *517*
   Negotiation   *518*
   Summary   *519*
INTERCULTURAL RELATIONS   519
   Migration and acculturation   *521*
   Summary   *523*
Chapter Summary   525
Suggestions for Further Reading   526

References   **527**
Glossary   **597**
Name Index   **609**
Subject Index   **627**

Notes on Contributors

Felix C. Brodbeck is Chair of Economic and Organizational Psychology at Ludwig-Maximilians Universitaet Muenchen, Germany. His main research interests are leadership, group performance, collective information processing, economic decision making, diversity and cross-cultural psychology. He has edited or authored several books and numerous research papers in the above areas.

Catrin Finkenauer is Professor at Clinical Child and Family Studies, VU University Amsterdam, The Netherlands. She is currently associate editor of *Personality and Social Psychology Bulletin*. Her research on interpersonal relationships includes basic research on relationship processes (e.g., trust, understanding) and applied research on interventions targeting children who have been witness to or a target of domestic violence and abuse.

Geoffrey Haddock is a Professor of Social Psychology at Cardiff University, UK. He has published widely on the topics of attitudes and social cognition. His current research focuses on affective and cognitive processes of evaluation.

Miles Hewstone is Professor of Social Psychology and Fellow of New College, Oxford University, UK. His main research topic is intergroup relations and the reduction of intergroup conflict, especially via intergroup contact, and he has edited or authored many books. He is founding co-editor (with Wolfgang Stroebe) of the *European Review of Social Psychology*, and has received numerous awards for his research.

Klaus Jonas has taught social and organizational psychology at universities in Germany, Austria and Switzerland. He is Professor of Social and Business Psychology at the University of Zurich, Switzerland. He has published on attitudes, stereotypes and human resource management. His current interests concern the influence of leadership on performance and satisfaction of subordinates.

Johan C. Karremans is Associate Professor at the Behavioural Science Institute (BSI) at the Radboud University Nijmegen, The Netherlands. His research mainly focuses on the processes that benefit or harm interpersonal relationships, especially in the face of relationship threat (e.g., conflict, attractive alternatives).

Sander L. Koole is Associate Professor of Clinical Psychology at the VU University, Amsterdam. His main research topics are self-regulation and emotion regulation. He co-edited the *Handbook of Experimental Existential Psychology*, which focuses on a new area of psychology that uses experimental methods to investigate how people are dealing with important life issues.

Barbara Krahé is Professor of Social Psychology at the University of Potsdam, Germany. Her research focuses on aggression and social cognition applied to legal decision-making. The second edition of her textbook, *The social psychology of aggression*, was published in 2013. She is a member of the International Society for Research on Aggression and was Associate Editor of its journal, *Aggressive Behavior*, from 2004 to 2012.

Mark Levine is a Professor of Social Psychology at the University of Exeter, UK. His research focuses on the role of social identity in pro-social and anti-social behaviour. His recent work has examined the role of group processes in the regulation of perpetrator, victim and bystander behaviour during aggressive and violent events.

Andrew G. Livingstone is Senior Lecturer in Social Psychology at the University of Exeter, UK, having previously held positions at the University of Stirling and Cardiff University. His research focuses on social identity, intergroup relations, and emotion. He is currently an associate editor of the *British Journal of Social Psychology*.

Gregory R. Maio is a Professor of Social Psychology at Cardiff University, UK. He has published widely on the topics of attitudes and social cognition. His current research focuses on the mental structure of social values, leading research at the Values in Action (ViA) Centre at Cardiff University.

Rachel Manning is a Senior Lecturer in Psychology at Anglia Ruskin University, UK. Her research interests include prosocial behaviours such as intervention in emergencies, charitable giving and volunteering.

Antony S. R. Manstead is Professor of Psychology at Cardiff University, UK, having previously held positions at the Universities of Sussex, Manchester, Amsterdam and Cambridge. He has been Editor or Associate Editor of several journals, the most recent case being *Psychological Science*. His research focuses on emotion, attitudes, and social identity.

Robin Martin is Professor of Organisational Psychology at Manchester Business School, University of Manchester. He has served on the faculties of the Universities of Aston, Queensland, Cardiff, Swansea and Sheffield. He conducts research in the area of social influence processes (especially majority and minority influence), workplace leadership, innovation and team working.

Carolyn C. Morf is Associate Professor of Personality Psychology at the University of Bern, Switzerland. Her research focuses on understanding self-regulatory processes through which individuals construct and maintain their desired self-views. She also examines the expression of these self-regulatory processes in personality (in particular narcissism). Her edited books include the *Handbook of Methods in Social Psychology (Sage, 2004)*.

Bernard A. Nijstad is Professor of Decision Making and Organizational Behavior at the University of Groningen, The Netherlands. His main research interests are individual and group creativity and individual and group decision-making.

Brian Parkinson lectures at Oxford University, UK. His research focuses on the interpersonal causes, effects and functions of emotion. His books include *Ideas and Realities of Emotion* (1995) and (with Fischer and Manstead) *Emotion in Social Relations* (2005). He was Editor of the *British Journal of Social Psychology* from 2004 to 2008 and Programme Chair for the International Society for Research on Emotion (ISRE) conference in 2011.

Louise Pendry is Senior Lecturer in Psychology at Exeter University, UK. She has published articles on stereotyping and social cognition. More recently, her research focuses on some applications of social cognition and stereotype activation/use (e.g., within the field of diversity training).

Stefan Schulz-Hardt is Professor of Industrial, Economic and Social Psychology at Georg-August-University Göttingen, Germany. He has published on group decision-making, escalation of commitment, stress in the workplace, and other topics. He is currently Associate Editor of the *Journal of Economic Psychology*.

Peter B. Smith is Emeritus Professor of Social Psychology at the University of Sussex, UK. His research has mostly been concerned with cross-cultural aspects of formal and informal influence processes, and with cross-cultural communication. He is author (with Fischer, Vignoles and Bond) of *Understanding Social Psychology Across Cultures*, and a former editor of the *Journal of Cross-Cultural Psychology*.

Russell Spears is Professor of Psychology at the University of Groningen, The Netherlands. His main research interests are in social identity processes with particular focus on the group emotions that play a role in intergroup relations. He has edited the *British Journal of Social Psychology* and (with Anne Maass) the *European Journal of Social Psychology*.

Wolfgang Stroebe, Emeritus Professor of Social Psychology at Utrecht University, is now at the University of Groningen, The Netherlands. He has published widely on topics of social and health psychology in scientific journals and written several books on these topics. His most recent interests have been the detection of fraud in science, the problem of replicability of psychological research, and the impact of gun ownership on homicide rates.

Nicole Tausch obtained her D.Phil at the University of Oxford in 2006. She is currently Lecturer in Social Psychology at the University of St Andrews, UK. Her research interests lie broadly in the areas of social identity, intergroup relations, prejudice, and collective action. She is a recipient of the British Psychological Society's Award for Outstanding Doctoral Research Contributions to Psychology, and is currently an associate editor of the *European Journal of Social Psychology*.

Daan van Knippenberg is Professor of Organizational Behavior at the Rotterdam School of Management, Rotterdam, The Netherlands. His research focuses on leadership, diversity, team performance, and creativity. Daan is Founding Editor of *Organizational Psychology Review* and an associate editor of *Academy of Management Journal*. He is a Fellow of the Society for Industrial and Organizational Psychology, and of the American Psychological Association.

Preface to Sixth Edition

In the competitive market for textbooks in any subject, a book that meets the needs of students and instructors for more than 25 years must be doing something right, in fact many things. Against stiff competition you have to evolve to survive. In this sixth edition we have once again extensively revised the material. And the fact that we have regularly undertaken such revisions has certainly contributed to the success of our book. The field of social psychology continues to expand, both in its material and in the number of countries in which it is taught, and any successful textbook will have to move with the times. As a result of the increasing complexity of our field, it has become impossible for any single person to be an expert on all the different areas of social psychology. The fact that we succeeded in persuading internationally leading experts on each of the various topics to contribute to this books guarantees a level of accuracy that would be impossible to achieve in a single author textbook or a book written by a small team of authors.

This bestselling textbook was always intended to appeal to instructors and to teach social psychology to students at universities throughout Europe and many other parts of the world. As judged by its longevity, its sales, and its translations (a dozen languages), we have succeeded. In this case 'we' refers not just to us as editors, but to our authors who are each experts on their topics and were willing to work with our necessarily tight editorial control in order to provide a well-integrated volume, in which the reader quickly knows what they will find in each chapter, where to find it, and how to use this valuable resource to the best, in order to provide an excellent course or to excel in their examinations.

Over the six editions we have never stood still. We have added and removed topics, and we have added and removed authors, the latter has helped to ensure that new perspectives are represented and material does not get outdated. Topics that remain are updated in each new edition. This edition provides students and instructors with the core of social psychology—chapters dealing with methods, social perception and attribution, social cognition, self and social identity, attitudes, social influence, aggression, prosocial behaviour, relationships, group processes and intergroup relations. But it also casts a look beyond the western perspective and includes a chapter on cultural social psychology, emphasizing that social psychology is a global science, but acknowledging the fact that replications of social psychological studies in other parts of the world often result in somewhat different findings.

Each new edition also provides an updated set of examples of relevant social-psychological phenomena, so that the reader can relate the material in each chapter to the events that they encounter in everyday life, read about in newspapers and on the internet, and see on their TV screens.

Other than coverage of the material, another feature of each new edition is that we have continuously made didactic improvements and added pedagogical aids to each new edition. Each chapter provides the reader with a very clear and comprehensive presentation of the central *theories*, *concepts*, *paradigms*, *results* and *conclusions* in each new area. In terms of structure, the reader will find that each chapter contains specific features, designed to improve learning and enhance the enjoyment of the task:

- A list of key concepts, consisting of the main terms that a student should know about each topic area.

- A 'route map' that provides a brief overview of the chapter, written in clear English.

- The definitions of each key concept are covered in each chapter, and provided in special glossary boxes in the margins to aid revision; they are also gathered together in an alphabetical glossary at the end of the book.

- The body of the text in each chapter is broken down into clear sections, and the reader is guided by subheadings throughout the chapter. We have sought to avoid long, uninterrupted passages of text, and to punctuate the text with figures, tables and occasional photographs.

- We have also provided brief biographies of 'leaders in the field', both classic and contemporary scholars from across the globe who have had a major impact on the research area covered in each chapter.

- Key theories are depicted in special 'theory boxes' to aid understanding of more complex processes.

- Each main section or subsection of the chapter begins with 'learning questions' – these are the major questions that the student should be able to answer having read the chapter – and ends with a summary.

- Each chapter ends with a summary and conclusions in the form of bullet points.

- A list of further reading is suggested, with a sentence indicating what the student will find in each source.

- Each chapter contains boxed features of three different types:

  - *Research close-up* Brief summaries of classic and contemporary research studies, explaining clearly why and how the research was done, what it found and what its implications are.

  - *Individual differences* Illustrative items from scales used to measure variables discussed in the text.

  - *Social psychology beyond the lab* Descriptions of some 'real life applications' of theory and research described in the chapter.

Features designed to aid learning and help both instructors and students do not end with the material *inside* the book. Extensive online resources are also provided on the web (www.wiley.com/college/hewstone), including a bank of over 1000 self-study and instructor test-bank questions, links to other useful websites, and PowerPoint presentations and flashcards.

As always when we complete a new edition, we find that we ourselves have also learned a great deal. Our authors have shared their wide knowledge and communicated so engagingly that we ourselves are encouraged to go and read more, as we hope readers of the book will be too. Such a large book cannot, of course, be completed without the help of others, whom we gratefully acknowledge here. First and foremost, we thank our authors for their excellent manuscripts and their willingness to go through repeated revisions in response to our editorial feedback. The final part of the long process from first draft to publication is of course seeing the manuscript typeset, proofread and published. We owe a debt to many in this process. We would like to thank Juliet Booker and Janis Soo for their superb production work, Jennifer Mair for her careful copy-editing, and Monika Allenbach, Isabelle Brunner, Gina Paolini and Vanessa Singer for their detailed editorial work, and in particular their diligence in checking the references in the list compiled at the back of the book. Joanna Tester has again brought to bear her unerring eye for detail as she saw the manuscript into proofs and this published volume. Finally, we thank Rachel New for her help in making edits to the final version.

Miles Hewstone, Oxford
Wolfgang Stroebe, Groningen & Utrecht
Klaus Jonas, Zürich

Guided Tour

CHAPTER HIGHLIGHTS

Key Terms are listed on each chapter opening page, highlighting the main topic areas for students.

KEY TERMS

- attribution theories
- authoritarian personality
- autokinetic effect
- balance theory
- Bennington study
- consistency theories
- covariation theory
- crisis in social psychology
- demand characteristics
- European Association of Social Psychology
- evolutionary social psychology
- experiment
- experimenter expectancy effects
- field experiment
- field theory
- laboratory experiment
- methodological individualism
- minimal group paradigm
- priming
- realistic conflict theory
- rebound effect
- scapegoat theory
- social cognition
- social facilitation
- social loafing
- social neuroscience

Chapter Outline reflects the coverage of each chapter, by main and subsection headings.

CHAPTER OUTLINE

INTRODUCTION 3

Some classic studies 3

A DEFINITION OF SOCIAL PSYCHOLOGY 6

The core characteristics of social psychology 6

THE UNIQUE PERSPECTIVE OF SOCIAL PSYCHOLOGY 7

The study of the individual and the social 7

A BRIEF HISTORY OF SOCIAL PSYCHOLOGY 10

The beginning 10
The early years 13
The years of expansion 14
The crisis years 17
Overcoming the crisis 19

SOCIAL PSYCHOLOGY IN EUROPE 19

SOCIAL PSYCHOLOGY TODAY 21

CHAPTER SUMMARY 23

A short outline of each chapter, written in clear English, is presented in the **Route Map of the Chapter**.

ROUTE MAP OF THE CHAPTER

Most textbooks introduce social psychology with examples of everyday experiences of social behaviour or even with a formal definition. We thought that a better way of familiarizing you with our discipline was to present some examples of classic studies. These should give you an impression of the research questions social psychologists address and of the methods they use to tackle these questions. Only then do we give a formal definition of social psychology and discuss the differences between social psychology and related areas. The second part of the chapter is devoted to the history of social psychology, which we trace from its starting years around 1900 until today. As our American colleagues like to point out, much of this history took place in the US. However, as we Europeans like to point out, this development was strongly influenced by European researchers, even before the establishment of social psychology in Europe during the last four decades.

ENHANCED LEARNING TOOLS

Each main section or subsection starts with a '**learning question**' (coloured purple in the printed book), major questions that the student should be able to answer after reading the chapter.

Each main section ends with a **Summary** to aid memorizing key segments of the content as students progress through the chapter.

Key Terms listed at the beginning of the chapter are printed in bold at the first point of use in the current chapter and appear with their **definition** at the first main point of discussion in the book. All Key Terms and definitions are collated and arranged alphabetically in the **Glossary** at the back of the book.

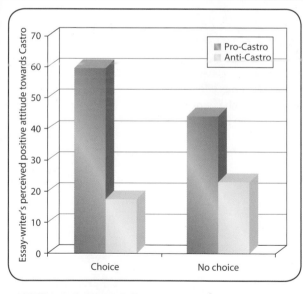

304　AN INTRODUCTION TO SOCIAL PSYCHOLOGY

thinking in terms of 'we' versus 'them' is promoted, by isolating new recruits from their families and friends, imposing strict secrecy and emphasizing the legitimacy of the terrorist organization. There is virtually no chance for people who have climbed up to this floor to withdraw and exit alive. Therefore, they move on to the *fifth floor*, which involves carrying out the terrorist act. In order to operate effectively on this floor, inhibitions against killing innocent people must be overcome, and this is achieved by two well-established psychological mechanisms: *categorization*, stressing the differentiation between ingroup and outgroup, and *distancing*, exaggerating the differences between the ingroup and the targets that are seen as the 'enemy'.

The staircase metaphor is useful for conceptualizing the process by which a small number of individuals from large groups of disaffected people living under adverse conditions end up committing acts of violence against innocent targets. At the same time, it provides some clues regarding the prevention of terrorism. Moghaddam (2005) points out that it is not enough to try and identify the individuals prepared to carry out terrorist acts before they get a chance to do so, because that would only make room for new people to step forward. Instead, terrorism can only be ended by reforming the conditions on the ground floor so that they are no longer perceived as unjust and hopeless by large parts of the population.

Summary

Intimate partner violence, sexual aggression, bullying and intergroup violence are widespread forms of aggression in everyday life. They can lead to lasting negative effects on the victims' psychological functioning and well-being. In research on intimate partner violence, the issue of whether men or women feature more prominently as perpetrators is controversial, but there is consistent evidence that women are more likely to be injured by an intimate partner than are men. Sexual aggression is perpetrated mostly by men against women. Bullying in school and the workplace is typically characterized by a power differential between perpetrator and victim. Some studies suggest that the experience of being bullied in school makes victims vulnerable to long-term psychological problems. In explaining aggression between groups, societal factors, such as perceived injustice, group factors, such as common norms, and individual factors, such as a lack of self-focused attention, play a role. The staircase model of terrorism considers the joint influence of these factors to explain terrorist violence.

PSYCHOLOGICAL PREVENTION AND INTERVENTION

What are effective strategies for preventing or reducing aggression?

It has become clear that aggression poses a serious threat to the health and well-being of individuals and the functioning of societies. Although the present chapter has focused on physical and psychological effects of aggression on the individual, it should also be remembered that the economic costs of interpersonal violence for a society as a whole are enormous. A report by the World Health Organization shows the financial consequences of different forms of violence (Waters et al., 2004). For example, it quotes data by Miller, Cohen, and Rossman (1993) who estimated the costs of rape in the United States in terms of medical treatment as well as impairment of mental health, productivity and quality of life at $47,000 per case. In a survey of over 3000 women in the United States, Rivara et al. (2007) found that annual health care costs were 19 per cent higher among victims of intimate partner violence than among non-victimized women. Based on a victimization rate of 44 per cent in their sample, they extrapolated that for every 100,000 women in the health care system, excess health care costs of $19.3 million are incurred each year as a result of intimate partner violence.

Given the dramatic effects of aggression and violence on individuals, social groups and communities at large, psychologists not only have to deal with the task of investigating how, when, and why aggressive behaviour is shown, they are also expected to propose ways of counteracting and preventing its occurrence. Aggressive behaviour is ultimately performed by individual actors. Therefore, an important aim of intervention efforts is to reduce the probability that a person will show aggressive behaviour, either in a specific situation or over time. Three main mechanisms have been discussed by which aggressive behaviour might, in principle, be prevented: **catharsis**, punishment, and the elicitation of incompatible responses.

> **catharsis** release of aggressive tension through symbolic engagement in aggressive behaviour.

Catharsis

It is widely believed that releasing aggressive tension through physical activity in sport or in symbolic ways,

---

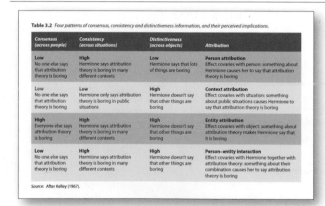

Table 3.2 *Four patterns of consensus, consistency and distinctiveness information, and their perceived implications.*

Consensus (across people)	Consistency (across situations)	Distinctiveness (across objects)	Attribution
Low No one else says that attribution theory is boring	**High** Hermione says attribution theory is boring in many different contexts	**Low** Hermione says that lots of things are boring	**Person attribution** Effect covaries with person: something about Hermione causes her to say that attribution theory is boring
Low No one else says that attribution theory is boring	**Low** Hermione only says attribution theory is boring in public situations	**High** Hermione doesn't say that other things are boring	**Context attribution** Effect covaries with situation: something about public situations causes Hermione to say that attribution theory is boring
High Everyone else says attribution theory is boring	**High** Hermione says attribution theory is boring in many different contexts	**High** Hermione doesn't say that other things are boring	**Entity attribution** Effect covaries with object: something about attribution theory makes Hermione say that it is boring
Low No one else says that attribution theory is boring	**High** Hermione says attribution theory is boring in many different contexts	**High** Hermione doesn't say that other things are boring	**Person–entity interaction** Effect covaries with Hermione together with attribution theory: something about their combination causes her to say attribution theory is boring

Source: After Kelley (1967).

FIGURE 3.9 *A football player adopting the 'archer's bow' posture, which is commonly used after being tackled.*

Source: From Morris & Lewis, 2010. © Dr Paul Morris.

FIGURE 3.3 *Correspondent inferences of essay-writer's attitudes.*

Source: Adapted from Jones & Harris, 1967, with permission from Elsevier.

The main chapter text is punctuated by **diagrams, graphs, tables and occasional photographs**, all designed to improve the reading and learning experience.

Key theories are made accessible in the text by way of **Theory Box** features to aid the understanding of more complex processes.

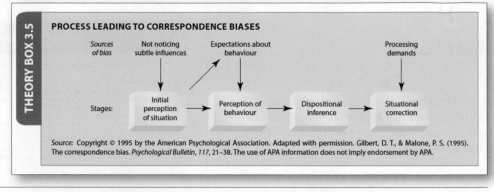

THEORY BOX 3.5

PROCESS LEADING TO CORRESPONDENCE BIASES

Sources of bias: Not noticing subtle influences — Expectations about behaviour — Processing demands

Stages: Initial perception of situation → Perception of behaviour → Dispositional inference → Situational correction

Source: Copyright © 1995 by the American Psychological Association. Adapted with permission. Gilbert, D. T., & Malone, P. S. (1995). The correspondence bias. *Psychological Bulletin, 117,* 21–38. The use of APA information does not imply endorsement by APA.

Brief biographies of **Leaders in the Field** are included, representing both classic and contemporary scholars from around the world, specific to the research area covered in each chapter.

LEADER IN THE FIELD

Daniel Gilbert (b. 1957) is Professor in Psychology at Harvard University. His academic career started inauspiciously at the age of 19 when his intention of studying creative writing in order to become a science fiction writer was thwarted because the class was full. The only available alternative was an Introduction to Psychology course. He still ended up as a best-selling author, but of non-fiction instead of fiction. The award-winning book in question (*Stumbling on Happiness*, 2006) drew on his influential research (with Timothy Wilson) into *affective forecasting*, which concerns people's often inaccurate predictions about their own emotional reactions to events (see Wilson & Gilbert, 2003). As for fulfilling his earlier ambition, he has also published short stories in science-fiction magazines. Of course, he is famous too for his innovative research on the correspondence bias.

Research Close-Ups provide brief summaries of pertinent research studies, both classic and contemporary, as an aid to explain why and how research was carried out and what the results implied.

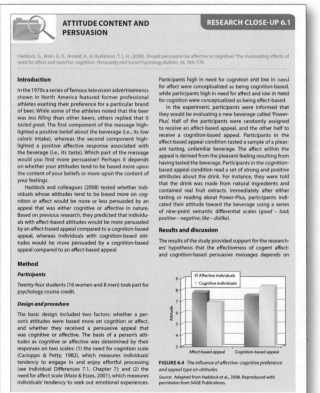

ATTITUDE CONTENT AND PERSUASION

RESEARCH CLOSE-UP 6.1

Haddock, G., Maio, G. R., Arnold, K., & Huskinson, T. L. H. (2008). Should persuasion be affective or cognitive? The moderating effects of need for affect and need for cognition. *Personality and Social Psychology Bulletin, 34,* 769–778.

Introduction

In the 1970s a series of famous television advertisements shown in North America featured former professional athletes exalting their preference for a particular brand of beer. While some of the athletes noted that the beer was *less filling* than other beers, others replied that it *tasted great*. The first component of the message highlighted a positive belief about the beverage (i.e., its low caloric intake), whereas the second component highlighted a positive affective response associated with the beverage (i.e., its taste). Which part of the message would you find more persuasive? Perhaps it depends on whether your attitudes tend to be based more upon the content of your beliefs or more upon the content of your feelings.

Haddock and colleagues (2008) tested whether individuals whose attitudes tend to be based more on cognition or affect would be more or less persuaded by an appeal that was either cognitive or affective in nature. Based on previous research, they predicted that individuals with affect-based attitudes would be more persuaded by an affect-based appeal compared to a cognition-based appeal, whereas individuals with cognition-based attitudes would be more persuaded by a cognition-based appeal compared to an affect-based appeal.

Method

Participants

Twenty-four students (16 women and 8 men) took part for psychology course credit.

Design and procedure

The basic design included two factors: whether a person's attitudes were based more on cognition or affect, and whether they received a persuasive appeal that was cognitive or affective. The basis of a person's attitudes as cognitive or affective was determined by their responses on two scales: (1) the need for cognition scale (Cacioppo & Petty, 1982), which measures individuals' tendency to engage in and enjoy effortful processing (see Individual Differences 7.1, Chapter 7); and (2) the need for affect scale (Maio & Esses, 2001), which measures individuals' tendency to seek out emotional experiences.

Participants high in need for cognition and low in need for affect were conceptualized as being cognition-based, while participants high in need for affect and low in need for cognition were conceptualized as being affect-based.

In the experiment, participants were informed that they would be evaluating a new beverage called 'Power-Plus'. Half of the participants were randomly assigned to receive an affect-based appeal, and the other half to receive a cognition-based appeal. Participants in the affect-based appeal condition tasted a sample of a pleasant tasting, unfamiliar beverage. The affect within the appeal is derived from the pleasant feeling resulting from having tasted the beverage. Participants in the cognition-based appeal condition read a set of strong and positive attributes about the drink. For instance, they were told that the drink was made from natural ingredients and contained real fruit extracts. Immediately after either tasting or reading about Power-Plus, participants indicated their attitude toward the beverage using a series of nine-point semantic differential scales (*good – bad; positive – negative; like – dislike*).

Results and discussion

The results of the study provided support for the researchers' hypothesis that the effectiveness of cogent affect- and cognition-based persuasive messages depends on

FIGURE 6.4 *The influence of affective–cognitive preference and appeal type on attitudes.*
Source: Adapted from Haddock et al., 2008. Reproduced with permission from SAGE Publications.

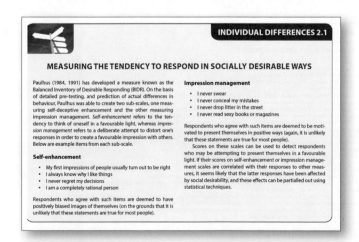

INDIVIDUAL DIFFERENCES 2.1

MEASURING THE TENDENCY TO RESPOND IN SOCIALLY DESIRABLE WAYS

Paulhus (1984, 1991) has developed a measure known as the Balanced Inventory of Desirable Responding (BIDR). On the basis of detailed pre-testing, and prediction of actual differences in behaviour, Paulhus was able to create two sub-scales, one measuring self-deceptive enhancement and the other measuring impression management. *Self-enhancement* refers to the tendency to think of oneself in a favourable light, whereas *impression management* refers to a deliberate attempt to distort one's responses in order to create a favourable impression with others. Below are example items from each sub-scale.

Self-enhancement

• My first impressions of people usually turn out to be right
• I always know why I like things
• I never regret my decisions
• I am a completely rational person

Respondents who agree with such items are deemed to have positively biased images of themselves (on the grounds that it is unlikely that these statements are true for most people).

Impression management

• I never swear
• I never conceal my mistakes
• I never drop litter in the street
• I never read sexy books or magazines

Respondents who agree with such items are deemed to be motivated to present themselves in positive ways (again, it is unlikely that these statements are true for most people).

Scores on these scales can be used to detect respondents who may be attempting to present themselves in a favourable light. If their scores on self-enhancement or impression management scales are correlated with their responses to other measures, it seems likely that the latter responses have been affected by social desirability, and these effects can be partialled out using statistical techniques.

Individual Differences are illustrative items from scales used to measure variables discussed in the text.

Social Psychology Beyond the Lab boxes feature various 'real-life applications' of theory and research applicable to the content of the current chapter.

SOCIAL PSYCHOLOGY BEYOND THE LAB 6.1

ATTITUDES AND PUBLIC OPINION SURVEYS

Given the importance of attitudes in understanding behaviour, it is not surprising that they have an enormous impact 'beyond the lab'. One area where attitudes and attitude measurement is very important is in the context of public opinion surveys. The use of public opinion surveys is widespread – across continents and across issues. For instance, public opinion surveys are often used to gauge the public's attitudes toward things like their national government, views on core social issues or policies (such as environmental attitudes or attitudes toward capital punishment), even to assess levels of happiness in a country and how happiness might change over time.

These opinion surveys will usually be carried out by public companies (e.g., the Gallup organization in the United States; IPSOS-MORI or YouGov in the United Kingdom) or through government organizations (e.g., the Office for National Statistics in the United Kingdom). Often, these surveys will be developed by individuals with a background in social psychology, and their methodology will almost certainly have been informed by advances made by social psychologists. Public opinion surveys might be completed over the phone, via post, or more recently, via the Internet.

One particularly interesting development has been the application of response time methodologies to public opinion surveys. Research by John Bassili and colleagues (e.g., Bassili, 1993, 1996; Bassili & Fletcher, 1991) has utilized computer-assisted telephone interviewing (CATI) to integrate contemporary attitudes research with public opinion surveys. The methodology involves the use of a computer clock that can provide millisecond accuracy in the timing of responses and a voice-recognition framework that converts an individual's responses into signals that trigger the clock after the interviewer asks a question. Using the CATI approach in a survey of Canadians' opinions, Bassili (1993) tested how two operationalizations of attitude strength, attitude accessibility and attitude certainty, might predict the discrepancy between an individual's voting intentions and their actual voting behaviour. The results showed that the response-time measure of accessibility was a significant predictor of the discrepancy between people's voting intentions and their actual voting behaviour. For example, the more accessible the attitude, the lower the discrepancy between voting intentions and voting behaviour.

END-OF-CHAPTER RESOURCES

CHAPTER SUMMARY

- *What is an attitude?* An attitude is an overall evaluation of an attitude object.
- *Can we have attitudes about anything?* Anything that can be evaluated along a dimension of favourability can be conceptualized as an attitude object.
- *What are the bases of attitudes?* Attitudes have affective, cognitive and behavioural antecedents. All three antecedents contribute to our overall evaluation of an object.
- *Is the structure of an attitude best considered to be one-dimensional or two-dimensional?* The two-dimensional perspective is advantageous as it allows for attitude ambivalence.
- *Why do we hold attitudes?* Attitudes serve a variety of functions, the most important of which is the object appraisal function.
- *Why is it useful to know the function of an attitude?* Knowing the function of an attitude is important because attempts to change an attitude are more likely to be successful when the persuasive appeal matches the attitude's function.
- *Does it matter if an attitude is strong or weak?* Yes – strong attitudes are more stable over time, more resistant to change and more likely to guide both information processing and behaviour.
- *What is the difference between explicit and implicit measures of attitude?* Explicit measures directly ask respondents to think about and report their attitude, whereas implicit measures do not.
- *Do explicit and implicit measures predict different types of behaviour?* Research has shown that explicit measures are more effective in predicting deliberative behaviour, whereas implicit measures are more effective in predicting spontaneous behaviour.
- *Do attitudes predict behaviour?* On the whole, attitudes do a reasonable job of predicting behaviour. The degree to which attitudes predict behaviour depends on a number of factors, including correspondence, the domain of behaviour, the strength of an attitude and person variables.
- *How do attitudes predict behaviour?* A number of models have been developed to understand how attitudes predict behaviour. The most influential models are the theory of planned behaviour and the MODE model.

A list of key learning points are presented in the **Chapter Summary** to help students consolidate their knowledge and understanding of the chapter's content.

SUGGESTIONS FOR FURTHER READING

Albarracín, D., Johnson, B. T., & Zanna, M. P. (Eds.). (2005). *Handbook of attitudes*. Mahwah, NJ: Erlbaum. This volume offers an advanced review of the field of attitudes research.

Cialdini, R. B. (2008). *Influence: Science and practice* (5th ed.). Boston, MA: Allyn & Bacon. This volume offers an accessible look at research on social influence.

Crano, W., & Prislin, R. (Eds.). (2009). *Attitudes and persuasion*. New York: Psychology Press. This volume reviews different streams of research on attitudes and attitude change.

Eagly, A. H., & Chaiken, S. (1993). *The psychology of attitudes*. Fort Worth, TX: Harcourt Brace Jovanovich. This volume provides a comprehensive review of research that laid the foundation for the progress that has been made in the past two decades.

Fazio, R. H., & Olson, M. A. (2003). Implicit measures in social cognition research: Their meaning and use. *Annual Review of Psychology, 54*, 297–327. This paper reviews advances that have been made concerning implicit measures of attitude.

Fazio, R. H., & Petty, R. E. (Eds.). (2007). *Attitudes: Structure, function, and consequences*. Hove, UK: Psychology Press. This volume comprises a collection of important published papers on attitude structure, attitude content and the attitude–behaviour relation.

Greenwald, A. G., Poehlman, T. A., Uhlmann, E., & Banaji, M. R. (2009). Understanding and using the Implicit Association Test: III. Meta-analysis of predictive validity. *Journal of Personality and Social Psychology, 97*, 17–41.

Haddock, G., & Maio, G. R. (Eds.). (2004). *Contemporary perspectives on the psychology of attitudes*. Hove, UK: Psychology Press. This volume reviews a number of contemporary research programmes on the psychology of attitudes.

Maio, G. R., Bell, D. W., & Esses, V. M. (1996). Ambivalence and persuasion: The processing of messages about immigrant groups. *Journal of Experimental Social Psychology, 32*, 513–536.

Maio, G. R., & Haddock, G. (2015). *The psychology of attitudes and attitude change*. London: Sage. This volume provides a comprehensive and accessible overview of research and theories relevant to the psychology of attitudes.

Maio, G. R., & Olson, J. M. (Eds.). (2000). *Why we evaluate: Functions of attitudes*. Mahwah, NJ: Erlbaum. This volume is a comprehensive examination of research on attitude functions.

Perloff, R. M. (2013). *The dynamics of persuasion: Communication and attitudes in the 21st century* (5th ed.). New York: Routledge. This volume highlights research on persuasion and social influence.

Petty, R. E., & Cacioppo, J. T. (1986a). *Communication and persuasion: Central and peripheral routes to attitude change*. New York: Springer. This volume highlights the research that was conducted in the development of the highly influential Elaboration Likelihood Model of persuasion.

Petty, R. E., Fazio, R. H., & Briñol, P. (Eds.). (2009). *Attitudes: Insights from the new implicit measures*. New York: Psychology Press. This volume highlights different research programmes regarding implicit measures of attitude.

Wittenbrink, B., & Schwarz, N. (Eds.). (2007). *Implicit measures of attitudes*. New York: Guilford. This volume provides an overview of different perspectives on the utility of implicit measures of attitude.

Each chapter ends with a list of **Suggestions for Further Reading** indicating key material found in each resource.

Accompanying Online Resources for Instructors and Students

BOOK COMPANION SITE FOR INSTRUCTORS

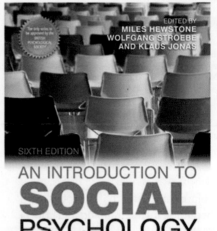

The Book Companion Site contains an extensive support package for instructors and can be found at **www.wiley.com/college/hewstone**.

On the website instructors will find:

- Test bank with over 1000 questions, including true/false, multiple choice and essay questions.
- Computerized test bank allowing instructors to create and print multiple versions of the test bank, as well as allowing users to customize exams by altering or adding new questions.
- PowerPoint presentations containing a combination of key concepts, examples, and figures and tables from the book.
- Links to the BBC Radio 4 'Mind Changers' series with contributions from the editors.

BOOK COMPANION SITE FOR STUDENTS

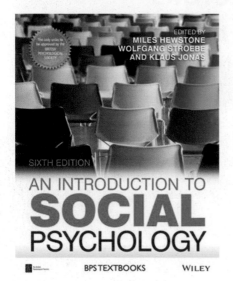

Welcome to the Student Companion Site for

An Introduction to Social Psychology, 6th Edition

Welcome to the Web site for **An Introduction to Social Psychology, 6th edition** edited by Miles Hewstone, Wolfgang Stroebe and Klaus Jonas. This Web site gives you access to the rich tools and resources available for this text. You can access these resources in two ways:

1. Using the menu at the top, select a chapter. A list of resources available for that particular chapter will be provided.

2. Using the menu at the top, select a resource. This will allow you to access a particular resource section. You will then have the option of selecting resources within the section or going directly to a specific chapter.

The *Introduction to Social Psychology* student website provides students with support material that will help develop their conceptual understanding of the material. The student website contains:

- Self-Study Quizzes including true/false, multiple choice and 'fill in the blank' questions to aid students' learning and self-study.

- Links to relevant journal articles that are referenced in the text to encourage further reading and critical analysis of the material.

- Flashcards showing key terms and definitions from the glossary.

- Links to the BBC Radio 4 'Mind Changers' series with contributions from the editors.

1 Introducing Social Psychology

WOLFGANG STROEBE, MILES HEWSTONE AND KLAUS JONAS

KEY TERMS

- attribution theories
- authoritarian personality
- autokinetic effect
- balance theory
- Bennington study
- consistency theories
- covariation theory
- crisis in social psychology
- demand characteristics

- European Association of Social Psychology
- evolutionary social psychology
- experiment
- experimenter expectancy effects
- field experiment
- field theory
- laboratory experiment
- methodological individualism

- minimal group paradigm
- priming
- realistic conflict theory
- rebound effect
- scapegoat theory
- social cognition
- social facilitation
- social loafing
- social neuroscience

CHAPTER OUTLINE

INTRODUCTION 3

   Some classic studies   3

A DEFINITION OF SOCIAL PSYCHOLOGY 6

   The core characteristics of social psychology   6

THE UNIQUE PERSPECTIVE OF SOCIAL PSYCHOLOGY 7

   The study of the individual and the social   7

A BRIEF HISTORY OF SOCIAL PSYCHOLOGY 10

   The beginning   10
   The early years   13
   The years of expansion   14
   The crisis years   17
   Overcoming the crisis   19

SOCIAL PSYCHOLOGY IN EUROPE 19

SOCIAL PSYCHOLOGY TODAY 21

CHAPTER SUMMARY 23

ROUTE MAP OF THE CHAPTER

Most textbooks introduce social psychology with examples of everyday experiences of social behaviour or even with a formal definition. We thought that a better way of familiarizing you with our discipline was to present some examples of classic studies. These should give you an impression of the research questions social psychologists address and of the methods they use to tackle these questions. Only then do we give a formal definition of social psychology and discuss the differences between social psychology and related areas. The second part of the chapter is devoted to the history of social psychology, which we trace from its starting years around 1900 until today. As our American colleagues like to point out, much of this history took place in the US. However, as we Europeans like to point out, this development was strongly influenced by European researchers, even before the establishment of social psychology in Europe during the last four decades.

INTRODUCTION

Some classic studies

How do social psychologists go about addressing research questions?

A proper textbook of social psychology should begin with the discussion of accepted definitions of the discipline. The reason we deviate from this safe course of action is that, when we ourselves began studying social psychology, we found these definitions rather incomprehensible. However, once we had finished the social psychology course and knew something about the subject, we could finally appreciate why social psychologists defined their discipline the way they did. Because presenting the definitions at the end of the book did not make much sense either, we decided on a compromise. We will first give you some examples of classic social psychology research to show you how social psychologists go about their studies. Then, in the next section, we present and discuss some definitions.

In 1954, Muzafer Sherif (see Leader in the Field, Muzafer Sherif, in Chapter 14), who was then Professor of Social Psychology at the University of Oklahoma (US), conducted one of a series of classic studies with 11- to 12-year-old boys, who had been sent to a remote summer camp at Robbers Cave State Park, Oklahoma. None of the boys knew each other before the study. They were divided into two groups, who stayed in cabins far apart from each other and did not know of each other's existence. For one week, each of the groups enjoyed the typical summer camp life, engaging in fun activities like camping out, transporting canoes over rough terrain to the water and playing various games. They had a great time. It is therefore not surprising that at the end of the week, group members had grown very fond of one another and the groups had developed strong group identities. Each chose a name for itself (the 'Rattlers' and the 'Eagles'), which they proudly displayed on shirts and flags.

At the end of the week, each of the groups was told that there was another group in the vicinity. As though acceding to the boys' requests, the staff arranged tournaments of games (e.g., touch football, baseball, tug of war) between the groups. The winning team would receive a cup, and members of the winning team would each be given a new penknife. The tournament started in the spirit of good sportsmanship, but as it progressed, hostilities between the groups began to develop. 'Soon members of each group began to call their rivals

"stinkers", "sneaks" and "cheats" . . . Near the end of this stage, the members of each group found the other group and its members so distasteful that they expressed strong preferences to have no further contact with them at all' (Sherif, 1967, p. 82).

What was the point of all of this? What can tales about boys in a summer camp tell us about real life? The answer is, a great deal. These Robbers Cave studies actually mark a turning point in the study of prejudice (i.e., dislike for members of an outgroup), because they challenged the then dominant view of prejudice as either an outflow of a prejudiced personality disposition (**authoritarian personality**; see Chapter 14) or as the result of displaced frustration (**scapegoat theory**). There was no indication that these boys had prejudiced personalities or needed scapegoats to displace their aggression. And yet, they developed strong dislikes for the members of the other group (the 'stinkers' and 'sneaks'), because they were competing with them for some valued good which only one of the two groups could attain. Sherif interpreted these findings as support for his **realistic conflict theory**, which assumed that intergroup hostility and intergroup prejudice are usually the result of a conflict of interest between groups over valued commodities or opportunities. Goals were the central concept in Sherif's theory: he argued that when two groups were competing for the same goal, which only one could achieve, there would be intergroup hostility.

Not surprising, you might say. After all, this is the reason why football supporters beat each other up every so often before and after games between their clubs. And yet, this is not the full story. Nearly two decades later, Henri Tajfel (see Leader in the Field, Henri Tajfel, in Chapter 14), then Professor of Social Psychology at Bristol University (UK), and colleagues conducted a series of studies that called into question the assumption that competitive goals are a necessary condition for the development of intergroup hostility (Tajfel, Billig, Bundy, & Flament, 1971). Participants in these studies were 14- to 15-year-old schoolboys, who all knew each other well and came to the psychology laboratory in

authoritarian personality personality syndrome characterized by a simplistic cognitive style, a rigid regard for social conventions and submission to authority figures (associated with prejudice towards minority groups and susceptibility to Fascism).

scapegoat theory a theory that holds that prejudice is due to aggression that is displaced towards members of an outgroup (scapegoats), because the group or set of circumstances that was the source of frustration is not within reach.

realistic conflict theory a theory developed by Sherif that holds that conflict and competition between groups over valued resources can create intergroup hostility and prejudice.

experiment a method in which the researcher deliberately introduces some change into a setting to examine the consequences of that change.

groups of eight to participate in an **experiment** (see Chapter 2) on visual perception. Their task was to estimate the number of dots that were flashed onto a screen. After completion of this task, they were told that they would also participate in a second experiment and, for the ease of coding, would be divided on the basis of the dot estimates they had just made. Half the boys were then (randomly) assigned to the 'under-estimators' group, the other half to the 'over-estimators' group. (In later studies, boys were often divided on the basis of their alleged preference for paintings by Klee or Kandinsky, an equally irrelevant criterion for boys of that age.) The boys then had to assign rewards to other individuals in real money. They did not know the identity of the other individuals, but only their code numbers and their group membership.

minimal group paradigm a set of experimental procedures designed to create groups based on essentially arbitrary criteria (with no interaction within or between them, and with no knowledge of who else belongs to each group) whose members show intergroup discrimination.

This experimental procedure became known as the **minimal group paradigm**. These groups were minimal, because they were created using arbitrary criteria, involved no interaction between members of the two groups, and group members had no knowledge of who belonged to the group. And yet Tajfel could show that members of these groups displayed intergroup discrimination. When asked to divide money between a member of their own group and a member of the other group, most boys gave consistently more money to members of their own group than to members of the other group (see Chapter 14). These studies were again quite innovative, because they showed that intergroup conflict was not an essential cause of intergroup discrimination (or at least ingroup favouritism). Apparently, the mere fact of division into groups was sufficient to trigger discriminatory behaviour.

You might now believe that you have some idea of what social psychology is all about and how social psychologists conduct their research. You might also think that the approach of Sherif was more in line with what you had expected, but that the studies by Tajfel, despite their artificiality, led to some interesting results. However, you will be somewhat premature in your confidence. A clearer and more appropriate picture of the field of social psychology will emerge after considering some additional studies, described below.

In 1994, Neil Macrae (then at Cardiff University) and colleagues studied people's ability to suppress their

prejudicial thoughts (Macrae, Bodenhausen, Milne, & Jetten, 1994). After all, there is a great deal of evidence that people acquire their prejudices quite early and may not be able to get rid of them later in life, even if these prejudicial thoughts have become inconsistent with their egalitarian values (Wilson, Lindsey, & Schooler, 2000). Thus, if people cannot forget their prejudicial thoughts, it would be good if, at least, they could inhibit them and prevent them from affecting their actions. As the studies by Macrae et al. (1994; see Chapter 4) show, this may be more difficult than one would think.

Participants in these studies were students. When they arrived at the laboratory, they were told that they were to participate in an investigation of people's ability to construct life event details from visual information. They were then presented with a colour photograph of a skinhead and were asked to write a short essay about a typical day in the life of this skinhead. Skinheads were chosen here not only because there is widespread prejudice against them, but also because, unlike prejudice towards other minority groups, expressing prejudice towards skinheads is not (yet) politically incorrect. Half of the participants were asked to suppress their prejudice against skinheads in writing this essay. They were told to try to write their essay without being influenced by their stereotypes about skinheads – that is, the beliefs they might have about the characteristics of skinheads in general. The other half (i.e., the control group) were not given this instruction.

After the participants had finished the first essay, they were given a photo of another skinhead and asked to write another essay about this second skinhead. This time, however, they were not given any instructions about suppressing stereotypes. Both essays were then

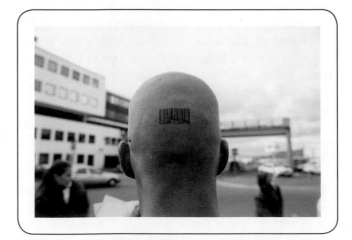

FIGURE 1.1 *How easy is it for people to suppress their prejudice towards skinheads?*

Source: © Brooks Walker. Used under licence from Getty Images.

rated by independent raters, who did not know whether a given essay had been written by a participant from either the experimental or the control group and who evaluated the extent to which writers expressed stereotypes about skinheads. With regard to the first essay, results were not very surprising. As one would expect of 'good' (i.e., obedient) participants, individuals who had been instructed to suppress their stereotypes in their first essay did so quite successfully. Their essays were much less stereotypic than the essays of the control group. However, the analysis of their second essays provided a striking finding: there was a **rebound effect** (see Chapter 4). The second essay of these 'suppressors' was more stereotypic than that of the control group. Thus, when people no longer tried to suppress their stereotypes, they showed a higher level of stereotypical thinking than if they had never tried to suppress their thoughts in the first place.

rebound effect where suppression attempts fail; used here to demonstrate how a suppressed stereotype returns to have an even greater impact upon one's judgements about a person from a stereotyped group.

Although these are fascinating results, Macrae and his colleagues were not satisfied with merely showing a rebound effect of stereotype suppression on thinking (see Chapter 4): they also wanted to know whether attempts to suppress one's stereotype would affect people's behaviour. They therefore conducted a second study. The first part of this study was identical to that of their first experiment. However, after having written an essay under either stereotype suppression or no-suppression instructions, participants were told that they would now go next door to meet the person depicted in the photograph (i.e., the skinhead). When they entered the room next door, there was a row of chairs standing next to each other, but no skinhead. However, on the first chair there was a denim jacket and bag. The experimenter told the participant that the other person must just have gone to the toilet and would return shortly and that the participant should sit down on one of the chairs in the meantime. The measure of interest in this case was the seating position, that is, how far the participant would choose to sit away from the skinhead he or she was supposed to meet. We would all acknowledge that the distance we keep from someone is an indication of our liking for that person (Macrae et al., 1994). And in line with the findings of the previous study, participants who had (successfully) suppressed their stereotype on writing the essay now chose a chair that was significantly further away from the skinhead than did individuals in the control group. Thus, the rebound effect of stereotype suppression affected not only thoughts, but also behaviour (but for

some constraints on the general effect, see Monteith, Sherman, & Devine, 1998).

As surprising as these findings were, the impact of stereotypes on behaviour was still restricted to the way the individual behaved towards a member of the group towards whom the stereotype was held. As we will see in the next experiment, the impact of stereotypes can be even more pervasive. This study was conducted by John Bargh (see Leader in the Field, John Bargh, in Chapter 4) and his colleagues (Bargh, Chen, & Burrows, 1996) at New York University (US). In the first part of this experiment, participants had to complete a 'scrambled sentence test' in which they had to form sentences from scrambled sets of words. For participants in the experimental group, these sentences contained words that were part of the (American) stereotype of the elderly, such as 'Florida', 'Bingo' and 'grey'. This procedure is known as '**priming**' (see Chapter 4), because these words will bring the elderly stereotype to participants' minds (i.e., make it more accessible), including characteristics of elderly people that were not even mentioned in the priming procedure.

priming activating one stimulus (e.g., bird) facilitates the subsequent processing of another related stimulus (e.g., wing, feather).

One such characteristic that is typically attributed to the elderly, but which was not mentioned in the priming procedure, is that elderly people move rather slowly. The researchers assumed that participants who were primed with the stereotype of the elderly would also think of 'moving slowly' as another salient characteristic of the elderly. It was further assumed that this thought would affect the participants' own behaviour. The researchers predicted that participants primed with the elderly stereotype would move more slowly than participants in the control condition who had been exposed to neutral primes. The experimenters then measured the time it took participants to walk from the experimental room to the nearest lift. In line with the hypothesis, participants who were primed with the elderly stereotype took significantly longer to reach the lift than did participants who had been primed with neutral words. It appears that thinking of the concept 'slow' influenced behaviour, and that consciousness did not play any part in this process, because participants were aware neither that they had been primed nor that they had been led to walk more slowly (see Research Close-Up 4.1 in Chapter 4).

We hope that reading about these studies has stimulated your interest in social psychology. If it has, you can read more about the first two studies in Chapter 14 (Prejudice and Intergroup Relations). The last two studies are discussed in Chapter 4 (Social Cognition).

Given that the research we have discussed so far is quite varied in its research questions, scope and methods, we now turn to a more general discussion of the nature of social psychology.

A DEFINITION OF SOCIAL PSYCHOLOGY

The core characteristics of social psychology

How do social psychologists define their discipline?

When social psychologists are called upon to define their discipline, they usually refer to the definition given by Gordon Allport (1954a) (see Leader in the Field, Gordon Allport, in Chapter 14) in his classic chapter on the history of social psychology, published in the second edition of the *Handbook of Social Psychology*: 'Social psychology is the attempt to understand and explain how the thoughts, feelings, and behaviours of individuals are influenced by the actual, imagined, or implied presence of other human beings' (p. 5). With 'imagined presence' Allport referred to the influence of reference persons (e.g., our parents) whose expectations might influence our behaviour. With the 'implied presence' he acknowledged the fact that much of our behaviour is shaped by social roles and cultural norms. This is quite a good definition, which can accommodate the studies that we have described earlier.

One characteristic of social psychology, which Allport implied but did not mention specifically, is the use of scientific methods. The scientific method of choice used in the studies we have just described was the experiment. We will discuss this method only briefly, because you will learn more about the experimental method in the chapter on methods (Chapter 2). Experiments are a method in which the researcher deliberately introduces some change into a setting to examine the consequences of that change. The typical procedure used in experiments is that conditions in which a change has been introduced (i.e., an independent variable manipulated) are compared to conditions in which this has not been the case, the so-called control group. By randomly assigning participants to either the experimental or control group, the researcher can be reasonably certain that any difference between the two groups was due to the manipulation of the independent variable.

Thus, Macrae and colleagues asked half their participants to suppress their stereotype of skinheads, and compared their thoughts and behaviour to those of a control group of individuals who had not been asked to suppress their stereotype. Bargh and colleagues compared the walking speed of participants who had been primed with the elderly stereotype with that of (control) participants who had not been primed. The study by Sherif is somewhat deficient in this respect, because he did not really have a proper control group. He compared the impact of the introduction of intergroup competition on group members' behaviour over time. The control conditions in the Tajfel experiment are difficult to explain without a more detailed description of the study. You may remember that Tajfel and colleagues assessed how the boys would divide money between a member of their own group and a member of the other group. As a control for ingroup bias, they simply reversed the alleged group membership of the two individuals between whom the money had to be divided.

Another methodological difference between the study by Sherif and those of the other researchers is that Sherif's study was a **field experiment** rather than a **laboratory experiment**: he used a natural setting (summer camp) to test his hypotheses. The other studies were all laboratory experiments which used settings that were specially created by the experimenter. For example, Macrae and colleagues led their participants to believe that they were in a study of people's ability to construct life event details from visual information. This is also an example of a darker aspect of social psychology, namely, that we often have to use deception to test our predictions. But if the participants in the study by Macrae and colleagues (1994) had known the real purpose of the study, this would have influenced their thoughts and behaviour and the results of such a study would have been meaningless. (We therefore often disregard the data of participants who guess the purpose of our experiments.) Field and laboratory experiments are not the only scientific methods used by social psychologists to test their hypotheses. You can read about other methods in Chapter 2 (Research Methods in Social Psychology).

Obviously, the use of scientific methods is not a characteristic that allows one to distinguish social psychology from other social sciences, as by definition all social sciences use methods they consider scientific, and for many of them, experiments are the method of choice. A more distinctive characteristic introduced by Allport is the fact

> **field experiment** a true randomized experiment conducted in a natural setting.

> **laboratory experiment** a study, conducted in the laboratory, in which the researcher deliberately introduces some change into a setting, while holding all other factors constant, to examine the consequences of that change.

that social psychology is concerned with social influence, and that it studies the impact of others on individuals' thoughts, feelings and behaviours. All the studies we described earlier tried to understand and explain how the thoughts, feelings and behaviours of their participants were influenced by the presence of other human beings. In the case of the study by Sherif, these human beings were mainly the members of the other group with whom the boys competed, although the members of their own groups also influenced the behaviour of these boys. In contrast to the Sherif study, where the others were actually present, the presence of others was imagined rather than real in the Tajfel study (recall that Allport's careful definition allowed for the impact of the *imagined* presence of others). Finally, in the studies by Macrae and by Bargh and colleagues, it was not really the presence of others that influenced participants' thoughts or behaviour, but the suppression or activation of their beliefs about other groups.

The studies by Macrae and Bargh are also good examples of an aspect of social psychological research that is less clearly emphasized in Allport's definition, namely, the fact that we are interested not only in the impact others have on our thoughts, feelings and behaviour, but also in the *cognitive processes* by which our thoughts, emotions and goals guide our understanding of the world around us and our actions. You can read more about this in Chapter 4 (Social Cognition).

A final characteristic of social psychology emphasized in Allport's definition is that social psychologists study the impact that the implied or actual presence of others has on the thoughts, feelings and behaviours of *individuals*. Thus, even when we study social groups, we examine the impact groups have on the individual group members. For example, in the classic study of conformity with group majorities, Asch (1956) examined the impact of the majority opinion on the judgements of individual participants (see Chapter 8). Similarly, Tajfel and colleagues (1971) studied the impact of the mere categorization of others into ingroup and outgroup on the way individuals distributed money between them. This emphasis on the individual is actually a very important point which had already been made by the elder brother of Gordon Allport, Floyd Allport, in his classic textbook of social psychology: 'There is no psychology of groups which is not essentially and entirely a psychology of individuals. Social psychology must not be placed in contradistinction to the psychology of the individual; it is a part of the psychology of the individual, whose behaviour it studies in relation to that sector of his environment comprised by his fellows' (F. Allport, 1924, p. 4). The emphasis on the individual does not deny the importance of the social context as a determinant of individual behaviour, but it rejects the existence of a group consciousness or a collective mind as separate from the minds of the individuals who comprise the group.

THE UNIQUE PERSPECTIVE OF SOCIAL PSYCHOLOGY

The study of the individual and the social

What differentiates social psychology from related disciplines such as personality psychology and sociology?

In addition to using examples of studies as well as a definition to illuminate the nature of social psychology, it might be helpful to contrast social psychological research to that of research in related disciplines. As in the previous section, we will use the example of an experimental study to clarify these differences. This study was conducted at a small elite college in the United States and was announced as an experiment on perception. The experimental sessions were held in a small classroom and eight participants attended each of the sessions. The participants, who were seated in two rows of four, were presented with sets of four lines of different length, a standard line and three comparison lines. Their task consisted of the comparison of the standard line with the three other lines, one of which was equal to the standard line. The comparison lines were numbered from 1 to 3, and the participants stated their judgements by calling out one of the numbers (see Figure 1.2).

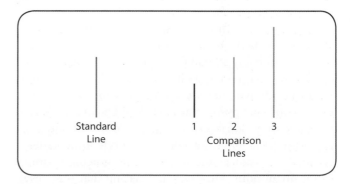

FIGURE 1.2 *Example of the stimulus pattern used in the conformity studies of Asch (1955).*

Source: Original data from Asch (1955), *Scientific American*, 193, 31–35.

Obviously, this was a simple experiment in visual discrimination in which the experimenter probably wanted to find out how accurately participants could differentiate between lines of different lengths and where the threshold lay at which people would begin to make mistakes. However, there is one feature of the experiment which does not fit with standard procedures in perception experiments – namely that participants judged these lines in groups. This would not have been a problem had the experimenter ensured that judgements were written down, to exclude the possibility that participants would be aware of each others' judgements. But in the present experiment, participants were asked to *call out* their judgements to the experimenter. This appears to be a serious methodological fault. Any determination of a difference threshold based on such data would be flawed, because participants might have been influenced by the earlier judgements that they overheard. Let us assume that the first participant calling out his judgements committed an error. The second participant, who might normally have given a correct response, might now have become uncertain and given the same erroneous response as the first participant. In this way, an experiment on perception might, in fact, have become a study of social influence.

Since we are concerned here with social psychology, it will not come as a surprise that the experimenter, a Professor of Social Psychology at Swarthmore College, Pennsylvania, was not really interested in measuring perceptual thresholds, but in the extent to which individuals would be influenced by a discrepant majority judgement. In fact, only one of the eight participants in each session was a 'naïve' participant; all the others were confederates of the experimenter and were instructed to give unanimous but wrong judgements on 12 out of the 18 trials. These judgements were so easy that participants who judged the stimuli in individual sessions made practically no incorrect judgements. And yet, when participants were exposed to the incorrect judgements of a unanimous majority, 36.8 per cent of their judgements were incorrect (Asch, 1955).

With this experimental setting, Asch created a situation that is familiar to most of us from everyday life. We have probably all had the experience of members of our group disagreeing with us on some issue, then having to decide whether we should go with the group or stick to our own position at the risk of becoming disliked or of looking foolish. Naturally, we do not usually disagree about the length of lines, but about some issue of greater importance, and often the disagreeing majority is not unanimous. However, the setting that was developed by Asch would allow us to manipulate all these variables, and most of them have indeed been investigated in subsequent research (for a review, see Allen, 1966).

Our decision to stick to our guns or go with the group will depend very much on how confident we are of the correctness of our own opinion, on how important a correct decision is for us and for the group, and on how well we know the other group members. We are probably also more willing to conform to a majority if we are confronted with a majority that is unanimous rather than divided. If we return to Gordon Allport's definition of social psychology, it is easy to see that the Asch experiment fits all of the characteristics: Asch used a laboratory experiment to study the social influence which a (false) majority judgement would have on the thoughts and behaviours (i.e., judgements) of individuals.

The Asch experiment also allows us to demonstrate the difference between social psychology and 'asocial' *general psychology*. If Asch had been interested in studying perceptual thresholds, he would have varied the difference in the lengths of his standard and comparison stimuli systematically, to assess the extent to which such variations affected perceptual judgements. The (perceptual) judgements would have remained the same, but they would now be investigated in relation to variations in the physical aspects of the stimuli, while keeping the social context constant. In contrast, Asch kept the physical stimulus constellation relatively constant and was interested in the effect that varying the social context (i.e., majority size and unanimity) had on perceptual judgements.

The Asch situation is also useful for demonstrating the difference between social and personality psychology. As a social psychologist, Asch was interested in the impact that characteristics of the social situation had on the thoughts and behaviours of his participants. Does the rate of conformity increase if we increase the number of majority members who give erroneous judgements? Does the conformity rate decrease if participants are allowed to give their judgements anonymously? Asch's approach is typical of social psychological research, which usually *manipulates* important aspects of the social context in order to assess the impact these changes have on the thoughts, feelings and behaviour of the target person.

Personality psychologists, on the other hand, might be less interested in the impact of the social context on behaviour and, instead, ask themselves why some participants are influenced by the erroneous judgements of the majority while others remain unaffected. Thus, the personality psychologist would be interested in the personality traits that are responsible for the fact that different individuals act differently in what is essentially the same social situation. The personality psychologist might test whether intelligent individuals are less likely than unintelligent ones to conform to majorities, or whether conformity is more prevalent among authoritarian rather than non-authoritarian personalities (see the discussion of the authoritarian personality in Chapter 14; Adorno, Frenkel-Brunswik, Levinson, & Sanford, 1950).

Personality psychologists would not, however, only address the question of individual differences as determinants of conformity; they would also want to know how these individual differences came about. Is it possible to relate differences in authoritarianism to differences in the way parents brought up their children, and what aspects of a person's upbringing determine his or her self-esteem? Thus, one could try to separate the disciplines of social and personality psychology as follows: individual behaviour is determined by three factors: (1) the biological constitution of individuals, (2) their acquired traits, and (3) the social and physical context. Whereas personality psychologists are mainly interested in studying how particular traits are acquired and how these traits influence the individual's behaviour, social psychologists study the impact of the social situation on individual behaviour.

Unfortunately, such a distinction would oversimplify the differences between social and personality psychology (for more details, see Krahé, 1992) because one of the central concepts of social psychology, namely social attitudes, is defined by many social psychologists (e.g., Eagly & Chaiken, 1993) as a tendency (i.e., individual disposition) to evaluate an attitude object positively or negatively (see Chapter 6). Even though social psychologists are mainly interested in studying how attitudes change in response to social influence attempts (see Chapters 7 and 8), they also use attitudes to predict individual behaviour (see Chapter 6). Furthermore, within social psychology, researchers have often been interested in studying individual difference variables, such as the degree to which individuals are prone to prejudice and susceptible to Fascist ideologies ('authoritarianism'; Adorno et al., 1950; see Chapter 14), or the degree to which individuals are oriented to situational cues or reactions of others ('self-monitoring'; Snyder, 1974).

Since there is a great deal of agreement that individual behaviour is influenced by personality traits (see Chapter 9 on aggression) as well as the social context, the two fields of personality psychology and social psychology are, in fact, difficult to separate. It is therefore not surprising that the leading social psychological journal is the *Journal of Personality and Social Psychology*, and that most American social psychologists are members of the Society of Personality and Social Psychology. However, there are subtle differences in focus. Social psychologists are typically interested in personality variables as *moderators*. They look for the extent to which the impact of an independent variable on a dependent variable is qualified by, or depends on, the level of an individual's score on a personality measure. For example, there is a higher correlation between attitudes and behaviour for 'low' than for 'high' self-monitors (Snyder & Kendzierski, 1982). Many of the chapters in this volume refer to such personality influences on social behaviour. Social psychologists also tend to emphasize that the impact of personality variables on social behaviour is weaker in 'strong' compared to 'weak' social situations (Mischel, 1977). Thus, social psychologists emphasize the power of strong social situations to relegate personality influences to the background. This occurs, for example, in experiments investigating helping in emergencies (Latané & Darley, 1976; see Chapter 10) and obeying an authority figure's orders to behave in immoral ways (Milgram, 1974; see Chapter 8).

After the difficulties we experienced in distinguishing social psychology from personality psychology, distinguishing it from neighbouring social sciences such as sociology might seem easy. It would appear that sociology differs from social psychology both in the issues it studies and in the level of analysis at which it addresses these issues. Unfortunately, things are again not that simple. First, there is quite a bit of overlap between the issues studied by social psychologists and those that interest sociologists. Thus, social groups and group norms are topics that are of equal interest to sociologists and social psychologists (see Chapter 12). The sociologist George Homans wrote one of the classic monographs on social groups (Homans, 1950) and the sociologists Hechter and Opp (2001) edited a volume that summarizes the important work of sociologists in the area of social norms.

Although there are sociological approaches that, influenced by the work of Talcott Parsons and Emile Durkheim, emphasize that sociological facts should not be explained through psychological processes (Vanberg, 1975), most sociologists would no longer accept this position. In fact, sociologists have made major contributions to the development of individualistic social psychological theories. Thus, the sociologists Homans (1961) and Blau (1964) have written monographs on exchange theory, a theory that has become central in social psychology through the classic *Social Psychology of Groups* written by the social psychologists Thibaut and Kelley (1959), but is now more frequently referred to as interdependence theory. The central tenet of this theory is that individuals interact with those others who provide the greatest rewards for the least costs (see Chapter 11). Thus, most sociologists agree with social psychologists in espousing what has been called **methodological individualism**, namely the assumption that even collective behaviour is essentially

methodological individualism the assumption that collective action must be explained by showing how it results from individual decisions and behaviour; collective behaviour is seen as essentially behaviour of the individuals who form the collective.

behaviour of the individuals who form the collective and therefore has to be explained in terms of rewards and costs of this behaviour to the individual (e.g., Klandermans, 1997). Even though there is a great deal of overlap between sociology and social psychology, there are also major differences in the way these areas approach social behaviour. Sociologists are more likely to trace social behaviour upwards to structural variables such as norms, roles or social class, whereas social psychologists will trace it downwards to the individual's goals, motives and cognitions. For example, both sociologists and social psychologists are interested in aggression and violence. Social psychologists have studied the cognitive and affective processes through which anger can, given the right contextual cues, explode in aggressive behaviour – that is, behaviour performed with the express intention of hurting another person (Chapter 9). Sociologists, on the other hand, have been more interested in why levels of aggression are higher in some societies or groups than in others. Why is the murder rate in the US so much higher than in Canada, even though guns are widely available in both countries? Since a possible difference could be the type of guns that are available in the two countries, with hunting rifles being more prevalent in Canada and hand guns or assault weapons more frequently held in the United States, the potential answer might lie in the aggressive images that will be activated by different types of weapons, leading us back to individual psychological processes. Thus, even though sociologists are more likely to link individual behaviour to social structural variables, while social psychologists are more likely to study individual processes, a combination of the two approaches might often provide a fuller explanation than either discipline can offer on its own.

A BRIEF HISTORY OF SOCIAL PSYCHOLOGY

The beginning

Who conducted the first experiment and who wrote the first textbook?

Authors who write about the history of a scientific discipline usually like to report dates that mark the origin of that discipline. Often these are the years in which the first textbooks or handbooks bearing the name of the discipline were published. In social psychology, 1908 is usually noted as the year when the first two textbooks of social psychology were published, one by a sociologist (Ross, 1908), the other by a psychologist (McDougall, 1908). However, since both texts cover very little material that we would consider social psychological these days, 1908 may not be the best choice for the birth year of social psychology.

One could also argue that using the date of the first textbook to mark the beginning of a discipline is questionable anyway, because it would be difficult to write a textbook about a discipline that did not already exist. There must first be relevant theorizing and research available with which to fill the pages of a textbook. It is probably for this reason that another date has become quite prominent in chapters on the history of social psychology, namely the date of (presumably) the first social psychological experiment, a study published in 1898 by Norman Triplett.

Triplett appeared to have been a fan of bicycle races. He was interested in the phenomenon whereby racing cyclists go faster when racing with others or when being paced than when riding alone, racing against the clock. Illustrating the research tool of 'archival analysis' (see Chapter 2), Triplett (1898) used records of the average speed of cyclists under these different conditions; he could indeed demonstrate that cyclists ride faster in competition or with pacers than when riding alone. However, as Triplett recognized, the shortcoming of this kind of quasi-experimental evidence is that different racers participate in different kinds of races and select those in which they do particularly well. The differences in speed between cyclists racing against the clock or racing in competition could therefore have been due to self-selection. To rule out this explanation, Triplett (1898) conducted an experiment in which schoolchildren performed a simple task (turning a fishing reel) either alone or in competition with another participant (see Research Close-Up 1.1). The experiment is usually cited as demonstrating the effects of what later became known as **social facilitation**, the phenomenon whereby the performance of simple tasks is facilitated by the presence of an audience or of others working on the same task (see Chapter 8). However, if you read the Research Close-Up, you will realize that his data do not warrant such a strong conclusion.

Although the study by Triplett (1898; reprinted in Smith & Haslam, 2012) had the elegance and clarity that

social facilitation an improvement in the performance of well-learned/easy tasks and a worsening of performance of poorly-learned/difficult tasks due to the presence of members of the same species.

TRIPLETT'S CLASSIC STUDY OF SOCIAL FACILITATION EFFECTS

RESEARCH CLOSE-UP 1.1

Triplett, N. (1898). The dynamogenic factors in pacemaking and competition. *American Journal of Psychology*, 9, 507–533.

Introduction

Triplett suggested several theoretical explanations for the superiority of cyclists who are paced or ride in a competition over those who ride alone. For example, there could be aerodynamic or psychological advantages for a racer who was paced or racing in a competition. However, Triplett was most interested in what he called 'dynamogenic factors', namely that 'the presence of another rider is a stimulus to the racer in arousing the competitive instinct; that another can thus be the means of releasing or freeing nervous energy from him that he cannot of himself release' (p. 516). His concept of nervous energy appears to be similar to the modern concept of arousal.

Method

Participants

Forty schoolchildren (14 boys, 26 girls) from 8 to 17 years participated in the study.

Design and procedure

The apparatus consisted of two fishing reels fixed to a wooden frame and placed sufficiently far apart so that two people could turn them side-by-side. A cord was looped from each of the fishing reels through corresponding wheels fixed to the opposite end of the frame, creating two closed circuits (like the circuit formed by the chain on a bicycle). A small white flag was sewn to each of the cords. By winding the fishing reel the flag traversed the course from the fishing reel to the wheel at the opposite end and back again. A trial consisted of four circuits of the course and the time taken for this performance was measured by stopwatch. After an initial practice session to become proficient with the apparatus, each participant performed

six test trials. Triplett created a somewhat complicated but quite ingenious design, with the sequence of alone and competition trials differing for Groups A and B in a systematic way (see Table 1.1).

The rationale behind these two sequences was that it eliminated practice as well as fatigue effects. Both effects are related to the number of trials performed by a participant (i.e., trial order). One would expect that during the first few trials performance improves due to practice. In later trials fatigue might set in and begin to slow down participants. Triplett controlled for both of these effects from trial 2 onwards by having the task performed under both conditions during each of the trials. As Strube (2005) who reanalysed Triplett's data pointed out, the first trial allows the assessment of individual differences in winding skill and provides a potential control for those differences in the statistical analyses. Trials 2 to 6 allow two basic kinds of comparisons, namely between groups and within subjects. Trial 2 is particularly important because both groups have equal practice but neither had previous experience with a coactor. Once participants had competed against a coactor, this experience might have influenced their performance in later alone conditions.

Results

Triplett categorized his participants into three groups on the basis of their performance during the various trials: those who were stimulated positively by competition and performed faster ($N = 20$), those who were 'overstimulated' and performed more slowly ($N = 10$), and those who were not affected ($N = 10$). From visual inspection of his data, Triplett concluded that his findings showed 'that the bodily presence of another contestant participating simultaneously in the race serves to liberate latent

Table 1.1 *Sequence of alone and competition trials for Groups A and B in Triplett's design.*

Trials:	1	2	3	4	5	6
Group A	alone	competition	alone	competition	alone	competition
Group B	alone	alone	competition	alone	competition	alone

energy not ordinarily available' (p. 533). This conclusion formed the basis of the myth reported in most textbooks that his study provided the first evidence for social facilitation. These days conclusions based on visual inspection of data are no longer accepted and journal editors require that researchers conduct (often extensive) statistical analysis of their results, and test how likely the results are to be due to chance. When Strube (2005) reanalysed Triplett's data more than a century after the publication of the original study using modern statistics, he found very little support for the original conclusion. Only one of several analyses resulted in a significant effect. This effect disappeared, however, when Strube eliminated the data of two left-handed participants, for whom the task would have been more difficult, as they were instructed to turn the wheel with their right hand. As you will learn in Chapter 8, the presence of others facilitates performance only for easy tasks, but inhibits performance with difficult tasks. Elimination of the left-handed participants should

therefore have strengthened rather than weakened the social facilitation effects. Strube concluded that 'the analysis of Triplett's data . . . indicate[s] barely a statistical hint of the social facilitation of performance to which his experiment has been credited' (2005, p. 280). This is quite different from the conclusions usually drawn in textbooks of social psychology.

Discussion

If significance tests had already been available and required by journal editors in 1898, Triplett's study might never have been published and historians of social psychology would have had to look elsewhere for the first experiment (Stroebe, 2012; Strube, 2005). It is nevertheless puzzling that Triplett failed to find clear evidence of social facilitation. After all, turning a fishing reel is a simple mechanical task and competition should clearly have facilitated performance.

became the hallmark of experimentation in social psychology, its historical significance has been challenged by scholars who doubted whether it really was the *first* social psychological experiment. For example, Haines and Vaughan (1979) have argued that there were other experiments before 1898 deserving to be called social psychological, such as studies on suggestibility by Binet and Henri (1894; see Stroebe, 2012). But social psychological experiments may have been performed even earlier by the French agricultural engineer Max Ringelmann, who between 1882 and 1887 conducted investigations into the maximum performance of workers pulling a load under different conditions (Kravitz & Martin, 1986). Although the comparison of individual and group performance was of only secondary interest to Ringelmann, he found the first evidence of productivity loss in groups, a phenomenon that was later named **social loafing** (see Chapter 13). Ringelmann found that eight men who pull at a rope together achieve only about 50 per cent of the pulling power that could be expected on the basis of their pulling measured individually. However, since Ringelmann only published this research in 1913, Triplett predates him, certainly as far as publication is concerned.

It is interesting to note that these early experiments were studies of an applied nature in areas which later

social loafing a motivation loss in groups that occurs when group members reduce their effort due to the fact that individual contributions to group performance are not identifiable.

became known as sports psychology and psychology of work performance. There were other studies of this nature available in other applied areas (e.g., Mayer, 1903; Moede, 1920) and it needed somebody to recognize that the study of the impact of the social context on performance was really a discipline by itself, namely, social psychology. It may then be justifiable to choose the date of the first textbook or handbook about a discipline as its 'origin' insofar as a discipline is characterized not only by its content, but also by its disciplinary identity. Thus, it is not sufficient that research that is vaguely social psychological has been conducted

LEADER IN THE FIELD

Floyd Henry Allport (1890–1978), the elder brother of Gordon Allport (see Leader in the Field, Chapter 14), received both his undergraduate degree (1914) and his PhD (1919) from Harvard University. His dissertation was based on his studies on social facilitation, a research area that had been suggested to him by Hugo Münsterberg, then Professor of Psychology at Harvard. In 1922 Allport obtained a position as Associate Professor of Social Psychology at the University of North Carolina at Chapel Hill. It was here that he began writing his *Social Psychology*, which was widely praised and adopted as a text. This book and his studies on the impact of the group on individual cognitive performance are his major contribution to social psychology. He retired from Syracuse University in 1956.

in the area of sports psychology or even agriculture. There needs to be somebody who pulls all this research together and declares the emergence of a new area (in which, incidentally, this applied research then becomes fundamental).

In our view, this was first achieved by Floyd Allport (1924), who in his textbook made several major contributions towards defining the field of social psychology (see Leader in the Field, Floyd Henry Allport). He declared the study of social behaviour as the subject of social psychology. He defined social behaviour as 'behavior in which the responses either serve as social stimuli or are evoked by social stimuli' (p. 148). As mentioned above, he postulated that social psychology 'is part of the psychology of the individual, whose behavior it studies in relation to that sector of the environment comprised by his fellows' (p. 4). He had noted earlier, in the same volume, 'For . . . only within the individual can we find the behavioral mechanisms and the consciousness which are fundamental in the interactions between individuals' (p. vi). Another contribution, which may be less embraced today, was his emphasis on the experimental method. Although the experimental method is still one of the major research tools of social psychologists, other research methods have become equally accepted these days. However, in Allport's time, the emphasis on experiments was probably essential for establishing the scientific respectability of social psychology. It would also have helped to distinguish it further from sociology, a discipline that still prefers surveys and field studies to conducting experiments. It is interesting, though, that with the exception of his chapter on the 'Response to social stimulation in groups', Allport (1924) did not review a great deal of experimental evidence of a social psychological nature.

Allport's conception of social psychology derived from his research on social facilitation (see Chapter 8). His experimental paradigm, which had the defining characteristics that he attributed to all social psychology research, had been developed 'in Germany by August Mayer, Meumann, Moede and others . . . prior to 1915'; Allport, 1919, p. 304). This strong German influence on his dissertation research is no coincidence, given that his dissertation supervisor was Hugo Münsterberg, a German psychologist who was then head of the psychology department at Harvard. Allport (1924, p. vii) acknowledges Münsterberg's influence in the preface to his book, where he writes, 'For the origins of my interest in social psychology I am indebted to the memory of Hugo Münsterberg. It was he who suggested the setting for my first experiment and who foresaw many of the possibilities which have been developed in this book.'

The early years

What were the key contributions to social psychology during the first half of the twentieth century?

It would be an exaggeration to claim that the publication of Floyd Allport's textbook stimulated an exponential growth in social psychological research immediately. In fact, not that many milestones are to be reported for the period before World War II. A rather doubtful one is the publication of the first *Handbook of Social Psychology* by Carl Murchison (1935). We call it doubtful because this handbook covers many topics which nobody would consider social psychological today, such as 'Population behavior of bacteria' or the 'Social history of the yellow man'. There are really only three chapters included in this volume that are truly social psychological in the sense that they would still be included in social psychology handbooks today: the chapter by Gordon Allport on attitudes, that by Dashiell on 'Experimental studies of the influence of social situation on the behaviour of individual human adults', and Cox Miles's chapter on gender differences. But there are also other chapters that could be part of a social psychology curriculum, even though they are not included in most modern handbooks. For example, there is a chapter on language by Esper, on age in human society by Miles, on material culture by Wissler, and on the physical environment by Shelford.

Three other significant events during this early period were the publication by Thurstone (1928) of a paper with the provocative title 'Attitudes can be measured', *The Psychology of Social Norms* by Sherif in 1936, and Newcomb's (1943) *Personality and Social Change*, a study of attitude formation in the student community of Bennington College (see Leader in the Field, Theodore Newcomb). Thurstone's article was remarkable because he described the first psychometrically sound method for the measurement of attitudes. Sherif's study became a classic, because he devised an experimental paradigm that allowed him to study the development of group norms in a laboratory situation (see Chapter 8). Participants in his study were repeatedly exposed to a stationary light source in a darkened room. Sherif made use of the fact that participants perceive this light source as moving (**autokinetic effect**) and that, if asked to judge the movement over repeated trials, they establish relatively stable individual norms. By putting individuals who had developed widely differing individual estimates into a group situation, Sherif could demonstrate that individuals in groups develop a joint and stable

> **autokinetic effect**
> perceptual illusion, whereby, in the absence of reference points, a stationary light appears to move.

Theodore Newcomb (1903–1984) received his undergraduate degree from Oberlin College in 1924 and entered Union Theological Seminary in New York intending to become a Christian Missionary (Converse, 1994). However, more attracted by the psychology courses taught at Columbia University across the road, he switched to psychology and received his PhD from Columbia in 1929. He joined Bennington College in 1934, a newly founded women's college that drew its students from the politically conservative 'upper crust' of Vermont society, but had a famously liberal atmosphere. His Bennington study of the change in attitudes that these young women underwent during their studies became a classic. Not only was the longitudinal design innovative at that time, but the study captured the interplay between individual and group processes and thus supported one of the central assumptions of social psychology. After a stint of wartime research, he became director of a joint doctoral programme of the departments of sociology and social psychology at the University of Michigan, where he stayed for the remainder of his career. Intrigued by the work of Fritz Heider (see Leader in the Field, Chapter 3), Newcomb developed his own interpersonal version of balance theory.

FIGURE 1.3 *How did Hitler's actions affect the development of social psychology?*

Source: © Dariush M. Used under licence from Shutterstock.

group norm, which they then maintain even when they continue to make their estimates again in individual situations.

Finally, Newcomb's **Bennington study** became a classic, because it is an ingenious longitudinal field study of social influence on a college campus. It maps out the way in which the political attitudes of students, all women who came from conservative homes, changed over time towards the liberal attitudes that were predominant on this college campus. Thus, it illustrates how individual beliefs and attitudes can be shaped by the group context, and thus supports one of the basic assumptions of social psychology. The study is particularly interesting because these students were followed up for 50 years, allowing researchers to demonstrate the stability of their attitude change over a lifetime (Alwin, Cohen, & Newcomb, 1991).

Bennington study a longitudinal field study of social influence showing how political attitudes of initially conservative female students changed over time towards the liberal attitudes that were predominant on this college campus.

The years of expansion

How did Adolf Hitler inadvertently further the development of social psychology in the US?

Somewhat tongue in cheek, Cartwright once wrote that the one person who most furthered the development of social psychology in North America was Adolf Hitler (Cartwright, 1979). This observation is correct insofar as Hitler's actions had an important impact on the development of social psychology in the US. World War II greatly stimulated interest in social psychological research. The Information and Education Branch of the US Army initiated surveys and experiments to assess the impact of army propaganda films on the morale of their soldiers. One social psychologist who became heavily involved in this work was Carl Hovland (see Leader in the Field, Carl Iver Hovland). Originally a learning theorist, Hovland became fascinated by the experimental study of the determinants of attitude change. The work he directed during his army years on experiments in mass communication was eventually published as one of the volumes of the *American Soldier* series under the editorship of the sociologist Stouffer (Hovland, Lumsdaine, & Sheffield, 1949).

After the war, Hovland returned to his academic career and founded the Yale Communication and Attitude Change programme. This programme attracted young

LEADER IN THE FIELD

Carl Iver Hovland (1912–1961) received his bachelor's and master's degrees from Northwestern University in 1932 and 1933. He then moved to Yale to work for his PhD under the prominent learning theorist Clark Hull. After finishing his dissertation in 1936, Hovland was invited to join the Yale faculty, of which he remained a member for the rest of his life. Hovland never abandoned his interest in learning theory. Even when he became fascinated by persuasion and attitude change during his wartime leave from Yale in the period from 1942 to 1945, he used learning theory principles as a theoretical perspective. His wartime research was published (with Lumsdaine and Sheffield) in 1949 in *Experiments in Mass Communication*. After returning to Yale, Hovland established the Yale Communication and Attitude Change programme, which he directed until his premature death in 1961. The research conducted there by Hovland and 30 students and co-workers over a 15-year period established the field of attitude change research as we know it today (Shepard, 1998).

 LEADER IN THE FIELD

Kurt Lewin (1890–1947) studied psychology and philosophy in Berlin. After fulfilling the formal requirements for a PhD in 1914 (a degree he received only in 1916), he volunteered for the army and spent the next four years fighting World War I (Marrow, 1969). He then returned to the University of Berlin to join the Gestalt psychologists Köhler and Wertheimer at the Institute of Psychology, where he stayed until his (permanent) move to the United States in 1933. The time at Berlin University was probably Lewin's most productive period. He attracted an international group of students, developed his field theory, which argued that behaviour is a function of both the person and the environment, and supervised a series of classic studies, mainly conducted by his students as part of their dissertation. These studies addressed fundamental issues of the psychology of motivation. Lewin's interest in social psychology developed only after his move to the United States (Marrow, 1969). In the US he first worked at Cornell University, then moved to the University of Iowa. During his 10 years at the University of Iowa (1935–1945) Lewin conducted some classic experimental studies in social psychology, such as the experiment on the impact of authoritarian and democratic leadership styles on group atmosphere and performance (Lewin, Lippitt, & White, 1939), which later stimulated research on participative leadership to overcome resistance to change (Coch & French, 1948). Lewin became more and more interested in social processes, and in 1944 he moved to the Massachusetts Institute of Technology, where he founded the Research Center for Group Dynamics.

researchers from a variety of universities and generated a stream of collaborative studies that defined attitude change research for decades to come (see Chapter 7). The programme resulted in the publication of four highly influential volumes on studies of the determinants of persuasion and attitude change. In the first of these volumes, Hovland, Janis, and Kelley (1953) explored the impact of communicator variables (e.g., prestige, credibility and expertise), communication variables (e.g., fear appeals) and context variables (e.g., salience of reference groups). Although the theoretical perspective of the programme was eclectic, Hovland himself was most comfortable with the view that attitude change was a special form of human learning (Jones, 1998).

A second action of the Hitler regime that advanced the development of social psychology in the US was the forced emigration of Jewish (e.g., Koffka, Lewin, Wertheimer) and even some non-Jewish (e.g., Köhler) academics from Germany. The most important of these émigrés for social psychology was undoubtedly Kurt Lewin, considered by many to be the most charismatic psychologist of his generation (Marrow, 1969). Lewin left the Berlin Psychological Institute in 1933 for the Department of Home Economics at Cornell University, to move in 1935 to the Iowa Child Research Station. In 1945 he established the Research Center for Group Dynamics at the Massachusetts Institute of Technology, which, after his premature death in 1947 at the age of 57 years, was moved to the University of Michigan (see Leader in the Field, Kurt Lewin).

It is difficult to understand today how and why Lewin became such a key figure in social psychology. As is the case today, the impact of a researcher in those days was mainly determined by three factors: (1) a great number

of publications in top journals; (2) the development of a theory, which stimulated a great deal of research; or (3) training of a stream of outstanding graduate students, who would later continue the work. Lewin did not score all that well on the first two criteria. Although Lewin's students were highly productive, he himself published only a few empirical studies in social psychology, the most well known being the study of autocratic and democratic leadership (Lewin et al., 1939), which initiated interest in the impact of leadership styles on group atmosphere and performance (see Chapter 13). His **field theory** provided a framework for looking at the forces (e.g., positive and negative valences) that influence the individual in a social situation. However, it did not lend itself easily to the derivation of testable hypotheses. Even his own empirical work was only very loosely related to that theory. And as Morton Deutsch (1968), one of Lewin's most eminent students, concluded two decades after Lewin's death: 'It cannot be said that field theory as a specific psychological theory has much current vitality. Nor can it be said that Lewin's specific theoretical constructs . . . are central to research now being carried out in social psychology' (p. 478). So how could Lewin become so influential? As Deutsch (1968) explains,

field theory a framework adopted by Kurt Lewin which represented the individual as an element in a larger system of social forces.

Lewin's 'impact is reflected instead in his general orientation to psychology, which has left its impression on his colleagues and students' (Deutsch, 1968, p. 478). Lewin believed that psychological events must be explained in psychological terms and that central processes in the 'life space' or psychological field of the individual such as cognition, motivation and goals are the proper focus of investigation. This theoretical perspective offered an exciting alternative to the behaviouristic theories that dominated psychology at that time. Furthermore, Lewin's approach to social psychology had two characteristics which were novel at the time. For him, a problem was only worth studying if addressing it would make a difference with regard to actual problems in the world (Festinger, 1980). Second, and more importantly, he insisted on studying such problems experimentally and on creating in the laboratory powerful situations that made a big difference (Festinger, 1980). Lewin instilled these ideas in his graduate students, and his impact on social psychology was mainly due to these graduate students, who, as a group, were highly influential during the second half of the twentieth century.

All these individuals shaped the field of experimental social psychology in the post-war period, but the most illustrious among them was undoubtedly Leon Festinger, whose theory of cognitive dissonance dictated the research agenda in social psychology during the 1960s and 1970s (Festinger, 1957; see also Chapter 7; Leader in the Field, Leon Festinger). The theory of

social comparison processes, which he had developed earlier (Festinger, 1954), had less of an immediate impact, but is still influential today (see e.g., Chapters 5, 8, 10 and 12).

Another important émigré was the Austrian, Fritz Heider (see Leader in the Field, Fritz Heider, in Chapter 3), although in this case Hitler cannot be blamed for his emigration. Heider came to the US in 1930 to work with Kurt Koffka, who was then at Smith College in Northampton, Massachusetts. He had initially planned to stay for only one year, but decided to remain when he fell in love with Grace Moore, whom he later married. He moved to the University of Kansas in 1947, where he remained until his retirement. His impact on the field is intriguing, because he was not a prolific writer, attracted few graduate students, and published no experimental research in social psychology. Yet he stimulated two of the theoretical traditions which dominated social psychology during the second half of the last century, namely **consistency theories** and **attribution theories**. With his paper on **balance theory** in 1946, Heider developed the notion central to consistency theories that inconsistency between our attitudes and beliefs creates tension in our cognitive system and a tendency to establish consistency. Although only a limited amount of research has been conducted to test Heider's balance theory, the theory stimulated the development of other consistency theories, most importantly the theory of cognitive dissonance.

With his paper on phenomenal causality, published in 1944, and his monograph *The Psychology of Interpersonal Relations*, published in 1958, Heider initiated another important theoretical perspective, namely attribution theory (see Chapter 3). Attribution theory is a social psychological theory about how individuals manage to infer the 'causes' underlying the behaviour of others, or even their own behaviour. In trying to interpret behaviour, we will typically attempt to disentangle the contribution of internal causes (e.g., personality traits, motivation) from external causes (e.g., situational factors). For example, if a mother learns that her son has received a poor grade in his first maths test, she will

consistency theories
a group of theories (see balance theory, cognitive dissonance theory) proposing that people prefer congruence or consistency among their various cognitions, especially among their beliefs, values, and attitudes.

attribution theories
a group of theories about how individuals manage to infer the 'causes' underlying the behaviour of others, or even their own behaviour.

balance theory a cognitive consistency theory that assumes that individuals strive to maintain consistency or balance (objects or persons perceived as belonging together are evaluated similarly) in their social perceptions.

 LEADER IN THE FIELD

Leon Festinger (1919–1990) completed his undergraduate studies at City College in New York, and his graduate research at the University of Iowa with Kurt Lewin (see Leader in the Field). After receiving his PhD in 1942, and a stint of wartime research, he rejoined Lewin and the newly formed Center for Group Dynamics at the Massachusetts Institute of Technology in 1945. In 1948, he moved with the Center to the University of Michigan, from there to the University of Minnesota in 1951, on to Stanford in 1955, and finally, in 1968, to the New School for Social Research in New York, where he stayed until his retirement (Schachter, 1994). During his period at MIT, Festinger, Schachter, and Back (1950) conducted their classic study of friendship patterns and residential proximity (see Chapter 11). Festinger (1950) published his first theoretical paper in social psychology on informal social communication and the process, via social comparison, of establishing the correctness of one's beliefs. These ideas were later elaborated in his paper on social comparison processes (Festinger, 1954). Soon afterwards, Festinger (1957) published the work for which he is best known, his theory of cognitive dissonance (see Chapter 7). It marked the end of his interest in social psychology, which shifted, first to the visual system and perception, then to archaeology and the history of religion.

wonder whether this poor result is due to lack of ability, lack of motivation or to an overly zealous maths teacher who gave too tough a test. Deciding between these alternatives will be important for her, because it will suggest different strategies to prevent this situation from happening again.

The impact of attribution theory in stimulating a great deal of research in the 1960s and 1970s is intriguing, because neither Heider's (1958) monograph nor his 1944 article was written in a way that would make it accessible or appealing to the average researcher in North America. There was also very little research to back up Heider's ideas. It is generally accepted that attribution theory became influential because three major figures in the field of social psychology – Edward Jones, Harold Kelley and Bernard Weiner – adopted it and translated it into a language that was more accessible to social psychologists and yielded clear, testable hypotheses (Jones & Davis, 1965; Kelley, 1967; Weiner, 1986). Probably most influential was Kelley's (1967) **covariation theory** (see Chapter 3). This model was appealing because Kelley argued that, in inferring causes of behaviour, our inference process would be analogous to conducting an analysis of variance, a statistical procedure highly familiar to social psychologists. Other influential adaptations of attribution theory were Jones and Davis's (1965) correspondent inference theory and Weiner's (1986) application of attribution theory to achievement motivation and emotion.

covariation theory proposes that observers work out the causes of behaviour by collecting data about comparison cases. Causality is attributed to the person, entity or situation depending on which of these factors covaries with the observed effect.

A final way in which Hitler influenced the development of social psychology is by stimulating interest in topics such as obedience and authoritarianism. Why did the German people accept such an authoritarian regime, and why did so many of them carry out commands they must have perceived as immoral even at the time? These questions stimulated some of the most influential research in social psychology: researchers studied the authoritarian personality (Adorno et al., 1950), the determinants of conformity (Asch, 1955) and obedience (Milgram, 1963). Lewin's interest in the effects of authoritarian and democratic leadership styles can be seen as an attempt to demonstrate the superiority of the democratic style, an attempt that was only partly effective because in his research autocratically led groups outperformed the democratic groups with regard to quantity of production, although democratic leadership produced more creative groups whose performance did not deteriorate so dramatically when the leader was removed (White & Lippitt, 1968).

The crisis years

How and why did the crisis in social psychology develop?

So far the history of social psychology appears to have been one of unmitigated success. Stimulated by World War II, social psychological research expanded enormously and there was soon no single psychology department at a top university that did not also have a strong social psychology unit. But just when social psychology was on the up and up, a **crisis in social psychology** developed that led to years of infighting about the right course one should follow. This crisis was probably initiated by two critical papers published in 1967 and 1973. The first of these two papers was a paper by Kenneth Ring entitled 'Experimental social psychology: Some sober questions about some frivolous values', published in the highly respected *Journal of Experimental Social Psychology*. In this paper, Ring contrasted the vision of Kurt Lewin of a social psychology that would contribute to the solution of important social problems with what he called the 'fun and games' attitude of the social psychology of his day. He argued that: 'Experimental social psychology today seems dominated by values that suggest the following slogan: 'Social psychology ought to be and is a lot of fun . . . Clever experimentation on exotic topics with zany manipulations seems to be the guaranteed formula for success . . . One sometimes gets the impression that an ever-growing coterie of social psychologists is playing (largely for another's benefit) a game of "can you top this?"' (pp. 116–17). Although Ring did not refer to any specific examples of this fun and games approach, his criticism was probably directed at some of the work conducted in tests of dissonance theory.

crisis in social psychology a crisis of confidence among social psychologists that started in the late 1960s and was overcome in subsequent decades. During the crisis years, social psychologists questioned the values, the methods and the scientific status of their discipline.

Ring, although a respected researcher, was not a very central figure in the social psychology of his time. Therefore, the paper stimulated some discussion but did not really have a serious impact on the field. However, in 1973, one of the golden boys of experimental social psychology, Kenneth Gergen, published an article entitled 'Social psychology as history' in the top journal of our discipline, the *Journal of Personality and Social Psychology*. As the title already suggests, Gergen's article was not an attack on the values directing social psychological research. Much more seriously, he questioned its scientific value. His two most important arguments were (1) that knowledge of social psychological principles could change our behaviour in ways which would negate these principles, and (2) that since the basic motives assumed by many of our theories are unlikely to be genetically determined, they might be affected by cultural change.

As an example of the first principle, Gergen argued that once groups were aware of their tendency to make extreme decisions (i.e., group polarization; see Chapter 8), they might consciously counteract this tendency in their decision-making. As an example of the second principle, Gergen used social comparison and dissonance theory. Social comparison theory assumes that people have a desire to evaluate themselves accurately and do this by comparing themselves to others. Gergen argued that one could easily imagine societies in which such a desire would not exist. Similarly, dissonance theory assumes a need for consistency, which not everybody might share. Gergen saw these problems as the main reason why, as he claimed, social psychological research often failed to be replicable, and hence did not result in a body of cumulative knowledge.

Most researchers these days would accept these arguments without questioning the scientific status of social psychology. With regard to Gergen's first point, we would argue that it would be difficult, even for a trained social psychologist, to keep in mind all situations in which our behaviour might be affected by others, to recognize all the relevant cues signalling such situations, and then to counteract the situational pressures. With regard to his second point, the jury is still out. There is increasing evidence that repeating the same social psychology study in different parts of the world often leads to rather different results (see Chapter 15). However, such variation does not necessarily challenge the assumption that there are universal social processes. After all, cultural differences might merely qualify such universal processes. For example, it is hard to imagine societies in which people do not engage in social comparison, because the evaluation of one's own abilities through social comparison is highly functional and essential for effective action. However, we do know that there are individual differences in the need for social comparison (Gibbons & Buunk, 1999), as there are in individual need for consistency (Cialdini, Trost, & Newsom, 1995). Since there are substantial individual differences within cultures, differences between cultures would not necessarily imply that the theories of social comparison or cognitive consistency should not apply to other cultures.

Gergen's (1973) critique would probably have been less effective had it not come at a time when the collective self-esteem of social psychologists had been undermined by other developments. For one, there was an attack on the usefulness of a concept that Allport (1935) had hailed as the most central concept of social psychology.

In a review of studies that empirically assessed the value of social attitudes in predicting behaviour, the sociologist Alan Wicker (1969) drew the following conclusion: 'Taken as a whole, these studies suggest that it is considerably more likely that attitudes will be unrelated or only slightly related to overt behavior than that attitudes will be closely related to actions' (p. 65). This conclusion was highly damaging, since social psychologists were interested in attitudes mainly because they expected them to predict behaviour. Since attitude change in most studies is assessed through an individual's self-rated position on some attitude dimension, the news that such ratings might be unrelated to behaviour was devastating.

A second development with a negative impact on the collective self-esteem of the scientific community of social psychologists was the publication of a series of papers that were highly critical of the experimental method (see Chapter 2). Thus, Martin Orne (1962) had suggested that most experimental situations contained **demand characteristics**, which would help research participants to guess the hypothesis to be tested in a given study. Since participants typically tried to be 'good subjects', Orne argued, they would then do their best to support these hypotheses.[1] Even more damaging was the suggestion of Robert Rosenthal (Rosenthal & Fode, 1963) that the expectations of the experimenter might influence the behaviour of research participants, even without their knowledge (**experimenter expectancy effect**). The impact of these expectations on the behaviour of research participants could, for example, be mediated by experimenters' reacting positively to responses that supported their hypotheses and negatively to responses that were inconsistent with expectations.

> **demand characteristics** cues that are perceived as telling participants how they are expected to behave or respond in a research setting; that is, cues that 'demand' a certain sort of response.

> **experimenter expectancy effect** produced unintentionally by the experimenter that increases the likelihood that participants will confirm the experimenter's hypothesis.

The reaction to these critical voices was the organization of numerous conferences in which the crisis was discussed, sometimes in rather heated language. Although these conferences resulted in a number of crisis books (e.g., Strickland, Aboud, & Gergen, 1976), they failed to bridge the theoretical and methodological chasm that separated the critics from mainstream social psychology. The critics finally founded their own social psychological schools, such as social constructionism in the United States (e.g., Gergen, 1999) and discourse analysis in the United Kingdom (e.g., Potter & Wetherell, 1987), which developed their own methodologies in an attempt to address these problems.

Overcoming the crisis

How was the crisis overcome?

In mainstream social psychology a number of developments were initiated, which over the years helped to alleviate some of the problems highlighted by these critics:

- Social psychologists began to demonstrate their ability to contribute to the solution of real-life problems by developing several applied areas, which contributed to resolving important societal problems. To mention only one such area, health psychology is an application of social psychology. One of the major research areas in health psychology is aimed at changing health-impairing behaviour patterns in our society (e.g., smoking, eating too much, drinking too much alcohol, practising unsafe sex). Social psychologists have helped to understand the reasons why people engage in these behaviours as well as to develop interventions aimed at changing them (Stroebe, 2011). The following chapters in this volume give many additional examples of how social psychology can be, and has been, applied to real social issues.

- The impression that social psychological research did not result in cumulative knowledge may have been the result of improper strategies of reviewing, a problem that was mostly resolved with the development of meta-analytic procedures (see Chapter 2). When reviewing research areas, researchers often erroneously concluded that support for a theory was missing or inconsistent, because few studies supported the theory by yielding significant results, whereas the majority of studies failed to find significant results. In the meantime, we have realized as a discipline (as has science, in general) that the failure to find significant results may simply have been due to conducting a study with an insufficiently large number of participants. If the effects we were looking for were small, this might have resulted in insignificant findings, even though the differences between conditions might all have been in the predicted direction. Since then, meta-analytic procedures have been developed which allow us to integrate statistically the results of independent studies of a given phenomenon, with a view to establishing whether the findings exhibit a pattern of relationships that is reliable across studies (Cooper & Hedges, 1994).

- We now know that attitudes are predictive of behaviour but that this relationship is often obscured in studies which employ inappropriate procedures in measuring the two components (see Chapter 6). As Ajzen and Fishbein (1977) demonstrated in their classic review, attitudes are related to behaviour if both components are assessed with measures that are both reliable and compatible. To be reliable, measures have to consist of multiple items rather than a single item. To be compatible, attitude and behaviour have to be assessed at the same level of specificity. Thus, if we want to predict whether people are likely to engage in physical exercise to improve their health, we should not measure their attitude towards their health, but their attitude towards engaging in physical exercise. The latter attitude is likely to be highly correlated with an aggregate measure of a variety of exercise behaviours (such as jogging, walking, going to the gym). If one wanted to predict specific exercise behaviour, such as whether an individual is likely to jog, one should measure his or her attitude towards jogging rather than towards physical exercise in general.

- Finally, social psychologists have tried to design their experimental manipulations in ways that would minimize the threat of demand characteristics and experimenter expectancy effects. Furthermore, the fact that many research participants do not even meet experimenters any more (because experiments are often run on the computer by computer programs) should certainly rule out experimenter expectancy effects. The depressing fact that most experiments do not work out the way they were expected to by the experimenter who designed them also appears to suggest that demand characteristics and experimenter expectancy effects cannot be all that powerful. Festinger (1980) most aptly expressed these feelings when he wrote: 'I've always wondered why, if these spurious experimenter effects were so strong, so many of my own experiments did not show the expected results' (p. 252).

SOCIAL PSYCHOLOGY IN EUROPE

How did social psychology develop in Europe?

Until the end of World War II, the development of social psychology as a discipline was restricted to the US. However, even before the influx of academic refugees in the 1930s, there had been a great deal of European influence on this development. For example, as mentioned earlier, F. Allport's (1924) work on social facilitation had been stimulated by one of his academic teachers at Harvard, the German Hugo Münsterberg, who in turn was familiar with similar work that had been done in Germany by Moede (1920). The experimental work of Bartlett (1932) in Britain on remembering can be viewed as a major precursor of contemporary research on social cognition. And finally, the theorizing underlying Sherif's (1936) studies of norm development is heavily influenced by Gestalt psychology.

However, even though there were individuals in Europe who conducted research that could be considered social psychological, there was no unitary social psychology. This situation continued into the 1960s, even though social psychology groups had been established at a number of European universities. But while there *was* social psychology in Europe, there was no *European social psychology*: there was no European collaboration, and most European researchers had not met each other, nor were they even aware of each other's work.

Obviously, a European network was not necessary for the development of a strong social psychology in some of the European countries where effective social psychology research groups already existed (e.g., Belgium, Britain, the Netherlands and Germany). However, in some other countries it would probably have taken many decades for social psychology to develop. Furthermore, since most of the European researchers met each other, if at all, only at conferences held in the US, without the foundation of a European association European social psychology would probably have remained a minor appendix of North American social psychology rather than developing its own theoretical perspective. Thus, the foundation of the European Association of Experimental Social Psychology was critical.

Given the dominance of North American social psychology at that time, even in Europe, it is no coincidence that it was again an American, John Lanzetta, who set things in motion in 1963. During a sabbatical year in London, Lanzetta, then Professor of Social Psychology at the University of Delaware, visited various social psychology groups in Europe. He was struck by the fact that many of these colleagues, though well informed about US social psychology, were not really aware of what was going on in the social psychology departments of neighbouring European countries. He decided to change this and raised funds for a first European Conference on Experimental Social Psychology, held in Sorrento, Italy, in 1963 (Moscovici & Marková, 2006; Nuttin, 1990). One of the main initiatives which emerged from this and two follow-up conferences was the foundation

of the European Association of Experimental Social Psychology (EAESP) in 1966. The European Association engaged in a number of regular activities, which had a great impact on the development of social psychology in Europe. These included:

- Summer schools for advanced students, taught by outstanding researchers.

- Publication of the *European Journal of Social Psychology* from 1970, which included most of the early research thought of (then at least) as typically 'European' (e.g., studies of intergroup relations or minority influence). Other key European publications were, first, the *European Monographs* series and, later, the *European Review of Social Psychology*. The first edition of the textbook you are reading now was published in 1988, in part to counteract the tendency of American textbooks to under-report the work of European social psychologists.

- The regular organization of conferences, including plenary meetings of the whole membership, and special East–West meetings (the latter were particularly effective forums at a time when travel and currency restrictions made it extremely difficult for social psychologists from Eastern and Western Europe to meet).

Membership of the **European Association of Social Psychology** (EASP), as it is known now after dropping 'experimental' from its name in 2008, has grown at a phenomenal rate, from fewer than 100 in 1970 to more than 1000 members in 2010. During this period, scientific development in social psychology also changed from being a one-sided enterprise, with American ideas being adopted in Europe, to a mutual development, with European ideas being taken up enthusiastically in the United States and ever-increasing collaboration leading to scientific growth. It is now accepted practice for prominent North American journals (*Journal of Personality and Social Psychology*, *Journal of Experimental Social Psychology* and *Personality and Social Psychology Bulletin*) to have at least one European editor, and likewise for the *European Journal of Social Psychology* to have non-European editors.

> **European Association of Social Psychology** (EASP) an association formed by European researchers in 1966 to further social psychology in Europe (originally named the European Association of Experimental Social Psychology (EAESP)).

Probably the two most important examples of European ideas influencing social psychology in the United States are research on intergroup behaviour and on minority influence. Although Henri Tajfel was not the first to conduct experimental research on intergroup behaviour (that honour goes to Sherif), he developed the paradigm (the *minimal group paradigm*) that turned intergroup behaviour into a major research area (see Chapter 14). The minimal group paradigm offered an easy and very economical procedure for the study of intergroup behaviour, but Tajfel and Turner (1979, 1986) developed from it a theoretical framework that could account for these findings, social identity theory (see Chapter 14).

The second theoretical innovation that was started in Europe and then accepted in the United States is research on minority influence. Social influence research in North America focused exclusively on conformity, that is, on explaining how majorities influence minorities. It was Moscovici who first pointed out that this type of theorizing could hardly explain social or religious innovations, where powerless minorities influenced powerful majorities (e.g., women's rights, Christianity). After Moscovici and his colleagues in Paris (e.g., Moscovici, Lage, & Naffrechoux, 1969) had published a number of studies demonstrating minority influence, and again with the development of a theory that could account for these effects, research on minority influence became a major research area both in the US and in Europe (Moscovici, 1976; see Chapter 8).

SOCIAL PSYCHOLOGY TODAY

What new theoretical perspectives have emerged during the last few decades?

In the 1980s most of the researchers who had contributed to modern social psychology, and who, as often as not, had come from the research centres directed by either Lewin or Hovland, were still alive and active (Cartwright, 1979). In the meantime, not only have many of these pioneers retired or died, but so also have most of the students whom they, in turn, had trained. The field has grown at an exponential rate. There are now chairs in social psychology at practically all major universities in the United States, in Europe, and in Australasia, and social psychologists number in the thousands rather than a few hundreds. Social psychology has also become an essential part of the psychology curriculum in these countries.

Not surprisingly, social psychology has also changed over these decades. Major scientific perspectives, such as consistency theory or attribution theory, have faded and

new perspectives, such as **social cognition**, **evolutionary social psychology** and **social neuroscience**, have emerged. Jones (1998) colourfully described these changing trends in research as 'band wagons and sinking ships' (p. 54).

Social cognition research is an application of principles of cognitive psychology to the area of social psychology (see Devine, Hamilton, & Ostrom, 1994). Unlike other psychological disciplines, social psychology has always placed a strong emphasis on how individuals internally represent their environment. Many of our theories have been labelled 'cognitive' (e.g., cognitive dissonance), and central concepts of social psychology (e.g., attitudes, beliefs, intentions) are cognitive constructs. It would thus appear a small step for social psychologists to borrow methods from cognitive psychology to study how social information is encoded and how the information is stored and retrieved from memory. This perspective has had a widespread influence across the field of social psychology, but is seen perhaps most clearly in changes to the way we theorize and do research in person perception (see Chapters 3 and 4), attitude change (Chapter 7), and prejudice and intergroup relations (Chapter 14).

Evolutionary social psychology (e.g., Burnstein & Branigan, 2001; Buss & Kendrick, 1998) is an application of evolutionary theory to social psychology. Evolutionary theory explains human behaviours, including differences in partner preference according to gender, from their reproductive value, that is, their value in producing offspring in our evolutionary past. Evolutionary psychology makes the basic assumption that if a given behaviour is (1) at least partly genetically determined and (2) increases the probability that an individual will produce offspring, the gene that determines this behaviour will become more prevalent in the gene pool of future generations. Evolutionary social psychologists have made important contributions to the study of interpersonal attraction (Chapter 11), helping and cooperation (Chapter 10) and aggression (Chapter 9). The development of evolutionary social psychology as an accepted research area in social psychology is surprising, as talking about genetic determinants of social behaviour was considered heresy in the decades following World War II

social cognition a large topic within social psychology concerned with understanding how we think about ourselves and other people and how the processes involved impact upon our judgements and behaviour in social contexts.

evolutionary social psychology is an application of evolutionary theory to social psychology.

social neuroscience an interdisciplinary field devoted to understanding how biological systems implement social processes and behaviour.

and the defeat of the race ideology of the Hitler regime. However, modern applications of evolutionary social psychology are less deterministic, less ideological and, most importantly, more solidly based on evolutionary theory than such earlier approaches.

Social neuroscience is the study of the neural correlates of social psychological phenomena (Cacioppo & Berntson, 2005; Ochsner & Lieberman, 2001). Building on huge recent advances in the use of non-invasive techniques for examining the functioning of the human brain, social neuroscience studies participants' brains while they are engaged in processing social information. There are two major approaches used by social neuroscience, namely *brain mapping* and *psychological hypothesis testing* (Amodio, 2010). Brain mapping studies (e.g., by functional magnetic resonance imaging, fMRI; see Figure 1.4a) attempt to identify the neural substrates of specific psychological processes. The hypothesis testing approach uses the results of brain mapping to test hypotheses about psychological variables. 'For example, a social psychologist, who studies intergroup prejudice might hypothesize that implicit racial bias is rooted in mechanisms of basic classical fear conditioning. To test this hypothesis, one might measure brain activity in the amygdala – a structure implicated in fear conditioning in many studies – while a participant completes a behavioural measure of implicit racial bias. In this case, the construct validity of the neural measure of fear conditioning . . . is already reasonably established . . . and the question concerns not the meaning of brain activation, but experimental effects among psychological variables' (Amodio, 2010, pp. 699–700).

Studies have already used such techniques to further our understanding of such disparate issues as the self (see Chapter 5), altruism (see Chapter 10), and racial prejudice (see Chapter 14). Some studies, for example, have examined changes in blood flow within the brain (using fMRI; Figure 1.4b) while people are shown race-relevant stimuli under different conditions. Such research has indicated that there is a link between social categorization and the amygdala. Phelps et al. (2000) showed, for example, that White participants' greater amygdala activation in response to Black versus White faces was significantly correlated with their implicit racial prejudice only when the faces were of unknown Black people, but not when they were of famous and well-liked Black and White individuals. These findings suggest that amygdala activation and behavioural responses of race evaluation are heavily shaped by social learning, and that familiarity with members of these groups can modulate bias. Thus, involvement of biological processes does not imply something fundamental and unchangeable. In fact, social neuroscience emphasizes that *social* variables can *influence*

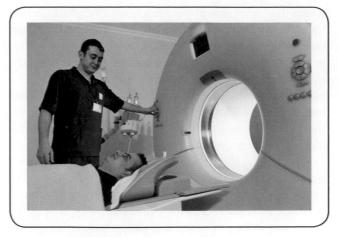

FIGURE 1.4(a) *Functional MRI scanning techniques have already been used to further our understanding of issues such as self, altruism and racial prejudice.*

Source: Image Copyright Levent Konuk. Used under licence from Shutterstock.com.

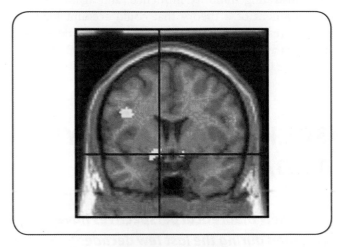

FIGURE 1.4(b) *An fMRI scan shows activation of the amygdala processing social, fear-related information.*

Source: Reproduced from Phelps et al. (2000) *Journal of Cognitive Neuroscience,* Massachusetts Institute of Technology Press with permission.

biological processes (Eberhardt, 2005; Phelps & Thomas, 2003). Furthermore, even if the neural correlates of prejudice can be identified, prejudice is a psychological construct and cannot be redefined as the activation of particular brain regions (Sherman, 2010).

Because brain mapping helps neuroscientists to understand the brain, whereas psychological hypotheses can usually be tested without using neural indicators, it can be argued that social psychology is much more useful in helping neuroscientists to understand the brain than neuroscience is in helping us to understand social psychological processes (Kihlstrom, 2010). As Kihlstrom (2010) nicely put it: 'Psychology without neuroscience is still the science of mental life, but neuroscience without psychology is just a science of neurons' (Kihlstrom, 2010, p. 762).

Despite some setbacks (see Stroebe, Postmes, & Spears, 2012), social psychology today is an exhilarating and thriving enterprise. Living up to Lewin's motto that nothing is as practical as a good theory, social psychologists are applying the understanding they have gained from their study of fundamental cognitive, emotional and motivational processes to the solution of real-life problems. As the chapters in this volume illustrate, they have contributed importantly to the development of applied areas ranging from health psychology, to organizational psychology (see Chapters 12 and 13), to resolving intergroup conflict (see Chapter 14). In the absence of systematic and controlled social psychological research in most areas, F. Allport (1924) had to rely heavily on speculation in his ambitious road map for social psychology as an empirical science. We hope that the readers of this textbook will appreciate the progress social psychologists have made in less than a century in replacing speculation with theory-guided empirical research.

CHAPTER SUMMARY

- *How can social psychology be defined?* Social psychology is often defined as the scientific attempt to understand and explain how thoughts, feelings and behaviours of individuals are influenced by the actual, imagined or implied presence of other human beings.

- *How does social psychology differ from other psychological disciplines?* One of the main differences is the focus on the impact of the characteristics of the social situation on thoughts and behaviour of individuals. Although social psychologists might also be interested in individual differences, they are usually concerned with individual differences in responses to characteristics of the social situation.

- *When was the first social psychology experiment conducted?* There are several candidates that could claim to have been the first experiment in social psychology, but all were conducted just before 1900.

- *When did the first textbook of social psychology appear?* The first textbook that covered topics which would still be considered social psychology today was written by Floyd Allport (1924).

- *Was there much social psychological research before World War II?* Although there was some important research conducted before World War II, most theorizing and research considered part of modern social psychology has been published since 1945.

- *What were the unintended effects of Hitler's actions on social psychology?* World War II created interest in social influence and attitude change. But the crimes of the Nazi regime also stimulated interest in issues such as conformity and obedience. Finally, the forced emigration of Jewish academics strongly shaped the development of social psychology in the US.

- *Who were the émigrés with the greatest influence on social psychology?* The most important émigré was Kurt Lewin. He attracted an illustrious group of students who shaped social psychology in the decades following World War II. Another influential émigré was the Austrian Fritz Heider, who left Europe for personal reasons. He stimulated two theoretical traditions, consistency theory and attribution theory, which dominated social psychology in the decades following World War II.

- *What were the causes of the crisis that developed in social psychology?* There were doubts raised about the societal relevance of social psychological research (i.e., frivolous values) as well as the scientific nature of our methods (i.e., the influence of demand characteristics, experimenter expectancy effects). These doubts were strengthened by the impression that our research did not result in cumulative knowledge and that attitudes did not predict behaviour. Finally it was questioned whether social psychological theories developed and tested in Western cultures (i.e., mainly in the US) would also apply to other cultures.

- *How was the crisis overcome?* Social psychology emerged from the crisis stronger than it was before. Some of the problems were overcome by theoretical or methodological improvements. Others resulted in the emergence of new research areas. For example, cultural social psychology was developed to assess the extent to which our theories are applicable across cultures (see Chapter 15). A strong applied social psychology was developed to demonstrate the societal relevance of social psychological theories and research.

- *What new theoretical perspectives have emerged during the last few decades?* Major scientific perspectives such as consistency theory or attribution theory have faded and new perspectives such as social cognition, evolutionary social psychology and social neuroscience have emerged.

NOTE

1. Early research reports referred to those who took part in psychological research as 'subjects'. It is now standard practice to refer to them as 'participants'.

SUGGESTIONS FOR FURTHER READING

Berscheid, E. (1992). A glance back at a quarter century of social psychology. *Journal of Personality and Social Psychology*, *63*, 525–533. A personal reflection by a leading scholar on developments in North America in the 25 years up to its publication.

Cartwright, D. (1979). Contemporary social psychology in historical perspective. *Social Psychology Quarterly*, *42*, 82–93. A lively attempt to put social psychology into historical perspective, famous for highlighting the 'influence' of Adolf Hitler.

Farr, R. M. (1996). *The roots of modern social psychology: 1872–1954*. Oxford: Blackwell. Scholarly treatment of the background to the modern era, with special reference to the relationship between social psychology and other social sciences.

Jahoda, G. (2007). *A history of social psychology: From the eighteenth-century enlightenment to the Second World War*. Cambridge, UK: Cambridge University Press. Another book that provides great insights into the history of ideas which finally led to the development of modern social psychology.

Kruglanski, A. W., & Stroebe, W. (Eds.). (2012). *Handbook of the history of social psychology*. New York: Psychology Press. Researchers, who have substantially contributed to central areas of social psychology, present their view of the development of their particular research area.

Moscovici, S., & Marková, I. (2006). *The making of modern social psychology: The hidden story of how an international social science was created*. Cambridge, UK: Polity. This book tells the fascinating story of how European social psychology was born.

Smith, J., & Haslam, S. A. (Eds.). (2012). *Social psychology: Revisiting the classic studies*. Thousand Oaks, CA: Sage. This book re-presents some of the classic studies in the field, reported in this and the following chapters (e.g., Triplett, Asch, Milgram), providing the background to each study, a summary of the main results and their impact, and a consideration of alternative interpretations and methodological issues.

2 Research Methods in Social Psychology

Antony S. R. Manstead and Andrew G. Livingstone

KEY TERMS

- confederate
- construct
- construct validity
- control group
- convergent validity
- cover story
- debriefing
- demand characteristics
- dependent variable
- discourse analysis
- experiment
- experimental confound
- experimental group
- experimental scenario

- experimenter
- expectancy effect
- external validity
- factorial experiment
- field experiment
- hypothesis
- implicit measures
- independent variable
- interaction effect
- internal validity
- Internet experiment
- main effect
- manipulation check
- mediating variable

- meta-analysis
- one-shot case study
- operationalization
- participants
- participant observation
- post-experimental enquiry
- post-test only control group design
- quasi-experiment
- quota sample
- random allocation
- reactivity
- reliability

- sampling
- simple random sample
- social desirability
- social neuroscience
- survey research
- theory
- triangulation
- true randomized experiment
- unobtrusive measures
- validity
- variable

CHAPTER OUTLINE

INTRODUCTION 27

  Summary 28

RESEARCH STRATEGIES 30

  Experiments and quasi-experiments 30
  Survey research 33
  Qualitative approaches 34
  Summary 36

A CLOSER LOOK AT EXPERIMENTATION IN SOCIAL PSYCHOLOGY 36

  Features of the social psychological experiment 36
  Experimental designs 38
  Threats to validity in experimental research 41

Social psychological experiments on the Internet 43
  Problems with experimentation 45
  Summary 46

DATA COLLECTION METHODS 47

  Observational methods 47
  Self-report methods 48
  Implicit and physiological methods 49
  Choosing a method 50
  Social neuroscience 51
  Summary 51

CHAPTER SUMMARY 51

ROUTE MAP OF THE CHAPTER

This chapter provides an overview of research methods in social psychology, from the development of theory to the collection of data. After describing three quantitative research strategies (experiments and quasi-experiments, and survey research), the chapter briefly discusses qualitative approaches, focusing on discourse analysis. There follows a description of the key elements of experimentation, as this is the most popular research method in social psychology. We also consider threats to validity in experimental research, and discuss problems with experimental research in social psychology. The final section of the chapter contains a description of different methods of data collection (observation, self-report, implicit, and physiological methods).

INTRODUCTION

How do social psychologists go about testing their theories?

Why should a chapter about the technical aspects of research methods come so early in this textbook? Why do we need to study research methods, rather than go directly to the real substance of social psychological phenomena and explanations for those phenomena? To answer these questions, we need to consider an even more fundamental question: Why do psychologists conduct research in the first place?

As social psychologists, we are of course interested in 'big' phenomena. What causes intergroup conflict? Why do people stereotype members of other groups? How do we form impressions of other people? Why do people behave differently when they are in a group? What leads people to change their attitudes? What factors influence whether close relationships succeed or fail? To answer these questions, we develop *theories*. For

> **theory** a set of abstract concepts (i.e., constructs) together with propositions about how those constructs are related to one another.

> **construct** an abstract theoretical concept (such as social influence).

> **variable** the term used to refer to the measurable representation of a construct.

example, we might want to develop a **theory** about the causes of intergroup conflict. In the first instance, this involves identifying **constructs** (abstract concepts, such as 'threat', or 'prejudice') or **variables** (a measurable representation of a construct, such as scores on questionnaire measures of threat perceptions or intergroup hostility) that we think are relevant to the question, and speculating about how these relate to one another. Crucially, our theories typically consist of propositions about *causal relationships* between constructs. In this way, we are not content with simply *describing* these 'big' phenomena; rather, we seek to *explain* them by identifying their antecedents. In developing a theory of intergroup conflict (see Chapter 14), we are not only interested in what conflict is like, but also in what causes it and how it might be reduced. For example, we might theorize that intergroup conflict is caused by feelings that the interests or well-being of one's own group are threatened by another group (see Branscombe, Ellemers, Spears, & Doosje, 1999).

We might initially base our theories on observation of real-life events, on intuition or on existing theories. But coming up with theories is only part of the story. Many other disciplines – such as philosophy, sociology, and anthropology – are concerned with the same issues and phenomena that interest social psychologists.

What helps to distinguish social psychology – and psychology as a whole – from these other disciplines is not simply the *type* of explanation we provide, but also a commitment to the *scientific method*, in which we test our theories against *evidence*. This introduces an essential characteristic of a theory: it must be *testable*. This means that we should be able to derive specific predictions (or hypotheses) from the theory concerning the relationship between two or more constructs, and to gather evidence that could support or contradict those predictions. If the data support the theory, it should be retained. However, if the data contradict the theory, it should be challenged and ultimately refuted. Existing theories should be replaced by new theories that can either (a) do a better job of accounting for the available data, (b) account for the data with fewer assumptions or core constructs (i.e., they are more parsimonious), (c) account for the existing data and *new* data, which the existing theory cannot account for, or (d) stimulate further research and more sophisticated theorization, helping us to ask better research questions and generate new hypotheses (for a general discussion of theories and theory evaluation, see Tzeng & Jackson, 1991).

Consider Janis's (1982) theory about the poor quality of decision-making that is apparent even in groups of competent and experienced persons – a phenomenon he termed 'groupthink' (see Chapter 8). Janis's (1982) theory consists of one set of concepts representing the antecedent conditions of poor group decision-making, another set representing the symptoms of groupthink, a third set representing symptoms of poor decision-making and a final set representing the process linking antecedent conditions to the symptoms of groupthink and poor decision-making (see Theory Box 2.1). One of the *antecedent conditions* is a 'cohesive group', a group whose members are psychologically dependent on the group. Because they are dependent on their group membership, they are more likely to conform to what they believe to be the consensual position in the group. An example *symptom* of groupthink is the presence of 'mind guards', a term Janis used to describe group members who take it on themselves to protect the group from information that questions the correctness or morality of an emerging decision. An example symptom of defective decision-making is failure to examine the risks of the preferred decision. Janis also specified how groupthink is brought about (i.e., the *mediating process*). In this case, the mediating process is a premature 'concurrence-seeking tendency', a powerful preference for agreement with fellow group members, before all these issues have been properly discussed. Thus antecedent conditions are linked to symptoms via a mediating process; we discuss the concept of mediation in more detail later in this chapter.

THEORY BOX 2.1

ANTECEDENT CONDITIONS, MEDIATING PROCESS AND SYMPTOMS OF GROUPTHINK IN JANIS'S (1982) THEORETICAL MODEL

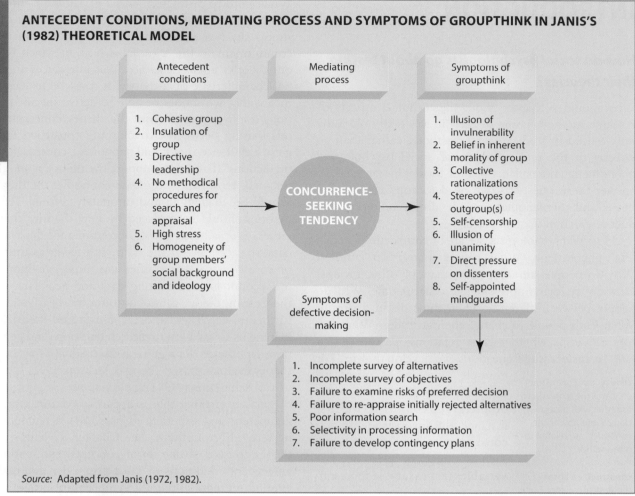

Source: Adapted from Janis (1972, 1982).

A prediction that we can derive logically from Janis's theory is that groups that are more cohesive should be more prone to making poor-quality decisions than groups that are less cohesive (see Research Close-Up 2.1). To the extent that the evidence is consistent with the prediction, we can be more confident in the theory from which we derived the prediction. Correspondingly, if the evidence is inconsistent with the prediction, we should be less confident in the underlying theory. Evidence might also reveal limits or *boundary conditions* to a predicted effect, showing that it only occurs under specific circumstances. An example of boundary conditions in relation to Janis's theory comes from research conducted by Postmes, Spears, and Cihangir (2001), who found that the effect of group cohesiveness on the quality of a group's decisions depended upon the *norm* of the group. Specifically, the quality of decisions was improved when the group had a norm of critical thinking compared to when it had a norm of maintaining consensus. In the light of this sort of evidence, the original theory may need to be modified, or even rejected entirely in favour of an alternative.

Now we can see why research methods are so important. They are the essential tools of our trade, providing a way of translating our ideas into actions, and of testing, challenging and improving our theories. The quality of our research depends not only on the quality of our theories, but on the quality of the research methods we use to test those theories.

Summary

Methods are the tools researchers use to test their theoretical ideas. These ideas can come from a variety of sources, but two that are quite common in social psychology are observations of real-life events and inconsistencies between previous research findings. A theory consists of a set of constructs linked together in a system, and specifies when particular phenomena should occur.

ARCHIVAL ANALYSES OF 'GROUPTHINK'

Janis, I. L. (1972). Victims of groupthink: A psychological study of foreign-policy decisions and fiascoes. Boston, MA: Houghton Mifflin.

Introduction

Janis's research on groupthink provides an excellent example of 'archival research', a research strategy that is not described or discussed elsewhere in the present chapter. In archival research the data come from archives – that is, from stored records of facts. 'Archival data may include such items as personal documents (letters or diaries), creative products (poems, paintings, essays), biographies or autobiographies, and histories or governmental records' (Simonton, 1981, p. 218). Janis (1972) decided to study in detail archival material relating to four major US foreign policy fiascoes: the Bay of Pigs invasion of Cuba in 1961; the decision to escalate the Korean War in 1950; the failure to be prepared for the attack on Pearl Harbor in 1941; and the decision to escalate the Vietnam War in 1964. Janis argues that in the case of each of these disastrous decisions, information was potentially or actually available to the policy-making groups that should have led them to different decisions.

Method

Janis's research took the form of careful scouring of all the documentary sources of information on the circumstances in which these faulty decisions were made. In his 1972 book *Victims of Groupthink*, Janis attempted to show how the archival data on each of these decisions can be regarded as forming a consistent social psychological pattern, the essence of which is shown in Theory Box 2.1. Janis (1982) published a second edition of his book in which he applied the notion of groupthink to the Watergate incident that ultimately led to US President Richard Nixon's resignation in 1974.

Later research

Tetlock (1979) conducted a more quantitative analysis of archival materials. He applied standardized procedures for analysing the content of public statements made by key decision-makers involved in the 'groupthink' and 'non-groupthink' decisions examined by Janis (1972). Tetlock was particularly interested in assessing the extent to which public statements made by key decision-makers reflected 'a tendency to process policy-relevant information in simplistic and biased ways' (p. 1317), and the extent to which these statements reflected 'a tendency to evaluate one's

own group highly positively and to evaluate one's . . . opponents highly negatively' (p. 1317).

To assess these two aspects of groupthink, Tetlock identified six key decision-makers who were intimately involved in five different foreign policy decisions, two of which were classified by Janis as 'non-groupthink', while he classified the other three as 'groupthink' decisions. He then randomly selected and analysed 12 paragraph-sized passages from the public statements made by each decision-maker at the time of each crisis. He found that the public statements of decision-makers in groupthink crises were significantly less complex than were the public statements of decision-makers in non-groupthink crises. He also found evidence that decision-makers in the groupthink crises gave more positive evaluations of their own political groups than did decision-makers in crises not characterized by groupthink. However, contrary to predictions, there was no difference between groupthink and non-groupthink decision-makers in terms of the intensity of negative evaluations of their political opponents. With the exception of this last finding, the results of Tetlock's study are consistent with Janis's conclusions, which were based on a more qualitative analysis of historical documents.

However, other archival research has been less supportive of Janis's theory. Peterson, Owens, Tetlock, Fan, and Martorana (1998) used archival methods to examine decision making of senior management groups in seven top US companies, such as Coca-Cola. They were interested in whether 'groupthink' symptoms were more characteristic of unsuccessful regimes than successful regimes. As Haslam (2004, p.102) summarizes, 'In contrast to Janis's **hypothesis**, groupthink symptoms appeared to be apparent in *all* group decision making and no more characteristic of the unsuccessful regimes than the successful ones.'

> **hypothesis** a prediction derived from a theory concerning the relationship between variables.

Discussion

A key advantage of the archival research strategy is that the evidence gleaned from archives is not distorted by **participants**' knowledge that researchers are investigating their behaviour. The behaviour took place in natural settings at an

> **participants** people who take part in a psychological study.

earlier time than that at which the behaviour was studied. There is, therefore, little or no chance that the behaviour could have been 'contaminated' by the research process. As Simonton (1981) put it, 'Because archival research exploits data already collected by others for purposes often very different from the intentions of the researcher, this methodology constitutes a class of "unobtrusive measures"' (p. 218). Offsetting this advantage are some disadvantages. The most obvious of these are (1) that the researcher is dependent on the quality of the archival information, which may not contain a good basis for assessing key variables, and (2) that even when associations between variables (such as the quality of a decision and the complexity of statements made by decision-makers) are found, it is unclear whether or how they are *causally* related.

RESEARCH STRATEGIES

What are the strengths and weaknesses of the principal research strategies available to the social psychologist?

Researchers who want to test their ideas and predictions have a range of different research strategies available to them. In this section we will consider experimental and quasi-experimental research, survey research and qualitative approaches.

Experiments and quasi-experiments

experiment a method in which the researcher deliberately introduces some change into a setting to examine the consequences of that change.

Experimental research is designed to yield causal information. The goal of an **experiment** is to see what happens to a phenomenon when the researcher deliberately modifies some feature of the environment in which the phenomenon occurs ('If I change variable B, will there be resulting changes in variable A?'). By controlling the variation in B, the researcher who finds that there are changes in A can draw causal conclusions. Instead of just knowing that more of variable A is associated with more of variable B, the experimental researcher discovers whether A increases when B is increased, decreases when B is reduced, remains stable when B is left unchanged and so on. Such a pattern of results would suggest that changes in B *cause* the changes in A.

quasi-experiment an experiment in which participants are not randomly allocated to the different experimental conditions (typically because of factors beyond the control of the researcher).

The experimental method has many variations. Two common variations are the **quasi-experiment** and the **true randomized experiment**. They differ with respect to the realism of the setting in which the data are collected and the degree of control that the researcher has over that setting. A quasi-experiment is typically conducted in a natural, everyday setting, one over which the researcher does not have complete control. The true randomized experiment, by contrast, is one in which the researcher has complete control over key features of the setting; however, this often involves a loss of realism.

true randomized experiment an experiment in which participants are allocated to the different conditions of the experiment on a random basis.

To grasp the key difference between a quasi-experiment and a true experiment, we need to consider further what is meant by the term experiment. Experiments are studies in which the researcher examines the effects of one class of variables (independent, or manipulated, variables) on another class of variables (dependent, or measured, variables). In a true randomized experiment the researcher has control over the independent variable *and* over who is exposed to this variable. Most importantly, the researcher is able to allocate research participants randomly to different conditions of the experiment (**random allocation**). In a quasi-experiment the researcher usually cannot control who is exposed to the independent variable. In a typical quasi-experiment, pre-existing groups of people are either exposed or not exposed to the independent variable.

random allocation (sometimes called *random assignment*) the process of allocating participants to groups (or conditions) in such a way that each participant has an equal chance of being assigned to each group.

Examples of each method may help to bring out the points of difference. Social psychologists interested in aggression have studied whether exposure to violent film and television material has an impact on the subsequent behaviour of the viewer (see Chapter 9). This can be done using true randomized experiments or quasi-experiments. An example of a true experiment on this issue is the study reported by Liebert and Baron (1972). Male and female children in each of two age groups were randomly allocated to one of two experimental conditions, one in which they viewed an excerpt from a violent television programme and another in which they viewed an exciting athletics race. Later both groups of children were ostensibly given the opportunity to hurt another child. Those who had seen the violent material were more likely to use this opportunity than were those who had seen the non-violent material. Because children had been randomly allocated to the violent and non-violent conditions, the observed difference can be attributed to the difference in type of material seen, rather than any difference in the type of children who saw the material.

An example of a quasi-experimental study of the same issue is the study reported by Black and Bevan (1992). They asked people to complete a questionnaire measure of their tendency to engage in aggressive behaviour under one of four conditions: while waiting in line outside a cinema to see a violent movie; while waiting in line to see a non-violent movie; having just seen a violent movie; and having just seen a non-violent movie. As can be seen in Figure 2.1, the researchers found that those waiting to see the violent film had higher aggression scores than those waiting to see the non-violent film; and also that those who had just seen the violent film scored higher than those waiting to see the violent film (although there was no difference in aggression scores between those who had just seen a non-violent movie and those waiting to see a

non-violent movie). These findings are consistent with the notion that viewing a violent movie increases the tendency to aggress, but the fact that participants were not allocated at random to the different conditions makes it impossible to rule out alternative explanations. For example, it may be that violent movies only increase aggressive tendencies among those who are attracted to view such movies in the first place.

Often the only way in which to conduct an experimental study of a social phenomenon is via a quasi-experiment. Ethical and practical considerations frequently make it impossible to allocate people randomly to different experimental conditions. If, like Stroebe, Stroebe, and Domittner (1988), you wish to study the effects of bereavement, for example, you obviously cannot randomly allocate research participants to a 'bereaved' and a 'non-bereaved' condition. The same applies in many other fields of research. Thus, the choice of research strategy is often a compromise between what is optimal and what is practicable. Fortunately, the sophistication of some quasi-experimental designs is such that it is possible to draw conclusions about causality with some confidence (Judd & Kenny, 1981a, b; West, Biesanz, & Pitts, 2000; see Leader in the Field, Charles M. Judd).

It is also possible to conduct a true experiment in a field setting, in which case it is referred to as a **field experiment** (see Chapter 1), which attempts to combine the control of a laboratory experiment with the realism of a quasi-experiment. An example of such a field experiment is given in Research Close-Up 2.2.

field experiment a true randomized experiment conducted in a natural setting.

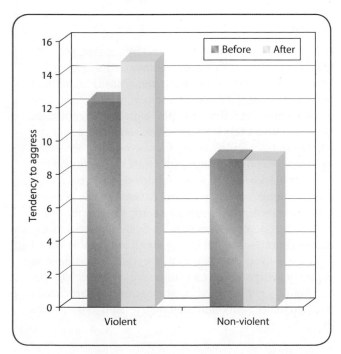

FIGURE 2.1 *Self-reported tendency to aggress, as a function of type of movie, and whether or not the respondent was waiting to see the movie or had just seen the movie.*

Source: Based on data reported by Black and Bevan (1992).

 LEADER IN THE FIELD

Charles M. Judd (b. 1946) is a leading scholar in the field of social cognition and stereotyping, but also an outstanding methodologist. He took his BA at Yale University, majoring in French, then studied theology at Union Theological Seminary, New York, before discovering a greater calling and pursuing graduate studies in psychology at Columbia University, where he obtained his PhD under Morton Deutsch. He began his teaching career at Harvard University, then moved to the University of Colorado, Boulder, where he has remained since 1986 (with the exception of two years at the University of California, Berkeley), and is now Professor of Distinction, College of Arts and Sciences. He is an expert on experimental design and analysis, and evaluation and quasi-experimental designs. He has contributed numerous highly influential articles on statistics (notably mediation and moderation analysis), has served as editor of many of the leading journals in the field, and received the 1999 Thomas M. Ostrom Award for Lifetime Contributions to Social Cognition Theory and Research. He was awarded the degree of Doctor Honoris Causa, Faculté de Psychologie et des Sciences de l'Education, Université Catholique de Louvain, Louvain-la-Neuve, Belgium, in 2006.

A FIELD EXPERIMENT TO STUDY HELPING BEHAVIOUR

Darley, J. M. & Batson, C. D. (1973). 'From Jerusalem to Jericho': A study of situational and dispositional variables in helping behavior. *Journal of Personality and Social Psychology*, 27, 100–108.

Introduction

The researchers were interested in testing the idea that one reason why bystanders do not come to the assistance of others, even when these others clearly need help, is that helping is costly. The particular 'cost' they studied in their research was time. To come to a stranger's assistance often involves a departure from your original plan. Such a departure can throw you off your schedule. The researchers also wanted to examine whether reminding people of the parable of the Good Samaritan, in which a passer-by does come to the assistance of a stranger in need of help, would influence willingness to give help. They tested these notions in a field experiment (see also Chapter 10). They also measured individual differences in religiosity, to see whether these would influence helping.

Method

The participants in the study were male seminary students (i.e., trainee priests) who believed that they were taking part in a study on 'religious education and vocations'. Each participant began the study in one building and was then asked to proceed to a second building to complete the study. Before leaving the first building, the participant was led to believe one of three things about the speed with which he should go to the other building: that there was no special hurry, that there was an intermediate degree of hurry, or that he was late for the second part of the study and should hurry up. This was the manipulation of the first variable, time pressure (no versus medium versus high degree of hurry). In the second part of the study, the participant expected to do one of two things: either talk about the parable of the Good Samaritan, or talk about job prospects for seminary students. This constituted the second manipulation: either having or not having the parable of the Good Samaritan made psychologically salient. The design of the study is shown in Figure 2.2.

On his way to the other building, the participant passed through an alley in which a person (the 'victim', but actually an accomplice of the experimenters) was sitting slumped in a doorway, head down, eyes closed. As the participant passed the victim, the latter coughed twice and groaned. The dependent variable in this field experiment was the extent to which the participant

	Degree of hurry		
Message	No	Medium	High
Good Samaritan			
Job prospects			

FIGURE 2.2 *Design of the Darley and Batson (1973) field experiment.*

did anything to help this person apparently in distress. The extent of the participant's helping behaviour was observed and coded.

Results

Helping was significantly influenced by the time pressure manipulation. The results are summarized in Figure 2.3. Those in the 'no hurry' condition were more helpful than those in the 'medium hurry' condition, who in turn were more helpful than those in the 'high hurry' condition. There was also a tendency for being reminded about the parable to have an influence; those who were reminded were more helpful than those who were not. Although this latter difference was correctly reported as not being statistically significant in Darley and Batson's paper, in a subsequent commentary on this research Greenwald (1975) noted that the observed trend provided some support for the hypothesis that thinking about the parable would increase helping but that further evidence was needed before drawing any firm conclusion. Individual differences in religiosity did not predict whether or not participants stopped to help, although they were related to the nature of the help given.

Discussion

Even those who have chosen to be trained in a vocation in which helping others is supposed to play a central

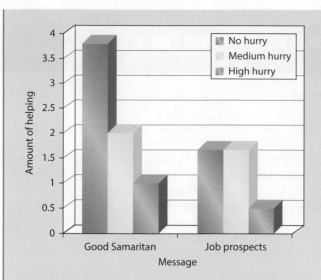

FIGURE 2.3 *Mean helping scores as a function of degree of hurry (no, medium, or high) and anticipated topic of talk (parable of Good Samaritan or job prospects for trainee priests).*

Source: Copyright © 1973 by the American Psychological Association. Adapted with permission. Darley, J. M. & Batson, C. D. (1973). 'From Jerusalem to Jericho': A study of situational and dispositional variables in helping behavior. *Journal of Personality and Social Psychology, 27,* 100–108. The use of APA information does not imply endorsement by APA.

role were affected by the time pressure variable. When they were in a hurry, even those trainee priests who thought that they were on their way to a discussion of the parable of the Good Samaritan were less likely to offer help to a stranger in need than were their counterparts who were in less of a hurry. From a methodological perspective, the neat thing about this field experiment is that it was conducted in a natural, everyday setting. Participants were randomly allocated to one of the six conditions of the experiment, so any differences found between these six conditions resulted, in principle, from the experimental manipulations. Thus internal validity was high (i.e., the researchers could be confident that changes in the independent variable *caused* changes in the dependent variable). But the fact that the setting of the experiment was such an everyday one means that this study also scores quite highly on realism (i.e., it has high external validity too). It is a good example of a field experiment.

Survey research

The practical and ethical considerations that can make quasi-experiments a useful strategy also apply more generally to **survey research** (Oppenheim, 1992; Schwarz, Groves, & Schuman, 1998; Visser, Krosnick, & Lavrakas, 2000). Surveys differ from experiments and quasi-experiments in that they focus on measuring existing levels of relevant variables, rather than manipulating them (see Social Psychology Beyond the Lab 2.1). Like experiments, survey designs are typically concerned with associations and/or cause-and-effect relationships between variables. However, the lack of control over independent – or *predictor* – variables means that it is virtually impossible to be certain about their causal role. For this reason, surveys often also measure other variables that can be taken into account in statistical analyses – that is, *controlled for* – in order to rule out possible alternative explanations for a relationship between a predictor variable and an outcome variable.

> **survey research** a research strategy that involves interviewing (or administering a questionnaire to) a sample of respondents who are selected so as to be representative of the population from which they are drawn.

An example of this strategy is provided by Pratto, Sidanius, Stallworth, and Malle (1994). They proposed that many different types of intergroup prejudice are predicted by a personality variable which they call *social dominance orientation,* or SDO (see Chapter 14). This variable reflects an individual's preference for unequal status relations between social categories. So, someone who scores high in SDO should be more sexist, and more likely to oppose equal rights for racial minorities. In support of this prediction, Pratto et al. (1994) found that SDO was indeed positively correlated with sexism, and negatively correlated with support for racial equality. However, they were also concerned that the relation between these variables and SDO could actually be due to the influence of another variable, such as political conservatism. If so, the argument that SDO is a unique predictor of prejudice would be greatly undermined. To test this possibility, Pratto et al. re-examined the correlations between prejudice and SDO while controlling for (or *partialling out*) the effect of political conservatism. The correlations remained significant, increasing their confidence that the role of SDO is not simply due to political conservatism.

SOCIAL PSYCHOLOGY BEYOND THE LAB 2.1

SURVEY RESEARCH

Descriptive survey designs focus on describing overall levels of relevant variables, such as the characteristics of one or more groups of people. Examples of descriptive survey designs include political opinion polls, market research and a census. Such descriptions can range from the simple (e.g., describing the percentage of people eligible to vote in a particular constituency who say that they intend to vote for a particular political candidate) to the more complex (e.g., describing the personal and social characteristics associated with use of recreational drugs among school-age children and teenagers).

Descriptive survey research is often concerned with large populations, such as all adults living in a particular community, region or country. To ensure that responses are *representative,* one could interview or collect completed questionnaires from the entire population in question (as is done in a census). In most cases, however, collecting data from all members of a population is simply not possible; even where it is possible, it is typically not cost-effective. The result is that the researcher has to choose which members of that population to survey. The process of selecting a subset of members is known as **sampling**.

> **sampling** the process of selecting a subset of members of a population with a view to describing the population from which they are taken.

> **simple random sample** a sample in which each member of the population has an equal chance of being selected and in which the selection of every possible combination of the desired number of members is equally likely.

Two main types of sampling are used in survey research: probabilistic and non-probabilistic. The most basic form of probabilistic sampling is the **simple random sample**. A simple random sample is one which satisfies two conditions: first, each member of the population has an equal chance of being selected; second, the selection of every possible combination of the desired number of members is equally likely. To explain the second condition, imagine that the population size is 10 (consisting of persons labelled A to J) and the sample size is two. There are 45 possible combinations of two members of the population (A + B, A + C, A + D, and so on, to I + J). In simple random sampling, each of these 45 possible combinations of two members has to be equally likely. In practice, of course, the sample size of a random sample (e.g., of the whole population of a country) is much larger than two and the process is much more complex. Researchers achieve random sampling by allocating numbers to each member of the population and using computer-generated random numbers to select a sample of the required size, a feature available on the web.

Because probability sampling is expensive and time-consuming, non-probability sampling is frequently used. The most common form of a non-probability sample is the **quota sample**. Here the objective is to select a sample that reflects basic attributes of the population. Such attributes might be age and sex. If you know the age and sex composition of the population concerned, you then ensure that the age and sex composition of the sample reflects that of the population. The term 'quota' refers to the number of people of a given type (e.g., females between the ages of 55 and 60) who have to be interviewed. The major advantage of quota sampling is that the interviewer can approach potential respondents until the quotas are filled without needing to recruit a specifically identified respondent. Some disadvantages of quota sampling are (1) that it is usually left to the interviewer to decide whom to approach in order to fill a quota, with the result that bias can enter into the selection process, and (2) that it is impossible to provide an accurate estimate of sampling error.

> **quota sample** a sample that fills certain prespecified quotas and thereby reflects certain attributes of the population (such as age and sex) that are thought to be important to the issue being researched.

Another strategy that can increase certainty regarding causal relationships in survey research involves taking measures of relevant variables at several points in time – a *longitudinal* survey design. The logic here is that if variable A at time 1 predicts variable B at time 2 (especially when controlling for differences in variable B at time 1), then we can be more certain that variable A has a causal effect on variable B.

Qualitative approaches

Traditionally, social psychological research – including the overwhelming majority of the research discussed in this book – has involved *quantitative* data analysis. That is, the data we analyse are represented as numbers. This makes our data amenable to statistical analyses, allowing researchers to say something about the *average* score on a variable (e.g., the *mean, median,* and/or *modal* score in a sample); the *range* of scores on a variable (e.g., the *variance* or *standard deviation*); and the *strength* and *reliability* of relations between two or more variables (e.g., through inferential tests such as *t*-tests, analysis of variance or regression). These analyses usually provide clear and interpretable outcomes, and moreover there is broad consensus among researchers about the meaning of these outcomes.

However, the quantitative approach is far from universal in social psychology. An alternative is *qualitative* analysis, in which data are typically textual rather than numerical, focusing on the content and meaning of the words and language used by participants. Qualitative approaches encompass a wide range of analytic techniques. Some of these are perfectly consistent with the philosophical assumptions that underpin quantitative research and the scientific method more generally. Among these assumptions is the belief that the phenomena in which we are interested represent an objective set of 'facts' that exist independently of the researcher's (or anyone else's) perspective on them. According to this view, the fact that many of the phenomena we study – such as an attitude – cannot be directly observed or measured simply means that we require sensitive and sophisticated research methods in order to study them. However, other qualitative approaches are more radical and explicitly reject these assumptions. What unifies qualitative approaches is a concern with the limitations of quantitative research of social phenomena, and the belief that qualitative techniques can provide additional, or even radically different insights (see Henwood, 1996).

The supposed limitations of quantitative techniques relate to the ways in which they potentially misrepresent and/or over-simplify phenomena and participants' perspectives on them. In particular, quantitative measures – especially *self-report* measures, which we discuss later – require the researcher to make assumptions regarding the range and content of possible responses, not to mention their *meaning* to participants. This is important, because a participant's understanding of a task or a questionnaire item may be quite different to that of the researcher. Moreover, the range of possible responses may not allow participants to communicate responses or perspectives that the researcher did not anticipate.

Several qualitative approaches help to address these concerns. At an early, exploratory stage of a research project, *content analysis* or *thematic analysis* of open-ended oral or written responses can shed light on potentially relevant factors. This approach can also be used to follow up quantitative analyses by exploring unexpected or ambiguous findings (see Livingstone & Haslam, 2008, for an example of the latter). Indeed, content analysis often

ultimately produces *quantitative* outcomes, because it allows the researcher to count occurrences of particular words, phrases or themes and conduct statistical analyses on the results. Alternatively, *grounded theory* focuses on systematically *generating* theory about a specific phenomenon in an inductive or 'bottom-up' manner, for example on the basis of exploratory interview data. Other techniques (e.g., *interpretative phenomenological analysis*) focus on revealing and interpreting the subjective meaning that participants attach to particular issues or events.

All of these techniques can complement or extend quantitative research. By contrast, other qualitative approaches such as forms of **discourse analysis** involve a more fundamental rejection of the assumptions that underlie quantitative and much qualitative research. Rather than searching for an objective, knowable set of 'facts' about social psychological phenomena, advocates of these approaches instead assume that there is no unique, valid interpretation of the world. Consequently, the focus of their research is on fine-grained features of everyday talk and interaction to explore how people actively construct particular interpretations of events. They might seek to show how, for example, racist or sexist attitudes arise not because of the beliefs or biases of the individual who expresses them, but rather as evaluations that emerge in the context of particular social interactions. Rather than being relatively fixed products of individual cognitive systems, such evaluations arise in the context of conversations and vary according to the particular social setting.

> **discourse analysis** a family of methods for analysing talk and texts, with the goal of revealing how people make sense of their everyday worlds.

An example of the use of discourse analysis is the study reported by Wetherell, Stiven, and Potter (1987). These researchers were interested in how male and female university students characterized employment opportunities for women. They reasoned that analysing how a group of 17 students talk about these issues would reveal the practical ideologies that are used to reproduce gender inequalities. The students were interviewed in a semi-structured way and their responses were transcribed and analysed. A benefit of this approach is that it enabled the researchers to identify contradictions in the way ordinary people talk about issues like gender inequality. Rather than having a single attitude, the students tended to endorse different positions at different points during the interview. Some of these positions were inconsistent with each other, but served specific ideological and strategic purposes at the particular point at which they were adopted.

Discourse analysis – and related approaches, such as conversation analysis – are not represented in the present volume, where the emphasis is on the strengths of approaches that assume the objective existence of the phenomena we study. Nevertheless, discourse analysis is an important and distinctive research tradition that typically approaches social phenomena in a different manner, and with different insights, to the majority of research covered in this volume. A recent (2012) special issue of the *British Journal of Social Psychology* provides a good indication of the type of research conducted by discourse analysts, and the philosophy behind the approach more generally. It is important to highlight that the assumptions of discourse analysis are also quite different from those of most qualitative research methods, which cover a very large range of different techniques, and which to a greater or lesser extent can complement the quantitative approaches outlined in this chapter.

The preceding overview of different research strategies makes it clear that one of the most important decisions to be made during the research process is which research strategy to adopt. It is worth pointing out that although some research strategies will be better suited than others to studying a given phenomenon, each and every strategy, however sophisticated its implementation, has its limitations. It is for this reason that one of the great pioneers of research methodology in the social sciences, Donald Campbell (see Leader in the Field, Donald T. Campbell), argued for **triangulation**. By this he meant that using multiple methods to study a given issue provides a better basis for drawing conclusions than does any single method. Because each method has its own strengths and weaknesses, using different methods helps the strengths of one method to compensate for the weaknesses of another (e.g., Fine & Elsbach, 2000).

> **triangulation** the use of multiple methods and measures to research a given issue.

 LEADER IN THE FIELD

Donald T. Campbell (1917–1996) is regarded as having been a master research methodologist. Campbell completed his undergraduate education at the University of California, Berkeley. After serving in the US Naval Reserve during World War II, he earned his doctorate from Berkeley and subsequently served on the faculties at Ohio State University, the University of Chicago, Northwestern, and Lehigh. He made lasting contributions in a wide range of disciplines, including psychology, sociology, anthropology, biology and philosophy. In social psychology he is best known for co-authoring two of the most influential research methodology texts ever published, *Experimental and Quasi-Experimental Designs for Research* (1966, with Julian C. Stanley) and *Quasi-Experimentation: Design and Analysis Issues for Field Settings* (1979, with Thomas D. Cook). Campbell argued that the sophisticated use of many approaches, each with its own distinct but measurable flaws, was required to design reliable research projects. The paper he wrote with Donald W. Fiske to present this thesis, 'Convergent and discriminant validation by the multitrait–multimethod matrix' (1959), is one of the most frequently-cited papers in the social science literature.

Summary

Research strategies are broad categories of research methods that are available to study social psychological phenomena. We began by noting that it often makes sense to study a phenomenon using more than one strategy. We identified three quantitative strategies (experiments and quasi-experiments, and survey research) before discussing qualitative research strategies.

A CLOSER LOOK AT EXPERIMENTATION IN SOCIAL PSYCHOLOGY

What are the main elements of a social psychological experiment?

Experimentation has been the dominant research method in social psychology, mainly because it is unrivalled as a method for testing theories that predict causal relationships between variables. Standard guides to research in social psychology (e.g., Aronson, Ellsworth, Carlsmith, & Gonzales, 1990; Aronson, Wilson, & Brewer, 1998) treat experimentation as the preferred research method. In fact there are some grounds for questioning the extent to which experimental studies provide unambiguous evidence about causation, as we shall see later.

We will first describe the principal features of the experimental approach to social psychological research. To assist this process of description, we will use Milgram's (1965; see Chapter 8) well-known study of obedience as an illustrative example.

Features of the social psychological experiment

The **experimental scenario** is the context in which the study is presented. In laboratory settings it is important to devise a scenario for which there is a convincing and well-integrated rationale, because the situation should strike participants as realistic and involving, and the experimental manipulations and the measurement process should not 'leap out' at the participant. In Milgram's study, participants were told that the study was an

> **experimental scenario** the 'package' within which an experiment is presented to participants.

investigation of the effects of punishment on learning. The participant was given, apparently at random, the role of 'teacher', while an accomplice of the experimenter posing as another participant (known as a **confederate**) took the role of 'learner'. The learner's task was to memorize a list of word pairs. The teacher's task was to read out the first word of each pair, to see whether the learner could correctly remember the second word, and to administer a graded series of punishments, in the form of electric shocks of increasing severity, if the learner failed to recall the correct word (which he had been instructed to do from time to time). This scenario was devised with a view to convincing the participant that the shocks were genuine (which they were not), and that the learner was actually receiving the shocks.

confederate an accomplice or assistant of the experimenter who is ostensibly another participant but who in fact plays a prescribed role in the experiment.

The **independent variable** is the one that is deliberately manipulated by the experimenter. All other aspects of the scenario are held constant, and the independent variable is changed systematically.

independent variable the variable that an experimenter manipulates or modifies in order to examine the effect on one or more dependent variables.

Operationalization refers to the way in which the variable is measured or manipulated in practice. In Milgram's research a key independent variable was the proximity of the 'learner' to the 'teacher'. In one condition, learner and teacher were in separate rooms; in a second condition, the teacher could hear the learner but could not see him; in a third condition, the teacher could both see and hear the learner's reactions; in a fourth condition, the teacher had to hold the learner's hand down on a metal plate in order for the shock to be delivered. All other aspects of the experimental setting were held constant, so that any variations in the teacher's behaviour in these four conditions should be attributable to the change in proximity between teacher and learner.

operationalization the way in which a theoretical construct is turned into a measurable dependent variable or a manipulable independent variable in a particular study.

The success of an experiment often hinges on the effectiveness of manipulations of the independent variable. By *effectiveness* we mean (1) the extent to which changes in the independent variable capture the essential qualities of the construct that is theoretically expected to have a causal influence on behaviour, and (2) the size of the changes that are introduced. For example, in Milgram's study, we should consider how well the four proximity conditions capture the construct of proximity. What is being manipulated, clearly, is *physical* proximity. Then there is the question of whether the changes between the

four conditions are sufficiently large to produce an effect. In this case it is hard to see how the proximity variable could have been manipulated more powerfully; an investigator who adopts weaker manipulations runs the risk of failing to find the predicted effects simply because the variations across levels of the independent variable are too subtle to have an impact. It has become standard practice in social psychological experiments to include among the measured variables one or more measures of the effectiveness of the manipulation; these are known as **manipulation checks**.

manipulation check a measure of the effectiveness of the independent variable.

Assessing whether an independent variable has had an effect requires the measurement of the participant's behaviour or internal state. This measured variable is known as the **dependent variable**, so called because systematic changes in this measured variable *depend upon* the impact of the independent variable. In Milgram's study, the dependent variable was the intensity of shocks in a 30-step sequence that the teacher was prepared to deliver. The results of Milgram's experiments are often expressed in terms of the percentage of participants who gave the maximum shock level (corresponding to 450 volts). The results of the Milgram (1965) study are shown in these terms in Figure 2.4. A key question to ask of any dependent variable is the extent to which it is a good

dependent variable the variable that is expected to change as a function of changes in the independent variable. Measured changes in the dependent variable are seen as 'dependent on' manipulated changes in the independent variable.

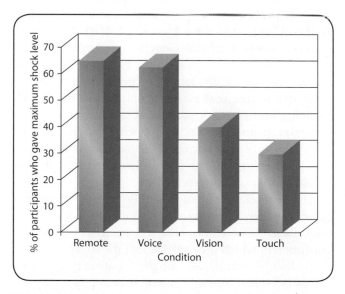

FIGURE 2.4 *Percentage of participants who administered the maximum shock level, and who were therefore deemed to be fully obedient.*

Source: Based on data reported by Milgram, 1965. Reproduction with permission from SAGE Publications.

measure of the underlying theoretical construct. In addition to this question of the 'fit' between a theoretical construct and the measured or dependent variable, the most important issue involved in designing dependent variables is what type of measure to use. We will discuss this in more detail below.

Laboratory experiments often involve deception, in the sense that the participant is misled about some aspect of the research. The extent of this deception can range from withholding information about the purpose of the research to misleading participants into thinking that the research is concerned with something other than its real purpose. The main reason for using deception is that participants would act differently if they were aware of the true objective of the study. If Milgram's participants had known that his was a study of obedience, we can be sure that the rate of disobedience would have been higher: the participants would have wanted to demonstrate their ability to resist orders to harm a fellow human.

Attitudes to the use of deception in social psychological research have changed during the past 45 years: misleading participants about the nature of an experiment is now viewed more negatively. The reason for this change is partly moral (i.e., where possible one should avoid deceiving someone else, whether or not in the context of an experiment) and partly practical (if participants are routinely misled about research, they will enter any future research in the expectation that they are going to be misled, which may influence their behaviour). Striking an appropriate balance between being completely honest with participants and wanting to study them free of the influence of their knowledge of the nature of the experiment is difficult. Psychological research conducted in universities in Europe, North America and Australasia is typically subject to prior approval by an ethics committee that evaluates and monitors research involving human participants, and national bodies such as the American Psychological Association (APA) and the British Psychological Society (BPS) have published guidelines concerning research using human participants that should be followed by researchers.

The key elements of the APA ethical principles (American Psychological Association, 2010) are as follows. First, most researchers will need to inform the institution in which they work about the study they plan to conduct. Second, those who participate in the research should provide informed consent, meaning that they are given an accurate account of what to expect and an opportunity to withdraw their participation. Special care needs to be taken when dealing with vulnerable groups like children or patients, and with groups over whom researchers may have power, such as students. Third,

deception should only be used in research when it can be scientifically justified and where no viable alternative is available. Fourth, research participants should be debriefed about the nature and purpose of the research, taking care to correct any misconceptions they may have. Finally, researchers should not fabricate or misreport any aspect of their data, and should take steps to correct or retract any mistakes in published reports as soon as they become aware of them. You will be able to find the guidelines for ethical research for your own country on the website of your national professional organization for psychology.

Consistent with these principles, one way to address the ethical issues that arise from the use of deception is by carefully **debriefing** participants. This is done at the end of the experimental session and involves informing the participant as fully as possible about the nature and purpose of the experiment, and the reason for any deception. In Milgram's study, for example, care was taken to assure participants that the 'shocks' they had administered were in fact bogus, and that the learner had not been harmed in any way; the reason for the deception was also carefully explained. The debriefing process should leave participants understanding the purpose of the research, satisfied with their role in the experiment, and with as much self-respect as they had before participating in the study.

> **debriefing** the practice of explaining to participants the purpose of the experiment in which they have just participated, and answering any questions the participants may have.

Experimental designs

When and why is it important to have a control condition in an experiment?

As we have seen, it is important that participants are allocated randomly to the different conditions of an experiment. Failure to achieve this goal constrains the researcher from concluding that observed differences between conditions in the dependent variable result from changes in the independent variable. We shall now examine more closely the issue of designing experiments in order to rule out alternative inferences as far as possible.

First consider a study that may *appear* to be an experiment but cannot properly be described as experimental. This is the **one-shot case study** (Cook & Campbell, 1979). To take a concrete example, imagine that a researcher wanted

> **one-shot case study** a research design in which observations are made on a group after some event has occurred or some manipulation has been introduced.

to know the effect of a new teaching method on learning. The researcher takes a class of students, introduces the new method, and measures the students' comprehension of the taught material. What conclusions can be drawn from such a design? Strictly speaking, none, for there is nothing with which the students' comprehension can be compared, so the researcher cannot infer whether the observed comprehension is good, poor or indifferent.

post-test only control group design an experimental design in which participants are randomly allocated to one of two groups; one group is exposed to the independent variable, another (the control group) is not.

experimental group a group of participants allocated to the 'experimental' condition of the experiment.

control group a group of participants who are typically not exposed to the independent variable(s) used in experimental research.

A simple extension of the one-shot design provides the *minimal requirements* for a true experimental study and is known as the **post-test only control group design**. Here there are two conditions. In the experimental condition participants are exposed to the manipulation (participants in this condition are known as the **experimental group**), and possible effects of the manipulation are measured. In the control condition participants are not exposed to the same treatment as participants in the experimental group (here the participants are known as the **control group**), but these participants are also assessed on the same dependent variable and at the same time point as the experimental group. Now the observation made in the experimental condition *can* be compared with something: the observation made in the control condition. So the researcher might compare one group of students who have been exposed to the new teaching method with another group who continued to receive the normal method, with respect to their comprehension of the course material. An important point is that participants are randomly allocated to the two conditions, ruling out the possibility that differences between the conditions are due to differences between the two groups of participants that were present before the new teaching method was implemented. So if the measure of students' comprehension differs markedly between the two conditions, it is reasonable to infer that the new teaching method caused this difference.

There are several other more sophisticated and complex designs, each representing a more complete attempt to rule out the possibility that observed differences between conditions result from something other than the manipulation of the independent variable (see Cook & Campbell, 1979). A very common design in social

psychological experiments is the **factorial experiment**, in which two or more independent variables are manipulated within the same study. The simplest case that can be represented is that in which there are two independent variables, each with two levels. Combining these, you have the design shown in Figure 2.5. A factorial design contains all possible combinations of the independent variables. In the design shown in Figure 2.5, each independent variable has two levels, resulting in four conditions. The main benefit of a factorial design is that it allows the researcher to examine the separate *and combined* effects of two or more independent variables. The separate effects of each independent variable are known as **main effects**. If the combined effect of two independent variables differs from the sum of their two main effects, this is known as an **interaction effect**.

factorial experiment an experiment in which two or more independent variables are manipulated within the same design.

main effect a term used to refer to the separate effects of each independent variable in a factorial experiment.

interaction effect a term used when the combination of two (or more) independent variables in a factorial experiment yields an effect that differs from the sum of the main effects.

To illustrate an interaction effect, let us consider Petty, Cacioppo, and Goldman's (1981) study of the effects of persuasive communications on attitude change. To test Petty and Cacioppo's (1986a) 'elaboration likelihood model', a theory of persuasion (see Chapter 7), these researchers manipulated two variables. The first was argument quality, i.e., whether the persuasive communication the participants read consisted of strong or weak arguments in favour of making the university examination system tougher. The second variable was involvement, i.e., whether the participants, who were students, thought that the university would introduce the tougher exam system next year, such that it would affect them personally (high involvement), or in the next decade, such that it would not affect them personally (low involvement). According to the elaboration likelihood model, argument

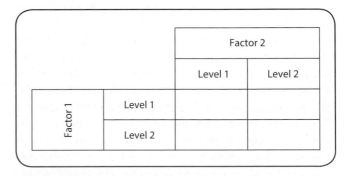

FIGURE 2.5 *Factorial experimental design involving two factors, each with two levels.*

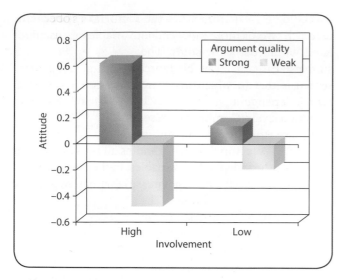

FIGURE 2.6 *Interaction between argument quality and involvement, showing that argument quality had a much stronger effect on attitudes when involvement was high.*

Source: Based on data reported by Petty, Cacioppo and Goldman, 1981.

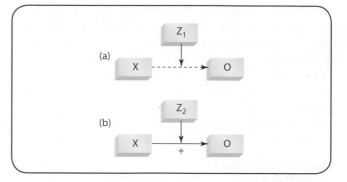

FIGURE 2.7 *(a) and (b) Diagram to illustrate the moderating influence of variable Z on the relationship between variables X and O. X only has an effect on O when Z has the value 2; (b) When Z has the value 1 (a), there is no effect of X on O.*

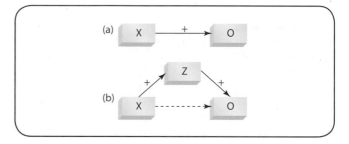

FIGURE 2.8 *(a) and (b) Diagram to illustrate that the effect of variable X on variable O is mediated by variable Z. When Z is not taken into account, X has a significant effect on O (a). Here X has a direct effect on O. When Z is taken into account (b), the effect of X on O is non-significant. Here X has an indirect effect on O, via Z.*

quality should have a stronger impact on attitudes when participants are involved with the message topic than when they are not. Figure 2.6 shows some of the key findings from the study by Petty et al. (1981). It can be seen that the effect of argument quality on attitudes was indeed much greater when involvement was high than when it was low. Because the predicted effect is an interaction, testing this prediction requires a factorial design.

An interaction effect is an instance of what is known more generally as *moderation*, in which the effect of one variable on another varies in strength depending on the level of a third variable. In other words, the role of the third variable is in determining *when* (under what conditions) the independent variable influences the dependent variable. In Figure 2.7, for example, the effect of variable X on variable O is moderated by variable Z. Specifically, X has an effect on O, but only when Z = 2 (Figure 2.7b). When Z = 1, X does not affect O (Figure 2.7a). It is important to distinguish moderation from another type of statistical relationship between three or more variables: namely, *mediation*.

To understand the concept of mediation, consider that the phenomena of interest to social psychologists often entail *chains* of events. If we strip this issue down to its bare essentials, we can ask whether variable X influences variable O *directly*, or whether the relation between X and O is mediated by another variable, Z. In other words, X may have an effect on O, but this is not a direct effect. Instead, X affects Z – the *mediating* variable – which in turn affects O (so, X affects O *via* Z). Researchers are therefore not only concerned with *if* or *when* X affects O: they are also concerned with *how* (through what process) X affects O.

In modern social psychological research, researchers therefore often attempt to measure **mediating variables** and then to conduct mediational analysis, for which there are well-established procedures (see Judd & Kenny, 1981a, b; Kenny, Kashy, & Bolger, 1998; Preacher & Hayes, 2004). By conducting an experiment we may establish that there is a causal relation between X and O; but we also measure Z, and find that the relation between X and Z is also very high, as is the relation between Z and O. We can then examine whether, once the X–Z and Z–O relationships are statistically taken into account, the originally established relationship between X and O becomes smaller, or disappears. This is the type of situation in which one can infer that the relationship between X and O is mediated by Z (Baron & Kenny, 1986; see Leader in the Field, David A. Kenny). This type of relationship is illustrated in Figure 2.8. In part (a), X has a direct, positive effect on O.

mediating variable a variable that mediates the relation between two other variables.

LEADER IN THE FIELD

David A. Kenny (b. 1946) took his undergraduate degree at the University of California, Davis, followed by both his MA and PhD at Northwestern University, where his adviser was the methodological pioneer, Donald T. Campbell (see previous Leader in the Field). He then taught at Harvard University, before moving to the University of Connecticut, where he is now Board of Trustees Distinguished Professor. He has published many influential methodological papers and books, and is interested in the study of naturalistic social behaviour and models of such behaviour. He has specialized in the analysis of dyadic processes (where each person's behaviour affects the other person's, with the result that they have to be treated as interdependent, rather than independent, pieces of data). His paper on moderation and mediation (co-authored with Reuben Baron; Baron & Kenny, 1986) is one of the most-cited articles in the field. He was honoured with the Donald T. Campbell Award by the Society of Personality and Social Psychology in 2006, and is a Fellow of the American Academy of Arts and Sciences.

In part (b), when the relationships between X and Z, and between Z and O, are taken into account, the direct effect of X on O becomes non-significant. Instead, the indirect effect of X on O via Z is positive and significant.

Threats to validity in experimental research

What is the difference between internal and external validity?

validity a measure is valid to the extent that it measures precisely what it is supposed to measure.

In a research context, **validity** refers to the extent to which one is justified in drawing inferences from one's findings. Experimental research attempts to maximize each of three types of validity: internal validity, construct validity and external validity.

internal validity refers to the validity of the inference that changes in the independent variable result in changes in the dependent variable.

Internal validity refers to the validity of the conclusion that an observed relationship between independent and dependent variables reflects a *causal* relationship, and is promoted by the use of a sound experimental design. We have already seen that the use of a control group greatly enhances internal validity, but even if one uses a control group there remain many potential threats to internal validity (Brewer, 2000; Cook & Campbell, 1979). Chief among these is the possibility that the groups being compared differ with respect to more than the independent variable of interest.

For example, let's assume that in Milgram's obedience research a different experimenter had been used for each of the four conditions described earlier, such that experimenter 1 ran all participants in one condition, experimenter 2 ran all participants in another condition, and so on. It might seem efficient to divide the work among different experimenters, but to do so in this way poses a major threat to the internal validity of the experiment. This is because the four conditions would no longer differ *solely* in terms of the proximity of the 'victim'; they would also have different experimenters running them. Thus the differing amounts of obedience observed in the four conditions *might* reflect the impact of the proximity variable, *or* the influence of the different experimenters (or, indeed, some combination of these two factors). The problem is that there would be an **experimental confound** between the physical proximity variable and a second variable, namely experimenter identity.

experimental confound when an independent variable incorporates two or more potentially separable components it is a confounded variable. When an independent variable is confounded, the researcher's ability to draw causal inferences is seriously compromised.

Even when we are confident that the relationship between X and O *is* a causal one, in the sense that internal validity is high, we need to consider carefully the nature of the constructs involved in this relationship. **Construct validity** refers to whether our independent or dependent variables adequately capture the constructs they are supposed to represent. Even if the researcher has reason to feel satisfied with the construct validity of the independent variable, there remains the question of whether the dependent variables actually assess what they were intended to assess. There are three main types of threat to the construct validity of dependent variables in social psychological experimentation: social desirability, demand characteristics and experimenter expectancy.

construct validity the validity of the assumption that independent and dependent variables adequately capture the abstract variables (constructs) they are supposed to represent.

Social desirability refers to the fact that participants are usually keen to be seen in a positive light, and may therefore be reluctant to provide honest reports of anything which they think would be regarded negatively. Equally, participants may 'censor' some of their behaviours so as to avoid being evaluated negatively. To the extent that a researcher's measures are affected by social desirability, they fail to capture the theoretical construct of interest.

social desirability refers to the fact that research participants are likely to want to be seen in a positive light and may therefore adjust their responses or behaviour in order to avoid being negatively evaluated.

An obvious way to reduce social desirability effects is to make the measurement process unobtrusive: if participants do not know what it is that is being measured, they will be unable to modify their behaviour.

An alternative strategy is to measure individual differences in the tendency to make socially desirable responses, and then to control for this statistically. Paulhus (1984, 1991) has developed a measure known as the Balanced Inventory of Desirable Responding (BIDR). This is a 40-item self-report questionnaire designed to measure the tendency to give socially acceptable or desirable responses. It consists of two sub-scales, one measuring *self-deceptive enhancement* and the other measuring *impression management*. Examples of items from each sub-scale are shown in Individual Differences 2.1. If scores on a self-report measure (like attitudes to an ethnic minority group) are correlated with BIDR scores, this suggests that self-reports are being biased in a socially desirable direction.

We should note, however, that it is better to try to eliminate completely the tendency to make socially desirable responses (rather than measuring it, and controlling for it statistically), simply because we do not know precisely what scales such as the BIDR measure.

Demand characteristics (see Chapter 1) are cues that unintentionally convey the experimenter's hypothesis to the participant. Individuals who know that they are being studied will often have hunches about what the experimenter is expecting to find. They may then attempt to provide the expected responses. When behaviour is enacted with the intention of fulfilling the experimenter's hypotheses, it is said to be a response to the demand characteristics of the experiment. Orne (1962, 1969) suggested ways of pinpointing the role demand characteristics play in any given experimental situation. For example, he advocated the use of **post-experimental enquiry**, in the form of an interview, preferably conducted by someone other than the experimenter, the object being to elicit from participants what they believed to be the aim of the experiment and the extent to which this affected their

> **demand characteristics** cues that are perceived as telling participants how they are expected to behave or respond in a research setting; that is, cues that 'demand' a certain sort of response.

> **post-experimental enquiry** a technique advocated by Orne (1962) for detecting the operation of demand characteristics. The participant is carefully interviewed after participation in an experiment, the object being to assess perceptions of the purpose of the experiment.

INDIVIDUAL DIFFERENCES 2.1

MEASURING THE TENDENCY TO RESPOND IN SOCIALLY DESIRABLE WAYS

Paulhus (1984, 1991) has developed a measure known as the Balanced Inventory of Desirable Responding (BIDR). On the basis of detailed pre-testing, and prediction of actual differences in behaviour, Paulhus was able to create two sub-scales, one measuring self-deceptive enhancement and the other measuring impression management. *Self-enhancement* refers to the tendency to think of oneself in a favourable light, whereas *impression management* refers to a deliberate attempt to distort one's responses in order to create a favourable impression with others. Below are example items from each sub-scale.

Self-enhancement

- My first impressions of people usually turn out to be right
- I always know why I like things
- I never regret my decisions
- I am a completely rational person

Respondents who agree with such items are deemed to have positively biased images of themselves (on the grounds that it is unlikely that these statements are true for most people).

Impression management

- I never swear
- I never conceal my mistakes
- I never drop litter in the street
- I never read sexy books or magazines

Respondents who agree with such items are deemed to be motivated to present themselves in positive ways (again, it is unlikely that these statements are true for most people).

Scores on these scales can be used to detect respondents who may be attempting to present themselves in a favourable light. If their scores on self-enhancement or impression management scales are correlated with their responses to other measures, it seems likely that the latter responses have been affected by social desirability, and these effects can be partialled out using statistical techniques.

behaviour. Clearly, researchers should do all they can to minimize the operation of demand characteristics, for example by using **unobtrusive measures**, that is, measures that are so subtle that participants are unaware of the fact that they are being taken, or by telling participants that the purpose of the experiment cannot be revealed until the end of the study and that in the meantime it is important that they do *not* attempt to guess the hypothesis. A **cover story** that leads participants to believe that the purpose of the study is something other than the real purpose is a widely used means of lessening the impact of demand characteristics.

> **unobtrusive measures** (also called *non-reactive measures*) measures that the participant is not aware of, and which therefore cannot influence his or her behaviour.

> **cover story** a false but supposedly plausible explanation of the purpose of an experiment; the intention is to limit the operation of demand characteristics.

Experimenter expectancy refers to the experimenter's own hypothesis or expectations about the outcome of the research. This expectancy can unintentionally influence the experimenter's behaviour towards participants in a way that increases the likelihood that they will confirm the experimenter's hypothesis. Rosenthal (1966) called this type of influence the **experimenter expectancy effect** (see Chapter 1). The processes mediating experimenter expectancy effects are complex, but non-verbal communication is centrally involved. An obvious way of reducing these effects is to keep experimenters 'blind' to the hypothesis under test, or at least blind to the condition to which a given participant has been allocated; other possibilities include minimizing the interaction between experimenter and participant, and automating the experiment as far as possible. Indeed, in much current social psychological research, the entire experiment, including all instructions to the participants, is presented via a computer. This obviously limits the opportunity for experimenters to communicate their expectancies (either verbally or non-verbally).

> **experimenter expectancy effect** effect produced unintentionally by the experimenter that increases the likelihood that participants will confirm the experimenter's hypothesis.

Even if the experimenter manages to avoid all these threats to internal and construct validity, an important question remains: to what extent can the causal relationship between X and O be generalized beyond the circumstances of the experiment? **External validity** refers to the generalizability of a finding beyond the circumstances in which it was observed by the researcher. One important feature of the experimental circumstances, of course, is the type of person who participates in the experiment. In many cases participants volunteer their

participation, and to establish external validity it is important to consider whether results obtained using volunteers can be generalized to other populations. There is a good deal of research on differences between volunteers and non-volunteers in psychological studies (see Rosenthal & Rosnow, 1975). The general conclusion is that there *are* systematic personality differences between volunteers and non-volunteers. Such findings are explained in terms of volunteers' supposedly greater sensitivity to and willingness to comply with demand characteristics. The external validity of studies based only on volunteers' behaviour is therefore open to question, and the solution to this problem is to use a 'captive' population, preferably in a field setting. One factor that limits the influence of this problem is the use of 'participant pools' in many psychology departments at large universities. Typically, these pools consist of first- and (sometimes) second-year undergraduate students who have to accumulate a set number of participant credits as part of their course. Thus, participants in studies that recruit from these pools are not, strictly speaking, volunteers.

> **external validity** refers to the generalizability of research findings to settings and populations other than those involved in the research.

Another criticism of social (and indeed other) psychological experiments is that the participants are often university students. Sears (1986) examined research articles published in major social psychology journals in 1985 and found that 74 per cent were conducted with student participants. Although students are certainly unrepresentative of the general population, being younger, more intelligent and more highly educated than the average citizen, this in itself is *not* necessarily a threat to the validity of the research. This is because the goal of much social psychological research is to understand the process(es) underlying a phenomenon (such as attitude change or stereotyping), rather than to describe the general population (a goal for which certain types of survey research are much better suited). In any case, there is often little reason to suppose that the processes underlying a phenomenon such as attitude change or stereotyping differ in some fundamental way between students and non-students.

Social psychological experiments on the Internet

What are the advantages and disadvantages of web-based experiments?

A relatively new development in psychological research is the use of the Internet to recruit and conduct

rarely uninvolved or detached. Rather, researchers exist in a power relationship with participants, in which they instruct participants what to do, and in turn the participant actively interprets the researcher's actions and infers and reacts to their intentions, often in complex ways that the researcher may not recognize, or simply choose to ignore (Spears & Smith, 2001).

What are the implications of these problems for the status of experimentation in social psychological research? It is important to note that defences of the experimental method have been every bit as staunch as its critiques (e.g., Tetlock, 1994). Moreover, many critics of the experimental approach do not advocate the abandonment of experimentation. For example, Gergen (1973) acknowledged that experiments would continue to play an important role in explaining the relationship between biological processes (such as physiological arousal) and social behaviour; that studies such as the Milgram experiment are useful for raising consciousness about the insidious nature of social influence; that experiments can increase the impact of theories by providing vivid demonstrations of conditions under which a theory makes successful predictions; and that experimentation can be useful to evaluate social reforms, such as the effectiveness of measures designed to conserve energy. Others (e.g., Spears & Smith, 2001) point out that recognizing the subjective, involved role of an experimenter – and the nuanced ways in which participants react – does not invalidate the experimental method; rather it can actually provide us with a richer and more complete understanding of the findings that emerge.

Summary

In this section we examined different aspects of the use of experimentation in social psychology. We began by describing the principal features of the social psychological experiment, before going on to discuss some common experimental designs. We then considered the main threats to validity in experimental research, such as demand characteristics and experimenter expectancy effects, before going on to describe how researchers are making increasing use of the Internet to conduct experiments. Finally, we considered some possible problems with the use of experiments in social psychological research.

FIGURE 2.9 *Racial distribution on Scottburgh's beachfront at 12.30 pm on 25 December 1999.*
Note: Each red circle = one 'black' person; each blue circle = one 'white' person; each yellow circle = one Indian person.
Source: From Dixon and Durrheim (2003), with permission from John Wiley & Sons. Photograph courtesy of Professor Durrheim.

DATA COLLECTION METHODS

What are the strengths and weaknesses of the principal data collection methods used in social psychological research?

Regardless of which research strategy has been adopted, investigators will need to decide upon the method or methods they will use to collect data. In quantitative research, data collection methods will involve the measurement of one or more variables. For example, in correlational designs researchers have to measure each of the variables that are expected to correlate. In experimental designs researchers need to measure the dependent variable. In either case, investigators are confronted with the task of translating a theoretical construct (for example, aggression) into a measurable variable (for example, willingness to harm someone). Any psychological measure should be both reliable and valid. **Reliability** here refers to the stability of the measure. If you measure an adult's height, the measurement will be highly stable from one day to the next and will also be independent of who is doing the measuring. A reliable measure is one that is not dependent on the time of measurement or on the person taking the measurement. However, a measure can be highly reliable yet low in validity. To pursue the height example, let us imagine that what you *really* want to measure is a person's weight. In the absence of a proper weighing scale you decide to measure height instead, because you do have a tape measure. Of course, height and weight are correlated with each other, so height may be a better estimate of weight than simple guesswork. But clearly, height is not especially valid as a measure of weight. So validity in this context refers to the extent to which the measured variable captures the construct you want to measure.

In social psychological research investigators typically adopt one or more of the following methods: observation, self-report, implicit, or physiological methods.

reliability the degree to which a measure is free from measurement error; a measure is reliable if it yields the same result on more than one occasion or when used by different individuals.

Observational methods

If the object of one's research is to collect information about social *behaviour*, an obvious means of doing so is by observation. Many behaviours of interest to social psychologists are detectable without sophisticated equipment and take place in public settings, which makes them suitable for observation. Although observational methods vary in kind from the informal and unstructured to the highly formal and structured, the object in each case is the same: to extract from the complex flux of social behaviour those actions that are of potential significance to the research question, and to record these actions over some period (Weick, 1985).

Sometimes the nature of the research setting or topic dictates that observation is conducted in a relatively informal and unstructured manner, with researchers posing as members of the group being observed. A classic example of research employing this method is Festinger, Riecken, and Schachter's (1956) study of the consequences of blatant disconfirmation of strongly held beliefs. The investigators identified a religious sect that predicted that the northern hemisphere would be destroyed by flood on a certain date. By joining that sect, members of the research team were able to observe what happened when the predicted events failed to materialize. Under such circumstances, observation clearly has to be covert and informal: if other sect members suspected that the researchers were not *bona fide* believers, the opportunity for observation would be removed. This type of observation is known as **participant observation**, and typically yields data that can be analysed qualitatively.

participant observation a method of observation in which the researcher studies the target group or community from within, making careful records of what he or she observes.

More formal methods of observation can be used when it is possible to record actions relevant to the research question without disrupting the occurrence of the behaviour. For example, naturally-occurring conversations are often the focus of discourse analysis and conversation analysis studies (e.g., Stokoe & Edwards', 2007, research on neighbour complaints and police interrogations). Observations of natural behaviour can also be analysed quantitatively. An example is Dixon and Durrheim's (2003) study of informal segregation on racial lines on a beach in post-apartheid South Africa. Their observational study charted the nature and extent of informal segregation by plotting the distribution of members of different racial categories in different areas of a Durban beach over time (Figure 2.9). In analysing this distribution, they noted that pairs and small groups of people tend to cluster together in areas the researchers subsequently termed 'umbrella spaces'. These spaces were typically marked by personal possessions and acted as regions in which typical beach activities took place. They coded the racial composition of groups of persons in a total of 2654 umbrella spaces during a defined time period. Over 99.9 per cent of these spaces were racially homogeneous, either exclusively 'white' ($N = 1949$; 73.4 per cent) or exclusively 'black' ($N = 705$; 26.6 per cent). The pattern was stable across time; during the entire observation period the researchers located only one integrated grouping on the beachfront. In this instance the failure to inform people that they were unwittingly participating in a research project is covered by the ethical code shown earlier (see reference in APA guidelines to 'naturalistic observations').

What these two examples have in common is the fact that the targets of the researchers' observations were unaware that they were being observed. Such observation overcomes a problem peculiar to any research that uses humans as participants, namely the tendency for the measurement process itself to have an impact on participants' behaviour, a phenomenon known as **reactivity**. It is well established that the knowledge that one is being observed can influence behaviour (see research on social facilitation effects, discussed in Chapter 8). Awareness of this problem has led many researchers to develop unobtrusive methods of observing and measuring behaviour. Webb, Campbell, Schwartz, and Sechrest (2000) compiled a useful sourcebook of methods of unobtrusive measurement.

reactivity a measurement procedure is reactive if it alters the nature of what is being measured.

The most formal type of observational method is one in which the researcher uses a predetermined category system for scoring social behaviour, producing data that can be analysed quantitatively. A well-known example of such a system is Bales's (1950) interaction process analysis (IPA), developed to study interaction in small social groups. Here the verbal exchanges between group members are coded in terms of 12 predetermined categories (e.g., 'requests information'; see Chapter 12). The scores of group members can then be used to determine (among other things) who is the leader of the group (see Bales & Slater, 1955). Further examples of observational coding schemes can be found in Bakeman (2000).

Observational methods of data collection have two main advantages over the self-report methods we shall consider below: first, they can often be made unobtrusively; second, even where the participant knows that his or her behaviour is being observed, enacting the behaviour is typically quite engrossing, with the result that participants have less opportunity to modify their behaviour than they would when completing a questionnaire. Nevertheless, there are some types of behaviour that are either difficult to observe directly (because they are normally enacted in private) or impossible to observe directly (because they took place in the past). Moreover, social psychologists are often interested in measuring people's *perceptions*,

cognitions or *evaluations*, none of which can be directly assessed simply through observation. For these reasons, researchers often make use of self-report methods.

Self-report methods

The essential feature of data collection using self-report methods is that questions about issues such as the participant's beliefs, attitudes and behaviour are put directly to the participant. The responses are self-report data. Self-report methods are usually quicker, cheaper and easier to use than observational methods. The researcher does not have to contrive a laboratory setting or find a natural setting in which to observe a behavioural response; furthermore, there is typically no need to train observers or to use recording equipment, because self-reports are usually recorded by the participant. Finally, as noted above, some of the variables that are of most significance to social psychologists are not directly observable. For these reasons, self-report methods are very common in social psychological research, and it is not unusual for studies to depend exclusively on self-report data.

There are two principal methods of collecting self-report data: the questionnaire and the interview. In the *questionnaire* method, participants are given a set of questions, along with instructions on how to record their answers (nowadays, this is often done by means of web-based surveys too). In the *interview* method, questions are put to the participant by an interviewer, who then records the participant's responses. Interviewing is particularly useful when there is reason to believe that the questions might be difficult to understand without clarification. A tactful and sensitive interviewer should be able to establish rapport and ensure that the respondent fully comprehends a question before answering. Another advantage of interviewing is that interviews can vary in terms of how 'structured' they are. Structured interviews follow a schedule that is fixed in terms of the number, wording and order of questions, and can involve asking participants to respond using questionnaire-style response options. In 'semistructured' interviews, the interviewer has a pre-defined series of topics to be covered in the interview, but he or she is able to vary the specific questions that are asked so that they are relevant to the unfolding discussion. Interviews can also be relatively unstructured, in which the researcher simply asks the participant to talk about a topic, without having pre-defined ideas about the specific issues that will arise. For example, researchers can use this method to elicit rich biographical narratives or 'life stories' from their participants (e.g., Hollway & Jefferson, 2005).

Downsides of interviewing are that it is costly in terms of time and money, and a poorly trained interviewer can easily bias the respondent's answers by hinting at a desired or socially acceptable response. By contrast, questionnaires are especially useful for gathering data from large numbers of participants with minimal expense, and the comparative anonymity of the process is preferable when the questions touch on sensitive issues. On the other hand, many people who are given questionnaires fail to complete and/or return them. Response rates for questionnaires sent by mail to randomly selected names and addresses vary between 10 and 50 per cent. Because there is always the danger that non-respondents differ systematically from respondents in some respect, low response rates are undesirable.

Devising a good questionnaire or interview schedule can be a difficult task. As with any psychological measure, the goal is to produce questions that are reliable and valid. Although there are many potential threats to reliability in the construction of questionnaires, the most serious is *ambiguity*: if a question is ambiguous, different respondents may interpret it differently and therefore provide answers to what is in effect a different question. The most serious threat to question validity is failure on the part of the investigator to have *specific objectives* for each question: the hazier the intent of the researcher in posing a particular question, the greater are the chances that it will fail to elicit information relevant to his or her objectives. However, there are other threats to reliability and validity that cannot easily be controlled. A simple rule-of-thumb is never to assume that answers to a single question will reliably or validly measure a construct. If two or more items are used to measure that construct, the factors that decrease reliability and validity of responses to any single question should cancel each other out, so a measure based on the average of the responses to the different items will be a more reliable measure of the underlying construct.

Because it is difficult to envisage all the potential pitfalls in questionnaire construction, there is no substitute for pilot work in which drafts of the final questionnaire are administered to participants whose answers and comments provide a basis for revision. Constructing an entirely fresh questionnaire can therefore be a time-consuming and painstaking process. Fortunately, there are collections of previously developed and pre-tested questionnaires, such as the one edited by Robinson, Shaver, Wrightsman, and Andrews (1991). It is worth checking such a source before setting out to construct an original questionnaire. If no suitable questionnaire already exists, the researcher should consult a text on questionnaire design such as the one by Oppenheim (1992) before devising a fresh questionnaire.

Self-report methods have several advantages. What are their drawbacks? Obviously it is not possible to collect self-report data completely unobtrusively: participants are aware that they are under investigation, and may modify their responses as a result of this awareness. In particular, there is ample opportunity for the respondent's answers to be influenced by motivational factors, such as social desirability. There is no simple solution to this difficulty, although there are steps that can be taken which reduce the scale of the problem. First, it is worth emphasizing to participants whenever possible that their responses are anonymous. Second, it is worth stressing the point that there are no right or wrong answers. Third, it is often possible to increase participants' motivation to respond truthfully by treating them as research accomplices rather than 'guinea-pigs'. Fourth, one could measure individual differences in the tendency to make socially desirable responses, and then control for these statistically. Fifth, one can validate self-report responses by checking them against reports provided by observers, who are unlikely to share the same biases as those making the self-reports (see Hewstone, Judd, & Sharp, 2011).

Implicit and physiological methods

A recent development in social psychological research methods has been the increasing use of methods for measuring perceptions, cognitions and evaluations that do not rely on self-report, thereby avoiding the disadvantages of the latter. Many of these methods are referred to as **implicit measures** (Greenwald & Banaji, 1995). Although not previously widely used, implicit measures have a long history in social psychology: Campbell (1950) published a classic paper on the indirect assessment of attitudes more than half a century ago.

> **implicit measures**
> measures of constructs such as attitudes that are unobtrusively assessed (e.g., by reaction time) so that participants are unaware of what is being assessed.

What is different about the modern use of implicit measures is that they usually take advantage of computer technology. Here computers are used not only for the presentation of experimental materials but also (and more importantly) for the precise measurement of various aspects of the participants' responses to these materials. An example of an implicit measure is the use of response latencies (i.e., how long it takes a participant to answer a particular question). Such measures can provide fresh insights into cognitive structures and processes.

For example, Mussweiler (2006) reported a series of studies in which he investigated whether behaving in a stereotyped way activates the corresponding stereotype. It is known that activating the stereotype of the elderly can induce people to walk more slowly (Bargh, Chen, & Burrows, 1996). Mussweiler wanted to examine whether the reverse is also true. Would walking more slowly activate the stereotype of the elderly? In one of his studies participants were instructed to walk at a speed determined by a metronome while listening to a story presented through headphones. The pace of walking was manipulated to be 30 paces per minute (slow) or 90 paces per minute (control). Participants then performed a lexical decision task, in which they had to judge as quickly and as accurately as possible whether strings of letters presented on a computer screen were words or non-words. Some of the real words were elderly-stereotypical (e.g., *forgetful*, *wise*) and others were not (e.g., *right*, *unclear*). Participants in the slow walking condition were faster to judge the elderly-stereotypical words than their counterparts in the control walking condition; however, they were no faster to make judgments about the non-stereotypical words. The advantage of using an implicit measure in this context is that participants simply are unaware of what it is that is being assessed in the lexical decision task, so the findings cannot be explained in terms of demand characteristics. Examples of the use of implicit measures to assess attitudes can be found in Chapter 6.

While implicit measures typically assess cognitive processes, *physiological* methods involve measuring biological markers or correlates of different psychological states. The logic here is that, like implicit measures and unlike self-report methods, it is very difficult for participants to fake or consciously modify physiological responses. The use of physiological methods in social psychology actually has a long history, for example in the use of galvanic skin response (a measure of psychological arousal) as an indicator of racial prejudice in interracial encounters (Cooper & Pollock, 1959; Rankin & Campbell, 1955). As physiological measurement techniques have become more sophisticated, their use in social psychological studies has become more common. Examples include the use of levels of cortisol – a hormone released when under stress – to supplement self-reported stress measures in Reicher and Haslam's (2006) BBC prison study (see Chapter 8), and the use of cardiovascular markers as indicators of perceived social threat (Scheepers, De Wit, Ellemers, & Sassenberg, 2012). A downside of physiological methods is that they can be expensive and technically demanding to use.

A major advantage of implicit and physiological methods is that they are not reactive. That is, they are not subject to biases such as social desirability and demand characteristics, because they tap processes that the respondent cannot control (and sometimes even operate outside awareness). However, it does not follow automatically that such measures have high validity. How does one know, for example, whether a fast reaction time reflects automatic stereotyping, as opposed to individual or group differences in lexical knowledge? To address questions such as this, one ideally needs to employ other methods (e.g., observational) that provide evidence that converges with the evidence provided by implicit and/or physiological methods. In principle such evidence helps to establish the **convergent validity** of different types of measure. Convergent validity is established when different operationalizations of the same construct produce the same results.

> **convergent validity** established by showing that different measures of the same construct (e.g., self-report, implicit, observation) are significantly associated with each other.

Another key advantage of implicit and physiological methods is that they can assess constructs and processes that may be outside the awareness of the individual. If people are not aware of having certain thoughts or feelings, they will by definition be unable to report them, even if they are highly motivated to be honest. The study of 'automatic' processes has become a key theme in social cognition research (see Bargh & Chartrand, 2000). Given that one of the attributes of an automatic process is that the individual is unaware of it, studying such a process requires the use of implicit measurement.

Choosing a method

Each of the data collection methods considered here has certain advantages and disadvantages. Although there are no hard-and-fast rules for choosing one type of method over another, two points should be borne in mind when judging the appropriateness of a method. First, the different types of method – observational, self-report, implicit, and physiological – can be used in conjunction with each other in many types of research. Second, they differ in terms of the type of information they yield. If observational, self-report, implicit, and physiological assessment of the same conceptual variable point to the same conclusion, this clearly enhances confidence in that conclusion. Furthermore, self-report methods often assess the outcome of a process; by using observational and implicit or physiological methods as well, the researcher can gain insight into the processes responsible for that outcome. A special quality of implicit and physiological methods is that they enable researchers to capture aspects of the individual's thoughts, feelings and behaviour that are beyond conscious control and therefore not susceptible to feigning.

Social neuroscience

social neuroscience
an interdisciplinary field devoted to understanding how biological systems implement social processes and behaviour.

Strictly speaking, **social neuroscience** is an interdisciplinary field of enquiry rather than a data collection technique, but we include it here because researchers who adopt a social neuroscience approach to studying social behaviour typically measure neural activity, in addition to observational, self-report, or implicit measures. So although social neuroscience involves much more than the use of measures of biological processes, it is the measurement of such processes that is the most distinctive characteristic of the social neuroscience approach. As Cacioppo and colleagues (2007, p. 101) put it, 'An assumption underlying social neuroscience is that all human social behavior is implemented biologically.' This assumption leads researchers who adopt this approach to study the 'social brain'. The most popular way to do this is by using functional magnetic resonance imaging (fMRI), a technique for studying the regions of the brain that are activated while people engage in tasks such as perceiving self and others, regulating their emotions, and thinking about social groups. The technique works by measuring the changes in blood flow that relate to neural activity.

Although the use of fMRI to study social behaviour is a relatively new endeavour and remains expensive in terms of equipment costs and training time, there is no doubt that its popularity will grow, as social psychologists become more familiar with the opportunities it affords and neuroscientists become increasingly motivated to study human social behaviour. To illustrate the potential for using fMRI to gain a better understanding of social psychological phenomena, consider a study by Harris and Fiske (2006). These researchers studied neural responses to 'extreme' outgroups, such as drug addicts and homeless people, groups who in terms of the stereotype content model (see Chapter 14) are seen as low in both warmth and competence (in contrast, for example, to the elderly, who are seen as high in warmth but low in competence, or rich people, who are seen as high in competence but low in warmth). It is known that there is an area of the brain, the medial prefrontal cortex (mPFC), which is activated during social cognition. Harris and Fiske found that the mPFC was activated by photographs depicting people belonging to all kinds of groups *except* those scoring low on both warmth and competence. Instead, viewing photographs of these groups activated the insula, a brain area associated with disgust. So the neural evidence from this study is consistent with the view that extreme outgroups are not thought about in the same way as members of other social groups (indeed, they may be seen as less than human; see Chapter 14).

Summary

This section examined the main data collection methods available to the social psychological researcher. These methods include observational, self-report, implicit, and physiological methods. We noted that each method has its own advantages and disadvantages, and that there is often a case for using more than one method in a given piece of research. We also noted the emergence of social neuroscience as a new interdisciplinary field of enquiry in which researchers use techniques such as brain imaging to study the neural bases of human social behaviour.

CHAPTER SUMMARY

- *What are research methods, and what is meant by methodology?* Research methods are the procedures a researcher uses to gather information, and *methodology* is a term used to refer to all aspects of the implementation of methods.

- *How do researchers test their theoretical predictions, and where do these predictions come from?* Information gathered using research methods is used to test the researcher's theoretical predictions. These predictions are derived from a theory. The theory is often generated through observation of real-life events or by trying to make sense of puzzling findings from previous research.

- *What research strategies are available?* We described three quantitative research strategies: quasi-experiments, true randomized experiments and survey research. Two key ways in which these strategies differ are in terms of (1) the degree to which one is able to generalize to a population and (2) the degree to which one can draw inferences about causality.

- *What are qualitative research methods?* These are methods that do not aim to provide numerical data. They tend to focus on textual and interpretative analysis, and are often used by researchers who believe that quantitative methods are unsuited to studying the phenomenon under investigation. Discourse analysis was identified as a popular qualitative approach. Discourse analysis emphasizes the importance of how social phenomena are constructed through discourse.

- *What are the main features of social psychological experiments?* We singled out the experiment for detailed discussion because of its prominence as a research strategy in social psychology during the last six decades. The main features of experimentation are the experimental scenario; the independent variable; the dependent variable; the manipulation check; and debriefing.

- *What is a true experimental design?* It is one that enables the researcher to infer that changes in the independent variable produce changes in the dependent variable. Such a design must therefore incorporate more than one condition, allowing the researcher to compare observations made under different conditions.

- *What is the minimal true experimental design?* It is the post-test only control group design, in which participants are randomly allocated to one of two conditions, only one of which involves being exposed to the manipulation. Several more complex designs are available, and of these the factorial design is very commonly used, mainly because of its ability to test predictions concerning interaction effects.

- *What is 'validity' in the context of research methods?* Drawing strong inferences from social psychological research depends on three types of validity: internal, construct and external. We identified confounding as a threat to internal validity; social desirability effects, demand characteristics and experimenter effects as threats to construct validity; and volunteer/non-volunteer differences as a threat to external validity.

- *Can the Internet be used as a way of collecting data?* The Internet has provided social (and other) psychologists with a new arena in which to conduct experiments, enabling them to reach larger and more diverse groups of participants. The evidence to date suggests that, despite the potential problems of web-based experiments, their results tend to parallel those obtained using conventional methods.

- *What are the possible disadvantages of experiments?* Some social psychologists have questioned the usefulness of experiments. We identified the cultural embeddedness of social behaviour, the fact that social behaviour is determined by multiple factors, and the ability of humans to modify their behaviour in the light of social psychological theories as grounds for questioning the assumption that experimentation generates cumulative knowledge of the laws governing social behaviour.

- *What are the principal ways in which data can be collected in social psychological research?* We identified several different methods: observation, self-report, implicit and physiological methods. Observational, implicit and physiological methods have the advantage of being less susceptible to social desirability effects, and can be made completely unobtrusive. However, observational methods are obviously limited to phenomena that can be observed and are not suited to the assessment of covert cognitive phenomena such as attitudes, causal attributions and stereotypes (see Chapters 3, 6, 7 and 14).

- *How can the 'covert' phenomena that are often of interest to social psychologists be studied?* To study such covert phenomena, researchers have traditionally relied on self-report methods, although there has been an increasing tendency to make use of implicit and even physiological methods, the goals of which are to reveal phenomena that may either be outside the awareness of the individual or be misreported in conventional self-report methods due to social desirability concerns.

- *Can the different ways of collecting data be used in conjunction?* There are obvious advantages in using these different types of method in conjunction with each other.

- *Do new ways of imaging brain activity have anything to offer social psychology?* Social psychologists and neuroscientists will make increasing use of techniques such as brain imaging in the search for a better understanding of the neural underpinnings of human social behaviour.

SUGGESTIONS FOR FURTHER READING

Aronson, E., Ellsworth, P. C., Carlsmith, J. M., & Gonzales, M. H. (1990). *Methods of research in social psychology* (2nd ed.). New York: McGraw-Hill. A comprehensive introduction to research methods in social psychology, with an emphasis on experimentation.

Cook, T. D., & Campbell, D. T. (1979). *Quasi-experimentation: Design and analysis issues for field settings*. Chicago: Rand McNally. An authoritative account of how to minimize threats to validity by careful research design.

Fiske, S. T., Gilbert, D. T., & Lindzey, G. (Eds.). (2010). *Handbook of social psychology* (5th ed., vol. 1). Hoboken, NJ: Wiley. The most recent edition of this essential handbook, containing contributions on experimentation (Chapter 2), non-experimental methods (Chapter 3), and data analysis (Chapter 4).

Greenberg, J., & Folger, R. (1988). *Controversial issues in social research methods*. New York: Springer. This book does a good job of presenting the debates surrounding key issues in research.

Greenwood, J. D. (1989). *Explanation and experiment in social psychological science: Realism and the social constitution of action*. New York: Springer. An interesting, critical treatment of the philosophical background to research methods.

Haslam, S. A., & McGarty, C. (2014). *Research methods and statistics in psychology* (2nd ed.). London: Sage. Second, revised edition of a highly accessible book written by social psychologists who believe that you cannot understand psychology unless you understand the process of conducting and interpreting psychological research.

Reis, H. T., & Judd, C. M. (Eds.). (2000). *Handbook of research methods in social and personality psychology*. New York: Cambridge University Press. State-of-the-art coverage of the key methodological issues in social and personality psychology.

3 Social Perception and Attribution

BRIAN PARKINSON

as comp
words w
ous' cam

primacy e
tendency
informatio
more influ
social perc
interpreta

Primacy
time pre
quickly a
higher; s
  Early
judgeme
rather th
students
and aske
as a 'war
a 'cold' p
learned a

summatio
ers add tog
of informat
a person; w
informatio
positive, ac
mildly posi
tion yields
tive impres

**implicit pe
theory** an
of ideas he
perceiver a
different tr
to be orgar
a person.

configural
a holistic ap
impression
implying th
ceivers activ
deeper mea
the bits of i
that they re
other peop

averaging
compute th
or unweigh
value of pie
mation abo
when other
is strongly p
tional mildl
information
positive imp

KEY TERMS

- actor–observer difference
- analysis of non-common effects
- attributional biases
- augmenting principle
- averaging
- causal attribution
- causal power
- causal schema
- central trait
- configural model

- consensus information
- consistency information
- correspondence bias
- correspondent inference theory
- covariation theory
- depressive realism
- discounting principle
- distinctiveness information
- false consensus bias
- implicit personality theory

- learned helplessness theory
- naïve scientist model
- peripheral trait
- primacy effect
- probabilistic contrast
- salience
- self-fulfilling prophecy
- self-serving attributional biases
- social perception
- summation

REVERSING THE ACTOR–OBSERVER EFFECT BY MANIPULATING PERSPECTIVE

RESEARCH CLOSE-UP 3.2

Storms, M. D. (1973). Videotape and the attribution process: Reversing actors' and observers' points of view. *Journal of Personality and Social Psychology, 27,* 165–175.

Introduction

Storms (1973) proposed that differences between actors' and observers' attributions depend partly on their different physical points of view: actors' attention is typically directed outwards towards the situation (including other actors), whereas observers' attention usually focuses on the observed person (i.e., the actor). Indeed, one explanation for the related correspondence bias is that actors are often the most dynamic and interesting objects in the environment and therefore attract observers' attention (and deflect it from other aspects of the situation; see Heider, 1958; Taylor & Fiske, 1978). The increasing availability of video technology in the early 1970s allowed Storms to manipulate actors' and observers' perspectives in order to assess the influence of this factor on situational and dispositional attributions.

Method

Participants

Thirty groups of four male students took part in this study. Two members of each group were randomly assigned the role of observers and the other two were assigned the role of actors.

Design and procedure

Stage 1. Actors were told to have a conversation to get to know one another while facing each other across a table. Each observer was seated next to one of the actors and instructed to observe the actor opposite him. Two video cameras were positioned so that each pointed at one of the actors (see Figure 3.7, Stage 1).

Stage 2. Participants in the video condition were shown the videotape of the recorded interaction after watching it in real time, but told that because only one camera had functioned correctly, they would only be able to see the visual image of one of the actors (coupled with audio from both sides of the conversation). Thus, one actor and one observer from each group saw a replay of the conversation from the same perspective as previously, while the other actor and observer saw the reversed perspective (i.e., the actor now saw his own face instead of the face of his interaction partner, and the observer saw the face of the actor that he had not observed during the actual conversation;

Stage 1 Bird's-eye view of get acquainted session (arrows indicate direction of attention)

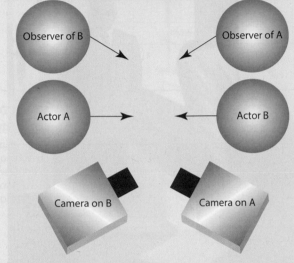

Stage 2 Bird's-eye view of video replay

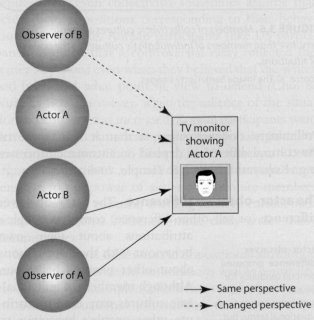

➤ Same perspective

---➤ Changed perspective

FIGURE 3.7 *The two stages of Storms's (1973) procedure.*

Source: Copyright © 1973 by the American Psychological Association. Reproduced with permission. Storms, M. D. (1973). Videotape and the attribution process: Reversing actors' and observers' points of view. *Journal of Personality and Social Psychology, 27,* 165–175. The use of APA information does not imply endorsement by APA.

see Figure 3.7, Stage 2). In the no-video condition, participants were told that none of the video equipment had worked and that the planned video replay would therefore not take place.

Measures

After Stage 2, actors rated their own friendliness, nervousness, talkativeness and dominance during the conversation, then rated the extent to which each of these behaviours had been caused by personal characteristics and by characteristics of the situation. Observers made corresponding ratings of the actors they had originally observed at Stage 1.

Results

Storms calculated difference scores by subtracting summed ratings of situational attribution for the four key behaviours from summed ratings of dispositional attribution. In the no-video and same-perspective conditions, actors' attribution scores were less dispositional (more situational) than observers' (see Figure 3.8). But in the reversed-perspective condition, observers' attribution scores were *less* dispositional (more situational) than actors'.

Discussion

This study demonstrates that actor–observer differences can be reversed by showing actors their own behaviour and showing observers the situation that actors are responding to (in this case, the other actor). A more general conclusion is also possible: that actors and observers tend to attribute greater causality wherever they pay more attention. Indeed, later studies (e.g., Taylor & Fiske, 1978) have shown that salient (attention-grabbing) factors tend to be seen as exerting more influence than non-salient factors.

One criticism of this study is that the usual actor–observer difference was not demonstrated (e.g., Gilbert &

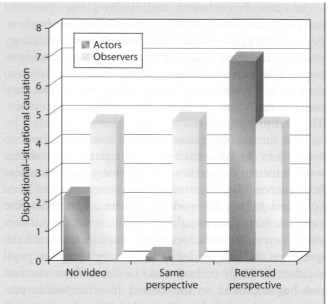

FIGURE 3.8 *Reversing the actor–observer difference following video replay.*

Source: Copyright © 1973 by the American Psychological Association. Adapted with permission. Storms, M. D. (1973). Videotape and the attribution process: Reversing actors' and observers' points of view. *Journal of Personality and Social Psychology, 27*, 165–175. The use of APA information does not imply endorsement by APA.

Malone, 1995). For example, analysis of the original ratings (separately assessing dispositional and situational attributions) rather than the difference scores used by Storms shows that actors were rated in equally dispositional terms by themselves and their observers across all conditions. However, the reported effect on situational attribution is theoretically interesting even if dispositional attribution is unaffected. The general implication is that we can correct for inattention to situational factors by manipulating attention.

they happen to be less appropriate (see Nisbett & Ross, 1980). The basic idea is that people's attributions are occasionally imperfect approximations of the causal structure of reality, but at least aim to represent that reality accurately. However, some kinds of bias are harder to explain in these terms. Self-serving attributional biases seem to represent a *motivated* distortion of what has happened in order to serve personal interests. Instead of being neutral observers of social events, we may sometimes interpret them in ways that suit us (or suit our ingroup more generally; Islam & Hewstone, 1993b, and see Chapter 14), allowing us to feel better about what has happened.

Let's assume that you have just done well in an exam. Your tendency may be to conclude that this reflects your innate ability (*self-enhancing bias*). However, if you do badly, perhaps you will decide that the questions were unfair or unusually difficult, or that the person sitting next to you in the examination hall was distracting you by sharpening his pencils so noisily (*self-protective bias*). More generally, you may be inclined to attribute positive outcomes to internal factors and negative outcomes to external factors, thus arriving at conclusions that maintain your positive self-image (e.g., Alicke & Sedikides, 2009, and see Chapter 5).

Some of the distinctions between different kinds of attributional process may also be clarified by evidence derived from brain-scanning. For example, Van Overwalle (2009) reviewed studies using fMRI to detect neural correlates of various kinds of social cognition and found that inferences about other people's goals, desires, and intention were associated with activation of the TPJ brain region, mentioned earlier, while inferences about longer-term dispositions were more likely to be associated with medial prefrontal cortex (mPFC) activation. Van Overwalle concluded that goal detection can utilize a 'where-to system' (a mechanism designed to pinpoint the direction taken by an observed action) that operates at a more perceptual, less abstract level than judgements about disposition which require integration of information.

AUTOMATIC AND CONTROLLED SOCIAL PERCEPTION

How much thought is involved in social perception and attribution?

Early theories of social perception (e.g., Asch, 1946) and attribution (e.g., Heider, 1958; Kelley, 1967) seemed to imply that people think long and hard before arriving at conclusions about other people and their behaviour. They apply best to those occasions when we treat other people's personalities and behaviours as puzzles that need to be solved carefully, for instance when actors do something unexpected or highly consequential.

Most everyday encounters with other people simply do not involve such a great deal of thought, and we often reach conclusions without really thinking about it. More recent theories correspondingly emphasize the automaticity and effortlessness of the cognitive processes that are involved. For example, Gilbert and Malone's (1995) ideas about automatic dispositional inference have parallels in accounts of stereotyping that suggest social categories relating to ethnic or minority groups may be directly activated in response to simple perceptual cues (e.g., Bargh, 1999, and see Chapter 4).

The idea that initial automatic attributions may subsequently be corrected using more controlled and effortful processing also relates to research into self-regulation of prejudice (see Monteith & Mark, 2005, and Chapter 4). Evidence suggests that stopping ourselves from applying unwarranted prejudices may face similar problems to adjusting dispositional inferences in response to situational information. For example, Fiske and Neuberg (1990) argue that automatic stereotyping is only followed by individuated impression formation when participants are sufficiently motivated to expend the additional cognitive effort. Further, Macrae, Bodenhausen, Milne, and Jetten (1994) showed that participants who had deliberately avoided thinking about a skinhead in prejudiced terms reverted to even more strongly stereotypical views once the requirement for self-control was removed (see Chapter 4). Evidently social perception and stereotyping depend on interactions and conflicts between controlled, systematic thinking and more automatic processes. Learning to detect unwanted effects of automatically activated conclusions is certainly possible if conditions are right (Monteith & Mark, 2005), but depends on systematic intervention and cooperative participants. Arriving at accurate and non-prejudicial social perceptions is not always a straightforward matter.

CHAPTER SUMMARY

- *How do we form impressions of what other people are like?* Information presented early in a sequence tends to be more influential (*primacy effect*), especially under time pressure. Information regarding 'central' personality traits, such as warmth, is given more weight, especially when it provides new and distinctive information.

- *Do the same processes of person perception operate when people meet face to face?* Information transmitted nonverbally can have more direct effects on impressions. We sometimes behave in ways that encourage other people to conform to our impressions of them (*self-fulfilling prophecies*).

- *What is attribution theory?* Attribution theory tries to explain how people work out the causes of events, particularly events involving other people.

- *How do people draw conclusions about the motives and dispositions guiding deliberate behaviour?* According to correspondent inference theory, observers compare the effects of a chosen option with those of a rejected option. Non-common effects reveal the actor's motivation and corresponding disposition.

- *How do people weigh up different possible causes?* According to *covariation theory*, lay perceivers conduct an informal statistical analysis to work out whether an observed effect correlates with the person, entity, or context.

- *What happens when there is insufficient information for covariation analysis?* People make use of prior knowledge about general principles of causation (*causal schemas*) or about specific people, objects, and events when deciding between possible causes.

- *How do people explain their successes and failures?* Weiner classified perceived causes of success and failure using three dimensions: locus (whether the cause is internal to the person or external), stability (whether the cause is stable or variable over time), and controllability (whether the person can influence the cause). Attributing failure to internal, stable, and uncontrollable causes reduces achievement motivation.

- *Are certain patterns of attribution associated with clinical depression?* Clinically depressed people often attribute negative outcomes to internal, stable and global (widely applicable) factors.

- *Do attributions shape our own emotions?* Schachter believed that emotions depend on attributing experienced physiological arousal to emotional situations. Although this is probably not true, the way that we interpret our emotions may be influenced by manipulating our explanations for bodily symptoms.

- *Are people more likely to attribute behaviour to internal or external causes?* In many situations, people from individualistic cultures underestimate the impact of situational causes of another person's behaviour (*correspondence bias*).

- *Why do people fall victim to correspondence biases?* Situational information may not be noticed, expectations about behaviour may distort interpretations, and people may not have the motivation and opportunity to correct automatic dispositional inferences.

- *Are correspondence biases inevitable?* Asking people to interpret the situation rather than the person may reverse correspondence biases under cognitive load. People from collectivistic cultures seem less susceptible to correspondence biases.

- *Do people favour internal attributions for their own behaviour?* According to the actor–observer difference, people are more likely to use external attributions for their own behaviour but internal attributions for other people's behaviour. However, these differences are not consistently found across the broad range of possible situations.

- *Are attributions motivated by self-interest?* Self-serving biases occur when people attribute positive outcomes to internal factors and negative outcomes to external factors.

- *Are attributions usually inaccurate?* Attributions usually lead to practically useful conclusions. Bias and error are probably restricted to special situations.

- *Are attributions different when explaining intentional behaviour?* For intentional behaviour, observers do not discount internal factors when external causes are detected. Explanations in terms of intentions take priority over other possible causes.

- *Do people try to be good scientists when making attributions?* Attributions are often motivated by practical concerns or conversational demands. Scientifically valid conclusions may not always suit our strategic purposes.

- *How hard do people typically think about the causes of behaviour?* Many attributions are made automatically. Controlled processing is only involved when what needs explaining is unexpected and important, and when there is sufficient motivation and opportunity to think about why something happened.

SUGGESTIONS FOR FURTHER READING

Dweck, C. S. (2006). *Mindset: The new psychology of success*. New York: Random House. Combines accessible descriptions of research findings from studies of attributions for success with relevant case studies to make a readable self-help book.

Fiske, S. T., & Taylor, S. E. (2013). *Social cognition: From brains to culture* (2nd ed.). London: Sage. Includes treatment of attribution theory within an overarching perspective on social cognition.

Försterling, F. (2001). *Attribution: An introduction to theories, research, and applications*. Hove, UK: Psychology Press. An accessible overview of attribution models and findings from Heider to the early twenty-first century.

Gladwell, M. (2005). *Blink: The power of thinking without thinking*. London: Penguin. A popular account of how quickly and automatically people reach conclusions about objects, events, and, of course, other people.

Hewstone, M. (1989). *Causal attribution: From cognitive processes to collective beliefs*. Oxford: Blackwell. A wide-ranging view of the field, including intrapersonal, interpersonal, intergroup and societal aspects of attribution.

Ross, L., & Nisbett, R. E. (1991). *The person and the situation: Perspectives of social psychology*. New York: McGraw-Hill. Highly readable introduction to the cognitive perspective on attributional bias and other aspects of social perception and inference.

Sloman, S. A. (2005). *Causal models: How people think about the world and its alternatives*. New York: Oxford University Press. A (mostly) non-technical introduction to some sophisticated ideas about causation, intentionality and how people reason using these concepts.

Weiner, B. (2006). *Social motivation, justice, and the moral emotions: An attributional approach*. Mahwah, NJ: Erlbaum. Weiner's (2006) book applies his ideas about attribution and motivation to issues relating to justice and to legal settings.

Zebrowitz, L. A. (1990). *Social perception*. Belmont, CA: Brooks. A thorough review of research into social perception that attempts to integrate ecological and cognitive approaches.

4 Social Cognition

LOUISE PENDRY

KEY TERMS

- accessibility
- accountability
- anchoring/adjustment heuristic
- automatic process
- availability heuristic
- base rate information
- categorization
- cognitive miser
- continuum model of impression formation

- controlled process
- dissociation model
- encoding
- goal
- goal dependent
- heuristic
- implicit goal operation
- individuating information
- lexical decision task
- outcome dependency

- priming
- probe reaction task
- rebound effect
- representativeness heuristic
- schema
- social cognition
- stereotype
- stereotype suppression

CHAPTER OUTLINE

INTRODUCTION 95

JUMPING TO CONCLUSIONS OR WORKING THINGS OUT
SLOWLY 95

THE AUTOMATIC PILOT WITHIN 96

    What makes a process automatic? 96

    The pervasive nature of social categorization 97

    Schemas: the next step in the process? 100

    *Making judgements when you don't have all the data:
cognitive heuristics 101*

    Why do we fall prey to judgemental heuristics? 104

    Schema activation and behaviour 105

    Summary 108

GOING THE EXTRA MILE: REGAINING COGNITIVE
CONTROL 108

    *Stereotype? What stereotype? How goals can stop the
stereotype being activated in the first place 108*

    *Quashing the effects of stereotype activation once it has
occurred 110*

    Summary 120

CHAPTER SUMMARY 121

ROUTE MAP OF THE CHAPTER

We inhabit a hectic social world. In any one day we can expect to deal with many other people. We may meet people for the first time, go out with old friends, find ourselves in a job interview trying to make a good impression on our prospective employer, or else queuing in a supermarket to pay for groceries, or waiting for a train on a busy platform. Even for those of us professing to live ordinary lives, no two days are exactly alike. So, precisely how do we navigate this complex social life? What social information grabs our attention? How do we organize and use it in our interactions with and judgements about others? These are some of the questions that interest social cognition researchers, and providing answers to them strikes at the very heart of understanding human mental life. In this chapter we investigate some of the ways in which we process social information in situations such as these. The chapter focuses especially on the distinction between the social processes and judgements we make that are often speedy and automatic 'gut reactions', such as categorization and heuristic processing, and those which may require more effort, deliberation and control (for example, forming more careful impressions of others and avoiding stereotyping).

INTRODUCTION

What is social cognition?

A core topic in social psychology is the study of **social cognition**, which is concerned with how we make sense of ourselves and others in our social world. Understanding how we select, store, remember and use social information can tell us a great deal about how we are able to successfully navigate what is a very complex social environment. As we go about our daily schedules, we are busy 'doing' social cognition for real. So, just what is it? Essentially, the study of social cognition promotes a deeper understanding of the mental processes that underlie human social behaviour (Fiske & Taylor, 1991). It sheds light on the steps people go through when thinking about others (Fiske, 2004).

social cognition a large topic within social psychology concerned with understanding how we think about ourselves and other people and how the processes involved impact upon our judgements and behaviour in social contexts.

If we think about it for just a moment, this has implications for a very broad range of human social phenomena and domains. What is especially intriguing about social cognition is that it taps into the kinds of questions we find ourselves asking. Questions such as:

- Why did I assume that the man at the coffee machine in the boardroom was the company director when he was in fact the secretary?

- Why did I assume that Dr Alex James would be male / white?

- Why is it that I expected Albert to be elderly?

- Why did it surprise me to discover that Hilda, my elderly neighbour, had a passion for car maintenance?

- Why did I take the time to talk to my new female work colleague and find myself subsequently re-evaluating my initially stereotypic impression of her?

The aim of this chapter is to pass on to you a little of what we have learned thus far about some of the main theoretical issues in the field (for more detail, see Bless, Fiedler, & Strack, 2004; Fiske & Taylor, 1991, 2013; Kunda, 1999; Moskowitz, 2005). This chapter will give you a flavour of some of the more established theories in the field, and consider both the classic and more contemporary research that such theories have generated in their quest to understand better the workings of the social mind.

JUMPING TO CONCLUSIONS OR WORKING THINGS OUT SLOWLY

Why is it so easy to jump to conclusions when making judgements about others?

Although the field of social cognition is extremely broad and vibrant, few researchers would deny that one recurring, overarching theme is the distinction between social thinking that is *fast and furious* and social thinking that is more *measured and precise*. Since the 1970s, significant developments in theory and methodology have meant that it is possible for us to now focus independently on these different types of thinking, that is, the influence of *unintentional* (i.e., unconscious) and *intentional* (i.e., conscious) processes in human thought and behaviour (Posner & Snyder, 1975). You might see this distinction encompassed in the term *dual-processing theories*. Or, to put it yet another way (and the way we will mainly refer to it hereafter), it refers to the contrast between **automatic** and **controlled processes**.

automatic process a process that occurs without intention, effort or awareness and does not interfere with other concurrent cognitive processes.

In this chapter, we focus primarily upon this distinction. Do we process information about others carefully and rationally, or do we instead make rash judgements on the spur of the moment? Understanding when and why we engage in automatic or controlled processing can tell us a lot about how we view our social world.

controlled process a process that is intentional, under the individual's volitional control, effortful and entailing conscious awareness.

To make this kind of distinction a little clearer, consider the following passage:

Simon tried to put nationalities to faces, according to stereotype. The group of brawny, over-tanned and over-jewelled men and women who had ordered Bordeaux rather than local wine should be German – prosperous, large and loud. Any table giving off a cloud of cigarette smoke should be French, just as a table of non-smokers, with more water than wine being drunk, should be Americans. The English loaded butter onto their bread and ordered the heaviest desserts. The Swiss ate neatly and kept their elbows off the table, alternating sips of wine and sips of water like clockwork. (Mayle, 1993, p. 234)

Simon's observations, taken from Peter Mayle's amusing book *Hotel Pastis*, may not strike us as particularly unusual. We may not endorse the national stereotypes conveyed in the passage quoted above, or we may at least question their accuracy, but somehow, we know exactly what Simon is talking about. Despite the perils of stereotypical thinking, it is something that we are apt to find irresistible (e.g., Brewer, 1988; Devine, 1989; Fiske & Neuberg, 1990).

Did Simon pause for even a moment to consider if his snap decisions were accurate? Did he stop to consider that in fact several of the French contingent were not actually smoking? Or that at least two of the English group were nibbling abstemiously on fruit salad (no cream)? No. The questions for social cognition researchers are: how and why did Simon respond in this manner? What processes led him to these conclusions? In social cognitive terms, the above illustration demonstrates several steps in a process that will be the focus of the next sections. Simon has:

- *Categorized* each of the people in the restaurant in terms of nationality (grouped them into discrete sets – here, nationalities – based upon perceived shared characteristics).

- *Activated* the *content* of these categories (what we term **schemas**: our expectancies about members of a category, here people belonging to such groups).

- Used a mental shortcut (rule of thumb) to pigeon-hole individuals according to how similar they are to typical members of a particular group (in line with the common stereotype that a large percentage of the British population eat unhealthily).

> **schema** a cognitive structure or mental representation comprising pre-digested information or knowledge about objects or people from specific categories, our expectancies about objects or groups, and what defines them.

Much of this occurred fairly spontaneously. Simon did not stop to deliberate more carefully. As we shall see, it is a fundamental tenet of social cognition research that we often process information in precisely this way, only moving beyond the obvious stereotype if motivated and able to do so (e.g., Fiske & Neuberg, 1990). Schemas such as those outlined above have a functional role to play in facilitating person perception. They are, as Bodenhausen (1990) has noted, a kind of cognitive shortcut, a simplifying rule of thumb or **heuristic** that serves us well a lot of the time, but not always (for more on heuristics, see later in this chapter, and also Chapter 7).

> **heuristic** a well-used, non-optimal rule of thumb used to arrive at a judgement that is effective in many but not all cases; stereotypes are often said to function as heuristics.

In this chapter, we will consider some of the research that speaks to the distinction between automatic and controlled processes: when, why and how do we engage in automatic versus controlled processing in person perception? By the end of this chapter you will be well equipped to provide preliminary answers to these questions.

THE AUTOMATIC PILOT WITHIN

Read the following passage:

> A father and his son were involved in a car accident in which the father was killed and the son was seriously injured. The father was pronounced dead at the scene of the accident and his body taken to a local morgue. The son was taken by ambulance to a nearby hospital and was immediately wheeled into an emergency operating room. A surgeon was called. Upon arrival, and seeing the patient, the attending surgeon exclaimed, 'Oh my God, it's my son!'
>
> Can you explain this?

So, how did you do? Many people find this question impossible to answer (based on lab class demonstrations over a number of years, often more than 40 per cent of students simply cannot do it; Pendry, Driscoll, & Field, 2007). Moreover, they are apt to generate a wide range of convoluted explanations (for example, the 'father' who was killed is a Catholic priest and the term 'son' is therefore being used rather loosely) other than the most obvious one (the surgeon is the boy's mother). Why do people have so much trouble and why do they generate such complex rationalizations? Essentially, they find it hard to overcome the automatically activated **stereotype** (i.e., surgeons are generally men; see Figure 4.1).

> **stereotype** a cognitive structure that contains our knowledge, beliefs and expectancies about some human social group.

As we shall see, this tendency to activate stereotypes automatically happens an awful lot. We will now pay some closer attention to why this occurs.

What makes a process automatic?

For a process to be considered automatic, several criteria are deemed necessary (e.g., Posner & Snyder, 1975): the process needs to occur without *intention*, *effort* or *awareness* and is *not expected to interfere with other concurrent cognitive processes*. For those of us who have been behind the wheel of a car for a few years, the act of changing

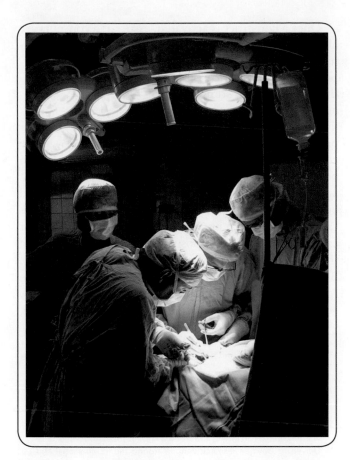

FIGURE 4.1 *Did you assume that these surgeons were men?*
Source: Image Copyright Brasiliao. Used under licence from Shutterstock.com.

gear would possibly meet these criteria. A controlled process, on the other hand, is one that is: *intentional, under the individual's volitional control, effortful* and *entails conscious awareness.* To continue the driving analogy, deciding whether it is safe to overtake on a busy motorway should (one would hope!) fulfil these criteria. Let us now consider how this automatic versus controlled distinction contributes to our understanding of the process of person perception. We will start by looking at social categorization.

The pervasive nature of social categorization

Almost every doctor who saw and examined me, labelled me a very interesting but also a hopeless case. Many told my mother very gently that I was mentally defective and would remain so . . . nothing could be done for me.

(Christy Brown, 1955, p. 10)

Christy Brown suffered from cerebral palsy and was considered mentally disabled until one day he snatched a piece of chalk from his sister and wrote some words with it. He went on to astound and defy the medical profession by becoming a widely acclaimed author, whose autobiography was made into a successful film, *My Left Foot.* Branded from birth as 'retarded and useless', he fought to overcome prejudice and ignorance. The consequences of **categorization** can, then, sometimes be rather unpalatable. Once we assign others to particular social categories, associated stereotypic information can dominate our judgements to a worrying degree. Nonetheless, it does seem unlikely that we can view others in total isolation from their obvious physical and social categories. This is the view adopted by many theorists who work in the area (e.g., Brewer, 1988; Fiske & Neuberg, 1990; Macrae & Bodenhausen, 2000), and we will now turn our attention to why they endorse such a position.

> **categorization** the tendency to group objects (including people) into discrete groups based upon shared characteristics common to them.

Categorization refers to the tendency we have to group objects (including people) into discrete groups, based upon shared characteristics. There are object categories for furniture, takeaway food and musical instruments, but also social categories for women, refuse collectors, children, rock stars and so on. It is a fundamental premise of the social cognition approach that such categories serve a very useful function (e.g., Allport, 1954b; Macrae, Milne, & Bodenhausen, 1994). Why do you think this is?

Consider the following thought experiment. Imagine a far-off planet, Zygon, a place where perceptual mechanisms and inferential strategies have evolved in a decidedly unearthly manner. One day, an inhabitant from Zygon lands her spaceship somewhere on planet Earth and begins her journey into the unknown. She will doubtless be faced with many new objects and life forms that we human beings would, effortlessly, be able to sort into people, buildings, animals, trees and so on. Not so the Zygonian. Devoid of the cognitive know-how to parse this new and complex social landscape into something more intelligible, she would eventually experience information overload. There would simply be too many stimuli to process, at least in any meaningful manner.

This ability to separate our social world into discrete social categories is therefore a vital adaptation that ensures we don't find ourselves in a similarly daunting position. Without it, each person we meet (or each object) would be unique and need to be treated accordingly. Imagine how much time and effort that would take. Stated simply, *categorization favours simplification,* which in turn renders the world a more orderly, predictable and controllable place.

So, having established why categorization is so useful, let's look in more detail at the evidence that it is an *automatic* process. In 1989, Devine published an influential article in which she argued that (1) knowledge about racial stereotypes is culturally shared, even by people who do not endorse such stereotypes, and (2) activation of this knowledge (i.e., stereotype activation) is an automatic process (see Leader in the Field, Patricia Devine). Recall that the criteria for a process to be automatic include that it is unconscious and does not require intention, attention or effort. If stereotype activation is truly automatic, this should mean that any time the appropriate cues are present (e.g., age, race or gender), stereotype activation should *invariably* result. So, how might this be tested empirically? Devine (1989, Study 2) used what is known as a **priming** paradigm (see Bargh & Pietromonaco,

> **priming** activating one stimulus (e.g., bird) facilitates the subsequent processing of another related stimulus (e.g., wing, feather).

1982). We need to dwell a moment on what priming is and why the priming paradigm is such a useful research tool to enable us to test Devine's hypothesis (and indeed, many other related research questions within social cognition).

When a construct is triggered in memory and made *temporarily accessible*, this is called priming and the stimulus that leads to this construct being triggered is called the prime (Moskowitz, 2005). In concrete terms, priming or activating one stimulus (e.g., horse) facilitates the way in which we subsequently process another related stimulus (e.g., mane, tail) via a process known as *spreading activation* (e.g., Neely, 1977; see Figure 4.2 for a schematic representation of this process).

Once a construct is activated, associated concepts are also triggered and attain a state of heightened **accessibility**, even if they were not directly primed initially. Such concepts therefore require some kind of cue to render them momentarily accessible. To use an analogy

> **accessibility** the extent to which information is easily located and retrieved.

proposed by Higgins, Bargh, and Lombardi (1985), these concepts are like a battery that is running low but can be recharged in certain circumstances (i.e., when the appropriate environmental trigger is present). It should be noted that other concepts, such as strongly held political beliefs, are often perpetually well charged (aided, for example, by repeated exposure to political arguments in the press, or political debates with like-minded friends). Being in a state of permanently high charge, they are routinely more accessible. These are termed *chronically accessible* concepts (for a detailed review, see Moskowitz,

 LEADER IN THE FIELD

Patricia Devine (b. 1959) spent her undergraduate years at the State University of New York, graduating in 1981, *summa cum laude*. This was followed by an MA (in 1983) and a PhD (in 1986) from Ohio State University. Devine's research centres around the intrapersonal and interpersonal challenges associated with prejudice in contemporary society. Her early work on the automatic and controlled components of stereotyping (1989) has been extremely influential in the field. Recent research concerns include the relation between explicit and implicit prejudice and the processes that regulate the use of stereotypes.

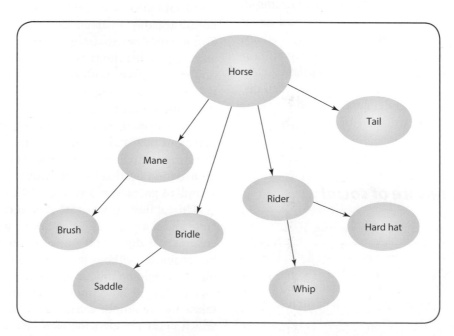

FIGURE 4.2 *Example of spreading activation.*

2005). Here, though, we focus primarily on how priming makes concepts temporarily accessible.

lexical decision task a cognitive measure of how quickly people classify stimuli as real words or nonsense words that enables researchers to assess if some categories of words are made more accessible as a result of an experimental manipulation/processing goal. Quicker responses to certain word categories indicate increased accessibility.

In one measure of accessibility, known as a **lexical decision task**, priming stimuli (e.g., words or pictures) are often presented on a computer, usually very quickly. Participants are then shown a letter string that may or may not be associated with the prime (and may or may not be a real word), and asked to decide if it is a real word or a non-word by pressing one of two computer keys. A priming effect is obtained when participants are shown to respond significantly faster to real words preceded by an associated prime (i.e., are quicker to respond to *wing* after being primed with *bird* than when not primed). The advantage of priming paradigms is that they usually indicate uncontrolled automatic processing. Participants' subsequent reaction times are not influenced by self-presentational strategies (i.e., wanting to show themselves in a certain, often socially desirable, light), as might be the case, say, with paper and pencil measures of stereotyping.

Now that we are clearer about how priming paradigms work and why they are so suited to the study of automatic processes within social cognition, let's return to Devine's work. In her experiment, primes related to a stereotype were presented outside of participants' conscious awareness. In order to do this, she presented the primes outside of participants' parafoveal field (i.e., out of their direct line of vision). The primes Devine used were terms related to the stereotype associated with Black people (i.e., labels such as *Blacks*, *Niggers*, and physical or trait characteristics including *poor*, *lazy*). The participants had been pre-tested for prejudice level: half were high in prejudice towards Black people, whereas half were low. This distinction forms an important part of Devine's experimental hypotheses, as we shall see later. Devine presented some participants with a high proportion (80 per cent) of ethnically associated words, and other participants with a much lower proportion (20 per cent).

Following the prime, in an ostensibly unrelated second experiment, participants read a brief scenario and were asked to form an impression of a target person who engaged in ambiguously hostile behaviours (after a paradigm originally developed by Srull & Wyer, 1980). Why hostile? Because pre-testing had indicated that hostility was a very strong feature of the Black stereotype (see also Duncan, 1976). None of the words used in the priming phase, however, was directly related to hostility. This is important, because it suggests that if the prime exerts the predicted effects upon interpretation of the ambiguous behaviour, it is due to automatic stereotype activation rather than simple priming of the hostile construct.

Let's consider what Devine predicted and found. Devine reported that those participants who received the high proportion of ethnic primes rated the target person in the story significantly more negatively (e.g., as more hostile and unfriendly) than did participants who received the low proportion of ethnic primes. Recall that Devine's view is that stereotypes are activated automatically. If this is so, then we should find that participants activate the Black stereotype in the priming phase of the study (unconsciously) and go on to use it (without awareness) in the second part of the study (when forming an impression of the target). This should translate into higher ratings of the target as hostile, following a Black prime.

What about the differing levels of prejudice among participants? This was a very neat twist: if these results are found in both high- and low-prejudice individuals, it is stronger evidence still that stereotype knowledge is culturally shared and that activation is indeed automatic. If the priming effect can be demonstrated even among individuals who do not endorse the stereotype, this is pretty good evidence that it happened automatically. If low-prejudice participants could have found some way of controlling this rather undesirable response, they surely would have done so, since it is clearly at odds with their beliefs. In fact, Devine found that participants' prior level of prejudice made little difference to how susceptible they were to the ethnic primes (for more on the studies in this paper, see Research Close-Up 4.3).

This study is one of a number that have investigated the so-called automaticity of stereotype activation (see also Banaji & Hardin, 1996; Perdue & Gurtman, 1990). The results seem to provide quite compelling evidence. Moreover, during the 1990s research in this area blossomed and the literature is now replete with evidence of the seeming automaticity of stereotype activation (for recent reviews see Bargh, 1999; Bodenhausen, Todd, & Richeson, 2009; Devine & Monteith, 1999).

So should we conclude that the case for the automaticity of stereotype activation is established beyond question? Perhaps not just yet. The situation regarding automaticity is actually rather complex, and researchers themselves are divided in terms of how it is best interpreted (see Bargh, 1999; Bodenhausen et al., 2009; Devine & Monteith, 1999). Moreover, recent research has provided some important qualifications to the debate, as we shall see later in this chapter. For now, we will note that stereotypes are often automatically activated. The question we now consider is this: once a stereotype category has been activated, what can happen next?

Schemas: the next step in the process?

Several years ago a British national daily newspaper ran an advertising campaign on television. The advertisements featured a skinhead running at speed towards a businessman. Figures 4.3a and 4.3b show two shots in the sequence; what do you think happened next?

Most people, when asked, assumed the next shot showed the skinhead mugging the businessman. He was instead rushing to save him from a large pile of falling bricks (see Figure 4.4).

The newspaper (*The Guardian*) used this example to illustrate its commitment to impartial reporting – the need to get the full picture. Here it serves a useful educational purpose: it potently depicts what can happen once

a category has been activated. Why did people jump to this conclusion? The answer lies in the spontaneous **encoding** of the situation. People see the skinhead, readily activate the pertinent skinhead schema (e.g., anarchic, violent) and arrive at the mistaken conclusion that he is probably about to behave aggressively. Encoding refers to how we translate what we see into a suitable format that can be readily stored in our mind (Fiske & Taylor, 1991).

> **encoding** the way in which we translate what we see into a digestible format to be stored in the mind.

This example illustrates that while it may be a useful strategy to leap to the first obvious conclusions when perceiving others, it is not always a sound one. The behaviour was somewhat *ambiguous*: there are many reasons why a person may be running in the direction of another. The important point is that, in this case, the activated schema *biased the interpretation of the behaviour* in line with the skinhead stereotype.

This tendency has been demonstrated in a number of laboratory experiments (e.g., Correll, Park, Judd, & Wittenbrink, 2002; Duncan, 1976; Payne, 2001). In an example reminiscent of the above real-world scenario, Correll et al. (2002) had participants play a video game in which they were shown photographs of young men in a range of settings (at a train station, in a park). Half were Black, half were White. Additionally, half were holding a gun, whereas the other half were holding harmless objects (mobile phone, camera). In the so-called 'Shooter Task' or 'Weapons-Identification Task,' participants had to press a button labelled 'Shoot' if the man in

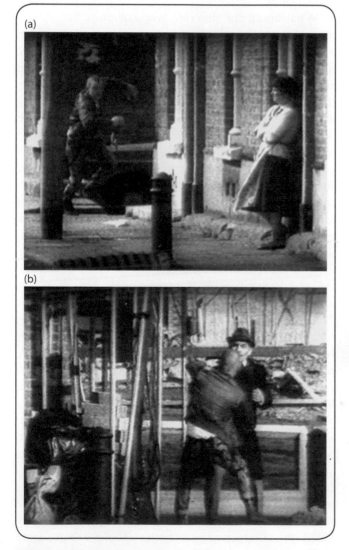

FIGURE 4.3 (a) and (b) *Two stills of a skinhead in* The Guardian *advertising campaign.*

Source: © Guardian News & Media Ltd 1986. Reproduced with permission.

FIGURE 4.4 *Final still of the skinhead in* The Guardian *campaign.*

Source: © Guardian News & Media Ltd 1986. Reproduced with permission.

the photo was carrying a gun, or press another button labelled 'Don't shoot' if he was not. They had just half a second to make each decision, so it really was a gut-reaction judgement. Points were awarded or deducted based upon whether participants made the correct judgements. Results showed that participants were most likely to hit 'Shoot' when the person was Black, regardless of whether they were holding a gun. This 'Shooter Bias' reveals how accessible schemas can bias the interpretation given to social events, especially when time (and processing capacity) are in short supply. (We now suggest you read Social Psychology Beyond the Lab 4.1 to see how this bias has been demonstrated beyond the laboratory setting.)

Let's now consider the schema topic in more detail. Once we have activated a category stereotype, we bring into play the *knowledge* contained within these structures: our schemas or stereotypes (Brewer, 1988; Fiske & Neuberg, 1990). Schemas are – stated simply – packets of pre-digested information we hold in our heads about objects or people from specific categories: our expectancies about objects or groups. As an illustration, consider the kinds of information that come to mind when the category 'woman' is activated. Such a person might be readily described as kind, gentle, nurturing and home-loving. Or perhaps one might instead consider a subcategory of this broad category, such as 'business woman' (ambitious, assertive, motivated, ruthless, wears designer suits, unpopular with colleagues). Clearly, several different types of information may be discerned, including, for example, knowledge about 'business women' (what they typically do and don't do) and value judgements about them (their likeability, popularity, etc.). However, a schema should not be misconstrued as a long list of separate unrelated items and attributes. Rather, it is a cognitive structure within which attributes are organized and relations between them perceived. Thus, we might perceive a relationship between the fact that 'business women' are ambitious and assertive, or perhaps between the observation that they are ruthless and not very popular (see Figure 4.5 for an illustration of such a schema).

So, a schema contains many different kinds of knowledge about a particular category. Armed with this knowledge, the process of impression formation is greatly facilitated, because schemas affect how quickly we perceive, notice and interpret available information (Fiske & Taylor, 1991; Kunda, 1999). We are apt to rely upon schemas for a number of reasons. Table 4.1 summarizes some of the main ones (from Fiske and Taylor, 1991).

In the following section we broaden the topic of cognitive shortcuts still further to see how other kinds of heuristic schematic processing can affect the judgements and decisions we make about others when there may be demands on our information processing capacities.

Making judgements when you don't have all the data: cognitive heuristics

Imagine that you have just started your degree course at a large London university. In your first tutorial meeting with your professor, you are introduced to the other students in your tutor group. One of them, Jez, has a deep

SOCIAL PSYCHOLOGY BEYOND THE LAB 4.1

IF THE FACE FITS. . . HOW JEAN CHARLES DE MENEZES CAME TO BE SHOT DEAD IN ERROR

In the wake of the London terrorist bombings of July 2005, police were following up a number of leads about the likely whereabouts of the bombers. An address found in one of the unexploded bags recovered by police led to close surveillance of a block of flats near Stockwell tube station in London. At 9.30 a.m., Brazilian-born Jean Charles de Menezes, an electrician, left the building following a call to fix a broken fire alarm. Believing him to be wearing clothing and behaving in a manner that aroused suspicions of his being a suicide bomber, and wanting to avert a further terrorist episode, the police followed him to Stockwell tube station, where he was shot dead. It was subsequently discovered that de Menezes was not carrying explosives and indeed was not connected in any way to the terrorist attack. The facts of the case have been the subject of ongoing debate, and inconsistencies in police statements have never been entirely resolved. Subsequent information suggests that the police may have jumped to conclusions based on the potential match between de Menezes and the Muslim terrorists. The de Menezes shooting highlights how schema use (here based upon physical appearance, clothing and behaviour) can have tragic consequences.

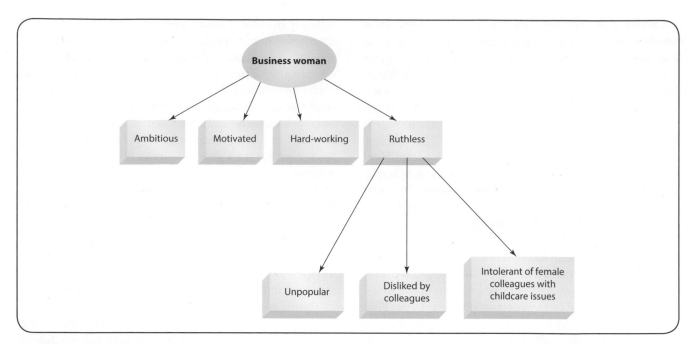

FIGURE 4.5 *Example of business woman schema.*

Table 4.1 *When do we rely upon schemas?*

Role schemas (that imply jobs or tasks people do) may dominate over traits (role schemas are more informative because they are richer and imply more associations)

Subtype schemas (business woman) may be used more than superordinate ones (woman) because they allow us to reconcile information that contradicts the broader superordinate level schema (women at work whose assertive behaviour contradicts their gender role may be viewed as business women)

Information presented early on can cue schemas (primacy) that help organize subsequent information

We use schemas that attract our attention (salience) because they set a person apart such as a male nurse in a ward with otherwise all female staff

We use schemas that have previously been primed (accessibility) because such information comes to mind easily and is readily available to us

We use schemas consistent with our current feelings (mood) because in most cases, our moods seem to cue mood-consistent schemas

We use schemas relevant to controlling our outcomes (power) because status hierarchies affect us whether we are high (leader) or low (minority group) in status

Source: Adapted from Fiske and Taylor (1991) *Social Cognition,* 2nd Edition. © The McGraw-Hill Companies.

tan, sun-bleached tousled locks, and is asking the tutor what facilities there are to store large surfing equipment in his hall of residence. Keen to get to know your fellow students and engage in friendly conversation, you say, 'Hi Jez. Let me guess. . . Are you maybe from Newquay or some other surfy place in the South West of England?' You base this hypothesis upon your knowledge of the common stereotype for surfers, which Jez seems to fit perfectly. This illustrates what is called the **representativeness heuristic**, a mental shortcut (rule of thumb) that we use in order to pigeonhole something/someone according to how similar it is to (or how representative it is of) a typical exemplar (here, the surfer stereotype; Kahneman & Tversky, 1972). It is one of several *judgemental heuristics* that allow us to make sense of large amounts of information in a relatively easy way.

> **representativeness heuristic** a mental shortcut whereby instances are assigned to categories on the basis of how similar they are to the category in general.

Yet, if you had access to the profile of students at this particular university, you would see that students from the South West are not very well represented: most students are drawn from the counties around London. If you were then told this, would you revise your initial opinion of Jez's likely origins? After all, you now know there are probably not that many students from the South West at this university. This information about the frequency of certain categories in the general population is called **base rate**

> **base rate information** information that gives us an idea about how frequent certain categories are in the general population.

information. If you were to give it due weight in your decision-making process, you might conclude that your original assumption was perhaps a bit hasty. The trouble is, and as decades of research have shown (see Gilovich & Savitsky, 2002), when we are faced with base rate information and seemingly conflicting exemplars, we often fail to take account of base rate information and are more influenced by representativeness information.

We don't only rely upon the representativeness heuristic when taking judgemental shortcuts. Say you are asked to estimate how many famous celebrities have succumbed to plastic surgery in the past few years. How would you go about calculating this? Would you, say, look at some comprehensive list compiled of the top one hundred celebrities and then systematically search for evidence about whether each of them had undergone plastic surgery before you made a cautious estimate? Or would you instead bring to mind (probably with very little trouble) the instances of celebrities whose faces are regularly splashed across the pages of the popular press who are well-known to have gone under the knife (Katie Price, Victoria Beckham, Angelina Jolie, Tom Cruise, Britney Spears, Cher, Tom Jones). And from this would you deduce that it is probably fairly commonplace for celebrities to indulge their desires for cosmetic self-enhancement? If you think you would probably have opted for this second 'quick and dirty' method, then you have just demonstrated for yourself the lure of the **availability heuristic**: you have based your judgement on how easily information comes to mind (Schwarz et al., 1991).

> **availability heuristic** a cognitive shortcut that allows us to draw upon information about how quickly information comes to mind about a particular event, to deduce the frequency or likelihood of that event.

Sometimes it works to our advantage, but at times it can let us down. Say for example that you are asked to guess how many high school students of your daughter's age prefer a particular, popular designer brand of clothing. Without really trying, you bring to mind numerous examples of male and female pre-teens you have seen hanging around in town, or friends of your daughter, all kitted out in hooded tops and sweatpants by this designer. It seems every young person is wearing this label. From this mental exercise, you may infer that the entire year group is equally addicted to the brand. And when you read in the press how over three-quarters of this age group own at least one item of clothing by this designer, you will feel your reliance on the availability heuristic was justified. Students of this age do clearly love this brand!

On the other hand, say you are asked how many women in their twenties are currently having babies. Without hesitation, you bring to mind numerous examples in your workplace of female colleagues in that age bracket who are either pregnant or off on maternity leave. From this you deduce that a high percentage of twenty-something women are reproducing right now. In fact, the higher numbers of women in your workplace are something of a blip that does not correlate that well with a falling birth-rate among this age group in the more general population. On this occasion, then, the availability heuristic has not provided an accurate estimate.

As a final illustration of another cognitive heuristic, imagine you are a judge deciding upon a prison sentence for a defendant who has been accused of rape. Obviously your decision ought to be made based upon a systematic review of the available evidence. What might surprise you, however, is that your decision about the length of the sentence could be very easily influenced by seemingly trivial factors. Say on your journey to the courtroom that day you had passed through roadworks with a series of 20 mph speed restrictions punctuating your journey. Could something as random as the temporary accessibility of an arbitrary number affect your decision? Might this number act as some kind of anchor, providing a numerical start point that you will probably not stray too far from when making your sentencing decision? Whilst this may sound a rather implausible scenario, research suggests such arbitrary anchors can exert a strong influence on later decisions.

Englich, Mussweiler, and Strack (2006) tested this idea in a real-life legal setting involving sentencing decisions made by experienced legal professionals. Participating legal experts were shown realistic case materials involving an alleged case of rape and asked to provide their sentencing decision based on their appraisal of the situation. Participants received one of three anchors: in one condition the anchor came from an irrelevant source (a journalist asking about the appropriateness of a certain sentencing decision); in a second condition they were told the anchor had been randomly chosen; and in a third condition, participants themselves randomly decided upon the anchor based on the toss of dice. In each case, the anchor was either high (three years) or low (one year). In all three conditions, the anchor constrained sentencing decisions, with participants assimilating their answer in the direction provided by the anchor. For example, in Study 1, participants provided with a high (three years) anchor reached a mean decision length of 33.38 months, whereas those provided with a low (one year) anchor suggested a mean decision length of 25.43 months (see Figure 4.6). Although one might expect (and indeed, hope) that experience and practice would reduce this tendency to be affected by arbitrary anchors,

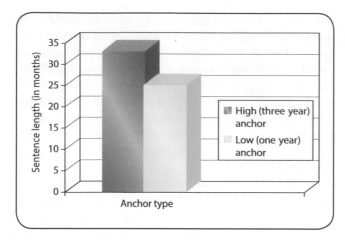

FIGURE 4.6 *Mean sentencing decisions (in months) as a function of different anchors.*

Source: From Englich et al. (2006) with permission from SAGE publications.

anchoring/adjustment heuristic a cognitive heuristic that makes us place weight upon initial standards/schemas (anchors) and as a result means we may not always adjust sufficiently far from these anchors to provide accurate judgements.

this was not the case. This result neatly illustrates what is known as the **anchoring/adjustment heuristic**. We now suggest you read Social Psychology Beyond the Lab 4.2 to see another demonstration of this cognitive heuristic.

Why do we fall prey to judgemental heuristics?

Judgemental heuristics such as these show us how cognitive shortcuts can exert a seductive influence upon our decision-making processes. Social cognition research can tell us a good deal about why they occur, and we will briefly consider some of the main findings here (for detailed reviews, see Fiske & Taylor, 2008; Moskowitz, 2005; Tversky & Kahneman 1974). We will consider each of the three main heuristics in turn: representativeness, availability and anchoring.

The representativeness heuristic is often used because we are unwilling to engage in the kind of effortful processing required to properly factor in base rate information, as noted above. We rely upon a fairly simple similarity judgement (e.g., Jez is more similar to the typical surfing dude than to the typical computer nerd). In addition, we may neglect to take proper account of sample size. In statistics it is well known that estimates drawn from large samples are more reliable than those drawn from small ones, yet we are often happy to make judgements via representativeness even if we base them on just a few exemplars. A third factor that may affect use of the representativeness heuristic is predictive value. When we hear information about a person second-hand, we should really pay heed to the source of that information in terms

SOCIAL PSYCHOLOGY BEYOND THE LAB 4.2

ANCHORING AND ADJUSTMENT AT WORK IN THE PROPERTY MARKET: MORE THAN JUST A PARLOUR TRICK?

Some researchers have suggested that the anchoring/adjustment heuristic is more likely to occur in lab settings where the information available is impoverished and not terribly realistic (Hogarth, 1981). Anxious to see if the lab findings generalized to more information-rich real-world settings, Northcraft and Neale (1987) asked experts (estate agents) and, for comparison, amateurs (students) to tour real properties that were for sale at the time and make judgements about their fair market value (FMV). As in the lab studies, and indeed reflecting common estate agent practice, all participants received an 'anchor' value in their information packs – here in the form of a guide price – which varied (low, moderately low, moderately high and high). As expected, participants' FMV estimates varied as a function of the guide price they received. For example, if provided with a guide

price of $65,900, estimates were $63,571 for students and $67,811 for estate agents. If the anchor value was higher ($83,900) estimates were $72,196 and $75,190, respectively. This was the case for both the 'experts' and 'amateurs' (although one might comment that the experts' valuations tended to be a little more optimistic and the students' a little more cautious!). The authors concluded that 'decision biases and heuristics are more than just parlour tricks and that they should play an important role in our understanding of everyday decision behaviour' (Northcraft & Neale, 1987, p. 96). Although a more realistic example, this research still provides an anchor, as opposed to letting people generate one for themselves. As we see in the next section, this distinction can have important implications for the prevalence of the anchoring/adjustment heuristic.

of its credibility. Imagine you hear a student describe a male housemate she has only just met as 'a bit antisocial', based solely upon his reclusive behaviour during Fresher's Week. Are you less inclined to believe this description is accurate than if you had heard a similar characterization from the housemate's best school friend who had garnered rather more evidence of her male friend's behaviours over several years? Ideally, we would give the second source more weight, but a lot of the time we do not (Fiske & Taylor, 2008). In sum, like much of the material in the first part of this chapter, the representativeness heuristic is another example of our tendency to prefer simple over more complex cognitive deliberations (that is, to behave as **cognitive misers**; Fiske & Taylor, 1991; 2008).

cognitive miser a view of people as being often limited in processing capacity and apt to take shortcuts where possible to make life simple.

Turning to the availability heuristic, it is perhaps best understood by thinking about how easily information springs to mind.

If information about the many instances of celebrities choosing plastic surgery pops into our heads with consummate ease, then we may conclude it is probably something that happens an awful lot. That is, we assume that volume of exemplars (*content*) correlates with its *ease of retrieval* (Schwarz et al., 1991). Another possibility is that we simply *feel* that if information comes to mind easily (or not) then it must say something about how frequent it actually is.

These two explanations (content versus feel) were considered in a study by Schwarz et al. (1991). People were first asked to recall six or twelve assertive behaviours they themselves had engaged in, and then had to judge their own assertiveness. Who do you think rated themselves as more assertive: those who had recalled six behaviours that confirmed this, or those who had to recall twelve behaviours? You might think the answer is easy, and that of course, those who provided more instances of their own assertiveness rated themselves as more assertive, but in fact this was not what was found. Those recalling only six assertive examples rated themselves as more assertive than those recalling twelve examples (by the way, these researchers also collected data on unassertiveness, and found the same pattern of results, such that those providing fewer examples of unassertive behaviour rated themselves as less assertive).

So, what is going on? Well, try this for yourself – how easy do you find listing twelve examples of your own assertive behaviour? The answer is probably 'not very'. You might easily come up with a few at first ('I said no to the extra workload my boss was trying to make me agree to', 'I stood up for a female colleague who was being bullied', 'I intervened when a group of youths were hassling an old lady in the shopping mall'), but you are likely to

falter soon after. So, what Schwarz et al. concluded was that it was the difficulty of retrieving examples that drove these effects. If you are struggling to get even four examples of assertive behaviour when you've been instructed to come up with twelve, you may be left thinking you are a pretty unassertive kind of person. What this study neatly shows, therefore, is that the feeling of difficulty/ease of retrieval can matter as much as absolute numbers (content).

Finally, the anchoring/adjustment heuristic is traditionally thought to occur because of a failure to properly adjust from an irrelevant value that provides an anchor (Tversky & Kahneman, 1974). More recently, though, the debate has broadened out to better understand why adjustments tend to be insufficient (Epley & Gilovich, 2006). Such research looks more closely at the processes that underpin the adjustment phase. In particular, Epley and Gilovich's (2006) studies explored why adjustment processes appear to differ when participants call upon their own, self-generated anchors when making judgements, as opposed to anchors provided by the experimenter. Past research (Epley, 2004; Epley & Gilovich, 2001) has found that where people generate their own anchors, these seem to function as a kind of judgemental heuristic and simplify what would otherwise be a quite complicated judgement. In such cases, adjustments seem to stop once participants feel they have reached a plausible value, and hence adjustments for self-generated anchors may be insufficient (in comparison to adjustments for experimenter-provided anchors). What this means in practice is that people who make judgements based on an anchor they have themselves generated typically do not move that far from it when providing their actual answer (that is they adjust less from their initial anchor). In sum, self-generated anchors may make appropriate adjustment less likely.

Schema activation and behaviour

Can we be primed to think, feel or behave in a certain way without even knowing it?

In the late 1990s, a number of articles appeared that demonstrated a very intriguing phenomenon: behavioural responses (e.g., walking slowly) can be automatically activated in response to an activated schema-relevant word (e.g., 'wrinkle'). (We now suggest that you read Research Close-Up 4.1.)

This same basic effect was subsequently demonstrated using a range of category stereotypes and trait concepts, and showed several behavioural consequences (e.g., performance on intelligence tasks, interpersonal behaviour, memory performance; for a review, see Dijksterhuis &

HOW DOES PRIMING AFFECT BEHAVIOUR?

RESEARCH CLOSE-UP 4.1

Bargh, J. A., Chen, M., & Burrows, L. (1996). Automaticity of social behavior: Direct effects of trait construct and stereotype activation on action. *Journal of Personality and Social Psychology, 71*, 230–244.

Introduction

This set of studies builds upon past priming research that demonstrates how a recently activated trait construct or stereotype, in an apparently unrelated context, can persist and exert an unintended effect upon the *interpretation of behaviour*. Here, the authors argue that *behavioural responses* to situations can also occur in response to an activated trait or stereotype prime. This rather disquieting suggestion is somewhat at odds with the prevailing assumption that behavioural responses to the social world are under conscious control. However, the authors reason that behavioural responses can be represented internally, just as are trait concepts and attitudes, and as such they should be capable of being activated automatically when triggering responses from the environment are present.

In three studies, the authors set out to put this hypothesis to the test. Here we focus on Study 2a: *Behavioural effects of activating the elderly stereotype*, in which participants were primed either with the elderly stereotype or with a neutral prime, and their subsequent walking speed was assessed. The authors hypothesized that elderly-primed participants would demonstrate significantly slower walking speeds in comparison to neutral-primed participants.

Method

Thirty male and female students participated in the study, which had a single factor (prime: elderly versus neutral) between-participants design.

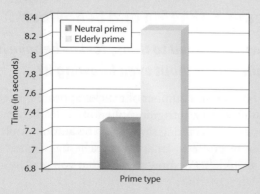

FIGURE 4.7 *Mean time (in seconds) needed to walk down a hallway as a function of prime type.*

Source: Copyright © 1996 by the American Psychological Association. Reproduced with permission. Bargh, J. A., Chen, M., & Burrows, L. (1996). Automaticity of social behavior: Direct effects of trait construct and stereotype activation on action. *Journal of Personality and Social Psychology, 71*, 230–244. The use of APA information does not imply endorsement by APA.

Participants were first asked to work on a scrambled sentence task under the guise of a language proficiency experiment. For each of 30 items, participants had to use the five words listed to construct a grammatically correct four-word sentence as quickly as possible. This task formed the priming phase, serving to activate (or not) the appropriate stereotype. Hidden within the scrambled sentences were words either relevant to the elderly stereotype (e.g., *grey, bingo, wrinkle*) or neutral, non-age-specific words. Importantly, elderly words associated with slowness (a common elderly stereotypic trait) were excluded from the elderly prime condition. After completing the task, participants were partially debriefed. A second experimenter then covertly recorded the amount of time participants took to walk down the corridor after leaving the laboratory. Finally, participants were fully debriefed.

Results

After the conclusion of the experiment, participants in the elderly priming condition walked down a hallway more slowly than neutral prime control participants (see Figure 4.7).

Discussion

These results, together with data from other studies reported in this article, provided compelling initial evidence in support of the authors' hypothesis. After participants were exposed to an elderly prime, they demonstrated motor behaviour in line with the activated stereotype (i.e., slower walking speeds). Importantly, the authors took care to exclude any references to time or speed in the stimulus materials, so the effect is not simply a result of trait priming. This suggests that the elderly-prime stimulus words instead activated the elderly stereotype in memory.

The take-home message is that social behaviour can be triggered automatically by relevant features of the stimulus environment and can occur without awareness. This finding is qualified somewhat by the observation that such effects only occur if participants have 'walking slowly' as part of their stereotype. It is further constrained by factors such as whether the prime generates behaviour that is relevant/possible in a particular situation (here, walking speed upon leaving the laboratory), and of course, whether a person is actually able to engage in the behaviour (a person with a broken leg and on crutches, for example, may be less affected by such a prime).

This paper spawned a great deal of interest and subsequent research and it remains a classic in this field.

Bargh, 2001; Leader in the Field, John Bargh). The priming methods can vary. For example, Bargh, Chen and Burrows (1996) used a scrambled sentence task to activate the elderly stereotype (see Research Close-up 4.1). Others have used subliminal word priming methods (Dijksterhuis, Aarts, Bargh, & Van Knippenberg, 2000), or have asked people to think/write about typical people of the categories (e.g., professors or secretaries; Dijksterhuis & Van Knippenberg, 1998), or have used photographs of target group members (e.g., punks or accountants; Pendry & Carrick, 2001). Moreover, the effect is not confined to stereotype activation. It has been shown to affect trait activation (Macrae & Johnston, 1998; see later in this chapter) and goal activation, as we shall now see (e.g., Holland, Hendriks, & Aarts, 2005; for a recent review, see Dijksterhuis, Chartrand, & Aarts, 2007).

For example, Holland, Hendriks and Aarts (2005) exposed participants to the recognizable scent of a cleaning product (although they did not know this was happening). The researchers hypothesized that the smell of the cleaning product would increase the accessibility of the concept of cleaning, and that this would guide participants' descriptions of future home activities (goal setting). Participants were asked to list five activities they wanted to do later that day. In the scent condition, 36 per cent listed cleaning as a goal, in comparison to only 11 per cent in the control (no smell) group. The authors suggest that this finding demonstrates that people use accessible representations of behavioural concepts to help them develop an appropriate **goal** (Holland et al., 2005; for a review see Custers & Aarts, 2005a). In other words, the cleaner prime promoted the goal of cleaning.

goal a positively valued behavioural end-state that encompasses the purposeful drive/motivation to engage in a behaviour/action/judgement.

So, why does it happen? According to Dijksterhuis et al. (2007), a number of concepts may be involved (see Theory Box 4.1). Initially, we need to either *think*

or *perceive* something (e.g., the smell of a cleaning product, reading words associated with the elderly). This is the '*input*' bit of their model. At the *output* end are what are termed motor programmes (which are what make us walk more slowly). In between input and output are three key elements that are ultimately responsible for the enactment of behaviour: traits, goals and behaviour representations. Nearly all social behaviour is said to be *mediated* by at least one (usually two) of these three variables, which means they are needed for the link between perception and behaviour to occur.

Traits are adjectival terms we use to describe general classes of behaviour. Often they are learned while we are young (Bargh, 2005). Most of us can recall instances where we have been praised by our parents (e.g., for being 'polite' when we remembered to say please and thank you) or chastised by them for rather less positive behaviour (e.g., being called 'naughty' when we drew on the walls of their newly painted bedroom). We are actually extremely quick to infer a trait from an observed behaviour (Winter & Uleman, 1984). As such, traits exert a very strong effect upon social behaviour, much of the time without our being aware of it (Dijksterhuis & Bargh, 2001).

Goals are what make our actions have an enduring purpose and can be described as positively valued behavioural end-states (Custers & Aarts, 2005). We may learn goals from experiencing the consequences of our behaviour (not submitting homework on time and getting a detention can lead us to develop a goal to schedule our work more carefully) or from liking the feeling that accompanies a behavioural endstate ('I like how it feels when I jump on the scales and have lost a few kilos, I'll keep on with my goal of dieting'; for more on goals, see Chapter 6).

The effect of both traits and goals on actual behaviour is mediated by behaviour representations (Dijksterhuis et al., 2007). In the Holland et al. (2005) study, participants primed with the scent of a cleaning product activated the means to achieve the goal: the behaviour representation of cleaning the house. In the Bargh et al. (1996) study, trait concepts probably activated behaviour representations. For example, activating the trait 'slow' probably results in activation of a behaviour representation such as 'linger' or 'dawdle'. Theory Box 4.1 provides a schematic representation of these routes.

The above findings on priming of behaviours and goals may at first seem somewhat surprising, but there is quite a lot of evidence accumulating in support of these results (for recent reviews see Bargh, 2005; Dijksterhuis & Bargh, 2001; Dijksterhuis et al., 2007). Research of this kind provides more evidence for the idea that much of our behaviour can occur without conscious awareness. Later in this chapter, though, we shall see that such effects are not inevitable.

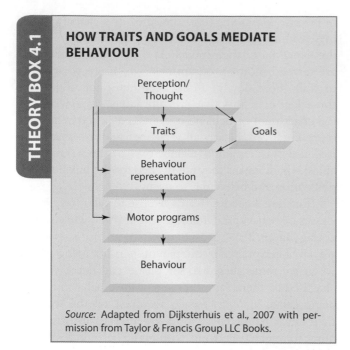

Source: Adapted from Dijksterhuis et al., 2007 with permission from Taylor & Francis Group LLC Books.

Summary

Thus far we have considered how social information can be activated automatically, and explored some of the consequences of this, in terms of stereotype activation, schemas and reliance on cognitive shortcuts such as heuristics. Taken to an extreme, such research can generate some seemingly pessimistic conclusions about how much we are in control of our person-perception faculties. If so much goes on without our awareness, are we forever at the mercy of our processing frailties? That is certainly one interpretation of this literature, although as we will see, such a view is far from the whole story.

GOING THE EXTRA MILE: REGAINING COGNITIVE CONTROL

What factors allow us to make more careful, considered judgements?

Recently a colleague recounted the following story. He had been introduced at a party to a staff member from another department, Computer Science. He recounted his tale thus: 'When I first saw him I thought, computer nerd! The geeky 70s clothes, the old-fashioned specs, the terrible hairstyle. The kind of guy who drives a Skoda and watches endless episodes of *Star Trek*. But after a few minutes of talking to him, I had to think again. This guy was wild. A real party animal, who drove an Audi TT and enjoyed bungee jumping in his spare time. I couldn't have been more wrong.' This illustration hints at the yawning gap that can exist between our initial category-driven impressions and the reality of what lies beyond. The colleague took the time to get beyond his initial impression. In this section we'll look at when and why, like this colleague, we may go this extra mile.

Stereotype? What stereotype? How goals can stop the stereotype being activated in the first place

In the wake of early research implying the inevitability of stereotype activation, researchers have documented a number of qualifications to this view. Let's consider an illustration of **implicit goal operation**, whereby implicit goals (linked to perceivers' individual motivation to behave in a certain way) can affect stereotype activation. (We now suggest that you read Research Close-Up 4.2.)

> **implicit goal operation** the process whereby a goal that enables people to regulate responses (e.g., to overcome stereotyping) is engaged without conscious awareness.

The research of Moskowitz et al. (1999) demonstrates how stereotype activation is affected by participants' implicit goals to behave in a certain way that may direct cognitive processing so as to prevent stereotype activation. Further research corroborates this viewpoint. Sassenberg and Moskowitz (2005) approached the notion of implicit goals from a different angle. Rather than looking at how people's chronic goals can effectively eliminate stereotype activation, they illustrated the generality of the 'implicit goals' argument by simply priming goal states. Previously, Sassenberg, Kessler and Mummendey (2004) had shown that by getting participants to think creatively (e.g., by describing three situations in which they themselves had been creative), it was possible to induce a 'think different' mindset in which original ideas were allowed to flourish and not be contaminated by a sense that one needs to somehow inhibit or suppress certain types of thought. This more creative process, they argued, might render the automatic associations of certain stimuli less likely. Applying this reasoning to stereotyping, Sassenberg and Moskowitz (2005) reasoned that a 'think different' mindset might also serve to reduce associations between stereotypic stimuli. They found that priming participants with implicit goals to be creative disrupted typical stereotypic associations

CAN IMPLICIT GOALS OVERRIDE STEREOTYPE ACTIVATION?

Moskowitz, G. B., Gollwitzer, P. M., Wasel. W., & Schaal, B. (1999; Study 3). Preconscious control of stereotype activation through chronic egalitarian goals. *Journal of Personality and Social Psychology, 77*, 167–184.

Introduction

In earlier studies in this paper, Moskowitz et al. demonstrated that there may be an effortless, preconscious form of cognitive control that in certain individuals prevents stereotype activation. Consider two people, Jack and Joe. Both would say they are low-prejudice, but whereas Jack would experience a feeling of incompleteness and self-disappointment upon learning that he had inadvertently acted in a stereotypic manner (and may want to do something about it), for Joe this realization would not be too troubling. Moskowitz et al. (1999) would view Jack as someone who chronically pursues egalitarian goals to be egalitarian, fair, tolerant and open-minded. Joe, on the other hand, would be more of a 'non-chronic egalitarian' in this respect. Do such differences in implicit goal states impact upon stereotype activation? Moskowitz et al. (1999, Study 3) investigated this very question. Methodologically, their design manipulated the length of time between a prime and the presentation of attributes; this is known as Stimulus Onset Asynchrony, or SOA.

Method

Seventy-eight male students participated in the study, which had a 2 (SOA: short versus long) x 2 (chronicity: chronic versus non-chronic egalitarians) x 2 (prime: men or women in photographs) x 2 (target attributes: stereotype-relevant versus irrelevant) design. The first two factors were between-participants, the last two were within-participants.

Participants were classified as chronic or non-chronic based upon responses to measures designed to assess commitment to egalitarian goals (here, with respect to fair treatment for women). In a second phase, participants saw photographs of men or women followed by an attribute, and were asked to pronounce this attribute as fast as possible. The attributes were either relevant to (e.g., 'loving') or irrelevant to (e.g., 'lonely') the stereotype of women, and they were presented either 200 ms (short SOA) or 1500 ms (long SOA) after the prime.

Results

Stereotype activation was demonstrated if participants were quicker to respond to stereotype-relevant attributes (e.g., loving) following stereotype-relevant primes (e.g., woman). Importantly, only non-chronics showed evidence

of such stereotype activation (see extreme left-hand bar in Figure 4.8, which shows faster reaction times to stereotypic words – 504 ms – for non-chronics following exposure to stereotypical primes). Participants with chronic goals failed to show this effect (see second bar from right in Figure 4.8, which shows slower reaction times to stereotype-relevant words – 554 ms – for chronic egalitarians following exposure to stereotypical primes).

Discussion

These results show that stereotype activation is goal-dependent, because participants who were chronic egalitarians did not show the usual effect of faster responses to category-relevant items after a category-relevant prime, whereas non-chronics did show this effect. This lack of activation could not, however, be due to conscious goals exerted on the part of chronics, because the difference between chronics and non-chronics was found even when attributes were presented 200 ms after the prime (conscious control is possible only after 600 ms have elapsed between the presentation of a prime and a stimulus). This led Moskowitz et al. (1999) to conclude that stereotype activation is not inevitable. For more on how goals affect stereotype control, see Moskowitz and Ignarri (2009).

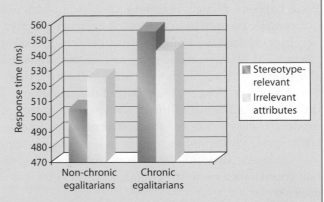

FIGURE 4.8 *Response times (ms) to target attributes at short (200 ms) Stimulus Onset Asynchrony.*

(conventional routes of thinking) and thereby implicitly controlled stereotypic responses.

These and several other studies temper the initially extreme conclusions reached about the inevitability and automaticity of stereotype activation. We now know that a wide range of target, perceiver and context-related factors can work to moderate stereotype activation. These include processing goals, training to negate stereotype activation, individual beliefs about prejudice/egalitarianism, accessibility of counterstereotypic exemplars, threats to perceiver self-esteem and available attentional capacity (Blair, Ma, & Lenton, 2001; de Lemus, Spears, Bukowski, Moya, & Lupiáñez, 2013; Kawakami, Dovidio, Moll, Hermsen, & Russin, 2000; Lepore & Brown, 1997; Macrae, Bodenhausen, Milne, Thorn, & Castelli, 1997; Moskowitz et al., 1999; Sinclair & Kunda, 1999).

goal dependent where an outcome is conditional upon a specific goal being in place (e.g., goal-dependent automatic stereotype activation).

Hence, category activation would appear to be **goal dependent** (Bargh, 1994), arising from the interplay of a range of cognitive, motivational and biological factors. In sum, evidence is accumulating that suggests it is sometimes possible to prevent stereotype activation (for more detail see Bargh, 1999; Blair, 2001; Bodenhausen et al., 2009; Devine & Monteith, 1999; Research Close-Up 4.3).

Quashing the effects of stereotype activation once it has occurred

Can we prevent automatically activated stereotypes from affecting our judgements?

What happens, though, in those situations in which it is not possible to prevent activation? If stereotype activation happens, and we would really rather it hadn't, what can we do? Most researchers agree that perceivers are able to exercise some degree of choice in their responses towards others (Fiske, 1989), provided they are *aware* of the potential influence of the stereotype, have sufficient *cognitive resources* available to exert control, and are in some way *motivated* not to respond in a stereotypic fashion (Devine & Monteith, 1999). If we fulfil these important criteria, then there are a number of strategies at our disposal.

In this section we consider several theoretical approaches that have furthered our understanding of the processes that may intervene following stereotype activation: Fiske and Neuberg's (1990) continuum model of impression formation; Devine's (1989) dissociation model of stereotyping; research on stereotype suppression (e.g., Macrae, Bodenhausen, Milne, & Jetten,

1994); and moderators of the perception–behaviour link (Dijksterhuis & Bargh, 2001).

Impression formation: the rocky road from category-based to individuated processing When forming impressions of others, we commonly rely upon two sources of information: (1) knowledge of a person's category membership (e.g., female, elderly, as we saw in the work reviewed earlier) and (2) **individuating information**, i.e., details of his or her personal characteristics (e.g., honest, forgetful). The persistent problem facing researchers has been to determine which of these contrasting sources of information contribute to the impressions derived (e.g., Brewer, 1988; Fiske & Neuberg, 1990).

individuating information information about a person's personal characteristics (not normally derived from a particular category membership).

Fiske and Neuberg's (1990) **continuum model of impression formation** provides one detailed answer to this puzzle. This model proposes that perceivers' evaluations of others fall somewhere along a continuum of impression formation, with category-based evaluations anchoring one end of the continuum and individuated responses the other. Constructed upon a number of theoretical premises, the model asserts that (1) category-based responses have priority; and (2) movement along the continuum, from category-based to individuated responses, is a function of interpretational, motivational and attentional factors (see Leader in the Field, Susan T. Fiske).

continuum model of impression formation views impression formation as a process going from category-based evaluations at one end of the continuum to individuated responses at the other, dependent on the interplay of motivational and attentional factors.

According to the model (and in line with much of the work we have already considered in this chapter), perceivers initially encounter a target and readily categorize him or her as a member of a particular social group. They then consider the personal relevance of the categorized target in the context of currently active concerns and goals. If the target is of little interest (e.g., the perceiver is merely passing a person in a street), then the impression formation process is short-circuited and resulting evaluations are predominantly category-based. If, however, the target is of at least minimal relevance (e.g., the target is an interviewer and the perceiver an interviewee hopeful of securing a new job), attentional resources are allocated to an appraisal of his or her personal attributes, and the protracted journey towards a more individuated impression begins. There are several stages at which processing can stop. An illustration of how this might work in practice in different situations is provided in Table 4.2.

Table 4.2 *Fiske and Neuberg's (1990) continuum model of impression formation: an illustration of how processing can stop at different stages.*

	Example	Example	Example
Initial categorization	Woman encountered in busy supermarket with a clutch of kids trailing behind: probably a mother *Processing stops here*, target is of no further interest/ perceiver is in a hurry	Person overheard in next office, has high-pitched voice: probably female Perceiver needs to know more (could be new work colleague), looks for more clues	Elderly person who is female called Hilda. Perceiver needs to know more (it's his prospective mother-in-law)
Confirmatory categorization		Person is applying make-up: definitely female Perceiver still not satisfied, processing continues	Hilda enjoys listening to rap music and visiting her grandchildren: not your average elderly woman; hard to confirm initial categorization as sufficient, perceiver carries on
Recategorization		Wait a minute, she is also carrying a briefcase and a palmtop organizer, so actually she is probably a *business woman* *Processing stops here*, perceiver is satisfied (realizes he will not be working with this business woman); recategorization will suffice	Hilda services her own car and likes spicy curries and flower arranging: defies an obvious recategorization, perceiver probes deeper
Piecemeal integration			This family-loving, elderly woman called Hilda enjoys loud modern music, calmer creative activities, is mechanically minded and thrives on a diet of chicken vindaloo and Bombay potatoes *Processing stops here*: target is not amenable to a categorical impression; perceiver satisfied with impression, although he has an extremely atypical mother-in-law

Source: Adapted from *Advances in Experimental Social Psychology*, Vol. 23, Fiske & Neuberg, A continuum of impression formation, from category-based to individuating processes, pp. 1–74, Copyright 1990, with permission from Elsevier.

Thus, initial categorization is relatively spontaneous, but the social perceiver will only stop here if the motivation to go further is lacking or if there are pressures (e.g., scarcity of time) conspiring against a more systematic appraisal of the evidence. Research on perceiver motivation and its effects on the impression formation process has resulted in the identification of several goals and task objectives that reliably elicit more individuated processing. Among the most important are (1) **outcome dependency** on a target (participants believe they will later meet the target and work together on a jointly judged task; Neuberg & Fiske, 1987; Pendry & Macrae, 1994); (2) perceiver **accountability** (perceivers believe they will have to justify their responses to a third party, and be held responsible for their impressions; Pendry, 1998; Tetlock, 1983); and (3) accuracy-set instructions (perceivers are instructed to be as accurate as possible; Kruglanski & Freund, 1983).

outcome dependency a motivational objective in which participants believe they will later meet a target and work together on a jointly judged task; shown to lead to less stereotypical target impressions.

accountability a processing goal whereby perceivers believe they will have to justify their responses to a third party and be held responsible for their impressions; this typically leads to less stereotypical impressions.

LEADER IN THE FIELD

Susan T. Fiske (b. 1952) obtained her PhD from Harvard in 1978. After a number of years, first at Carnegie Mellon and then at the University of Massachusetts (Amherst), she moved to Princeton. In the course of her career she has amassed many prestigious awards, including (with Shelley Taylor; *see Leader in the Field, Chapter 5*) the 2003 Thomas Ostrom Award from the Person Memory Interest Group for work in social cognition. A past president of the American Psychological Society (2002–2003), she has published numerous articles, book chapters and books. Her current research focuses upon how stereotyping, prejudice and discrimination are encouraged or discouraged by social relationships, such as cooperation, competition and power.

While differing on a number of counts, these motivational factors all share a common feature: they increase perceiver involvement with the target and encourage more individuated impressions. However, motivation to engage in controlled processing may on its own be insufficient if cognitive resources are depleted. For example, Pendry and Macrae (1994, Study 1) led participants to believe they would meet and interact with Hilda, an elderly female. Half the participants were also made outcome-dependent: they stood to gain £20 for their joint performance with Hilda on a word-puzzle task. The remaining participants would work with Hilda, but their outcome would not depend on her performance. All participants received the same information about Hilda, half of which (12 items) was stereotypic, half of which was counter-stereotypic.

While reading the profile, half the participants performed a resource-depleting concurrent mental task (digit rehearsal); the others simply read the profile. To assess their impressions, all participants were asked to rate six personality traits (three pre-tested as stereotypic and three as counter-stereotypic with respect to elderly females) for how characteristic they were of Hilda. Pendry and Macrae predicted and found that the formation of an individuated impression was contingent upon participants being both motivated (here, by being outcome-dependent) and having full processing capacity (i.e., not being required to rehearse the digits while forming the impression).

In a second study, Pendry and Macrae (1994) sought to establish whether participants who are outcome-dependent rather than outcome-independent devote a greater proportion of their attentional capacity when forming an impression of a target. The idea that motivated perceivers allocate more attention to processing information is a fundamental premise of Fiske and Neuberg's model, although support for it at that time was somewhat limited.

To test this hypothesis, Pendry and Macrae (1994, Study 2) used what is called a **probe reaction task** (PRT; see Bargh, 1982). Participants were instructed to optimize their performance on the impression formation task and to use their remaining attentional capacity to respond to a probe stimulus that was presented in addition to the main task (i.e., turning off a randomly illuminated light bulb icon that appeared several times on a computer screen while the impression task was being performed). Importantly, this probe reaction task was not a method of resource depletion (like the digit rehearsal task). That is, its purpose was not to divert attentional resources away from the primary impression formation task and make the process harder. Rather, it assessed what attention was not being used in the primary task (i.e., how much attention was left over). If more involving motivational goals do entail greater attention to the target, then we should expect that participants under these conditions would have less attention left over to switch off the light bulb quickly. This translates into slower reaction times on this measure for outcome-dependent participants. This is indeed what the study found (see Figure 4.9).

This research provides evidence for the view that motivated involvement with a target can lead to more controlled processing (and hence less stereotypic impressions; Neuberg & Fiske, 1987). More than this, it suggests that the extent to which we are able to go beyond initial, category-based impressions will be dependent upon the interplay between motivational and attentional factors.

> **probe reaction task** a simple reaction time task that assesses residual attentional capacity, that is, the amount of attention that is left over from performing the primary task. This task does not take away attention from the primary task (it is not a resource depleting task).

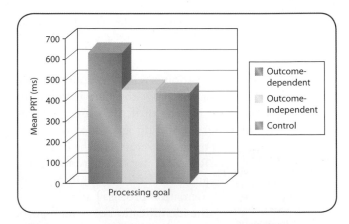

FIGURE 4.9 *Participants' mean probe reaction times (PRTs) (milliseconds) as a function of processing goal.*

Source: Reprinted from Pendry & Macrae (1994), Study 2, with permission from Elsevier

In sum, once attention is depleted, our ability to systematically process information about others, even if we are motivated to do so, may be diminished (for more on this topic, see Fiske, Lin, & Neuberg, 1999; Gawronski, Ehrenberg, Banse, Zukova, & Klauer, 2003).

Replacing stereotypic thoughts with egalitarian responses As we saw earlier, Devine's (1989) paper provided some initial evidence for the automaticity of ste-

dissociation model proposes that two different processes can occur independently, and that one does not inevitably follow from the other (e.g., Devine's proposed dissociation between automatic and controlled processes in stereotyping).

reotype activation. Devine's thesis did not, however, stop there. In her **dissociation model** of stereotyping, she argued that automatic and controlled processes may be dissociated. What this means is that automatic activation of a stereotype does not inevitably lead to stereotypic responding. We now suggest that you read Research

Close-Up 4.3, and look at Theory Box 4.2 for a schematic overview of Devine's model.

Later research echoes this general sentiment. For example, Monteith (1993) has shown that when people are committed to being non-prejudiced and their behaviour appears to violate these standards, they feel guilty, become self-focused (direct attention towards the self) and direct their efforts at reducing this discrepancy to ensure it does not happen again. Hence, Monteith (1993) found that low-prejudice participants provided unfavourable (i.e., non-stereotypic) evaluations of jokes about gay people, but only if they had been made to realize that in an earlier phase of the experiment they had (without realizing it) acted in a prejudiced fashion. Research of this nature relies upon classifying participants based upon their scores on a prejudice scale which is constructed so as to minimize social desirability effects (e.g., Modern Racism Scale: McConahay, Hardee, & Batts, 1981).

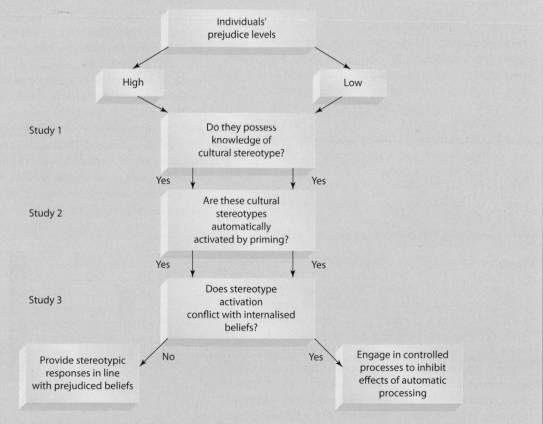

THEORY BOX 4.2

DEVINE'S (1989) AUTOMATIC AND CONTROLLED COMPONENTS OF PREJUDICE MODEL

Individuals' prejudice levels

High → Low

Study 1 — Do they possess knowledge of cultural stereotype?

Yes — Yes

Study 2 — Are these cultural stereotypes automatically activated by priming?

Yes — Yes

Study 3 — Does stereotype activation conflict with internalised beliefs?

No → Provide stereotypic responses in line with prejudiced beliefs

Yes → Engage in controlled processes to inhibit effects of automatic processing

Source: Copyright © 1989 by the American Psychological Association. Reproduced with permission. Devine, P. G. (1989). Stereotypes and prejudice: Their automatic and controlled components. *Journal of Personality and Social Psychology, 56,* 5–18. The use of APA information does not imply endorsement by APA.

WHAT ARE THE AUTOMATIC AND CONTROLLED COMPONENTS OF STEREOTYPES AND PREJUDICE?

RESEARCH CLOSE-UP 4.3

Devine, P. G. (1989, Study 3). Stereotypes and prejudice: Their automatic and controlled components. *Journal of Personality and Social Psychology, 56,* 5–18.

Introduction

In her first study in this series, Devine demonstrated that all participants, whether high or low in prejudice, were equally knowledgeable of the cultural stereotype of Black individuals. The second study demonstrated that when participants' ability to consciously monitor stereotype activation was prevented, all participants responded in line with the activated stereotype (as we saw earlier). However, Devine's theoretical model proposes a dissociation between automatic and controlled processes. In essence, this means that once a stereotype has been activated automatically, a stereotypic response is not inevitable. When participants have time and motivation to correct for initially stereotypic thoughts, they will do so. Later in the paper (Study 3) she set out to demonstrate this.

Method

The design involved a simple one-way comparison between participants low versus high on prejudice. Sixty-seven White students took part in the study. Participants were divided into high-prejudice ($N = 34$) and low-prejudice ($N = 33$) groups based on a median split of scores on the Modern Racism Scale (MRS; McConahay et al., 1981).

Participants were run in small groups. First, they were asked to list as many alternative labels as possible for the social group Black Americans (to include slang terms). This served to activate participants' cognitive representations of Black people. Following the label-generation task, they were asked to list their honest thoughts about the racial group of Black people, under anonymous conditions. Afterwards, they completed the seven-item MRS.

Results

The proportion of pejorative and non-pejorative labels arising from the label-generation task was computed for each participant. A comparison between high- and low-prejudice participants revealed no significant differences in terms of the proportion of pejorative labels generated in the first phase. Then the researchers coded participants' responses to the thought-listing task in terms of valence (positive or negative) and whether the thought concerned a belief about the group or was instead a trait description. Thus, four different kinds of thoughts were coded (positive trait, negative trait, positive belief, negative belief). Examples of positive traits included 'brothers' and 'Afro Americans', whereas negative traits covered terms such as 'coons' and 'spear-chuckers'. For responses coded instead as 'beliefs', these included 'Affirmative action will restore historical inequalities' (positive) and 'Blacks are free loaders' (negative).

Analyses of the frequencies of different types of thoughts listed by participants revealed that high-prejudice participants more often listed negative traits than each of the other three types of thoughts (which did not differ from each other). However, low-prejudice participants listed positive belief thoughts more often than the other three types of thoughts (which did not differ from each other). These results can be seen in Figure 4.10.

Discussion

This study demonstrated that low-prejudice participants were able to provide non-stereotypic and egalitarian descriptions about black people, because in this more deliberate thought-listing paradigm, participants were more inclined to think carefully about what they said, and how this would fit with their prejudice-relevant self-concepts. As such, they produced very few pejorative thoughts. Devine would argue that this shows that these participants overcame the automatically activated stereotype and replaced it with thoughts more in keeping with their nonprejudiced beliefs. As such, Study 3 appears to qualify the rather pessimistic conclusions highlighted by the first two studies in the paper.

It should be noted, though, that subsequent research has questioned some of the conclusions drawn from this research (see Lepore & Brown, 1997). Whilst later research has qualified some of the original findings, this remains an extremely influential and widely-cited paper in the field.

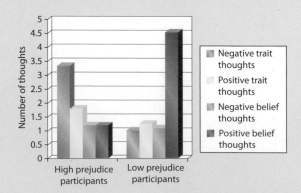

FIGURE 4.10 *Thought listing (labels used to describe African Americans) by High and Low prejudice participants.*

What research of this kind demonstrates is that it is possible to regulate stereotypic responding if (1) we are aware of the possibility of unconscious prejudicial influence, (2) we are sufficiently motivated (here, by virtue of a desire to appear unprejudiced), and (3) we have the required time available to do so (see Macrae & Bodenhausen, 2000).

In a more recent demonstration of how the consequences of stereotype activation need not be inevitable, Sim, Correll and Sadler (2013) revisited the 'shooter bias' paradigm outlined earlier (Correll, Park, Judd, & Wittenbrink, 2002). Recall how Correll et al. found that participants were more likely to shoot at a male target if he was Black, compared with White, regardless of whether he was holding a gun. Sim et al. reasoned that such a bias may be linked to perceiver expertise and training. In Study 1, undergraduates in the training condition were given considerable practice in the First Person Shooter Task (FPST) prior to commencing the study proper in order to familiarize themselves with the task and to gain experience in how to complete it accurately. Novices (untrained undergraduates) did not receive this training (but performed an observational computer task). Police officers were already deemed to be experts as other research shows the shooter bias is less pronounced in this occupational group, so they received no FPST training (see Correll, Park, Judd, & Wittenbrink, Sadler, & Keesee, 2007). Next, participants (either novice or trained undergraduates or experienced police officers) were given newspaper articles that focused on either Black or White criminals. This served to make racial stereotypes accessible. Then all participants completed the FPST. Results showed that novices were more prone to the shooter bias after reading the Black criminal article than were either trained undergraduates or experienced police officers. In other words, novices were far more influenced by more accessible racial stereotypes, and this impacted on their performance in the FPST, whereas experts and trained police officers were able to exert greater control over these stereotypes in terms of their subsequent actions in the FPST.

Whilst these findings do provide a note of optimism, it is worth noting that later studies in this series provided some qualifications. When the training context or nature of on-the-job experiences reinforced the association between Black individuals and danger, training did not appear to reduce bias. It is possible then, that in some contexts (e.g., neighbourhoods with a high incidence of Black crime) race may become a relevant cue and still be used by experts. To be maximally effective, Sim et al. (2013) argue that training of police officers needs to focus on non-racial information.

The idea that people can be effectively trained to overcome the consequences of stereotype activation is one that has been noted elsewhere in more applied settings such as medical training and diversity training situations (e.g., Pendry, Driscoll & Field, 2007; Stone & Moskowitz, 2011). When treating minority groups, white medical doctors have been shown to rely upon automatically activated stereotypes to guide their interaction, consultation and diagnostic procedures (Moskowitz, Stone, & Childs, 2012). This can have deleterious consequences, in terms of both unconscious negative non-verbal behaviours towards members of minority groups, and physicians' reliance on stereotypes to guide diagnosis. Stone and Moskowitz (2011) argue that commonly used training methods to overcome bias in medical decision-making, such as cultural competence training (i.e., encouraging physicians to tailor delivery to meet patients' social, cultural and linguistic needs), do not routinely overcome this problem. Instead they advocate the use of training programmes that teach about implicit bias. Such programmes first allow participants to actually experience implicit bias for themselves (e.g., by engaging in an Implicit Association Test which measures our unconscious association between groups of stimuli such as racial categories and positive or negative stereotypic traits; Greenwald, McGhee, & Schwartz, 1998; see Chapter 6, this volume). This is followed by presentation of data on implicit bias research and education about strategies that may reduce implicit bias. Strategies that have been shown to be effective in laboratory settings include pursuing egalitarian goals, identifying common identities, counter-stereotyping and perspective taking (Blair & Banaji, 1996; Moskowitz, Salomon, & Taylor, 2000). Stone and Moskowitz reason that such training may make medical professionals increasingly mindful of their own implicit biases and encourage activation of more egalitarian goals (cf. Monteith, 1993; Pendry et al., 2007). Testing these ideas in more applied settings will be an important development in the future.

There are several more general issues of note here which suggest we exercise caution when considering how easy it is to control activated stereotypes. For example, we may not always be aware of the unfelt influence of the stereotype (Bargh, 1999; Wilson & Brekke, 1994). Also, as we have seen, time or processing capacity limitations can impede even the most motivated perceiver (Pendry & Macrae, 1994). It is possible, too, that even if we are motivated to control stereotypic reactions, attempts at control can backfire for an altogether different reason, as we shall now see.

Stereotype suppression: pushing the unwanted thought out of mind (if not always out of sight)

Imagine you have just encountered an elderly woman in the supermarket. She looms large as you enter the fruit and vegetable aisle, thwarting your speedy passage to secure an aubergine by inconveniently standing right in front of you, consulting her shopping list. 'Dithery old biddy, it must be pension day!', you catch yourself thinking, and then you chastise yourself. You think, 'I really must stop this, she is no more in my way than anyone else, she is just rather older than most'. You try to banish such stereotypic thoughts and proceed to the dairy aisle. There, you encounter another elderly female. She is also in your way, but this time she's carefully weighing up the prices of different cheeses as you wait to extricate the last packet of Parmesan from the depleted shelf above her. How do you react to this second elderly female? Are you successfully able to suppress the elderly stereotype?

stereotype suppression the act of trying to prevent an activated stereotype from impacting upon one's judgements about a person from a stereotyped group.

There has been a great deal of interest in precisely this topic: does **stereotype suppression** work?

The research was stimulated by Wegner's (1994) ironic processes of mental control model. Wegner termed these processes *ironic* because they result in exactly the opposite of what the suppression instructions were intended to achieve (e.g., instructions to suppress stereotyping actually *increase* stereotyping). According to Wegner, when we try to suppress unwanted thoughts, two mental processes result. First, the intentional operating process (IOP) begins to search for thoughts that can serve as distractors (to distract us from thinking about the thing we don't want to think about). Let's use the example of trying not to think about an ex-partner to illustrate these processes, and then relate these to the process of stereotype suppression. What Wegner suggests is that the IOP looks for evidence that you are thinking, not about your ex-partner (unwanted thought), but about other things (the essay that is due in next week, the party invite you have received). At the same time, a second, ironic monitoring process (IMP) kicks in, searching for evidence of

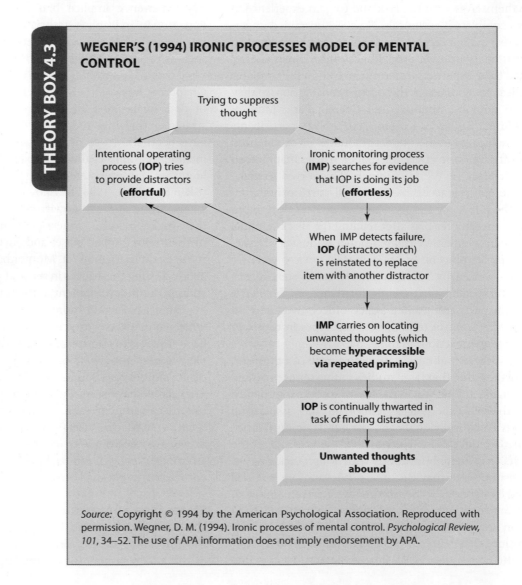

THEORY BOX 4.3

WEGNER'S (1994) IRONIC PROCESSES MODEL OF MENTAL CONTROL

Trying to suppress thought

Intentional operating process (**IOP**) tries to provide distractors (**effortful**)

Ironic monitoring process (**IMP**) searches for evidence that IOP is doing its job (**effortless**)

When IMP detects failure, **IOP** (distractor search) is reinstated to replace item with another distractor

IMP carries on locating unwanted thoughts (which become **hyperaccessible via repeated priming**)

IOP is continually thwarted in task of finding distractors

Unwanted thoughts abound

Source: Copyright © 1994 by the American Psychological Association. Reproduced with permission. Wegner, D. M. (1994). Ironic processes of mental control. *Psychological Review, 101,* 34–52. The use of APA information does not imply endorsement by APA.

the unwanted thoughts (the romantic meals you used to enjoy with your ex, the gifts you received from him or her, the beach holiday you'd planned to take together in the Seychelles). In order to identify these unwanted thoughts, the IMP has to hold at some preconscious level the very thoughts one wants to suppress. Here's the important point: the IOP is a cognitively demanding process. To use the terminology we employed earlier, it entails controlled thinking. However, the IMP is thought to operate in an automatic manner.

So what happens next? Because the IMP (the process that spots signs of suppression failure) can operate in the absence of cognitive resources, it is free to run mental riot even when resources are depleted, constantly searching for signs of failure. To continue the above example, this means it can very easily and repeatedly locate instances of your thinking about the unwanted thought (i.e., your ex-partner, all the good times you had). Recall earlier we learned that constructs that were frequently activated (primed) become more accessible. Well, that is pretty much what is hypothesized to happen here. The unwanted thoughts on which the IMP is focusing receive a healthy dose of priming and, without the IOP, become even more accessible. In other

rebound effect where suppression attempts fail; used here to demonstrate how a suppressed stereotype returns to have an even greater impact upon one's judgements about a person from a stereotyped group.

words, a **rebound effect** is demonstrated. Essentially, we end up thinking even *more* about our ex-partner than we would have done had we not been trying to suppress such thoughts in the first place! The implication for stereotype suppression is that, under certain circumstances, the more people try to suppress stereotypes, the less successful they will be. See Theory Box 4.3 for a summary of this process.

Macrae and colleagues (1994) reported a series of experiments that demonstrate this rebound effect. In their first study, participants were asked to write about a day in the life of a skinhead, with a photo as a prompt (the study purportedly investigated people's ability to construct life event details from visual information). Half were told to avoid stereotypic thoughts about skinheads (i.e., suppress stereotype) while writing the passage, half were not. Later, they were shown another skinhead photograph and asked to write a second passage. This time no 'skinhead suppression' instructions were given. The researchers hypothesized that if the 'suppression' participants experienced repeated stereotype priming in the first phase, then they might show evidence of a rebound effect in the second phase. As a result, their passages should be more stereotypic in the second phase. This is indeed what Macrae et al. found (see Figure 4.11).

Two additional studies provide further support for this finding. In a second study, the rebound effect was demonstrated in a different way (behavioural reactions). After participants had initially suppressed (or not) the stereotype of skinheads, they were taken to an adjacent room where they were to meet the skinhead depicted in the photograph. They were led to believe that the skinhead had just stepped out of the room for a moment, and that he had left his belongings on one of the chairs. The authors reasoned that if rebound effects are revealed in overt behaviour, this would manifest itself in 'suppress' participants seeking to maintain a greater social distance from the skinhead. This would result in these participants electing to sit further away from a skinhead's belongings in the second phase than participants who were not instructed to suppress. Results confirmed these predictions.

The final study used a lexical decision task to demonstrate that participants who were suppressing a stereotype about a skinhead later showed faster responses to traits related to the skinhead stereotype. This finding suggests that the initial suppression phase resulted in the stereotype becoming hyperaccessible. Later research developed these preliminary findings, in particular by showing that heightened self-focus (being made aware of oneself, for example by being visible in a mirror or on video camera) can cause suppression to occur in

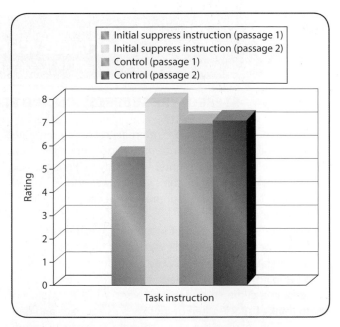

FIGURE 4.11 *Ratings of passage stereotypicality as a function of task instruction.*

Source: Copyright © 1994 by the American Psychological Association. Reproduced with permission. Macrae, C. N., Bodenhausen, G. V., Milne, A. B., & Jetten, J. (1994). Out of mind but back in sight: Stereotypes on the rebound. *Journal of Personality and Social Psychology, 67*, 808–817. The use of APA information does not imply endorsement by APA.

a spontaneous fashion (e.g., Macrae, Bodenhausen, & Milne, 1998; see Leader in the Field, Neil Macrae).

This tendency for suppressed thoughts to return later with greater ferocity is not confined to stereotyping. It has also been demonstrated in other domains, such as the legal setting. For example, in mock jury settings, participants may not appropriately discount a defendant's confession when deciding upon a verdict, even when they have been informed that the confession was coerced, the judge ruled the evidence inadmissible, and, importantly, even when participants report that the evidence has not swayed their decisions (Kassin & Sukel, 1997; for a review, see Steblay, Hosch, Culhane, & McWethy, 2006; for a further example, we now suggest that you read Social Psychology Beyond the Lab 4.3).

Although these results paint a fairly convincing picture, several years and a handful of studies later some caveats are in order that pertain to methodological issues and concerns about external validity (for a review, see Monteith, Sherman, & Devine, 1998). Consider the stereotypes used in these early studies. Skinheads (and in other studies, hairdressers, supermodels and construction workers) may not be groups for whom we feel a great need to suppress stereotypes (in comparison to, say, Black people, gay people or women). Stereotyping certain

LEADER IN THE FIELD

Neil Macrae (b. 1963) gained all his qualifications at the University of Aberdeen [BSc (1987), PhD (1990), DSc (2006)]. After working in several universities in the UK and US, he returned to Scotland in 2005, where he is currently Professor of Social Cognition at the University of Aberdeen. Macrae has published widely in the fields of social cognition and social cognitive neuroscience. He has received several prestigious career awards over the years (BPS Spearman Medal, APA Early Career Award, EAESP Jaspars Award, SESP Career Trajectory Award, EAESP Kurt Lewin Award, Royal Society-Wolfson Fellowship), he is a Fellow of the Royal Society of Edinburgh (FRSE) and also a Fellow of the British Academy (FBA). His current research interests focus upon person perception and mental time travel.

groups may not carry the same potential penalties or condemnation. Also, people differ in terms of the extent to which they endorse or avoid stereotyping. Where stereotypes refer to more stigmatized groups about whom people are likely to be less openly prejudiced (e.g., gays), rebound effects are weakened among participants low in prejudice towards this group (e.g., Monteith, Spicer, & Tooman, 1998). However, participants high in prejudice demonstrate the same rebound effects we saw earlier.

SOCIAL PSYCHOLOGY BEYOND THE LAB 4.3

STEREOTYPE SUPPRESSION AND REBOUND EFFECTS IN THE COURTROOM

In the courtroom jurors are often instructed to disregard inadmissible evidence, but what impact does this have upon their later judgements? In a study by Peters, Jelicic, and Merckelbach (2006) this question was addressed with respect to stereotype suppression. Dutch participants played the role of mock jurors and were first shown a photo of either a group of immigrant (negative prime) or Dutch (neutral prime) individuals, and under the guise of an unrelated experiment, were asked to rate each face on a sympathy scale. Next they were told that they would be reading a crime story, and half were told they ought not to think of specific stereotypes such as age, race and gender when reading the story (thought suppression condition), whereas the other half were simply told they would be reading a crime story. The story was an article about a group of young people who had acted in a violent manner towards a victim. Their race was never specified. Later, participants had to decide whether statements were either *old*

(they had been in the original article) or *new* (they were not present in the original story). The researchers then looked at the errors in participants' recollections. Peters et al. found that participants who had been primed with the immigrant photograph and instructed to suppress stereotypes made more stereotype-consistent recognition errors (that is, they 'remembered' more information in line with the racial stereotype) in comparison to the other conditions. The researchers conclude that forget/suppress instructions can actually foster the creation of false memories. In this case, it seemed to create a rebound effect, such that stereotypical memories were more likely to be found. Although this is still a lab-based study, the implications of this research for real-life legal settings are important. It is often the case that jurors are instructed to disregard statements as 'inadmissible evidence', and this type of research shows quite powerfully how the very instruction to do so can backfire when that information is related to stereotypes.

Several reasons are advanced for these differences (see Monteith et al., 1998). It may be that people low in prejudice are more motivated to avoid prejudiced reactions (Dunton & Fazio, 1997; see Individual Differences 4.1 for more details on the scale used; Wyer, 2007); or that they are more practised in trying to rid themselves of stereotypic thoughts (Kawakami et al., 2000). Perhaps they have faster access to replacement (i.e., non-stereotypic) thoughts (e.g., Blair & Banaji, 1996); or they may be more motivated to form individuated impressions of others (e.g., Fiske & Neuberg's, 1990, continuum model mentioned previously). Finally, they may possess a goal state

that encourages them to create a particular desirable state of mind (e.g., chronic egalitarian goals, as in the research by Moskowitz et al., 1999, we saw earlier) as opposed to suppressing an unfavourable one (stereotypes).

There is also a cultural qualification that is worth noting. For example, Zhang and Hunt (2008) demonstrated how stereotype rebound effects are less pervasive among Chinese participants, because collectivist cultures such as the Chinese place greater emphasis on inhibiting personal beliefs and on maintaining group harmony, and so are better practised in inhibition (see Chapter 15 for more on cultural influences on social psychology). In sum,

INDIVIDUAL DIFFERENCES 4.1

MOTIVATION TO CONTROL PREJUDICED REACTIONS SCALE

Researchers have noted that direct, self-report measures of racial attitudes (such as the Modern Racism Scale, MRS) may not always be a valid assessment of true attitudes. Fazio, Jackson, Dunton, and Williams (1995) noted that for some people completing the MRS, there may exist a motivation to control prejudiced reactions, and that this can affect responses. Dunton and Fazio's (1997) Motivation to Control Prejudiced Reactions Scale sought to isolate and assess the factors that explain such a motivation. The scale items were developed to assess different kinds of motivation. Responses to items are given on a scale of −3 (*strongly disagree*) to +3 (*strongly agree*) with a higher score indicative of a stronger motivation to control prejudice. (Note that items followed by (R) are reverse-scored).

After administering the scale to several samples of undergraduate students, the researchers isolated certain distinct motivational factors. First, some items provided checks on whether participants' reluctance to reveal negative reactions to black individuals was related to a desire to conform to societal norms to not appear prejudiced (see, e.g., items 1, 6, 12, and 14). Second, some items assessed an internal motivation to control prejudice (that is, a concern with appearing prejudiced to oneself; see, e.g., items 3, 10, 11, 13, and 15); taken together, these two motivations (whether reflecting a private or public concern with not appearing prejudiced) reflect '*concern with acting prejudiced*'. Finally, since either of the above motivations could be linked to an individual's sensitivity regarding whether certain verbal expressions or behaviour may offend others, several items also assessed one's willingness to refrain from showing thoughts, feelings or behaviour that might offend or lead to dispute (see, e.g., items 2, 4, 9, and 16). This latter factor therefore reflects '*restraint to avoid dispute*'.

The authors found that the extent to which people are prepared to express racial prejudice was moderated by the extent to which they reported being motivated to avoid prejudiced reactions. As such, this measure provides a useful insight into how prejudicial judgements and behaviours may be controlled.

1. In today's society it is important that one not be perceived as prejudiced in any manner.
2. I always express my thoughts and feelings, regardless of how controversial they might be. (R)
3. I get angry with myself when I have a thought or feeling that might be considered prejudiced.
4. If I were participating in a class discussion and a Black student expressed an opinion with which I disagreed, I would be hesitant to express my own viewpoint.
5. Going through life worrying about whether you might offend someone is just more trouble than it's worth. (R)
6. It's important to me that other people not think I'm prejudiced.
7. I feel it's important to behave according to society's standards.
8. I'm careful not to offend my friends, but I don't worry about offending people I don't know or don't like. (R)
9. I think that it is important to speak one's mind rather than to worry about offending someone. (R)
10. It's never acceptable to express one's prejudices.
11. I feel guilty when I have a negative thought or feeling about a Black person.
12. When speaking to a Black person, it's important to me that he/she not think I'm prejudiced.
13. It bothers me a great deal when I think I've offended someone, so I'm always careful to consider other people's feelings.
14. If I have a prejudiced thought or feeling, I keep it to myself.
15. I would never tell jokes that might offend others.
16. I'm not afraid to tell others what I think, even when I know they disagree with me. (R)
17. If someone who made me uncomfortable sat next to me on a bus, I would not hesitate to move to another seat. (R)

Source: Dunton & Fazio, 1997, with permission from SAGE Publications.

the extent to which rebound effects occur is dependent upon a variety of factors – of which only a few could be illustrated here.

The link between social perception and social behaviour is not inevitable Earlier we saw some intriguing demonstrations of the link between stereotype activation (e.g., priming participants with elderly traits) and behaviour (e.g., participants walking more slowly). This seems quite compelling evidence for the inevitability of stereotype activation (and as we saw, the effect extends to trait and goal activation also). Subsequent research has, however, enabled us to paint a more balanced picture. It appears that while this effect does often occur, there are several factors which, when present, modify the typical pattern of results.

Many of the studies demonstrating the automatic effects of schema activation upon behaviour fail to take into account the potentially moderating effect of both factors inside the person (perceivers' motivations and goals) and factors outside the person (characteristics of the environment). Macrae and Johnston's (1998) paper neatly fills this gap. In the first study, participants were either primed (or not) with the construct of helpfulness by means of a scrambled sentence task. That is, for those in the 'helpfulness' prime condition, two thirds of the scrambled sentences contained words associated with helpfulness (e.g., aided, provided, encouraging). For those in the control condition, these critical 'helpfulness' words were replaced with words that were not associated with helping in any way.

As they were preparing to leave the experimental room to move to an adjacent laboratory, the experimenter dropped her belongings on the floor, including a number of pens. Importantly, in one condition the pens were leaking badly, but in the other condition they were not. What Macrae and Johnston predicted and found was that participants were more likely overall to help following the helpful prime, but only when the pens were normal (helping was high in both help prime and control prime conditions: 93.7 per cent and 68.7 per cent, respectively). But the prime had no effect when the pens were leaky. Apparently, the thought of helping to pick up the pens and getting covered in ink was a strong disincentive to help in both priming conditions (help prime: 6.2 per cent and control prime: 12.5 per cent). In the second study, participants were again primed with the construct of helpfulness. In addition, they were told they were either on time or late. Again, as they got up to leave, the experimenter dropped her belongings, including some pens (none of which was leaking). While participants primed with helpfulness were more inclined to help, this tendency was notably decreased for participants led to

believe they were running late. (For additional studies on helping behaviour, see Chapter 10.)

These findings imply that the typical effects of perception upon behaviour are dominated by current processing goals, when the behaviours needed to attain the goals are at odds with those implied perceptually (i.e., even though primed with helpfulness, the costs of being helpful in terms of getting covered in ink or being late serve to override the effects of the prime). Hence, behavioural control is viewed as a battle between activated schemas and various environmental cues and internal goal states either promoting or inhibiting the occurrence of certain action patterns (Shallice, 1988).

The effects of priming on automatic social behaviour seem also to be eliminated when participants' self-focus is increased (for more on effects of self-focus, see Chapter 5). Dijksterhuis, Bargh and Miedema (2000) primed participants with the politician stereotype (or did not). Half were seated in front of a mirror (high self-focus), half were not. Later they were all asked to write an essay about nuclear testing. Pre-testing had established that an aspect of the politician stereotype is that they are notoriously long-winded. Hence, the researchers hypothesized that the politician prime would result in longer essays. This was true, but only for participants in the low self-focus condition. Participants seated in front of a mirror did not show the effect.

So why does self-focus diminish the effects of the prime? The researchers argue that self-focus has been shown to activate what are termed *action tendencies* (Carver & Scheier, 1981). The action tendencies that self-focus can make more salient and accessible are certain norms, behavioural standards and goals. Here self-focus effectively serves to prevent the execution of an undesirable behaviour (being long-winded). Under conditions of self-focus, usual effects of perception on behaviour can be eliminated.

So, the situation regarding the seemingly automatic effects of schema activation upon behaviour is rather more elaborate than was first thought. In many cases the effects of stereotypes and other schemas upon behaviour are far from inevitable (for more on this topic, see Dijksterhuis & Bargh, 2001; Dijksterhuis et al., 2007).

Summary

In this section, we have seen how implicit goals can exert control over stereotype activation. Moreover, we may still be able to rescue the situation even if stereotypes have been activated, provided we are aware of the potential influence of the activated stereotype, are motivated not to stereotype and are cognitively able to do so. So, the picture may be less bleak than we might have feared.

CHAPTER SUMMARY

In this chapter we have given a broad overview of what social cognition research is like, what questions it asks, and what methods it uses to understand how we process social information, and why we sometimes do so quite superficially, and at other times in greater detail.

- *Why is social cognition research important?* Social cognition research has provided us with some important theoretical clues about how we process and organize social information and how we use it in our interactions with and judgements about others.

- *What is the difference between automatic and controlled processes?* Automatic processes are those that occur without intention, effort or awareness and are not expected to interfere with other concurrent cognitive processes. Controlled processes are intentional, under an individual's volitional control, effortful and entail conscious awareness.

- *What are schemas and how do they affect our judgements and behaviour?* Often, stereotype activation can occur automatically. Once a category is activated, we can bring into play the knowledge contained within these structures (schemas). Schemas affect how quickly we perceive and interpret available information, and impact on subsequent processes of judgement and memory. They can also impact upon our behaviour, as shown by research into the perception–behaviour link.

- *What are cognitive heuristics and when do we rely on them in our judgements?* Cognitive heuristics are mental shortcuts that readily enable us to process large amounts of information. Some of the main cognitive heuristics include representativeness (judging something based on how good a fit it is to our expectations about how it should look), availability (judging something based upon how easily information comes to mind) and anchoring/adjustment (generating an initial start point for a judgement and failing to correct appropriately from it). We rely upon such heuristics because they provide speedy and often good enough decisions and thus avoid more effortful processing.

- *Why are goals important in the study of social cognition?* Researchers have demonstrated that perceivers' goals can impact greatly upon the way social information is processed and equally, can be affected by subtle primes that unconsciously activate goal pursuit. For example, implicit goal activation has been shown to affect the degree to which stereotypes are activated, and priming methods (e.g., priming participants with a cleaner smell) can lead participants to activate implicit goals in line with such primes (e.g., to tidy their homes).

- *When and why do we process social information more systematically?* We may, under certain circumstances and if certain goals are in place, process information more systematically. If we do engage in automatic processing, we may nonetheless engage in several strategies to overcome automatically activated constructs (such as stereotypes). For example, we may engage in a more complex appraisal of the available information (individuated impression formation), replace stereotypic thoughts with more egalitarian ones or attempt to suppress the stereotype.

- *What does the field conclude about the automatic/controlled distinction in stereotyping?* Some researchers, such as Bargh (1999), consider that stereotype activation is more inevitable than we might like. Others, like Devine and Monteith (1999), take a more cautious view, arguing that control appears to be possible, at least some of the time. Over time, evidence is accumulating to suggest this latter view is a more appropriate position.

NOTE

Now that you have reached the end of this chapter, you are in a better position to provide answers to some of the questions posed at the beginning. Let's revisit them and then recap on what we have covered.

- Why did I assume that the man at the coffee machine in the boardroom was the company director when he was in fact the secretary?
- Why did I assume that Dr Alex James would be male and White?
- Why is it that I expected Albert to be elderly?

Answers Automatic stereotype activation or representativeness heuristic. Categories like gender, race and age are readily activated in the presence of a person from or a name associated with these groups; equally, the person in each example possessed characteristics that made you think he or she was representative of a particular category (e.g., the man in the boardroom was wearing a suit, Albert is a name typically associated with older men).

- Why did it surprise me to discover that Hilda, my elderly neighbour, had a passion for car maintenance?

Answer We used the representativeness heuristic. Other aspects of Hilda's character seemed representative of how most old ladies behave. We expect, and often seek out, information that is consistent with our stereotypes. An elderly female's penchant for wielding the spanner violates our well-established expectancies of what little old ladies typically do.

- Why did I take the time to talk to my new female work colleague and find myself subsequently re-evaluating my initially stereotypic impression of her?

Answer When we are motivated by a particular goal – for example we need to get along with someone, or because we are low in prejudice towards members of that group – and have the cognitive resources available – we are able to move beyond initial category-based impressions to form more individuated ones.

SUGGESTIONS FOR FURTHER READING

Bargh, J. A. (1999). The cognitive monster: The case against the controllability of automatic stereotype effects. In S. Chaiken & Y. Trope (Eds.), *Dual-process theories in social psychology* (pp. 361–382). New York: Guilford. A spirited and utterly engaging defence of the inevitability of stereotype activation.

Bodenhausen, G. V., Todd, A. R., & Richeson, J. A. (2009). Controlling prejudice and stereotyping: Antecedents, mechanisms, and contexts. In T. D. Nelson (Ed.), *Handbook of prejudice, stereotyping, and discrimination* (pp. 111–135). New York: Psychology Press. A fascinating, engaging and up to date review of the literature surrounding stereotype control.

Custers, R., & Aarts, H. (2005). Beyond priming effects: The role of positive affect and discrepancies in implicit processes of motivation and goal pursuit. In W. Stroebe & M. Hewstone (Eds.), *European review of social psychology* (Vol. 16, pp. 257–300). Hove, UK: Psychology Press. This article develops and considers an interesting framework for understanding the non-conscious activation of goal-directed behaviour.

Devine, P. G., & Monteith, M. J. (1999). Automaticity and control in stereotyping. In S. Chaiken & Y. Trope (Eds.), *Dual-process theories in social psychology* (pp. 339–360). New York: Guilford. A slightly more even-handed debate on the same topic.

Dijksterhuis, A., & Bargh, J. A. (2001). The perception–behavior expressway: Automatic effects of social perception on social behavior. In M. P. Zanna (Ed.), *Advances in experimental social psychology* (Vol. 33, pp. 1–40). San Diego, CA: Academic Press. This chapter brings together much of the recent literature on this topic and attempts to deepen our understanding of the mechanisms that may underlie the effects.

Dijksterhuis, A., Chartrand, T. L., & Aarts, H. (2007). Effects of priming and perception on social behavior and goal pursuit. In J. A. Bargh (Ed.), *Social psychology and the unconscious: The automaticity of higher mental processes* (pp. 51–131). New York: Psychology Press. This chapter develops the ideas outlined in Dijksterhuis and Bargh's (2001) earlier chapter and incorporates more recent work on goal pursuit.

Fiske, S. T., & Taylor, S. E. (1991). *Social cognition* (2nd ed.). New York: McGraw-Hill. This is the classic text on the topic, with extensive coverage of a wide range of issues within the discipline.

Fiske, S. T., & Taylor, S. E. (2013). *Social cognition: From brains to culture* (3rd ed.). New York: Sage. An updated version of the above, this text incorporates both the classic ideas and the more contemporary ones that have emerged in the last decade or so.

Kahneman, D. (2011). *Thinking, fast and slow*. New York: Farrar, Straus and Giroux. A readable overview of the Nobel laureate's ground-breaking research on human decision-making, especially the use of cognitive heuristics.

Macrae, C. N., & Bodenhausen, G. V. (2000). Social cognition: Thinking categorically about others. *Annual Review of Psychology, 51*, 93–120. A thorough, readable overview of the literature.

Monteith, M. J., Sherman, J. W., & Devine, P. G. (1998). Suppression as a stereotype control strategy. *Personality and Social Psychology Review, 2*, 63–82. A clear, considered and interesting review of the literature.

Moskowitz, G. B. (2005). *Social cognition: Understanding self and others*. New York: Guilford. Engagingly written and comprehensive in scope.

Moskowitz, G. B., & Ignarri, C. (2009). Implicit volition and stereotype control. In W. Stroebe & M. Hewstone (Eds.), *European review of social psychology* (Vol. 20, pp. 97–145). Hove, UK: Psychology Press. This article reviews work that looks at how the pursuit of goals can elicit control of stereotyping.

5 The Self

CAROLYN C. MORF AND SANDER L. KOOLE

KEY TERMS

- delay of gratification
- desired selves
- ego depletion
- identity negotiation
- implicit egotism
- implicit self-esteem
- independent versus interdependent self
- introspection
- reflected appraisals

- self-assessment motive
- self-awareness
- self-concept
- self-construals
- self-determination theory
- self-enhancement
- self-esteem
- self-handicapping
- self-perception theory
- self-presentation

- self-reference effect
- self-regulation
- self-schemas
- self-verification
- self-worth contingencies
- social comparison
- sociometer theory
- terror management theory
- working self-concept

CHAPTER OUTLINE

INTRODUCTION 125

WHERE SELF-KNOWLEDGE COMES FROM 126

Through our own observation: personal sources 126

Through the help of others: social sources 129

Experiencing a coherent self: autobiographical memories and the self as narrative 131

Summary 132

THE ORGANIZATIONAL FUNCTION OF THE SELF: THE SELF AS MENTAL REPRESENTATION 133

The nature of the self-concept 133

The nature of self-esteem 136

Cultural and gender influences on self-knowledge 140

The neural underpinnings of self-knowledge 143

Summary 145

THE MOTIVATIONAL FUNCTIONS OF THE SELF 145

Know thyself: the self-assessment motive 146

Bigger, better, faster, stronger: the self-enhancement motive 146

The puzzle of low self-regard: self-verification 153

Why do we self-enhance? 154

The pros and cons of pursuing self-esteem 156

Summary 157

THE REGULATORY FUNCTIONS OF THE SELF: THE SELF IN CONTROL 157

Self-awareness theory 159

Self-regulation theory 160

The consequences of self-regulation 164

Escaping the self 165

Autonomous self-regulation as a resource 166

Summary 166

SELF STABILITY AND CHANGE 167

CHAPTER SUMMARY 168

ROUTE MAP OF THE CHAPTER

In this chapter we elaborate theory and research findings regarding the key aspects of the self. Throughout, we focus on the social nature of the self. First, we consider where self-knowledge comes from and explore both its personal and social sources. In tandem, we reflect on the accuracy (or lack thereof) of this self-knowledge. Second, we discuss the organization and content of the self in terms of self-concept and self-esteem and consider how these structures guide our processing of social information – both in general and in the cultural arena in which they transpire. In the third section, we expand on the motives that drive the self to achieve the selves we desire. Fourth, we look at the regulatory functions of the self and how it enables us to pursue our goals and aspirations. The chapter closes by discussing identity negotiation processes and by considering to what extent the self can change.

INTRODUCTION

What makes the self social?

In May 2002 the 13-year-old Christina Long was strangled inside a car in a mall parking lot in Westchester County (Connecticut, US) after having sex with a man nearly twice her age, whom she had met on the Internet. Who was Christina Long? By most outward signs she was a virtuous and well-adjusted person: at her Catholic girls' school, Christina was an honour student, making good grades, and she was popular, serving as co-captain of the cheerleading squad, in addition to being an altar girl. What her family and friends did not know, however, was that Christina also had another life. At night she logged onto the Internet, where she used a provocative screen name (LongToohot4u), flirting and routinely having sex with partners she met in chat rooms. Which was Christina's real self then? The one that came out at night or the one she was during the day? Or, were both selves different sides of her? And if so, how do they fit together?

These are intriguing questions that probably all of us face at one time or another. And even if for most of us the divergences between our self-experiences are not as great as they were for Christina, we are all aware of different aspects of our self in different social contexts (with best friend, with mother, with new date), different moods, and at different times. This highlights a key aspect of the self: the self that is expressed and experienced is highly variable and socially contextualized. The latter means that you develop a sense of who you are through your interactions with others – from your experiences in these interactions, from how others react and respond to you, the values and attitudes you acquire in these interactions, and the meanings you bestow on these experiences.

Thus the self is shaped through an active social construal process. We do not just passively absorb and integrate social feedback, but rather we actively interpret and might even create it. We create our social realities by choosing whom we interact with, the behaviours and demeanour we portray, the clothes and make-up we wear, what we post on Facebook and by selecting the groups we belong to. Although in adolescents there may be some more active experimenting with who one is (deliberately 'trying on' different identities with different people), this construal process is usually subtle and we are not highly cognizant of it most of the time.

Another central theme throughout this chapter is that these **self-construals** are motivated. We have certain goals for how we want to be and for how we want to be seen by others. Do you want others to think of you as generous, smart and fun-loving? Then you will behave accordingly. You will also avoid doing things that do not fit with how you see yourself and you will feel bad if you slip up and nevertheless do something that clashes with your self-views (such as being nasty to a friend). Nevertheless, you are not unlimited in the self or identity that you can construct – you are limited on the one hand by your biology (e.g., your temperament), and on the other hand by your social experiences (e.g., your early attachment histories, your culture) and the skills and abilities you bring to bear on these experiences.

> **self-construals** a person's views and knowledge about him- or herself is shaped through an active construal process that plays out in interaction with the social environment. This process is motivated by how one would like to see oneself.

The self and its diverse expressions thus evolve through 'doing' (behaving and interpreting) in the social world. This is the *agentic* aspect of the self, or what William James (1890, 1950) long ago referred to as the 'I' (see Leader in the Field, William James). It is the active part of the self; the power we have to shape our functioning and life circumstances. But the self is not just a doer; the self also has a 'being' aspect, what James labelled the

LEADER IN THE FIELD

William James (1842–1910) was an American psychology pioneer and philosopher. Brother of the novelist Henry James, he was born in New York City and received his education from tutors and private schools in the US and Europe. After studying painting and then switching to scientific studies, he finally changed to the Harvard School of Medicine and received his MD in 1869. He never started to practise medicine, but travelled to Germany after finishing his studies in search of a cure for his severe depression. There he was inspired by psychologists and philosophers and decided to become a psychologist. Back at Harvard he started teaching psychology and established the first American psychology laboratory in 1874. He later wrote, 'I never had any philosophic instruction, the first lecture on psychology I ever heard being the first I ever gave' (Perry, R. B., 1948, 1996, p. 78). James published his masterwork *The Principles of Psychology* in 1890. His chapter entitled 'The Consciousness of Self', is typically considered the beginning of the modern account of the self in psychology. James foreshadowed in this chapter much of how we conceive of the self today, and the topics he defined still set much of the contemporary research agenda, including the feelings and emotions of the self, the diverse aspects of self, self-esteem, the self-as-knower and known – the I and the Me, and how these two come to work together to create a sense of continuity in the stream of consciousness.

'me'. 'Being' refers to the descriptive or object aspect of the self. These are your beliefs and feelings about yourself – the things you would list, when asked to describe yourself – and your self-esteem. Therefore, another key aspect of the self is that it is an elaborate knowledge and feeling structure – an intricate organized system of beliefs, values, feelings, expectations and goals. This ever-evolving dynamic system emerges through the doing aspect of the self, but it also guides and constrains the construal process (see Morf & Mischel, 2012, for a more detailed discussion). As a result, as James argued, the agent and object, the 'I' and 'me', are inseparable – they come to be known together in the same stream of consciousness. Hence, although we see ourselves as distinct entities and perhaps think of the self as something highly personal, the self is a social construct – formed through our interactions with other people (see Theory Box 5.1).

In this chapter, we elaborate on these key aspects of the self and examine the research findings that support them. We first consider where self-knowledge comes from. We explore both personal (e.g., self-reflection) and social (e.g., social comparisons) sources and reflect on the accuracy of this self-knowledge. Second, we discuss the organization and content of the self – the self as a knowledge and feeling structure – and how this structure guides our processing of social information. In the third section, we expand on the motivational operations in our efforts to construct and maintain our **desired selves** (e.g., self-enhancement, self-verification). Fourth, we examine the regulatory functions of the self: how the self enables us to plan our actions and pursue our goals and aspirations. Throughout, we also look at cross-cultural differences.

> **desired selves** contain our potential (possible selves), as well as the wishes and aspirations (ideal self), and the duties and obligations (ought self) that we, or significant others, hold for us.

The chapter closes with a discussion of identity negotiation processes and by contemplating the question to what degree we are 'hostage' to our selves, or that change may be possible.

WHERE SELF-KNOWLEDGE COMES FROM

How do we know ourselves?

If I ask you who you are, you readily start describing yourself. You probably feel you know who you are and know it better than anyone else. You experience a stable sense of yourself as a distinct being, a person with an identity. But how do we know ourselves? Where do our selves come from? How accurate is our self-knowledge? This section examines the various forces that shape one's self-knowledge and contribute to our sense of self. These forces can be highly personal; for example, when you self-reflect, observe your own behaviour, or put together your life experiences in meaningful autobiographical stories. But as you will see, to a large extent our selves are shaped interpersonally through our experiences in interacting with others: their judgements about us, the social roles we play, how we compare to other people, and the relationships and cultures we live in. We also examine throughout how well we actually know ourselves. The section ends with a discussion about how we come to experience a unified and coherent sense of self.

Through our own observation: personal sources

Introspection and self-reflection   One way to know yourself is to look inward: you reflect on and try to inspect your internal states, both mental and emotional. While this kind of **introspection** perhaps seems like the

THEORY BOX 5.1

SELF AND SOCIAL ENVIRONMENT

The self is formed through its interactions with other individuals and groups within the social world, which also contains cultural rules and norms.

Source: Adapted and simplified from Morf, Torchetti, & Schürch, 2011 with permission of John Wiley & Sons.

introspection the process by which one observes and examines one's internal states (mental and emotional) for behaving in a certain way.

simplest and most obvious way to achieve self-knowledge – after all, you have access to this information like no one else – it turns out to be quite problematic. When people introspect about the reasons for their internal states or behaviours, the information produced is often inaccurate (Wilson & Dunn, 2004). There are a number of reasons for this. One is that, because people are constantly processing lots of information simultaneously, and much of it automatically without conscious awareness, they often are not aware of the most immediate causes of their thoughts or behaviours.

In a now classic study, Wilson and Nisbett (1978) asked female shoppers in a large shopping centre to rate the quality of nylon stockings displayed on a rack – unbeknownst to the participants, the nylons were in fact all identical. The results showed that although female shoppers claimed to have picked which stockings to buy based on softness or workmanship, they in fact simply chose the ones they saw last (see Figure 5.1). Interestingly, people not only do not know how their mind works, they are also rather unaware of being unaware. People seem to make up reasons on the spot for their preferences and actions that simply fit the situation, without realizing that they do not correspond to an internal personal state. For example, in one study participants were shown photograph pairs of women and asked in each to choose the one they found more attractive. Later, when asked to explain the reasons for their choices, they readily gave plausible causes ('she's radiant'; 'I like her earrings'), even though they were on some trials presented with inaccurate information about their choices (i.e., they were shown their less preferred choice) (Johansson, Hall, Sikström, & Olsson, 2005).

Introspection can sometimes even reduce the accuracy of self-knowledge. Many studies show that the more people analyse the reasons for how they feel, the less their attitudes correspond to their behaviours (Wilson, 2002). When it comes to complex choices, such as which room to rent or which plane ticket or car to buy, those who deliberated less during the purchase were later on more satisfied with their purchase, than those who were more analytical (Dijksterhuis, Bos, Nordgren, & Van Baaren, 2006). These findings imply that perhaps those who analysed less had more intuitive access to what they really like or care about – a process that got disrupted by conscious thought.

A second reason why introspection is limited is because people are commonly motivated to keep unwanted thoughts and experiences out of memory or consciousness. These thoughts, however, nevertheless affect their behaviours (see also Chapter 4). Macrae and colleagues (Macrae, Bodenhausen, Milne, & Jetten, 1994) asked participants to avoid stereotypical thinking while writing about a 'skinhead'. Although this thought suppression was successful (the written descriptions contained less stereotypical thoughts, compared to a control group without instructions to suppress), participants' stereotypes still influenced their behaviours in the end. When expecting to meet such an individual, those in the suppression condition sat significantly further away from the seat the 'skinhead' had evidently occupied moments earlier (as seen by the fact that he had left some of his clothes on the chair). This study thus highlights that we have very limited self-insight about those aspects of the self we wish were not true about us.

A third problem, which we will return to later, when discussing the motivational functions of the self, is that people tend to overestimate their positive aspects (Dunning, 2005). Most people think they are better than average – be it on attractiveness, their personality traits, skills or competence, although that is obviously statistically impossible (Alicke & Govorun, 2005). Moreover, a landmark review by Taylor and Brown (1988) concluded that most psychologically healthy individuals harbour a number of positive illusions about the self (see Leader in the Field, Shelley E. Taylor). These illusions range from positive self-illusions of control, of prospects for success, and of good judgements (Armor & Taylor, 1998; Roese & Olson, 2007). Such illusions may be a good thing to some degree, as they help us feel better and thus engage in more active coping (Taylor et al., 1992). However, they will also get in our way, when a more accurate self-view would be helpful, for example when choosing the job or partner that best suits our inclinations, or when self-improvement or self-change would be advantageous (Dunning, Johnson, Ehrlinger, & Kruger, 2003; Robins & Beer, 2001).

Does introspection help us understand our self then? Yes, to some degree: We know *what* we feel and think,

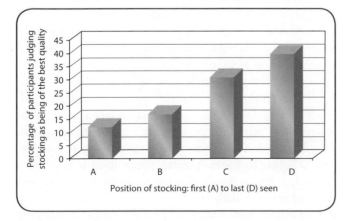

FIGURE 5.1 *Position effects on judgements of the quality of consumer goods (stockings).*

Source: Data from Wilson & Nisbett, 1978; Expt. 2.

LEADER IN THE FIELD

Shelley E. Taylor (b. 1946) received her BA from Connecticut College in 1968 and her PhD from Yale University in 1972. She was Associate Professor at Harvard University until 1979 and then moved to the University of California, Los Angeles, where she is currently Distinguished Professor of Social Psychology. Shelley Taylor's research has made important contributions to several different areas in social psychology. Besides health psychology, social support research and social neuroscience, her work also focuses on social cognition, especially on social comparisons, 'positive illusions' and self-enhancement. Examples of 'positive illusions' are overly positive self-perceptions, illusion of personal control and unrealistic optimism about the future. These illusory beliefs are commonly understood as effects of self-enhancement (i.e., a desire to maximize the positivity of one's self-views) and have been found to be largely beneficial (however, see the section on the *Pros and Cons of Pursuing Self-Esteem* in this chapter for a somewhat contrasting view). Overall her work, for which she has received numerous awards from varied areas in psychology (including the Distinguished Scientist Award of the American Psychological Association), has been dedicated to exploring the socioemotional resources and protective processes that have biological and/or psychological benefits, especially when people have to face stress. Taylor was elected to the American Academy of Arts and Sciences in 2003.

and we can potentially learn more about ourselves that way. Writing about our life experiences seems to help us gain better understanding (see Pennebaker & Chung, 2011, for a review), as does imagining ourselves in a situation and trying to simulate the emotions we might experience then (e.g., Carver & Scheier, 1981; Fazio, Chen, McDonel, & Sherman, 1982). On the other hand, as we saw, because we tend to try to push certain experiences away, and because we cannot consciously attend to everything we process, introspection provides very limited self-knowledge, especially when it comes to *why* we think or feel something.

Self-perception theory To the extent that internal states are ambiguous or difficult to interpret, Bem's **self-perception theory** (1972) suggests that people can infer these states by observing their own behaviour – just as we would as outside observers. Have you ever noticed after the fact, for example, that you suddenly started doing something you previously thought was not really of interest to you, like going to the gym or watching football on TV? And you then concluded that it must be more important and more enjoyable to you after all. Or, you may suddenly find yourself smiling and whistling to yourself after a big presentation in a seminar class, only to conclude that you are very relieved and therefore must

self-perception theory the theory assumes that when inner states are ambiguous, people can infer these states by observing their own behaviour.

have been much more stressed by it than you had previously realized. When making these inferences, we also take into account the conditions under which the behaviour occurs, and we only attribute behaviour to internal states if the situation alone seems insufficient to have caused the behaviour (see also Chapter 3). For example, you will not assume you love cleaning your room if your roommate obliges you to do it. Therefore, just like outside observers, we take account of situational pressures, including rewards and punishments.

This points to a very important application of self-perception theory as it relates to motivation. People can engage in activities for either extrinsic (praise, esteem, money) or intrinsic (interest, challenge, enjoyment) reasons. Extrinsically motivated activities are ones we do as a means to an end – in order to obtain tangible rewards or to avoid punishment (like cleaning your room). In contrast, intrinsically motivated activities are things like hobbies, where we do them for the sake of the activity itself – for the fun of it. For example, if you are a student who is intrinsically motivated, you will work day and night on your term paper, and on weekends, just because you are interested in the topic, even when you know the paper already fulfils the minimum requirements. But the question now is what happens if you get very high marks or your term paper is highly praised by your professor? Common sense might suggest that this should enhance your motivation. Self-perception theory, however, predicts the danger of an overjustification effect: the intrinsic motivation may diminish, because the activity has become associated with an external reward (see also Chapter 7). You may stop writing on weekends, or entirely stop working more than necessary. The reward has undermined your motivation. Many studies have confirmed this overjustification effect in both children and adults and in many settings (Deci & Ryan, 1985; Lepper & Greene, 1978).

This creates a serious dilemma: how do we – as teachers, parents, employers – manage this trade-off between intrinsic and extrinsic rewards in order to keep people motivated? A crucial factor seems to be how the reward is perceived. A key issue is that it is perceived as sincere and non-coercive. As such, rewards tend to work better if they are in the form of verbal praise, are unexpected, come as a surprise afterwards, and are seen as a special 'bonus' for superior performance (Covington, 2000; Eisenberger & Cameron, 1996; Henderlong & Lepper, 2002). Trying to foster intrinsic motivation is important not only because it makes activities more enjoyable and people are more likely to perform them, but also because it tends to increase the quality of the work. A study by Amabile (1996) had art experts rate art works and found that artists' commissioned work was judged to be of lesser quality than their non-commissioned work. An implication of this research is that paying children for good grades, although it is widely practised by some parents, may be quite problematic, at least for those who are already highly intrinsically motivated. This is because the financial reward risks replacing intrinsic motivation (doing things for the pleasure of doing them) with extrinsic motivation (doing things to get concrete rewards).

In sum, just like introspection, self-perception has its limits also and for some of the same reasons. Many factors contribute to our behaviour, and it is easy to become confused about which are the most important. We sometimes underestimate less obvious situational factors and other times overestimate them. As noted previously, lots of information processing is done automatically without conscious awareness, thus it makes sense that we often misattribute the causes to what most readily springs to mind (see Chapter 4 on the availability heuristic).

Through the help of others: social sources

A primary source of self-knowledge comes from other people. We learn a great deal about ourselves through observing how other people react toward us or from what they directly tell us, as well as from comparing ourselves and our views with those of others (see Srivastava, 2012).

Attachment processes and social appraisal The first relationship we have in life is with our primary caregiver, usually our mother. Our very first sense of who we are begins to develop through these earliest interactions in infancy. According to attachment theory (see also Chapter 11), we come to learn about our lovability and worth, as we experience how our mother cares for us and responds to our needs (Bowlby, 1969). Caregiving that is consistent and appropriately responsive to the infants' needs plants the seeds for a positive self-concept; whereas caregiving that is neglectful and unresponsive, or even abusive, teaches children that they are not worthy and that others cannot be trusted (Hazan & Shaver, 1994). This can be the foundation for a negative self-concept and low self-esteem. These early so-called 'working models' of both self and others (our expectations about how they are likely to behave toward us) become a lens through which we interpret and react to other people's responses throughout our lives (Hazan & Shaver, 1987).

The rudiments of the self thus develop through these early attachment processes even before we have conscious self-awareness. Later in life, we internalize other people's appraisals of us through more cognitively reflected processes. The sociologist Charles Horton Cooley (1902) suggested that other people's reactions to us serve as a mirror in which we see ourselves. He called this the 'looking-glass self': Through observing others' reactions, you imagine how they perceive and judge you. These **reflected appraisals** are then internalized into your self-concept and guide future behaviour. If you think others think well of you, you too will have a positive view of yourself and act accordingly. Mead (1934) added that most of what we know about the self comes from taking on the perspective of what he called the 'generalized other' – a combination of perspectives of all others involved in the activity. This idea that we learn who we are through seeing ourselves through the eyes of others has been tested in many studies, but has been found to be only partially correct (see Tice & Wallace, 2003, for a review). While it is true that people see themselves the way they *believe* that other people see them, research shows that there is usually not a good match with others' *actual* evaluations (Shrauger & Schoeneman, 1979).

> **reflected appraisals** inferences regarding others' appraisals of us that we gain by observing other people's reactions towards us.

Why is it that our own self-views are often quite different from the views our family members or friends have of us? This is because there is an asymmetry in the types of information available to us and others, and in the motivations related to its detection and use (Vazire, 2010). As a result, other-perceptions tend to be more accurate for highly observable traits, whereas self-perceptions are better for internal traits (e.g., feelings). On the other hand, we also have a self-protection bias, which limits our ability to detect accurately how other people view us – especially when these views differ from our own (see Kenny & DePaulo, 1993, for a review). Others contribute to this by not always being straightforward and hiding their negative assessments, so as not to hurt someone's feelings. Another reason is that, as with any theory, we have a confirmation bias. We are more likely to pay attention to instances in which others share and agree with our views, as opposed to when they do not (White, Brockett, & Overstreet, 1993). And finally, even if we do sometimes pick up on discrepant or even negative reactions from others, we are not always receptive to such feedback (Greenwald, 1988). Who wants to know, for example, that others think they are socially inept – lacking in social competences and graces? In general, although we do incorporate some of other people's feedback into our self-views, we are also biased in how we process information about ourselves – hearing what we like and what fits with our own self-conception, while ignoring or rejecting what does not fit. Thus, feedback from others is rarely adopted one-to-one.

Social comparison Another influential source through which the self is actively shaped is through comparing our traits, abilities, or opinions with those of others (see also Chapter 8). If you race down a ski slope in 23 seconds, you have no idea what that means, until you know how it compares with other racers' times. In his theory

social comparison a process of comparing oneself with others in order to evaluate one's own abilities and opinions.

of **social comparison**, Festinger (1954) proposed that when people are uncertain of their abilities or opinions – when objective standards are missing – then they evaluate themselves through comparisons with similar others. You will not obtain very useful information about your tennis ability if you compare yourself with Roger Federer (unless you are yourself a pro). Instead, you need to compare yourself with people of the same general ability, or those with similar training and background (Suls, Martin, & Wheeler, 2002; Suls & Wheeler, 2000). Social comparison processes are pervasive, because many facts about the self are such that they carry little information until you use others as a benchmark (Mussweiler, Rüter, & Epstude, 2006).

Indeed, social comparisons seem to be so important that we will use this information even when objective standards are available. We judge our ability to be better if we have a low score that is above average than when we have a high score that is below average (Klein, 1997). We make these comparisons automatically, without thinking and often without being aware of it (Gilbert, Price, & Allan, 1995). Social comparisons sometimes also serve motivational purposes. In this case, we often compare ourselves with others who are better or worse, instead of similar to us. If you want to get better at tennis, then you will compare upward to someone just better enough to inspire you and show you how to reach the next level (Blanton, Buunk, Gibbons, & Kuyper, 1999). Alternatively, if you are feeling really low, because things are not going well for you, you might remind yourself of people who are worse off than you – a downward social comparison, to make yourself feel better (Taylor & Lobel, 1989).

Maintaining, regulating and expanding the self in interpersonal relationships

Our sense of who we are is also shaped in more subtle ways through our ongoing interactions with significant relationship partners. This is true even when the other person is not around – we imagine what the other person might say or do, how they would see us. They act like a 'private audience', with whom we carry on internal conversations, or for whom we put on performances (Baldwin & Holmes, 1987). Sometimes we do this explicitly, maybe even arguing with and trying to convince the other person in our minds. But at other times we might not even be aware that these audiences are influencing us. In a study by Baldwin and colleagues (Baldwin, Carrell, & Lopez, 1990), for example, Catholic women were exposed to a subliminal priming procedure.

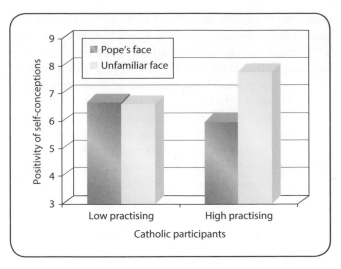

FIGURE 5.2 *Overall self-conceptions as a function of subliminal primed faces.*

Source: Data from Baldwin, Carrell, & Lopez, 1990; Study 2. Reproduced by permission of Elsevier.

They saw brief flashes of light that, unbeknownst to them, contained images of a disapproving face either of the Pope or of a – to them unknown – psychologist (Robert Zajonc). Subsequently, they evaluated themselves as less moral and more anxious, if they had been exposed to the Pope, as opposed to the unknown psychologist, but *only* if they were practising Catholics (see Figure 5.2). Personally significant others thus shape who we are and our sense of appropriate behaviour.

In interacting with our significant others we develop and store in memory relational schemas – mental models that contain typical interaction and feeling patterns we have, when interacting with the other person (see Baldwin, 1992, for a review). These mental models have far-reaching implications, because they are triggered not only by the specific other person, but also by any feature that reminds one of that person (Andersen & Chen, 2002). So, if a new acquaintance has some resemblance to an earlier important relationship figure in your life like your father, you may start behaving and feeling towards that new person in a similar (positive or negative) way as you did towards your father.

New close relationships not only 'reactivate' old behavioural patterns, they can also contribute to growth by introducing novel features into one's self-knowledge. In a prospective longitudinal study Aron, Paris, and Aron (1995) asked students five times over ten weeks to indicate if they had fallen in love and to make open-ended lists of self-descriptive terms (e.g., athletic, outgoing, studious). Students who had recently fallen in love showed increased diversity in their self-descriptions – they literally expanded the self to include features of their new relationship partner in their own self-concepts. Such changes are sustained over time, with people becoming more confused about which traits belong to them and which to their partners (Mashek, Aron, & Boncimino, 2003). In short, together our past and new relationships with significant others in our lives are an important source of who we are.

Social identity   People's social identities (see Chapter 14) are an extension of the relational self. We incorporate not only significant others into our self-concepts, but also the social groups we identify with – our gender, ethnicity, religion, profession, political membership and so on. Do you get upset if someone makes a derogatory comment regarding members or practices of your ethnic group? Or do you feel proud when a member of your country wins an international competition? Then these are your social identities. People derive feelings of worth and who they are both from their personal qualities, as well as from associations with the groups they value and to which they attach emotional significance. The focus on social identity emerged in post-World War II Europe driven primarily by the desire to understand the psychological basis of intergroup discrimination (see Tajfel, Jaspars, & Fraser, 1984), but its scope and influence have since reached much beyond that (e.g., Hogg, 2012).

Social identity theory formulated by Tajfel and Turner (1979, 1986) provides a framework about how people connect to their wider social network and derive self-knowledge and meaning from their group memberships. A key assumption is that people have a need for positive social identity and are thus strongly motivated toward contrasting their ingroups (groups to which they feel they belong) favourably with any outgroups (Tajfel & Turner, 1979, 1986). This can have the negative consequence of intergroup discrimination and conflict. On the positive side, however, this raises an ingroup member's self-esteem and can positively shield one from external discrimination if one is of a low-status or otherwise disadvantaged group (Abrams & Hogg, 1988; Rubin & Hewstone, 1998). This may at least partially explain the perhaps surprising finding that many members of low status groups do not display low self-esteem or a negative self-concept (Branscombe, Schmitt, & Harvey, 1999).

Self-categorization theory, which emerged from social identity theory, also divides the world into 'us' and 'them', but does not assume that this is a motivated process, rather simply a fact of life that happens automatically at the perceptual level (Turner, 1985; Turner & Reynolds, 2011). Self-categorization theory is, in a sense, a broader framework than social identity theory, in that it focuses on the shifting between and interplay of both personal and social identity. Personal identity refers to individual trait-like self-attributes which define the individual as a unique person different from other (ingroup) persons (e.g., 'I am

generous'). Social identity refers to self-views that define the individual in terms of shared similarities with members of the social groups they care about in contrast to other social groups (e.g., 'we psychologists understand people better than physicists do') (see also Chapter 14). Sometimes your personal identity is more important, and at other times your social identity is. Self-categorization theory suggests that when your group identity becomes focal, your personal identity decreases in importance – indeed you undergo a 'depersonalization' process, such that you see yourself as highly similar to, in effect as interchangeable with, other group members (Klein, Spears, & Reicher, 2007). When this shift occurs, you will act more in line with your social than your personal identity (e.g., when participating in a group demonstration).

In conclusion, social sources crucially contribute to our self-knowledge – be that from direct feedback in dyadic interactions, our interpretations of how others see us, or our group identifications. Which of his or her many identities is most salient for an individual at any time will vary according to the social context and according to the extent to which a person values each self-view.

Experiencing a coherent self: autobiographical memories and the self as narrative

Has the preceding section left you wondering how it is even possible that we can come to experience a unitary and coherent self, given that it is so diverse in different contexts and highly dependent on social relations? How is it that, despite the fact that we realize that we can be quite a different person in different situations and with different people, we still know it is 'me' and always the same 'me'? There are several mechanisms that allow us to experience a subjectively unified self; they all involve our private thoughts and feelings, and our phenomenological sense of self (i.e., the self we experience).

Autobiographical memories   Our autobiographical memories are the recollections of the sequences of events in our lives and how we experienced them (Williams, Conway, & Cohen, 2008). These include lifetime periods, such as your school time, the time you lived at your parents' home, or more specific events, like when you lost an important person in your life, or when you won a competition. These memories shape who we are by connecting the past to the present and giving us a sense of continuity. You may even engage in a kind of 'mental time travel' by imagining the self in the past and experiencing sensory-perceptual details of what it was like then

(Conway, 2005). Some memories are more vivid than others, and those are remembered more readily. For example, many 'first-time' experiences are vivid – your first kiss, the first time you travelled to a foreign country on your own, or when you moved into your own apartment. We also have so-called 'flash-bulb' memories, like a vivid snapshot of a moment or circumstance in which something highly emotional happened (Brown & Kulik, 1977), when we remember where we were and what exactly we were doing at the time. Many people, for example, can remember where they were, what they did and felt, when Princess Diana died; most of us have similar memories for when we heard about 9/11, or saw it on TV.

Autobiographical memories may be more or less accurate, most likely containing a little of both: objective accuracy as well as biased reconstruction (Ross & Sicoly, 1979). Just like any other information about the self, we revise it in line with our self-concept and often to reflect favourably on us. The more vivid the memory, the more resistant it is to forgetting. The good news is that for most of us our positive memories in general are more vivid and thus more resistant to forgetting; while negative memories fade faster (D'Argembeau, Comblain, & Van der Linden, 2003). This is even more true for people with high self-esteem, although the reverse is true for depressives (Blaney, 1986).

Self as narrative People weave together these autobiographical memories in stories they tell about themselves and their lives. They construct these self-narratives to make meaning out of the events they experience, to integrate their goals, make sense of conflict, and to explain how and why they change over time (McAdams, 2008a). Like any story, these life narratives have *settings, scenes, characters, plots* and *dominant themes*. Perhaps unlike a story though, they have no predetermined storyline or ending; they are ever evolving – being changed and/ or redirected as we move through life (e.g., Josselson, 2009). As such, they are very subjective and highly selective, as the meanings and values attributed to scenes are dependent on the individual him- or herself and the culture in which he or she lives. Although two stories are never alike, there are some common dominant themes. McAdams's research finds that American narratives often involve redemption – successfully overcoming a negative event in one's life (McAdams, 2008b). A typical example would be the redemptive life story of Oprah Winfrey: 'I grew up a little Negro child who felt so unloved and so isolated – the emotion I felt most as a child was loneliness – and now the exact opposite has occurred for me in adulthood' (p. 24). Stories such as these in general enable people to feel satisfied and content with their lives.

Across cultures, stories take on somewhat different 'flavours'. Asian narratives, for example, tend to be less self-focused. Instead of being about individual experiences (one's own role and emotions in events) as found for European American adults, autobiographical memories of Chinese participants focused more on social and historical events and within those on the social interactions and significant others in the stories (Wang & Conway, 2004). This difference is not surprising, as it reflects the differences between the cultural norms of both societies (see also Chapter 15). We can conclude that autobiographical narratives are shaped by the cultural norms from which individuals derive meaning for their lives.

Together, both autobiographical memories and self-narratives show the role of construal in the social self: the stories we create about ourselves are ultimately who we are – a point we will come back to throughout this chapter. In constructing this self-knowledge, we rely both on self-reflection processes and also on our more subjective experiences of self. The latter may be particularly important in gaining a sense of coherence and continuity in our selves (Conway, Singer, & Tagini, 2004).

Summary

The self is shaped and known through multiple sources: personal, relational, and social. Introspection and self-perception are both personal sources that involve reflecting on the self. Introspection entails trying to look inward to gain access to your inner thoughts and feelings, whereas self-perception involves observing and drawing inferences from your behaviours. But information gained through personal sources is often highly inaccurate due to both errors in information processing and motivational biases. Interpersonally we learn about ourselves by observing how other people, especially our significant others, react toward us. We use these reactions like a mirror in which we can see ourselves. This mirror too, however, is distorted – our perceptions of others' views of us, and how they really view us, do not match up very well. Another important source of self-knowledge comes through social comparisons and through our belonging to social groups. Of course, the results of these evaluations depend on the people we compare or associate ourselves with – thus this knowledge too is biased.

Together, all these sources highlight the active construal aspect of the self. Self-processes are highly subjective (and not always very accurate). In this sense, the self is neither fictional, nor true, but rather constructed within constraints. It is also highly variable and context dependent. But there exists a phenomenological sense of continuity.

THE ORGANIZATIONAL FUNCTION OF THE SELF: THE SELF AS MENTAL REPRESENTATION

How is the self represented in the mind?

So far we have spoken about where self-knowledge comes from and how we come to know who we are. But what is the nature of this self-knowledge? Where and what is the raw material of our self-knowledge? What kind of information does it contain and how is it organized? In essence, whereas the development and expressions of our selves take place mostly in the social arena, the raw material of the self is represented and organized in our minds. In this section, we discuss two types of represented self-knowledge: the cognitive representation in the self-concept, and the affective evaluation of the self – our self-esteem. We also consider cultural differences in content and organization of self-knowledge, and current work by neuroscientists examining the brain activities that underlie self-related processing of information.

The nature of the self-concept

self-concept the cognitive representation of our self-knowledge consisting of a sum total of all beliefs we have about ourselves. It gives coherence and meaning to one's experience, including one's relations to other people.

Our **self-concept** involves a network of beliefs we have about ourselves. It is a collection of the content of our self-experiences, including our characteristics, our social roles, our values, goals, and even our fears – everything we use when asked to describe who we are.

Self-schemas and information processing The elements of our self-concept, the specific beliefs by which we define ourselves, are our **self-schemas**. Self-schemas are mental structures that help us organize past experiences and guide the processing of new self-relevant information. The concept was introduced in a landmark paper by Markus (1977), in which she showed that having a particular self-schema in some domain (e.g., extraversion, independence) will affect how we deal with information in important ways (see Leader in the Field, Hazel R. Markus). In one study she had people rate themselves on a number of attributes related to the dimensions of

self-schemas mental structures that help us organize and guide the processing of self-related information.

 LEADER IN THE FIELD

Hazel R. Markus (b. 1949) was born in London, England and received her BA in Psychology from California State University at San Diego in 1970 and a PhD in Psychology from the University of Michigan (Ann Arbor) in 1975, where she then worked as Assistant Professor, Associate Professor and Professor of Psychology until 1994. Currently she is the Davis-Brack Professor in the Behavioral Sciences at Stanford University. Her research focuses on the socio-cultural shaping of self. A significant contribution of Hazel Markus to social psychology was the introduction of the concept of 'self-schema' that she describes as the cognitive representation of the self that organizes self-knowledge and guides self-relevant information-processing. She is also a pioneer in the research on how cultural contexts (e.g., ethnicity, race, gender, social class) shape and reflect emotions, cognitions and motivations of individuals, with a particular interest in self-relevant processes (see the section on Cultural and gender influences on self-knowledge later in this chapter). She has received numerous awards for her work, including the Distinguished Scientist Award of the American Psychological Association. Markus was elected to the American Academy of Arts and Sciences in 1994.

independence–dependence (e.g., individualistic–conforming, assertive–submissive) and also state how important each aspect was to their self-definition. She identified participants as being 'schematic' (i.e., having a self-schema) on independence or dependence if they considered the related terms as highly descriptive and important to their self-concept. People who rated the terms as not particularly descriptive or unimportant to their self-concepts were considered 'aschematic'. The latter people appear to lack a self-schema on that dimension.

In another laboratory session a few weeks later, Markus found that schematic participants judged schema-congruent traits as true or not true of themselves much more quickly and more confidently than did aschematics. Schematics also more easily remembered past behaviours consistent with the trait, and were more likely to reject new information that contradicted their self-view. So, if being sociable is central to your self-concept, you are quick to decide that going out with lots of people describes you and staying home reading a book does not; you will also easily recall many instances when you were the centre of attention, and you will not believe someone who tells you that you are shy. Thus we process information that is relevant to our self-concept quickly and we remember it well.

The reason for this is one of the most basic and widely researched phenomena in the self-concept literature: the **self-reference effect** (Higgins & Bargh, 1987; Klein & Kihlstrom, 1986; Kuiper & Rogers, 1979). This refers to the fact that information related to the self is processed more thoroughly and more

self-reference effect the tendency to process and remember self-related information better than other information.

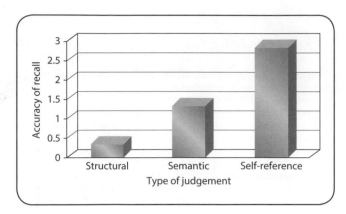

FIGURE 5.3 *Accuracy of recall as a function of type of judgement task.*

Source: Data from Rogers, Kuiper, & Kirker, 1977; Exp 1. Copyright © 1977 by the American Psychological Association. Reproduced with permission. Rogers, T. B., Kuiper, N. A., & Kirker, W. S. (1977). Self-reference and the encoding of personal information. *Journal of Personality and Social Psychology, 35,* 677–688. The use of APA information does not imply endorsement by APA.

deeply, and thus recalled better, than other information. Initial studies on the effect (Rogers, Kuiper, & Kirker, 1977) asked participants to make different types of judgements about trait adjectives, for example their structural properties (small or large font?), their semantic meaning (does x mean the same as y?), or their self-descriptiveness (does it describe you?). Later on, participants were given a surprise recall test asking them to remember as many of the original words as possible. As you probably guessed, findings showed the self-reference effect (see Figure 5.3): participants remembered best those adjectives for which they had rated their self-descriptiveness relative to those for which they had made other types of judgements. The implication is that to the extent that you personalize how you understand or memorize things and events around you, the more you will elaborate on them and the easier they will be to remember. This is true even if you do not agree with them. Even if participants denied the trait-descriptiveness of an adjective (i.e., said 'no' to the question whether the trait described them), they recalled it better later on.

The self-reference effect illustrates that the self is, so to speak, your home base from the position of which everything else is assessed and classified. Not surprisingly then, our self-schemas also play an important role in how we process information about other people. When judging someone else's performance, we often spontaneously compare it with our own (Dunning & Hayes, 1996). Or in judging other people's personalities, we do so according to their similarity or dissimilarity to our own (Dunning & McElwee, 1995; Dunning, Perie, & Story, 1991). How do you decide how studious or how

athletic someone else is? By comparing them with your own studiousness or athleticism (Dunning & Cohen, 1992). Moreover, your most valued traits are also the most important in judging other people (Lewicki, 1983). If generosity and open-mindedness are aspects you value highly in yourself, you will also notice and pay attention to these dimensions (or lack thereof) in others and judge them accordingly.

Active versus stored self-schemas No doubt then, our self-concept is at the centre of how we process everything that transpires around us. But not all of our mass of self-knowledge is active all of the time. In any situation, only a smaller subset is directly relevant and thus activated to guide our behaviour. This is called the **working self-concept** (Markus & Kunda, 1986). When you are at a party, for example, your easy-going, jolly and maybe wild side of the self may be activated; whereas when meeting with your professor, your intellectual, conscientious and more restrained self comes out. This is similar to when you Google information on the web – only a subset of information becomes available for use, that which is relevant to your current search term. This highlights the importance of the working self-concept, because, once activated, it is what determines your behaviour, rather than the full self-concept, or any other aspect of yourself, even an important one, if it is not currently 'turned on'. A crucial question therefore, to which a great deal of current research is devoted, is what turns on certain aspects of the self for different people at different times and in different situations.

Some factors are determined by the situational context and are similar for most people. For example, if someone has a religious side, it is more likely to be activated in church than in an amusement park. Another important general situational factor is distinctiveness: if something sets you apart, or makes you unique, in your immediate environment, then this aspect of yourself is more likely to become activated. For example, a friend recently went to what she thought was a mixed gender sauna, only to discover one man after another coming in (she had mistakenly gone into the men's sauna). She became acutely aware of herself as a woman, and her gender became more important to her self-concept than it usually would (and certainly more than if she had been in a group of all women). McGuire and colleagues' (McGuire & McGuire, 1988; McGuire, McGuire, & Cheever, 1986) research programme testing distinctiveness theory showed that the spontaneous self-concepts of children typically consist of attributes which are uncommon or unique in their social

working self-concept
subset of relevant self-knowledge that is activated and guides our behaviour in a given situation.

environment. For example, age is more salient for children who are younger than their classmates, or ethnicity if they are from a minority group within the school.

In addition to these more general aspects of situations, there are also large individual differences, as to which parts of the self-concept are activated in response to which situational cues. This depends on which domains are especially important to an individual. Imagine, for example, the following scenario in an experiment conducted by Downey and Feldman (1996). After a short initial task with another participant, you are informed by the experimenter that the other participant does not want to continue with the second part. How do you react to this event? In the study, some participants simply assumed the other must have run out of time; others, however, felt upset and assumed they were the reason for the other person's departure. These latter participants were individuals high on rejection sensitivity – people for whom fear of being rejected is a highly salient theme in their self-concept, and this aspect thus became activated in the current ambiguous situation (see Figure 5.4). Their rejection sensitivity, however, did not become activated when the situation was unambiguous; for example, when the experimenter informed participants that they had run out of time to complete the second half of the study (control condition). Altogether, what these studies on the power of the working self-concept show is that our sense of who we are is dramatically shaped by the current situation, but also influences our interpretation of it.

Actual, ideal and possible selves

Thus far we have talked only about self-beliefs that we hold about ourselves in the present. Our self-concepts also include, however, our desired selves: our goals, our hopes and fears, our ideals and standards. What are the selves you imagine for yourself in the future? What are your ideas for what you would like to become, or are afraid of becoming and want to avoid? These are your possible selves (Markus & Nurius, 1986). They exert a motivational function – perhaps you are studying, because you have a future image of yourself as a career counsellor, or perhaps you watch your diet to avoid becoming fat. Other types of desired self-schemas are ideal and ought selves (Higgins, 1987; Higgins, Klein, & Strauman, 1985). In contrast to your actual self – who you truly believe you currently are – the ideal self represents your (or your significant others') wishes and hopes for how you would like to be. Our ought selves refer to those aspects we (or our significant others) feel it is our duty or obligation to meet. Discrepancies between our actual and our ideal or ought selves have been shown to have implications for a person's emotional and motivational experiences (Higgins, Bond, Klein, & Strauman, 1986; Strauman, 1992; Strauman &

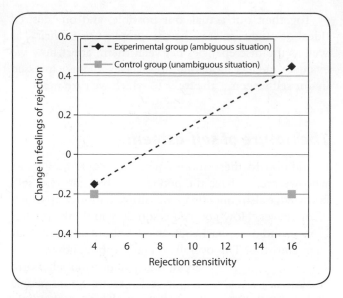

FIGURE 5.4 *Change in feelings of rejection from pre-interaction to post-manipulation as a function of rejection sensitivity and experimental condition.*

Source: Copyright © 1996 by the American Psychological Association. Reproduced with permission. Downey, G., & Feldman, S. I. (1996). Implications of rejection sensitivity for intimate relationships. *Journal of Personality and Social Psychology, 70,* 1327–1343. The use of APA information does not imply endorsement by APA.

Higgins, 1988; see Theory Box 5.2). Ideal selves motivate us to work actively to attain our aspirations, and when we fall short of achieving them, we experience sadness, disappointment and depression. When we, for example, fail an examination which we had very much hoped to pass, we might feel disappointed and depressed. By contrast, our ought selves motivate us to avoid negative outcomes (e.g., punishment), and we feel anxiety, guilt and worry to the extent that we fail to meet our duties and obligations. When we, for example, did not help a friend or stranger in a situation in which we think we ought to have helped morally, we might feel guilty about that.

Implicit and explicit self-knowledge

A final important distinction is that while some of the knowledge in our self-concept is explicit or conscious, a lot of it is implicit – that means, outside of awareness. Explicit self-beliefs come about through reflection or deliberate thought process, and these beliefs are thus controllable. Implicit aspects of the self, in contrast, are beliefs about ourselves that are below our awareness. As a result, they are much less controllable and more automatic than explicit self-beliefs (Devos, Huynh, & Banaji, 2012). Despite this automaticity, however, implicit self-knowledge is neither necessarily more accurate nor more authentic (Nosek, Greenwald, & Banaji, 2007). The two are different aspects of the same self-system that conjointly influence our thoughts, emotions and behaviours.

Together, our actual, our possible, and our desired (ideal or ought) selves – be they implicit or explicit – as well as the discrepancies between them, affect how we evaluate and feel about our 'now' selves. This is expressed in our self-esteem – the topic to which we turn next.

The nature of self-esteem

In addition to these more cognitive representations of who we are, or have the potential to become, our self-knowledge also contains an overall evaluation or appraisal of ourselves. How good a person do you think you are? How proud or embarrassed are you about some of your characteristics? This overall evaluation about how we feel about our qualities and self-worth is our **self-esteem**. Some people are higher in self-esteem than others, which means that they see themselves in more strongly positive terms and have fewer negative self-views (e.g., see Leary & MacDonald, 2003, for a review). They also are more confident that they will be able to succeed at their goals and are more optimistic that things will generally go their way. In contrast, people with low self-esteem see themselves in less positive ways and are more doubtful about their abilities and qualities. On one hand these overall general self-evaluations are the sum total of how you feel about yourself in a variety of domains – from appearance to particular accomplishments (e.g., in school or athleticism), to social abilities

self-esteem the overall evaluation that we have of ourselves along a positive—negative dimension.

(e.g., Marsh, 1990). At the same time, and equally important, our global feelings of self-esteem direct 'top down' how we feel about our more specific self-views (Brown, Dutton, & Cook, 2001). Thus, a person with high global self-esteem is more likely to see themselves as intelligent, competent, likeable and good looking than someone with lower self-esteem, even when objective evidence suggests they are both equal on those dimensions.

Trait and state self-esteem   Trait self-esteem captures how you feel about yourself generally overall and typically most of the time – and, it is what we refer to when we say someone has high or low self-esteem. Individual Differences 5.1 presents a commonly used self-esteem scale to measure these differences between people, both at a trait and state level.

Studies have shown that trait self-esteem remains fairly stable across the life course, despite some general age shifts during stages of development. On average, self-esteem is relatively high in childhood, drops during adolescence (particularly for girls), rises gradually throughout adulthood, then declines again in old age (Robins & Trzesniewski, 2005). These developmental changes notwithstanding, individuals tend to maintain their ordering relative to one another: individuals who have relatively high self-esteem at one point in time tend to have relatively high self-esteem years later. However, despite the overall long-term stability, just like our self-schemas that are not all always activated at any one time, so too does our momentary experienced self-esteem fluctuate from time to time depending on contextual factors.

THEORY BOX 5.2

SELF AND SOCIAL ENVIRONMENT

Affective consequences of discrepancies between actual and ideal or ought self-guides.

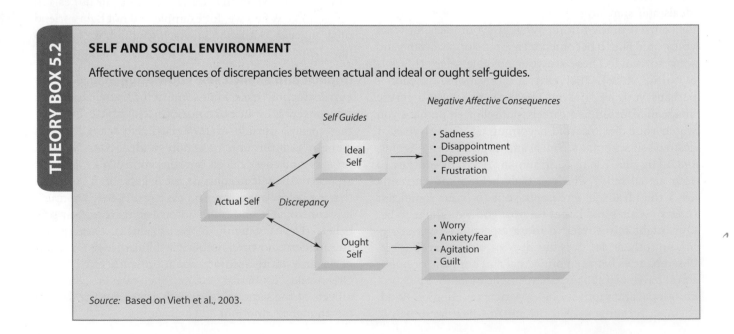

Source: Based on Vieth et al., 2003.

State self-esteem refers to these variable self-evaluations that change in response to temporary experiences – successes and failures, interpersonal praise or criticism. Thus, similar to the self-concept more broadly, there are temporary contextual shifts in self-esteem. In an experiment by Leary, Tambor, Terdal, and Downs (1995), for example, some participants learned that they were being excluded from a group task based on personal preferences of the other group members, who had ranked all potential participants based on personal essays. Not surprisingly, these participants experienced decreased state self-esteem in contrast to other participants who had been excluded based on a random procedure justified by the experimenter as needed by the experimental design (see Figure 5.5). In contrast, those who were included for the same reasons showed the opposite pattern: state self-esteem for those included based on group preferences was comparatively somewhat higher than for those who were randomly selected (even if this difference was not statistically significant).

In addition, some people's self-esteem is overall less stable and as a result fluctuates more highly in response to daily experiences (Kernis, Cornell, Sun, Berry, & Harlow, 1993). Self-esteem instability reflects fragile self-esteem and sets people up to experience diminished psychological well-being in a number of ways. People with unstable self-esteem are especially sensitive to and concerned about potential self-esteem threats: they will, for example, react to negative performance feedback with elevated anger, hostility and defensiveness. They also feel less autonomous and less self-determined, and are more likely to experience depressive symptoms in response to hassles (see Kernis & Goldman, 2003, for a review).

Contingencies of self-worth Which situations matter? Just as individuals differ in which situations activate certain aspects of their self-concepts, they also differ in which life domains are important to their self-esteem. Crocker and colleagues have shown, for example, that for some people their looks are more important, whereas for others their self-esteem hinges more on their academic achievements, and for yet others it may be the approval from others or the relationships with their family members, or alternatively their cultural or religious values (Crocker & Wolfe, 2001). Think for a moment about which setbacks and successes most affect your self-esteem. Your state self-esteem will rise and fall depending on the domains in which you are psychologically most invested – or in other words, those upon which your self-esteem is contingent. Thus, to the degree that you can structure your life such that you can excel in those domains that matter to you, your self-esteem will benefit. Turn to Research Close-Up 5.1 to learn how this was examined in an interesting field study by Crocker, Sommers, and Luhtanen (2002).

Another way to aid your self-esteem may be to try to modify the importance of some of your **self-worth contingencies**. It turns out that more internal contingencies, such as virtue, are associated with less distress than more external contingencies, such as physical appearance or approval from others (Crocker & Luhtanen, 2003). In general, the less your self-esteem depends on attaining specific external outcomes (approval, grades) and the more it can rely on internal reinforcers (interest, autonomy), the more genuine is your self-esteem and the more you will be buffered against setbacks (Deci & Ryan, 1995; Kernis, Lakey, & Heppner, 2008). A final point is that it is best not to stake one's self-worth exclusively on one domain (Linville, 1987). The more one derives one's sense of self-worth from multiple areas, the less one's self-esteem suffers when things are not going well in one domain. For example, in a study on recent relationship break-up, individuals with a high number of interrelated self-aspects (high self-complexity) experienced much less distress and fewer coping problems than individuals low on self-complexity (Smith & Cohen, 1993).

> **self-worth contingencies** domains – both internal (e.g., virtue) and external (e.g., power) – on which we stake our self-worth.

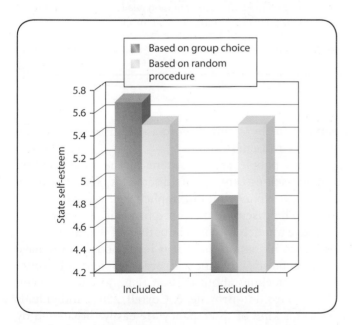

FIGURE 5.5 *Level of state self-esteem as a function of group choice vs. random procedure.*

Source: Data from Leary, Tambor, Terdal, & Downs, 1995; Expt. 3. Copyright © 1995 by the American Psychological Association. Reproduced with permission. Leary, M. R., Tambor, E. S., Terdal, S. K., & Downs, D. L. (1995). Self-esteem as an interpersonal monitor: The sociometer hypothesis. *Journal of Personality and Social Psychology, 68*, 518–530. The use of APA information does not imply endorsement by APA.

THE MEASUREMENT OF SELF-ESTEEM

Self-esteem refers to one's overall evaluation of oneself as a person, i.e., more specific assessments concerning one's adequacy in different areas of life are blended into a global judgement. The Rosenberg Self-Esteem Scale (RSES, Rosenberg, 1965), which is characterized by being easy and quick to administer, and having high face-validity (Blascovich & Tomaka, 1991), presents one of the most widely used self-report instruments for measuring self-esteem.

Instruction

Using the scale below, indicate your agreement with each of the following statements.

1 Strongly disagree   2 Disagree   3 Agree   4 Strongly agree

1. I feel that I am a person of worth, at least on an equal plane with others.
2. I feel that I have a number of good qualities.
3. All in all, I am inclined to feel that I am a failure.*
4. I am able to do things as well as most other people.
5. I feel I do not have much to be proud of.*
6. I take a positive attitude toward myself.
7. On the whole, I am satisfied with myself.
8. I wish I could have more respect for myself.*
9. I certainly feel useless at times.*
10. At times I think I am no good at all.*

The RSES is typically scored using a 4-point format (as shown above), with answers usually coded 1–4, thus resulting in a scale range of 10–40, with higher scores representing higher self-esteem (Blascovich & Tomaka, 1991; although some authors use different scales).

The RSES contains an equal number of positively and negatively worded items. Thus, to determine your score, first reverse the scoring for the five negatively worded items (3, 5, 8, 9 & 10) as follows: 1 = 4, 2 = 3, 3 = 2, 4 = 1. Then add up your scores across the 10 items to see where your total score falls between 10 and 40. There are no discrete cut-off points to delineate high and low self-esteem, but as has been shown in various adolescent and adult samples, mean scores on the RSES are typically somewhat above the midpoint, converging at around 30 (e.g., in an intercultural study, Schmitt & Allik, 2005, obtained a mean value of 30.85, SD = 4.82 across 53 nations).

The wording of the RSES as presented above is appropriate when self-esteem is measured as a trait, i.e., a characteristic of one's personality that remains relatively stable over time. However, self-esteem can also be construed as a state, in this case referring to how individuals feel about themselves at a given moment, which must be specified in the item wording. Thus, when self-esteem is conceived of as dynamic and changeable, as opposed to something more constant, question phrasing needs to be adjusted to indicate the point of time referred to ('at the moment', 'right now').

Note: * indicates a reverse-scored item.

Implicit and explicit self-esteem Just as self-beliefs come in both explicit and implicit forms, so does self-esteem. We have both conscious and unconscious feelings of positivity or negativity toward ourselves. This is particularly tricky to measure – how does one get information about something that people do not know themselves? This requires rather ingenious methods. One of these is the name-letter effect (Koole, Dijksterhuis, & Van Knippenberg, 2001; Koole & Pelham, 2003; Nuttin, 1985, 1987): to the extent that people have a greater preference for the letters of their own name, more than other people like these letters, the higher is their **implicit self-esteem**. Another commonly used measure is the Implicit Association Test (IAT; Greenwald & Farnham, 2000). See Individual Differences 5.2, which describes this clever method that enables one to measure implicit

> **implicit self-esteem** the positivity of a person's automatic or nonconscious evaluation of him- or herself.

self-esteem by a timed word-association without the person's awareness.

Some people are consistent in their explicit and implicit self-esteem, others discrepant, such that they have high explicit, but low implicit, self-esteem, or vice versa. The case of coexistence of positive explicit and negative implicit feelings about the self is a rather interesting combination, in that it leads people to behave in a 'defensive' manner in order to fend off these negative feelings about the self (e.g., Jordan, Spencer, Zanna, Hoshino-Browne, & Correll, 2003). Individuals with this kind of discrepancy are easily threatened by negative feedback and they will do anything to reduce its impact on the self (Epstein & Morling, 1995). For instance, they might blame the test writer for writing a bad test; they will put down or even aggress against people who outperform them (Bushman & Baumeister, 1998; Morf & Rhodewalt, 1993). The opposite discrepancy – high implicit self-esteem

CONTINGENCIES OF SELF-WORTH: SELF-WORTH RISES AND FALLS IN RESPONSE TO IMPORTANT LIFE EVENTS

RESEARCH CLOSE UP 5.1

Crocker, J., Sommers, S. R., & Luhtanen, R. K. (2002). Hopes dashed and dreams fulfilled: Contingencies of self-worth and graduate school admissions. *Personality and Social Psychology Bulletin, 28,* 1275–1286.

Introduction

William James (1890, 1950) proposed that global state self-esteem – our general evaluation of self-worth – fluctuates around a typical level depending on positive or negative events in domains on which one's self-worth is based. Crocker and colleagues (2002) set out to test this hypothesis in a naturalistic setting involving significant life events as successes or failures unfold over time. Specifically, their study involved senior college students applying for master's and doctoral programmes. Would their self-esteem increase on days they received an acceptance to a graduate school? And would their self-esteem decrease in turn after receiving a rejection, relative to their global self-esteem (on days without decisions)? And is the boost or decline in self-esteem greater for those students who base their self-esteem more strongly on academic competence? In other words, they assessed the degree to which within-person changes in self-esteem can be linked to specific events in the person's life. They hypothesized that the magnitude of these changes would depend on the importance of the academic domain to the person's self-esteem.

Method

Participants

The participants were 37 college seniors, applying to master's and doctoral programmes. They were recruited through advertisements in the campus newspapers and through e-mail to the honours undergraduate mailing list. Participants were paid $50 for their participation.

Design and procedure

At the beginning of the study, participants completed the Rosenberg Trait Self-Esteem Scale (Rosenberg, 1965) and the contingency of self-worth measure (Crocker & Wolfe, 2001). The latter distinguishes between eight domains on which people can base their self-esteem (e.g., academic competence, appearance, others' approval, or virtue). An example from the academic domain is: 'My self-esteem gets a boost when I get a good grade on an exam or paper'. Then, for a two-month period, participants completed a web-based questionnaire twice a week on a regular schedule of their own choosing, as well as on any day when they received official notifications from graduate schools. The web-based questionnaire also contained an adapted state version of the Rosenberg Self-Esteem Scale (see Individual Differences 5.1), consisting of 10 items rated on a scale from 1 (*strongly disagree*) to 7 (*strongly agree*), and asking for their self-worth feelings on that day.

This field study had a quasi-experimental design, as there was no random assignment to conditions. It involved a naturally occurring event: acceptances versus rejections from graduate schools, which were compared to baseline days (no decision letters). Contingency of self-worth was analysed as a continuous variable from low to high.

Results

Figures 5.6a and 5.6b show the main results. As predicted, students with highly academic contingent self-worth showed a boost of self-esteem on days of acceptance, compared to baseline days (days without a decision), while the self-esteem of students with low academic contingency remained unchanged. Also, as expected, on days of rejection the self-esteem of students with highly academic contingent self-worth decreased more than that of students with low contingency of self-esteem on academics. These fluctuations within people occurred above and beyond large differences between people in overall stable self-esteem.

Discussion

These results show that for those senior students who based their self-esteem strongly on academics, acceptance to or rejection from a graduate school had a stronger impact on their daily self-esteem than for those students whose self-worth was not contingent on academics. Crocker and colleagues (2002) therefore concluded that fluctuations in self-esteem are due, at least in part, to positive and negative events in domains on which people stake their self-worth. Thus, more than a century after William James published his work about the nature of self-esteem, this study provides support for one of his key predictions: while trait self-esteem may remain relatively stable over the life span, there are fluctuations around this typical level reflecting those domains on which one has staked one's self-worth.

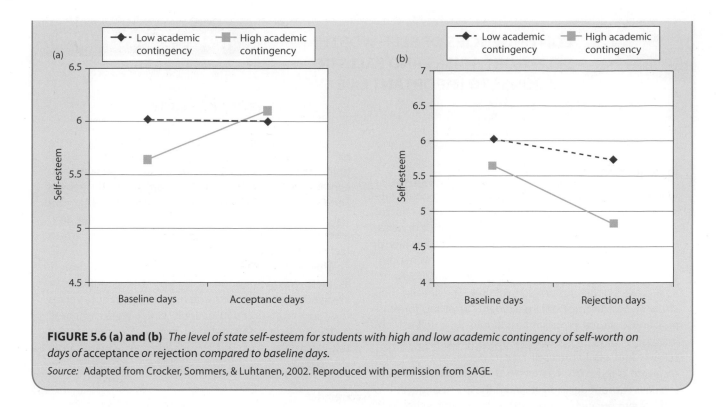

FIGURE 5.6 (a) and (b) *The level of state self-esteem for students with high and low academic contingency of self-worth on days of* acceptance *or* rejection *compared to baseline days.*

Source: Adapted from Crocker, Sommers, & Luhtanen, 2002. Reproduced with permission from SAGE.

together with low explicit self-esteem – has been shown to be related to social anxiety disorder (e.g., Schreiber, Bohn, Aderka, Stangier, & Steil, 2012). Individuals with consistent explicit and implicit self-esteem, in contrast, are more secure and have less need to be defensive (Kernis, 2003).

Cultural and gender influences on self-knowledge

In the section on the origins of self-knowledge, we saw how strongly our selves are shaped by our interpersonal experiences and environments. It will come as no surprise therefore that culture and gender also exert their influence. If you are a person who by heritage or through migration identifies with two (or more) cultures yourself, then you know immediately what we mean. Are you one kind of person when with your family and another when with your friends or at school? Are your two 'selves' compatible, or do they confuse you at times, or even seem in conflict with one another? Cultures vary in how similar or different they are in their conceptualizations of the individual and his or her role in society, and thus in the social selves that they encourage (see Chapter 15). These different conceptions of self in turn shape our perceptions of the world,

our motivations and our emotional reactions to events (Triandis, 1989, 1995).

Independent versus interdependent selves The most studied contrasting dimension in self-construal first put forward by Markus and Kitayama (1991) involves the **independent versus interdependent self** (see Theory Box 5.3, and also Chapter 15). The independent self, widespread in the Western world, in particular northwestern Europe and North America, emphasizes autonomy, individualism, and uniqueness – what makes the self distinct from others. In contrast, the interdependent self, more prevalent among East Asians (or other more collectivistic cultures – *see Chapter 15*) construes the self as fundamentally connected to others and embedded in society, and thus emphasizes relationship harmony and what connects the self to others and groups. When Westerners are asked to describe themselves, they are more likely to use abstract trait adjectives (e.g., smart), whereas East Asians are more likely to describe social relationships or group identities (e.g., college student) (see Trafimow, Triandis, & Goto, 1991).

> **independent versus interdependent self** while the independent self emphasizes autonomy and individualism and defines the self via internal attributes like traits, an interdependent self stresses the connection to others and defines the self in terms of relationships with others.

INDIVIDUAL DIFFERENCES 5.2

MEASURING IMPLICIT SELF-ESTEEM WITH THE IMPLICIT ASSOCIATION TEST

Procedure

The self-esteem IAT (Implicit Association Test) measures self-esteem at an implicit level; that is, the test does not require aware-ness of one's self-esteem and is not subject to conscious control. The basic idea behind the IAT technique is that knowledge about the self has an associative structure. The IAT measures implicit associations between categories of items by assessing how easily those categories are mapped onto each other.

The IAT involves several steps (see Figure 5.7). Participants are presented with words on a computer screen one at a time and must

Example Step 1

Example Step 2

Example Step 3

Example monitor for Step 4 not shown.

Example Step 5

	Category labels	Sample items	Category labels
Step 1: practice block (20 trials)	not me		me
	○	self	●
	●	other	○
Step 2: practice block (20 trials)	unpleasant		pleasant
	○	joy	●
	●	vomit	○
Step 3: practice block (20 trials) critical block (40 trials)	unpleasant or not me		pleasant or me
	○	self	●
	○	joy	●
	●	other	○
	●	vomit	○
Step 4: practice block (20 trials)	me		not me
	●	self	○
	○	other	●
Step 5: practice block (20 trials) critical block (40 trials)	unpleasant or me		pleasant or not me
	●	self	○
	○	joy	●
	○	other	●
	●	vomit	○

FIGURE 5.7 *Categorization tasks for five steps of the self-esteem Implicit Association Test (IAT). Black dots indicate the correct response. The IAT effect is the difference in response times between Steps 3 and 5. (IAT: a full description of the IAT is given in Chapter 6.)*

decide as quickly as possible to which of four categories each word belongs by hitting a key on the keyboard. Latencies are measured and averaged for each task variation. In the first two steps, participants practise how to categorize two different target concepts ('me' or 'not me' and 'pleasant' or 'unpleasant' attributes) using specific keys. Thus, for example, when the word presented below is 'other', the participant has to press the left key ('not me'), but when the word is 'self' the participant has to press the right key ('me'). The procedure is analogous for unpleasant/pleasant attributes (see Step 2).

Step 3 is the first critical trial. Here participants are asked to map the four categories ('me' and 'not me' targets, 'pleasant' and 'unpleasant' attributes) onto just two responses (these are the same keys as they were assigned to in the practice steps: for example 'me+pleasant' to the right key and 'not me+unpleasant' to the left key). Thus, for example, when the word presented below is 'other', the participant has to press the left key ('not me'), but when the word is 'joy', the participant has to press the right key ('pleasant'). The fourth step provides practice that reverses the assignments of either the target or attribute concepts learned on Steps 1 and 2 (here shown for 'me' and 'not me' targets). This is followed by the next critical step (Step 5), in which pairings of

the categories from Step 3 are switched (e.g., 'me+unpleasant' to the left key and 'not me+pleasant' to the right key). Thus, for example, when the word presented below is 'self', the participant has to press the left key ('me'), and when the word is 'vomit', the participant also has to press the left key ('unpleasant').

Implicit self-esteem is measured in the form of an IAT score, computed as the average speed difference between the two critical steps (Step 5 minus Step 3). The IAT score measures how much easier it is for participants to categorize self items with pleasant attributes than self items with unpleasant attributes; the higher the score the higher the person's implicit self-esteem. Due to the implicit assessment of automatic associations, the IAT makes it extremely difficult, if not impossible, for participants to intentionally control or conceal their self-evaluations.

To try out the IAT for implicit self-esteem (and other implicit measures) for yourself, visit the IAT Project Implicit® homepage, where links to online tests as well as detailed information are provided. After taking the test, you will be provided with your test score and short feedback to help interpret your automatic tendency to associate certain categories (e.g., yourself with 'good' versus 'bad').

THEORY BOX 5.3

INDEPENDENT VERSUS INTERDEPENDENT CONCEPTUAL REPRESENTATIONS OF THE SELF

Core concepts (bold Xs) are representations of the self that are most elaborated in memory and most accessible when thinking about the self. For those with interdependent self-construals these core concepts are at the intersection between the self and others, whereas for those with independent construals of the self the inner attributes are most important. Xs not shown in bold represent non-core concepts.

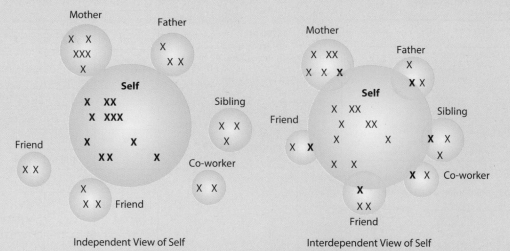

Source: From Markus & Kitayama, 1991. Reproduced with permission from Taylor and Francis.

As you might imagine, self-views for someone with an independent self are more consistent across social contexts than they are for someone with an interdependent self who sees the self in more relational terms (e.g., Choi & Choi, 2002; Tafarodi, Lo, Yamaguchi, Lee, & Katsura, 2004). In one study, Japanese and Americans were asked to fill out 20 sentences beginning with 'I am. . .' within

different contexts (e.g., peer, higher-status partner). This study found that Japanese were less consistent across contexts in their self-descriptions than were Americans (Kanagawa, Cross, & Markus, 2001). Nevertheless, interdependent selves are consistent within specific relationships and highly stable over time (English & Chen, 2007). Hence, even if the Japanese reported a different self with mother than with romantic partner, within the same relationship, they stayed the same. Therefore, it is not that interdependents' selves shift willy-nilly across contexts, nor do they lack authenticity, but rather, they have a different kind of self-concept consistency – one in which their selves remain consistent within specific relational contexts. To see such cultural differences, researchers have to adjust their 'cultural glasses' to open their minds to another culture's perspective.

Coupled with these different self-views are also different motivations and feelings about the self. We have already mentioned that most people like to think about themselves as better than average (Alicke & Govorun, 2005) and to entertain positive self-illusions of probable success (Taylor & Brown, 1988). This is, however, primarily true of those with an independent self-view; whereas individuals with interdependent self-views value modesty and self-criticism (Heine, Lehman, Markus, & Kitayama, 1999). As a result, East Asians tend to score lower than Westerners on traditional self-esteem scales. This difference, however likely, does not reflect that individuals with an interdependent self feel worse about themselves, but rather, as we will see later in the chapter, that what contributes to

self enhancement motivation to enhance the positivity of our self-conceptions, often over what would be objectively warranted. Achieved by various strategies (e.g., self-serving attributions, basking in reflected glory, positive self-presentations).

positive self-regard and how **self-enhancement** is expressed varies across these cultural groups.

To the extent that cultural differences in self-esteem are due to differences in modesty, these cultural differences should be stronger for reports of self-competence than for reports of affective self-regard. Consistent with this, East Asians report equally positive self-feelings toward themselves (lack of shame, pride) as do North Americans, even though East Asians report less positive self-competence (Cai, Brown, Deng, & Oakes, 2007). Moreover, members of East-Asian cultures score as high as Westerners on positivity towards the self on implicit measures (Cai et al., 2011; Kitayama & Uchida, 2003; Yamaguchi et al., 2007). For instance, Japanese individuals show enhanced liking for their own name letters (Kitayama & Karasawa, 1997), and are faster to pair self-related words with positive rather than negative words (Yamaguchi et al., 2007). In short, although there are differences in reported explicit self-esteem across cultures, these do not seem to reflect real differences in underlying self-esteem.

Gender Similar differences in the self can also be found between genders: women tend to develop more interdependent selves and link their self-esteem more to interdependent qualities (Cross, Bacon, & Morris, 2000; Cross & Madson, 1997). Men, in contrast, develop more independent selves and link their self-esteem more to their independent qualities (Josephs, Markus, & Tafarodi, 1992). These differences can be explained through gender-specific socialization practices, by which girls are taught to prioritize the qualities that align them with others, whereas boys are encouraged to develop qualities that distinguish them from others (e.g., Spence, Deaux, & Helmreich, 1985). To answer the question whether men and women also differ in global self-esteem, Kling and colleagues analysed the data of 216 studies and two nationally representative American data sets (Kling, Hyde, Showers, & Buswell, 1999). They found only small differences between genders, wherein men reported slightly higher self-esteem than women.

Individual differences and contextual variability

Although culture (of which gender can perhaps be thought of as a special case) has a pervasive impact on the self, it is important to highlight that there are still individual differences, even within cultures. In any culture (or within gender), there are individuals who are more or less independent or interdependent than others (Oyserman, Coon, & Kemmelmeier, 2002). That is, there are interdependent men or Westerners, just as there are independent women or East Asians. In addition, no one is just independent or just interdependent, but a bit of both. In fact the degree of independence or interdependence respectively, can be influenced by the context. For example, a study by Trafimow and colleagues (Trafimow, Silverman, Fan, & Law, 1997) with Chinese students from Hong Kong (who spoke English as a second language), found that filling out a 'Who am I?' test either in English or in Chinese importantly influenced the outcome. Students who took the test in English reported more personal traits, whereas students who took the test in Chinese focused more on social relations. This phenomenon of changing the self in response to situational cues is called *cultural frame switching*. Individuals who live with (at least) two cultures are experts in both of them. They have more than one set of cultural tools to interpret the world, or in other words two cultural meaning systems (DiMaggio, 1997; Shore, 1996) and will switch between them depending on the situational demands (e.g., Hong, Benet-Martínez, Chiu, & Morris, 2003).

The neural underpinnings of self-knowledge

Is there something special about how the brain processes and represents information relevant to the self? With the recent advance of neuroimaging techniques, the past two decades have seen a surge of research trying to identify the neurological correlates of self-knowledge (Figure 5.8). The hope is to be able to understand the mechanisms through which people develop representations of self (versus others), how we come to feel a sense of agentic action, and what processes give rise to experiencing a unitary self. Although our understanding of the neural basis of the self is just beginning, progress has been made on the neural correlates of various aspects of self-processing – both from studying the impaired, injured brain and from imaging the healthy brain.

The bulk of the initial neuroscience research on the self was directed at understanding whether encoding information about the self is carried out by different brain regions than encoding information about other people. Many studies now converge to show that the medial prefrontal cortex (mPFC) is involved in self-referential processing (see Beer, 2012, for a review). For example, there is increased activation in the mPFC related to the self-reference effect described earlier, where we encode information in relation to the self more deeply compared to information related to political figures or syllabic structure (e.g., Craik et al., 1999; Kelley et al., 2002). The mPFC also plays a role when making self-descriptiveness judgements of personality characteristics (Macrae, Moran, Heatherton, Banfield, & Kelley, 2004), when people observe their own face (Keenan, Wheeler, Gallup, & Pascual-Leone, 2000), or when they

determine self-ownership of objects (Kim & Johnson, 2010). Interestingly, the mPFC has also been shown to be sensitive to the cultural differences in self-construal we talked about earlier. One study asked both Japanese and American participants to rate the self-descriptiveness of trait adjectives either in general, or in a particular context (e.g., 'How casual are you when you talk to your mother') (Chiao et al., 2009). Participants who identified with individualistic values showed greater mPFC activation for self-descriptiveness judgements made in general, whereas those for whom collectivistic values were more important had heightened mPFC activation for self-judgements in a particular context.

Does this mean, then, that the mPFC is the 'self' component in the brain? The answer is a firm 'no'. For one thing, a number of regions other than the mPFC have also been shown to be involved in self-related processing (e.g., Klein, 2004). And with regard to the mPFC, the problem is that in other studies the mPFC has also been shown to be activated when processing information about other people, especially close others (e.g., Ochsner et al., 2005), or when we try to take on another person's perspective (Pfeifer et al., 2009), or try to infer their mental state (Mitchell, Banaji, & Macrae, 2005). It appears then that the mPFC is more broadly involved in general social cognition processes and is not unique to the self. In fact, it may be that when we make inferences about the self as an object this may be no different from

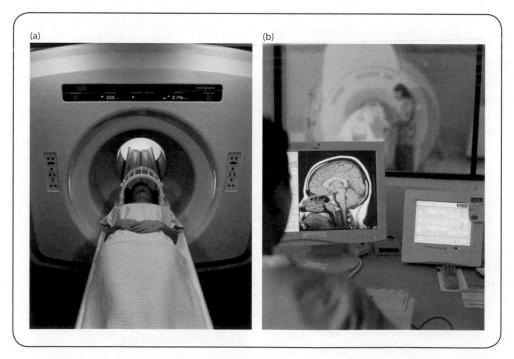

FIGURE 5.8 (a) and (b) *Due to the recent advance of neuroimaging techniques, the past two decades have seen a surge of research trying to identify the neurological correlates of self-knowledge.*

Source: (a) © Charles Thatcher. Used under licence from Getty Images; (b) © Stewart Cohen. Used under licence from Getty Images.

when we process information about other things. In synthesizing neuroimaging results from a large number of studies, Legrand and Ruby (2009) argue that self-relatedness information processing involves a wide cerebral network, the activity of which can be explained by basic cognitive processes common to all tasks.

As already hinted at by William James, however, there is more to the self than its objective aspect. The self also encompasses a sense of personal agency: the experience that we are the cause and origin of our own thoughts and action. This perspective is unique to the self. Legrand and Ruby (2009) argue that self-specificity may be found here and will come in the form of making the relation between one's own actions and their consequences in the social world. Consistent with this idea, initial brain imaging studies investigated a sense of agency by examining those brain mechanisms responsible for comparing predicted and actual action-effects. In one such study (Spengler, Von Cramon, & Brass, 2009), for example, participants first learned an arbitrary action–effect pairing: they had to press a button as quickly as possible when a white square appeared alternating between the use of either their index or middle finger. Immediately thereafter either a red or blue box appeared, and these colours were systematically mapped on to either of the two fingers. Later on, in the scanner, participants again had to press a button as soon as a white square appeared, and were then presented on some trials with matching and on other trials with non-matching action–effects (i.e., the finger–colour combination they had learned or the opposite).

Following each event, participants had to judge whether they themselves had produced the effects (i.e., the squares), or whether these had been computer-generated. Results revealed that participants showed a decreased sense of agency for mismatched trials, or in other words, when previously learned action–effects were altered and did not meet the internal prediction. These same trials also mapped on to increased neural activation of the temporal parietal junction (TPJ), a brain area responsible for monitoring the correspondence (or lack thereof) between internal predictions with external events. A recent meta-analysis of studies on the neural correlates of agency concluded that TPJ activation is present in external-agency attribution ('not me'). Self-agency in contrast seems to be marked by activations in the premotor and primary somatosensory cortex (Sperduti et al., 2011). Self-specificity thus seems to derive from integration of (motor) command of one's actions and the sensory consequences we experience in the social world.

In conclusion, the important point to be made is that there is no specific 'self' region in the brain. The self cannot be localized as a neural entity, but rather is informed by a set of interrelated, functionally independent systems interacting in complex ways (e.g., Klein, Lax, & Gangi, 2010).

Summary

The self-concept can be described as the collection of the content of all our self-experiences, including our characteristics, our social roles, our values, our goals, our fears and so on. This self-knowledge can be categorized into two types: the cognitive representation in the self-concept – our self-schema – and the affective evaluation of the self – our self-esteem. The self-schemas help organize and guide the information processing of self-relevant contents and often function as a reference for judging others. These schemas exert their influence both at the explicit and at the implicit level, and they contain a range of actual, desired (ideal and ought), and possible self-beliefs. At any one time, it is not the entire self-concept that is driving our feelings, thoughts and behaviours, but rather the active or working self-concept – whatever aspect of the self-concept is applicable to the current situation. Self-esteem can be considered a feeling toward oneself based on an overall evaluation about our qualities and worth. It can be described at the trait or at the state level and – as with the self-schemas – it can influence us explicitly or implicitly. In addition, different domains can be differentially important for the self-esteem of different people. Culture and gender shape both our self-concept and our self-esteem. Finally, there is no specific 'self' region in the brain.

THE MOTIVATIONAL FUNCTIONS OF THE SELF

To what extent are we motivated to find out the truth about ourselves versus preferring positive distortions?

The beginning of the twenty-first century has seen an unprecedented rise of talent shows as a popular genre of reality TV. Popstars, the Idols series, The X-Factor and the Got Talent series and the like have drawn hundreds of millions of viewers around the world. Although there are many variations on the theme, talent shows inevitably feature a jury of experts who provide feedback to the contestants about their performance. Indeed, a major part of what is shown on TV focuses on contestants' reactions to the jury's feedback, which are typically highly emotional. Positive feedback makes contestants act euphorically, by jumping up and down, shouting, crying with joy and so on. Negative feedback often shatters contestants, bringing to them tears of sadness, or making them lash out in anger.

Modern talent shows exploit something that social psychologists have long known, namely, the fact that people care deeply about information that pertains to the self. Indeed, most of us are all too eager to find out what kind of traits, talents and abilities we possess. This basic curiosity may explain the widespread appeal of horoscopes, popular magazines, psychological tests and training programmes that are designed to help us on the road to self-discovery. But how sincere are we in our quest for self-knowledge? Are we genuinely motivated to find out the truth about who we are? Or do we merely seek to confirm our preconceived ideas about ourselves?

Know thyself: the self-assessment motive

According to Socrates, a Greek philosopher who lived between 470 and 399 BC, accurate self-knowledge represents the highest human virtue. From this perspective, most of us should try to reach an understanding of the self that is as accurate and objective as possible. This striving is also known as the **self-assessment motive**.

self-assessment motive striving to reach an accurate and objective understanding of the self.

To the extent that we are driven by self-assessment motives, we should be eager to perform tests or tasks that provide us with a maximum amount of objective information about ourselves. For instance, if we truly want to know how smart (or dumb) we are, we should prefer a scientifically validated IQ test over our own subjective impression of our intelligence. In line with the self-assessment perspective, several studies have shown that people prefer high diagnostic tasks, that is, tasks that can clearly tell them whether they have a certain trait or ability, over low diagnostic tasks (Trope, 1983, 1986).

However, there is a catch here. If we were purely interested in developing an accurate understanding of the self, we should be equally motivated to learn about our desirable and undesirable qualities. Most of us are indeed eager to learn about our desirable traits and abilities, which make us look good (Sedikides, 1993). But what about our undesirable traits and weaknesses? Here, research findings are mixed. Some studies have shown that people are equally interested to hear about their desirable and undesirable qualities (Strube, Lott, Lê-Xuân-Hy, Oxenberg, & Deichmann, 1986; Trope,

1980). However, other studies have found that people are primarily interested in obtaining accurate information about their strengths rather than about their weaknesses (Brown, 1990; Strube & Roemmele, 1985). It thus appears that our motivation to learn about our weaknesses is not as reliable as our motivation to learn about our strengths. Although the self-assessment motive seems intuitively plausible, this motive is of only limited use in explaining how most of us process information about the self (Sedikides, 1993).

Bigger, better, faster, stronger: the self-enhancement motive

Our refusal to learn about our weaknesses is readily understandable in terms of the *self-enhancement motive*, which refers to our desire to enhance the positivity of our self-conceptions or protect the self from negative information (Sedikides & Strube, 1997). The self-enhancement motive is central to classic and contemporary psychological theories that assume that people have a basic need to view themselves positively, or a need for self-esteem (e.g., James, 1890, 1950; Rogers, 1951; Steele, 1988). According to the self-enhancement view, our need for self-esteem leads us to focus on information that has favourable implications for the self and to avoid information that has unfavourable implications for the self.

Self-enhancing illusions One important way in which we self-enhance is revealed through the kinds of beliefs that we adopt. As noted earlier, Taylor and Brown (1988) concluded that most psychologically healthy individuals entertain many positive illusions about the self. The most obvious kind of positive illusion is the superiority bias, which means that we tend to hold unrealistically positive views of the self. For instance, we display a pervasive tendency to see the self as better than others. We judge positive personality attributes to be more descriptive of ourselves than of the average person, but regard negative personality attributes as less descriptive of ourselves than of the average person (Alicke, 1985; Brown, 1986). We further judge ourselves more favourably compared to more objective standards, such as external observers (Lewinsohn, Mischel, Chaplin, & Barton, 1980). One particularly striking demonstration of this self-enhancing illusion was provided by Epley and Whitchurch (2008). These researchers took a facial photograph of each person in a group of participants and used a computerized morphing procedure to make the photographs look more or less attractive (see Figure 5.9). Participants were found to identify the attractively enhanced photo of themselves more readily as their own

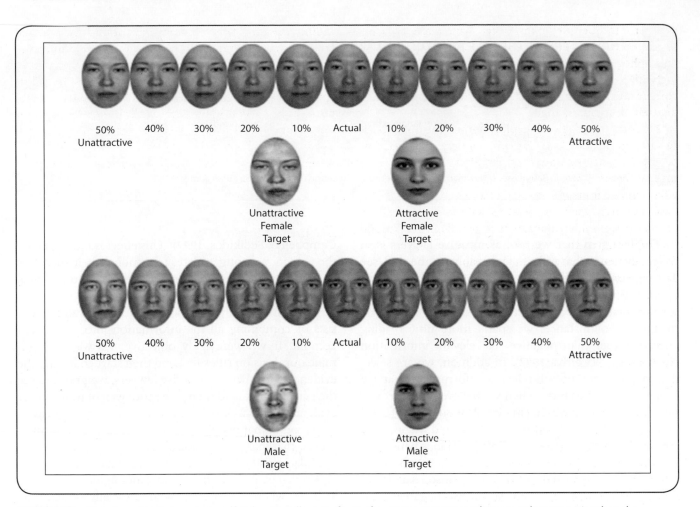

FIGURE 5.9 *Stimuli used to demonstrate self-enhancing illusions: faces of participants were made more or less attractive than the actual photograph using a computer program.*

Source: From Epley & Whitchurch, 2008; Expt. 1. Reproduced with permission from SAGE publications.

face than the photo of their actual face. Thus, it appears that we are prone to regard our own facial image as being more desirable than it actually is.

Self-enhancement biases can be found in many other beliefs that we hold about ourselves (Roese & Olson, 2007). For instance, we often display unrealistic optimism, holding overly positive expectations of what the future might bring (Armor & Taylor, 1998). Those of us who are romantically involved further display couple-serving bias, believing that our own romantic relationship is superior to that of others (Buunk, 2001; Rusbult, Van Lange, Wildschut, Yovetich, & Verette, 2000). Likewise, we are prone to ingroup favouritism, believing that our own group is superior to other groups (Hewstone, Rubin, & Willis, 2002; Mullen, Brown, & Smith, 1992). Self-enhancement may also take on less obvious forms. For instance, consider the false consensus effect (Ross, Greene, & House, 1977), which refers to our beliefs that others' opinions are more similar to ours than is actually the case. This effect can be seen as

a subtle form of self-enhancement, in that it allows us to think that our own opinions enjoy more popular support than they actually do (McGregor, Nail, Marigold, & Kang, 2005).

Self-enhancing information processing How can we sustain self-enhancing beliefs even when they are contradicted by reality? An underlying reason is that the ways in which we process information are also self-enhancing. Indeed, there is much evidence that our reasoning processes are biased to support conclusions that are favourable to the self. This process is an example of motivated reasoning (Kunda, 1990). Importantly, we are not at liberty to believe whatever we want merely because we want to. Instead, we maintain an 'illusion of objectivity' (Pyszczynski & Greenberg, 1987) by selectively searching for and combining information that supports our desired conclusions. We thus act as if we are intuitive lawyers who are trying to make the best case for a particular, preselected conclusion (Baumeister & Newman, 1994).

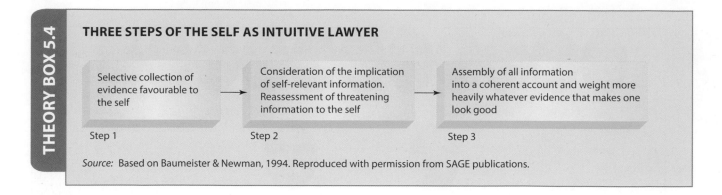

The first step that we take as intuitive lawyers is to collect evidence that reflects favourably on the self (see Theory Box 5.4 for the three steps of the self as intuitive lawyer). We are highly selective in the kinds of self-relevant information we attend to and in what we choose to ignore. For instance, we spend more time reading positive rather than negative self-relevant information (Baumeister & Cairns, 1992). In addition, we are selective in the kinds of self-relevant information that we remember. For instance, when we believe that extroversion is favourable, we quickly recall memories of situations in which we acted in an extroverted manner. By contrast, when we believe that introversion is beneficial, we quickly recall memories of situations in which we acted in an introverted manner (Sanitioso, Kunda, & Fong, 1990). Likewise, when we receive negative feedback about the self, we hardly attend to this information (Green, Sedikides, & Gregg, 2008; Sedikides & Green, 2004), so that we easily forget negative self-relevant information. Conversely, we spend much time reflecting on positive feedback about the self, so that we recall positive self-relevant information very well.

The second step that we take as intuitive lawyers is to consider the implications of self-relevant information and to reassess them, if these implications are threatening to the self. For instance, Liberman and Chaiken (1992) found that regular coffee drinkers were more critical than other individuals of research reports suggesting a link between caffeine consumption and a potentially fatal disease. In a related vein, studies have shown that people become more critical of the validity of psychological tests when the test results are disagreeable to them personally (Pyszczynski, Greenberg, & Holt, 1985; Wyer & Frey, 1983). Our tendency to explain away information that threatens the self may also explain why we tend to assign different causes to successes and failures. Many studies have observed such self-serving attributional biases (see Chapter 3): we take credit for our triumphs, while blaming the circumstances for our personal failures (Miller & Ross, 1975; see also

Campbell & Sedikides, 1999). This effect is illustrated by the tendency among athletes to attribute their successes to their personal qualities and their failures to bad luck (Mullen & Riordan, 1988).

The third step that we take as intuitive lawyers consists of combining all the information into a coherent account. If we were truly objective, we would determine our decision rules first and then start collecting the evidence. However, as intuitive lawyers, we prefer to see the evidence first and then give more weight to whatever evidence makes us look good. Indeed, Dunning and associates found that people attach the most weight to those criteria that make them look best (Dunning, Meyerowitz, & Holzberg, 1989). For instance, a student who is good at maths is likely to define competence in terms of maths abilities, whereas a student who is socially skilled may place more emphasis on social abilities. An unfortunate consequence of our idiosyncratic definitions of our abilities is that we tend to remain unaware of our incompetence (Dunning et al., 2003). Self-enhancement motives may thus be an important barrier to self-improvement.

Implicit self-enhancement More generally, we seem to be mostly unaware of the extent to which our thinking is influenced by self-enhancement motives (Baumeister & Newman, 1994; Kunda, 1990; Tesser, 2000). One reason for this lack of awareness may be self-deception. If we openly acknowledge that we are self-enhancing, this may undermine our very efforts to convince ourselves that we are endowed with favourable qualities. Another reason why self-enhancement motives may operate outside of awareness is that these motives are driven by basic affective processes. Successful self-enhancement leads to positive affect and failed self-enhancement leads to negative affect (Roese & Olson, 2007; Tesser, 2000). This affective feedback may guide how we are considering information about the self, even when we have little or no awareness of this process. For instance, learning that we just made an embarrassing mistake may trigger a brief bout of negative feelings, which prompts us to look for a circumstance that could excuse our incompetent behaviour. It is well-established that much of our affective life occurs outside of awareness (Berridge & Winkielman, 2003; Chartrand, Van Baaren, & Bargh, 2006; Zajonc, 1998). For this reason, self-enhancement processes may similarly be driven by unconscious processes.

In a groundbreaking article, Greenwald and Banaji (1995) observed that persons or objects that are associated with the self are often evaluated more positively. For instance, we evaluate mundane objects like pens and mugs more favourably when we happen to own them (Beggan, 1992). Likewise, we evaluate people more favourably when they share their date of birth with us (Miller, Downs, & Prentice, 1998) or when we are photographed together with them (Burgess, Enzle, & Morry, 2000). As noted earlier, we even like the letters of our name more than other people like these letters (Koole & Pelham, 2003; Nuttin, 1985, 1987). These examples illustrate that we evaluate self-associated objects more positively, even when this association is purely arbitrary. As such, it appears that we are not fully aware of how the self enhances our evaluations of self-associated objects. This tendency to gravitate toward people, places and things that resemble the self is referred to as **implicit egotism** (Pelham, Carvallo, & Jones, 2005).

> **implicit egotism** non-conscious or automatic positive evaluation of self-associated objects.

Self-presentation and self-enhancement So far we have portrayed self-enhancement as a process that largely takes place between the ears. However, it is important to recognize that self-enhancement has widespread influence on our interactions with other people. Anthropologists like Joseph Campbell (1949) and Ernest Becker (1973) observed that all cultures around the world and throughout history have developed some kind of value system that allows people to gain a feeling that they are a person of worth. If this is correct, then self-enhancement motives may explain why most of us are striving hard every day to live up to the norms of our society by, for instance, dressing according to the latest fashion, getting a university degree, acting as responsible citizens and so on.

THEORY BOX 5.5

SELF-PRESENTATION STRATEGIES

	Attributions sought	Emotion to be aroused	Prototypical actions
Self-Promotion	Competent (effective, 'a winner')	Respect (awe, deference)	• Talk proudly about your experience or education. • Make people aware of your accomplishments.
Ingratiation	Likeable	Affection	• Take an interest in your colleague's personal lives to show them that you are friendly. • Use flattery and favours to make your colleagues like you more.
Exemplification	Worthy (suffers, dedicated)	Guilt (shame, emulation)	• Try to appear like a hard-working, dedicated employee to make others feel less worthy than you. • Stay at work late so people will know you are hard-working.
Intimidation	Dangerous (ruthless, volatile)	Fear	• Be intimidating with coworkers when it will help you get your job done. • Let others know that you can make things difficult for them if they push you too far.
Supplication	Helpless (handicapped, unfortunate)	Nurturance (obligation)	• Act like you know less than you do so people will help you out. • Pretend not to understand something to gain someone's help.

Source: Bolino & Turnley (1999) table adapted with permission from SAGE Publications Ltd. Also adapted with permission of Taylor and Francis, from Jones, E. E., & Pittman, T. S. (1982). Toward a general theory of strategic self-presentation. In J. M. Suls (Ed.), *Psychological perspectives on the self* (Vol. 1, pp. 231–262). Hillsdale, NJ: Erlbaum. Permission conveyed through Copyright Clearance Center, Inc.

The importance of self-enhancement motives for our everyday behaviour is highlighted by research on self-presentation. **Self-presentation** refers to the ways in which we try strategically to manage the impressions we are communicating to an audience (Jones & Pittman, 1982). The audience can be either imagined or real. We present ourselves in many different ways to different people and for many different reasons (Jones & Pittman, 1982). Study Theory Box 5.5 to learn about different types of self-presentational strategies people use when trying to evoke specific attributions and emotions in their audience. As you can see, these are quite varied and can run from acting helpless ('supplication') to obtain nurturance and help, to excessive flattery ('ingratiation') to get others to like one. Nevertheless, our primary objective in self-presentation is to convey a favourable image of the self to others. Some of the more direct ways in which we may self-present are by dressing smartly, smiling, and telling others about our important achievements (Wicklund & Gollwitzer, 1982). Self-presentation may also be directed at covering up our inadequacies. For instance, we may make excuses for socially unskilled behaviour (Snyder & Higgins, 1988).

> **self-presentation** a range of strategies that we adopt in order to shape what others think of us.

Another tactic is **self-handicapping** (Jones & Berglas, 1978). In this sophisticated form of self-presentation, we create an impediment that makes good performance unlikely, but that will allow a positive interpretation of the performance outcome regardless. For instance, in one study, participants were given the opportunity to practise more, or less, for an upcoming battery of intelligence tests (Tice & Baumeister, 1990). If participants did not engage in much practice, they would have an external explanation for not performing well. If participants then did poorly, this would not mean that they had to infer that they were incompetent. However, if participants then did well, they succeeded in spite of sub-optimal circumstances. The inference therefore is that one must have really high ability. Augmenting ability attributions after success has been shown to be characteristic primarily of individuals high in self-esteem (Rhodewalt, Morf, Hazlett, & Fairfield, 1991).

> **self-handicapping** the tendency to engage in self-defeating behaviours in order to provide a subsequent excuse for failure and augment ability attributions in the case of success.

In other words, through these and other forms of self-handicapping, our self-image is always well off. However, self-handicapping comes at the expense of a lower chance of succeeding, and of finding out just how good we really are. Research suggests that we indeed use various kinds of self-handicapping tactics, such as alcohol use, drug use, test anxiety and procrastination (Tice, 1991; Tucker, Vuchinich, & Sobell, 1981; Zuckerman, Kieffer, & Knee, 1998). Turn to Research Close-Up 5.2 now to learn about an important gender difference in self-handicapping behaviour.

Notably, we do not always self-present by speaking favourably about ourselves. Indeed, direct self-praise is often frowned upon and invites negative reactions from our social environment (Paulhus, 1998). We therefore self-present in a tactical manner, in ways that elude direct disapproval from others. For instance, we may strengthen our ties with successful others, a strategy known as 'basking in reflected glory' ('BIRGing', Cialdini et al., 1976). For example, you may wear the scarf or shirt of your local sports team after they won a match. Through this association you get a boost to your self-esteem. We further make sure that we present ourselves in a more modest fashion when we are among friends (Tice, Butler, Muraven, & Stillwell, 1995). We will have future interactions with our friends, so that they are better able to verify our claims about ourselves. Furthermore, we do not self-enhance as much when doing so comes at the expense of close others. For instance, self-serving bias in attributions becomes attenuated when we are among close others.

Sedikides and colleagues (Sedikides, Campbell, Reeder, & Elliot, 1998) induced closeness experimentally in one study by having participants engage in a structured self-disclosure task (they were asked to discuss questions that became progressively more personal – for example, from 'How old are you' to 'Tell me one thing that most people do not know about you'). Next, they engaged in a creativity task – either with the person they had become close to, or they were switched to a new person (distant) – and were then provided with success versus failure feedback on the creativity test. Following this feedback, participants were asked to attribute the outcome (success or failure) to themselves or the partner along a continuum. Findings revealed that participants took more credit for the dyad's success and less responsibility for failure if they were with a distant other participant (this is the typical self-serving attribution effect). However, close participants took neither greater responsibility for the dyad's success, nor lower responsibility for failure – they self-attributed responsibility for either outcome somewhere in-between the distant other conditions (see Figure 5.10). We display this gracious attributional pattern because we have a positive impression of close others and expect them to reciprocate our self-effacing response. Indeed, when close others display more self-serving responses, our responses become as self-enhancing as with non-close others (Sedikides et al., 1998). In sum, our self-presentations are highly tactical and sensitive to the specific requirements of the social context.

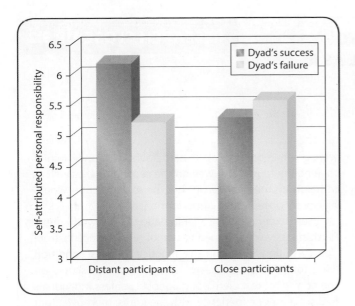

FIGURE 5.10 *Self-attributed personal responsibility as a function of closeness to other participants and success versus failure feedback.*

Source: Copyright © 1998 by the American Psychological Association. Adapted with permission. Sedikides, C., Campbell, W. K., Reeder, G. D., & Elliot, A. J. (1998). The self-serving bias in relational context. *Journal of Personality and Social Psychology, 74,* 378–386 Excerpt 1. The use of APA information does not imply endorsement by APA.

Pancultural self-enhancement Although Western cultures emphasize individualistic values such as personal freedom and self-expression, many non-Western cultures emphasize more collectivistic values such as conformity and fitting in with the group (Triandis, 1989; see Chapter 15). Heine and associates have suggested that self-enhancement motives are only applicable to individuals who have been socialized within individualistic societies (Heine et al., 1999). As discussed earlier in the chapter, in collectivistic cultures individuals are more likely to have an interdependent conception of the self, which may render them less motivated to affirm positive views of the self. Research has confirmed that East Asians, as representatives of collectivistic cultures, typically have self-views that are only moderately positive, and much weaker self-enhancement biases than North Americans, at least in their self-reports. Indeed, several studies have found evidence for a self-critical bias among Japanese individuals. For instance, one experiment found that Japanese students were more easily convinced that their performance was below average than were Canadian students (Heine, Takata, & Lehman, 2000).

Cultural psychologists have thus challenged the universality of the self-enhancement motive. But this challenge has itself been challenged. First, people may be most likely to self-enhance on dimensions that are consistent with our cultural roles (Sedikides, Gaertner, & Toguchi, 2003). Accordingly, a number of studies have found that members of individualistic cultures self-enhance mostly on individualistic traits indicating personal effectiveness (e.g., independent, unique, leader). Members of collectivistic cultures, in contrast, self-enhance mostly on collectivistic traits signifying social connectedness (e.g., respectful, compliant, loyal) (Gaertner, Sedikides, & Chang, 2008; Sedikides et al., 2003). Second, self-evaluations by members of collectivistic cultures may be more influenced by norms that emphasize modesty. Norms towards modesty appear to be stronger in East Asia than in the West (Cai et al., 2007). Such modesty norms typically prohibit boasts about one's accomplishments.

Third, as mentioned earlier, members of East-Asian cultures do show significant positivity towards the self on implicit measures (Cai et al., 2011; Kitayama & Uchida, 2003; Yamaguchi et al., 2007). At first glance, the co-existence of explicit self-criticism and implicit self-regard seems paradoxical. However, various theorists have suggested that one's own self-critical remarks are usually met with sympathy and compassion in interdependent cultures (Cai et al., 2011; Kitayama & Uchida, 2003). Consequently, self-critical East Asians are likely to develop positive associations towards the self, even when (or paradoxically, because) their explicit comments about the self are negative. Consistent with this, explicit modesty is positively associated with implicit self-esteem among members of Eastern cultures, but not among members of Western cultures (Cai et al., 2011). Cai and colleagues (2011) showed this using the implicit association test (IAT) described earlier as an implicit measure of self-esteem. With this method, the researchers found the expected association between enacting modest behaviour and high implicit self-esteem for Asian participants, but not for American participants. Moreover, this was despite Asians reporting low explicit self-esteem. In short, within different cultural contexts, different 'roads' may lead to positive self-regard.

To summarize, there are important differences between cultures that shape both norms for self-presentation and the kinds of qualities people aspire to. These cultural differences lead to striking differences in how East Asians present themselves relative to Westerners. Nevertheless, when appropriately measured, self-enhancement tendencies can be observed equally among members of both Eastern and Western cultures. Self-enhancement thus appears to be a universal human motive.

WOMEN ARE LESS LIKELY TO USE EFFORT WITHDRAWAL AS A SELF-HANDICAP

McCrea, S. M., Hirt, E. R., & Milner, B. J. (2008). She works hard for the money: Valuing effort underlies gender differences in behavioral self-handicapping. *Journal of Experimental Social Psychology*, *44*, 292–311.

Introduction

If individuals worry about failing on a specific task, they sometimes create or claim obstacles in order to have an excuse for possible failing. Hereby they can protect their self-esteem and preserve an impression of ability. This strategy is called self-handicapping. Claimed self-handicaps, in which individuals only state that an obstacle exists (e.g., stress), can be distinguished from behavioural self-handicaps, in which individuals actually create obstacles (e.g., withdraw practice effort). This distinction is important, as it is related to a gender difference in self-handicapping: both men and women have been found to use claimed self-handicaps, but it is predominantly men who engage in behavioural self-handicapping (Hirt, Deppe, & Gordon, 1991). In their study, McCrea and colleagues further analysed this gender difference and tested a possible explanation for it. They hypothesized that, compared to men, women might place more value on exerting effort and thus would be less likely to curtail it. Only the results of Study 3 are reported here.

Method

Participants

The participants were 188 introductory psychology students (92 male and 96 female). They received research credits in return for their participation.

Design and procedure

Before starting the actual experiment, participants completed two questionnaires: (1) a 'worker scale', which measured how hard the students reported that they work (e.g., 'I work hard to be successful at whatever I do.'); and (2) a 'prescriptive effort norm scale', which measured how highly they value effort (e.g., 'I admire people who work hard.').

Participants first completed a computerized 15-item multiple-choice analogy test that they believed to be a traditional test for verbal intelligence. The items chosen were particularly difficult. After completing this task, the computer displayed a message informing participants that they had scored 12 out of 15 items correct, and that this score placed them in the top 10% of college students. They were further told that they would be expected to score highly on a subsequent nonverbal test as well, and that the researchers would compare their two scores to see if they matched this high expectation. These instructions

were given in order to make participants feel uncertain of their ability to perform well on the second test, as well as to heighten the impression that the experimenter would be closely observing their performance.

The experimental manipulation followed next. Participants were assigned to one of two practice instruction conditions: those in the 'practice matters' condition were told that past research had shown that scores on the nonverbal test were not diagnostic, unless individuals had some prior experience with the items; moreover, that without such practice they would score lower than their actual intelligence would warrant. Those in the 'practice doesn't matter' condition were told that past research had shown that practice had no effect on scores on the test. Participants in both conditions were then given a chance to practise prior to the test. All participants received a practice booklet with 18 items and were allowed to practise for as long (or as little) as they liked. The time participants spent practising was surreptitiously recorded, along with the number of practice items completed. Afterwards, they completed the 15-item test.

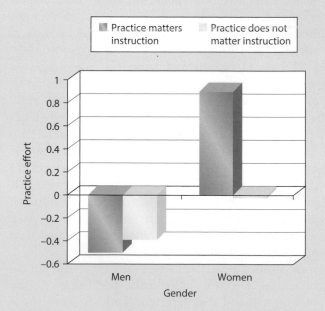

FIGURE 5.11 *Practice effort as a function of instruction and gender. Note: Practice effort was computed as an index of time spent practising and number of items completed.*

Source: From McCrea, Hirt, & Milner, 2008; Expt. 3. Reproduced with permission from Elsevier.

The experiment thus had a 2-factor design: 2 (gender: male vs. female) X 2 (degree to which effort withdrawal could serve as a self-handicap: low/'practice doesn't matter' vs. high/'practice matters').

Results

The results provided support for the hypothesis. Figure 5.11 shows the gender differences in behavioural self-handicapping: only men reduced their effort in the 'practice matters' condition, whereas women practised significantly more. In the 'practice doesn't matter' condition, there was no significant gender difference. Further analyses revealed that the gender difference was due in part to women's reporting being harder workers, as well as their placing more value on effort.

Discussion

The results of this study confirmed the gender difference in behavioural self-handicapping found in earlier studies. Moreover, the authors also provided an explanation for that effect. Women value effort more highly and reported that they invested more in working harder than did men. Therefore, women do not engage in effort withdrawal as a self-handicapping behaviour – the costs of this behavioural self-handicapping would be too high for women. The authors speculate that the difference between men and women in their evaluation of work and effort could be an expression of a greater pressure to adhere to norms. Future studies are needed to further explicate this gender difference, as it was not completely explained by the scales measured in this study.

The puzzle of low self-regard: self-verification

Most of us view the self in largely positive terms. Most, but not all, of us. A small but distinct number of individuals are inclined to view the self in more neutral, if not negative, terms. These individuals represent an intriguing psychological puzzle. Are these individuals somehow immune to self-enhancement needs? Or do these individuals still have the desire to self-enhance, but does something keep them from doing so?

A research programme led by Swann and associates (Swann & Buhrmester, 2012) goes a long way towards resolving the puzzle of individuals with low self-regard (see Leader in the Field, William B. Swann). According to these researchers, our stable self-views are tied to feelings that the world is meaningful and coherent. A stable and coherent view of ourselves and the world is crucial, because it allows us to organize our experience, predict future events, and guide social interaction. Our

self-verification motivation to affirm firmly held self-beliefs, arising from a desire for stable and coherent self-views.

desire for stable and coherent self-views gives rise to the **self-verification** motive, a motivation to affirm our firmly held beliefs about ourselves. For those of us with positive self-views (who are in the majority), affirming positive self-views jointly serves self-verification and self-enhancement motives. However, for those of us with negative self-views (a sizeable minority), there is a fundamental conflict between self-verification and self-enhancement motives. Affirming positive self-views feels good on one level, because it fulfils self-enhancement needs. However, doing so does not feel right, because

it compromises the feelings of coherence that drive our self-verification motives (Swann & Buhrmester, 2012).

The self-verification perspective holds that people will fight to maintain stable self-views even when these self-views are negative, so that maintaining them is psychologically painful (Swann & Buhrmester, 2012). In line with this provocative idea, studies have shown that people gravitate towards self-verifying interaction partners (e.g., Hixon & Swann, 1993; Robinson & Smith-Lovin, 1992; Swann, Stein-Seroussi, & Giesler, 1992). For instance, one study asked participants with positive and negative self-views to pick one of two potential partners to get to know better over an

 LEADER IN THE FIELD

William B. Swann (b. 1952) received his BA from Gettysburg College in 1974 and his PhD from the University of Minnesota in 1978. Since then he has worked at the University of Texas at Austin, where he is Professor of Social and Personality Psychology. He is best known for his research on self-verification: the theory assumes that people prefer others to see them consistent with their own firmly held beliefs and feelings about themselves (both negative and positive). Another focus of Swann's work is on the process of identity negotiation: the processes through which people in relationships reach mutual agreements regarding 'who' each person is. Once these agreements have been reached, people are expected to remain faithful to their identities. These agreements establish what people expect of one another, and thus determine the way they relate and, in turn, keep the relationship together. In a 2004 survey, Professor Swann was listed among the top 30 most-cited authors published in *Journal of Personality and Social Psychology*, and in a 2006 survey in *Dialogue*, among the top 30 most-cited authors in social psychology textbooks.

interaction of two to three hours (Swann et al., 1992). These potential partners had allegedly provided their evaluations of participants' personality profiles. One partner expressed a very favourable impression of the participant; the other expressed a somewhat negative impression. As it turned out, most participants chose a partner whose evaluation of them matched their own self-views (see Figure 5.12). This means that participants with positive self-views preferred interaction partners who had favourable impressions of them. However, perhaps more surprisingly, participants with negative self-views preferred interaction partners who had unfavourable impressions of them. Importantly, these self-verification tendencies occur not just in the laboratory, but have also emerged in real-life relationships, such as marriage, friendships and work teams (see Swann & Buhrmester, 2012). Self-verification strivings occur equally for men and women and both for specific self-views (e.g., intelligence, sociability) and global self-worth. People are particularly likely to seek self-verifying feedback for self-views that are confidently held, important or extreme (see Swann & Buhrmester, 2012, for a review).

Do people with negative self-views relish negative feedback about the self? Or have they simply stopped caring about the self? The answer to both questions is negative. Instead, individuals with a negative self-view feel deeply torn upon receiving negative evaluations. On the one hand, these individuals like to hear others say good things about them. This positive reaction to self-enhancing feedback is characteristic for the first, automatic reaction of individuals with negative self-views (Swann, Hixon, Stein-Seroussi, & Gilbert, 1990). On the other hand, however, individuals feel that self-enhancing feedback does not describe them very accurately. Consequently, individuals with negative self-views feel more understood by interaction partners who evaluate them negatively. This preference for negative but self-verifying feedback only emerges when people have sufficient time and attentional resources to think about their decision, otherwise people prefer positive feedback, regardless of how self-verifying it is (Swann et al., 1990). In sum, individuals with negative self-views still have self-enhancement tendencies, but these tendencies may be overruled by more deliberate strivings for self-verification.

Why do we self-enhance?

In a classic study, Peterson and Seligman (1987) examined how members of the Baseball Hall of Fame from 1900–1950 explained their successes and failures. The results showed that players lived significantly longer to the extent that they provided self-serving explanations of good and bad events (i.e., attributed success to themselves and failure to specific circumstances). This striking finding is consistent with other studies showing that self-enhancement tendencies are positively associated with mental and physical health (Taylor, Kemeny, Reed, Bower, & Gruenewald, 2000). This pattern is not only observed in the West, but also in Eastern cultures, which promote modesty and self-criticism among their members (Gaertner et al., 2008). Moreover, although these findings are correlational, there is also evidence that affirming positive self-views can directly cause health benefits (Creswell et al., 2005, 2007).

Sociometer theory In what way is self-enhancement beneficial to our health? This question relates to the deeper reasons why we are driven to self-enhance. Why is it so important to us to think well of ourselves? In addressing these questions, Leary and associates have emphasized the interpersonal functions of having positive feelings towards the self (Leary et al., 1995). According to Leary, our feelings of self-esteem signal the degree to which we feel acceptance or rejection by other members of our social group. When we experience

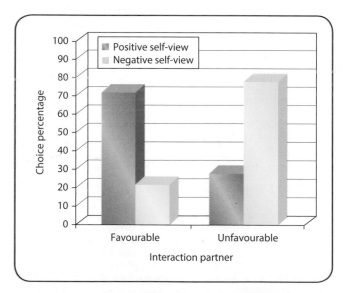

FIGURE 5.12 *Percentage of participants who chose favourable versus unfavourable interaction partners depending on positivity of participants' own self-view.*

Source: Data copyright © 1992 by the American Psychological Association. Reproduced with permission. Swann, W. B., Jr., Stein-Seroussi, A., & Giesler, R. B. (1992). Why people self-verify. *Journal of Personality and Social Psychology, 62,* 392–401. The use of APA information does not imply endorsement by APA.

rejections from others, our self-esteem drops, which motivates us to restore our social standing through various self-enhancing behaviours. When we feel accepted, we maintain our positive sense of self-esteem. Feelings of self-esteem may thus act as a 'sociometer' (a kind of social barometer) that helps us to keep track of our social status.

The **sociometer theory** has inspired a great deal of research on the effects of social exclusion on self-esteem.

> **sociometer theory** a theory that posits that our self-esteem functions as a signal of the degree to which we feel accepted or rejected by other people.

However, its assumptions have proven surprisingly difficult to confirm. A relatively recent meta-analysis that combined almost 200 relevant studies found no evidence that social exclusion has a negative impact on self-esteem (Blackhart, Nelson, Knowles, & Baumeister, 2009). Moreover, the same exclusion manipulations that failed to influence self-esteem did have effects on other variables, such as impairing one's ability to self-regulate (Baumeister, DeWall, Ciarocco, & Twenge, 2005) or producing a substantial reduction in prosocial behaviour (Twenge, Baumeister, DeWall, Ciarocco, & Bartels, 2007). These findings call into question whether self-esteem is directly linked to our perceived level of belongingness. More generally, the absence of effects of exclusion on self-esteem poses a major challenge to the sociometer model.

Terror management theory

An alternative perspective on the psychological functions of self-esteem is provided by **terror management theory** (Greenberg, Solomon, & Pyszczynski, 1997).

> **terror management theory** a theory that assumes that people cope with the fear of their own death by constructing worldviews that help to preserve their self-esteem.

Inspired by existential thinkers like Otto Rank and Ernest Becker, terror management theory proposes that our human self-awareness greatly magnifies our potential for anxiety, because it allows us to realize that our own death is inevitable. To manage this existential anxiety, we become invested in our culture, which provides our existence with meaning and order. Culture also provides us with ways of achieving immortality, either literally through religious beliefs about an afterlife, or symbolically by identifying with values that transcend our individual existence (e.g., justice, love or science). To achieve literal or symbolic immortality, we must maintain the values that are proscribed by our culture. To the extent that we are effective at this, we will experience a sense of self-esteem. Terror management theory thus suggests that the ultimate reason why we self-enhance is because

having a positive self helps us to overcome our deepest existential fears.

Research has provided strong evidence for the basic tenets of terror management theory (see Pyszczynski, Greenberg, Solomon, Arndt, & Schimel, 2004, for an overview). First, affirming positive beliefs about the self reduces death anxiety (Greenberg et al., 1993) and helps to put thoughts about death out of the mind (Schmeichel & Martens, 2005). Second, reminding people of death (i.e., increasing mortality salience) leads to stronger self-enhancement strivings. For instance, in one study, Israeli soldiers were reminded of either death or of a neutral topic (Taubman Ben-Ari, Florian, & Mikulincer, 1999). Risky driving is for many people a means to show off, test their limits, or compete with other drivers (Taubman Ben-Ari, 2000). According to terror management theory, concerns with death should motivate the individuals reminded of their death to engage in more risky driving. In line with this prediction, the results showed that reminders of death led to more dangerous driving manoeuvres (as assessed through self-report and on a driving simulator), particularly among soldiers who took pride in their driving ability.

Likewise, death reminders increase the appeal of high-status items (e.g., a Lexus car) and materialism among people living in capitalist cultures, which emphasize financial success as a source of self-worth (Rindfleisch, Burroughs, & Wong, 2009). Notably, these effects are not paralleled by reminders of other aversive topics, such as failing an important exam, or uncertainty. Third, suggesting to people that there is scientific proof for an afterlife reduces the impact of mortality salience on self-enhancement strivings (Dechesne et al., 2003). After being asked to write down the first thing that came to mind when thinking about death or a control topic (watching television), participants read an article presenting scientific arguments for or against the existence of an afterlife. When reading an article arguing for no life after death, participants showed the typical mortality salience effect of more positive self-ratings when reminded about death relative to the control group. However, when participants read an article containing scientific arguments for a life after death, this self-enhancement following death reminders disappeared (see Figure 5.13).

Taken together, there is impressive support for the terror management functions of self-enhancement. Although self-enhancement is logically unrelated to the problem of death, self-enhancement psychologically protects us against death anxiety. Consequently, one major reason why we self-enhance is that doing so helps us to cope more effectively with existential concerns.

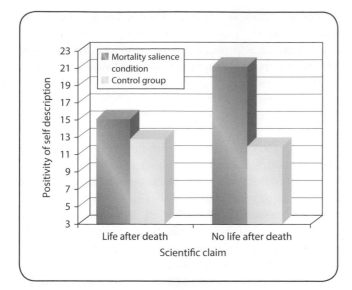

FIGURE 5.13 *Self-enhancement striving (positivity of self-description) as a function of mortality salience condition and scientific claim about the existence of life after death.*

Source: Data copyright © 2003 by the American Psychological Association. Reproduced with permission. Dechesne, M., Pyszczynski, T., Arndt, J., Ransom, S., Sheldon, K. M., Van Knippenberg, A., & Janssen, J. (2003). Literal and symbolic immortality: The effect of evidence of literal immortality on self-esteem striving in response to mortality salience. *Journal of Personality and Social Psychology, 84,* 722–737. The use of APA information does not imply endorsement by APA.

The pros and cons of pursuing self-esteem

People self-enhance in order to support and bolster their self-esteem and to squelch existential fears. But to what degree are self-enhancement and high self-esteem a good thing? On one hand, high self-esteem is linked to many positive outcomes: people with high self-esteem are more resilient to stress, setbacks and depression; they are more optimistic about their futures and have more self-confidence; all round, they feel good about themselves (Baumeister, Campbell, Krueger, & Vohs, 2003; Bonanno, Rennicke, & Dekel, 2005; Taylor, Lerner, Sherman, Sage, & McDowell, 2003). However, this is not the whole story. People with high self-esteem also often take large and inappropriate risks, ranging from unsafe sexual behaviour to substance abuse or even delinquency (Baumeister et al., 2003). High self-esteem is also associated with stronger ingroup bias and more prejudice (Aberson, Healy, & Romero, 2000; Crocker & Schwartz, 1985). Moreover, when people feel their self-esteem is threatened, they often react by lashing out – putting others down or aggressing against them (Bushman & Baumeister, 1998; Bushman et al., 2009; Morf & Rhodewalt, 1993). In this light, unjustifiably inflated self-esteem is

FIGURE 5.14 *Narcissists display grossly inflated self-views yet have a fragile self-esteem.*

particularly problematic, as it is capricious, and thus easily challenged or threatened.

A special case of grossly inflated self-views yet fragile self-esteem comes in the form of narcissism (Akhtar & Thomson, 1982; Morf & Rhodewalt, 2001; Morf, Torchetti, & Schürch, 2011; see Figure 5.14). The syndrome of narcissism was originally developed by psychiatrists to describe a personality disorder that they observed in some of their clients who displayed a pervasive pattern of a grandiose sense of self and a lack of empathy for others (American Psychiatric Association, 1994). But social psychologists too have been interested in narcissism and have studied weaker forms of this personality trait in nonclinical samples (see Morf, Torchetti, & Schürch, 2011, for a review). Their more empirical research has confirmed that narcissists in the nonclinical range similarly hold sky-high opinions of themselves, yet simultaneously have disparaging views of others. Others are of interest to them not for their own sake, but merely as vehicles for the narcissists' own self-enhancement. Narcissists brag, show off, want others to admire them; they also compete with others and exert power over them in order to assert their superiority (Buss & Chiodo, 1991; Campbell & Foster, 2007; Wallace & Baumeister, 2002). While these behaviours sometimes get narcissists what they want, they also backfire at times and undermine the narcissists' self-enhancement efforts (see Morf, Horvath, & Torchetti, 2011, for a review).

For example, in new groups, narcissists' self-enhancement brings them admiration and they are often chosen as leaders, but once their bluff has been discovered, the admiration turns into dislike and rejection (Brunell et al., 2008; Judge, LePine, & Rich, 2006; Paulhus, 1998). Some studies have questioned whether a hidden negative self-view (Bosson et al., 2008) underlies narcissists' self-enhancement efforts. However, some recent studies using implicit measures (see the section on implicit self-esteem of this chapter) have indeed confirmed the role of latent worthlessness in narcissistic responding (Horvath & Morf, 2009; Morf, Horvath, & Zimmermann, 2011). Thus, narcissistic individuals might harbour latent feelings of self-doubt, despite their highly favourable reported self-views at the explicit level (e.g., Horvath & Morf, 2009; Jordan et al., 2003; also see Gregg & Sedikides, 2010, for an in-depth discussion). It appears then that easily activated latent feelings of worthlessness are part of the psychological makeup of narcissists. As a result, narcissists show the types of defensive behaviours talked about earlier, when explicit and implicit self-beliefs are at odds. They cannot help themselves, it seems, from constantly pushing their self-esteem (Baumeister & Vohs, 2001).

Turn now to Social Psychology Beyond the Lab 5.1 to learn about the link between threatened egotism and violence.

Hence there clearly are risks to raising self-esteem, especially if it is not based on actual deeds and thus unwarranted. Moreover, when we should take these risks depends on the context. Although there clearly are many interpersonal advantages to modesty and humility (Sedikides, Gregg, & Hart, 2007), both modesty and self-enhancement must always be seen in the context in which they transpire. Being excessively modest in a job interview is unlikely to get one an executive position; correspondingly, being overly self-enhancing when a friend just failed a test is not going to seal the friendship. All told, then, pursuing self-esteem is a mixed bag, and one has to take into account that there are many different kinds of high self-esteem.

When high self-esteem is genuine, people feel secure and thus are less angered by or reactive to criticism (Kernis, 2003). They also do not care about being the centre of attention, or overtrumping others. Secure self-esteem is rooted in feeling good about who one is, and is not contingent on external sources (Crocker & Park, 2004; Kernis et al., 2008). Importantly, the upshot is that the less one's focus is on self-image, and the more it is on developing one's competence, relationships and autonomy, the more likely it is that one will build a solid base for genuine self-esteem (see Deci & Ryan, 1995). Only people high on genuine self-esteem may also be high on self-compassion. Self-compassion means being kind toward oneself and mindful that failure is part of human experience, rather than overly self-critical (Neff, 2003).

Offering the same (mental) health benefits as self-esteem, self-compassion comes with fewer negatives (Terry & Leary, 2011). Thus, while 20 years ago researchers were advocating trying to increase self-esteem in schools, it may be self-compassion on which they focus in the near future.

Summary

We care deeply about any information that pertains to the self. Intuitively, one might expect that we are driven by a self-assessment motive and therefore mainly want to develop an accurate understanding of the kind of person we are. However, the available evidence indicates that we usually prefer to self-enhance, by seeking positive information about the self and by processing it in a self-serving way. Self-enhancement mainly operates implicitly and is found in culturally-appropriate forms in many different parts of the world. Besides presenting oneself toward others in a favourable way, self-enhancement helps in coping with existential anxieties. Nevertheless, we are also inclined to self-verify, by seeking information that supports our pre-existing ideas about the self. Given that most of our self-views are positive, self-enhancement and self-verification motives push us in the same direction most of the time, although people with low self-regard prefer to self-verify their negative self-beliefs. Finally, although high self-esteem is associated with a range of positive outcomes, it also can come with costs – especially when self-esteem is inflated and contingent upon external sources. Genuine self-esteem and self-compassion, in contrast, offer important health benefits.

THE REGULATORY FUNCTIONS OF THE SELF: THE SELF IN CONTROL

....

How does the self regulate our behaviour so that we can plan effectively and pursue our goals and aspirations?

Before you read any further, take a look at yourself in the mirror. What goes through your mind as you are doing this? Perhaps your thoughts initially turn to your outward appearance, such as whether your shirt makes you look slimmer, the urgency with which you need a new haircut, or if you have blackheads on your nose. But

SOCIAL PSYCHOLOGY BEYOND THE LAB 5.1

THREATENED EGOTISM AND VIOLENCE

On July 22, 2011, the 32-year-old Norwegian Anders Breivik detonated a car bomb in downtown Oslo, killing eight people and critically wounding 10 others. Two hours later, Breivik appeared dressed as a police officer at a Labour Party of Norway youth camp. Here, Breivik shot 69 attendees and injured 66 before he surrendered to the police and was taken into custody. Subsequent investigations suggest that Breivik had acted alone, meticulously planning his attacks years in advance.

What could drive an individual like Breivik to plan and commit acts of unspeakable violence towards other human beings? Traditionally, many psychologists have believed that violence and aggression are caused by low self-esteem (e.g., Levin & McDevitt, 1993; Staub, 1989; see Chapter 9 *on aggression*). In the last decade or so, however, this view has been challenged. An influential review by Baumeister, Smart, and Boden (1996) found little evidence that individuals with low self-esteem are particularly aggressive. In fact, these researchers found more support for the opposite pattern, such that individuals with high self-esteem tend to be the aggressors. For instance, murderers, rapists, wife beaters, violent youth gangs and aggressive nations are all characterized by strongly held views of their own superiority. Moreover, aggressive tendencies increase when people's self-esteem has recently been boosted (e.g., by drinking alcohol), and decrease after people experienced a drop in self-esteem (e.g., by decreases in social status). Baumeister and associates referred to these patterns as the 'dark side' of high self-esteem.

The notion of a dark and violent side of high self-esteem fits with what is currently known about the Breivik case. Just a few hours before his attacks, Breivik uploaded a document on the Internet that disclosed many details about himself. Among other things, he stated that he was 'very proud' of his Viking heritage, boasted of his business ventures as 'successful' and described his personality as 'optimistic, pragmatic, ambitious, creative and hard-working'. As such, Breivik obviously possessed very favourable views of himself.

Should we now embrace the theory that high self-esteem causes aggression? No, that would be too simple. A groundbreaking study by Kernis and associates showed that individuals with high self-esteem display considerable variability in aggressive behaviour (Kernis, Grannemann, & Barclay, 1989). These researchers measured self-esteem at different points in time so that they could simultaneously consider both the level and the stability of self-esteem. The results showed that individuals with unstable high self-esteem had the highest levels of anger and aggressive behaviour. By contrast, individuals with stable high self-esteem had the lowest levels of anger and aggression. Individuals with stable and unstable low self-esteem fell between these extremes. These findings suggest that there are two types of individuals with high self-esteem: some are hot-tempered and aggressive, while others are slow to anger and non-aggressive.

The puzzling mix of people that profess to have high self-esteem has led researchers to search for constructs that might separate the aggressive and non-aggressive subtypes. One construct that has proven useful in this regard is narcissism. As previously noted, narcissists distinguish themselves by exaggerated self-importance; they demand admiration and are prone to exhibitionistic behaviour. Furthermore, they expect special treatment and are inclined to exploit others. At the same time, they are highly reactive to threats to self-esteem, and respond to such threats with feelings of rage, defiance, shame and humiliation (see Morf & Rhodewalt, 2001; Morf, Torchetti, & Schürch, 2011 for reviews). Several pieces of information about Anders Breivik indeed seem to fit with a narcissistic personality.

First, note that his Internet manifesto disclosed many details about his personal life, including his family background, education, employment history and even his hobbies and favourite sports. Breivik's apparent eagerness to publicize a slew of rather trivial personal facts is consistent with a narcissistic preoccupation with the self. The manifesto indicates further that Breivik thought of himself in highly elevated and heroic terms, as he identified himself with an order of knights that was linked to the old Christian crusaders. In addition, Breivik appeared to be fascinated by his own physical appearance, as his manifesto ended with a series of pictures of him posing in several fancy and outlandish outfits (e.g., a Masonic formal outfit, a diving suit). Finally, it is worth noting that Breivik conveyed some awareness of his self-preoccupation, acknowledging that his chief character flaw was 'a relatively inflated ego' and that others generally perceived him as arrogant.

Narcissistic tendencies have similarly been observed among other perpetrators of mass violence, such as the widely publicized shootings at Columbine and Virginia Tech (Twenge & Campbell, 2003). No doubt these cases are extreme and might be considered pathological. But research has shown that narcissists, even in the normal range, display aggressive tendencies, particularly when their positive self-views are threatened. For instance, in two laboratory studies, participants were either praised or insulted by a confederate posing as another participant (Bushman & Baumeister, 1998). Later on, participants received an opportunity to aggress against the confederate (or another person) by subjecting him or her to an aversive blast of loud noise. Both studies showed that participants who had high narcissism scores and had been insulted displayed the greatest aggression – in other words, when their ego was threatened. Notably, narcissists did not aggress when they had received praise, and only aggressed against the person who had insulted them. Narcissists are thus not generally or indiscriminately aggressive. A number of field studies have since confirmed the link between narcissism and violent behaviour in more naturalistic settings (e.g., Barry, Frick, Adler, & Grafeman, 2007; Bushman, Bonacci, Van Dijk, & Baumeister, 2003).

Hence, although narcissists endorse highly positive views about themselves, these self-views seem to be rather fragile and easily challenged. Accordingly, the egotism of narcissists might be a surface layer that conceals more basic insecurities – a notion that has been confirmed in some recent studies (e.g., Horvath & Morf, 2009; Jordan et al., 2003; also see Gregg & Sedikides, 2010, for an in-depth discussion). Do latent self-doubts then explain the aggressive outbursts among narcissists? On the non-behavioural level, Morf and colleagues showed that after subliminal activation of worthlessness, narcissistic men reacted faster to aggression-related words, while the accessibility of aggression even decreased for less narcissistic participants (Morf, Horvath, & Zimmermann, 2011).

This indicates that in narcissists the concept of aggression is directly triggered by the concept of worthlessness. Research on aggressive behaviour of individuals with high explicit and low implicit self-esteem provides similar results. For instance, they are more prone to discriminate against outgroup members (Jordan, Spencer, & Zanna, 2005) and are less forgiving towards someone who has offended them (Eaton, Struthers, Shomrony, & Santelli, 2007). Furthermore, teenagers with high explicit and low implicit self-esteem were rated by teachers as significantly more aggressive than their fellow-students (Sandstrom & Jordan, 2008). Taken together, this work suggests important parallels in aggressive responding among narcissists and individuals with high explicit and low implicit self-esteem.

At this point we want to emphasize the importance of distinguishing between extreme and pathological cases of narcissism and more common subclinical varieties of narcissism and threatened egotism. Most everyday narcissists do not display extreme violence and do not lash out against innocent others. Even though they tend to be interpersonally exploitative and abrasive, many narcissists are nonetheless successful and psychologically healthy (Kernberg, 1975; Morf, Horvath, & Torchetti, 2011; Sedikides, Rudich, Gregg, Kumashiro, & Rusbult, 2004). Continued ongoing scientific efforts to unravel the links between having an inflated ego, threatened egotism and aggression will hopefully bring us closer to understanding what leads to the actions of individuals like Anders Breivik, and, even more important, to ways of preventing such disasters.

---

if you are like most people, your thoughts may quickly turn inwards, to your personal goals and the expectations that others have of you, and whether you are living up to those expectations. Indeed, many scholars of the self have observed that self-reflection often leads people to think about their goals and aspirations. The self thus enables people to plan their actions more effectively, and this is among the major adaptive advantages of having a self (Higgins, 1996; Pyszczynski, Greenberg, & Solomon, 1999; Sedikides & Skowronski, 1997).

Self-awareness theory

When you are turning your attention inward, you become the object of your own consciousness. This intriguing state of self-focus may arise when you are looking at yourself in a mirror (Hass & Eisenstadt, 1990). However, self-focus may also be increased by other factors that lead you to pay more attention to yourself. For

instance, you are likely to become more self-focused when you see a video recording of yourself, hear an audio recording of your own voice, when your name is mentioned, when you somehow experience yourself as different from the people around you, or when you are writing about yourself (Macrae, Bodenhausen, & Milne, 1998; Silvia & Duval, 2001; Silvia & Eichstaedt, 2004). Self-focus also tends to become increased in public situations, when you realize that your actions are being monitored by an audience (Baumeister, 1984).

So how does self-focus influence behaviour? According to Duval and Wicklund's (1972) classic theory of objective **self-awareness**, focusing attention on the self motivates people to assess how well they are living up to norms for appropriate behaviour and to act more in accordance with these norms. For instance, as you become self-focused, you may think of the hours of reading that you still have to do in order to prepare for your social psychology class. If

self-awareness a psychological state in which one's attention is directed at the self.

THEORY BOX 5.6

CAUSES AND EFFECTS OF SELF-AWARENESS

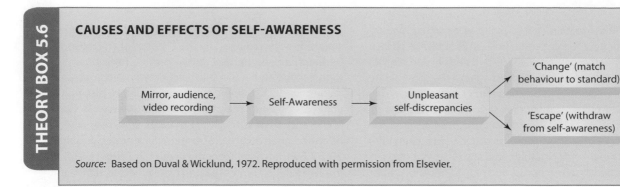

Source: Based on Duval & Wicklund, 1972. Reproduced with permission from Elsevier.

this assessment reveals that you are falling short of the norm, self-focus will give rise to negative feelings (e.g., feeling guilty for not having done enough reading). These negative feelings, in turn, will motivate you to change your behaviour – you may go to the library in order to complete your readings (see Theory Box 5.6).

This notion has been confirmed in over a hundred empirical studies (for a review, see Silvia & Duval, 2001). One study, for example, showed that self-focus can make people work harder at a difficult task, especially when their attention is directed at their performance (Dana, Lalwani, & Duval, 1997). Other studies have shown that self-focus can lead people to offer more assistance to a person with a legitimate request for help (Gibbons & Wicklund, 1982; see Chapter 10 on helping). Yet other studies found that self-focus leads people to suppress socially undesirable stereotypes (Macrae et al., 1998). Notably, the effects of self-focus also depend upon your self-efficacy, or your beliefs about whether you are capable of acting in a certain manner to achieve certain goals (Bandura, 1977a, b). For instance, imagine that your parents expect you to do well in maths at school. If your self-efficacy is high, you believe that you are capable of mastering your maths lessons. In this case, high self-focus will lead you to invest more time and effort in studying maths. By contrast, if your self-efficacy is low, you believe that you are unable to master maths no matter how hard you try. In the latter case, self-focus will lead you to invest less time and effort in studying maths (see Carver, Blaney, & Scheier, 1979). The effects of self-focus are therefore quite flexible, and depend upon your beliefs about what you can realistically accomplish.

Self-regulation theory

self-regulation the process of controlling and directing one's behaviour in order to achieve desired thoughts, feelings, and goals.

Self-focus makes us more inclined to regulate our behaviour. In this sense, self-focus is closely connected with **self-regulation**, or the control 'of the self by the self'

(Baumeister, Schmeichel, & Vohs, 2007). But what does this mean? Should we think of the self as a 'homunculus' or little man in our head that takes charge of what we do or feel? Or is it possible to understand self-regulation in terms of a concrete mechanism or psychological process?

Carver and Scheier (1981, 1998) developed a compelling answer to these questions by relating self-focus to a more general understanding of self-regulation. Their approach builds on the notion of a cybernetic system (Miller, Galanter, & Pribram, 1960). An everyday example of such a system is the room thermostat, which turns the heating on or off whenever the local temperature passes a preset value. In its simplest form, a cybernetic system consists of a TOTE loop, an acronym for 'test-operate-test-exit' (see Theory Box 5.7). In the initial test phase, you compare current circumstances to a standard. For instance, you may wonder whether you have been generous enough to your friends. If there is a discrepancy, you enter a phase of operation and take steps to reduce the discrepancy. For instance, if you fear you have been too much of a tightwad, you may decide to throw a party for your friends. Then comes another test, to see whether you have met the standard or not. Can you now say that you are a generous person? If not, the system continues to operate until you have reached the standard. Perhaps you find that generosity is not just about material things, so you really should spend more time with your friends. Finally, when you meet the standard, the system exits the TOTE loop and the cycle ends. The cybernetic theory of self-regulation thus proposes that we self-regulate by monitoring how we live up to standards, and, when we fall short, by taking action to bring us closer to these standards.

Self-regulatory standards The first part of self-regulation means that we adopt some kind of standard, which may be a personal goal, social norm, expectations of others and the like. Self-regulatory standards may be formulated relatively broadly or more specifically. According to Carver and Scheier (1981, 1998) self-regulatory standards

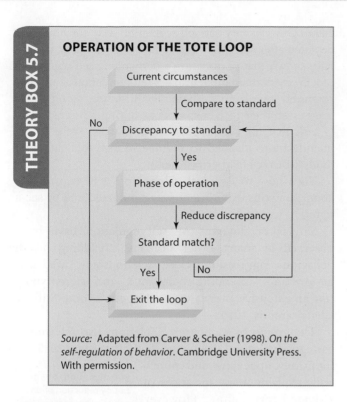

OPERATION OF THE TOTE LOOP

THEORY BOX 5.7

Current circumstances

↓ Compare to standard

No

Discrepancy to standard ←

↓ Yes

Phase of operation

↓ Reduce discrepancy

Standard match?

Yes ↓ | No

Exit the loop

Source: Adapted from Carver & Scheier (1998). *On the self-regulation of behavior.* Cambridge University Press. With permission.

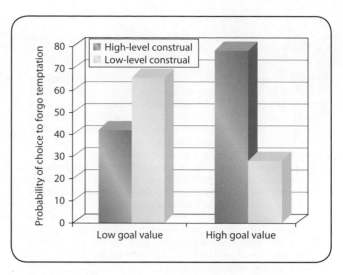

FIGURE 5.15 *Probability of choice to forego temptation as a function of goal importance and construal level.*

Source: Data from Fujita & Roberts, 2010; Expt. 1. Reprinted with permission from Elsevier.

may operate on four different levels. At the highest level are system concepts, which consist of the personal characteristics that describe the kind of person we want to be (including the ideal and ought selves discussed earlier). For example, most of us want to be generous, responsible and honest individuals. System concepts give rise to the next lower level – principles, which consist of global behavioural aspirations. For instance, we can become a generous person by adhering to the principle that we should give and share what we have with other people. Principles state values, and are still free of behavioural content, in that they are applicable to many kinds of behaviour. The specific behaviours that we perform are prescribed by programmes or scripts (the next lower level). For example, to adhere to one's principle of sharing with others, one might donate money to charity or leave a large tip at a restaurant. Finally, programmes such as donating money to charity lead to even more specific goals or sequences at the lowest level. Sequences consist of motor control goals that are typically executed without conscious supervision. For instance, the behavioural programme of leaving a tip might be enacted by the sequence of opening one's wallet and taking out a five Euro note.

In most situations we like to think of our goals in abstract, high-level terms (what Carver and Scheier would call system concepts and principles). For example, most individuals reading this chapter will think of it as 'studying psychology' rather than 'staring at letters'.

Linking our behaviour to abstract goals renders what we are doing more meaningful (Vallacher & Wegner, 1987). Because the self is closely associated with higher-level meanings, more abstract goals are more strongly connected with the self. Indeed, research suggests that self-regulation improves when we think more abstractly about our goals (Fujita, Trope, Liberman, & Levin-Sagi, 2006; Schmeichel & Vohs, 2009). For instance, relative to those who are thinking of their lower-level goals, people who are thinking of their higher-level goals are more willing to delay immediate gratification to obtain a larger reward, display greater physical endurance, and are better able to resist temptations (Fujita et al., 2006). Specifically, when induced to engage in higher-level thinking (think 'why I try to maintain my health', versus 'how'), participants chose to forgo temptation by committing to a healthy food regimen in advance, at least if their goal to improve their health was high (see Figure 5.15; Fujita & Roberts, 2010). In this way they were able to protect their goals from anticipated temptations. Conversely, individuals who fail at self-regulation often tend to think of their goals in more low-level, concrete terms (Schmeichel & Vohs, 2009; Twenge, Catanese, & Baumeister, 2003). Thus, when you are reading this text, you would do better to think of it as 'learning about human nature' instead of 'looking at letters'.

Monitoring The second part of self-regulation is that we start monitoring our behaviour. According to Carver and Scheier (1981, 1998) this monitoring function is facilitated by self-awareness, which leads us to assess the

LEADER IN THE FIELD

Roy F. Baumeister (b. 1953) is currently the Eppes Eminent Professor of Psychology at Florida State University. He completed his PhD in social psychology from Princeton in 1978, under the supervision of Ned Jones, a social psychologist renowned for his research on attribution and self-presentation. After a postdoctoral fellowship at the University of California at Berkeley, Baumeister worked at Case Western Reserve University from 1982 to 2003. Baumeister's research spans a wide range of topics in self and identity. His early research focused on the nature of self-presentational behaviour when someone is constrained by a reputation. He also examined the question of why people underperform in public situations, a phenomenon known as 'choking under pressure'. His subsequent work explored how the desire to escape self-awareness explains many paradoxical and seemingly self-destructive behaviours such as suicide, masochism and binge eating. Baumeister has further investigated self-esteem, which led him to conclude that the benefits of high self-esteem are often exaggerated (see Social Psychology Beyond the Lab 5.1). Since the mid-1990s, Baumeister and associates have developed the model of ego depletion, which proposes that self-regulation draws upon limited energy resources (see Research Close-Up 5.3). Baumeister has received many honours, and the Institute for Scientific Information lists him among the handful of most-cited psychologists in the world.

self's standing with regard to relevant standards. To test this notion, these researchers asked participants to copy complex figures from a photograph, while their self-focus was either experimentally heightened (by a mirror or the presence of an experimenter) or not. In the self-focus conditions, participants more often checked whether their drawing matched the standard of the photograph. Related experiments have shown that self-focus led individuals to seek out information about performance norms. Directing attention to the self thus leads us to monitor more closely whether our behaviour is in accordance with standards. The role of monitoring in self-regulation is further supported by neuroscience findings. Specific brain regions – like the anterior cingulate cortex – monitor whether we should step up our self-regulatory efforts (Amodio, Devine, & Harmon-Jones, 2008; Botvinick, Braver, Barch, Carter, & Cohen, 2001; Inzlicht & Gutsell, 2007).

Self-regulatory strength If you have ever followed a diet or tried to give up smoking, you can verify how hard self-regulation can be. Translating our self-regulatory standards into actual behaviour is thus the third important aspect of self-regulation. Common sense relates self-regulation to 'willpower' or 'strength of character'. Research by Baumeister and associates indicates that such notions may actually have a kernel of truth (see Leader in the Field, Roy F. Baumeister). These researchers suggest that self-regulation functions like a strength or a muscle that draws upon limited energy resources (Muraven & Baumeister,

2000). Our capacity for self-regulation may thus become depleted after sustained use. In line with this idea, studies have shown that performing a demanding self-regulation task in one domain often impairs self-regulation in another ostensibly unrelated domain. For instance, dieters who suppressed their facial expressions during a funny movie (a task that uses self-regulatory resources) were subsequently more inclined to indulge in tasty but fattening foods (Vohs & Heatherton, 2000).

Turn now to Research Close-Up 5.3 to learn more about how this experiment was conducted and to see a figure of its results.

Similar breakdowns of self-regulation have been observed in many other domains, including health behaviour, aggression, close relationships, academic performance, spending behaviour, and stereotyping (for an extensive overview, see Hagger, Wood, Stiff, & Chatzisarantis, 2010).

The notion of regulatory depletion, also referred to as '**ego depletion**' (Muraven & Baumeister, 2000), is intuitively appealing and potentially explains many instances of self-regulatory failure. However, the effects of regulatory depletion are often hard to distinguish from a lack of monitoring. Indeed, several studies have found that so-called 'regulatory depletion' effects disappear when people are encouraged to monitor their actions more closely. Such monitoring may be promoted by providing people with regular performance feedback (Wan & Sternthal, 2008) and increasing self-awareness (Alberts, Martijn, & De Vries, 2011). These findings are difficult to explain in terms of energy depletion, because increased monitoring might be expected to use up even more energy. Many of the effects in regulatory depletion studies may thus be due to poor monitoring rather than energy depletion. Increasing monitoring therefore may be a promising route to increase self-regulatory capacity.

> **ego depletion** a temporary reduction of one's self-regulatory capacities due to restricted energy resources after sustained self-control efforts.

Are self-regulatory breakdowns inevitable when we have to self-regulate for extended periods of time? Although the strength model (Muraven & Baumeister, 2000) suggests a pessimistic answer to this question, other models leave room for optimism. In the 1980s, Billy Ocean wrote a hit song with the lines, 'When the going gets tough, the tough get going'. In line with this idea, performing an initial self-regulatory task can sometimes lead to increases in self-regulatory performance (Converse & DeShon, 2009; Dewitte, Bruyneel, & Geyskens, 2009; Jostmann & Koole, 2006, 2007). For instance, when a dieting person has to resist a tasty but fattening food on one occasion, this person tends to be better at declining a sugary snack on a subsequent

DIETING IS DISRUPTED AFTER HAVING RESISTED EARLIER FOOD TEMPTATIONS

Vohs, K. D., & Heatherton, T. F. (2000). Self-regulatory failure: A resource depletion approach. *Psychological Science, 11*, 249–254.

Introduction

Ego depletion theory holds that self-regulation draws upon a limited energy resource that allows people to control unwanted impulses and desires (Muraven & Baumeister, 2000). According to this perspective, an active effort to control behaviour in one domain depletes regulatory resources and hence leads to diminished capacity for self-regulation in other domains. Vohs and Heatherton (2000) investigated whether this ego depletion model can be applied to chronic dieters. Prior research on ego depletion had only examined artificial self-regulatory tasks that were implemented during an experimental session (e.g., squeezing a handgrip). Dieting is a more naturalistic and very common form of self-regulation in everyday life. At the same time, dieting is a very challenging task, given that long-term weight loss is extremely difficult to achieve. We summarize only the first study of this paper, and briefly refer to the results of the other two studies in the discussion below.

Method

Participants

One hundred female students participated in the experiment. They were labelled as either chronic dieters ($N = 36$) or nondieters ($N = 64$) on the basis of their scores on a scale designed to measure tendencies for restrained eating (Herman & Polivy, 1980).

Design and procedure

To ensure that participants' eating behaviour was not influenced by their prior food consumption, they were instructed not to eat for two hours before the experiment. Participants arrived individually and were asked to watch a neutral video about the daily activities of Bighorn sheep. The experimental manipulations took place while participants were watching the video.

The experiment had two manipulations. The first manipulation was meant to create differences in temptation level. An array of tasty snacks (Doritos, Skittles, M&Ms and salted peanuts) was placed either within arm's reach of the participants or across the room (approximately three metres away). Pilot research had shown that being seated next to tasty snacks is highly tempting for chronic dieters, but does not influence their mood or self-esteem. The second manipulation was meant to create differences in the need for self-regulation. Half of the participants were told that they could help themselves to the snack. This 'help yourself' instruction placed the burden of responsibility on the participants themselves, and hence placed greater demands on their capacity for self-regulation. The other participants were told that the snacks were being used in a different experiment later that day and asked not to touch them. The 'don't touch' instruction placed constraints on participants' behaviour, so that the level of temptation should not matter in this group, as self-regulatory demands were low. Thus, this experiment had a 3-factor design: 2 (type of dieters: chronic versus nondieters) X 2 (level of temptation: low versus high) X 2 (self-regulatory demand: low versus high).

After watching the video, participants rated their mood and were taken to another room to taste and rate ice cream flavours for 10 minutes. For this task, participants were seated in front of three flavours of ice cream. The ice cream was presented in very large containers that prevented the experimenter from seeing how much the participants ate. As the experimenter left the room, she added, 'By the way, help yourself to any ice cream you want; we have tons in the freezers.' The measure of self-regulatory ability was the amount of ice cream eaten by the participants. The latter was assessed by weighing the ice cream containers before and after participants had tasted and rated the ice cream.

Results

The results showed that the eating behaviour of chronic dieters was significantly influenced by the experimental manipulations (see Figure 5.16). Dieters in the high temptation condition ate more ice cream than dieters in the low temptation condition. However, this effect only occurred in the 'help yourself' group (high self-regulatory demand) when participants were responsible themselves for their snacking behaviour. In the 'don't touch' group (low self-regulatory demand), temptation level had no effect on eating behaviour of dieters.

The eating behaviour of nondieters was not influenced by the experimental manipulations. In addition, the experimental manipulations had no effects on mood.

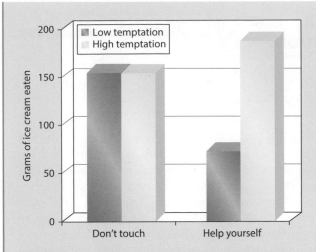

FIGURE 5.16 *Effects of temptation level and availability condition on eating behaviour of chronic dieters.*

Note: Data for nondieters are not shown in this graph.; *Source:* Data from Vohs & Heatherton, 2000; Expt. 1. Reprinted with permission from SAGE publications.

Discussion

These results demonstrate that resisting food temptations can make it harder for chronic dieters to restrain their eating behaviour in another, subsequent context.

This effect fits very well with the model of ego depletion (Muraven & Baumeister, 2000). The ego depletion model is a general model of self-regulation that extends far beyond the domain of eating behaviour. Consequently, the model would predict that the depleting effects of dieting might carry over, not just to eating behaviour, but also to other forms of behaviour that require self-regulation. In line with this, the second study by Vohs and Heatherton (2000) showed that resisting food temptations also leads chronic dieters to display poorer self-regulation on a task that was unrelated to food intake, namely persistence on word puzzles. The ego depletion model further predicts that chronic dieters might suffer from depletion by other activities that require self-regulation. This prediction was tested in a third study by Vohs and Heatherton, which asked chronic dieters either to suppress their emotions or to let their emotions flow naturally during an emotion-eliciting film clip. The results showed that emotion suppression led chronic dieters to eat more ice cream during the taste-rating test. Taken together, the research by Vohs and Heatherton sheds important new light on the dynamics of self-regulation. Their research helps us to understand better why many of us often find it difficult to control our impulses in everyday life.

occasion (Dewitte et al., 2009). This is because we can adapt better to a series of self-regulatory tasks when these are all in the same domain (Dewitte et al., 2009). Similarly, providing people with more time to adjust themselves to increases in self-regulatory demands leads to enhanced self-regulation, rather than the deteriorations predicted by the depletion model (Converse & DeShon, 2009). The impact of additional self-regulatory demands may thus depend on how well we can adapt to changes in self-regulatory demands (Koole, Jostmann, & Baumann, 2012). As long as we can adapt to the situation, we can respond to more demanding situations by stepping up our self-regulatory efficiency. Similarly, motivation seems to be an important factor that can increase self-control (Kross & Mischel, 2010), and this is even true after ego-depletion (Baumeister & Vohs, 2007). It is only when we are no longer capable of such adaptive responding that our self-regulation breaks down.

The consequences of self-regulation

Our capacity for self-regulation is associated with a wide range of desirable outcomes. In the 1960s, Mischel and colleagues (Mischel, Ebbesen, & Zeiss 1972; Mischel, Shoda, & Rodriguez, 1989) in a landmark study

developed the **delay of gratification** paradigm, in which a child is confronted with a choice between a small immediate reward (e.g., one cookie) and a more valuable but delayed reward (two cookies). In numerous follow-up studies, preschool ability to wait (i.e., to delay gratification) was shown to predict consequential later outcomes in adulthood. These range from higher grades in college, better ability to cope with stress, higher self-worth and self-esteem, less physical and verbal aggression, as well as less drug abuse, and less psychopathology (see Mischel, et al., 2011 for a review). Therefore, delay of gratification appears to be an important early-life marker for long-term adaptive mental and physical development and health.

> **delay of gratification** the ability to resist the temptation of an immediate reward and wait for a later larger reward.

Given these benefits, we may wonder if we can ever engage in too much self-regulation. The answer appears to be 'yes'. There are at least two ways in which even our best attempts to self-regulate may backfire. First, in high-pressure sports settings, such as during penalty kicks or championship games, well-trained athletes often perform much more poorly than usual (e.g., Dohmen, 2008; Jordet, 2009; Wright, Voyer, Wright, & Roney, 1995). This pattern of *choking under pressure* tends to occur when those athletes are highly self-focused (Baumeister, 1984;

Baumeister & Showers, 1986). It appears that self-focus leads people to pay increased attention to their behaviour and to control their behaviour in a step-by-step fashion. Attention at this step-by-step level disrupts the execution of well-learned or proceduralized skills (Beilock & Carr, 2001).

A second drawback of self-regulation is that it can lead us to get stuck in negative emotions. Recall that when we self-regulate, we compare the self against standards for appropriate behaviour. Most of the time, we do not completely live up to these standards. Consequently, the self-regulation of behaviour inevitably evokes negative affect (Higgins, 1987; see Fejfar & Hoyle, 2000, for a meta-analytic overview). When we experience a series of setbacks and failures, focusing on our shortcomings will contribute to the onset and maintenance of depression (Pyszczynski & Greenberg, 1987). In such cases, it may well be adaptive to cease further attempts at self-regulation. Indeed, people who were able to disengage from unattainable goals were found to display fewer depressive symptoms (Wrosch & Miller, 2009) and improved immune functioning (Miller & Wrosch, 2007). Thus, despite the many advantages that self-regulation brings, it is healthy to abandon further attempts at self-regulation when our goals turn out to be unrealistic.

Escaping the self

In light of the negative affect that can be invoked by focusing on the self, we may sometimes be motivated to avoid self-aware states. The upshot of this desire for self-avoidance can be either seemingly paradoxical or self-destructive behaviours, as well as highly adaptive self-regulation. On the negative end for instance, it may foster alcohol abuse. Experiments have shown that consuming alcohol lowers self-awareness (Hull, Levenson, Young, & Sher, 1983). See Figure 5.17, which shows the relative frequency of self-focus statements while delivering a speech ('what I like and dislike about my body and physical appearance'), relative to other-focused (external) or 'other' (nonfocused) statements following alcohol consumption, as compared to a placebo (tonic). Alcohol clearly reduced the frequency of self-statements. Moreover, individuals with chronically high self-awareness are at greater risk of developing drinking problems (Hull & Young, 1983). Another behaviour that may be driven by escapist motives is binge eating (Heatherton & Baumeister, 1991). Dieting individuals frequently engage in periods of disinhibited eating, or eating binges. Such eating binges may be an unintended effect of these individuals' ambitious dieting goals, which may give rise to the need to escape self-awareness. Escapist needs may be met by eating binges, which lead awareness to shift away from the self towards the immediate experience of strong physical sensations. Finally, the need to escape self-awareness may lead people to commit the ultimate form of self-destructive behaviour, namely suicide. Suicidal individuals are often highly self-focused and tend to hold unrealistically high expectations of themselves (Baumeister, 1990). Moreover, experimental studies have shown that thoughts of suicide often automatically spring to mind when people realize they are falling short of an important personal standard (Chatard & Selimbegović, 2011).

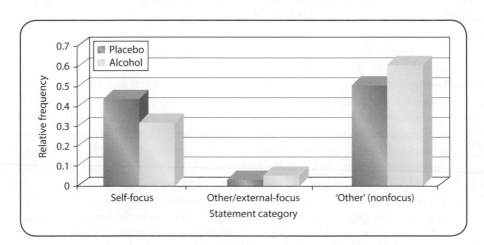

FIGURE 5.17 *Frequency of self-focus statements relative to others as a function of alcohol vs. placebo.*

But there are also less dramatic strategies to decrease the threat that can originate from self-focus. Kross and colleagues examined the positive effects of self-distancing for self-regulation. For example, they found that analysing negative interpersonal experiences from a self-distanced perspective decreases negative emotions (Kross, Ayduk, & Mischel, 2005) and even blood pressure (Ayduk & Kross, 2008). In addition, spontaneous self-distancing led to better problem-solving behaviour and less reciprocation of negativity during conflicts among couples in ongoing relationships (Ayduk & Kross, 2010). Self-distancing can thus facilitate self-reflection in ways that adaptively and consequentially influence people's thoughts, feelings, and behaviour —both in the short and long term. Hence, whether 'escaping' the self ultimately is harmful or helpful may well depend on why people do it: if they self-distance in order to be able to focus on their feelings without becoming overwhelmed, rather than simply trying to avoid their feelings altogether, successful self-regulation may result.

Autonomous self-regulation as a resource

In the foregoing paragraphs, we have characterized self-regulation in somewhat ambivalent terms. On the one hand, self-regulation is an adaptive process that allows us to strive for meaningful goals and act in accordance with social norms. On the other hand, self-regulation (and the self-awareness that supports it) may deplete our energies, and an excessive emphasis on controlling our natural impulses may lead to anxiety, depression, binge eating, and even suicide. This mixture of findings seems puzzling. How can self-regulation be at once adaptive and associated with severe psychological problems?

One way to resolve this paradox is suggested by Ryan and Deci (2008; see also Deci & Ryan, 1985, 2000). According to their **self-determination theory**, people's

self-determination theory a motivational theory that accounts for people's reasons for self-regulation: if self-regulation is motivated by external pressure it is effortful and can lead to psychological conflict. However, if self-regulation is freely chosen it is much more efficient without being depleting.

reasons for regulating their behaviour shape how they go about the self-regulation process. In some situations, people engage in self-regulation because they feel pressured to do so by others, like their peers or authorities. Because such external pressures are often at odds with what people truly want, this type of self-regulation tends to be effortful, energy-depleting and laden with psychological conflict. At other times, however, people may choose to engage in self-regulation of their own accord, because regulating their behaviour is fully compatible with their own needs and interests. When self-regulation is thus freely chosen and autonomous, it is likely to be more harmonious and efficient.

Studies indeed suggest that self-regulation demands more energy when it is externally motivated rather than driven by intrinsic, autonomous motivations (Muraven, Gagné, & Rosman, 2008, Experiment 1). Ryan and Deci (2008) have gone even further, by suggesting that autonomous self-regulation may boost the overall energy available to the self. This notion was partly inspired by observations that people's reported energy levels and vitality increase markedly over the weekend (Sheldon, Ryan, & Reis, 1996). Follow-up studies in which participants were paged multiple times a day and asked to report on their feelings showed that this 'weekend effect' was statistically explained by the enhanced autonomy that people experienced over the weekend (Ryan, Bernstein, & Brown, 2010). Thus the enhanced freedom that comes with weekends may allow people to replenish their energies. Similar results have been observed for their recreational activities such as playing video games and skilled sports (see Ryan & Deci, 2008, for a review). In addition, the pursuit of intrinsic life goals, such as relationships, personal growth and serving the community is associated with greater self-reported vitality across different cultures, including the US and South Korea (Kasser & Ryan, 1996; Kim, Kasser, & Lee, 2003). By contrast, people who adopt many extrinsic life goals, such as money, fame or image display reduced vitality relative to people who adopt fewer extrinsic life goals. Taken together, it appears that freely chosen autonomous self-regulation may maintain or even enhance people's energies and vitality.

Summary

The self is an active agent that guides and regulates our actions. According to self-awareness theory, when our attention is focused on the self, we monitor our behaviour more closely. Self-focus thus promotes self-regulation, by leading us to act more in accordance with our personal goals and prevailing social norms. Self-regulation generally promotes adaptive and socially responsible behaviour and thus contributes to mental and physical development and health. Nevertheless, self-regulation can deplete our limited energy resources when it has to be sustained over a longer period. In addition, increased self-focus can interfere with well-practised routines and lead us to get stuck in negative emotions. To prevent these problems, we may relax our efforts at self-regulation by avoiding self-aware states. Escapist behaviours may range from alcohol consumption to binge eating and even suicide. Alternatively, we may reduce the negative sides of self-regulation when we engage in self-distancing to 'cool' our focus on negative emotions or in autonomous self-regulation – when we self-regulate in the service of intrinsic life goals, such as relationships or personal growth.

SELF STABILITY AND CHANGE

To what degree can the self change, and through what process(es)?

We have seen in this chapter that the self is our 'home base' that guides all of our actions – it colours how we interpret the world, the interaction partners we choose and how we present ourselves. Are we hostage to this self then? Or, alternatively, to what degree can the self change, and how? The answer to this question can be found in another fact that has also been amply demonstrated throughout the chapter: the self is a social product (e.g., Stryker & Vryan, 2003). We learn who we are through our interactions with others, but at the same time we influence how these others react to us by behaving toward them in certain ways – ways that are driven by how we view (or would like to view) ourselves, our goals for ourselves, our values. In other words, there is a continual reciprocal interaction between what William James (1890, 1950) called the 'doing' (behaving and interpreting) and the 'being' (descriptive) aspects of the self – the agent and the object (or what we would nowadays call the mental representation of the self). And, because the agent is acting in the social world and being met by other similarly acting selves of other individuals, there is room for change.

We engage in what Swann and colleagues refer to as an **identity negotiation** process (e.g., Swann & Bosson, 2008; Swann, Johnson, & Bosson, 2009). We establish who we are through ongoing mutual give-and-take interactions with other individuals, and eventually come to a 'working agreed-upon consensus' between both (or multiple) people (see also

identity negotiation a process by which we establish who we are through mutual give-and-take interactions with others.

Goffman, 1959). This negotiation process allows for shifts in the self. These shifts can be more minor, as occurs when people enter new jobs or new relationships, or they can be more dramatic, as when people move to entirely new and foreign environments, or experience a serious illness. A lot of the time, these shifts occur subtly due to factors out of our control, simply due to the fact that other individuals do not always respond to us in ways that are fully commensurate with our self-views. For example, if you just started a new higher status job and people begin treating you with much more respect, with time your self-views and self-esteem may adjust upward. At other times we deliberately influence the process and try to produce change in ourselves. As dramatically illustrated in our introductory example of Christina Long, people can – and do – put on different identities. Someone may also enter therapy to effect a specific desired change.

What are the processes through which this change comes about? Although any one of these aspects can set off the process, in essence, three things have to come together: we have to change our behaviour, others have to come to consistently respond differently toward us, and we have to come to believe the new self-view(s). Many studies underscore the paramount importance of the social environment in constructing and supporting a new self-view (Schlenker, 2012). Harter (1993) for example has shown that a child's self-esteem is most likely to change when the child's social network changes through a move to a new school or new town. In an important study, Tice (1992) showed that self-presentational behaviour has the biggest impact on private self-views if performed in front of an audience. In this study, she asked students to portray themselves in a specific way (either as extroverted or introverted, randomly assigned). Half of them were being watched by another person (public condition), the other half spoke in a private room into a tape recorder. Later, students were asked to rate their own personalities on trait adjectives. As predicted, those who had self-presented in front of an audience endorsed the self-view they had previously enacted more strongly than those who self-presented in an anonymous condition. Importantly, this private self-view showed up not only in self-report, but also in behaviour. Participants were later asked to wait in a waiting room, in which there was another person. Figure 5.18 shows the distance at which participants seated themselves relative to the other person. As can be seen, those who had previously been in the public condition acted in line with the self-view presented earlier, whereas there was no effect for those in the

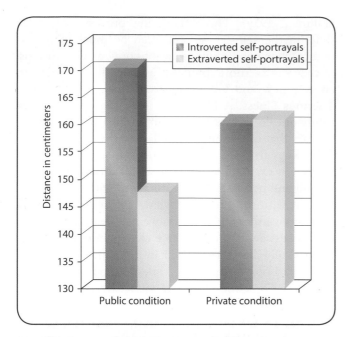

FIGURE 5.18 *Mean distance participants sat from the confederate as a function of prior self-portrayal (introverted versus extroverted) and publicity of self-presentation (audience versus private).*

Source: Data copyright © 1992 by the American Psychological Association. Reproduced with permission. Tice, D. M. (1992). Self-concept change and self-presentation: The looking glass self is also a magnifying glass. *Journal of Personality and Social Psychology, 63,* 435–451. The use of APA information does not imply endorsement by APA.

private condition. Participants who had self-presented as being extroverted in public sat much closer to the other person than anyone else, and they were also significantly more likely to initiate a conversation.

Many processes contribute to these internalizations of public behaviours. First, we engage in biased scanning – retrieving evidence from memory that fits the self-view (Jones, Rhodewalt, Berglas, & Skelton, 1981). Second, we engage in the self-perception process (Bem, 1972) discussed earlier: we observe our behaviour and assume it accurately reflects who we are. Third, we get 'caught up' in the role we are enacting (Gergen, 1971). Fourth, making a public commitment to a behaviour enlists future action to back it up (e.g., Schlenker & Wowra, 2003). That is, people will match their self-presentations to their performances when these performances are publicly known (although they will present themselves positively regardless of prior performances if these are unknown to others). Finally, if behaviour is widely discrepant from original self-views, then a cognitive dissonance process may set in (see Chapter 7 on attitude change), requiring us to adjust our self-views to reduce the discomfort experienced from behaving in an inconsistent manner (Aronson, 1969).

In conclusion, for any major change to take hold, an internalization process needs to take place – there has to be a genuine change of your own views of your self. For these to remain permanent, they also have to become integrated into your self-narratives – you have to revise your self-story to fit the new version – and importantly, you have to enlist the social environment to support them. Any one of these factors alone does not suffice. We are neither at the mercy of our self-views, nor of our social environment: the self is constructed, maintained and changed through a transactional process both in the mind and within a social reality.

CHAPTER SUMMARY

- *Why is the self 'social'?* The self we experience and express is highly variable and dependent on social circumstances. The self is constructed, maintained and changed through our interactions with others.

- *What are the personal sources of self-knowledge and how accurate are they?* Reflecting and observing ourselves is a means to gain insight into ourselves. However, these sources of self-knowledge may be inaccurate, as we cannot consciously attend to automatic processes, and we tend to push away unwanted information.

- *What are the interpersonal sources of self-knowledge and how accurate are they?* The things that others tell us about ourselves, their reactions toward us, as well as the comparisons we draw between others and ourselves, permit us to learn much about our self. Furthermore, interactions with significant others as well as belonging to social groups shape our views of ourselves. These sources too, however, can be biased.

- *How do we gain a coherent self?* Autobiographical memories as well as self-narratives – that we construe in line with our self-concept – help create a coherent and continuous sense of the self.

- *What is meant by self-concept?* The self-concept is the cognitive representation of our self-knowledge, and consists of characteristics that we use for describing us. These self-beliefs are stored in self-schemas that organize and guide the processing of self-relevant information. They encompass actual, ideal and possible selves, and they come in both explicit and implicit forms.

- *What is self-esteem?* Self-esteem is the evaluative component of self-knowledge and consists of an overall appraisal of our self. It is conceived as either a trait or a state, and people can differ in which life domains are important to their self-esteem. As with the self-concept, self-esteem too can come in both the explicit and the implicit form.

- *What is the influence of culture on the self?* Cultures differ in their conceptualization of the individual and of his or her role in society. Therefore, cultural differences, as for example between independent and interdependent self-construals, shape our perceptions, motivations and emotional reactions.

- *Do we prefer true or positively distorted self-information?* Although there is evidence for the self-assessment motive (i.e., the desire to learn objective information), we are primarily driven by the self-enhancement motive (i.e., the desire to enhance the positivity of the self and to protect it from negative information).

- *What strategies do we adopt when we self-enhance?* There are intrapersonal strategies, like the superiority bias and the self-serving attributional bias. But self-enhancement also influences our interpersonal self-presentation and encompasses, among other strategies, dressing smartly, talking about achievements, self-handicapping or basking in reflected glory.

- *What is self-verification?* Self-verification is the desire to affirm our firmly held self-views. As long as these self-views are positive, self-enhancement and self-verification go in the same direction. But people with low self-regard prefer to self-verify their negative self-beliefs instead of self-enhancing.

- *Why do we self-enhance?* Self-enhancement is beneficial for our physical and mental health. Sociometer theory suggests that positive self-feelings are desirable because our self-esteem signals the degree of social belongingness. Terror management theory has received more empirical support – it proposes that self-enhancement helps us cope with existential fears.

- *Is high self-esteem good?* High self-esteem is associated with many positive things, such as, for example, higher resiliency to stress and depression. At the same time, it is linked with undesirable outcomes like more risky behaviour of various types and – in the case where someone feels threatened – aggression. High self-esteem seems desirable to the extent that it is genuine and not contingent on external sources. Similarly, self-compassion has a lot of positive effects on well-being and health and without negative side-effects.

- *How does the self regulate our behaviour?* Self-regulation can be thought of as a cybernetic system, where actual circumstances are monitored and compared to self-regulatory standards. When these are not met, actions are taken to reduce the discrepancy between desired and actual states.

- *Should we self-regulate?* In general self-regulation helps us resist temptation and therefore pursue long-term goals more successfully. Sometimes self-regulation strategies can deplete one's resources and have unwanted deleterious consequences. The challenge is to conserve one's resources, not to over-control, and to preserve a focus on personal growth.

- *Can the self change?* As the self is a social product, changing it is also socially determined. In the process of negotiating our identity in mutual interactions with others, for changes to take hold we need to change our behaviour, believe the new self-views and enlist others to consistently respond towards us differently.

SUGGESTIONS FOR FURTHER READING

Baer, J., Kaufman, J. C., & Baumeister, R. F. (2008). *Are we free? Psychology and free will*. New York: Oxford University Press. This book reviews experimental and theoretical work by researchers from all branches of psychology interested in investigating humans' free will.

Baumeister, R.F., & Tierney, J. (2011). *Willpower: Rediscovering the greatest human strength*. New York, N. Y.: Penguin Press. This book shows how to focus our strengths, resist temptation, and redirect our lives.

Dunning, D. (2005). *Self-insight. Roadblocks and detours on the path to knowing thyself*. New York: Psychology Press. An accessibly written book, dealing with frequently encountered human shortcomings in trying to evaluate and know oneself.

Feinberg, T. E., & Keenan, J. P. (Eds.). (2005). *The lost self. Pathologies of the brain and identity*. New York: Oxford University Press. A compilation of contributions from acknowledged experts in the fields of philosophy, cognitive neuroscience, neurology and psychology, grouped to provide an exploration of the neurobiology of the self.

Harter, S. (1999). *The construction of the self. A developmental perspective*. New York: Guilford. This book analyses the emergence of individuals' unique sense of self as a result of cognitive and social construction processes, and provides a theoretical background for this development.

Heatherton, T. F. (2011). Neuroscience of self and self-regulation. *Annual Review of Psychology, 62*, 363–390. This article reviews recent social neuroscience research on the psychological components that support the human capacity for self-regulation.

James, W. (1961). The Self. In G. Allport (Ed.), *Psychology: The briefer course* (pp. 159–191). Cambridge, MA: Harvard University Press. (Original work published 1892.) James's original chapter on the self is a classic – a 'must-read', as James's notions of the self have proven fundamental to modern conceptualizations and continue to influence our present understandings of the construct. It is a captivating read too!

Kernis, M. H. (Ed.). (2006). *Self-esteem issues and answers. A sourcebook of current perspectives*. New York: Psychology Press. This volume summarizes the current status of knowledge on the topic in an engaging and readable format, shedding light on what is known about the functioning of self-esteem, while simultaneously giving the reader a sense of the complexities involved in the concept.

Leary, M. R. (2004). *The curse of the self: Self-awareness, egotism, and the quality of human life*. New York: Oxford University Press. The author illustrates the idea that human sufferings (e.g., depression, anxiety and other negative emotions) in part could be seen as emerging from the human capacity of self-reflection and egocentrism.

Morf, C. C., & Mischel, W. (2012). The self as a psycho-social dynamic processing system: Toward a converging science of selfhood. In M. R. Leary & J. P. Tangney (Eds.), *Handbook of self and identity* (2nd ed., pp. 21–49). New York: Guilford. This chapter expands on the ideas of the self as a coherent, organized, yet dynamic system and elaborates on the self-construction process presented in this chapter.

Sedikides, C., & Skowronski, J. J. (1997). The symbolic self in evolutionary context. *Personality and Social Psychology Review, 1*, 80–102. The authors take an interesting perspective on the symbolic self by evaluating the adaptive value of this human capacity and tracing its emergence back to evolutionary pressures.

Wilson, T. D. (2002). *Strangers to ourselves: Discovering the adaptive unconscious*. Cambridge, MA: Harvard University Press. This book examines the evolution of the idea of the unconscious, the ways in which it operates, and how our actions – rather than our thoughts – help us to know ourselves.

6 Attitudes

GEOFFREY HADDOCK AND GREGORY R. MAIO

KEY TERMS

- affective component of attitudes
- attitude
- attitude functions
- attitude–behaviour relation
- attitudinal ambivalence
- behavioural component of attitudes
- cognitive component of attitudes
- cognitive dissonance
- ego-defensive function

- evaluative conditioning
- explicit measures of attitude
- implementation intentions
- implicit measures of attitude
- mere exposure effect
- MODE model
- multicomponent model of attitude
- object appraisal function
- one-dimensional perspective of attitudes

- perceived behavioural control
- self-efficacy
- self-monitoring
- self-perception theory
- social adjustment function
- theory of planned behaviour
- theory of reasoned action
- two-dimensional perspective on attitudes
- utilitarian function
- value-expressive function

task, participants completed another puzzle task in which participants had to find words that were hidden within the puzzle. The researchers were interested in determining whether the unobtrusive priming of the goal of achievement would lead participants to perform better (i.e., achieve more) compared to participants who had not been previously primed with the goal of achievement. Bargh and colleagues (2001) found that participants who had been unobtrusively primed with achievement performed better in locating hidden words than control participants.

You might wonder whether researchers have integrated work on implementation intentions, habits, and goals. Indeed, a number of researchers have considered the links among these constructs. For instance, Webb, Sheeran, and Luszczynska (2009) assessed the degree to which implementation intentions are effective in eliciting behaviour change in the face of unwanted habitual behaviour. These researchers found that implementation intentions were especially effective when individuals' habits were weaker rather than stronger. In a different line of research, Neal, Wood, Labrecque, and Lally (2012) explored the conditions that are most likely to trigger habitual behaviour. These researchers found that people often perceive their habits to be guided by goals, and that moderately strong habits can be influenced automatically by individuals' goals.

The MODE model Not all behaviour is deliberative and planned. Quite often we act spontaneously without consciously thinking of what we intend to do. When our behaviour is spontaneous, the theory of planned behaviour may not provide a proper conceptualization of behavioural prediction (see Fazio, 1990). In an attempt to uncover how attitudes influence spontaneous behaviour, Fazio (1990) developed the **MODE model** of attitude–behaviour relations. MODE refers to Motivation and Opportunity as DEterminants of behaviour.

> **MODE model** a model of attitude–behaviour relations in which motivation and opportunity are necessary to make a deliberative consideration of available information.

At a basic level, the MODE model suggests that, if individuals have *both* sufficient motivation *and* opportunity, they may base their behaviour on a deliberative consideration of the available information. However, when either the motivation or the opportunity to make a reasoned decision is low, only attitudes that are highly accessible will predict spontaneous behaviour. A number of studies by Fazio and colleagues have supported the MODE model (see e.g., Sanbonmatsu & Fazio, 1990; Schuette & Fazio, 1995). For example, Schuette and Fazio (1995) considered how attitude accessibility and motivation influence the extent to which people

process information in a biased way. Schuette and Fazio asked university students to evaluate two research studies on the effectiveness of the death penalty as a crime deterrent. One study supported the idea that capital punishment is an effective crime deterrent; the second study reached the opposite conclusion. Before participants looked at the studies, Schuette and Fazio manipulated the accessibility of each participant's attitude toward the death penalty. Some participants expressed their attitude once (low accessibility), whereas others expressed their attitude six times (high accessibility). To manipulate motivation, some participants were told that their conclusions would be compared to those made by an expert panel. Participants in the low motivation condition did not receive this information.

The results revealed that the relation between individuals' prior attitude and their judgement about the study depended on both the accessibility of the participants' attitude and their level of motivation. Participants evaluated the articles in line with their own attitude when their attitude was highly accessible and their motivation was low. In this case, their highly accessible attitude served as a cue that biased their perceptions. However, when participants were highly motivated, or when they had expressed their attitude only once, attitudes were not correlated with evaluations of the studies. In these conditions, being motivated can lead individuals to overcome the potential biases of their attitude, even if it is accessible. When respondents are not motivated, expressing an attitude just once does not make it sufficiently accessible for it to influence their perceptions.

The RIM model Another model relevant to the link between attitudes and behaviour has been developed by Strack and Deutsch (2004). Their *reflective–impulsive model* (RIM) proposes that behaviour is controlled by two interacting systems: a reflective system that guides and elicits behaviour via a reasoned consideration of available information, and an impulsive system that guides and elicits behaviour through more automatic associative links. The reflective system can be seen as involving processes that resemble how people respond to explicit measures of attitude, whereas the impulsive system involves processes that bear greater resemblance to implicit measures of attitude. Indeed, Strack and Deutsch suggest that the reflective system should have a greater influence on deliberative behaviour, while the impulsive system should have a greater influence on spontaneous behaviour. Consistent with the ideas proposed in the RIM model, studies have demonstrated that explicit and implicit measures of attitude predict different types of behaviour (as discussed earlier in the chapter).

Summary

On the whole, attitudes do a reasonable job of predicting behaviour. The degree to which attitudes predict behaviour depends upon factors such as the level of correspondence across measures, the domain of behaviour, attitude strength and personality factors. The theory of reasoned action and its extension, the theory of planned behaviour, have received strong support as models for predicting deliberate behaviour. The MODE model suggests that motivation and opportunity are necessary to make a deliberative consideration of available information. The RIM model proposes that behaviour is controlled by two interacting systems: a reflective system and an impulsive system.

CHAPTER SUMMARY

- *What is an attitude?* An attitude is an overall evaluation of an attitude object.

- *Can we have attitudes about anything?* Anything that can be evaluated along a dimension of favourability can be conceptualized as an attitude object.

- *What are the bases of attitudes?* Attitudes have affective, cognitive and behavioural antecedents. All three antecedents contribute to our overall evaluation of an object.

- *Is the structure of an attitude best considered to be one-dimensional or two-dimensional?* The two-dimensional perspective is advantageous as it allows for attitude ambivalence.

- *Why do we hold attitudes?* Attitudes serve a variety of functions, the most important of which is the object appraisal function.

- *Why is it useful to know the function of an attitude?* Knowing the function of an attitude is important because attempts to change an attitude are more likely to be successful when the persuasive appeal matches the attitude's function.

- *Does it matter if an attitude is strong or weak?* Yes – strong attitudes are more stable over time, more resistant to change and more likely to guide both information processing and behaviour.

- *What is the difference between explicit and implicit measures of attitude?* Explicit measures directly ask respondents to think about and report their attitude, whereas implicit measures do not.

- *Do explicit and implicit measures predict different types of behaviour?* Research has shown that explicit measures are more effective in predicting deliberative behaviour, whereas implicit measures are more effective in predicting spontaneous behaviour.

- *Do attitudes predict behaviour?* On the whole, attitudes do a reasonable job of predicting behaviour. The degree to which attitudes predict behaviour depends on a number of factors, including correspondence, the domain of behaviour, the strength of an attitude and person variables.

- *How do attitudes predict behaviour?* A number of models have been developed to understand how attitudes predict behaviour. The most influential models are the theory of planned behaviour and the MODE model.

SUGGESTIONS FOR FURTHER READING

Albarracín, D., Johnson, B. T., & Zanna, M. P. (Eds.). (2005). *Handbook of attitudes*. Mahwah, NJ: Erlbaum. This volume offers an advanced review of the field of attitudes research.

Cialdini, R. B. (2008). *Influence: Science and practice* (5th ed.). Boston, MA: Allyn & Bacon. This volume offers an accessible look at research on social influence.

Crano, W., & Prislin, R. (Eds.). (2009). *Attitudes and persuasion*. New York: Psychology Press. This volume reviews different streams of research on attitudes and attitude change.

Eagly, A. H., & Chaiken, S. (1993). *The psychology of attitudes*. Fort Worth, TX: Harcourt Brace Jovanovich. This volume provides a comprehensive review of research that laid the foundation for the progress that has been made in the past two decades.

Fazio, R. H., & Olson, M. A. (2003). Implicit measures in social cognition research: Their meaning and use. *Annual Review of Psychology, 54*, 297–327. This paper reviews advances that have been made concerning implicit measures of attitude.

Fazio, R. H., & Petty, R. E. (Eds.). (2007). *Attitudes: Structure, function, and consequences*. Hove, UK: Psychology Press. This volume comprises a collection of important published papers on attitude structure, attitude content and the attitude–behaviour relation.

Greenwald, A. G., Poehlman, T. A., Uhlmann, E., & Banaji, M. R. (2009). Understanding and using the Implicit Association Test: III. Meta-analysis of predictive validity. *Journal of Personality and Social Psychology, 97*, 17–41.

Haddock, G., & Maio, G. R. (Eds.). (2004). *Contemporary perspectives on the psychology of attitudes*. Hove, UK: Psychology Press. This volume reviews a number of contemporary research programmes on the psychology of attitudes.

Maio, G. R., Bell, D. W., & Esses, V. M. (1996). Ambivalence and persuasion: The processing of messages about immigrant groups. *Journal of Experimental Social Psychology, 32*, 513–536.

Maio, G. R., & Haddock, G. (2015). *The psychology of attitudes and attitude change*. London: Sage. This volume provides a comprehensive and accessible overview of research and theories relevant to the psychology of attitudes.

Maio, G. R., & Olson, J. M. (Eds.). (2000). *Why we evaluate: Functions of attitudes*. Mahwah, NJ: Erlbaum. This volume is a comprehensive examination of research on attitude functions.

Perloff, R. M. (2013). *The dynamics of persuasion: Communication and attitudes in the 21st century* (5th ed.). New York: Routledge. This volume highlights research on persuasion and social influence.

Petty, R. E., & Cacioppo, J. T. (1986a). *Communication and persuasion: Central and peripheral routes to attitude change*. New York: Springer. This volume highlights the research that was conducted in the development of the highly influential Elaboration Likelihood Model of persuasion.

Petty, R. E., Fazio, R. H., & Briñol, P. (Eds.). (2009). *Attitudes: Insights from the new implicit measures*. New York: Psychology Press. This volume highlights different research programmes regarding implicit measures of attitude.

Wittenbrink, B., & Schwarz, N. (Eds.). (2007). *Implicit measures of attitudes*. New York: Guilford. This volume provides an overview of different perspectives on the utility of implicit measures of attitude.

7 Strategies of Attitude and Behaviour Change

Wolfgang Stroebe

KEY TERMS

- cognitive dissonance theory
- cognitive response model
- counterattitudinal behaviour
- distraction
- dual-process theories of persuasion
- heuristic processing
- heuristic-systematic model (HSM)
- intrinsic motivation
- need for cognition
- need for cognitive closure
- reactance theory
- subliminal advertising
- systematic processing
- thought-listing

CHAPTER OUTLINE

INTRODUCTION 203

PERSUASION 203

Theories of systematic processing 203
Summary 207
A dual-process theory of persuasion 207
Summary 216
Changing implicit attitudes 216
Summary 217
Advertising as applied persuasion 217
Summary 224

INCENTIVE-INDUCED ATTITUDE CHANGE 224

*Counterattitudinal behaviour
  and attitude change* 225
*Some paradoxical effects of incentives
  and sanctions* 228
*Further limitations of the effectiveness
  of incentive-induced change* 229
Summary 229

CHAPTER SUMMARY 230

ROUTE MAP OF THE CHAPTER

This chapter discusses two strategies of attitude and behaviour change, namely persuasion and the use of incentives (e.g., taxation, legal sanctions). We will discuss when, how and why persuasion results in attitude and behaviour change and review empirical studies that have been conducted to assess the validity of these theoretical interpretations. Finally, we will apply these theories to the area of advertising. The second part of the chapter will focus on the use of incentives. Instead of relying on the uncertain effects of persuasion to induce people to use seatbelts or give up smoking, governments often employ legal sanctions or taxation to influence behaviour directly. These strategies are quite effective in influencing behaviour, but it is much less clear whether they can also result in attitude change.

INTRODUCTION

The notion of using social psychological knowledge to change attitudes and to influence behaviour conjures up visions of advertising executives planning mass media campaigns to sell cars, refrigerators, alcoholic drinks or margarine. And this vision is certainly not incorrect. However, social psychology is equally useful in persuading people to change unhealthy behaviour patterns such as smoking, drinking or engaging in unsafe sex. In fact, one of the most effective campaigns in recent times, achieving substantial changes in attitudes and behaviour, has probably been the war against smoking. It began in 1964 with the publication of the report of the United States Surgeon General's Advisory Committee on Smoking and Health (USDHEW, 1964). The persuasive information on the substantial health impairment suffered by smokers was quickly adopted by the news media and thus reached a wide audience. The material not only persuaded many smokers to stop, it also convinced politicians that it was time to act and, some years later, compulsory health warnings were introduced on tobacco advertisements and cigarette packets. Finally, in the 1980s, Federal cigarette tax was doubled and various states introduced additional excise taxes on cigarettes. Largely as a result of this anti-smoking campaign, smoking is now generally recognized as a health risk and an addiction. Moreover, especially in the US, smoking has declined substantially. (See Figure 7.1.)

This chapter focuses on the two major strategies of attitude and behaviour change, namely (1) the use of *persuasion*, and (2) the use of *incentives* or *sanctions*. In each section, we will discuss the effectiveness of these strategies and use the major theories in the literature to analyse the psychological processes that are responsible for their impact.

PERSUASION

Persuasion involves the use of communications to change the beliefs, attitudes and behaviour of others. Research on persuasion received a big boost during World War II when the American army looked for strategies to counteract enemy propaganda and to boost the morale of their own troops (Hovland, Lumsdaine, & Sheffield, 1949). After the war, Carl Hovland, the director of the mass communication programme within the US Army's information and education division, assembled a group of eminent researchers at Yale University (e.g., Abelson, Janis, Kelley, McGuire, Rosenberg) and this group was instrumental in making the study of persuasion and attitude change one of the central areas of social psychology.

Theories of systematic processing

Is attitude change determined by how well we understand and remember persuasive arguments?

Before 1980, most of the theories of persuasion and attitude change emphasized **systematic processing**. They assumed that attitude change was mediated by the message recipient's detailed processing of the persuasive arguments contained in the communication; that is to say, processing of the message arguments was the means by which persuasive arguments had their effect on attitudes (see Chapter 2 for discussion of mediating variables). The two most influential theories of systematic processing have been the information processing model (McGuire, 1969, 1985) and the cognitive response model (e.g., Greenwald, 1968; Petty, Ostrom & Brock, 1981).

> **systematic processing** thorough, detailed processing of information (e.g., attention to the arguments contained in a persuasive communication); this kind of processing relies on ability and effort.

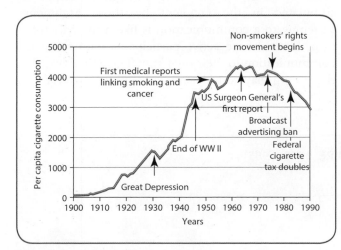

FIGURE 7.1 *Per capita cigarette consumption per year among adults, and major smoking and health events in the US, 1900–1990.*

Source: Based on Novotny, Romano, Davis, & Mills, 1992.

The information processing model of persuasion

The paradigm proposed by McGuire (1969, 1985) provides a useful framework for thinking about the stages involved in the processing of persuasive communications. According to this model, the persuasive impact of a message is the product of at least five steps: (1) attention; (2) comprehension; (3) yielding; (4) retention; and (5) behaviour (see Theory Box 7.1). For example, the ultimate objective of speeches given on television by politicians is to get the members of the audience to vote for their party. If viewers use the break between programmes to go to the bathroom (failure to attend) the appeal will not result in attitude change. Even if viewers attend to the communication, it will have little impact if they find the arguments too complex (failure to comprehend) or if they do not accept the communicator's conclusions and, as a result, do not change their beliefs and attitudes (failure to yield). But even if the candidate manages to persuade the audience, this will be of no use if viewers change their attitudes again before election day (failure to retain) or if bad weather keeps them away from the ballot box (failure to act). Since the message receiver must go through each of these steps if the communication is to have the ultimate persuasive impact, and since it is unlikely that the probability of any given step will be maximal, McGuire's framework offers one explanation of why it is often difficult to induce behaviour change through information campaigns.

In social psychological studies, the impact of a communication is typically assessed immediately following exposure to the message. Thus, our analysis is restricted to the first three steps of the chain. Moreover, attention and comprehension have usually been combined into a single step of reception of the message content in order to simplify measurement. Thus McGuire's model can be reduced to a two-step version, which states that the probability of a communication resulting in change

of beliefs and attitudes is the joint product of reception and acceptance (yielding) (see Leader in the Field, William J. McGuire).

Few studies have supported the claim that the reception of message arguments determines attitude change. In general, message reception, when measured by the recall of message arguments, is not found to correlate significantly with attitude change (see Eagly & Chaiken, 1993). This failure to find significant correlations between argument recall and attitude change raised doubts about McGuire's two-step model, in particular the role of attention to and comprehension of the arguments presented in persuasive communications. Even more critical for the model was the fact that it lacked specific theoretical principles that would allow one to predict the factors that affect acceptance and to understand the processes that mediate the relationship between acceptance and attitude change. The cognitive response model provides such a theory.

The cognitive response model: a theory of yielding

The **cognitive response model** of persuasion was developed by Greenwald and his colleagues at Ohio State University, partly to explain the non-significant correlation between argument recall and attitude change (Greenwald, 1968; Petty, Ostrom & Brock, 1981; see Leader in the Field, Anthony Greenwald). According to this model, it is not the reception of arguments that mediates attitude change, but the thoughts (cognitive responses) stimulated in the recipient by those arguments. Listening to a communication is like a mental discussion. Listeners are active participants who relate the communication to their own knowledge. In doing this, the person may consider much cognitive material that

> **cognitive response model** assumes that attitude change is mediated by the thoughts, or 'cognitive responses', which recipients generate as they receive and reflect upon persuasive communications.

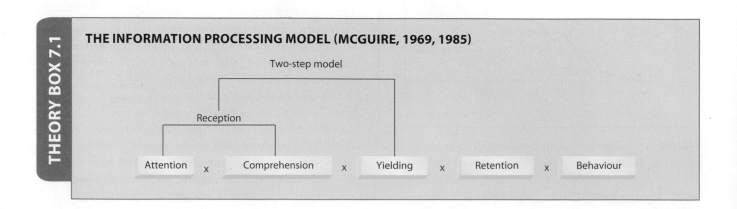

THEORY BOX 7.1

THE INFORMATION PROCESSING MODEL (MCGUIRE, 1969, 1985)

Two-step model

Reception

Attention x Comprehension x Yielding x Retention x Behaviour

LEADER IN THE FIELD

William J. McGuire (1925–2008) was born in New York City, US. After a brief stint in the army, he studied psychology at Fordham University, where he received his BA (1949) and MA (1950). He then spent a year as a Research Fellow at the University of Minnesota at the time Festinger was there (see Leader in the Field, Chapter 1). In 1951 he went to Yale University for his PhD, which he received in 1954. He stayed on at Yale for four more years, and after holding positions at various other universities (Illinois, Columbia and San Diego) he returned to Yale as Professor of Psychology in 1971, remaining there until his retirement in 1999. Bill McGuire dominated research on attitudes and attitude change until the 1980s. During his early time at Yale, he was a member of the famous Yale Communication and Attitude Change Program headed by Carl Hovland (see Leader in the Field, Chapter 1). When he returned to Yale ten years after the death of Hovland, he continued the research tradition of the Yale program. He made numerous empirical and theoretical contributions to the area, and also authored the highly influential chapters on attitudes and attitude change in the second and third editions of the *Handbook of Social Psychology* (McGuire, 1969, 1985).

 LEADER IN THE FIELD

Anthony Greenwald (b. 1939) received his BA from Yale University in 1959 and his MA from Harvard University in 1961. In 1963 he completed his PhD, also at Harvard, under the supervision of Gordon Allport (see Leader in the Field, Chapter 14). After a two year Postdoctoral Fellowship at the Educational Testing Service, he moved to the psychology department at Ohio State University, where he remained until 1986. During this time he developed the cognitive response approach that revolutionized attitude change theory. The cognitive response model assumed that all persuasion was basically self-persuasion, in that external messages triggered favourable or unfavourable thoughts that were ultimately responsible for persuasion or resistance. After more than 20 years on the faculty of Ohio State University, Greenwald moved to the University of Washington in 1986, where he worked on such topics as subliminal persuasion and the self. Perhaps his second most important contribution to attitudes was the introduction of the *implicit association test* or IAT as a means of assessing automatic evaluations.

is not contained in the communication itself to generate thoughts for or against the arguments presented in the communication. It is these self-generated thoughts and not the presented arguments *per se* which mediate attitude change. Messages persuade if they evoke predominantly favourable thoughts, and they fail to persuade if they evoke predominantly unfavourable thoughts. Thus, the impact of persuasion variables on attitude change does not depend on the extent to which they facilitate argument reception, but on the extent to which they stimulate individuals to generate their own favourable or unfavourable thoughts about the information presented.

On first reading, this does not appear to be a very impressive theory. It is also not terribly new. Writing in 1949, Hovland, Lumsdaine, and Sheffield had already suggested that audiences may resist persuasion by going over their own arguments against the position during exposure to the communication. Hovland and Weiss (1951) later emphasized that the best way to study internal processes of attitude change was to have respondents verbalize their thoughts as they responded to the communication. However, although cognitive responses were everybody's favourite concept to be invoked when non-obvious findings of persuasion studies had to be explained (e.g., Festinger & Maccoby, 1964), research on the role of cognitive responses as mediators of persuasion had been hampered by the absence of accepted measures of self-generated thinking.

One major methodological contribution of the Ohio State researchers to the study of persuasion was therefore the development of a measure of cognitive

responses: **thought-listing** (Greenwald, 1968; Osterhouse & Brock, 1970). This enabled them to assess the processes assumed to mediate attitude change. With this thought-listing task recipients of a message are asked to list the thoughts they had while listening. These thoughts are later categorized into those that are favourable or unfavourable to the position advocated by the message. Thoughts that do not fit either of these categories (e.g., neutral or irrelevant thoughts) are not considered.

> **thought-listing**
> a measure of cognitive responses; message recipients are asked to list all the thoughts that occurred to them while being exposed to a persuasive message.

The second major contribution of the Ohio State researchers was theoretical. Previous conceptualizations of cognitive responses had focused only on the production of counterarguments that *reduce* persuasion (e.g., Festinger & Maccoby, 1964). In an important theoretical contribution, Petty, Wells, and Brock (1976) broadened the concept of cognitive responses by arguing that strong and well-argued messages are likely to produce predominantly favourable thoughts which should *enhance* persuasion.

This extended cognitive response model accounts for a number of inconsistent findings in the attitude change literature. Thus, it helps to explain why there is often not a significant correlation between argument recall and attitude change. If it is the thoughts stimulated by arguments and not the arguments themselves that are responsible for attitude change, then there is no reason to expect that the message arguments that a recipient remembers would be related to attitude change. What one would expect, however, is a significant correlation between the extent to which these thoughts are favourable or unfavourable towards the arguments presented by the communicator and the amount of attitude change. The newly developed thought-listing measure enabled researchers to test (and to support) this assumption (e.g., Osterhouse & Brock, 1970).

Another inconsistency resolved by the cognitive response approach related to findings of research on the impact of **distraction** on attitude change. We have probably all had the experience of being distracted while listening to some communication. The station on our car radio might have faded in the middle of a broadcast, or the people next to us might have started a loud conversation. Since being distracted whilst listening to a communication should impair reception, one would expect distraction to reduce the persuasive impact of a communication. Although some studies reported findings consistent with this prediction (e.g., Haaland & Venkatesan, 1968), others found distraction to strengthen the persuasive impact of a communication (e.g., Festinger & Maccoby, 1964).

distraction while listening to a persuasive communication, individuals are distracted by having to perform an irrelevant activity or by experiencing sensory stimulation irrelevant to the message.

According to the cognitive response model, such discrepant results are to be expected. Distraction reduces the recipient's ability to generate cognitive responses to a message. The impact of distraction on attitude change should therefore depend on the favourability of the thoughts produced by a message (Petty et al., 1976). If these dominant thoughts are mainly unfavourable and critical of the argumentation, distraction should enhance persuasion. However, for messages that elicit predominantly favourable thoughts that are supportive of the argumentation, distraction should work to inhibit persuasion.

But how can we manipulate the favourability of a listener's dominant thoughts? Since we have put so much emphasis on self-generated thoughts as a mediator of persuasion in this section, it is easy to forget that these thoughts are cognitive responses to persuasive arguments and are therefore likely to be influenced by the *quality* of these arguments. Thus, communications which present several strong arguments (e.g., arguments which are coherent, logical and compelling) are likely to elicit cognitive responses which are predominantly favourable to the position argued, whereas messages consisting mainly of weak arguments should elicit predominantly unfavourable responses. This process is illustrated in Theory Box 7.2.

Petty and colleagues (1976, Experiment 1) exposed students to messages arguing for an increase in tuition fees at their university. These communications

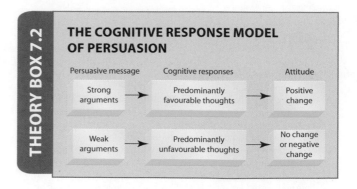

consisted of either very strong or very weak arguments. Distraction was manipulated by having participants record visual stimuli (briefly flashed on a screen at a rate of 0, 4, 12 or 20 flashes per minute) while listening to the message. In line with predictions, increases in distraction enhanced persuasion for the message that consisted of weak arguments, but reduced persuasion for the message containing strong arguments (Figure 7.2). The participants' thought-listing data provided support for the assumption that both the increase and the decrease in persuasion were due to thought disruption. In the case of weak arguments, the distraction manipulation decreased recipients' ability to generate counterarguments to the weak message; in the case of strong arguments, distraction reduced the number of favourable thoughts participants were able to generate to that version of the message.

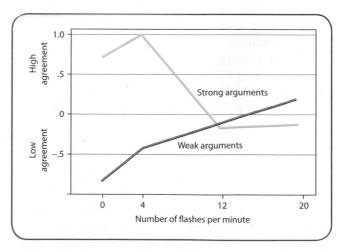

FIGURE 7.2 *Mean level of agreement (shown as z-scores) in relation to argument quality and level of distraction.*

Source: Copyright © 1976 by the American Psychological Association. Adapted with permission. Petty, R.E., Wells, G.L., & Brock, T.C. (1976). Distraction can enhance or reduce yielding to propaganda: Thought disruption versus effort justification. *Journal of Personality and Social Psychology, 34,* 874–884. The use of APA information does not imply endorsement by APA.

Summary

McGuire's information processing theory shares with the cognitive response model of Greenwald (1968) the assumption that persuasive arguments have to be processed systematically in order to influence beliefs and attitudes. However, whereas McGuire assumed further that change of beliefs and attitudes was a function of how well we understood and remembered the persuasive arguments, the cognitive response model assumes that it is not the arguments, but the respondents' thoughts generated in response to arguments, which determine change.

A dual-process theory of persuasion

Do people sometimes change their attitudes without systematic processing of persuasive arguments, and what factors determine intensity of processing?

That attitude change is mediated by detailed processing of the arguments may strike one as a plausible way to analyse the psychological processes that mediate persuasion. After all, is there any other way to be persuaded, if not through the arguments contained in a persuasive communication? However, if we think of the hundreds of advertisements we are exposed to every day, we might become doubtful. Does anybody really think about the arguments contained in advertisements about soft drinks or toothpaste? Do these advertisements even contain arguments? And yet surely if people were not influenced by them, these companies would not spend millions on their advertising budgets.

These are the types of questions that we will address in our discussion of the heuristic-systematic model, one of the **dual-process theories of persuasion**. Dual-process theories are an extension of the cognitive response model. Their major theoretical contribution is twofold: (1) In contrast to the cognitive response model, which assumes that attitude change is always mediated by argument-relevant thinking, dual process theories acknowledge that recipients may sometimes take shortcuts and accept or reject the recommendation of a communicator without scrutinizing the arguments presented in support of that recommendation. (2) Dual process theories also specify the conditions under which people will engage in each of

dual-process theories of persuasion theories of persuasion postulating two modes of information processing, systematic and non-systematic. Modes differ in the extent to which individuals engage in content-relevant thoughts and critical evaluation of the arguments contained in a message.

these processes. There are two dual-process theories of persuasion, the **heuristic-systematic model (HSM)** (e.g., Chaiken, 1980; Chaiken, Liberman & Eagly, 1989; Chen & Chaiken, 1999; see Leader in the Field, Shelly Chaiken) and the elaboration likelihood model (ELM; Petty & Cacioppo, 1986a, b; Petty & Wegener, 1999; see Leader in the Field, Richard E. Petty).

heuristic-systematic model (HSM) attitude change to persuasive communications is mediated by heuristic and/or systematic processing: when motivation and ability are high, systematic processing is likely; when they are low, individuals rely on heuristic cues.

LEADER IN THE FIELD

Richard E. Petty (b. 1951) received his BA in political science and psychology from the University of Virginia in 1973. He then moved to Ohio State University for his graduate studies, where he received his PhD in 1977. He began his academic career the same year at the University of Missouri, from where, after a sabbatical at Yale in 1986, he returned to Ohio State in 1987. Since 1998 he has been Distinguished University Professor at Ohio State University. At Ohio State he began a fruitful collaboration with fellow PhD student John Cacioppo (see Leader in the Field, Chapter 6). At that time persuasion research was plagued by inconsistencies in empirical findings, which could not be explained by available theoretical models. In their attempt to reconcile these conflicting findings Petty and Cacioppo developed the idea of the two routes to persuasion at the same time at which Chaiken proposed the related distinction between systematic and heuristic processing. The main difference is that Petty and Cacioppo also include other processes (e.g., evaluative conditioning, self-perception) at the low-effort end of their processing continuum. It is probably fair to say that Petty has taken over the mantle of Bill McGuire (see Leader in the Field, this chapter) as the dominant figure in the area of attitude and attitude change research.

LEADER IN THE FIELD

Shelly Chaiken (b. 1949) studied mathematics at the University of Maryland (College Park) and received her BA in 1971. She then became a graduate student in social psychology at the University of Massachusetts (Amherst), where she received her MS in 1975 and her PhD in 1978. After brief spells at the University of Toronto and Vanderbilt University, she moved to New York University as Professor of Psychology in 1985, where she stayed until 2005, when she retired. At the University of Massachusetts, she did her graduate studies with Alice Eagly (see Leader in the Field, Chapter 6) and developed the idea for the heuristic-systematic model during her work for her PhD. She continued her close collaboration with Eagly even after her PhD and co-authored *The Psychology of Attitudes* with her in 1993, which has been the defining book on that topic for many years. She has published numerous empirical articles testing and extending her heuristic-systematic model. In 1999 she also edited (jointly with Yaacov Trope) an important volume on *Dual-process Theories in Social Psychology*.

Because there is so much overlap between these two theories in their core assumptions we will focus on just one model, the HSM, in this chapter. We choose this model because it explores in greater detail the possible interplay of systematic and non-systematic modes, and because it considers a variety of motives or goals for both heuristic and systematic processing.

The heuristic-systematic model (HSM) The HSM distinguishes two modes of persuasion, which form the endpoints of a continuum of processing intensity. One mode, systematic processing, is identical to the processes assumed by the cognitive response model. Systematic processing involves careful and thoughtful consideration of the arguments presented in support of a position. The second mode reflects the fact that people often change their attitudes without thinking about the arguments contained in a communication, because the issue is not very important or because they lack time or knowledge to evaluate the arguments contained in a communication. Under these conditions, individuals will engage in heuristic processing.

heuristic processing assessing the validity of a communication through reliance on heuristics; that is, simple rules like 'statistics don't lie', 'experts can be trusted', 'consensus implies correctness', rather than through evaluation of arguments.

Heuristic processing (Theory Box 7.3b) focuses on some simple decision rules that people use to judge the validity of messages. For example, people may have learned from previous experience that statements by experts tend to be more accurate than statements by non-experts. They may therefore apply the rule 'experts can be trusted' when the communicator seems to be an expert (Eagly & Chaiken, 1993). Or they may have learned to trust people they like and, on finding a communicator likeable, they will apply the 'liking–agreement' heuristic, such as 'people agree with people they like' or 'people I like usually have correct opinions' (Eagly & Chaiken, 1993).

The probability that a recipient will critically evaluate arguments contained in a message and engage in systematic processing is determined by both *processing motivation* and *processing ability*. Processing motivation is important because such thoughtful scrutiny requires time and effort. Processing ability is important because, in order to be able to critically evaluate arguments, a person needs both issue-relevant knowledge and sufficient time. For example, if a computer salesperson gives us a highly technical sales pitch about the advantages of a computer they are trying to sell to us, we will not be able to evaluate these arguments if we lack the necessary computer knowledge. But even if we have the necessary knowledge, we might not be able to think about these arguments if we have no time

THEORY BOX 7.3

HEURISTIC-SYSTEMATIC MODEL OF CHAIKEN (E.G., CHAIKEN ET AL., 1989): (A) SYSTEMATIC PROCESSING; (B) HEURISTIC PROCESSING

to do so, because we have to come to a decision immediately. If, however, individuals are motivated and able to think about the arguments contained in a communication, they will engage in systematic processing. However, sometimes recipients may not be motivated (e.g., the issue is trivial) or able (e.g., they have no time or lack the knowledge) to engage in an extensive process of message evaluation. Under these conditions attitudes will typically be based on heuristic processing although other low-effort attitude change mechanisms (e.g., evaluative conditioning, mere exposure, self-perception) may also be involved.

The interplay of processing modes. It was originally assumed that the heuristic and systematic processing modes were compensatory: the more individuals relied on systematic processing, the less they would use heuristic processing (and vice versa). If individuals are motivated to scrutinize message arguments and are able to do so, they base their decision on their evaluation of these arguments and should have no need for short-cuts and the use of heuristic processing. More recently, it has been accepted that individuals do not necessarily disregard the informational value of heuristic cues once they have begun to engage in systematic processing, because heuristic cues might add valuable information. Thus, according to this perspective, individuals might rely to some extent on heuristic processing even under high processing intensity. One condition under which this is likely to happen is when the persuasive information is ambiguous and thus open to different interpretations (Bohner, Moskowitz, & Chaiken, 1995). Under such conditions, the heuristic information might bias the interpretation of the information contained in the arguments (the so-called 'bias hypothesis'). Recipients might then give more weight to arguments that are consistent with the recommendation made by a source that is credible than by a source that is not credible. A study by Chaiken and Maheswaran (1994; Research Close-Up 7.1) provides support for the bias hypothesis.

Multiple motives. So far we have described the information processing underlying attitude change as a relatively objective and unbiased activity. The original version of the HSM postulates a single motive: people are motivated to hold correct attitudes. This accuracy motivation determines the processing goal, namely to assess the validity of persuasive messages. More recently, dual process theories have been extended to incorporate two further motives or goals for heuristic and systematic processing (Bohner et al., 1995; Chaiken et al., 1989). Whereas accuracy motivation encourages objective and unbiased information processing, the other two motives are assumed to bias the processing of persuasive

information; that is, to induce individuals to hold particular preferred attitude positions.

One class of motives likely to bias information processing has been labelled *defence motivation*. The processing goal of defence-motivated individuals is to confirm the validity of preferred attitude positions and to disconfirm the validity of positions that are not preferred (Eagly & Chaiken, 1993). A number of conditions can motivate individuals to defend their present attitudinal position, such as vested interest or a need for consistency. For example, a person who had just spent a great deal of money on buying a camera of brand X would not like to hear that brand X cameras are unreliable and overpriced. Similarly, if a position being argued is inconsistent with other beliefs a person holds quite firmly, accepting this new position would violate that person's need for consistency. For example, a member of the American Rifle Association, who strongly believes that people need guns to defend themselves, would be unwilling to accept evidence that gun ownership doubles the risk of becoming the victim of violence (Stroebe, 2013).

A second class of motives likely to bias information processing has been termed *impression motivation*. This motive refers to the desire to express attitudes that are socially acceptable. It is assumed to be aroused in influence settings, in which the identities of significant audiences are salient or when people must communicate their attitudes to others who may have the power to reward or punish them. The processing goal of impression-motivated recipients is to assess the social acceptability of alternative positions in order to accept attitudinal positions that will please or appease potential evaluators. For example, a trade union activist will be unwilling to accept the necessity of increasing the pension age to 67, even though he might find some of the arguments in favour of an increase difficult to reject. The incorporation of impression motivation links dual-process theories to theories of social influence such as the model of Deutsch and Gerard (1955) discussed in Chapter 8. This model postulates that group members may accept opinions from other members either because they believe them to be valid (informational social influence), or because they think that acceptance of these beliefs will make them more accepted as group members (normative social influence). Informational social influence should predominate in settings that arouse accuracy motivation, whereas normative social influence should occur under conditions that arouse impression motivation.

Assessing processing intensity There are two strategies that allow researchers to assess the extent to

HOW HEURISTIC PROCESSING CAN BIAS SYSTEMATIC PROCESSING

RESEARCH CLOSE-UP 7.1

Chaiken, S., & Maheswaran, D. (1994). Heuristic processing can bias systematic processing: Effects of source credibility, argument ambiguity, and task importance on attitude judgment. *Journal of Personality and Social Psychology*, 66, 460–473.

Introduction

Dual-process theories regard systematic processing as more effortful and capacity limited than heuristic processing. Initially, they therefore assumed that heuristic processing predominates when processing ability and motivation are low, whereas systematic processing becomes the dominant mode when processing ability and motivation are high. The heuristic-systematic model does not assume a trade-off between these processing modes. Instead, it assumes that both processing modes affect persuasion at the high-effort end of the processing continuum, whereas only heuristic processing dominates at the low-effort end. Since systematic processing usually provides much more information than heuristic processing, the effect of heuristic processing on persuasion will often be obscured (*attenuation hypothesis*). However, there are conditions under which this will not be the case. For example, when the persuasion information is ambiguous and thus amenable to differential interpretations, the expectancies established by the individual's processing of heuristic cues can bias the interpretation of the message content (*bias hypothesis*). The present experiment manipulated task importance, source credibility and message ambiguity to test this hypothesis. With an ambiguous message and high task importance, source credibility was expected to positively bias systematic processing when credibility was high and to negatively bias systematic processing when credibility was low.

Method

Participants

Three hundred and sixty-seven students participated in this study.

Design and procedure

Participants were told that they would read and give their opinions about a new telephone answering machine, the 'XT-100'. They then read a four-page booklet that contained the manipulations of source credibility, message type and task importance. A questionnaire that assessed participants' attitudes and other dependent measures followed.

Independent variables

Source credibility. The information was attributed either to the sales staff of a supermarket chain (low credibility) or to a respected consumer report magazine (high credibility).

Message type. The product description compared the XT-100 with two competing brands on six product attributes, and asserted that the XT-100 was superior to those brands. The recommendation was based either on strong arguments (superior on important attributes), weak arguments (superior on unimportant attributes) or, in the ambiguous condition, on some arguments in favour of and some against the XT-100.

Task importance. Participants were told either that they were part of a small selected group being canvassed by the producers of the XT-100 to decide whether the machine should be sold in their area (high task importance), or that they were part of a very large group to be canvassed and that the machine would only be sold outside the state in which the respondent lived (low task importance).

Dependent variables

Attitudes. Participants rated the extent to which they would consider buying the XT-100, their favourability towards it and the extent to which they regarded it a good product.

Cognitive responses. Participants were given three minutes to list their thoughts about the product or product description. Two independent raters then coded these thoughts according to whether (a) they related to the source or to the product attributes, and (b) whether they expressed positive, negative or neutral evaluations of source or product.

Manipulation checks. Participants were asked to indicate their level of motivation to read the product description, their perception of the credibility of the source, and the extent to which the product description contained positive or negative features.

Results

Results supported predictions. Under low task importance, attitudes were mainly determined by source credibility

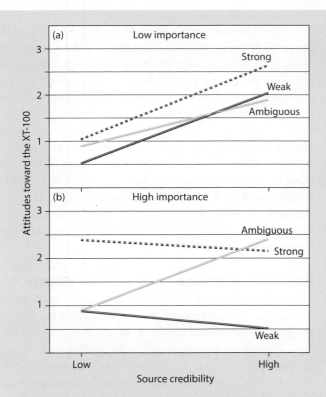

FIGURE 7.3(a) and (b) *Attitudes towards the XT-100 as a function of task importance (low versus high), source credibility (low versus high) and message type (strong versus ambiguous versus weak). Theoretical and actual range of attitude scores was −4 to 4, where higher numbers imply more positive attitudes.*

Source: Copyright © 1994 by the American Psychological Association. Adapted with permission. Chaiken, S., & Maheswaran, D. (1994). Heuristic processing can bias systematic processing: Effects of source credibility, argument ambiguity, and task importance on attitude judgment. *Journal of Personality and Social Psychology, 66,* 460–473. The use of APA information does not imply endorsement by APA.

(Figure 7.3a). Under high task importance and unambiguously strong or weak messages, attitudes were mainly determined by argument quality, an effect mediated by systematic processing. However, respondents under high task importance who had received an ambiguous message showed a strong source credibility effect, despite high levels of systematic processing (Figure 7.3b). Under these conditions, source credibility influenced the valence of the thoughts. Participants thought more positively about the attributes of the XT-100 when source credibility was high rather than low. No such bias occurred when the message was unambiguous. Thus, source credibility exerted a direct influence through heuristic processing when the task was unimportant. When the task was important, but the message ambiguous, source credibility exerted an indirect effect on attitudes by biasing systematic processing.

Discussion

Results under low task importance as well as under high task importance with an unambiguously strong or weak message replicated previous research. Evidence for the bias hypothesis comes from respondents in the high task importance condition, who were exposed to an ambiguous message. Although these motivated participants displayed evidence for systematic processing, their attitudes were mainly affected by source credibility. Analysis of their cognitive responses revealed that source credibility exerted an indirect effect by positively biasing systematic processing when credibility was high and negatively biasing systematic processing when credibility was low.

which recipients of a message engage in systematic message processing. One method, which was mentioned earlier, is the thought-listing technique. With this method, individuals are asked to list the thoughts they had while listening to a communication. Analysis of these thoughts focuses only on thoughts about the arguments contained in the message and more specifically the number of favourable and unfavourable thoughts stimulated by these arguments. If attitude change is due to systematic processing, then recipients of a message should have generated numerous thoughts about the arguments contained in the message. In other words, the greater the intensity of processing, the more message-relevant thoughts should have been produced. In addition, if these thoughts were responsible for the attitude change, there

should be a relationship between the overall favourability of these thoughts and the amount of attitude change. If people only generated negative thoughts about the message (e.g., 'all nonsense'; 'totally inconsistent with what I know about this issue') they would be unlikely to change their attitude in line with the position advocated. Sometimes they might even change in the negative direction. In contrast, if they respond with many favourable thoughts about the arguments contained in the message (e.g., 'this makes a lot of sense'; 'it fits with a good newspaper comment I read recently'), they are likely to change their attitude towards the advocated position. Therefore, a favourability index based on thought-listing (e.g., ratio of favourable thoughts to total number of relevant thoughts) should be correlated with or act as a mediator of attitude change under systematic processing. In contrast, if people changed their attitudes simply because they thought that the communicator was an expert and/or because the issue was not particularly important anyway, they should produce few message-relevant thoughts and these thoughts should be unrelated to the extent of their attitude change.

An even more powerful tool to assess the degree to which message recipients engage in systematic processing is the variation of argument quality. With this technique, recipients are exposed to communications that consist of either strong or weak arguments. (The categorization of arguments as strong or weak is decided beforehand on the basis of pilot research.) Exposure to strong arguments should stimulate predominantly favourable thoughts about the message in recipients who engage in systematic processing. As a result, there should also be significant attitude change. On the other hand, if arguments are weak, systematic processing should produce predominantly unfavourable thoughts about the message, and therefore very little attitude change. The less recipients are motivated and able to think about the arguments contained in a message (i.e., to engage in systematic processing), the weaker should be the effect of a manipulation of argument quality on the favourability of a recipient's message-relevant thoughts and, as a consequence, also on the extent to which these arguments induce attitude change. The combined use of both thought-listing (as one of the dependent measures) and manipulation of argument quality (as one of the independent variables) therefore provides a valid tool for diagnosing the extent to which individuals engage in systematic processing of the content of a message.

Processing ability and attitude change Variation in processing ability should affect information processing mainly when individuals are motivated to process a message. Thus, studies of variables that influence processing ability have typically used issues that were highly relevant to the students who were the recipients of these communications (e.g., a planned increase in tuition fees, or a proposed change in the college exam system). Among the most important variables influencing a person's ability to systematically process persuasive arguments are distraction and message repetition. Since we have considered research on distraction earlier, we will focus here on message repetition. In contrast to distraction, which reduces processing ability, (moderate) argument repetition should provide recipients with more opportunity for cognitively elaborating a communication. Thus, repetition should enhance attitude change for messages consisting of strong arguments and reduce attitude change for weak messages. Cacioppo and Petty (1989) tested this hypothesis by exposing respondents either one or three times to a message that contained either strong or weak persuasive arguments. Consistent with their predictions, increasing exposure to the same message led to higher agreement with high-quality messages, but led to decreased agreement with low-quality messages. However, the positive impact of repetition on high-quality messages will only occur if recipients are motivated to think about the communication (Claypool, Mackie, Garcia-Marques, McIntosh, & Udal, 2004). Furthermore, when messages are repeated too often, boredom sets in, which can result in rejection of even high-quality arguments in high-relevance messages (Cacioppo & Petty, 1979).

Processing motivation and attitude change The most influential determinant of a person's motivation to think about the arguments contained in a message is the perceived *personal relevance* of the communication. Only if the issue is important to them personally should recipients of a communication be motivated to critically evaluate the arguments contained in a message. With low involvement, when the issue of the communication is of little relevance, recipients are likely to rely on heuristic cues to assess the validity of the position advocated by the communication.

Petty, Cacioppo, and Goldman (1981) tested these predictions experimentally. They exposed college students to an attitude-discrepant communication advocating major changes to the college examination system. This communication, on a topic of great importance to students, contained either strong or weak arguments and was attributed either to a source with high expertise (the Carnegie Commission on Higher Education) or to one with low expertise (a class at a local high school). The researchers manipulated personal relevance by informing students either that these changes were going to be instituted the following year and would thus affect them personally, or that they would take effect only in 10 years' time. Petty and colleagues (1981) predicted that when students believed that the changes would affect their own fate (high personal relevance), they should be motivated to scrutinize the arguments and to engage in issue-relevant thinking. For these highly involved students, argument quality would be a major factor in persuasion. Students who believed that these changes would only be instituted long after they had left the university (low personal relevance) would not be motivated to think a great deal about the communication. Instead, they would use heuristic rules such as 'experts can be trusted' to assess the validity of the advocated position.

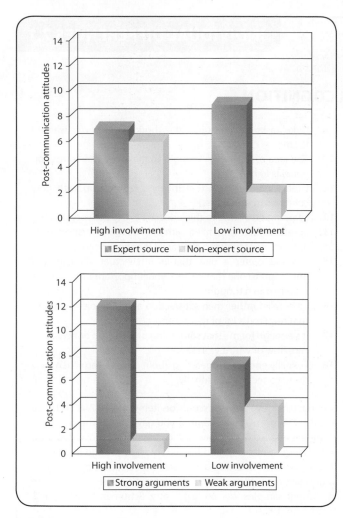

FIGURE 7.4 *Interactive effect of involvement and source expertise on post-communication attitudes (upper panel); Interactive effect of involvement and argument quality on post-communication attitudes (lower panel).*

Source: Copyright © 1981 by the American Psychological Association. Reproduced with permission. Petty, R. E., Cacioppo, J. T., & Goldman, R. (1981). Personal involvement as a determinant of argument-based persuasion. *Journal of Personality and Social Psychology, 41*, 847–855. The use of APA information does not imply endorsement by APA.

The results strongly supported these predictions (Figure 7.4). As Figure 7.4 (upper panel) shows, the nature of the source was a significant determinant of attitudes only for the low-involvement participants. For the highly involved participants it did not make a difference whether the communication came from an expert or a non-expert source, they formed their attitude based on their evaluation of the arguments. As Figure 7.4 (lower panel) shows, for high involvement participants argument quality was a significant factor: they were much more influenced by strong than by weak arguments. In contrast, under low involvement, the effect of argument quality was not significant.

Individual differences in processing motivation

The extent to which individuals scrutinize message arguments is affected not only by situational factors but also by individual differences in their motivation to think about persuasive communications. For example, people who frequently engage in and enjoy effortful cognitive activity (those high in **need for cognition**) should be more likely to form attitudes on the basis of the arguments contained in a communication than are people who are low in need for cognition. Cacioppo and Petty (1982) constructed a scale to measure need for cognition (see Individual Differences 7.1). Since need for cognition reflects a cognitive motivation rather than an intellectual ability, it correlates only moderately with verbal intelligence ($r = .24$; Cacioppo, Petty, Feinstein, & Jarvis, 1996). Consistent with expectations, argument quality affected attitude change mainly for individuals with high rather than low need for cognition. A study by Haugtvedt and Petty (1992) further demonstrated that attitude change in respondents with a high need for cognition was more persistent over time and more resistant against counter-argumentation than in individuals with low need for cognition.

The **need for cognitive closure** is another individual difference variable that has been shown to influence the intensity with which individuals process information (Klein & Webster, 2000; Kruglanski & Webster, 1996; Webster & Kruglanski, 1994). It refers to the individual's need for a definite answer to a question, any answer as opposed to confusion and ambiguity. Two highly related tendencies are assumed to underlie this need, namely 'urgency', that is the need to arrive at closure quickly, and 'permanency', that is the need to remain at closure once it has been achieved. These two tendencies are assumed to be separated by a demarcation point, namely the point at which a belief 'crystallizes' and turns from a conjecture to a firm 'fact' (Kruglanski & Webster, 1996). During the 'urgency' phase, before a belief crystallizes, individuals will be relatively open to persuasion attempts, because such attempts should accelerate closure. Once a belief has crystallized, the 'permanency' tendency kicks in, and individuals will be reluctant to engage in further information processing and will be resistant to persuasive arguments (Kruglanski & Webster, 1996). The need for cognitive closure is assumed to reflect a stable

> **need for cognition**
> an individual difference variable which differentiates people according to the extent to which they enjoy thinking about arguments contained in a communication.

> **need for cognitive closure** refers to the desire of individuals for a definite answer to a question – any answer, as opposed to uncertainty; the need reflects an individual difference variable, but can also be situationally induced.

THE NEED FOR COGNITION

This scale (short version by Cacioppo, Petty, & Kao, 1984) assesses need for cognition, the tendency of individuals to engage in and enjoy effortful cognitive endeavours (Cacioppo et al., 1996). When exposed to a persuasive message, people high in need for cognition are assumed to engage in more content-relevant thinking (i.e., systematic processing) than individuals low in need for cognition.

Instructions: Indicate to what extent each statement is characteristic of you, using the following response alternatives:

1 = *extremely uncharacteristic of me (not at all like me)*
2 = *somewhat uncharacteristic of me*
3 = *neither uncharacteristic nor characteristic of me*
4 = *somewhat characteristic of me*
5 = *extremely characteristic of me*

1. I would prefer complex to simple problems.
2. I like to have the responsibility of handling a situation that requires a lot of thinking.
3. Thinking is not my idea of fun.
4. I would rather do something that requires little thought than something that is sure to challenge my thinking ability.
5. I try to anticipate and avoid situations where there is a likely chance I will have to think in depth about something.
6. I find satisfaction in deliberating hard and for long hours.
7. I only think as hard as I have to.
8. I prefer to think about small, daily projects to long-term ones.

9. I like tasks that require little thought once I've learned them.
10. The idea of relying on thought to make my way to the top appeals to me.
11. I really enjoy a task that involves coming up with new solutions to problems.
12. Learning new ways to think doesn't excite me very much.
13. I prefer my life to be filled with puzzles that I must solve.
14. The notion of thinking abstractly is appealing to me.
15. I would prefer a task that is intellectual, difficult and important to one that is somewhat important but does not require much thought.
16. I feel relief rather than satisfaction after completing a task that required a lot of mental effort.
17. It's enough for me that something gets the job done; I don't care how or why it works.
18. I usually end up deliberating about issues even when they do not affect me personally.

Scoring: First, reverse your scores on items 3, 4, 5, 7, 8, 9, 12, 16 and 17. On any of these items, if you gave a 1 to the question, change it into a 5. If you gave a 2, change it into a 4; if you gave a 4, change it into a 2; and if you gave a 5, change it into a 1. If you gave a 3, leave it as a 3. Scores are added, and the higher your score, the higher your need for cognition. The median score in student samples was 60 (e.g., Petty, Schumann, Richman, & Strathman, 1993).

individual difference that is mostly measured with the Need for Closure Scale, a 42-item scale developed by Webster and Kruglanski (1994). (A shortened version of this scale has recently been proposed and validated by Roets and Van Hiel, 2011; see Individual Differences 7.2.) These scales show a moderately negative correlation with need for cognition (e.g., $r = -.28$; Webster & Kruglanski, 1994).

A study by Klein and Webster (2000) provides some support for these assumptions. Participants in their study were given promotional material about a new telephone answering machine. The information varied both in length (three versus nine arguments) and in the quality of the arguments that were presented (strong versus weak). Results showed that attitudes of individuals high in need for closure were more affected by the number of arguments than by argument quality, whereas low need for closure individuals were more likely to be affected

by argument quality. Since the length of a communication can be considered a heuristic cue (Chaiken, 1980), these findings are consistent with the assumption that individuals high in need for closure rely on heuristic cues rather than scrutiny of arguments. In contrast, the fact that argument quality influenced attitudes of individuals who are low in need for cognitive closure suggests that they formed their attitude based on scrutiny of the content of the communication.

The existence of stable individual differences between people in their need for cognitive closure does not preclude the possibility that this need is also influenced by situational factors. One of the situational factors known to heighten need for closure is time pressure. Suppose you are going on a vacation and you decide to buy a camera at the airport, because your old camera has just been stolen on the train. If you have ample time before your plane leaves, you will look at

INDIVIDUAL DIFFERENCES 7.2

THE NEED FOR COGNITIVE CLOSURE

The need for cognitive closure refers to people's wish for a definite answer to a question – any answer, as opposed to uncertainty. The scale shown here is a brief 15-item version (Roets & Van Hiel, 2011) of the original 42-item Need for Closure Scale (Webster & Kruglanski,1994). Try the scale yourself. You have to indicate the extent to which you endorse each item by responding to a 6-point Likert scale, ranging from 1 (*completely disagree*) to 6 (*completely agree*). If you score 57 or above, your need for cognitive closure is above average.

1. I don't like situations that are uncertain.
2. I dislike questions that could be answered in many different ways.
3. I find that a well-ordered life with regular hours suits my temperament.
4. I feel uncomfortable when I don't understand the reason why an event occurred in my life.
5. I feel irritated when one person disagrees with what everyone else in the group believes.
6. I don't like to go into a situation without knowing what I can expect from it.
7. When I have made a decision, I feel relieved.
8. When I am confronted with a problem, I'm dying to reach a solution very quickly.
9. I would quickly become impatient and irritated if I could not find a solution to a problem immediately.
10. I don't like to be with people who are capable of unexpected actions.
11. I dislike it when a person's statement could mean many different things.
12. I find that establishing a consistent routine enables me to enjoy life more.
13. I enjoy having a clear and structured mode of life.
14. I do not usually consult many different opinions before forming my own view.
15. I dislike unpredictable situations.

a range of different cameras, have all their advantages and disadvantages explained and then select one that promises to be most suitable for your needs. In contrast, if you have only 10 minutes before boarding starts, you have to rely on heuristic cues to reach your decision. You might choose the camera recommended by the salesperson ('experts know what is good'), you might rely on the price–quality heuristic and buy their most expensive camera, or the camera of a brand that is familiar to you (i.e., 'if I have heard of this brand, it must be good').

Processing intensity and stability of change

Persuasion induced by systematic processing is more persistent over time than persuasion induced by heuristic processing. High levels of issue-relevant cognitive activity are likely to require frequent accessing of the attitude and the related knowledge structure. This activity should therefore increase the number of linkages between structural elements, making the attitude schema more internally consistent, enduring and also more resistant to counterarguments. Attitude formation or change that is based on systematic processing should therefore result in stronger attitudes (Krosnick, Boninger, Chuang, Berent, & Carnot, 1993). There are

four key manifestations of strong attitudes (Krosnick & Petty, 1995; see also Chapters 6 and 8): strong attitudes are more persistent over time (e.g., Haugtvedt & Petty, 1992; Petty & Cacioppo, 1986a, b); they are more resistant to counterattitudinal appeal (Petty, Haugtvedt & Smith, 1995); they are more likely to influence information processing (Houston & Fazio, 1989; Lord, Ross & Lepper, 1979); and they are more likely to guide behaviour (Holland, Verplanken, & Van Knippenberg, 2002; Martin, Martin, Smith, & Hewstone, 2007).

In contrast, attitudes formed via non-systematic processing tend to be relatively weak. This means they do not persist over time, are unlikely to resist counterpersuasion, do not guide information processing and do not predict behaviour. However, as Eagly and Chaiken (1993) pointed out, heuristic processing could also result in enduring attitude change if the cue became associated with the attitude and remained salient over time (for example, I might persistently recall that my drinking two glasses of wine a day was recommended by my trusted physician). Nonetheless, such an attitude would be vulnerable to counter-propaganda, because it lacks elaborate cognitive support. Beyond the fact that my physician recommended it, I would have no rationale for supporting the habit.

Summary

Dual-process theories of persuasion such as the HSM assume that attitude change does not have to be a result of a critical evaluation of the arguments contained in a message, but can also be determined by attitude change processes that do not require systematic message processing such as heuristic processing or evaluative conditioning. The extent of systematic message processing depends on processing motivation and ability. More systematic processing is assumed to result in stronger attitudes.

Changing implicit attitudes

The theories of attitude change that we have discussed so far make no distinction between implicit and explicit attitudes. And yet, as we saw in Chapter 6, there is extensive evidence for these two types of attitudes. Furthermore, practically all research conducted to test these theories assessed attitude change with self-report measures, which would reflect explicit attitudes. Thus, we know a great deal about how to change attitudes reflected by explicit measures, but very little about achieving change on implicit measures.

Dual-process models contrast attitude change based on systematic processing of arguments with low-effort processes that are not based on argument scrutiny. It would therefore be tempting to assume that systematic processing – as a process based on extensive deliberation – should result in change of explicit but not implicit attitudes. Evaluative conditioning and mere exposure, on the other hand, should produce changes in implicit but not in explicit attitudes. As appealingly elegant as such a 'matching hypothesis' would be, we already know that it cannot be correct. After all, studies demonstrating the effectiveness of mere exposure (e.g., Zajonc, 1968) and evaluative conditioning (e.g., Staats & Staats, 1958) as methods of attitude change were published years before the first measures of implicit attitudes appeared in print (e.g., Fazio, Jackson, Dunton, & Williams, 1995; Greenwald, McGhee, & Schwartz, 1998). Thus, until recently all such demonstrations of attitude change were based on explicit measures of attitudes.

However, in the meantime, ample evidence has been accumulated to indicate that evaluative conditioning can change implicit attitudes. For example, in a conditioning study in which one of two Pokemon cartoon characters was consistently paired with positively valenced words and images, and the other with words and images of negative valence, Olson and Fazio (2001) demonstrated that this conditioning did not only influence self-reports of attitudes towards these cartoon characters, but also attitudes assessed with an implicit measure (IAT). Similarly, Dijksterhuis (2004) reported that repeated association of the word 'I' with either positive or negative trait terms resulted in a change of implicitly measured self-esteem, even when the stimuli were presented subliminally. Finally, Houben, Havermans, and Wiers (2010) used an evaluative conditioning paradigm to unobtrusively change alcohol-related attitudes and drinking behaviour of their participants. The repeated association of alcohol-related words with negative pictures resulted in a change in alcohol-related implicit attitudes (measured with an IAT) in the experimental compared to the control condition. Furthermore, participants in the experimental condition also reported lower alcohol consumption in the following week, compared to their drinking at baseline.

Most surprising, however, from a matching perspective, is evidence that systematic processing of persuasive communications can also change implicit attitudes. Briñol, Petty, and McCaslin (2009) demonstrated this in a set of studies they conducted. In one of these studies, participants received strong or weak persuasive arguments in favour of a new policy to integrate more African-American professors into the university. In addition, personal relevance was manipulated by informing students that this policy would be implemented either next year in their own university or in 10 years in a different university. Implicit racial attitudes were assessed with an IAT. Consistent with earlier findings on explicit measures (e.g., Petty et al., 1981), argument quality had greater impact on implicit attitudes when personal relevance was high.

In a second study, participants were exposed to strong or weak arguments in favour of including more vegetables in their diet (Briñol et al., 2009). To manipulate personal relevance, the information was either included in an article about health behaviour that (presumably) had consequences for academic performance or formed part of an article about plant properties. In addition, participants had to list their thoughts about the communications. As in the previous study, argument quality affected implicit attitudes (IAT) mainly under high personal relevance. More importantly, however, under conditions of high relevance, the impact of argument quality on implicit attitudes was mediated by the valence of the thoughts. Thus, the extent to which attitudes are systematically processed influences the magnitude of attitude change on implicit as well explicit measures.

Several theoretical models have been proposed that offer explanations of how implicit and explicit attitudes are changed (Fazio, 1990, 2007; Petty, Briñol, & DeMarree, 2007; Wilson, Lindsey, & Schooler, 2000). The earliest of these models, the MODE model (see Chapter 6) offers an elegant explanation that is well supported by empirical evidence (for reviews, see Fazio, 1990, 2007). We will use this model for explaining change of implicit and explicit attitudes.

According to the MODE model, attitudes are *associations* between a given attitude object and a given summary evaluation of the object. These evaluations can be based on appraisals of the attributes of the attitude object, as assumed by expectancy-value theories. They can also reflect emotional reactions evoked by the attitude object and associated with it through evaluative conditioning. Finally, they can derive from one's past behaviour. Thus, attitudes are one form of knowledge, namely evaluative knowledge, and are as such represented in memory. 'Just as we associate "bread" with "butter" and "doctor" with "nurse", we can associate "yuck" with cockroaches, or a sense of ecstatic delight with chocolate or single-malt scotch' (Fazio, 2007, p. 609). This conception of the attitude construct is largely consistent with the attitude definition offered in Chapter 6.

The associations between the attitude object and the evaluative response can vary in strength and therefore also in their accessibility in memory. At the weak end of the continuum from weak to strong associations, people have to construct an attitude when exposed to the attitude object. Thus, when asked their attitude towards eating more vegetables, they have to think about what they know about vegetables to come up with their attitude towards including more vegetables in their diet. Moving along this strength dimension, attitudes become sufficiently accessible for the mere perception of the attitude object to *automatically* trigger the evaluative response. Thus, just seeing vegetables on the menu, they respond positively without deliberation. It is these automatic evaluative responses that are captured by implicit measures of attitudes. Because these object-evaluation associations can be based on beliefs as well as on conditioned responses, they can be influenced by deliberative as well as automatic processes. The MODE model can therefore explain why explicit, as well as implicit, attitudes can be influenced not only by persuasive communications, but also by evaluative conditioning or frequency of exposure.

But if implicit and explicit measures are influenced by the same processes, why are such measures often hardly related? The reason for such discrepancies according to the MODE model is that implicit measures only (or mainly) reflect the automatically triggered evaluative response (i.e., the object-evaluation association), whereas self-reports of attitudes are often affected by additional factors (e.g., social desirability; political correctness). If individuals are not motivated to misrepresent their attitude, or if they are unable to do so (e.g., because they have to respond quickly), their attitudes measured

with implicit measures should be highly correlated with attitudes assessed with explicit measures. To test this assumption, Fazio and colleagues (1995; Experiment 4) used a measure of individual motivation to control racial prejudice in addition to an explicit and an implicit measure of prejudice. Consistent with predictions, they found that the less participants were motivated to control their prejudice the more their scores on the two measures of racial prejudice were related.

Summary

Because most early research on persuasion used explicit measures of attitudes, this section discussed strategies of change that influence implicit attitudes. As we have argued, there is no support for a 'matching hypothesis'. Research shows that implicit attitudes can be changed by processes based on extensive deliberation, as well as processes that do not require deliberation (e.g., evaluative conditioning, mere exposure). These findings are interpreted in terms of the MODE model.

Advertising as applied persuasion

Is subliminal advertising possible?

In the course of this chapter, we have already related some of the findings of persuasion studies to advertising. However, those of you who think of advertising as a powerful force that creates consumer needs and shapes the competition in markets today might have been slightly disappointed by our discussion of persuasion techniques. After all, it is hard to imagine that the processes we discussed here can have powerful effects like creating the image of the Marlboro Man, or helping to propel Absolut Vodka in the US from an inconsequential brand with fewer than 100,000 bottles sold in 1980 to become America's leading premium vodka brand with a sales volume of 40 million litres in 2006 (Figure 7.5). You might suspect that other factors have been at work (e.g., marketing, pricing strategy) or that there is some secret ingredient, a 'silver bullet' persuasion strategy that we have not discussed so far.

Subliminal advertising One candidate for such a weapon, albeit not a very secret one, is **subliminal advertising**. The term 'subliminal' refers to the presentation of a message so briefly (or faintly) that it is below the threshold of awareness. Subliminal advertising was made notorious in 1957 through publicity surrounding

> **subliminal advertising** advertising slogans that are presented so briefly (or faintly) that they are below the threshold of awareness.

FIGURE 7.5 *Advertising helped propel Absolute Vodka from an inconsequential brand to become America's leading premium vodka.*

Source: © The Absolut Company AB. Used under permission from The Absolut Company AB. ABSOLUT® VODKA. ABSOLUT COUNTRY OF SWEDEN VODKA & LOGO ABSOLUT, ABSOLUT BOTTLE DESIGN AND ABSOLUT CALLIGRAPHY ARE TRADEMARKS OWNED BY THE ABSOLUT COMPANY AB.

James Vicary's claim (see Social Psychology Beyond the Lab 7.1). People became so upset by the idea that they could be manipulated without their awareness that subliminal advertising has subsequently been legally banned in Australia and the UK. In the US it was forbidden by the broadcasting authority (Pratkanis & Aronson, 2001).

The fear of subliminal advertising was fuelled by the great powers people attributed to this procedure. People seemed to believe that being unaware of an influence attempt also meant that they could be induced to act in ways that were against their own interest. These fears appeared to have been influenced by Freudian thinking about the unconscious. People seemed to assume that subliminal advertising would trigger repressed motives and pass by the conscious control of behaviour. This kind of assumption must have led the police department of the town of Wichita, Kansas in 1978 to try to catch a serial killer by inserting the subliminal message 'contact the chief' into a news broadcast (Gibson, 2005). Since the killer was only apprehended in 2005, and not because of self-incrimination, the subliminal commands appear to have been ineffective.

While the presentation of visual messages is subliminal due to the brief exposure time, back-masking has been used to produce auditory messages assumed to be subliminal. With back-masking messages are recorded *backwards* on a tape that is otherwise recorded forwards. The method was allegedly first used by the Beatles in 1966, but then taken over by many other rock bands.

SOCIAL PSYCHOLOGY BEYOND THE LAB 7.1

THE BIRTH OF SUBLIMINAL ADVERTISING

On September 12, 1957, James Vicary, a market researcher, gave a press conference that became known around the world. He announced the formation of a new corporation, the *Subliminal Projection Company*, formed to exploit a major breakthrough in advertising, namely subliminal advertising. Vicary described the results of a six-week test conducted in a New Jersey movie theatre. Two slogans were flashed over the film for the duration of three thousands of one second at five second intervals, urging viewers to 'drink Coke' and to 'eat popcorn'. Vicary claimed that this subliminal advertising resulted in increases of 57.5 per cent in popcorn and of 18.1 per cent in Coke sales over the six-week period.

Newspapers around the world reported Vicary's announcement, triggering waves of protest about this subliminal brainwashing. People became so upset by

the idea that they could be manipulated without their awareness that laws banning subliminal advertising were subsequently introduced in Australia and the UK, with severe penalties for those who disobeyed. In the US subliminal advertising was not legally banned, but the Federal Communication Commission will revoke a company's broadcasting licence if the use of subliminal messages is proven (Pratkanis & Aronson, 2001).

At first Vicary refused to release any of his data. However, when the uproar continued, Vicary admitted in an interview to *Advertising Age* in 1962 that his claim had been a hoax, he had never done the study (Pratkanis & Aronson, 2001). The irony is that under certain conditions, this type of manipulation could have had an effect, as we will show below.

In another example of irrational beliefs about the effects of subliminal messages, there were court cases against rock bands accused of having inserted subliminal messages into their songs. In one trial against the rock band Judas Priest, the subliminal message 'do it' was considered responsible for two suicides. Fortunately for the rock group, the judge did not accept this argument. The W.V. Grant Evangelist Association even offered 'Subliminal Neckties' with the word 'Jesus saves' repeatedly, imperceptibly embedded in the necktie. When a Christian wore this 'Eagle Neckwear', he was told, he would be reaching virtually everyone who looked at him and leaving the message that Jesus saves imprinted on their subconscious mind.

In 2000 subliminal messages even entered the US presidential race. One Republican advertising spot spliced the word 'rats' into a segment about Democratic candidate Al Gore (Stroebe, 2012). Although 'rats' was part of a clearly visible line, 'bureaucrats decide', the less than flattering four-letter word ('rats') appeared on the screen 30 ms before the rest of the word 'bureaucrats'. Republican candidate George W. Bush claimed it was an accident, but television affiliates quickly withdrew the commercial.

While people do not want to be manipulated against their will, they quite like the idea of their willpower being buttressed by subliminal suggestion. American consumers appear to spend more than $50 million annually on audiotapes that contain subliminal messages to help them to improve their self-esteem, their memory and their study habits, or to help them to lose weight and stop smoking (Pratkanis & Aronson, 2001).

Studies of the effectiveness of self-help tapes have found no evidence of any effects. Greenwald, Spangenberg, Pratkanis, and Eskenazi (1991) conducted a study in which they measured participants' self-esteem and memory and then presented them with tapes that, according to the manufacturers, contained subliminal messages that should either improve self-esteem ('I have high self-worth and high self-esteem') or memory ('My ability to remember and to recall is increasing daily'). Crosscutting the manipulation of the subliminal content of the tapes, half the respondents were led to believe that they listened to the memory tape, the other half that they listened to the self-esteem tape. Respondents took the tapes home and listened to them daily for five weeks. When their self-esteem and their memory were reassessed on their return to the laboratory, no improvements could be detected. It is interesting, though, that those participants who thought that they had received the memory tape (regardless of whether they really had been given the memory tape or had been given the self-esteem tape) believed that their memory had improved. Similarly,

respondents who believed that they had received the self-esteem tape reported substantial improvements in their self-esteem. Thus, whereas the actual content of the tapes had no effect whatsoever, the *assumed* content resulted in a 'placebo effect'. Participants believed that their memory (or their self-esteem) had improved, even though, objectively, there had been no improvements at all. Obviously, such beliefs guarantee satisfied customers and the continued sales of self-help tapes.

That these subliminal messages were ineffective is hardly surprising (see Chapter 4 on Social Cognition). First, subliminal verbal primes have to consist of one or perhaps two (very short) words to be effective, and not of whole sentences. Second, while there is support for effects of subliminal visual priming, there is no evidence for priming effects of messages that have been recorded backwards (e.g., Kreiner, Altis, & Voss, 2003). Third, successful priming does nothing more than increase the accessibility of the primed concept and of thoughts related to that concept. Thus, even if it were possible to subliminally prime sentences like, 'My ability to remember is increasing daily' or 'I have high self-worth', they would be unlikely to improve our memory or our self-esteem.

Coca-Cola is a relatively short brand name and thus meets the first condition for a subliminal prime. Thus, if clever advertising technicians developed a technique that enabled them to successfully prime movie or TV audiences, could Coca-Cola sales be improved through subliminal priming? This would depend on a number of conditions. First, it would depend on the thoughts members of the audience associate with Coca-Cola. If they find it too sweet a drink, priming will not change their opinion. On the other hand, if they associate it with great taste and great thirst-quenching qualities, then priming might make them want to have a Coke, but only if they are thirsty at that particular moment. Finally, as we will discuss, priming effects would depend on the mood induced by the film into which the primes are embedded. You should now stop and read Research Close-Up 7.2, which describes an experiment by Karremans, Stroebe, and Claus (2006) that investigates these issues. More recently, Bermeitinger et al. (2009) conceptually replicated the findings of Karremans and colleagues, demonstrating the effect of subliminal advertising on actual consumption behaviour.

It is interesting to note that in the Karremans et al. study, the dependence of the priming effect on thirst (i.e., prime × thirstiness interaction) was strongest for participants who only drank Lipton Ice infrequently. The authors did not report this effect, because it was not significant. However, some years later, Verwijmeren, Karremans, Stroebe, and Wigboldus (2011) demonstrated in a replication of the Karremans et al. study that

SUBLIMINAL ADVERTISING

Karremans, J. C., Stroebe, W., & Claus, J. (2006). Beyond Vicary's fantasies: The impact of subliminal priming on brand choice. *Journal of Experimental Social Psychology, 42*, 792–798.

Introduction

Because short brand names can be primed subliminally, it should be possible to influence the choice of different brands with subliminal messages. However, Karremans and colleagues reasoned that certain conditions had to be met for subliminal priming to affect choice. First, because priming merely increases the cognitive accessibility of the primed concept, product priming will only be effective if people really like the product. For example, subliminal advertising is unlikely to induce people to drink Coca-Cola if they do not like its taste. Second, brand priming will only be influential if people really have a need for the advertised product. Thus, even if people like the taste of Coca-Cola, priming will not induce them to choose it if they are not thirsty. And finally, since the Coca-Cola company spends millions each year on advertising and thus on keeping the brand cognitively highly accessible, subliminal advertising of this brand might not be very effective, because it is already at the forefront of most people's minds.

Based on pretesting, Karremans et al. selected Lipton Ice (a type of iced tea) as a brand that is liked, considered thirst-quenching and yet is not highly cognitively accessible. They conducted two experiments to test the hypothesis that subliminally priming the brand name of Lipton Ice (rather than the brand of a popular mineral water) would increase choice of Lipton Ice, but only in participants who are thirsty. Since the only difference between the two experiments was that thirst was rated in the first, but manipulated in the second experiment, and since both studies confirmed the hypothesis, we present only Experiment 2 here.

Method

Participants and design

One hundred and five male and female students participated and were randomly assigned to one of the conditions of the 2 (thirst: thirsty versus non-thirsty) $\times$ 2 (prime: Lipton Ice versus control) between-participants design.

Procedure

Participants were seated in a cubicle behind a computer and were told that they would be participating in a number of unrelated experiments. The first task for half of the participants was a 'tongue detection' task, with which thirst was manipulated. These participants were given a very salty sweet that had a letter on one side, and had to detect the letter with their tongue. They were given one minute for this task. It was assumed that the salty taste and the post-ingestive effect of the salt would increase thirst. Next, participants had to perform a visual detection task, in which they were presented with letter sequences and had to detect small letters interspersed in sequences of capital letters. In fact this task was designed to subliminally prime half of the participants with Lipton Ice and the other half with a control nonsense letter string ('Npeic Tol'). The primes were presented 25 times, but each time for only 23 ms, so that participants were not aware of them. The letter sequence was preceded and followed by a string of Xs ('XXXXXX'), supposedly to help participants to focus on the task. In fact, the string of Xs served as pre- and post-masks. The post-mask is particularly important, because it blocks the visual memory of the prime through visual stimulation. Next, participants were asked to take part in a study on consumer behaviour. First, they were asked which brand of soft drink they would prefer, if they were offered a drink now. Two brand names (Lipton Ice and the control brand) appeared, one on the left and one on the right of the screen, and participants had to push a key on the left or right to indicate their preferred brand. Lipton Ice appeared half of the time on the right, the other half on the left. Next, participants had to rate their intention to drink Lipton Ice, using two rating scales (e.g., 'If you were sitting on a terrace now, how likely would you be to drink Lipton Ice?': 1 – *not at all likely*, to 7–*very likely*).

Results and discussion

The experiment resulted in a significant main effect for the Lipton Ice prime on choice. Participants in the Lipton

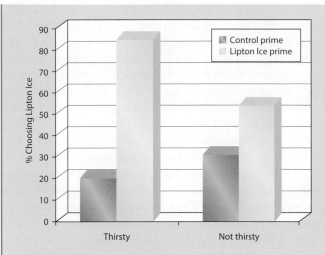

FIGURE 7.6 *Percentage of participants choosing Lipton Ice as a function of thirst and prime.*

Source: Karremans et al., 2006, Study 2. Reproduced with permission of Elsevier.

Ice prime condition were significantly more likely (69 per cent) to choose Lipton Ice than participants in the control prime condition (25 per cent). However, this main effect was moderated by a significant prime × thirstiness interaction, with thirsty participants being more strongly affected by the Lipton Ice prime than non-thirsty participants. The equivalent interaction was significant for the measure of intention to drink Lipton Ice. Thus, when offered a choice between a brand of mineral water or Lipton Ice, participants who had been primed with Lipton Ice were significantly more likely to choose it over the mineral water, but mainly if they were thirsty (Figure 7.6). Under these conditions they also expressed greater intentions to choose Lipton Ice in a hypothetical situation (if they were now sitting on a terrace and ordering a drink).

the interaction between priming and thirst was moderated by the extent to which participants were habitual drinkers of Lipton Ice. Priming worked only for thirsty individuals who did not drink Lipton Ice regularly: it had no effect on habitual consumers of Lipton Ice. This finding supports our assumption that subliminal advertising will mainly be effective for brands that are not highly cognitively accessible. For brands like Coca-Cola, that are, for most consumers, already at the 'top of the head', subliminal advertising is unlikely to have an effect.

In the studies reported so far, the subliminal primes were embedded in either a letter search task or a computer game (see, for example, Research Close-Up 7.2). With both these tasks, the experimenter can determine beforehand which point of the monitor viewers will be focusing on. This is not the case when subliminal primes are embedded in a film. Although a study by Cooper and Cooper (2002) demonstrated the effectiveness of subliminally presenting product primes in a film, they could only show an effect on thirst ratings and not on product choice.

A further complication when embedding brand primes in a film is that the emotions evoked by the film might 'rub off' on the brand name. From what we know about evaluative conditioning, we could expect that repeated subliminal exposure to a brand name would only increase choice of that brand if the brand is presented in a positive context (i.e., in a film that evokes

positive emotions). When presented in the context of a film that evokes negative emotions, the negative affect should become attached to the brand. Thus, embedding subliminal brand primes in a film that evokes negative emotions might even decrease the likelihood that the primed brand would be chosen afterwards.

Now let us return to Vicary's claim about subliminal advertising in the New Jersey movie theatre. Would he have succeeded with his subliminal messages to increase Coca-Cola sales if he had tried? It is not terribly likely. His exposure time was extremely short. He would also have had a greater chance if he had used a less widely advertised brand. It would also have depended on the film that was shown in that theatre. Since he embedded his primes in a comedy film, it might have worked. If it had been a sad film, however, it might even have had adverse effects. What we do know, however, is that subliminal advertising will not induce people to act against their will. It will not even help them to buttress their sagging willpower.

Matching advertising messages to consumer goals For advertising to be optimally effective, marketers need to match their message to the goals consumers are likely to pursue in purchasing a particular product. In this section, we will first present a typology of the goals consumers pursue in buying goods. We will then present a typology of consumer goods and discuss the relationship between these two typologies (see Stroebe & Keizer, in press, for a more extended discussion). Finally, we will discuss how marketing experts can match their messages to consumer goals.

A typology of consumer goals Goods are acquired as a means to achieve some goal. Goals are outcomes that are both desirable and perceived as attainable. In terms of a purely utilitarian perspective, one would expect that consumers buy goods or services simply for the function they are supposed to serve (e.g., cars for driving, watches for knowing the time). This is certainly true for products such as toothpaste, washing powder or dishwashers. But many other goods have a significance that goes beyond their utilitarian function. Although people buy cars to be more mobile, or watches to know the time, this is often not the only purpose. Otherwise there would be no market for Rolls Royce cars or Rolex watches. There are cheaper and no less comfortable means to move from A to B, and a cheap digital Quartz watch will keep time just as well as an expensive gold mechanical Rolex watch (Chronocentric, 2012).

So why do people spend considerable amounts of money to buy some expensive product when a cheaper one would serve as well? The reason is that the goods people buy often also have an identity-expressive function. They convey meaning through which people communicate something about themselves to others (Govers & Shoormans, 2005; McCracken, 1986). As Belk (1988) argued, one cannot hope to understand consumer behaviour without understanding the meanings consumers attach to the goods they purchase. However, people do not only choose certain brands to *express* their identity, owning these products also helps them to be the kind of person they want to be. Thus goods often have a second identity-related function, namely identity formation. Our possessions are not only a reflection of our identity, they are also a major *contributor* to it (Belk, 1988). 'To a large degree, we are what we have and possess' (Tuan, 1980, p. 472).

How do goods acquire the kind of surplus meaning that helps them to serve identity-related functions? Most of the products people purchase are branded. Thus, 'Apple', 'Rolex', 'Mercedes' or 'BMW' are brand names with a meaning established through large advertising budgets. The jeans teenagers wear often display some brand name. A 'brand is a label with which to identify an individual product and to differentiate it from that of its competitors' (Fennis & Stroebe, 2010, p. 304). The beliefs and evaluations associated with the brand name constitute the brand image. One aspect of this brand image is the 'brand personality'. The brand personality consists of a set of human characteristics that people associate with a brand (Aaker, 1997). It reflects the stereotypic image of the typical user of the brand, an image created by advertising, but also influenced by our experience with people who use the brand. The stereotypic drivers of a BMW have characteristics that differentiate them from the typical owner of a Volvo. Whereas stereotypical BMW drivers are sporty types, who derive pleasure from driving, the typical Volvo driver is (or used to be) a family person for whom safety is an important value. And the people who buy a BMW or a Volvo make that decision partly because they either aspire to be such a person or because they think that they already are such a person and want to express this identity. Thus one of the factors that determines a consumer's attitude towards a particular brand is the extent to which the perceived personality of the brand is consistent with a consumer's self-concept (Aguirre-Rodriguez, Bosnjak & Sirgy, 2012).

It is important to note, however, that people differ in the extent to which they value the identity-related functions of goods. Some people only care about the utilitarian function of a product and are uninterested in the impression they make on others. These are people who dress sensibly rather than fashionably, who drive a Golf rather than a Mini and prefer wearing a cheap digital Quartz watch even if they could afford a time piece by Cartier or Rolex. One could also argue that this typology of consumer goals is incomplete, because it overlooks the important fact that people also purchase goods for their intrinsic value, namely the enjoyment these goods provide. Thus, even though people might prefer the Mini over the Golf partly for self-expressive reasons, they are also likely to have been attracted by the sporty feel of the Mini and the driving pleasure it provides.

A typology of consumer goods One important dimension on which consumer goods vary, and that is related to the different goals consumers pursue in acquiring goods, is the distinction between thinking and feeling goods (Tellis, 2004). Thinking goods are products such as washing machines, electric toothbrushes, razors or hairdryers that mainly serve utilitarian goals. The important attributes of these products are performance, reliability and quality. Consumers try to choose thinking products that do a good job at a reasonable price.

In contrast, feeling goods, such as paintings, jewellery, wine or designer clothes are evaluated primarily in terms of personal preference. The important attributes of feeling goods are taste, flavour and design. It is difficult to think of a utilitarian goal served by jewellery. And even though people may sometimes drink a glass of wine to quench their thirst, there are better and cheaper beverages to serve this purpose. It is important to consider thinking and feeling goods not as different categories but as endpoints of a continuum. Although there are pure thinking goods (e.g., toothpaste, washing machine) and pure feeling goods (e.g., paintings, jewellery), most feeling products also serve utilitarian goals and most thinking goods serve identity-related goals. For example, cars would be categorized as thinking goods and are certainly judged with regard to performance, reliability and quality. And yet for years BMW used the slogan 'Freude am Fahren', which, loosely translated, refers to 'driving pleasure'. And in their advertisements they often depict their cars in front of expensive hotels, pictures that appeal to identity-related goals.

A second important dimension on which consumer goods vary is the level of involvement required from a consumer making a purchase (Vaughn, 1980). At the low involvement end are repetitive, routine or habitual choices such as the purchase of household cleaning products, toiletries or dairy products. These decisions require little information-search or deliberation, because they are made repeatedly and involve relatively small sums of money. At the high involvement end are decisions about infrequently bought and expensive goods, such as automobiles, cameras or even houses. These decisions are involving, because the costs of making the wrong decision are quite high. Therefore, these decisions require a great deal of information search and deliberation.

Matching the message to the product Because the position of a good on the continuum from thinking to feeling goods is related to the consumer goals the purchase is likely to satisfy, this position will influence whether an advertisement will target more utilitarian as compared to more identity-related goals. Whereas messages emphasizing the utilitarian values of a product are effective with thinking goods, such messages are likely to be ineffective when advertising a feeling product. In other words, one would expect that in order to have maximum impact, advertising messages have to match the function that is predominantly served by a product.

Support for this hypothesis comes from a study by Shavitt (1990), who presented participants with four pairs of ads about four products. Two were thinking products (coffee, air conditioner) and two were feeling products (greeting cards, perfume). Fictitious brands of each product category were then advertised with either a utilitarian or an identity-related appeal. An example of a utilitarian appeal would be 'The delicious, hearty flavour of aroma from Sterling Blend coffee comes from a blend of freshest coffee beans'. Identity-related appeals included arguments such as 'The coffee you drink says something about the type of person you are' (p. 136). Consistent with predictions, the utilitarian message resulted in the most positive attitude for thinking products, whereas the identity-related message was most effective for feeling products.

Appeals to identity-expressive motives work best if they are not too explicit. For example, if advertisements for the phenomenally expensive Rolex watch were to state explicitly that ownership of a Rolex is a sign of great wealth, many people might be deterred from buying a Rolex. Because even though they might buy a Rolex watch exactly for that reason, they would not want this to be obvious to others. Advertisers therefore often use pictures to appeal to self-expressive or identity goals. Thus, with mixed feeling/thinking products, the text of advertisements typically conveys (utilitarian) performance information, whereas the pictures appeal to the identity-related motives of consumers. For example, the text in car advertisements provides information about performance and reliability, whereas the pictures show the car in beautiful exotic environments, with beautifully elegant people, or in front of chic hotels. All of these pictorial cues suggest that the owners of such cars move in elevated circles. With goods that are nearly exclusively feeling goods, such as designer clothes or jewellery, advertisements are likely to contain hardly any text, but pictures of beautiful people wearing the clothes or the jewellery.

Whereas the position of a product on the thinking to feeling dimension determines the type of message that is most effective, the involvement dimension determines the consumers' motivation to process the information contained in an advertisement. Although the degree of involvement has no clear implications for the advertising of feeling goods, it is an important determinant of the strategies advertisers use for thinking goods: They will rely on persuasive arguments to advertise high involvement thinking goods. In contrast, product endorsements by experts or celebrities will be preferred for low involvement thinking goods. We have all seen the actor who, dressed like a dentist (i.e., expert), praises the qualities of a particular toothpaste or toothbrush.

Support for this hypothesis comes from a study by Petty, Cacioppo and Schumann (1983) that was essentially a conceptual replication of the Petty et al. (1981) study described earlier. Petty and colleagues (1983) used a simulated advertising context, exposing participants to different versions of an advertisement about a fictitious brand of disposable razors (Edge Disposable Razors) and also manipulating personal relevance. The four versions of the ad varied in terms of two factors, namely the quality of arguments supporting the brand (strong, weak) and the celebrity status of the featured endorser of Edge (celebrity, average citizen).

The strong arguments mentioned the 'unsurpassed sharpness' due to a 'new advanced honing method' or the reduced risk of cuts 'due to a specially chemically formulated coating'. Weak arguments stated that the razor was designed 'with the bathroom in mind' or 'floats on water with a minimum of rust'. The person endorsing the product was either a famous athlete or a citizen of a small city in California. Personal relevance was manipulated by leading participants in the high relevance condition to believe that they would be allowed to choose a brand of disposable razor at the end of the study *and* that the Edge razor would be marketed in their area. Under low personal relevance, participants were not promised a choice of disposable razors and were informed that the Edge razors would not be marketed in their area. The main dependent measure was their attitude towards the razor brand.

Personal relevance should determine whether respondents based their attitude towards the razor mainly on the arguments contained in an advertisement or on the celebrity status of the endorser. With high processing motivation as a result of high personal relevance, respondents should be more persuaded when arguments are of high rather than low quality. Since these respondents would form their attitude based on the arguments presented, the celebrity status of the endorser should make little difference. In contrast, with low processing motivation due to low personal relevance, they should base their attitude on the status of the endorser. They should be more persuaded when the endorser is a celebrity figure rather than an average citizen. In line with predictions, and replicating the findings of the Petty et al. (1981) study described earlier, celebrity status influenced attitudes mainly under conditions of low personal relevance, whereas argument quality was mainly effective under high involvement conditions.

Instead of using endorsements by celebrities or experts to advertise low involvement thinking goods, one can also try to use emotional appeals to increase the personal relevance of a product. For example, one could try to induce guilt feelings in parents who neglect their children's welfare by not making them brush their teeth with toothpaste X. Alternatively, one could use fear appeals (Das et al., 2003; De Hoog et al., 2005). This latter approach was taken by Gerald Lambert, who in 1922 hired an advertising agency to improve the sluggish sales of Listerine, at the time a product used as an antiseptic in surgery and to fight throat infections (Pratkanis & Aronson, 2001). Seeking a wider market, Lambert decided to promote it as a mouthwash. The problem was that nobody in those days really used a mouthwash. Furthermore, accusing people of having

'bad breath' would not have been a popular message. Thus, the ads for Listerine used the obscure medical term 'halitosis' instead of 'bad breath'. The slogans of this famous campaign played on people's fear of being rejected by their social environment. 'Even your best friend won't tell you. Listerine is good for halitosis.' Or, 'Often a bridesmaid . . . never a bride.'

The campaign was extremely effective, turning Listerine into a household name. An analysis of TV commercials indicates that marketers are aware of these matching principles. Choi, Yoon, Paek and Reid (2012) categorized 1356 TV commercials according to whether the message was mainly utilitarian or mainly value-expressive and related this categorization to a classification of products based on the thinking/feeling dimension. Consistent with matching principles, advertisements for feeling goods used mainly value-expressive messages, whereas advertisements for thinking goods used mainly utilitarian messages. These effects occurred independent of levels of involvement.

Summary

In this section we discussed, first, the feasibility of subliminal advertising. There is by now substantial evidence that subliminal messages can influence brand choice, but only under specific conditions, namely for products that are not highly accessible and which are needed to satisfy an active goal. We then discussed the relationship between the type of product advertised and the type of appeal most effective for such products. We introduced the distinction between feeling and thinking products, and argued that for feeling products appeals to self-expressive or identity-related goals are most appropriate, whereas persuasive arguments about utilitarian qualities are most effective with thinking products.

INCENTIVE-INDUCED ATTITUDE CHANGE

Does the use of incentives (e.g., taxation, legal sanctions) constitute an effective strategy of attitude and behaviour change?

Powerful institutions often influence behaviour directly through incentives or legal sanctions rather than relying on the uncertain effects of persuasion. For example, in 1975 when Swedish drivers could not be persuaded to use their seatbelts, the government introduced a law that made seatbelt use compulsory for front-seat passengers in private cars. The introduction of this law increased the frequency of seatbelt use from 30 per cent to 85 per cent within a few months (Fhanér & Hane, 1979). Similarly, in New York, where seatbelt use ranged from 10 to 20 per cent prior to the introduction of a seatbelt law in 1984, it increased to 45–70 per cent after the law came into force in early 1985. The introduction of these laws also resulted in substantial reductions in the deaths of vehicle occupants (Robertson, 1986).

Governments can also use taxation to reduce the occurrence of undesirable behaviour patterns. There is ample evidence that the demand for alcoholic drinks and cigarettes, like the demand for most commodities, responds to changes in price and income (see Stroebe, 2011). A review of available research from several countries concluded that, all other things being equal, a rise in alcohol prices generally led to a drop in the consumption of alcohol, whereas an increase in the income of consumers generally led to a rise in alcohol consumption. There is similar evidence for smoking (Stroebe, 2011).

Thus, there is ample evidence that use of incentives is an effective strategy of behaviour change. It is also likely that incentive-induced behaviour change results in a change in attitudes towards the behaviour. According to the value-expectancy models discussed in the previous chapter, one's attitude towards a given behaviour reflects the perceived consequences of engaging in that behaviour. Therefore, changes in the price of, for example, alcoholic drinks should influence one's attitude towards *buying* alcoholic drinks. It should have no effect, however, on one's attitude towards *drinking* them. Consequently, although a marked increase in the price of alcoholic drinks is likely to induce people to buy fewer of them, they might drink at their old level of consumption when not constrained by price (e.g., at a party where drinks are freely available). Furthermore, should alcohol prices come down again, people's attitude towards buying alcoholic drinks would again become more positive.

With regard to the effectiveness of legal sanctions, governments have the added problem that, to be effective, these sanctions may require continuous monitoring. It would therefore be desirable if the behaviour change induced by legal sanctions resulted in a change in attitudes. In the following sections we will discuss conditions under which incentive-induced behaviour change might lead to attitude change.

Counterattitudinal behaviour and attitude change

One condition for attitude change following **counterattitudinal behaviour** could be that individuals find performing that behaviour much less aversive than they had anticipated. For example, seatbelt users in the 1980s, who reluctantly used their belts because of the sanctions threatened by the law, may have found them much less restrictive than they anticipated. Thus, they may have realized that their negative attitude towards seatbelt use was unjustified. This attitude change is likely to have been accompanied by a process of habit formation. Over time, putting on their seatbelts may have become habitual for most people. Thus, what was originally a conscious action, requiring cognitive resources and performed purely to avoid being sanctioned, may have turned into effortless and automatic behaviour. There is evidence that behaviour becomes habitual if it is performed frequently and in contexts that are likely to be stable. Thus, when we live for many years in the same place, we develop many habits that we have to abandon when we move (Ouellette & Wood, 1998). We would further argue that behaviour is unlikely to become habitual if it is effortful and associated with negative consequences. However, all is not lost if performing the behaviour is really as unpleasant as anticipated, because **cognitive dissonance theory** (Festinger, 1957) would still lead us to expect that people will change their attitudes in the direction of greater consistency with their behaviour, at least under certain well-specified conditions.

> **counterattitudinal behaviour** behaviour (usually induced by monetary incentives or threats) which is inconsistent with the actor's attitude or beliefs.

> **cognitive dissonance theory** assumes that dissonance is an aversive state which motivates individuals to reduce it (e.g., by changing beliefs, attitudes or behaviour, and searching for consonant, or avoiding dissonant, information).

Cognitive dissonance theory According to cognitive dissonance theory, individuals who are induced to behave in a way that is discrepant with their attitude will experience cognitive dissonance (Festinger, 1957). Dissonance is an aversive state (i.e., unpleasant, like hunger or thirst), which motivates individuals to reduce it. This motivation will be stronger the greater the dissonance. One way to reduce dissonance is to change one's attitude towards the behaviour.

To explain this prediction, we will have to describe cognitive dissonance theory in more detail. Whenever an individual chooses between alternative courses of action, there have to be reasons that justify the chosen action (consonant cognitions), otherwise the person would not have made that particular choice. However, there are usually also reasons that would have argued for choosing the rejected alternative (dissonant cognitions). The more reasons there are that would have justified choosing the rejected alternative, and the more important these reasons are, the greater will be the dissonance the person experiences and the greater the pressure to reduce it. For example, if Susan buys a car and decides on a Mini over a Golf, the sporty image and feel of the car would be consonant cognitions. However, the Golf would probably have cost less, had a larger luggage compartment and a more comfortable ride. These qualities of the Golf, which Susan gave up by choosing the Mini, will contribute to her cognitive dissonance (i.e., dissonant cognitions). Since, once made, choices are difficult to reverse (especially choices involving expensive purchases), the most likely means for her to reduce dissonance is to persuade herself that the Mini is even more fun and the Golf more bourgeois than she always thought. There is empirical evidence that people's evaluations of two objects are more discrepant some time after a choice between them than before the choice took place (e.g., Brehm, 1956).

If drivers use seatbelts to avoid paying a fine, their behaviour is not completely voluntary. And yet, since they could have decided to risk the fine, it is still a free decision. It is in this situation where dissonance theory makes its most counterintuitive prediction. Since the threatened sanctions are consonant cognitions for those who comply with the law, dissonance would be greater the less severe these sanctions. If death was the penalty for not using one's seatbelt, few seatbelt users would feel dissonance. On the other hand, if the penalty was $1, people who comply would probably feel considerable dissonance. After all, a fine of $1 is not a very substantial justification to engage in behaviour that one did not really want to engage in. Thus, if an individual behaves in a counterattitudinal manner to avoid a penalty or gain some benefit,

dissonance will be greater if either the penalty or the benefits are small rather than large.

Festinger and Carlsmith (1959) tested these predictions in their classic experiment. Participants had to perform two dull motor tasks for an hour and were then asked, under some pretext, whether they would be willing to tell the next participant that the experimental task was really interesting. They were offered either $20 or $1 for agreeing to do this (in effect, telling a lie, although the experimenters did not present it in those terms). According to cognitive dissonance theory, participants who had been offered $20 should have less difficulty in justifying their behaviour than individuals who received only $1; after all, $20 was then (and still is) a large sum of money. Participants in the $20 condition should therefore experience less cognitive dissonance and less need to reduce it than those who had only been offered $1 for telling a lie (see Theory Box 7.4). In line with these predictions, Festinger and Carlsmith found that, when asked afterwards to indicate how enjoyable they had found the two motor tasks, participants in the $1 condition rated them more enjoyable than did individuals who had been paid $20, or than individuals in the control group who had merely rated the motor tasks without having been asked to describe it as interesting (Figure 7.7).

Festinger and Carlsmith intuitively built two features into their experimental situation that, though not specified by the original version of the theory, turned out to be essential for dissonance arousal. First, since the experimenter's request was not ostensibly part of the experiment, participants were free to refuse the request and thus experienced high freedom of choice and therefore felt responsible for their behaviour. However, since most people are absolute suckers when it comes to refusing requests made in face-to-face situations (see Chapter 8), Festinger and Carlsmith did not have to worry that many participants would refuse, even in the $1 condition. Second, since the target of the lie (actually

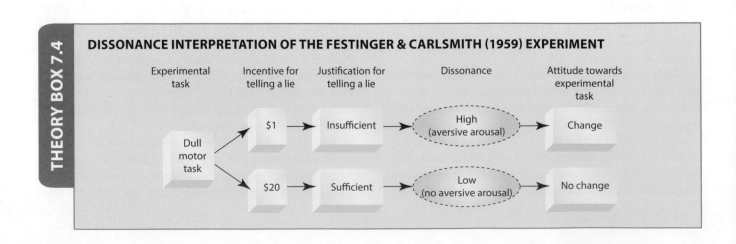

THEORY BOX 7.4

DISSONANCE INTERPRETATION OF THE FESTINGER & CARLSMITH (1959) EXPERIMENT

Experimental task	Incentive for telling a lie	Justification for telling a lie	Dissonance	Attitude towards experimental task
Dull motor task	$1	Insufficient	High (aversive arousal)	Change
	$20	Sufficient	Low (no aversive arousal)	No change

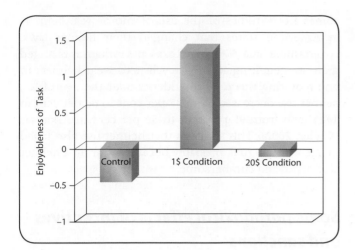

FIGURE 7.7 *Ratings of task enjoyableness by condition.*

Source: Copyright © 1959 by the American Psychological Association. Adapted with permission. Festinger, L., & Carlsmith, J. M. (1959). Cognitive consequences of forced compliance. *Journal of Abnormal and Social Psychology, 58,* 203–210. The use of APA information does not imply endorsement by APA.

a confederate of the experimenters) had indicated that she had originally not intended to participate in the experiment because of an exam, the participants' behaviour led to aversive consequences. After all, by telling a lie, the participant persuaded the other person to engage in a boring task instead of preparing for an exam. Both freedom of choice (Linder, Cooper, & Jones, 1967) and negative consequences (Cooper & Worchel, 1970) are necessary for counterattitudinal behaviour to arouse dissonance.

Self-perception theory Dissonance theory provoked some controversy in its heyday. The major challenge to the dissonance interpretation came from *self-perception*

theory (Bem, 1965, 1972). This theory assumes that people often do not know their own attitudes and, when asked about them, are in the same position as an outside observer (see Chapters 5 and 6). As we have learned in the discussion of attribution theory (see Chapter 3), people usually infer attitudes of others from relevant instances of past behaviour. Thus, when asked to state their attitude towards the motor task, participants in Festinger and Carlsmith's experiment would have remembered that they told another participant that the task was interesting. They would have used this knowledge as information about their own attitude towards the task, unless there were reasons to *discount* their own behaviour as a source of information. Being paid a large sum of money to behave in a certain way is a good reason to discount one's behaviour as a source of information about one's attitude. Thus, when paid $20, they would probably discount their own behaviour as source of information and evaluate the experimental task merely on the basis of how they remembered it (i.e., as boring). Self-perception theory can thus account for Festinger and Carlsmith's findings without referring to unpleasant, aversive states and clashing cognitions (see Theory Box 7.5).

It is now generally accepted that the two theories should be regarded as complementary formulations, with each theory being applicable to its own specialized domain (Fazio, Zanna, and Cooper, 1977; Stroebe & Diehl, 1988). According to Fazio, Zanna, and Cooper (1977), self-perception theory accurately characterizes attitude change in the context of mildly discrepant behaviour where the individual argues for a position close to his or her own initial attitude. Fazio and colleagues term such behaviour *attitude-congruent*, and define it as any position that is still acceptable to an

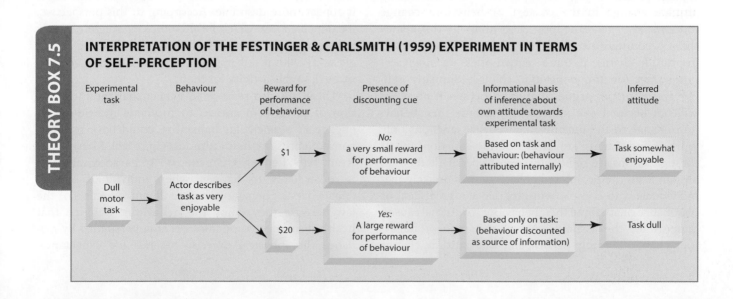

THEORY BOX 7.5

INTERPRETATION OF THE FESTINGER & CARLSMITH (1959) EXPERIMENT IN TERMS OF SELF-PERCEPTION

individual, even though it may not be in accordance with his or her actual attitude. For example, people who believe that all atomic power stations should be closed down immediately would probably also find acceptable the position that no new atomic power stations should be built and the existing ones should be phased out within 10 years. However, these opponents of atomic power stations would find completely unacceptable the argument that we need new atomic power stations to ensure future energy needs. Since it can be assumed that individuals are motivated to put considerably more cognitive effort into justifying their action if it is counterattitudinal rather than attitude-congruent, this integration is consistent with expectations from dual-process theories: low-involvement individuals (those still behaving in an attitude-congruent manner, hence exerting little effort in justification) should rely predominantly on heuristic processes (Stroebe & Diehl, 1988).

Dissonance, self-perception and the use of incentives Will people who smoke less or drink less because of taxation-induced price increases also change their attitudes towards smoking or drinking? Individuals who smoke less because cigarette prices have increased, or drink less because alcohol prices have gone up, may experience some dissonance. After all, their decision to reduce their consumption of cigarettes or alcohol will be the result of a decision about how to allocate their income. They would have been able to consume at the old level if they had decided to reduce *other* expenses (on food, vacations, etc.). Like all freely made choices, such a decision is likely to result in cognitive dissonance, and one of the ways to reduce dissonance would be to persuade oneself that one was better off by smoking and drinking less.

It is more doubtful whether dissonance or self-perception processes play an important role in mediating attitude change in the context of behaviour change induced by legal sanctions. According to dissonance theory, counterattitudinal behaviour will only result in attitude change if the incentive offers an *insufficient justification* for the behaviour change. Similarly self-perception theory argues that the processes it proposes will not occur if the individuals attribute their behaviour change to the incentive. Since legal sanctions only work if individuals are aware of the sanction and if these sanctions are *sufficiently severe* to persuade them to abstain from the prohibited behaviour, it is unlikely that individuals who comply will experience a great deal of dissonance or attribute their behaviour to internal causes. Support for the assumption that this type of behaviour change is rarely accompanied by attitude change

comes from studies of the use of motorcycle helmets in American states that changed their helmet laws. For example, in 1997 when Texas and Arkansas changed their law requiring all motorcyclists to wear helmets to one requiring this only for riders under the age of 21, helmet use decreased from 97 per cent to 66 per cent in Texas and from 97 per cent to 51 per cent in Arkansas (Waller, 2002). This suggests that helmet use also failed to become habitual, probably because wearing a helmet is effortful and cumbersome.

Some paradoxical effects of incentives and sanctions

Unfortunately, some evidence suggests that legal sanctions or positive incentives can have paradoxical effects on attitudes, with sanctions making the behaviour seem more attractive and positive incentives decreasing the attractiveness of the behaviour they stimulate. There seems to be some truth in the old saying that forbidden fruits are the sweetest, at least for those fruits that had originally been freely available. According to **reactance theory** (Brehm, 1966), the elimination of behavioural freedom should result in reactance, a motivational state directed towards the re-establishment of this behavioural freedom. Obviously, the most direct form of re-establishing the threatened or lost freedom would be to exercise it. Reactance will therefore frequently result in an intensified form of the behaviour that has been sanctioned. However, regardless of whether or not one violates the sanctions, reactance will increase the motivation to engage in the sanctioned behaviour and thus make it appear more desirable. According to this perspective, introducing a law which forbids smoking might not only induce smokers to smoke whenever they think they can get away with it – it might also make smoking an even more desirable activity for them.

> **reactance theory**
> reactance is an aversive state caused by restriction of an individual's freedom of choice over important behavioural outcomes. Reactance is assumed to motivate the individual to re-establish the restricted freedom.

There are also reasons to expect that the introduction of positive incentives to motivate individuals to engage in a particular behaviour could have negative consequences on their attitudes (e.g., Deci, Koestner, & Ryan, 1999; Lepper & Greene, 1978). Paradoxically, this is most likely to happen when individuals already engaged in the behaviour before the introduction of the law because they enjoy the behaviour. Imagine that health insurance companies became persuaded by evidence that physical exercise extends life expectancy, reduces illness risk and saves health costs. They therefore decided to offer financial rewards (i.e., reduced premiums) for individuals who jogged regularly. This might induce many people to jog who would not have done so otherwise. But at the same time, it might also undermine the motivation of people who enjoy jogging and are already jogging regularly. At least, this is the prediction one would derive from research on the effects of external (e.g., monetary) rewards on **intrinsic motivation** and performance. Intrinsically motivated behaviours are performed out of interest and because they are enjoyed. Research has demonstrated that both enjoyment and performance of an intrinsically enjoyable task can decrease once people have been given some reward for performing that task (e.g., Deci et al., 1999; Lepper & Greene, 1978).

> **intrinsic motivation** behaviour is said to be intrinsically motivated if people perform it because they enjoy it. This enjoyment is sufficient to produce the behaviour and no external reward is required. In fact, external rewards (e.g., financial contributions) are likely to reduce intrinsic motivation.

Further limitations of the effectiveness of incentive-induced change

Since people are rarely interested in attitude change as an end in itself, but rather as a means to changing behaviour, influencing behaviour through monetary incentives or legal sanctions would seem to be the most effective of the strategies discussed in this chapter. As we have seen, there is ample evidence to support this notion. Seatbelt laws succeeded not only in substantially increasing seatbelt use, they also resulted in a change in attitudes towards seatbelt use, at least among those who complied (Fhanér & Hane, 1979). In view of the apparent effectiveness of incentive-induced behaviour change, one wonders why people still bother with persuasion.

There are actually a number of considerations to be taken into account. The most obvious is lack of power. Only governments have the power to enact laws, and even they are constrained in the use of this power. For example, although the behavioural factors that are detrimental to people's health (e.g., smoking, overuse of alcohol) are well known, governments rely on persuasion as well as legal action to change behaviour.

An additional constraint on strategies of influence based on the use of monetary incentives or legal sanctions is that these strategies can only be used for behaviour that can be monitored. Thus, while efficient for publicly identifiable behaviour such as seatbelt use or speeding, positive or negative incentives are difficult to apply if the behaviour that one wishes to influence is difficult to monitor objectively. For example, in the area of race relations, governments can eliminate some of the objective and observable instances of discrimination (e.g., by introducing quotas for employment of members of racial minorities), but they cannot force people to be nice to members of outgroups, to invite them to their homes or let their children marry one of them. This is one of the reasons why the American Supreme Court mandated the end of segregated schooling. Since they could not outlaw prejudice, they attempted to reduce it by increasing interracial contact (see Chapter 14).

Finally, the effectiveness of legal sanctions is likely to depend on the acceptance of the law and on individual perception that violation of the law is associated with a high risk of sanction. For example, it is quite likely that the introduction of the law making seatbelt use compulsory would not have been effective had people not accepted that such a law was in their own best interests. In fact, without the persuasion campaigns that made it widely known that the wearing of seatbelts substantially reduced the risk of injuries in traffic accidents, it is unlikely that such a law would have been introduced. Similarly, the increases in Federal cigarette tax that occurred in the US during the 1970s and 1980s would not have been possible without the anti-smoking campaign. The anti-smoking campaign in the US also illustrates the fact that persuasion and incentive-related strategies do not preclude each other and are probably most effective when used in combination. Thus, the anti-smoking campaign resulted in a non-smoking ethos that was probably responsible for the legislative successes of the non-smokers' rights movements during the 1970s and 1980s.

Summary

Powerful institutions often use incentives or legal sanctions rather than persuasion to influence behaviour. There is evidence that such strategies are often effective in changing behaviour. It is less clear, however, whether these strategies also achieve a change in relevant attitudes. For incentive-induced counterattitudinal behaviour to induce dissonance, the incentive has to be relatively small and not sufficient to justify the behaviour. Because large incentives would justify the behaviour, there would be no need to reduce dissonance through attitude change. However, the effect of the introduction of penalties for non-use of seatbelts suggests that even small incentives can sometimes result in behaviour change.

CHAPTER SUMMARY

- *What are the major strategies of attitude and behaviour change?* This chapter discussed two major strategies, namely persuasion and the use of incentives (e.g., taxation, legal sanctions).

- *What is the difference between the early theories of persuasion and the more recent dual-process theories?* Early theories of persuasion (information processing model, cognitive response theory) focused on persuasion resulting from the systematic processing of the semantic content of persuasive messages. More recently, dual-process theories (e.g., HSM) have accepted that people often adopt attitudes on bases other than their systematic processing of arguments. Dual-process theories integrate theories of systematic processing and persuasion processes that are based on low-effort processes (e.g., heuristic processing) and they specify the conditions under which people engage in each of these processes.

- *When do people engage in systematic processing of message arguments?* According to dual-process theories such as the HSM, individuals will engage in systematic processing of message arguments only if they are *motivated* and *able* to do so.

- *What are the factors that determine processing motivation?* Processing motivation is determined by situational factors such as personal relevance of the attitude issue and by individual difference variables such as need for cognition.

- *What are the factors that determine processing ability?* Processing ability is determined by factors such as time, absence of distraction or message repetition. Whenever individuals are unmotivated or unable to engage in systematic processing of message content, they base their decision of whether to accept or reject a persuasive communication on low-effort processing.

- *Does subliminal advertising work?* The effectiveness of subliminal advertising depends on the product and the need state of the target of the advertising. Subliminally advertising Lipton Ice was effective for participants who were not habitual drinkers of this brand, and who were thirsty.

- *How does effective advertising work?* For advertising to be optimally effective, marketers need to match their message to the goals consumers pursue in purchasing a particular product: some goods are bought to satisfy utilitarian goals (e.g., toothpaste, washing machine), others to satisfy identity-related goals (e.g., jewellery).

- *How does matching work?* The position of goods on the continuum from thinking to feeling goods is related to the consumer goals a purchase is likely to satisfy. Therefore advertisers will target more utilitarian goals for thinking goods and identity-related goals for feeling goods. For thinking goods, the degree of involvement (e.g., importance of a purchase) will determine whether marketers will rely mainly on persuasive arguments or use product endorsements by experts or celebrities.

- *Are incentives useful for influencing attitudes and behaviour?* Governments may use taxation or legal sanctions to make certain behaviours like smoking, drinking alcohol or the non-use of seatbelts more costly to individuals. Such strategies have been effective in promoting the targeted behaviour, but less successful in also inducing attitude change.

- *Can incentives and persuasion be used jointly?* Since private acceptance of these government strategies is likely to aid compliance, we argued that the use of incentives *and* of persuasive appeals should be considered as complementary rather than competing strategies.

SUGGESTIONS FOR FURTHER READING

Bohner, G., & Dickel, N. (2011). Attitudes and attitude change. *Annual Review of Psychology, 62*, 391–417. A state-of-the-art review of the field of attitude research.

Chen, S., & Chaiken, S. (1999). The heuristic-systematic model in its broader context. In S. Chaiken & Y. Trope (Eds.), *Dual-process theories in social psychology* (pp. 73–96). New York: Guilford. This chapter presents the most recent version of the heuristic-systematic model and reviews research conducted to test the theory.

Fennis, B. M., & Stroebe, W. (2010). *The psychology of advertising*. Hove, UK: Psychology Press. A comprehensive, state-of-the-art review of the psychological findings on the impact of advertising. It discusses this research in the context of recent developments in the fields of social and consumer psychology.

Maio, G. R., & Haddock, G. (2010). *The psychology of attitudes and attitude change*. London: Sage. A well-written introduction. A comprehensive and accessible overview of theories and empirical findings in the area of attitude change.

Petty, R. E., Fazio, R. H., & Briñol, P. (Eds.). (2009). *Attitudes: Insights from the new implicit measures*. New York: Psychology Press. This book contains chapters by leading researchers reviewing theorizing and research on the topic of implicit measures of attitudes.

Petty, R. E., & Wegener, D. T. (1999). The elaboration likelihood model: Current status and controversies. In S. Chaiken & Y. Trope (Eds.), *Dual-process theories in social psychology* (pp. 41–72). New York: Guilford. This chapter presents the most recent version of the elaboration likelihood model and reviews research conducted to test the theory.

8 Social Influence

MILES HEWSTONE AND ROBIN MARTIN

KEY TERMS

- autokinetic effect
- compliance
- conformity
- consistency
- conversion
- deindividuation
- descriptive norms
- door-in-the-face technique
- evaluation apprehension

- foot-in-the-door technique
- group polarization
- groupthink
- informational influence
- injunctive norms
- innovation
- lowballing technique
- majority influence
- minority influence

- normative influence
- norms
- obedience to authority
- referent informational influence
- self-categorization theory
- social comparison
- social facilitation
- social influence
- whistle blowing

HOW NORM VIOLATION PROMOTES ANTISOCIAL BEHAVIOUR

RESEARCH CLOSE-UP 8.1

Keizer, K., Lindenberg, S., & Steg, L. (2008). The spreading of disorder. *Science, 322*, 1681–1685.

Introduction

The so-called 'broken windows theory' of crime (Kelling & Wilson, 1982) emphasizes the role of norms in causing petty crime. This criminological theory argues that by removing signs of disorder such as broken windows, litter, and graffiti, we could simultaneously remove triggers of disorderly and petty criminal behaviour. Keizer, Lindenberg, and Steg (2008) conducted six elegant field experiments that provided the first causal evidence in support of this theory.

Theoretically, their studies build on the earlier work of Cialdini and colleagues (Cialdini, Reno, & Kallgren, 1990), which had shown the importance of injunctive norms (which refer to the approval or disapproval of a particular kind of behaviour) and descriptive norms (which simply describe a particular behaviour common in a setting). Whereas injunctive norms provide information about which behaviour is most appropriate in a given situation (e.g., the 'don't litter' norm), descriptive norms affect behaviour simply because they provide information about which behaviour is most common in that situation. Thus, injunctive norms concern what one *should* do in a certain situation, whereas descriptive norms concern what *is* the case in that situation.

The studies by Keizer et al. cleverly addressed what happens when injunctive and descriptive norms are in conflict. For example, do more people litter in a setting where the anti-graffiti norm (an injunctive norm) is in conflict with the descriptive norm (i.e., a setting in which it is common for people to spray the walls with graffiti)? We will summarize only the first study in this paper, but refer briefly to the results of some of the other studies in the discussion, below. All the studies were controlled field experiments, conducted in common public places in the town of Groningen, in The Netherlands.

Method

Participants

One hundred and fifty-four members of the public (*N* = 77 in each of the two conditions) were observed when they came to collect their parked bicycles.

Design and procedure

The experiment compared two conditions, both staged in the same alley located in a shopping area, where people commonly parked their bicycles. A conventional sign clearly indicated that graffiti was prohibited (i.e., injunctive norm disapproving of graffiti). In an 'order' condition, the walls of the alley were clean, whereas in a 'disorder' condition they were sprayed with graffiti. Participants in the study (who were unaware that they were being observed) were people who came to collect their parked bicycles. However, prior to collecting their bicycle, the experimenters had, unobserved, attached a fake advertising flyer to the handlebars of their bicycle in such a way that the participants had to remove it before they could easily use their handlebars. There were, however, no litter bins in the alley, thus the cyclists could only follow the 'no littering' norm by taking the flyer with them. The experimenters simply counted how many cyclists littered (counted as either throwing the flyer on the ground, or hanging it on another bicycle) in the two conditions.

Results

The effect of violating the graffiti norm on the extent of littering was substantial and highly significant. Of the participants in the order (no graffiti) condition, 33 per cent littered, compared with 69 per cent of the participants in the disorder (graffiti) condition (see Figure 8.4).

Discussion

This study showed very clearly that violating the anti-graffiti norm doubled the extent of littering. Studies 2 to 6 confirmed these findings, using a variety of norms

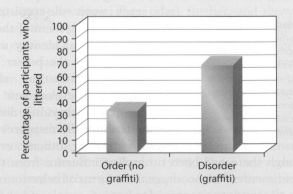

FIGURE 8.4 *Percentage of participants littering as a function of order versus disorder.*

Source: Data from Keizer, Lindenberg, & Steg, 2008; Study 1.

and behaviours. Studies 5 and 6 even showed that the presence of graffiti (whether on a public post box, or in the area around the post box) substantially increased the proportion of participants who *stole* an envelope clearly containing a five Euro note (which the experimenters had left dangling tantalizingly in the opening of the post box!), compared with a 'clean' control condition. The researchers also ruled out alternative explanations (e.g., it was unlikely that people littered more in some conditions simply because they calculated that they were less likely to be arrested for this, because police in the town generally turned a blind eye to littering).

Based on this impressive evidence the researchers concluded that the most likely explanation for this overall set of results was that one form of 'disorder' (e.g., graffiti) actually encouraged a different form of 'disorder' (e.g., littering, or stealing), because the violation of one norm (e.g., not to spray graffiti) weakened conformity to the other norm (not to litter, not to steal). The researchers concluded by referring to the policy implications of their findings, including the need for early detection of signs of disorder, and prompt intervention to prevent the spread of other forms of disorder as norms for appropriate behaviour are inhibited.

forms (deliberate influence), this is a good place to ask *why* people are influenced by others. As we have indicated, some forms of influence are low-level, rather trivial effects (e.g., social facilitation), which do not appear to be driven by motives. Other forms of influence are much more interesting, because they illustrate some of the fundamental goals that guide human social behaviour, and their underlying motives.

One of the earliest theoretical analyses of this question was that of Festinger (1950). Focusing on task-oriented groups with face-to-face communication, he argued that norm-formation as well as norm-following were outcomes of pressures towards uniformity within the group. Uniformity itself serves two functions of group membership, *social reality testing* and *group loco-motion*. When we follow established social norms, we are confident that our behaviour is appropriate, correct and socially desirable – we have subjective validity (Turner, 1991). Although we can test the subjective validity of some beliefs against physical reality ('Is this water hot? I will put a thermometer in it to check'), other beliefs can only be tested against social reality ('What is my opinion towards euthanasia? I will see what my friends believe'). Agreement with other members of the relevant group (be it immediate task group or wider reference group) by comparing our views with theirs (Festinger, 1954) provides us with subjective validity for our beliefs (see also Chapters 5 and 12 on social comparison theory). (See Individual Differences 8.1 for a scale that assesses the tendency to make social comparisons.)

Social comparison (see Chapter 5) is most likely to occur in situations that are novel, ambiguous or objectively unclear (Sherif, 1936; Tesser, Campbell, & Mickler, 1983), and when people are unsure, they are

most likely to look to, and be guided by, the beliefs and behaviours of *similar* others. Thus, social reality testing is the consensual validation of beliefs through social comparison. This is seen as necessary for the group to reach its desired goals, what Festinger (1950) called *group locomotion*. Coordination of goals and activities among group members is necessary for the group to move, as a group, effectively and efficiently in the direction it wants or needs to go. Consider conformity, going along with the group (which we introduced in Chapter 1 and will return to in more detail below). Even though it tends to have negative connotations in Western, individual societies (Markus & Kitayama, 1994), conformity can help us to achieve group goals quickly and easily (Cialdini & Trost, 1998). Think for a few seconds how chaotic society would be in the complete absence of conformity.

Festinger suggested that opinion discrepancies within groups elicit pressures towards uniformity, which produces communication between members of the group. Uniformity is achieved by group members convincing others to move towards their position, by themselves shifting towards the position held by others, or by redefining the group by rejecting those members who disagree (see Levine, 1989; Turner, 1991).

Deutsch and Gerard (1955) proposed a simple but highly significant analysis of motives for social influence. They argued that people agree with others for *normative* or *informational* reasons. **Normative influence** presumes a need for social approval or harmony with others, and occurs when people conform to the positive expectations of others – they avoid behaving in ways that will lead to social

normative influence influence based on conforming to the positive expectations of others: people avoid behaving in ways that will lead to social punishment or disapproval.

INDIVIDUAL DIFFERENCES 8.1

MEASURING THE TENDENCY TO COMPARE OURSELVES WITH OTHERS

Social comparison refers to the use of others as points of reference to evaluate our abilities, or to show us what we should be thinking or feeling. This comparison may be considered relatively automatic (Gilbert, Giesler, & Morris, 1995), but occurs most often when we are uncertain about what to think or feel, during periods of stress, novelty or change and in situations that foster competition. Gibbons and Buunk (1999) developed a scale to measure the tendency to make social comparisons as an individual difference variable. The scale addresses the three specific underlying motives for comparison that have been generally accepted in the literature on social comparison: self-evaluation, self-improvement and self-enhancement (Taylor, Wayment, & Carrillo, 1996; Wood, 1989). The scale's 11 items capture the tendency to compare with others concerning life accomplishments, how well one has done at something, social skills, popularity, how one approaches a task, mutual opinions, experiences, problems and situations, or to learn more about something.

You can assess your own tendency to make social comparisons by completing the 11-item scale, below, which is preceded by the instructions:

'Most people compare themselves from time to time with others. For example, they may compare the way they feel, their opinions, their abilities, and/or their situations with those of other people. There is nothing particularly "good" or "bad" about this type of comparison, and some people do it more often than others. We would like to find out how often you compare yourself with other people. To do that we would like to ask you to indicate how much you agree with each statement below, by using the following scale.'

The scale ranges from *I disagree strongly* (1) to *I agree strongly* (5).

1. I often compare how my loved ones (boy or girlfriend, family members, etc.) are doing with how others are doing.
2. I always pay a lot of attention to how I do things compared with how others do things.
3. If I want to find out how well I have done something, I compare what I have done with how others have done.
4. I often compare how I am doing socially (e.g., social skills, popularity) with other people.
5. I am not the type of person who compares often with others. (*reversed*)
6. I often compare myself with others with respect to what I have accomplished in life.
7. I often like to talk with others about mutual opinions and experiences.
8. I often try to find out what others think who face similar problems as I face.
9. I always like to know what others in a similar situation would do.
10. If I want to learn more about something, I try to find out what others think about it.
11. I *never* consider my situation in life relative to that of other people. (*reversed*)

Gibbons and Buunk (1999) reported data on various samples, including five samples of students in the Netherlands (*N* = 3200 total). The mean score (after reverse-scoring items 5 and 11) was 37.93, so if you score clearly lower than this score your tendency to make social comparisons is lower than average, whereas if you score clearly higher than this score your tendency to make social comparisons is higher than average.

---

punishment or disapproval. The main goal, then, is to build and maintain satisfactory relationships with others, and accuracy becomes correspondingly less important (Prislin & Wood, 2005). **Informational influence** presumes a need to reduce uncertainty, and involves accepting the information obtained from others as evidence about reality. The main goal in this case is to make accurate and valid judgements.

> **informational influence** influence based on accepting the information obtained from others as evidence about reality.

Notwithstanding the impact Deutsch and Gerard's framework has had on the whole social influence literature, Prislin and Wood (2005) have criticized the interpretation of it, which emphasizes only whether people

are (public settings) or are not (private settings) under *surveillance*. According to a simplistic application of the normative–informational distinction, social influence based on normative influence is temporary, and evidenced in public settings, but not maintained in private settings in which judgements do not have social consequences; whereas informational influence yields enduring change in judgements, and holds in both private and public settings. In contrast to this view, Prislin and Wood emphasize that normative motives can, in fact, have informational consequences that hold up later in time, and in private settings.

One way to integrate these different approaches to understanding *why* social influence occurs is to highlight four major motives (Cialdini & Trost, 1998; see also Prislin & Wood, 2005): 'effective action', 'building and maintaining relationships', 'managing the self concept' and 'understanding'. This approach emphasizes the goals of both the *target* of influence and the influencing *agent*. Thus, for example, a participant in Sherif's autokinetic studies could have shifted his or her estimate of how much the point of light appeared to move, in the direction of the group norm, in order to facilitate the group working effectively, to gain approval and acceptance from others in the group, to avoid a self-conception as someone who is different or deviant, or to believe that he or she now sees things more accurately. But the target also yields to informational social influence, because he or she takes the behaviour of others as information about reality or wants to be accepted by the group.

We will return to these goals throughout the remainder of this chapter. We emphasize, here, that individuals will process the information available in social situations so as to meet whatever goal is salient. Thus, depending on whether the focus is on action, relationships, the self concept or understanding, the target of social influence will focus information processing on its implications for behavioural effectiveness, social relations, the desired view of the self or the validity of the available information. Each of these goals can also be addressed in various ways (see Lundgren & Prislin, 1998; Prislin & Wood, 2005). When the implications are important, people can address the relevant goal(s) through careful thought and systematic analysis, yielding change that endures across time and settings. Or, when the goals are less compelling, and people have less need to be confident in their judgements, they can meet them through less systematic, more heuristic strategies (see Chapter 7 on dual-route models of attitude change).

Summary

When we look at why social influence occurs, we see some of the fundamental motives that direct human social behaviour. Pressures toward uniformity and agreement among group members help us to validate social beliefs and guide the group towards its goals. We can also agree with others because we wish to be liked (or to avoid being disliked), or because we accept information from others as evidence about how things 'really are'. Ultimately, we are influenced by others so that we behave effectively, build and maintain relationships with others, manage our own self-concept and understand the social world more effectively.

DELIBERATE SOCIAL INFLUENCE

Inducing compliance

What are the main techniques of inducing compliance, and how and when do they work?

Compliance refers to a particular kind of response whereby the target of influence acquiesces to a request from the source of influence (Cialdini & Trost, 1998), but typically 'gives in' to the request without a true change of attitude. The request may be explicit or implicit, but the target recognizes that he or she is being pressured to respond in a desired way. We emphasize that even though these forms of influence may appear relatively mild, all are based on *requests*, they are also all quite manipulative, and you are likely to encounter them in your interactions with skilled professional salespeople – so beware! But they can also be used for positive ends, as in eliciting donations to charity. (As you will see later, the term *compliance* is also used more generally in the research on conformity, to refer to change in public behaviour to match a norm, but without corresponding change on a private level.) We consider, below, the three main techniques of inducing compliance.

> **compliance** a response whereby the target of influence acquiesces to a request from the influence source (also refers to change in behaviour to match a norm without change on a private level).

The door-in-the-face technique   In the **door-in-the-face technique** (also known as a 'reciprocal concessions' procedure), the requester begins with an extreme request that is almost always refused (e.g., 'Can you lend me £20?'). The requester, upon the initial request being declined, then retreats to a more moderate request, in fact the one that the requester had in mind all along (e.g., 'Can you lend me £5?'). By acting in this way, the requester hopes that the concession from an extreme to a moderate request will encourage the target of the request to make a similar, reciprocal, concession and move from initial refusal of the larger request to acceptance of the smaller one (e.g., Cialdini et al., 1975).

> **door-in-the-face technique** compliance technique in which the requester begins with an extreme request that is almost always refused, then retreats to a more moderate request, which he or she had in mind all along (also known as a 'reciprocal concessions' procedure).

This technique works effectively in commercial settings (e.g., Fennis, 2008), and is widely used in fundraising. For example, after refusing a larger request for a donation, people are much more likely than before to give any contribution (Reingen, 1978). It has also been used to solicit blood donors (Cialdini & Ascani, 1976). Researchers first asked people to take part in a long-term donor programme. When that request was declined, the requester asked for a one-time donation. Again, compliance with the small request was significantly greater after refusal of the large request (50 per cent), than in a control condition, in which people were asked only to perform the smaller favour (32 per cent). You can even use this technique on your lecturers! Harari, Mohr, and Hosey (1980) found that if students asked faculty members to spend 15 to 20 minutes talking to them about an issue of interest, some 59 per cent of the faculty agreed. But as many as 78 per cent acquiesced if they had first been asked for a much bigger favour (giving two hours a week of help to the student for the rest of the semester), which they had of course refused.

The success of this technique relies on two interlinked explanations. First, when the salesperson makes a concession, it is normative for the consumer to *reciprocate*, at least to some extent, which he or she does by accepting the concession. The tactic is much less effective if the time between the two requests is perceived as too long (Cann, Sherman, & Elkes, 1975), if the two requests are made by two different people (Snyder & Cunningham, 1975), and if the first request is excessive (Schwarzwald, Raz, & Zvibel, 1979). Second, when the target (e.g., the consumer, faced with a salesperson) makes a concession, he or she has re-established *equity* with the salesperson. The motives underlying compliance of this sort include our desire to build and maintain social relationships, but also our wish to view ourselves as, for example, generous (Brown & Smart, 1991) or consistent (Cialdini, Trost, & Newsom, 1995).

The foot-in-the-door technique

The **foot-in-the-door technique** adopts the reverse strategy, with the requester first asking for a small favour that is almost certain to be granted, and then following this up with a request for a larger, related favour (Freedman & Fraser, 1966). For example, a car salesperson may ask a potential buyer to test drive a car. Compliance to the critical request (buying the car) will be enhanced if the customer can first be made to comply with the initial, smaller request. The requester uses initial compliance as a means of committing the target to behave in a

foot-in-the-door technique compliance technique in which the requester first asks for a small favour that is almost certain to be granted, then follows this up with a request for a larger, related favour.

way that is consistent with it, and there is plentiful evidence that people are suckers for this approach (see Beaman, Cole, Preston, Klentz, & Steblay, 1983, for a review), which is frequently used by telemarketers (see Fennis & Stroebe, 2010). In a dramatic example, housewives were much more likely to allow a team of five or six men into their homes for two hours to go through their household products after they had answered a couple of questions about the kinds of soaps they used, than when no such smaller request was made in advance (Freedman & Fraser, 1966). It can also be used for charitable donations: respondents who had agreed to accept and wear a small lapel pin promoting a local charity were also more likely to give money to that charity when approached at a later point in time (Pliner, Hart, Kohl, & Saari, 1974).

The success of this technique relies on the general idea of consistency (Cialdini & Trost, 1998; Cialdini et al., 1995). Thus, the person who agreed to wear the lapel pin will wish to behave consistently when contacted later. This is closely linked to an explanation in terms of self-perception theory (see Chapter 7). For example, the car-buying customer may infer from his or her behaviour that he or she is the kind of person who drives that sort of car.

Lowballing

In the **lowballing technique**, which Cialdini and Trost (1998, p. 178) refer to as one of the 'more unsavoury' techniques, compliance to an initial attempt is followed by a more costly and less beneficial version of the same request (Cialdini, Cacioppo, Bassett, & Miller, 1978). For example, a car dealer may induce the customer to decide on a particular model of car by offering a low price for it, or an attractive trade-in deal on the customer's old vehicle. Then, after the decision has been made, the dealer goes back on the deal, giving some reason why the car is no longer available at the originally agreed price. Really unscrupulous dealers may even strengthen the customer's commitment, by allowing him or her to arrange financing, or even take the car home overnight (Joule, 1987).

lowballing technique compliance to an initial attempt is followed by a more costly and less beneficial version of the same request.

This technique seems to rely on the target, even though he or she has been duped, feeling an unfulfilled obligation to the requester. The target is also already psychologically committed to the purchase, and so proceeds anyway. The technique is primarily effective when used by a single requester (Burger & Petty, 1981), and when the target freely makes the initial commitment (Cialdini et al., 1978; see Chapter 7 on cognitive dissonance theory). Although we have thus far treated lowballing as a rather negative technique, we should also note that it has been used successfully for more noble causes, such as getting people to give more money to a charitable cause (Fennis, Janssen, & Vohs, 2009).

Integration These techniques of inducing compliance rely on general principles such as equity, reciprocity and self-consistency (for further principles, and an application of these techniques to advertising, see Fennis & Stroebe, 2010, Chapter 7). One other general principle guiding induced compliance concerns perceived rewards and costs. People are not quite the suckers that these phenomena may imply, and in general they are likely to comply with a request for help if the costs are low, but not if costs are high (Cialdini & Goldstein, 2004). Under low costs they may display relative 'mindlessness' (Langer, Blank, & Chanowitz, 1978), for example not listening carefully to the exact words of a requester who asks to jump ahead of them in the queue for the photocopier machine, with the lame excuse that they 'have to make some copies'. However, when the requester asks to copy a larger number of pages (implying costs for the target, who will have to hang around and wait), then the requester's words are listened to carefully, and compliance only follows a convincing justification (e.g., 'I have to visit my sick mother in hospital').

The influence of numerical majorities and minorities

How and when do numerical majorities and minorities exert influence?

Whereas strategies for inducing compliance involve interpersonal influence, social influence is also a key phenomenon in small groups. The first studies to examine the conditions under which an individual yields or conforms to a numerical majority were conducted by Solomon Asch (e.g., Asch, 1951, 1956; see Levine, 1999, and Leyens & Corneille, 1999, for commentaries on the impact of Asch's research). The 'Asch experiments' have become a classic in the literature, and we have already

innovation see minority influence.

majority influence (conformity) social influence resulting from exposure to the opinions of a majority, or the majority of one's group.

described the basic paradigm (see Chapter 1; and Jetten & Hornsey, 2012). In this section we will, first, review the main findings from the Asch paradigm, and then consider when and why people conform. Next, we introduce minority influence and **innovation**, the

situation in which either an individual or a group in a numerical minority can influence the majority. Finally, we review the major theoretical approaches to explain both **majority influence** and **minority influence**.

minority influence (innovation) situation in which either an individual or a group in a numerical minority can influence the majority.

Majority influence: the Asch paradigm and beyond Asch (1956) began his famous work expecting to show that people were *not* as suggestible as was generally believed at that time (see Leader in the Field, Solomon E. Asch). He also believed that the norm-following behaviour shown in Sherif's (1936) studies could be attributed to the ambiguous nature of the autokinetic stimulus. He contended that when unambiguous stimuli were used, and where there was a clearly correct answer, people would remain independent of the group's inaccurate judgements. As you will see, the results turned out rather differently.

Asch used a task in which groups of participants were shown two cards. On one card were three lines of different lengths, with each line having a number. The second card contained just one line (the standard line) that was of the same length as one of the three lines on the first card. The participant's task was simply to state publicly which of the three lines was the same length as the standard line. This task was repeated 18 times, and on each trial different cards were shown, using different lengths of lines. In a control condition, in which participants performed alone with no group influence, over 99 per cent of the responses were correct, showing that the task was simple and unambiguous.

What Asch did next was very interesting. He had participants perform the task publicly, answering aloud, in groups of six to nine. He arranged that all the participants (all were male), except one, would be confederates of the experimenter – that is, they were instructed by the experimenter to give a set pattern of answers, some of which were clearly incorrect. In some studies, the confederates all gave the wrong answer to the task. In addition, the seating arrangement was such that the naïve participant always gave his answers last-but-one. In other words, the naïve participant heard several people give the same wrong answer before he was required to give his own response. Asch's research question was, how would the naïve participant respond when faced with a consistent majority giving an (obviously) incorrect response? In fact, Asch found that the naïve participants gave the same incorrect response as the majority on 36.8 per cent of occasions.

It might be easy to brush aside these findings and assert that participants were just publicly agreeing with the majority. Yet, such behaviour does not only occur in public responses. In one variation of the study (Asch, 1956) a situation was arranged so that the naïve participant believed he had arrived too late and so could write down his responses while the other group members (the confederates) still gave their responses aloud. The rate of conforming to the majority fell to 12.5 per cent, but this is still much higher than when no confederates were present (0.7 per cent). Or one might argue that such conformity was found when participants made decisions about the length of lines, which had no real consequences, but would not be found for more important judgements, such as moral decisions. Yet, Kundu and Cummins (2013) reported a pronounced effect of conformity when they studied moral decisions using the Asch paradigm.

Subsequent studies on **conformity** tended to move away from Asch's paradigm, which was costly and time-consuming, because each naïve participant had to be tested alongside a group of confederates. Instead, using the Crutchfield (1955) paradigm, there are no confederates and the numerical majority is implied through feedback about other people's responses. Each participant sits in a separate cubicle (with no visual or verbal contact) and they all respond to the task via response switches. In addition, the response of each other group member is displayed on each participant's console. Each participant believes that they are receiving the responses of the group members but, in fact, they are not; the response pattern can be programmed by the experimenter to show either agreement or disagreement with other participants.

conformity see majority influence.

There is now plentiful evidence that social influence has a significant effect even when the actions of the other people are not directly observed (e.g., Nolan, Schultz, Cialdini, Goldstein, & Griskevicius, 2008). More recently still, most studies of conformity have abandoned the group context completely, and participants receive feedback concerning other people's responses in summary form (e.g., being told that 82 per cent of the population hold a particular attitude). Comparison between different paradigms shows reliable differences, with conformity rates being highest in face-to-face situations (e.g., Levy, 1960). This is not surprising, as literally facing the majority increases normative pressures to conform. But face-to-face group pressure is not essential for longer-term change, whether it is due to informational or normative influence. A recent study which investigated social influence via interlinked computers in a network reported that conformity was still evident three weeks after the study (Heerdink, van Kleef, Homan, & Fischer, 2013).

In a clever recent study Mori and Arai (2010) replicated Asch's paradigm without the use of confederates, by colouring the tops of the stimulus lines in either green or magenta. The participants, Japanese students, wore one of two types of polarizing sunglasses to view the stimuli which, unknown to them, filtered either green or magenta, to make the lines appear longer or shorter (so the majority was created simply by having the larger number of participants wearing glasses with the same-coloured filter). Results from this paradigm showed that women conformed to the majority, but men did not. Future replications will be needed, however, to ascertain whether this difference from Asch's results is due to a change of paradigm, cultural differences (see Chapter 15), or both.

When do people conform? Asch's first studies were followed by many variants. Among the most important factors found to influence the level of conformity are group size, unanimity and social support, and culture.

In terms of the numerical size of the majority, conformity increased quite dramatically as the number of majority members (faced with a minority of one) increased from one to three, but the influence of additional members was minimal (Asch, 1951; see Figure 8.5). However, results are rather inconsistent (see Gerard, Wilhelmy, & Conolley, 1968; Reis, Earing, Kent, & Nezlek, 1976). A crucial factor to avoid the levelling off of conformity after the third participant seems to be that the members of the majority must be seen to be independent, and not simply 'sheep' (Wilder, 1977); once that is the case, there is a linear increase in conformity as group size increases (Gerard et al., 1968).

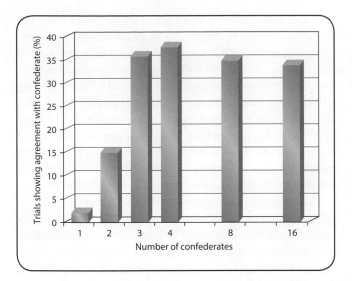

FIGURE 8.5 *Percentage of errors as a function of number of confederates.*

Source: Based on Asch, 1951.

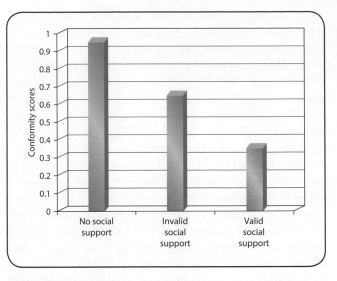

FIGURE 8.6 *Conformity in the absence and in the presence of social support.*

Source: Based on Allen & Levine, 1971. Reproduced with permission of Elsevier.

In one study Asch arranged for one of the confederates, who responded before the naïve participant, to give the correct answer. The level of conformity by the naïve participant dropped dramatically – but was this due to the correct respondent breaking the majority's unanimity, or his giving the naïve participant 'social support' for the correct answer? Another of Asch's studies was designed to answer this question, and showed that breaking the majority's unanimity was most important. When he had one of the confederates deviate from the majority, but by giving a different incorrect answer, this broke unanimity, but did not give the naïve participant a supporter. The results showed that the rates of conformity by the naïve participant reduced to nearly the same level as when there had been a social supporter. Genuine social support does, however, have a value over and above breaking unanimity when social influence concerns attitudes and opinions rather than unambiguous stimuli (see Allen, 1975, for a review). The true value of the social supporter is in providing a valid and independent assessment of reality (see Allen, 1975). Using the Asch task, Allen and Levine (1971) varied whether the participant had social support, and what type of support. In one of their two support conditions the social support was 'invalid', because the supporter was wearing spectacles with thick lenses. Although giving correct answers, this supporter could not possibly be perceived as a valid source of information on a visual-discrimination task. The results, shown in Figure 8.6, indicate that, although invalid support was better than none, valid social support was clearly most effective.

Finally, Bond and Smith (1996) conducted a meta-analysis of nearly 100 studies using the Asch conformity paradigm, and found greater acceptance of others' judgements in collectivistic cultures (which tend to subordinate individual goals to group goals) than in individualistic cultures (which tend to place an emphasis on individual goals and achievement; see Chapter 15). Indeed, the impact of culture was much greater than any other moderator of group influence, including the size of the majority. A number of potential reasons have been given for cultural differences in conformity. Many of these are based upon ecological or economic factors that vary across countries and shape cultural norms for conformity (Van de Vliert, 2009).

Why do people conform? In post-experimental interviews conducted by Asch (see Asch, 1987) participants gave a number of reasons why they yielded to the majority. Some thought the majority was wrong, but went along with them simply to feel they belonged to the group and to avoid being ostracized. Others thought that the majority must be right, as they were the only person to see the task differently, i.e., 'several pairs of eyes' are more likely to be correct than the one pair of the naïve participant.

These different reasons given for yielding to the majority map closely onto theoretical accounts of conformity. The most popular explanation for conformity is based upon Festinger's perspective on small group behaviour, which we described earlier in this chapter. Group members are cognitively and socially dependent on each other (Festinger, 1950), because opinion uniformity helps them to validate their opinions (social reality) and to move the group towards its goals (group locomotion).

Explanations for the Asch studies also relied on Deutsch and Gerard's (1955) distinction between normative and informational social influence, introduced earlier. If conformity is related to the desire to be liked (normative influence) and the desire to be right (informational influence) then factors that affect these desires should increase the likelihood of conformity. In terms of normative social influence, conformity should be greater when people believe they are part of a group than when they do not. Making the group salient will increase people's desire to be part of the group and therefore increase conformity. This was shown in the study by Deutsch and Gerard (1955) that used the Asch paradigm. They found that conformity increased when participants were told they were part of a group, and that the best-performing groups in the study would win a prize, compared to a condition in which no such information was given. On the other hand, conformity decreased when participants' responses were anonymous (via the Crutchfield apparatus discussed earlier). In terms of informational influence, factors that increase the credibility of the majority as a valid source of reality (e.g., status and expertise) lead to more conformity (Kiesler & Kiesler, 1969). Also, factors that weaken the credibility of the majority as a valid source of information reduce conformity (e.g., breaking the majority consensus as shown above; Allen & Levine, 1971). What exactly Asch's studies showed continues to be debated by social psychologists. As Hodges and Geyer (2006) pointed out, multiple strategies may underlie participants' behaviour (e.g., the typical pattern of varying responses between dissent and agreement might be a deliberate, strategic attempt to appear cooperative).

Traditionally, researchers have distinguished between private acceptance and public compliance by showing that influence persists (a) in the absence of the influencing group or (b) when participants respond anonymously. However, Wood (2000) has criticized the use of anonymous responding as a measure of private acceptance, and in their meta-analysis of the Asch paradigm, Bond and Smith (1996) found no difference in levels of agreement when participants knew their responses would be known by the majority compared to when they did not. Zaki, Schirmer, and Mitchell (2011) used a social neuroscience approach to try to distinguish true modification of judgements from mere public compliance. Using a task in which participants privately rated the attractiveness of faces, they found that participants conformed to false feedback about ratings of their peers. They rated faces as more attractive when they had received feedback that peers rated the faces higher than they had, compared

to when they had received feedback that peers rated the faces lower than they had. Most interestingly, neuroimaging showed that this social influence was accompanied by activity in two brain regions – the nucleus accumbens and the orbitofrontal cortex – associated with coding subjective value. When participants viewed faces that they believed had been rated more positively by their peers than by themselves, there was greater activity in these regions than when they viewed faces rated less positively by their peers. Klucharev et al. (2009), also adopting a neuroscience approach, found that conflict with group opinion triggered a neuronal response in two other specific areas, the rostral cingulate zone and the ventral striatum. They concluded that social conformity is linked to error-monitoring at the neural level, which signals the danger of our responses, and hence us, being 'too different' from others.

More generally, we can understand conformity by considering three main goals that it can serve (Cialdini & Goldstein, 2004; Cialdini & Trost, 1998). A shift towards a group consensus can allow the individual (1) to believe that he or she now sees things more accurately; (2) to gain the approval and acceptance of positively-viewed others; and (3) to avoid a self-concept as different, deviant or as refusing to compromise for the good of the group.

Minority influence and innovation Research on conformity focused on the ability of the majority to influence the individual, and therefore neglected the possibility that the individual (or minority) could influence the majority. According to Festinger's account that was the dominant early explanation of conformity, minorities lack the resources to make majority members dependent on them. Minorities, by definition, lack power, status and numerical size, and therefore do not have the means to enforce normative or informational influence.

Yet history is replete with examples of individuals and minorities who, through their actions, have had a tremendous impact upon the majority in society. It was this observation by the French social psychologist, Serge Moscovici (1976, 1980), that led to a theoretical re-shaping of the area. Moscovici argued that if social influence only relied upon conformity to the majority, then it would be difficult to see how groups would change, new ideas develop and innovation might occur. Moscovici argued that minorities are distinctive – they stand out from the crowd – and from this distinctiveness they can create conflict within the majority by challenging the dominant majority view, and in so doing offer a new and different perspective. Since people wish to avoid conflict, they will often dismiss the minority position by attributing its deviancy to some underlying, undesirable psychological dimension (Papastamou, 1986). For example, the minority might be seen as 'crazy', 'biased' or 'provocative' in an attempt to explain its deviant view. Indeed, if one considers many 'successful' minorities (such as, Galileo, Freud and Copernicus or, more recently, politicians representing the Green Party, who have moved from the margins to the mainstream of politics), they often suffered ridicule and rejection by the majority before their views became accepted.

In order to overcome people's inclination to reject the deviant minority, the minority must adopt a particular style of behaviour that communicates to the majority that the minority is sure of, and committed to, its position. Moscovici termed this the minority's behavioural style and he emphasized, above all, **consistency**: the need

> **consistency** a behavioural style indicating that the same position is maintained across time; seen as central to minority influence.

for the minority to respond with the same response to the same issue over time. Moscovici, Lage, and Naffrechoux (1969) demonstrated these ideas experimentally. They presented groups of six female participants with a series of slides that were unambiguously blue and differed only in their light intensity. To each slide, every participant was required to say aloud the colour of the slide. In a control condition, participants not exposed to influence named the colour of the slide as 'blue' on almost all trials (99.75 per cent). However, in one condition the group contained two confederates (a numerical minority), who were seated such that they gave their responses, aloud, before the naïve participants, and were instructed to call the blue slides 'green' on every trial. When this occurred the naïve participants also called the slide green on 8.42 per cent of occasions, and this was significantly higher than in the control condition (0.25 per cent) that had no confederates. The importance of the minority responding consistently was shown in a third condition of the experiment, where the confederates were inconsistent (they responded randomly green to only some of the slides, and blue to others). When the minority was inconsistent, the percentage of green responses from the naïve participants fell to 1.25 per cent, which was not different from the control condition (see Figure 8.7). It is clear that for a minority to be successful it must respond consistently (see also Nemeth, Swedlund, & Kanki, 1974).

Theoretical approaches to majority and minority influence

There are currently two broad explanations for majority–minority influence phenomena, each of which subsumes several theories (Levine & Moreland, 1998). We term these the 'conflict' and 'social categorization' approaches.

Moscovici (1976, 1980) argued that conflict was the critical factor underlying influence. According to him, all

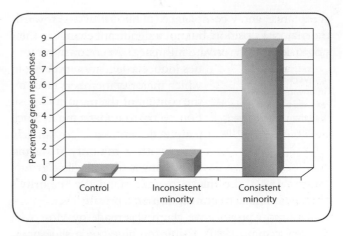

FIGURE 8.7 *Percentage green responses given by majority participants in the experiment by Moscovici, Lage, and Naffrechoux (1969).*

MOSCOVICI'S (1980) CONVERSION THEORY

- Majority influence
  - generates **comparison** process (focus on relationship between source and target)
  - conflict is resolved by overt compliance to majority position in **public**, and/or
  - on **direct** measures without further consideration of the issue
- Minority influence
  - triggers **validation** process (closer attention to the issue)
  - target is unlikely to agree with minority in public, for fear of being labelled 'deviant'
  - but cognitive processing of minority message can lead to conversion in **private** and/or **indirect** attitude change

forms of influence, whether from a majority or minority, result in conflict and individuals are motivated to reduce that conflict. However, Moscovici's (1980) dual-process 'conversion theory' argues that people employ different processes, with different outcomes, depending on whether the source of the conflict is a majority or a minority (see Theory Box 8.2). Moscovici proposed a contrast between two types of process, *comparison* and *validation*, which has some similarities to Deutsch and Gerard's (1955) distinction between normative and informational influence. Moscovici argued that majorities induce a comparison process, in which the target of influence focuses on the discrepancy between his or her position and that advocated by the majority. The minority targets, because they wish to gain the majority's acceptance, show compliance (public influence) towards the majority position, but not a significant change in their original position (private influence). In contrast, minorities induce a validation process, in which majority members focus on the content of the minority's position, to try to understand it. Since people do not wish to publicly agree with a minority (to avoid identifying with a deviant group, Mugny, 1982), the quest to understand the minority's position can lead to **conversion** on a private level.

conversion a change in private response after exposure to influence by others; internalized change; a change in the way one structures an aspect of reality.

The most provocative claim was made by Moscovici and Personnaz (1980). Using the blue-green slide paradigm, they claimed that if a minority consistently responded that a blue slide was 'green', then even though they could not bring that participant to accept that direct influence, they would exert influence on an indirect and private level. In this case the indirect level was the chromatic complementary after-image of the slide. The after-image is what one sees when one views a white screen after viewing a coloured slide; the after-image of blue is yellow-orange, and of green it is red-purple. Of course, the experimenters did not tell participants that different colours were linked to different after-images, and it is assumed that participants were ignorant of this too.

Moscovici and Personnaz did indeed find that when minority-influenced participants reported what colour after-image they saw on a white screen, they tended to see the after-image of a blue slide as more red-purple (complementary colour for green) than did majority-influenced and no-influence control participants, consistent with the idea that they had begun to see the slide as the minority saw it, as 'green'. However, despite the novelty of the study, the claim that a minority can cause a perceptual conversion is implausible, given what we know about the physiology of after-images. There have also been failures to replicate, and the study has been criticized on methodological grounds (see Martin & Hewstone, 2001a, 2012, for a discussion).

A much less contentious way of measuring indirect influence is to measure influence on a target attitude, and on an indirectly-related attitude. For example, Pérez and Mugny (1987) exposed participants to a counter-attitudinal pro-abortion message that was attributed to either a majority or minority source. The researchers then measured participants' attitudes towards both the target issue, abortion, and an indirectly-related issue, birth control. Although the issue of birth control had not been mentioned in the source's message, it is related to it at a superordinate level (i.e., someone who is pro-abortion would also tend to be pro-birth control). While the minority had little impact on the direct abortion

issue, it had a large impact on the birth control issue – participants had become more favourable to birth control. This was not found when the source was a majority. This result shows that the impact of the minority was low on direct attitudes (presumably because participants did not want to identify publicly with the minority) but the minority had a 'hidden impact' (Maass & Clark, 1984) on a related indirect attitude (see also Alvaro & Crano, 1997).

Moscovici's theory has received partial support from an extensive meta-analysis by Wood, Lundgren, Ouellette, Busceme, and Blackstone (1994). Overall, they reported that majorities had greater influence than minorities on both public measures and direct measures responded to in private. Minorities were, however, equally or more influential than majorities on indirect measures responded to in private.

An important recent development in this area has been the increased use of theory and methodology derived from the persuasion literature (see Chapter 7) to understand majority and minority influence. Specifically, researchers have drawn a parallel between Moscovici's concepts of comparison and validation and the distinction between non-systematic and systematic processing made in models of persuasion (the elaboration likelihood model and the heuristic–systematic model) (see Maass & Clark, 1983; Martin & Hewstone, 2001b). Thus, studies have manipulated source status (majority versus minority) and argument quality (strong versus weak arguments). This design allows the researcher to investigate which source is associated with systematic processing; if processing is systematic, there should be greater persuasion by the strong than the weak message, as well as more message-congruent thoughts, and these thoughts should mediate attitude change. There is, however, disagreement amongst researchers concerning which source condition (minority or majority) should elicit the most cognitive scrutiny of the message, with some advocating superior message processing associated with a minority (e.g., Moscovici, 1980), others advocating this for the majority (e.g., Mackie, 1987), and still others proposing that both a majority and minority can lead to message processing under different circumstances (e.g., Baker & Petty, 1994).

Martin and Hewstone (2008) have developed a theoretical framework that accounts for these inconsistent results. Based on Petty and Cacioppo's (1986a, b) elaboration likelihood model, it is termed the 'source context elaboration model' (see also Crano & Chen, 1998; De Dreu & De Vries, 1993; De Vries, De Dreu, Gordijn, & Schuurman, 1996), and now has extensive empirical support (see Martin & Hewstone, 2008, for a review). Essentially this approach makes two broad sets of predictions concerning (a) the types of processes underlying majority and minority influence and when they occur, and (b) the consequences for attitudes following majority and minority influence.

The first set of predictions states that the effects of source status (majority versus minority) vary along an elaboration continuum (the extent to which the situation allows or encourages elaboration of the source's message). When the elaboration demands are low (e.g., the topic is low in personal relevance), message recipients do not process the source's arguments, and attitudes can be guided through simple heuristics (such as the consensus heuristic, 'the majority is more likely to be right than the minority'). When elaboration demands are high (e.g., the topic is high in personal relevance), then people will attend to, and process, arguments from both the majority and the minority source, and there should be attitude change to the message containing strong than weak arguments in each case. However, most influence situations to which people are exposed are not characterized by either very low or high processing demands but, rather, are located at an intermediate level. In this situation, Martin and Hewstone proposed that Moscovici's (1980) conversion theory should apply – that is, systematic processing of only the minority arguments.

Martin, Hewstone, and Martin (2007, Experiment 2) presented participants with a set of typed strong or weak anti-voluntary euthanasia arguments, and assessed both thoughts generated and attitudes. Portions of the arguments were repeated alongside the original message (the selected text). The level of message elaboration was manipulated by asking participants to conduct one of three tasks on the selected text. In the low elaboration condition participants were asked simply to check whether the selected text was written in the same font type and size as the original message. This task should result in only shallow message processing, and therefore there should be no effect of argument quality. However, the majority source, operating via a consensus heuristic, should have greater impact on attitudes than the minority source. In the intermediate elaboration condition participants were asked to check the spelling of words in the selected text. This task requires semantic processing of single words, and Martin et al. predicted message processing only for the minority source, due to its distinctiveness leading to message validation (cf. Moscovici, 1980). Finally, in the high elaboration condition participants were asked to paraphrase some highlighted portions of the presented texts in different words but to convey the same meaning as the original text. This task requires semantic processing of sentences, and Martin et al. therefore predicted that strong arguments (regardless of majority/minority support)

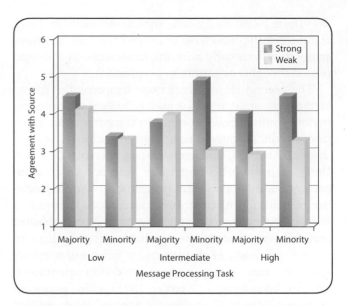

FIGURE 8.8 *Agreement as a function of numerical size of source, argument quality and level of message processing task.*
Source: Based on Martin et al., 2007; Expt. 2, with permission from SAGE.

would have greater impact on the reported attitudes than weak arguments.

Results for attitudes (agreement with source) confirmed the authors' hypotheses (see Figure 8.8). In the low elaboration condition, the only reliable effect was for source status, with the majority having more influence than the minority. The lack of an argument quality effect suggests the source status main effect was due to non-elaborative processing. In the intermediate elaboration condition, there was a reliable interaction between source status and argument quality, showing a difference between strong and weak messages for the minority but not majority source. Finally, in the high elaboration condition there was an argument quality effect for *both* majority and minority sources, showing participants had engaged in elaborative processing for both sources.

The pattern of results for message-congruent thoughts complemented the attitude data. In the low elaboration condition there were no reliable effects, consistent with the claim that attitudes were guided by heuristic cues and not by elaboration of the source's arguments. In the intermediate elaboration condition there was a reliable interaction between source status and argument quality that mirrored the pattern found for attitudes. Finally, in the high elaboration condition, the only reliable finding was for argument quality. Further evidence that the argument quality effect was due to elaborative processing comes from the finding that the proportion of message-congruent thinking in both the intermediate and high elaboration conditions mediated the effects found on attitude scores (see Horcajo, Petty, & Briñol, 2010, who have examined the role of source status in differentially affecting confidence in message-related thoughts as a route to persuasion).

The second set of predictions concerns the nature of the attitudes that are formed following majority and minority influence. According to the persuasion literature, attitudes formed through systematic processing are 'strong' (Krosnick, Boninger, Chuang, Berent, & Carnot, 1993) in terms of being more resistant to counter-persuasion, more persistent over time, and more predictive of behaviour than attitudes formed via nonsystematic processing. Martin and Hewstone have published consistent evidence showing that minorities lead to 'strong' attitudes, in that attitudes following minority influence were more resistant to counter-persuasion (Martin, Hewstone, & Martin, 2003), more persistent over time (Martin, Hewstone, & Martin, 2008) and better predictors of behaviour (Martin, Martin, Smith, & Hewstone, 2007) compared to attitudes formed following majority influence. Turn now to Research Close-Up 8.2, which summarizes the evidence that minority-instigated attitudes are more resistant to counter-persuasion.

There is also support for the conflict explanation of majority–minority influence from Nemeth's (1986, 1995) research and her convergent–divergent theory (see Leader in the Field, Charlan Jeanne Nemeth). According to Nemeth, majority versus minority status does not affect the *amount* of thinking about the message, but the *type* of thinking and the focus of thoughts. She has consistently found that majorities produce a narrow focus on the message they present, whereas minorities produce a broader focus on new information and attitudinal positions. Her explanation for this effect is that learning that the majority has a different position to oneself creates stress, particularly if the majority is physically present, and stress is known to narrow the focus of attention. Specifically, exposure to majority influence leads to message-relevant, convergent thinking, which yields uncreative solutions to problems. In contrast, exposure to minority influence leads to issue-relevant, divergent thinking, producing creative problem-solving solutions (e.g., Maass & Volpato, 1994; Mucchi-Faina, Maass, & Volpato, 1991; Nemeth & Kwan, 1985). Consistent with this view, exposure to majority dissent is more helpful than exposure to minority dissent when a task requires convergent thinking, while minority dissent is more effective on tasks requiring divergent thinking (Nemeth, Mosier, & Chiles, 1992).

In an illustrative study of how minorities lead to more creative task performance Nemeth and Wachtler (1983) conducted a study involving an embedded figures test (see Figure 8.10). Participants had to identify if a standard

LEADER IN THE FIELD

Charlan Jeanne Nemeth (b. 1941) was born in St. Louis, Missouri. She received her BA in Mathematics from Washington University in St. Louis in 1963, an MA in Social Psychology from the University of Wisconsin-Madison in 1965, and a PhD in Psychology from Cornell University in 1968 (where her advisors were Len Berkowitz (see Leader in the Field, Chapter 9) and Steve Jones). One year after her PhD, she spent a year working with two of the founding fathers of European Social Psychology, Henri Tajfel (Bristol; see Leader in the Field, Chapter 14) and Serge Moscovici (Paris; see Leader in the Field, this chapter). She is currently professor in the Department of Psychology, University of California, Berkeley. For most of her professional career she has studied small group decision-making with an emphasis on the ways in which such decisions can be made 'better', more correct and more creative. Her work on the value of dissent has been broadly applied in the law as it pertains to jury decision-making, and in business as it pertains to corporate cultures of innovation.

figure was contained (or embedded) within a set of comparisons. The participants were led to believe that either a numerical majority (four out of six group members) or a numerical minority (only two out of six members) supported a particular answer. When people were exposed to a majority view, they followed that majority answer exactly (i.e., they identified the standard figure in other figures, but in the same orientation as the majority source had, for example stimulus U in Figure 8.10), or they performed as they would alone. However, when people were exposed to a minority view, they detected more instances of the standard figure, including correct answers that were not proposed by the minority (i.e., they identified the standard figure in more other figures, and both in the same orientation as the minority source had done, and when inverted, or rotated; e.g., stimuli I and R in Figure 8.10). These results show improved task performance as a result of exposure to minority rather than majority dissent.

Research has recently investigated the nature of the arguments *generated by* individuals who find themselves in either a numerical majority or minority (Kenworthy, Hewstone, Levine, Martin, & Willis, 2008). Because they are outnumbered, numerical minorities must necessarily take multiple perspectives – both their own as well as that of the numerical majority – in order to reduce the threat of invalidation. By contrast, numerical majorities will be less motivated to adopt others' perspective and to think in novel and creative ways to defend their position, because their opinion has the weight of consensus (see Levine & Russo, 1995). In three studies Kenworthy et al. (2008) showed that being in a numerical minority led to the generation of arguments that were rated more original and convincing (by judges blind to experimental

MINORITY SOURCES INDUCE STRONGER ATTITUDES

Martin, R., Hewstone, M., & Martin, P. Y. (2003). Resistance to persuasive messages as a function of majority and minority source status. *Journal of Experimental Social Psychology, 39*, 585–593.

Introduction

As the main text of the chapter explains, Moscovici's (1980) conversion theory predicts that minority influence leads to greater message processing than does majority influence. This paper reports three studies that take a different, and novel, approach to examining this hypothesis. We describe one study here. In this study the participants were exposed to two messages that argued different positions in relation to the same topic. The messages were delayed in time, and participants completed attitude measures after each message. The first message (initial message) argued a pro-euthanasia position, while the second argued the opposite, anti-euthanasia position (counter-message).

If attitudes following the initial message had been formed from processing the message in detail, then these attitudes should resist the second counter-message. Active processing of the arguments in the initial message (i.e., thinking of issues in agreement with the message) should provide individuals with arguments to resist the attack from the second counter-message. If, however, the attitudes formed following the first message were *not* based upon detailed message processing, then these attitudes should be influenced by (or yield to) the second message.

The authors predicted that if minority influence leads to greater message processing, as proposed by Moscovici (1980), then attitudes formed following exposure to a minority should be more resistant to a second counter-message than are attitudes formed following majority influence.

Method

Participants and design

The participants were 69 undergraduate students at a British university (25 males and 44 females) who were randomly assigned to one of two conditions (majority versus minority support of initial message).

Stimulus materials

The topic of the message was the legalization of voluntary euthanasia (i.e., the right to end life if suffering from a terminal illness). Pre-testing had shown that the participants were moderately in favour of voluntary euthanasia. Two messages were employed which used strong and persuasive arguments that were either against (initial message) or in favour of (counter-message) voluntary euthanasia.

Procedure

Participants were tested in groups of between two and five. The study had five stages. First, participants rated their attitude towards voluntary euthanasia on a 9-point scale from 1 – *totally disagree* to 9 – *totally agree* (pre-test). Second, they were informed that a recent survey at their university showed that either 82 per cent (majority) or 18 per cent (minority) of students were in favour of legalizing voluntary euthanasia. They then read several arguments that summarized the majority or minority position in favour of voluntary euthanasia (initial message) (note, the researchers presented the same arguments in each condition, only the majority/minority label changed). Third, participants' attitudes towards voluntary euthanasia were measured again on the same 9-point scale employed in the first booklet (post-test I: initial message). Fourth, participants were then shown arguments that conveyed the opposite perspective to the initial message; that is, against voluntary euthanasia (counter-message). Fifth, participants rated their attitude towards voluntary euthanasia for a third time on the 9-point scale (post-test II: counter-message).

Results

Scores on the attitude scale were reverse-coded so that high scores indicated greater influence to the initial message while low scores indicated greater influence to the counter-message. As can be seen from Figure 8.9, the participants were influenced by both the majority and minority, as there was a significant change in attitudes between pre-test and post-test I: initial message, in the direction of the source of influence. The amount of change in the majority and minority conditions was the same. At this stage, it appears that the majority and minority led to the same amount of influence, but the results for the counter-message show this was derived from different processes.

The prediction was that attitudes following majority influence would result from compliance, without thinking about the message arguments in detail and, therefore, these attitudes should yield to a counter-message. This is what happened in the majority condition, as the scores

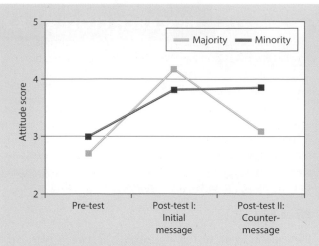

FIGURE 8.9 *Mean attitudes as a function of majority versus minority source and pre-test, post-test 1 (initial message) and post-test II (counter-message).*

Note: Greater agreement with the source of the first message is reflected by *high* scores on the initial message and *low* scores on the counter-message. Resistance is measured by the difference between the initial message and the counter-message – the smaller the difference, the greater the resistance. The figure shows that when the source of the initial message is a majority, scores revert to the baseline at post-test II. In contrast, when the source of the initial message is a minority, scores resist counter influence (post-test II remains at the level of post-test I).

Source: Data from Martin, Hewstone, & Martin, 2003. Reproduced with permission of Elsevier.

following the counter-message (post-test II) were significantly lower than scores following the initial message (post-test I). In fact, in the majority condition, attitudes

following the counter-message reduced to the same level as the pre-test attitude; this suggests that the attitude change to the initial message was only superficial, as attitudes returned to their pre-test level when exposed to the counter-message.

By contrast, the prediction was that attitudes following minority influence would be due to detailed evaluation of the minority's arguments, and this should enable participants to resist the counter-message. Again, this is what happened. There was no difference in attitude scores between the initial message (post-test I) and the counter-message (post-test II), showing that participants had not changed their attitude (i.e., had resisted) when exposed to the second message.

Discussion

This is the first investigation of resistance to persuasion in the context of majority and minority influence and it offers a new demonstration, consistent with Moscovici's (1980) conversion theory, of greater message processing induced by a minority, compared with a majority, source. However, the authors acknowledge that majorities can, and often do, encourage systematic message processing but in situations that encourage message elaboration. This was shown in another study where participants were told, before they read the majority message, that they would later be asked to recall the arguments contained in it (this procedure should encourage message processing). With these instructions, attitudes following majority influence also resisted the counter-message (Martin, Hewstone, & Martin, 2008).

condition and hypotheses of the experiment) than those produced by participants in the numerical majority condition. For a broader analysis of how minority status affects how people think, feel, and relate to others, see Butera and Levine (2009). We will return to the value of dissent within groups later, in the section on group decision-making. There we see that an over-emphasis on harmony and consensus, and a failure to encourage and attend to diverse viewpoints, can lead to disastrous decision-making.

Whereas the dependence and conflict approaches focus on intragroup processes, the social categorization account focuses on intergroup *and* intragroup processes (Mugny, 1982; Mugny & Pérez, 1991; Turner, Hogg, Oakes, Reicher, & Wetherell, 1987). Mugny and Pérez argue that minority influence occurs if identification with the source is compatible with a positive social identity (essentially, the extent to which one feels positive about membership of a group; see Chapter 14).

According to this view, minorities categorized as outgroups have little direct influence, but can have indirect influence if they induce a validation process (see also Mugny, Butera, Sanchez-Mazas, & Pérez, 1995; Pérez & Mugny, 1996; Quiamzade, Mugny, Falomir-Pichastor, & Butera, 2010), whereas minorities categorized as ingroups can produce direct influence, because the target of influence identifies with the source of influence. (See also research by Crano and colleagues suggesting that ingroup minorities are evaluated in a more open-minded way, e.g., Alvaro & Crano, 1997; Crano & Alvaro, 1997; Crano & Chen, 1998).

The impact of group identification on social influence also lies at the heart of the **self-categorization theory** analysis

self-categorization theory theory explaining how the process of categorizing oneself as a group member forms social identity and brings about various forms of both group (e.g., group polarization, majority–minority influence) and intergroup (e.g., intergroup discrimination) behaviours.

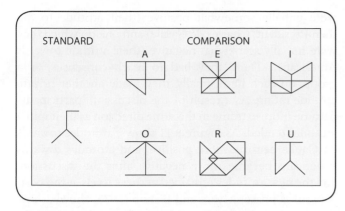

FIGURE 8.10 *Stimuli used by Nemeth and Wachtler (1983).*

Source: Nemeth & Wachtler, 1983. Reproduced with permission of John Wiley & Sons, Ltd.

of majority and minority influence (see Turner, 1991). According to self-categorization theory (for a fuller account see Chapters 5 and 14), individuals identify with a particular group and conform to a prototypical group position. This form of social influence is termed **referent informational influence**. The prototypical position maximizes both similarities between ingroup members and differences between ingroup and outgroup (Hogg, Turner, & Davidson, 1990; Mackie, 1986). Self-categorization theory predicts that social influence will occur only if three conditions are met: (1) the target perceives that the source disagrees with his or her position; (2) the source and target are perceived as members of the same group; and (3) the source's position is prototypical of the group norm (i.e., it is most typical of the ingroup, and least typical of the outgroup; Van Knippenberg, Lossie, & Wilke, 1994).

> **referent informational influence** individuals identify with a particular group and conform to a prototypical group position.

People have a need to hold attitudes consistent with their social identities, and according to self-categorization theory people adopt ingroup positions to reduce subjective uncertainty about their responses. Disagreement with others categorized as similar to the self, however, conveys subjective uncertainty, and motivates people to resolve the discrepancy by means of mutual social influence. David and Turner (1996, 1999) provided evidence for self-categorization theory. They found majority compliance and minority conversion only when the source of influence was categorized as similar to the target of influence; when the source was characterized as being dissimilar to the target of influence there was no direct or indirect influence (see also Gordijn, Postmes, & De Vries, 2001).

To summarize, there is clear support for Moscovici's (1980) proposal that we should study the influence of minorities as well as majorities. However, there is mixed support for his theory, as there is for self-categorization theory's prediction that only ingroup minorities will have an impact. There is evidence that both majorities and minorities can instigate detailed processing of their messages, under specific circumstances, and that both ingroup and outgroup minorities can exert influence; typically, however, the influence of ingroup minorities will be greater, and it will be shown primarily on indirect private measures of influence and on measures of divergent thinking.

One final observation we make about research on minority influence is that how and where we do research may have underestimated the impact of minorities (Hewstone & Martin, 2010). For example, while the meta-analysis carried out by Wood et al. (1994) found that minority influence is more likely to be indirect rather than direct, is more frequently found in private rather than public contexts, and tends to be delayed rather than immediate, this may not be the case when we study influence processes in freely-interacting groups, which allow for reciprocal exchange between minority and majority members, and especially when consensus must be reached (see Smith & Tindale, 2010). Research conducted using freely-interacting groups has shown that the presence of a minority source of influence brings about a change in how the group considers and treats the evidence before it (see Schulz-Hardt, Frey, Lüthgens, & Moscovici, 2000), and, generally, this is associated with an improvement in the group's products or decisions (e.g., Brodbeck, Kerschreiter, Mojzisch, Frey, & Schulz-Hardt, 2002; see Chapter 13). However, as indicated above, the issue of level of influence is particularly important in freely-interacting groups where social pressures to conform will be greater. For example, Sinaceur, Thomas-Hunt, Neale, O'Neill and Haag (2010) found that minority factions, in a group decision-task, led majority individuals to be more accurate on private post-group discussion judgements than on public group discussion judgements. This effect only occurred, however, when the minorities were seen as experts at the task. Minorities may also have more impact outside the laboratory, in organizations for example (Grant & Patil, 2012). Whereas empirical studies in our laboratories show that minorities, compared with majorities, are rarely able to exert direct influence in changing the views of others, Aime and Van Dyne (2010) argue that the study of groups in organizations provides a more balanced view of the impact of minorities and majorities on issues that are important to group functioning. For example, research by De Dreu and colleagues (e.g., De Dreu & West, 2001), using diverse work groups, has shown that minority dissent stimulates the consideration of multiple perspectives in a decision-making task and enhances group creativity (see also Park & DeShon, 2010). Given that much of our social interaction now takes place online, it will also be a topic for future research to investigate whether factors originally thought to play a role in face-to-face communication will also prove important when working in virtual groups or in groups dispersed geographically (see Bazarova, Walther, & McLeod, 2012).

Group decision making

Why do groups make more extreme decisions than individuals?

Group polarization Imagine that you get together with a group of friends and discuss your favourite lectures. If you reach a group decision on, say, your evaluation of the social-psychology course, is it likely to be the average of your individual views? In fact, although this was originally thought to be how groups made decisions, through research on norm formation such as the work of Sherif (1936) discussed earlier, research has

group polarization
tendency to make decisions that are more extreme than the average of group members' initial positions, in the direction already favoured by the group.

shown that far from an 'averaging' process, group discussion is associated with a 'polarizing' process. **Group polarization** refers to the tendency to make decisions that are more extreme than the average of group members' initial positions, in the direction already favoured by the group. Individual members' private opinions then converge on this polarized decision. Although many of the relevant studies demonstrate *attitude* polarization we emphasize that, consistent with our description of the field of social influence in general, the same phenomenon has been demonstrated for many kinds of judgements and decisions, including stereotypes, interpersonal impressions and jury decisions (see Lamm & Myers, 1978, and Social Psychology Beyond the Lab 8.1). There is plentiful empirical evidence for group polarization, and it has a broad impact on social and political life (see Sunstein, 2009).

The phenomenon of group polarization was first demonstrated by Moscovici and Zavalloni (1969) (see Leader in the Field, Serge Moscovici). They had small groups of French high-school students first write down in private their attitudes towards two topics, one on which they

were initially somewhat positive (their attitude to the then-President, Charles de Gaulle) and one on which they were initially somewhat negative (their attitude towards Americans). Then, they had to reach consensus, as a group, on each item; finally, they made another private attitude rating. As a result of the discussion, participants became more extreme in the same direction as their initial attitudes tended. As Figure 8.11 shows, attitudes towards de Gaulle became more positive, and attitudes towards Americans became more negative after the discussion, and the new attitudes remained at these levels at the post-consensus phase. Myers and Bishop (1970) showed how this process can polarize racial attitudes, as those who discuss their attitudes with like-minded others become more prejudiced if they are already inclined in that direction, but less prejudiced if they are inclined to be more liberal (see Figure 8.12). This provides a neat demonstration of a process that promotes extremism (see Sunstein, 2009).

There are three main explanations for this effect – persuasive arguments, social comparison, and self-categorization – which we will, first, review and then integrate (see Theory Box 8.3).

Persuasive arguments As the discussion in a group unfolds, individuals typically learn something from each other; the discussion allows for an exchange of knowledge, opinions, and, above all, *arguments*, as group members try to convince one another (Burnstein & Vinokur, 1977). Vinokur and Burnstein (1974) highlighted three kinds of information that circulate among members of a group: information that (1) expresses a view pro or contra the issue; (2) contains some novelty (which is intrinsically persuasive); and (3) has cogency (the ability to

LEADER IN THE FIELD

Serge Moscovici (1925–2014) was born in Romania to Jewish parents. Following systematic discrimination, including exclusion from high school, he was a victim of the 1941 Bucharest pogrom, and was interned in a Nazi forced labour camp. He made his way secretly to France, where he studied psychology at the Sorbonne. His professional career has been spent at the Ecole des Hautes Etudes en Sciences Sociales, Paris, with visiting appointments in Princeton, and at the New School for Social Research, New York. He became director of the Laboratoire Européen de Psychologie Sociale (European Laboratory of Social Psychology) at the Maison des Sciences de l'Homme, Paris. His ground-breaking contributions to the study of social influence comprise the very first experimental studies of both group polarization and minority influence. He was one of the giants of European social psychology, as well as one of its founding fathers, whose impact on the discipline would be hard to exaggerate.

SOCIAL PSYCHOLOGY BEYOND THE LAB 8.1

JURY DECISION-MAKING

Although we have focused on experimental studies of social influence in this chapter, there is no shortage of examples of these phenomena in the real world, nor of applications of the relevant theory and research. One prime example is the work of juries, a group of 12 laypeople who, primarily in countries with English common-law traditions, decide on culpability in criminal trials or liability in civil trials. An average of 390,000 British citizens serve as jurors each year (Waller, Hope, Burrowes, & Morrison, 2011). These groups make important, sometimes literally life-and-death, decisions. But they are often quite homogeneous – famously described by British judge, Lord Devlin, as 'middle aged, middle minded and middle class' – and illustrate several of the phenomena discussed in this chapter.

Social psychologists have studied juries for many years, typically using an experimental trial-simulation methodology (because, for legal reasons, researchers are not permitted direct access to jurors' decisions). While this may appear to be a fundamental weakness of the relevant research, because the laboratory analogue cannot exactly reproduce the pressures and responsibilities of a real jury, Kerr (1995) notes that laboratory and jury groups are similar in that they are both *ad hoc* collections of people who, initially, do not know each other.

Although some key aspects of how juries operate involve individual decision-making tendencies and biases (involving the *juror*, rather than the *jury*, see Hastie, 1993), social psychologists have focused on jury deliberation processes (e.g., Hastie, Penrod, & Pennington, 1983; Stasser, Kerr, & Bray, 1982). Many of the phenomena considered in this chapter (and the two chapters in this volume that deal with group dynamics, Chapters 12 and 13) can be seen at work in juries. Here we will highlight some of those relating to social influence, focusing on group polarization, majority influence and minority influence.

Juries clearly show group polarization. A classic legal source noted that verdicts handed down are more extreme than the individual jury members' initial judgements, but always in the same direction as the initial judgements (Kalven & Zeisel, 1966). Moreover, bias found in individual jurors' judgements (e.g., attention paid to pre-trial publicity) tends to be accentuated by deliberating juries (Stasser et al., 1982). Myers and Kaplan (1976) studied this issue experimentally, by forming mock juries that had to determine the guilt of defendants. Via a manipulation of the strength of the evidence, some groups already initially favoured conviction, while other groups initially favoured acquittal. Discussions within each of these kinds of groups led to a polarization of these initial tendencies (see also Hastie et al., 1983). Subdividing the group of 12 into smaller groups for part of the deliberation process might be one way to weaken this tendency to polarize. Waller, Hope, Burrowes, and Morrison (2011) compared decision-making in mock juries that were and were not subdivided, and found that individuals in the subdivided groups reported more equal contribution of group members and less inhibition about contribution to the group discussion.

Juries also illustrate majority influence, because initial, pre-deliberation majorities nearly always prevail in the criminal courts (Kalven & Zeisel, 1966). Moreover, social psychologists studying juries emphasize that jury deliberation involves more than simple persuasion (i.e., informational influence) and, in fact, there is a strong normative component (Kerr, 1995).

Smith and Tindale (2010) demonstrate that once it achieves a two-thirds majority, the majority view tends to determine the outcome of the jury decision process (Davis, 1980; Tindale & Davis, 1983). They note, however, that, overall, jurors who support acquittal tend to be more influential than those who support conviction (Davis, Kerr, Stasser, Meek, & Holt, 1977; Kerr & MacCoun, 1985; Tindale, Davis, Vollrath, Nagao, & Hinsz, 1990), most likely because the not-guilty verdict is in keeping with social norms. Therefore, even if seven members of a twelve-person jury favour guilty at the beginning of their deliberation, the final verdict is more likely than not to be defined by the five-person minority favouring not guilty; thus minority influence is at work too.

The 'reasonable doubt' criterion used in law requires that jurors vote for conviction only in the event that they cannot generate any reasonable doubts concerning the defendant's guilt. Therefore, arguing in favour of acquittal is often much easier than is arguing in favour of conviction, because only one reasonable doubt needs to be generated in order to validate the acquittal position. Consistent with this notion, Kerr and MacCoun (1985) found that minority factions favouring acquittal were not influential when the reasonable doubt criterion was replaced by a 'preponderance of the evidence' criterion. Under this latter criterion, neither verdict is inherently easier to validate, and, therefore, majority factions tend to prevail.

Banned, as you are, from ever actually observing a jury deliberate, you could at least take a well-justified break from your studies of social influence to watch the classic film *Twelve Angry Men* (directed by Sidney Lumet, 1957). This film illustrates the strong normative component within juries, as the majority attempts to coerce opposed and undecided jurors. But, most famously, it demonstrates minority influence, as the main protagonist (played by Henry Fonda) succeeds in overturning an 11-to-1 jury favouring a guilty judgement. Or you could read Grove's (1998) interesting account of what it is like to serve on a jury, *The Juryman's Tale*. A recent study (Waller et al., 2011) argued that a 12-person jury constitutes an artificially large 'conversational group' and is likely to exclude some people. Using mock juries they found that participants subdivided into three subgroups of four individuals reported that they had contributed more to the decision-making process, and felt less inhibited from taking part in the discussion, than individuals in groups of 12. It did not, however, change the verdicts.

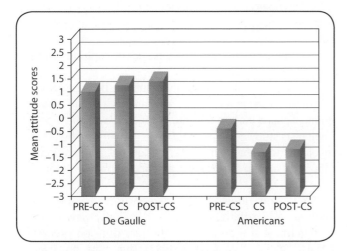

FIGURE 8.11 *Group polarization: attitudes towards de Gaulle and towards Americans in pre-consensus, consensus and post-consensus conditions.*

Source: Data copyright © 1969 by the American Psychological Association. Reproduced with permission. Moscovici, S., & Zavalloni, M. (1969). The group as a polarizer of attitudes. *Journal of Personality and Social Psychology, 12,* 125–135. The use of APA information does not imply endorsement by APA.

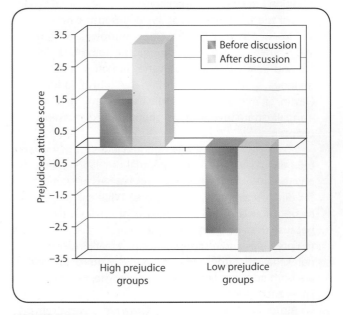

FIGURE 8.12 *Group polarization in high and low prejudice groups as a function of discussion.*

Source: From Myers, D. G., & Bishop, G. D. (1970). Discussion effects on racial attitudes. *Science, 169,* 778–779. Reprinted with permission from AAAS.

persuade). During the exchange of arguments, each individual is likely to learn novel reasons for holding the consensual view, whereby attitudes become more extreme; indeed, arguments consistent with the dominant tendency are rated more persuasive than those that contradict it, and the greater the number of arguments related to their initial position, the more group members polarize (Burnstein, Vinokur, & Trope, 1973). Discussion also provides an opportunity for individuals both to repeat their own views and to hear those views repeated by others; repetition contributes to the shift towards more extreme judgements (Brauer & Judd, 1996; Brauer, Judd, & Gliner, 1995).

Three lines of evidence support the persuasive arguments approach, also called the informational approach, because it argues that polarization is based on informational social influence (Deutsch & Gerard, 1955). First,

polarization is correlated with the ratio of pro versus con arguments available to group members; second, polarization can be produced by manipulating this ratio; and third, polarization increases with the novelty and validity of the arguments that group members hear (Kaplan & Miller, 1977; Vinokur & Burnstein, 1978). Thus, this explanation is essentially parallel to that offered by cognitive theories of persuasion (see Chapter 7): a group member's attitude is a function of the number and persuasiveness of pro and contra arguments recalled from memory when he or she formulates this position (Eagly & Chaiken, 1993).

Social comparison An alternative account of group polarization is based on social comparison theory (Festinger, 1954). It is also known as the normative

THEORY BOX 8.3

WHAT PRODUCES GROUP POLARIZATION? THREE MAIN THEORIES

A group member:

- Hears *arguments* from other group members
  1. Persuasive arguments theory
- Learns the *position* of other group members
  2. Social comparison theory
- Is more influenced by ingroup than outgroup members
  3. Self-categorization theory
- Together, these 3 processes lead to:
  4. More polarized attitudes following group discussion (more extreme, in the same direction)

explanation for polarization, because it contends that polarization is due to normative influence (Deutsch & Gerard, 1955; see above). According to this view, group members tend to compare themselves with others, and have a need to view themselves positively and gain approval from others (Goethals & Zanna, 1979; Myers & Lamm, 1976). Moreover, they wish to be different from other group members, but in a socially desirable direction; so, after learning others' positions, they shift to an even more extreme position themselves (Myers, 1978).

The main line of support for this explanation is that group polarization can be brought about, quite simply, by learning of other group members' attitudinal *positions*. Participants who received information about the distribution of other group members' positions before they made their own decisions took more extreme positions than those unaware of other group members' positions (Myers, Bach, & Schreiber, 1974). They did so, moreover, without ever hearing others' arguments, and only when they were informed about the distribution of opinions held by all other members of the group, not simply when they were informed of the group average (Myers & Kaplan, 1976).

Self-categorization A more recent normative account of group polarization acknowledges the importance of both persuasive arguments *and* members' positions, but in addition emphasizes that group membership is essential to group polarization (Turner, 1991). Polarization arises from tendencies to accentuate similarities between members of one's own group, but to differentiate from members of outgroups. Consistent with this view, polarization is enhanced by reference to an outside group

(Doise, 1969), which emphasizes the ingroup–outgroup division. Indeed, even in the absence of actual discussion between members of the same group, members' attitudes shift towards a perceived ingroup norm that best defines the group in contrast to the relevant outgroup (Hogg, Turner, & Davidson, 1990).

Whereas the earlier accounts define the group norm as the *average* position of all the group's members, and view polarization as movement beyond that norm, the self-categorization account argues that the group norm can be more extreme than the average position, and polarization can reflect movement *towards* that norm. For example, a group of conservative students may share the view that taxes should be reduced, but when they think of a comparison group (such as socialist students) who do not share this view, then they may polarize even further in their support for taxation. According to self-categorization theory (which we introduced earlier in the section on majority–minority influence), individuals identify with a particular group and conform to a prototypical group position, a position that defines views held in their group. Prototypes are individual representations of group norms, and they are formed by making comparisons, both within the group and between groups, which maximize the perceived difference between the two groups (see earlier section on minority influence). Thus, group members perceive the group's position to be more extreme than it actually is, based on the average of the group members' responses. This referent informational influence helps to define the ingroup as different from the outgroup (Hogg et al., 1990; Mackie, 1986). Interestingly, group members are more comfortable and more vocal when their opinions differ from the average group member's opinion in the direction of the group prototype, than if their opinions differ in the opposite direction (Miller & Morrison, 2009; Morrison & Miller, 2008).

There are three main lines of empirical support for the self-categorization account of group polarization. First, polarization produced by listening to a group discussion, or learning others' positions, depends on participants believing that they are members of the *same* group (i.e., ingroup members), and not a competing group (i.e., outgroup members) (Mackie & Cooper, 1984; Turner et al., 1987; Turner, Wetherell, & Hogg, 1989). Listeners also perceive the content of the discussion to be more polarized when they think the discussants are ingroup members than when they do not (Mackie, 1986). Second, polarization is mediated by group members' perceptions of the ingroup's position (Turner et al., 1989). Third, intergroup attitudinal polarization is more extreme (ingroup and outgroup positions are further apart) when group membership is more salient or members identify more strongly with their group (e.g., Mackie, 1986; Mackie & Cooper, 1984; Turner et al., 1989).

Integration It has long been acknowledged that informational and normative approaches appear to work together to produce group polarization (Kaplan & Miller, 1987). Can we say which theory best accounts for the data? In fact, they each contribute something distinctive. Isenberg's (1986) meta-analysis, which predates the self-categorization account, reported significant effect sizes for both the normative account and, especially, the persuasive-arguments account. Which kind of influence is more important depends on the context. Kaplan (1987) concluded that normative influence was more likely with judgemental issues, a group goal of harmony, person-oriented group members and public responses, whereas informational influence was more likely with intellective issues, a group goal of making a correct decision, task-oriented group members and private responses. The self-categorization account builds on the other two approaches, because it contends that *arguments* from other ingroup members will be more persuasive than those of outgroup members, and that learning the *positions* held by different ingroup members will be more persuasive than learning about the positions of outgroup members.

Groupthink Part of the explanation for research activity on group polarization is the potentially serious implications of polarization for decision-making in natural settings (Eagly & Chaiken, 1993). Such decisions are typically made by groups composed of like-minded participants (e.g., councils, committees, juries, the cabinets of ruling governments), and the processes involved may lead the groups to make decisions which are incorrect, unwise or, in the worst case, disastrous. This is most evident in the case of **groupthink**, a syndrome of poor group decision-making in which members of a cohesive ingroup strive for unanimity at the expense of a realistic appraisal of alternative courses of action (Janis, 1982; see Theory Box 8.4). Groupthink does not necessarily arise from group polarization, but it is an extreme form of problems associated with the failure to exchange information (or, at least, different views) among group members (Levine & Moreland, 1998). In essence, groupthink constitutes an extreme form of normative influence, where the norm to reach and maintain consensus and harmony within the group completely eliminates any informational influence that could show how disastrous the group's intended decision is likely to be.

> **groupthink** a syndrome of poor group decision-making in which members of a cohesive ingroup strive for unanimity at the expense of a realistic appraisal of alternative courses of action.

The concept of groupthink (which alludes to 'Big Brother's' attempt to control the way people think, in George Orwell's 1949 novel, *Nineteen Eighty-Four*) has received a great deal of popular attention, because it claims to explain a series of US foreign-policy fiascos, including the calamitous Bay of Pigs invasion of Cuba (1961) and the escalation of the Vietnam War (1964–1967). Janis applied work on group decisions to elite political settings by carrying out a series of case studies, in which he researched government records, political

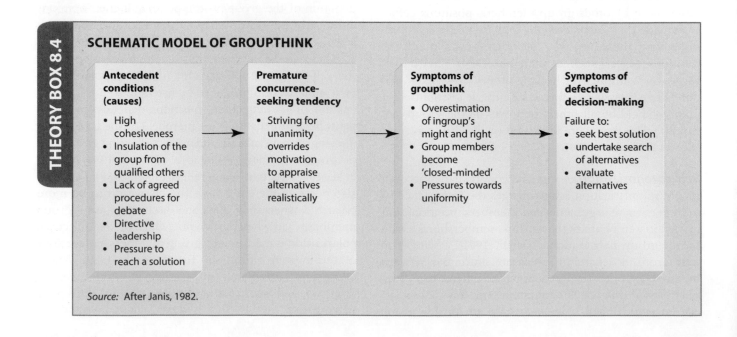

THEORY BOX 8.4

SCHEMATIC MODEL OF GROUPTHINK

Antecedent conditions (causes)
- High cohesiveness
- Insulation of the group from qualified others
- Lack of agreed procedures for debate
- Directive leadership
- Pressure to reach a solution

→

Premature concurrence-seeking tendency
- Striving for unanimity overrides motivation to appraise alternatives realistically

→

Symptoms of groupthink
- Overestimation of ingroup's might and right
- Group members become 'closed-minded'
- Pressures towards uniformity

→

Symptoms of defective decision-making
Failure to:
- seek best solution
- undertake search of alternatives
- evaluate alternatives

Source: After Janis, 1982.

diaries and politicians' accounts of these turbulent periods (see also Raven, 1974; 't Hart, 1990). According to Janis, the main causes of groupthink include high cohesiveness, insulation of the group from external critics, opinionated leadership, lack of agreed procedures for debate and pressure to reach a solution. Specifically, Janis (1982) claimed that high cohesiveness in interaction with a stressful situation leads to groupthink; this outcome will be more likely the more structural weaknesses are present in the group (e.g., insulation, directive leadership and lack of agreed decision-making procedures).

In turn, some of the main characteristics of groupthink decision-makers are that they are more prone to jump to premature conclusions, dismiss contradictory information, bolster preferred options, suppress dissent within the group and display excessive optimism about the outcomes (Tetlock, 1998). Such decision-making is, moreover, not restricted to foreign-policy issues. Esser and Lindoerfer (1989) argued that the ill-fated decision to launch the *Challenger* space shuttle in 1986 (in which seven astronauts died, as the shuttle exploded 58 seconds after lift-off) had many of the hallmarks of groupthink (see also Starbuck & Farjoun, 2005). In a recent analysis of policy mistakes by British governments, political scientists King and Crewe (2013) give several examples. These include the failed attempt in 1990 to introduce a 'poll tax' or 'Community Charge' (a per capita fixed-amount tax imposed on every person of voting age, independent of their income, which led to a series of riots). King and Crewe (2013) refer to the government's 'review team' for this policy as 'almost a parody of Irving Janis's face-to-face groups indulging in group-think' (p. 256). Its leader showed no interest in engaging with two nominated outside assessors, who were sceptical of the policy. It minimized contact with outsiders, other than the Prime Minister, Margaret Thatcher, whose idea the new tax was! The poll tax review team failed to appraise realistically alternative options, and did not notice the risks involved.

Popular as the notion of groupthink is, its empirical support is rather weak. Analysis of case studies, often based on content analysis of available records, does show increased rigidity and more simplistic thinking among decision-makers involved in groupthink decisions, compared to more favourable outcomes (Tetlock, 1979). Herek, Janis, and Huth (1987) also reported a negative association between the number of symptoms of groupthink and the quality of the decision. But there is little evidence that cohesiveness alone, or in combination with other supposed antecedents, contributes to defective decision-making. As Tetlock (1998) also points out, one can quite easily find successful political decisions

in cases with evidence of groupthink (e.g., Churchill suppressed dissent in cabinet meetings in 1940–1941 when some group members advocated a negotiated peace with Hitler), but also instances in which vigilant decision-making failed to prevent disastrous outcomes (e.g., President Jimmy Carter's failed mission to rescue hostages from Iran in 1980, despite his encouragement of open debate).

Laboratory studies are even less supportive, perhaps because it is difficult, if not impossible, to create in the laboratory true analogues of highly-cohesive, insulated groups, working under high pressure to make decisions with massive political consequences (Esser, 1998; Mullen, Anthony, Salas, & Driskell, 1994). Manipulations of groupthink have generally not produced poor-quality discussions and decisions (Flowers, 1977; Leana, 1985), and groupthink has been found in groups with either high- or low-cohesiveness (see Aldag & Fuller, 1993; Turner, Pratkanis, Probasco, & Leve, 1992).

There are, also, fundamental weaknesses of the groupthink model. It does not allow precise predictions, it is difficult to operationalize the concept (must all the characteristics of groupthink be present to define it as such?), and it is often only applied after-the-fact. Haslam (2004) concludes that, in organizational settings, all group decision-making includes some element of so-called groupthink symptoms (see Peterson, Owens, Tetlock, Fan, & Martorana, 1998). Faced with this lack of supportive evidence, Aldag and Fuller (1993) proposed a more general, but also more complex, group problem-solving model (see also 't Hart, Stern, & Sundelius, 1997). It includes many of the features discussed by Janis, but also others. For example, it allows for cohesiveness to play a role, but it is seen as just one aspect of *group structure* (see Chapter 12) which, along with *decision characteristics* and *decision-making context*, determine *emergent group characteristics* (e.g., perceptions that the ingroup is moral and unanimous in its opinions); these characteristics, in turn, affect *decision process characteristics* (e.g., how carefully objectives are surveyed, and whether alternatives are generated), leading ultimately to *outcomes*. We present a simplified version of this model in Figure 8.13.

Despite the critiques of the concept of groupthink, it has proven a remarkably attractive notion to not only scholars but also policy analysts. In their wide-ranging book *The Blunders of our Governments*, King and Crewe (2013) devote a chapter to the topic, concluding, 'other things being equal, cohesion and mutual loyalty are desirable properties in any human group. Nevertheless, group-think is a barrier to successful decision making more often than not. It renders blundering more probable' (p. 267).

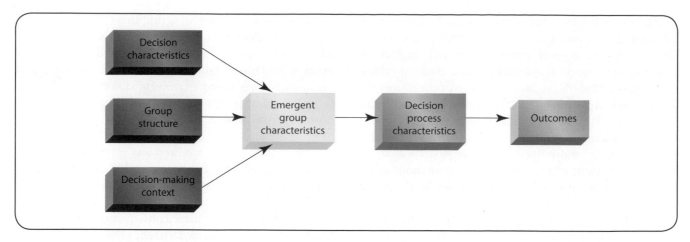

FIGURE 8.13 *Simplified general problem-solving model.*

Source: After Aldag & Fuller, 1993. Copyright © 1993 by the American Psychological Association. Adapted with permission. Aldag, R. J., & Fuller, S. R. (1993). Beyond fiasco: A reappraisal of the groupthink phenomenon and a new model of group decision processes. *Psychological Bulletin, 113*, 533–552. The use of APA information does not imply endorsement by APA.

Obedience to authority

What are the main situational determinants of obedience to authority?

As we have seen in this chapter, social influence emanates from many sources, often group members of equal status to the target of influence. Research on **obedience to authority**, which began with Stanley Milgram's (1963) famous research, addresses a different form of influence, namely obedience to a source who is not an equal, but an authority figure (see Leader in the Field, Stanley Milgram). Obedience, here, is defined as complying with orders from a person of higher social status within a defined hierarchy or chain of command (Miller, 1995). It is often an example of the functioning of legitimate power, whereby an internalized framework of norms, values, customs and procedures specifies that such influence is appropriate (Turner, 1991; e.g., we are told to 'do as your parents/teachers/senior officers tell you'). The motives underlying obedience are diverse, including respect for the expertise of authority and fear of the consequences of disobedience. In the following sections we will (1) outline Milgram's paradigm and initial results; (2) review some of the findings on the situational determinants of obedience; (3) evaluate the theoretical analysis of obedience; (4) consider ethical issues and alternatives to the Milgram paradigm for studying obedience; and (5) introduce the phenomenon of disobedience.

obedience to authority complying with orders from a person of higher social status within a defined hierarchy or chain of command.

 LEADER IN THE FIELD

Stanley Milgram (1933–1984) earned his Bachelor's degree at Queens College, New York in 1954, but in political science: he never took a psychology course as an undergraduate. He completed his PhD at Harvard University, and taught at Yale University and the New School for Social Research, New York. Although best known for his research on obedience, Milgram also studied conformity, life in cities, and did pioneering work on nonreactive measures. His research across many diverse fields is characterized by its phenomenological approach, the salience of moral issues and the importance he attached to situational determinants of social behaviour. Milgram has recently received the honour of a full-length biography, entitled *The Man who Shocked the World: The Life and Legacy of Stanley Milgram* (Blass, 2004).

Milgram's obedience paradigm The classic research was conducted by Milgram (1963, 1974), who intended that his experimental research should help to understand better how the Nazi Holocaust (and all the individual acts of obedience involved in that systematic annihilation) could have taken place (Figure 8.14). Milgram was, specifically, fascinated with the trial in Jerusalem of the arch-architect of the 'final solution', Adolf Eichmann, as reported by the philosopher Hannah Arendt (1965) in her book *Eichmann in Jerusalem: A Report on the Banality of Evil*. If such evil were 'banal', or unexceptional, then would most people show destructive obedience? Prior to his research Milgram doubted it, and indeed his first study was intended to be the 'baseline', a situation in which few people would obey. Later research was then to manipulate key variables and investigate their impact

FIGURE 8.14(a) and (b) *Milgram's research into obedience was originally intended to help us understand how the Nazi Holocaust could have taken place.*

Source: (a) © Bruno De Hogues. Used under licence from Getty Images; (b) Image copyright rhfletcher. Used under licence from Shutterstock.com.

on rates of obedience (see Milgram, 1963, 1974; see also Blass, 1999, 2000; Miller, Collins, & Brief, 1995), and to replicate the main findings with comparable obedience rates across a range of cultures (Blass, 2012).

We have already referred to some details of this notorious research to lay out principles of research methodology (see Chapter 2). Now we go into more detail, highlighting crucial aspects of the research, and referring to some of the 18 studies reported by Milgram in his 1974 book. For his first study Milgram recruited 40 male participants via newspaper advertisements (for a study on memory, with no mention made of obedience) to take part in a study at Yale University. At the laboratory, the investigator explained that a teacher–learner scenario would be used, and participants were led to believe that roles had been determined by chance. In fact, it was always arranged such that the 'learner' was the experimental confederate, and he was instructed to make errors on the task in a predetermined way. The experimenter explained that, by means of a simulated shock generator, the participant (as 'teacher') was to deliver increasingly more intense electric shocks to the 'learner' each time he made a mistake on the learning task (participants were informed that the shocks were extremely painful, but that they would cause no permanent damage; Milgram, 1963). In fact, no shocks were delivered, but the impact of the experimental scenario was so high that all participants believed that they were shocking the learner.

The learner was strapped into a chair and electrodes were fixed to his wrists. The teacher was taken to a different room, where he was instructed to punish the learner's first mistake with a shock of 15 volts, increasing in intensity by a further 15 volts with every new mistake. A shock generator in front of him showed the teacher 30 buttons, and clear verbal labels, ranging from '15V', through '60V' ('slight shock'), to '120V' ('moderate shock'), and finally to '450V' ('danger: severe shock XXX'). In a clever touch, at the onset of the study Milgram ensured that all participants experienced the reality of a relatively low-intensity electric shock (45 volts), so that they could not later claim that they had not believed they were really shocking the victim.

Milgram, a dramatist as much as an experimenter (see Blass, 1992), carefully *scripted* the whole scenario, down to the detail of having the experimenter wear a *grey* lab coat (indicating that he was a mere technician, rather than, as is frequently *mis*reported, a white coat, which might have signified that he was a higher-status physician or scientist). The victim's responses followed a predetermined series, rising in intensity with the level of shock: 'Ugh' (75, 90, 105 volts); 'Hey, this really hurts' (120 volts); 'Experimenter, get me out of here! I won't be in the experiment any more! I refuse to go on' (150 volts); screams of agony (270 volts); screams and refusal to answer (300, 315 volts); intense and prolonged agonized scream (330 volts). Likewise, the experimenter used a graded set of commands ('prods') to keep the teacher going: 'Please continue'; 'The experiment requires that you continue'; 'It is absolutely essential that you continue'; and 'You have no other choice, you *must* go on.' In this way Milgram ensured that his experimental scenario had a very high impact on participants without sacrificing control over the situation.

The results of this baseline study were staggering. Far from the minimal level of obedience expected, no participant stopped before administering a 300 volt shock. Across the sample, maximal obedience was shown by 26 of 40 respondents: 65 per cent. By comparison, in a later study, when participants were free to choose any shock level, only 2 out of 40 participants exceeded the 150 volts level, and 28 never went beyond 75 volts. Rather surprisingly, when Milgram moved the location of the study from a laboratory at a prestigious university to a room in a run-down building located in a nearby city, away from the university, he still found evidence for obedience (although the rate dropped from 65 per cent to 48 per cent).

Situational determinants of obedience

The main thrust of Milgram's subsequent studies was to explore variation in the rate of obedience across different social situations. In various conditions, for example, Milgram manipulated the proximity of the victim, the authority of the experimenter and the behaviour of peers.

Four conditions varied the physical (and emotional) proximity of the victim. In one condition he pounded heavily on the wall separating his room from the teacher's; in another the participant heard his crying and shouting (as described earlier). In two other conditions the teacher and the victim were actually in the same room; in one condition, the teacher not only heard but also saw the victim; in the other condition, the teacher had to hold the victim's hand down on a shock plate. The obedience rates corresponding to these four conditions of increasing proximity are shown in Figure 8.15. Maximal obedience fell from 65 per cent of the participants to 30 per cent. Milgram also found that the duration of the shock given decreased with increasing proximity.

Milgram also varied the authority of the experimenter and how much control he exerted. This was hugely influential. When the experimenter was absent from the participant's room and gave his orders over the telephone, maximal obedience dropped to 21 per cent (a number of participants said over the phone that they were giving higher shocks than they in fact did!). In another variation, the experimenter had to leave the room before instructing the participant to increase shock levels. He handed over his authority to a second participant who was present, and who would only have to record the learner's reaction times. This second participant then came up with the idea of increasing the shock level with every error and, throughout the learning session, he insisted that the teacher applied his rules. Only 20 per cent of the participants obeyed the equal-status authority to the end. In addition, when a participant refused to obey and the 'authority' decided that he would administer the shocks himself, a number of participants physically attacked the experimenter or tried to unplug the shock generator. Participants did not, however, show such heroism when the authority was the scientist in a lab coat.

Two experimental variations investigated the role of peer pressure. In the first there were three co-teachers, the participant and two confederates. The first confederate presented the task, the second recorded the learner's responses, and the participant administered the shocks. The first confederate refused to continue at 150 volts, and was joined by the second confederate at 210 volts. Their refusal had a dramatic effect on the participants: only 10 per cent were maximally obedient, compared with 65 per cent when no peer was present (see Figure 8.16). In contrast, if the teacher, who administered the learning task, was accompanied by a co-teacher who gave the shocks, 92 per cent of the participants continued to the end of the experiment.

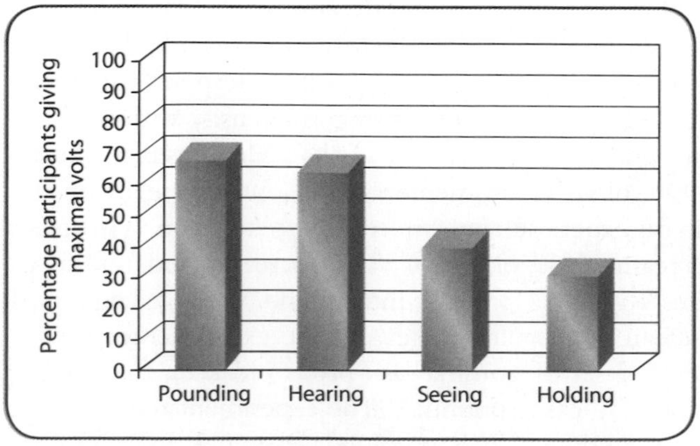

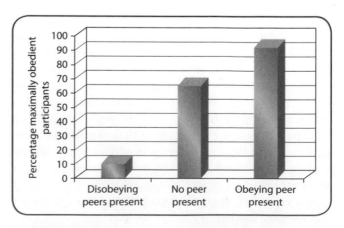

FIGURE 8.15 *Obedience as a function of physical proximity.*
Source: Data from Milgram, 1974.

FIGURE 8.16 *Obedience as a function of peer behaviour.*
Source: Data from Milgram, 1974.

Why do people obey? It is not convincing to argue that the participants (a majority of whom obeyed to high levels across most studies) were sadists. In one study by Milgram participants *chose* their own level of shock, and they opted for very low-level shocks. Surely sadists would have seized their opportunity here? Participants also appeared to be distressed by the experience, often appearing tense, displaying nervous laughter, sweating profusely and even begging the experimenter to stop. This evidence tends to rule out both the possibility that participants were sadists, and the claim that they did not believe Milgram's cover story. Milgram's own theoretical analysis of obedience included four factors, which have received varying levels of support (see Theory Box 8.5).

First, and rather descriptively, Milgram argued for the importance of socio-cultural factors. We grow up in a society in which we learn (indeed, we are taught) to obey authorities, beginning with parents and school teachers, and ending with police officers. Moreover, we expect those authority figures to be legitimate and trustworthy.

Second, and more persuasively, Milgram pointed to 'binding factors', the subtle creation of psychological barriers to disobedience. He used the notion of 'entrapment' to refer to the experimenter's gradual increase in punishment levels ordered, rather than beginning with an outrageous demand which most participants would probably have refused. This approach can be seen as an instance of the 'foot-in-the-door' technique for obtaining compliance (Freedman & Fraser, 1966) discussed earlier, and this subtle progression towards destructive obedience may be crucial in helping us to understand how ordinary individuals can ultimately commit acts of evil (see Browning, 1992; Darley, 1992; Kelman & Hamilton, 1990; Miller, 1986).

Third, Milgram argued that the subordinate in a hierarchical system does not accept personal responsibility for his or her actions, but allocates this responsibility to someone higher up in the organization. He referred to this as an 'agentic shift', where the obedient participants switch off their own conscience and see themselves as *agents* for carrying out a more senior person's wishes. This, of course, is a convenient, self-serving account used by many perpetrators of evil, such as the former Iraqi torturer's statement that 'I was following orders. Saddam [Hussein] is responsible' (reported in *The Observer*, 14 May 2006). Empirical support for this notion is, however, weak (see Nissani, 1990; Waller, 2002). Mantell and Panzarella (1976), in a replication of Milgram's research conducted in Germany, reported no relationship between participants' degree of obedience and their post-experimental assignment of responsibility. In his own post-experimental interviews Milgram asked participants to use a 'responsibility clock' to divide up responsibility between the experimenter, themselves and the victim. He did not, however, find that obedient participants assigned more responsibility to the experimenter. In fact, both obedient and disobedient participants attributed almost equal responsibility to the experimenter, which contradicts the claim that obedient participants somehow pass responsibility up the 'chain of command'. However, disobedient participants saw themselves as more responsible (and the learner-victim as less responsible) than did the obedient participants, whereas obedient participants assigned relatively less responsibility to themselves and relatively more responsibility to the learner-victim than did disobedient participants (see Milgram, 1974, Appendix II).

Consistent with this view is recent evidence suggesting that there is more to Milgram's experiments than at first meets the eye (see Russell's fascinating 2010 analysis of documents from Milgram's personal archive at Yale University, and his analysis of how Milgram's original idea evolved into a paradigm that 'worked'). Further problems in relation to Milgram's 'agentic shift' hypothesis come from a qualitative analysis of tape recordings and transcripts from two of Milgram's studies by Gibson (2013), who specifically focused on the experimenter's use of the four prods to encourage participants to continue to give the shocks. He found that participants often argued with the experimenter about the continuation of the study. The analysis throws into question Milgram's description of his manipulations, and shows that the experimenter did not simply give orders that had to be obeyed but that he also gave responses that constituted '*arguments* designed to *convince and persuade*' (p. 305). This shows the importance of the relationship between the authority figure and person who obeys is critical, and that it is one that involves negotiation through social influence processes. This has led some scholars to focus on the

---

THEORY BOX 8.5

WHY DO WE OBEY?

- **Sociocultural perspective**
  - We learn to obey authority and expect to encounter legitimate, trustworthy authority
- **Binding factors**
  - Subtle creation of psychological barriers to disobedience; gradual increase in punishment levels in Milgram's research is a means of 'entrapment'
- **Responsibility**
  - **The agentic shift**: The subordinate in a hierarchical system does not accept personal responsibility for his or her actions but allocates responsibility to an individual
- **Situational factors**
  - Some situations are so 'strong' that they dominate individual differences in personality, and make us behave

Source: Based on data in Milgram, 1974.

role of identification between the teacher and learner and to question whether the Milgram experiments show not obedience but the use of power to lead to identification-based followership (see Reicher & Haslam, 2011; Reicher, Haslam, & Smith, 2012).

Fourth, and finally, Milgram's whole research programme placed huge emphasis on the power of the situation, something that is fundamental to the study of social psychology (see Chapter 1). His findings suggest that destructive obedience is well within the behavioural repertoire of most people (Miller, 1986), and he emphasized the power of the situation rather than personality factors. There is, in fact, some evidence of influential personality variables. Individuals who hold authoritarian beliefs are more likely to obey authorities (Elms & Milgram, 1966; Kelman & Hamilton, 1990), and participants high in empathic concern expressed a reluctance to continue with the procedure earlier than did participants lower on this trait, although they were not actually more likely to refuse to continue (in a study that stopped at the 150 volt level; Burger, 2009). Notwithstanding some evidence for personality variables, Milgram's paradigm highlights the power of the situation. To acknowledge this fact, however, is not to exonerate the perpetrators of evil deeds and adopt a morally condoning attitude towards them (Miller, Gordon, & Buddie, 1999). Harm-doing, which may well have been instigated by situational factors initially, demands self-regulation processes that definitely involve the actor-person himself (see Bandura, 1999). Hence Blass (1991) underlined the complexities of predicting obedience, arguing for both personality and situational factors, which should be studied in interaction.

Ethical issues and alternatives to the Milgram paradigm Milgram's research has become the most famous of all experiments in social psychology (it spawned TV programmes, films, a play, and even a song by Peter Gabriel, *We Do What We're Told*). It speaks to the darkest side of human nature, and has been used in attempts to understand better phenomena such as genocide (Staub, 1989) and war crimes (Bourke, 1999). But it also became infamous, generating controversy, centred on ethical issues (see Baumrind, 1964; Miller, 1986; see also Chapter 2). Milgram was severely criticized for inducing suffering in his participants. Using a procedure that would be impossible to replicate today given ethical guidelines for research, he induced stress and anxiety in his participants and, among those who did obey, guilt about how they had behaved. Indeed, the furore caused by Milgram's studies led to the putting in place of strict ethical guidelines for research that operate today. Whilst Milgram states that all participants received post-experimental briefing about the procedures (what Milgram refers to as 'dehoaxing'), Nicholson (2011) analysed Milgram's post-experimental interviews and questioned how effective this technique was. Nicholson reports that many of Milgram's participants did not know that they had not delivered real shocks until some time after the study and, in some cases, weeks later. Indeed, one participant reported that they had been searching the *New Haven Register*'s death notices to see if their 'learner' was listed! Even if participants had been informed that they had not given real shocks, many reported extremely high levels of anxiety following the study in the belief that they were personally capable of such destructive obedience.

No contemporary study could inform participants that, although blatantly untrue, 'It is absolutely essential that you continue', or 'You have no other choice, you *must* go on'. Indeed, the furore caused by this research is credited with generating regulations that control the use of human participants in psychological research. More generally, some of the questions you may care to consider are: could the participants' psychological suffering be dealt with in normal debriefing? How would participants react, on learning that they were – apparently – capable of heinous acts in response to orders? Should the experiment have ever been carried out? Is the research sufficiently important to justify such deception of, and stress experienced by, participants? To what extent was the criticism triggered by the results, rather than the research itself?

It is, of course, because of the ethical issues that arose from Milgram's studies that research using exactly the same paradigm he used can no longer be conducted. However, other milder forms of obedience can be, and have been, researched. Burger (2009) did actually conduct a partial replication of Milgram's paradigm in 2006, in which he protected the well-being of participants (in accordance with ethical guidelines). He had participants follow the Milgram paradigm up to the 150 volt level. On the basis that 79 per cent of Milgram's participants who exceeded this point went all the way to the maximal shock level, he estimated that the rate of full obedience at 150 volts in his 2006 sample (70 per cent) was only slightly lower than Milgram's at 150 volts, 45 years earlier (82.5 per cent), a difference that is not statistically significantly.

Other research has explored obedience in less damaging and more ethically acceptable contexts, which can still investigate psychological processes in obedience, but simply not in the Milgram paradigm. The first alternative may strike you, in fact, as just as ethically dubious as Milgram's study. Sheridan and King (1972) conducted a conceptual replication of Milgram in which, rather than have participants ordered to give imagined shocks to a fake human victim, they gave actual shocks to a real canine victim, 'a cute, fluffy puppy' (p. 165) when it made errors on a discrimination task. The levels of actual shocks (ranging from 15–75 volts to 300–450 volts) were designed to create 'responses such as running, howling, and yelping, without, however, doing the [puppy] any serious harm' (p. 165). At the highest level (the shock indicator showed 300–450 volts, but the puppy actually received 800 volts at 1 milliamps) the actual voltage level was sufficient to produce 'continuous barking and howling' (p. 165). Under these conditions male and female participants showed maximal levels of obedience of comparable and higher levels, respectively, than in Milgram's paradigm.

Obedience has also been studied in the context of asking a participant to disrupt a job interview in the name of scientific research (Meeus & Raaijmakers, 1986, 1995). Another fascinating field study (Gamson, Fireman, & Rytina, 1982) telephoned volunteers to ask if they were willing to take part in various kinds of research, including research in which they would be misled about its purpose until later. Having agreed, participants were asked to go to a nearby hotel, in which they were asked to act in an unethical and damaging way towards an innocent victim in order to help a legal case on behalf of a large oil company against an individual. Under these conditions 25 per cent of participants fully complied with the request.

Finally, Slater et al. (2006) conducted a conceptual replication of Milgram's paradigm in an immersive virtual environment, in which a virtual human was to be shocked, with increasing voltage, for her mistakes in a series of memory tests. The virtual victim responded in comparable ways to Milgram's actual learner-victim, and participants responded – even at the physiological level (assessed by their galvanic skin responses) – as if she were actually real; they also responded with high levels of obedience. Two conditions were compared: 'visible' (in which the learner was seen and heard throughout, and responded to shocks with increasing signs of discomfort); and 'hidden' (in which the learner was only seen and heard briefly, at the start of the study, and thereafter responded through text). There was some evidence that participants showed a stronger desire to stop in the visible condition. These promising initial results suggest that virtual reality might provide a methodology by which future research on obedience could be conducted in a more ethically acceptable manner.

Disobedience Another valuable perspective on Milgram's research is whether the results are, in fact, so surprising. Later critics suggested that the experimenter may have played a more active role in instigating obedience than is evident from Milgram's (1965) early report (perhaps inducing obedience through demand characteristics; see Chapter 2), and that the evidence of *disobedience* is itself remarkable (35 per cent of the participants defied the experiment at some point, and disobedient participants gave shocks of shorter duration). Early resistance seems crucial (only 17 per cent of those showing early signs of protest delivered shocks of more than 150 volts), a claim substantiated by re-analysis of some of Milgram's data.

Packer (2008) conducted a meta-analysis of data from eight of Milgram's obedience experiments, and reported that disobedience was most likely at 150 volts. This was the point at which the learner-victim supposedly receiving the shocks first asked to be released. Packer further reports that, across the studies, as obedience decreased, disobedience at 150 volts (but at no other level) increased. He concludes his analysis by proposing that disobedience is not simply associated with increasing expressions of pain on the part of the learner-victim. Rather, the 150 volt point is a 'critical decision point' (p. 301) at which participants acknowledged that the learner's right to terminate the experiment should override their obedience to the experimenter. Bocchiaro and Zimbardo (2010), using an administrative obedience paradigm based on Meeus and Raaijmakers (1986), also reported that disobedience at the victim's first request to be released was crucial. Interestingly, this evidence highlighting the importance of early resistance is consistent with Rochat and Modigliani's (1995) historical study of French citizens who, under Nazi rule during World War II, refused to persecute war refugees in the village of Le Chambon. Those who resisted, resisted early.

Whistle blowing is a specific form of disobedience, occurring when people report corruption or unethical practice within an organization (Miceli, Near, & Dworkin, 2008; Near & Miceli, 1985). Although Bocchiaro, Zimbardo and Van Lange (2012) have recently outlined an experimental paradigm for the study of whistle blowing, most research has been in the form of field studies (e.g., Miceli, Dozier, & Near, 1991). Such behaviour is relatively rare, not least because a significant proportion of whistle blowers are subjected to harassment from senior members of the organization, ostracism from peers (Glazer & Glazer, 1989; MacNamara, 1991; Miceli & Near, 1992) and are very likely to lose their jobs (Alford, 2001). Whistle blowers are, in effect, critics of the ingroup, who are generally damned for their temerity (see Hornsey, 2005). There is evidence from the medical

whistle blowing a specific form of disobedience, in which people report corruption or unethical practice within an organization.

domain suggesting that willingness to blow the whistle declines with time in training (Goldie, Schwartz, McConnachie, & Morrison, 2003). Apparently medical students learn to keep quiet by seeing the retaliation meted out to whistle blowers (Bolsin, 2003). Yet such courageous action is necessary, whether to stop scientific fraud (Stroebe, Postmes, & Spears, 2012), medical malpractice (as in the case of the anaesthetist who blew the whistle on a senior surgeon responsible for abnormally high mortality rates in paediatric heart surgery at a hospital in Bristol, UK during the 1990s; see Boseley, July 2012), or mistreatment of prisoners of war (as in the case of the Navy dog handler who refused to be drawn into the abuse of Iraqi prisoners in Abu Ghraib prison; see Greenberg & Dratel, 2005). Yet as a rule such 'moral rebels' rarely receive the respect and support they deserve (Monin, Sawyer, & Marquez, 2008).

Research on obedience in perspective Whatever your view of Milgram's experiments (ethically acceptable – or not?; due to demand characteristics – or not?), every social psychologist should read and have an opinion about Milgram's research on obedience (see Blass, 1992). Subsequent studies in different countries and with various paradigms have demonstrated the generality of the effect he first demonstrated (e.g., Mantell, 1971; Meeus & Raaijmakers, 1986, 1995; Shanab & Yahya, 1978), and highlighted the importance of obedience in a range of settings, including military, medical and organizational contexts (see Brief, Dukerich, & Doran, 1991), and financial scandals that clearly involved an element of obedience or 'wilful blindness' (Heffernan, 2011; Swartz & Watkins, 2003; Toffler & Reingold, 2003). For example, in medical settings blind obedience of nurses to physicians' orders can lead to medication errors and even fatal consequences (Hofling, Brotzman, Dalrymple, Graves, & Pierce, 1966; Lesar, Briceland, & Stein, 1997; Rank & Jacobson, 1977).

Milgram specifically sought to extend Asch's conformity experiment to 'something more consequential than judging lengths of lines' (Blass, 1992, p. 286). In this he was hugely successful; destructive obedience is more widespread than most of us would ever have imagined. This research can, however, provide only part of the explanation for the excesses of the Third Reich, which Milgram set out to understand (see Miller, 2004). The Nazi Holocaust included many acts that were not simply acts of obedience to authority (see Johnson & Reuband, 2005; Newman & Erber, 2002). One of the most famous case histories is Browning's (1992) historical analysis of the massacre in July 1942 of some 1,500 Jewish civilians in the Polish village of Józefów by men of the Nazi Reserve Police Battalion 101 – in the title of Browning's book, *Ordinary Men*. However this was not a matter of simple obedience, but also included 'argumentation' backed up by physical threats (Navarick, 2012). As Berkowitz (1999) argued, the slaughter of millions of Jews and other 'undesirables' in the Holocaust cannot be reduced to the 'central dynamic' of obedience alone. Milgram's research does not represent many significant features of the Holocaust, including well-documented sadism and the individual psychology of those who initiated the barbaric policy, thus questioning his 'banality of evil' thesis (Haslam & Reicher, 2007, 2008).

Summary

The study of deliberate social influence introduces some of the most celebrated experiments ever carried out by social psychologists. We began by considering three main techniques of inducing compliance, based on requests – the door-in-the-face, the foot-in-the-door, and lowballing. Next, we reviewed the literature on majority versus minority social influence, showing how the field has moved from a narrow focus on majority influence only, to an understanding that both majorities and minorities can be influential and in various ways. We then reported on the tendency of groups to polarize individual members' views, and linked this to some of the extreme consequences of social influence in groups, as seen in groupthink. Finally, we reviewed research on obedience to authority, including Milgram's classic research, the ethical issues it raises and the phenomenon of whistle blowing.

CHAPTER SUMMARY

- *What are the main types of influence, and how can they be best understood?* This chapter discussed two main types of social influence, 'incidental' and 'deliberate,' and sought to understand them in terms of fundamental motives.

- *What is meant by social influence?* Social influence refers to change of attitudes, beliefs, opinions, values and behaviour, as a result of being exposed to other individuals' attitudes, beliefs, opinions, values and behaviour.

- *What is meant by incidental social influence?* Incidental social influence refers to situations in which people are influenced, although there has been no explicit attempt to influence them (e.g., social facilitation and inhibition effects).

- *How does the presence of other people affect task performance?* People are influenced by the presence or implied presence of others, which tends to improve performance on simple/well-learned tasks, but worsen performance on complex/novel tasks.

- *What are social norms, and why are they important? Social norms are rules and standards that guide behaviour.* They can be descriptive or injunctive; we can infer them from other people's behaviour, and they can be easily established and transmitted.

- *What drives social influence?* Social influence is driven by some of the fundamental motives directing human social behaviour. Ultimately, we are influenced by others so that we behave effectively, build and maintain relationships with others, manage our own self-concept, and understand the social world more effectively.

- *What are the main types of deliberate social influence?* Deliberate social influence includes inducing compliance with requests, the influence of numerical majorities and minorities, group decision-making and obedience to authority.

- *What are the main strategies for inducing compliance, and how do they work?* There is evidence for three main strategies of inducing compliance – door-in-the-face, foot-in-the-door, and lowballing – that rely greatly on general principles such as equity, reciprocity and self-consistency.

- *Are we only influenced by majorities, or can minorities also have an impact?* Both numerical majorities and minorities can exert influence, and the major explanations concern conflict and social categorization. Majorities tend to have greater influence on public and direct measures, but minorities can be more effective on indirect, private measures.

- *Overall, is conformity a 'good' or a 'bad' thing?* Conformity is a rather ambivalent concept. The very existence of a society depends on it, but it can be a force for good (e.g., encouraging donations to charity) as well as for bad (e.g., tyranny of the majority), and even evil (e.g., following others and behaving immorally).

- *What impact do groups have on decision-making?* Groups tend to polarize decisions, due to normative, informational and referent influence. Groupthink is proposed as an extreme form of poor decision-making, but its empirical and theoretical basis is rather weak.

- *When and why do we obey?* Obedience to authority is primarily driven by situational factors, but we still lack a clear explanation of why it occurs. Research on this topic poses important ethical questions, and more recent work on whistle blowing underlines the moral importance of disobedience.

SUGGESTIONS FOR FURTHER READING

Allen, V. L. (1975). Social support for nonconformity. In L. Berkowitz (Ed.), *Advances in experimental social psychology* (Vol. 8, pp. 1–43). New York: Academic Press. A detailed account of theory and research with respect to the factors leading to a reduction in conformity to a majority.

Anderson, N. B. (Ed.). (2009). Obedience – then and now [Special issue]. *American Psychologist, 64*(1), whole issue. A special issue on obedience, including a 2006 replication of Milgram and critical commentaries on what this later study does, and does not, actually tell us.

Asch, S. E. (1956). Studies of independence and conformity: A minority of one against a unanimous majority. *Psychological Monographs, 70*, 70. This text presents Asch's own account of his famous conformity experiments. The best way to learn about these studies is to read them firsthand.

Baron, R. S., & Kerr, N. L. (2003). *Group process, group decision, group action* (2nd ed.). Buckingham, UK: Open University Press. Extends the material presented in this chapter on social facilitation, majority and minority influence, and group decision-making.

Cialdini, R. B., & Trost, M. R. (1998). Social influence: Social norms, conformity, and compliance. In D. T. Gilbert, S. T. Fiske, & G. Lindzey (Eds.), *Handbook of social psychology* (4th ed., Vol. 2, pp. 151–192). Boston, MA: McGraw-Hill. Authoritative source, especially good on norms and compliance strategies.

Janis, I. L. (1972). *Victims of groupthink: A psychological study of foreign-policy decisions and fiascoes*. Boston, MA: Houghton Mifflin. Janis's original presentation of groupthink, illustrated with case materials showing disastrous decision-making in the area of foreign policy.

Martin, R., & Hewstone, M. (Eds.). (2010). *Minority influence and innovation: Antecedents, processes and consequences*. Hove, UK: Psychology Press (Taylor & Francis). An overview of contemporary theoretical approaches to and applications of minority influence.

Milgram, S. (1974). *Obedience to authority: An experimental view*. New York: Harper & Row. Compelling and readable overview of Milgram's own programme of 18 experiments, and the furore they unleashed.

Miller, A. G., Collins, B. E., & Brief, D. E. (1995). Perspectives on obedience to authority: The legacy of the Milgram experiments. *Journal of Social Issues, 51*, 1–19. A journal special issue on reactions to Milgram's obedience research and subsequent theory and research on obedient and defiant behaviour.

Sunstein, C. R. (2009). *Going to extremes: How like minds unite and divide*. New York: Oxford University Press. A readable guide to how group polarization impacts on social and political life, encouraging people to adopt extremism in their attitudes and behaviour.

Turner, J. C. (1991). *Social influence*. Buckingham, UK: Open University Press. A scholarly overview of the whole field, with a sophisticated theoretical analysis from the perspective of self-categorization theory.

9 Aggression

BARBARA KRAHÉ

KEY TERMS

- aggression
- Aggression Questionnaire (AQ)
- aggressive cues
- aggressive scripts
- bullying
- catharsis
- cognitive neo-associationist model
- collective violence
- Conflict Tactics Scales (CTS)
- cyberbullying
- direct aggression
- direct reinforcement
- displaced aggression
- excitation transfer theory

- frustration–aggression hypothesis
- General Aggression Model (GAM)
- geographic regions approach
- habituation
- heat hypothesis
- hormones
- hostile aggression
- hostile attribution bias
- indirect aggression
- instrumental aggression
- intergroup aggression
- interpersonal aggression
- intimate partner violence
- media violence–aggression link

- mobbing
- modelling
- peer nominations
- physical aggression
- post-traumatic stress disorder (PTSD)
- relational aggression
- sexual aggression
- staircase model
- steam boiler model
- terrorism
- time periods approach
- trait aggressiveness
- violence
- weapons effect

SUGGESTIONS FOR FURTHER READING

Anderson, C. A. (2001). Heat and violence. *Current Directions in Psychological Science*, *10*, 33–38. Concise summary of the evidence and theoretical explanations of the link between hot temperatures and aggression.

Anderson, C. A., Berkowitz, L., Donnerstein, E., Huesmann, L. R., Johnson, J. D., Linz, D., Malamuth, N. M., & Wartella, E. (2003). The influence of media violence on youth. *Psychological Science in the Public Interest*, *4*, 81–110. A comprehensive and critical review of the evidence on the influence of media violence on aggression, particularly among young media users.

Anderson, C. A., & Bushman, B. J. (1997). External validity of 'trivial' experiments: The case of laboratory aggression. *Review of General Psychology*, *1*, 19–41. A thought-provoking analysis of the way in which different measurement strategies in aggression research complement and cross-validate each other.

Archer, J. (2000). Sex differences in aggression between heterosexual partners: A meta-analytic review. *Psychological Bulletin*, *126*, 651–680. A comprehensive review of the evidence based on the Conflict Tactics Scales (CTS) to address gender differences in intimate partner violence.

Flannery, D. J., Vazsonyi, A. T., & Waldman, I. D. (Eds.). (2007). *Cambridge handbook of violent behavior and aggression*. New York: Cambridge University Press. A comprehensive and up-to-date collection of papers with a focus on criminality and violence.

Geen, R. G. (2001). *Human aggression* (2nd ed.). Buckingham, UK: Open University Press. An introductory text providing an overview of definitions, theories and forms of aggression.

Goldstein, A. P. (2002). *The psychology of group aggression*. Chichester, UK: Wiley. Examines different forms and dynamics of aggression between social groups.

Horvath, M., & Brown, J. (Eds.). (2009). *Rape: Challenging contemporary thinking*. Cullompton, UK: Willan. A collection of topical papers examining sexual violence from an interdisciplinary perspective.

Johnson, M. P., & Ferraro, K. J. (2000). Research on domestic violence in the 1990s: Making distinctions. *Journal of Marriage and the Family*, *62*, 948–963. Provides a conceptual analysis of different forms and patterns of intimate partner violence and shows how this differentiation may be useful for understanding gender differences.

Kirsh, S. J. (2012). *Children, adolescents, and media violence* (2nd ed.). Thousand Oaks, CA: Sage. Fun to read. Addresses all the facets of young people's attraction to violent media and the potential risks involved.

Koss, M. P., White, J. W., & Kazdin, A. E. (Eds.) (2011). *Violence against women and children* (Vol. 2: Navigating solutions). Washington, DC: American Psychological Association. Together with the companion volume by White, Koss, and Kazdin (see below), this book presents the current knowledge about the problem and prevention of violence against women and children brought together by three leading experts in the field.

Krahé, B. (2013). *The social psychology of aggression* (2nd ed.). Hove, UK: Psychology Press. Textbook that provides an introduction to theories, methods and topics in social psychological aggression research.

Meier, B. P., & Wilkowski, B. M. (2013). Reducing the tendency to aggress: Insights from social and personality psychology. *Social and Personality Psychology Compass*, *7*, 343–354. Discusses different strategies for preventing and reducing aggressive behaviour.

Moghaddam, F. M. (2006). *From the terrorists' point of view*. Westport, CT: Praeger. The book provides a more elaborate account of the staircase model described in this chapter and outlines possible ways of diminishing the threat of terrorism.

Ruback, R. B., & Thompson, M. P. (2001). *Social and psychological consequences of violent victimization*. Thousand Oaks, CA: Sage. A clear and comprehensive review of the impact of violence from the victims' perspective.

Victoroff, J., & Kruglanski, A. W. (Eds.). (2009). *Psychology of terrorism*. New York: Psychology Press. Up-to-date collection of papers addressing many facets of this pressing worldwide problem.

White, J. W., Koss, M. P., & Kazdin, A. E. (Eds.), *Violence against women and children* (Vol. 1: Mapping the terrain). Washington, DC: American Psychological Association. Companion volume to Koss et al. (2012; see above).

10 Prosocial Behaviour

MARK LEVINE AND RACHEL MANNING

KEY TERMS

- altruism
- arousal: cost–reward model
- audience inhibition
- bystander effect
- coefficient of relatedness (*r*)
- common ingroup identity model
- diffusion of responsibility
- empathic concern

- empathy
- evaluation apprehension
- helping behaviour
- impulsive helping
- kin selection
- negative-state-relief model
- pluralistic ignorance
- proportion of shared genes

- prosocial behaviour
- prosocial personality
- public goods game
- reciprocal altruism
- self-efficacy
- strong reciprocity
- volunteerism

CHAPTER OUTLINE

INTRODUCTION 311

PROSOCIAL BEHAVIOUR, HELPING AND ALTRUISM 312

Definitions 312
The altruism–egoism debate 313
Prosocial behaviours 316
Summary 317

WHY PEOPLE DON'T HELP 317

A decision-making model of bystander behaviour 319
Summary 323

WHY PEOPLE DO HELP 323

The costs and rewards of helping 323
Groups, identity and prosocial behaviour 325
Helping outgroups 326
Social identity and the bystander effect 328
Social identity, emotion and bystander intervention 329
Summary 329

ISSUES IN RESEARCHING PROSOCIAL BEHAVIOUR 330

Violence and helping 330
Gender and helping 331
Long-term, sustained helping behaviours 332
Summary 336

EVOLUTION, GENES AND HELPING 336

When helping is not self-interested 338
Summary 339

THE SOCIAL NEUROSCIENCE OF HELPING 339

Summary 340

HELPING IN THE REAL WORLD 340

Selfish vs. altruistic behaviour in
life-threatening emergencies 341
Summary 344

CHAPTER SUMMARY 344

ROUTE MAP OF THE CHAPTER

The topic of prosocial behaviour covers a wide range of phenomena and can be studied in a variety of ways. In this chapter we consider different kinds of prosocial behaviour, and explore theories of why people help (and who they help) at several different levels. We consider prosocial behaviour at the intra-individual level (are there biological mechanisms which affect helping?), the interpersonal level (how does the relationship between helper and recipient affect helping?), and the group level (what do we know about helping within and between groups?). We also explore how situational factors affect helping, and reveal how the social context is key to the understanding of many forms of helping behaviours. In addition we explore a range of different prosocial behaviours, from instant acts of physical courage in emergency situations to long-term commitments to a particular cause or a specific person. In the course of exploring these topics we reveal the wide range of inventive and creative research methods used by researchers in this area. The chapter also looks at some of the key 'big picture' questions about prosocial behaviour. For example, we ask whether helping can ever be truly selfless. We also ask if prosocial behaviour necessarily has positive effects. In the course of the chapter we consider some amazing examples of human prosocial behaviour. We discover that human cooperative behaviour is something of an evolutionary puzzle. Unlike other creatures, humans frequently cooperate with strangers, often in large groups and even in the absence of personal or reputational gain. By studying prosocial behaviour we have the opportunity to explore some of the things that make us uniquely human.

INTRODUCTION

The study of prosocial behaviour allows psychologists to explore basic questions about human nature, the kinds of questions that philosophers have been asking for centuries. These include questions of whether humans are fundamentally selfish or selfless by nature, or whether humans are ultimately good or bad. Take for example the way in which ordinary people have responded to natural disasters and emergencies over the last decade. Unfortunately there have been many such events to choose from, including the Japanese earthquake and tsunami (2011), the Haiti earthquake (2010; Figure 10.1), the Asian tsunami (2005), Hurricane Katrina in the US (2005), the Kashmir earthquake (2005) or the Iran earthquake (2003).

The first thing to note is that many ordinary people donated huge amounts of money to the relief funds set up after these disasters. People donated money to help strangers they will never meet, strangers who would never be able to thank them for the help they had given. This kind of behaviour is a puzzle to those who think that humans are only concerned with their own self-interest, and to those who believe that humans only feel ties to a small band of close family and kin. By giving money in this way, humans demonstrate the capacity to feel a sense of **empathy** with others in distress and a willingness to help others, even when it is not clear that they will benefit in return. All of this suggests that we possess a powerful capacity for good.

> **empathy** the experience of understanding or sharing the emotional state of another person.

And yet . . . not all of us help and, even when we do, we don't help everybody equally or all the time.

FIGURE 10.1 *Haitian people standing amongst the ruins of collapsed buildings after the 2010 earthquake.*

Source: © Design Pics/Reynold Mainse. Used under licence from Getty Images.

For example, according to figures from the Centre for Research on the Epidemiology of Disasters (CRED) at the Catholic University of Louvain (in Belgium), more than a hundred times as many people died in the Haiti earthquake (222,570 deaths) than as a result of Hurricane Katrina (1833 deaths). However, despite the huge difference in death tolls and the vast disparity in the wealth of the respective countries, researchers at the Centre on Philanthropy at Indiana University discovered that Americans gave much more to the American disaster ($5.3 billion) than they did to Haiti ($1.45 billion). Compare both of these with responses to the earthquake in the Pakistan controlled area of Kashmir. Here 73,338 people lost their lives, but Americans gave much less – $630 million – to the appeal. Of course, it is not only in America that these kinds of patterns can be found. In 2000, people in Switzerland gave their (relatively) wealthy fellow citizens 74 million Swiss Francs following a landslide in the canton of Wallis in which 13 people died, but gave less – 9 million Swiss Francs – to Iranian victims of the 2003 earthquake in the city of Bam, in which 26,796 people died.

How do we explain the differences? Why do we seem more willing to help some people than others? Is it simply to do with the relative publicity that the different disasters get? Or are important psychological processes at work?

In his book, *The Life You Can Save*, the philosopher and ethicist Peter Singer (2009) poses the following conundrum: if you saw a small child drowning in a pond, you would do all you could to save them; it wouldn't be an acceptable excuse to say that you did not save the child because you did not want to ruin a new pair of shoes, or couldn't afford to have your clothes cleaned. Everybody would try to save the child. And yet, UNICEF, the United Nations International Children's Emergency Fund, estimates that about 24,000 children die every day from preventable, poverty-related causes. They could be saved if the billion people in the world that live very comfortable lives could be persuaded to give; Singer argues that if you have ever spent money on buying a drink when water is freely available from a tap, then you are one of those people with money to spare. It sounds easy, but in practice, people can always think of reasons not to do it. Even when we have the means, and it wouldn't cost us much to do it, we can be reluctant to help.

Contrast this with the workers who volunteered to stay behind at the stricken Fukushima nuclear reactor after the Japanese earthquake and tsunami. With the radiation at potentially lethal levels, and the reactor in danger of meltdown, 50 workers volunteered to remain when conditions became so dangerous that most workers were evacuated. Dubbed the 'Fukushima 50', they fought to bring the reactor under control in life-threatening conditions. Some workers said they volunteered because they were single men with no children, and thus were more able to face the risks than those who had dependants relying on them. Others said they did so because they felt a sense of responsibility to their fellow workers. Yet others felt a duty to protect their fellow citizens and to preserve the reputation of Japan. Whatever the reasons, conditions at the Fukushima plant meant that people were putting their lives in danger to protect others.

In these few examples we see some of the key questions, conundrums and dilemmas that animate research on prosocial behaviour. The aim of this chapter will be to explore the wide range of psychological research that touches on prosocial behaviour in all its forms. In doing so we will encounter the key social psychological theories of helping, the methods used to explore these theories, and examine work at the cutting edge of contemporary research on prosocial behaviour.

PROSOCIAL BEHAVIOUR, HELPING AND ALTRUISM

Does pure altruism exist?

As the examples above demonstrate, we are seemingly surrounded with opportunities for helping. However, before we look at the various social psychological accounts of these phenomena, it is useful to begin by thinking about the nature of the phenomena themselves. What do we mean by the terms 'prosocial behaviour' or 'helping'? Examples of the contrasting reactions to the emergency/disaster situations noted above highlight some of the different circumstances that seemingly require the help of others. There is, evidently, a vast range of situations that may elicit helping. Clearly this raises an additional challenge to social psychologists. Therefore, before we begin to work through the various ways in which social psychologists have approached the issue of understanding prosocial behaviour, we might first consider what we mean by prosocial behaviour itself. As we will see, much of the thinking about what constitutes prosocial behaviour focuses either on particular forms or types of behaviours, or on the motivations behind such behaviours. At a more general level, we might also begin to consider whether it is possible to develop a single theory, model or approach which can account for all the different behaviours that might be encapsulated by the term 'prosocial behaviour'.

Definitions

As Bierhoff (2002) has pointed out, the terms **helping behaviour**, **prosocial behaviour** and **altruism** are frequently used interchangeably. However, distinct definitions for each are available. Piliavin (see Leader in the Field, Jane Allyn Piliavin, later in this chapter) and her colleagues have defined helping behaviour as 'an action that has the consequence of providing some benefit to or improving the well-being of another person' (Dovidio, Piliavin, Schroeder, & Penner, 2006, p. 22).

This definition makes helping behaviour the most inclusive term. Bierhoff (2002) argues that the definition of prosocial behaviour is narrower because 'helping' is not considered as 'prosocial behaviour' if the act is motivated by professional obligations. An example of helping behaviour that would not be considered prosocial behaviour would be a nurse caring for a patient, as this behaviour is performed as part of their job. Furthermore, Piliavin, Dovidio, Gaertner, and Clark (1981) point to the fact that what is considered to be prosocial behaviour is culturally dependent. They therefore suggest that prosocial behaviour is 'defined by society as behaviour generally beneficial to other people and to the ongoing social system', and go on to state that 'a great deal of disagreement regarding what is really prosocial action can occur depending on where one stands' (p. 4).

This point has been highlighted by a number of different researchers. For example, Grzelak and Derlega (1982) have suggested that there may be some positive aspects to social behaviour that we might ordinarily consider 'negative': for example, although social conflict may involve some injury, or even loss of life, it may also help to improve the living conditions of many people; see Chapter 14. Similarly, Huston and Korte (1976) have challenged the seemingly unproblematic subscription of many social psychologists to the moral tradition represented by the parable of the Good Samaritan. They point to cross-cultural variation to suggest that in some contexts, endangering oneself and thereby one's 'kin' is in itself a transgression. Thus, giving help may not necessarily be experienced as positive from the position of the person giving help. In parallel to

helping behaviour actions that are intended to provide some benefit to or improve the well-being of others.

prosocial behaviour refers to behaviour defined by society as beneficial to other people; it excludes behaviour that is motivated by professional obligations, and may be driven by more selfish (egoistic) and/or more selfless (altruistic) motivations.

altruism refers to behaviour carried out to benefit others without anticipation of external rewards; it is driven by exclusively empathic motivation.

this, Grzelak and Derlega (1982) have also questioned the notion of prosocial behaviour in terms of whether these assumed positive forms of behaviour are indeed experienced as positive by the recipient. In line with this suggestion, Nadler (see Leader in the Field, Arie Nadler, later in this chapter) has conducted a programme of research that empirically demonstrates the potential negative impact of helping on the recipient of the help. We will return to Nadler's work towards the end of this chapter.

Finally, the term *altruism* is the most constrained – and the most contested. Altruism is usually reserved for cases in which the helper tries to improve the welfare of the other person *as an end in itself*. In other words, altruism should normally refer to acts that in no way benefit the help-giver (thus, for example, the acts should not bring social approval or reduce personal distress at witnessing pain in others). Piliavin (2009) defines altruism as behaviour that is carried out in order to benefit others without anticipation of rewards from external sources.

What is most contentious about the definition of altruism is the problem of defining the motivations that are believed to lie behind it. The definition of altruism implies a clear separation between self and other. Actions must be 'selfless' to qualify as altruistic. However, as we have seen from psychological research on the self (see Chapter 5) the concept of the self is contested. There is no clear agreement on how we might separate self from other, and there is a body of research on the idea of self–other overlap (see Chapter 11). This has contributed to debates on whether 'pure' (or selfless) altruistic behaviour can ever exist. More specifically, it has lead to an intense debate about the motivations that may (or may not) lie behind helping behaviour. As we will see, researchers have argued over the degree to which helping can be explained by altruistic or egoistic concerns.

 LEADER IN THE FIELD

C. Daniel Batson (b. 1943) obtained his PhD in Psychology from Princeton in 1972 (he also holds a PhD in Theology). He has spent most of his career at the University of Kansas, where he is currently Emeritus Professor; he is also Adjunct Professor at the University of Tennessee. Batson famously developed the empathy-altruism hypothesis during his sustained attempt to experimentally test for the existence of true altruistic motivation for helping. Using a range of ingenious experimental procedures, Batson has sought to distinguish the egoistic and altruistic motivational systems, and has highlighted empathy as a possible source of the altruistic motivation systems. More recently, Batson and his colleagues have begun to examine the alternative motivations of principlism and collectivism in more detail.

The altruism–egoism debate

Obviously, if it's help you're after, you may not be concerned with why you are helped, only that you are (or not, as the case may be). Moreover, as others have pointed out (Piliavin et al., 1981), the final outcome of a particular helping situation might be reached from a number of different starting points, and in a number of different ways. But the question of what motivates helping is one that has concerned a range of psychologists. Is the goal of helping to benefit others, or to benefit ourselves? In social psychology, one of the main distinctions is between egoistically motivated helping and altruistically motivated helping – although, as Batson (1994) has suggested, there are other motives for prosocial action, which he calls *principlism* (acting to uphold a principle), and *collectivism* (acting to benefit a group).

A considerable amount of research has highlighted the contrast between egoistic and altruistic helping. For example, using data from the World Values Survey – a survey of 13,584 voluntary workers in 33 countries – Van de Vliert, Huang and Levine (2004) conducted a factor analysis that revealed a two-factor structure in motivations for doing unpaid voluntary work. Items loading on an 'egoistic' motivations factor were: 'time on my hands, wanted something worthwhile to do'; 'purely for personal satisfaction'; 'for social reasons, to meet people'; and 'to gain new skills and useful experience'. The five items loading on an altruistic motivations factor were: 'a sense of solidarity with the poor and disadvantaged'; 'compassion for those in need'; 'identifying with people who were suffering'; 'religious beliefs'; and 'to help give disadvantaged people hope and dignity'. When checking the cross-national equivalence of the two constructs, egoistic motivations and altruistic motivations, these researchers reported fairly consistent findings cross-nationally.

Demonstrating whether behaviours are motivated egoistically or altruistically is both a theoretical and methodological challenge. Research addressing this issue has utilized ingeniously designed experiments that have required the careful consideration of how to distinguish egoistic from altruistic helping (see Research Close-Up 10.1). One of the key researchers in this field is Batson (see Leader in the Field, C. Daniel Batson). Batson and his colleagues have developed the empathy-altruism hypothesis in their attempts to demonstrate the existence of helping that is motivated by altruistic rather than egoistic concerns. This is not to suggest that we can claim that all helping is motivated altruistically. Rather, altruism is a possible underlying motivation. According to the empathy-altruism hypothesis, it is the feeling of empathy, specifically, that evokes altruistic motivation.

EMPATHY LEADS TO ALTRUISTIC HELPING

Batson, C. D., Duncan, B. D., Ackerman, P., Buckley, T., & Birch, K. (1981). Is empathic emotion a source of altruistic motivation? *Journal of Personality and Social Psychology, 40*, 290–302.

Introduction

There are real difficulties in identifying underlying motivations, or being able to say precisely why someone acted as they did. Seemingly altruistic motives might sometimes be ultimately interpreted as egoistic ones. For example, you may have helped someone in order to relieve their distress, but this was, in turn, in order to alleviate the unpleasant feelings you experienced through knowing someone was in need, because you yourself would feel bad if you did nothing. This study began by dealing with the issue of how to differentiate between behaviours that are egoistically motivated and behaviours that are altruistically motivated. Egoistic helping is conceptually distinguished from altruistic helping in terms of the 'end state goal' of each: for egoistic helping it is increasing the helper's own welfare; for altruistic helping it is increasing the other's welfare. In order to distinguish empirically between egoistic and altruistic helping, the behavioural correlates of these two forms of helping are considered. The egoistically motivated bystander can alleviate their personal distress in seeing another person suffer by either helping, or by leaving: both achieve the same end state goal. If leaving is made harder (or the 'costs' of leaving are increased), then the egoistically motivated bystander is more likely to help. If leaving is easier, the egoistically motivated bystander is less likely to help (and more likely to leave). In contrast, for the altruistically motivated bystander, the end state goal can only be achieved by helping, therefore making leaving harder will have no impact on their likelihood of helping.

Method

Participants

In their first study, 44 female students at the University of Kansas took part in the study. Eleven participants were assigned to each of four conditions (four additional participants were excluded from the analysis because they did not believe that the scenario used in the experiment was real). Participants had previously completed a personal values and interest questionnaire.

Design and procedure

In the study, participants observed a confederate, Elaine, taking part in what they were told was a learning experiment. Participants were also told that Elaine would receive electric shocks at random intervals during the experiment. A 2 (difficulty of escape: easy versus difficult) × 2 (similarity of victim: similar versus dissimilar) between-groups design was used. Difficulty of escape was manipulated by telling participants that they needed to observe either the first two or all ten of the trials. Similarity of victim was manipulated by giving participants a copy of a 'personal values and interests' questionnaire and telling them that it was Elaine's. By creating two versions of the questionnaire, Elaine could be presented as having either similar or dissimilar values and interests to the participant. Based on the work of Stotland (1969) and Krebs (1975), this similarity manipulation was used as an indirect manipulation of empathic emotion – more similar victims would elicit greater empathy. As the experiment took place, Elaine was seen to be having considerable difficulty in taking part, and went on to explain that she had experienced difficulty in reaction to electric shocks in the past. The experimenter then asked the participant if she would be willing to take over Elaine's role. The dependent measure was the willingness (or not) of the participant to trade places with Elaine.

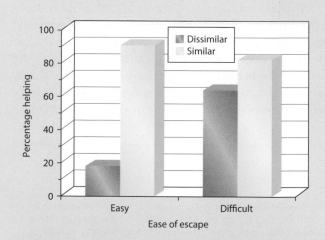

FIGURE 10.2 *Percentage of participants who helped Elaine depending on similarity to victim and ease or difficulty of escape.*

Results

There was a significant escape × similarity interaction: the proportion of participants willing to take Elaine's place in the easy-escape, dissimilar-victim condition was much lower than in the other three conditions (see Figure 10.2).

Discussion

As the manipulation of empathic emotion in this study was indirect, a second experiment was conducted in order to manipulate it more directly. This second study replaced the similarity manipulation with a manipulation of arousal attribution. Participants were given a placebo drug that they were told would (depending on the experimental condition) induce feelings similar to **empathic concern** or to personal distress. Researchers

> **empathic concern** an emotional state consisting of emotions such as compassion, warmth and concern for another person.

argued that participants who could attribute their feelings of personal distress to the drug were more likely to act out of empathic concern, while those who could attribute their feelings of empathic concern to the drug were more likely to act out of personal distress. After receiving the placebo and the instructions, participants watched Elaine receiving electric shocks. The results of both studies supported the predictions of the empathy-altruism hypothesis (see Theory Box 10.1): when participants believed that Elaine was similar to them (and therefore empathized with her, as in study 1), or when they believed they were acting out of feelings of empathic concern (as in study 2), they helped her regardless of whether escape was easy or difficult. Participants who believed that Elaine was dissimilar to themselves (and therefore did not empathize with her, as in study 1), or who perceived their response to Elaine receiving shocks as personal distress (as in study 2), helped more often if it was difficult to leave the experiment.

We are dealing with a fairly fundamental issue here – is it possible to demonstrate definitively the existence of helping that is not motivated by egoistic concerns? There are also difficult challenges posed in trying to demonstrate which motivations (singly, or together) ultimately drive behaviour. It is therefore perhaps not surprising that other scholars have challenged Batson's position that altruistically motivated helping does exist. One of the leaders of this challenge has been Cialdini, with whom Batson had a lengthy debate throughout the 1970s and 1980s. Cialdini's alternative position was based on the **negative-state-relief model** of helping behaviour. This approach suggests that witnessing someone in need creates an unpleasant mood in the observer, who is thus motivated to act to relieve this unpleasant mood. Helping will occur in reaction to the suffering or need of another person, but is motivated on the basis of alleviating one's own negative mood. Therefore actions are based on self-interest, with no possibility for truly altruistically motivated helping.

> **negative-state-relief model** this model argues that human beings have an innate drive to reduce their own negative moods; helping behaviour can elevate mood – thus in this model people help for egoistic rather than altruistic reasons.

Cialdini and his colleagues have argued, therefore, that seeing a victim suffering causes participants to feel sadness, and that it is this sadness that leads people to help (see Theory Box 10.2). Research in support of the negative-state-relief model has suggested, for example, that participants in the 'high-empathy' conditions of experiments such as Batson et al. (1981) also feel increased sadness, and that it is this sadness, and not empathy, that

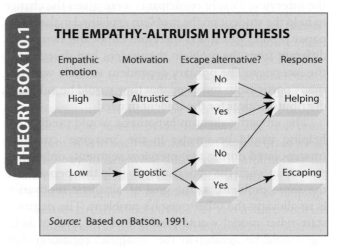

THEORY BOX 10.1

THE EMPATHY-ALTRUISM HYPOTHESIS

Source: Based on Batson, 1991.

predicts helping (Cialdini et al., 1987). Although a meta-analysis by Carlson and Miller (1987) suggested that there was no support for the negative-state-relief model, this has in turn been disputed by Cialdini and colleagues (Cialdini & Fultz, 1990).

While there may be no straightforward resolution to these seemingly diametrically opposed positions, Piliavin (2009) suggests that the 'coup de grâce to Cialdini's position' (p. 213) came when its supporters, Dovidio and colleagues, carried out an experiment anticipating that they would find support for purely egoistically motivated helping. In Dovidio, Allen, and Schroeder's (1990) study, participants were asked to listen to a taped interview from a college radio station. Participants in an 'imagine' condition were instructed to think about how the person in the interview felt as they listened to the broadcast, whereas participants in an 'observe' condition were instructed to

THE IMPACT OF BYSTANDERS ON HELPING IN AN EMERGENCY

Darley, J. M., & Latané, B. (1968). Bystander intervention in emergencies: Diffusion of responsibility. *Journal of Personality and Social Psychology, 8,* 377–383.

Introduction

When other people are present in an emergency, the norms that favour the helping of a victim can be weakened, as each individual bystander is aware that there are others present who could help. Although each bystander may not know what the others are doing, the responsibility for helping – as well as the potential blame for not helping – is shared amongst those present. No single person is solely responsible for helping, and therefore each person is less likely to help. When only one bystander is present in an emergency situation, the full responsibility for helping rests with that individual. In addition, when a bystander knows that other people are present in an emergency situation, but cannot see them, he or she might reasonably assume that someone else has already helped the person in need. This leads to the hypothesis that the more bystanders present in an emergency, the less likely (or less quickly) any individual bystander will intervene to help.

Method

Participants

Thirteen male and 59 female students at New York University took part in the experiment as part of a class requirement.

Design and procedure

Participants arrived at the experiment in a long corridor containing doors that opened off into several small rooms. Each participant was shown into one of these rooms, seated at a table and told that they would take part in a discussion about personal problems experienced by college students in a high-pressure, urban environment. Participants were told that the discussion would take place via an intercom system in order to guarantee the anonymity of participants (although this was in fact to allow a tape recorded simulation of the other participants and the emergency). Moreover, participants were told that in order to ensure that the discussion was not inhibited by the presence of outside listeners, the experimenter would not be listening to the discussion (whereas the true purpose of this instruction was to ensure that the experimenter, who would be perceived as responsible, was not considered to be present in the emergency situation).

As the experimenter would not be present as far as the participants understood, they were told that each person would take turns to talk, presenting their problem to the group. Each person would then comment in turn on what had been talked about, and then there would be a free discussion. Only one participant could be heard at any one time, as each participant's microphone would only be switched on for two minutes, and at the same time all other microphones would be switched off (so that, when an emergency arose, participants could not hear what other people present were doing or saying, or discuss the emergency with them). Once the instructions had been given, the discussion began.

The first person to speak was the future 'victim'. He talked about the difficulty he had in adjusting to his studies and to life in New York City. He also mentioned that he was prone to seizures. The discussion then moved round the other people, including the real participant who spoke last in each cycle. When it was the future victim's next turn, his speech became louder and incoherent, he began to choke and then went quiet. Judges who listened to the tape estimated that it was evident that the victim had collapsed 70 seconds after the signal for his turn in the discussion. The victim's turn was cut off 125 seconds after the signal for him to speak. The time between the beginning of the victim's apparent seizure and when the participant left the cubicle to help was recorded by the experimenter, which constituted the main dependent variable. If the participant did not leave their room within six minutes, the experimenter terminated the experiment. The participant was then told the true nature of the experiment, at which point any emotions aroused in the emergency situation were dealt with. Participants then filled out a questionnaire on their thoughts and feelings during the experiment, along with several measures of personality.

The main independent variable was the number of other people that the participant was told were also part of the discussion group – who the real participant could also hear as part of the discussion. There were three main conditions: a two-person group (which contained only the real participant and the future victim), a three-person group (which contained the real participant, the future victim and the sound of one additional confederate), and a six-person group (which contained the real participant, the future victim and the sound of four additional confederates).

Results

The data from two participants who did not perceive the seizure as real were excluded from the study. The number of bystanders perceived by the participant to be present in the emergency situation had a strong effect on the level of participants leaving their room and reporting the emergency. Eighty-five per cent of participants who thought that they were the only person witnessing the victim's seizure reported it before the victim's turn was cut off on the intercom, compared to 62 per cent of participants who thought that one other person was present, and 31 per cent of those who thought that there were four other witnesses to the emergency (see Figure 10.4). Every participant in the two-person condition, versus 62 per cent of the participants in the six-person conditions, reported the emergency at some point. At every point in time over the duration of the emergency situation, more participants in the two-person condition had responded than in the three-person condition, and more in the three-person condition had responded compared to the six-person condition. All participants who reported the emergency to the experimenter did so within three minutes of the seizure. No significant correlations were found between speed of reporting and any of the personality measures.

Discussion

The results support the authors' hypothesis that the presence of other bystanders in an emergency situation would reduce feelings of personal responsibility and reduce the speed with which the participants reported the emergency, a social psychological process they termed the diffusion of responsibility. An awareness of four other bystanders who could help the victim (in the six-person condition) led to less helping than an awareness of no or one other bystander. Those participants who did not report the emergency did not appear apathetic at the end of the experiment. They often showed concern for the victim, and physical signs of nervousness suggesting they were in a state of indecision and conflict regarding what they should do, rather than having decided not to help.

In a second experiment Latané and Darley (1968) identified additional ways in which the presence of others had an impact on bystanders' reactions to an emergency. In this experiment, they examined participants' reactions to an emergency that unfolded as they sat in a room filling in a questionnaire. Participants were all male students at Columbia University in New York City who had been recruited to take part in a study on 'problems involved in life at an urban university'. When they arrived they were directed to a waiting room and asked to complete a preliminary questionnaire. However, as they were doing this, the room began to fill with a visible (but harmless) white smoke. The researchers then noted whether participants left the room to report the smoke, and measured the length of time that it took them to do so. The experiment was terminated after six minutes if participants had still failed to raise the alarm.

In different experimental conditions, participants were either on their own in the room or there with two others. Moreover, sometimes the others were naïve participants and sometimes they were confederates who had been instructed to ignore the smoke and remain passive. The results indicated that when people were on their own most of them (75 per cent) raised the alarm, but that when they were with others only 38 per cent did so. Participants also responded much more quickly in the former condition. For example, after two minutes, 55 per cent of the participants in the alone condition had reported the smoke, but only 12 per cent of the three-person groups had done so. After four minutes, 75 per cent of the participants in the alone condition had reported the smoke, but the reporting rate in the 3-person groups was still at 12 per cent (the reporting rate for 3-person groups rose to 38 per cent in the final two minutes). Moreover, when the other people in the room were confederates who remained passive throughout the unfolding drama, then participants were also likely to be passive, with only 10 per cent raising the alarm in this condition (a small minority helped immediately while the rest remained passive throughout).

Latané and Darley proposed that social influence processes could account for the inaction of bystanders in emergencies such as this. The presence of other bystanders is, they suggested, a key feature of understanding bystander behaviour.

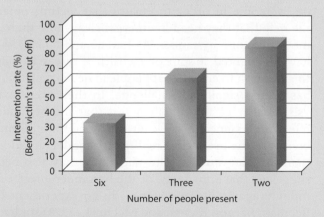

FIGURE 10.4 *Helping as a function of number of people present.*

Note: Criterion of helping shown is reporting before victim's turn is cut off.

Source: Copyright © 1968 by the American Psychological Association. Reproduced with permission. Darley, J. M., & Latané, B. (1968). Bystander intervention in emergencies: Diffusion of responsibility. *Journal of Personality and Social Psychology, 8,* 377–383. The use of APA information does not imply endorsement by APA.

this, we often look at them, and they look at us, as each of us tries to work out what to do. In doing so, we inadvertently become models of inaction for each other (see discussion of modelling in Chapter 9). This process suggests that the appropriate response to the emergency is therefore to do nothing. The situation has become socially defined as a non-emergency, which lessens the likelihood of helping, thereby inaction becomes normative for the situation. This process may occur at step 2 of the decision-making model, where the bystander decides if the event is an emergency or not. He or she may look to others to define the situation, in which case pluralistic ignorance may occur if there are other people present.

Audience inhibition This third social psychological process also decreases the likelihood of bystanders helping. When other bystanders are present, individuals become aware that the other people present would see their intervention attempt. This results in anxiety, which decreases the individual likelihood of intervention, particularly in unfamiliar situations in which the individual bystander is unsure of what to do or of whether their intervention attempt will be successful. This may be due to a belief that they lack the ability to intervene successfully. There is also a chance that the bystander has misinterpreted the situation as an emergency when, in fact, it is not one – intervention would therefore risk additional embarrassment in front of an audience. As such, this process can be seen as a form of **evaluation apprehension** (see Chapter 8), whereby people become concerned that, as they perform a task, they are being evaluated by

evaluation apprehension a learned response to the presence of others when performing a task, whereby the performer experiences arousal when anticipating evaluation by these others (can affect social facilitation, and also helping behaviour.

others present. This process may occur at step 5 of the model, where the bystander decides whether or not to implement the intervention. At this stage you may be concerned with how others might perceive you, and anticipate possible embarrassment as a result – in other words, the process of audience inhibition may lead to you not helping.

The more that these inhibitory processes are activated, the less likely it is that helping will occur. Latané and Darley (1976) demonstrated this in an experiment using five different conditions. Each condition varied according to whether the participant believed there were other bystanders present or not, and which communication channels were available between the bystanders. In the condition with the lowest number of inhibitory factors (condition 1), participants were alone

in a room watching (via a monitor) a person receiving electric shocks and falling on the floor. In the condition with the highest number of inhibitory factors (condition 5), participants could see, and be seen by, another bystander. The other bystander was a confederate who, in the relevant conditions, could be seen by the participant responding passively to the emergency. Thus, in the condition with the largest number of inhibitory factors, the participant was aware of the presence of others, could see another inactive bystander, and also knew that their own actions would be seen by the other bystander. As expected, those participants in the alone condition helped the most. Those who knew of another bystander but couldn't see or be seen by them (condition 2) helped slightly less. This was followed by the one-way communication conditions (seeing but not being seen, or not seeing but being seen; conditions 3 and 4), with those people who could see the other bystander and be seen by them helping the least. The greater number of channels of communication led to more social inhibition, suggesting that the three processes identified are independent and operate additively.

The bystander effect is robust and has been replicated many times (see meta-analysis of 53 articles by Fischer et al., 2011), although researchers have also demonstrated some of the limitations of the effect, suggesting, for example, that the effect does not hold in situations of high potential danger for both victim and bystanders (Fischer, Greitemeyer, Pollozek, & Frey, 2006). One of the key challenges for this research, which demonstrates the power of situational factors in bystander behaviour, is how the bystander effect might be overcome in order to ensure that victims obtain the help that they need in emergencies where there is more than one bystander. As Latané and Nida (1981) have highlighted, in spite of a wealth of research, using this research to ensure that people in need receive help has been a significant challenge. In their meta-analysis, Fischer et al. (2011) suggest that the bystander effect has lessened in size over time, and that this may be due to the use of less realistic bystander situations than in older studies. Alternatively, it has also been suggested that knowledge of the bystander effect may militate against its occurrence. In an experiment by Beaman, Barnes, Klentz, and McQuirk (1978) students were told about the bystander effect, including the three inhibition processes, in a lecture. In a seemingly unrelated subsequent study, when confronted with an emergency in the presence of a passive confederate, students who had learned about the bystander effect were more likely to offer help to a victim than students who had not learned about the bystander effect.

This might suggest that providing people with more information about the bystander effect might help to lessen its impact.

Alternatively, given that the audience inhibition process is particularly strong when bystanders feel that they lack competence to provide help, it has been suggested that various forms of training may help to overcome the bystander effect – in fact, the presence of others may facilitate helping when a bystander feels that they are competent to provide help (Schwartz & Gottlieb, 1976). This highlights the role of **self-efficacy** (see Chapter 6) in helping: if a bystander feels that they are able to help, then helping is more likely. However, it has been pointed out that a feeling of responsibility is a more important predictor of helpfulness, although a sense of competence can contribute to feelings of responsibility (Bierhoff, 2002).

> **self-efficacy** beliefs about one's ability to carry out certain actions required to attain a specific goal (e.g., that one is capable of following a diet, or to help someone).

Summary

The bystander effect is one of the most robust in social psychology: one of the key reasons why people don't help is because of the presence of others. As the number of fellow bystanders to an emergency increases, so responsibility for helping is diffused amongst all those present: individual bystanders therefore feel less personally responsible and are less likely to intervene. Bystanders appear to react passively to emergencies, inadvertently creating a passive model for others. And fear of negative evaluation of one's own potential helping behaviour is an additional barrier to helping. The challenge remains in terms of understanding what makes people help, as opposed to not help.

WHY PEOPLE DO HELP

What are the underlying motivations of prosocial behaviour?

In the previous section we looked at some of the factors that inhibit or prevent people from helping. This approach tends to focus on the disruptions to individual cognitive decision-making. In this section we will look at a range of different approaches that have attempted to explain why people *do* help. These approaches take a different kind of focus. Rather than emphasizing individual cognitive processes, they explore the role of physiology, emotion and group processes.

The costs and rewards of helping

In contrast to Latané and Darley's focus on explaining why people *do not* help, Piliavin and colleagues, contemporaries of Latané and Darley, set out to explain why people *do* help. Their 'subway train studies' (e.g., Piliavin, Rodin, & Piliavin, 1969), which involved the researchers staging emergency incidents on the subway trains of New York and then observing rates of intervention, provided some of the earliest bystander intervention studies that challenge the bystander effect. In one of the studies of Piliavin et al. a 'victim' (one member of a team of students who ran the field experiments) would stagger and collapse on a subway car while other members of the team recorded how many people helped. The trials were run with either black or white 'victims', all of whom were male. In some of the trials the 'victim' smelled of alcohol and carried a bottle wrapped tightly in a brown bag ('drunk' condition), while on other trials the 'victim' appeared sober and carried a black cane ('cane' condition).

The researchers recorded the number of people who came to the victims' assistance, and were surprised to find that helping was often at ceiling level, regardless of the number of other people present. Piliavin et al. (1969) reported that helping was offered by at least one bystander in 100 per cent of trials for all victims in the 'cane' condition, and for white victims in the 'drunk' condition; helping was shown in 73 per cent of trials for black victims in the 'drunk' condition. None of the bystanders left the subway car on any of the trials, but some people did leave the area in the immediate vicinity of the victim, particularly on the 'drunk' trials. Piliavin et al. concluded that, in their real-life 'laboratory on wheels', there was no strong relationship between number of bystanders and speed or likelihood of help. There was, however, a tendency for black individuals to help black victims, and for white individuals to help white victims. This tendency was particularly evident when the victim was drunk rather than if they carried a cane. The longer the emergency went on without any intervention, the more people were likely to move away.

Inspired by numerous stories of emergency intervention where bystanders put themselves in considerable personal danger, Piliavin and colleagues developed a model of emergency intervention called the **arousal: cost–reward model**. In part this

> **arousal: cost–reward model** suggests that observing an emergency creates a sense of arousal in the bystander, which becomes increasingly unpleasant. Bystander responds by considering costs and rewards of helping or not helping.

model addressed the suggestion that the decision-making model of bystander intervention proposed by Latané and Darley did not incorporate a specific motivational construct in order to explain the movement of people through the suggested decisions. The model developed by Piliavin et al. has two main components: a central motivational construct, that of *vicarious arousal*, and a cognitive, decision-making component regarding the calculation of *costs and rewards of actions* (Piliavin et al., 1981, p. 6; see Leader in the Field, Jane Allyn Piliavin).

The original formulation of the arousal: cost–reward model proposes that observing an emergency creates a state of arousal in the bystander. This arousal becomes more unpleasant as it increases, but can be reduced by a response that is selected on the basis of cost and reward considerations (see Theory Box 10.4, panel (a)). Costs and rewards are comprised of two different categories, depending on whether the bystander helps or whether the victim receives no help (Piliavin et al., 1981; Piliavin, Piliavin, & Rodin, 1975). The costs associated with the bystander helping come in forms such as loss of time, physical danger and effort expenditure. The potential rewards for helping include raised self-esteem, thanks from the victim, praise, honour and glory. The costs associated with the victim not receiving any help include continued unpleasant empathic arousal, self-blame, public censure and loss of rewards that would have followed had the bystander helped (Piliavin et al., 1981). The potential rewards associated with not helping relate primarily to the continuation of activities (Piliavin et al., 1969). In the original model, situational factors in an emergency situation were proposed to either stimulate or not stimulate arousal in the bystander; severe, clear emergencies, where the bystander witnesses the distress of another person and which happen close to a bystander were proposed to

stimulate the most arousal. If they do not stimulate arousal, then no response is given. If they do stimulate arousal, this will be interpreted differently in different situations. Cost/reward calculations will subsequently occur and lead to a response that might include direct or indirect intervention, escape or a reinterpretation of the situation (see Theory Box 10.4).

One study illustrating how costs can impact on helping behaviour comes from the work of Darley and Batson (1973), and has already been discussed in Chapter 2 (see Research Close-Up 2.2, Chapter 2). Participants who were told that they were in a hurry offered less help than participants who were not in a hurry, thus the personal cost of being late led to less helping.

Piliavin and colleagues went on to develop their original model further to include a range of additional constructs (see Theory Box 10.4, panel (b)). Rather than a sequence of processes, they suggested that different processes can occur simultaneously, allowing for cyclical effects. In the revised model, the researchers added bystander characteristics (trait factors such as competence and personal norms; state factors such as mood and attention) and personal characteristics of the victim (such as their similarity to the helper) as factors that contribute to the emergency intervention process. They also emphasized the importance of the attribution of the cause and nature of the arousal felt by the bystander in an emergency situation, the role of empathy felt towards victims as a possible form of arousal, and the point that in extreme emergencies costs may only be attended to partly, or not at all (Piliavin et al., 1981). Thus, in some emergency situations – characterized in terms of their clarity, reality, prior knowledge of the victim and physical orientation of the bystander to the emergency – a response consisting of **impulsive helping** may occur, when the bystander's attention is completely focused on the victim. Such situational, bystander and victim characteristics can lead to high levels of arousal, which can lead directly to a response that does not rely on the consideration of potential costs and rewards.

The general expansion of the arousal: cost–reward model additionally includes the concept of 'we-ness' as it relates to the bystander–victim relationship. Piliavin et al. (1981) suggest that a sense of 'we-ness' between the bystander and victim increases the likelihood of intervention, as it differentially impacts on the associated costs and rewards of helping. They suggest that helping responses towards victims perceived as 'we-group' are innate in human beings, whereas

> **impulsive helping**
> immediate, non-deliberative form of helping that does not appear to involve a conscious decision-making process, and in which the helper does not attend to the presence of other bystanders.

LEADER IN THE FIELD

Jane Allyn Piliavin obtained her PhD from Stanford University in 1962, and is currently Conway-Bascom Professor Emerita of Sociology and Women's Studies at the University of Wisconsin-Madison. Together with Irving Piliavin, she developed the influential arousal: cost–reward model of helping behaviour in emergency situations. Her interest in helping behaviour subsequently led her to shift focus from isolated incidents of helping towards the study of long-term, repeated help-giving. This work has highlighted the importance of roles, and the development of an altruistic identity. Various aspects of her work, particularly in the area of blood donation, have fed into public policy.

THEORY BOX 10.4

ORIGINAL AND REVISED AROUSAL: COST-REWARD MODEL

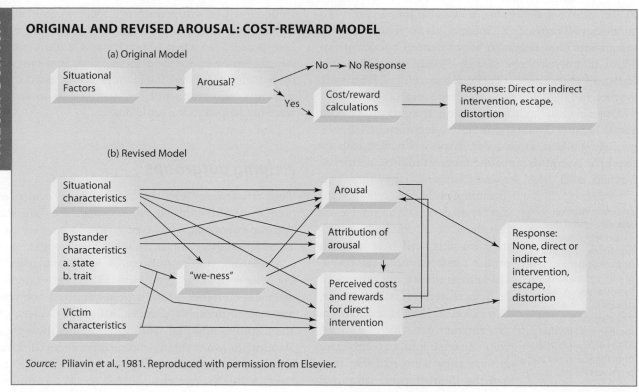

Source: Piliavin et al., 1981. Reproduced with permission from Elsevier.

socialization seeks to eliminate these forms of impulsive or immediate helping. In clear emergency situations this innate response can happen very quickly, and therefore 'beat' the slower, socialized response that attempts to eliminate them. 'We-ness' is proposed to increase the likelihood of intervention, as it increases the benefits and reduces the costs of helping: a bystander may be more confident of the consequences of helping a victim with whom she or he felt a sense of 'we-ness', and therefore the relative costs of helping would be reduced. 'We-ness' is also proposed to increase the arousal felt by the bystander, and increase the costs of the victim receiving no help. Subsequently, these researchers have begun to draw on social identity approaches in order to consider the group-based features of helping (e.g., Dovidio, Piliavin, Gaertner, Schroeder, & Clark, 1991). It is to this aspect of helping – the role of group level explanations of behaviour – that we now turn.

Groups, identity and prosocial behaviour

The traditional focus of the social psychology of prosocial behaviour has been on how people relate to each other as individuals rather than as members of social groups. Thus, researchers have considered *individual*

decision-making processes (Latané & Darley, 1970), *individual* emotions (Batson et al., 1981), or the characteristics of relationships between *individual* helpers and the recipients of help (Clark, Mills, & Corcoran, 1989). Until recently there had been very little focus on the role of group processes in helping (but see Hornstein, 1976, for an exception). In fact, if groups were considered at all, they were usually assumed to have a negative effect on people's willingness to help. The classic concepts of *diffusion of responsibility* or *pluralistic ignorance* both seem to suggest that groups impact negatively on an individual's ability to behave prosocially at the appropriate time.

In recent years, however, researchers have begun to move away from seeing the influence of the group in a wholly negative light. This shift in focus has been the result of collaborations between researchers interested in helping behaviour, on the one hand, and researchers interested in group processes and intergroup relations on the other (see Stürmer & Snyder, 2010). The group processes literature is concerned with how people act as members of their social groups, rather than in terms of their individual characteristics. The key insight from this work is that individuals can think and act as group members, and that when a group or social identity is salient, then behaviour is shaped by the norms and the values of the group. This group identity can sometimes lead to antisocial behaviour, but it can also lead to prosocial behaviour (Postmes & Spears, 1998). Thus, helping researchers have begun to be influenced by ideas from Social Identity Theory (Tajfel, 1978a, 1982a) and Self Categorization Theory (Turner, Hogg, Oakes, Reicher, & Wetherell, 1987) (see also Chapters 5 and 14).

Dovidio and colleagues, using insights from both Social Identity Theory and Self Categorization Theory, have shown how groups can shape willingness to help. Using the **common ingroup identity model** (Gaertner & Dovidio, 2000, 2008; see also Chapter 14) they show that if members of different groups can be made to see themselves as members of a common group, then hostility and bias between groups can be reduced and proso-cial behaviour towards others can be increased. For example, Dovidio et al. (1997) conducted an experiment in which students were divided into two arbitrary groups: they were told that they had the kind of personality that 'overestimates' or 'underestimates'. They then spent some time in a group of three 'underestimators' or a group of three 'overestimators'. Having done this they were then placed in one of two conditions: a 'common superordinate identity' condition, or a 'two-group' condition. In the common superordinate identity condition groups of underestimators and overestimators were put together, but all participants were asked to wear the same colour university sweatshirt, and to sit around a table with a member of the other group on either side of them (i.e., in an A, B, A, B pattern). In the two-group (separate identity) condition, overestimators wore a sweatshirt of one colour and sat on one side of the table, while under-stimators wore a sweatshirt of another colour and sat on the other side of the table. All participants then worked together on a decision-making task. After the task had been completed, participants were separated, and when they were on their own, they were given an opportunity to help an ingroup or an outgroup member. The help request was in the form of an appeal to help with recruit-ment of participants for a study, and to help put post-ers around the university campus. Participants were much more likely to help an outgroup person if they had been in the common ingroup identity condition (see also Chapter 14 for how re-categorizing former ingroups and outgroups can promote better intergroup relations). Similar group processes can be seen in the study by Levine, Prosser, Evans, and Reicher (2005) (see Research Close-Up 10.3) in which football fans were primed to see themselves in terms of their team identity (Manchester

> **common ingroup identity model** this model seeks to reduce bias between groups by changing the nature of categorization from ingroups versus out-groups to a single, more inclusive identity. The model harnesses the forces of ingroup favour-itism to reduce bias and promote helping.

United fans) or a superordinate identity (football fans). Participants failed to help a stranger identified as a Liverpool FC fan when a Manchester United identity was salient, but extended help to the Liverpool fan when a more inclusive football fan identity was salient. However, strangers who could not be identified as football fans were not helped to the same degree.

Helping outgroups

Thus far we have seen that there is good evidence that people are likely to help others when they are seen as ingroup members. However, it would be a mistake to assume that there is a single social identity mechanism – a simple 'ingroup favouritism' – which underlies help-ing behaviour at the group level. Take, for example, the extensive literature which uses helping as a non-reactive measure of prejudice (Saucier, Miller, & Doucet, 2005): some studies find that white participants show ingroup favouritism, while others find no differences (Bickman & Kamzan, 1973), or even outgroup favouritism (Dutton & Lake, 1973). Saucier et al. (2005) reveal a complex pic-ture of the way white participants offer help to white and black victims. They argue that white people are less likely to help black people in situations where failure to help can clearly be attributed to something other than race, or in situations of high emergency where interven-tions are potentially very costly.

Faced with this rich complexity of ingroup and outgroup helping, a social identity approach does not imply that the salience of social identity always results in ingroup favouritism. Rather, the suggestion is that when social identity is salient, people will act in terms of the norms and values of the group. Some identities may contain norms to 'look after your own'. Other identities (like some religious identities, for example) might have norms that encourage members to help outgroup mem-bers even more than ingroup members. When thinking about groups and helping, it is important to distinguish between helping based on ingroup inclusion and helping based on ingroup norms. Take, for example, the work of Reicher and colleagues on Holocaust rescue – in par-ticular the rescue of Bulgarian Jews. Reicher, Cassidy, Wolpert, Hopkins, and Levine (2006) show that, unlike most countries in Europe under the influence of the Nazis during the Second World War, Bulgaria managed to resist German demands to deport Jews to the concen-tration camps (Denmark was the only other country to do so successfully).

Reicher et al. analysed key documents (including political speeches, open letters and official statements) from influential people and organizations (including

THE IMPACT OF SOCIAL IDENTITY ON EMERGENCY HELPING

Levine, M., Prosser, A., Evans, D., & Reicher, S. D. (2005). Identity and emergency intervention: How social group membership and inclusiveness of group boundaries shape helping behavior. *Personality and Social Psychology Bulletin, 31*, 443–453.

Introduction

This research uses football fans to study the effect of social identity on helping behaviour in 'real life' emergencies. The paper explores the hypothesis that bystanders are more likely to help victims of an emergency when the victims are seen as fellow ingroup members. However, the paper also acknowledges that group boundaries are not fixed. It seeks to demonstrate that, by changing the way people think about their own social identity, we can extend the boundaries of the ingroup. By extending the boundaries of the ingroup it becomes possible to increase the range of people who are helped.

Two experiments were conducted. Manchester United football fans were recruited to take part in both experiments. In Study 1 they were primed to think about themselves in terms of their Manchester United social identity. However, in Study 2 they were primed to think about themselves in terms of a more inclusive social identity – as a football fan (rather than a Manchester United fan).

In both experiments, participants were exposed to an accident. While they were walking across a university campus, a stranger came jogging along, then tripped and fell, and appeared to be hurt. The stranger was sometimes wearing a Manchester United football shirt, sometimes a Liverpool FC football shirt, and sometimes an ordinary unbranded sports shirt. It was predicted that, when Manchester United identity was salient (Study 1), participants would help the stranger wearing a Manchester United shirt more often than when the stranger wore a Liverpool or plain shirt. However, when football fan identity was salient (Study 2) they were expected to help as much when the stranger wore either a Manchester United or a Liverpool shirt, but not when the stranger wore a plain shirt.

Method

Participants

Thirty-five male participants aged between 18 and 21 (who were self-identified Manchester United fans) participated in Study 1. Twenty-nine male Manchester United fans (aged between 18 and 21) participated in Study 2.

Design and procedure

In both studies, participants came to the psychology department of an English university and were placed in a small cubicle. In Study 1 they completed a questionnaire and wrote an essay about how much they loved being a Manchester United fan. In Study 2 they completed a questionnaire and wrote an essay about how much they loved being a football fan. After this first stage, they left the cubicle and were asked to walk on their own to another building to watch a video about football fans. While they were walking, an accident was staged in front of them. A confederate, who was a stranger to the participants, came running along, tripped, fell, and cried out in pain while holding on to his ankle. The confederate was sometimes wearing a Manchester United shirt, sometimes a Liverpool FC shirt, and sometimes an ordinary unbranded sports shirt. Three hidden observers (who were blind to the hypothesis of the study) watched the behaviour of each participant and rated his behaviour independently. They rated the amount and form of helping using measures adapted from Darley and Batson's (1973) 'Good Samaritan' study explained above. Participants were also questioned by a member of the research team when they reached their destination (but before they were debriefed) about anything they may have witnessed on their journey. This was to ensure that they had witnessed the event and that they had recognized the appropriate football shirt in the appropriate condition.

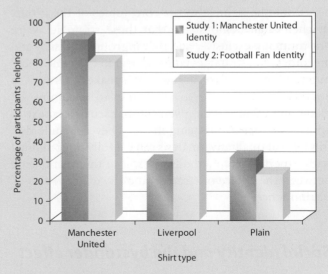

FIGURE 10.5 *Effects of inclusivity of social identities on rates of helping.*

Results

In Study 1, when the Manchester United social identity was salient, participants were significantly more likely to help when the victim wore a Manchester United shirt than either a Liverpool or a plain shirt; see Figure 10.5. In Study 2, when football fan social identity was salient, participants were equally likely to help when the victim wore either a Liverpool shirt or a Manchester United shirt, but not when he wore a plain shirt.

Discussion

The results confirm the hypothesis that people are more likely to help strangers when they see some signs of common group membership in the person in need. However, the study also shows that group boundaries are not fixed, and by getting people to think about themselves in terms of more inclusive social identities we can increase the range of people who are helped. The findings are particularly interesting because Manchester United and Liverpool fans have a strong historical rivalry. This rivalry has been known to result in intergroup violence. And yet, simply by changing the level at which people identify, Manchester United fans can be encouraged to extend a helping hand to those they might otherwise feel antagonistic towards. This suggests that a way to increase feelings of responsibility for the welfare of others is to promote social identities that are as inclusive as possible.

politicians, lawyers, and the church). By conducting a systematic qualitative analysis of the way arguments were constructed and deployed in the texts, they showed that the Bulgarian political elite based their resistance to German demands on two main strategies. The first strategy was to argue that Jews were Bulgarians, and thus to deport a Jew was to deport a Bulgarian. They termed this an 'ingroup inclusion' strategy, and it could be achieved because the nature of Bulgarian identity was constructed in civic rather than racial terms. The second strategy was to argue that it violated the values of Bulgarian identity to allow Jews to be deported. Reicher et al. termed this an 'ingroup norm' strategy. The argument here was that it was fundamentally 'unBulgarian' to allow such a fate to befall any group, and so to stand back and allow the deportation to happen would be a threat to the core values of the group. Reicher et al. demonstrate that these strategies were not mutually exclusive, and that ingroup inclusion and ingroup norm strategies could appear in the same document. However, they argue that speakers tended to emphasize one strategy over another to maximize the likelihood of influence given the particular context in which the appeal was being made. They conclude that this kind of qualitative analysis can usefully be combined with experimental methods to explore the relationship between the choice of strategy and the effectiveness of the influence.

Social identity and the bystander effect

The social identity tradition has also been applied to the behaviour of bystanders in emergencies. Levine and colleagues have argued that the bystander effect (the idea that bystanders are more likely to intervene when alone than when in the presence of others) is a partial story. Using insights from the social identity and self-categorization theories, they suggest that the key to bystander behaviour in the presence of others is not simply the number of other bystanders, but rather the psychological relationship between the bystanders. For example, Levine, Cassidy, and Jentzsch (2010) conducted experiments in which they asked (university student) participants to imagine they were with one other person, or many other people, in a public place. The public places were settings like a restaurant or a cinema. The experiment followed the design of Garcia, Weaver, Moskowitz, and Darley (2002) who had shown that simply imagining the presence of others led to a decrease in willingness to donate money – something they called the 'implicit bystander effect'. However, Levine et al. varied who the others were imagined to be. Depending on the experimental condition, the others were imagined as strangers, friends or group members (i.e., students). As part of the experiment, participants were asked about willingness to donate money to charity and willingness to volunteer time to take part in further psychology experiments.

Results showed that when the others were imagined as friends, increasing group size resulted in a reduction in the amount people were willing to donate to charity, or the hours they were prepared to volunteer to help the psychology department. This was the same finding as in Garcia et al. However, when the others were imagined as strangers, increasing group size resulted in an increase in donation intention and an increase in willingness to volunteer for experiments. When the others were imagined as students, increasing group size did not affect willingness to donate money, but did lead to an increase in volunteering for the experiments. Levine et al. (2010) argue that this pattern of results suggests something more complex than the traditional bystander effect. It is the combination of who the others are believed to be (i.e., the psychological relationship between bystanders), the context in which the presence of others is imagined, and the kind of helping behaviour which is proposed, that shapes the nature of bystander behaviour.

Levine, Cassidy, Brazier, and Reicher (2002) have also shown that the social identity relationships between bystander and fellow bystander can shape willingness to intervene in an emergency. Fellow bystanders are more influential when they are seen as ingroup members rather than outgroup members. Moreover, social identity and group size can interact to promote as well as inhibit helping in emergencies. For example, Levine and Crowther (2008) showed that, when gender identities were salient, and men and women witnessed an incident of public domestic violence, group size could have different effects. In this experiment, participants watched CCTV footage of an attack by a man on a woman (on a public street) while they sat on their own, or in groups of three. The group conditions were comprised of either three men, or three women, or were groups with a male majority or a female majority. After they watched the footage, participants were asked to say how likely they would be to intervene if they saw an incident like this in real life. Men were more likely to say they would intervene when they had watched the footage on their own rather than in the presence of other men. This is the classic bystander effect. However, for women, the presence of other women led to an increased readiness to help. They were more likely to express an intention to intervene when in an all-female group than when on their own. This runs contrary to the traditional bystander effect. When groups contained both men and women, then co-presence had different effects for the men and the women. When men were in the minority, they were more likely to say they would intervene. However, when women were in the minority, they were significantly less likely to say they would intervene.

Taken together, these studies suggest that it is the way people understand the psychological relationships between bystanders, rather than the simple presence of others, that is key to understanding bystander behaviour.

Social identity, emotion and bystander intervention

In addition to the work on how the salience, boundaries and contents of social identities shape helping behaviour, research has also explored the role of identity processes at the intersection of emotion and helping. For example, Stürmer and colleagues (Stürmer, Snyder, Kropp, & Siem, 2006; Stürmer, Snyder, & Omoto, 2005) argue that much of the literature on emotion and helping is limited by an individualistic or interpersonal focus. By introducing insights from the social identity tradition, they were able to demonstrate that social identity relationships moderate empathy-motivated helping. Stürmer and colleagues conducted research on longer-term helping and volunteering (for example volunteers in community-based HIV/AIDS service organizations) and argued that it is not that people are more likely to help ingroup members than outgroup members, but rather that ingroup and outgroup helping can be explained by different psychological pathways.

Using data from a large-scale project on the psychological aspects of volunteerism in a community-based AIDS service organization, they compared a sample of (male and female) heterosexual and homosexual volunteers who were all serving as 'buddies' or 'home-helps' to male homosexual HIV/AIDS patients. Using self-defined sexual orientation as a proxy measure of ingroup/outgroup status, they looked at the behaviours, motivations and emotions that volunteers expressed in their relationship to the person they were volunteering to help. Results showed that empathy with the client tended to be a strong predictor of helping in homosexual volunteers, while liking or attraction was a strong predictor of help when volunteers were heterosexual.

Summary

There are several levels at which the motivation to help others can be understood. Evidence shows that people help as a way of dealing with the emotional and physiological costs of being in an emergency situation. People also help because of their psychological connections to others. When we see people as members of a common ingroup then we are more likely to help them. Outgroup members can be helped too. However, when ingroup members are helped it is based on feelings of empathy. When outgroup members are helped, feelings of liking or warmth towards the outgroup member are usually the key. Finally, when social identities are salient, then the presence of other people does not always lead to inhibition of helping (the traditional bystander effect). When the norms and values of an identity promote helping, then having other group members around can enhance the expression of the identity and thus lead to greater helping.

ISSUES IN RESEARCHING PROSOCIAL BEHAVIOUR

What effect do violence and gender have on willingness to help?

Thus far we have seen a range of work focusing on why people help and why they don't help. One of the most impressive features of this work is the attempt to study *actual helping behaviour* – as opposed to methods that ask about hypothetical helping situations, or ask about intentions to act. The inventive and cleverly choreographed behavioural studies that established the bystander effect are good examples of this. Despite the achievements of laboratory research on helping behaviour, Cherry (1995), in her critique of the bystander tradition, makes an important observation. She argues that when Latané and Darley went into the lab to study bystander behaviour in the light of the story of the 38 witnesses, they neglected two key features of the original event – violence and gender. By concentrating only on the number of bystanders they ignored much of what was socially meaningful about the behaviour of the bystanders. Cherry argues that this neglect was a result of 'culturally embedded theorizing' (p. 16). Latané and Darley were working at a time when society in general was not sensitized to the problem of male violence (see Chapter 9) or the gendered nature of helping behaviour.

A contributing factor to this omission must also have been the practical and ethical difficulties associated with researching violence. It is logistically very difficult to create a violent incident in a laboratory context that is both believable to participants and can be reproduced with the degree of consistency required for experimental designs. At the same time, exposing participants to violence in experimental settings raises a number of ethical challenges. These include considerations of the deception and distress that participants might be exposed to (see the discussion of ethical issues in Chapter 2). Some researchers have, however, managed to overcome these difficulties to the satisfaction of the ethical review committees in their universities, and the research they have produced has suggested some important new directions for research on prosocial behaviour.

Violence and helping

In research that does explore the behaviour of bystanders to violent (rather than non-violent) emergencies, the bystander-effect explanation seems to work less well.

While the presence of others can sometimes inhibit intervention, more often than not, the presence of others tends to enhance the likelihood of intervention in violent emergencies. This research tends not to be traditional laboratory research, given the difficulties of simulating violence in a laboratory. For example, Harari, Harari, and White (1985) conducted a field experiment in which they staged an 'attempted rape' on the grounds of a university campus. Participants were divided into those in groups (defined as students walking close together, rather than being in intact groups in order to 'reduce experimental contamination', p. 635), and those who were alone. While they were walking along, they saw a female student (a confederate of the experimenters) being grabbed by a male confederate who jumped out from behind a bush and attempted to drag the female student away while she struggled and called for help. Harari et al. found that 85 per cent of participants in groups intervened, whereas 65 per cent of participants who were alone intervened. Moreover, 80 per cent of interventions were direct (an indirect intervention route was offered via a campus security officer in the distance).

In similar fashion, Schreiber (1979) also set up a violent emergency outside of the lab, using a procedure that would be unlikely to receive ethical approval today (not least given the number of high-profile school shootings). Schreiber used his own lecture class to simulate a shooting incident on campus. Every year for six years, Schreiber had a confederate intruder rush into his lecture room, shout at, scuffle with and then shoot a 'victim' in the class. The victim then fell on the floor 'covered in blood', while the instructor 'simulated an emotional state of intense fear and yelled' (p. 245). In the six years, only two people intervened directly, and both of these had some expertise in dealing with violence (one was a probation officer, the other an American football player). However, 14 people did try to get help, and these indirect interveners came from the larger lecture classes rather than the smaller lecture classes.

Using a less ethically controversial method, Wells and Graham (1999) explored the reactions of bystanders to aggressive bar-room incidents. They conducted systematic observations of 12 bars, then conducted a series of telephone interviews in which people talked about violent incidents in bars. In addition to their observation that third parties became involved in almost 50 per cent of incidents, they found that aggressive interventions served to increase the violence, while non-aggressive interventions decreased it. Their research showed that the nature and form of third-party behaviour is important to the outcome of violent incidents. In other words, understanding the nature of the violence requires more than just the study of the perpetrator and the victim.

In contrast to these examples that make use of direct observations of people's behaviour in violent situations, Christy and Voigt (1994) extended the study of bystanders and violence to consider responses to public episodes of child abuse. They gave an 80-item questionnaire to 269 people who self-reported that they had witnessed an event of child abuse. Almost half the sample reported having witnessed child abuse in a public rather than a private place. However, of those who were bystanders to public violence towards children, only one out of four witnesses acted to intervene. Of those who did intervene, direct interveners, in addition to feeling greater certainty about taking action, had more often witnessed abuse and were themselves more likely to have been abused as children, compared to indirect interveners.

Levine (1999) used yet another method to study bystander responses to violence towards children. He examined the court transcripts of the trial of two 12-year-old boys (Jon Venables and Robert Thompson) for the abduction and murder of two-year-old James Bulger in Liverpool in 1993. In an echo of the Kitty Genovese story, 38 witnesses were called at the trial, all of whom had encountered James and his abductors on the walk around Liverpool before his eventual murder. Levine argues that the traditional five-step cognitive decision-making model did not fit with the witnesses' accounts of why they failed to intervene. Witnesses *did* notice that James was injured and in distress, they *did* think that some kind of intervention might be warranted, and they *did not* explain their failure to act in terms of diffusion of responsibility or pluralistic ignorance. Instead, they did not intervene because they assumed, or were told by the older boys, that James was their brother. Levine argues that invoking 'the family' as a way of making sense of the relationship between the bystanders and the boys made it psychologically difficult for bystanders to act. Strangers are not supposed to approach or become involved with children from other families. This is particularly true for men, given current scares over the risk posed to children by 'predatory paedophiles'. However, Levine argues that it was not inevitable that the category of 'the family' should have come to dominate the interactions between bystanders and the boys. If the bystanders had constructed their encounter as one between adults and children (rather than family and non-family members) – and acted as though adults have responsibility for the welfare of all children – then they might have been more likely to intervene (Figure 10.6). (See the previous section on groups, identity and prosocial behaviour for other examples of how changing the group identity can change willingness to intervene.)

For ethical and practical reasons it can be difficult to examine bystander intervention in violent emergencies; however, developments in technology, and their application in social psychological research, can help us to address this issue. Recent research has been conducted in immersive virtual reality (Slater, Rovira, Southern, Swapp, Zhang, Campbell, & Levine, 2013) in order to examine bystander responses to a violent attack by one person on another. In this experiment, the participants were all Arsenal Football Club supporters, and the victim of the attack was either a fellow Arsenal supporter (ingroup) or a general football fan but not a fan of Arsenal (group irrelevant). This was established through conversation and by the shirt worn by the avatar (either an Arsenal shirt, or a red sports shirt without any team affiliation). In line with previous work from a social identity perspective, more attempts at physical and verbal intervention (coded by researchers from video recordings) were made by participants in the ingroup condition than in the group irrelevant condition. In addition, the researchers asked participants the extent to which they believed victims looked to them for help. For participants in the ingroup condition, the level of intervention was higher if they believed the victim was looking to them for help.

Gender and helping

Some studies have specifically looked at the role of gender in violent situations. Using simulated 'attacks' (male on female; male on male; female on male; female on female),

FIGURE 10.6 *Levine (1999) argues that witnesses in the James Bulger murder case did not intervene because they assumed, or were told by the older boys, that James was their brother, and it is a widely held belief that strangers are not supposed to approach or become involved with children from other families.*

Source: © Getty Images. Used under licence from Getty Images.

Borofsky, Stollak, and Messé (1971) demonstrated that intervention (attempting to stop the fight, or speaking directly to those involved) was at its lowest for male bystander participants when a man attacked a woman (see Table 10.1). Female participants showed low rates of intervention overall, with only two out of 21 female participants intervening during the whole experiment (although less than half – 10 – of the 21 male participants intervened). Shotland and Straw (1976) also reported a series of experiments that involved a staged fight between a man and a woman in the presence of a bystander. The incident was characterized as involving either a husband-and-wife couple, or two strangers. In the 'married' condition, the woman was overheard shouting, 'I don't know why I ever married you'; in the 'strangers' condition, the woman was overheard shouting, 'I don't know you'. Shotland and Straw's experiments showed that bystanders were more likely to intervene in an attack on a woman by a man if they believed the couple were strangers than if they were married. If the bystanders were unsure of the nature of the relationship between the man and the woman, they were more likely to infer an intimate connection, and were therefore less likely to intervene.

While Cherry's (1995) analysis points to the importance of gender in the study of bystander intervention, and notes that gendered violence generally shows a different pattern of results from the classic research on bystander intervention, a consideration of gender often manifests itself in the analysis of differential rates of helping for men and women. Eagly and Crowley (1986), for example, provided a meta-analysis of gender differences in helping behaviour research. While they found, in general, that men helped more than women in the range of studies that they reviewed, they pointed out that this was due to the focus in the literature on short-term encounters between strangers, highlighting the way in which a large proportion of the research in the

area has focused on particular forms of helping behaviour. Thus, Eagly and Crowley argued that the differential rates of helping by men and women were a product of the form of the studies themselves and the specific helping behaviours that they have studied. In particular, they argued that behaviours prescribed by the female gender role are more often shown in long-term close relationships that do not tend to feature in the bystander literature. They suggest that such behaviours include caring for the personal and emotional needs of others, delivering routine forms of personal service, and facilitating the progress of others toward their goals (Eagly & Crowley, 1986, p. 284). Behaviours that are prescribed by the male gender role, on the other hand, consist of the type of non-routine, risky acts of rescuing others that often feature in bystander experiments (see also Eagly, 2009).

In a questionnaire study of intervention in drunk driving situations, Rabow, Newcomb, Monto, and Hernandez (1990) asked participants about their past experiences of seeing and reacting to someone they thought was too drunk to drive. Rabow et al. found that rates of intervention (doing something to stop the person from driving) reported by men and women did not differ significantly; although more women than men reported intervening: 57 per cent compared to 43 per cent, this difference was not statistically significant. Rabow et al. used Eagly and Crowley's (1986) analysis to suggest that, when bystanders have had no prior training and when those present are not strangers (laboratory studies typically involve strangers), women are as likely to intervene as men, perhaps even more so.

Eagly and Crowley (1986) suggested that this bias towards the kinds of helping behaviours prescribed by the male gender role was due to the dominance of the experimental paradigm in social psychological research, particularly during the 1970s. They argued that manipulating independent variables and assigning participants randomly to conditions, which are defining features of experimentation (see Chapter 2) can generally only be accomplished in the context of short-term encounters with strangers. The difficulty of using the experimental method to explore long-term helping behaviours has meant that there has been relatively less interest in them. There is now, however, a growing body of research that has looked at longer-term helping, to which we now turn.

Table 10.1 *Percentage of men and women intervening as a function of victim and perpetrator gender.*

Perpetrator gender	Victim gender	Participant Gender	
		Male	*Female*
Male	Male	80%	0%
	Female	0%	25%
Female	Male	67%	0%
	Female	57%	20%

Source: Borofsky et al., 1971. Reproduced with permission from Elsevier.

Long-term, sustained helping behaviours

As the study of helping behaviour has developed in the years following its original impetus in the 1960s, various forms of helping behaviours have been studied. For example, Piliavin and her colleagues have shifted focus from the arousal: cost–reward model of helping towards a consideration of roles and the longer-term context of helping behaviour (e.g., Callero, Howard, & Piliavin, 1987; Grube & Piliavin, 2000; Lee, Piliavin, & Call, 1999). This more recent work draws from Identity Theory (Stryker, 1980), a sociological theory which suggests that we have different role identities which, taken together, make up the self (see also Chapter 5). Note that Identity Theory is a distinct approach from Social Identity Theory, which is covered in Chapter 14. While Social Identity Theory focuses on intergroup relations and group processes, and their implications for identity, Identity Theory focuses on the notion of roles and their relationship to behaviour. These role identities are related to social structure, and influence behaviour as different roles relate to different expectations. Moreover, the more a person voluntarily performs a particular role, the more likely it is that their identity will develop in relation to the behaviours involved in that performance. Piliavin and her colleagues have used this perspective to look at a series of long-term helping behaviours in order to examine how such behaviours come to be sustained. Lee et al. (1999), for example, demonstrated how their model of blood donation, based on identity theory, was also applicable to volunteering and charitable donation. The model, developed on the basis of longitudinal studies of the antecedents and consequences of role-identity as a blood donor, suggests that perceived expectations, parental modelling, personal norms, past behaviour and role-identity as a donor predict the intention to donate (time, money and blood).

The research of Lee et al. (1999) was based on the National Charity Survey, a telephone interview survey based in New York City involving 1002 respondents. They asked questions about participants' perceptions of others' expectations concerning donating blood, money and time. For each of the different helping behaviours – donating blood, money and time – the participants were asked about: (1) others' expectations (whether other people expected them to donate); (2) modelling (whether their parents donated); (3) past receipt of help (whether they or someone close to them had previously received help); (4) personal norms (how often they thought other people should donate); (5) past behaviour (i.e., how many times they had donated blood, money or time over the past year); (6) role identity (whether the behaviour was an important part of who they are); and (7) behavioural intention (how likely it was that they would donate each of the goods in the next 12 months). The researchers tested the model that they had developed with blood donation and found that, while there were some differences, the model was applicable to all three forms of

donation. The authors noted some differences, however, between the different types of helping: for example, in comparison to other forms of donation, past behaviour was more important to blood donation and role identity was more important to donating time (i.e., volunteering). This work usefully highlights both the precursors to helping and the longer term effects of helping on the helper, beyond the specific helping situation, and also demonstrates how a model developed in one area of helping can be applied to different areas.

An alternative approach that looks at long-term helping behaviour, and specifically **volunteerism**, comes from the work of Omoto and Snyder (2010). These researchers have developed the volunteer process model, which examines the antecedents, experiences and consequences of volunteer behaviour. This model proposes that these antecedents, experiences and consequences of volunteer activity operate at different levels of analysis: *individual* (e.g., individual decisions regarding involvement in volunteering, and associated individual level psychological processes); *interpersonal* (e.g., the dynamics of relationships between volunteers and the various other people they come into contact with as a result of their volunteering); *organizational* (e.g., the issues faced by volunteer-related organizations in recruiting and retaining volunteers); and *societal* (e.g., the relationships between volunteers and broader social structures and collective dynamics); see Figure 10.7. This growing body of work has largely examined volunteering for AIDS-related organizations in the US.

> **volunteerism** when individuals give time and effort willingly without expecting rewards.

The volunteer process model emphasizes how volunteerism is a process that develops over time, and involves the decision to get involved in volunteering, seeking out volunteering opportunities, undertaking volunteer activities, and ultimately ceasing volunteer activities. Antecedents of volunteering have been identified in a range of studies. Personality and dispositional factors, such as empathic concern, and motivational factors, such as a concern for community, together with particular life circumstances, such as levels of social support, have been found to predict involvement in volunteering (e.g., Omoto & Snyder, 1993; Omoto, Snyder, & Martino, 2000). In terms of volunteer experiences, researchers have found that volunteers become increasingly connected to the people in receipt of their volunteering work ('clients'). In one study, after six months of volunteers working in a buddy programme in an AIDS service organization, 76 per cent of volunteers had been introduced to the members of their clients' social network, and 52 per cent of clients had been introduced to volunteers' own social networks (Omoto & Snyder, 2010).

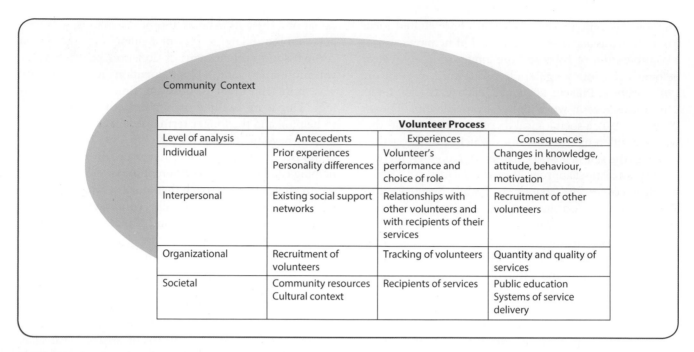

FIGURE 10.7 *Volunteer process model in a community context.*

Source: From Omoto & Snyder, 2002, 2010. Reproduced by permission of SAGE and John Wiley & Sons Ltd.

The consequences of volunteering have been illustrated, for example, in a study that found that 28 per cent of volunteers had recruited another volunteer after six months of volunteering. In addition, as volunteers become increasingly connected to a 'community of shared concerns' (Omoto & Snyder, 2010, p. 233), so too does their participation in other forms of prosocial action increase (e.g., charitable giving and social activism). While this work has thus far been primarily focused on individual level processes, it has also begun to look at community processes, and how the concern about and connections to community can help to both motivate and sustain volunteer behaviours. Thus, a psychological sense of community – for example, a community of people concerned with HIV – has been found to motivate volunteerism, to be an important feature of volunteers' experiences, and to be enhanced through volunteering. Those people reporting a stronger psychological sense of community have been found to undertake prosocial behaviours more frequently, feel psychologically healthier, and to be intent on undertaking more prosocial action in the future.

Another area of research that has focused specifically on longer term forms of helping – and in particular those which carry a significant amount of risk for the helper – is the study of those individuals who helped Jews during World War II. Some researchers have referred to this as 'courageous resistance' (Shepela et al., 1999), whereas others have attempted to isolate an 'altruistic personality' through the study of those involved (e.g., Oliner & Oliner, 1992); we return to the issue of personality below. While there is no clear consensus regarding the explanation of these acts of helping, research suggests that all such helpers tended to share a world view in which victims were seen as part of a common moral community with themselves (e.g., all human beings), and felt obliged to help members of that community who were in need (Reicher et al., 2006). This suggestion illustrates how research in this particular area of prosocial behaviour shows some theoretical and conceptual similarities to research in other areas of helping, which have begun to highlight the role of a sense of shared group membership in the helping process, and also illustrates a possible link between explanations of different forms of helping.

Looking at longer-term helping, rather than helping in emergency situations, has thus raised additional possibilities for research, including the notion of identifying a **prosocial personality**. While earlier researchers had rejected the possibility of identifying reliable personality factors to predict helping, Penner (2002) has suggested that this was due to the focus on helping in emergency situations, and a narrow focus on specific types of helping behaviours. In response, Penner and colleagues (Penner, Fritzsche, Craiger, & Freifeld, 1995) developed the Prosocial Personality Battery (PSB); see Individual Differences 10.1. Penner and Finkelstein (1998) have defined a prosocial personality orientation as 'an

prosocial personality
an enduring tendency to think about the rights and welfare of others, to feel concern and empathy, and to act in a way that benefits them.

MEASURING THE PROSOCIAL PERSONALITY

Penner et al. (1995) developed the Prosocial Personality Battery (PSB) to measure people's tendency to think about the welfare and rights of other people, to feel concern and empathy for them and to act in a way that benefits them. There are two versions of the PSB: one has 56 items, the other (a short form) has 30 items. The 30-item questionnaire has very similar psychometric properties to the longer form. The PSB has two factors: other-oriented empathy and helpfulness. People scoring highly on other-oriented empathy are likely to experience empathy, and to feel concern about and responsibility for the welfare of others. People who score highly on helpfulness are more likely to report a history of helpful activities, and are also unlikely to experience self-oriented discomfort when seeing someone else in distress.

Below we present 22 items from the Prosocial Personality Battery (short form). These 22 items make up the other-oriented empathy factor. These include items measuring *social responsibility*, *empathetic concern*, *perspective taking*, *other-oriented moral reasoning* and *mutual concerns moral reasoning*. The items are all answered on a 5-point scale with the endpoints 1 (*strongly disagree*) and 5 (*strongly agree*). As you will see, some items are followed by an (R). This means that they are reverse scored when the questions are combined to make up a sub-scale.

Social responsibility

1. When people are nasty to me, I feel very little responsibility to treat them well. (R)
2. I would feel less bothered about leaving litter in a dirty park than in a clean one. (R)
3. No matter what a person has done to us, there is no excuse for taking advantage of them.
4. With the pressure for grades and the widespread cheating in school nowadays, the individual who cheats occasionally is not really as much at fault. (R)
5. It doesn't make much sense to be very concerned about how we act when we are sick and feeling miserable. (R)
6. If I broke a machine through mishandling, I would feel less guilty if it was already damaged before I used it. (R)
7. When you have a job to do, it is impossible to look out for everybody's best interest. (R)

Empathetic concern

8. When I see someone being taken advantage of, I feel kind of protective towards them.

9. Other people's misfortunes do not usually disturb me a great deal. (R)
10. When I see someone being treated unfairly, I sometimes don't feel very much pity for them. (R)
11. I am often quite touched by things that I see happen.

Perspective taking

12. I sometimes find it difficult to see things from the 'other person's' point of view. (R)
13. I sometimes try to understand my friends better by imagining how things look from their perspective.
14. If I'm sure I'm right about something, I don't waste much time listening to other people's arguments. (R)
15. I believe that there are two sides to every question and try to look at them both.
16. When I'm upset at someone, I usually try to 'put myself in their shoes' for a while.

Other-oriented moral reasoning

17. My decisions are usually based on my concern for other people.
18. I choose a course of action that maximizes the help other people receive.
19. My decisions are usually based on concern for the welfare of others.

Mutual concerns moral reasoning

20. My decisions are usually based on what is the most fair and just way to act.
21. I choose alternatives that are intended to meet everybody's needs.
22. I choose a course of action that considers the rights of all people involved.

The data from Penner et al. (1995), based on a large US sample, showed the following mean scores for each of the separate scales (after reverse-scoring items marked R): social responsibility ($M = 4.18$, SD = 0.52), empathetic concern ($M = 3.30$, SD = 0.54), perspective taking ($M = 4.28$, SD = 0.64), other-oriented moral reasoning ($M = 4.28$, SD = 0.71), and mutual concerns moral reasoning ($M = 3.84$, SD = 0.56). You can compare your own score with any of these mean scores, to see if you tend to score higher or lower on each scale than average.

enduring tendency to think about the welfare and rights of other people, to feel concern, and empathy, and to act in a way that benefits them' (p. 526). The Prosocial Personality Battery comprises two factors: other-oriented empathy and helpfulness. Research has suggested that a range of

behaviours correlate with one or both of these factors including speed of response in simulated emergencies, the frequency of everyday acts of helping, the frequency of helping co-workers, the willingness to mentor co-workers, and the willingness to be an organ donor (Penner, 2002).

In addition, Penner (2002) suggests that his model of the prosocial personality is quite similar to Oliner and Oliner's (1992) description of the personality traits of the gentiles who rescued Jews during the Nazi Holocaust.

This consideration of longer-term helping situations has highlighted a number of dynamic models that attempt to explain why people first become involved in such sustained prosocial behaviours, how they are sustained, and what the consequences of the behaviours are for those undertaking these behaviours. While the question remains as to whether a single theory is sufficient to explain all types of helping behaviours, what is clear is the importance of the role of identity in both long and short term helping.

Summary

In this section we have seen the advantages and disadvantages of laboratory research that looks at helping behaviour. The early research by Latané and Darley had the advantage of looking at real-life helping behaviours rather than self-report measures. However, it also neglected important aspects of helping situations, in particular violence and gender. Later researchers used a variety of methods – including field experiments, observational methods, analysis of court documents, and most recently virtual reality simulations – to explore these absences. This research revealed that bystanders to violence might act differently to the way they do in other emergencies. It also showed the importance of gender – not only in violent emergencies, but also in the way researchers think about helping in general. The focus on gender led to research on longer-term sustained helping behaviours rather than short-term emergency helping. The study of long-term helping behaviours has included an interest in volunteerism and the study of the effects of volunteer behaviour on the volunteer and the person in need.

EVOLUTION, GENES AND HELPING

....

What is the difference between the 'coefficient of relatedness' and the 'proportion of shared genes', and which is the more important factor in whom we help most?

In considering why people do help each other, we have so far considered a number of theoretical frameworks that have arisen from social psychological research.

In particular we have already seen the debates between social psychologists on the question of whether humans can be truly altruistic. This debate has been about whether humans are responding to their own discomfort and distress, or the discomfort and distress of others. However, there is another level at which the question of human altruism has been considered. Evolutionary biologists have also been concerned with the question of altruism because human cooperation is an evolutionary puzzle. Unlike other animals, humans frequently cooperate with genetically unrelated strangers, often in large groups, with people they will never meet again, and in circumstances where the reputation gains for helping are small or absent (Fehr & Gächter, 2002). The focus of this research is concerned with what Penner et al. (2005) would call the micro-level of analysis, which they argue is underrepresented in psychological helping research.

Early research in this area of evolutionary biology suggested that what appears to be altruism – that is, personal sacrifice on behalf of others – is really just behaviour that serves self-interest in the long run. This idea was based on a gene-centred approach to understanding human behaviour. From the gene's point of view, evolutionary success depends on leaving the maximum number of copies of itself behind in the population. Richard Dawkins, in his book *The Selfish Gene* (1976, 1989), described humans as 'survival machines – robot vehicles blindly programmed to preserve the selfish molecules known as genes . . . this selfishness will usually give rise to selfishness in individual behaviour' (p. 1).

According to this view, when we help others, we must be doing so because of some, self-interested, motivation. The first explanation for why this might happen came in the form of *inclusive fitness theory* (Hamilton, 1964). Hamilton extended Charles Darwin's classic version of natural selection, which had, until this point, focused on genetic inheritance through transmission to direct offspring only. Hamilton argued that, because close relatives of an organism shared some identical genes, the idea of reproductive fitness could be extended beyond immediate offspring to include the wider network of an organism's kin (thus the theory is 'inclusive'). Using mathematical principles, and applying a cost-benefit analysis to the evolutionary 'problem' of altruism, Hamilton demonstrated that the general theory of the evolutionary emergence of genes also applies to the genes that underlie altruistic behaviour. He showed how the idea of a **coefficient of relatedness** (*r*) can be used to explain how genes for altruism

coefficient of relatedness (*r*) between two individuals can be calculated by knowing how many steps removed individuals are from a common ancestor (e.g., coefficients of relatedness between children–parents and grandchildren–grandparents are .5 and .25, respectively).

emerge, and what the limits of this altruistic behaviour might be. For example, assuming there is reproductive benefit to the species as a whole of a parent sacrificing their own interests to favour their own child, then a gene that causes its possessor to give parental care will leave more copies of itself than a gene which promotes child neglect. More children survive to continue the altruism gene line. In other words, this gene for parental care comes to be naturally selected.

'Hamilton's rule', as it has come to be known, suggests that the costs (or *c*) of altruism must be balanced with benefits (or *b*) to blood relatives in order for natural selection to favour the gene or genes for altruism (Dugatkin, 2007). Because blood relatives may also carry the gene for altruism (as expressed by the *coefficient of relatedness, or r*), then the benefits to blood relatives of the altruist can outweigh the costs to the altruist themselves. Given the nature of genetic transfer of information (we receive half of our genome from each of our parents), the likelihood of passing on this gene to an offspring would be 50 per cent (the likelihood of a grandchild receiving this gene would then be 25 per cent, reducing to 12.5 per cent in a great grandchild, and so on). Similarly, it becomes possible to calculate this coefficient of relatedness between siblings or between cousins – in fact between any combination of family members. For example, siblings with the same mother and father share half their genetic inheritance and thus have a coefficient of relatedness of .5 (or 50 per cent). First cousins (i.e., those whose parents are siblings) will have a coefficient of relatedness of .125 (or 12.5 per cent) – while each cousin will have an *r* of .25 (or 25 per cent) in their relationship to the common grandparent.

The importance of the degree of genetic relatedness to altruism is captured nicely in a quote attributed to the famous British geneticist and evolutionary biologist J. B. S Haldane. When asked if he would give his life to save a drowning brother, he is reputed to have said, 'No, but I would to save two brothers or eight cousins' (quoted in McElreath & Boyd, 2007, p. 82). Of course, the logic of this approach is that there is no gene-level self-interest in helping unrelated strangers, and so we are less likely to do so. Thus, using the *coefficient of relatedness* as a mathematical principle for determining relatedness, the degree of altruism towards others can be predicted.

Hamilton's model for the evolution of altruism, then, suggests that when $r \times b > c$, then natural selection will favour the gene for altruism (Dugatkin, 2007). The cost of altruism can be outweighed by the benefit, but this benefit will be weighted by the probability (*r*) that the recipient carries the gene for altruism. The more distant the relatedness, the less likely it is that the recipient also carries the gene for altruism, and therefore less overall

benefit will be accrued; the cost to the altruist will not be outweighed by the benefit. Therefore a gene for altruism is less likely to evolve, and altruism in a population will be less likely. However, when the overall benefit (weighted by *r*) outweighs the cost, then a gene for altruism may evolve.

From the point of view of genetic selection, the coefficient of relatedness matters much more at the beginning of the evolutionary process, when the gene underlying kin altruism first emerges and begins to become selected. However, once these genes evolve and spread, they end up in most individuals in a species. For example, everywhere you look today, in human and animal societies, parental care seems to be the norm. However, the fact that everybody employs the same strategy does not mean that the evolutionary advantage of selectively helping kin goes away. Rather it becomes an *evolutionarily stable strategy* (Dawkins, 1979) that continues to outperform strategies of random acts of helping other unrelated strangers. In other words, **kin selection** continues to offer evolutionary advantage – which is why it does not die out.

In understanding the role of kin selection in altruism, it is important not to mistake *coefficient of relatedness* with **proportion of shared genes**. Park (2007) points out that this is a common mistake in most social psychology textbooks. Hamilton's (1964) inclusive fitness theory is *not* saying that we help others because we share a large proportion of our genes with them. After all, by some measures, humans share 99 per cent of their genes, and there is a 98 per cent genetic overlap between humans and chimpanzees. There is no easy way to divide humans by the amount of genetic material they share. In other words, it is a mistake to characterize the idea of kin selection as something that says that we help genetically similar individuals. We are all genetically similar to each other. Hamilton's mechanism for explaining altruistic behaviour is the degree of relatedness to others specifically *in respect of the altruism gene*. All remaining genes in our bodies are completely irrelevant to the discussion.

This misunderstanding has occasionally been worked up into theories that propose differences in helping based on genetic similarity (cf. Rushton's, 1989, Genetic Similarity Theory, which argues that individuals tend to be more altruistic to individuals who are genetically similar to themselves – even if they are not kin – and less altruistic

> **kin selection** (also known as *inclusive fitness theory*) proposes that we have evolved to favour people who are genetically related to us, and are more likely to help close relatives (kin) than strangers.

> **proportion of shared genes** refers to the amount of genetic material shared by humans (and animals); humans have an almost identical proportion of shared genes with any randomly selected other human being.

Hein et al. found that willingness to help the ingroup member was related to activation in the anterior insula (AI) region of the brain – and to post-experimental self-report measures that showed higher empathic concern. The anterior insula is one of the areas that has previously been identified as central to empathy-related brain responses (Singer & Lamm, 2009). At the same time, not helping the outgroup members was best predicted by activation in the nucleus accumbens (NAcc) region of the brain (see Figure 10.8). NAcc activation has previously been observed in studies in which people derive pleasure from the misfortune of others (Singer et al., 2006). This suggests that watching an outgroup member receive pain could be processed in a reward-related manner.

On the basis of these results, Hein et al. suggested that this kind of fMRI study reveals the possibility of two types of motivational systems that underlie helping behaviour: activation in the AI when witnessing suffering indicates empathy-based motivation and an increased willingness to help; activation in the NAcc suggests empathy is absent and helping is withheld. Moreover, Hein et al. showed that there is an ingroup bias in empathy-related AI responses and ingroup helping. We are more likely to respond to an ingroup member's pain with an empathy-related response. However, if an outgroup member was evaluated positively then his suffering elicited AI (empathy-based) rather than NAcc (pleasure-related) activation, and he was likely to receive help despite his outgroup membership. These findings are an interesting companion to the work of Stürmer and colleagues (see the section on identity, emotion and helping). Stürmer et al. argue that the motivations for helping ingroup and outgroup members are different. Helping ingroup members is motivated by empathy, while helping outgroup members is motivated by feelings of liking or attraction (Stürmer et al., 2005; Stürmer et al., 2006).

Summary

Recent advances in technologies to study the brain have begun to reveal the neural correlates of different kinds of helping behaviour. Different areas of the brain seem to be activated when we help others, and when we refrain from helping. This activation seems to occur in centres that are associated with empathy (when we help ingroup members) and pleasure (when we fail to help outgroup members). These findings may indicate different brain activation systems for different kinds of helping behaviour. These are exciting new areas of research with the potential to transform our understanding of human prosociality.

HELPING IN THE REAL WORLD

Is it always good to help?

At first sight it might seem as though the motivation to help others must always be a good thing. In fact, in much of this chapter we have explored attempts to understand why people help in order that we might increase the likelihood that people will help. However, it turns out that not all helping behaviour has positive outcomes – and, even when intentions may be noble, some helping can harm the receivers of help.

Nadler (e.g., 2002), who has conducted extensive research in the context of the intractable Arab–Israeli conflict, points out that all helping (both interpersonal and intergroup) involves power relations. Put another way, Nadler argues that helping, almost by definition, occurs between unequals. A person or group who has superior resources directs them towards another person or group who are in need. If the helper and the recipient are in an unequal relationship, then helping can signal caring and generosity on the part of the helper, but it can also remind the recipient of their dependence and weakness. This threat to personal or group esteem can sometimes lead the recipient to resist or reject the help (Nadler & Fisher, 1986; see Leader in the Field, Arie Nadler).

For example, Nadler and Saguy (2004) show how attempts by the Israeli government to offer assistance to Palestinian groups were often rejected on the grounds that they would perpetuate Palestinians' economic, academic or cultural dependence on Israelis. Palestinians were upset when Israelis assumed they knew what kind of help was required without asking, or offered Palestinians help without asking if they needed it. Nadler refers to this kind of helping as 'assumptive' help, and demonstrates that assumptive help can be bad for

    LEADER IN THE FIELD

Arie Nadler (b. 1947) obtained his PhD from Purdue University in 1976, and is currently Professor of Social Psychology at Tel-Aviv University. He holds the Argentina Chair for Research of Psychology of Conflict and Cooperation, and was co-founder of the Tami Steinmetz Center for Peace Research at Tel-Aviv University. Nadler's work has questioned the taken-for-granted notion that helping others is universally positive. In his work, Nadler has highlighted the importance of power relations, and demonstrated how helping relations can be seen as unequal social relations, given the ability of the helper to help. Thus, those who are dependent on help may subsequently be seen as having lower status and lacking in power.

the personal self-worth or collective self-esteem of the recipient (Halabi, Dovidio, & Nadler, 2008).

In addition to assuming they know what is required, powerful groups can harm those they attempt to help by offering some kinds of help and not others. As the Chinese proverb says, 'Give a man a fish and he will eat for a day, teach a man to fish and he will eat for a lifetime'. Similarly, Nadler identifies two kinds of helping, *dependency-orientated help* and *autonomy-orientated help*. Dependency-orientated help consists of providing the recipient with the full solution to the problem. It treats recipients as though they are unable to contribute towards solving their problems and, furthermore, reinforces their dependency on the powerful group. By contrast, autonomy-orientated help consists of providing recipients with the tools to solve the problem on their own. It treats recipients as resourceful, and assumes that, once they acquire the appropriate tools, they will be able to tackle their own difficulties.

For Nadler, the way help is offered, and the kind of help that is offered, tells us much about status relations between individuals and groups. He has developed the Intergroup Helping as Status Relations (IHSR) model (Nadler, 2002) to show how groups can use helping behaviour to preserve or challenge their status with respect to a relevant outgroup. The model makes specific predictions about the kinds of help high-status groups will offer and the kinds of help low-status groups will seek. For example, when relations between groups are perceived as stable and legitimate, then low-status groups are happy to receive dependency-orientated help from high-status groups (see also the summary of social identity theory in Chapter 14). However, when relations are seen as illegitimate and unstable, the politics of helping become very tense. High-status groups are motivated to withhold autonomy-orientated help and promote dependency-orientated help as a way of trying to counter the threat of the low-status group. High-status groups try to use helping to secure their own dominant social position – rather than to meet the needs of the less well-off. Nadler and colleagues refer to this as *defensive helping* (Nadler, Harpaz-Gorodeisky, & Ben-David, 2009). At the same time, the low-status group becomes less willing to receive dependency-orientated help and more motivated to seek autonomy-orientated help. When low-status groups reject offers of help they are often seen as irrational or ungrateful. However, it is usually because they perceive the kind of help on offer as being dependency-orientated and designed to undermine their ability to take control of their own destiny. Nadler's keen eye for the politics of the Israeli–Palestinian conflict has allowed him to demonstrate that groups arrange power and status relations not only through negative behaviours like discrimination and hostility, but also through seemingly positive behaviours like helping.

Selfish vs. altruistic behaviour in life-threatening emergencies

While, as we have seen, debates continue regarding whether human beings are essentially selfish or altruistic by nature, it is often claimed that human beings' essential selfishness is revealed in emergency or life-threatening situations. Take the example of a fire in a crowded place. The common conception – fuelled by plotlines for Hollywood disaster movies – is that people try to save themselves at the expense of others. They rush to the exits, trampling others underfoot, in a single-minded attempt to save their own life. Viewed in this way, people look like selfish actors who have produced a situation of mass panic. Because everyone is looking after him- or herself, they don't cooperate, and become increasingly competitive in a way that produces irrational or aggressive behaviour. This idea of the panicked crowd has a long history. High death tolls in the Iroquois Theatre fire in Chicago in 1903 (in which 600 people died) and the Cocoanut Grove Theatre fire in Boston in 1942 (in which 492 died) have both been attributed to foolish overreactions to the fire. These events were always presented as classic cases of mass panic.

However, more recently, social psychologists have begun to change their minds about what really happens in emergencies. For example, Chertkoff and Kushigian (1999) studied the Cocoanut Grove fire in detail and discovered that physical obstructions and not mass panic were responsible for the loss of life. Deaths were caused by blocked exits and poor building design (such as doors which opened inwards rather than outwards). The club owner was found guilty of involuntary manslaughter and new fire regulations were developed to stop this happening again. However, the myth of the panicked crowd persisted.

Frey, Savage, and Torgler (2010) looked at survival rates from two of the greatest maritime disasters in history, the sinking of the *Titanic* and the *Lusitania* (see also Social Psychology Beyond the Lab 10.2). They studied passenger and survival lists from both ships and controlled for the effect of gender, age, ticket class, nationality and type of family relationship. They found that children were more likely to survive than adults on the *Titanic*, but more likely than adults to die on the *Lusitania*. Women were more likely than men to survive on the *Titanic*, but less likely to survive than men on the *Lusitania*. Frey et al. suggest that these differences in survival rates can be explained by the behaviour of the men. When there was a fair amount of time

SOCIAL PSYCHOLOGY BEYOND THE LAB 10.2

UNDERSTANDING BEHAVIOUR IN LIFE-THREATENING EMERGENCIES

While it is possible to simulate many things in a laboratory setting, it would be impossible (for ethical and practical reasons) to create conditions in which people truly felt that their lives were in danger. And yet, when trying to answer questions about whether humans are fundamentally self-interested or whether they can behave in a truly altruistic fashion, it is how people act in these extreme situations that is of profound interest to psychologists. In the absence of evidence, there is a danger we may fall back on anecdote or prejudice. One manifestation of this is the myth of mass panic in crowd emergencies. For a long time the common-sense assumption about behaviour in life-threatening emergencies was that it was almost always marked by selfish, panic-stricken behaviour in which individuals tried to save themselves. However, recent innovative research, exploring data from real life emergencies, has begun to paint alternative pictures of how humans behave under life-threatening conditions.

For example, Frey et al. (2010) conducted a fascinating analysis of the survival rates from two of the most catastrophic marine disasters in history – the sinking of the *Titanic* and the *Lusitania*. These were both enormous ships, built with similar designs, that sank within three years of each other with a similar loss of life (a death rate of 68.7 per cent for the *Titanic* and 67.3 per cent for the *Lusitania*). Frey et al. were able to use the sinking of these two ships as a kind of 'natural experiment'. The key difference between the two disasters was the time it took for each ship to sink. The *Lusitania* went under in 18 minutes, while the *Titanic* stayed afloat for 2 hours and 40 minutes. Frey et al. compared and contrasted survival rates, while controlling for factors such as the number of men, women and children on board each ship, the social class of the passengers, where they were likely to be located on the ship and the number and size of family groups. Some interesting differences emerged. Children were 14.8 per cent more likely to survive than adults on the *Titanic*, but on the *Lusitania* they were 5.3 per cent less likely to do so. Women were 53 per cent more likely to survive than men on the *Titanic*, but 1.1 per cent less likely to do so on the *Lusitania*. Frey et al. argue that these different survival rates suggest that – on the *Titanic* at least – social norms rather than self-interest seemed to govern people's behaviour. On the *Titanic*, compared with the *Lusitania*, men were more likely to help women and children into the lifeboats, and so their

survival rates were higher than would be expected. On the *Lusitania*, where time was scarce, individual self-interest seems to have predominated, and women and children were less likely to have survived. Frey et al. propose that, in emergencies that unfold over a longer period of time, socially determined behavioural patterns have time to re-establish themselves after the shock of the original emergency. The fact that there was time available to evacuate the ship in the case of the *Titanic* meant that prosocial behaviour predominated. However, in the rapidly sinking *Lusitania*, Frey et al. suggest that short-term flight impulses may have dominated behaviour, leading to more self-interested and selfish behaviour amongst the men and less concern for the welfare of women and children. Of course, this kind of analysis tells us very little about people's own understanding of their behaviour in these emergencies. Frey et al. did not have any data from the passengers on the ships themselves: they could only extrapolate from the patterns of survival to the kinds of behaviours which might have resulted in the different survival rates.

In a different kind of non-laboratory approach, Drury and colleagues (Drury, Cocking, & Reicher, 2009; Drury & Reicher, 2010) analysed the behaviour of people in another kind of emergency, namely the aftermath of a terrorist attack. They collected evidence from survivors of the bomb attacks on the London Underground (and a London bus; see Figure 10.9) on 7 July 2005. More specifically, they collected data from a variety of different sources, which all contained

FIGURE 10.9 *Devastation after the London terrorist attacks in July 2005.*

Source: © AFP/Stringer. Used under licence from Getty Images.

accounts of the events from the perspectives of both survivors and witnesses. These included contemporaneous
newspaper accounts (from 18 newspapers) that reported
a range of statements from eyewitnesses and survivors. In
addition Drury et al. established a collection of 127 personal
accounts that were given to official reviews, BBC websites,
blogs, message boards, books and a radio documentary.
Finally, they recruited primary respondents (people who had
been in the bombings and were prepared to be interviewed
directly). The primary respondents were recruited through
newspaper advertisements – and from advertisements on
the websites of support groups. Fifteen interviews were
done online and 12 interviews were conducted face-to-face.

All this data from the three sources was then transcribed and prepared for analysis. The data was coded and
subjected to a thematic analysis. The researchers looked
for themes like 'panic' or 'helping'. Based on this analysis,
Drury et al. showed that the term 'panic' was used by a
few witnesses and survivors, but mostly by commentators
who did not witness events directly. Descriptions from the
survivors tell the opposite story. Rather than selfishness
and competition, mutual helping and concern predominated. In fact, helping seemed to take place despite the
fact that people felt they were in personal danger, rather
than because they felt out of danger once the first bomb
had gone off.

after the original shock of the emergency (as there was
on the *Titanic*) then there was a chance for social norms
to re-establish themselves. The norm of 'women and
children first' became established and increased the survival rate for those categories. However, when there was
no time (as in the sinking of the *Lusitania*) then more self-
interested and selfish behaviour predominated and male
survival rates were higher. This suggests that responses
to emergencies can be shaped by social norms rather
than panic, and that normative behaviour can become
strongly established if time allows.

This idea of the response to rapidly unfolding emergencies was also studied by two fire safety researchers
(Proulx & Fahy, 2003) who analysed ordinary people's
responses and behaviours in the aftermath of plane
strikes on the twin towers of New York City's World
Trade Center on 11 September 2001. Fires were raging
on the upper floors of the 110-storey towers and the only
way out was down the stairwells. Based on interviews
with firefighters and other emergency staff, as well as
survivor testimony, Proulx and Fahy found that there
was none of the mass panic that many emergency planners expect to see in a disaster. Instead, they showed that
people behaved sensibly and displayed a solidarity that
was a valuable asset. They knew they were in danger but
they were not screaming and trampling each other. They
waited in line in the packed stairwells, taking turns and
helping those that needed help. Some individuals even
put themselves in greater danger to free obstructions
that were preventing others from escaping. Of course,
there were a few individuals who looked after themselves
and ignored others in distress, but they were few and far
between. Because of this orderly evacuation and these
unofficial rescue efforts, most people below the impact
zones managed to get out of the buildings alive.

In similar fashion, Drury and colleagues (Drury,
Cocking, & Reicher, 2009; Drury & Reicher, 2010)
showed that the response of ordinary people to the
bombing of the London transport system on 7 July 2005
was also marked by a sense of togetherness and solidarity. In a coordinated terrorist attack, four bombs were
detonated (three on Underground trains and one on a
bus) during the morning rush hour. Those on the trains
were left in the dark, surrounded by the dead and injured,
and in fear that there might be further explosions. In a
series of interviews with survivors, including 90 people
who were on the trains, Drury and colleagues found that
there was no panic. People helped each other by tend-
ing to the injured, offering emotional support and sharing water. They did not flee in a frantic attempt to save
themselves. In fact, most of the interviewees described
a strong sense of togetherness in the face of the emergency. They talked about feelings of unity, affinity and
togetherness, and contrasted this with the kinds of feelings they would normally experience in the presence of
others on a crowded commuter train.

Drury and colleagues suggest that emergencies
produce a sense of common fate amongst the victims,
and that this in turn leads to a sense of shared identity
(Turner et al., 1987). Ordinary commuters sharing a train
carriage on a normal workday may be physically close –
but psychologically distant. In fact, the very presence of
other strangers may make them think more about themselves as individuals. However, when the emergency
strikes, and seems to affect everyone equally, then their
identity can change to include others. People shift from
thinking about 'me' to 'us'. This leads to greater mutual
helping and mutual support.

Drury et al. (2009) went on to look at behaviour in
a range of emergency situations, including disasters in

football stadiums, music festivals and sinking ships. They showed that the same pattern applies. All the crowds seemed to display some sense of unity when the emergency began, even if they began as fragmented groups; those who reported a greater sense of common fate showed higher levels of shared identity; those with higher shared identity were more likely to talk about examples of shared helping. Based on their extensive work in this area, Drury and Reicher (2010) conclude that behaviour in emergencies is not radically different from behaviour in everyday situations. When an emergency happens, people continue to observe social norms, act in terms of their social values and remember their humanity. They do not turn into savages desperate to escape. In fact, these researchers argue that 'disasters bring out the best – not the *beast* – in people' (p. 65).

Summary

Looking at the complexities of helping in the real world helps to deepen our understanding of helping behaviour. Not all helping is good – even when the motivations behind it are noble. To understand the true effects of helping, we need to ask what kind of help is being offered and who is likely to benefit. We also need to challenge prevailing myths about human nature. Research on real-life emergencies has shown that disasters do not always or necessarily bring out the selfish survivalist in humans. Rather, the evidence is that people tend to help each other – even at the potential cost of their own lives. These ideas are helping to change the way policy-makers and practitioners think about human helping behaviour in emergency situations.

CHAPTER SUMMARY

- *Why study prosocial behaviour?* The study of prosocial behaviour allows psychologists to explore basic questions about human nature. These include questions of whether humans are fundamentally selfish or selfless by nature, or whether humans are ultimately good or bad.

- *What is prosocial behaviour?* Various terms are used to define the subject matter in the area of prosocial behaviour. What is considered to be prosocial can be seen to be culturally dependent, but prosocial behaviour is essentially behaviour that is defined as beneficial to other people, but not carried out as part of an obligation.

- *What kinds of phenomena do researchers in this area study?* Research in this area covers many different kinds of behaviours, ranging from short-term helping in emergencies, everyday acts of helping, through to long-term, sustained helping where the helper may put themselves in a position of considerable danger.

- *What role does altruism play?* There is empirical support for the existence of altruistically motivated helping. Research looking at the empathy-altruism hypothesis has shown that feelings of empathy can lead to helping which has the end goal of increasing another person's welfare.

- *What determines helping in emergency situations?* Situational factors are important determinants of behaviour in emergency situations. Latané and Darley's work on the bystander effect has demonstrated the influence of the presence of others on bystander behaviour in emergencies, with a particular focus on why people do not help.

- *What role does arousal play in emergency situations?* Research that looks at why people do help has suggested that unpleasant arousal is created in an emergency situation, and that people will seek to reduce this arousal as a result of considering the costs and rewards of helping and not helping.

- *How do group processes shape helping behaviour?* Group processes have been highlighted as important across a range of helping behaviours. While these have sometimes been presented as impacting negatively on helping, a range of contemporary research has begun to highlight how our psychological connection to others can have a positive impact on helping.

- *What methods are used in helping research?* A wide range of methods has been used to study prosocial behaviours. While the use of laboratory settings has a number of advantages, research using alternative methods has provided novel insights into the factors impacting on bystander behaviour.

- *Are there gender differences in helping?* While it seems that men may help more than women, this may be a result of the kinds of helping situations that have been studied. When we study helping in long-term, close relationships, women tend to help more.

- *Why do people volunteer?* Work on the psychology of volunteerism has shown the importance of identity processes for volunteer behaviour.

- *Does evolution make us selfish?* Research from evolutionary biology has suggested that helping is not entirely selfishly motivated, and that humans will punish selfish behaviours in others.

- *What do we know about brain activation and helping behaviour?* Research from social neuroscience has helped us to identify some of the neural correlates of prosocial behaviours.

- *Is helping always good?* Prosocial behaviours are not always positive, both from the perspective of the giver and the receiver of help. Contemporary research on receiving help, for example, has demonstrated the importance of power relations in helping situations.

- *Do we behave selfishly in emergencies?* Disasters do not bring out the selfish nature of humans. Evidence from real-world disasters suggests that people in such emergencies tend to help each other, even when their own lives are in danger.

SUGGESTIONS FOR FURTHER READING

Batson, C. D. (2011). *Altruism in humans*. New York: Oxford University Press. A timely and useful overview of theory and research on the empathy-altruism hypothesis.

Bierhoff, H. W. (2002). *Prosocial behaviour*. Hove, UK: Psychology Press. Presents a wide range of research on the psychology of prosocial behaviour in its many different forms.

Dovidio, J. F., Piliavin, J. A., Schroeder, D. A., & Penner, L. A. (2006). *The social psychology of prosocial behavior*. Mahwah, N.J: Erlbaum. An authoritative overview of the field by a quartet of the leading North American scholars and researchers in this area.

Fischer, P., Krueger, J. I., Greitemeyer, T., Vogrincic, C., Kastenmüller, A., Frey, D., Heene, M., Wicher, M., & Kainbacher, M. (2011). The bystander-effect: A meta-analytic review on bystander intervention in dangerous and non-dangerous emergencies. *Psychological Bulletin, 137*, 517–537. A recent meta-analysis of the classic bystander effect, setting out the limitations of the effect in different emergency situations and pointing to different explanations of their findings.

Penner, L. A., Dovidio, J. F., Piliavin, J. A., & Schroeder, D. A. (2005). Prosocial behavior: Multilevel perspectives. *Annual Review of Psychology, 56*, 365–392. A useful review article that integrates a range of research to set out the different levels of analysis involved in a broad range of prosocial phenomena.

Piliavin, J. A., Dovidio, J. F., Gaertner, S. L., & Clark, R. D., III. (1981). *Emergency intervention*. New York: Academic Press. This book presents a wide range of research relating to the arousal: cost–reward model of intervention in emergencies, and also gives an insight into how such models are developed over time.

Stürmer, S., & Snyder, M. (Eds.). (2010). *The psychology of prosocial behavior: Group processes, intergroup relations, and helping*. Chichester, UK: Wiley-Blackwell. An edited volume that presents a range of contemporary perspectives on different forms of prosocial behaviour.

11 Attraction and Close Relationships

JOHAN C. KARREMANS AND CATRIN FINKENAUER

KEY TERMS

- attachment theory
- communal relationship
- companionate love
- derogation of alternatives
- disclosure reciprocity
- equity theory
- evolutionary social psychology

- exchange relationship
- forgiveness
- investments
- mere exposure effect
- misattribution of arousal
- need to belong
- passionate love

- perceived partner responsiveness
- relationship commitment
- relationship superiority
- self-disclosure
- similarity–attraction effect
- social support
- willingness to sacrifice

compelling example of the effect of attachment differences in coping with stressful situations. In this study, heterosexual dating couples were unobtrusively videotaped while they were sitting in a waiting room. The couple had been told that the woman would soon participate in a task that is known to 'arouse considerable anxiety and distress in most people'. Before the experiment began, both members of the couple had completed a questionnaire, which included measures of attachment style. The ratings of the videos revealed several interesting findings. Secure women sought out more support from their partner as their level of displayed anxiety – as observed by the raters of the videos – increased. In contrast, women with an insecure attachment style (specifically, avoidant women) tended to seek *less* support from the partner as their level of anxiety increased. Put differently, secure women relied on their partners (i.e., trusted their partners) in an attempt to relieve the distress, while avoidant women did not rely on their partners, apparently not viewing their partners as what is sometimes called a *safe haven*. In addition, securely attached men provided more support when their partners displayed more signs of distress, while avoidant men were less inclined to do so. Thus, attachment style differences affect both support seeking and giving.

Summary

People have a strong and natural tendency to be around others, to form and maintain close relationships, and to prevent exclusion from others. Belongingness with others benefits both psychological and physical well-being, while being excluded from others can literally hurt. By providing social support, close others can help us to deal with stress, although individual differences in attachment styles cause individuals to rely on others to varying degrees. Overall, the important message of the chapter so far is: relationships *do* matter.

INTERPERSONAL ATTRACTION

When and why do we experience interpersonal attraction?

Now that we have established the importance of interpersonal relationships in people's lives, the remainder of the chapter will – more or less – follow the course of a relationship, starting at the beginning: with whom, and under what circumstances, do we form interpersonal relationships? What factors determine interpersonal attraction?

The benefits of physical attractiveness

In most cases, the first impression one has when meeting a new person is based on the other person's physical appearance. Does appearance matter? Probably you have heard people claim that, for them, it's only what's on the 'inside' that matters when judging another person – not the outside (perhaps you are even one of these people?). That, of course, is a noble sentiment; however, scientific evidence suggests otherwise. Consider the following research findings. Schoolteachers judge attractive pupils as more intelligent, and accordingly give them higher grades (Clifford & Walster, 1973). Attractive people raise more money for charity in their collecting boxes (Chaiken, 1979). For both men and women, each point increase on an attractiveness scale ranging from 1 to 5 is associated with an average increase in annual income of more than US $2000 (Frieze, Olson, & Russell, 1991). Judges tend to give lower sentences to attractive people (Downs & Lyons, 1991). In parallel with these findings, Kampe, Frith, Dolan, and Frith (2001) demonstrated that reward systems in the brain are activated when attractive people turn their gaze on you. This is just a selection of many other similar findings that suggest the benefits of being attractive (for an overview, see Langlois et al., 2000). One of the most remarkable, perhaps even disturbing, findings in this area is that mothers who have attractive babies (as judged by outside observers) tend to behave differently toward their child compared to mothers of unattractive babies: they are more playful and display more affectionate behaviour toward the child, both shortly after birth as well as three months later (Langlois, Ritter, Casey, & Sawin, 1995).

What is beautiful is good

There is thus little doubt that appearance does matter when judging other people. But why is attractiveness so important? Why do we even care about someone's

among p
ers. Even
guish bet
and una
faces (La
although
about wl
different
not attra
Wu, 1995

Thus,
beholder
who is ar
assess att
In other
attractive
differ fro
such feat
identified
people o
tally crea
other fac
which is
attractive
& Musse
tiveness,
attractive
1999). Re
about the
ple, som
be fully e
are also
ageness a
beauty (C

Other
called ho
high che
These fac
of oestro
tend to b
ciated wi
a large jav

Of co
size and
both mer
Tasker, &
torso has
ders – ar
& Tovée
have a p
waist-to-l
ter findin
gists in

LEADER IN THE FIELD

Ellen S. Berscheid (b. 1936) is a Regents Professor at the University of Minnesota, where she received her PhD in 1965. Berscheid has made numerous and highly influential contributions in the field of relationship science. She is particularly interested in problems associated with relationship satisfaction and stability, relationship cognition, and emotional experiences within relationships, especially love and sexual desire. In 1974, Berscheid was at the centre of controversy when she was awarded a large research grant by the National Science Foundation in the US for her work on why and how people fall in love. Senator Proxmire of Wisconsin regarded this as 'wasteful federal funding of research'. The scientific community has been more positive about her work: she is the recipient of several prestigious awards, such as the Donald T. Campbell Award for Distinguished Research in Social Psychology from the Society of Personality and Social Psychology, and the Distinguished Scientist Award from the Society of Experimental Social Psychology.

looks? One reason is that we assume that people who are attractive also have nice personalities, as shown by Dion, Berscheid, and Walster (1972; see Leader in the Field, Ellen S. Berscheid). They asked participants to rate pictures of attractive and unattractive people on a number of personality characteristics. Attractive (as compared to unattractive) people were rated as more friendly, sociable and trustworthy, and also as more competent. The researchers called this the 'what is beautiful is good' stereotype. Later studies replicated these effects, demonstrating that both children and adults are judged as being more sociable and competent when they are more attractive. Similar effects have even been found when making personality judgements about attractive and unattractive people when the pictures were shown for only a tenth of a second (Locher, Unger, Sociedade, & Wahl, 1993). Even within 100 milliseconds, attractive people are judged to be more friendly and skilful, illustrating the pervasiveness of the stereotype.

The important question, of course, is whether there is some truth to this: are attractive people indeed 'better' people? Do attractive and unattractive individuals behave differently? Langlois and her colleagues (Langlois et al., 2000) analysed the results of over 100 studies that examined whether attractiveness was associated with differences in traits and behaviours. They reported that, on average, attractive people were more extroverted, had higher self-confidence, and possessed better social skills. So, yes, attractive people have, on average, somewhat more outgoing and social personalities. Langlois and colleagues concluded that, apparently, beauty is not only skin deep.

It is unlikely though that attractive people are born more sociable and friendly than unattractive people. What else explains why attractiveness tends to be correlated with social skills? Recall the study discussed above, showing that

mothers behave more affectionately towards attractive than unattractive babies (Langlois et al., 1995). A little later in life, attractive children in preschool are treated significantly more favourably by their peers and their teachers than are less attractive children. This continues in adult life, when attractive individuals get more attention and receive more help and cooperation from others than do less attractive individuals (for an overview of the effects of attractiveness across the life span, see Langlois et al., 2000). No wonder attractive people become the more sociable people that most of us assume they are! It is easy to imagine how getting positive attention and responses from other people induces a person to behave in a positive and kind manner in return. In other words, attractive people often confirm the 'what is beautiful is good' stereotype by reciprocating the favourable responses they get from others. This is another example of the self-fulfilling prophecy, as discussed in Chapter 3. Snyder, Tanke, and Berscheid (1977) provided support for this idea in a very elegant experiment, which you can read about in Research Close-Up 11.2.

Scholars in the field of **evolutionary social psychology** provide another – not incompatible – explanation for the important role of attractiveness in our judgements about and behaviours toward other people. They argue that in our evolutionary past attractiveness reflected good health (Buss, 1995). Humans who were attracted to specific features in a potential mate that were positively associated with health and chances of procreation success, were more likely to reproduce. However, although attractiveness may have marked health in our evolutionary history, there is little evidence that attractiveness is related to health and fertility in current times, at least not in Western societies (Weeden & Sabini, 2005). In line with the 'what is beautiful is good' stereotype, however, people do think that attractive people are healthier, as shown in a study by Kalick, Zebrowitz, Langlois, and Johnson (1998). Participants in this study rated the attractiveness of a number of individuals shown in photographs, and also how healthy they thought these individuals were. While participants thought that more attractive individuals were also healthier, this was in fact not the case, as revealed from their medical files.

> **evolutionary social psychology** an approach that explains human behaviour and preferences based on their 'reproductive value'; that is, their value in producing offspring.

The features that determine physical attractiveness

Before turning to the question of what *is* considered attractive, the question arises whether people agree about who is, and who is not, attractive? The answer is 'yes'. Of course, people do not always and completely expect your friends, parents and siblings to be responsive, and you expect to disclose information to them, yet you would probably not expect the same from your children. Indeed, as we have mentioned earlier, vertical or complementary relationships involve unequal exchanges of benefits. Parents provide care and children receive care; family members of disabled people provide support and help, disabled people receive support and help (hopefully; see also Chapter 10 on the potentially unequal relationship between help-givers and help-recipients). Similarly, responsiveness and disclosure reciprocity are unequal in complementary relationships. Commonly, children disclose to their parents, but parents do not necessarily reciprocate their children's disclosure to avoid burdening them with their worries and fears (Amato & Afifi, 2006; Finkenauer et al., 2004). Also, parents typically may not expect children to be responsive to their needs, while children expect parents to be responsive to their needs, wishes and desires.

Relationship ending

As we have discussed in this and the previous section, maintenance processes, disclosure and responsiveness are at the heart of happy, harmonious and lasting relationships. It is not surprising that relationships become conflictual or even end when one of these ingredients is lacking. This is illustrated in a study by Markman (1981), who followed 90 couples from the time when they planned to get married till five and a half years later. In the initial phase of the study, couples completed a self-report questionnaire on their satisfaction with the relationship and rated the intensity of any problems they experienced in their relationship. They were also asked to discuss their major problem area by taking turns in both the discloser and the listener role. During this discussion, the couples rated their partner's responsiveness to their disclosure on a scale, ranging from 'super negative' to 'super positive'. At a one-year follow-up, initial satisfaction was positively associated with current marital adjustment, and problem intensity was negatively associated with adjustment. There was no association with the initial ratings on partner's responsiveness. However, at the later follow-ups (two and a half and five years later), only the ratings of partners' responsiveness during the communication predicted current marital adjustment. Those couples that had indicated – before getting married – that partner responsiveness was more positive were more likely to be satisfied with their marriage five years later. In contrast, those couples that had indicated that partner responsiveness was negative became distressed over time. Thus, a simple rating of the quality of

communication in the couple was able to predict marital distress five years later, suggesting that it is less important what couples argue about than how they argue and how they respond to each other.

And if a relationship ends, be it a romantic relationship, friendship or family relationship, this can have a strong impact on the partners involved. Of course, in some cases, such as the battered women in Research Close-Up 11.3, partners may be better off when they end a relationship. Still, on average, people who have been divorced suffer strong declines in their mental and physical health, both in the short and long term (Richards, Hardy, & Wadsworth, 1997). The end of a marriage not only results in the loss of economic resources, but may also involve the loss of a social network (Sbarra, Law, & Portley, 2011). And perhaps most importantly, the end of a marriage or a long-term (romantic) relationship is such a painful process because it often entails the end of an attachment bond. Indeed, partners often form a strong emotional attachment that cannot easily be dissolved or replaced. This is also one of the reasons why people generally find it so difficult to end a relationship. Individuals with an anxious/ambivalent attachment style especially have a hard time dealing with break-up, because it often confirms and reinforces their anxiety about being abandoned (Davis, Shaver, & Vernon, 2003). Furthermore, as we have seen in this chapter, early relationship experiences – including the dissolution of a relationship – may importantly affect our expectations about future relationships. For example, a troublesome romantic break-up may erode an individual's trust in potential future relationship partners, and it may therefore be harder to find a new partner. Most research findings suggest that the decline and dissolution of a long-term relationship is generally associated with suffering for one partner, and in most cases both partners. We can therefore only hope that the science of relationships can contribute, if only a little, to building better relationships.

Summary

People have many different relationships. In relationships people influence and affect each other, they are interdependent. In close relationships people are more interdependent than in superficial relationships: close relationship partners have a stronger and more frequent impact on each other. Disclosure and perceived partner responsiveness play a key role in the formation and maintenance of all relationships. By disclosing information about themselves and by being responsive to each other's needs, people maintain their relationships and signal that they accept and care about each other.

agi
wh
wit
an

CHAPTER SUMMARY

- *What are the benefits of interpersonal relationships?* Our relationships with others are associated with both psychological and physical well-being, partly because partners often help us to deal more effectively with stress. In contrast, lacking relationships with others has detrimental consequences for an individual's well-being.

- *Why do we form relationships with others?* Evolutionary psychologists argue that we form relationships with others because in our evolutionary past relationships with others provided us with many survival and reproductive benefits. That's why we have an innate *need to belong*. Relatedly, attachment theory states that people have a natural tendency to form attachment bonds with others, because others help them to deal with threatening situations.

- *Do all people rely on other people to an equal extent?* It appears that, among both children and adults, differences in *attachment styles* exist. The majority of people are *securely* attached, and they are comfortable with contact and intimacy with others. However, people with an *insecure* attachment style are, for different reasons, less comfortable with intimacy and close contact. Such differences in attachment style explain to an important extent how people respond to their relationship partners – including the romantic partner.

- *Does physical attractiveness matter?* There is abundant evidence that how we evaluate and behave towards others is strongly influenced by attractiveness: we *do* judge a book by its cover. One of the reasons for this is the existence of a 'what is beautiful is good' stereotype, which entails that people tend to believe that attractive others are friendly, sociable, and competent. There seems to be some truth to this as a result of self-fulfilling prophecies: because people assume that attractive people are friendly, they will treat attractive others positively, which in turn will elicit friendly behaviour on the part of the attractive others.

- *Is physical attractiveness entirely in the eye of the beholder?* The answer to this question is no. People generally show more consensus than disagreement about what is attractive, both within and across cultures. There are also objective physical features that determine attractiveness, such as symmetry, averageness, and so-called hormone-markers (high cheekbones, soft skin for females; large jaw and prominent eyebrows and cheekbones for males).

- *Physical attractiveness is surely not the only factor determining why we are attracted to others. What other factors are there?* First, we of course have to be in the proximity of others to even have a chance to get to like them. And we tend to like those who are physically close to us, partly because familiarity breeds liking. We also like those who are similar to us. Finally, the conditions under which we meet others can have a strong influence on attraction. In arousing situations, people may misattribute their arousal to a person they meet.

- *What is love, actually?* Brain-imaging studies show that people who are in love have a strong craving to be with the other person – comparable, at least in the brain, to an addictive craving as observed in smoking or drug addiction. However, love does not only refer to the initial stage of being madly in love. According to Sternberg's triangular theory of love, over the course of a relationship different types of love can be distinguished, consisting of a combination of different levels of passion, intimacy, and commitment.

- *What makes people strongly committed to remain in a relationship?* According to equity theory, partners are satisfied as long as there is a balance between what both partners put into (costs), and get out of (rewards), the relationship. However, relationship stability also depends on the extent to which partners perceive that there may be better alternatives to the relationship, and on how much partners have already invested in the relationship. This is summarized in the investment model, which predicts that partners are strongly committed to maintaining their relationship as long as they are highly satisfied with the relationship, the quality of alternatives is low, and they have invested much in the relationship.

- *Is relationship commitment thus directly related to the stability of the relationship?* Relationship commitment predicts relationship stability *because* relationship commitment instigates behaviours and thoughts that benefit relationship functioning, such as forgiveness, accommodation, and the derogation of alternatives. Such 'pro-relationship acts' in turn breed trust and commitment in the other partner, who in turn will be more likely to act in a pro-relationship manner.

- *What type of relationships do people have?* Relationships are characterized by the fact that relationship partners are interdependent: what one person does, affects the other person. Relationships differ on a variety of dimensions. In exchange relationships, partners ensure equitable benefits; in communal relationships, both partners' concern is to be responsive to each other. The most important voluntary relationships are friendships. They are beneficial for people's well-being throughout their life span and have important functions in the development of social skills and competencies.

- *How do people maintain their relationships?* Disclosing information about oneself is one of the most important processes to increase intimacy and closeness in relationships, especially when the disclosure is directed at a specific relationship partner. Disclosure signals that the relationship is special and that the other person plays a unique role in the life of the discloser.

- *Why do relationships end?* Often relationships end when partners fail to be responsive to each others' needs. Not being responsive causes people to feel that the other does not care about them.

SUGGESTIONS FOR FURTHER READING

Berscheid, E., & Regan, P. C. (2005). *The psychology of interpersonal relationships*. Upper Saddle River, NJ: Prentice-Hall. A comprehensive introduction to research on relationships, for anyone interested in the basic knowledge of relationships.

Bradbury, T. N., & Karney, B. R. (2010). *Intimate relationships*. New York: Norton & Company. This book provides an excellent overview of research on intimate relationships, mostly on romantic, friends, and family relations.

Fisher, H. (2004). *Why we love: The nature and chemistry of romantic love*. New York: Holt. A popular-science book providing an evolutionary and neuroscientific view on love.

Fletcher, G. J. O. (2002). *The new science of intimate relationships*. Oxford, UK: Blackwell. An accessible book about what science tells us about love, sex, and friendship.

Mashek, D. J., & Aron, A. (2004). *Handbook of closeness and intimacy*. Mahwah, NJ: Erlbaum. A scholarly book that summarizes the central processes in relationships, written by some of the most active and recognized relationship researchers.

Miller, R. S., & Perlman, D. (2008). *Intimate relationships*. New York: McGraw-Hill. An introductory book to the science of relationships, with many illustrations of the relevance of relationship science to the readers' everyday lives.

Regan, P. C. (2008). *The mating game: A primer on love, sex, and marriage*. Thousand Oaks, CA: Sage. This book offers a view on relationships from a purely evolutionary viewpoint.

Reis, H. T., & Rusbult, C. E. (2004). *Key readings on close relationships*. Washington, DC: Taylor & Francis. In this book you can read a collection of some of the 'classic' articles in the history of relationship science.

Swami, V., & Furnham, A. (2008). *The psychology of physical attraction*. New York: Routledge. Offers an overview of scholarly work on physical beauty, culture, evolution, and other aspects of human attractiveness.

Vohs, K. D., & Finkel, E. J. (Eds.). (2006). *Self and relationships: Connecting intrapersonal and interpersonal processes*. New York: Guilford. This book provides an overview of research that integrates people's internal worlds and their close relationships.

Williams, K. D. (2001). *Ostracism: The power of silence*. New York: Guilford. Written by one of the leading researchers in this field, this book provides a comprehensive examination of the roots and consequences of ostracism.

12 Group Dynamics

BERNARD A. NIJSTAD AND DAAN VAN KNIPPENBERG

KEY TERMS

- cohesion
- emotional contagion
- entitativity
- expectation states theory
- group
- group commitment
- group socialization

- initiation
- interpersonal cohesion
- need to belong
- role
- role transition
- socio-emotional behaviours
- speaking hierarchy

- staffing level
- status
- task behaviours
- task cohesion
- transactive memory

Kerr, 2003). These three perspectives are complementary rather than mutually exclusive.

Following Darwin's theory of evolution, the *sociobiological perspective* (e.g., Bowlby, 1958) emphasizes the adaptive value of forming groups. Forming groups enables humans (and other social animals) to deal more effectively with enemies or predators, and allows cooperation in areas such as raising children, farming or hunting. Earlier in our evolutionary history, when food was often scarce and enemies and predators were dangerous, forming groups had a significant evolutionary advantage. A predisposition to form groups increased the chances of survival of the individual and, through the evolutionary principle of natural selection, this predisposition was selected and passed on to later generations. This human predisposition to form and maintain stable, strong and positive relationships with others is called the **need to belong** (see Chapter 11) (Baumeister & Leary, 1995). Baumeister and Leary argued that this human need is innate and universal. Indeed, evidence indicates that the tendency to form groups is found across all cultures and situations, suggesting that this tendency is evolutionarily 'built in'.

need to belong the intrinsic motivation to affiliate with others and be socially accepted.

According to the *cognitive perspective*, groups help us to understand our world. *Social comparison theory* (Festinger, 1954; see Chapters 5 and 8) argues that people want to hold accurate views of the world. They can do this by validating their beliefs either against 'physical reality' (e.g., 'Will this glass crack if I hit it with a hammer?') or against 'social reality' (e.g., 'I like this new music; I wonder what my friends think about it?'). People turn to others especially for beliefs for which there is no physical reality (e.g., preferences). Building on these ideas, *social identity theory* (e.g., Tajfel & Turner, 1979, 1986; see Chapters 5 and 14) and *self-categorization theory* (Turner, Hogg, Oakes, Reicher, & Wetherell, 1987; see Chapters 5 and 14) argue that people define themselves and others partly in terms of group membership. These theories propose that seeing oneself and others as members of groups helps to reduce uncertainty and make sense of our world (e.g., Hogg, 2007; Hogg & Abrams, 1993). Being a member of a group often provides guidelines for the way we should behave and think. If you think about the Ajax football fans we started this chapter with, their behaviour is clearly guided by their group membership and the behaviours thought to be appropriate for that group (see the later discussion of group norms). Further, seeing other people as members of specific groups helps to interpret their behaviour: knowing that the people in the subway are Ajax fans makes it much easier to understand what is going on.

A *utilitarian perspective* argues that people derive benefits from groups. *Social exchange theory* (e.g., Thibaut & Kelley, 1959; see Chapter 11; also Leader in the Field, John Walter Thibaut) argues that social relations (including those within groups) help to fulfil the individual's needs and often take the form of exchange processes. These exchanges might involve material goods (e.g., borrowing a tool, selling your car) or interpersonal helping (e.g., helping a friend move house), but also psychological 'goods' such as love, friendship or approval. Enduring exchange relations between two or more people are more effectively organized when people form a (more or less stable) group. Thus, groups exist because they facilitate mutually beneficial social exchange.

Social exchange theory argues that social relations involve costs as well as benefits, and as long as the benefits exceed the costs, the relation will yield a 'profit'. There is much evidence that people are unhappy about relations if they feel that they invest more in them (e.g., time) than they get back (e.g., approval) (e.g., Le & Agnew, 2003; see also Chapter 11). Furthermore, satisfaction with an exchange relationship depends on the degree to which there are alternative relationships that yield more profit. Thus, people join groups because they derive benefits from their group membership. People may leave groups (if possible) when they are unhappy about the benefits relative to the costs of group membership, or when alternative groups exist that have a better cost–benefit ratio (also see Rusbult & Farrell, 1983). In general, people will leave groups when better alternatives are available, including the option of being alone.

Types of groups, entitativity and group functions

As we noted earlier, our definition of groups is relatively broad, and many types of groups may be included.

 LEADER IN THE FIELD

John Walter Thibaut (1917–1986) was born in Marion, Ohio. He studied philosophy at the University of North Carolina. During World War II he came into contact with psychology when he was assigned to the Aviation Psychology Program. In 1946 he moved to the Massachusetts Institute of Technology to study with Kurt Lewin (see Leader in the Field, Chapter 1). After Lewin's death in 1947, Thibaut moved to the University of Michigan, where he received his PhD. His subsequent career took him to Boston University, Harvard University and back to the University of North Carolina. Thibaut is best known for his 1959 book (co-authored with Harold Kelley; see Leader in the Field, Chapter 3) *The Social Psychology of Groups*. In that book, Thibaut and Kelley laid out the foundations of social exchange theory, arguing that social relations take the form of social exchange processes.

Table 12.1 *Characteristics of different types of groups.*

Characteristic	Type of group (examples)			
	Intimacy group (family members, friends, romantic partners)	Task group (jury members, cast of a play, sports team)	Social category (women, black people, Americans)	Loose association (people at a bus stop, at the cinema, living in same area)
Interaction	High	Moderate/High	Low	Low
Importance	High	Moderate/High	Low	Low
Common goals	High	Moderate/High	Low	Low
Common outcomes	High	Moderate/High	Low	Low
Similarity	High	Moderate	Low	Low
Duration	Long	Moderate	Long	Short
Permeability	Low	Moderate	Low	High
Size	Small	Small	Large	Moderate
Entitativity	High	High	Moderate	Low

Source: Data copyright © 2000 by the American Psychological Association. Adapted with permission. Lickel, B., Hamilton, D. L., Wieczorkowska, G., Lewis, A., Sherman, S. J., & Uhles, A. N. (2000). Varieties of groups and the perception of group entitativity. *Journal of Personality and Social Psychology, 78*, 223–246. The use of APA information does not imply endorsement by APA.

However, there are different types of groups with different characteristics. Further, some groups seem more 'groupy' than other groups, a phenomenon often referred to as the **entitativity** of groups. Campbell (1958) coined the new word 'entitativity' to refer to the degree to which a collection of people is perceived as being bonded together in a coherent unit.

entitativity the degree to which a collection of people is perceived as being bonded together in a coherent unit.

So, what different types of groups can we distinguish? Lickel et al. (2000) wondered whether people spontaneously distinguish between different types of groups. They provided their participants (American and Polish students) with a sample of 40 different groups, such as 'members of a family', 'black people', 'members of a jury' and 'people in line at a bank'. Participants had to rate these different groups on eight dimensions: degree of interaction among members; importance of group members to each other; common goals and common outcomes for group members; similarity among group members; duration; permeability (how easy it is to join or leave the group); and size. The groups were also rated on the degree to which the group really was a group (group entitativity). After they had done the ratings, participants were asked to sort the 40 groups into different categories using their own individual criteria, including as many or as few categories as they wanted.

Lickel et al. (2000) found that some of their 40 groups were consistently sorted into one common category, whereas other groups were consistently sorted into other categories. Further, groups that were sorted into the same category were also rated similarly on the eight dimensions. Lickel et al. identified four types of groups: intimacy groups; task groups; social categories; and loose associations. In Table 12.1 we give a summary of their findings and some examples of the different types of groups. As can be seen in the table, the types of groups differed along the different dimensions. For example, intimacy groups (e.g., a family) were rated to have high levels of interaction, were seen as important, had common goals and outcomes, had a high degree of similarity, were of long duration and low permeability and were fairly small. Social categories (e.g., women), in contrast, were rated to have low levels of interaction, were rated low on importance of members to each other, with low levels of common goals and outcomes, and low member similarity, and were rated to be of long duration, low in permeability, and large.

speculate that this might be one reason why some people are drawn towards extremist groups. Social uncertainty may lead to higher levels of self-uncertainty and thus to the greater appeal of very entitative groups, perhaps including extremist or fundamentalist groups, who clearly distinguish themselves from other groups. Indeed, there is some evidence for this suggestion. Hogg, Meehan, and

Farquharson (2010) studied Australian students' support for a group proposing extremist action against a planned rise in payment of tuition fees (upfront rather than after graduation), such as a campus blockade. They found that support for the extremist group, but not for a group proposing more moderate action, increased when students' self-uncertainty was primed.

INDIVIDUALS IN GROUPS: THE INDIVIDUAL LEVEL OF ANALYSIS

What stages of group socialization can be distinguished and what factors determine role transitions?

In this section we consider the individual within the group: that is, we focus on the individual level of analysis. In particular, we discuss Moreland and Levine's (1982) model of group socialization, which is shown in Theory Box 12.1 (see also Leaders in the Field, John M. Levine and Richard L. Moreland). **Group socialization** may be

group socialization the efforts of the group to assimilate new members to existing group norms and practices.

defined as the process through which the group tries to assimilate members to existing group norms and practices. As defined in Chapter 8, *norms* refer to belief systems about how (not) to behave, which guide behaviour and reflect group members' shared expectations about typical or desirable activities. In a later section of this chapter group norms are discussed more extensively. Here, the focus is on Moreland and Levine's model, which is applicable to groups that exist for comparatively long periods of time and have direct interaction between members, but which experience changes in membership. Examples would include a sports team, a team within an organization or a student society (i.e., many intimacy groups and task groups).

Moreland and Levine's model distinguishes five stages of group membership: investigation, socialization, maintenance, resocialization and remembrance. According to the model, moving from one stage to the next involves a **role transition**. Thus, moving from prospective member

role transition a change in the relation between a group member and a group.

(the stage of investigation) to new member (the stage of socialization) involves the role transition of entry. Further role transitions

are acceptance (from new member to full member), divergence (from full member to marginal member) and exit (from marginal member to ex-member). As can be seen in Theory Box 12.1, the five different stages differ in the degree of **group commitment** – in other words, the degree to which a group member

group commitment a psychological bond of a group member with the group and its goals including the desire to maintain group membership.

has a psychological bond with the group and its goals and wishes to maintain group membership. Group commitment increases gradually as people become full members, after which it decreases towards the point at which individuals wish to leave the group (although this may not always happen).

Role transitions occur as a result of evaluation processes in which the group and the individual evaluate

 LEADERS IN THE FIELD

John M. Levine (b. 1942) and **Richard L. Moreland** (b. 1951) have worked together on issues around group dynamics for more than three decades. Their collaboration started when Moreland joined the University of Pittsburgh in 1978 after receiving his PhD from the University of Michigan in that same year. Levine had worked in Pittsburgh since 1969, immediately after receiving his PhD from the University of Wisconsin. One of the first papers they wrote together was their highly influential article on group socialization that is discussed in the text. After this paper, they continued publishing on group socialization, and also worked on topics such as newcomer influence, collaboration, group composition, group commitment and group loyalty. They are also widely known for their efforts to summarize progress in the field of group dynamics in book chapters and books, such as their 1990 paper on Progress in Small Group Research that appeared in the *Annual Review of Psychology* (Levine & Moreland, 1990), their chapter on Small Groups in the *Handbook of Social Psychology* (Levine & Moreland, 1998), and a chapter on the history of small group research (Levine & Moreland, 2012). In fact, their collaboration has been so close that they have occasionally been erroneously introduced as John Moreland and Dick Levine, about which they note: 'The fact that we are flattered by such introductions says a lot about why we continue to collaborate' (Levine & Moreland, 2004, p. 170). Apart from their collaborative work, Levine is also known for his research on minority influence and newcomers, and Moreland has done important work in the area of shared cognition and transactive memory (see later in this chapter).

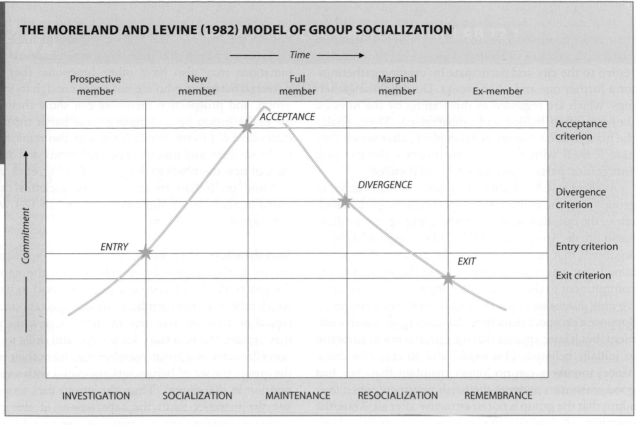

THE MORELAND AND LEVINE (1982) MODEL OF GROUP SOCIALIZATION

one another's 'rewardingness', or the extent to which the group is rewarding for the member and to which the member is valued by the group. When the group is rewarding for members, they will try to enter the group or maintain group membership (i.e., feel group commitment). Similarly, when a group values a (prospective) member, the group will encourage the person to become or stay a member of the group (i.e., the group is committed to the member). This is related to our earlier discussion of social exchange processes and the benefits people can derive from them (e.g., to gain social approval or receive help or material goods). Indeed, according to Moreland and Levine (1982), group commitment is a function of the past, present and expected future rewardingness of the group, compared to the rewardingness of alternative groups. In the remainder of this section, we consider the key stages shown in Theory Box 12.1.

Joining a group and group socialization: becoming a full member

Investigation In the stage of investigation, groups look for people who might make a contribution to the attainment of group goals. Task groups will often search for people who have the required skills and abilities, whereas intimacy groups will tend to emphasize compatibility (e.g., similarity) with the existing membership. Prospective members, on the other hand, will look for groups that may potentially fulfil their needs. For example, when you have just moved to a new city to start college, you will probably try to identify specific groups that might help to fulfil your social needs. Thus, you might join a student society, hoping to find people with whom you can start a new, positive and stable relation (i.e., fulfil your need to belong). Another example of how groups fulfil members' needs is discussed in Research Close-Up 12.1.

Entry and initiation When the level of group commitment (i.e., the mutual commitment between the group and the prospective member) reaches an entry criterion, a role transition will occur: *entry*. Entry is often marked by some ritual or ceremony that makes it clear that the relation between the group and the (prospective) member has changed. In an organization, this may take the form of a welcome speech, and in social groups it may be a party. At other times the entry or **initiation** ritual can be quite unpleasant and painful for the prospective member.

initiation the role transition of entry into a group, often accompanied by some ritual.

Lodewijkx and Syroit (1997) studied initiation into a Dutch sorority (a student society for female students).

The major way in which groups and members try to increase the rewardingness of their relationship is through role negotiation. Thus, the member tries to occupy the role within the group that best satisfies his or her needs, whereas the group tries to assign roles to members in such a way that the group's goals can be best achieved. One of the more important roles within the group is that of group leader (see Chapter 13). However, there are often other roles that need to be fulfilled within groups, such as those of 'recruiter' (who identifies and evaluates prospective members) and 'trainer' (who has a role during the socialization of new members). The relation between the group and the member will be rewarding, and group commitment will remain high to the degree that role negotiations are successful. We examine what it means to 'be in a group' in more detail in the next section, where we discuss norms, roles and status.

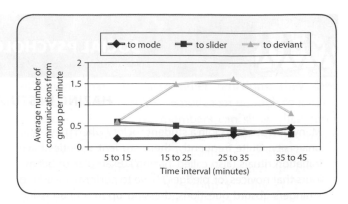

FIGURE 12.2 *Communications directed towards the mode, slider and deviant over time.*

Source: Copyright © 1951 by the American Psychological Association. Adapted with permission. Schachter, S. (1951). Deviation, rejection, and communication. *Journal of Abnormal and Social Psychology, 46,* 190–207. The use of APA information does not imply endorsement by APA.

Leaving a group: divergence and exit

Divergence After a time, group members may lose interest in the group, for example because they are dissatisfied with their role in the group, or because they have identified other groups that are more rewarding. On the other hand, group commitment of the group to its members may decline when members fail to live up to group expectations. For example, members may not perform well in their role, or may violate important group norms. This will lead the group to re-label these members as marginal members or deviates. The group might, for instance, no longer give marginal members full information, or other group members might exclude marginal members from informal cliques (e.g., they are no longer asked to come along for a drink after work). Often considerable pressure is exerted on deviates to realign or even to leave the group (especially if the group is overstaffed).

Schachter (1951) experimentally demonstrated the pressure that is exerted on deviates. He had groups discuss a delinquency case, in which the life history of a juvenile delinquent was provided, and groups had to decide on a punishment for a minor crime. In each of the experimental groups there were confederates playing different roles: the 'mode' who accommodated to the group's average judgement, the 'slider' who initially took an extreme position (e.g., a very harsh punishment) but then moved towards the group norm, and the 'deviate', who also took an extreme position, but maintained it throughout the discussion. Initially, the group discussion was primarily aimed at the two deviating members (the slider and the deviate) in each group, trying to change their minds. When it became apparent that the deviates

would not change, the groups eventually excluded them, refusing to talk to them and ignoring their contributions (see Figure 12.2). After the discussion, deviates were also liked less than other group members.

Resocialization and exit Divergence might be followed by a period of resocialization. In this period, the group might try to persuade marginal members not to leave, or they might try to accommodate to the wishes of marginal members (e.g., give them a different role). Similarly, group members may try to convince the group not to expel them, and might try to assimilate to the group's expectations again. This might result in re-entry to the group when successful. However, when resocialization fails, group members may reach an exit criterion and leave the group. As with other role transitions, this may involve some ritual, such as a goodbye speech or a party.

According to Moreland and Levine's (1982) model of group socialization, voluntary exit from a group becomes more likely when there are alternative groups that are more attractive. An example would be a football player who leaves a club to play in a rival team because of higher earnings. However, sometimes group members will resist temptation, and remain loyal to their group despite the presence of a (perhaps) more attractive group. One factor appears to be identification: the more people identify with their group, the more positive they perceive their group to be, and the less likely they are to leave the group (even when the group has performed poorly in the past; see Van Vugt & Hart, 2004). You can measure your level of identification with a group by responding to the questions in Individual Differences 12.1.

MEASURING IDENTIFICATION

Instruction

Think of a group of which you are a member. Then answer the following questions on a scale from 1 (*completely disagree*) to 4 (*neutral*) to 7 (*completely agree*) with this group in mind.

Items

1. I feel strongly affiliated with this group.
2. Other groups can learn a lot from us.
3. Belonging to this group is an important part of my identity.
4. In times of trouble, the only way to know what to do is to rely on my group's leader(s).
5. I am glad to contribute to this group.
6. Compared to other groups of this kind, this group is particularly good.
7. It is important to me that I view myself as a member of this group.
8. All group members should respect the customs, the institutions and the leaders of this group.
9. I am strongly committed to this group.
10. Relative to other groups, we are a very moral group.
11. It is important to me that others see me as a member of this group.
12. It is disloyal to criticize this group.
13. I like to help this group.
14. This group is better than other groups in all respects.
15. When I talk about the group members, I usually say 'we' rather than 'they'.
16. There is usually a good reason for every rule and regulation that the group leader(s) propose.

Source: Adapted from Roccas, Sagiv, Schwartz, Halevy, and Eidelson (2008), with permission from SAGE Publications Ltd.

Scoring

This questionnaire is taken from Roccas, Sagiv, Schwartz, Halevy, and Eidelson (2008). These authors argue that there are four basic dimensions underlying identification: *importance* ('How much do I view the group as part of who I am?'), *commitment* ('How much am I willing to benefit the group?'), *superiority* ('How much do I view my group as superior to other groups?') and *deference* ('How much do I honour, revere, and submit to the group's norms, symbols and leaders?').

Add up your answers to questions 3, 7, 11, and 15 to compute an *importance* score.

Add up your answers to questions 1, 5, 9, and 13 to compute a *commitment* score.

Add up your answers to questions 2, 6, 10, and 14 to compute a *superiority* score.

Add up your answers to questions 4, 8, 12 and 16 to compute a *deference* score.

Then divide all four scores by four (the number of items per scale) to get a minimum score of 1 and a maximum score of 7.

Norms

The test was filled out by American and Israeli university students, who were asked to report how much they identified with their nation. Based on both samples, you can interpret your scores as follows:

On *importance* a score lower than 4.3 would be low, a score of 5.4 would be average and a score higher than 6.5 would be high.

On *commitment* a score lower than 3.9 would be low, a score of 5.0 would be average and a score higher than 6.1 would be high.

On *superiority* a score lower than 2.9 would be low, a score of 4.0 would be average and a score higher than 5.1 would be high.

On *deference* a score lower than 1.9 would be low, a score of 3.0 would be average and a score higher than 4.1 would be high.

In some cases, the group may expel a member, which can be quite a painful experience. For example, an employee might be fired or a church member might be excommunicated. Research has shown that social exclusion from groups has enormous negative effects on excluded members. Consider the following situation. You are invited to come to the psychology lab to participate in an experiment and are asked to wait in a waiting room until the experiment starts. In that room two other participants are also waiting (they are, in fact, confederates of the experimenter). One of them has brought a tennis ball and playfully throws it to the

other participant. That participant joins in and throws the ball to you. For a while, the three of you play this ball-tossing game. After some time, however, the other participants no longer throw the ball to you, but only to each other, and this goes on for several minutes. How would you feel?

Williams (2001) reports extensive evidence concerning the power of social exclusion. Using the ball-tossing game (and other situations), he found that social exclusion produces severe negative moods and anger, and leads to lower ratings on belongingness and self-esteem. Further, Eisenberger, Lieberman, and Williams (2003) found that exclusion quite literally is a form of 'social pain'. These researchers had participants play a computerized version of the ball-tossing game while lying in an fMRI (functional magnetic resonance imaging) brain scanner. Using the fMRI scanner, the researchers could identify which brain areas were active during social exclusion. Participants were led to believe that, by pushing a button, they could throw a (virtual) ball to another participant, who could then throw the ball back to them or to a third participant. In fact, there was only one real participant, and the computer was programmed in such a way that this participant received the ball nine times, after which the ball was no longer thrown to him or her. While being excluded from the game, an fMRI brain scan was made. Eisenberger et al. (2003) found that social exclusion activates an area in the brain (the anterior cingulate cortex) that is normally activated when a person is in physical pain. Furthermore, the level of activation of that brain area was correlated with participants' reports of distress.

Remembrance The last stage of the Moreland and Levine model is remembrance (see Theory Box 12.1). In this stage, the ex-member and the group retrospectively evaluate each other. Thus, remaining group members will evaluate the ex-member's contributions to the group and will maintain some degree of commitment to the ex-member if these contributions are seen as positive. Similarly, ex-members look back on their time with the group with either fond or bitter memories. In extreme cases, ex-members may even try to destroy their former group in an act of revenge. Workplace shootings, in which employees who had been dismissed shot their boss or former colleagues, are extreme examples. One such incident happened in Kansas City, US, in 2004, where a man who had been laid off several months earlier killed five former colleagues and wounded two more before taking his own life. Such events are, of course, extreme, and occur very rarely.

Summary

Individuals move through different phases of group membership (prospective member, new member, full member, marginal member and ex-member). These stages of group membership differ in the degree of group commitment of the group and the member to each other. Moving from one stage to the next involves a role transition, and role transitions can both be extreme (e.g., severe initiation rituals) and have a large impact on members (e.g., after exit).

GROUP DEVELOPMENT AND STRUCTURE: THE GROUP LEVEL OF ANALYSIS

How do group interaction, structure, norms, status and roles develop?

In the previous section we discussed the (changing) relation of the group member with the group. In this section we explore the group level of analysis. First, we discuss how groups themselves can also change over time. Second, groups have certain characteristics, such as norms to govern their behaviour and a group structure, in which some members have more **status** than others, or in which different members occupy different roles in the group. These issues are examined below. It should be noted that this section is mainly relevant for groups with direct (usually face-to-face) interaction.

> **status** evaluation of a role by the group in which a role is contained or defined.

Group development

Some groups are formed for a special reason and end after a given time. Examples include therapy groups, project teams and the group of students in a psychology seminar. These groups will generally develop: the interaction patterns among group members change over time. Further, there may be similarities in the way different groups develop. The basic idea is that every group faces specific challenges and has specific goals, and these challenges and goals change over time. This, in turn, has consequences for the way group members interact with each other, as well as for group performance and the rewardingness of the group to its members.

Tuckman (1965) and Tuckman and Jensen (1977) introduced a classic five-stage model of group development: forming, storming, norming, performing and adjourning (see Theory Box 12.2). In the first stage, when the group is *forming*, group members feel insecure because they do not know each other and do not know what is expected of them. As a consequence, interactions are usually polite and inhibited. In this first stage, people get to know each other and develop a shared identity as members of the same group. This might happen at the beginning of a psychology seminar: students still feel insecure, engage in polite conversation, and the

THEORY BOX 12.2

THE FIVE STAGES OF GROUP DEVELOPMENT

Forming	Storming	Norming	Performing	Adjourning
Group members get to know each other: high uncertainty	Group members resist influence: disagreement and high conflict	Group members share a common purpose: high friendship and cohesion	Group members work together towards their goal: performance-oriented relations	Group members leave the group: feelings of accomplishment or failure, sometimes grief or relief

Source: Based on information reported in Tuckman & Jensen, 1977.

atmosphere is quite subdued. Once people have got to know each other, they enter the second stage (*storming*). The challenge in the second stage is to develop a group structure. Here issues of leadership and influence are at stake, and as group members may compete about different roles in the group, there may be conflicts and disagreements. Most groups will overcome this, and when a group structure and group roles have been established, they can move on to the third stage, *norming*. In this stage, group members develop close ties, and come to agree upon the group's goals and develop norms that govern group interaction. Once this has been achieved, the group enters the *performing* stage. Because group structure and group norms have been established, the group's efforts can be directed towards achieving the group's task. Although it is probably still necessary to engage in behaviours to maintain a positive atmosphere in the group, most activities will be task-related. The final stage of group development is *adjourning*. When the task has been accomplished or is abandoned, the group will end. This might be associated either with feelings of accomplishment or with feelings of disappointment (dependent, of course, on task success).

According to the Tuckman and Jensen (1977) model, the different stages of group life should be characterized by different interaction patterns within the group. But how can we establish whether this really is true? To answer that question, it is necessary to code group interactions into specific categories and see whether certain types of behaviour are more frequent in the early or the later stages of group life. Probably the best-known coding system of group interaction is Bales's (1950) *interaction process analysis* (IPA; see also Bales & Slater, 1955; Chapter 2; and Leader in the Field, Robert F. Bales). IPA

task behaviours behaviours during group interactions that are directed at task completion.

makes the basic and important distinction between **task behaviours** (all behaviours directed at task

LEADER IN THE FIELD

Robert F. Bales (1916–2004), a pioneer in the development of systematic methods of group observation and measurement of interaction processes, received his BA and MS degrees in sociology from the University of Oregon. He received his PhD in sociology in 1945, and was appointed Professor of Social Relations in 1957, retiring in 1986. During the 1944–1945 academic year, Bales spent a formative year as Research Associate at the Section on Alcohol Studies at Yale University. His research on the interactions in therapeutic group settings for alcohol addicts formed the basis for his first and classic book, *Interaction Process Analysis: A Method for the Study of Small Groups*, published in 1950. Bales hoped that by studying the interaction of many such groups he would discover recurring patterns that might help to understand and to predict the functioning of problem-solving groups. His interaction process analysis proved an extremely useful tool for studying group interaction, group member roles and group development. This research reflected his conception of social psychology as the scientific study of social interaction within the group, and group activity – rather than individual activity – as the primary unit of analysis. With this research programme Bales sought to integrate the psychological and sociological sources of social psychology.

completion) and **socio-emotional behaviours** (all behaviours directed at interpersonal relations within the group). In the socio-emotional domain it further distinguishes

socio-emotional behaviours behaviours during group interactions that are directed at interpersonal relations.

between positive and negative behaviours. According to Bales, task-related behaviour is necessary for task completion, but can lead to conflicts when people disagree. In order not to disturb the functioning of the group, socio-emotional behaviour is necessary to restore group harmony. The coding system of IPA is shown in Figure 12.3. As can be seen in the figure, the scheme distinguishes between 12 different categories, divided into socio-emotional behaviours that are positive, task-related behaviours (which are emotionally neutral) and negative socio-emotional behaviours.

Socio-emotional behaviour, positive	1. Shows solidarity, raises other's status, gives help, reward.
	2. Shows tension release, jokes, laughs, shows satisfaction.
	3. Agrees, shows passive acceptance, understands, concurs, complies.
Task behaviour, neutral	4. Gives suggestions, directions, implying autonomy for other.
	5. Gives opinion, evaluates, analyses, expresses feelings and wishes.
	6. Gives orientation, information, repeats, clarifies, confirms.
	7. Asks for orientation, information, repetition, confirmation.
	8. Asks for opinion, evaluation, analysis, expression of feeling.
	9. Asks for suggestion, direction, possible ways of action.
Socio-emotional behaviour, negative	10. Disagrees, shows passive rejection, formality, withholds help.
	11. Shows tension, asks for help, withdraws out of the field.
	12. Shows antagonism, deflates other's status, defends or asserts self.

FIGURE 12.3 *The coding scheme of Interaction Process Analysis.*

Source: Based on information reported in Bales (1950).

Now, according to the Tuckman and Jensen (1977) stage model, these 12 categories of behaviour should occur to differing degrees in the different stages of group life. The forming stage should be characterized by much positive socio-emotional behaviour, whereas in the storming stage more negative socio-emotional behaviour should occur. In the norming stage, there should be both positive socio-emotional behaviour and task-related behaviour, and the performing stage should be dominated by task-related behaviour. Is this what really happens? At a general level, the answer seems to be 'yes'. For example, Wheelan, Davidson and Tilin (2003) found time together to be negatively related to socio-emotional behaviours (the longer the group was together, the *fewer* of these behaviours); time together was also positively related to task-related behaviours (the longer the group was together, the *more* of these behaviours). More about group development can be found in Wheelan (1994).

On the other hand, stage models such as Tuckman and Jensen's can easily be criticized as an oversimplification of reality. Some groups, for example, may never have a storming stage, whereas other groups are in conflict continuously. Further, groups may sometimes return to a previous stage instead of progressing to the next as the model would assume. Finally, it will often be impossible to establish which stage the group is in, and the assumption that the different stages are qualitatively different from each other is difficult to maintain. Rather, different activities occur in each stage, although they

may vary in intensity. Most researchers would therefore argue that there are no abrupt changes in the way group members interact with each other, but rather that these changes occur gradually and that one can see this as a gradual development of groups over time.

On being similar: norms, shared cognition and cohesion

Group norms Group norms are belief systems about how (or how not) to behave, which guide behaviour but without the force of laws, and which reflect group members' shared expectations about typical or desirable activities. Some norms are prescriptive, and prescribe which attitudes, behaviour and beliefs are and are not appropriate in the context of the group; other norms are descriptive, and merely describe which behaviour is typical within the group (see Chapter 8). Norms serve as guides for attitudes and behaviour and in that way perform an important regulatory function. Group members tend to conform to group norms (i.e., think and act in accordance with group norms), either because group norms are internalized – that is, become part of the individual's belief and value system (Turner, 1991) – or because group norms are enforced by the (anticipated) reaction of other group members to normative and anti-normative behaviour (Deutsch & Gerard, 1955).

Because of this adherence to group norms, groups function more smoothly with than without norms. For instance, if everybody adheres to group norms, other group members' behaviour becomes more predictable and therefore can be anticipated. In that sense, group norms help regulate group interaction. Group norms are also an important source of information about social reality. Often, people rely on what many people see as valid and true as an accurate reflection of (social) reality. Another important function of norms is that conformity to group norms illustrates one's group commitment – it shows that one is 'a good group member' (cf. Hollander, 1958; see also Chapter 8). A particularly dramatic illustration of the power of group norms can be found in Social Psychology Beyond the Lab 12.2.

This is not to say, however, that all group members always conform to group norms. Individual group members may show deviant behaviour. If they do, however, they are likely to run into the negative responses of their fellow group members, even to the extent that they may be excluded from the group (Schachter, 1951). Because social exclusion is a highly unpleasant experience (see Williams, 2001, earlier in this chapter), such pressures to conform to group norms tend to be quite effective in many situations. Thus, groups may enforce and maintain their group norms.

As already noted in the discussion of group development, groups develop group norms relatively early in their existence (Tuckman, 1965). This does not mean that group norms do not change. Norms may change over time. This change may occur because the environment of the group changes. It may also occur because the membership of the group changes. New members tend to be socialized into the group and its norms (Moreland & Levine, 1982), but they may also introduce changes to the group. Indeed, as research on minority influence shows (see Chapter 8), if the conditions are right a deviant minority may convert a whole group towards a different way of thinking. Group norms should therefore be seen on the one hand as enforcing their own maintenance, and on the other as subject to change over time and situations. Group norms are thus both an influence on group process and an outcome of group process.

Socially shared cognition and affect An aspect of groups that has received more attention in recent years is shared cognition (Salas & Fiore, 2004; Tindale & Kameda, 2000). Over time, groups may develop a shared understanding of different aspects of group life, such as the tasks the group performs, the role of each member in the group, and each member's particular knowledge, skills and abilities. For each individual group member, such understanding is important, but when it is shared within the group it has the added advantage of setting the stage for smooth coordination, communication and cooperation, because all group members have a similar understanding of what they are supposed to do and who does what. Socially shared cognitions, when accurately reflecting the demands faced by the group, may therefore improve group functioning and performance (Van Ginkel & Van Knippenberg, 2008).

A nice illustration of the influence of shared cognition is found in work on **transactive memory**. Transactive memory refers to shared knowledge about how information is distributed in the group. Rather than having all the information themselves, group members know who knows what and whom to ask for information about specific things (Wegner, 1987). Transactive memory makes it possible for groups to operate efficiently and adequately, because it helps locate information and 'the right person for the job' (see also Chapter 13). Indeed, shared cognition in the form of a transactive memory system has been positively related to group performance in a number of studies (DeChurch & Mesmer-Magnus, 2010, for a meta-analysis). For an illustration of the benefits of transactive memory, see Research Close-Up 12.2.

> **transactive memory** a system of knowledge available to group members with shared awareness of each other's expertise, strengths and weaknesses.

Groups may share not only cognition but also emotions (George, 1990). A classic study by Schachter and Singer (1962) already demonstrated that people can catch one another's emotional states. Participants in that study received an injection of epinephrine, which causes bodily reactions that also occur when in an emotional state, such as increased heart rate and palpitation. When participants were not informed about these bodily effects (they were told that they had received an injection of vitamins and thus were uncertain why they experienced these symptoms), they were found to be strongly influenced by the emotions of another person present in the room (a confederate of the experimenter), who acted either euphorically or angrily. Thus, participants reported higher levels of euphoria when the confederate acted euphorically, and higher levels of anger when the confederate acted angrily. More recently, the idea that people can catch one another's moods and emotions has also been examined in a group context, and there is emerging evidence that groups may come to share emotions, and that these shared emotions affect group functioning (Kelly & Spoor, 2013, for an overview). Barsade (2002), for instance, studied **emotional contagion**, which is the transfer of moods and emotions among

> **emotional contagion** the transfer of moods and emotions among people in a group.

THE IMPORTANCE OF KNOWING WHO KNOWS WHAT

Moreland, R. L., & Myaskovsky, L. (2000). Exploring the performance benefits of group training: Transactive memory or improved communication? *Organizational Behavior and Human Decision Processes, 82*, 117–133.

Introduction

Transactive memory – shared awareness of the expertise of each of the group members – should help groups perform better. Knowing who knows what helps to locate the knowledge and expertise necessary to deal with the task at hand within the group, helps to coordinate efforts by assigning tasks to those members with most expertise for these tasks, and reduces potential problems due to disagreements. But how are these transactive memory systems formed, and do they actually benefit performance? Moreland and Myaskovsky argued that groups with members that were trained as a group for a task, rather than as separate individuals, would benefit from this because watching each other in action during training would allow the group to develop transactive memory. However, also simply telling group members (who were trained individually) which group member is good at which task should have similar beneficial effects. Only groups whose members were trained individually and who do not receive feedback about the group members' expertise should do relatively poorly.

Method

One hundred and eighty-nine students were assigned to three-person groups. These groups were assigned to three different conditions in a between-subjects design. They were assigned either to an individual training condition, a group training condition or a feedback condition in which group members learned individually about other group members' expertise (i.e., which would also allow for the formation of transactive memory).

The group task was to assemble a radio with as few errors as possible. To that end, group members were first trained in the assembly task. Depending on condition, this training was given to the group as a whole or to individual group members. In the feedback condition, individually trained group members later learned about each other's expertise via written feedback. Subsequently, they performed the group task (i.e., assembling a radio). This group interaction was videotaped, and independent coders rated the observed behaviour on the tapes for indicators of transactive memory: *specialization*, with group members focusing on their own expertise; *coordination*

of task efforts along expertise lines; and *trust* in each other's expertise (as evidenced in less argument about areas of expertise).

Results

As predicted, groups whose members were trained as a group or received feedback about other members' expertise made fewer assembly errors than groups with members who were trained individually (see Figure 12.4). This pattern of results was mirrored in the transactive memory measure (a combination of specialization, coordination and trust), and further analysis suggested that the greater transactive memory was the underlying process that brought about the better performance of group-trained and feedback groups.

Discussion

This study illustrates the importance of transactive memory to group performance: groups are better able to use their expertise and engage in better-coordinated efforts the more they have a shared awareness of who knows what. The study also shows that this awareness may be achieved through a shared training experience, as well as through specific feedback about group members' areas of expertise.

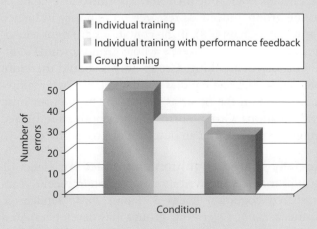

FIGURE 12.4 *Number of errors as a function of training condition.*

Source: Based on Moreland & Myaskovsky, 2000, with permission from Elsevier.

SOCIAL PSYCHOLOGY BEYOND THE LAB 12.2

JONESTOWN

On 18 November 1978 more than 900 men, women and children died in a mass suicide/murder in Jonestown, a jungle encampment in Guyana, South America. Most of them drank, or were forced to drink, a fruit punch that had been laced with cyanide and tranquillizers. Parents first gave it to their children, then drank it themselves (Figure 12.5). How could this have happened? Why did a whole group of people resort to this desperate measure? Strict adherence to group norms is part of the answer.

The people of Jonestown were members of a religious cult, called the People's Temple. The cult was founded in the US by James Warren Jones and had moved to the jungle encampment in Guyana in the mid-1970s. There, the members of the cult had to work hard in the fields and lived in isolation from the outside world. Immediately before the tragedy, US Congressman Ryan had visited Jonestown with some journalists, investigating accusations that people were being held there against their will. Eighteen people indeed wanted to leave with Ryan. However, cult members attacked them at the airstrip as they were leaving, killing the congressman, three journalists and one defector, and wounding 12 others. Back in

Jonestown, Jones proclaimed that the 'end had come', and that in this extreme situation 'revolutionary suicide' was their only option. The members of the People's Temple obeyed, committing mass suicide and killing those who were unable or unwilling to kill themselves (including children and the elderly). The dramatic story of Jonestown is described in the 1980 book *Black and White* by Shiva Naipaul.

To begin to understand why they chose death, one must first realize that the members of the People's Temple were socialized to accept the norms of the cult. One of the more important norms was loyalty to the group, a norm that was quite strictly enforced. Moreover, the cult's leadership was extremely autocratic – whatever the cult's leader, Jones, decreed was group normative and had to be obeyed (see Hogg & Van Knippenberg, 2003, for a discussion of leaders as embodying group norms). Second, the members of the People's Temple lived in isolation from the outside world and had no contacts with relatives or others outside Jonestown. One implication of their isolation was that an end to Jonestown would imply a loss of all their current social ties. It also implied that the people of the Jonestown commune were only in contact with like-minded people. As this chapter shows, one function of groups is to provide us with knowledge of our social and physical world. In isolation, people may even begin to believe bizarre things, such as the concept of 'revolutionary suicide'. The members of the cult, for example, believed that an end to Jonestown would mean not only an end to the promised land they had believed in, but also facing torture and imprisonment by the US government. When faced with the grim prospect of losing all social ties, all hopes, everything they believed in, and of being tortured and imprisoned, several of them saw no reason to live. Those that were less inclined to go down with the cult on Jones's bidding were trapped by the strong conformity to group norms of their fellow cult members, who forced them into partaking in the mass suicide.

Although the Jonestown case is clearly extreme, and fortunately very rare, it does illustrate the power of the social group (and of an autocratic leader). It is one of social psychology's goals to understand these tragedies and hopefully prevent them in the future.

FIGURE 12.5 *Members of the People's Temple at Jonestown, Guyana, committed mass suicide in 1978. They were socialized to accept the cult's norms, especially group loyalty.*

Source: PA Images. Reproduced with permission.

people in a group. Barsade had groups discuss a fictional business case, in which they had to distribute bonuses among employees. Unknown to the real participants, one of the group members was a confederate (a drama student) who was trained to show either positive or negative emotions during the exercise (through facial expressions, tone of voice and so on). Barsade found evidence for emotional contagion: group members' moods became more similar to the confederate's mood. Further, when the confederate showed positive emotions, the group discussion was more cooperative and less conflict occurred. In a similar vein, Sy, Coté, and Saavedra (2005) showed that the affect displayed by the leader of a group transferred to the members of the group and affected group performance: groups performed better when the leader displayed positive affect than when the leader displayed negative affect.

Group cohesion   Group **cohesion** (or 'cohesiveness') is the force that binds members to the group and induces them to stay with the group (Festinger, 1950). Group cohesion is assumed to be important to group functioning, because it helps to keep the group together and motivates group members to

> **cohesion** the force that binds members to the group.

exert themselves on behalf of the group. Evidence for this proposition is mixed, however, and research suggests that it is useful to distinguish between types of cohesion. **Task cohesion** refers to the shared commitment to the group's tasks, while **interpersonal cohesion** refers to the attraction to the group. As a meta-analysis by Mullen and Copper (1994) shows,

> **task cohesion** cohesion based on attraction of group members to the group task.

> **interpersonal cohesion** cohesion based on liking of the group and its members.

only task cohesion is (positively) related to group performance. Further, cohesion may not always improve performance, as can be seen in Research Close-Up 12.3.

On being different: status and roles

Whereas norms make group members' behaviour more alike, there are also clear differences between group members in the way they behave and the position they have in the group. Take a football team for instance. Clearly, different players have different roles, defined by their position on the field (goalkeeper, defender, forward). Besides these formal roles, there will also be informal roles. For example, a more experienced team member (even though not formally the team captain) may have more influence on the other players than a newcomer, and another team member may always take the initiative to reconcile people after an argument.

Earlier we discussed Bales's (1950) interaction process analysis (IPA). It appears that IPA is a useful tool for looking at status and roles inside a group: it is possible to keep track of the 12 different types of behaviour (see Figure 12.3) for each group member, to see whether there are differences among group members. Research using IPA (or other coding systems) to code behaviour in freely interacting groups has revealed a number of important insights. A good overview of these insights can be found in one of the most influential books on group dynamics, McGrath's (1984) *Groups: Interaction and performance* (see Leader in the Field, Joseph E. McGrath). We will discuss two of these findings now.

First, some group members talk more than others, and the discrepancy increases with the size of the group. Thus, groups develop a **speaking hierarchy** (Bales, 1953) in which members higher in the hierarchy talk more than

> **speaking hierarchy** hierarchy within a group based on who talks most.

those lower in the hierarchy. For example, Figure 12.7 shows the speaking hierarchy found by Stephan (1952), which depicts the percentage of time a group member was talking in different-sized groups. For example, the person talking most in an eight-person group talked about 20 per cent of the time, while the person talking least talked only about two per cent of the time. Further, people who talk more are usually seen as more influential. Later research has shown that group members do not distribute their participation evenly throughout the discussion, but rather that contributions are concentrated

LEADER IN THE FIELD

Joseph E. McGrath (1927–2007) was one of the most influential people in the field of group dynamics. This is the case not only because of his own research and writing, but also because he was an excellent mentor who supervised a number of graduate students who later became well-known researchers themselves (for example Richard Hackman, Janice Kelly, Andrea Hollingshead and Linda Argote). McGrath received his PhD from the University of Michigan in 1955, and worked at the University of Illinois from 1960 until his retirement in 1997 (after which he remained active as a researcher until his death). He has published a number of influential books, but one of his best-known is the 1984 book entitled *Groups: Interaction and Performance*. This book provides an excellent summary and integration of work on group dynamics as well as work on group performance (see Chapter 13, this volume). McGrath was especially interested in change of groups over time, and believed that research should emphasize the dynamics of groups, rather than just looking at snapshot pictures of groups in the lab. In his later work McGrath studied the differences between face-to-face versus computer-mediated communication. McGrath was also famous for the poems that he wrote on his work as a mentor and researcher, which he referred to as 'doggerels'. About mentoring of students he wrote, for example: 'So what I best could do for them/Was not to scorn nor flatter/But rather to convince them that/Their own ideas matter.'

GROUP COHESIVENESS LEADS TO BETTER PERFORMANCE WHEN THE GROUP ACCEPTS PERFORMANCE GOALS

Podsakoff, P. M., MacKenzie, S. B., & Ahearne, M. (1997). Moderating effects of goal acceptance on the relationship between group cohesiveness and productivity. *Journal of Applied Psychology, 82,* 974–983.

Introduction

Does group cohesion lead to better performance? Podsakoff and colleagues argued that higher cohesion does not always lead to better performance. They argued that the relationship between cohesiveness and performance should depend on the group's acceptance of performance goals. If the group accepts the performance goals of the organization, cohesiveness should be positively related to group performance. If, however, the group does not accept performance goals, then cohesiveness is expected to be unrelated (or even negatively related) to performance.

Method

The study participants were 218 members of 40 work crews at a paper mill in the US. Crews consisted of 5.25 members on average, most participants were male (96 per cent), and their average age was 39. These participants responded to questions in a standardized questionnaire, and performance data was also collected from company records. The design was correlational (i.e., correlations were computed among measured variables, and no manipulations were involved), and analyses were performed at the group level.

Two measures were obtained through a questionnaire distributed among the work crew members: group cohesiveness and acceptance of the performance goals of the company. Thus, all group members individually rated their perception of group cohesiveness and their acceptance of performance goals. Performance of each crew was obtained from company records. It consisted of the amount of paper produced as a percentage of total machine capacity.

Results

Figure 12.6 shows the results. As predicted, group cohesion and group goal acceptance interacted in predicting

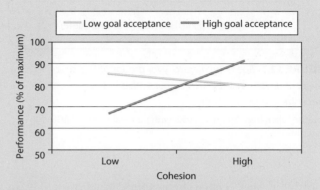

FIGURE 12.6 *The relation between cohesion and performance for crews low and high in goal acceptance.*

Source: After Podsakoff, MacKenzie, & Ahearne, copyright © 1951 by the American Psychological Association. Adapted with permission. Podsakoff, P. M., MacKenzie, S. B., & Ahearne, M. (1997). Moderating effects of goal acceptance on the relationship between group cohesiveness and productivity. *Journal of Applied Psychology, 82,* 974–983. The use of APA information does not imply endorsement by APA.

task performance. When groups were relatively accepting of performance goals, the relationship between group cohesion and group performance was positive. However, when groups were not accepting of performance goals, the relationship between group cohesion and performance tended to be negative.

Discussion

This study illustrates that group cohesion does not necessarily motivate performance. Rather, it motivates group members to exert themselves for causes that are seen as important to the group (see Van Knippenberg & Ellemers, 2003). When group members do not accept the company's performance goals, higher cohesion will generally not improve performance.

in periods of high activity (Dabbs & Ruback, 1987). Thus, if a person has spoken recently, he or she is more likely to speak again. Often this takes the form of a dyadic exchange, in which two group members alternate speaking turns. When this happens, we say that the group is in a *floor* position (i.e., two group members 'hold the floor';

Parker, 1988). Parker found that four-person groups were in a floor position no less than 61 per cent of their time, much more than would be expected if all group members contributed equally.

Second, research using IPA has found that some people are consistently more task-oriented (i.e., they engage

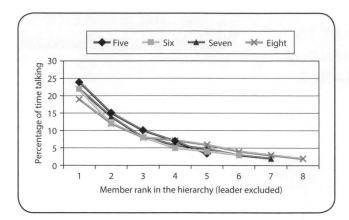

FIGURE 12.7 *Speaking hierarchy for groups of five, six, seven, and eight members. (Member rank is based on percentage of time talking.)*

Source: Taken from Stephan, 1952, with permission from SAGE publications.

mostly in task-related behaviours, categories 4–9 in Figure 12.3), whereas others are more relationship-oriented (i.e. they engage more in socio-emotional behaviours) (Slater, 1955). The former type of person has been labelled the *task specialist* and the latter the *socio-emotional specialist*: clearly a case of (informal) role differentiation. It further appeared that these two group members interacted with each other quite frequently, and much more than would be expected according to chance (i.e., they were often in a floor position). Finally, the task specialist was seen as most influential, but he or she was liked less than the socio-emotional specialist.

Who talks most in the group and who takes which role is dependent on personality and individual abilities. For example, an extroverted person will probably talk more than an introverted person. However, this is not the whole story: there are other factors that determine who is more and who is less influential. The most comprehensive theory about status in groups is **expectation states theory** (Berger, Rosenholtz, & Zelditch, 1980). This deals with the issue of how status structures emerge in groups and how they are shaped by the outside status of group members (see Ridgeway, 2001, for an overview of the theory and the evidence for it). A simplified graphical depiction of the theory is presented in Theory Box 12.3.

> **expectation states theory** argues that status differences within a group result from different expectations that group members have about each other.

Expectation states theory is applicable to groups in which members strive for a common goal or perform a common task. It assumes that several inequalities within a group, such as inequalities in participation and influence, are highly correlated because they are all derived from *performance expectations*. That is, because of specific characteristics of group members, other group members form expectations about the usefulness of each group member's contributions. These expectations then serve as a self-fulfilling prophecy: the greater the expectations, the more likely a person is to speak up, offer suggestions and be evaluated positively by the others. The lower the expectations, the less likely it is that these things happen. The important question, then, is: what determines these performance expectations?

The theory assumes that performance expectations are influenced by so-called *status characteristics*. A distinction is drawn between *diffuse* status characteristics (not necessarily related to the group task), including, for example, gender, age and race, and *specific* status characteristics, such as skills and abilities (i.e., characteristics that are necessary for the group task and previous task success).

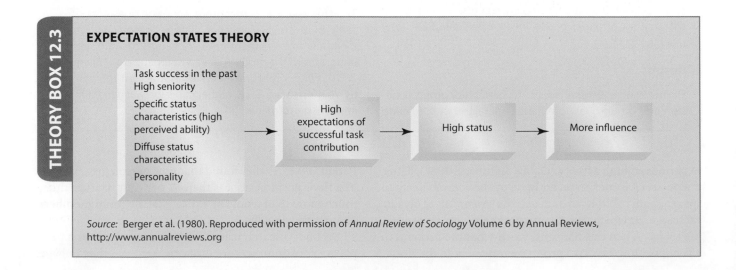

THEORY BOX 12.3

EXPECTATION STATES THEORY

Source: Berger et al. (1980). Reproduced with permission of *Annual Review of Sociology* Volume 6 by Annual Reviews, http://www.annualreviews.org

These characteristics carry certain cultural expectations about competencies. For example, women have stereotypically been seen as less competent than men (especially on tasks that are more 'masculine'; e.g., Pugh & Wahrman, 1983), and more senior people may be seen as more competent (up to a certain age) than younger people (Freese & Cohen, 1973). Similarly, higher expectations are formed for people who are more experienced, have a higher status in society more generally, or have a relevant area of expertise. Obviously, these expectations may sometimes be false (e.g., a woman may in fact be more competent than a man), but they nevertheless affect people's status in the group and the amount of influence they have. The reason is that expectations need to be explicitly falsified before they lose their influence, and as long as they are not falsified, they continue to have their effect in a self-fulfilling way. There is extensive evidence supporting the theory. For example, Driskell and Mullen (1990) found that characteristics of group members affected their status and power through the expectations of other group members (for more evidence, see Ridgeway, 2001).

In general, having differentiated roles and status positions in a group will be beneficial for coordination and performance because it is clear who is responsible for what (cf. our discussion of transactive memory, earlier in this chapter). However, this is the case only when roles and status positions are accepted within the group. If not, fierce power struggles may take place, in which individuals compete for desirable positions within the group. Recent work suggests that these power struggles may severely undermine effective coordination and performance (Bendersky & Hays, 2012; Greer & Van Kleef, 2010). Such power struggles may take place early in the existence of the group (e.g., in the storming phase), but are also more likely in groups that consist of members who all have a high status position in society (e.g., groups of senior managers): it seems to be that the powerful fight among each other in these groups (Greer & Van Kleef, 2010).

Summary

Groups develop over time, in the sense that their interaction patterns change. Further, some processes cause group members to become more similar to each other, both in terms of their behaviour (as prescribed by group norms) and in terms of their cognitions and emotions. Finally, differences between group members may also emerge, for which expectation states theory offers a theoretical account. We now turn to the last level of analysis: the contextual or intergroup level.

GROUPS IN THEIR ENVIRONMENT: THE INTERGROUP LEVEL OF ANALYSIS

In what ways does the (intergroup) context affect intragroup behaviour?

Going back to our opening example of the football fans, it is clear that these people do not always behave in this way. They are also supporters of their team when the team is not playing, but it is the context of the match that draws them together and that brings out their behaviour in the subway station. Playing against another team renders these supporters' affiliation with their favourite team salient and evokes the quite uniform behaviour that clearly identifies them as a group.

What holds for these supporters holds for all groups. Groups do not live in isolation. Other groups are part of the environment in which groups function. Understanding the psychology of groups therefore requires studying the influence of the *intergroup context* on the thoughts, feelings and behaviour of group members. Part of this involves the study of intergroup relations – the way group members think, feel and act towards members of other groups (see Chapter 14). The intergroup context may, however, also affect intragroup processes, and that is the issue we focus on here.

The intergroup context and the salience of group membership

The fact that individuals are members of a specific group does not mean that this group membership is always at the forefront of their minds. Self-categorization as a group member needs to be cognitively activated, or rendered *salient*, for the group membership to exert its influence on people's self-definition (see Chapter 5). Once salient, group membership then influences group members' attitudes and behaviour via this self-definition (i.e., social identity; see Turner et al., 1987; also Chapters 8 and 14). An important influence of the intergroup context is that of rendering group membership salient. Exposure to other groups in a sense 'reminds' us of our own group memberships. Especially in the context of an intergroup confrontation of some kind, this may work to render group membership a salient influence on group members' thoughts, feelings and behaviour. Such confrontations may involve explicit competition, as in sports or in the political arena, or competition for scarce goods (e.g., customers, funding), but may also involve more implicit forms of competition, such as competition for social status (e.g., 'which is the most important department within an organization?', 'which street gang has the toughest reputation?').

These processes are well illustrated in a study by James and Greenberg (1989). They conducted two experiments in which they had students from their university work on a task solving anagrams. The task objective was to solve as many anagrams as possible, and participants' performance on the task (i.e., the number of anagrams solved) was the main dependent variable of interest. James and Greenberg argued that students would be more motivated, and therefore perform better, when their university membership was made salient in the context of a comparison between students from their university and students from another university.

James and Greenberg experimentally manipulated the extent to which students' affiliation to their university was salient. In their first experiment, they manipulated group membership salience by letting participants work in a room that was painted either white (low salience condition) or red and blue (the colours of the university: high salience condition). All participants were led to believe that the experiment was part of a larger study comparing the performance of students from their university with that of students from a 'rival' university. As expected, participants in the high group membership salience condition (red-and-blue room) solved more anagrams than did participants in the low group membership salience condition.

In their second experiment, James and Greenberg aimed to show that this effect would only be found in the presence of intergroup comparison and not in the absence of this intergroup comparison. In order to demonstrate this, they manipulated not only group membership salience but also the presence or absence of the comparison with the other university. Intergroup comparison was manipulated by telling half of the participants that their performance would be compared with that of the rival university (as in the first study), whereas the other half did not receive this instruction. This time, salience was manipulated by giving participants a practice anagram that solved either as *wildcats*, which referred to their university mascot (high salience condition), or as *beavers*, which had no relevance for university membership (low salience condition). Results indicated that group salience had no effect when the intergroup comparison was absent, but that group salience led to

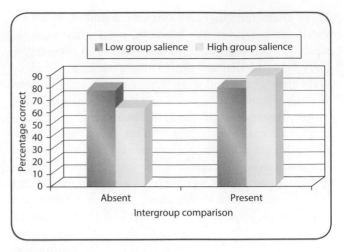

FIGURE 12.8 *Percentage of anagrams solved correctly as a function of ingroup salience and comparison condition.*

Source: Based on James & Greenberg, 1989, with permission from SAGE Publications.

higher (and the highest) performance when intergroup comparison was present (see Figure 12.8).

What this study shows is that group membership needs to be salient to affect behaviour, but that the context in which it is rendered salient affects whether and how group membership salience translates into behaviour (for more on this issue, see Haslam, 2004; Van Knippenberg, 2000). In the intergroup context created by James and Greenberg (1989), performing well could help establish that one's own group was superior to the comparison group. Because salient group memberships reflect on how we see ourselves, the relative standing of our group vis-à-vis other groups (i.e., are we 'better'?) reflects on how good or bad we can feel about ourselves. Obviously, then, we prefer our groups to compare favourably to other groups, and are willing to contribute actively to our group achieving such a favourable comparison (Tajfel & Turner, 1979). In the situation created by James and Greenberg, this led individuals for whom group membership was made salient in the context of intergroup comparison to work harder. In other situations, intergroup comparisons may have different effects: see Social Psychology Beyond the Lab 12.3 for an illustrative example.

An important influence of the intergroup context on group members is, thus, that it may render group membership salient, and may increase the likelihood that this salient self-categorization will be translated into attitudes and behaviour. The intergroup context may also affect group members' perceptions of their own group, and by doing so may affect attitudes and behaviour that are contingent on these perceptions. This is an issue that is addressed next.

SOCIAL PSYCHOLOGY BEYOND THE LAB 12.3

THE OLD FIRM, AND MANY, MANY MORE . . .

Intergroup comparison and intergroup competition may invite group members to give of their best to outperform the other group. Some intergroup comparisons are more important to groups than others, however, and these comparisons in particular motivate efforts on behalf of the group to put the group in a favourable light vis-à-vis the other group.

One only needs to look around to see examples of this in everyday life. People in many countries find it easy to identify 'rival cities' – Melbourne and Sydney in Australia, Amsterdam and Rotterdam in The Netherlands, Lisbon and Porto in Portugal, etc. Sport is also full of such examples, where one opponent in particular is associated with such feelings of intergroup rivalry. As a case in point, consider Celtic and Glasgow Rangers, two football clubs from Glasgow, Scotland. Their rivalry is so intense (at least in part because it also captures antagonism between Catholics and Protestants) that a match between Celtic and Rangers even goes by a nickname – 'The Old Firm'. For both Celtic and Rangers, winning The Old Firm is perhaps the most important goal in the season, and hooliganism reaches its peak around these matches, suggesting that supporters, and especially hooligans, feel likewise (for a book on football club rivalry, see Giles Goodhead's (2004) *Us versus Them: Journeys to the World's Greatest Football Derbies*).

Such rivalries may be observed at all levels between all kinds of groups – nations, cities, organizations, universities, sport clubs, etc. What all such intergroup comparisons have in common is that they render group membership highly salient and motivate group members to outperform the other group. This may inspire great things such as superior athletic performance, but also outright undesirable behaviour such as hooliganism, as well as more silly expressions of intergroup rivalry such as an unwillingness to pronounce the other group's name (a widespread custom in the Dutch city of Rotterdam, for instance, is to not pronounce the name of Amsterdam, but rather to refer to the city simply by its telephone area code, '020').

A recent paper has empirically examined the causes and consequences of rivalry among college-level basketball teams in the US (Kilduff, Elfenbein, & Staw, 2010). Kilduff and colleagues defined rivalry as a subjective competitive relation between two actors that entails increased psychological involvement and perceived stakes of competition, independent of the objective characteristics of the situation. Such rivalry was more likely when teams were geographically proximal, more similar (e.g., similar previous performance), had often had competitive encounters before, and had a history of competition (e.g., with many close games). The consequence of rivalry was that team members were willing to put more effort into the game, which mainly showed up as improved defensive performance (e.g., more blocked shots). Thus, intergroup competition with a rival seems especially motivating, and even more so than 'ordinary competition'.

The intergroup context, group perceptions and social influence

Part of what defines a group is the distinction between who is 'in' and who is 'out'. Groups exist by virtue of their members, but also by the fact that there are some people who are *not* members of the group and may indeed be members of *other* groups. Accordingly, people's perceptions of their membership groups are affected by the comparison between their own group and other groups, and group members' perceptions of their group are also contingent on what differentiates their group from other groups (Turner et al., 1987). Put differently, we ascribe characteristics to ourselves and to our groups on the basis of our perception that we possess these characteristics to a greater degree than others. For example, we will only come to the conclusion that the members of our group are intelligent if we perceive our group to be more intelligent than some other groups. Indeed, such social comparison processes for evaluating ourselves permeate social life (see Chapter 14 for further detail on intergroup social comparison). The important point for our present discussion is that if the intergroup context changes, comparison groups may change, and as a consequence our perceptions of our group may change.

Take, for instance, the case of political parties. Members of a party that is the most conservative within a country's political spectrum will probably think of their party as conservative. However, when a new party emerges that is perceived to be more conservative, the attribute 'conservative' may become less suited to distinguish the party from other parties, and party members' perceptions of their party may change to emphasize other characteristics of their party. Or consider, for example, the discussion about Turkey's prospective membership of the European Union. In contrast to the other countries of the European Union, the largest religious denomination in Turkey is Islam rather than Christianity. This fact seems to have highlighted the shared roots in Christianity of the current EU countries in the perception of many parties taking part in the discussion – an attribute that until now never really seemed at the forefront of perception within the European Union.

Changes in the intergroup context may occur because old groups disappear from the scene (e.g., a competitor goes bankrupt) or new groups emerge, or because an existing group becomes more relevant as a comparison group (as in the example of Turkey and the European Union) or less relevant as a comparison group (e.g., because a competing firm focuses more on other markets than competing directly with one's own firm in the same market). Such changes may affect which attributes of the group are salient (i.e., what differentiates the group from relevant other groups), but they may also alter our perception of a given attribute of the group.

Take the example of a group of psychology students who think of themselves as intelligent. In comparison to most groups in society, this makes sense and greater intelligence may indeed be a feature distinguishing psychology students from other groups. Imagine, however, that this group finds itself in a context where comparison with a group of the proverbial rocket scientists becomes relevant. Intelligence is still a salient attribute – indeed, rocket science is invoked in everyday language to indicate levels of complexity and sophistication requiring the highest levels of intelligence and expertise – but the psychology students will find that they no longer distinguish themselves through superior intelligence. Rather, intelligence is what distinguishes rocket scientists from other groups, and psychology students may be invited to see the intelligence of their own group as modest at best.

Summary

The intergroup context may both affect the salience of group membership and inform group members' behaviour within this wider context. This context of intergroup relations can influence perceptions of group norms that may feed into attitudes and behaviour.

CHAPTER SUMMARY

- *When can we say that a group exists?* A group exists when two or more people define themselves as members of a group.

- *Why do people join groups?* The reasons why people form, join and distinguish groups are sociobiological (evolutionarily built in, for self-preservation), cognitive (to gain understanding of our world) and utilitarian (to gain benefits).

- *Are there different types of groups, and how do they differ from each other?* Different types of groups, such as task groups, intimacy groups, social categories and loose associations, differ on a number of important dimensions such as group entitativity, importance, shared objectives and which needs these groups are likely to fulfil.

- *How does group membership change over time?* Group members move through the different stages of group membership (prospective member, new member, full member, marginal member and ex-member) separated from each other by role transitions, and these different stages are characterized by different levels of commitment.

- *How can harsh initiation rituals be explained?* The role transition of entry can be marked by a harsh transition ritual. A classic explanation for these rituals is given by dissonance theory, which argues that such rituals increase commitment to the group. However, as we have seen, severe initiations often do *not* increase liking, and have other functions than increasing commitment.

- *What determines how easy it is to become a group member?* An important determinant of group openness is staffing level: it is easier to become a full member of an understaffed as compared to an overstaffed group.

- *What are the consequences of exclusion from groups?* Social exclusion from groups can lead to quite severe anger and depression.

- *How do groups change over time?* Groups develop over time, because the challenges they face and the goals they have change. Tuckman's classic theory distinguishes five stages: forming, storming, norming, performing and adjourning.

- *How can we systematically observe group interactions?* Interaction process analysis is a useful coding scheme for group interactions and makes a basic distinction between socio-emotional and task behaviours.

- *How does being in a group affect memory and emotions?* Through shared experiences, groups develop shared cognitions, such as transactive memory systems (i.e. knowing who knows what) and shared emotions.

- *What is the role of group cohesion?* Cohesion can be based on attractiveness of the group (interpersonal cohesion) or on attractiveness of the group task (task cohesion). In general, cohesion motivates group members to exert effort for causes that are important to the group.

- *How do status and role differences develop within groups?* Expectation states theory explains the emergence of a status structure in a group. It argues that certain status characteristics lead to performance expectations that subsequently lead to differences in status and influence.

- *How does the intergroup context influence intragroup behaviour?* The presence of other groups can make group membership salient. As a consequence, group members will be more strongly influenced by their group membership.

SUGGESTIONS FOR FURTHER READING

Haslam, S. A. (2004). *Psychology in organisations: The social identity approach* (2nd edn.). London: Sage. A detailed review of the influence of group norms and intergroup context on attitudes and behaviour in groups.

Hogg, M. A., & Van Knippenberg, D. (2003). Social identity and leadership processes in groups. In M. P. Zanna (Ed.), *Advances in experimental social psychology* (Vol. 35, pp. 1–52). San Diego, CA: Academic Press. An analysis of the relationship between group norms and leadership, showing how leaders may be influential by being seen to embody what is group-normative.

Levine, J. M. (Ed.). (2013). *Frontiers of social psychology: Group processes*. Hove, UK: Psychology Press. A recent collection of papers, dealing with several issues addressed in this chapter (e.g., affective processes and social identity in groups).

Lickel, B., Hamilton, D. L., & Sherman, S. J. (2001). Elements of a lay theory of groups: Types of groups, relational styles, and the perception of group entitativity. *Personality and Social Psychology Review, 5*, 129–140. An in-depth discussion of types of groups and 'lay theories' about them (i.e., how lay people look at groups).

McGrath, J. E. (1984). *Groups: Interaction and performance*. Englewood Cliffs, NJ: Prentice Hall. Provides a very good overview of early findings in group dynamics and group performance research.

Moreland, R. L., & Levine, J. M. (1982). Socialization in small groups: Temporal changes in individual–group relations. In L. Berkowitz (Ed.), *Advances in experimental social psychology* (Vol. 15, pp. 137–192). New York: Academic Press. An extensive discussion of group socialization.

Nijstad, B. A. (2009). *Group performance*. Hove, UK: Psychology Press. Gives a more in-depth discussion of various topics dealt with in this chapter.

Peltokorpi, V. (2008). Transactive memory systems. *Review of General Psychology, 12*, 378–394. Gives a recent and comprehensive overview of the literature on transactive memory systems and other forms of shared cognition.

Ridgeway, C. L. (2001). Social status and group structure. In M. A. Hogg & R. S. Tindale (Eds.), *Blackwell handbook of social psychology: Group processes* (pp. 352–375). Oxford: Blackwell. A good summary of the research on expectation states theory.

Tindale, R. S., & Kameda, T. (2000). Social sharedness as a unifying theme for information processing in groups. *Group Processes & Intergroup Relations, 3*, 123–140. A straightforward statement of the importance and effects of the social sharedness of cognition and psychological states in groups.

Wheelan, S.A. (1994). *Group process: A developmental perspective*. Boston, MA: Allyn & Bacon. A discussion of group development that examines different stages of group life.

13 Group Performance and Leadership

Stefan Schulz-Hardt and Felix C. Brodbeck

KEY TERMS

- brainstorming
- cognitive restriction
- cognitive stimulation
- contingency approaches
- coordination losses
- dispensability effect
- eureka effect
- group composition
- group leadership
- group learning
- group performance management
- group synchronization
- group task types
- group-to-group transfer

- group-to-individual-in-group transfer
- group-to-individual transfer
- hidden profile
- individual capability gains and losses
- individual-to-individual transfer
- Köhler effect
- laissez-faire leaders
- leader traits
- leaderless groups
- leadership behaviour
- leadership effectiveness
- leadership (in organizations)
- leadership style

- motivation losses and gains
- nominal group
- potential group performance (group potential)
- production blocking
- Ringelmann effect
- shared or team leadership
- social compensation
- social competition
- social loafing
- sucker effect
- team awareness
- transactional leaders
- transformational (charismatic) leaders

Brodbeck, F. C. (2008). Leadership in organisations. In N. Chmiel (Ed.), *An introduction to work and organisational psychology: A European perspective*. (2nd ed., pp. 281–304). Oxford: Blackwell Publishing. A concise and up-to-date account of leadership theory and practice from a work and organizational psychology perspective. A good way quickly to catch up with what leadership theory and research is about.

Larson, J. R., Jr. (2010). *In search of synergy in small group performance*. New York: Psychology Press. This highly informative and well-written book builds on the methodological thoroughness offered by Steiner's seminal 1972 book (see below), improves on it and brings it together with the current state of empirical research in group performance.

Nijstad, B. A. (2009). *Group performance*. Hove, UK: Psychology Press. A comprehensive, well-written, easy-to-understand and, nevertheless, challenging and up-to-date introduction to the field of group performance processes.

Pierce, J. L., & Newstrom, J. W. (2002). *Leaders & the leadership process: Readings, self-assessments and applications*. Boston, MA: McGraw-Hill. In addition to concise descriptions of leadership theory and practice, this textbook contains many excerpts of classic theoretical and research-oriented papers, as well as self-assessments, practical applications and useful further readings in the domain of leadership.

Steiner, I. D. (1972). *Group processes and productivity*. New York: Academic Press. Steiner's book remains *the* classic and pioneering analysis of group performance on various tasks. Although over 40 years old, many insights from this book are still highly relevant, and some of them still await their realization in group performance research.

Turner, M. E. (2001). *Groups at work: Theory and research* Mahwah, NJ: Erlbaum. This book's social psychological and organizational perspectives on the fundamental topics of group performance research offer a useful tool for students and researchers who are interested in the organizational application of group performance research, and for practitioners who want to learn more about the theoretical basis of groups and group performance.

Witte, E. H., & Davis, J. H. (Eds.). (1996). *Understanding group behavior* (Vol. 1 and 2). Mahwah, NJ: Erlbaum. These two volumes contain a series of insightful papers from well-known group researchers. They are particularly valuable to readers who would like to broaden the scope from 'pure' group performance research to many other facets of intragroup and intergroup behaviour that are nevertheless relevant for group performance.

Yukl, G. A. (2012). *Leadership in organizations* (8th ed.). Upper Saddle River, NJ: Prentice Hall. This classic book contains a comprehensive review of leadership theories and research. New editions appear regularly.

14 Prejudice and Intergroup Relations

RUSSELL SPEARS AND NICOLE TAUSCH

KEY TERMS

- accentuation effect
- authoritarian personality
- contact hypothesis
- decategorization
- ethnocentrism
- extended contact hypothesis
- group emotions
- group identification
- illusory correlation effect
- ingroup bias
- ingroup reappraisal

- intergroup anxiety
- jigsaw classroom
- mutual differentiation
- negative interdependence
- outgroup bias
- outgroup homogeneity effect
- positive differentiation
- positive interdependence
- positive–negative asymmetry
- prejudice
- principle–implementation gap

- recategorization
- relative deprivation
- self-esteem hypothesis
- social dominance orientation
- social identity
- social reality constraints
- superordinate goals

CHAPTER OUTLINE

INTRODUCTION 441

PERSONALITY APPROACHES TO PREJUDICE 443

The authoritarian personality 443

Prejudice and a desire for social dominance 444

Authoritarianism and social dominance orientation as
ideologies 445

Summary 448

THE COGNITIVE APPROACH TO PREJUDICE 449

Outgroup homogeneity,
stereotyping and prejudice 449

Illusory correlation: a cognitive account of prejudiced
stereotype formation 450

Developments and integrations 451

Summary 453

GROUP APPROACHES TO PREJUDICE 453

Intragroup processes, ingroup
bias and prejudice 453

Intergroup explanations of prejudice and discrimination 454

The individual's relation to the group: group identification
and its components 458

Elaborating the intergroup level 461

Integrative intergroup theories 466

Can emotions help to explain the variety and intensity
of prejudice? 468

Summary 471

PSYCHOLOGICAL INTERVENTIONS TO REDUCE PREJUDICE
AND IMPROVE INTERGROUP RELATIONS 472

The 'contact hypothesis' 472

Varying levels of categorization 476

Psychological processes involved in intergroup contact
and prejudice reduction 480

Other prejudice-reduction techniques 482

The wider implications of prejudice reduction 483

Summary 485

CHAPTER SUMMARY 486

ROUTE MAP OF THE CHAPTER

This chapter presents a number of different explanations for prejudice and discrimination between groups. These range from individual level explanations in terms of personality and individual differences, and in terms of the cognitive mechanisms associated with social categorization and stereotyping processes, to more group level explanations focusing on the relations between groups. At the group level, behaviour that favours one's own group can be beneficial to the individual, and when realistic conflicts arise between groups, prejudice can reflect and reinforce one's group interests. However, realistic conflicts are not the only source of prejudice at the intergroup level. For example, social identity theory introduces additional psychological factors underlying ingroup bias, such as the motive to make one's group positively distinct from others. We also consider a range of additional group-level threats that can help to explain prejudice and discrimination. The trend to provide a more detailed analysis of the specific relations between groups, able to explain specific forms of prejudice, is continued by a focus on the role of different group emotions in this process. Finally we present a range of ways in which practitioners and policy-makers can try to reduce prejudice (such as increasing intergroup contact) and consider the strengths and limitations of these different approaches.

INTRODUCTION

Prejudice and discrimination can take many forms, from the extreme to the almost banal. The Holocaust, the genocides in Cambodia and Rwanda (Figure 14.1), and 'ethnic cleansing' in the former Yugoslavia, are clear examples of the extreme forms. A man who leaps to the aid of a woman who seems to be having problems with her computer can also be accused of a form of prejudice, although he (or even she) might not recognize it as such. These very different examples convey the importance, but also the diversity, of prejudice, and the difficult task facing social psychologists who want to explain it, as well as propose solutions.

In many ways the study of prejudice has become more complex than it seemed in the early days of social psychology. Much of the research on prejudice back then was conducted in the US, on White people's attitudes towards Black people. Overt racial prejudice was quite a

FIGURE 14.1 *The Rwandan Genocide in 1994 was a mass murder of an estimated 800,000 people.*

Source: © Travel Ink. Used under licence from Getty Images.

clear-cut issue, conforming to the classic definition of a negative or derogatory attitude towards a group. Since those days the nature of prejudice has changed, or at least expanded, but so has the nature of social psychology and the explanations we offer. The changes in prejudice are both good and bad. Although prejudice towards ethnic minorities, women, gays and lesbians (to name a few) is nowhere near as blatant as it used to be, this does not mean it has disappeared, although in many cases it does seem to have become less accepted in society. This shift is also reflected in some of the concepts in current use in social psychology: terms like 'modern' racism, 'aversive' racism, the 'new racism' (versus the old fashioned kinds) and 'subtle' or 'benevolent' prejudice (versus the blatant and hostile forms). Without getting bogged down in definitions just yet, these distinctions all convey a shift to more nuanced and less open forms of prejudice and bigotry. As Bob Dylan once sang, *The times, they are a-changin'*.

However, it would also be premature to celebrate: change is not necessarily always a sign of progress. If societal norms have rendered prejudice less acceptable, they may also have forced some forms of prejudice underground (see Chapter 4) while not always necessarily eliminating its causes. Subtle prejudices may also be more sophisticated. This may make some of the 'modern' forms of prejudice more difficult to detect and to challenge, and attempts to suppress prejudice can backfire or rebound if underlying motives remain. Moreover, some of the examples of the atrocities provided at the start of this chapter were perpetrated recently, showing that it is clearly not the case that the extreme forms of prejudice have disappeared entirely either. Despite many social changes, then, 'old fashioned' forms of prejudice and **ethnocentrism** are alas still relevant, albeit less common than they once were.

> **ethnocentrism** the tendency to judge ingroup attributes as superior to those of the outgroup and, more generally, to judge outgroups from an ingroup perspective.

Extreme forms of intergroup hostility are not always straightforward either. The Norwegian right-wing extremist who in July 2011 embarked on a 'crusade' against Muslims and multiculturalism espoused a blatant white supremacist form of prejudice that has fortunately become less common. And yet his killing spree was directed mainly at *white* Norwegians, his own ethnic ingroup who he apparently saw as part of his problem in political terms. Clearly the question of who the ingroup and outgroup are, who the 'us and them' are, is not always straightforward, but also an important *psychological* issue, and a question of ideology.

In this chapter we try to recognize and understand the diverse forms that prejudice can take, in a world that is perhaps more diverse, in Europe at least, than early social psychology textbooks focusing on the American context might suggest. To be sure, gender, 'race' and sexuality are important dimensions on which prejudice operates across the globe, but many others, especially those around nationality and ethnicity, are quite specific to local context, especially in a continent as diverse as Europe. Moreover, we cannot assume that prejudice around the same groups and categories will be the same everywhere. In some countries and cultures social norms against sexism and homophobia may be better developed than in others, and the same group may be a perpetrator of prejudice or a victim, depending on the local context.

While recognizing the diversity in prejudice and the importance of the normative context in which it occurs, we do not, however, think that our accounts have to be purely descriptive, or determined in each case by unique historical factors. One strength of a social psychological approach to prejudice is that it aims to provide theoretical explanations that might apply to a range of different groups and contexts at different times, while trying to do justice to the differences.

As the nature of prejudice has changed, social psychology has not stood still either. As the theories and techniques have developed, so has the very concept of prejudice itself. Consider again the classic definition of prejudice as a negative attitude towards a group. It has become clear that this is rather inadequate as a way of defining prejudice that captures all its forms. Take our example of the man who goes to help the woman with a computer problem. On the surface, such behaviour could be classified in other areas of psychology as an example of helping or prosocial behaviour (see Chapter 10). However, socially aware readers will also detect the sensitivity in this situation: the woman might be quite competent to sort out her computer herself, and may feel patronized by the implication that she is not able to do so (a useful 'thought experiment' when considering gender equality is to consider how a man would feel if a woman offers him help in this context!). That some women might welcome such offers of help only complicates the issue further. This can be seen as an example of 'benevolent sexism' (Glick & Fiske, 1996), an ostensibly positive or helpful orientation that nevertheless reflects or reinforces less positive views of women at least on important dimensions like competence. The example of benevolent prejudice reinforces the point that the old fashioned definition of prejudice, though useful to a point, will not suffice. Instead we propose a working definition of

prejudice as an attitude or orientation towards a group (or its members) that devalues it directly *or* indirectly, often to the benefit of the self or own group.

> **prejudice** an attitude or orientation towards a group (or its members) that devalues it directly *or indirectly*, often to the benefit of the self or own group.

Rather than getting bogged down in debates about whether men who open doors for women are really being sexist, it is perhaps more useful to see how this could reflect more general processes that might benefit one group over the other in the long run: it may be that some men are happy to open the door to the company canteen to women, but not the door to the company boardroom. In this chapter we present theoretical explanations for prejudice that try to make sense of the functions it can serve, however banal or extreme its form. When we think of more extreme examples of prejudice, such as the atrocious acts of the Norwegian extremist, Anders Breivik, it is all too easy to write off such behaviour as *evil*. Although this attribution may be an understandable way of coping with such crises, it does not explain anything. Our job as social psychologists is at least to *try* to explain such behaviour.

In order to give our journey through the field some structure we take an approach that is roughly chronological, starting with classic approaches to prejudice and finishing with more contemporary explanations that do more justice to its diversity. At the same time, and overlapping with this, we structure our treatment in terms of the *levels* of explanation that have been offered for prejudice. One important dimension distinguishing different approaches concerns the level of analysis, or whether the *individual* or *group* should form the central explanatory focus: does prejudice primarily stem from processes within individuals, or from relations between groups?

We start with the more individual-level explanations (personality-based, cognitive), moving on to more group-based explanations. Personality-based explanations arose in the heyday of psychoanalysis in the 1930s and 1940s, and saw personal needs and motives as primary. Although the psychodynamic theories went out of vogue, the interest in individual differences (and motives) has remained. With the cognitive revolution in the 1970s, explanations emphasized the cognitive mechanisms and functions of social categorization and stereotyping common to all of us that could underlie prejudice (see also Chapter 4). Although these approaches clearly differ, they both share a focus on the individual.

In contrast, group-level approaches focus on the perceiver, as well as the target, as a member of a group, with group-level needs and interests. Intergroup explanations have benefited from the legacy of both the personality and cognitive traditions, and incorporate both motivational and cognitive processes. The group level of analysis makes the way we conceptualize prejudice more complex, but also more amenable to its diverse forms and the different contexts in which it can arise. The complex social relations between groups provide the opportunity for diverse comparisons and perceptions, which extend the negative (and positive) reactions to target groups in a number of different emotional directions (e.g., people can respond to members of different outgroups with feelings of fear, anger or even admiration) resulting in quite different feelings of prejudice and different discriminatory responses (e.g., avoidance, confrontation, paternalism). A key element that remains, in line with the modern definition, is that prejudice often serves the perceiver's interests in some way, and this is a recurring theme at all levels of explanation that indeed helps *to explain*.

All of these different levels have something to contribute to the explanation of prejudice, and although some may make more sense in some contexts than others, in many cases more than one level may be relevant. We are not saying that one level of explanation is inherently correct or superior. Take again the emotive example of the Norwegian extremist. It is hard to believe that individual-level factors such as personality did not play a central role in his case (see Chapter 5, Social Psychology beyond the Lab 5.1). Indeed, individual difference accounts may, reassuringly, help to explain why such atrocious acts remain extremely unusual – because there is something special about this individual. Nevertheless, this individual, however far from our social reality he was, clearly saw the world through a prism of 'us and them', involving very strong 'ingroup' loyalties and 'outgroup' enmities. Social categorization processes, social stereotypes and the identities and animosities of the intergroup level may all have played a crucial part here, and at the very least formed the setting in which his personal pathology played itself out (and indeed egalitarian *societal* norms against prejudice might ironically even have *contributed* to the force of the individual-level explanation in this case, by exacerbating a personal sense of resentment). When it comes to explaining prejudice in the modern world, it is not a case of 'one size fits all'. In many cases we may need to draw on many levels of explanation to make full sense of prejudice, and also to explain how it can vary so widely between and within groups. We consider, first, the individual-level explanations that start us on this road.

PERSONALITY APPROACHES TO PREJUDICE

Is there a prejudiced personality?

People differ in terms of their attitudes towards social groups. More interestingly, it seems that attitudes towards a range of social groups are often correlated: people who have negative attitudes towards one outgroup also tend to have negative attitudes towards other outgroups (Allport, 1954b). This is most evident in the case of the outright bigot, who dislikes, for example, Black people, Jews and homosexuals, three quite different groups. The generality of prejudice suggests that prejudiced beliefs may somehow be rooted within an individual's personality. So is there such a thing as a 'prejudiced personality'? In this section we introduce two facets of personality investigated by social psychologists, the authoritarian personality and social dominance orientation.

The authoritarian personality

The monstrous events that took place in Nazi Germany, in particular the Holocaust, led many scholars to believe that prejudice must be an aberration of human psychology. Surely, these actions could not have been those of *normal* men and women? Theoretical models were therefore developed that explained prejudice as a manifestation of a particular pathological personality. The most well-known of these models was proposed by Adorno, Frenkel-Brunswik, Levinson, and Sanford (1950), who suggested that individuals' social and political attitudes, and in particular their susceptibility to Fascist ideas, are expressions of deep-seated aspects of their personality that can be traced back to early childhood experiences. Their theory was heavily influenced by psychodynamic theory, which was very popular at the time. Psychodynamic theory was developed from Sigmund Freud's work on psychoanalysis. It posits that all human behaviour can be explained by the dynamic interplay of conscious and unconscious motivations. Unpleasant or unacceptable impulses are dealt with through a variety of defence mechanisms, such as the (often unconscious) displacement of negative feelings and impulses from a powerful object towards a less powerful and less threatening one (e.g., kicking your dog when you are angry at your boss).

Adorno and colleagues (1950) believed that similar processes are involved in the development of a prejudiced personality. They suggested that an overly strict upbringing, concerned with obedience to parents and conformity to conventional norms, can lead to conflicting feelings of admiration and aggression towards the parents. Rather than targeting hostile impulses directly at the parents, who are viewed as powerful and able to retaliate, these negative feelings are likely to be displaced and directed at weaker targets or 'scapegoats', such as minority groups against whom derogation and even aggression are socially sanctioned. Adorno et al. (1950) proposed that this personality syndrome would be reflected in a person's social attitudes, simplistic thinking (e.g., intolerance of ambiguity), a rigid regard for social conventions and deference to authority figures. Adorno and colleagues referred to this constellation of traits as the **authoritarian personality**.

authoritarian personality personality syndrome characterized by a simplistic cognitive style, a rigid regard for social conventions and submission to authority figures (associated with prejudice towards minority groups and susceptibility to Fascism).

To test their ideas that this personality syndrome would be linked to a variety of prejudices and was rooted in early childhood experiences, Adorno et al. (1950) constructed a personality inventory to assess the central aspects of this syndrome; it was called the 'F-scale', as it was designed to measure susceptibility to Fascist ideas. This measure contained a number of subscales, including authoritarian submission, conventionalism (the desire to adhere to ingroup norms) and authoritarian aggression (intolerance of those who violate conventional values). The scale, together with a number of other scales measuring different forms of prejudice, was then completed by a large sample (about 2000 adults) of White Californians. Lending support to the idea that personality factors are involved in prejudiced attitudes, F-scale scores were found to correlate positively with various forms of prejudice (e.g., anti-Semitism, general ethnocentrism). To provide support that this personality pattern was indeed related to strict parenting, a subset of participants who scored either very high or very low on the F-scale were then invited for in-depth clinical interviews that examined the participants' early childhood experiences. These interviews seemed to support the theory of Adorno et al. (1950), as those participants who had high scores on the F-scale (unlike low scorers) tended to idealize their parents, and indicated that their parents demanded strict obedience and imposed harsh punishments.

Although *The Authoritarian Personality* (1950) was highly influential and stimulated much empirical research, interest in the concept soon waned. This was partly due to a number of damaging methodological criticisms (the use of unrepresentative samples, potential interviewer biases in the clinical interviews and the fact that items were positively framed and open to response bias, whereby respondents tended to agree with items). More fundamentally, however, researchers started to move away from psychodynamic explanations of social phenomena (see Brown, 2010).

Research on the F-scale, and on the idea of a 'prejudiced personality', thus declined in the 1960s and 1970s. However, it was revived by Altemeyer (1981), who refined the measurement of authoritarianism and reconceptualized it as *right-wing authoritarianism*. According to Altemeyer, right-wing authoritarians tend to have highly conventional attitudes and display a high degree of submission to the established authorities in their society, such as government officials and traditional religious leaders. They also show high levels of aggression in the name of these authorities, in particular towards deviants, and are willing to help the government persecute almost any outgroup (Altemeyer, 1998). Rather than viewing the origins of right-wing authoritarianism as displaced aggression towards punitive parents, Altemeyer saw a social environment that reinforced obedience, conventionalism and aggression as a more direct determinant, and emphasized the role of social learning processes, in particular during adolescence. In short, the basis for right-wing authoritarianism lay now in attitudes and norms rather than in personality. Altemeyer (1981, 1998) developed several versions of the right-wing authoritarianism scale, which, like the original scale of authoritarianism, includes three subscales: authoritarian submission, conventionalism and authoritarian aggression. This scale has been widely used and predicts a range of social attitudes, including support for harsh punishment of lawbreakers such as the death penalty, support for aggressive military force, acceptance of the infringement of civil liberties, and prejudice towards various social groups, including homosexuals and racial and ethnic outgroups.

Prejudice and a desire for social dominance

Research on individual differences in prejudice received further attention due to the introduction of another dimension that seems to explain individual variation in prejudice, namely **social dominance orientation** (Pratto, Sidanius, Stallworth, & Malle, 1994). The concept of social dominance orientation is grounded in *social dominance theory* (Sidanius & Pratto, 1999), which proposes that forming group-based hierarchies is a universal human tendency and that most

social dominance orientation an individual difference variable that captures a desire for hierarchical group relations.

societies are therefore organized hierarchically (e.g., in terms of ethnicity, class, gender). Central to the theory is that the hierarchical social order is maintained through individual and institutional discrimination, often justified with the help of so-called 'legitimizing myths'. Legitimizing myths are consensually held values, attitudes, beliefs or cultural ideologies that provide moral and intellectual justification for group inequality, or even the oppression of some groups by others. Such legitimizing myths can include forms of prejudice such as racism and sexism (e.g., the societal dominance of White men can be justified by encouraging the belief in the intellectual inferiority of Black people and women), but also ideas that seem progressive on the surface. An example of such a hierarchy-enhancing legitimizing myth is the ideology of meritocracy, which proposes that outcomes in society – such as wealth, jobs, and power – should be allocated according to merit (e.g., abilities) rather than based on irrelevant factors such as gender, ethnicity or class. Although true meritocracy should increase social justice and group equality, the belief that meritocracy exists, and that those who have power, wealth and status deserve their rewards, while those who are poor have themselves to blame, ignores the fact that people from different social backgrounds do not have the same opportunities to succeed. Thus, the belief that meritocracy exists can serve to legitimize social inequality and help to maintain the (hierarchical) status quo.

So how do we capture people's orientations towards group hierarchy versus group equality? Pratto and colleagues developed the social dominance orientation scale to assess such individual differences (Pratto et al., 1994; see Individual Differences 14.1).

If social dominance orientation assesses the degree to which people support or oppose hierarchical group relations, and if hierarchy-enhancing 'legitimizing myths' help to maintain hierarchical social systems, then the two should be closely linked. This is indeed the case. There is extensive evidence that people higher in social dominance orientation are also more sexist, racist and prejudiced towards immigrants, as well as a range of other social groups (see Pratto, Sidanius, & Levin, 2006, for a review). Moreover, there is also evidence that people high in social dominance orientation are more likely to believe in the notion that people's income reflects their competence (i.e., that income allocation is meritocratic) and to oppose progressive policies to advance the cause of members of minority groups, such as affirmative action, women's rights programmes and social policies assisting the poor (Pratto et al., 1994).

Thus, like right-wing authoritarianism, social dominance orientation can explain individual differences in prejudice. But are right-wing authoritarianism and social dominance orientation related? These variables may seem similar, in that people high in right-wing authoritarianism and people high in social dominance orientation both display high levels of prejudice. But research has shown that there are a number of differences between these two dimensions that suggest that they do not have the same psychological roots (see Altemeyer, 1998). For example, unlike right-wing authoritarians, 'social dominators' do not particularly endorse submitting to authorities, nor do they value conventions or tradition (unless it serves their goals). They are also less religious, more likely to be male and more likely to be Machiavellian (manipulative of others for their personal gain) compared to people high in right-wing authoritarianism. Further evidence that these dimensions are different is that right-wing authoritarianism and social dominance orientation are only weakly correlated, and seem to explain different segments of the variance in prejudice (but together they sometimes explain over 50 per cent of the variance in prejudice against a variety of outgroups; Altemeyer, 1998).

So social dominators and right-wing authoritarians are not necessarily the same people. In combination, however, they could make a 'lethal union' (Altemeyer, 1998). According to Altemeyer, people high in social dominance orientation, who desire both intergroup hierarchy and interpersonal dominance, would make good candidates for dominant leaders who are likely to try to maximize their power even if that involves acting unethically. People high in right-wing authoritarianism, on the other hand, exemplify the submissive follower who would unquestioningly support their leader's decisions (see Son Hing, Bobocel, Zanna, & McBride, 2007).

Authoritarianism and social dominance orientation as ideologies

Although individual difference variables like right-wing authoritarianism and social dominance orientation explain a substantial amount of variation in prejudice, the question remains whether personality variables can really provide explanations for the uniformity and extent of prejudiced beliefs found in societies such as Nazi Germany or South Africa during the Apartheid era (Figure 14.2). Is it likely that millions of people share the same dysfunctional personality structure or specific individual orientation (Billig, 1976)? The social psychologist in you probably doubted this already. As you will already know, people's opinions and behaviours are strongly influenced by the social context, in particular the opinions and behaviours of other people around them (see Chapter 8).

THE SOCIAL DOMINANCE ORIENTATION SCALE (PRATTO ET AL., 1994)

Social dominance theory (Sidanius & Pratto, 1999) proposes that societies contain ideologies that each may promote or attenuate hierarchy at that time. Individual differences in the extent to which these competing ideologies are accepted are conceptualized as social dominance orientation. This scale, developed by Pratto et al. (1994), measures the extent to which individuals have a strong desire to promote or reduce intergroup hierarchies.

Instructions for completion

Below is a series of statements with which you may either agree or disagree. For each statement, please indicate the degree of your agreement/disagreement by circling the appropriate number from '1' to '7'.

		Strongly Disagree					Strongly Agree	
1.	Some groups of people are just more worthy than others.	1	2	3	4	5	6	7
2.	In getting what your group wants, it is sometimes necessary to use force against other groups.	1	2	3	4	5	6	7
3.	It's OK if some groups have more of a chance in life than others.	1	2	3	4	5	6	7
4.	To get ahead in life, it is sometimes necessary to step on other groups.	1	2	3	4	5	6	7
5.	If certain groups of people stayed in their place, we would have fewer problems.	1	2	3	4	5	6	7
6.	It's probably a good thing that certain groups are at the top and other groups are at the bottom.	1	2	3	4	5	6	7
7.	Inferior groups should stay in their place.	1	2	3	4	5	6	7
8.	Sometimes other groups must be kept in their place.	1	2	3	4	5	6	7
9.	It would be good if all groups could be equal.	1	2	3	4	5	6	7
10.	Group equality should be our ideal.	1	2	3	4	5	6	7
11.	All groups should be given an equal chance in life.	1	2	3	4	5	6	7
12.	We should do what we can to equalize conditions for different groups.	1	2	3	4	5	6	7
13.	We should increase social equality.	1	2	3	4	5	6	7
14.	We would have fewer problems if we treated different groups more equally.	1	2	3	4	5	6	7
15.	We should strive to make incomes more equal.	1	2	3	4	5	6	7
16.	No one group should dominate in society.	1	2	3	4	5	6	7

Instructions for scoring

Items 9–16 (which should *not* be presented in a block, as they are shown here) should be reverse coded. How does your score compare to that of other undergraduate students? In a recent study by Jetten and Iyer (2010), first-year undergraduate students at a British university were asked to complete this scale. Their average score in the first year of their studies was quite low (*M* = 2.64, which is below the scale midpoint of 4). To find out whether your score is high or low, you can compare it to this sample. A score

≥3.75 (which is the mean plus one standard deviation in this sample) would be relatively high, a score ≤1.53 (the mean minus one standard deviation) would be relatively low.

Pettigrew (1958) illustrated the importance of the social context in a cross-cultural study in which he compared samples from South Africa and the southern United States (both segregated along racial lines at the time) with samples in the northern United States. He showed that, although levels of authoritarianism in the samples did not differ, racial prejudice was lower in the northern US compared to both the southern US and South Africa. This suggested that personality is not sufficient in explaining racial prejudice and that social context (e.g., whether or not someone lives in a racist society) has to be taken into account. Pettigrew (1958) also measured individual differences in social conformity (e.g., 'A good group member should agree with the other members') in the South African sample. This allowed him to test more directly whether conformity to social norms played a role in prejudice. As expected, those respondents who scored high on the social conformity scale were more prejudiced than those who had low scores.

FIGURE 14.2 *Racist sign on a bus during the Apartheid era in South Africa.*

Source: © De Agostini. Used under licence from Getty Images.

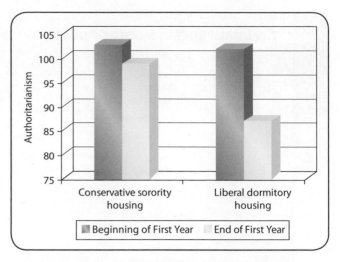

FIGURE 14.3 *Changes in authoritarianism over one year at college as a function of social norms in housing.*

Source: Copyright © 1957 by the American Psychological Association. Adapted with permission. Siegel, A. E., & Siegel, S. (1957). Reference groups, membership groups, and attitude change. *Journal of Abnormal and Social Psychology, 55,* 360–364. The use of APA information does not imply endorsement by APA.

You might also wonder whether individual differences like authoritarianism and social dominance orientation really represent enduring personality characteristics, or whether these variables themselves vary as a function of social context. Siegel and Siegel (1957) assessed women college students in the United States at the beginning and end of their first year at college and compared their level of authoritarianism. The women were assigned to either sorority or dormitory housing. At this college, sororities (social organizations for female undergraduates in North America) at the time were more conservative in their attitudes, while dormitories had more liberal norms. Importantly, these housing allocations were made on a random basis, ensuring that self-selection could not account for any of the findings. The results were striking (see Figure 14.3). While the two groups did not differ in authoritarianism at the beginning of the college year, the women assigned to the more liberal housing showed a significant drop in their levels of authoritarianism at the end of the year. Thus, it seems that authoritarianism changed as a function of social context.

More recently, a study by Guimond, Dambrun, Michinov, and Duarte (2003) investigated the possibility that social dominance orientation would change due to group context. They compared junior (first-year) and senior (third- and final-year) students studying an elite subject (Law) with students who studied a less prestigious subject (Psychology). Social dominance theory suggests that people from dominant groups will show higher levels of social dominance orientation than people from subordinate or lower-status groups, because they benefit most from group hierarchy and are therefore most motivated to justify it. For example, lawyers (the group into which law students are socialized) tend to have more high-powered positions in society than do other

professional groups such as psychologists. Consistent with the idea that members of dominant groups show higher levels of social dominance orientation, Guimond et al. found that the law students generally scored higher on social dominance orientation than the psychology students, even at the beginning of their studies, suggesting that levels of social dominance orientation might help to determine the subject of study and career chosen. Interestingly, these group differences were particularly pronounced among students in the senior years. This suggests that group socialization (over time) affects levels of social dominance orientation.

Research also suggests that threats in one's social environment affect these individual differences. In one study among a sample of New Zealand students, Duckitt and Fisher (2003) provided their participants with scenarios that described the future of New Zealand as either relatively stable and secure (the 'low threat' condition), or as likely to involve a rise in crime, violence and social conflict (the 'high threat' condition). They then measured right-wing authoritarianism and social dominance orientation. Results indicated that participants in the threat condition reported higher levels of right-wing authoritarianism. There was also a small increase in social dominance orientation in the threat condition.

So if variables such as authoritarianism and social dominance orientation are not entirely stable dispositions, then what are they? A recent theoretical model reconceptualized these variables as *ideological beliefs*, determined in part by personality dimensions, but also

THE DUAL PROCESS MODEL OF DUCKITT AND COLLEAGUES

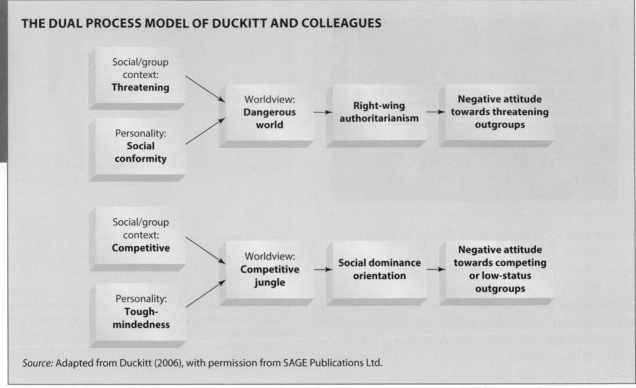

Source: Adapted from Duckitt (2006), with permission from SAGE Publications Ltd.

by group relations in a given social context. Duckitt and colleagues (Duckitt, 2001, 2006; Duckitt, Wagner, Du Plessis, & Birum, 2002) proposed a dual process model (see Theory Box 14.1) in which right-wing authoritarianism and social dominance orientation represent two independent dimensions of social attitudes that express different motivational goals. Right-wing authoritarianism is generated by a view that the world is a dangerous and threatening place, and results in support for measures that establish and maintain societal control, stability and cohesion. Such a world view is brought about by the actual presence of threats in the social context (e.g., the perceived prevalence of crime, as in Duckitt & Fisher's, 2003, experiment). In addition, according to the model, individuals high on the personality dimension of social conformity are predisposed to view the world in this way. The goal motivation linked to social dominance orientation, on the other hand, is that of asserting power and group dominance, and social dominance orientation is predicted by a view that the world is a ruthlessly competitive jungle. This world view is activated in a social context characterized by high levels of inequality and competition over power and status, and is more likely to be held by individuals who are tough-minded.

Thus, the model suggests that these two world views (the world as a dangerous place, or a competitive jungle) are relatively stable reflections of personality and socialization, but are also influenced by the actual social situations. The different goal motivations linked to right-wing authoritarianism and social dominance orientation further suggest that these individual differences should predict prejudice towards different kinds of groups. Because right-wing authoritarianism expresses a threat-driven motivation to establish security and maintain social order, people high in this should dislike groups that threaten these values. Social dominance orientation, on the other hand, should predict negative attitudes towards outgroups that compete for power or are subordinate, which activate the desire to establish or maintain dominance. Consistent with this view, Duckitt (2006) demonstrated that right-wing authoritarianism predicts prejudice towards groups that violate conventions (e.g., rock stars, drug dealers), while social dominance orientation predicts prejudice towards subordinate groups (e.g., disabled people).

Summary

In this section we examined personality approaches to prejudice and discussed two personality dimensions (right-wing authoritarianism and social dominance orientation) that have been linked to high levels of prejudice. We showed that these two dimensions are strong and independent predictors of prejudice and related social attitudes. We also demonstrated, however, that the view that prejudice is a stable personality dimension is not tenable. We showed that social factors play an important role in shaping individual levels of prejudice, and that these individual difference variables are themselves influenced by the social context. We gave an overview of a recent theoretical development (the dual process model) that reframed right-wing authoritarianism and social dominance orientation as ideological orientations that are determined by both personality and social context.

THE COGNITIVE APPROACH TO PREJUDICE

Can we explain prejudice purely by cognitive processes?

The cognitive approach to prejudice arose partly in reaction to the earlier psychodynamic explanations discussed previously, but also earlier socio-cultural explanations that saw stereotypes and prejudice as a product of the images we learn from our environment. In an influential volume that brought together many examples of this approach, Hamilton (1981) explained that one aim was to see how far researchers could push the idea that the basis for prejudice was purely cognitive; just because prejudice entailed affective reactions, it did not mean that it had an affective or motivational basis. This was the era (in the 1970s and 1980s) in which research had rejected the influence of psychodynamic principles, and social psychology was increasingly influenced by theories and models in cognitive psychology and the judgement and decision-making literature. The dominant information processing models had also moved away from the idea (and ideal) that we were perfect and rational information processors, to the notion that there are limits on perception and cognition that encouraged various cognitive shortcuts or 'heuristics' and 'biases' (see Chapter 4). Within social psychology this 'meta-theory' provided a fertile ground for researchers looking to explain prejudice and stereotyping in terms of biased cognitive processes.

accentuation effect when (social) categories are correlated with a continuous dimension (e.g., skin colour, eye shape) there is a judgemental tendency to overestimate *similarities* within, and *differences* between the categories on this dimension.

Tajfel's earlier work on **accentuation effects** in categorization processes (e.g., Tajfel & Wilkes, 1963) formed a basis for understanding social categorization processes, and why people might exaggerate differences between groups and similarities within them. For example, if we take a 'racial' categorization (e.g., White people versus Black people, European versus African) we can identify skin colour as a dimension that is broadly correlated with this categorization. Having said this, there is clearly also a broad range of skin colours within these categories (i.e., the darkest European may even be darker in skin colour than the lightest-skinned African). However, the judgemental effect of this correlation between category and colour is such that people are likely to overestimate the *similarity* of skin colours *within* the categories and to overestimate the *differences* in skin colour *between* the categories (see e.g., Corneille, Huart, Becquart, & Brédart, 2004).

The accentuation explanation of categorization effects was important in showing how certain features attributed to stereotyping might occur, namely perceiving greater similarities *within* groups (group homogeneity), than *between* them. Since Allport's classic volume, *The Nature of Prejudice* (1954b), one aspect of stereotyping that has been related to prejudice was 'overgeneralization', namely the tendency to see members of a category as like each other ('They are all the same'). Evidence of such accentuation or overgeneralization provides a further dimension to our conceptualization of prejudice: reduced variability within the group may be seen as a form of prejudice (or at least stereotyping), which is different from the *negative evaluation* of the group or its members. Put another way, if a Caucasian European says, 'Asians all look alike to me', this is not the same as saying, 'I don't like Asians'. (Although both can be seen as a form of prejudice.)

On its own the accentuation principle does not explain *negative* affective prejudice towards an outgroup (unless negativity is already correlated with group membership), nor indeed any tendency to perceive them as *more* homogeneous than the ingroup. We now consider some cognitive mechanisms that can result in prejudice towards outgroups in terms of judgements of 'them' being more homogeneous and more negative than views of 'us'.

Outgroup homogeneity, stereotyping and prejudice

One strand of the cognitive approach to stereotyping and prejudice has focused on perceptions of group variability, and specifically the idea that prejudice involves us having more homogeneous perceptions of outgroups than ingroups (the **outgroup homogeneity effect**). Many different explanations for this effect have been proposed. One obvious possibility concerns 'selective exposure', the argument that we simply know more people from the ingroup, and therefore have a more variable sample to draw upon when forming impressions of the ingroup. While this may be true, it is interesting that outgroup homogeneity has also been found in the case of gender,

outgroup homogeneity effect a tendency to see the outgroup as more homogeneous than the ingroup.

as in a classic study by Park and Rothbart (1982). They showed evidence for more homogeneous and stereotypic perceptions of the opposite gender, yet selective exposure seems unlikely to be the process driving biased group perceptions in this case, at least for most adults, who will know many people of both genders. Park and Rothbart suggested that the way we structure and encode information about ingroups and outgroups may be important here, and subsequent research has shown that we are more likely to distinguish subgroups within the ingroup, whereas we treat the outgroup simply as 'them' (Park, Ryan, & Judd, 1992). Consider, for example, the many subgroups you recognize within your own university (e.g., the athletes, the workaholics, the Christians, the drinkers), yet when you think of a rival university, you do not think of them in this more differentiated manner.

The comparative context is important too. Haslam and Oakes (1995) pointed to an asymmetry in the way we typically see ingroup members and outgroup members that could help to explain perceptions of outgroup homogeneity. As we have seen, the social categorization process means we are likely to accentuate within-category similarities and between-category differences in an intergroup context, which should make both ingroup and outgroup seem relatively homogeneous. However, much of the time we will interact with people from our ingroup (e.g., people from our own university, or our own country) without the outgroup being present or salient at all (i.e., an *intra*group context). In this context we would expect the tendency to accentuate within-group similarities to be weak or absent: we are more likely to see people as unique individuals (there is no outgroup to compare and contrast our group to, after all). By contrast, when we interact with outgroup members, this is very likely to make the intergroup context salient (e.g., 'We British are different from you French'). When we put these two contexts together, the asymmetry in how we normally see the ingroup versus the outgroup is likely to result in us bringing to mind more homogeneous perceptions of the outgroup than the ingroup overall.

Research also suggests that there may be circumstances in which the *ingroup* is seen as more homogeneous than the outgroup, and that this is not necessarily always a bad thing (Simon, 1992; see also *The individual's relation to the group: group identification and its components*, and Theory Box 14.2, later in this chapter). For example, if the dimension of judgement is positive (e.g., 'intelligence'), ingroup homogeneity might be good (e.g., you are happy when recruiters, for example, see students from your university as all being highly intelligent). Homogeneity of viewpoints within the group might also reflect consensus and solidarity (e.g., political conservatives share the view that liberty is a fundamental value, while socialists share the view that equality is more important). Overall, despite some early attempts to link prejudice with more homogeneous impressions of outgroups, the evidence that this always happens, and is prejudicial, is rather mixed.

Illusory correlation: a cognitive account of prejudiced stereotype formation

The classic example of a purely cognitive explanation for how prejudiced beliefs about *evaluative* group differences could be formed comes from the research on the **illusory correlation effect** by Hamilton and Gifford (1976). They identified a mechanism that could, they argued, account for how negative beliefs about ethnic minorities might develop, even in the absence of any relation between the group and negative attributes, or indeed any prior *expectations* about such group differences. Such expectations can themselves also lead to the perception of stereotypic differences; the extensive literature on 'schema' effects (see Chapter 4) shows how expectations can bias perception in line with established stereotypes. But how can we explain how these expectations are formed in the first place? Hamilton and Gifford presented participants with a series of slides of individual behaviours performed by members of two groups, Group A (the larger 'majority' group), and Group B (the smaller 'minority' group) – see Figure 14.4.

Behaviours differed in terms of their valence (e.g., 'M. R., a member of Group A, helped the old lady across the road'; 'R. A., a member of Group B cheated in an

illusory correlation effect the tendency to perceive a relationship that does not actually exist, or to perceive one that does exist as stronger than it actually is; in group terms the erroneous tendency to associate one group more with one stereotypic or evaluative dimension than another.

	Positive Behaviours	Negative Behaviours
Group A (Majority)	16	8
Group B (Minority)	8	4

FIGURE 14.4 *Illusory correlation paradigm.*

Source: Based on Hamilton & Gifford, 1976, with permission from Elsevier.

exam'). As you can see from Figure 14.4, there were twice as many behaviours describing Group A (the majority group) as Group B (the minority group), and the majority of behaviours for each group were positive (but, crucially, in equal proportions). This distribution reflects the fact that negative behaviours tend to be infrequent, and we also encounter minorities less frequently than the majority group. However, because the *proportion* of positive to negative behaviours is equal in both groups, there is no objective *correlation* between group membership and the valence of the behaviours. After the slide show was over, participants were presented with the behaviours again, but without group labels, and asked to remember whether they came from Group A or B. They were also asked to make ratings of members of the groups on positive and negative traits, and estimate what percentage of positive and negative behaviours came from members of Groups A and B.

On all measures participants associated Group B with the more negative behaviours or traits. Why? This finding could not be explained by a tendency to evaluate smaller groups more negatively because, in a second experiment, where negative behaviours were now in a majority for both groups, more *positive* stereotyping of the minority group resulted. Hamilton and Gifford explained this finding in terms of the higher accessibility in memory of the most distinctive combination – infrequent behaviours in the numerically distinctive group. A distinctive combination that 'stands out', influencing memory and judgement, is an example of the 'availability heuristic', the tendency to predict the frequency of an event based on how easily it can be brought to mind (Tversky & Kahneman, 1973; see Chapter 4).

Subsequent research has considered alternative explanations for this effect. Some have focused on different memory mechanisms (Fiedler, 1991; Smith, 1991). Others have argued that there are real (evaluative) differences between the groups conveyed in the data that are then *accentuated* (see e.g., Klauer & Meiser, 2000; McGarty, Haslam, Turner, & Oakes, 1993). Perhaps more relevant to the rationale of the cognitive approach, however, is evidence that the illusory correlation effect is eliminated when participants are categorized as members of one of the target groups (e.g., the minority group, Group B) themselves (Schaller & Maass, 1989). It seems that motivational factors deriving from group membership can override this cognitive bias (see intergroup explanations below).

Developments and integrations

Cognitive misers Chapter 4 goes into some of the cognitive processes underlying prejudice in more detail.

Consistent with the cognitive approach, research developing the 'cognitive miser' metaphor has argued that one reason we stereotype is to simplify social perception, easing our information processing burden (we are 'cognitive misers'). A study by Macrae, Milne, and Bodenhausen (1994) provides a nice illustration of this argument. In this experiment participants were asked to form an impression of a person based on traits characteristic of them, presented on a computer (e.g., clever, caring). This was the primary task. At the same time they listened on headphones to a series of facts about a novel topic: the secondary task. When forming the impression (the primary task), participants were able to remember *more* facts about the novel topic (the secondary task), *if* the traits of the target person were also accompanied by a stereotype-consistent category label (e.g., 'Doctor' for the traits 'clever' or 'caring'). Following the cognitive miser rationale, it seems that the Doctor stereotype saved cognitive resources by helping to encode the information (Doctors tend to be caring and clever) leaving more attention free for the other task. However, this only seems to work when the information fits the stereotype. Yzerbyt, Rocher, and Schadron (1997) showed that when information about a target person was stereotype *inconsistent* (e.g., 'Skinhead' in the case of 'caring' and 'clever'), activating the stereotype actually *impaired* performance on the secondary task. In this case *resolving* the inconsistency between target and stereotype consumed more cognitive resources. In short, it seems that activating stereotypes is not always energy-saving.

Explicit versus implicit prejudice, indirect measures and social neuroscience As well as offering a level of explanation for prejudice, the cognitive approach has been especially innovative and influential in improving *how* we measure prejudice, with implications for how we conceptualize it. Recall that, as we wrote in the introduction to this chapter, many forms of prejudice have become more subtle and less blatant than they used to be. This does not necessarily mean that prejudice is disappearing (would that it were so!) but this is, at least in part, because social norms have changed, making expressions of prejudice less socially acceptable. However, if the underlying causes and functions of prejudice remain, people may simply become better at hiding or suppressing it. Under these conditions it is particularly important to use measures that get around this. We have already introduced implicit measures in our earlier chapter on attitudes (see Chapter 6).

The distinction between implicit and explicit bias is theoretically important, as well as for methodological reasons. Many dual-process models make a distinction between processes that tend to be efficient, automatic and less under our intentional and conscious control, and those that are more conscious and deliberative (e.g., Fazio & Olson, 2003; Fiske & Neuberg, 1990; see Chapters 4 and 6). The influential model of prejudice developed by Devine (1989) is perhaps the most well-known example of a dual-process approach as applied to stereotyping and prejudice. She argued that we all have access to prejudiced stereotypes in our culture (e.g., about Black people) and that these tend to be activated automatically and outside of our control, although low-prejudiced people are consciously motivated to counter this prejudice. This is discussed extensively in Chapter 4, so we will not go into further details here (see also the critique of her model by Lepore & Brown, 1997, discussed there).

The more general point to make here is that explicit and implicit measures of prejudice do not necessarily measure the same thing, and are (therefore) not always highly correlated (Amodio & Devine, 2006; Correll, Judd, Park, & Wittenbrink, 2010; Karpinski & Hilton, 2001). Because implicit measures are more suited to getting around social desirability concerns, it would be tempting to conclude as a result that implicit measures are therefore *better* than explicit measures. This conclusion would be unwarranted, however. Some have argued also that, just because we might have certain associations (that affect our response on implicit measures), this does not necessarily mean that we endorse these associations and any prejudice based on them (e.g., Karpinski & Hilton, 2001). Amodio (2008) also warns that implicit measures have not proven to be strong or reliable predictors of explicit intergroup behaviour. In a recent review Gawronski and Payne (2010) point out that social desirability is only one dimension on which implicit and explicit measures differ, and may not be the most important. For example, we cannot explain the finding that lower-educated people tend to be more prejudiced by the simple assumption that better-educated people are more sensitive to norms of social desirability, as some have supposed. Wagner and Zick (1995) used a bogus pipeline procedure to reduce socially desirable responses. The bogus pipeline is a fake physiological procedure designed to give participants the idea that experimenters have insights into their true feelings and thoughts (rather like a polygraph or lie detector), which therefore encourages the participants to respond truthfully (Jones & Sigall, 1971). Wagner and Zick found that the education effect was just as strong when they used the bogus pipeline (i.e., when effect of social desirability should be reduced) as when they did not use it. It would therefore be premature to discard explicit measures of prejudice and always to prefer implicit ones.

Different implicit measures also differ in *what* they measure; they have their own strengths and weaknesses, and some appear to be more implicit than others. For example, Vanman, Saltz, Nathan, and Warren (2004) used activity in the facial muscles associated with smiling and frowning (electromyography, or EMG) as an implicit measure of prejudice in White Americans towards Black people (i.e., more frowning, less smiling). They compared this implicit measure with another widely used measure, the Implicit Association Test or IAT (see Chapter 6), a reaction time measure. Vanman et al. found that such EMG activity reliably predicted White participants' racial bias against Black applicants, compared with White applicants, in a hiring decision. Responses on the IAT, however, did not predict this discrimination. In short, it seems that the White participants were more able to control their IAT responses than their facial expressions. So although implicit measures definitely add to our methodological toolkit, they need to be assessed and used on their merits. They do not necessarily provide a magic bullet, but do help to provide a more complete picture of prejudice (see Chapter 2 on research methods).

As well as distinguishing between implicit and explicit forms of prejudice, the developments in implicit measures have also allowed researchers to distinguish between prejudice and *stereotyping* at the implicit level. Various researchers had noted that stereotyping is not necessarily always prejudiced (e.g., Oakes, Haslam, & Turner, 1994). For example, we can have positive stereotypes about other groups, and also our own, and these do not have to reflect benevolent prejudice. It is therefore important to distinguish the evaluative and descriptive dimensions of stereotypes (Wittenbrink, Judd, & Park, 1997). A study by Amodio and Devine (2006) makes a good case for this point at the implicit level using the Implicit Association Test (see Chapter 6). They demonstrated both implicit evaluative bias (i.e., prejudice) towards Black Americans by White Americans, but also, independently, implicit *stereotyping* of these groups. One of the most interesting findings here, however, was that implicit stereotyping and implicit prejudice were *not* related (e.g., $r = .06$ in Study 1). This finding is important for evaluating the cognitive approach, that prejudice results from cognitive biases, and that stereotyping processes explain prejudice (rather than the reverse). Indeed, some recent research suggests stereotypes can develop to justify pre-existing prejudice, rather than causing it (Crandall, Bahns, Warner, & Schaller 2011). Ironically then, developments within social cognition research using implicit measures have tended to *weaken* the claim that prejudice results primarily from cognitive processes, and point to a stronger and relatively independent affective or emotional basis to prejudice. For example, a meta-analysis of 57 studies on racial attitudes and discrimination showed emotional prejudices to be *twice* as strongly related to discrimination than stereotypes and beliefs about these groups (Talaska, Fiske, & Chaiken, 2008). We return to a focus on emotions later in this chapter.

Another methodological innovation that follows the logic of implicit measurement even further 'upstream' concerns the developments in neuroscience that allow us to locate brain activity associated with social information processing (see also Chapter 1). This has opened up the field of 'social neuroscience' (Amodio & Frith, 2006; Blakemore, Winston, & Frith, 2004). In particular, the technique of functional magnetic resonance imaging (fMRI) locates the brain activity that can shed light on the processes, and the brain regions, involved in ingroup bias and prejudice (see e.g., Amodio, 2008; Amodio & Frith, 2006, for reviews). Other techniques, such as research using event-related potentials (ERPs), are better designed to measure the time course of brain activity in the cortex than their localization in the brain (e.g., *when* there is a specific neural response following presentation of a stimulus). Although these neuroscience measures can also be seen as indirect measures that are not under voluntary cognitive control, in some ways they provide a more *direct* window on process that is less mediated by language and self-reports. However, once again research using these techniques takes us beyond the cognitive approach, and also provides many important insights into the motivational and emotional bases of prejudice and discrimination. Moreover, as we argue shortly, just because processes relating to prejudice take place in the brain, this does not necessarily mean that they correspond to the *individual* level of analysis.

Summary

Although designed to capitalize on our cognitive limitations, the cognitive approach may also have some limitations of its own, and offers perhaps only a partial explanation of prejudice. First of all, the cognitive emphasis on social categorization and stereotyping processes as forming the basis for prejudice tends to neglect the possibility that motivation (and prejudice itself) may influence categorization and stereotyping. Moreover, we cannot assume that stereotypes are necessarily prejudiced by definition (after all, we can have stereotypes about our own groups!). The passions aroused in prejudice mean that the presence of motivation may often play a key role in *producing* as well as overriding prejudice (in contrast to Devine's approach). Although culture, cognition and personality all offer accounts of *how* prejudice might occur, it is also not always clear that they offer compelling explanations of *why* it occurs or *where* it comes from. Shifting the explanation to another level (the societal or the individual level) should not disguise this. To address this question it is now appropriate to consider the level of the phenomenon of prejudice itself: the (inter)group level.

GROUP APPROACHES TO PREJUDICE

Can prejudice be explained at the (inter) group level, or does it reduce to individual self-interests?

Prejudice is directed at groups. When we analyse the word 'prejudice', it means *pre-judging* someone, judging them before the facts are known, typically on the basis of some known group features (i.e., stereotypes). But if prejudice is about seeing and judging people *as members of groups*, it is perhaps odd that so much research on this topic views the phenomenon from the perspective of the individual's psychology and functioning. The previous sections focused on individual differences, and on the sort of cognitive processes that affect us all, as two approaches to explaining prejudice that both operate at the level of the individual. We now consider explanations at the level of the group, by focusing first on the relation of members to their own group (intragroup approaches) and then to explanations that refer more explicitly to the relation of the ingroup to the outgroup (intergroup approaches).

Intragroup processes, ingroup bias and prejudice

From a group perspective, one way to understand why people come to dislike or even hate others because of their group membership is to understand their relationship to their own group. Like other primates, we live in groups. Anthropologists, evolutionary psychologists and behavioural ecologists have emphasized the benefits of group living (see also Chapter 12). In earlier times the group provided considerable benefits in terms of security from other individuals and groups, but also in terms of cooperation within the group. Evolutionary theorists have proposed that genes that support cooperation and group living might be selected for and give the individuals (or more precisely their genes) an advantage (Dunbar, Barrett, & Lycett, 2005). Although 'group selection' (the idea that groups replicate and survive for the good of the group or species as a whole) has been discredited as a mechanism of evolution (e.g., Dawkins, 1976), 'group living' and all the traits and tendencies that contribute to that still confer many advantages (Dunbar et al., 2005; Sober & Wilson, 1998). Groups not only help to promote our safety, security and survival, they also help us to fulfil other needs, including esteem and respect, which are important to our position within the group. The need to be esteemed and respected by others can be seen as aspects of a general need to belong and to feel valued by others (Baumeister & Leary, 1995). One influential account of self-esteem and its functions, the 'sociometer theory' (Leary, Tambor, Terdal, & Downs, 1995) argues that self-esteem provides us with a 'barometer' of the extent to which others accept us, and groups are one important source of this acceptance (see also Chapter 5 for sociometer model).

Returning to our focus on prejudice, what do these group benefits mean for our understanding of prejudice? If we recognize that groups can be good for individuals, is it possible to explain prejudice against outgroups merely through the benefits that the *ingroup* can provide to individuals? We might call this an 'intragroup' explanation of prejudice, because it looks inward to the benefits the ingroup provides, rather than at any threats that the outgroup may pose. A key argument is that we favour other ingroup members in our behaviour because there is an expectation of reciprocity within ingroups that we might not get from outgroups (Gaertner & Insko, 2000; Rabbie, Schot, & Visser, 1989; Yamagishi & Kiyonari, 2000; see also Chapter 10). Although expectations of greater reciprocity within the ingroup could help to explain some behaviour that favours the ingroup (and we return to this below), it does not so easily explain attitudes or behaviour that *derogate* the outgroup. To understand this we may need to move to the intergroup level, which we now consider.

Intergroup explanations of prejudice and discrimination

If prejudice occurs primarily between groups, surely it makes sense to search for 'intergroup' explanations? One typical reaction to this idea is 'Maybe, but our job as psychologists means getting inside the head, which is after all located within the individual'. While this is true, if we follow this line of reasoning too dogmatically the intergroup level of analysis might be seen as more the domain of sociology. It would be a mistake, however, to relinquish the intergroup level of analysis completely to other social sciences, and a great loss to (social) psychology. Two famous social psychologists, Donald Campbell and Muzafer Sherif (see Leader in the Field, Muzafer Sherif) realized this point, and were independently responsible, with their colleagues, for one of the first intergroup explanations of prejudice and discrimination: *realistic conflict theory.*

The key idea of realistic conflict theory is that prejudice and discrimination reflect real conflicts of interests

between groups that are in competition for valued but scarce resources (like wealth, but also status and prestige). The most famous example of this explanation is the 'boys camp' study conducted by Sherif and his colleagues at Robbers Cave, Oklahoma (Sherif, Harvey, White, Hood, & Sherif, 1961), which we have already outlined in Chapter 1. For their field study, Sherif et al. capitalized on the common practice in America for parents to send their children away to camp for the summer. In this case well-adjusted white middle-class boys, around 12 years old, who did not know each other beforehand, were selected to take part, minimizing the chance that personality factors or pre-existing loyalties or conflicts could play a role. In the first phase the boys formed separate groups (named the 'Eagles' and the 'Rattlers'), unaware of each other. In the second phase the experimenters introduced the groups and set up a series of competitions between them (e.g., tug-of-war, making a hut from available materials) in which only one group would win a prize (a so-called zero-sum conflict). As predicted, this led to conflict between the groups. This was only reduced in the third phase of the experiments, which gave the boys tasks that could only be achieved by the groups cooperating (e.g., to pull a truck with their food supplies out of the mud) – Figure 14.5. As we will see again later, such **superordinate goals** (goals which can *only* be achieved by the groups pooling their resources and working together) can be important in reducing prejudice and conflict between groups.

> **superordinate goals**
> goals that can only be achieved by two groups working together cooperatively, to mutual benefit.

The boys camp studies clearly qualify as an intergroup explanation, because the boys' interests are bound up with their own group (just as in the intragroup explanation described earlier), but they are also negatively related to the interests of the outgroup. In other words there is a

   LEADER IN THE FIELD

Muzafer Sherif (1906–1978) was born in Turkey and moved to the US to study at Harvard. At Yale he worked with Carl Hovland (*see Leader in the Field, Chapter 1*) on an influential approach to social judgement processes and how these were affected by one's own attitude and involvement in the topic, before settling at the University of Oklahoma. He also conducted pioneering research on social influence and norm formation, and developed a paradigm of influence using the autokinetic effect (see Chapter 8). However, he has perhaps become best known for his research on the Robbers Cave boys camp studies (1961), which became a cornerstone of realistic conflict theory (see also related research by Donald Campbell (*see Leader in the Field, Chapter 2*) and his associates). This theoretical approach remains one of the most powerful explanations of intergroup conflict.

FIGURE 14.5 (a) and (b) *(a) The Rattlers compete against the Eagles in tug-of-war contest: they copy the Eagles' strategy of digging in by sitting down when the going gets tough; (b) now they are on the same side in the tug-of-war: the Rattlers and Eagles combine their efforts to start the truck.*

Source: Images from *The Robbers Cave Experiment* © 1998 by Muzafer Sherif. Published by Wesleyan University Press. Reprinted by permission of Wesleyan Press.

> **positive interde-**
> **pendence** a situation in
> which there are positive
> bonds between individu-
> als or groups character-
> ized by cooperation,
> reciprocity and mutual
> benefits.

positive interdependence within the ingroup but a **negative interdependence** with the outgroup. When the superordinate goals, which could only be achieved together, were introduced, this negative interdependence between groups transformed into a positive interdependence between groups.

The realistic conflict explanation of prejudice, like the intragroup explanation based on reciprocity or positive interdependence within the group, depends to a large degree on *self-interest* resulting from tangible rewards. In other words, to the extent that one's own group benefits, individual members of the group are likely to benefit also. Although this is a powerful explanation of intergroup behaviour, one could rightly ask whether this is a truly intergroup explanation after all. That is, if group interests correspond with individual interests (just as with the intragroup explanation earlier), maybe the intergroup explanation can be *reduced* to the individual level of interest and explanation? Although engaging in conflict can also be dangerous and costly, a more persuasive example of the intergroup level of explanation would be one in which individual self-interest is ruled out. This is one key feature of the so-called *minimal group paradigm* developed by Tajfel, Billig, Bundy, and Flament (1971), which they designed to go beyond the realistic conflict approach. See Research Close-Up 14.1 to read about this paradigm, which we suggest you do now.

As we have already hinted in the section on *intra*group explanations, some researchers have argued that the findings of the minimal group studies (although they ensured that rewards were never allocated directly to the self), did not entirely rule out self-interest. A key argument here is that people may still have *expectations* of positive interdependence and reciprocity: they expect other ingroup members to reward them, so it makes rational sense to reward others in the ingroup too (e.g., Gaertner & Insko, 2000; Rabbie et al., 1989). Indeed, research that measures perceived ingroup reciprocity, or explicitly manipulates dependence on the ingroup for rewards, confirms that these are powerful predictors of ingroup favouritism in minimal groups (Gaertner & Insko, 2000; Rabbie et al., 1989; Stroebe, Lodewijkx, & Spears, 2005).

So does this mean that evidence of minimal **ingroup bias** is not evidence of an intergroup explanation after all? Maybe not. The *maximum difference* strategy (see Figure 14.6 in Research Close-Up 14.1), in which group members maximize the difference in rewards given to the ingroup versus the outgroup, even at a cost to the ingroup in terms of absolute rewards, looks much more like an intergroup strategy that takes into account (antagonistic) relations with the

> **negative**
> **interdependence** a
> situation in which bonds
> between individuals or
> groups are characterized
> by conflicts of interests,
> often leading to antago-
> nism or *realistic conflict*.

> **ingroup bias** behav-
> iours or evaluations that
> favour the ingroup over
> the outgroup; ingroup
> favouritism treats the
> ingroup more positively,
> outgroup derogation
> treats the outgroup less
> positively (e.g., in giving
> fewer rewards) or more
> negatively (e.g., in giving
> punishments).

outgroup. This argument does not mean that self-interest is entirely ruled out, but use of the *maximum difference* strategy does reflect *group* interests.

So evidence for the intergroup level of explanation seems to be strengthened by the results from the minimal group paradigm as well as realistic conflict theory. Although the mechanism for the minimal ingroup bias, and specifically maximum difference, remains unclear, we go into some of the proposed explanations below. However, the first general lesson of the minimal group studies was to demonstrate that the individual level of analysis was not the whole story. This paradigm was instrumental in showing the need for a concept of self at the group level that speaks to group interests (in contrast to purely individual self-interest) to match the intergroup level of explanation. So was born the concept of *social identity*, which emerged out of the minimal group research and led later to the development of *social identity theory* (Tajfel & Turner, 1979; see below).

Now recall our question of whether explaining behaviour in psychological terms is possible when we consider intergroup behaviour (there is no psychology, at the level of the group as a whole, after all). So how is a psychology of groups possible, given that experience is always individually based? The concept of **social identity** offers one answer to this conundrum. Tajfel (1978b) defined social identity as that part of the self-concept corresponding to our knowledge of our group membership and the value and emotional significance we attach to this (see Leader in the Field, Henri Tajfel). Social identities refer to groups or social categories in the social world (e.g., women, Scots, overestimators, etc.) so it is clearly part of the intergroup level of social reality. However, because this identity can be an *important part of how we see ourselves*, it is also part of our own psychological make-up, and can therefore help to explain intergroup behaviour.

As Tajfel's definition makes clear, we can have strong commitment to, and identification with, these social identities. People who support 'their' football team, people who join a demonstration to protest at education cuts, against the invasion of Iraq, or in solidarity with the plight of Palestinians in Gaza, arguably all do this because of a commitment to a group and its cause and not just out of individual self-interest. The view that 'psychology is about individuals and sociology about groups' therefore reflects a mistaken understanding of disciplinary boundaries. The idea that psychology applies only to the individual level of analysis reflects rather a *philosophical* position, sometimes called 'methodological individualism' (Schumpeter, 1908). The concept of social identity opens up a different way of thinking about intergroup relations, less focused on individual functions.

> **social identity** that part of our self-concept corresponding to group memberships, and the value and emotional significance attached to these memberships.

Evidence for social identity and ingroup bias from social neuroscience

Quite recently research in social neuroscience has been instructive in addressing the question of whether there is a social level of self associated with the ingroup that could help to explain ingroup bias. In one study Volz, Kessler, and Von Cramon (2009) used the technique of functional magnetic resonance imaging (fMRI), which is able to localize brain activity, to address this question. The area of the brain that is associated with processing information relevant to the self is the medial prefrontal cortex (mPFC), and previous research has shown that this area is especially active when the individual self-concept is implicated (see e.g., Macrae, Moran, Heatherton, Banfield, & Kelley, 2004; see Chapter 5). In their study Volz et al. categorized participants according to the minimal group procedure based on a bogus perceptual test (foreground versus background figure perceivers). While their brain activity was being monitored, participants then engaged in a number of reward distribution tasks, similar to the Tajfel matrices, designed to measure strategies of fairness and intergroup discrimination on trials that involved allocating rewards to ingroup and outgroup members (mixed trials; see also Tajfel et al., 1971).

LEADER IN THE FIELD

Henri Tajfel (1919–1982) was born to a Jewish family in Wloclawek, northern Poland and was studying in Paris when World War II broke out. Had he not concealed his Polish identity when the Nazis invaded, he would most likely have perished in the concentration camps instead of becoming a French prisoner of war. After the war he worked to resettle refugees before settling in Britain, where he studied psychology as a mature student at Birkbeck College and received his PhD from London University in 1954. He moved later to the chair at Bristol University, creating an influential research group there through the 1970s. His early research on categorization and social judgement (see *accentuation* effect) formed an important foundation for social identity theory, which he developed at Bristol with John Turner (see Leader in the Field, John Turner, later in this chapter). His wartime experiences certainly coloured his understanding of intergroup relations and prejudice. Although the significance of social identity could not have been clearer from this experience, Tajfel had to create this concept in order to open up a field previously individualistic in its focus. His influence in developing social psychology in Europe both theoretically and institutionally, as one of the founding fathers of the *European Journal of Social Psychology* and the European Association of Social Psychology, provides a lasting legacy in Europe and beyond.

THE MINIMAL GROUP PARADIGM

Tajfel, H., Billig, M. G., Bundy, R. P., & Flament, C. (1971). Social categorization and intergroup behaviour. *European Journal of Social Psychology, 1,* 149–178.

Introduction

The purpose of these seminal experiments was to probe the minimal conditions for creating discrimination or ingroup bias. Previous research had shown that intergroup discrimination depended on realistic conflicts of interests between groups (Sherif et al., 1961) or some sense of inter-dependence or common fate within the group (Rabbie & Horwitz, 1969). It is not entirely clear why Tajfel and colleagues thought that stripping away such factors would reveal any evidence of bias, but it is good that they did! In the introduction they refer to the role of categorization as providing order and meaning, harking back to Tajfel's pioneering article on cognitive aspects of prejudice (Tajfel, 1969). However the important point of these studies was first to establish the minimal basis for discrimination as a phenomenon.

So what are minimal groups? Tajfel et al. spelled out the minimal criteria as including the following:

1. No face-to-face interaction (within or between groups).
2. Complete anonymity.
3. Respondents should not personally gain from their responses (to rule out self-interest).
4. A strategy designed to differentiate between groups should be in competition with rational/utilitarian principles of obtaining the maximum benefit for all, and also gaining most for the ingroup in absolute terms. In other words, for this strategy it is not important if *we get less* than we could, so long as *we get more than them.*
5. Responses should be made as important and real as possible (i.e., involve concrete rewards rather than some form of evaluation).

With these principles Tajfel et al. developed two innovative procedures relating to (a) the *social categorization process* and (b) the measurement of *reward allocations,* which are key features of the minimal group paradigm. These are highly influential and still widely used.

Method

Participants

Participants were Bristol schoolboys aged 14–15 years (*N* = 64, Experiment 1; *N* = 48, Experiment 2).

Procedure: 'mere' social categorization

Social categorization was established in two different ways. In Experiment 1 the schoolboys were categorized by means of a dot estimation procedure: they were asked to estimate the number of dots projected on a screen, presented for a fraction of a second. On the basis of 40 of these trials the boys were told that they were either in a group of *under-estimators* (i.e., a group who under-estimated the number of dots) or a group of *over-estimators*. In fact, they were assigned randomly to these categories. In Experiment 2 the now-famous preference for the paintings of Klee versus Kandinsky was used. Here participants indicated their aesthetic preferences for a series of 12 paintings (six by each painter) designated as 'A' or 'B' for each paired choice (although in fact some pairs contained two by the same painter). Once again actual assignment to categories was random.

Participants then completed the reward matrices anonymously in separate cubicles.

Measures: the Tajfel matrices

Tajfel et al. developed a series of reward matrices that could be used to test for 'minimal' ingroup bias. Each matrix consisted of a row of paired numbers with (for example) the upper number of each pair corresponding to what a specific member of the ingroup would receive, if chosen, and the lower number going to a specific outgroup member. The first point to note is that Tajfel et al. therefore tried to rule out *self-interest* by requiring that rewards were allocated to a *specific* ingroup and outgroup member (and *not the groups as a whole*) so that these rewards would never get back to the allocators themselves (criterion 3). The matrices were designed to distinguish between different allocation strategies (criterion 4). These included *fairness* (equal allocation to ingroup and outgroup), *maximum joint profit* (MJP), *maximum ingroup profit* (MIP), and *maximum difference* (i.e., in favour of the ingroup; MD). See Figure 14.6 for a simplified version illustrating these different strategies (Van Leeuwen, 2000).

The design of the matrices allowed the preferences for different strategies to be tested against each other (referred to as 'pull scores'). Perhaps the most theoretically interesting strategy is the maximum difference strategy (see criterion 4) because, when contrasted with the maximum ingroup profit strategy, this could mean giving

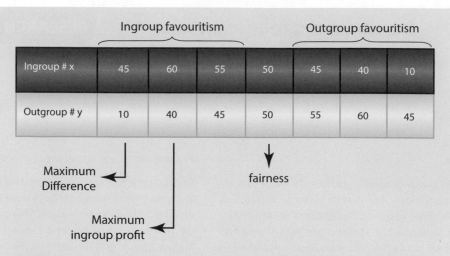

FIGURE 14.6 *The different response strategies on the Tajfel matrices (note: this has been adapted and simplified for illustrative purposes).*
Source: From van Leeuwen, 2000, with permission from Dr E. van Leeuwen.

fewer rewards to the ingroup in absolute terms in order to ensure that the ingroup gets more than the outgroup.

Results

Summarizing the key findings across the studies a first point, often overlooked, is that a substantial percentage of participants opt for a fairness strategy in allocating rewards to ingroup versus outgroup (almost 20 per cent in Experiment 1). Experiment 2 showed that preference for MD was stronger than MIP, which in turn was stronger than MJP. In other words, there was a preference for reward allocations that *maximized the difference* in favour of the ingroup, even at the cost in absolute terms to the ingroup. This can also be seen as a form of *derogation* toward the outgroup.

Discussion

The results of these first minimal group studies were extremely provocative, because they seem to show that no conflict of interest, and indeed no self-interest at all, is necessary for people to discriminate on behalf of their group. In the paper Tajfel et al. proposed a 'generic' norm explanation for the discrimination, suggesting that there is a basic norm of competitiveness within Western societies that leads people to discriminate in favour of their own group. However, this explanation fell from favour, partly because a similar case can be made for a fairness norm (because there was clear evidence that this strategy was widely used too). The 'social identity' explanation would only emerge later.

Very similarly to the original minimal group studies, Volz et al. were able to distinguish participants who predominantly chose fairness strategies, and those who were more discriminatory in their responses. Crucially, the participants who showed more ingroup bias, also showed greater activation for those areas associated with the self and thus predicted to relate also to social identity (i.e., areas located in the medial prefrontal cortex). Those engaged in fairness, however, showed no such activation. Moreover, four participants who were found *not* to identify with their group (they scored below the midpoint of a group identification measure) also showed no such activation of the mPFC, whereas four randomly selected participants who identified with their group *did*. This evidence suggests that our group self or social identity is indeed very much part of the self-concept, as Tajfel originally claimed, and just as much as is the individual self. The fact that some group identification is necessary for

this social self to become activated is also evidence that a certain level of group identification is essential to social identity. Before we consider aspects of the intergroup context that might help us to explain discrimination further, it is now useful to examine in more detail the nature of group identification, as our bridge to the group, and how we conceptualize and measure this.

The individual's relation to the group: group identification and its components

What is group identification and can it explain prejudice?

Following Tajfel's definition of social identity as our psychological bridge to the group, it is possible to

group identification
the degree to which people see themselves in terms of a group membership (group-level self-definition) and the degree of value and emotional attachment to the group (group-level self-investment).

further conceptualize and indeed measure **group identification** as the strength of this bridge. This may also be useful in helping to predict and explain prejudice and ingroup bias. At first sight, focusing on individual differences in group identification sounds reminiscent of other individual difference approaches to prejudice we considered earlier (e.g., right-wing authoritarianism), which we associated more with individual level explanations. An important difference here is that measures of group identification relate directly to the ingroup (and thus the group level), while allowing for individual variations in this link (helping to explain individual variation). Identification may also vary as a function of the social context in which group identities become salient. For example, even people who normally only identify weakly with their nationality may become more passionate about their country when the Olympics or the football World Cup comes round every four years. Put another way, group identification may be an outcome (or dependent variable) influenced by the social context as well as an input (or independent variable).

Recall Tajfel's definition of social identity as the knowledge of our group memberships and the value and emotional significance attached to these. This points to (at least) two different dimensions of group identification. Leach and colleagues (Leach et al., 2008) developed a scale to measure and validate the (componential) structure of group identification that fits well with Tajfel's definition. This research employed response items used in a range of previous research (in which participants rated their agreement on 7-point Likert scales: *strongly agree* to *strongly disagree*) to test a model of the structure of group identification. The first two studies, using Dutch psychology students, examined three different group identities (as Dutch, as Europeans, as students of the University of Amsterdam). For these different group identities the same hierarchical structure for group identification was found in each case (see Theory Box 14.2). This confirmed the general distinction between a self-definition dimension of group identification and a self-investment dimension, at the upper level of the hierarchy, that in turn include further components at the lower level. The self-definition dimension comprises two components: individual self-stereotyping as a group member (e.g., 'I am similar to the average ingroup member'); and ingroup homogeneity (e.g., 'Ingroup members have a lot in common'). The self-investment dimension comprises three components: solidarity (e.g., 'I feel a bond with the group'); satisfaction (e.g., 'I feel glad to

be in the group'); and centrality (e.g., 'This group is an important part of who I am'). Further studies confirmed the *construct, discriminant* and *predictive validity* of the scales (see Chapter 2).

Group identification is important because it makes clear that group membership is not just an objective matter, but is also *psychological* and subjective. This point makes groups a topic for social psychologists and not just sociologists. It can help to explain how different people might react to similar situations differently. If group identification is a measure of our relation to the group, perhaps it is an obvious candidate to help explain prejudice? And perhaps it is more relevant to the intergroup context than other individual difference variables? Whereas ideological factors such as authoritarianism and social dominance orientation are clearly *about* the intergroup context, group identification more specifically locates *us in* the intergroup context and gives us investment in our group.

So could group identification perhaps explain prejudice and ingroup bias? There is some evidence that this may indeed be the case. A series of studies by Bourhis and his collaborators has shown that high group identifiers generally show more ingroup bias in the minimal group paradigm. For example, in one study Gagnon and Bourhis (1996) showed that high group identifiers with their minimal ingroup discriminated more against the outgroup, and that group identification was actually a better predictor of discrimination in this study than expectations of ingroup-reciprocity. However some scholars have criticized this research because group identification was measured *after* discrimination, making the causal direction unclear (see Gaertner & Insko, 2000; Stroebe et al., 2005).

Some researchers have made a claim for a *general* link between ingroup identification and ingroup bias (e.g., Hinkle & Brown, 1990), but this has also been disputed (Turner, 1999). Although group identification may predict prejudice and ingroup bias under certain conditions, there are problems with seeing it as a general predictor of ingroup bias or prejudice. A first question is, how does group identification arise? What causes it (which would just defer the question of what causes prejudice and raise the problem of circularity of explanation)? Moreover, does it necessarily follow that 'I like *us*, therefore I dislike *them*'? Put more graphically, Brewer (1999) has argued that 'ingroup love' is different from 'outgroup hate'; ingroup favouritism is not the same as outgroup derogation. In fact, the evidence from the minimal group paradigm shows that when the Tajfel matrices are used to distribute penalties or punishments rather than rewards, then the typical ingroup bias effect (or outgroup derogation, as implied by the punishments) tends to reduce or disappear (and it is debatable whether the maximum

THEORY BOX 14.2

GROUP-LEVEL SELF-DEFINITION AND SELF-INVESTMENT: A HIERARCHICAL MULTICOMPONENT-MODEL OF INGROUP IDENTIFICATION

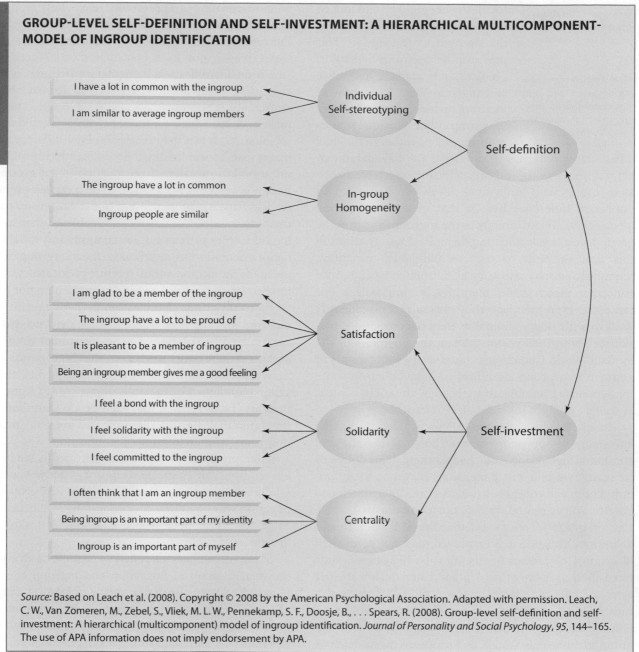

Source: Based on Leach et al. (2008). Copyright © 2008 by the American Psychological Association. Adapted with permission. Leach, C. W., Van Zomeren, M., Zebel, S., Vliek, M. L. W., Pennekamp, S. F., Doosje, B., . . . Spears, R. (2008). Group-level self-definition and self-investment: A hierarchical (multicomponent) model of ingroup identification. *Journal of Personality and Social Psychology*, 95, 144–165. The use of APA information does not imply endorsement by APA.

difference strategy is true derogation where it involves the allocation of positive rewards). Mummendey and Otten (1998) refer to this finding as the **positive–negative asymmetry**, namely the tendency to show more ingroup bias when allocating positive resources (e.g., rewards) than negative ones (e.g., punishments). One explanation for this asymmetry is that punishment or outgroup derogation is *harsher* than ingroup favouritism, and less normatively accepted, especially when there is little overt justification for

positive–negative asymmetry evidence that people show more ingroup bias when distributing positive rewards than punishment or penalties.

discrimination as in the minimal group paradigm (see *Threats to group values* later in this chapter).

Such findings tend to support Brewer's conclusion that the minimal group paradigm (despite the maximum difference effect) provides at best weak evidence for derogation of the outgroup. So, although ingroup identification (like ingroup reciprocation) can play a role in understanding prejudice, it does not easily explain more extreme forms of prejudice and discrimination on its own. However, as we shall see, the concept of identification is central to understanding social identity and the group level of explanation: we need a certain level of identification to see ourselves as group members and thus to generate minimal ingroup bias. Group identification can also be an important *moderator* variable, working in combination with other factors to explain individual differences in prejudice or discrimination. We now turn to different aspects of the intergroup context that can produce the threats that help to motivate and explain prejudice and discrimination, especially in its stronger forms.

Elaborating the intergroup level

How do threats posed by the outgroup help to explain prejudice and discrimination?

We now incorporate *relations* with the outgroup more explicitly into our theorizing. One way to think about this is to consider the outgroup posing a range of *threats* to the ingroup, with prejudice and discrimination forming ways of coping with these threats. Considering these threats also introduces some of the key intergroup theories of prejudice and discrimination.

Threats to group existence Perhaps the most serious threat one could imagine at the intergroup level is a threat to the very existence of one's group. Fortunately examples of genocide are rare (although alas not rare enough) but milder degrees of threat (e.g., to group security) are also relevant. Although such threats can be manifest in the antagonism or aggression of the outgroup, outgroups can also pose a threat to group security for other reasons. One interesting recent evolutionary account for the emergence of xenophobia (fear of foreigners) is the threat of disease and infection they might pose (e.g., Faulkner, Schaller, Park, & Duncan, 2004). Faulkner et al. showed in four correlational studies that people who were more chronically worried about their vulnerability to disease were also more likely to show xenophobic attitudes to unfamiliar immigrant groups (i.e., those who could be seen to pose a potential disease threat). They also demonstrated this experimentally. In two experiments they presented participants with evidence for the ease with which bacteria are transmitted (or, in a control condition, evidence concerning the ease with which accidents occur). Crossed with this manipulation, the Canadian participants then either expressed their attitudes towards a familiar immigrant outgroup (e.g., Scottish, Taiwanese) or an unfamiliar immigrant outgroup (e.g., Nigerian, Mongolian). Results confirmed the prediction that attitudes to the *unfamiliar* immigrant outgroup were particularly hostile when participants were also exposed to the disease salient condition.

We now turn to a very different kind of theory, which also concerns threats to our existence. According to *terror management theory* (Greenberg, Solomon, & Pyszczynski, 1997), being reminded of our own mortality can evoke intense existential angst, causing us to seek reassurance that our lives have meaning through a retreat into familiar cultural values and groups. One of the predicted consequences is increased ingroup favouritism (Castano, Yzerbyt, Paladino, & Sacchi, 2002; Solomon, Greenberg, & Pyszczynski, 1991). Although mortality salience is a threat at the individual level, threats to the group's existence could be just as likely to evoke group-level responses, and perhaps more so. Research confirms that a sense of group continuity (i.e., that the group will still exist when you die) can be very important to group esteem (Sani, 2008) and fulfil the need to belong. Events that physically threaten the safety of some members of the group, or attacks on its icons (e.g., flag burning) could invoke potentially powerful motives and defence mechanisms. The 9/11 and subsequent suicide attacks by Al Qaida terrorists are examples that can be interpreted as threats to Western culture and values that evoke such defensive reactions (Figure 14.7).

FIGURE 14.7 *The 9/11 and subsequent suicide attacks by Al Qaida terrorists are examples that can be interpreted as threats to Western culture and values that evoke defensive reactions.*

Source: © Steve Winter. Used under licence from Getty Images.

Other more common examples of existential threat are likely to be experienced by minority groups, especially where their identity relies on group attributes that might be under threat, such as a minority language. For example, Livingstone, Spears, Manstead, and Bruder (2009) showed that the Welsh-speaking minority within Wales (where only 20 per cent of Welsh people speak their heritage language) were more likely to justify a violent campaign of arson attacks on holiday homes owned by the English in their Welsh homeland. Historically the English had tried to eradicate the Welsh language, which explains both the relatively low percentage of people who speak it today, and why Welsh speakers might feel existential threat. Indeed this effect was strongest for Welsh speakers who felt their Welsh identity to be vulnerable (i.e., under threat) and who also perceived the relationship with England to be unfair or illegitimate. This interaction was absent for Welsh people who do not speak Welsh, who are less likely to see their Welsh identity in terms of the Welsh language, and therefore experience less existential threat.

Threats to resources: realistic and relative

As we have already seen in realistic conflict theory, one of the most powerful explanations for prejudice between groups is that outgroups are seen to threaten our interests, especially when we are in conflict or competition for the same valued resources (Sherif et al., 1961; see also Esses, Jackson, Dovidio, & Hodson, 2005, for a more recent application). Clearly material factors are important in explaining intergroup conflicts. However, the minimal group studies showed that realistic threats are not necessary for discrimination, and the idea that threats are not always objective, but often more subjective, is also well made by **relative deprivation** theory (Runciman,

> **relative deprivation** a resentful feeling that the self or ingroup is worse off than the other or outgroup.

1966). The key idea here is that what we *have*, as groups as well as individuals, depends not just on objective circumstances, but on how we feel we are doing *compared to others*. In other words, even if we are doing quite well in objective, material terms, if we think others are doing better, we are likely to feel relatively deprived. For example, when Germany was reunified after the collapse of the former Soviet bloc, suddenly there were strong reasons for the former East Germans ('Ossis') to compare their lot with the more economically successful former West Germany ('Wessis'). The outcome of this comparison resulted in a clear feeling of relative deprivation for those in the East, and led to realistic conflicts over resources, such as the view that more future jobs and investment should go to East rather than West Germany (Mummendey, Kessler, Klink, & Mielke, 1999).

Threats to group status and esteem

If relative deprivation theory focuses on what your group lacks compared to others, social identity theory (Tajfel & Turner, 1979) emphasizes more generally how your group *is*, compared to others. A key theme in social identity theory is that people compare their own group with other groups and seek to differentiate their own group positively, thereby providing a positive social identity and sense of group worth. Making social comparisons with higher status groups on valued dimensions is therefore likely to be quite threatening, because this implies a low status and negative social identity. Social identity theory proposes that groups will strive to attain (or maintain) positive identity, and to positively differentiate their group from these outgroups. **Positive differentiation** is closely related to the concept of ingroup bias, and involves making the group positively different from a comparison outgroup on available dimensions of comparison. This could entail discrimination (as in the reward allocations of the minimal group paradigm),

> **positive differentiation** involves making the group positively different from a comparison outgroup on available dimensions of comparison (e.g., by means of more positive evaluations or reward allocations) (see also *ingroup bias*).

but it could also involve evaluative ratings that are less discriminatory (e.g., 'We are kinder than them'; 'We are more moral than them').

Note that if status is seen as a valued resource, then realistic conflict theory could also explain ingroup bias. But remember that realistic conflict was more or less ruled out of the minimal group studies, and it is here that the social identity explanation has a theoretical advantage. The idea that groups are motivated to differentiate themselves positively from outgroups, to gain a positive social identity, became a cornerstone of social identity theory that was used to explain the minimal group bias effects. Positive differentiation also helps to explain why group members might choose the maximum difference strategy in the minimal group paradigm (see Research Close-Up 14.1), which is not easy to explain by ingroup reciprocity.

The idea that positive differentiation enhances esteem through a positive identity has become known as the **self-esteem hypothesis** (Abrams & Hogg, 1988; Oakes & Turner, 1980). Research has generally been supportive of this idea (Aberson, Healy, & Romero, 2000; Rubin & Hewstone, 1998), although early studies suffered from methodological problems,

> **self-esteem hypothesis** the prediction that ingroup bias will lead to an increase in group level self-esteem or satisfaction.

and often conceptualized self-esteem in individualistic or global terms, against the spirit of the group-level explanation of social identity theory.

A study by Hunter, Platow, Howard, and Stringer (1996) addressed some of these methodological shortcomings, including the criticism that much previous research had been conducted on minimal groups, where it is more difficult for a meaningful level of group identification and group-esteem to develop (see Theory Box 14.2). Hunter et al. could not have chosen more meaningful and involved groups: Catholic and Protestant school pupils in Northern Ireland in the 1990s during the height of the conflict, known as 'The Troubles'. The design of this study involved a between-participants factor with two conditions. In the experimental condition, participants had the opportunity to show ingroup bias, and in the control condition they did not. For all participants, self-esteem was assessed twice (on several domains of self-esteem), three weeks apart; but for those in the experimental condition only, the opportunity to show ingroup bias was provided between the first and second assessments of self-esteem. Three weeks after the first esteem measurement session pupils in the *experimental* condition rated the ingroup (pupils from their own school) and outgroup (pupils at a school for the opposite religion in the same town) on a subset of six of the specific domains of self-esteem (i.e., honesty, mathematical, academic, verbal and physical ability, and physical appearance) and overall evaluation. Then pupils in both experimental and control conditions rated themselves on all the different domains of esteem once again (i.e., including the six domains rated in the experimental condition). This repeated measures design allowed for the assessment of *changes* in *state* self-esteem (after the opportunity for ingroup bias or not).

Results from the experimental condition showed that participants generally rated their ingroup higher on all dimensions (i.e., ingroup bias), although the ingroup was rated especially high on physical ability, and the outgroup lower on honesty (a clear sign of the distrust between Protestants and Catholics during The Troubles). Self-esteem increased in the experimental condition only, on four of the six dimensions (honesty, academic ability, verbal ability and physical appearance), but global self-esteem was unaffected by the opportunity to discriminate. Hunter et al. speculated that the specific dimensions on which self-esteem was enhanced were the ones that were the most important and relevant to pupils' identity, although they did not provide independent evidence for this. However, this research does seem to show that ingroup bias can enhance self-esteem on some key specific dimensions of group identity without necessarily improving global esteem.

If low status is threatening to our sense of esteem and undermines a positive social identity, we might expect low-status groups to be particularly likely to show ingroup bias. However, this does not always seem to be the case, as confirmed in a meta-analysis of research by Mullen, Brown, and Smith (1992). Mullen et al. found more evidence for ingroup favouritism among low-status groups outside the laboratory than those created in the laboratory. One reason for this is the role of **social reality constraints**: the point that when groups have a low status, they may feel that claiming a better position for themselves, especially on the status-defining dimension, is not justified or legitimate. This is particularly likely in laboratory studies, where status is manipulated, because there is little scope, and perhaps little motivation, to contest status feedback just received. However, this can happen in naturally occurring groups too. For example, in the study by Hunter et al. (1996) discussed above, ingroup bias was *weaker* among the *Catholic* than the *Protestant* pupils in their research, probably reflecting the lower status of this group in Northern Ireland at the time.

> **social reality constraints** evidence that the outgroup is clearly better on a certain dimension can make ingroup bias on that dimension difficult to justify.

However, many naturally occurring groups with lower status do not always accept their lower status position (i.e., they perceive it as illegitimate). Remember that the Catholic pupils in the study carried out by Hunter et al. still showed ingroup bias (just less than the Protestants). To go back to another example, many East Germans ('Ossis') would not accept their group as being inferior, despite their economic disadvantages. Indeed esteem and group identification is often just as high (if not higher) in disadvantaged groups as those with higher status, and the threat to identity of low status can often strengthen solidarity with one's group (Ellemers, Spears, & Doosje, 2002). The issue of status legitimacy is a part of the more complete social identity theory that we discuss further below.

In many real-life intergroup comparisons, groups will differ on many different dimensions, providing opportunities for groups to rate their own group as better on certain dimensions but the other group as better on others (see also Hewstone & Brown, 1986). For example, psychology students might rate themselves as more sociable but less intelligent than physics students. In this way both groups can claim a positive identity (without challenging social reality constraints). In social identity theory this is called a 'social creativity' strategy: the groups are not challenging the outgroup by means of direct competition (i.e., ingroup bias, discrimination), but are simply favouring dimensions that allow for positive differentiation. However, it is also possible to see how the use of this strategy, instead of eliminating prejudice and discrimination, could just perhaps make it more subtle. If psychology students choose to emphasize their sociability over intelligence, and physics students do the reverse, physics students may still claim they are somehow better by arguing that intelligence is a more important dimension than being sociable. Research by Mummendey and Schreiber (1984) makes exactly this point, and referred to this strategy as 'different but better'! (See Leader in the Field, Amélie Mummendey.)

This example points to a problem of this social creativity strategy for low status groups: they will typically find it difficult to claim superiority on the status-defining dimension (such as competence), yet this will often be the most important and valued one (Ellemers, 1993). Discriminating in terms of reward allocations may then be a more viable route to a positive identity because of social reality constraints on the status-defining dimension. Indeed, in line with relative deprivation theory, it can be easier to justify better rewards if you feel your group has been unfairly denied ('We need and deserve more resources!'). When faced with identity-based threats in terms of low status or resources, social identity theory makes similar predictions to realistic conflict and relative deprivation theories. A key difference is the motive for such behaviour. According to social identity theory, discrimination would address an attempt to gain a positive identity rather than competing for material resources for their own sake.

Threats to group value(s) Other kinds of threat to identity less obviously involve esteem, but do imply a threat to values central to the ingroup identity. We see this most clearly in the case of conflicting ideological or religious values. The most salient current example is perhaps the relation of radical Islam to the more secular or Christian Western world. This theme goes back to ideas of similarity – attraction (e.g., Byrne & Wong, 1962; see Chapter 11) and belief congruence (e.g., Rokeach & Rothman, 1965), which proposed that simply having different beliefs and values could be a basis for prejudice towards outgroups. This idea has re-emerged in the *integrated threat theory* (e.g., Stephan, Diaz-Loving, & Duran, 2000); Stephan and colleagues coined the term 'symbolic threat' to refer to group values that threaten the ingroup's way of life (albeit more ideologically than physically).

Although group values different from those of the ingroup may become the target of prejudice, more optimistically group norms and values can also be a source of tolerance and reduced discrimination, to the extent that they may prescribe *less* prejudice and discrimination in themselves. 'Political correctness' could be seen as one such norm that, at least where values are followed, would lead to less prejudice and discrimination. Indeed such norms are not necessarily contradictory to the social identity approach, because they can become valued dimensions of identity. For example, in contrast to the Al Qaida example, many religions – including Muslim, Christian and Buddhist – are against discrimination ('Love thy neighbour. . .' is a theme that recurs in all three religions, as well as many others).

An influential theoretical account of group norms is provided by *self-categorization theory*, developed by John Turner and his collaborators (Turner, Hogg, Oakes, Reicher, & Wetherell, 1987; see Leader in the Field, John Turner). In this framework the concept of social identity was more explicitly distinguished from personal identity (the 'individual self'), and related to social influence processes (see Chapter 8). A key point here is that when group identities are valued (see group identification earlier in this chapter) and become salient in an intergroup context, we are likely to conform willingly to the norms associated with our group. We are also likely to see ourselves and others in terms of group attributes (e.g., stereotypes, norms), a process referred to as 'depersonalization' (see also the self-definition component of group identification earlier, and accentuation effects). Conformity to group norms that distinguish ingroup from outgroup is motivated and regulates group behaviour: what to do and what *not* to do. A good example of this is the so-called 'black sheep effect' (Marques, Yzerbyt, & Leyens, 1988) in which ingroup members who deviate from ingroup norms are judged even *more* harshly than outgroup members who show exactly the same behaviour. This is an interesting exception to ingroup favouritism: typically ingroup members would be judged more

 LEADER IN THE FIELD

Amélie Mummendey (b. 1944) was born in Bonn, where she also received her Masters in psychology, followed by her PhD from the University of Mainz in 1970. For many years Mummendey was Professor at the University of Münster, building up an influential group of researchers and starting an annual series of research meetings on intergroup relations. When she moved to the chair at the University of Jena she maintained this initiative, and the Jena conference continues to this day. The group at Jena, under her leadership, became one of the most prolific centres for research on intergroup relations in Europe. She also inaugurated the International Graduate College (in collaboration with other European universities), which trained numerous social psychologists who have also become key figures in the field. Mummendey's early research focused on aggression, but her contributions to the social identity approach have been particularly notable. These include much research and theorizing on the processes underlying intergroup discrimination, but also tolerance between groups. These contributions include research on the 'different but better' differentiation strategy, the 'positive–negative asymmetry' and the ingroup projection model.

positively than outgroup members. Instead this harsher judgement of an ingroup transgression can be seen as a form of 'policing' of ingroup behaviour that might otherwise reflect badly on the ingroup image.

If there are group norms about discrimination being bad or antisocial, will discrimination harm esteem rather than enhance it? There is indeed some evidence of this (Branscombe & Wann, 1994; Scheepers, Spears, Manstead, & Doosje, 2009). Research also shows that, where the group has a norm of being fair and not discriminating, stronger identification with the group can actually increase *fairness* rather than discrimination (e.g., Jetten, Spears, & Manstead, 1997). These findings also help to explain why discrimination that actually involves derogating the outgroup is perhaps less common than examples of ingroup enhancement (see also Mummendey & Otten, 1998; Perdue, Dovidio, Gurtman, & Tyler, 1990). An explanation for this *positive–negative asymmetry* is the thought that harming others may indeed damage the ingroup image (Reynolds, Turner, & Haslam, 2000). These examples provide reassuring reminders that prejudice and discrimination are not *inevitable* consequences of group membership or group identification.

Threats to group distinctiveness If too much difference from an outgroup can be a problem, then it seems that too much similarity with an outgroup can be too! Have you ever had the experience when travelling with your friends abroad that the locals get your nationality wrong? You might be Dutch but they think you are German. You might be Italian but they think you are Spanish or French. You might be British but they think you are American. These identity confusions can be irritating (and apparently some more than others). But why? It is not that students are necessarily prejudiced towards the groups they are confused with (at least we hope not). There are actually two closely related threats to identity contained in these examples (see Ellemers et al., 2002). First, people like to be seen in terms of identities important to them (see 'centrality', a component of group-level self-investment in Theory Box 14.2). Being seen in terms of other identities, especially erroneous ones, can evoke 'categorization threat' (see also Flores & Huo, 2013). But that is not the whole story. We also do not like it when another group is so similar to ours, because it undermines the very essence of what our group is that makes us different and special. Hence a Dutch or a Swiss German student may be more irritated when he or she is seen as German, rather than as French or American. In other words, we tend to be most sensitive when the other group actually *is* similar to our own, in terms of attributes or stereotypes. Groups that are too similar to our own can therefore threaten the unique identity of the group: 'distinctiveness threat'. Some have even argued that having a distinctive group identity is even more fundamental than avoiding a negative one. For example, Mlicki and Ellemers (1996) found that 'complaining' is an important self-stereotype of Polish identity, and though apparently negative, something that Poles will often emphasize (see Leader in the Field, Naomi Ellemers; also self-verification versus self-enhancement in relation to the personal self, Chapter 5).

Positive differentiation (also in the form of discrimination) can restore or even create group distinctiveness. Now remember the social identity explanation for the minimal ingroup bias effect, namely that people try positively to differentiate their group in order to create a *positive group distinctiveness* (and not just enhance the ingroup; see e.g., Tajfel, 1982b). This distinctiveness motive had been largely forgotten in research on minimal groups that had largely concentrated on the self-esteem hypothesis. However, because participants in the minimal group paradigm lack information about the groups (precisely because they are minimal!) this may also create distinctiveness threat (Spears, Jetten, Scheepers, & Cihangir, 2009). Spears et al. (2009) decided to put this idea to the test. In one experiment they categorized participants according to the classic procedure based on preferences for Klee or Kandinsky (see Research Close-Up 14.1). As expected, the typical ingroup bias effect was found in this condition. However, in another condition they simply added the information that people who prefer Klee tend to be extroverts, whereas those who prefer Kandinsky tend to be introverts (or vice versa to counterbalance). In this condition ingroup bias was virtually eliminated. An explanation is that making the minimal group identities more meaningful (introvert versus extrovert) provided a distinctive group identity, making it unnecessary to *create* this identity by means of positive differentiation (this interpretation was supported by follow-up studies). In a meta-analysis, Jetten, Spears, and Postmes (2004) also found that high identifiers with the ingroup were particularly likely to respond to distinctiveness threat (i.e., comparison with *similar* outgroups) by differentiating more. The more invested you are in your group, the more important it is to distinguish it from similar outgroups.

Brewer (1991) developed a slightly different conception of distinctiveness threat in *optimal distinctiveness theory*. She proposed that individuals have two fundamental needs: a need to integrate or affiliate (the need to belong: Baumeister & Leary, 1995), but also a need to differentiate oneself from others; a distinctiveness motive. She argued that groups that are relatively small in size (and thus distinctive), such as numerical minorities, optimally meet these two needs.

Smaller and numerically distinctive groups may particularly value their group identity for other reasons also (it turns out that minorities often identify more strongly with their group identity than do majorities; see Leonardelli, Pickett, & Brewer, 2010). If minorities do not have power or resources, their identity may

assume more importance and they may be particularly sensitive to being assimilated into the same category as the majority group, especially as this identity confusion may happen more often than the reverse (think again of the German 'Ossis'). It is no accident that the examples we chose at the start of this section tended to focus on the sensitivities of the *smaller* group of the two. Larger and more dominant groups need not worry too much about distinctiveness threat, because they will be confronted with it less often (e.g., Americans are not often called Canadians). It is also easier for them to dominate, especially in superordinate categories that contain them both.

This insight provided the inspiration for another explanation for discrimination known as the *ingroup projection model* (Mummendey & Wenzel, 1999). You will recall that emphasizing superordinate goals and interests is one method to *reduce* conflict and discrimination, according to realistic conflict theory. However, the ingroup projection model suggests that this may not always work. If one group is dominant in size and status, they will typically set the agenda for what counts as normative or 'prototypical' for the superordinate category that includes both subgroups (i.e., their norms are projected onto the superordinate group). Thus, the English may be seen as more typically British than the Welsh or Scots. In Germany, West Germans are seen as more typically German than East Germans are (especially by Wessis themselves!). West Germans may then feel justified in discriminating more against East Germans, because they see Ossis as less typical of the German norms and ideals than Wessis (see Waldzus, Mummendey, Wenzel, & Boettcher, 2004). So although numerical group distinctiveness may provide some benefits to identity definition, it could also make your group more vulnerable to discrimination by the powerful majority.

Integrative intergroup theories

How do beliefs about our position in the social hierarchy help to explain discrimination?

The repertoire of threats groups encounter helps to explain many cases of intergroup differentiation and discrimination. However, some theories cannot be reduced to a list of threats, but combine, in more complex and integrative ways, some of these explanatory principles with an analysis of the social structure (the status hierarchy, or intergroup power relations), and our beliefs and feelings about our position in this structure. In this section we consider theories that provide a more detailed analysis of how prejudice and discrimination can relate to dynamics structured by status and power between groups (see also realistic conflict theory and relative deprivation theory, already discussed).

Socio-structural theories We have already introduced social identity theory (Tajfel & Turner, 1979) in relation to a number of forms of identity threat (esteem, status, distinctiveness). These threats to identity do not occur in a 'social vacuum', but reflect the position of people in the social structure. As we saw above, groups disadvantaged by low status are likely to feel threatened. However, this threat is just a starting point: social identity theory was developed in large part to explain *how and why* low-status groups cope with this situation, because (as we have already noted) discrimination and ingroup bias does not *always* result. Whether people respond to this threat with direct discrimination towards the rival group, for example, depends on whether the status relation is seen as legitimate or illegitimate and as stable or unstable (and so open to change). Tajfel and Turner (1979) referred to social comparison between groups in a status hierarchy that highlights the illegitimacy and instability of the situation as 'insecure'; insecure social comparisons encourage low-status groups to imagine how things could be better (called 'cognitive alternatives to the status quo'). It is under these conditions that social identity theory predicts most intergroup conflict (and thus discrimination). It follows that conflict and discrimination will not *always* result from status differences (an important difference from realistic conflict theory).

Although the *absence* of discrimination may seem like a good thing, social conflict can, at least sometimes, be important and necessary if social change is to occur. Take the 'Arab Spring', the wave of popular democratic uprisings that swept across many Arab countries in 2011. Few would argue that these uprisings and mass protests reflect the operation of prejudice and discrimination (at least in the conventional pejorative sense), but they certainly reflect conflict and social change. This is why it is important to take into account power and legitimacy when thinking about prejudice and discrimination: the ingroup bias of the powerless may not be the same, or have the same aims and functions, as that of the advantaged. Whereas low-status groups may be competing to change the status quo, high-status groups may use ingroup bias to reflect and legitimize their superior position, bolstering group esteem (see Scheepers, Spears, Doosje, & Manstead, 2006a, b, for some evidence of these different functions). So as well as offering a group explanation of prejudice and discrimination, social identity theory is also a theory of social change. We will address this issue in more detail in the next section, where we show that prejudice reduction strategies can sometimes

work against social change and the interests of low-status groups (Dixon, Levine, Reicher, & Durrheim, 2012; Saguy, Tausch, Dovidio, & Pratto, 2009).

A second powerful factor that can contribute to the stability of the status quo is what we might call the 'ideology of individualism', or individual mobility. If social change is not feasible, another route to a positive identity is to move into the high-status group. Of course this depends on mobility being possible (i.e., *permeable* group boundaries). Clearly this is only an option that can be tried by the few rather than the many (it is unrealistic to think of one group moving into the other en masse). In short, this is an *individual* strategy that changes nothing in the status relations between the groups. However, the ideology of individualism (the 'American dream' that anyone can make it rich, for example) is remarkably potent. Research by Wright and colleagues has shown that even very limited ('token') mobility is enough to deflect low-status group members from engaging in more group-level strategies for social change (Wright, Taylor, & Moghaddam, 1990). In one of their experiments Wright et al. showed that even a very small chance (e.g., 5 per cent) that a low-status group member could gain promotion to the high-status group was sufficient to stop people in this group engaging in collective social change strategies that might give a chance for fairer outcomes for all. Intergroup strategies only became likely when no mobility at all was possible. In other words there is a tendency to think selfishly if there is a chance of promotion, however meagre, to the higher status group ('everyone for themselves'). This idea is well illustrated in Reicher and Haslam's (2006) recreation of the classic Stanford Prison Study (see Chapter 8), filmed for the BBC television in the UK. In this experiment one of the most militant and disruptive 'prisoners' became much less militant when there was the prospect of becoming one of the guards (Reicher & Haslam, 2006).

These additional dimensions to social identity theory point to the importance of ideological factors relating to beliefs about the social structure that can moderate our reactions to realistic conflicts and identity threats. Indeed Tajfel referred to an ideological continuum of beliefs about the social structure from complete individual mobility at one end (e.g., the American dream that anyone with the right effort and ability can make it to the top) to social change beliefs at the other (e.g., that 'revolution' is necessary to gain intergroup equality). If you are focused on individual mobility you are not really thinking about your group's disadvantage so much as *your own personal* disadvantage. This is therefore a strategy associated with low identifiers and the individual level. We can now put together the various elements of social identity theory (see Theory Box 14.3).

SOCIAL IDENTITY THEORY: HOW LOW-STATUS GROUPS COPE WITH DISADVANTAGE/IDENTITY THREAT

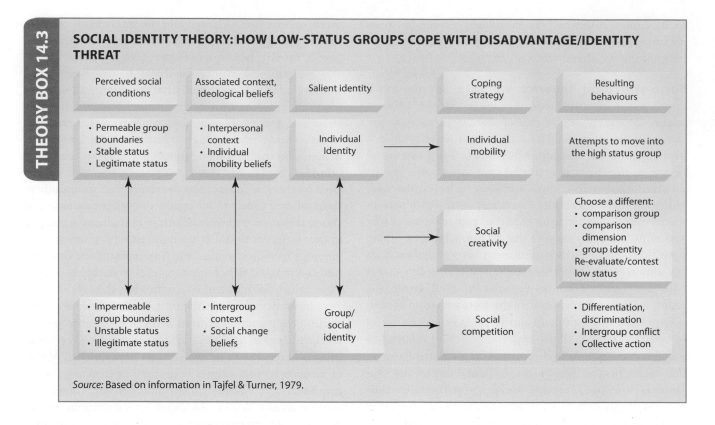

Source: Based on information in Tajfel & Turner, 1979.

The idea that we *do not always* discriminate or show prejudice towards outgroups is just as important as explaining discrimination itself. Any complete theory of intergroup conflict needs to be able to explain when and why it occurs, but also *when it does not*. Another approach that emphasizes the possibility that discrimination in favour of one's own group does not always occur is *system justification theory* (Jost & Banaji, 1994). This approach goes further than social identity theory in arguing that at least some members of low-status groups are actually *motivated* to justify the system in which differences in status and power exist. Thus, both social identity theory and system justification theory can explain **outgroup bias** towards high-status groups: the tendency to rate the outgroup as better, typically on the status-defining dimension. However, whereas social identity theory predicts this when low status is stable and legitimate, making ingroup bias and claims to high status difficult to sustain (see social reality constraints), system justification theory argues that some low-status group members are *motivated* to defend the existing social hierarchy in the system (but see Brandt, 2013, for a recent empirical challenge to this theory).

These more integrative and group-level theories of intergroup relations reveal how complex prejudice and discrimination are. As we noted in the introduction, as

outgroup bias a tendency to favour the outgroup over the ingroup in terms of evaluations or reward allocations.

the prevalence of blatant forms of racism, sexism and prejudice has receded, one of the growth areas of prejudice research has focused on subtler and even benevolent forms of prejudice (e.g., Glick & Fiske, 1996). According to this view, positive views and stereotypes of outgroups can also be prejudicial, especially when they reinforce the disadvantaged positions of low-status groups. Seeing Black people as great athletes, or women as good cooks and so on, despite being apparently positive, makes such groups prisoners of stereotypes that can prevent them competing in higher-status domains. Nor do these apparently positive stereotypes always benefit the group anyway (have you noticed how many top TV chefs are men rather than women?).

Can emotions help to explain the variety and intensity of prejudice?

Intergroup emotion theories In recent years emotion-based approaches have led the way in explaining the diverse forms of contemporary prejudice. Dijker (1987), who examined the different profiles of prejudice towards different ethnic minority groups in The Netherlands (e.g., Turkish, Moroccans, Surinamese) had shown that there was much to be gained in distinguishing prejudice in terms of the specific emotion reactions that specific outgroups may elicit. A number of approaches followed that used emotion theories to understand the different forms prejudice can take and the different functions it might fulfil. The first and best known is *intergroup emotion theory* (Smith, 1993). Classical emotion theories propose that emotions can be characterized not just by different feelings (e.g., anger, fear, contempt), but also in terms of the 'appraisals' that typically produce these states and the 'action tendencies' that follow from them. Appraisals are cognitions that assess the specific relevance of the situation for the perceiver (Lazarus, 1991). Appraisals address such questions as: 'Is this person a threat to me?' (a primary appraisal); 'Can I cope with this threat in some way?' (a secondary or coping appraisal). Different appraisals can lead to distinctively different emotions. Emotions also have characteristic 'action tendencies' associated with them (Frijda, 1986). Thus, fear is likely to result in more avoidance, whereas anger is likely to result in approach behaviour (e.g., confrontation, conflict). Appraising a member of another group as a physical threat, especially if the self is weak, may lead to feeling fear, and the action tendency to avoid members of the group in general. In contrast, a sense of being wronged by the other, along with an appraisal of strength, may lead to anger, and the action tendency of approach and confrontation.

The new insight was to argue that we could experience such emotions not as individuals but as group members: **group emotions**. Intergroup emotion theory is grounded in the social identity approach, and group identification is generally predicted to intensify these emotions. Thus, if football fans of a rival team threaten me outside the football ground because I am wearing the scarf of my team, this may evoke a group-based emotion (e.g., fear or anger). However, in such cases there is always the possibility that emotions could be appraised and felt personally *or* as a group member ('Is it me, personally, or is it *we* that feel this?'). Group emotions become perhaps more clear-cut when we experience them *vicariously*, on behalf of a fellow ingroup member. This is nicely illustrated in a study by Gordijn, Wigboldus, and Yzerbyt (2001), in which participants at one university (the University of Amsterdam) reacted to news that students at another university in The Netherlands (the University of Leiden) were angry about the plans of the authorities there to introduce stricter study requirements (e.g., higher workload, admissions exams). Only when the Amsterdam students were categorized as *students* (i.e., part of the same category as the Leiden students) did they show high

group emotions
emotions experienced as members of social groups rather than as individuals, reflecting appraisals of events in terms of group level concerns and coping resources.

levels of anger at the proposal (i.e., above the scale midpoint). Their anger was reduced when they were part of a *different* category to the victims (i.e., based on university affiliation: Amsterdam versus Leiden; see Figure 14.8). This example shows that group-based emotions are felt on behalf of fellow group members, and not personally, because these plans to change the study requirements did not affect the Amsterdam students directly.

The idea of emotional prejudice is powerful because it allows us to distinguish many different *types* of prejudice that depend on the relation between groups. Prejudices such as racism might be quite different to sexism and homophobia (try to think of the different appraisals and resulting emotions that might underlie any prejudice in these cases). Simply focusing on negative attitudes does not allow us to distinguish between these types of prejudice. Indeed, there may be many different kinds of racial prejudice, and this will not only depend on features of the target outgroup, but also aspects of the ingroup. Because the members of the ingroup may vary in their appraisals depending on their own characteristics, appraisals and emotions may even vary within the ingroup. For example, women and the elderly may experience more physical threat and therefore feel more fear towards certain groups than do young men.

A further advantage of the group emotion approach to prejudice is that it is better able to explain more extreme and intense forms of prejudice, such as outgroup derogation, than some earlier theories that focus

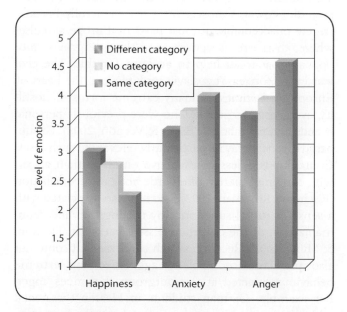

FIGURE 14.8 *Happiness, anxiety and anger experienced by Amsterdam students as a function of the categorization of the students from Leiden (different, no, or same category).*

Source: Gordijn, Wigboldus, & Yzerbyt, 2001, with permission from SAGE Publications Ltd.

more on explaining ingroup favouritism (Brewer's point about 'outgroup hate'). You could say group emotions put the passion into prejudice. One example of a malicious emotional prejudice is the emotion of 'intergroup *schadenfreude*' (Leach, Spears, Branscombe, & Doosje, 2003). German students will know *schadenfreude* as the pleasure people can experience when they see someone having an accident or slip up (think of those cheesy home video TV shows). However, this pleasure can turn nasty at the intergroup level. Following the writing of the philosopher Nietzsche, Leach et al., argued that experiencing group *schadenfreude* can provide a source of 'imaginary revenge' towards a bitter rival, especially when your own group is threatened by a sense of inferiority (see the discussion of status threats earlier). To test this idea, Leach et al. measured Dutch students' reactions to Germany being knocked out of the World Cup by Croatia in 1998 (a *schadenfreude* opportunity for the Dutch). The sense of inferiority was manipulated in two ways in a 2 × 2 between-participants design. The Dutch students were reminded (or not) that the Netherlands had never won the World Cup before (a *chronic* inferiority threat). In a second manipulation they were reminded (or not) of the game in which Brazil had knocked out the Dutch team in this tournament (an *acute* inferiority threat). Dutch pleasure at the German loss (*schadenfreude*) was indeed significantly higher after exposure to both these threats compared to control conditions.

Although, as we noted in the introduction, blatant prejudice towards most groups has thankfully become largely unacceptable in most parts of Europe and elsewhere, there are exceptions, and the intergroup emotion approach can help to account for this. The civil war in the former Yugoslavia took place in the heart of Europe, and witnessed many extreme forms of hostility, even between people who were previously personal friends and neighbours (Esses & Vernon, 2008). Group-based *contempt* may be particularly relevant in such cases. Contempt is a less constructive emotion than anger; with contempt there is often little hope of reconciliation (Fischer & Roseman, 2007), and it is also associated with a sense of moral superiority by the ingroup and dehumanization of the outgroup (Esses, Veenvliet, Hodson, & Mihic, 2008). Recent research confirms that contempt also predicts more violent, aggressive and extreme behaviour directed at the outgroup than does anger. For example, German students in Hessen threatened with the introduction of study fees from the local state government were more likely to support violent action, such as rioting, the more contempt they felt towards the authorities (Tausch et al., 2011).

We do not need wars or riots to find more extreme examples of prejudice in our midst, however. One group that seems to attract high levels of prejudice across Europe is the Roma people (sometimes pejoratively referred to as 'gypsies'). This is especially true in Romania, where prejudice and discrimination towards the Roma is blatant and even socially accepted. Why is this so? Intergroup emotion theory might help us to understand why. As we have already seen, anger and fear can underlie distinct forms of emotional prejudice. Roma people seem to attract anger because many see them as not working or contributing to the economy, but depending on state benefits (contempt is also relevant here). However, in Romania, unlike in other countries in Europe, the Roma people also represent a very sizeable ethnic group, and consequently they are more likely to be seen as a source of threat (e.g., regarding street crime). This unusual but potent combination of group-based anger *and* fear helps to explain the especially blatant prejudice towards the Roma in Romania.

The intergroup-emotion approach to prejudice has spawned a rich programme of research, and many theoretical frameworks have now emerged to fill in the gaps and explain the wide variety of emotional prejudice (e.g., Cottrell & Neuberg, 2005; Iyer & Leach, 2008; Yzerbyt & Kuppens, 2009). We finally elaborate one approach that has been particularly influential in delineating different forms of prejudice. The *stereotype content model* of Fiske, Cuddy, Glick, and Xu (2002) focuses on two key appraisal dimensions of *competence* and *warmth* that are commonly used to judge others. The warmth dimension relates to how competitive the group is (cold being more competitive). Considering groups as either high or low on each of these dimensions results in four quadrants (see Theory Box 14.4). The combination of high competence and high warmth is the most positive, and leads to positive emotions like admiration. It tends to be where we find the ingroup, but also respected outgroups (e.g., Black professionals). When groups are rated low on both of these dimensions, then disgust, contempt and anger can arise and characterize what Fiske et al. call 'contemptuous prejudice'. A typical group in this cell is homeless people, and also the Roma people from our earlier example. The combination of high warmth and low competence might attract more positive emotions like sympathy and pity. However, this superficially positive reaction conceals the 'paternalistic prejudice'. Benevolent sexism also falls into this category.

One compelling example of benevolent sexism, and its effects, comes from recent research by Becker, Glick, Ilic, and Bohner (2011). Think back to the example at

THEORY BOX 14.4

THE STEREOTYPE CONTENT MODEL

Four types of outgroup, combinations of status and competition, and corresponding forms of prejudice as a function of perceived warmth and competence.

		Competence	
Warmth		**Low**	**High**
High		Paternalistic prejudice Low status, not competitive Pity, sympathy E.g., women (benevolent sexism)	Admiration High status, not competitive E.g., ingroup, allies
Low		Contemptuous prejudice Low status, competitive Contempt, disgust, anger E.g., homeless, Roma people	Envious prejudice High status, competitive Envy, jealousy E.g., Jews, bankers

Source: Copyright © 2002 by the American Psychological Association. Adapted with permission. Fiske, S. T., Cuddy, A. J. C., Glick, P., & Xu, J. (2002). A model of (often mixed) stereotype content: Competence and warmth respectively follow from perceived status and competition. *Journal of Personality and Social Psychology, 82*, 878–902. The use of APA information does not imply endorsement by APA.

the beginning of this chapter of the man offering to help the woman with her computer problem. How could this positive act of helping be considered as prejudice by the man, and of any harm to the woman? Well, Becker and her colleagues found that women who accepted help from men tended to be seen as warm but incompetent, whereas those that declined it were viewed as competent but cold. To coin a phrase, the authors concluded that women were 'damned if they did and damned if they didn't'. The helping man, on the other hand, did not suffer any of these drawbacks but was viewed as both warm and competent in his benevolence. So even the man that means well (and thinks of himself as chivalrous rather than benevolently sexist) may ironically not be doing the woman he helps any favours in the eyes of others.

Other examples of benevolent prejudice are stereotypes towards the disabled and the elderly. The combination of high competence and low warmth presents a very different kind of threat to the perceiver and one potentially more dangerous. This has been characterized as 'envious prejudice'; anti-Semitic bigotry towards Jews provides a good example of this form of prejudice (Glick, 2008). In the recent financial crisis bankers are another example (although their competence could also be questioned!).

Summary

In this section we examined the value of taking a group-level approach to prejudice and discrimination. As group animals who derive many benefits from our memberships of groups there may be good reasons to trust and favour ingroups over outgroups. Prejudice and discrimination are targeted at outgroups, so it also makes sense to explain these in intergroup terms and by analysing the threats the outgroup can pose. The concept of social identity has been particularly useful, because it refers not only to the target of prejudice, but also captures the sense of self that makes us part of the ingroup. This is not to deny a role for individual explanations of prejudice and discrimination, but they may become less relevant than intergroup factors in intergroup settings. Differences in group identification and group-relevant appraisals also help to explain variations in prejudice at the group level. However, intergroup factors also explain why group members do not always show prejudice and discrimination (e.g., social reality constraints, group norms), and tolerance and fairness can also boost group-esteem, and be strengthened by group identification when normative. With this more optimistic point in mind we now turn to the tricky but important issue of how prejudice and discrimination can be reduced.

settings confirm the positive effect of institutional support (Landis, Hope, & Day, 1984; Morrison & Herlihy, 1992; Parker, 1968).

Allport's (1954b) contact hypothesis has been highly influential, inspiring a vast amount of empirical research, as well as the development of his initial propositions into a fully-fledged theory (see Hewstone & Swart, 2011; Tropp, 2012; Tropp & Mallett, 2011, for summaries of recent contact research). His ideas contributed to the US Supreme Court's decision to outlaw racially segregated schools, and have been applied widely in the 'real world' as part of interventions to improve intergroup relations.

jigsaw classroom a cooperative teaching method designed to reduce prejudice in diverse classrooms.

One particularly successful intervention is the so-called **jigsaw classroom**, a cooperative teaching method designed to reduce prejudice in diverse classrooms (e.g., Aronson & Patnoe, 1997; see Social Psychology Beyond the Lab 14.1).

So can we be confident that (appropriate) contact reduces prejudice? Early reviews (e.g., Amir, 1976; Cook, 1984) often reached conflicting conclusions. One of the most contentious issues was whether the effects of contact would actually *generalize* from the encountered outgroup members to the outgroup as a whole. This question is crucial when considering the effectiveness of intergroup contact as a tool to improve intergroup relations on a wider scale.

Furthermore, critics were also concerned about the necessity of Allport's (1954b) optimal contact conditions (see also Stephan, 1987): the long list of necessary conditions may be difficult to meet in real life, and contact under less than optimal conditions might increase prejudice. To address these concerns, and to provide a more systematic review of the contact literature, Pettigrew and Tropp (2006) carried out a meta-analysis of over 500 studies, conducted over five decades, that had examined the relation between intergroup contact and prejudice. They found a highly significant negative relation between contact and prejudice across studies, suggesting that contact is associated with reduced prejudice. In fact, only a small percentage of studies suggested that contact is associated with increased prejudice.

Keep in mind that many of the studies included in the meta-analysis were cross-sectional, meaning that they often used questionnaires which measured levels of contact with outgroup members and attitudes towards the outgroup at the same point in time. In cross-sectional studies, it is never clear whether the negative relation between contact and prejudice indicates that contact reduces prejudice, or whether less prejudiced people simply engage in more contact. To complicate things more, a significant association between two variables can

also be due to their correlation with a third, unknown (or unmeasured) variable, which causes variation in both variables. For example, if less-educated people tend to be more prejudiced as well as live in areas where contact is less likely to occur, then education could explain a negative relation between contact and prejudice. Thus, the best way of establishing a causal link between contact and prejudice is to conduct an experiment, either in the field, such as the housing experiments described earlier (Deutsch & Collins, 1951; Wilner et al., 1955) or in the laboratory (e.g., see Wilder's, 1984 study, described later). Longitudinal studies, which measure contact and prejudice at different points in time and examine the relation of contact to *changes* in prejudice, are also helpful to rule out alternative causal relations. A number of such studies have been conducted in recent years (e.g., Swart, Hewstone, Christ, & Voci, 2011; Tausch et al., 2010; Van Laar, Levin, Sinclair, & Sidanius, 2005) and tend to suggest that contact does indeed predict reductions in prejudice over time.

Let us return to the importance of Allport's (1954b) optimal contact conditions. Of the studies included in Pettigrew and Tropp's (2006) meta-analysis, some fully met allport's optimal contact conditions, others only partially fulfilled them, and some studies did not fulfil them at all. This allowed Pettigrew and Tropp to test how important Allport's conditions are. Interestingly, the significant relation between contact and prejudice emerged irrespective of whether Allport's contact conditions were present, although studies that fulfilled the conditions showed stronger effects. The authors therefore concluded that Allport's original contact conditions are not *necessary* for positive contact effects to occur, but that they are *facilitating* conditions that are likely to make contact more effective.

Pettigrew and Tropp (2006) were also able to address the question of whether contact effects generalize from the encountered group member to the group as a whole. They did this by comparing the effect sizes of contact obtained for ratings of individual outgroup members with effects sizes obtained for ratings of the outgroup as a whole. Because effect sizes for outgroup ratings were not significantly smaller than effect sizes for ratings of individuals, Pettigrew and Tropp concluded that contact effects typically do generalize. But this does not yet answer the question of *when* the positive effects of contact are most likely to generalize to the outgroup as a whole.

This issue was examined in a study by Wilder (1984). In this study, female students recruited from two rival colleges (Douglas College and Rutgers College) interacted with a member of the other college (who was actually a confederate). The two groups had fairly complementary stereotypes of one another. While Rutgers

SOCIAL PSYCHOLOGY BEYOND THE LAB 14.1

THE JIGSAW CLASSROOM

The jigsaw classroom is a learning technique that was developed by Aronson and his graduate students. It was first used in schools in Austin, Texas, in 1971, shortly after schools in the city were desegregated and children from different ethnic backgrounds were for the first time taught together in the same classroom. Aronson was called by a school superintendent just a few weeks after desegregation and asked to help improve the increasingly hostile interracial relations at the school (tension between groups had built up over the weeks, culminating in fights between the youngsters). After observing classes for a few days, Aronson and his students concluded that the hostility between the different ethnic groups was fuelled by a competitive climate in the classroom, where students worked individually and competed for the teacher's approval and grades. They decided that, to improve relations, this competitive climate needed to be transformed into a cooperative one. So they started to develop the jigsaw technique.

This is how it works: a class is divided into smaller task groups of six children from different ethnic backgrounds. A lesson is divided into six parts and each student is assigned one part of the material. For example, the first time the jigsaw technique was applied, fifth-graders were asked to learn about the life of Eleanor Roosevelt, and her biography was divided into six segments (e.g., her childhood, her family life, her work as First Lady and so on). Each student in a group was assigned one of these segments to prepare, and asked to report what they learned to the other members of the group, who did not have any other access to this information. In short, each group member contributed a unique piece of the jigsaw puzzle. The jigsaw process thus facilitates interaction among all students in the class, leading them to value each other as contributors to their common task. It encourages engagement with members of other ethnic groups by giving them an essential part to contribute. Note that this technique fulfils many of Allport's (1954b) conditions for optimal contact: the children work cooperatively towards a common goal, each member is vital to achieving the common task, ensuring equal status of majority and minority children, and the interaction receives institutional support from the school.

The jigsaw technique has now been used in schools for 40 years and its effectiveness has been demonstrated in a number of studies in which children were randomly assigned to either a jigsaw classroom or a traditional classroom (e.g., see Aronson & Patnoe, 1997). These studies have consistently shown that the children taught in jigsaw classrooms not only come to like each other more, but also perform better in exams and have higher self-esteem compared to children taught in traditional classrooms. Moreover, a number of studies have also shown that the children do not just come to like their outgroup classmates more, but also come to like the other ethnic groups in general more – that is, they become less prejudiced. Thus, the effects of the jigsaw classroom *generalize* from individual group members to the outgroup as a whole. We will discuss the important issue of generalization, and the conditions under which it is most likely to occur, in greater detail later in the text.

To learn more about the jigsaw classroom, visit Elliot Aronson's 'jigsaw.org' website.

women viewed Douglas women as being overly concerned with their appearance, conservative and studious, Douglas women perceived Rutgers women as liberal and interested in having fun at the expense of their studies. Moreover, pre-tests confirmed that both groups were biased in favour of the ingroup; they preferred their own college over the other college. The crucial question examined in Wilder's study was not just whether positive contact could affect views of the outgroup, but whether the effects of contact on overall outgroup attitudes would depend on the typicality of the encountered 'exemplar'.

Wilder thus varied whether the outgroup member behaved and dressed in a manner that was either typical or atypical of the outgroup. For example, for participants from Rutgers University, in the typical outgroup member condition, the confederate introduced herself as a Douglas student, was dressed neatly and wore make-up, looked at her diary to check if the experiment clashed with a meeting of her conservative political club and mentioned that she hoped the experiment would be brief because she had a lot of studying to do. She thus fulfilled the stereotypes Rutgers women had of Douglas women (neatness, conservatism and studiousness). When the confederate posed as a Rutgers woman, she wore faded jeans and a baggy T-shirt, looked at her diary to check if the experiment clashed with a meeting of her liberal political club and mentioned that

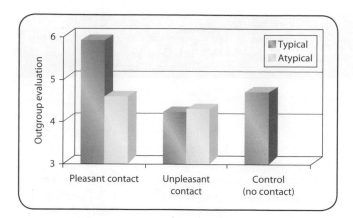

FIGURE 14.10 *Outgroup evaluation as a function of typicality of outgroup member and quality of contact.*

Source: Adapted from Wilder, 1984, with permission from Elsevier.

she hoped the experiment would be brief because she needed to get ready for a party. In the atypical condition, the Douglas student dressed and behaved like a typical Rutgers student and vice versa. The interaction consisted of a number of problem-solving tasks during which the confederate then acted in either a positive or negative manner (she supported or rejected the participant's ideas in a number of problem-solving tasks), rendering the contact either pleasant or unpleasant. As one would expect, participants' ratings of the outgroup were more positive when the confederate behaved in a positive and cooperative manner. Importantly, however, the extent to which the contact experience generalized to evaluations of the outgroup as a whole depended on the outgroup member's typicality. Only when the encountered outgroup member was typical did the positive contact experience generalize to the outgroup as a whole (see Figure 14.10).

This finding suggested that contact effects are most likely to generalize to the outgroup when the outgroup member is viewed as representative (cf. Rothbart & John, 1985), for which there is now extensive evidence (see Brown & Hewstone, 2005). We return to the issue of generalization in the next section, where we address the role of levels of categorization in prejudice reduction.

Varying levels of categorization

Does changing the structure of categories reduce prejudice?

The question of whether to approach prejudice from an individual or group perspective also has implications for how best to implement contact as a prejudice-

reduction strategy. Researchers have developed three distinct theoretical models that examine the nature of cognitive group representations during contact, and which is more effective. Although each of these models was based on the social identity / self-categorization approach (Tajfel & Turner, 1979; Turner et al., 1987), each draws quite different conclusions about how contact should be structured in order to reduce prejudice. Keep in mind that while these models were initially concerned with intergroup contact interventions, many of the ideas and questions put forward by these approaches apply more widely, in particular to the question of how relations between majority and minority groups should be managed in society. For example, is intergroup harmony in diverse societies best achieved by taking a 'colour-blind' approach and treating everyone as an individual? Or should we promote multiculturalism in which group differences are acknowledged and appreciated? As you will see, the answer is not that simple (see Rattan & Ambady, 2013, for a recent review of these contrasting approaches).

Three models of contact The **decategorization** approach (e.g., Brewer & Miller, 1984) recommends reducing the salience of intergroup boundaries during contact by inducing two cognitive processes: 'differentiation' (making distinctions between individual outgroup members); and 'personalization' (stressing the uniqueness of each individual outgroup member). This can be achieved by promoting opportunities to get to know each other and by encouraging the disclosure of intimate personal information during contact (e.g., Ensari & Miller, 2002). This approach is consistent with Allport's (1954b) suggestion that contact should be intimate and allow for real acquaintance with outgroup members. Brewer and Miller suggested that the attention to idiosyncratic information would result in less attention being paid to category-based stereotypical information. They believed that the repeated use of individual information would reduce the usefulness of the category in future interactions, and thereby have generalized effects (less prejudiced reactions to outgroup members in general).

Support for the effectiveness of personalized contact comes from a series of experiments (e.g., Bettencourt, Brewer, Croak, & Miller, 1992) in which experimentally created groups were brought together to work on a cooperative task. Participants were instructed to focus

decategorization
reducing the salience of intergroup boundaries through personalized contact; attention to idiosyncratic rather than category-based information about outgroup members should, over time, reduce the usefulness of the category, and reduce prejudice.

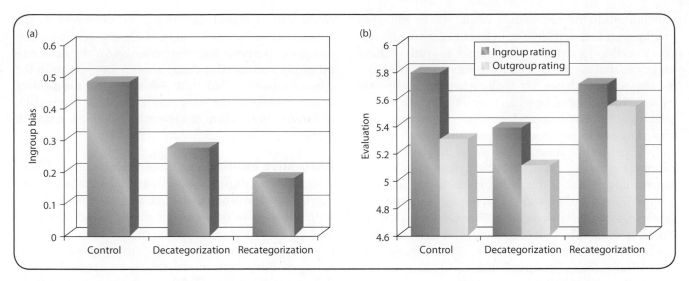

FIGURE 14.11 (a) and (b) *(a) Ingroup bias as a function of categorization; (b) Ingroup evaluation and outgroup evaluation as a function of categorization.*

Source: Copyright © 1989 by the American Psychological Association. Adapted with permission. Gaertner, S. L., Mann, J., Murrell, A., & Dovidio, J. F. (1989). Reducing intergroup bias: The benefits of recategorization. *Journal of Personality and Social Psychology, 57*, 239–249. The use of APA information does not imply endorsement by APA.

either on personal characteristics (person-oriented condition) or on the task at hand (task-oriented condition). These studies demonstrated that participants in the person-oriented condition show less bias in the allocation of rewards to ingroup and outgroup members compared to participants in the task-oriented condition. This was true even when participants were asked to allocate rewards to an outgroup member whom they had not encountered before and who was presented on a video screen. This finding provided evidence that the effects of personalized contact generalize to the outgroup as a whole.

The idea that personalized contact reduces prejudice is also supported by research on intergroup friendships. Pettigrew (1997) demonstrated that people who had an outgroup friend expressed less prejudice towards the outgroup as a whole than did people who only had an outgroup neighbour or coworker, but not a friend. Compared to other forms of contact, friendship also emerged as the strongest predictor of reduced prejudice in Pettigrew and Tropp's (2006) meta-analysis.

The decategorization approach suggests that people should interact with members of other groups as individuals and refrain from using social categories. But is this realistic? As we discussed earlier, groups fulfil important human needs, and social identities form valued parts of the self, so people might be reluctant to give up or ignore their group memberships. Rather than aiming to eliminate the use of social categories altogether, the

recategorization approach (also referred to as the *common ingroup identity model*; Gaertner, Mann, Murrell, & Dovidio, 1989; see also Chapter 10) proposes that prejudice can be reduced by transforming cognitive group representations from two groups ('us' and 'them') to one inclusive social entity ('we').

Several studies have now shown that recategorization results in reduced ingroup bias (see Gaertner & Dovidio, 2000). Interestingly, a study by Gaertner et al. (1989) showed that recategorization reduces bias in a different way to decategorization (i.e., conditions that encourage participants to interact as individuals). This is shown in Figure 14.11. While decategorization and recategorization resulted in similar amounts of reduction in *bias* (see Figure 14.11a), decategorization reduced bias by making evaluations of former *ingroup* members *less* positive, while recategorization reduced bias by making evaluations of former *outgroup* members *more* positive, compared to the control condition in which participants interacted as members of different groups (see Figure 14.11b).

Although the empirical support for the benefits of recategorization is wide-ranging, many of the studies testing this model were conducted in the laboratory. This raises the question of whether a superordinate identity can overcome powerful ethnic and racial categorizations that are an important part of people's

recategorization
recommends replacing salient ingroup–outgroup distinctions at a subordinate level with a common ingroup identity at a superordinate level that includes both former ingroup and outgroup members.

self-concepts in the 'real world'. Would you be willing to give up your national identity in favour of a broader category such as 'European'? A number of authors have suggested that there may be strong resistance to changes in category boundaries, especially when the groups are engaged in hostilities, or when they differ in size, power or status. Remember our discussion earlier about the importance of identifying with optimally distinct groups and the perils of distinctiveness threat. Minority group members may be particularly reluctant to accept a superordinate identity if it is dominated by the majority group (Simon, Aufderheide, & Kampmeier, 2001). For example, as we discussed earlier, East Germans ('Ossis') would be more reluctant to identify with Germans than would West Germans ('Wessis'). The *categorization* model (also called **mutual differentiation** model; Hewstone & Brown, 1986) presents a viewpoint that differs sharply from the decategorization and recategorization approaches. This model suggests that, rather than reducing the salience of the original categories, group affiliations should be made salient during contact. This encourages the problematic relationship between the ingroup and outgroup to be addressed directly, reducing the risk that the outgroup members encountered are psychologically distanced from the outgroup, which could inhibit generalization (Rothbart & John, 1985).

> **mutual differentiation** (or *categorization approach to improving intergroup relations*) making group affiliations salient during contact to give members of the respective groups distinct but complementary roles.

But how should positive intergroup contact be structured? Hewstone and Brown (1986) recommend that, in order to maintain social identities and positive distinctiveness, but to avoid intergroup comparisons in the interaction, the contact situation should be structured so that members of the respective groups have distinct but complementary roles to contribute towards the achievement of a common goal. Mutual strengths should be recognized and equally valued, which can be achieved by ensuring that the ingroup and the outgroup are rated on independent dimensions (Mummendey & Schreiber, 1984). Thus, this approach does not seek to change the original category structure, but aims to transform the level of interdependence between the two groups from negative to positive (i.e., from a competitive to a more cooperative relationship). Both the role of category salience in the generalization of contact effects and the advantage of letting participants work on different task dimensions have been empirically supported (Brown & Wade, 1987; Deschamps & Brown, 1983; Van Oudenhoven, Groenewoud, & Hewstone, 1996). Nonetheless, this approach also has drawbacks. Making category memberships salient

could lead to biased perception and behaviour in the contact situation, and might therefore reinforce stereotypical perceptions (Neuberg, 1996). An emphasis on group memberships may also create anxiety in the contact situation and thus risk the generalization of negative affect to the outgroup as a whole (Greenland & Brown, 1999; Islam & Hewstone, 1993a; Stephan & Stephan, 1985).

Integrative models The three theoretical models of categorization during contact (decategorization, recategorization and mutual differentiation) make different suggestions as to how contact should be structured to be most beneficial. Each of the models is supported by empirical evidence and each has advantages and disadvantages. But which model should be applied? Rather than viewing these models as competing positions, researchers have begun to see them as complementary approaches and have started to integrate them.

For example, Pettigrew (1998) combined them into a three-stage longitudinal model. He suggested that, because initial intergroup interactions are often formal and characterized by anxiety, decategorization should optimally happen first. Personalized contact would reduce this initial anxiety and lead to interpersonal liking. The social categories should be made salient in the next step in order to achieve generalization of positive affect to the outgroup as a whole. Recategorization into a superordinate category may then happen later, leading to maximum reduction in prejudice. Pettigrew (1998) realized, however, that the final stage of recategorization may be difficult if original group memberships are not easily abandoned. In this case, group members may prefer to maintain mutual recognition as separate groups, but also to acknowledge that they share a common group identity at a superordinate level (e.g., the English, Welsh and Scots who are all also British). This has been referred to as a *dual identity* (Gaertner & Dovidio, 2000) or *dual categorization* (Hornsey & Hogg, 2000) model. A dual identity model, in which both the original subgroup identities and a superordinate identity are made salient, has now been supported in several experimental studies (see Research Close-Up 14.2). Dual identification is the most beneficial strategy for members of minority groups, resulting, for example, in less 'acculturative stress' (the stress of moving to a different culture) among immigrants (Berry, Kim, Minde, & Mok, 1987) and less ingroup bias (Gaertner, Rust, Dovidio, Bachman, & Anastasio, 1996; González & Brown, 2006). It seems to be less successful, however, in reducing prejudice among members of numerical majority groups (González & Brown, 2006). Figure 14.13 presents a schematic representation of the different models.

THE BENEFITS OF DUAL CATEGORIZATION

Hornsey, M. J., & Hogg, M. A. (2000). Subgroup relations: A comparison of mutual intergroup differentiation and common ingroup identity models of prejudice reduction. *Personality and Social Psychology Bulletin, 26*, 242–256.

Introduction

In this article, Hornsey and Hogg wanted to examine what happens when naturalistic groups are asked to forsake a valued subgroup identity in favour of a superordinate identity. They were sceptical about the applicability of a common ingroup identity in the real world and hypothesized that making a superordinate category salient at the expense of a valued subgroup identity is likely to result in distinctiveness threat. This would consequently lead to greater bias towards the outgroup in order to reassert the subgroup identity. They proposed a new integrative model that suggested that dual categorization (making both the subgroup and superordinate group identity salient at the same time) would be the most effective way of reducing bias. The research was conducted in the context of different subject groups within a university in Australia.

Method

Participants

Participants were 191 undergraduate students ($N = 119$ females, $N = 72$ males) who studied either a maths/science ($N = 83$) or humanities ($N = 108$) subject. They participated individually.

Procedure and design

Participants were told that the local government was planning to build a recreational park and it was their task to choose 10 out of a list of 30 objects and services that they considered to be essential for its success. In an individual condition there was no mention of any category (i.e., neither the subgroup nor the superordinate identity was salient); participants were told that the government was interested in the opinions of *ordinary individuals*. In the superordinate category condition participants were told that the government was interested in the opinions of *university students* and was planning to compare them to the opinions of town planners. A piece of cardboard with their university logo formed a visible reminder of their superordinate category. In the subordinate group condition, participants were told that the government was interested in comparing the responses of *humanities*

and maths/science students. They were asked to circle their faculty area and, depending on their subject, to use either a blue or red pen to complete the questionnaire. In a final condition, participants were given the instructions for the superordinate condition followed by the instructions for the subordinate condition, making both their subcategory and the superordinate category salient. This yielded a 2 (subgroup: salient versus not salient) × 2 (superordinate group: salient versus not salient) between-subjects design.

Measures

Participants completed a manipulation check (they indicated the extent to which their thoughts were drawn to their faculty and their university membership while completing the task, in order to assess the salience of the two categories), a measure of their identification with their subgroup (i.e., their faculty) and a measure of ingroup bias at the subgroup level (the extent to which they would like to work with members of their own and the other faculty in an alleged subsequent task).

Results

A 2 (subgroup: salient versus not salient) × 2 (superordinate group: salient versus not salient) between-subjects analysis of variance revealed a significant interaction between subgroup salience and superordinate group salience. Figure 14.12a shows that the highest level of bias occurred in the condition in which the superordinate, but not the subordinate, group was salient. Participants also showed stronger identification with their subgroup in this condition (see Figure 14.12b). In contrast, participants in the condition in which both the superordinate and the subordinate category were salient showed relatively low levels of bias.

Discussion

Categorizing people exclusively at the superordinate group level (as recommended by the recategorization model) can threaten the distinctiveness of subgroup identities. In this example, people may not want to be seen simply as 'students', but wish to hold on to their valued identities as either maths/science or humanities students. This can result in a need to reassert the original group boundaries by increasing identification and expressing bias in favour of their subgroup. This distinctiveness threat can be avoided when the original subgroup identities are preserved within the common superordinate identity (i.e., dual categorization).

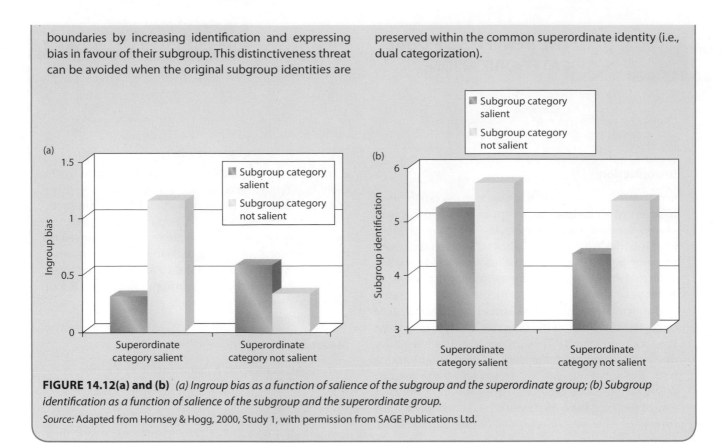

FIGURE 14.12(a) and (b) *(a) Ingroup bias as a function of salience of the subgroup and the superordinate group; (b) Subgroup identification as a function of salience of the subgroup and the superordinate group.*

Source: Adapted from Hornsey & Hogg, 2000, Study 1, with permission from SAGE Publications Ltd.

Psychological processes involved in intergroup contact and prejudice reduction

Which psychological processes play a role in prejudice reduction?

Understanding the psychological processes involved in prejudice reduction is important because it can enable researchers to design optimal interventions that target these processes specifically. In the case of face-to-face intergroup contact, which may often be difficult to achieve in real life, such knowledge can help to identify alternative or supplementary interventions with similar psychological effects (see below). Researchers examining prejudice reduction generally, and intergroup contact specifically, have therefore paid a great deal of attention to the issue of *process* in recent years.

Allport (1954b) did not really specify the psychological 'driving forces' of prejudice reduction through contact. He suggested, however, that negative stereotypes and attitudes towards outgroups are often due to a lack of information or erroneous information about a group, and that contact would provide an opportunity to correct these assumptions. Research on knowledge acquisition as

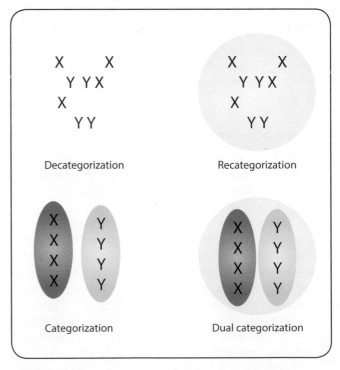

FIGURE 14.13 *Schematic representations of the decategorization, recategorization, categorization and dual categorization models.*

Source: Adapted from Brewer, 2003, with permission.

a potential explanatory variable (or 'mediator') has found some limited support for this idea (Stephan & Stephan, 1985). While increased knowledge about the outgroup explains at least part of the reduction in prejudice (Pettigrew & Tropp, 2008), more recent work has emphasized the importance of affective processes. Contact seems to impact more strongly on affective than on cognitive variables, having a greater effect on attitudes than stereotypes (Tropp & Pettigrew, 2005), and it seems to have its effects predominantly via its impact on affective processes (Brown & Hewstone, 2005; Swart, Hewstone, Christ, & Voci, 2011). Moreover recent research suggests an important asymmetry in this regard, in so far as negative contact seems to predict increased prejudice more strongly than positive contact reduces it (Barlow et al., 2012). This highlights once again the crucial importance of the quality of the contact.

Much of this research has focused on **intergroup anxiety**, a negative affective state felt when anticipating or experiencing contact with an outgroup. Intergroup anxiety stems from the expectation of negative consequences for oneself during intergroup interactions, such as embarrassment or rejection, and may be exacerbated by negative outgroup stereotypes, a history of intergroup conflict or a high ratio of outgroup to ingroup members (Stephan & Stephan, 1985; see also Greenland, Xenias, & Maio, 2012, for a recent elaboration of the different dimensions of intergroup anxiety). Because anxiety is accompanied by a narrowed attention focus and information-processing biases, it can undermine the positive effects of contact (e.g., Wilder & Shapiro, 1989). High levels of intergroup anxiety may also lead to the avoidance of contact altogether (Plant & Devine, 2003; Shelton & Richeson, 2005) or render any interaction awkward (Shelton, 2003). Because this negative affective state is linked to outgroup members, it is strongly associated with negative outgroup attitudes. Much research has shown that successful contact helps to overcome these apprehensions; reduced anxiety is a key mediator in the negative relationship between contact and prejudice (e.g., Islam & Hewstone, 1993a).

In addition to reducing negative anxiety, contact can also promote positive affective ties and increase empathy. Empathy can broadly be defined as the experience of understanding or sharing the emotional state of another person (see Chapter 10), and includes both emotional (empathic concern) and cognitive (perspective taking) facets (Davis, 1994). Research has shown

intergroup anxiety a negative affective state experienced when anticipating future, or experiencing actual, contact with an outgroup member, stemming from the expectation of negative consequences for oneself during intergroup interactions.

that empathy has beneficial effects on attitudes and behaviour (Stephan & Finlay, 1999). Several studies have shown that contact positively affects both cognitive and affective components of empathy, which partially explains how contact has an effect on prejudice reduction (Harwood, Hewstone, Paolini, & Voci, 2005; Tam, Hewstone, Harwood, Voci, & Kenworthy, 2006). A meta-analysis specifically on mediators of contact effects highlighted the role of increased empathy and reduced intergroup anxiety as the key mechanisms through which intergroup contact reduces prejudice (Pettigrew & Tropp, 2008).

A final mechanism we consider here is that of **ingroup reappraisal**. Pettigrew (1997) suggested that meaningful intergroup contact can help people to realize that ingroup norms, customs and lifestyles are not inherently superior to those of outgroups. In fact, this process would be expected to reduce prejudice towards *all* outgroups, leading to a wide generalization of contact effects. Several studies support this idea. For example, Pettigrew (1997) demonstrated that respondents who had contact with members of nationally represented minority groups (e.g., Germans' contact with people of Turkish descent) were also more accepting of other national groups that are less represented in that country (e.g., Algerians; see also Van Laar et al., 2005). Pettigrew (2009) labelled this form of generalization the 'secondary transfer effect' of intergroup contact. The 'transfer' is also not confined to outgroups that are similar to each other (e.g., across national groups, in the case above). Tausch et al. (2010) showed, for example, that contact across the sectarian divide in Northern Ireland (i.e., Catholics meeting Protestants and vice versa) promoted not only more positive attitudes towards the religious outgroup, but also towards racial minorities. Tausch et al. reported secondary transfer effects across multiple intergroup contexts, and showed that they were not due to socially desirable responding (i.e., someone giving politically correct positive responses to one outgroup also giving such positive responses to other outgroups). They also provided longitudinal evidence for this secondary transfer effect, showing that contact with the other community predicted reduced racial prejudice over time.

In sum, research has successfully identified some of the key psychological processes involved in how intergroup contact reduces prejudice. As we will see next, these processes can also be set in motion by techniques other than direct face-to-face contact.

ingroup reappraisal realization that ingroup norms, customs and lifestyles are not inherently superior to those of outgroups; this process is implicated in the generalization of positive contact effects to other outgroups.

Other prejudice-reduction techniques

Can prejudice be reduced by interventions other than contact?

Although face-to-face intergroup contact has been most widely researched as a prejudice-reduction intervention, actually arranging contact can involve serious practical obstacles. Different social groups often live highly segregated lives. This is particularly the case when there is a history of conflict and when there are strong social norms against intergroup interactions. Social psychologists are aware of these obstacles and have developed a number of approaches that do not require direct interaction, utilizing channels such as the Internet or other media to achieve widespread exposure (Amichai-Hamburger & McKenna, 2006).

Providing stereotype-disconfirming information about the outgroup Following Allport's (1954b) view that prejudice can result from erroneous stereotypes, research has investigated the effects of providing different types of stereotype-disconfirming information on outgroup perceptions. Several models of stereotype change have been tested: a *bookkeeping model*, whereby stereotype change happens gradually via the accumulation of stereotype-inconsistent information; a *conversion model*, which envisages radical change in response to a single piece of dramatic disconfirming information; and a *subtyping model*, whereby stereotype-inconsistent information creates a subtype and the outgroup stereotype becomes more complex (Weber & Crocker, 1983). Subtyping is also a means by which stereotypes are maintained in the face of disconfirmation, because a new subtype can be viewed as unrepresentative of the group, leaving the stereotype more or less unchanged (see Hewstone, 1994, for a review). Overall, there is some evidence that stereotypes change according to the bookkeeping model (e.g., the more interesting accountants we meet, the less we stereotype accountants as boring), and the conversion model (e.g., one really engaging accountant can sometimes change our view of the entire group), but the evidence is strongest for subtyping (e.g., if we encounter several accountants who are interesting people, but also love playing with numbers – and are therefore typical – then we are most likely to revise our prejudice that all accountants are boring; e.g., Johnston & Hewstone, 1992).

Extended contact The **extended contact hypothesis** (Wright, Aron, McLaughlin-Volpe, & Ropp, 1997) proposes that the *mere knowledge* that an ingroup member has a close relationship with an outgroup member can improve outgroup attitudes. Thus, people can experience intergroup contact indirectly (see Dovidio, Eller, & Hewstone, 2011, for a recent review). In one experimental study, Wright et al. (1997) first created negative intergroup attitudes by letting two groups in the laboratory compete with each other. They then asked *one* member from each group to engage in friendship-building exercises with the other group. The two participants believed that this exercise was part of another study. It involved disclosing increasingly personal information to each other, an exercise that was previously shown to result in high interpersonal closeness among strangers (Aron, Aron, Tudor, & Nelson, 1991). The remaining participants were asked to complete a number of unrelated questionnaires during that time. After the task was finished the groups were reunited and the experimenter encouraged participants to tell each other about the tasks they had just performed. Wright and colleagues found that outgroup attitudes improved after the friendship-building task, even among participants who themselves had *not* participated in the friendship building task. Thus, they provided evidence that extended contact can indeed improve attitudes. But *how* or *why* does extended contact reduce prejudice? Wright and colleagues suggested that one important mechanism concerns perceived group norms. As mentioned earlier, group norms do not always support intergroup interactions. Observing successful intergroup interactions, however, signals that engaging with outgroup members is acceptable to both the ingroup and the outgroup. Learning about intergroup contact would then also reduce the observers' anxiety about interacting with outgroup members in the future.

The extended contact hypothesis has now received substantial support in a variety of intergroup contexts. Evidence has also accrued about how and when it works: extended contact effects are mediated by reduced intergroup anxiety (e.g., Paolini, Hewstone, Cairns, & Voci, 2004), and by changing both ingroup and outgroup norms (e.g., Turner, Hewstone, Voci, & Vonofakou, 2008). Extended contact seems to be most effective for people who have few opportunities for direct contact (e.g., Christ et al., 2010). It has also been successfully applied in school settings: school children who learned about an intergroup friendship via a story expressed less prejudice (Cameron & Rutland, 2006). Extended contact can also happen via the media; Schiappa, Gregg, and Hewes (2005) showed that watching television programmes that portrayed intergroup contact (e.g., the American TV show *Will and Grace*, which portrays a gay man as a main

> **extended contact hypothesis** mere knowledge that an ingroup member has a close relationship with an outgroup member can improve outgroup attitudes.

character) reduced levels of prejudice towards the target groups featured.

Perspective-taking and empathy induction

Interventions that attempt to promote perspective-taking and empathy typically involve role-playing and the presentation of information from the outgroup's perspective. For example, Clore and Jeffery (1972) instructed participants to assume the role of a disabled person by travelling about in a wheelchair for an hour. This exercise significantly improved attitudes toward disabled people, an effect that was still found four months later. Galinsky and Moskowitz (2000) presented their participants with a photo of an elderly person and asked them to imagine what a day in their life would be like. Compared to the two control groups, which received no further instructions or were asked to suppress the stereotype, participants in the perspective-taking condition showed reduced stereotyping of elderly people in a subsequent task (see also Finlay & Stephan, 2000).

The wider implications of prejudice reduction

Does prejudice reduction result in more equal societies?

It is important to evaluate the effects of prejudice-reduction interventions not just in terms of whether they successfully reduce prejudiced attitudes, but also in terms of whether they promote good intergroup relations more generally. An implicit assumption in much of the research we have talked about in this section has been that reducing prejudice among members of the socially dominant group would result in reduced discrimination against members of minority or disadvantaged groups, thereby increasing group equality (see Wright & Lubensky, 2009). Consequently, this research has predominantly examined the effects of interventions on members of advantaged groups, and used prejudiced beliefs and feelings as the primary outcome variables. Less is known about how these interventions affect members of minority groups. Given both that attitudes do not always predict behaviour (see Chapter 6) and that dominant groups are motivated to maintain their power (Sidanius & Pratto, 1999), we might be sceptical about the effects of contact and prejudice reduction on wider societal change. Indeed, some researchers have argued that reducing prejudice does not necessarily address or eliminate intergroup inequality (Jackman & Crane,

1986). As we have emphasized earlier in our discussion of social identity theory, members of low-status groups also have an important role to play in bringing about societal change (e.g., through collective action). Thus, conflict, such as the current uprising in the Arab world, is therefore not always a bad thing and can lead to real societal change in the long run.

Recently a number of researchers have started to consider these issues. This research suggests that the link between reduced prejudice and political attitudes and actual behaviour is not clear-cut. For example, Dixon, Durrheim, and Tredoux (2007) found that while White South Africans were in favour of equality *in principle*, they tended to oppose interventions that would help to achieve this goal in practice, such as school quotas, affirmative action and land restitution. They termed this phenomenon the **principle–implementation gap**. Indeed, White South Africans' contact with Black South Africans had a weaker effect on attitudes towards specific pro-Black policies than it did on reducing prejudice towards Black people.

> **principle–implementation gap** acceptance of racial equality in principle is accompanied by resistance to specific policies that would bring about such racial equality.

Experimental research assessing the causal effect of positive intergroup contact on attitudes and actual discriminatory behaviour also suggests that, although positive contact improves advantaged group members' attitudes towards the disadvantaged, this does not reduce discrimination (Saguy et al., 2009; see Research Close-Up 14.3). Ironically, positive contact experiences can also lead members of disadvantaged groups to become *less* aware of intergroup inequalities (Dixon et al., 2012; Dixon, Tropp, Durrheim, & Tredoux, 2010; Saguy et al., 2009), to be less supportive of policies aimed at promoting equality (Dixon et al., 2007; 2012; Sengupta & Sibley, 2013), and to be less willing to engage in collective action on behalf of their group (Tropp, Hawi, van Laar, & Levin, 2012; Wright & Lubensky, 2009; but see also Becker, Wright, Lubensky, & Zhou, 2013).

Overall, these recent findings suggest that research on interventions to improve intergroup relations needs to go beyond using prejudice reduction as the sole indicator of the success of the intervention, and to assess more consequential outcomes, such as actual behaviour and support for policies. In other words actions (continued discrimination) speak louder than words (reduced prejudice). Moreover, interventions should also address the needs of members of disadvantaged groups to ensure that interventions do not compromise realizing their group goals.

IRONIC CONSEQUENCES OF INTERGROUP CONTACT

Saguy, T., Tausch, N., Dovidio, J. F., & Pratto, F. (2009). The irony of harmony: Intergroup contact can produce false expectations for equality. *Psychological Science, 20*, 114–121.

Introduction

The authors suggested that beyond improving attitudes toward the outgroup, positive contact can also reduce disadvantaged-group members' awareness of intergroup inequalities and raise their expectations that the advantaged group would treat them fairly. These expectations could, in turn, reduce disadvantaged group members' motivation to engage in actions aimed at achieving social change toward group equality. An experiment examined the causal effect of positive intergroup contact (i.e., that emphasized commonalities between groups rather than group differences) on (a) disadvantaged-group members' attitudes toward the outgroup, (b) attention to inequality, and (c) expectations of fair treatment by the outgroup. The researchers also measured advantaged-group members' outgroup attitudes, awareness of inequality and their actual resource allocation between groups.

Method

Participants

Participants were 210 undergraduate students ($N = 126$ females, $N = 84$ males). Each experimental session involved a mixed-gender group of six students.

Procedure and design

Participants were randomly assigned to one of two three-person groups. They were then told that there was another group and that each group would be asked to make one of two decisions: one group (the powerful, advantaged group) would be asked to decide how to distribute 10 credits (a valued resource) between the groups and the other group (the disadvantaged group) would be asked to decide how to distribute 10 marbles (not valued) between the groups. Participants were then told that, before making their decisions, the two groups would have the chance to meet. To manipulate type of contact, the groups were either asked to discuss things the groups had in common in the session (e.g., 'Similar steps the groups went through in this study'; the *commonality-focused contact condition*) or aspects of the experiment on which the groups

differed (e.g., 'Differences between the tasks the groups will do next'; *differences-focused contact condition*). Thus, the study involved a 2 (group position: advantaged versus disadvantaged) × 2 (contact type: commonality-focused versus differences-focused) factorial design.

Measures

The participants then completed a number of questionnaires measuring their awareness of the intergroup inequality and their attitudes towards the other group. Participants in the disadvantaged group were also asked to estimate the number of credits they expected to receive from the advantaged group. Finally, members of the advantaged group were asked to distribute the 10 credits between the two groups.

Results

As expected, both the advantaged and the disadvantaged groups were less aware of intergroup inequality in the commonality-focused contact, compared to the difference-focused contact, condition (see Figure 14.14a). In line with predictions, intergroup attitudes were more positive in the commonality-focused contact condition. Disadvantaged group members expected to receive significantly more credits from the advantaged group in the commonality-focused compared to the differences-focused condition. There was, however, no significant difference between the two contact conditions in terms of the actual distribution of credits by the advantaged group, who discriminated against the disadvantaged group in each case. Figure 14.14b shows the number of credits expected and the number of credits received.

Discussion

This study demonstrated that although positive commonality-focused contact improves intergroup attitudes this does not translate into less discrimination. Rather, commonality-focused contact made both groups *less aware* of the intergroup inequality, and raised the disadvantaged groups' hopes about the credits they would receive, an expectation that proved to be false. In fact, the advantaged group discriminated in favour of their ingroup in both contact conditions. A second, correlational study investigated whether these expectations for equal treatment have implications for disadvantaged group members' support for social change. This study surveyed Arabs in Israel (a socially disadvantaged group), and showed that more positive intergroup contact with Jews (the advantaged group) was associated with perceptions of Jews as more fair, which in turn predicted decreased support for social change. It is therefore critical to recognize that intergroup harmony per se does not necessarily translate into intergroup equality.

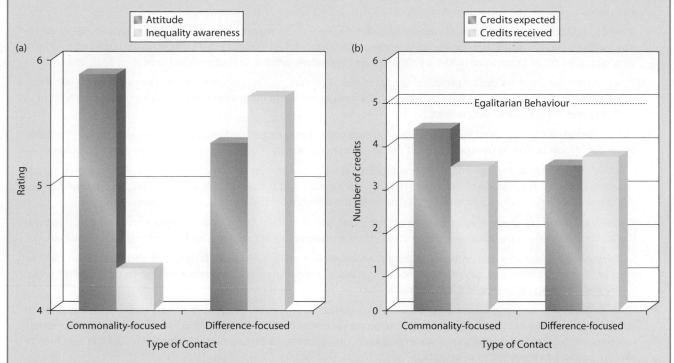

FIGURE 14.14(a) and (b) *(a) Outgroup attitudes and awareness of inequality across groups as a function of contact type; (b) Number of credits (out of 10) expected by the disadvantaged group and number of credits received from the advantaged group as a function of contact type.*

Source: Adapted from Saguy, T., Tausch, N., Dovidio, J. F., & Pratto F. (2009). The irony of harmony: Intergroup contact can produce false expectations for equality. *Psychological Science, 20,* 114–121. © SAGE Publications, reprinted with permission.

Summary

In this section we have shown that contact between members of opposing groups is an effective tool for reducing prejudice, especially if it takes place under favourable conditions. We presented three cognitive models of intergroup contact that make different suggestions about how contact should be structured to achieve generalized prejudice reduction; recent integrations of these models seem to be particularly effective. We also demonstrated that prejudice reduction involves a number of cognitive and affective mechanisms, such as increased knowledge, reduced intergroup anxiety, increased empathy and a reappraisal of the ingroup. We discussed how interventions other than direct intergroup contact, such as perspective-taking exercises or extended contact, can also promote these processes. We concluded this section by suggesting that interventions to improve intergroup relations need to go beyond measuring prejudice to assess the consequences of interventions for intergroup equality more generally.

CHAPTER SUMMARY

- *What is prejudice?* Prejudice is traditionally defined as a negative attitude towards an outgroup, but can also emphasize ostensibly positive aspects of a group. It typically functions to the perceiver's advantage, even when it implies a positive perception of the outgroup.

- *How do we explain prejudice?* Prejudice can be explained at both individual and group levels. At the individual level, personality and individual difference approaches help to explain variation in prejudice between people. Group-level explanations are well placed to explain the social nature of prejudice.

- *Is there a prejudiced personality?* People who are prejudiced against one outgroup are often prejudiced against others. Right-wing authoritarianism and social dominance orientation have been linked to prejudice. However, social norms play a role in shaping prejudice, and individual difference variables are themselves influenced by the social context.

- *How can cognitive processes explain prejudice?* Cognitive processes can explain how we come to see members of a social category as very like each other, and how prejudiced beliefs might form, but motivational processes can also be important in inhibiting prejudice, and also in causing it.

- *Can intragroup processes account for prejudice towards outgroups?* It may make good (evolutionary) sense to favour members of our own group, but on its own this does not provide a strong explanation of why we might actively derogate outgroups.

- *Can conflicts of interest at the intergroup level be reduced to individual self-interest?* Realistic conflicts of interest between groups provide a powerful explanation of intergroup hostility, but ingroup bias still occurs in minimal groups, and expectations of ingroup reciprocity cannot explain why people maximize the difference in reward allocations between groups.

- *What (other) threats to group identity from an outgroup can help to explain discrimination?* Threats to the ingroup include threats to its very existence, threats to group-esteem, threats to the values of the group, and threats to group distinctiveness.

- *So are prejudice and discrimination between groups inevitable?* Not at all. Intergroup factors can also help to explain the *absence* of discrimination (e.g., under conditions of legitimacy, and social reality constraints, or when it goes against group norms and threatens the image of the ingroup).

- *What do group emotions add to our understanding of prejudice?* Group emotions specify threats to the ingroup, through appraisals of how the outgroup affects it, and the appropriate response. The role of group identification in how intensely emotions are felt helps to explain variation in prejudice. Group emotions (e.g., contempt, *schadenfreude*) can also help to explain the more extreme forms of prejudice.

- *How can prejudice be reduced?* Intergroup contact is one of the most-widely applied interventions to reduce prejudice. Contact effects are most likely to generalize to the outgroup as a whole when the encountered group members are typical of the outgroup.

- *Does changing the level of categorization reduce prejudice?* Changing group representations in different ways (through decategorization, recategorization, and mutual differentiation) has been shown to reduce prejudice, but in different ways. A dual-categorization approach (making both the original categories and a superordinate category salient) is an effective way of reducing prejudice while avoiding the pitfalls of distinctiveness threat.

- *Can prejudice be reduced by interventions other than direct contact?* Prejudice reduction can also be set in motion by other techniques, such as presenting stereotype disconfirming information, extended contact, and inducing empathy and perspective taking.

- *Does prejudice reduction result in more equal societies?* Recent findings suggest that this is not necessarily the case. Ironically, positive contact experiences can lead members of disadvantaged groups to become *less* aware of intergroup inequalities and less willing to engage in collective action on behalf of their group.

SUGGESTIONS FOR FURTHER READING

Brown, R. (2010). *Prejudice: It's social psychology* (2nd ed.). Chichester, UK: Wiley-Blackwell. A detailed overview of intergroup phenomena and their explanations.

Dovidio, J. F., Gaertner, S. L., & Saguy, T. (2009). Commonality and the complexity of 'we': Social attitudes and social change. *Personality and Social Psychology Review, 13*, 3–20. Examines the role of collective identities in the development of prejudice and inequality and in interventions to improve attitudes towards other groups and in inhibiting or facilitating social change.

Ellemers, N., Spears, R., & Doosje, B. (2002). Self and social identity. *Annual Review of Psychology, 53,* 161–186. Provides an overview of different identity threats and coping strategies that develop and extend the social identity approach.

Hewstone, M., Rubin, M., & Willis, H. (2002). Intergroup bias. *Annual Review of Psychology, 53,* 575–604. A comprehensive overview of the literature on ingroup bias.

Otten, S., Sassenberg, K., & Kessler, T. (Eds.). (2009). *Intergroup relations: The role of motivation and emotion.* New York: Psychology Press. This volume contains a number of state-of-the-art summaries of research programmes, some of which are referred to in this chapter (e.g., Yzerbyt & Kuppens on group-based emotions and prejudice, and Spears et al. on the minimal group paradigm).

Scheepers, D., Spears, R., Doosje, B., & Manstead, A. S. R. (2006b). The social functions of in-group bias: Creating, confirming, or changing social reality. In W. Stroebe & M. Hewstone (Eds.), *European review of social psychology* (Vol. 17, pp. 359–396). Hove, UK: Psychology Press. Provides an analysis of the different functions served by ingroup bias, contrasting low and high status groups.

Son Hing, L. S., & Zanna, M. P. (2010). Individual differences. In J. F. Dovidio, M. Hewstone, P. Glick, & V. M. Esses (Eds.), *Handbook of prejudice, stereotyping and discrimination* (pp. 163–178). London: Sage. A good overview of current thinking on the role of individual differences in prejudice.

Tausch, N., & Hewstone, M. (2010). Intergroup contact. In J. F. Dovidio, M. Hewstone, P. Glick, & V. M. Esses (Eds.), *Handbook of prejudice, stereotyping and discrimination* (pp. 544–560). London: Sage. A recent comprehensive overview of research on intergroup contact.

Tiedens, L. Z., & Leach, C. W. (Eds.). (2004). *The social life of emotions.* Cambridge, MA: Cambridge University Press. An edited collection of various perspectives on the field of intergroup emotions, also as applied to prejudice.

15 Cultural Social Psychology

PETER B. SMITH

KEY TERMS

- acculturation
- acquiescent responding
- back-translation
- better than average effect
- bicultural identity
- bicultural identity integration
- cognitive styles

- cross-cultural replication
- cultural masculinity–femininity
- culture
- display rules
- eco-cultural theory
- embeddedness versus autonomy

- hierarchy versus egalitarianism
- individualism–collectivism
- mastery versus harmony
- nation-level factor analysis
- power distance
- self-construals
- uncertainty avoidance

CHAPTER OUTLINE

INTRODUCTION 491

CULTURE AND CULTURAL DIFFERENCES 491

Defining culture 492

Nations as cultures 493

Measuring culture 494

Overcoming methodological challenges 496

Summary 499

CULTURE AND COGNITION 500

Summary 503

CULTURE AND SELF-CONSTRUAL 503

Cross-cultural variation in self-enhancement 504

Self-construal as an explanation of cultural differences 506

Self-construal over time 507

Summary 508

INTERPERSONAL RELATIONS 509

Prosocial behaviour with strangers 509

Intimate relationships 509

Summary 510

GROUP PROCESSES 511

Summary 513

INTERGROUP RELATIONS 515

Group honour 517

Negotiation 518

Summary 519

INTERCULTURAL RELATIONS 519

Migration and acculturation 521

Summary 523

CHAPTER SUMMARY 525

ROUTE MAP OF THE CHAPTER

When the same social psychology study is repeated in different parts of the world it often comes up with different results. This chapter provides a model of cultural differences that can explain why this is not just a failure of experimenters' expertise. Drawing on studies that have been discussed in many of the earlier chapters in this book, it shows that cultural variations can benefit social psychologists rather than handicap them. By identifying the social behaviours that are particularly salient in different parts of the world, we can take account of causal factors that have been given insufficient attention within mainstream social psychology. We can also test which social psychological phenomena are universal and which occur only in some parts of the world.

INTRODUCTION

Wen Hua Wang's family moved to the United Kingdom when she was young. She quickly formed a bond with two other Chinese girls at school and they all did well. Wen Hua gained admission to a respected university. She finds the courses very interesting, attends all the lectures and takes copious notes. She wonders why the British students are not so committed to learning, and why some of them speak to the professor in such familiar and disrespectful ways. On group projects, she is reluctant to speak up and it seems difficult for her to find a role for herself. She would like to speak more with the professor because she is sure that he will be able to help her.

- Why is Wen Hua so strongly motivated?
- Why does she think that familiarity with the professor is disrespectful?
- Why is she reluctant to take the lead in groups?
- Why does she think the professor is the best source of help?

Wen Hua is experiencing a mild case of what has been colloquially described as 'culture shock'. In the early years of her life she has been socialized to think of herself and others around her in ways that differ from those among whom she now finds herself. Her attitudes, values and beliefs were typical of those found in Chinese societies, but now they are more unusual. She feels a strong bond between herself and those close to her, especially her family. When she attends to her studies she does so because she feels that her success will enhance the reputation of her family as much as her own reputation. She places a high value on establishing harmonious relations with others. In situations where she is unsure how to behave, she keeps to herself for fear of embarrassing others or losing face by showing ignorance or tactlessness. In the presence of those who are older or more senior, she feels it is important to give them respect.

This chapter will first provide some examples of what has happened when researchers have attempted to repeat social psychological studies, typically conducted originally in North America, in other parts of the world. There can be many reasons why different results are obtained in any one instance, but overall there is good reason to believe that cultural differences are involved. Psychologists have been interested in culture since the earliest beginnings of the discipline. Wilhelm Wundt established one of the world's first psychology laboratories in Leipzig, Germany in 1879. Between 1911 and 1920, he published ten volumes entitled *Völkerpsychologie* (normally translated as 'folk psychology'), which included discussion of differing cultures around the world. More recently psychologists have discussed cultural differences in terms of variations in attitudes, values and beliefs. These variations can contribute to our understanding of the concept of culture if we take them into account. In the remainder of this chapter, we examine studies that are relevant to issues that have been discussed in preceding chapters, particularly in relation to social cognition, self-concept, personal relationships, group behaviour and intergroup relations. In each of these areas we will show how attention to cultural differences can enrich our understanding of social psychological processes.

CULTURE AND CULTURAL DIFFERENCES

What is culture and why should we study it?

The opening chapter of this book discusses some of the best-known and frequently discussed social psychology experiments. Most of these experiments were conducted in the United States and some in the United Kingdom. What would happen if they were repeated somewhere else in the world? We can answer this question, because there have been attempts at **cross-cultural replication** of all these studies, some of them many times. Consider first an early study of group dynamics that was published by Schachter (1951). In this study, Schachter set up a series of student discussion groups. Unknown to most group members, each group contained an accomplice of the experimenter. The accomplice (the 'deviate') was instructed to take up a position opposed to the views of the majority and stick to his position. Schachter predicted that the deviate would over time receive less and less attention and be rejected by the group, which is just what he found among his US respondents.

A few years later, Schachter and seven colleagues (1954) reported on the results of a slightly different version of this study that was conducted in seven different European nations. In this case, groups of 11-year-old schoolboys were asked to decide which of several model aeroplanes to build. The results were complex and not at all as the experimenters had predicted. The groups in France did almost all reach agreement and did reject the deviate, as predicted. However, many of the groups in Belgium, West Germany (as it was then known) and the UK did not reach agreement at all, and ratings on a 7-point scale as to whether the deviate should leave the group varied greatly between nations, as shown in Figure 15.1. Furthermore, in a minority of the British and German groups, the deviate's viewpoint was accepted, so that he had in fact become the leader. There are many

> **cross-cultural replication** a test of whether the results of a study are the same if it is repeated as exactly as possible in another cultural context.

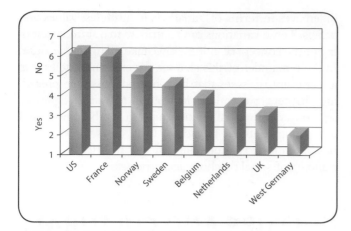

FIGURE 15.1 *Should the deviate stay in the group?*

Source: Based on Schachter et al., 1954, with permission from SAGE Publications Ltd.

possible reasons for the variations in these particular results. For instance, the accomplices may not all have behaved in exactly the same way. The US study differed from the European ones, but even within Europe there were large differences. We need to see whether they are typical.

Figure 15.2 shows that some other classic social psychological studies have also yielded differing results when conducted in other parts of the world, while others have yielded evidence of universal effects. For instance, the studies by Ekman and his colleagues (1987) have established that six basic emotions are conveyed by the same facial expressions in all locations that were sampled. In most replications of classic studies, an effect somewhat similar to that reported in the US *is* obtained, but its magnitude varies by location. Part of the reason for this variability is that it is extremely difficult to set up exactly the same study in different parts of the world. The local context can give differing meanings to the same procedures. There may also be something unusual about these particularly famous studies. To test this possibility, two Israeli psychologists selected six lesser-known studies that had nonetheless been published in top US journals, and attempted to replicate their results in Israel (Amir & Sharon, 1987). Five of the original studies had used students and one had used school students. Amir and Sharon replicated all six studies using similar populations. In some cases the replication sample was smaller, in others it was larger. The original six US studies had yielded 37 significant effects. Amir and Sharon also found 37 significant effects, but only 25 of them replicated the US results. Twelve were new effects not found in the US. So, of the 49 results overall, only 25 were common to both nations. Clearly, there is a substantial problem, particularly bearing in mind that there are many nations in the world that are more different from the US than is Israel.

Defining culture

To understand the reasons why results vary between locations even when differences in the methods and samples used are minimized, we need a definition of

Classic study	Effect found	Replications	Effect found
Lewin, Lippitt, & White (1939) US boys clubs	Democratic leadership preferred	Meade (1985) Boys clubs in India, Hong Kong, Hawaii, US	Autocratic leaders preferred in Hong Kong and in India
Asch (1956) US students and adults	37% conformity	Studies in 16 other nations (see Bond & Smith, 1996)	From 6% conformity in France to 58% among Fijian Indians
Milgram (1963) US adults	65% fully obedient	Studies in eight other nations (see Smith & Bond, 1998)	From 16% to 95% fully obedient
Ekman (1972) Students in 5 nations	Correct identification of 6 basic emotions from US photos	Ekman et al. (1987) 14 cultural groups sampled using photos drawn from all locations	Anger, joy, sadness, disgust, surprise and fear are portrayed in the same way everywhere
Zimbardo, Maslach, & Haney (2000) US students roleplaying a prison	Destructive authority achieved	Reicher & Haslam (2006) UK adults	Destructive authority overthrown

FIGURE 15.2 *Replications of some famous studies.*

Source: Based on Smith, Bond, & Kağıtçıbaşı, 2006.

culture a social system that is characterized by the shared meanings that are attributed to people and events by its members.

culture. A good definition is one that focuses on the way in which people give meaning to what goes on around them, because any particular social practice can have different meanings in different locations. For instance, if I maintain very steady eye contact with you, or come very close to you, that would be interpreted as friendly in some parts of the world and as rude or hostile in others. So if we are trying to understand social behaviours in different parts of the world, we do best to focus on the meanings attributed to events. As Rohner (1984) put it, culture is 'the totality of . . . learned meanings maintained by a human population, or by identifiable segments of a population, and transmitted from one generation to the next' (pp. 119–120).

As discussed in other chapters of this book, people interpret the meanings of the behaviours that they encounter. A social system can be said to have a culture when the members of that system *agree* with one another about the meaning of what is going on around them. The concept of culture can be applied to families, teams, organizations and nations. Within larger social systems we would not expect to find a total consensus on meanings, and there will typically be subcultures defined for instance by age, gender, social class, location, profession, religion and ethnicity. Despite this it can still be useful to consider nations as cultures, because there are numerous historical, political, linguistic and climatic factors that encourage a continuity of shared perspective. One of the pioneers of cultural psychology, Hofstede has an apt and more incisive definition of culture as '. . . the collective programming of the mind that distinguishes the members of one category of people from another' (Hofstede, 2001, p. 9). This is not a reformulation of F. Allport's (1924) 'group mind' theory (which argued for the existence of a group consciousness or a collective mind, as separate from the minds of the individuals who comprise the group; see Chapter 1); it is a statement that all of us are engaged in a continuing negotiation of meaning with those around us.

Nations as cultures

It is relatively easy to see how the actions of one person can influence the emergent culture of a newly formed small group. When we think about the cultures of larger social entities, it is clear that the majority of influence will be in the other direction; the individual will be encouraged to assign meanings to events through interactions with others who have a shared history of exposure to particular types of climate, child-rearing, educational system, political history, media exposure and employment opportunities. All of these elements may change over time, but they will not change fast because so many people are elements within the system that they comprise. The proposal that cultural variations around the world are derived from the demands imposed by differing types of physical environment is known as **eco-cultural theory**. The way in which variations in physical environment can lead to different types of subsistence, which in turn generate different types of institution, different socialization practices, and therefore different psychological attributes is summarized in broad outline in Theory Box 15.1. We examine more specific aspects of eco-cultural theories later.

eco-cultural theory a theory that proposes that different forms of culture have arisen as adaptations to differing environmental challenges to survival.

THEORY BOX 15.1

CREATION OF CULTURES

Ecological Context: e.g., Climate, Landscape, Natural Resources

↓

Institutions: e.g., Agriculture, Hunting, Mining, Military Activity

↓

Societal Practices: e.g., Family Structure, Intergroup Relations, Gender Roles

↓

Socialization Processes: e.g., Child Rearing, Schooling, Work Socialization

↓

Psychological Outcomes: e.g., Cognitive Style, Values, Beliefs, Behaviours

Source: Based on Smith, Bond, & Kağitçibaşi, 2006.

This approach was based on Schwartz's theoretical proposition that people everywhere will develop values relating to three basic problems, namely *survival as an individual, coordination of social interaction* and the *welfare and survival of groups*. He predicted that in all cultures people's values will cluster together in relation to these three needs, although cultures will vary in how strongly different values are endorsed. His individual-level studies confirmed that most values of individuals can be classified into the same set of clusters no matter where in the world the data are collected. Next, he conducted a nation-level analysis of his data in the same way as Hofstede had done, using only the values that he had found to have consistent meanings. Three dimensions emerged, each of which matches one of the three basic needs that he had identified. He named these as **embeddedness versus autonomy**, **hierarchy versus egalitarianism** and **mastery versus harmony**, as shown in Figure 15.4.

Finally, Schwartz (2004) used these dimensions to plot the comparative positioning of the nations that he had sampled. Examples of the nations scoring highest and lowest on each dimension are shown in Figure 15.5 (Schwartz, 2004). Schwartz's contrast between values that he summarized as embeddedness and values summarized as autonomy parallels Hofstede's dimension of individualism–collectivism. The individualistic European nations

embeddedness versus autonomy characteristic of a culture in which relations with one's long-term membership groups are prioritized, rather than emotional and intellectual separateness from others.

hierarchy versus egalitarianism characteristic of a culture in which inequality is accepted and deference is given to one's seniors, rather than granting equality to all people.

mastery versus harmony characteristic of a culture in which achievement is sought and esteemed, rather than harmony with nature.

in his sample are here shown as endorsing autonomy values. In contrast, the US scores higher on mastery. His contrast between hierarchy and egalitarianism values parallels Hofstede's dimension of power distance. Schwartz's third dimension, mastery versus harmony, is not, however, close to Hofstede's remaining dimensions. See also Social Psychology Beyond the Lab 15.1, which illustrates a practical application of value differences.

These two large-scale research projects have provided what one might consider as a provisional psychological map of the world. Each project used different methods at different times and with different respondents who were drawn from a different range of nations, but the dimensions that they identified correlate quite well with each other. They provide us with a basis from which we can begin to investigate why studies in different parts of the world can yield different results. However, we cannot treat the scores for individual nations like an independent variable in an experiment. A nation's culture is both a cause and an effect of the psychological processes that occur within it, as shown in Theory Box 15.2. We can use the scores to interpret the results of studies, but we need to return to experimental methods before we can be sure about causal relationships. Before looking at some cross-cultural studies, we must first consider some distinctive problems of research method that cross-cultural researchers have needed to overcome.

Overcoming methodological challenges

In looking at cross-cultural studies, it is useful to evaluate them in terms of how well they have overcome six key difficulties that researchers face. First, we must consider the problem of language. Where respondents use different first languages, accurate translation is essential. To be sure of

Basic need	Group survival	Social coordination	Individual survival
Dimension	Embeddedness versus autonomy	Hierarchy versus egalitarianism	Mastery versus harmony
Typical values endorsed at positive pole	Social order National security Respect tradition Honouring elders	Social power Wealth Authority	Daringness Ambition Choosing one's own goals Social recognition
Typical values endorsed at negative pole	Curiosity Enjoying life Pleasure Freedom	Honesty Equality Helpfulness Social justice	Protecting the environment Unity with nature World at peace

FIGURE 15.4 *Values defining nation-level dimensions identified by Schwartz (1994).*

Source: Based on information reported in Schwartz (1994).

Dimension	Embeddedness versus autonomy	Hierarchy versus egalitarianism	Mastery versus harmony
Highest scoring nations	Ghana Nigeria South Africa Philippines Malaysia	Uganda Zimbabwe Namibia Thailand Ghana	China Zimbabwe Korea Hong Kong USA
Lowest scoring nations	Switzerland (Francophone) Canada (Francophone) France East Germany West Germany UK Denmark Austria Netherlands	Italy Spain Sweden Norway Finland West Germany East Germany Slovenia	Italy Spain Sweden Norway Finland Estonia Slovenia West Germany

FIGURE 15.5 *Nation-level scores based on Schwartz's value survey (2004). Note: The German data were collected before reunification.*

Source: Based on data reported in Schwartz (1994).

back-translation translation of a research questionnaire that has already been translated from one language to a second language back into the original language by a translator who has not seen the original version.

adequacy, a **back-translation** of a translated questionnaire into the original language must be made by a second translator who has not seen the original. Use of local languages enhances validity. If English language versions are used with respondents for whom English is not their first language, their responses are found to become more like those obtained from respondents whose first language is English (Harzing, 2005). The use of English encourages people to respond in ways that they have learned are typical of English speakers, rather than in ways that are more typical of their own culture. This is an instance of unintended experimental priming.

Second, even after successful translation, measures may have different psychometric properties in different contexts, because words often have different emotional overtones in different languages. For instance, in Schwartz's studies it emerged that the meaning of 'true friendship' varies across cultures (Schwartz & Sagiv, 1995). In Japan, 'true friendship' was seen as associated with 'belonging', whereas in Western samples it was associated with 'mature love'. Thus, the Japanese associate friendship with inclusion, but Westerners link it with intimacy. A good study is one that can demonstrate the reliability and validity of its measures (see Chapter 2) in each of the cultures that is sampled.

Third, respondents to questionnaires in different parts of the world differ systematically in how they use response scales. A particularly acute problem in cross-cultural studies is that in some cultures it is normative to express one's opinions by agreeing or disagreeing, while in others it is desirable to take a more neutral stance. If researchers do not control for differences in **acquiescent responding**, comparisons of mean scores from different cultures will be meaningless. Both Hofstede and Schwartz used such controls, so

acquiescent responding a tendency for a respondent to agree with all items on scales measuring attitudes, beliefs or values, even those that contradict one another.

THEORY BOX 15.2

PROCESSES FAVOURING CULTURAL CONTINUITY

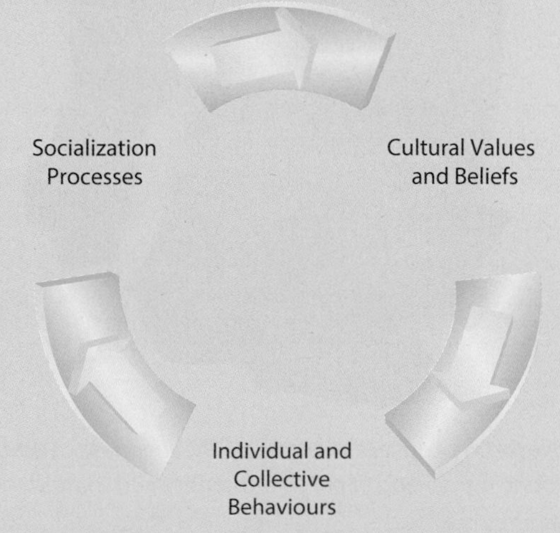

Socialization Processes

Cultural Values and Beliefs

Individual and Collective Behaviours

Source: Based on Smith, Fischer, Vignoles, & Bond (2014).

SOCIAL PSYCHOLOGY BEYOND THE LAB 15.1

ADVERTISEMENTS SUSTAIN CULTURAL VALUES

Cultures are defined in terms of shared meanings. Advertisers are also interested in creating shared meanings when they seek to establish brand images for their products within particular markets. How do these two fields of interest relate to one another? Within the US, Aaker (1997) identified the types of brand images that exist by asking respondents to evaluate advertisements on rating scales representing personality dimensions. She found five types of US brand images. These could be summarized as sincerity, excitement, competence, sophistication and ruggedness. Ruggedness was defined by US raters in terms of 'outdoorness', masculinity, toughness and 'westernness'. Examples would be advertisements for Levi jeans, Harley-Davidson motorcycles and Marlboro cigarettes.

Aaker, Benet-Martínez, and Garolera (2001) replicated this study in Japan and in Spain. In Japan, four of these images were also found, but there were no products emphasizing

ruggedness. Instead, there was a brand image that focused on peacefulness. The advertisements illustrating peacefulness were characterized by Japanese raters as shy, mild mannered, peaceful, naïve, dependent and childlike (Figure 15.6a). In Spain, sincerity, excitement and sophistication were again found, but the competence and ruggedness images were replaced by a brand image focused on passion. The advertisements illustrating passion were characterized by Spanish raters as fervent, passionate and intense, but also spiritual, mystical and Bohemian (Figure 15.6b). The authors argue that there is a reciprocal relationship between culture and brand images. Exposure to particular brand images can be thought of as a series of attempts at priming by advertisers. Where the prime accords with one of the types of value preferences that Schwartz identified in different nations, the advertisement is more likely to be effective. Repeated use of brand images by advertisers will also influence the maintenance or change of cultural values.

(a)

(b)

FIGURE 15.6 (a) and (b) *Cultural icons exemplifying culturally distinctive forms of advertisements: (a) The Japanese geisha, exemplifying mildness, dependence and peacefulness; and (b) Flamenco dancing, a blend of passion, intensity and spirituality.*

Source: (a) © Serika; (b) © Mad Pushup. Both images used under licence from Shutterstock.

we can trust their mean scores. Figure 15.7 illustrates the extent of cultural variation in acquiescence along 5-point rating scales in a study that sampled 43 nations. The scores for acquiescence were created by averaging each respondent's ratings on 68 scales, where it is logically impossible for respondents to endorse all the survey items. A score above 3.0 indicates a tendency to agree with items, while one below 3.0 indicates a tendency to disagree with them. The mean scores from the UK and Thailand differ by .9, which is 20 per cent of the entire scale, large enough to distort the meaning of any uncorrected comparison between nations.

A fourth priority is to be aware of the cultural subjectivity of the labels that we use for the topics that social psychologists study. For instance, in Chapters 1 and 8 we follow the usual practice of describing Asch's (1956) line judgement study as a study of conformity. Yet the phenomenon actually being studied is behavioural change in a setting in which other people have given obviously incorrect answers. Within a collectivist culture, that same behaviour might be described as tact or sensitivity in saving others from embarrassment, rather than as conformity.

Fifth, while it is convenient to study cultural differences by sampling people from different national cultures, we need to be aware that nations differ from one another in many ways. We should be most impressed by studies that have included a check on whether the respondents in the study do actually endorse the values or other measures of cultural orientation that are typical of their nation. This is equivalent to the manipulation check that experimentalists employ. We should be even more impressed by studies that show that the differences found between two

samples disappear if the measure of cultural orientation is statistically controlled. This would indicate that we can not only describe cultural differences, but that we can also explain how they bring about their effects. Several studies of this kind are discussed later in this chapter.

Finally, you will have noted in earlier chapters that psychologists try where possible to use experimental methods, so that that they can establish causal relationships between their variables. There are practical limitations on the extent to which cultural differences can be studied experimentally, but the increasing number of *bicultural* people in the world has opened up the possibility of experimental cultural studies. We can test whether the behaviour of bicultural individuals changes in the ways that our theories predict when they are primed to focus on one or the other of their alternative cultural identities. Studies of this type have high potential in testing the cultural validity of social psychological theories.

Summary

Most social psychological studies have been conducted in just a few rather distinctive nations of the world. Results from studies done elsewhere can test and improve the universal validity of social psychological theories. Cultural differences between large-scale groupings such as nations can be mapped by examining patterns of shared values and beliefs. These maps can be used to test why the results of studies vary. Valid cross-cultural studies must overcome methodological challenges posed by

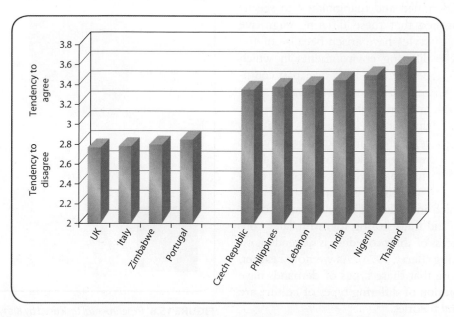

FIGURE 15.7 *Highest and lowest scoring nations on a measure of acquiescent responding to questionnaires.*
Source: Based on Smith, 2004.

differences between languages, response styles and the multiple ways in which nations differ from one another.

CULTURE AND COGNITION

What are cognitive styles and how are they related to culture?

In the preceding section we considered the contrast between individualistic cultures and collectivistic cultures. There are many factors that can contribute to the creation and maintenance of this contrast. For instance, individualistic nations are predominantly rich, whereas collectivistic nations have until recently been less so (Hofstede, 2001). In this section we focus on basic psychological processes that may also underlie this contrast. Nisbett (2003) has proposed that members of Western nations tend to process information in analytic ways, whereas members of East Asian nations tend to process information in holistic ways. What do we mean by the terms *analytic* and *holistic* in this context? Faced with some situation or problem, an analytic thinker would seek to identify a key element in the situation and focus on its effect on what goes on around it (for instance, the behaviour of a star football player). A holistic thinker would be more likely to give equal attention to each of the elements in the situation, and their interrelationships (for example, the way that the team as a whole played). A psychological experiment is a good example of the analytic perspective, because one key factor is identified and manipulated to see its effect. Nisbett reasoned that these differing **cognitive styles** have arisen because of the differing environments in which people have lived over past centuries. Historically, survival in some environments has been dependent upon skills in hunting, which is typically an individual activity that requires picking out targets from their background. In other environments, survival has depended on agriculture, which involves rapidly harvesting crops at particular times and then storing them for later consumption. The success of this procedure is dependent on collaborative working (Berry, 1976). As we noted earlier, theories that propose that these types of demands have influenced the evolution of differing types of culture are known as *eco-cultural* theories.

Many studies have confirmed the existence of this type of cultural difference in information-processing styles

cognitive styles people with an analytic style focus on the main element within information that they are processing; people with a holistic style focus on the relations between the different elements in information that they are processing.

(Nisbett, Peng, Choi, & Norenzayan, 2001). For instance, Japanese and American students were shown a series of images on a screen, each showing a line drawn within a box, as illustrated in Figure 15.8 (Kitayama, Duffy, Kawamura, & Larsen, 2003). The box at the top of the figure contains a line that is one-third of the height of the square. Respondents were next shown a new smaller or larger blank box similar to the ones shown in the lower part of the figure, but with no line drawn inside it. Without any longer being able to see the original, they were then asked to draw a line in the new box that was either in proportion to the original one in the upper box, or that was the same length as the original one (shown in the box in the upper part of the figure). The lines actually drawn in the two lower boxes show, respectively, the correct length of the line drawn proportionately (left box) and exactly (right box). This procedure is known as the 'line and frame test'. As expected, Americans were better at exact reproduction of the line, while Japanese were better at proportional reproduction of the line. Thus, the Japanese had noted the contexts of the lines, while the Americans had not. In studies of recognition and recall, Japanese and American students were shown underwater scenes and pictures of wildlife (Masuda & Nisbett, 2001). They were then shown a second set of pictures in which some changes had been made. Japanese were much better at noticing changes in the animals' contexts, and also in detecting whether they had been shown a particular animal before, so long as it was in the same context as before.

Since there is evidence for a contrast in cognitive styles, it can be expected to influence the results of studies

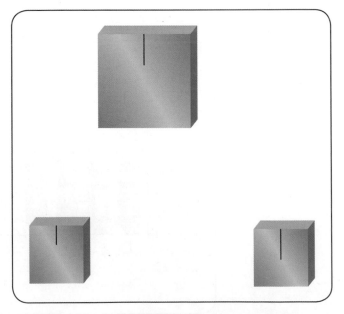

FIGURE 15.8 *Experimental task used by Kitayama et al. (2003).*

Source: Adapted from Kitayama et al. (2003) with permission from SAGE Publications.

concerning social perception. As discussed in Chapter 3, many studies on causal attribution (typically using American students as participants) have yielded evidence in favour of correspondence bias. In other words, people in these experiments explain another person's behaviour more in terms of their personal traits than in terms of the circumstances in which the behaviour occurs. Norenzayan, Choi, and Nisbett (2002) gave Americans and Koreans various kinds of information about some fictitious characters and asked them to predict how these characters would behave in future. The Koreans drew more on the information concerning circumstances, whereas the Americans drew more on the characters' past behaviour. However, when no circumstantial information was provided, both Korean and US respondents were equally willing to predict future behaviour on the basis of past behaviour. Similarly, Miyamoto and Kitayama (2002) found that even when their respondents were told that an individual's behaviour had been constrained by role requirements, both Japanese and Americans did show correspondence bias.

These results are important, because they indicate that although cultural differences in cognitive styles do exist, they do not derive from differences in ability to make particular types of judgement. A change in experimental instructions can cause Asians to make judgements that are similar to Americans' judgements. It is better to think of these cultural differences as learned habits, ways of processing information that are particularly useful in a given kind of cultural context. Analytic thinking can be especially valuable, not just to hunters, but also to those living in contemporary individualistic cultures; holistic thinking can be distinctively useful, not just to rice farmers, but to those living in contemporary industrialized collectivist cultures.

Differences in cognitive style can also lead to inferences about the actions of others that have direct implications for the contrast between individualism and collectivism. Morris and Peng (1994) compared American high-school children of either European descent or Chinese descent. They were shown videos depicting images of fish of various colours swimming around. A blue fish was further to the right on the screen than the others and moved in a slightly different direction. As Figure 15.9 shows, European Americans attributed the blue fish's moves to both internal and external forces, whereas the Chinese Americans saw external forces as much more important. Americans commented more frequently that the blue fish was influencing the others. Chinese commented more frequently that the other fish were influencing the blue fish. This study shows how the European American children attributed individualistic motives to the blue fish, whereas the Chinese Americans saw the fish's movements in terms of response to the group.

Nisbett (2003) identified these variations as a contrast between 'Western' nations and 'East Asian' nations. Later

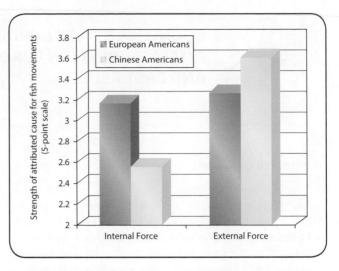

FIGURE 15.9 *What causes the blue fish to move?*

Source: Copyright © 1994 by the American Psychological Association. Adapted with permission. Morris, M. W., & Peng, K. (1994). Culture and cause: American and Chinese attributions for social and physical events. *Journal of Personality and Social Psychology, 67,* 949–971. The use of APA information does not imply endorsement by APA.

studies show us that these labels are too global. The contrast may have more to do with individualism and collectivism than with East versus West. Kitayama, Ishii, Imada, Takemura, and Ramaswamy (2006) compared two samples from within Japan. The northern island of Hokkaido has a population descended from pioneer settlers, in contrast to the more southerly Honshu island. Kitayama et al. expected that, just as was the case in the United States, pioneers colonizing new areas would be more individualistic than those who had chosen to stay in more settled areas. They therefore predicted, and found, that their Hokkaido sample would show high correspondence bias, whereas the Honshu sample would not. Uskul, Kitayama, and Nisbett (2008) administered the line and frame test to three samples in Eastern Turkey, namely farmers, herdsmen and fishermen. They reasoned that herding and fishing are more individualistic activities than farming, which requires more collective action. Consistent with eco-cultural theory, the farmers did best at judging the relative line lengths. The herdsmen did better at judging absolute lengths.

The studies discussed in this section have made no reference to Europe. To put this right, now is a good time to look at Research Close-Up 15.1.

How do the studies in this section match up to the criteria for good cross-cultural studies that were outlined in the preceding sections? On most criteria they do very well. They used experimental methods, mostly with behaviours as dependent measures. However, they did not include any direct measures of cultural differences. The predictions as to what effects would be found are based on suggested differences between American and

COGNITIVE STYLES IN NORTH AMERICA, WESTERN EUROPE AND EAST ASIA

Kitayama, S., Park, H., Sevincer, A. T., Karasawa, M., & Uskul, A. K. (2009). A cultural task analysis of implicit independence: Comparing North America, Western Europe, and East Asia. *Journal of Personality and Social Psychology, 97*, 236–255.

Research question

Over the past ten years, Kitayama and his colleagues have pioneered the study of cultural differences in cognitive styles, focusing exclusively on data from the US and from East Asia. These studies have provided increasingly detailed tests of the hypothesis originally proposed by Markus and Kitayama (1991) that cognitive styles differ in cultures characterized as independent or interdependent. These concepts are discussed in the next section of this chapter. In this study, Kitayama et al. sought to understand the distinctiveness of their earlier findings by also including European respondents. They also wanted to know whether the cognitive styles that they had postulated exist uniformly across each cultural group, or whether each style is restricted to just some members of each group.

Design and procedure

Students in Germany, the UK, the US and Japan completed four of the empirical tasks that had been developed in earlier studies. The design of the first task was 4 (nationalities) X 2 (vignette type). Respondents read brief vignettes in which people had engaged in socially desirable and in socially undesirable behaviours. The sequence of vignette type was reversed for half of the respondents. They were asked to rate the extent to which these people's behaviour was due to their dispositions or to the context, and whether these behaviours would have been different if the dispositions or context were different. This task is essentially the same as that used by Norenzayan, Choi, and Nisbett (2002) discussed earlier. It yields a measure of correspondence bias.

The second task was the line and frame test also described earlier, as shown in Figure 15.8. Here, the design was 4 (nations) X 2 (type of judgement required). In some trials, respondents were asked to reproduce the absolute length of lines, and in other trials they were asked to reproduce the line in proportion to the size of the box in which it was to be placed. The sequence of trials was counterbalanced. This task yields a measure of analytic versus holistic cognition.

In the third task, the students were given a list of everyday social situations. The design was 4 (nations) X 2 (situation type). Situations were either social (e.g., 'having a positive interaction with friends') or not social (e.g., 'being caught in a traffic jam'). The participants were asked to think of the last time they were in each of these kinds of situations, and then to record which of a list of emotions they had experienced. This task gives measures of the frequency of socially engaging emotions and of socially disengaging emotions. Engaging emotions are those that necessarily do involve others, such as feeling friendly, ashamed or guilty. Disengaging emotions are these that do not necessarily involve other people, such as pride, frustration and anger.

The fourth task had a correlational design. The students from each nation rated their level of general happiness in each situation. This rating was correlated with their overall frequency of engaging and disengaging emotions to see which contributed more to overall happiness. Where happiness is more strongly correlated with engaging emotions, Kitayama et al. refer to it as *social* happiness. Where happiness is more strongly correlated with disengaging emotions, they call it *personal* happiness.

Results

Consistent with earlier results and as shown in Figure 15.10, the Americans showed more correspondence bias, more analytic cognitive style, more frequent disengaging emotions and happiness that was more personal than social. There were no significant differences between the results from Germany and those from the UK. The scores for the European students were intermediate between those from the US and Japan, but they nonetheless differed significantly from the Japanese and US results in almost all comparisons. Germans showed less correspondence bias than Americans, and both European samples showed more correspondence bias than did the Japanese. Europeans had a cognitive style that was more holistic than Americans, but more analytic than the Japanese. They reported more socially engaging emotions than Americans and more disengaging emotions than Japanese. British students gave more emphasis to social happiness than Americans did, but less than Japanese. German students gave more emphasis to social happiness than Americans did, and did not differ from the Japanese in this respect.

These results are obtained by comparing contrasts between samples on each of the separate tasks. The researchers also computed correlations between the results for the four tasks within each country's sample. The correlations found were very low. In other words, the people who scored highest on correspondence bias were not the same people who scored highest on analytic cognition or frequently experiencing personal rather than social emotions.

Implications

This important study has several implications. First of all, it confirms that we should not assume that results obtained in US studies will be replicable in Europe. In this case, the results for Europeans differed about equally from the US results and from the Japanese results. So, we should see differences in cognitive style in terms of variations along a spectrum, not as mutually exclusive.

Second, the low correlations between the different cognitive style indicators give us a new and fuller way of looking at culture. The models of culture provided by Hofstede (2001) and Schwartz (2004) suggest that cultures have a relatively homogeneous set of values and beliefs. Kitayama adds to that by proposing that a cultural context offers a range of opportunities to act and think in particular ways. These opportunities will be taken up by different types of people from within that culture. The effects obtained in a study typically will represent an interaction between the cultural context and individuals' personalities and preferences. Thus, when we look at a culture, we will find culturally distinctive phenomena, but not every individual will show all phenomena.

Study	USA	UK	Germany	Japan
Mean bias toward dispositional attribution (7-point rating scales)	1.2	1.2	1.1	.4
Mean greater accuracy on the holistic task than the relative task (in millimetres)	1.4	5.5	4.0	7.0
Mean greater frequency of disengaging emotions than engaging emotions (6-point rating scales)	.52	.24	.16	−.46
Greater personal happiness than social happiness (difference between correlation coefficients)	.16	.00	−.15	−.38

FIGURE 15.10 *Scores obtained in the four tasks by Kitayama et al. (2009). The scores in each row can be compared with one another, but the tasks are measured in different ways, so comparing scores within columns is not meaningful.*

Source: Copyright © 2009 by the American Psychological Association. Adapted with permission. Kitayama, S., Park, H., Sevincer, A. T., Karasawa, M., & Uskul, A. K. (2009). A cultural task analysis of implicit independence: Comparing North America, Western Europe, and East Asia. *Journal of Personality and Social Psychology, 97,* 236–255. The use of APA information does not imply endorsement by APA.

Japanese cultures that were first advanced in a classic paper by Markus and Kitayama (1991). We discuss the nature of these differences, and attempts by other researchers to measure them directly, in the next section.

Summary

Faced with the complexity of information available to them, members of individualistic cultures tend to focus on what they see as the central feature of any set of stimuli. Members of collectivistic cultures tend to take more account of the surrounding context. These differing cognitive styles affect the ways in which the behaviour of others is interpreted. Members of individualistic cultures more readily interpret the behaviours of others in terms of fixed qualities such as personality. Members of collectivistic cultures expect less consistency of behaviour, and interpret variations in terms of contextual constraints such as roles.

Cognitive styles can find expression in a variety of ways, so that there is a diversity of effects even within a single culture. Cognitive styles are habits induced by cultural socialization, and can be temporarily reversed experimentally.

CULTURE AND SELF-CONSTRUAL

Can the ways that we think about ourselves explain cultural variations in behaviour?

The paper mentioned earlier (Markus & Kitayama, 1991) was a review, which provided a further development of Markus's earlier work on **self-construal** (see Chapter 5; also Leader in the Field, Shinobu Kitayama). Their proposal

LEADER IN THE FIELD

Shinobu Kitayama (b. 1957) grew up in Japan and obtained his Bachelor's and Master's degrees from the University of Kyoto. Obtaining his PhD from the University of Michigan in 1987, he taught subsequently at the University of Oregon and at Kyoto University. In 2003 he returned to the University of Michigan, where he directs the Centre for Culture and Cognition. He has been a key figure in opening up and developing studies in social cognition that contrast North America and East Asia. Jointly with Hazel Markus (see Leader in the Field, Chapter 5), he made the case for the contrasting effects of independence and interdependence. His more recent studies draw on his rich and first-hand understanding of both Japanese and US culture. He is Co-editor of the *Handbook of Cultural Psychology* (2007).

self-construals a person's views and knowledge about him- or herself is shaped through an active construal process that plays out in interaction with the social environment. This process is motivated by how one would like to see oneself.

was that while people in the US tend to think of themselves as independent agents, people in Japan are more likely to think of themselves as *inter*dependent with those around them. This proposal can be seen as a special case of the differences in cognitive style considered in the preceding section, and was quickly taken as a formulation that could be applied more widely than just to the US and Japan. As illustrated in Chapter 5, Theory Box 5.3, an interdependent self is a likely consequence of being socialized within a collectivist culture.

Markus and Kitayama did not attempt to measure self-construal, but they showed that by assuming that there is a contrast between independence in the US and interdependence in Japan, they could explain a wide variety of differences in the results of studies comparing aspects of motivation, emotion and cognition in these two nations.

Numerous measures of self-construal have been created by other researchers. The best known has been that developed by Singelis (1994), which is given in full in Individual Differences 15.1. Try filling out your responses to his scale before you read any further. Subsequent studies have cited this scale more than 500 times, hence many researchers have found it useful. Some studies using the scale are discussed later.

Before going further, it is worth looking at some of the weaknesses of the Singelis self-construal scale, because these can illustrate what divides a good cross-cultural study from a poor one. All the items on the scale are positively worded, so someone who is high in acquiescent responding is likely to get high scores on both scales. This does not matter if you compare your own scores on the two scales, because your acquiescence is the same for both sets of questions. However, if the average score from one nation is compared with that from another nation, the result can

be very misleading. For instance, Oyserman, Coon, and Kemmelmeier (2002) concluded that there is no difference between the average scores from the US and Japan, which is not what we would expect on the basis of the large-scale surveys by Hofstede (1980) and Schwartz (2004). In a later analysis Schimmack, Oishi, and Diener (2005) pointed out that Oyserman et al. had taken no account of the possible presence of acquiescent responding in the studies that they reviewed. Schimmack et al. showed that when they discounted acquiescence using the techniques employed by Hofstede, the expected differences between the US, Japan and other nations were found.

A second difficulty with the Singelis scale is that many of the items tapping interdependence refer to 'your group'. As we saw in the previous section, people from collectivist cultures are much more aware of the context in which their relationships occur. When filling out the items, you may have wondered which group these items were referring to. Interdependent people would find it especially difficult to answer these items without knowing which group is being referred to. Some researchers have explored this issue more directly. English and Chen (2007) asked European American and Asian American students to rate themselves in four different situations (in class, at the gym, at a party and in the cafeteria). There was much more difference between the ways that the Chinese Americans rated their attributes in these situations than there was for the European Americans. When the test was repeated two months later, there was good consistency for self-descriptions in the same situations over time. This is important, because it shows that the Asian Americans' inconsistency across situations at the same time was not just because they did not have a clear sense of themselves. English and Chen conclude that Asian Americans have an 'if-then' view of self ('If I am in class, then I am like this'). Tafarodi, Lo, Yamaguchi, Lee, and Katsura (2004) asked students whether their 'inner self' remains the same in different situations. In the Canadian sample, 72 per cent said that it did, but only 36 per cent of Japanese and 28 per cent of Hong Kong Chinese said so. We need to consider how differences of this magnitude may affect the conclusions drawn by social psychologists from research conducted only within Western cultural groups. Let us now try to do this, by looking at attributions for success and failure.

Cross-cultural variation in self-enhancement

Chapter 5 describes studies that show how we have a bias toward interpreting events around us in ways that enhance our self-image (Miller & Ross, 1975). If East

INDEPENDENT VERSUS INTERDEPENDENT SELF-CONSTRUAL

Please indicate how much you agree or disagree with each of the statements below as a description of yourself, using the response scale presented below.

1. My personal identity, independent of others, is very important to me.
2. My relationships with those in my group are more important to me than my personal accomplishments.
3. I enjoy being unique and different from others.
4. My happiness depends on the happiness of those in my group.
5. Being able to take care of myself is a primary concern for me.
6. I am careful to maintain harmony in my group.
7. Speaking up during a class or meeting is not a problem for me.
8. I would sacrifice my self-interests for the benefit of the group.
9. Having a lively imagination is important to me.
10. I will stay in a group if they need me, even if I am not happy with the group.
11. I'd rather say 'no' directly than risk being misunderstood.
12. I should consider my parents' advice when making education or career plans.
13. I am comfortable being singled out for praise or rewards.
14. I respect decisions made by my group.
15. I am the same person at home as I am at college.
16. If my brothers or sisters fail, I feel responsible.
17. I act the same way no matter who I am with.
18. I have respect for the authority figures with whom I interact.
19. I feel comfortable using someone's first name soon after I meet him or her.
20. I would offer my seat on the bus to my professor.
21. I prefer to be direct and forthright when dealing with people that I have first met.

22. I respect people who are modest about themselves.
23. I value being in good health above everything.
24. Even when I strongly disagree with group members, I avoid an argument.

1 = Strongly disagree
2 = Disagree
3 = Slightly disagree
4 = Neutral
5 = Slightly agree
6 = Agree
7 = Strongly agree

These items comprise the self-construal scale developed by Singelis (1994). Odd-numbered items refer to independence and even-numbered items refer to interdependence. You can calculate your scores for independent and for interdependent self-construal by taking the average of your ratings on odd- and even-numbered items respectively. Higher scores indicate a stronger self-construal. Whether your scores are high or low compared to others will depend on what your nationality is. Singelis (1994) reported mean independence of 5.1 for European Americans and 4.6 for Asian Americans. He found mean interdependence of 4.4 for European Americans and 4.9 for Asian Americans. Depending upon your own degree of acquiescent responding, you may find that both your scores are above these means, or both may be below them. It can be more informative to compare on which of the two scales you scored higher.

Source: The self-construal scale: Singelis, T. M. (1994). The measurement of independent and interdependent self-construals. *Personality and Social Psychology Bulletin, 20,* 580–591. © SAGE Publications, reprinted with permission.

Asians do not have such a strong sense of inner self, would they have less need for self-enhancement? Finding a satisfactory answer to this question has proved difficult, because the type of measure that is used influences the answer obtained. Heine, Lehman, Markus, and Kitayama (1999) noted that East Asians consistently score lower than North Americans on measures of self-esteem. They also show a larger gap between ratings of how they are and how they would like to be, and they react to success and failure in ways that differ from those found in North American studies. While North Americans tend to take credit for success and find excuses for failure, Japanese are more prone to attribute success to luck or help from others and take the blame for failure. These findings

suggest that East Asians may have a much weaker need for self-enhancement.

Other researchers have used a different measure of self-enhancement and obtained different results. Sedikides, Gaertner, and Toguchi (2003) asked Japanese and American students to estimate the percentage of people who were better than them on various abilities. This method yields what is known as the **better than average effect** (BAE). In other words, more than 50 per cent of people think that they are better than average on most criteria. Sedikides et al. found the BAE was just as strong among Japanese as

> **better than average effect** the finding that more than 50 per cent of participants report themselves to be better than average on a variety of criteria.

it was among Americans. They concluded that the need for self-enhancement is universal. How can this contradiction between results obtained with different methods be explained?

In the study by English and Chen (2007) it was found that, just like self-construal, self-enhancement measured by BAE varied much more between situations among Chinese Americans than among Europeans. This implies that for those with interdependent self-construal, some situations may elicit self-enhancement more than others. We may be able to understand the conflicting results if we can identify the nature of these situations. A study by Kurman (2003) focused on the role of modesty. She wanted to determine whether modesty was associated with low self-enhancement in all cultures or just in collectivist ones, where modesty norms are likely to be stronger. She first asked Singapore Chinese and urban Israeli high school students to rate how important modesty was to them. They also completed a self-construal measure. As would be expected from Hofstede's (1980) data (see Figure 15.3), the Israelis were more independent than the Singaporeans. In both samples, Kurman found that greater endorsement of modesty was associated with low self-enhancement, as measured by BAE. So, this effect may be general to all cultures, but we would expect that in cultures where modesty is more favoured, such as those in Asia, there will be fewer situations in which self-enhancement occurs.

Kurman's results help to explain how different methods give contradictory research findings, but they still leave open the question of whether the self-enhancement motive is or is not universal. Muramoto (2003) used an indirect procedure to determine whether Japanese respondents value self-enhancement, even though they express themselves modestly. She asked Japanese students to recall occasions when they had succeeded or failed. As expected, they attributed successes to others and blamed themselves for failures. However, Muramoto also asked them to rate how their friends and family would evaluate these successes and failures. Here she found that the Japanese students believed that friends and family would give them credit for successes and blame them less for failures. Further ratings showed that those people who received these kinds of support from family and friends felt that they were better understood by them. So the Japanese do wish for self-enhancement, but the cultural preference for modesty leads them to conceal this motive. This series of studies illustrates an important conclusion about the value of cross-cultural psychology. Studies may initially show contrasting results from different parts of the world, but if we investigate the reasons for these differences we can discover what is truly universal and what causes universal effects to be expressed more strongly in some locations than in others.

Self-construal as an explanation of cultural differences

Self-construal is a quality of the individual. Culture is defined as a widely shared set of meanings. So, we should expect that some behaviours can be explained in terms of the ways that individuals think about themselves, while others will be more influenced by the shared cultural context. An example of the first kind of effect is shown by a cross-cultural study of embarrassment. Singelis, Bond, Sharkey, and Lai (1999) asked students in Hong Kong, Hawaii (Asian Americans and European Americans) and mainland US to rate how embarrassed they would be in a series of different situations. They found that those with more interdependent self-construals expected to be more embarrassed and had lower self-esteem. Furthermore, when comparing the four samples, those samples with higher mean interdependence were the ones in which there was a higher mean expectation of being embarrassed.

In contrast, in Kurman's (2003) study, no relationship was found between self-construal and self-esteem, which is likely to be associated with self-enhancement. As already discussed, low self-enhancement is associated with greater endorsement of modesty. The difference between these two results is likely to be because of the difference between being embarrassed, which is a private emotion, and self-enhancement, which involves public actions. Public actions will be much more affected by the shared attitudes and norms that define a culture. Matsumoto, Yoo, and Fontaine (2008) have surveyed the endorsement in 32 nations of what they call **display rules** – in other words, norms about whether emotions should be expressed in public. As expected, nations in East Asia and elsewhere that score higher on collectivism score low on endorsement of display rules, and the nations that score highly on individualism, such as the US, score highly on endorsement of display rules. Figure 15.11 shows that there are also substantial variations within Europe in endorsement of emotional expression.

> **display rules** cultural understandings as to whether emotions should be expressed openly.

Cross-cultural psychologists have until now given more direct attention to individual attributes such as values and self-construals than to the social norms that prevail in different cultural contexts. However, values and norms are often interwoven: the perception by individuals that certain values are shared by those around them frequently provides the basis for what can become normative. Complementing Matsumoto et al.'s study of specific norms about emotional display, Gelfand et al. (2011) have surveyed respondents in 33 nations as to how

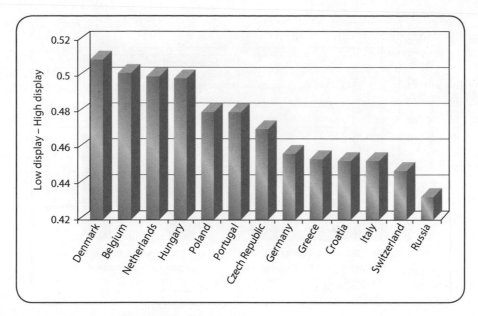

FIGURE 15.11 *Nations scoring highest and lowest on emotional display.*

Source: Based on Matsumoto et al., 2008, with permission from SAGE Publications.; *Note:* Scores for non-European nations (some of which scored very low) are deliberately excluded. The scores are for overall expressiveness, which correlated most strongly with expressions of surprise and happiness.

strong (tight versus loose) local social norms in general are perceived to be, and how much individuals would be punished if they deviated from these norms. Pakistan, Malaysia and India scored highest on tightness and the Ukraine, Estonia and Hungary scored highest on looseness. This dimension of cultural variation was found to be independent of individualism–collectivism. We may expect that self-construals will be more strongly predictive in contexts where actions are private and norms are loose than in contexts where actions are public and norms are tight.

Self-construal over time

In Chapter 5 it was also noted that we typically see our self as having continuity through our lifespan. Consistent with this view, in this chapter we have discussed the types of self-construal that predominate in individualist and collectivist cultures. However, from Chapter 14 you will understand that through an average day we may think of ourselves in a variety of different ways, depending on our affiliations with different groups and different activities. So, can independence and interdependence vary over time? Trafimow, Triandis, and Goto (1991) were the first to show that they can (see Leader in the Field, Harry C. Triandis). They asked a group of students in the US to spend two minutes thinking of all the things that they had in common with their family (interdependent prime

 LEADER IN THE FIELD

Harry C. Triandis (b. 1926) grew up on the Greek island of Corfu. During World War II the local schools were closed and he taught himself by reading the *Encyclopaedia Britannica*. He obtained a first degree in engineering in Canada, but transferred his interest to psychology, gaining a PhD in social psychology from Cornell University in 1958. Moving to the University of Illinois, he developed a cross-cultural perspective on the use of the semantic differential questionnaire to map the meaning of concepts. His early understanding that cultural differences are best thought of as differences in assigned meanings was summarized in *The Analysis of Subjective Culture* (1972). He pioneered the development of a network of cross-cultural psychologists, was one of the first presidents of the International Association for Cross-Cultural Psychology, and was the Chief Editor of the *Handbook of Cross-Cultural Psychology*. More recently his many publications did much to popularize interest in individualism and collectivism. Many of his former students at the University of Illinois are now leading contemporary cross-cultural psychologists.

condition). Another group of students was asked to spend two minutes thinking of all the things that make them different from others (independent prime condition). The groups included both European Americans and Chinese Americans. Respondents were then asked to complete an open-ended measure of self-construal, in which they are asked to complete the phrase 'I am . . .' 20 times. Judges then coded the open-ended responses for independent and interdependent self-descriptions.

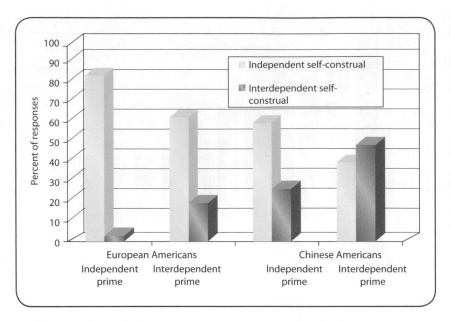

FIGURE 15.12 *Self-construals in response to priming.*

Source: Based on Trafimow et al., 1991. Copyright © 2009 by the American Psychological Association. Adapted with permission. Trafimow, D., Triandis, H. C., & Goto, S. G. (1991). Some tests of the distinction between the private self and the collective self. *Journal of Personality and Social Psychology, 60,* 649–655. The use of APA information does not imply endorsement by APA.

Figure 15.12 shows the results. In both groups, the independent prime is associated with a higher score on independent self-construal and the interdependent prime is associated with a higher score on interdependent self-construal. However, comparing the results on the left- and right-hand sides of the figure, it is clear that the European Americans remained more independent than the Chinese Americans in both conditions, and the Chinese Americans were still more interdependent in both conditions.

If scores on independence and interdependence can be changed by two minutes of experimental priming, how can these concepts be of any use in explaining cultural differences? There are two kinds of answer to this question. First, we need to be aware that priming occurs not only in psychology experiments: there are many aspects of a culture that are likely to continually prime members of the culture to construe themselves in particular ways. An ever-present example is the language that is spoken. Correct usage of most of the languages spoken in the more individualist nations of the world requires the inclusion of the pronoun 'I' when speaking about oneself. Many of the languages spoken in more collectivist nations permit one to drop the pronoun 'I' (Kashima & Kashima, 1998). Some languages, for example Arabic, do not even have a direct linguistic representation of the pronoun 'I'. So customary language use can prime self-construal of oneself as independent or interdependent. So too can adherence to cultural norms, that is to say the conventionally accepted types of response to one's behaviours typically received from other members of one's cultural group. For instance, an individual in a given culture would be aware of the local emotional display rules discussed earlier. In these ways, cultures can be constantly created and recreated through millions of interpersonal interactions, rather than having a fixed and static nature.

A second consequence of the finding that self-construal can be primed experimentally is that we can use experimental methods to investigate some aspects of cultural differences. Some examples are discussed in the final section of this chapter.

Summary

A key way in which cultures differ is in whether they encourage individuals to think of themselves as relatively independent of others or as interdependent with those to whom they are close. Independence is associated with a need to see oneself positively. Interdependence is associated with a need to maintain harmonious relations with others through publicly expressed modesty. Cultural differences are partly explained by differences in self-construal and partly by shared norms. Self-construals are changeable but are continually elicited by salient aspects of culture, such as language use and behavioural norms.

INTERPERSONAL RELATIONS

How do people relate to people whom they meet, and form relationships with them, in different cultural contexts?

In preceding sections we have seen that people from different cultures tend to have different values and to think of themselves in different ways. We would therefore expect these differences to be reflected in how they communicate with each other. However, we cannot simply describe cultural contrasts in communication style because, as we have seen in earlier sections, people with interdependent self-construals will adapt their behaviour depending on the social context. Gudykunst et al. (1992) compared the reported communication experiences of students in Hong Kong, Japan, the US and Australia. Respondents from the US and Australia did not make any distinction between communication with members of their ingroup and their outgroup. However, those from Japan and Hong Kong did make such a distinction. When communicating with ingroup members they reported feeling more similar, having more shared networks, more questioning of each other and more feeling that they could understand one another without being explicit.

These contrasts have been further explored by Verkuyten and Masson (1996), who studied same-sex adolescent friendships among ethnic groups living in The Netherlands. Independent self-construal was higher among Dutch respondents and those from Spain, Italy and the former Yugoslavia. Interdependent self-construal was higher among Moroccan and Turkish respondents. The authors found that interdependence predicted feeling closer to one's best friend, but having a smaller number of other friends. Interdependence also predicted having more rules about how to speak to third parties about one's best friend. This study is useful because it not only identifies cultural contrasts, but also shows how self-construal measures can explain the contrasts that are found.

Prosocial behaviour with strangers

If people from collectivist nations distinguish between ingroup and outgroup relationships, it makes sense to discuss each type of relationship separately. In Chapter 10 prosocial behaviours were discussed. How do cultural differences affect the tendency to help a stranger in distress? Levine, Norenzayan, and Philbrick (2001) compared bystander helpfulness in 23 nations. They trained

accomplices to create three separate situations on the streets of a major city in each nation. In the first situation, each accomplice dropped a pen while walking past a single stranger. In the second situation, as a pedestrian approached, the accomplice appeared to have hurt their leg and was struggling to pick up a pile of magazines that they had dropped. In the third situation, the accomplice was dressed as a blind person and was waiting for a green light at a pedestrian crossing. The proportion of helpful responses across these three emergencies was positively correlated and was therefore combined into a single index. As Figure 15.13 shows, there was a large variation between nations.

This study provides a first indication of cultural variations in prosocial behaviour, but because few other measures were collected, it leaves many possible explanations of this effect untested. Helpfulness to strangers was unrelated to differences in individualism and collectivism, but was higher in less rich nations and those scoring higher on Schwartz's (2004) measure of embeddedness (Knafo, Schwartz, & Levine, 2009).

Intimate relationships

We can expect that the ways in which intimate relationships are created will reflect the prevailing cultural context. Buss (1989) asked 9500 students in 37 nations to rate the desirability of 18 qualities in a future opposite-sex romantic partner. Across the sample as a whole, men said they would prefer partners whom they perceived as young, healthy and beautiful, while women would prefer partners whom they saw as ambitious, industrious and having high earning potential (see Chapter 11 for discussion of the possible evolutionary basis for such partner choices). There were also substantial variations in preferences across nations. The greatest variability was found in preference for pre-marital chastity, which was more strongly required by respondents in collectivist nations (Buss et al., 1990). In a collectivist culture, a female partner's lack of chastity would be a threat to the honour of her whole group. We discuss this in a later section. Shackelford, Schmitt, and Buss (2005) made a further study of this dataset, using factor analysis to identify four dimensions that could be used to summarize the variation across nations. The first of these dimensions contrasted the presence of love as a precondition for a relationship, with emphasis on status and financial prospects. Figure 15.14 shows the nations scoring at either extreme of this dimension. Preference for a relationship based on love was found to be strongest in more wealthy nations, which tend to be those that are individualistic rather than collectivistic. See also

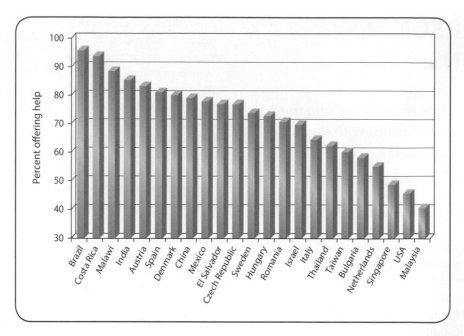

FIGURE 15.13 *Prosocial behaviour across countries.*

Source: Based on Levine et al., 2001, with permission from SAGE Publications.

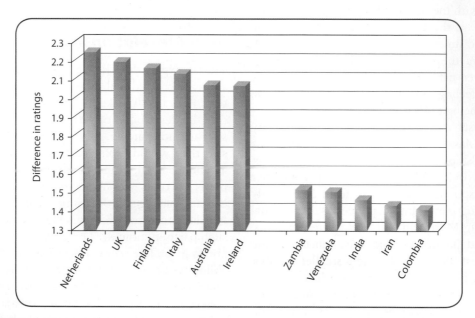

FIGURE 15.14 *Preference for love more than for status and financial prospects as a precondition for a relationship.*

Source: Based on Shackelford et al., 2005, with permission from Elsevier.

Social Psychology Beyond the Lab 15.2, which gives some examples of how partner preferences are typically expressed in the UK and India.

The studies of partner preference provide an example of a field in which we find both universality for some variables and cultural variations for other variables. Gender differences are universal, but preferred partner qualities vary in strength between cultures. For a similar pattern of results, see the discussion of cultural effects on aggression in Chapter 9.

Summary

Our cultural background affects the way that we speak to others and to what extent we distinguish between relating to strangers and relating to friends. Social relationships within collectivistic cultures are more exclusive of outsiders and require less explicit communication. Choice of intimate partners is influenced not just by the personal qualities of the partners, but also by the attributes of the families from which they are drawn.

SOCIAL PSYCHOLOGY BEYOND THE LAB 15.2

THE IDEAL PARTNER FITS WITH CULTURAL NORMS

What qualities are important in seeking a partner? In the UK, personality traits and interests are emphasized. In India, caste, family status, qualifications and sometimes horoscopes are more salient. Note how in the UK individuals advertise themselves, whereas in India it is often the family rather than the individual that seeks a partner. Note also that one of the UK advertisements is for a homosexual partner.

United Kingdom	India
Lots of energy and a lust for life. Eccentric, kind-hearted female, 35, 5'9", loves singing, dancing, reading and travel; would like to meet confident pragmatic, hard-working male, 33–38, who likes a joke and a hearty laugh.	**Smart,** very handsome Brahmin boy, 31, 180 cm, BE, MBA, own established business, monthly income six figures, send biodata and photo (must).
Attractive 39yo black male speaks five languages would like to meet female, similar age for long-term relationship. Likes walking by the sea, food, cooking and travel.	**Delhi-based** Punjabi Khatri family seeks professionally qualified girl from educated family for IT, MBA, 29 years, 5'7" working manager in leading company.
New here, looking around. I am a 32yo male seeking an honest, balanced fun female 25–34 with good sense of humour.	**Hindu girl,** 23, 160 cm, BTech working professional software engineer, only child, father senior bank executive, mother legal professional, seeks preferably BTech, MBA, below 28 from educated family. Caste no bar.
Tall, blonde, incredible hunk, 27, attractive handsome young male would like to meet older non-scene, distinguished gentleman, 65+, hopefully leading to friendship and relationship.	**Beautiful** working girl in Delhi sought for handsome Uttar Pradesh Khatri boy, born 3.2.1980 /3.15 am, 5'3", employed in a reputable company.

Sources: The Guardian (London), April 2010; *Sunday Times of India*, matrimonials, March 2010.

GROUP PROCESSES

How does collectivism affect group behaviours?

Asch's (1956) classic study of how groups influence the individual's behaviour has been described in Chapters 1 and 8. We might expect that the effects found would depend on the cultural context in which the study is conducted. Bond and Smith (1996) reported a meta-analysis of the 133 published replications and extensions of this study. Ninety-seven of these replications were conducted within the United States, and even within the US there was substantial variation in the level of conformity that was found. Bond and Smith were principally interested in what happened when the study was repeated elsewhere, and they found that replications had been conducted in another 16 nations. But when an experiment is repeated, it is very difficult to match exactly the ways the original study was done. To try to compare studies cross-culturally, they first studied in more detail variations across studies conducted in one country. Bond

and Smith determined how much the varying results obtained within the US were associated with the differences in procedures and samples in these studies. They found the strongest variations were caused by three factors: (1) the size of the majority that gave false answers; (2) the relative lengths of the lines that were used; and (3) whether the majority were from an outgroup or not. These results were then used as statistical controls for these same sources of variation in examining the studies conducted elsewhere. The results obtained from differing regions of the world are shown in Figure 15.15. To test possible reasons for the contrasting results from different nations, Bond and Smith correlated the measures of national difference provided by Hofstede (1980) and Schwartz (2004) with the scores for conformity. They found that conformity was highest in the nations grouped in the figure as 'Rest of the World', where Hofstede's collectivism and Schwartz's embeddedness values are most strongly endorsed. Thus, conformity was highest in societies in which people emphasize their links with others and their long-term membership groups.

If members of collectivist cultures conform more frequently, then we may expect their behaviour to differ when they are in groups compared to when they are

SOCIAL LOAFING IN CHINA, THE US AND ISRAEL

RESEARCH CLOSE-UP 15.2

Earley, P. C. (1993). East meets West meets Mideast: Further explorations of collectivistic versus individualistic work groups. *Academy of Management Journal, 36,* 319–348.

Research question

Social loafing is the phenomenon in which group members work less hard when they are in a group compared to when they are on their own. It has been frequently identified in studies conducted in the US. The process is fully described in Chapter 13 (see Research Close-Up13.1). Earley tested the hypothesis that respondents' attitudes toward interdependence would affect the extent to which social loafing would occur. He predicted that those who favour interdependence (referred to as collectivists) would work hardest when working with members of their ingroup. He was also concerned to establish the extent to which social loafing occurs in real work groups as much as it does in short-term groups of students brought together for the purpose of the experiment.

Design and procedure

Participants were full-time managers who were attending training courses. The design was 3 (nationalities) × 3 (experimental conditions). The sample comprised 45 Israelis, 60 mainland Chinese and 60 Americans from the United States. All participants were given a simulated 'in-basket' of paperwork tasks on which to work. In the *individual* condition they were told that they should expect to complete 20 items within an hour. In the *ingroup collective* condition they were told that they were working in a team of 10 and that the other team members were people from the same region of the country who had been selected to be similar to one another and to have many common interests. The team was expected to complete 200 items within the hour. In the *outgroup collective* condition they were told that they were working in a team of 10 and that the other group members were from different regions of the country and would have little in common. They were also expected to complete 200 items within the hour. In fact, all participants were working individually. Participants also completed a questionnaire measuring their attitudes toward independence (individualism) and interdependence (collectivism). The dependent measure was the number of tasks completed per person.

Results

Scores from each nation were first standardized, so that the means for each nation were equivalent. This enables the researchers to analyse the results for the sample as a whole without reference to nationality and without distortion from other sources of difference between the samples. Earley then divided his sample between those who had endorsed independence and those who had endorsed interdependence. As Figure 15.17 shows, individualists completed significantly fewer tasks when they believed that they were working in either of the collective conditions versus individually. Collectivists completed significantly *more* tasks in the ingroup collective condition than in either of the other experimental conditions.

Pooling the results across nations ignores the fact that most of the individualists would be in the US sample and most of the collectivists would be in the Chinese sample. Therefore it is useful also to test the hypothesis separately for each nation's data. When this is done unstandardized data can be used. The results are shown in Figure 15.18, but note that the samples from each nation were quite small.

Implications

This is one of the most striking cross-cultural studies that has been conducted. The results show that social loafing is not just reduced in differing cultural contexts – it is

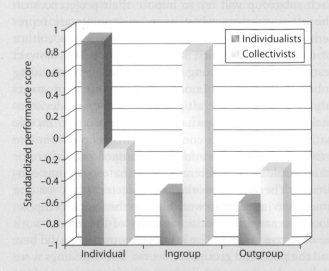

FIGURE 15.17 *Social loafing in three experimental conditions.*

Source: Reproduced from Earley (1993) by permission of the Academy of Management.

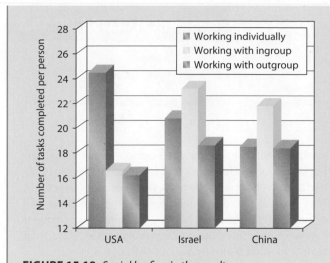

FIGURE 15.18 *Social loafing in three cultures.*
Source: Based on information reported in Earley, 1993.

actually reversed. Collectivists do not loaf in groups: they work harder. In an earlier study, Earley (1989) found the same result when he sampled managers who were actually at work, not in a simulated work setting. Of course there could be many reasons why a study conducted in the US, Israel and China could come up with contrasting results. By measuring participants' attitudes toward independence and interdependence directly, Earley was able to show that he could explain why the results came out as they did. If we look at these results through Western eyes, we might say that collectivists work harder in groups because of conformity pressures. However, this does not answer the question of why there might be norms favouring hard work in collectivist groups. A better explanation is to say that in collectivist cultures one's interdependent identity is inextricably linked with one's group, so that hard work enhances one's identity, just as working hard individually does for an individual.

INTERGROUP RELATIONS

How does collectivism affect relations with outgroups?

As has been discussed in Chapters 12 and 14, social identity theory has played a major role in the development of social psychology. It has, however, been developed and tested mostly within the predominantly more individualistic national cultures that provide the heartland of social psychology. What happens when group memberships are a more permanent and central element in one's identity, as occurs within collectivist cultures and within ethnic minority subcultures in individualistic nations? People high in interdependence may need to use different ways from those who are more independent to maintain a positive comparison between their ingroup and relevant outgroups.

The minimal group paradigm pioneered by Tajfel, Billig, Bundy, and Flament (1971; *see Research Close-Up 14.1*) was first tested with 11-year-old schoolchildren. Consider the study conducted in New Zealand by Wetherell (1982). Wetherell compared the responses of three separate samples of 8-year-old children: New Zealanders of European origin, Maoris (who are indigenous to New Zealand) and Samoan immigrants to New Zealand. The European New Zealanders responded to being arbitrarily assigned to a group by maximizing the difference between ingroup rewards and outgroup rewards, just as has been repeatedly found in earlier

studies based on the study carried out by Tajfel et al. However, the Samoans tried to maximize the rewards of both the ingroup and the outgroup, while the results for Maoris were intermediate between the other two samples. On the face of it, the Samoan results in particular appear contradictory to social identity theory, because the Samoans did not try to enhance the status of their own group. In trying to understand the results, Wetherell wondered whether the collectivist culture of Samoans led them to perceive fellow-Samoans, whether categorized as 'ingroup' or 'outgroup' by the experimenters, as, in fact, 'ingroup members', and the white experimenter as the outgroup. She also noted that the giving of gifts is highly esteemed in Samoan culture, so that a Samoan might achieve higher status for the ingroup by giving gifts to others. It is also possible that as young immigrants, the Samoan children did not fully understand the culturally strange procedures in which the white experimenter was asking them to participate. A more exact test of the extent to which the minimal group paradigm gives similar results in different cultures has been provided by Falk, Heine and Takemura (2014). Japanese adults were found to significantly favour their arbitrarily-assigned ingroup, but this effect was less strong than among Canadian adults.

In order to test reasons for these varying results, studies are required that focus on intergroup relations and also include measures of cultural relevance, such as independence and interdependence. Research Close-Up 15.3 describes some findings of this kind, which do support the cross-cultural validity of social identity theory, but which also show some culturally variable effects.

SOCIAL IDENTITY IN CHINA AND THE US

RESEARCH CLOSE-UP 15.3

Chen, Y.-R., Brockner, J., & Katz, T. (1998). Toward an explanation of cultural differences in in-group favoritism: The role of individual versus collective primacy. *Journal of Personality and Social Psychology, 75*, 1490–1502.

Research question

Chen and her colleagues were interested to see how members of a team would react to adverse feedback when they were in a collectivist cultural context rather than an individualist context. If one's group identity is more fixed and salient than it is in the nations where social identity theory was first formulated, how would the different types of identity management strategies proposed by Tajfel and Turner (1986) be affected?

As discussed in Chapter 14, social identity theory specifies social mobility, social creativity and social competition as three ways in which a group member might seek to retain a positive identity, even where their group is evaluated poorly. The theory also states the circumstances in which each of these options will be employed. Where group boundaries are permeable and the group is poorly evaluated, a group member might opt for social mobility – in other words, leave the group. This option would be attractive to someone with an independent self-construal. In collectivist cultures where group boundaries are not so permeable, would respondents whose group is poorly evaluated find alternative ways to preserve their group affiliation, and would these strategies be followed especially by those who endorse interdependence? Tajfel and Turner's theory suggests that they would choose social competition or social creativity – that is to say, either comparing their group favourably with others or changing the basis of comparison with other groups. Chen et al. did not make a specific prediction as to which strategy their more collectivist respondents would employ.

Design and procedure

The design was a 2 (nation: China/US) × 2 (individual feedback: success/failure) × 2 (team feedback: success/failure) experiment. Participants were 292 students at Peking University in China and 80 students at Columbia University in the US. After filling out an attitude survey and a measure of independence/interdependence, participants were told that they had been assigned to a team whose members held similar attitudes to one another on a variety of issues. They were then given brief descriptions of 10 romantic couples that were said to have been prepared by clinical psychologists. They were asked to predict whether each couple would still be together after a year, and were told that successful prediction was an indicator of intellectual and interpersonal competence. After completing this task, participants received feedback that told them either that they had done well or poorly on the task (experimental factor 1). They were also told that their team had either done well or poorly (experimental factor 2). Finally, as dependent measures, they rated the performance of themselves, their team and other teams on various scales.

Results

Chinese respondents mostly scored higher on interdependence and US respondents mostly scored higher on independence. The findings of interest concern the ways in which respondents handled the failure feedback compared to the success feedback. Among the Americans, those who were told that they had done well individually, but their team had done poorly, gave their team much lower ratings. However, in the same situation among the Chinese there was no such decrease in ingroup ratings. Instead, they rated the performance of outgroup teams significantly more negatively. Figure 15.19 shows that the

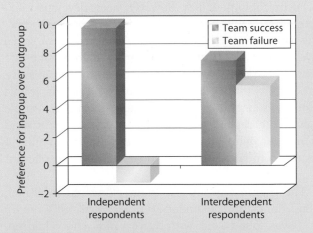

FIGURE 15.19 *Ingroup preference when receiving individual success feedback.*

Source: Based on Chen, Brockner, & Katz (1998). Copyright © 1998 by the American Psychological Association. Adapted with permission. Chen, Y.-R., Brockner, J., & Katz, T. (1998). Toward an explanation of cultural differences in in-group favoritism: The role of individual versus collective primacy. *Journal of Personality and Social Psychology, 75*, 1490–1502. The use of APA information does not imply endorsement by APA.

same pattern of results is obtained when the data are analysed in terms of independence–interdependence rather than in terms of nationality. Chen et al. used a 7-item measure of 'individual versus collective primacy', derived from several different measures of independent and interdependent self-construal, including some of the items in the Singelis (1994) scales (see Individual Differences 15.1). Thus, they found that of all the possible reasons why Americans and Chinese might behave differently in this experiment, the self-construal scores provide a sufficient explanation.

Implications

American respondents were clearly employing Tajfel and Turner's (1986) social mobility strategy. In effect they were saying, 'If this team is no good, then I don't wish to be part of it.' For them, it was more important to preserve a positive individual identity than a positive group identity. In contrast, the Chinese response was more like, 'If our team did poorly, then the others must have done even worse.' This is consistent with Tajfel and Turner's social competition strategy. By adjusting the basis of comparison in this way, they could preserve a positive team identity. In a similar study conducted later, Chen, Brockner, and Chen (2002) showed that when outgroup teams were said to have done better than one's own team, interdependent respondents still rated their own team positively, while independent respondents did not. These studies thus give cross-cultural support to social identity theory, but show that identity strategies do vary in ways that reflect variations in individualism–collectivism. However, the results of both these studies rest on a brief and previously unknown measure of independence and interdependence that requires fuller development to ensure its validity.

Group honour

As we have seen, many studies of individualistic and collectivistic cultures have focused on the US and East Asia. However, issues relevant to collectivism are important within intergroup relations in all parts of the world. The need to maintain the honour of one's group in relation to others is salient not just among the more collectivist immigrant communities within nations in northern Europe, but also in the more collectivist nations of southern Europe, and as we shall see, even in the southern states of the US. Rodriguez Mosquera, Manstead, and Fischer (2002a) compared understandings of the concept of honour in the Netherlands and in Spain, by comparing students' responses to Schwartz's (1992) value survey. As Schwartz had done in his earlier study, Rodriguez Mosquera et al. defined meanings of values by examining the extent to which endorsing one value was correlated with endorsing other values. In the Netherlands, honour was more strongly associated with endorsement of independent values such as *self-respect* and *achieving more than others*. In contrast, in Spain honour was more strongly associated with interdependent values such as *loyalty* and *honesty*. In a further study, Rodriguez Mosquera, Manstead, and Fischer (2002b) asked Dutch and Spanish students to imagine their response to a series of scenarios in which insults were received. The Spanish students reported feeling more threatened and more ashamed when family honour was insulted, whereas the Dutch reported more shame and anger when their autonomy and assertiveness were under threat.

Cultures in which honour is defined interdependently can be expected to show evidence of vigorous defence of the honour of one's group. For instance, Semin and Rubini (1990) compared students' reports of insults used most frequently in northern Italy with those used in southern Italy. Southern Italy has a culture that is much more collectivistic than northern Italy (Capozza, Brown, Aharpour, & Falvo, 2006). Favoured insults in northern Italy were more frequently focused on characterizing the insulted individual, for instance in terms of sexual expletives or of undesirable traits ('You're stupid'; 'You're a cretin'). In Sicily, in the south, insults were more frequently targeted at the individual's group membership, especially their family. Examples included: 'I wish a cancer on you and all your relatives'; 'Your sister is a cow'; 'You are queer and so is your father'; 'You are a communist'; and insults based on references to incest.

Historically, the nations around the Mediterranean such as Spain, Italy and Turkey have been characterized as honour cultures, but defence of group honour is likely to be a salient value in many of the cultures that have been classified as collectivistic. Leung and Cohen (2011) suggest it is useful to distinguish collectivistic cultures that seek to preserve face (such as those in East Asia) from those that seek to preserve honour (such as those in South Asia and the Mediterranean region). Even within the United States the relatively more collectivist values of the southern states are associated with acceptance of more aggressive responding to uphold the honour of one's group than in the northern US. For instance, Nisbett and Cohen (1996) mailed a job application letter to potential employers that had supposedly been written by someone convicted of a killing in an honour-related incident. Companies in the south and west of the US more often responded favourably to the application than did those in the more individualistic north of the US. Honour killings continue to be reported in the press in many nations where perceived female sexual infidelity is seen as a major threat to the honour of the group.

Negotiation

In fields such as diplomacy and business it is frequently necessary to engage in negotiation with representatives of groups whose cultures may differ from one's own. The differing values espoused within individualist and collectivist cultures make it likely that tasks of this kind will be approached in different ways. Morris et al. (1998) compared the approaches to negotiation used by business students from India, Hong Kong, the Philippines and the US. Preferred negotiation styles were characterized as either competing or avoiding conflict. The Americans were more competitive, while the Hong Kong Chinese were more avoidant. Respondents also completed Schwartz's (1992) measure of individuals' values. Morris et al. were able to show that the differences between the samples in competitiveness were associated with differences in how much respondents endorsed achievement values, while the differences in avoidance were associated with differences in how much tradition and conformity values were endorsed.

Thus, we can see that measures that are useful in defining cultural differences can help to predict some of the difficulties that will arise when people from differing cultures negotiate with one another. However, this study does not tell us how they are likely to cope with these difficulties. Successful negotiation across cultures is likely to require adaptations in one's behaviour. We can gain a better understanding of these adaptations by looking at more detailed analyses. Adair and Brett (2005) constructed a complex one-hour-long simulation of a commercial negotiation. This enabled analyses of actual negotiation behaviours over time rather than simple summaries of negotiation style. Adair and Brett examined the extent to which intercultural negotiators modified their behaviour compared to those negotiating with others from their own culture. There were two intracultural experimental conditions and one intercultural condition. The collectivist intracultural negotiations comprised dyads drawn from Russia, Japan, Hong Kong and Thailand. The individualist intracultural

negotiations comprised dyads from Germany, Israel, Sweden and the US. In all of these instances, each dyad comprised two people from the same nation. In the intercultural dyads, some US negotiators were pitted against Japanese negotiators, while others negotiated with Hong Kong Chinese. The negotiations were audiotaped, transcribed and coded into a series of predetermined categories. In order to examine the sequential development of the negotiations, the transcripts were divided into quarters.

In studies that use a complex content analysis of this kind, the numbers of dyads from each individual nation is necessarily low, so Adair and Brett analysed the results for all individualist dyads in contrast to the results for all collectivist dyads. Negotiators from the individualistic nations showed more direct exchange of information through questions (e.g., 'We could offer 40 per cent upfront') and answers (e.g., 'We couldn't possibly accept that offer'). Only during the last quarter did they make actual offers focused on a possible agreement. Negotiators from collectivistic nations used indirect information exchange more frequently. In other words, they made a mixture of offers and more generally phrased persuasive arguments (e.g., 'Everyone knows our company makes the finest products and we plan to continue introducing new ones') during the early stages, and inferred what must be the more important priorities of the other party from the relatively indirect responses (e.g., 'This deal is very important for me. I'm up for promotion and the budget is really tight') that they obtained to their offers. In the intercultural dyads, the collectivistic negotiators were found to have adopted the more direct information exchange that is favoured by individualistic negotiators. The individualistic negotiators did not adapt their behaviour. The intercultural negotiations achieved less joint gain (measured in dollars) than both the collectivist and the individualist intracultural negotiations.

This study tells us two things. First, it is consistent with expectation that the negotiators from collectivist cultures take more account of their context, and therefore it is they who adapt their behaviour more during intercultural negotiation. Secondly, this adaptation is only partially effective, because information exchange and the making of offers have different meanings in differing contexts. Early offers in collectivist cultures can serve well as an exploratory device among those who understand their purpose, but they are likely to be misunderstood by negotiators from cultures in which direct communication is favoured. Being an effective negotiator cross-culturally requires not only being willing to adapt one's behaviour, but also an awareness of how the other party will interpret

SOCIAL PSYCHOLOGY BEYOND THE LAB 15.3

THE POLITICAL PERILS OF CROSS-CULTURAL NEGOTIATION

The costs of failing to understand the intentions of parties from other cultural contexts is nowhere more apparent than in the field of international negotiation. The US dropped the atomic bombs on Hiroshima and Nagasaki in Japan in 1945 after the Japanese had responded to a US ultimatum for unconditional surrender using the ambiguous word *mokusatsu*, which can mean 'silent contempt', 'ignore' or 'we need more time'. In this instance, it was translated as 'ignore'. However, the Japanese emperor had already agreed to surrender: conflicts within his government needed to be resolved before they were ready to respond.

More recently, it is said that the 1990 conflict in Kuwait was precipitated because US Secretary of State James Baker spoke softly to Tariq Aziz, the Iraqi foreign minister, presenting him with a letter indicating that the US would intervene militarily if Iraq did not withdraw following their invasion of Kuwait (Kimmel, 1994). Consistent with Western styles of communication, the letter was task-oriented, impersonal, definite and time-limited. An Arab understanding of threats would be that they are only meant seriously if delivered extravagantly and emphatically. Aziz would have favoured a slower-paced and less focused building up of trust between the two parties.

The United Nations Climate Change Conference held in Copenhagen in 2009 was regarded by most parties as a failure. Many factors contributed to that, but it provided numerous instances of cultural differences in negotiation style and the way in which these may have affected the outcome (Lynas, 2009). President Obama delayed his arrival at the conference until his advisers judged that there was a possibility of agreement with the Chinese. When he arrived he joined the group of predominantly Western leaders who were attempting to rescue the stalled negotiations. However, the Chinese and Indian governments sent only middle-ranking protocol officers to these meetings, thereby preventing the flexibility that might have been possible within a meeting of heads of state. Obama reacted by leaving these meetings and having two one-to-one negotiations with Chinese premier Wen Jiabao, thus illustrating his preference for direct communication. He returned from the second of these meetings announcing agreement on certain points. The Chinese responded by introducing new demands into the group discussions through their protocol officers, thus regaining control of the negotiation. Obama responded by once more seeking out the Chinese, and this time found them engaged in an alternative negotiation with a small group of key non-Western nations. Obama joined these negotiations uninvited, and a new agreement was announced. The new and rather modest deal was, in turn, much criticized by nations that had not been a party to any of these discussions, but was eventually accepted. Chinese indirectness had proved most effective in achieving the goals that they desired, but there would have been no agreement at all without the more direct initiatives of several Western leaders.

those behaviours (see Social Psychology Beyond the Lab 15.3).

on more specific concepts such as independence and interdependence.

Summary

Members of groups within collectivist cultures give high priority to preserving their group's status. This leads them to seek harmony with ingroup members through indirect communication, and to defend their group robustly when interacting with outgroup members. These effects are broadly consistent with social psychological theories developed through sampling of members of individualist cultures, but in order to explain the particular ways in which collectivist group status is upheld in more collectivistic cultures, we need to draw

INTERCULTURAL RELATIONS

Will globalization mean the end of cultural differences?

In recent decades there have been unprecedented levels of contact between cultural groups located in different parts of the world. This has occurred through the globalization of the media, through short-term visits by tourists, students and business people and through long-term relocation by migrants and refugees. During this same period, almost all nations have become more affluent, although inequalities persist both within and between nations. Short-term population movements have most often been from individualist nations to collectivist nations, whereas the long-term population movements have mostly been in the reverse direction. The principal source of evidence as to the correlates of all this geographic mobility is provided by data collected by the World Values Survey. Initiated within a small range of nations in the early 1980s, this survey now provides information from more than 90 nations on endorsement of a wide variety of values and behaviours. The data have been collected from representative samples within each nation every few years. This makes it possible to gain a broad overview of the extent of global cultural change.

Inglehart and Baker (2000) analysed endorsement of World Values Survey items that they had found to make up a dimension of what they defined as 'post-materialist' values. Initially these authors defined a post-materialist as someone who tends to agree with survey items that can be summarized as these five statements:

- My self-expression and quality of life are more important than my economic and physical security.
- I am happy.
- Homosexuality is justifiable.

- You can trust most people.
- I have signed one or more petitions.

Subsequent research identified many additional survey items that post-materialists agree with. These items support gender equality, tolerance of minorities, recycling, state support for the needy and new technologies. When data from the 1980s was compared with that from the 1990s, a substantially increased percentage of those classified as post-materialists was found in 19 of 21 nations. The magnitude of these changes for some of these nations can be seen in Figure 15.20. The lower part of the figure shows the percentage of post-materialists *minus* the percent of materialists in each nation in 1980. The negative percentages in this part of the figure show that in 1980 there were more materialists than post-materialists in all European nations except Finland. For instance, in Italy, there were almost 40 per cent more materialists than post-materialists. The upper part of the table shows the *change* over the following decade. For instance, Italy shows a gain of post-materialists of around 45 per cent, so that by 1990 there were slightly more Italians classified as post-materialists than as materialists. Of course, respondents at these two points in time were not the same people. We do not know whether these changes have occurred through people actually changing their values, or through the replacement of populations as generations succeeded one another. Nonetheless, it appears that values that in the past were more characteristic of just a few of the most individualistic nations are becoming more widespread. These

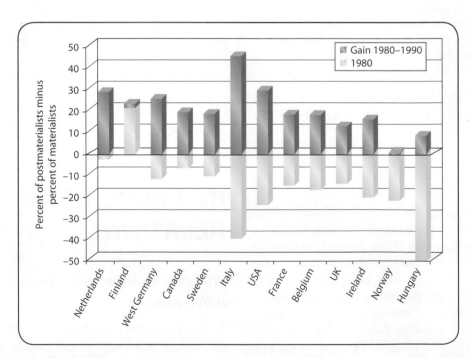

FIGURE 15.20 *Percentage of post-materialists minus percentage of materialists, 1980 and increase to 1990.*
Source: Based on data reported in Inglehart, 1997.

changes characterize the profile of nations as a whole, not all individuals. In each nation, there remain many individuals who would not be classified as post-materialists.

Inglehart and Oyserman (2004) explored these results and found that the nation-level scores for post-materialism correlate strongly with Hofstede's (1980) measures of individualism and Schwartz's (2004) measures of autonomy. However, they note that the profiles of nations with differing historical, religious and political systems remain distinctive. What we are seeing is a global trend in value endorsement, not a convergence toward a single profile of 'modern' or Western values. The profiles of values endorsed for instance in East Asian nations, in the former Soviet bloc, in Islamic nations, in Latin America, in predominantly Protestant Europe, in predominantly Catholic Europe and in the Anglo nations each remain distinctive, but with rather more post-materialists in almost all nations. As Figure 15.20 also shows, the changes are happening just as much in nations that were already individualistic, such as the US, as they are in other nations that were not individualistic in times past.

Over the past several decades the great majority of nations have experienced economic growth (International Monetary Fund, 2005). The nations within which endorsement of post-materialist values has risen have been those experiencing increasing prosperity. World Values Survey data has also shown a movement *away* from post-materialist values within the much smaller number of nations that have suffered economic decline, such as the former Soviet bloc nations of Eastern Europe. Thus, future economic crises might engender a reversal of current value changes.

Migration and acculturation

One major source of cultural change is the current migration of large numbers of people from collectivist cultures in Asia, Africa and the Caribbean to more individualistic cultures in Europe, North America and Australasia. Social psychologists have a role to play in explaining the

challenges that are raised by this process and in contributing to their resolution. **Acculturation** is a term that was defined some time ago as the process whereby two cultural groups that come into contact with one another cause changes in one or both parties (Redfield, Linton, & Herskovits, 1936). These changes may be in values, in behaviours and in how one feels about oneself. Although it is clear that increasing immigration does currently have a major political and social impact on the culture of individualistic nations, social psychological research has mostly been focused on the choices faced by immigrants and their descendents, leaving most of the study of changes in the nations receiving migrants to political scientists. As illustrated by Theory Box 15.3, Berry (1997) has emphasized that migrant acculturation is not simply a process whereby migrants must choose the extent to which they wish to adopt the values and behaviours of the majority culture (see Leader in the Field, John Berry). They also face choices as to how much of their culture of origin they wish to sustain. In addition, they will experience varying degrees of preference from majority culture members for each of the acculturation modes that are illustrated in Theory Box 15.3.

Most studies have shown that migrants favour the integration mode, that is to say participating in the majority culture, while also retaining the values and behaviours associated with their identity of origin (Sam & Berry, 1997). However, this preference is not always reciprocated by the majority population. For instance, Van Oudenhoven, Prins, and Buunk (1998) found that Moroccan and Turkish immigrants in the Netherlands favoured integration, but that Dutch majority respondents were more favourable to assimilation. One way in which migrants may adapt to this contrast in preferences is illustrated by Arends-Toth and Van de Vijver (2003), who found that while the Dutch majority favoured assimilation both at work and at home, Turkish migrants in the Netherlands favoured integration at work and separation at home. Look now at Individual

> **acculturation** the process whereby two cultural groups that come into contact with one another cause changes in one or both parties.

THEORY BOX 15.3

BERRY'S TYPOLOGY OF ACCULTURATION MODES

Preferences	Retain original identity and group characteristics	Lose original identity and group characteristics
Valuable to join the larger society	Integration	Assimilation
Not valuable to join the larger society	Separation	Marginalization

Note: The preferences refer to the individual's preferences for him- or herself.
Source: Based on Berry, 1997, with permission from John Wiley & Sons.

LEADER IN THE FIELD

John Berry (b. 1939) grew up in Canada but completed his PhD at the University of Edinburgh in the UK. His dissertation was focused on the cultural adaptations of the Inuit and Cree nations to differing environments in Northern Canada. This led to his early formulation of eco-cultural theory. He was a founding member of the International Association for Cross-Cultural Psychology and was the Principal Editor of the second edition of the *Handbook of Cross-Cultural Psychology*. He has also co-authored the first published textbook for the field of cross-cultural psychology as a whole. During the past three decades he has developed his model of acculturation processes, supervised the dissertations of many researchers now active in this field and assisted the Canadian government in the development of their policies relating to immigration.

Differences 15.2 to see how acculturation attitudes have most often been measured.

The conditions predisposing positive outcomes for intergroup contact have been discussed in Chapter 14. In relation to migration, particularly critical groups are the first- and second-generation children of immigrants, who experience socialization both by their family of origin and by the culture of the nation within which they have been born. First-generation children arrive as migrants, while second-generation children are born within their new nation or residence. Berry, Phinney, Sam, and Vedder (2006) conducted a cross-sectional survey of more than 5000 first- and second-generation adolescents in 13 nations. Their European samples included both former colonial nations (France, Germany, The Netherlands, Portugal and the UK) and other nations that have recently received many migrants (Finland, Norway and Sweden). In each nation, one or more ethnic minorities were sampled, as well as a sample of non-migrants. Scores for better migrant adjustment showed a weak but positive association with the integration mode. For instance, those scoring high on integration were higher on measures of positive adjustment such as life satisfaction and self-esteem, and lower on psychological problems, poor school adjustment and behaviour problems, than those who scored lower on integration. These results were much more strongly affected by respondents' specific ethnicity than by the particular host nation within which they were living. For instance, as noted before, apart from work relations, Turkish migrants quite often favour separation rather than integration. Consequently, they score higher on adjustment in nations where there is a substantial Turkish community. Conversely, Vietnamese migrants favour integration and their adjustment is therefore less influenced by the presence or absence of other Vietnamese.

One reason why the relationship between the integration mode of adjustment and measures of adjustment is not stronger may be because the concept of integration is

too broadly defined. Favouring integration implies a **bicultural identity** and there are differing ways of sustaining a bicultural identity, some of which may have better consequences than others. An immigrant or any person who is descended from more than one cultural background has two cultural identities available. **Bicultural identity integration** is present when a person sees their alternate identities as compatible with one another. To explore this issue, look now at Research Close-Up 15.4.

> **bicultural identity** seeing oneself as having simultaneous membership of two culturally-distinct groups.

> **bicultural identity integration** present when a person sees their alternate identities as compatible with one another.

The priming study by Benet-Martínez, Leu, Lee, and Morris (2002) (see Research Close-Up 15.4) was conducted in the US, but there is no reason to expect differing results with European respondents. For instance, Verkuyten and Pouliasi (2002) compared the impact of priming on bicultural Greek children growing up in the Netherlands with control groups of monocultural Greek children living in Greece and Dutch children living in the Netherlands. The bicultural children were primed either by showing them Dutch icons (e.g., windmills, the national flag) or by showing them Greek icons (e.g., the Acropolis, the national flag). They were then presented with a series of tasks in which they had to provide reasons for events that had occurred.

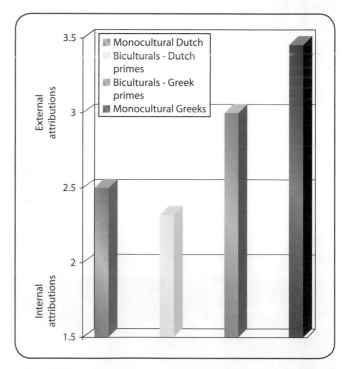

FIGURE 15.21 *Attributions made by primed and unprimed Greek and Dutch children.*

Source: Based on Verkuyten & Pouliasi, 2002, with permission from SAGE Publications.

INDIVIDUAL DIFFERENCES 15.2

ATTITUDES TO ACCULTURATION

Below are the items used in the research by Berry et al. (2006). You can complete them whether you are a member of an ethnic minority or a member of the majority in your nation. If you are a minority member, 'ethnic' in the items below refers to your own group. If you are a majority group member, take the phrase 'ethnic group' as referring to the most salient ethnic minorities within your nation. 'National' refers to your nation. Please indicate how much you agree or disagree with each of the statements, using the response scale presented below.

1. I feel that [ethnic group] should adapt to national cultural traditions and not maintain those of their own.
2. I would rather marry an [ethnic] than a national.
3. I feel that [ethnic group] should maintain their own cultural traditions but also adapt to those of this nation.
4. I would rather marry a national than an [ethnic].
5. I would be just as willing to marry a national as an [ethnic].
6. I feel that it is not important for [ethnic group] either to maintain their own cultural traditions or to adapt to those of this nation.
7. I feel that [ethnic group] should maintain their own cultural traditions and not adapt to those of this nation.
8. I would not like to marry either a national or an [ethnic].
9. It is more important to me to be fluent in [ethnic language] than in the national language.
10. It is more important to me to be fluent in the national language than in [ethnic language].
11. It is important to me to be fluent in both the national language and [ethnic language].
12. It is not important to me to be fluent either in [ethnic language] or the national language.

13. I prefer social activities that involve both national members and [ethnic] members.
14. I prefer to have only national friends.
15. I prefer to have only [ethnic] friends.
16. I prefer social activities that involve nationals only.
17. I prefer to have both national and [ethnic] friends.
18. I don't want to attend either national or [ethnic] activities.
19. I prefer social activities that involve [ethnic group] members only.
20. I don't want to have either national or [ethnic] friends.

1 = Strongly disagree
2 = Somewhat disagree
3 = Not sure/neutral
4 = Somewhat agree
5 = Strongly agree

Calculate your scores as follows: assimilation is the mean of items 1, 4, 10, 14 and 16. Integration is the mean of items 3, 5, 11, 13 and 17. Separation is the mean of items 2, 7, 9, 15 and 19. Marginalization is the mean of items 6, 8, 12, 18 and 20. In the sample of Berry et al. as a whole, mean scores for minority respondents were 2.20 for assimilation, 3.93 for integration, 2.59 for separation and 1.78 for marginalization. Means for majority members were 2.59, 3.69, 2.37 and 2.28 respectively. Thus, on average, as in other studies, all respondents favoured integration, but minority respondents did so more strongly, while majority respondents also favoured assimilation.

Source: This scale reproduced from Berry et al. (2006). Immigrant youth in cultural transition: Acculturation, identity and adaptation across national contexts.

The first task also used the video of a fish swimming ahead of a group of other fish developed by Morris and Peng (1994), described earlier in this chapter. Later questions concerned reasons for the behaviour of hypothetical schoolchildren. For example, one question was, 'One day a child is late for school. What could be the reason?' The results of these various tasks were combined to yield an index of internal versus external attribution. As Figure 15.21 shows, the researchers found that those children who had been primed with Dutch icons made more internal attributions, while those children primed with Greek icons made more external attributions. The figure also shows the means for attributions made by the monocultural Dutch and the monocultural Greek children. The difference between the mean for the Dutch children and the bicultural people who had been primed with Dutch icons was not significant. Nor was the difference between the mean for monocultural Greek children and the bicultural

people who had been primed with Greek icons. Thus, the full extent of the difference between the data from more individualistic Dutch and from the more collectivistic Greeks was reproduced through experimental priming.

Summary

Increased wealth and population mobility have been associated with global changes in values toward increased individualism and post-modern values. However, these changes are directional rather than converging on the values of any pre-existing culture. Migration and intermarriage are creating increasing numbers of bicultural individuals. Bicultural identity integration appears to be associated with optimal acculturation. Experimental priming of bicultural people is creating opportunities to integrate cultural perspectives with other areas of research in social psychology.

BICULTURAL IDENTITY INTEGRATION   RESEARCH CLOSE-UP 15.4

Benet-Martínez, V. L., Leu, J., Lee, F., & Morris, M. W. (2002). Negotiating biculturalism: Cultural frame switching in biculturals with oppositional versus compatible cultural identities. *Journal of Cross-Cultural Psychology, 33*, 492–516.

Research question

Given the increasing frequency of biculturalism in many nations, Benet-Martínez and her colleagues were interested in alternate ways of handling bicultural identities. How does someone think and feel if they perceive their identities as incompatible with one another? Do compatible identities facilitate cultural integration? Can experimental methods illuminate these issues? The authors tested two main hypotheses about how individuals who are low versus high on identity integration respond when faced with an attribution task. First, because their identities are not in conflict, those who are high on identity integration were expected to respond to a US prime by making the more internal attributions that are typical of Americans, and to a Chinese prime by making the more external attributions that are typical of Chinese. Second, and in contrast, because of the identity conflict that they experience, respondents low in identity integration were expected to respond defensively, making external attributions in response to the US primes and internal attributions in response to the Chinese primes.

Design and procedure

The study used a 2 (type of identity integration) × 2 (type of prime) between-subjects design. Participants were 176 young Chinese Americans (mean age 16) who had all lived in China for at least five years and in the US for at least another five years. The sample was split between those who were low or high on bicultural identity integration (BII). The primes were either American (e.g., Mickey Mouse, a cowboy, the Statue of Liberty); Chinese (e.g., the Summer Palace in Beijing, a rice farmer, the Great Wall); or control items unrelated to culture. Participants first received one of these primes, then viewed a series of videos showing a fish moving ahead of a group of other fish; this task was first used by Morris and Peng (1994), and was discussed earlier in this chapter. They were asked to rate the extent to which 'the one fish is being influenced by the group' (e.g., being chased, teased or pressured by others) and to rate the extent to which 'the one fish is influenced by some internal trait' (such as independence, personal objective or leadership). Next, each participant was asked to make a single rating of the extent to which they perceived themself as a Chinese who lives in America, rather than as a Chinese American. This provided a measure distinguishing between low and high bicultural identity integration. Finally, participants also completed the measure of Berry's four acculturation modes (see Individual Differences 15.2).

Results

The predictions were supported. The left-hand side of Figure 15.22 indicates the results for respondents with low bicultural identity integration (BII). These data show the reverse pattern of attributions from those that were found by Morris and Peng (1994). With the Chinese primes these participants made more internal attributions, and with the American primes they made more external attributions. In contrast, the results for the respondents with high BII, shown on the right of the figure, replicate the results of Morris and Peng, as shown earlier in Figure 15.9. Despite the differing effects for high and low identity integration, both groups scored equally high on Berry's measure of integration.

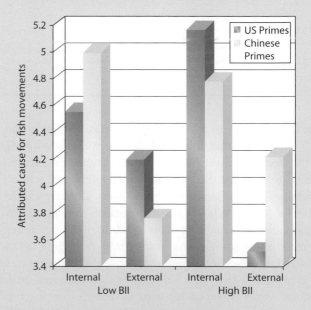

FIGURE 15.22 *Attributions made by bicultural people high and low in identity integration.*

Note: BII denotes bicultural identity integration.
Source: Based on Benet-Martínez et al., 2002, with permission from SAGE Publications.

Implications

This study has two important implications. First, the concept of bicultural identity integration can advance our understanding of the processes of acculturation. Berry's (1997) favoured concept of the integration mode of acculturation is broadly defined and can encompass quite different types of person. Someone with low bicultural integration is in some ways like a person who has a kind of split personality. Whichever personal identity they choose to express at a particular time, they place themselves on the outside of the other identity. The study by Benet-Martínez et al. supports the view that low BII people feel the need to compensate for that 'outsideness'. So, a low BII Chinese American responds to a Chinese prime by emphasizing their Americanness, and to an American prime by emphasizing their Chineseness. A high BII person does not feel the need to do this, and that facilitates their relations with others. For instance, in later studies by the same group, Mok, Morris, Benet-Martínez, and Karakitapoğlu-Aygün (2007) have shown that high BII Chinese Americans tend to have networks of friends of varying ethnicity, many of whom also know each other. Those with low BII have two separate networks of friends who do not know each other.

A second implication of this study is that it extends the potential of experimental priming as a way of understanding cultural aspects of social psychology. Bicultural people may have more ready access to alternate identities than monocultural people, and this makes them distinctively useful to researchers. Furthermore, the effects found from priming studies with bicultural people may be parallel to those found when comparing mean differences between monocultural groups. If the effects are found to be parallel, then the prospects for establishing causal links between the various factors involved in the creation and maintenance of cultures are bright.

CHAPTER SUMMARY

- *What is culture and why should we study it?* A culture is a social system that is characterized by the shared meanings that are attributed to people and events by its members. Nations around the world have cultures that are sufficiently different that social psychological studies may yield different results in different locations.

- *What are cognitive styles and how are they related to culture?* Analytic cognitive styles are more prevalent within individualistic nations, while holistic cognitive styles are more typical in collectivist cultures. Environmental challenges and contemporary languages and norms serve to create and sustain these differences.

- *Can the ways in which we think about ourselves explain cultural variations in behaviour?* Individual-level measures of independent and interdependent self-construal provide a focused way of testing explanations for the cultural differences in social behaviour that have been found. We discussed the case of the student Wen Hua at the start of this chapter. If we were to measure her self-construal and values, we would probably find that she scores high on interdependence and endorses embeddedness, hierarchy and mastery values.

- *How do social relations and relationship formation vary across different cultural contexts?* Members of collectivist cultures prioritize long-term ingroup relationships. They distinguish more sharply the ways that they behave in different types of relationship than do members of individualist cultures. In a collectivist culture, even intimate relationships between individuals are construed in terms of their relevance to group identities. Wen Hua finds it difficult to make new relationships because she is no longer in touch with her ingroup.

- *How does collectivism affect group behaviours?* In a collectivist culture, identity is derived from group memberships. To sustain that group's harmony and integrity, Wen Hua will work hard, communicate indirectly, respect status and conform more. In uncertain circumstances, Wen Hua seeks guidance from the senior figure and shows respect by working hard and not showing dissent.

- *How does collectivism affect relations with outgroups?* In a collectivist culture, group memberships are not open to change. An individual will therefore seek to enhance the esteem of his or her group by finding ways to compare it favourably with others. When interacting with people from outgroups, they will defend themselves against any threat to their group's honour.

- *Will globalization mean the end of cultural differences?* Greater prosperity and mobility have induced a global trend toward post-modern values, but differences between cultural groups are persisting. Migrant acculturation and intermarriage are creating an increasing proportion of bicultural people. Experimental priming of bicultural people provides a way in which investigation of cultural differences can directly enrich the validity of the findings of mainstream social psychology.

SUGGESTIONS FOR FURTHER READING

Chiu, C.-Y., & Hong, Y.-Y. (2006). *Social psychology of culture*. New York: Psychology Press. This text emphasizes studies that use experimental methods and make comparisons between North Americans and East Asians.

Heine, S. J. (2012). *Cultural psychology* (2nd ed.). New York: Norton. This recent text also emphasizes comparisons between North America and East Asia.

Hofstede, G. H. (2001). *Culture's consequences: Comparing values, behaviors, institutions and organizations across nations* (2nd ed.). Thousand Oaks, CA: Sage. Detailed description of Hofstede's pioneering project.

International Association for Cross-Cultural Psychology (not dated). *Online readings in psychology and culture*. Retrieved from http://scholarworks.gvsu.edu/orpc. Free access to 100 articles discussing all areas of cross-cultural psychological research, with contributions from many of the leading figures in the field.

Kitayama, S., & Cohen, D. (Eds.). (2007). *Handbook of cultural psychology*. New York: Guilford. Interdisciplinary perspectives on the evolution of culture.

Smith, P. B., & Best, D. L. (Eds.). (2009). *Cross-cultural psychology* (four volumes). London: Sage. Seventy-three of the most influential papers in the field reprinted in full.

Smith, P. B., Fischer, R., Vignoles, V.L., & Bond, M. H. (2013). *Understanding social psychology across cultures: Engaging with others in a changing world*. London: Sage. This text develops much more fully the perspective taken in the present chapter.

Ward, C. A., Bochner, S., & Furnham, A. (2001). *The psychology of culture shock*. Hove, UK: Routledge. This is the leading textbook that addresses the issues of migration, acculturation and intercultural contact.

References

Aaker, J. L. (1997). Dimensions of brand personality. *Journal of Marketing Research, 34,* 347–356.

Aaker, J. L., Benet-Martínez, V., & Garolera, J. (2001). Consumption symbols as carriers of culture: A study of Japanese and Spanish brand personality constructs. *Journal of Personality and Social Psychology, 81,* 492–508.

Aarts, H., & Dijksterhuis, A. (2000). Habits as knowledge structures: Automaticity in goal-directed behavior. *Journal of Personality and Social Psychology, 78,* 53–63.

Abbey, A., Zawacki, T., Buck, P. O., Clinton, A. M., & McAuslan, P. (2004). Sexual assault and alcohol consumption: What do we know about their relationship and what types of research are still needed? *Aggression and Violent Behavior, 9,* 271–303.

Abelson, R. P. (1995). Attitude extremity. In R. E. Petty & J. A. Krosnick (Eds.), *Attitude strength: Antecedents and consequences* (pp. 25–42). Mahwah, NJ: Erlbaum.

Aberson, C. L., Healy, M., & Romero, V. (2000). Ingroup bias and self-esteem: A meta-analysis. *Personality and Social Psychology Review, 4,* 157–173.

Abrams, D., & Hogg, M. A. (1988). Comments on the motivational status of self-esteem in social identity and intergroup discrimination. *European Journal of Social Psychology, 18,* 317–334.

Abramson, L. Y., Metalsky, G. I., & Alloy, L. B. (1989). Hopelessness depression: A theory-based subtype of depression. *Psychological Review, 96,* 358–372.

Abramson, L. Y., Seligman, M. E., & Teasdale, J. D. (1978). Learned helplessness in humans: Critique and reformulation. *Journal of Abnormal and Social Psychology, 87,* 49–74.

Adair, W. L., & Brett, J. M. (2005). The negotiation dance: Time culture and behavioural sequences in negotiation. *Organization Science, 16,* 33–51.

Adams, J. S. (1963). Towards an understanding of inequity. *Journal of Abnormal and Social Psychology, 67,* 422–436.

Adorno, T. W., Frenkel-Brunswik, E., Levinson, D. J., & Sanford, R. N. (1950). *The authoritarian personality.* New York: Harper.

Aguirre-Rodriguez, A., Bosnjak, M., & Sirgy, M. J. (2012). Moderators of the self-congruity-effect on consumer decision-making: A meta-analysis. *Journal of Business Research, 65,* 1179–1188.

Aime, F., & Van Dyne, L. (2010). Bringing social structure to both sides of an issue: How proximal and distal ties interact with minority and majority positions to affect influence in workgroups. In R. Martin & M. Hewstone (Eds.), *Minority influence and innovation: Antecedents, processes and consequences* (pp. 313–340). Hove, UK: Psychology Press.

Ainsworth, M. D. S., Bell, S. M., & Stayton, D. (1974). Infant–mother attachment and social development. In M. P. M. Richards (Ed.), *The integration of the child into a social world* (pp. 99–135). London: Cambridge University Press.

Ajzen, I. (1991). The theory of planned behavior. *Organizational Behavior and Human Decision Processes, 50,* 179–211.

Ajzen, I., & Fishbein, M. (1977). Attitude-behavior relations: A theoretical analysis and review of empirical research. *Psychological Bulletin, 84,* 888–918.

Ajzen, I., & Madden, T. J. (1986). Prediction of goal-directed behavior: Attitudes, intentions, and perceived behavioral control. *Journal of Experimental Social Psychology, 22,* 453–474.

Akhtar, S., & Thomson, J. A., Jr. (1982). Overview: Narcissistic personality disorder. *American Journal of Psychiatry, 139,* 12–20.

Albarracín, D., Johnson, B. T., Fishbein, M., & Muellerleile, P. A. (2001). Theories of reasoned action and planned behavior as models of condom use: A meta-analysis. *Psychological Bulletin, 127,* 142–161.

Albarracín, D., Johnson, B. T., & Zanna, M. P. (Eds.). (2005). *Handbook of attitudes.* Mahwah, NJ: Erlbaum.

Albarracín, D., & Wyer, R. S., Jr. (2000). The cognitive impact of past behavior: Influences on beliefs, attitudes, and future behavioral decisions. *Journal of Personality and Social Psychology, 79,* 5–22.

Alberts, H. J. E. M., Martijn, C., & De Vries, N. K. (2011). Fighting self-control failure: Overcoming ego depletion by increasing self-awareness. *Journal of Experimental Social Psychology, 47,* 58–62.

Aldag, R. J., & Fuller, S. R. (1993). Beyond fiasco: A reappraisal of the groupthink phenomenon and a new model of group decision processes. *Psychological Bulletin, 113,* 533–552.

Alford, C. F. (2001). *Whistleblowers: broken lives and organizational power.* Ithaca, NY and London: Cornell University Press.

Alicke, M. D. (1985). Global self-evaluation as determined by the desirability and controllability of trait adjectives. *Journal of Personality and Social Psychology, 49,* 1621–1630.

Alicke, M. D., & Govorun, O. (2005). The better-than-average effect. In M. D. Alicke, D. A. Dunning, & J. I. Krueger (Eds.), *The self in social judgment* (pp. 85–106). New York: Psychology Press.

Alicke, M. D., & Sedikides, C. (2009). Self-enhancement and self-protection: What they are and what they do. In W. Stroebe & M. Hewstone (Eds.), *European review of social psychology* (Vol. 20, pp. 1–48). Hove, UK: Psychology Press.

Allen, V. L. (1965). Situational factors in conformity. In L. Berkowitz (Ed.), *Advances in experimental social psychology* (Vol. 2, pp. 133–175). New York: Academic Press.

Allen, V. L. (1975). Social support for nonconformity. In L. Berkowitz (Ed.), *Advances in experimental social psychology* (Vol. 8, pp. 1–43). New York: Academic Press.

Allen, V. L., & Levine, J. M. (1971). Social support and conformity: The role of independent assessment of reality. *Journal of Experimental Social Psychology, 7,* 48–58.

Allport, F. H. (1919). Behavior and experiment in social psychology. *Journal of Abnormal Psychology, 14,* 297–306.

Allport, F. H. (1924). *Social psychology.* Boston, MA: Houghton Mifflin.

Allport, G. W. (1935). Attitudes. In C. Murchison (Ed.), *Handbook of social psychology* (pp. 798–844). Worcester, MA: Clark University Press.

Allport, G. W. (1954a). The historical background of modern social psychology. In G. Lindzey (Ed.), *Handbook of social psychology* (2nd ed., Vol. 1, pp. 3–56). Reading, MA: Addison-Wesley.

Allport, G. W. (1954b). *The nature of prejudice.* Reading, MA: Addison-Wesley.

Allport, G. W. (1961). *Pattern and growth in personality.* Oxford: Holt, Rinehart and Winston.

Allport, G. W. (1968). *The person in psychology: Selected essays.* Boston, MA: Beacon.

Alnuaimi, O. A., Robert, L. P., & Maruping, L. M. (2010). Team size, dispersion, and social loafing in technology-supported teams: A perspective on the theory of moral disengagement. *Journal of Management Information Systems, 27,* 203–230.

Alonso-Arbiol, I., Balluerka, N., Shaver, P. R., & Gillath, O. (2008). Psychometric properties of the Spanish and American versions of the ECR Adult Attachment Questionnaire: A comparative study. *European Journal of Psychological Assessment, 24,* 9–13.

Altemeyer, B. (1981). *Right-wing authoritarianism.* Winnipeg, Canada: University of Manitoba Press.

Altemeyer, B. (1998). The other 'authoritarian personality'. In M. P. Zanna (Ed.), *Advances in experimental social psychology* (Vol. 30, pp. 47–92). San Diego, CA: Academic Press.

Altman, I., & Taylor, D. A. (1973). *Social penetration: The development of interpersonal relationships.* New York: Holt, Rinehart and Winston.

Alvaro, E. M., & Crano, W. D. (1997). Indirect minority influence: Evidence for leniency in source evaluation and counterargumentation. *Journal of Personality and Social Psychology, 72,* 949–964.

Alwin, D. F., Cohen, R. L., & Newcomb, T. M. (1991). *Political attitudes over the life span: The Bennington women after fifty years.* Madison, WI: University of Wisconsin Press.

Amabile, T. M. (1996). *Creativity in context: Update to the social psychology of creativity.* Boulder, CO: Westview.

Amato, P. R., & Afifi, T. D. (2006). Feeling caught between parents: Adult children's relations with parents and subjective well-being. *Journal of Marriage and Family, 68,* 222–235.

American Psychiatric Association. (1994). *Diagnostic and statistical manual of mental disorders* (4th ed.). Washington, DC: Author.

American Psychological Association. (2010). *Ethical principles for psychologists and code of conduct* (2002, amended June 1, 2010).

Amichai-Hamburger, Y., & McKenna, K. Y. A. (2006). The contact hypothesis reconsidered: Interacting via the Internet. *Journal of Computer-Mediated Communication, 11,* 825–843.

Amir, Y. (1976). The role of intergroup contact in change of prejudice and intergroup relations. In P. A. Katz (Ed.), *Towards the elimination of racism* (pp. 245–308). New York: Pergamon.

Amir, Y., & Sharon, I. (1987). Are social psychological laws cross-culturally valid? *Journal of Cross-Cultural Psychology, 18,* 383–470.

Amodio, D. M. (2008). The social neuroscience of intergroup relations. In W. Stroebe & M. Hewstone (Eds.), *European review of social psychology* (Vol. 19, pp. 1–54). Hove, UK: Psychology Press.

Amodio, D. M. (2010). Can neuroscience advance social psychological theory? Social neuroscience for the behavioral social psychologist. *Social Cognition, 28,* 695–716.

Amodio, D. M., & Devine, P. G. (2006). Stereotyping and evaluation in implicit race bias: Evidence for independent constructs and unique effects on behavior. *Journal of Personality and Social Psychology, 91,* 652–661.

Amodio, D. M., Devine, P. G., & Harmon-Jones, E. (2008). Individual differences in the regulation of intergroup bias: The role of conflict monitoring and neural signals for control. *Journal of Personality and Social Psychology, 94,* 60–74.

Amodio, D. M., & Frith, C. D. (2006). Meeting of minds: The medial frontal cortex and social cognition. *Nature Reviews Neuroscience, 7,* 268–277.

Andersen, S. M., & Chen, S. (2002). The relational self: An interpersonal social-cognitive theory. *Psychological Review, 109,* 619–645.

Anderson, C. A. (1989). Temperature and aggression: Ubiquitous effects of heat on occurrence of human violence. *Psychological Bulletin, 106,* 74–96.

Anderson, C. A. (2001). Heat and violence. *Current Directions in Psychological Science, 10,* 33–38.

Anderson, C. A., Anderson, K. B., Dorr, N., DeNeve, K. M., & Flanagan, M. (2000). Temperature and aggression. In M. P. Zanna (Ed.), *Advances in experimental social psychology* (Vol. 32, pp. 63–133). New York: Academic Press.

Anderson, C. A., Berkowitz, L., Donnerstein, E., Huesmann, L. R., Johnson, J. D., Linz, D., ... Wartella, E. (2003). The influence of media violence on youth. *Psychological Science in the Public Interest, 4*, 81–110.

Anderson, C. A., & Bushman, B. J. (1997). External validity of 'trivial' experiments: The case of laboratory aggression. *Review of General Psychology, 1*, 19–41.

Anderson, C. A., & Bushman, B. J. (2002). Media violence and the American public revisited. *American Psychologist, 57*, 448–450.

Anderson, C. A., Bushman, B. J., & Groom, R. W. (1997). Hot years and serious and deadly assault: Empirical tests of the heat hypothesis. *Journal of Personality and Social Psychology, 73*, 1213–1223.

Anderson, C. A., & Dill, K. E. (2000). Video games and aggressive thoughts, feelings, and behavior in the laboratory and in life. *Journal of Personality and Social Psychology, 78*, 772–790.

Anderson, C. A., Gentile, D. A., & Buckley, K. E. (2007). *Violent video game effects on children and adolescents: Theory, research, and public policy.* New York: Oxford University Press.

Anderson, C. A., Shibuya, A., Ihori, N., Swing, E. L., Bushman, B. J., Sakamoto, A., ... Saleem, M. (2010). Violent video game effects on aggression, empathy, and prosocial behavior in Eastern and Western countries: A meta-analytic review. *Psychological Bulletin, 136*, 151–173.

Anderson, N. B. (Ed.). (2009). Obedience – then and now [Special issue]. *American Psychologist, 64*(1).

Anderson, N. H. (1981). *Foundations of information integration theory.* New York: Academic Press.

Archer, J. (2000). Sex differences in aggression between heterosexual partners: A meta-analytic review. *Psychological Bulletin, 126*, 651–680.

Archer, J. (2004). Sex differences in aggression in real-world settings: A meta-analytic review. *Review of General Psychology, 8*, 291–322.

Archer, J., Birring, S. S., & Wu, F. C. W. (1998). The association between testosterone and aggression in young men: Empirical findings and a meta-analysis. *Aggressive Behavior, 24*, 411–420.

Archer, J., & Coyne, S. M. (2005). An integrated review of indirect, relational, and social aggression. *Personality and Social Psychology Review, 9*, 212–230.

Archer, J., & Lloyd, B. B. (2002). *Sex and gender* (2nd ed.). New York: Cambridge University Press.

Archer, J., & McDaniel, P. (1995). Violence and gender: Differences and similarities across societies. In B. R. Ruback & N. A. Weiner (Eds.), *Interpersonal violent behaviors: Social and cultural aspects* (pp. 63–87). New York: Springer.

Arends-Tóth, J., & Van de Vijver, F. J. R. (2003). Multiculturalism and acculturation: Views of Dutch and Turkish Dutch. *European Journal of Social Psychology, 33*, 249–266.

Arendt, H. (1963). *Eichmann in Jerusalem: A report on the banality of evil.* New York: Viking.

Argyle, M. (1991). *Cooperation: The basis of sociability.* London: Routledge.

Armitage, C. J., & Conner, M. (2001). Efficacy of the theory of planned behaviour: A meta-analytic review. *British Journal of Social Psychology, 40*, 471–499.

Armor, D. A., & Taylor, S. E. (1998). Situated optimism: Specific outcome expectancies and self-regulation. In M. P. Zanna (Ed.), *Advances in experimental social psychology* (Vol. 30, pp. 309–379). San Diego, CA: Academic Press.

Arnold, M. B. (1960). *Emotion and personality (Volume 1): Psychological aspects.* New York: Columbia University Press.

Aron, A., & Aron, E. N. (1986). *Love and the expansion of self: Understanding attraction and satisfaction.* Washington, DC: Hemisphere.

Aron, A., Aron, E. N., Tudor, M., & Nelson, G. (1991). Close relationships as including other in the self. *Journal of Personality and Social Psychology, 60*, 241–253.

Aron, A., Paris, M., & Aron, E. N. (1995). Falling in love: Prospective studies of self-concept change. *Journal of Personality and Social Psychology, 69*, 1102–1112.

Aronson, E. (1969). The theory of cognitive dissonance: A current perspective. In L. Berkowitz (Ed.), *Advances in experimental social psychology* (Vol. 4, pp. 1–34). New York: Academic Press.

Aronson, E., Ellsworth, P. C., Carlsmith, J. M., & Gonzales, M. H. (1990). *Methods of research in social psychology* (2nd ed.). New York: McGraw-Hill.

Aronson, E., & Mills, J. (1959). The effect of severity of initiation on liking for a group. *Journal of Abnormal and Social Psychology, 59*, 177–181.

Aronson, E., & Patnoe, S. (1997). *The jigsaw classroom: Building cooperation in the classroom* (2nd ed.). New York: Longman.

Aronson, E., Wilson, T. D., & Brewer, M. B. (1998). Experimentation in social psychology. In D. T. Gilbert, S. T. Fiske, & G. Lindzey (Eds.), *Handbook of social psychology* (4th ed., Vol. 1, pp. 99–142). Boston, MA: McGraw-Hill.

Asch, S. E. (1946). Forming impressions of personality. *Journal of Abnormal and Social Psychology, 41*, 258–290.

Asch, S. E. (1951). Effects of group pressure upon the modification and distortion of judgments. In H. Guetzkow (Ed.), *Groups, leadership and men* (pp. 177–190). Pittsburgh, PA: Carnegie.

Asch, S. E. (1955). Opinions and social pressure. *Scientific American, 193*, 31–35.

Asch, S. E. (1956). Studies of independence and conformity: A minority of one against a unanimous majority. *Psychological Monographs, 70*, 1–70.

Asch, S. E. (1987). *Social psychology.* New York: Oxford University Press.

Atkins, C. J., Kaplan, R. M., & Toshima, M. T. (1991). Close relationships in the epidemiology of cardiovascular disease. In W. H. Jones & D. Perlman (Eds.), *Advances in personal relationships* (Vol. 3, pp. 207–231). London: Jessica Kingsley.

Averill, J. R., Malmstrom, E. J., Koriat, A., & Lazarus, R. S. (1972). Habituation to complex emotional stimuli. *Journal of Abnormal Psychology, 80*, 20–28.

Avolio, B. J. (1999). *Full leadership development: Building the vital forces in organizations.* Thousand Oaks, CA: Sage.

Ayduk, O., & Kross, E. (2008). Enhancing the pace of recovery: Self-distanced analysis of negative experiences reduces blood pressure reactivity. *Psychological Science, 19*, 229–231.

Ayduk, O., & Kross, E. (2010). From a distance: Implications of spontaneous self-distancing for adaptive self-reflection. *Journal of Personality and Social Psychology, 98*, 809–829.

Back, M. D., Schmukle, S. C., & Egloff, B. (2008). Becoming friends by chance. *Psychological Science, 19*, 439–440.

Baer, J., Kaufman, J. C., & Baumeister, R. F. (2008). *Are we free?: Psychology and free will.* New York: Oxford University Press.

Bakeman, R. (2000). Behavioral observation and coding. In H. T. Reis & C. M. Judd (Eds.), *Handbook of research methods in social and personality psychology* (pp. 138–159). New York: Cambridge University Press.

Baker, S. M., & Petty, R. E. (1994). Majority and minority influence: Source-position imbalance as a determinant of message scrutiny. *Journal of Personality and Social Psychology, 67*, 5–19.

Baldwin, M. W. (1992). Relational schemas and the processing of social information. *Psychological Bulletin, 112*, 461–484.

Baldwin, M. W., Carrell, S. E., & Lopez, D. F. (1990). Priming relational schemas: My advisor and the Pope are watching me from the back of my mind. *Journal of Experimental Social Psychology, 26*, 435–454.

Baldwin, M. W., & Holmes, J. G. (1987). Salient private audiences and awareness of the self. *Journal of Personality and Social Psychology, 52*, 1087–1098.

Bales, R. F. (1950). *Interaction process analysis: A method for the study of small groups.* Cambridge, MA: Addison-Wesley.

Bales, R. F. (1953). The equilibrium problem in small groups. In T. Parsons, R. F. Bales, & E. A. Shils (Eds.), *Working papers in the theory of action* (pp. 111–161). New York: Free Press.

Bales, R. F., & Slater, P. E. (1955). Role differentiation in small decision-making groups. In T. Parsons & R. F. Bales (Eds.), *Family, socialization, and interaction process* (pp. 259–306). Glencoe, IL: Free Press.

Banaji, M. R., & Hardin, C. D. (1996). Automatic stereotyping. *Psychological Science, 7*, 136–141.

Bandura, A. (1977a). Self-efficacy: Toward a unifying theory of behavioral change. *Psychological Review, 84*, 191–215.

Bandura, A. (1977b). *Social learning theory.* Englewood Cliffs, NJ: Prentice Hall.

Bandura, A. (1983). Psychological mechanisms of aggression. In R. G. Geen & E. I. Donnerstein (Eds.), *Aggression: Theoretical and empirical reviews* (Vol. 1, pp. 1–40). New York: Academic Press.

Bandura, A. (1999). Moral disengagement in the perpetration of inhumanities. *Personality and Social Psychology Review, 3*, 193–209.

Bandura, A., Ross, D., & Ross, S. A. (1961). Transmission of aggression through imitation of aggressive models. *Journal of Abnormal and Social Psychology, 63*, 575–582.

Bandura, A., Ross, D., & Ross, S. A. (1963). Vicarious reinforcement and imitative learning. *Journal of Abnormal and Social Psychology, 67*, 601–607.

Barber, J. P., Abrams, M. J., Connolly-Gibbons, M. B., Crits-Christoph, P., Barrett, M. S., Rynn, M., & Siqueland, L. (2005). Explanatory style change in supportive-expressive dynamic therapy. *Journal of Clinical Psychology, 61*, 257–268.

Bargh, J. A. (1982). Attention and automaticity in the processing of self-relevant information. *Journal of Personality and Social Psychology, 43*, 425–436.

Bargh, J. A. (1994). The four horsemen of automaticity: Awareness, intention, efficiency, and control in social cognition. In R. S. Wyer Jr. & T. K. Srull (Eds.), *Handbook of social cognition* (2nd ed., Vol. 1, pp. 1–40). Hillsdale, NJ: Erlbaum.

Bargh, J. A. (1999). The cognitive monster: The case against the controllability of automatic stereotype effects. In S. Chaiken & Y. Trope (Eds.), *Dual-process theories in social psychology* (pp. 361–382). New York: Guilford.

Bargh, J. A. (2005). Bypassing the will: Toward demystifying the nonconscious control of social behavior. In R. R. Hassin, J. S. Uleman, & J. A. Bargh (Eds.), *The new unconscious* (pp. 37–58). New York: Oxford University Press.

Bargh, J. A., & Chartrand, T. L. (2000). The mind in the middle: A practical guide to priming and automaticity research. In H. T. Reis & C. M. Judd (Eds.), *Handbook of research methods in social and personality psychology* (pp. 253–285). New York: Cambridge University Press.

Bargh, J. A., Chen, M., & Burrows, L. (1996). Automaticity of social behavior: Direct effects of trait construct and stereotype activation on action. *Journal of Personality and Social Psychology, 71*, 230–244.

Bargh, J. A., Gollwitzer, P. M., Lee-Chai, A., Barndollar, K., & Trötschel, R. (2001). The automated will: Nonconscious activation and pursuit of behavioral goals. *Journal of Personality and Social Psychology, 81*, 1014–1027.

Bargh, J. A., & Pietromonaco, P. (1982). Automatic information processing and social perception: The influence of trait information presented outside of conscious awareness on impression formation. *Journal of Personality and Social Psychology, 43*, 437–449.

Barlow, F. K., Paolini, S., Pedersen, A., Hornsey, M. J., Radke, H. R. M., Harwood, J., ... Sibley, C. G. (2012). The contact caveat: Negative contact predicts increased prejudice more than positive contact predicts reduced prejudice. *Personality and Social Psychology Bulletin, 38*, 1629–1643.

Barnett, O. W., Miller-Perrin, C. L., & Perrin, R. D. (2011). *Family violence across the lifespan* (2nd ed.). Thousand Oaks, CA: Sage.

Baron, R. A., & Richardson, D. R. (1994). *Human aggression* (2nd ed.). New York: Plenum.

Baron, R. M., & Boudreau, L. A. (1987). An ecological perspective on integrating personality and social psychology. *Journal of Personality and Social Psychology, 53*, 1222–1228.

Baron, R. M., & Kenny, D. A. (1986). The moderator-mediator variable distinction in social psychological research: Conceptual, strategic, and statistical considerations. *Journal of Personality and Social Psychology, 51*, 1173–1182.

Baron, R. S., & Kerr, N. L. (2003). *Group process, group decision, group action* (2nd ed.). Buckingham, UK: Open University Press.

Barry, C. T., Frick, P. J., Adler, K. K., & Grafeman, S. J. (2007). The predictive utility of narcissism among children and adolescents: Evidence for a distinction between adaptive and maladaptive narcissism. *Journal of Child and Family Studies, 16*, 508–521.

Barsade, S. G. (2002). The ripple effect: Emotional contagion and its influence on group behavior. *Administrative Science Quarterly, 47*, 644–675.

Bartholomew, K. (1990). Avoidance of intimacy: An attachment perspective. *Journal of Social and Personal Relationships, 7*, 147–178.

Bartholow, B. D., & Anderson, C. A. (2002). Effects of violent video games on aggressive behavior: Potential sex differences. *Journal of Experimental Social Psychology, 38*, 283–290.

Bartlett, F. C. (1932). *Remembering. A study in experimental and social psychology*. Cambridge, MA: Cambridge University Press.

Bass, B. M. (1985). *Leadership and performance beyond expectations*. New York: Free Press.

Bass, B. M. (2008). *The Bass handbook of leadership: Theory, research, and managerial applications* (4th ed.). New York: Free Press.

Bass, B. M., & Avolio, B. J. (1994). *Improving organizational effectiveness through transformational leadership*. Thousand Oaks, CA: Sage.

Bassili, J. N. (1993). Response latency versus certainty as indexes of the strength of voting intentions in a CATI survey. *Public Opinion Quarterly, 57*, 54–61.

Bassili, J. N. (1996). The 'how' and 'why' of response latency measurement in survey research. In N. Schwarz & S. Sudman (Eds.), *Answering questions: Methodology for determining cognitive and communicative processes in survey research* (pp. 319–346). San Francisco, CA: Jossey-Bass.

Bassili, J. N., & Fletcher, J. F. (1991). Response-time measurement in survey research: A method for CATI and a new look at nonattitudes. *Public Opinion Quarterly, 55*, 331–346.

Batson, C. D. (1991). *The altruism question: Toward a social-psychological answer*. Hillsdale, NJ: Erlbaum.

Batson, C. D. (1994). Why act for the public good? Four answers. *Personality and Social Psychology Bulletin, 20*, 603–610.

Batson, C. D. (2011). *Altruism in humans*. New York: Oxford University Press.

Batson, C., Batson, J., Singlsby, J., Harrell, K., Peekna, H., & Todd, R. (1991). Empathic joy and the empathy-altruism hypothesis. *Journal of Personality and Social Psychology, 61*, 413–426.

Batson, C. D., Duncan, B. D., Ackerman, P., Buckley, T., & Birch, K. (1981). Is empathic emotion a source of altruistic motivation? *Journal of Personality and Social Psychology, 40*, 290–302.

Baum, A. (1990). Stress, intrusive imagery, and chronic distress. *Health Psychology, 9*, 653–675.

Baumeister, R. F. (1984). Choking under pressure: Self-consciousness and paradoxical effects of incentives on skillful performance. *Journal of Personality and Social Psychology, 46*, 610–620.

Baumeister, R. F. (1990). Suicide as escape from self. *Psychological Review, 97*, 90–113.

Baumeister, R. F. (1991). *Escaping the self: Alcoholism, spirituality, masochism, and other flights from the burden of selfhood*. New York: Basic Books.

Baumeister, R. F., & Cairns, K. J. (1992). Repression and self-presentation: When audiences interfere with self-deceptive strategies. *Journal of Personality and Social Psychology, 62*, 851–862.

Baumeister, R. F., Campbell, J. D., Krueger, J. I., & Vohs, K. D. (2003). Does high self-esteem cause better performance, interpersonal success, happiness, or healthier lifestyles? *Psychological Science in the Public Interest, 4*, 1–44.

Baumeister, R. F., Catanese, K. R., & Wallace, H. M. (2002). Conquest by force: A narcissistic reactance theory of rape and sexual coercion. *Review of General Psychology, 6*, 92–135.

Baumeister, R. F., DeWall, C. N., Ciarocco, N. J., & Twenge, J. M. (2005). Social exclusion impairs self-regulation. *Journal of Personality and Social Psychology, 88*, 589–604.

Baumeister, R. F., & Leary, M. R. (1995). The need to belong: Desire for interpersonal attachments as a fundamental human motivation. *Psychological Bulletin, 117*, 497–529.

Baumeister, R. F., & Newman, L. S. (1994). Self-regulation of cognitive inference and decision processes. *Personality and Social Psychology Bulletin, 20*, 3–19.

Baumeister, R. F., Schmeichel, B. J., & Vohs, K. D. (2007). Self-regulation and the executive function: The self as controlling agent. In A. W. Kruglanski & E. T. Higgins (Eds.), *Social psychology: Handbook of basic principles* (2nd ed., pp. 516–539). New York: Guilford.

Baumeister, R. F., & Showers, C. J. (1986). A review of paradoxical performance effects: Choking under pressure in sports and mental tests. *European Journal of Social Psychology, 16,* 361–383.

Baumeister, R. F., Smart, L., & Boden, J. M. (1996). Relation of threatened egotism to violence and aggression: The dark side of high self-esteem. *Psychological Review, 103,* 5–33.

Baumeister, R. F., & Tierney, J. (2011). *Willpower: Rediscovering the greatest human strength.* New York: Penguin Press.

Baumeister, R. F., & Vohs, K. D. (2001). Narcissism as addiction to esteem. *Psychological Inquiry, 12,* 206–210.

Baumeister, R. F., & Vohs, K. D. (2007). Self-regulation, ego depletion, and motivation. *Social and Personality Psychology Compass, 1,* 115–128.

Baumrind, D. (1964). Some thoughts on ethics of research: After reading Milgram's 'Behavioral Study of Obedience'. *American Psychologist, 19,* 421–423.

Baxter, L. A. (1987). Self-disclosure and relationship disengagement. In V. J. Derlega & J. H. Berg (Eds.), *Self-disclosure: Theory, research, and therapy* (pp. 155–174). New York: Plenum.

Bazarova, N. N., Walther, J. B., & McLeod, P. L. (2012). Minority influence in virtual groups: A comparison of four theories of minority influence. *Communication Research, 39,* 295–316.

Beaman, A. L., Barnes, P. J., Klentz, B., & McQuirk, B. (1978). Increasing helping rates through information dissemination: Teaching pays. *Personality and Social Psychology Bulletin, 4,* 406–411.

Beaman, A. L., Cole, C. M., Preston, M., Klentz, B., & Steblay, N. M. (1983). Fifteen years of foot-in-the-door research: A meta-analysis. *Personality and Social Psychology Bulletin, 9,* 181–196.

Becker, E. (1973). *The denial of death.* New York: Free Press.

Becker, J. C., Glick, P., Ilic, M., & Bohner, G. (2011). Damned if she does, damned if she doesn't: Consequences of accepting versus confronting patronizing help for the female target and male actor. *European Journal of Social Psychology, 41,* 761–773.

Becker, J. C., Wright, S. C., Lubensky, M. E., & Zhou, S. (2013). Friend or ally: Whether cross-group contact undermines collective action depends what advantaged group members say (or don't say). *Personality and Social Psychology Bulletin, 39,* 442–455.

Beer, J. S. (2012). A social neuroscience perspective on the self. In M. R. Leary & J. P. Tangney (Eds.), *Handbook of self and identity* (2nd ed.). New York: Guilford.

Beer, J. S. (in press). Self-evaluation and self-knowledge. In S. T. Fiske & C. N. Macrae (Eds.), *Sage handbook of social cognition.* New York: Sage.

Beggan, J. K. (1992). On the social nature of nonsocial perception: The mere ownership effect. *Journal of Personality and Social Psychology, 62,* 229–237.

Beilock, S. L., & Carr, T. H. (2001). On the fragility of skilled performance: What governs choking under pressure? *Journal of Experimental Psychology: General, 130,* 701–725.

Belk, R. W. (1988). Possessions and the extended self. *Journal of Consumer Research, 15,* 139–168.

Belknap, J., Fisher, B. S., & Cullen, F. T. (1999). The development of a comprehensive measure of the sexual victimization of college women. *Violence Against Women, 5,* 185–214.

Bell, D. W., & Esses, V. M. (2002). Ambivalence and response amplification: A motivational perspective. *Personality and Social Psychology Bulletin, 28,* 1143–1152.

Bem, D. J. (1965). An experimental analysis of self-persuasion. *Journal of Experimental Social Psychology, 1,* 199–218.

Bem, D. J. (1972). Self-perception theory. In L. Berkowitz (Ed.), *Advances in experimental social psychology* (Vol. 6, pp. 1–62). New York: Academic Press.

Bendersky, C., & Hays, N. A. (2012). Status conflict in groups. *Organization Science, 23,* 323–340.

Benet-Martínez, V. L., Leu, J., Lee, F., & Morris, M. W. (2002). Negotiating biculturalism: Cultural frame switching in biculturals with oppositional versus compatible cultural identities. *Journal of Cross-Cultural Psychology, 33,* 492–516.

Bentall, R. P., & Fernyhough, C. (2008). Social predictors of psychotic experiences: Specificity and psychological mechanisms. *Schizophrenia Bulletin, 34,* 1012–1020.

Bentall, R. P., Kinderman, P., & Kaney, S. (1994). The self, attributional processes and abnormal beliefs: Towards a model of persecutory delusions. *Behaviour Research and Therapy, 32,* 331–341.

Ben-Ze'ev, A. (2004). *Love online: Emotion on the Internet.* Cambridge, MA: Cambridge University Press.

Berger, C. R., & Calabrese, R. J. (1975). Some explorations in initial interaction and beyond: Toward a developmental theory of interpersonal communication. *Human Communication Research, 1,* 99–112.

Berger, J., Rosenholtz, S. J., & Zelditch, M. (1980). Status organizing processes. *Annual Review of Sociology, 6,* 479–508.

Berkman, L. F., & Syme, S. L. (1979). Social networks, host resistance, and mortality: A nine year follow-up study of Alameda County residents. *American Journal of Epidemiology, 109,* 186–204.

Berkowitz, L. (1993). *Aggression: Its causes, consequences, and control.* Philadelphia, PA: Temple University Press.

Berkowitz, L. (1999). Evil is more than banal: Situationism and the concept of evil. *Personality and Social Psychology Review, 3,* 246–253.

Berkowitz, L., & LePage, A. (1967). Weapons as aggression-eliciting stimuli. *Journal of Personality and Social Psychology, 7,* 202–207.

Bermeitinger, C., Goelz, R., Johr, N., Neumann, M., Ecker, U. K. H., & Doerr, R. (2009). The hidden persuaders break into the tired brain. *Journal of Experimental Social Psychology, 45,* 320–326.

Berridge, K. C., & Winkielman, P. (2003). What is an unconscious emotion? The case for unconscious 'liking'. *Cognition and Emotion, 17,* 181–211.

Berry, D. S., & McArthur, L. Z. (1986). Perceiving character in faces: The impact of age-related craniofacial changes on social perception. *Psychological Bulletin, 100,* 3–18.

Berry, J. W. (1976). *Human ecology and cognitive style: Comparative studies in cultural and psychological adaptation.* New York: Wiley.

Berry, J. W. (1997). Immigration, acculturation and adaptation. *Applied Psychology: An International Review, 46,* 5–34.

Berry, J. W. et al. (Eds.). (1997). *Handbook of cross-cultural psychology* (2nd ed., 3 vols.). Boston: Allyn and Bacon.

Berry, J. W., Kim, U., Minde, T., & Mok, D. (1987). Comparative studies of acculturative stress. *International Migration Review, 21,* 491–511.

Berry, J. W., Phinney, J. S., Sam, D. L., & Vedder, P. (2006). *Immigrant youth in cultural transition: Acculturation, identity and adaptation across national contexts.* Mahwah, NJ: Erlbaum.

Berscheid, E. (1985). Interpersonal attraction. In G. Lindzey & E. Aronson (Eds.), *Handbook of social psychology* (3rd ed., Vol. 2, pp. 413–484). New York: Random House.

Berscheid, E. (1992). A glance back at a quarter century of social psychology. *Journal of Personality and Social Psychology, 63,* 525–533.

Berscheid, E., & Regan, P. C. (2005). *The psychology of interpersonal relationships.* Upper Saddle River, NJ: Prentice Hall.

Berscheid, E., & Reis, H. T. (1998). Attraction and close relationships. In D. T. Gilbert, S. T. Fiske, & G. Lindzey (Eds.), *Handbook of social psychology* (4th ed., Vol. 2, pp. 193–281). Boston, MA: McGraw-Hill.

Berscheid, E., Snyder, M., & Omoto, A. M. (1989). The Relationship Closeness Inventory: Assessing the closeness of interpersonal relationships. *Journal of Personality and Social Psychology, 57,* 792–807.

Berscheid, E., & Walster, E. (1974). Physical attractiveness. In L. Berkowitz (Ed.), *Advances in experimental social psychology* (Vol. 7, pp. 158–215). New York: Academic Press.

Bessière, K., Kiesler, S., Kraut, R., & Boneva, B. S. (2008). Effects of Internet use and social resources on changes in depression. *Information, Communication & Society, 11,* 47–70.

Bettencourt, B. A., Brewer, M. B., Croak, M. R., & Miller, N. (1992). Cooperation and the reduction of intergroup bias: The role of reward structure and social orientation. *Journal of Experimental Social Psychology, 28,* 301–319.

Bettencourt, B. A., & Miller, N. (1996). Gender differences in aggression as a function of provocation: A meta-analysis. *Psychological Bulletin, 119,* 422–447.

Betzig, L. (1989). Causes of conjugal dissolution: A cross-cultural study. *Current Anthropology, 30,* 654–676.

Bickman, L., & Kamzan, M. (1973). The effect of race and need on helping behavior. *Journal of Social Psychology, 89,* 73–77.

Bieneck, S., & Krahé, B. (2011). Blaming the victim and exonerating the perpetrator in cases of rape and robbery: Is there a double standard? *Journal of Interpersonal Violence, 26,* 1785–1797.

Bierhoff, H. W. (2002). *Prosocial behaviour.* Hove, UK: Psychology Press.

Billig, M. (1976). *Social psychology and intergroup relations.* London: Academic Press.

Binet, A., & Henri, V. (1894). De la suggestibilité naturelle chez les enfants [The natural suggestibility of children]. *Revue Philosophique, 38,* 337–347.

Birnbaum, M. H. (2000). Introduction to psychological experiments on the Internet. In M. H. Birnbaum (Ed.), *Psychological experiments on the Internet* (pp. 3–34). San Diego, CA: Academic Press.

Biro, S., & Leslie, A. M. (2007). Infants' perception of goal-directed actions: Development through cue-based bootstrapping. *Developmental Science, 10,* 379–398.

Björkqvist, K., Lagerspetz, K. M., & Kaukiainen, A. (1992). Do girls manipulate and boys fight? Developmental trends in regard to direct and indirect aggression. *Aggressive Behavior, 18,* 117–127.

Black, S. L., & Bevan, S. (1992). At the movies with Buss and Durkee: A natural experiment on film violence. *Aggressive Behavior, 18,* 37–45.

Blackhart, G. C., Nelson, B. C., Knowles, M. L., & Baumeister, R. F. (2009). Rejection elicits emotional reactions but neither causes immediate distress nor lowers self-esteem: A meta-analytic review of 192 studies on social exclusion. *Personality and Social Psychology Review, 13,* 269–309.

Blackwood, N. J., Bentall, R. P., Ffytche, D. H., Simmons, A., Murray, R. M., & Howard, R. J. (2003). Self-responsibility and the self-serving bias: An fMRI investigation of causal attributions. *Neuroimage, 20,* 1076–1085.

Blair, I. V. (2001). Implicit stereotypes and prejudice. In G. B. Moskowitz (Ed.), *Cognitive social psychology: The Princeton Symposium on the legacy and future of social cognition* (pp. 359–374). Mahwah, NJ: Erlbaum.

Blair, I. V., & Banaji, M. R. (1996). Automatic and controlled processes in stereotype priming. *Journal of Personality and Social Psychology, 70,* 1142–1163.

Blair, I. V., Ma, J. E., & Lenton, A. P. (2001). Imagining stereotypes away: The moderation of implicit stereotypes through mental imagery. *Journal of Personality and Social Psychology, 81,* 828–841.

Blakemore, S. J., Winston, J., & Frith, U. (2004). Social cognitive neuroscience: Where are we heading? *Trends in Cognitive Sciences, 8,* 216–222.

Blaney, P. H. (1986). Affect and memory: A review. *Psychological Bulletin, 99*, 229–246.

Blankenship, K. L., & Wegener, D. T. (2008). Opening the mind to close it: Considering a message in light of important values increases message processing and later resistance to change. *Journal of Personality and Social Psychology, 94*, 196–213.

Blanton, H., Buunk, B. P., Gibbons, F. X., & Kuyper, H. (1999). When better-than-others compare upward: Choice of comparison and comparative evaluation as independent predictors of academic performance. *Journal of Personality and Social Psychology, 76*, 420–430.

Blascovich, J., & Tomaka, J. (1991). Measures of self-esteem. In J. P. Robinson, P. R. Shaver, & L. S. Wrightsman (Eds.), *Measures of personality and social psychological attitudes* (Vol. 1, pp. 115–160). San Diego, CA: Academic Press.

Blass, T. (1991). Understanding behavior in the Milgram obedience experiment: The role of personality, situations, and their interactions. *Journal of Personality and Social Psychology, 60*, 398–413.

Blass, T. (1992). The social psychology of Stanley Milgram. In M. P. Zanna (Ed.), *Advances in experimental social psychology* (Vol. 25, pp. 277–329). San Diego, CA: Academic Press.

Blass, T. (1999). The Milgram paradigm after 35 years: Some things we now know about obedience to authority. *Journal of Applied Social Psychology, 29*, 955–978.

Blass, T. (Ed.). (2000). *Obedience to authority: Current perspectives on the Milgram paradigm*. Mahwah, NJ: Erlbaum.

Blass, T. (2004). *The man who shocked the world: The life and legacy of Stanley Milgram*. New York: Basic Books.

Blass, T. (2012). A cross-cultural comparison of studies of obedience using the Milgram paradigm: A review. *Social and Personal Psychology Compass, 6/2*, 196–205.

Blau, P. M. (1964). *Exchange and power in social life*. New York: Wiley.

Bless, H. (2001). The consequences of mood on the processing of social information. In A. Tesser & N. Schwarz (Eds.), *Blackwell handbook of social psychology: Intraindividual processes* (pp. 391–412). Oxford: Blackwell.

Bless, H., Bohner, G., Schwarz, N., & Strack, F. (1990). Mood and persuasion: A cognitive response analysis. *Personality and Social Psychology Bulletin, 16*, 331–345.

Bless, H., Fiedler, K., & Strack, F. (2004). *Social cognition: How individuals construct social reality*. New York: Psychology Press.

Bocchiaro, P., & Zimbardo, P. G. (2010). Defying unjust authority: An exploratory study. *Current Psychology, 29*, 155–170.

Bocchiaro, P., Zimbardo, P. G., & Van Lange, P. A. M. (2012). To defy or not to defy: An experimental study of the dynamics of disobedience and whistle-blowing. *Social Influence, 7*, 35–50.

Bodenhausen, G. V. (1990). Stereotypes as judgmental heuristics: Evidence of circadian variations in discrimination. *Psychological Science, 1*, 319–322.

Bodenhausen, G. V., Todd, A. R., & Richeson, J. A. (2009). Controlling prejudice and stereotyping: Antecedents, mechanisms, and contexts. In T. D. Nelson (Ed.), *Handbook of prejudice, stereotyping, and discrimination* (pp. 111–135). New York: Psychology Press.

Bohner, G., & Dickel, N. (2011). Attitudes and attitude change. *Annual Review of Psychology, 62*, 391–417.

Bohner, G., Moskowitz, G. B., & Chaiken, S. (1995). The interplay of heuristic and systematic processing of social information. In W. Stroebe & M. Hewstone (Eds.), *European review of social psychology* (Vol. 6, pp. 33–68). Chichester, UK: Psychology Press.

Bohner, G., & Wänke, M. (2002). *Attitudes and attitude change*. Hove, UK: Psychology Press.

Bolino, M. C., & Turnley, W. H. (1999). Measuring impression management in organizations: A scale development based on the Jones & Pittman Taxonomy. *Organizational Research Methods, 2*, 187–206.

Bolsin, S. N. (2003). Whistle blowing. *Medical Education, 37*, 294–296.

Bonanno, G. A., Rennicke, C., & Dekel, S. (2005). Self-enhancement among high-exposure survivors of the September 11th terrorist attack: Resilience or social maladjustment? *Journal of Personality and Social Psychology, 88*, 984–998.

Bond, C. F., & Titus, L. J. (1983). Social facilitation: A meta-analysis of 241 studies. *Psychological Bulletin, 94*, 265–292.

Bond, R., & Smith, P. B. (1996). Culture and conformity: A meta-analysis of studies using Asch's (1952b, 1956) Line Judgment Task. *Psychological Bulletin, 119*, 111–137.

Bonner, B. L., Silito, S. D., & Baumann, M. R. (2007). Collective estimation: Accuracy, expertise, and extroversion as sources of intra-group influence. *Organizational Behavior and Human Decision Processes, 103*, 121–133.

Bornstein, R. F. (1989). Exposure and affect: Overview and meta-analysis of research, 1968–1987. *Psychological Bulletin, 106*, 265–289.

Borofsky, G. L., Stollak, G. E., & Messé, L. A. (1971). Sex differences in bystander reactions to physical assault. *Journal of Experimental Social Psychology, 7*, 313–318.

Boseley, S. (July, 2012). Failure to implement children's heart surgery reforms 'has cost lives'. *The Guardian*. Retrieved from http://theguardian.com/society/2012/jul/04/failure-childrens-heart-surgery-reforms

Bosson, J. K., Lakey, C. E., Campbell, W. K., Zeigler-Hill, V., Jordan, C. H., & Kernis, M. H. (2008). Untangling the links between narcissism and self-esteem: A theoretical and empirical review. *Social and Personality Psychology Compass, 2*, 1415–1439.

Botvinick, M. M., Braver, T. S., Barch, D. M., Carter, C. S., & Cohen, J. D. (2001). Conflict monitoring and cognitive control. *Psychological Review, 108*, 624–652.

Bourke, J. (1999). *An intimate history of killing: Face-to-face killing in the twentieth century*. London: Granta.

Bower, G. H. (1981). Mood and memory. *American Psychologist, 36*, 129–148.

Bowers, D. G., & Seashore, S. E. (1966). Predicting organizational effectiveness with a four-factor theory of leadership. *Administrative Science Quarterly, 11*, 238–263.

Bowlby, J. (1958). The nature of the child's tie to his mother. *International Journal of Psychoanalysis, 39,* 350–373.

Bowlby, J. (1969). *Attachment and loss: Attachment* (Vol. 1). London: Hogarth.

Bowlby, J. (1982). *Attachment and loss: Attachment* (Vol. 1, 2nd ed.). New York: Basic Books.

Bowling, N. A., & Beehr, T. A. (2006). Workplace harassment from the victim's perspective: A theoretical model and meta-analysis. *Journal of Applied Psychology, 91,* 998–1012.

Bradbury, T. N., & Karney, B. R. (2010). *Intimate relationships.* New York: Norton.

Bradford, D. L., & Cohen, A. R. (1984). *Managing for excellence: The guide to developing high performance in contemporary organizations.* New York: Wiley.

Brandt, M. J. (2013). Do the disadvantaged legitimize the social system? A large-scale test of the status–legitimacy hypothesis. *Journal of Personality and Social Psychology, 104,* 765–785.

Branscombe, N. R., Ellemers, N., Spears, R., & Doosje, B. (1999). The context and content of social identity threat. In N. Ellemers, R. Spears, & B. Doosje (Eds.), *Social identity: Context, commitment, content* (pp. 35–58). Oxford: Blackwell.

Branscombe, N. R., Schmitt, M. T., & Harvey, R. D. (1999). Perceiving pervasive discrimination among African Americans: Implications for group identification and well-being. *Journal of Personality and Social Psychology, 77,* 135–149.

Branscombe, N. R., & Wann, D. L. (1994). Collective self-esteem consequences of outgroup derogation when a valued social identity is on trial. *European Journal of Social Psychology, 24,* 641–657.

Brauer, M., & Judd, C. M. (1996). Group polarization and repeated attitude expressions: A new take on an old topic. In W. Stroebe & M. Hewstone (Eds.), *European review of social psychology* (Vol. 7, pp. 173–207). Chichester, UK: Psychology Press.

Brauer, M., Judd, C. M., & Gliner, M. D. (1995). The effects of repeated expressions on attitude polarization during group discussions. *Journal of Personality and Social Psychology, 68,* 1014–1029.

Brehm, J. W. (1956). Postdecision changes in the desirability of alternatives. *Journal of Abnormal and Social Psychology, 52,* 384–389.

Brehm, J. W. (1966). *A theory of psychological reactance.* New York: Academic Press.

Brennan, K. A., Clark, C. L., & Shaver, P. R. (1998). Self-report measurement of adult attachment. In J. A. Simpson & W. S. Rholes (Eds.), *Attachment theory and close relationships* (pp. 46–76). New York: Guilford.

Brewer, M. B. (1988). A dual process model of impression formation. In T. K. Srull & R. S. Wyer Jr. (Eds.), *Advances in social cognition* (Vol. 1, pp. 1–36). Hillsdale, NJ: Erlbaum.

Brewer, M. B. (1991). The social self: On being the same and different at the same time. *Personality and Social Psychology Bulletin, 17,* 475–482.

Brewer, M. B. (1999). The psychology of prejudice: Ingroup love or outgroup hate? *Journal of Social Issues, 55,* 429–444.

Brewer, M. B. (2000). Research design and issues of validity. In H. T. Reis & C. M. Judd (Eds.), *Handbook of research methods in social and personality psychology* (pp. 3–16). New York: Cambridge University Press.

Brewer, M. B. (2003). *Intergroup relations.* Buckingham, UK: Open University Press.

Brewer, M. B., & Miller, N. (1984). Beyond the contact hypothesis: Theoretical perspectives on desegregation. In M. B. Brewer & N. Miller (Eds.), *Groups in contact: The psychology of desegregation* (pp. 281–302). Orlando, FL: Academic Press.

Brief, A. P., Dukerich, J. M., & Doran, L. I. (1991). Resolving ethical dilemmas in management: Experimental investigations of values, accountability, and choice. *Journal of Applied Social Psychology, 21,* 380–396.

Briñol, P., & Petty, R. E. (2003). Overt head movements and persuasion: A self-validation analysis. *Journal of Personality and Social Psychology, 84,* 1123–1139.

Briñol, P., & Petty, R. E. (2008). Embodied persuasion: Fundamental processes by which bodily responses can impact attitudes. In G. R. Semin & E. R. Smith (Eds.), *Embodiment grounding: Social, cognitive, affective, and neuroscientific approaches* (pp. 184–207). Cambridge, MA: Cambridge University Press.

Briñol, P., Petty, R. E., & McCaslin, M. J. (2009). Changing attitudes on implicit versus explicit measures: What is the difference? In R. E. Petty, R. H. Fazio, & P. Briñol (Eds.), *Attitudes: Insights from the new implicit measures* (pp. 285–326). New York: Psychology Press.

Brodbeck, F. C. (2008). Leadership in organisations. In N. Chmiel (Ed.), *An introduction to work and organisational psychology: A European perspective* (2nd ed., pp. 281–304). Oxford: Blackwell.

Brodbeck, F. C., & Greitemeyer, T. (2000a). A dynamic model of group performance: Considering the group members' capacity to learn. *Group Processes & Intergroup Relations, 3,* 159–182.

Brodbeck, F. C., & Greitemeyer, T. (2000b). Effects of individual versus mixed individual and group experience in rule induction on group member learning and group performance. *Journal of Experimental Social Psychology, 36,* 621–648.

Brodbeck, F. C., Kerschreiter, R., Mojzisch, A., Frey, D., & Schulz-Hardt, S. (2002). The dissemination of critical, unshared information in decision making groups: The effects of pre-discussion dissent. *European Journal of Social Psychology, 32,* 35–56.

Brodbeck, F. C., Kerschreiter, R., Mojzisch, A., & Schulz-Hardt, S. (2007). Group decision making under conditions of distributed knowledge: The information asymmetries model. *Academy of Management Review, 32,* 459–479.

Brown, C. (1955). *My left foot.* Oxford: Simon & Schuster.

Brown, J. D. (1986). Evaluations of self and others: Self-enhancement biases in social judgments. *Social Cognition, 4,* 353–376.

Brown, J. D. (1990). Evaluating one's abilities: Shortcuts and stumbling blocks on the road to self-knowledge. *Journal of Experimental Social Psychology, 26,* 149–167.

Brown, J. D., Dutton, K. A., & Cook, K. E. (2001). From the top down: Self-esteem and self-evaluation. *Cognition and Emotion, 15,* 615–631.

Brown, J. D., & Smart, S. A. (1991). The self and social conduct: Linking self-representations to prosocial behavior. *Journal of Personality and Social Psychology, 60,* 368–375.

Brown, R. (1999). *Group processes* (2nd ed.). Oxford: Blackwell.

Brown, R. (2010). *Prejudice: It's social psychology* (2nd ed.). Chichester, UK: Wiley-Blackwell.

Brown, R., & Abrams, D. (1986). The effects of intergroup similarity and goal interdependence on intergroup attitudes and task performance. *Journal of Experimental Social Psychology, 22,* 78–92.

Brown, R., & Fish, D. (1983). The psychological causality implicit in language. *Cognition, 14,* 237–273.

Brown, R., & Hewstone, M. (2005). An integrative theory of intergroup contact. In M. P. Zanna (Ed.), *Advances in experimental social psychology* (Vol. 37, pp. 255–343). San Diego, CA: Academic Press.

Brown, R., & Kulik, J. (1977). Flashbulb memories. *Cognition, 5,* 73–99.

Brown, R., & Wade, G. (1987). Superordinate goals and intergroup behaviour: The effect of role ambiguity and status on intergroup attitudes and task performance. *European Journal of Social Psychology, 17,* 131–142.

Browning, C. R. (1992). *Ordinary men: Reserve police battalion 101 and the final solution in Poland.* New York: HarperCollins.

Brunell, A. B., Gentry, W. A., Campbell, W. K., Hoffman, B. J., Kuhnert, K. W., & DeMarree, K. G. (2008). Leader emergence: The case of the narcissistic leader. *Personality and Social Psychology Bulletin, 34,* 1663–1676.

Bruner, J. S., & Tagiuri, R. (1954). The perception of people. In G. Lindzey (Ed.), *Handbook of social psychology* (Vol. 2, pp. 634–654). Reading, MA: Addison-Wesley.

Buhrmester, D., & Prager, K. (1995). Patterns and functions of self-disclosure during childhood and adolescence. In K. J. Rotenberg (Ed.), *Disclosure processes in children and adolescents* (pp. 10–56). New York: Cambridge University Press.

Buhrmester, M., Kwang, T., & Gosling, S. D. (2011). Amazon's Mechanical Turk: A new source of inexpensive, yet high-quality, data? *Perspectives on Psychological Science, 6,* 3–5.

Bunderson, J. S., & Sutcliffe, K. M. (2003). Management team learning orientation and business unit performance. *Journal of Applied Psychology, 88,* 552–560.

Bureau of Justice Statistics. *National Crime Victimization Survey.* Retrieved from http://bjs.ojp.usdoj.gov/content/pub/pdf/ipvus.pdf

Burger, J. M. (2009). Replicating Milgram: Would people still obey today? *American Psychologist, 64,* 1–11.

Burger, J. M., & Petty, R. E. (1981). The low-ball compliance technique: Task or person commitment? *Journal of Personality and Social Psychology, 40,* 492–500.

Burgess, M., Enzle, M. E., & Morry, M. (2000). The social psychological power of photography: Can the image-freezing machine make something of nothing? *European Journal of Social Psychology, 30,* 613–630.

Burks, V. S., Laird, R. D., Dodge, K. A., Pettit, G. S., & Bates, J. E. (1999). Knowledge structures, social information processing, and children's aggressive behavior. *Social Development, 8,* 220–236.

Burns, J. M. (1978). *Leadership.* New York: Harper & Row.

Burnstein, E., & Branigan, C. (2001). Evolutionary analyses in social psychology. In A. Tesser & N. Schwarz (Eds.), *Blackwell handbook of social psychology: Intraindividual processes* (pp. 3–21). Oxford: Blackwell.

Burnstein, E., & Vinokur, A. (1977). Persuasive argumentation and social comparison as determinants of attitude polarization. *Journal of Experimental Social Psychology, 13,* 315–332.

Burnstein, E., Vinokur, A., & Trope, Y. (1973). Interpersonal comparison versus persuasive argumentation: A more direct test of alternative explanations for group-induced shifts in individual choice. *Journal of Experimental Social Psychology, 9,* 236–245.

Bushman, B. J. (2002). Does venting anger feed or extinguish the flame? Catharsis, rumination, distraction, anger, and aggressive responding. *Personality and Social Psychology Bulletin, 28,* 724–731.

Bushman, B. J., & Baumeister, R. F. (1998). Threatened egotism, narcissism, self-esteem, and direct and displaced aggression: Does self-love or self-hate lead to violence? *Journal of Personality and Social Psychology, 75,* 219–229.

Bushman, B. J., Baumeister, R. F., & Stack, A. D. (1999). Catharsis, aggression, and persuasive influence: Self-fulfilling or self-defeating prophecies? *Journal of Personality and Social Psychology, 76,* 367–376.

Bushman, B. J., Baumeister, R. F., Thomaes, S., Ryu, E., Begeer, S., & West, S. G. (2009). Looking again, and harder, for a link between low self-esteem and aggression. *Journal of Personality, 77,* 427–446.

Bushman, B. J., Bonacci, A. M., Van Dijk, M., & Baumeister, R. F. (2003). Narcissism, sexual refusal, and aggression: Testing a narcissistic reactance model of sexual coercion. *Journal of Personality and Social Psychology, 84,* 1027–1040.

Bushman, B. J., & Cooper, H. M. (1990). Effects of alcohol on human aggression: An integrative research review. *Psychological Bulletin, 107,* 341–354.

Bushman, B. J., & Geen, R. G. (1990). Role of cognitive-emotional mediators and individual differences in the effects of media violence on aggression. *Journal of Personality and Social Psychology, 58,* 156–163.

Bushman, B. J., Ridge, R. D., Das, E. H., Key, C. W., & Busath, G. L. (2007). When God sanctions killing: Effect of scriptural violence on aggression. *Psychological Science, 18,* 204–207.

Bushman, B. J., & Whitaker, J. L. (2010). Like a magnet: Catharsis beliefs attract angry people to violent video games. *Psychological Science, 21,* 790–792.

Buss, A. H., & Perry, M. (1992). The Aggression Questionnaire. *Journal of Personality and Social Psychology, 63,* 452–459.

Buss, A. H., & Warren, W. L. (2000). *The Aggression Questionnaire Manual.* Los Angeles, CA: Western Psychological Service.

Buss, D. M. (1989). Sex differences in human mate preferences: Evolutionary hypotheses tested in 37 cultures. *Behavioral and Brain Sciences, 12,* 1–49.

Buss, D. M. (1995). Evolutionary psychology: A new paradigm for psychological science. *Psychological Inquiry, 6,* 1–30.

Buss, D. M., Abbott, M., Angleitner, A., Asherian, A., Biaggio, A., Blanco-Villasenor, A., ... Deraad, B. (1990). International preferences in selecting mates: A study of 37 cultures. *Journal of Cross-Cultural Psychology, 21,* 5–47.

Buss, D. M., & Chiodo, L. M. (1991). Narcissistic acts in everyday life. *Journal of Personality, 59,* 179–215.

Buss, D. M., & Kendrick, D. T. (1998). Evolutionary social psychology. In D. T. Gilbert, S. T. Fiske, & G. Lindzey (Eds.), *The handbook of social psychology* (4th ed., Vol. 2, pp. 982–1026). Boston, MA: McGraw-Hill.

Butera, F., & Levine, J. M. (Eds.). (2009). *Coping with minority status: Responses to exclusion and inclusion.* New York: Cambridge University Press.

Buunk, B. P. (2001). Perceived superiority of one's own relationship and perceived prevalence of happy and unhappy relationships. *British Journal of Social Psychology, 40,* 565–574.

Buunk, B. P., & Van der Eijnden, R. J. J. M. (1997). Perceived prevalence, perceived superiority, and relationship satisfaction: Most relationships are good, but ours is the best. *Personality and Social Psychology Bulletin, 23,* 219–228.

Byrne, D. (1971). *The attraction paradigm.* New York: Academic Press.

Byrne, D., Ervin, C. R., & Lamberth, J. (1970). Continuity between the experimental study of attraction and real-life computer dating. *Journal of Personality and Social Psychology, 16,* 157–165.

Byrne, D., & Wong, T. J. (1962). Racial prejudice, interpersonal attraction, and assumed dissimilarity of attitudes. *Journal of Abnormal and Social Psychology, 65,* 246–253.

Cacioppo, J. T., Amaral, D. G., Blanchard, J. J., Cameron, J. L., Carter, C. S., Crews, D., ... Quinn, K. J. (2007). Social neuroscience: Progress and implications for mental health. *Perspectives on Psychological Science, 2,* 99–123.

Cacioppo, J. T., & Berntson, G. G. (Eds.). (2005). *Social neuroscience.* New York: Psychology Press.

Cacioppo, J. T., Gardner, W. L., & Berntson, G. G. (1997). Beyond bipolar conceptualizations and measures: The case of attitudes and evaluative space. *Personality and Social Psychology Review, 1,* 3–25.

Cacioppo, J. T., Hughes, M. E., Waite, L. J., Hawkley, L. C., & Thisted, R. A. (2006). Loneliness as a specific risk factor for depressive symptoms: Cross-sectional and longitudinal analyses. *Psychology and Aging, 21,* 140–151.

Cacioppo, J. T., Marshall-Goodell, B. S., Tassinary, L. G., & Petty, R. E. (1992). Rudimentary determinants of attitudes: Classical conditioning is more effective when prior knowledge about the attitude stimulus is low than high. *Journal of Experimental Social Psychology, 28,* 207–233.

Cacioppo, J. T., & Petty, R. E. (1979). Effects of message repetition and position on cognitive response, recall, and persuasion. *Journal of Personality and Social Psychology, 37,* 97–109.

Cacioppo, J. T., & Petty, R. E. (1982). The need for cognition. *Journal of Personality and Social Psychology, 42,* 116–131.

Cacioppo, J. T., & Petty, R. E. (1989). Effects of message repetition on argument processing, recall, and persuasion. *Basic and Applied Social Psychology, 10,* 3–12.

Cacioppo, J. T., Petty, R. E., Feinstein, J. A., & Jarvis, W. B. G. (1996). Dispositional differences in cognitive motivation: The life and times of individuals varying in need for cognition. *Psychological Bulletin, 119,* 197–253.

Cacioppo, J. T., Petty, R. E., & Kao, C. F. (1984). The efficient assessment of need for cognition. *Journal of Personality Assessment, 48,* 306–307.

Cacioppo, J. T., Priester, J. R., & Berntson, G. G. (1993). Rudimentary determinants of attitudes: Arm flexion and extension have differential effects on attitudes. *Journal of Personality and Social Psychology, 65,* 5–17.

Cai, H., Brown, J. D., Deng, C., & Oakes, M. A. (2007). Self-esteem and culture: Differences in cognitive self-evaluations or affective self-regard? *Asian Journal of Social Psychology, 10,* 162–170.

Cai, H., Sedikides, C., Gaertner, L., Wang, C., Carvallo, M., Xu, Y., ... Jackson, L. E. (2011). Tactical self-enhancement in China: Is modesty at the service of self-enhancement in East Asian culture? *Social Psychological and Personality Science, 2,* 59–64.

Cairns, E., Kenworthy, J., Campbell, A., & Hewstone, M. (2006). The role of in-group identification, religious group membership and intergroup conflict in moderating in-group and out-group affect. *British Journal of Social Psychology, 45,* 701–716.

Callero, P. L., Howard, J. A., & Piliavin, J. A. (1987). Helping behavior as role behavior: Disclosing social structure and history in the analysis of prosocial action. *Social Psychology Quarterly, 50,* 247–256.

Calvert-Boyanowsky, J., & Leventhal, H. (1975). The role of information in attenuating behavioral responses to stress: A reinterpretation of the misattribution phenomenon. *Journal of Personality and Social Psychology, 32,* 214–221.

Cameron, L., & Rutland, A. (2006). Extended contact through story reading in school: Reducing children's prejudice toward the disabled. *Journal of Social Issues, 62,* 469–488.

Campbell, D. T. (1950). The indirect assessment of social attitudes. *Psychological Bulletin, 47,* 15–38.

Campbell, D. T. (1958). Common fate, similarity, and other indices of the status of aggregates of persons as social entities. *Behavioral Science, 3,* 14–25.

Campbell, D. T., & Fiske, D. W. (1959). Convergent and discriminant validation by the multitrait–multimethod matrix. *Psychological Bulletin, 56,* 81–105.

Campbell, D. T., & Stanley, J. C. (1966). *Experimental and quasi-experimental designs for research.* Chicago: Rand McNally.

Campbell, J. (1949). *The hero with a thousand faces.* New York: Pantheon.

Campbell, J. D., & Fehr, B. (1990). Self-esteem and perceptions of conveyed impressions: Is negative affectivity associated with greater realism? *Journal of Personality and Social Psychology, 58,* 122–133.

Campbell, J., & Stasser, G. (2006). The influence of time and task demonstrability on decision making in computer-mediated and face-to-face groups. *Small Group Research, 37,* 271–294.

Campbell, W. K., & Foster, J. D. (2007). The narcissistic self: Background, an extended agency model, and ongoing controversies. In C. Sedikides & S. J. Spencer (Eds.), *The self* (pp. 115–138). New York: Psychology Press.

Campbell, W. K., & Sedikides, C. (1999). Self-threat magnifies the self-serving bias: A meta-analytic integration. *Review of General Psychology, 3,* 23–43.

Canary, D. J., Stafford, L., Hause, K. S., & Wallace, L. A. (1993). An inductive analysis of relational maintenance strategies: Comparisons among lovers, relatives, friends, and others. *Communication Research Reports, 10,* 5–14.

Cann, A., Sherman, S. J., & Elkes, R. (1975). Effects of initial request size and timing of a second request on compliance: The foot in the door and the door in the face. *Journal of Personality and Social Psychology, 32,* 774–782.

Cannon, W. B. (1927). The James-Lange theory of emotions: A critical examination and an alternative theory. *American Journal of Psychology, 39,* 106–124.

Capozza, D., Brown, R., Aharpour, S., & Falvo, R. (2006). A comparison of motivational theories of identification. In R. Brown & D. Capozza (Eds.), *Social identities: Motivational, emotional and cultural influences* (pp. 51–72). Hove, UK: Psychology Press.

Carlson, M., Marcus-Newhall, A., & Miller, N. (1990). Effects of situational aggression cues: A quantitative review. *Journal of Personality and Social Psychology, 58,* 622–633.

Carlson, M., & Miller, N. (1987). Explanation of the relation between negative mood and helping. *Psychological Bulletin, 102,* 91–108.

Carré, J. M., McCormick, C. M., & Mondloch, C. J. (2009). Facial structure is a reliable cue of aggressive behavior. *Psychological Science, 20,* 1194–1198.

Cartwright, D. (1979). Contemporary social psychology in historical perspective. *Social Psychology Quarterly, 42,* 82–93.

Carver, C. S., Blaney, P. H., & Scheier, M. F. (1979). Reassertion and giving up: The interactive role of self-directed attention and outcome expectancy. *Journal of Personality and Social Psychology, 37,* 1859–1870.

Carver, C. S., & Scheier, M. F. (1981). *Attention and self-regulation: A control-theory approach to human behavior.* New York: Springer.

Carver, C. S., & Scheier, M. F. (1998). *On the self-regulation of behavior.* New York: Cambridge University Press.

Castano, E., Yzerbyt, V., Paladino, M. P., & Sacchi, S. (2002). I belong, therefore, I exist: Ingroup identification, ingroup entitativity, and ingroup bias. *Personality and Social Psychology Bulletin, 28,* 135–143.

Cate, R. M., Lloyd, S. A., Henton, J. M., & Larson, J. H. (1982). Fairness and reward level as predictors of relationship satisfaction. *Social Psychology Quarterly, 45,* 177–181.

Chaiken, S. (1979). Communicator physical attractiveness and persuasion. *Journal of Personality and Social Psychology, 37,* 1387–1397.

Chaiken, S. (1980). Heuristic versus systematic information processing and the use of source versus message cues in persuasion. *Journal of Personality and Social Psychology, 39,* 752–766.

Chaiken, S., & Baldwin, M. W. (1981). Affective-cognitive consistency and the effect of salient behavioral information on the self-perception of attitudes. *Journal of Personality and Social Psychology, 41,* 1–12.

Chaiken, S., Liberman, A., & Eagly, A. H. (1989). Heuristic and systematic information processing within and beyond the persuasion context. In J. S. Uleman & J. A. Bargh (Eds.), *Unintended thought* (pp. 212–252). New York: Guilford.

Chaiken, S., & Maheswaran, D. (1994). Heuristic processing can bias systematic processing: Effects of source credibility, argument ambiguity, and task importance on attitude judgment. *Journal of Personality and Social Psychology, 66,* 460–473.

Chaiken, S., & Trope, Y. (Eds.). (1999). *Dual process theories in social psychology.* New York: Guilford.

Chartrand, T. L., Van Baaren, R. B., & Bargh, J. A. (2006). Linking automatic evaluation to mood and information processing style: Consequences for experienced affect, impression formation, and stereotyping. *Journal of Experimental Psychology: General, 135,* 70–77.

Chatard, A., & Selimbegović, L. (2011). When self-destructive thoughts flash through the mind: Failure to meet standards affects the accessibility of suicide-related thoughts. *Journal of Personality and Social Psychology, 100,* 587–605.

Chen, S., & Chaiken, S. (1999). The heuristic-systematic model in its broader context. In S. Chaiken & Y. Trope (Eds.), *Dual-process theories in social psychology* (pp. 73–96). New York: Guilford.

Chen, S., Shechter, D., & Chaiken, S. (1996). Getting at the truth or getting along: Accuracy- versus impression-motivated heuristic and systematic processing. *Journal of Personality and Social Psychology, 71*, 262–275.

Chen, Y.-R., Brockner, J., & Chen, X.-P. (2002). Individual-collective primacy and in-group favouritism: Enhancement and protection effects. *Journal of Experimental Social Psychology, 38*, 482–491.

Chen, Y.-R., Brockner, J., & Katz, T. (1998). Toward an explanation of cultural differences in in-group favoritism: The role of individual versus collective primacy. *Journal of Personality and Social Psychology, 75*, 1490–1502.

Cheng, P. W. (1997). From covariation to causation: A causal power theory. *Psychological Review, 104*, 367–405.

Cheng, P. W., & Novick, L. R. (1990). A probabilistic contrast model of causal induction. *Journal of Personality and Social Psychology, 58*, 545–567.

Chernyshenko, O. S., Miner, A. G., Baumann, M. R., & Sniezek, J. A. (2003). The impact of information distribution, ownership, and discussion on group member judgment: The differential cue weighting model. *Organizational Behavior and Human Decision Processes, 91*, 12–25.

Cherry, F. E. (1995). *The 'stubborn particulars' of social psychology: Essays on the research process.* London: Routledge.

Chertkoff, J. M., & Kushigian, R. H. (1999). *Don't panic: The psychology of emergency egress and ingress.* Westport, CT: Praeger.

Chhokar, J. S., Brodbeck, F. C., & House, R. J. (2008). *Culture and leadership across the world: The GLOBE book of in-depth studies of 25 societies.* Mahwah, NJ: Erlbaum.

Chiao, J. Y., Harada, T., Komeda, H., Li, Z., Mano, Y., Saito, D., … Iidaka, T. (2009). Neural basis of individualistic and collectivistic views of self. *Human Brain Mapping, 30*, 2813–2820.

Chiu, C.-Y., & Hong, Y.-Y. (2006). *Social psychology of culture.* New York: Psychology Press.

Choi, H., Yoon, H. J., Paek, H. J., & Reid, L. N. (2012). Thinking and feeling products and utilitarian and value-expressive appeals in contemporary TV advertisements: A content analytic test of functional matching in the FCB model. *Journal of Marketing Communications, 18*, 91–111.

Choi, H.-S., & Levine, J. M. (2004). Minority influence in work teams: The impact of newcomers. *Journal of Experimental Social Psychology, 40*, 273–280.

Choi, I., & Choi, Y. (2002). Culture and self-concept flexibility. *Personality and Social Psychology Bulletin, 28*, 1508–1517.

Choi, I., & Nisbett, R. E. (1998). Situational salience and cultural differences in the correspondence bias and actor-observer bias. *Personality and Social Psychology Bulletin, 24*, 949–960.

Choi, I., Nisbett, R. E., & Norenzayan, A. (1999). Causal attribution across cultures: Variation and universality. *Psychological Bulletin, 125*, 47–63.

Christ, O., Hewstone, M., Tausch, N., Wagner, U., Voci, A., Hughes, J., & Cairns, E. (2010). Direct contact as a moderator of extended contact effects: Cross-sectional and longitudinal impact on outgroup attitudes, behavioral intentions, and attitude certainty. *Personality and Social Psychology Bulletin, 36*, 1662–1674.

Christy, C. A., & Voigt, H. (1994). Bystander responses to public episodes of child abuse. *Journal of Applied Social Psychology, 24*, 824–847.

Chronocentric (2012). http://www.chronocentric.com/watches/accuracy.shtml

Cialdini, R. B. (2008). *Influence: Science and practice* (5th ed.). Boston, MA: Allyn & Bacon.

Cialdini, R. B., & Ascani, K. (1976). Test of a concession procedure for inducing verbal, behavioral, and further compliance with a request to give blood. *Journal of Applied Psychology, 61*, 295–300.

Cialdini, R. B., Borden, R. J., Thorne, A., Walker, M. R., Freeman, S., & Sloan, L. R. (1976). Basking in reflected glory: Three (football) field studies. *Journal of Personality and Social Psychology, 34*, 366–375.

Cialdini, R. B., Cacioppo, J. T., Bassett, R., & Miller, J. A. (1978). Low-ball procedure for producing compliance: Commitment then cost. *Journal of Personality and Social Psychology, 36*, 463–476.

Cialdini, R. B., & Fultz, J. (1990). Interpreting the negative mood-helping literature via 'mega'-analysis: A contrary view. *Psychological Bulletin, 107*, 210–214.

Cialdini, R. B., & Goldstein, N. J. (2004). Social influence: Compliance and conformity. *Annual Review of Psychology, 55*, 591–621.

Cialdini, R. B., Kallgren, C. A., & Reno, R. R. (1991). A focus theory of normative conduct: A theoretical refinement and reevaluation of the role of norms in human behavior. In M. P. Zanna (Ed.), *Advances in experimental social psychology* (Vol. 24, pp. 201–234). San Diego, CA: Academic Press.

Cialdini, R. B., Reno, R. R., & Kallgren, C. A. (1990). A focus theory of normative conduct: Recycling the concept of norms to reduce littering in public places. *Journal of Personality and Social Psychology, 58*, 1015–1026.

Cialdini, R. B., Schaller, M., Houlihan, D., Arps, K., Fultz, J., & Beaman, A. L. (1987). Empathy-based helping: Is it selflessly or selfishly motivated? *Journal of Personality and Social Psychology, 52*, 749–758.

Cialdini, R. B., & Trost, M. R. (1998). Social influence: Social norms, conformity, and compliance. In D. T. Gilbert, S. T. Fiske, & G. Lindzey (Eds.), *Handbook of social psychology* (4th ed., Vol. 2, pp. 151–192). Boston, MA: McGraw-Hill.

Cialdini, R. B., Trost, M. R., & Newsom, J. T. (1995). Preference for consistency: The development of a valid measure and the discovery of surprising behavioral implications. *Journal of Personality and Social Psychology, 69*, 318–328.

Cialdini, R. B., Vincent, J. E., Lewis, S. K., Catalan, J., Wheeler, D., & Darby, B. L. (1975). Reciprocal concessions procedure for inducing compliance: The door-in-the-face technique. *Journal of Personality and Social Psychology, 31*, 206–215.

Cini, M. A., Moreland, R. L., & Levine, J. M. (1993). Group staffing levels and responses to prospective and new members. *Journal of Personality and Social Psychology, 65,* 723–734.

Clark, M. S., & Mills, J. (1979). Interpersonal attraction in exchange and communal relationships. *Journal of Personality and Social Psychology, 37,* 12–24.

Clark, M. S., Mills, J., & Corcoran, D. M. (1989). Keeping track of needs and inputs of friends and strangers. *Personality and Social Psychology Bulletin, 15(4),* 533–542.

Claypool, H. M., Mackie, D. M., Garcia-Marques, T., McIntosh, A., & Udal, A. (2004). The effects of personal relevance and repetition on persuasive processing. *Social Cognition, 22,* 310–335.

Clifford, M. M., & Walster, E. (1973). The effect of physical attractiveness on teacher expectation. *Sociology of Education, 46,* 248–258.

Clore, G. L., Bray, R. M., Itkin, S. M., & Murphy, P. (1978). Interracial attitudes and behavior at a summer camp. *Journal of Personality and Social Psychology, 36,* 107–116.

Clore, G. L., & Jeffery, K. M. (1972). Emotional role playing, attitude change, and attraction toward a disabled person. *Journal of Personality and Social Psychology, 23,* 105–111.

Clore, G. L., Schwarz, N., & Conway, M. (1994). Cognitive causes and consequences of emotion. In R. S. Wyer & T. K. Srull (Eds.), *Handbook of social cognition* (2nd ed., Vol. 1, pp. 323–417). Hillsdale, NJ: Erlbaum.

Coan, J. A., Schaefer, H. S., & Davidson, R. J. (2006). Lending a hand: Social regulation of the neural response to threat. *Psychological Science, 17,* 1032–1039.

Coch, L., & French, J. R. P., Jr. (1948). Overcoming resistance to change. *Human Relations, 1,* 512–532.

Cohen, E. (1984). The desegregated school: Problems of status, power, and interethnic climate. In N. Miller & M. Brewer (Eds.), *Groups in contact: The psychology of desegregration* (pp. 77–96). New York: Academic Press.

Cohen, E. G., & Lotan, R. A. (1995). Producing equal-status interaction in the heterogeneous classroom. *American Educational Research Journal, 32,* 99–120.

Cohen, J. (1988). *Statistical power analysis for the behavioral sciences* (2nd ed.). Hillsdale, NJ: Erlbaum.

Cohen, L. E., & Felson, M. (1979). Social change and climate rate trends: A routine activity approach. *American Sociological Review, 44,* 588–608.

Cohen, S., & Wills, T. A. (1985). Stress, social support, and the buffering hypothesis. *Psychological Bulletin, 98,* 310–357.

Coie, J. D., & Dodge, K. A. (1998). Aggression and antisocial behavior. In W. Damon & N. Eisenberg (Eds.), *Handbook of child psychology* (5th ed., pp. 779–862). New York: Wiley.

Collins, N. L., & Feeney, B. C. (2000). A safe haven: An attachment theory perspective on support-seeking and caregiving in adult intimate relationships. *Journal of Personality and Social Psychology, 78,* 1053–1073.

Collins, N. L., & Miller, L. C. (1994). Self-disclosure and liking: A meta-analytic review. *Psychological Bulletin, 116,* 457–475.

Collins, W. A., Maccoby, E. E., Steinberg, L., Hetherington, E. M., & Bornstein, M. H. (2000). Contemporary research on parenting: The case for nature and nurture. *American Psychologist, 55,* 218–232.

Conger, J. A., & Kanungo, R. N. (1987). Toward a behavioral theory of charismatic leadership in organizational settings. *Academy of Management Review, 12,* 637–647.

Conger, J. A., & Kanungo, R. N. (1998). *Charismatic leadership in organizations.* Thousand Oaks, CA: Sage.

Converse, P. D., & DeShon, R. P. (2009). A tale of two tasks: Reversing the self-regulatory resource depletion effect. *Journal of Applied Psychology, 94,* 1318–1324.

Converse, P. E. (1994). *Theodore Mead Newcomb. Biographical memoirs* (Vol. 64, pp. 322–338). Washington, DC: National Academies Press.

Conway, M. A. (2005). Memory and the self. *Journal of Memory and Language, 53,* 594–628.

Conway, M. A., Singer, J. A., & Tagini, A. (2004). The self and autobiographical memory: Correspondence and coherence. *Social Cognition, 22,* 491–529.

Cook, K. (2014). *Kitty Genovese: The murder, the bystanders, the crime that changed America.* New York: Norton.

Cook, S. W. (1984). Cooperative interaction in multiethnic contexts. In M. B. Brewer & N. Miller (Eds.), *Groups in contact: The psychology of desegregation* (pp. 155–185). Orlando, FL: Academic Press.

Cook, T. D. (1979). Meta-analysis and the integrative research review. In C. Hendrick & M. S. Clark (Eds.), *Research methods in personality and social psychology* (Vol. 11, pp. 142–163). Newbury Park, CA: Sage.

Cook, T. D., & Campbell, D. T. (1979). *Quasi-experimentation: Design and analysis issues for field settings.* Chicago: Rand McNally.

Cooley, C. H. (1902). *Human nature and the social order.* New York: Scribner.

Cooper, H. M. (1989). *Integrating research: A guide for literature reviews.* Newbury Park, CA: Sage.

Cooper, H. M., & Hedges, L. V. (Eds.). (1994). *The handbook of research synthesis.* New York: Sage.

Cooper, J., & Cooper, G. (2002). Subliminal motivation: A story revisited. *Journal of Applied Social Psychology, 32,* 2213–2227.

Cooper, J., & Worchel, S. (1970). Role of undesired consequences in arousing cognitive dissonance. *Journal of Personality and Social Psychology, 16,* 199–206.

Cooper, J. B., & Pollock, D. A. (1959). The identification of prejudicial attitudes by the galvanic skin response. *Journal of Social Psychology, 50,* 241–245.

Corneille, O., Huart, J., Becquart, E., & Brédart, S. (2004). When memory shifts toward more typical category exemplars: Accentuation effects in the recollection of ethnically ambiguous faces. *Journal of Personality and Social Psychology, 86,* 236–250.

Correll, J., Judd, C. M., Park, B., & Wittenbrink, B. (2010). Measuring prejudice, stereotypes and discrimination. In J. F. Dovidio, M. Hewstone, P. Glick, & V. M. Esses (Eds.), *Handbook of prejudice, stereotyping and discrimination* (pp. 45–62). London: Sage.

Correll, J., Park, B., Judd, C. M., & Wittenbrink, B. (2002). The police officer's dilemma: Using ethnicity to disambiguate potentially threatening individuals. *Journal of Personality and Social Psychology, 83,* 1314–1329.

Correll, J., Park, B., Judd, C. M., Wittenbrink, B., Sadler, M. S., & Keesee, T. (2007). Across the thin blue line: Police officers and racial bias in the decision to shoot. *Journal of Personality and Social Psychology, 92,* 1006–1023.

Cottrell, C. A., & Neuberg, S. L. (2005). Different emotional reactions to different groups: A sociofunctional threat-based approach to 'prejudice'. *Journal of Personality and Social Psychology, 88,* 770–789.

Cottrell, N. B. (1968). Performance in the presence of other human beings: Mere presence, audience, and affiliation effects. In E. C. Simmel, R. A. Hoppe, & G. A. Milton (Eds.), *Social facilitation and imitative behavior* (pp. 91–110). Boston, MA: Allyn & Bacon.

Cottrell, N. B. (1972). Social facilitation. In C. G. McClintock (Ed.), *Experimental social psychology* (pp. 185–236). New York: Holt, Rinehart and Winston.

Covington, M. V. (2000). Goal theory, motivation, and school achievement: An integrative review. *Annual Review of Psychology, 51,* 171–200.

Coyne, J. C., & De Longis, A. (1986). Going beyond social support: The role of social relationships in adaptation. *Journal of Consulting and Clinical Psychology, 54,* 454–460.

Coyne, J. C., Rohrbaugh, M. J., Shoham, V., Sonnega, J. S., Nicklas, J. M., & Cranford, J. A. (2001). Prognostic importance of marital quality for survival of congestive heart failure. *American Journal of Cardiology, 88,* 526–529.

Coyne, S. M., Padilla-Walker, L. M., & Howard, E. (2013). Emerging in a digital world: A decade review of media use, effects, and gratifications in emerging adulthood. *Emerging Adulthood, 1,* 125–137.

Craig, W., Harel-Fisch, Y., Fogel-Grinvald, H., Dostaler, S., Hetland, J., Simons-Morton, B., … Pickett, W. (2009). A cross-national profile of bullying and victimization among adolescents in 40 countries. *International Journal of Public Health, 54,* 216–224.

Craik, F. I. M., Moroz, T. M., Moscovitch, M., Stuss, D. T., Winocur, G., Tulving, E., & Kapur, S. (1999). In search of the self: A positron emission tomography study. *Psychological Science, 10,* 26–34.

Crandall, C. S., Bahns, A. J., Warner, R., & Schaller, M. (2011). Stereotypes as justifications of prejudice. *Personality and Social Psychology Bulletin, 37,* 1488–1498.

Crano, W., & Prislin, R. (Eds.). (2009). *Attitudes and persuasion.* New York: Psychology Press.

Crano, W. D., & Alvaro, E. M. (1997). The context/comparison model of social influence: Mechanisms, structure, and linkages that underlie indirect attitude change. In W. Stroebe & M. Hewstone (Eds.), *European review of social psychology* (Vol. 8, pp. 175–202). Chichester, UK: Wiley.

Crano, W. D., & Chen, X. (1998). The leniency contract and persistence of majority and minority influence. *Journal of Personality and Social Psychology, 74,* 1437–1450.

Crawford, M. T., & Salaman, L. (2012). Entitativity, identity, and the fulfillment of psychological needs. *Journal of Experimental Social Psychology, 48,* 726–730.

Creswell, J. D., Lam, S., Stanton, A. L., Taylor, S. E., Bower, J. E., & Sherman, D. K. (2007). Does self-affirmation, cognitive processing, or discovery of meaning explain cancer-related health benefits of expressive writing? *Personality and Social Psychology Bulletin, 33,* 238–250.

Creswell, J. D., Welch, W. T., Taylor, S. E., Sherman, D. K., Gruenewald, T. L., & Mann, T. (2005). Affirmation of personal values buffers neuroendocrine and psychological stress responses. *Psychological Science, 16,* 846–851.

Crick, N. R., & Grotpeter, J. K. (1995). Relational aggression, gender, and social-psychological adjustment. *Child Development, 66,* 710–722.

Crocker, J., & Luhtanen, R. K. (2003). Level of self-esteem and contingencies of self-worth: Unique effects on academic, social, and financial problems in college students. *Personality and Social Psychology Bulletin, 29,* 701–712.

Crocker, J., & Park, L. E. (2004). The costly pursuit of self-esteem. *Psychological Bulletin, 130,* 392–414.

Crocker, J., & Schwartz, I. (1985). Prejudice and ingroup favoritism in a minimal intergroup situation: Effects of self-esteem. *Personality and Social Psychology Bulletin, 11,* 379–386.

Crocker, J., Sommers, S. R., & Luhtanen, R. K. (2002). Hopes dashed and dreams fulfilled: Contingencies of self-worth and graduate school admissions. *Personality and Social Psychology Bulletin, 28,* 1275–1286.

Crocker, J., & Wolfe, C. T. (2001). Contingencies of self-worth. *Psychological Review, 108,* 593–623.

Cross, S. E., Bacon, P. L., & Morris, M. L. (2000). The relational-interdependent self-construal and relationships. *Journal of Personality and Social Psychology, 78,* 791–808.

Cross, S. E., & Madson, L. (1997). Models of the self: Self-construals and gender. *Psychological Bulletin, 122,* 5–37.

Crump, M. J. C., McDonnell, J. V., & Gureckis, T. M. (2013). Evaluating Amazon's Mechanical Turk as a tool for experimental behavioral research. *PLoS One, 8,* 1–18.

Crutchfield, R. S. (1955). Conformity and character. *American Psychologist, 10,* 191–198.

Cruz, M. G., Henningsen, D. D., & Smith, B. A. (1999). The impact of directive leadership on group information sampling, decisions, and perceptions of the leader. *Communication Research, 26,* 349–369.

Culbertson, K. A., & Dehle, C. (2001). Impact of sexual assault as a function of perpetrator type. *Journal of Interpersonal Violence, 16,* 992–1007.

Cunningham, J. A., Strassberg, D. S., & Haan, B. (1986). Effects of intimacy and sex-role congruency on self-disclosure. *Journal of Social and Clinical Psychology, 4,* 393–401.

Cunningham, M. R., Roberts, A. R., Barbee, A. P., Druen, P. B., & Wu, C.-H. (1995). 'Their ideas of beauty are, on the whole, the same as ours': Consistency and variability in the cross-cultural perception of female physical attractiveness. *Journal of Personality and Social Psychology, 68,* 261–279.

Cunningham, W. A., Preacher, K. J., & Banaji, M. R. (2001). Implicit attitude measures: Consistency, stability, and convergent validity. *Psychological Science, 12,* 163–170.

Custers, R., & Aarts, H. (2005a). Beyond priming effects: The role of positive affect and discrepancies in implicit processes of motivation and goal pursuit. In W. Stroebe & M. Hewstone (Eds.), *European review of social psychology* (Vol. 16, pp. 257–300). Hove, UK: Psychology Press.

Custers, R., & Aarts, H. (2005b). Positive affect as implicit motivator: On the nonconscious operation of behavioral goals. *Journal of Personality and Social Psychology, 89,* 129–142.

Cutrona, C. E. (1996). *Social support in couples: Marriage as a resource in times of stress.* Thousand Oaks, CA: Sage.

Dabbs, J. M., Jr., & Ruback, B. R. (1987). Dimensions of group process: Amount and structure of vocal interaction. In L. Berkowitz (Ed.), *Advances in experimental social psychology* (Vol. 20, pp. 123–169). San Diego, CA: Academic Press.

Dainton, M., & Aylor, B. (2002). Routine and strategic maintenance efforts: Behavioral patterns, variations associated with relational length, and the prediction of relational characteristics. *Communication Monographs, 69,* 52–66.

Dana, E. R., Lalwani, N., & Duval, T. S. (1997). Objective self-awareness and focus of attention following awareness of self-standard discrepancies: Changing self or changing standards of correctness. *Journal of Social and Clinical Psychology, 16,* 359–380.

D'Argembeau, A., Comblain, C., & Van der Linden, M. (2003). Phenomenal characteristics of autobiographical memories for positive, negative, and neutral events. *Applied Cognitive Psychology, 17,* 281–294.

Darley, J. M. (1992). Social organization for the production of evil. *Psychological Inquiry, 3,* 199–218.

Darley, J. M., Jr., & Batson, C. D. (1973). 'From Jerusalem to Jericho': A study of situational and dispositional variables in helping behavior. *Journal of Personality and Social Psychology, 27,* 100–108.

Darley, J. M., & Latané, B. (1968). Bystander intervention in emergencies: Diffusion of responsibility. *Journal of Personality and Social Psychology, 8,* 377–383.

Das, E. H. H. J., De Wit, J. B. F., & Stroebe, W. (2003). Fear appeals motivate acceptance of action recommendations: Evidence for a positive bias in the processing of persuasive messages. *Personality and Social Psychology Bulletin, 29,* 650–664.

David, B., & Turner, J. C. (1996). Studies in self-categorization and minority conversion: Is being a member of the out-group an advantage? *British Journal of Social Psychology, 35,* 179–199.

David, B., & Turner, J. C. (1999). Studies in self-categorization and minority conversion: The in-group minority in intragroup and intergroup contexts. *British Journal of Social Psychology, 38,* 115–134.

Davidov, M., & Grusec, J. E. (2006). Multiple pathways to compliance: Mothers' willingness to cooperate and knowledge of their children's reactions to discipline. *Journal of Family Psychology, 20,* 705–708.

Davidson, A. R., & Jaccard, J. J. (1979). Variables that moderate the attitude-behavior relation: Results of a longitudinal survey. *Journal of Personality and Social Psychology, 37,* 1364–1376.

Davis, D., Shaver, P. R., & Vernon, M. L. (2003). Physical, emotional, and behavioral reactions to breaking up: The roles of gender, age, emotional involvement, and attachment style. *Personality and Social Psychology Bulletin, 29,* 871–884.

Davis, J. H. (1980). Group decision and procedural justice. In M. Fishbein (Ed.), *Progress in social psychology* (Vol. 1, pp. 157–229). Hillsdale, NJ: Erlbaum.

Davis, J. H., Kerr, N. L., Stasser, G., Meek, D., & Holt, R. (1977). Victim consequences, sentence severity, and decision processes in mock juries. *Organizational Behavior and Human Performance, 18,* 346–365.

Davis, M. H. (1994). *Empathy: A social psychological approach.* Boulder, CO: Westview.

Dawkins, R. (1976). *The selfish gene.* Oxford: Oxford University Press.

Dawkins, R. (1979). Twelve misunderstandings of kin selection. *Zeitschrift für Tierpsychologie, 51,* 184–200.

Dawkins, R. (1989). *The selfish gene.* New York: Oxford University Press.

DeChurch, L. A., & Mesmer-Magnus, J. R. (2010). The cognitive underpinnings of effective teamwork: A meta-analysis. *Journal of Applied Psychology, 95,* 32–53.

De Dreu, C. K. W., & De Vries, N. K. (1993). Numerical support, information processing and attitude change. *European Journal of Social Psychology, 23,* 647–662.

De Dreu, C. K. W., & West, M. A. (2001). Minority dissent and team innovation: The importance of participation in decision making. *Journal of Applied Psychology, 86,* 1191–1201.

De Hoog, N., Stroebe, W., & De Wit, J. B. F. (2005). The impact of fear appeals on processing and acceptance of action recommendations. *Personality and Social Psychology Bulletin, 31,* 24–33.

de Lemus, S., Spears, R., Bukowski, M., Moya, M., & Lupiáñez, J. (2013). Reversing implicit gender stereotype activation as a function of exposure to traditional gender roles. *Social Psychology, 44*, 109–116.

De Vries, N. K., De Dreu, C. K. W., Gordijn, E., & Schuurman, M. (1996). Majority and minority influence: A dual role interpretation. In W. Stroebe & M. Hewstone (Eds.), *European review of social psychology* (Vol. 7, pp. 145–172). Chichester, UK: Wiley.

De Wolff, M. S., & Van Ijzendoorn, M. H. (1997). Sensitivity and attachment: A meta-analysis on parental antecedents of infant attachment. *Child Development, 68*, 571–591.

Dechesne, M., Pyszczynski, T., Arndt, J., Ransom, S., Sheldon, K. M., Van Knippenberg, A., & Janssen, J. (2003). Literal and symbolic immortality: The effect of evidence of literal immortality on self-esteem striving in response to mortality salience. *Journal of Personality and Social Psychology, 84*, 722–737.

Deci, E. L., Koestner, R., & Ryan, R. M. (1999). A meta-analytic review of experiments examining the effects of extrinsic rewards on intrinsic motivation. *Psychological Bulletin, 125*, 627–668.

Deci, E. L., & Ryan, R. M. (1985). *Intrinsic motivation and self-determination in human behavior.* New York: Plenum.

Deci, E. L., & Ryan, R. M. (1995). Human autonomy: The basis for true self-esteem. In M. H. Kernis (Ed.), *Efficacy, agency, and self-esteem* (pp. 31–49). New York: Plenum.

Deci, E. L., & Ryan, R. M. (2000). The 'what' and 'why' of goal pursuits: Human needs and the self-determination of behavior. *Psychological Inquiry, 11*, 227–268.

Delgado, M. R., Frank, R. H., & Phelps, E. A. (2005). Perceptions of moral character modulate the neural systems of reward during the trust game. *Nature Neuroscience, 8*, 1611–1618.

Demir, M., & Özdemir, M. (2010). Friendship, need satisfaction, and happiness. *Journal of Happiness Studies, 11*, 243–259.

Dennis, A. R., & Valacich, J. S. (1993). Computer brainstorms: More heads are better than one. *Journal of Applied Psychology, 78*, 531–537.

DeRosa, D. M., Smith, C. L., & Hantula, D. A. (2007). The medium matters: Mining the long-promised merit of group interaction in creative idea generation tasks in a meta-analysis of the electronic group brainstorming literature. *Computers in Human Behavior, 23*, 1549–1581.

Deschamps, J.-C., & Brown, R. (1983). Superordinate goals and intergroup conflict. *British Journal of Social Psychology, 22*, 189–195.

DeShon, R. P., Kozlowski, S. W. J., Schmidt, A. M., Milner, K. R., & Wiechmann, D. (2004). A multiple-goal, multilevel model of feedback effects on the regulation of individual and team performance. *Journal of Applied Psychology, 89*, 1035–1056.

Deutsch, M. (1968). Field theory in social psychology. In G. Lindzey & E. Aronson (Eds.), *Handbook of social psychology* (2nd ed., pp. 412–487). Reading, MA: Addison-Wesley.

Deutsch, M., & Collins, M. E. (1951). *Interracial housing: A psychological evaluation of a social experiment.* Minneapolis, MI: University of Minnesota Press.

Deutsch, M., & Gerard, H. B. (1955). A study of normative and informational social influences upon individual judgment. *Journal of Abnormal and Social Psychology, 51*, 629–636.

Devine, P. G. (1989). Stereotypes and prejudice: Their automatic and controlled components. *Journal of Personality and Social Psychology, 56*, 5–18.

Devine, P. G., Hamilton, D. L., & Ostrom, T. M. (Eds.). (1994). *Social cognition: Impact on social psychology.* San Diego, CA: Academic Press.

Devine, P. G., & Monteith, M. J. (1999). Automaticity and control in stereotyping. In S. Chaiken & Y. Trope (Eds.), *Dual-process theories in social psychology* (pp. 339–360). New York: Guilford.

Devos, T., Huynh, Q.-L., & Banaji, M. R. (2012). Implicit self and identity. In M. R. Leary & J. P. Tangney (Eds.), *Handbook of self and identity* (2nd ed., pp. 155–179). New York: Guilford.

Dewitte, S., Bruyneel, S., & Geyskens, K. (2009). Self regulating enhances self-regulation in subsequent consumer decisions involving similar response conflicts. *Journal of Consumer Research, 36*, 394–405.

Diehl, M., & Stroebe, W. (1987). Productivity loss in brainstorming groups: Toward the solution of a riddle. *Journal of Personality and Social Psychology, 53*, 497–509.

Diener, E. (1980). Deindividuation: The absence of self-awareness and self-regulation in group members. In P. B. Paulus (Ed.), *Psychology of group influence* (pp. 209–242). Hillsdale, NJ: Erlbaum.

Diener, E. (1984). Subjective well-being. *Psychological Bulletin, 95*, 542–575.

Dijker, A. J. M. (1987). Emotional reactions to ethnic minorities. *European Journal of Social Psychology, 17*, 305–325.

Dijksterhuis, A. (2004). I like myself but I don't know why: Enhancing implicit self-esteem by subliminal evaluative conditioning. *Journal of Personality and Social Psychology, 86*, 345–355.

Dijksterhuis, A., Aarts, H., Bargh, J. A., & Van Knippenberg, A. (2000). On the relation between associative strength and automatic behavior. *Journal of Experimental Social Psychology, 36*, 531–544.

Dijksterhuis, A., & Bargh, J. A. (2001). The perception-behavior expressway: Automatic effects of social perception on social behavior. In M. P. Zanna (Ed.), *Advances in experimental social psychology* (Vol. 33, pp. 1–40). San Diego, CA: Academic Press.

Dijksterhuis, A., Bargh, J. A., & Miedema, J. (2000). Of men and mackerels: Attention, subjective experience and automatic social behavior. In H. Bless & J. P. Forgas (Eds.), *The message within: The role of subjective experience in social cognition and behavior* (pp. 37–51). Philadelphia, PA: Psychology Press.

Dijksterhuis, A., Bos, M. W., Nordgren, L. F., & van Baaren, R. B. (2006). On making the right choice: The deliberation-without-attention effect. *Science, 311,* 1005–1007.

Dijksterhuis, A., Chartrand, T. L., & Aarts, H. (2007). Effects of priming and perception on social behavior and goal pursuit. In J. A. Bargh (Ed.), *Social psychology and the unconscious: The automaticity of higher mental processes* (pp. 51–131). New York: Psychology Press.

Dijksterhuis, A., & Van Knippenberg, A. (1998). The relation between perception and behavior, or how to win a game of Trivial Pursuit. *Journal of Personality and Social Psychology, 74,* 865–877.

Dill, K. E., Anderson, C. A., Anderson, K. B., & Deuser, W. E. (1997). Effects of aggressive personality on social expectations and social perceptions. *Journal of Research in Personality, 31,* 272–292.

DiMaggio, P. (1997). Culture and cognition. *Annual Review of Sociology, 23,* 263–287.

Dindia, K. (1994). The intrapersonal-interpersonal dialectical process of self-disclosure. In S. Duck (Ed.), *Dynamics of relationships* (pp. 27–57). Thousand Oaks, CA: Sage.

Dion, K., Berscheid, E., & Walster, E. (1972). What is beautiful is good. *Journal of Personality and Social Psychology, 24,* 285–290.

Dirks, K. T. (1999). The effects of interpersonal trust on work group performance. *Journal of Applied Psychology, 84,* 445–455.

Dishion, T. J., & Nelson, S. E. (2007). Male adolescent friendships: Relationship dynamics that predict adult adjustment. In R. C. M. E. Engels, M. Kerr, & H. Stattin (Eds.), *Friends, lovers and groups: Key relationships in adolescence* (pp. 11–32). Chichester, UK: Wiley.

Dixon, J., & Durrheim, K. (2003). Contact and the ecology of racial division: Some varieties of informal segregation. *British Journal of Social Psychology, 42,* 1–23.

Dixon, J., Durrheim, K., & Tredoux, C. (2007). Intergroup contact and attitudes toward the principle and practice of racial equality. *Psychological Science, 18,* 867–872.

Dixon, J., Levine, M., Reicher, S., & Durrheim, K. (2012). Beyond prejudice: Are negative evaluations the problem and is getting us to like one another more the solution? *Behavioral and Brain Sciences, 35,* 411–425.

Dixon, J., Tropp, L. R., Durrheim, K., & Tredoux, C. (2010). Let them eat harmony: Prejudice-reduction strategies and attitudes of historically disadvantaged groups. *Current Directions in Psychological Science, 19,* 76–80.

Dodge, K. A. (1980). Social cognition and children's aggressive behavior. *Child Development, 51,* 162–170.

Dohmen, T. J. (2008). Do professionals choke under pressure? *Journal of Economic Behavior and Organization, 65,* 636–653.

Doise, W. (1969). Intergroup relations and polarization of individual and collective judgments. *Journal of Personality and Social Psychology, 12,* 136–143.

Dollard, J., Doob, L. W., Miller, N. E., Mowrer, O. H., & Sears, R. R. (1939). *Frustration and aggression.* New Haven, CT: Yale University Press.

Dooley, J. J., Pyzalski, J., & Cross, D. (2009). Cyberbullying versus face-to-face bullying: A theoretical and conceptual review. *Zeitschrift für Psychologie, 217,* 182–188.

Dovidio, J. F. (1995). With a little help from my friends. In G. G. Brannigan & M. R. Merrens (Eds.), *The social psychologists: Research adventures* (pp. 98–113). New York: McGraw-Hill.

Dovidio, J. F., Allen, J. L., & Schroeder, D. A. (1990). Specificity of empathy-induced helping: Evidence for altruistic motivation. *Journal of Personality and Social Psychology, 59,* 249–260.

Dovidio, J. F., Eller, A., & Hewstone, M. (2011). Improving intergroup relations through direct, extended and other forms of indirect contact. *Group Processes & Intergroup Relations, 14,* 147–160.

Dovidio, J. F., Gaertner, S. L., & Saguy, T. (2009). Commonality and the complexity of 'we': Social attitudes and social change. *Personality and Social Psychology Review, 13,* 3–20.

Dovidio, J. F., Gaertner, S. L., Validzic, A., Matoka, K., Johnson, B., & Frazier, S. (1997). Extending the benefits of recategorization: Evaluations, self-disclosure, and helping. *Journal of Experimental Social Psychology, 33,* 401–420.

Dovidio, J. F., Kawakami, K., Johnson, C., Johnson, B., & Howard, A. (1997). On the nature of prejudice: Automatic and controlled processes. *Journal of Experimental Social Psychology, 33,* 510–540.

Dovidio, J. F., Piliavin, J. A., Gaertner, S. L., Schroeder, D. A., & Clark, R. D., III. (1991). The arousal: cost-reward model and the process of intervention: A review of the evidence. In M. S. Clark (Ed.), *Prosocial behavior* (pp. 86–118). Thousand Oaks, CA: Sage.

Dovidio, J. F., Piliavin, J. A., Schroeder, D. A., & Penner, L. (2006). *The social psychology of prosocial behavior.* Mahwah, NJ: Erlbaum.

Downey, G., & Feldman, S. I. (1996). Implications of rejection sensitivity for intimate relationships. *Journal of Personality and Social Psychology, 70,* 1327–1343.

Downs, A. C., & Lyons, P. M. (1991). Natural observations of the links between attractiveness and initial legal judgments. *Personality and Social Psychology Bulletin, 17,* 541–547.

Driskell, J. E., & Mullen, B. (1990). Status, expectations, and behavior: A meta-analytic review and test of the theory. *Personality and Social Psychology Bulletin, 16,* 541–553.

Drury, J., Cocking, C., & Reicher, S. (2009). Everyone for themselves? A comparative study of crowd solidarity among emergency survivors. *British Journal of Social Psychology, 48,* 487–506.

Drury, J., & Reicher, S. D. (2010). Crowd control. *Scientific American Mind, 21,* 58–65.

Dryer, D. C., & Horowitz, L. M. (1997). When do opposites attract? Interpersonal complementarity versus similarity. *Journal of Personality and Social Psychology, 72,* 592–603.

Duck, S., Rutt, D. J., Hurst, M. H., & Strejc, H. (1991). Some evident truths about conversations in everyday relationships: All communications are not created equal. *Human Communication Research, 18,* 228–267.

Duckitt, J. (2001). A dual-process cognitive-motivational theory of ideology and prejudice. In M. P. Zanna (Ed.), *Advances in experimental social psychology* (Vol. 33, pp. 41–113). San Diego, CA: Academic Press.

Duckitt, J. (2006). Differential effects of right wing authoritarianism and social dominance orientation on outgroup attitudes and their mediation by threat from and competitiveness to outgroups. *Personality and Social Psychology Bulletin, 32,* 684–696.

Duckitt, J., & Fisher, K. (2003). The impact of social threat on worldview and ideological attitudes. *Political Psychology, 24,* 199–222.

Duckitt, J., Wagner, C., Du Plessis, I., & Birum, I. (2002). The psychological bases of ideology and prejudice: Testing a dual process model. *Journal of Personality and Social Psychology, 83,* 75–93.

Duffy, S. M., & Rusbult, C. E. (1986). Satisfaction and commitment in homosexual and heterosexual relationships. *Journal of Homosexuality, 12,* 1–23.

Dugatkin, L. A. (2007). Inclusive fitness theory from Darwin to Hamilton. *Genetics, 176,* 1375–1380.

Dunbar, R. I. (2009). The social brain hypothesis and its implications for social evolution. *Annals of Human Biology, 36,* 562–572.

Dunbar, R. I. M., Barrett, L., & Lycett, J. (2005). *Evolutionary psychology: A beginner's guide.* Oxford: Oneworld.

Duncan, B. L. (1976). Differential social perception and attribution of intergroup violence: Testing the lower limits of stereotyping of Blacks. *Journal of Personality and Social Psychology, 34,* 590–598.

Dunn, J. (2004). *Children's friendships: The beginnings of intimacy.* Oxford: Wiley-Blackwell.

Dunning, D. (2005). *Self-insight: Roadblocks and detours on the path to knowing thyself.* New York: Psychology Press.

Dunning, D., & Cohen, G. L. (1992). Egocentric definitions of traits and abilities in social judgment. *Journal of Personality and Social Psychology, 63,* 341–355.

Dunning, D., & Hayes, A. F. (1996). Evidence for egocentric comparison in social judgment. *Journal of Personality and Social Psychology, 71,* 213–229.

Dunning, D., Johnson, K., Ehrlinger, J., & Kruger, J. (2003). Why people fail to recognize their own incompetence. *Current Directions in Psychological Science, 12,* 83–87.

Dunning, D., & McElwee, R. O. B. (1995). Idiosyncratic trait definitions: Implications for self-description and social judgment. *Journal of Personality and Social Psychology, 68,* 936–946.

Dunning, D., Meyerowitz, J. A., & Holzberg, A. D. (1989). Ambiguity and self-evaluation: The role of idiosyncratic trait definitions in self-serving assessments of ability. *Journal of Personality and Social Psychology, 57,* 1082–1090.

Dunning, D., Perie, M., & Story, A. L. (1991). Self-serving prototypes of social categories. *Journal of Personality and Social Psychology, 61,* 957–968.

Dunton, B. C., & Fazio, R. H. (1997). An individual difference measure of motivation to control prejudiced reactions. *Personality and Social Psychology Bulletin, 23,* 316–326.

Dutton, D. G., & Aron, A. P. (1974). Some evidence for heightened sexual attraction under conditions of high anxiety. *Journal of Personality and Social Psychology, 30,* 510–517.

Dutton, D. G., & Lake, R. A. (1973). Threat of own prejudice and reverse discrimination in interracial situations. *Journal of Personality and Social Psychology, 28,* 94–100.

Duval, S., & Wicklund, R. A. (1972). *A theory of objective self awareness.* New York: Academic Press.

Dweck, C. S. (2006). *Mindset: The new psychology of success.* New York: Random House.

Dweck, C. S., Chiu, C.-Y., & Hong, Y.-Y. (1995). Implicit theories and their role in judgments and reactions: A world from two perspectives. *Psychological Inquiry, 6,* 267–285.

Eagly, A. (2009). The his and hers of prosocial behaviour: An examination of the social psychology of gender. *American Psychologist, 64,* 644–658.

Eagly, A. H., & Chaiken, S. (1993). *The psychology of attitudes.* Fort Worth, TX: Harcourt Brace Jovanovich.

Eagly, A. H., & Crowley, M. (1986). Gender and helping behavior: A meta-analytic review of the social psychological literature. *Psychological Bulletin, 100,* 283–308.

Eagly, A. H., & Steffen, V. J. (1986). Gender and aggressive behavior: A meta-analytic review of the social psychological literature. *Psychological Bulletin, 100,* 309–330.

Earley, P. C. (1989). Social loafing and collectivism: A comparison of the United States and the People's Republic of China. *Administrative Science Quarterly, 34,* 565–581.

Earley, P. C. (1993). East meets West meets Mideast: Further explorations of collectivistic versus individualistic work groups. *Academy of Management Journal, 36,* 319–348.

Earley, P. C., & Mosakowski, E. (2000). Creating hybrid team cultures: An empirical test of international team functioning. *Academy of Management Journal, 43,* 26–49.

Easterlin, R. A. (2003). Explaining happiness. *Proceedings of the National Academy of Science, 100,* 11176–11183.

Eastwick, P. W., & Finkel, E. J. (2008). Sex differences in mate preferences revisited: Do people know what they initially desire in a romantic partner? *Journal of Personality and Social Psychology, 94,* 245–264.

Eastwick, P. W., Finkel, E. J., Mochon, D., & Ariely, D. (2007). Selective vs. unselective romantic desire: Not all reciprocity is created equal. *Psychological Science, 18,* 317–319.

Eaton, A. A., Majka, E. A., & Visser, P. S. (2008). Emerging perspectives on the structure and function of attitude strength. In W. Stroebe & M. Hewstone (Eds.), *European review of social psychology* (Vol. 19, pp. 165–201). Hove, UK: Psychology Press.

Eaton, J., Struthers, C. W., Shomrony, A., & Santelli, A. G. (2007). When apologies fail: The moderating effect of implicit and explicit self-esteem on apology and forgiveness. *Self and Identity, 6,* 209–222.

Eberhardt, J. L. (2005). Imaging race. *American Psychologist, 60,* 181–190.

Edwards, D., & Potter, J. (1993). Language and causation: A discursive action model of description and attribution. *Psychological Review, 100,* 23–41.

Eisenberger, N. I. (2012). The pain of social disconnection: Examining the shared neural underpinnings of physical and social pain. *Nature Reviews Neuroscience, 13,* 421–434.

Eisenberger, N. I., Lieberman, M. D., & Williams, K. D. (2003). Does rejection hurt? An fMRI study of social exclusion. *Science, 302,* 290–292.

Eisenberger, R., & Cameron, J. (1996). Detrimental effects of reward: Reality or myth? *American Psychologist, 51,* 1153–1166.

Ekman, P. (1972). Universals and cultural differences in facial expressions of emotion. In J. Cole (Ed.), *Nebraska Symposium on Motivation* (Vol. 19, pp. 207–283). Lincoln, NE: University of Nebraska Press.

Ekman, P., Friesen, W. V., O'Sullivan, M., Chan, A., Diacoyanni-Tarlatzis, I., Heider, K., … Ricci-Bitti, P. E. (1987). Universals and cultural differences in the judgments of facial expressions of emotion. *Journal of Personality and Social Psychology, 53,* 712–717.

Elizur, Y., & Mintzer, A. (2003). Gay males' intimate relationship quality: The roles of attachment security, gay identity, social support, and income. *Personal Relationships, 10,* 411–435.

Ellemers, N. (1993). The influence of socio-structural variables on identity management strategies. In W. Stroebe & M. Hewstone (Eds.), *European review of social psychology* (Vol. 4, pp. 27–57). Chichester, UK: Wiley.

Ellemers, N., Spears, R., & Doosje, B. (2002). Self and social identity. *Annual Review of Psychology, 53,* 161–186.

Elms, A. C., & Milgram, S. (1966). Personality characteristics associated with obedience and defiance toward authoritative command. *Journal of Experimental Research in Personality, 1,* 282–289.

Englich, B., Mussweiler, T., & Strack, F. (2006). Playing dice with criminal sentences: The influence of irrelevant anchors on experts' judicial decision making. *Personality and Social Psychology Bulletin, 32,* 188–200.

English, T., & Chen, S. (2007). Culture and self-concept stability: Consistency across and within contexts among Asian Americans and European Americans. *Journal of Personality and Social Psychology, 93,* 478–490.

Ensari, N., & Miller, N. (2002). The out-group must not be so bad after all: The effects of disclosure, typicality, and salience on intergroup bias. *Journal of Personality and Social Psychology, 83,* 313–329.

Epley, N. (2004). A tale of Tuned Decks? Anchoring as adjustment and anchoring as activation. In D. J. Koehler & N. Harvey (Eds.), *The Blackwell handbook of judgment and decision making* (pp. 240–256). Oxford, England: Blackwell.

Epley, N., & Gilovich, T. (2001). Putting adjustment back in the anchoring and adjustment heuristic: Differential processing of self-generated and experimenter-provided anchors. *Psychological Science, 12,* 391–396.

Epley, N., & Gilovich, T. (2006). The anchoring-and-adjustment heuristic. *Psychological Science, 17,* 311–318.

Epley, N., & Whitchurch, E. (2008). Mirror, mirror on the wall: Enhancement in self-recognition. *Personality and Social Psychology Bulletin, 34,* 1159–1170.

Epstein, S., & Morling, B. (1995). Is the self motivated to do more than enhance and/or verify itself? In M. H. Kernis (Ed.), *Efficacy, agency, and self-esteem* (pp. 9–29). New York: Plenum.

Erdmann, G., & Janke, W. (1978). Interaction between physiological and cognitive determinants of emotions: Experimental studies on Schachter's theory of emotions. *Biological Psychology, 6,* 61–74.

Erez, M., & Somech, A. (1996). Is group productivity loss the rule or the exception? Effects of culture and group-based motivation. *Academy of Management Journal, 39,* 1513–1537.

Esser, J. K. (1998). Alive and well after 25 years: A review of groupthink research. *Organizational Behavior and Human Decision Processes, 73,* 116–141.

Esser, J. K., & Lindoerfer, J. S. (1989). Groupthink and the space shuttle Challenger accident: Toward a quantitative case analysis. *Journal of Behavioral Decision Making, 2,* 167–177.

Esses, V. M., Haddock, G., & Zanna, M. P. (1993). Values, stereotypes, and emotions as determinants of intergroup attitudes. In D. M. Mackie & D. L. Hamilton (Eds.), *Affect, cognition, and stereotyping: Interactive processes in group perception* (pp. 137–166). San Diego, CA: Academic Press.

Esses, V. M., Jackson, L. M., Dovidio, J. F., & Hodson, G. (2005). Instrumental relations among groups: Group competition, conflict, and prejudice. In J. F. Dovidio, P. Glick, & L. A. Rudman (Eds.), *On the nature of prejudice* (pp. 225–243). Oxford: Blackwell.

Esses, V. M., Veenvliet, S., Hodson, G., & Mihic, L. (2008). Justice, morality, and the dehumanization of refugees. *Social Justice Research, 21*, 4–25.

Esses, V. M., & Vernon, R. A. (Eds.). (2008). *Explaining the breakdown of ethnic relations: Why neighbors kill.* Oxford: Blackwell.

Exum, M. L. (2006). Alcohol and aggression: An integration of findings from experimental studies. *Journal of Criminal Justice, 34*, 131–145.

Falk, C. F., Heine, S., & Takemura, K. (2014). Cultural variation in the minimal group effect. *Journal of Cross-Cultural Psychology, 45*, 265–281.

Fantz, R. L. (1963). Pattern vision in newborn infants. *Science, 140*, 296–297.

Farr, R. M. (1996). *The roots of modern social psychology: 1872–1954.* Oxford: Blackwell.

Faulkner, J., Schaller, M., Park, J. H., & Duncan, L. A. (2004). Evolved disease-avoidance mechanisms and contemporary xenophobic attitudes. *Group Processes & Intergroup Relations, 7*, 333–353.

Faulmüller, N., Mojzisch, A., Kerschreiter, R., & Schulz-Hardt, S. (2012). Do you want to convince me or to be understood? Preference-consistent information sharing and its motivational determinants. *Personality and Social Psychology Bulletin, 38*, 1684–1696.

Fazio, R. H. (1990). Multiple processes by which attitudes guide behavior: The MODE model as an integrative framework. In M. P. Zanna (Ed.), *Advances in experimental social psychology* (Vol. 23, pp. 75–109). San Diego, CA: Academic Press.

Fazio, R. H. (1995). Attitudes as object-evaluation associations: Determinants, consequences, and correlates of attitude accessibility. In R. E. Petty & J. A. Krosnick (Eds.), *Attitude strength: Antecedents and consequences* (pp. 247–282). Hillsdale, NJ: Erlbaum.

Fazio, R. H. (2000). Accessible attitudes as tools for object appraisal: Their costs and benefits. In G. R. Maio & J. M. Olson (Eds.), *Why we evaluate: Functions of attitudes* (pp. 1–36). Mahwah, NJ: Erlbaum.

Fazio, R. H. (2007). Attitudes as object-evaluation associations of varying strength. *Social Cognition, 25*, 603–637.

Fazio, R. H., Chen, J. M., McDonel, E. C., & Sherman, S. J. (1982). Attitude accessibility, attitude-behavior consistency, and the strength of the object-evaluation association. *Journal of Experimental Social Psychology, 18*, 339–357.

Fazio, R. H., Jackson, J. R., Dunton, B. C., & Williams, C. J. (1995). Variability in automatic activation as an unobtrusive measure of racial attitudes: A bona fide pipeline? *Journal of Personality and Social Psychology, 69*, 1013–1027.

Fazio, R. H., & Olson, M. A. (2003). Implicit measures in social cognition research: Their meaning and use. *Annual Review of Psychology, 54*, 297–327.

Fazio, R. H., & Petty, R. E. (Eds.). (2007). *Attitudes: Their structure, function, and consequences.* Hove, UK: Psychology Press.

Fazio, R. H., & Williams, C. J. (1986). Attitude accessibility as a moderator of the attitude-perception and attitude-behavior relations: An investigation of the 1984 presidential election. *Journal of Personality and Social Psychology, 51*, 505–514.

Fazio, R. H., Zanna, M. P., & Cooper, J. (1977). Dissonance and self-perception: An integrative view of each theory's proper domain of application. *Journal of Experimental Social Psychology, 13*, 464–479.

Feeney, J. A. (2002). Attachment, marital interaction, and relationship satisfaction: A diary study. *Personal Relationships, 9*, 39–55.

Fehr, E., & Camerer, C. F. (2007). Social neuroeconomics: The neural circuitry of social preferences. *Trends in Cognitive Sciences, 11*, 419–427.

Fehr, E., & Gächter, S. (2002). Altruistic punishment in humans. *Nature, 415*, 137–140.

Feinberg, T. E., & Keenan, J. P. (Eds.). (2005). *The lost self: Pathologies of the brain and identity.* New York: Oxford University Press.

Fejfar, M. C., & Hoyle, R. H. (2000). Effect of private self-awareness on negative affect and self-referent attribution: A quantitative review. *Personality and Social Psychology Review, 4*, 132–142.

Fennis, B. M. (2008). Persuasion pleasure and selling stress: The role of non-verbal communication in consumer influence settings. *Advances in Consumer Research, 35*, 797–798.

Fennis, B. M., Janssen, L., & Vohs, K. D. (2009). Acts of benevolence: A limited-resource account of compliance with charitable requests. *Journal of Consumer Research, 35*, 906–924.

Fennis, B. M., & Stroebe, W. (2010). *The psychology of advertising.* Hove, UK: Psychology Press.

Ferguson, C. J. (2002). Media violence: Miscast causality. *American Psychologist, 57*, 446–447.

Ferguson, C. J. (2007). Evidence for publication bias in video game violence effects literature: A meta-analytic review. *Aggression and Violent Behavior, 12*, 470–482.

Festinger, L. (1950). Informal social communication. *Psychological Review, 57*, 271–282.

Festinger, L. (1954). A theory of social comparison processes. *Human Relations, 7*, 117–140.

Festinger, L. (1957). *A theory of cognitive dissonance.* Stanford, CA: Stanford University Press.

Festinger, L. (1980). *Retrospections on social psychology.* New York: Oxford University Press.

Festinger, L., & Carlsmith, J. M. (1959). Cognitive consequences of forced compliance. *Journal of Abnormal and Social Psychology, 58*, 203–210.

Festinger, L., & Maccoby, N. (1964). On resistance to persuasive communications. *Journal of Abnormal and Social Psychology, 68*, 359–366.

Festinger, L., Riecken, H. W., & Schachter, S. (1956). *When prophecy fails.* Minneapolis, MN: University of Minnesota Press.

Festinger, L., Schachter, S., & Back, K. (1950). *Social pressures in informal groups: A study of human factors in housing.* New York: Harper.

Fhanér, G., & Hane, M. (1979). Seat belts: Opinion effects of law-induced use. *Journal of Applied Psychology, 64,* 205–212.

Fiedler, K. (1991). The tricky nature of skewed frequency tables: An information loss account of distinctiveness-based illusory correlations. *Journal of Personality and Social Psychology, 60,* 24–36.

Fincham, F. D. (2000). The kiss of the porcupines: From attributing responsibility to forgiving. *Personal Relationships, 7,* 1–23.

Fincham, F. D., Paleari, F. G., & Regalia, C. (2002). Forgiveness in marriage: The role of relationship quality, attributions, and empathy. *Personal Relationships, 9,* 27–37.

Fine, G. A., & Elsbach, K. D. (2000). Ethnography and experiment in social psychological theory building: Tactics for integrating qualitative field data with quantitative lab data. *Journal of Experimental Social Psychology, 36,* 51–76.

Finkel, E. J., Rusbult, C. E., Kumashiro, M., & Hannon, P. A. (2002). Dealing with betrayal in close relationships: Does commitment promote forgiveness? *Journal of Personality and Social Psychology, 82,* 956–974.

Finkenauer, C., Engels, R. C. M. E., Branje, S. J. T., & Meeus, W. (2004). Disclosure and relationship satisfaction in families. *Journal of Marriage and Family, 66,* 195–209.

Finkenauer, C., Kubacka, K. E., Engels, R. C. M. E., & Kerkhof, P. (2009). Secrecy in close relationships: Investigating its intrapersonal and interpersonal effects. In T. D. Afifi & W. A. Afifi (Eds.), *Uncertainty, information management, and disclosure decisions: Theories and applications* (pp. 300–319). New York: Routledge.

Finlay, K., & Stephan, W. G. (2000). Reducing prejudice: The effects of empathy on intergroup attitudes. *Journal of Applied Social Psychology, 30,* 1720–1737.

Fischer, A. H., & Roseman, I. J. (2007). Beat them or ban them: The characteristics and social functions of anger and contempt. *Journal of Personality and Social Psychology, 93,* 103–115.

Fischer, P., & Greitemeyer, T. (2006). Music and aggression: The impact of sexual-aggressive song lyrics on aggression-related thoughts, emotions, and behavior toward the same and the opposite sex. *Personality and Social Psychology Bulletin, 32,* 1165–1176.

Fischer, P., Greitemeyer, T., Pollozek, F., & Frey, D. (2006). The unresponsive bystander: Are bystanders more responsive in dangerous emergencies? *European Journal of Social Psychology, 36,* 267–278.

Fischer, P., Krueger, J. I., Greitemeyer, T., Vogrincic, C., Kastenmüller, A., Frey, D., ... & Kainbacher, M. (2011). The bystander-effect: A meta-analytic review on bystander intervention in dangerous and non-dangerous emergencies. *Psychological Bulletin, 137,* 517–537.

Fishbein, M. (1963). An investigation of the relationship between beliefs about an object and the attitudes towards that object. *Human Relations, 16,* 233–240.

Fishbein, M. (1967). Attitude and the prediction of behavior. In M. Fishbein (Ed.), *Readings in attitude theory and measurement* (pp. 477–492). New York: Wiley.

Fishbein, M., & Ajzen, I. (1975). *Belief, attitude, intention, and behavior.* Reading, MA: Addison-Wesley.

Fisher, H. E. (2004). *Why we love: The nature and chemistry of romantic love.* New York: Holt.

Fisher, H. E., Aron, A., & Brown, L. L. (2006). Romantic love: A mammalian brain system for mate choice. *Philosophical Transactions of the Royal Society B, 361,* 2173–2186.

Fiske, S. T. (1989). Examining the role of intent: Toward understanding its role in stereotyping and prejudice. In J. S. Uleman & J. A. Bargh (Eds.), *Unintended thought* (pp. 253–283). New York: Guilford.

Fiske, S. T. (2004). *Social beings: Core motives in social psychology.* Chichester, UK: Wiley.

Fiske, S. T., Cuddy, A. J. C., Glick, P., & Xu, J. (2002). A model of (often mixed) stereotype content: Competence and warmth respectively follow from perceived status and competition. *Journal of Personality and Social Psychology, 82,* 878–902.

Fiske, S. T., Gilbert, D. T., & Lindzey, G. (Eds.). (2010). *Handbook of social psychology* (5th ed., Vol. 1). Hoboken, NJ: Wiley.

Fiske, S. T., Lin, M., & Neuberg, S. L. (1999). The continuum model: Ten years later. In S. Chaiken & Y. Trope (Eds.), *Dual-process theories in social psychology* (pp. 231–254). New York: Guilford.

Fiske, S. T., & Neuberg, S. L. (1990). A continuum of impression formation, from category-based to individuating processes: Influences of information and motivation on attention and interpretation. In M. P. Zanna (Ed.), *Advances in experimental social psychology* (Vol. 23, pp. 1–74). New York: Academic Press.

Fiske, S. T., & Taylor, S. E. (1991). *Social cognition* (2nd ed.). New York: McGraw-Hill.

Fiske, S. T., & Taylor, S. E. (2008). *Social cognition: From brains to culture* (3rd ed.). New York: McGraw-Hill.

Fiske, S. T., & Taylor, S. E. (2013). *Social cognition: From brains to culture* (2nd ed.). London: Sage.

Flannery, D. J., Vazsonyi, A. T., & Waldman, I. D. (Eds.). (2007). *Cambridge handbook of violent behavior and aggression.* New York: Cambridge University Press.

Fletcher, G. J. O. (2002). *The new science of intimate relationships.* Oxford: Blackwell.

Flores, N. M., & Huo, Y. J. (2013). 'We' are not all alike: Consequences of neglecting national origin identities among Asians and Latinos. *Social Psychological and Personality Science, 4,* 143–150.

Flowers, M. L. (1977). A laboratory test of some implications of Janis's groupthink hypothesis. *Journal of Personality and Social Psychology, 35,* 888–896.

Forgas, J. P., Bower, G. H., & Moylan, S. J. (1990). Praise or blame? Affective influences on attributions for achievement. *Journal of Personality and Social Psychology, 59*, 809–819.

Försterling, F. (2001). *Attribution: An introduction to theories, research, and applications*. Hove, UK: Psychology Press.

Forsyth, D. R. (1995). Norms. In A. S. R. Manstead & M. Hewstone (Eds.), *Blackwell encyclopedia of social psychology* (pp. 412–417). Oxford: Blackwell.

Fraley, R. C., & Shaver, P. R. (2000). Adult romantic attachment: Theoretical developments, emerging controversies, and unanswered questions. *Review of General Psychology, 4*, 132–154.

Fraley, R. C., Waller, N. G., & Brennan, K. A. (2000). An item response theory analysis of self-report measures of adult attachment. *Journal of Personality and Social Psychology, 78*, 350–365.

Freedman, J. L., & Fraser, S. C. (1966). Compliance without pressure: The foot-in-the-door technique. *Journal of Personality and Social Psychology, 4*, 195–202.

Freeman, J. B., & Ambady, N. (2011). A dynamic interactive theory of person construal. *Psychological Review, 118*, 247–279.

Freese, L., & Cohen, B. P. (1973). Eliminating status generalization. *Sociometry, 36*, 177–193.

Freud, S. (1920). *Beyond the pleasure principle*. New York: Bantam.

Frey, B. S., Savage, D. A., & Torgler, B. (2010). Interaction of natural survival instincts and internalized social norms exploring the Titanic and Lusitania disasters. *Proceedings of the National Academy of Sciences of the United States of America, 107*, 4862–4865.

Frieze, I. H. (2000). Violence in close relationships-development of a research area: Comment on Archer (2000). *Psychological Bulletin, 126*, 681–684.

Frieze, I. H., & Davis, K. E. (Eds.). (2002). *Stalking: Perspectives on victims and perpetrators*. New York: Springer.

Frieze, I. H., Olson, J. E., & Russell, J. (1991). Attractiveness and income for men and women in management. *Journal of Applied Social Psychology, 21*, 1039–1057.

Frijda, N. H. (1986). *The emotions*. Cambridge, MA: Cambridge University Press.

Frost, J. H., Chance, Z., Norton, M. I., & Ariely, D. (2008). People are experience goods: Improving online dating with virtual dates. *Journal of Interactive Marketing, 22*, 51–61.

Fujita, K., & Roberts, J. C. (2010). Promoting prospective self-control through abstraction. *Journal of Experimental Social Psychology, 46*, 1049–1054.

Fujita, K., Trope, Y., Liberman, N., & Levin-Sagi, M. (2006). Construal levels and self-control. *Journal of Personality and Social Psychology, 90*, 351–367.

Funder, D. C. (1987). Errors and mistakes: Evaluating the accuracy of social judgment. *Psychological Bulletin, 101*, 75–90.

Furman, W., & Bierman, K. L. (1984). Children's conceptions of friendship: A multimethod study of developmental changes. *Developmental Psychology, 20*, 925–931.

Gaertner, L., & Insko, C. A. (2000). Intergroup discrimination in the minimal group paradigm: Categorization, reciprocation, or fear? *Journal of Personality and Social Psychology, 79*, 77–94.

Gaertner, L., Sedikides, C., & Chang, K. (2008). On pancultural self enhancement: Well-adjusted Taiwanese self-enhance on personally valued traits. *Journal of Cross-Cultural Psychology, 39*, 463–477.

Gaertner, S. L., & Dovidio, J. F. (2000). *Reducing intergroup bias: The common ingroup identity model*. Philadelphia, PA: Psychology Press.

Gaertner, S. L., & Dovidio, J. F. (2008). Addressing contemporary racism: The common ingroup identity model. In C. Willis-Esqueda (Ed.), *Nebraska Symposium on Motivation: Motivational aspects of prejudice and racism* (Vol. 53, pp. 111–133). New York: Springer.

Gaertner, S. L., Mann, J., Murrell, A., & Dovidio, J. F. (1989). Reducing intergroup bias: The benefits of recategorization. *Journal of Personality and Social Psychology, 57*, 239–249.

Gaertner, S. L., Rust, M. C., Dovidio, J. F., Bachman, B. A., & Anastasio, P. A. (1996). The contact hypothesis: The role of a common ingroup identity on reducing intergroup bias among majority and minority group members. In J. L. Nye & A. M. Brower (Eds.), *What's social about social cognition?* (pp. 230–260). Thousand Oaks, CA: Sage.

Gagnon, A., & Bourhis, R. Y. (1996). Discrimination in the minimal group paradigm: Social identity or self-interest? *Personality and Social Psychology Bulletin, 22*, 1289–1301.

Galinsky, A. D., & Moskowitz, G. B. (2000). Perspective-taking: Decreasing stereotype expression, stereotype accessibility, and in-group favoritism. *Journal of Personality and Social Psychology, 78*, 708–724.

Gamson, W. A., Fireman, B., & Rytina, S. (1982). *Encounters with unjust authority*. Homewood, IL: Dorsey.

Gansberg, M. (1964, March 27). 37 who saw murder didn't call the police. *New York Times* (p. 1).

Garcia, S. M., Weaver, K., Moskowitz, G. B., & Darley, J. M. (2002). Crowded minds: The implicit bystander effect. *Journal of Personality and Social Psychology, 83*, 843–853.

Gawronski, B. (2004). Theory-based bias correction in dispositional inference: The fundamental attribution error is dead, long live the correspondence bias. In W. Stroebe & M. Hewstone (Eds.), *European review of social psychology* (Vol. 15, pp. 183–217). Hove, UK: Psychology Press.

Gawronski, B., Ehrenberg, K., Banse, R., Zukova, J., & Klauer, K. C. (2003). It's in the mind of the beholder: The impact of stereotypic associations on category-based and individuating impression formation. *Journal of Experimental Social Psychology, 39*, 16–30.

Greer, L. L., & Van Kleef, G. A. (2010). Equality versus differentiation: The effects of power dispersion on group interaction. *Journal of Applied Psychology, 95,* 1032–1044.

Gregg, A. P., & Sedikides, C. (2010). Narcissistic fragility: Rethinking its links to explicit and implicit self-esteem. *Self and Identity, 9,* 142–161.

Greitemeyer, T., & Osswald, S. (2009). Prosocial video games reduce aggressive cognitions. *Journal of Experimental Social Psychology, 45,* 896–900.

Greitemeyer, T., & Schulz-Hardt, S. (2003). Preference-consistent evaluation of information in the hidden profile paradigm: Beyond group-level explanations for the dominance of shared information in group decisions. *Journal of Personality and Social Psychology, 84,* 322–339.

Grice, H. P. (1975). Logic and conversation. In P. Cole & J. L. Morgan (Eds.), *Syntax and semantics* (Vol. 3, pp. 41–58). New York: Academic Press.

Griffin, R. S., & Gross, A. M. (2004). Childhood bullying: Current empirical findings and future directions for research. *Aggression and Violent Behavior, 9,* 379–400.

Grove, T. (1998). *The juryman's tale.* London: Bloomsbury.

Grube, J. A., & Piliavin, J. A. (2000). Role identity, organizational experiences, and volunteer performance. *Personality and Social Psychology Bulletin, 26,* 1108–1119.

Grzelak, J., & Derlega, V. J. (1982). Cooperation and helping behavior: An introduction. In V. J. Derlega & J. Grzelak (Eds.), *Cooperation and helping behavior: Theories and research* (pp. 2–15). New York: Academic Press.

Gudykunst, W. B., Gao, G., Schmidt, K. L., Nishida, T., Bond, M. H., Leung, K., ... Barraclough, R. A. (1992). The influence of individualism-collectivism, self-monitoring, and predicted-outcome value on communication in ingroup and outgroup relationships. *Journal of Cross-Cultural Psychology, 23,* 196–213.

Guerin, B. (1993). *Social facilitation.* Cambridge, MA: Cambridge University Press.

Guimond, S., Dambrun, M., Michinov, N., & Duarte, S. (2003). Does social dominance generate prejudice? Integrating individual and contextual determinants of intergroup cognitions. *Journal of Personality and Social Psychology, 84,* 697–721.

Haaland, G. A., & Venkatesan, M. (1968). Resistance to persuasive communication: An examination of the distraction hypotheses. *Journal of Personality and Social Psychology, 9,* 167–170.

Hackman, J. R., & Morris, C. G. (1975). Group tasks, group interaction process, and group performance effectiveness: A review and proposed integration. In L. Berkowitz (Ed.), *Advances in experimental social psychology* (Vol. 8, pp. 45–99). New York: Academic Press.

Haddock, G., & Carrick, R. (1999). How to make a politician more likeable and effective: Framing political judgments through the numeric values of a rating scale. *Social Cognition, 17,* 298–311.

Haddock, G., & Maio, G. R. (Eds.). (2004). *Contemporary perspectives on the psychology of attitudes.* Hove, UK: Psychology Press.

Haddock, G., Maio, G. R., Arnold, K., & Huskinson, T. (2008). Should persuasion be affective or cognitive? The moderating effects of need for affect and need for cognition. *Personality and Social Psychology Bulletin, 34,* 769–778.

Haddock, G., Rothman, A. J., Reber, R., & Schwarz, N. (1999). Forming judgments of attitude certainty, intensity, and importance: The role of subjective experiences. *Personality and Social Psychology Bulletin, 25,* 771–782.

Haddock, G., Zanna, M. P., & Esses, V. M. (1993). Assessing the structure of prejudicial attitudes: The case of attitudes toward homosexuals. *Journal of Personality and Social Psychology, 65,* 1105–1118.

Hagger, M. S., Wood, C., Stiff, C., & Chatzisarantis, N. L. D. (2010). Ego depletion and the strength model of self-control: A meta-analysis. *Psychological Bulletin, 136,* 495–525.

Haines, H., & Vaughan, G. M. (1979). Was 1898 a great date in the history of experimental social psychology? *Journal of the History of the Behavioral Science, 15,* 323–332.

Halabi, S., Dovidio, J. F., & Nadler, A. (2008). When and how do high status group members offer help: Effects of social dominance orientation and status threat. *Political Psychology, 29,* 841–858.

Hall, P. A., Zehr, C. E., Ng, M., & Zanna, M. P. (2012). Implementation intentions for physical activity in supportive and unsupportive environmental conditions: An experimental examination of intention–behavior consistency. *Journal of Experimental Social Psychology, 48,* 432–436.

Hamilton, D. L. (Ed.). (1981). *Cognitive processes in stereotyping and intergroup behavior.* Hillsdale, NJ: Erlbaum.

Hamilton, D. L., & Gifford, R. K. (1976). Illusory correlation in interpersonal perception: A cognitive basis of stereotypic judgments. *Journal of Experimental Social Psychology, 12,* 392–407.

Hamilton, V. L. (1980). Intuitive psychologist or intuitive lawyer? Alternative models of the attribution process. *Journal of Personality and Social Psychology, 39,* 767–772.

Hamilton, W. D. (1964). The genetical evolution of social behaviour. *Journal of Theoretical Biology, 7,* 1–52.

Han, H. A., Czellar, S., Olson, M. A., & Fazio, R. H. (2010). Malleability of attitudes or malleability of the IAT? *Journal of Experimental Social Psychology, 46,* 286–298.

Haney, C., Banks, C., & Zimbardo, P. (1973). Interpersonal dynamics in a simulated prison. *International Journal of Criminology and Penology, 1,* 69–97.

Harari, H., Harari, O., & White, R. V. (1985). The reaction to rape by American male bystanders. *Journal of Social Psychology, 125,* 653–658.

Harari, H., Mohr, D., & Hosey, K. R. (1980). Faculty helpfulness to students: A comparison of compliance techniques. *Personality and Social Psychology Bulletin, 6*, 373–377.

Harker, L., & Keltner, D. (2001). Expressions of positive emotions in women's college yearbook pictures and their relationship to personality and life outcomes across adulthood. *Journal of Personality and Social Psychology, 80*, 112–124.

Harmon-Jones, E., Amodio, D. M., & Harmon-Jones, C. (2009). Action-based model of dissonance: A review, integration, and expansion of conceptions of cognitive conflict. In M. P. Zanna (Ed.), *Advances in experimental social psychology* (Vol. 41, pp. 119–166). San Diego, CA: Academic Press.

Harris, L. T., & Fiske, S. T. (2006). Dehumanizing the lowest of the low: Neuroimaging responses to extreme out-groups. *Psychological Science, 17*, 847–853.

Harris, L. T., Todorov, A., & Fiske, S. T. (2005). Attributions on the brain: Neuro-imaging dispositional inferences, beyond theory of mind. *Neuroimage, 28*, 763–769.

Harter, S. (1993). Causes and consequences of low self-esteem in children and adolescents. In R. F. Baumeister (Ed.), *Self-esteem: The puzzle of low self-regard* (pp. 87–116). New York: Plenum.

Harter, S. (1999). *The construction of the self: A developmental perspective*. New York: Guilford.

Hartup, W. W. (1996). The company they keep: Friendships and their developmental significance. *Child Development, 67*, 1–13.

Hartup, W. W., & Stevens, N. (1997). Friendships and adaptation in the life course. *Psychological Bulletin, 121*, 355–370.

Harwood, J., Hewstone, M., Paolini, S., & Voci, A. (2005). Grandparent-grandchild contact and attitudes toward older adults: Moderator and mediator effects. *Personality and Social Psychology Bulletin, 31*, 393–406.

Harzing, A. W. (2005). The use of English questionnaires in cross-national research: Does cultural accommodation obscure cross-national differences? *International Journal of Cross Cultural Management, 5*, 213–224.

Haslam, S. A. (2004). *Psychology in organisations: The social identity approach* (2nd ed.). London: Sage.

Haslam, S. A., & McGarty, C. (2003). *Research methods and statistics in psychology*. London: Sage.

Haslam, S. A., & McGarty, C. (2014). *Research methods and statistics in psychology* (2nd ed.). London: Sage.

Haslam, S. A., & Oakes, P. J. (1995). How context-independent is the outgroup homogeneity effect? A response to Bartsch and Judd. *European Journal of Social Psychology, 25*, 469–475.

Haslam, S. A., & Reicher, S. D. (2007). Beyond the banality of evil: Three dynamics of an interactionist social psychology of tyranny. *Personality and Social Psychology Bulletin, 33*, 615–622.

Haslam, S. A., & Reicher, S. D. (2008). Questioning the banality of evil. *Psychologist, 21*, 16–19.

Hass, R. G., & Eisenstadt, D. (1990). The effects of self-focused attention on perspective-taking and anxiety. *Anxiety Research, 2*, 165–176.

Hassebrauck, M. (1993). Die Beurteilung der physischen Attraktivität [The evaluation of physical attractiveness]. In M. Hassebrauck & R. Niketta (Eds.), *Physische Attraktivität* (pp. 29–60). Göttingen, Germany: Hogrefe.

Hastie, R. (1993). *Inside the juror*. New York: Cambridge University Press.

Hastie, R., Penrod, S., & Pennington, N. (1983). *Inside the jury*. Cambridge, MA: Harvard University Press.

Hatfield, E., & Rapson, R. L. (1993). *Love, sex, and intimacy: Their psychology, biology, and history*. New York: HarperCollins.

Haugtvedt, C. P., & Petty, R. E. (1992). Personality and persuasion: Need for cognition moderates the persistence and resistance of attitude changes. *Journal of Personality and Social Psychology, 63*, 308–319.

Hawker, D. S. J., & Boulton, M. J. (2000). Twenty years' research on peer victimization and psychosocial maladjustment: A meta-analytic review of cross-sectional studies. *Journal of Child Psychology and Psychiatry, 41*, 441–455.

Hazan, C., & Shaver, P. R. (1987). Romantic love conceptualized as an attachment process. *Journal of Personality and Social Psychology, 52*, 511–524.

Hazan, C., & Shaver, P. R. (1994). Attachment as an organizational framework for research on close relationships. *Psychological Inquiry, 5*, 1–22.

Heatherton, T. F. (2011). Neuroscience of self and self-regulation. *Annual Review of Psychology, 62*, 363–390.

Heatherton, T. F., & Baumeister, R. F. (1991). Binge eating as escape from self-awareness. *Psychological Bulletin, 110*, 86–108.

Hechter, M., & Opp, K. D. (Eds.). (2001). *Social norms*. New York: Sage.

Hedges, L. V., & Olkin, I. (1985). *Statistical methods for meta-analysis*. New York: Academic Press.

Heerdink, M. W., van Kleef, G. A., Homan, A. C., & Fischer, A. H. (2013). On the social influence of emotions in groups: Interpersonal effects of anger and happiness on conformity versus deviance. *Journal of Personality and Social Psychology, 105*, 262–284.

Heffernan, M. (2011). *Wilful blindness: Why we ignore the obvious at our peril*. New York: Simon & Schuster.

Hehman, E., Leitner, J. B., & Gaertner, S. L. (2013). Enhancing static facial features increases intimidation. *Journal of Experimental Social Psychology, 49*, 747–754.

Heider, F. (1944). Social perception and phenomenal causality. *Psychological Review, 51*, 358–374.

Heider, F. (1946). Attitudes and cognitive organization. *Journal of Psychology: Interdisciplinary and Applied, 21*, 107–112.

Heider, F. (1958). *The psychology of interpersonal relations*. New York: Wiley.

Heider, F., & Simmel, M. (1944). An experimental study of apparent behavior. *American Journal of Psychology, 57*, 243–259.

Hein, G., Silani, G., Preuschoff, K., Batson, C. D., & Singer, T. (2010). Neural responses to ingroup and outgroup members' suffering predict individual differences in costly helping. *Neuron, 68*, 149–160.

Heine, S. J. (2012). *Cultural psychology* (2nd ed.). New York: Norton.

Heine, S. J., Lehman, D. R., Markus, H. R., & Kitayama, S. (1999). Is there a universal need for positive self-regard? *Psychological Review, 106*, 766–794.

Heine, S. J., Takata, T., & Lehman, D. R. (2000). Beyond self-presentation: Evidence for self-criticism among Japanese. *Personality and Social Psychology Bulletin, 26*, 71–78.

Henchy, T., & Glass, D. C. (1968). Evaluation apprehension and the social facilitation of dominant and subordinate responses. *Journal of Personality and Social Psychology, 10*, 446–454.

Henderlong, J., & Lepper, M. R. (2002). The effects of praise on children's intrinsic motivation: A review and synthesis. *Psychological Bulletin, 128*, 774–795.

Hendrick, S. S. (1981). Self-disclosure and marital satisfaction. *Journal of Personality and Social Psychology, 40*, 1150–1159.

Henrich, J., Heine, S. J., & Norenzayan, A. (2010). The weirdest people in the world? *Behavioral and Brain Sciences, 33*, 61–83.

Henry, R. A., Strickland, O. J., Yorges, S. L., & Ladd, D. (1996). Helping groups determine their most accurate member: The role of outcome feedback. *Journal of Applied Social Psychology, 26*, 1153–1170.

Henwood, K. L. (1996). Qualitative inquiry: Perspectives, methods and psychology. In J. T. E. Richardson (Ed.), *Handbook of qualitative research methods for psychology and the social science* (pp. 25–40). Leicester, UK: Blackwell.

Herek, G. M. (1986). The instrumentality of attitudes: Toward a neofunctional theory. *Journal of Social Issues, 42*, 99–114.

Herek, G. M., Janis, I. L., & Huth, P. (1987). Decision making during international crises: Is quality of process related to outcome? *Journal of Conflict Resolution, 31*, 203–226.

Herman, C. P., & Polivy, J. (1980). Restrained eating. In A. J. Stunkard (Ed.), *Obesity* (pp. 208–225). Philadelphia, PA: Saunders.

Hersh, S. M. (2004). *Chain of command*. London: Penguin.

Herskovits, M. J. (1948). *Man and his works: The science of cultural anthropology*. New York: Knopf.

Hertel, G., Kerr, N. L., & Messé, L. A. (2000). Motivation gains in performance groups: Paradigmatic and theoretical developments on the Köhler effect. *Journal of Personality and Social Psychology, 79*, 580–601.

Hertel, G., Niemeyer, G., & Clauss, A. (2008). Social indispensability or social comparison: The why and when of motivation gains of inferior group members. *Journal of Applied Social Psychology, 38*, 1329–1363.

Hewstone, M. (1989). *Causal attribution: From cognitive processes to collective beliefs*. Oxford: Blackwell.

Hewstone, M. (1994). Revision and change of stereotypic beliefs: In search of the elusive subtyping model. In W. Stroebe & M. Hewstone (Eds.), *European review of social psychology* (Vol. 5, pp. 69–109). Chichester, UK: Wiley.

Hewstone, M., & Brown, R. (1986). Contact is not enough: An intergroup perspective on the 'contact hypothesis'. In M. Hewstone & R. Brown (Eds.), *Contact and conflict in intergroup encounters* (pp. 1–44). Oxford: Blackwell.

Hewstone, M., Judd, C. M., & Sharp, M. (2011). Do observer ratings validate self-reports of intergroup contact?: A round-robin analysis. *Journal of Experimental Social Psychology, 47*, 599–609.

Hewstone, M., & Martin, R. (2010). Minority influence: From groups to attitudes and back again. In R. Martin & M. Hewstone (Eds.), *Minority influence and innovation: Antecedents, processes and consequences* (pp. 365–394). Hove, UK: Psychology Press.

Hewstone, M., Rubin, M., & Willis, H. (2002). Intergroup bias. *Annual Review of Psychology, 53*, 575–604.

Hewstone, M., & Swart, H. (2011). Fifty-odd years of inter-group contact: From hypothesis to integrated theory. *British Journal of Social Psychology, 50*, 374–386.

Higgins, E. T. (1987). Self-discrepancy: A theory relating self and affect. *Psychological Review, 94*, 319–340.

Higgins, E. T. (1996). Knowledge activation: Accessibility, applicability, and salience. In E. T. Higgins & A. W. Kruglanski (Eds.), *Social psychology: Handbook of basic principle* (pp. 133–168). New York: Guilford.

Higgins, E. T., & Bargh, J. A. (1987). Social cognition and social perception. *Annual Review of Psychology, 38*, 369–425.

Higgins, E. T., Bargh, J. A., & Lombardi, W. J. (1985). Nature of priming effects on categorization. *Journal of Experimental Psychology: Learning, Memory, and Cognition, 11*, 59–69.

Higgins, E. T., Bond, R. N., Klein, R., & Strauman, T. (1986). Self-discrepancies and emotional vulnerability: How magnitude, accessibility, and type of discrepancy influence affect. *Journal of Personality and Social Psychology, 51*, 5–15.

Higgins, E. T., Klein, R., & Strauman, T. (1985). Self-concept discrepancy theory: A psychological model for distinguishing among different aspects of depression and anxiety. *Social Cognition, 3*, 51–76.

Hilton, D. J. (1988). Logic and causal attribution. In D. J. Hilton (Ed.), *Contemporary science and natural explanation: Commonsense conceptions of causality* (pp. 33–65). Brighton, UK: Harvester.

Hilton, D. J. (1990). Conversational processes and causal explanation. *Psychological Bulletin, 107*, 65–81.

Hilton, D. J., McClure, J., & Sutton, R. M. (2010). Selecting explanations from causal chains: Do statistical principles explain preferences for voluntary causes? *European Journal of Social Psychology, 40*, 383–400.

Hilton, D. J., & Slugoski, B. R. (1986). Knowledge-based causal attribution: The abnormal conditions focus model. *Psychological Review, 93*, 75–88.

Hinde, R. A. (1979). *Towards understanding relationships*. London: Academic Press.

Hinduja, S., & Patchin, J. W. (2010). Bullying, cyberbullying, and suicide. *Archives of Suicide Research, 14*, 206–221.

Hinkle, S., & Brown, R. (1990). Intergroup comparisons and social identity: Some links and lacunae. In D. Abrams & M. A. Hogg (Eds.), *Social identity theory: Constructive and critical advances* (pp. 48–70). London: Harvester Wheatsheaf.

Hirt, E. R., Deppe, R. K., & Gordon, L. J. (1991). Self-reported versus behavioral self-handicapping: Empirical evidence for a theoretical distinction. *Journal of Personality and Social Psychology, 61*, 981–991.

Hixon, J. G., & Swann, W. B., Jr. (1993). When does introspection bear fruit? Self-reflection, self-insight, and interpersonal choices. *Journal of Personality and Social Psychology, 64*, 35–43.

Hodges, B. H., & Geyer, A. L. (2006). A nonconformist account of the Asch experiments: Values, pragmatics, and moral dilemmas. *Personality and Social Psychology Review, 10*, 2–19.

Hoeksema-Van Orden, C. Y. D., Gaillard, A. W. K., & Buunk, B. P. (1998). Social loafing under fatigue. *Journal of Personality and Social Psychology, 75*, 1179–1190.

Hoel, H., Rayner, C., & Cooper, C. L. (1999). Workplace bullying. In C. L. Cooper & I. T. Robertson (Eds.), *International review of industrial and organizational psychology* (pp. 195–230). New York: Wiley.

Hofling, C. K., Brotzman, E., Dalrymple, S., Graves, N., & Pierce, C. M. (1966). An experimental study in nurse-physician relationships. *Journal of Nervous and Mental Disease, 143*, 171–180.

Hofstede, G. H. (1980). *Culture's consequences: International differences in work-related values*. Beverly Hills, CA: Sage.

Hofstede, G. H. (1991). *Cultures and organizations: Software of the mind*. Maidenhead, UK: McGraw-Hill.

Hofstede, G. H. (2001). *Culture's consequences: Comparing values, behaviors, institutions and organizations across nations*. Thousand Oaks, CA: Sage.

Hogarth, R. M. (1981). Beyond discrete biases: Functional and dysfunctional aspects of judgmental heuristics. *Psychological Bulletin, 90*, 197–217.

Hogg, M. A. (2007). Uncertainty-identity theory. In M. P. Zanna (Ed.), *Advances in experimental social psychology* (Vol. 39, pp. 69–126). San Diego, CA: Academic Press.

Hogg, M. A. (2012). Social identity and the psychology of groups. In M. R. Leary & J. P. Tangney (Eds.), *Handbook of self and identity* (2nd ed., pp. 502–519). New York: Guilford.

Hogg, M. A., & Abrams, D. (1993). Towards a single process uncertainty reduction model of social motivation in groups. In M. A. Hogg & D. Abrams (Eds.), *Group motivation: Social psychological perspectives* (pp. 173–190). New York: Harvester Wheatsheaf.

Hogg, M. A., Meehan, C., & Farquharson, J. (2010). The solace of radicalism: Self-uncertainty and group identification in the face of threat. *Journal of Experimental Social Psychology, 46*, 1061–1066.

Hogg, M. A., Sherman, D. K., Dierselhuis, J., Maitner, A. T., & Moffitt, G. (2007). Uncertainty, entitativity, and group identification. *Journal of Experimental Social Psychology, 43*, 135–142.

Hogg, M. A., Turner, J. C., & Davidson, B. (1990). Polarized norms and social frames of reference: A test of the self-categorization theory of group polarization. *Basic and Applied Social Psychology, 11*, 77–100.

Hogg, M. A., & Van Knippenberg, D. (2003). Social identity and leadership processes in groups. In M. P. Zanna (Ed.), *Advances in experimental social psychology* (Vol. 35, pp. 1–52). San Diego, CA: Academic Press.

Holland, R. W., Hendriks, M., & Aarts, H. (2005). Smells like clean spirit: Nonconscious effects of scent on cognition and behavior. *Psychological Science, 16*, 689–693.

Holland, R. W., Verplanken, B., & Van Knippenberg, A. (2002). On the nature of attitude—behavior relations: The strong guide, the weak follow. *European Journal of Social Psychology, 32*, 869–876.

Hollander, E. P. (1958). Conformity, status, and idiosyncrasy credit. *Psychological Review, 65*, 117–127.

Hollway, W., & Jefferson, T. (2005). Panic and perjury: a psychosocial exploration of agency. *British Journal of Social Psychology, 44*, 147–163.

Homans, G. C. (1950). *The human group*. New York: Harcourt.

Homans, G. C. (1961). *Social behavior: Its elementary forms*. New York: Harcourt.

Hong, Y.-Y., Benet-Martínez, V., Chiu, C.-Y., & Morris, M. W. (2003). Boundaries of cultural influence: Construct activation as a mechanism for cultural differences in social perception. *Journal of Cross-Cultural Psychology, 34*, 453–464.

Hood, W. R., & Sherif, M. (1962). Verbal report and judgment of an unstructured stimulus. *Journal of Psychology: Interdisciplinary and Applied, 54*, 121–130.

Horcajo, J., Petty, R. E., & Briñol, P. (2010). The effects of majority versus minority source status on persuasion: A self-validation analysis. *Journal of Personality and Social Psychology, 99*, 498–512.

Hornsey, M. J. (2005). Why being right is not enough: Predicting defensiveness in the face of group criticism. In W. Stroebe & M. Hewstone (Eds.), *European review of social psychology* (Vol. 16, pp. 301–334). Hove, UK: Psychology Press.

Hornsey, M. J., & Hogg, M. A. (2000). Subgroup relations: A comparison of mutual intergroup differentiation and common ingroup identity models of prejudice reduction. *Personality and Social Psychology Bulletin, 26*, 242–256.

Hornstein, H. A. (1976). *Cruelty and kindness: A new look at aggression and altruism*. Englewood Cliffs, NJ: Prentice Hall.

Horvath, M., & Brown, J. (Eds.). (2009). *Rape: Challenging contemporary thinking*. Cullompton, UK: Willan.

Horvath, S., & Morf, C. C. (2009). Narcissistic defensiveness: Hypervigilance and avoidance of worthlessness. *Journal of Experimental Social Psychology, 45*, 1252–1258.

Horwitz, S. K., & Horwitz, I. B. (2007). The effects of team diversity on team outcomes: A meta-analytic review of team demography. *Journal of Management, 33*, 987–1015.

Houben, K., Havermans, R. C., & Wiers, R. W. (2010). Learning to dislike alcohol: Conditioning negative implicit attitudes toward alcohol and its effect on drinking behavior. *Psychopharmacology, 211*, 79–86.

House, R. J. (1971). A path goal theory of leader effectiveness. *Administrative Science Quarterly, 16*, 321–338.

House, R. J. (1996). Path-goal theory of leadership: Lessons, legacy, and a reformulated theory. *Leadership Quarterly, 7*, 323–352.

House, R. J., Hanges, P. J., Javidan, M., Dorfman, P. W., & Gupta, V. (Eds.). (2004). *Leadership, culture, and organizations: The GLOBE study of 62 societies*. Thousand Oaks, CA: Sage.

House, R. J., & Mitchell, T. R. (1974). Path-goal theory of leadership. *Journal of Contemporary Business, 3*, 81–97.

House, R. J., Spangler, W. D., & Woycke, J. (1991). Personality and charisma in the US presidency: A psychological theory of leader effectiveness. *Administrative Science Quarterly, 36*, 364–396.

Houston, D. A., & Fazio, R. H. (1989). Biased processing as a function of attitude accessibility: Making objective judgments subjectively. *Social Cognition, 7*, 51–66.

Hovland, C. I., Janis, I. L., & Kelley, H. H. (1953). *Communication and persuasion: Psychological studies of opinion change*. New Haven, CT: Yale University Press.

Hovland, C. I., Lumsdaine, A. A., & Sheffield, F. D. (1949). *Experiments on mass communication*. Princeton, NJ: Princeton University Press.

Hovland, C. I., & Weiss, W. (1951). The influence of source credibility on communication effectiveness. *Public Opinion Quarterly, 15*, 635–650.

Huesmann, L. R. (1998). The role of information processing and cognitive schema in the acquisition and maintenance of habitual aggressive behavior. In R. G. Geen & E. Donnerstein (Eds.), *Human aggression: Theories, research, and implications for policy* (pp. 73–109). New York: Academic Press.

Huesmann, L. R., & Eron, L. D. (Eds.). (1986). *Television and the aggressive child: A cross-national comparison*. Hillsdale, NJ: Erlbaum.

Huesmann, L. R., & Guerra, N. G. (1997). Children's normative beliefs about aggression and aggressive behavior. *Journal of Personality and Social Psychology, 72*, 408–419.

Huesmann, L. R., & Miller, L. S. (1994). Long-term effects of the repeated exposure to media violence in childhood. In L. R. Huesmann (Ed.), *Aggressive behavior: Current perspectives* (pp. 153–186). New York: Plenum.

Huesmann, L. R., Moise-Titus, J., Podolski, C.-L., & Eron, L. D. (2003). Longitudinal relations between children's exposure to TV violence and their aggressive and violent behavior in young adulthood: 1977–1992. *Developmental Psychology, 39*, 201–221.

Hüffmeier, J., & Hertel, G. (2011). When the whole is more than the sum of its parts: Group motivation gains in the wild. *Journal of Experimental Social Psychology, 47*, 455–459.

Hüffmeier, J., Kanthak, J., & Hertel, G. (2013). Specifity of partner feedback as moderator of group motivation gains in Olympic swimmers. *Group Processes and Intergroup Relations, 16*, 516–525.

Hull, J. G., Levenson, R. W., Young, R. D., & Sher, K. J. (1983). Self-awareness-reducing effects of alcohol consumption. *Journal of Personality and Social Psychology, 44*, 461–473.

Hull, J. G., & Young, R. D. (1983). The self-awareness-reducing effects of alcohol: Evidence and implications. In J. M. Suls & A. G. Greenwald (Eds.), *Psychological perspectives on the self* (Vol. 2, pp. 159–190). Hillsdale, NJ: Erlbaum.

Hunter, J. A., Platow, M. J., Howard, M. L., & Stringer, M. (1996). Social identity and intergroup evaluative bias: Realistic categories and domain specific self-esteem in a conflict setting. *European Journal of Social Psychology, 26*, 631–647.

Huntsinger, J. R., & Smith, C. T. (2009). First thought, best thought: Positive mood maintains and negative mood degrades implicit-explicit attitude correspondence. *Personality and Social Psychology Bulletin, 35*, 187–197.

Huskinson, T., & Haddock, G. (2004). Individual differences in attitude structure: Variance in the chronic reliance on affective and cognitive information. *Journal of Experimental Social Psychology, 40*, 82–90.

Huston, M., & Schwartz, P. (1995). The relationships of lesbians and of gay men. In J. T. Wood & S. Duck (Eds.), *Under-studied relationships: Off the beaten track* (pp. 89–121). Thousand Oaks, CA: Sage.

Huston, T. L., & Korte, C. (1976). The responsive bystander: Why he helps. In T. Lickona (Ed.), *Moral development and behavior: Theory, research, and social issues* (pp. 269–283). New York: Holt, Rinehart and Winston.

Ingham, A. G., Levinger, G., Graves, J., & Peckham, V. (1974). The Ringelmann effect: Studies of group size and group performance. *Journal of Experimental Social Psychology, 10*, 371–384.

Inglehart, R. (1997). *Modernization and postmodernization: Cultural, economic, and political change in 43 societies*. Princeton, NJ: Princeton University Press.

Inglehart, R., & Baker, W. E. (2000). Modernization, cultural change, and the persistence of traditional values. *American Sociological Review, 65*, 19–51.

Inglehart, R., & Oyserman, D. (2004). Individualism, autonomy and self-expression: The human development syndrome. In H. Vinken, J. Soeters, & P. Ester (Eds.), *Comparing cultures: Dimensions of culture in a comparative perspective* (pp. 74–96). Leiden, NL: Brill.

International Association for Cross-Cultural Psychology (not dated). *Online Readings in Psychology and Culture*. Retrieved from http://scholarworks.gvsu.edu/orpc

International Monetary Fund (2005). *World economic outlook database*. Washington, DC. Retrieved from www.imf.org/external/pubs/ft/weo/2005/01/data/dbginim.cfm

Inzlicht, M., & Gutsell, J. N. (2007). Running on empty: Neural signals for self-control failure. *Psychological Science, 18*, 933–937.

Isenberg, D. J. (1986). Group polarization: A critical review and meta-analysis. *Journal of Personality and Social Psychology, 50*, 1141–1151.

Islam, M. R., & Hewstone, M. (1993a). Dimensions of contact as predictors of intergroup anxiety, perceived out-group variability, and out-group attitude: An integrative model. *Personality and Social Psychology Bulletin, 19*, 700–710.

Islam, M. R., & Hewstone, M. (1993b). Intergroup attributions and affective consequences in majority and minority groups. *Journal of Personality and Social Psychology, 64*, 936–950.

Ito, T. A., Miller, N., & Pollock, V. E. (1996). Alcohol and aggression: A meta-analysis on the moderating effects of inhibitory cues, triggering events, and self-focused attention. *Psychological Bulletin, 120*, 60–82.

Iyer, A., & Leach, C. W. (2008). Emotion in inter-group relations. In W. Stroebe & M. Hewstone (Eds.), *European review of social psychology* (Vol. 19, pp. 86–125). Hove, UK: Psychology Press.

Jackman, M. R., & Crane, M. (1986). 'Some of my best friends are black…': Interracial friendship and Whites' racial attitudes. *Public Opinion Quarterly, 50*, 459–486.

Jacobs, R. C., & Campbell, D. T. (1961). The perpetuation of an arbitrary tradition through several generations of a laboratory microculture. *Journal of Abnormal and Social Psychology, 62*, 649–658.

Jacobson, R. P., Mortensen, C. R., & Cialdini, R. B. (2011). Bodies obliged and unbound: Differentiated response tendencies for injunctive and descriptive social norms. *Journal of Personality and Social Psychology, 100*, 433–448.

Jahoda, G. (2007). *A history of social psychology: From the eighteenth-century enlightenment to the Second World War*. Cambridge, UK: Cambridge University Press.

James, K., & Greenberg, J. (1989). In-group salience, intergroup comparison, and individual performance and self-esteem. *Personality and Social Psychology Bulletin, 15*, 604–616.

James, W. (1884). What is an emotion? *Mind, 9*, 188–205.

James, W. (1950). *The principles of psychology, Vol. 1, Chapter X: The consciousness of self* (pp. 291–401). New York: Dover. (Original work published 1890).

James, W. (1961). *Psychology: The briefer course, Chapter XII: The self* (pp. 159–191). Cambridge, MA: Harvard University Press. (Original work published 1892).

Janis, I. L. (1972). *Victims of groupthink: A psychological study of foreign-policy decisions and fiascoes*. Boston, MA: Houghton Mifflin.

Janis, I. L. (1982). *Groupthink* (2nd ed.). Boston, MA: Houghton Mifflin.

Janis, I. L., & Mann, L. (1977). *Decision making: A psychological analysis of conflict, choice, and commitment*. New York: Free Press.

Jetten, J., & Hornsey, M. J. (2012). Conformity: Revisiting Asch's line-judgment studies. In J. R. Smith & S. A. Haslam (Eds.), *Social psychology: Revisiting the classic studies* (pp. 76–90). London: Sage.

Jetten, J., & Iyer, A. (2010). Different meanings of the social dominance orientation concept: Predicting political attitudes over time. *British Journal of Social Psychology, 49*, 385–404.

Jetten, J., Spears, R., & Manstead, A. S. R. (1997). Strength of identification and intergroup differentiation: The influence of group norms. *European Journal of Social Psychology, 27*, 603–609.

Jetten, J., Spears, R., & Postmes, T. (2004). Intergroup distinctiveness and differentiation: A meta-analytic integration. *Journal of Personality and Social Psychology, 86*, 862–879.

Johansson, P., Hall, L., Sikström, S., & Olsson, A. (2005). Failure to detect mismatches between intention and outcome in a simple decision task. *Science, 310*, 116–119.

Johnson, A. L., Crawford, M. T., Sherman, S. J., Rutchick, A. M., Hamilton, D. L., Ferreira, M. B., & Petrocelli, J. V. (2006). A functional perspective on group memberships: Differential need fulfillment in a group typology. *Journal of Experimental Social Psychology, 42*, 707–719.

Johnson, B. T., & Eagly, A. H. (2000). Quantitative synthesis of social psychological research. In H. T. Reis & C. M. Judd (Eds.), *Handbook of research methods in social and personality psychology* (pp. 496–528). London: Cambridge University Press.

Johnson, D. J., & Rusbult, C. E. (1989). Resisting temptation: Devaluation of alternative partners as a means of maintaining commitment in close relationships. *Journal of Personality and Social Psychology, 57*, 967–980.

Johnson, E. A., & Reuband, K.-H. (2005). *What we knew: Terror, mass murder and everyday life in Nazi Germany*. New York: Basic Books.

Johnson, J. T., Jemmott, J. B., & Pettigrew, T. F. (1984). Causal attribution and dispositional inference: Evidence of inconsistent judgments. *Journal of Experimental Social Psychology, 20*, 567–585.

Johnson, M. H., Dziurawiec, S., Ellis, H., & Morton, J. (1991). Newborns' preferential tracking of face-like stimuli and its subsequent decline. *Cognition, 40,* 1–19.

Johnson, M. H., & Morton, J. (1991). *Biology and cognitive development: The case of face recognition.* Oxford: Blackwell.

Johnson, M. P., & Ferraro, K. J. (2000). Research on domestic violence in the 1990s: Making distinctions. *Journal of Marriage and Family, 62,* 948–963.

Johnson, R. D., & Downing, L. L. (1979). Deindividuation and valence of cues: Effects on prosocial and antisocial behavior. *Journal of Personality and Social Psychology, 37,* 1532–1538.

Johnson, T. J., Feigenbaum, R., & Weiby, M. (1964). Some determinants and consequences of the teacher's perception of causation. *Journal of Educational Psychology, 55,* 237–246.

Johnston, L., & Hewstone, M. (1992). Cognitive models of stereotype change: Subtyping and the perceived typicality of disconfirming group members. *Journal of Experimental Social Psychology, 28,* 360–386.

Joinson, A. N. (2003). *Understanding the psychology of Internet behaviour.* Basingstoke, UK: Palgrave Macmillan.

Jones, E. E. (1998). Major developments in five decades of social psychology. In D. T. Gilbert, S. T. Fiske, & G. Lindzey (Eds.), *Handbook of social psychology* (4th ed., Vol. 1, pp. 3–57). Boston, MA: McGraw-Hill.

Jones, E. E., & Berglas, S. (1978). Control of attributions about the self through self-handicapping strategies: The appeal of alcohol and the role of underachievement. *Personality and Social Psychology Bulletin, 4,* 200–206.

Jones, E. E., & Davis, K. E. (1965). From acts to dispositions: The attribution process in person perception. In L. Berkowitz (Ed.), *Advances in experimental social psychology* (Vol. 2, pp. 219–266). New York: Academic Press.

Jones, E. E., & Harris, V. A. (1967). The attribution of attitudes. *Journal of Experimental Social Psychology, 3,* 1–24.

Jones, E. E., & Nisbett, R. E. (1972). The actor and the observer: Divergent perceptions of the causes of behavior. In E. E. Jones, D. E. Kanouse, H. H. Kelley, R. E. Nisbett, S. Valins, & B. Weiner (Eds.), *Attribution: Perceiving the causes of behavior* (pp. 79–94). Morristown, NJ: General Learning Press.

Jones, E. E., & Pittman, T. S. (1982). Toward a general theory of strategic self-presentation. In J. M. Suls (Ed.), *Psychological perspectives on the self* (Vol. 1, pp. 231–262). Hillsdale, NJ: Erlbaum.

Jones, E. E., Rhodewalt, F., Berglas, S., & Skelton, J. A. (1981). Effects of strategic self-presentation on subsequent self-esteem. *Journal of Personality and Social Psychology, 41,* 407–421.

Jones, E. E., & Sigall, H. (1971). The bogus pipeline: A new paradigm for measuring affect and attitude. *Psychological Bulletin, 76,* 349–364.

Jordan, C. H., Spencer, S. J., & Zanna, M. P. (2005). Types of high self-esteem and prejudice: How implicit self-esteem relates to ethnic discrimination among high explicit self-esteem individuals. *Personality and Social Psychology Bulletin, 31,* 693–702.

Jordan, C. H., Spencer, S. J., Zanna, M. P., Hoshino-Browne, E., & Correll, J. (2003). Secure and defensive high self-esteem. *Journal of Personality and Social Psychology, 85,* 969–978.

Jordet, G. (2009). Why do English players fail in soccer penalty shootouts? A study of team status, self-regulation, and choking under pressure. *Journal of Sports Sciences, 27,* 97–106.

Josephs, R. A., Markus, H. R., & Tafarodi, R. W. (1992). Gender and self-esteem. *Journal of Personality and Social Psychology, 63,* 391–402.

Josselson, R. (2009). The present of the past: Dialogues with memory over time. *Journal of Personality, 77,* 647–668.

Jost, J. T., & Banaji, M. R. (1994). The role of stereotyping in system-justification and the production of false consciousness. *British Journal of Social Psychology, 33,* 1–27.

Jostmann, N. B., & Koole, S. L. (2006). On the waxing and waning of working memory: Action orientation moderates the impact of demanding relationship primes on working memory capacity. *Personality and Social Psychology Bulletin, 32,* 1716–1728.

Jostmann, N. B., & Koole, S. L. (2007). On the regulation of cognitive control: Action orientation moderates the impact of high demands in Stroop interference tasks. *Journal of Experimental Psychology: General, 136,* 593–609.

Joule, R. V. (1987). Tabacco deprivation: The foot-in-the-door technique versus the low-ball technique. *European Journal of Social Psychology, 17,* 361–365.

Jourard, S. M. (1971). *The transparent self.* New York: Van Nostrand Reinhold.

Judd, C. M., & Kenny, D. A. (1981a). *Estimating the effects of social interventions.* London: Cambridge University Press.

Judd, C. M., & Kenny, D. A. (1981b). Process analysis: Estimating mediation in treatment evaluations. *Evaluation Review, 5,* 602–619.

Judge, T. A., Bono, J. E., Ilies, R., & Gerhardt, M. W. (2002). Personality and leadership: A qualitative and quantitative review. *Journal of Applied Psychology, 87,* 765–780.

Judge, T. A., Colbert, A. E., & Ilies, R. (2004). Intelligence and leadership: A quantitative review and test of theoretical propositions. *Journal of Applied Psychology, 89,* 542–552.

Judge, T. A., LePine, J. A., & Rich, B. L. (2006). Loving yourself abundantly: Relationship of the narcissistic personality to self- and other perceptions of workplace deviance, leadership, and task and contextual performance. *Journal of Applied Psychology, 91,* 762–776.

Judge, T. A., & Piccolo, R. F. (2004). Transformational and transactional leadership: A meta-analytic test of their relative validity. *Journal of Applied Psychology, 89,* 755–768.

Judge, T. A., Piccolo, R. F., & Ilies, R. (2004). The forgotten ones? The validity of consideration and initiating structure in leadership research. *Journal of Applied Psychology, 89,* 36–51.

Kafetsios, K., & Nezlek, J. B. (2002). Attachment styles in everyday social interaction. *European Journal of Social Psychology, 32,* 719–735.

Kahneman, D. (2011). *Thinking, fast and slow.* New York: Farrar, Straus and Giroux.

Kahneman, D., & Tversky, A. (1972). Subjective probability: A judgment of representativeness. *Cognitive Psychology, 3,* 430–454.

Kalick, S. M., Zebrowitz, L. A., Langlois, J. H., & Johnson, R. M. (1998). Does human facial attractiveness honestly advertise health? Longitudinal data on an evolutionary question. *Psychological Science, 9,* 8–13.

Kalven, H., & Zeisel, H. (1966). *The American jury.* Boston, MA: Little, Brown.

Kampe, K. K. W., Frith, C. D., Dolan, R. J., & Frith, U. (2001). Reward value of attractiveness and gaze. *Nature, 413,* 589.

Kanagawa, C., Cross, S. E., & Markus, H. R. (2001). 'Who am I?' The cultural psychology of the conceptual self. *Personality and Social Psychology Bulletin, 27,* 90–103.

Kaplan, K. J. (1972). On the ambivalence-indifference problem in attitude theory and measurement: A suggested modification of the semantic differential technique. *Psychological Bulletin, 77,* 361–372.

Kaplan, M. F. (1987). The influencing process in group decision making. In C. Hendrick (Ed.), *Review of personality and social psychology* (Vol. 8, pp. 189–212). Thousand Oaks, CA: Sage.

Kaplan, M. F., & Miller, C. E. (1977). Judgments and group discussion: Effect of presentation and memory factors on polarization. *Sociometry, 40,* 337–343.

Kaplan, M. F., & Miller, C. E. (1987). Group decision making and normative versus informational influence: Effects of type of issue and assigned decision rule. *Journal of Personality and Social Psychology, 53,* 306–313.

Karpinski, A., & Hilton, J. L. (2001). Attitudes and the Implicit Association Test. *Journal of Personality and Social Psychology, 81,* 774–788.

Karremans, J. C., & Aarts, H. (2007). The role of automaticity in determining the inclination to forgive close others. *Journal of Experimental Social Psychology, 43,* 902–917.

Karremans, J. C., Stroebe, W., & Claus, J. (2006). Beyond Vicary's fantasies: The impact of subliminal priming and brand choice. *Journal of Experimental Social Psychology, 42,* 792–798.

Karremans, J. C., & Van Lange, P. A. M. (2004). Back to caring after being hurt: The role of forgiveness. *European Journal of Social Psychology, 34,* 207–227.

Karremans, J. C., & Van Lange, P. A. M. (2008). Forgiveness in personal relationships: Its malleability and powerful consequences. In W. Stroebe & M. Hewstone (Eds.), *European review of social psychology* (Vol. 19, pp. 202–241). Hove, UK: Psychology Press.

Kashima, E. S., & Kashima, Y. (1998). Culture and language: The case of cultural dimensions and personal pronoun use. *Journal of Cross-Cultural Psychology, 29,* 461–486.

Kasser, T., & Ryan, R. M. (1996). Further examining the American dream: Differential correlates of intrinsic and extrinsic goals. *Personality and Social Psychology Bulletin, 22,* 280–287.

Kassin, S. M. (1979). Consensus information, prediction, and causal attribution: A review of the literature and issues. *Journal of Personality and Social Psychology, 37,* 1966–1981.

Kassin, S. M., & Sukel, H. (1997). Coerced confessions and the jury: An experimental test of the 'harmless error' rule. *Law and Human Behavior, 21,* 27–46.

Katz, D. (1960). The functional approach to the study of attitudes. *Public Opinion Quarterly, 24,* 163–204.

Katzenstein, G. (1996). The debate on structured debate: Toward a unified theory. *Organizational Behavior and Human Decision Processes, 66,* 316–332.

Kawachi, I., & Berkman, L. F. (2001). Social ties and mental health. *Journal of Urban Health, 78,* 458–467.

Kawakami, K., Dion, K., & Dovidio, J. F. (1998). Racial prejudice and stereotype activation. *Personality and Social Psychology Bulletin, 24,* 407–416.

Kawakami, K., Dovidio, J. F., Moll, J., Hermsen, S., & Russin, A. (2000). Just say no (to stereotyping): Effects of training in the negation of stereotypic associations on stereotype activation. *Journal of Personality and Social Psychology, 78,* 871–888.

Keating, C. F., Pomerantz, J., Pommer, S. D., Ritt, S. J., Miller, L. M., & McCormick, J. (2005). Going to college and unpacking hazing: A functional approach to decrypting initiation practices among undergraduates. *Group Dynamics: Theory, Research, and Practice, 9,* 104–126.

Keenan, J. P., Wheeler, M. A., Gallup, G. G., Jr., & Pascual-Leone, A. (2000). Self-recognition and the right prefrontal cortex. *Trends in Cognitive Sciences, 4,* 338–344.

Keizer, K., Lindenberg, S., & Steg, L. (2008). The spreading of disorder. *Science, 322,* 1681–1685.

Kelley, H. H. (1950). The warm-cold variable in first impressions of persons. *Journal of Personality, 18,* 431–439.

Kelley, H. H. (1967). Attribution theory in social psychology. In D. Levine (Ed.), *Nebraska Symposium on Motivation* (Vol. 15, pp. 192–238). Lincoln, NE: University of Nebraska Press.

Kelley, H. H. (1972). Causal schemata and the attribution process. In E. E. Jones (Ed.), *Attribution: Perceiving the causes of behavior* (pp. 151–174). Morristown, NJ: General Learning Press.

Kelley, H. H. (1997). The 'stimulus field' for interpersonal phenomena: The source of language and thought about interpersonal events. *Personality and Social Psychology Review, 1,* 140–169.

Kelley, H. H., & Thibaut, J. W. (1978). *Interpersonal relations: A theory of interdependence.* New York: Wiley.

Kelley, W. M., Macrae, C. N., Wyland, C. L., Caglar, S., Inati, S., & Heatherton, T. F. (2002). Finding the self? An event-related fMRI study. *Journal of Cognitive Neuroscience, 14,* 785–794.

Kelling, G. L., & Wilson, J. Q. (1982). Broken windows. *Atlantic Monthly, 249,* 29–38.

Kelly, A. E., & McKillop, K. J. (1996). Consequences of revealing personal secrets. *Psychological Bulletin, 120,* 450–465.

Kelly, J. B., & Johnson, M. P. (2008). Differentiation among types of intimate partner violence: Research update and implications for interventions. *Family Court Review, 46,* 476–499.

Kelly, J. R., & Spoor, J. R. (2013). Affective processes. In J. M. Levine (Ed.), *Frontiers of social psychology: Group processes.* Hove, UK: Psychology Press.

Kelman, H. C., & Hamilton, V. L. (1989). *Crimes of obedience: Toward a social psychology of authority and responsibility.* New Haven, CT: Yale University Press.

Kenny, D. A., & DePaulo, B. M. (1993). Do people know how others view them? An empirical and theoretical account. *Psychological Bulletin, 114,* 145–161.

Kenny, D. A., Kashy, D. A., & Bolger, N. (1998). Data analysis in social psychology. In D. T. Gilbert, S. T. Fiske, & G. Lindzey (Eds.), *Handbook of social psychology* (4th ed., Vol. 1, pp. 233–265). Boston, MA: McGraw-Hill.

Kenworthy, J. B., Hewstone, M., Levine, J. M., Martin, R., & Willis, H. (2008). The phenomenology of minority-majority status: Effects on innovation in argument generation. *European Journal of Social Psychology, 38,* 624–636.

Kernberg, O. F. (1975). *Borderline conditions and pathological narcissism.* New York: Aronson.

Kernis, M. H. (2003). Toward a conceptualization of optimal self-esteem. *Psychological Inquiry, 14,* 1–26.

Kernis, M. H. (Ed.). (2006). *Self-esteem issues and answers: A sourcebook of current perspectives.* New York: Psychology Press.

Kernis, M. H., Cornell, D. P., Sun, C. R., Berry, A., & Harlow, T. (1993). There's more to self-esteem than whether it is high or low: The importance of stability of self-esteem. *Journal of Personality and Social Psychology, 65,* 1190–1204.

Kernis, M. H., & Goldman, B. M. (2003). Stability and variability in self-concept and self-esteem. In M. R. Leary & J. P. Tangney (Eds.), *Handbook of self and identity* (pp. 106–127). New York: Guilford.

Kernis, M. H., Grannemann, B. D., & Barclay, L. C. (1989). Stability and level of self-esteem as predictors of anger arousal and hostility. *Journal of Personality and Social Psychology, 56,* 1013–1022.

Kernis, M. H., Lakey, C. E., & Heppner, W. L. (2008). Secure versus fragile high self-esteem as a predictor of verbal defensiveness: Converging findings across three different markers. *Journal of Personality, 76,* 477–512.

Kerr, N. L. (1983). Motivation losses in small groups: A social dilemma analysis. *Journal of Personality and Social Psychology, 45,* 819–828.

Kerr, N. L. (1995). Juries. In A. S. R. Manstead & M. Hewstone (Eds.), *Blackwell encyclopedia of social psychology* (pp. 343–345). Oxford: Blackwell.

Kerr, N. L., & Bruun, S. E. (1983). Dispensability of member effort and group motivation losses: Free-rider effects. *Journal of Personality and Social Psychology, 44,* 78–94.

Kerr, N. L., & MacCoun, R. J. (1985). The effects of jury size and polling method on the process and product of jury deliberation. *Journal of Personality and Social Psychology, 48,* 349–363.

Kiesler, C. A., & Kiesler, S. B. (1969). *Conformity.* Reading, MA: Addison-Wesley.

Kihlstrom, J. F. (2010). Social neuroscience: The footprints of Phineas Gage. *Social Cognition, 28,* 757–783.

Kilduff, G. J., Elfenbein, H. A., & Staw, B. M. (2010). The psychology of rivalry: A relationally dependent analysis of competition. *Academy of Management Journal, 53,* 943–969.

Kim, K., & Johnson, M. K. (2010). Extended self: Medial prefrontal activity during transient association of self and objects. *Social Cognitive and Affective Neuroscience, 7,* 199–207.

Kim, Y., Kasser, T., & Lee, H. (2003). Self-concept, aspirations, and well-being in South Korea and the United States. *Journal of Social Psychology, 143,* 277–290.

Kimmel, P. R. (1994). Cultural perspectives on international negotiations. *Journal of Social Issues, 50,* 179–196.

King, A., & Crewe, I. (2013). *The blunders of our governments.* London, UK: Oneworld.

Kirsh, S. J. (1998). Seeing the world through Mortal Kombat-colored glasses: Violent video games and the development of a short-term hostile attribution bias. *Childhood: A Global Journal of Child Research, 5,* 177–184.

Kirsh, S. J. (2006). *Children, adolescents, and media violence* (1st ed.). Thousand Oaks, CA: Sage.

Kirsh, S. J. (2012). *Children, adolescents, and media violence* (2nd ed.). Thousand Oaks, CA: Sage.

Kitayama, S., & Cohen, D. (Eds.). (2007). *Handbook of cultural psychology.* New York: Guilford.

Kitayama, S., Duffy, S., Kawamura, T., & Larsen, J. T. (2003). Perceiving an object and its context in different cultures: A cultural look at new look. *Psychological Science, 14,* 102–206.

Kitayama, S., Ishii, K., Imada, T., Takemura, K., & Ramaswamy, J. (2006). Voluntary settlement and the spirit of independence: Evidence from Japan's 'northern frontier'. *Journal of Personality and Social Psychology, 91,* 369–384.

Kitayama, S., & Karasawa, M. (1997). Implicit self-esteem in Japan: Name letters and birthday numbers. *Personality and Social Psychology Bulletin, 23,* 736–742.

Kitayama, S., Park, H., Sevincer, A. T., Karasawa, M., & Uskul, A. K. (2009). A cultural task analysis of implicit independence: Comparing North America, Western Europe, and East Asia. *Journal of Personality and Social Psychology, 97,* 236–255.

Kitayama, S., & Uchida, Y. (2003). Explicit self-criticism and implicit self-regard: Evaluating self and friend in two cultures. *Journal of Experimental Social Psychology, 39,* 476–482.

Klandermans, B. (1997). *The social psychology of protest.* Oxford: Blackwell.

Klauer, K. C., & Meiser, T. (2000). A source-monitoring analysis of illusory correlations. *Personality and Social Psychology Bulletin, 26,* 1074–1093.

Klein, C. T. F., & Webster, D. M. (2000). Individual differences in argument scrutiny as motivated by need for cognitive closure. *Basic and Applied Social Psychology, 22,* 119–129.

Klein, O., Spears, R., & Reicher, S. (2007). Social identity performance: Extending the strategic side of SIDE. *Personality and Social Psychology Review, 11,* 1–18.

Klein, S. B. (2004). The cognitive neuroscience of knowing one's self. In M. S. Gazzaniga (Ed.), *The cognitive neurosciences* (3rd ed., pp. 1077–1089). Cambridge, MA: MIT Press.

Klein, S. B., & Kihlstrom, J. F. (1986). Elaboration, organization, and the self-reference effect in memory. *Journal of Experimental Psychology: General, 115,* 26–38.

Klein, S. B., Lax, M. L., & Gangi, C. E. (2010). A call for an inclusive approach to the social cognitive neurosciences. *Social Cognition, 28,* 748–756.

Klein, W. M. (1997). Objective standards are not enough: Affective, self-evaluative, and behavioral responses to social comparison information. *Journal of Personality and Social Psychology, 72,* 763–774.

Klinesmith, J., Kasser, T., & McAndrew, F. T. (2006). Guns, testosterone, and aggression: An experimental test of a mediational hypothesis. *Psychological Science, 17,* 568–571.

Kling, K. C., Hyde, J. S., Showers, C. J., & Buswell, B. N. (1999). Gender differences in self-esteem: A meta-analysis. *Psychological Bulletin, 125,* 470–500.

Klohnen, E. C., & Luo, S. (2003). Interpersonal attraction and personality: What is attractive: Self similarity, ideal similarity, complementarity, or attachment security? *Journal of Personality and Social Psychology, 85,* 709–722.

Klomek, A. B., Sourander, A., Niemela, S., Kumpulainen, K., Piha, J., Tamminen, T., … Gould, M. S. (2009). Childhood bullying behaviors as a risk for suicide attempts and completed suicides: A population-based birth cohort study. *Journal of the American Academy of Child and Adolescent Psychiatry, 48,* 254–261.

Klucharev, V., Hytönen, K., Rijpkema, M., Smidts, A., & Fernández, G. (2009). Reinforcement learning signal predicts social conformity. *Neuron, 61,* 140–151.

Knafo, A., Schwartz, S. H., & Levine, R. V. (2009). Helping strangers is lower in embedded cultures. *Journal of Cross-Cultural Psychology, 40,* 875–879.

Kobayashi, C., Glover, G. H., & Temple, E. (2006). Cultural and linguistic influence on neural bases of 'Theory of Mind': An fMRI study with Japanese bilinguals. *Brain and Language, 98,* 210–220.

Köhler, O. (1926). Kraftleistungen bei Einzel- und Gruppenarbeit [Physical performance in individual and group situations]. *Industrielle Psychotechnik, 3,* 274–282.

Koole, S. L., Dijksterhuis, A., & Van Knippenberg, A. (2001). What's in a name: Implicit self-esteem and the automatic self. *Journal of Personality and Social Psychology, 80,* 669–685.

Koole, S. L., Jostmann, N. B., & Baumann, N. (2012). Do demanding conditions help or hurt self-regulation? *Social and Personality Compass, 6,* 328–346.

Koole, S. L., & Pelham, B. W. (2003). On the nature of implicit self-esteem: The case of the name letter effect. In S. J. Spencer, S. Fein, M. P. Zanna, & J. M. Olson (Eds.), *Motivated social perception: The Ontario Symposium* (Vol. 9, pp. 93–116). Mahwah, NJ: Erlbaum.

Koss, M. P., Abbey, A., Campbell, R., Cook, S., Norris, J., Testa, M., … White, J. (2007). Revising the SES: A collaborative process to improve assessment of sexual aggression and victimization. *Psychology of Women Quarterly, 31,* 357–370.

Koss, M. P., Bailey, J. A., Yuan, N. P., Herrera, V. M., & Lichter, E. L. (2003). Depression and PTSD in survivors of male violence: Research and training initiatives to facilitate recovery. *Psychology of Women Quarterly, 27,* 130–142.

Koss, M. P., White, J. W., & Kazdin, A. E. (Eds.). (2011). *Violence against women and children* (Vol. 2: *Navigating solutions*). Washington, DC: American Psychological Association.

Krahé, B. (1992). *Personality and social psychology: Towards a synthesis*. London: Sage.

Krahé, B. (2001). *The social psychology of aggression* (1st ed.). Hove, UK: Psychology Press.

Krahé, B. (2013). *The social psychology of aggression* (2nd ed.). Hove, UK: Psychology Press.

Krahé, B., & Berger, A. (2005). Sex differences in relationship aggression among young adults in Germany. *Sex Roles, 52*, 829–838.

Krahé, B., & Bieneck, S. (2012). The effect of music-induced mood on aggressive affect, cognition, and behavior. *Journal of Applied Social Psychology, 42*, 271–290.

Krahé, B., Bieneck, S., & Möller, I. (2005). Understanding gender and intimate partner violence from an international perspective. *Sex Roles, 52*, 807–827.

Krahé, B., & Möller, I. (2004). Playing violent electronic games, hostile attributional style, and aggression-related norms in German adolescents. *Journal of Adolescence, 27*, 53–69.

Krahé, B., Möller, I., Huesmann, L. R., Kirwil, L., Felber, J., & Berger, A. (2011). Desensitization to media violence: Links with habitual media violence exposure, aggressive cognitions and aggressive behavior. *Journal of Personality and Social Psychology, 100*, 630–646.

Krahé, B., Schütze, S., Fritsche, I., & Waizenhöfer, E. (2000). The prevalence of sexual aggression and victimization among homosexual men. *Journal of Sex Research, 37*, 142–150.

Krahé, B., Waizenhöfer, E., & Möller, I. (2003). Women's sexual aggression against men: Prevalence and predictors. *Sex Roles, 49*, 219–232.

Kraus, S. J. (1995). Attitudes and the prediction of behavior: A meta-analysis of the empirical literature. *Personality and Social Psychology Bulletin, 21*, 58–75.

Kravitz, D. A., & Martin, B. (1986). Ringelmann rediscovered: The original article. *Journal of Personality and Social Psychology, 50*, 936–941.

Krebs, D. (1975). Empathy and altruism. *Journal of Personality and Social Psychology, 32*, 1134–1146.

Kreiner, D. S., Altis, N. A., & Voss, C. W. (2003). A test of the effect of reverse speech on priming. *Journal of Psychology: Interdisciplinary and Applied, 137*, 224–232.

Krosnick, J. A., Betz, A. L., Jussim, L. J., & Lynn, A. R. (1992). Subliminal conditioning of attitudes. *Personality and Social Psychology Bulletin, 18*, 152–162.

Krosnick, J. A., Boninger, D. S., Chuang, Y. C., Berent, M. K., & Carnot, C. G. (1993). Attitude strength: One construct or many related constructs? *Journal of Personality and Social Psychology, 65*, 1132–1151.

Krosnick, J. A., & Petty, R. E. (1995). Attitude strength: An overview. In R. E. Petty & J. A. Krosnick (Eds.), *Attitude strength: Antecedents and consequences* (pp. 1–24). Hillsdale, NJ: Erlbaum.

Kross, E., Ayduk, O., & Mischel, W. (2005). When asking 'why' does not hurt: Distinguishing rumination from reflective processing of negative emotions. *Psychological Science, 16*, 709–715.

Kross, E., & Mischel, W. (2010). From stimulus control to self-control: Towards an integrative understanding of the processes underlying willpower. In R. R. Hassin, K. Ochsner, & Y. Trope (Eds.), *Self control in society, mind, and brain* (pp. 428–446). New York, NY: Oxford University Press.

Krug, E. G., Dahlberg, L. L., Mercy, J. A., Zwi, A. B., & Lozano, R. (2002). *World report on violence and health*. Retrieved May 30, 2010, from http://whqlibdoc.who.int/hq/2002/9241545615.pdf

Kruglanski, A. W. (1989). *Lay epistemics and human knowledge: Cognitive and motivational bases*. New York: Plenum.

Kruglanski, A. W., & Freund, T. (1983). The freezing and unfreezing of lay-inferences: Effects on impressional primacy, ethnic stereotyping, and numerical anchoring. *Journal of Experimental Social Psychology, 19*, 448–468.

Kruglanski, A. W., & Stroebe, W. (Eds.). (2012). *Handbook of the history of social psychology*. New York: Psychology Press.

Kruglanski, A. W., & Webster, D. M. (1996). Motivated closing of the mind: 'Seizing' and 'freezing'. *Psychological Review, 103*, 263–283.

Kruglanski, A. W., Webster, D. M., & Klem, A. (1993). Motivated resistance and openness to persuasion in the presence or absence of prior information. *Journal of Personality and Social Psychology, 65*, 861–876.

Krull, D. S. (1993). Does the grist change the mill? The effect of the perceiver's inferential goal on the process of social inference. *Personality and Social Psychology Bulletin, 19*, 340–348.

Kuiper, N. A., & Rogers, T. B. (1979). Encoding of personal information: Self-other differences. *Journal of Personality and Social Psychology, 37*, 499–514.

Kunda, Z. (1990). The case for motivated reasoning. *Psychological Bulletin, 108*, 480–498.

Kunda, Z. (1999). *Social cognition: Making sense of people*. Cambridge, MA: MIT Press.

Kundu, P., & Cummins, D. D. (2013). Morality and conformity: The Asch paradigm applied to moral decisions. *Social Influence, 8*, 268–279.

Kunst-Wilson, W. R., & Zajonc, R. B. (1980). Affective discrimination of stimuli that cannot be recognized. *Science, 207*, 557–558.

Kurman, J. (2003). Why is self-enhancement low in certain collectivist cultures? An investigation of two competing explanations. *Journal of Cross-Cultural Psychology, 34*, 496–510.

Kuzmanovic, B., Bente, G., von Cramon, D. Y., Schilbach, L., Tittgemeyer, M., & Vogeley, K. (2012). Imaging first impressions: Distinct neural processing of verbal and nonverbal social information. *Neuroimage, 60*, 179–188.

Kuzmanovic, B., Jefferson, A., Bente, G., & Vogeley, K. (2013). Affective and motivational influences in person perception. *Frontiers in Human Neuroscience, 7*, article 266.

Lalljee, M., & Abelson, R. P. (1983). The organisation of explanations. In M. Hewstone (Ed.), *Attribution theory: Social and functional extensions* (pp. 65–80). Oxford: Blackwell.

Lalljee, M., Lamb, R., Furnham, A., & Jaspars, J. (1984). Explanations and information search: Inductive and hypothesis-testing approaches to arriving at an explanation. *British Journal of Social Psychology, 23*, 201–212.

Lamm, H., & Myers, D. G. (1978). Group-induced polarization of attitudes and behavior. In L. Berkowitz (Ed.), *Advances in experimental social psychology* (Vol. 11, pp. 145–195). New York: Academic Press.

Landis, D., Hope, R. O., & Day, H. R. (1984). Training for desegregation in the military. In N. Miller & M. B. Brewer (Eds.), *Groups in contact: The psychology of desegregation* (pp. 257–278). Orlando, FL: Academic Press.

Landry, S. H., Smith, K. E., & Swank, P. R. (2006). Responsive parenting: Establishing early foundations for social, communication, and independent problem-solving skills. *Developmental Psychology, 42*, 627–642.

Langer, E. J., Blank, A., & Chanowitz, B. (1978). The mindlessness of ostensibly thoughtful action: The role of 'placebic' information in interpersonal interaction. *Journal of Personality and Social Psychology, 36*, 635–642.

Langlois, J. H., Kalakanis, L., Rubenstein, A. J., Larson, A., Hallam, M., & Smoot, M. (2000). Maxims or myths of beauty? A meta-analytic and theoretical review. *Psychological Bulletin, 126*, 390–423.

Langlois, J. H., Ritter, J. M., Casey, R. J., & Sawin, D. B. (1995). Infant attractiveness predicts maternal behaviors and attitudes. *Developmental Psychology, 31*, 464–472.

Langlois, J. H., Ritter, J. M., Roggman, L. A., & Vaughn, L. S. (1991). Facial diversity and infant preferences for attractive faces. *Developmental Psychology, 27*, 79–84.

Langlois, J. H., Roggman, L. A., & Musselman, L. (1994). What is average and what is not average about attractive faces? *Psychological Science, 5*, 214–220.

LaPiere, R. T. (1934). Attitudes versus actions. *Social Forces, 13*, 230–237.

Larson, J. R., Jr. (2010). *In search of synergy in small group performance*. New York: Psychology Press.

Larson, J. R., Jr., & Christensen, C. (1993). Groups as problem-solving units: Toward a new meaning of social cognition. *British Journal of Social Psychology, 32*, 5–30.

Larson, J. R., Jr., Christensen, C., Abbott, A. S., & Franz, T. M. (1996). Diagnosing groups: Charting the flow of information in medical decision-making teams. *Journal of Personality and Social Psychology, 71*, 315–330.

Larson, J. R., Jr., Christensen, C., Franz, T. M., & Abbott, A. S. (1998). Diagnosing groups: The pooling, management, and impact of shared and unshared case information in team-based medical decision making. *Journal of Personality and Social Psychology, 75*, 93–108.

Larson, J. R., Jr., Foster-Fishman, P. G., & Franz, T. M. (1998). Leadership style and the discussion of shared and unshared information in decision-making groups. *Personality and Social Psychology Bulletin, 24*, 482–495.

Larson, J. R., Jr., Foster-Fishman, P. G., & Keys, C. B. (1994). Discussion of shared and unshared information in decision-making groups. *Journal of Personality and Social Psychology, 67*, 446–461.

Latané, B., & Darley, J. M. (1968). Group inhibition of bystander intervention in emergencies. *Journal of Personality and Social Psychology, 10*, 215–221.

Latané, B., & Darley, J. M. (1970). *The unresponsive bystander: Why doesn't he help?* New York: Appleton-Century-Crofts.

Latané, B., & Darley, J. M. (1976). Help in a crisis: Bystander response to an emergency. In J. W. Thibaut, J. T. Spence, & R. C. Carson (Eds.), *Contemporary topics in social psychology* (pp. 309–332). Morristown, NJ: General Learning Press.

Latané, B., & Nida, S. (1981). Ten years of research on group size and helping. *Psychological Bulletin, 89*, 308–324.

Latané, B., Williams, K., & Harkins, S. (1979). Many hands make light the work: The causes and consequences of social loafing. *Journal of Personality and Social Psychology, 37*, 822–832.

Laughlin, P. R., & Sweeney, J. D. (1977). Individual-to-group and group-to-individual transfer in problem solving. *Journal of Experimental Psychology: Human Learning and Memory, 3*, 246–254.

Laurenceau, J.-P., Feldman Barrett, L., & Pietromonaco, P. R. (1998). Intimacy as an interpersonal process: The importance of self-disclosure, partner disclosure, and perceived partner responsiveness in interpersonal exchanges. *Journal of Personality and Social Psychology, 74*, 1238–1251.

Laurenceau, J.-P., Feldman Barrett, L., & Rovine, M. J. (2005). The interpersonal process model of intimacy in marriage: A daily-diary and multilevel modeling approach. *Journal of Family Psychology, 19*, 314–323.

Lazarus, R. S. (1991). *Emotion and adaptation*. New York: Oxford University Press.

Le, B., & Agnew, C. R. (2003). Commitment and its theorized determinants: A meta-analysis of the investment model. *Personal Relationships, 10*, 37–57.

Leach, C. W., Spears, R., Branscombe, N. R., & Doosje, B. (2003). Malicious pleasure: Schadenfreude at the suffering of another group. *Journal of Personality and Social Psychology, 84*, 932–943.

Leach, C. W., Van Zomeren, M., Zebel, S., Vliek, M. L. W., Pennekamp, S. F., Doosje, B., … Spears, R. (2008). Group-level self-definition and self-investment: A hierarchical (multicomponent) model of in-group identification. *Journal of Personality and Social Psychology, 95*, 144–165.

Leana, C. R. (1985). A partial test of Janis' groupthink model: Effects of group cohesiveness and leader behavior on defective decision making. *Journal of Management, 11*, 5–18.

Leary, M. R. (2004). *The curse of the self: Self-awareness, egotism, and the quality of human life*. New York: Oxford University Press.

Leary, M. R., & MacDonald, G. (2003). Individual differences in trait self-esteem: A theoretical integration. In M. R. Leary & J. P. Tangney (Eds.), *Handbook of self and identity* (pp. 401–418). New York: Guilford.

Leary, M. R., Tambor, E. S., Terdal, S. K., & Downs, D. L. (1995). Self-esteem as an interpersonal monitor: The sociometer hypothesis. *Journal of Personality and Social Psychology, 68*, 518–530.

LeBon, G. (1896). *The crowd: A study of the popular mind*. London: T. Fisher Unwin.

Lee, L., Piliavin, J. A., & Call, V. R. A. (1999). Giving time, money, and blood: Similarities and differences. *Social Psychology Quarterly, 62*, 276–290.

Lefkowitz, M. M., Eron, L. D., Walder, L. O., & Huesmann, L. R. (1977). *Growing up to be violent*. New York: Pergamon.

Legrand, D., & Ruby, P. (2009). What is self-specific? Theoretical investigation and critical review of neuroimaging results. *Psychological Review, 116*, 252–282.

Lemay, E. P., Jr., Clark, M. S., & Feeney, B. C. (2007). Projection of responsiveness to needs and the construction of satisfying communal relationships. *Journal of Personality and Social Psychology, 92*, 834–853.

Leonardelli, G. J., Pickett, C. L., & Brewer, M. B. (2010). Optimal distinctiveness theory: A framework for social identity, social cognition, and intergroup relations. In M. P. Zanna & J. M. Olson (Eds.), *Advances in experimental social psychology* (Vol. 43, pp. 63–113). San Diego, CA: Academic Press.

Lepore, L., & Brown, R. (1997). Category and stereotype activation: Is prejudice inevitable? *Journal of Personality and Social Psychology, 72*, 275–287.

Lepper, M. R., & Greene, D. (1978). *The hidden costs of reward: New perspectives on the psychology of human motivation*. Oxford: Erlbaum.

Lepper, M. R., Greene, D., & Nisbett, R. E. (1973). Undermining children's intrinsic interest with extrinsic reward: A test of the 'overjustification' hypothesis. *Journal of Personality and Social Psychology, 28*, 129–137.

Lesar, T. S., Briceland, L., & Stein, D. S. (1997). Factors related to errors in medication prescribing. *Journal of the American Medical Association, 277*, 312–317.

Leung, A. K. Y., & Cohen, D. (2011). Within- and between-culture variation: Individual differences and the cultural logics of honor, face and dignity cultures. *Journal of Personality and Social Psychology, 100*, 507–526.

Levin, J., & McDevitt, J. (1993). *Hate crimes: The rising tide of bigotry and bloodshed*. New York: Plenum.

Levine, J. M. (1989). Reaction to opinion deviance in small groups. In P. B. Paulus (Ed.), *Psychology of group influence* (2nd ed., pp. 187–231). Hillsdale, NJ: Erlbaum.

Levine, J. M. (1999). Solomon Asch's legacy for group research. *Personality and Social Psychology Review, 3*, 358–364.

Levine, J. M. (Ed.). (2013). *Frontiers of social psychology: Group processes*. Hove, UK: Psychology Press.

Levine, J. M., Choi, H.-S., & Moreland, R. L. (2003). Newcomer innovation in work teams. In P. B. Paulus & B. A. Nijstad (Eds.), *Group creativity: Innovation through collaboration* (pp. 202–224). New York: Oxford University Press.

Levine, J. M., & Moreland, R. L. (1990). Progress in small group research. *Annual Review of Psychology, 41*, 585–634.

Levine, J. M., & Moreland, R. L. (1998). Small groups. In D. T. Gilbert, S. T. Fiske, & G. Lindzey (Eds.), *Handbook of social psychology* (4th ed., Vol. 1, pp. 415–469). Boston, MA: McGraw-Hill.

Levine, J. M., & Moreland, R. L. (2004). Collaboration: The social context of theory development. *Personality and Social Psychology Review, 8*, 164–172.

Levine, J. M., & Moreland, R. L. (2012). A history of small group research. In A. W. Kruglanski & W. Stroebe (Eds.), *Handbook of the history of social psychology* (pp. 383–405). New York: Psychology Press.

Levine, J. M., & Russo, E. (1995). Impact of anticipated interaction on information acquisition. *Social Cognition, 13*, 293–317.

Levine, M. (1999). Rethinking bystander nonintervention: Social categorization and the evidence of witnesses at the James Bulger murder trial. *Human Relations, 52*, 1133–1155.

Levine, M., Cassidy, C., Brazier, G., & Reicher, S. (2002). Self-categorization and bystander non-intervention: Two experimental studies. *Journal of Applied Social Psychology, 32*, 1452–1463.

Levine, M., Cassidy, C., & Jentzsch, I. (2010). The implicit identity effect: Identity primes, group size, and helping. *British Journal of Social Psychology, 49*, 785–802.

Levine, M., & Crowther, S. (2008). The responsive bystander: How social group membership and group size can encourage as well as inhibit bystander intervention. *Journal of Personality and Social Psychology, 95*, 1429–1439.

Levine, M., Prosser, A., Evans, D., & Reicher, S. (2005). Identity and emergency intervention: How social group membership and inclusiveness of group boundaries shape helping behavior. *Personality and Social Psychology Bulletin, 31*, 443–453.

Levine, R. V., Norenzayan, A., & Philbrick, K. (2001). Cross-cultural differences in helping strangers. *Journal of Cross-Cultural Psychology, 32*, 543–560.

Levy, L. (1960). Studies in conformity behavior: A methodological note. *Journal of Psychology: Interdisciplinary and Applied, 50*, 39–41.

Lewicki, R. J. (1983). Lying and deception: A behavioral model. In M. H. Bazerman & R. J. Lewicki (Eds.), *Negotiating in organizations* (pp. 68–90). Beverly Hills, CA: Sage.

Lewin, K. (1948). *Resolving social conflicts*. New York: Harper & Row.

Lewin, K., Lippitt, R., & White, R. K. (1939). Patterns of aggressive behavior in experimentally created 'social climates'. *Journal of Social Psychology, 10*, 271–299.

Lewinsohn, P. M., Mischel, W., Chaplin, W., & Barton, R. (1980). Social competence and depression: The role of illusory self-perceptions. *Journal of Abnormal Psychology, 89*, 203–212.

Lewinsohn, P. M., Steinmetz, J. L., Larson, D. W., & Franklin, J. (1981). Depression-related cognitions: Antecedent or consequence? *Journal of Abnormal Psychology, 90*, 213–219.

Leyens, J. P., & Corneille, O. (1999). Asch's social psychology: Not as social as you may think. *Personality and Social Psychology Review, 3*, 345–357.

Liberman, A., & Chaiken, S. (1992). Defensive processing of personally relevant health messages. *Personality and Social Psychology Bulletin, 18*, 669–679.

Lickel, B., Hamilton, D. L., & Sherman, S. J. (2001). Elements of a lay theory of groups: Types of groups, relational styles, and the perception of group entitativity. *Personality and Social Psychology Review, 5*, 129–140.

Lickel, B., Hamilton, D. L., Wieczorkowska, G., Lewis, A., Sherman, S. J., & Uhles, A. N. (2000). Varieties of groups and the perception of group entitativity. *Journal of Personality and Social Psychology, 78*, 223–246.

Lickel, B., Miller, N., Stenstrom, D. M., Denson, T. F., & Schmader, T. (2006). Vicarious retribution: The role of collective blame in intergroup aggression. *Personality and Social Psychology Review, 10*, 372–390.

Lieberman, J. D., Solomon, S., Greenberg, J., & McGregor, H. A. (1999). A hot new way to measure aggression: Hot sauce allocation. *Aggressive Behavior, 25*, 331–348.

Liebert, R. M., & Baron, R. A. (1972). Some immediate effects of televised violence on children's behavior. *Developmental Psychology, 6*, 469–475.

Likert, R. (1932). A technique for the measurement of attitudes. *Archives of Psychology, 22*, 55.

Linder, D. E., Cooper, J., & Jones, E. E. (1967). Decision freedom as a determinant of the role of incentive magnitude in attitude change. *Journal of Personality and Social Psychology, 6*, 245–254.

Lindsay, J. J., & Anderson, C. A. (2000). From antecedent conditions to violent actions: A general affective aggression model. *Personality and Social Psychology Bulletin, 26*, 533–547.

Linville, P. W. (1987). Self-complexity as a cognitive buffer against stress-related illness and depression. *Journal of Personality and Social Psychology, 52*, 663–676.

Livingstone, A., & Haslam, S. A. (2008). The importance of social identity content in a setting of chronic social conflict: Understanding intergroup relations in Northern Ireland. *British Journal of Social Psychology, 47*, 1–21.

Livingstone, A. G., Spears, R., Manstead, A. S. R., & Bruder, M. (2009). Illegitimacy and identity threat in (inter)action: Predicting intergroup orientations among minority group members. *British Journal of Social Psychology, 48*, 755–775.

Locher, P., Unger, R., Sociedade, P., & Wahl, J. (1993). At first glance: Accessibility of the physical attractiveness stereotype. *Sex Roles, 28*, 729–743.

Lodewijkx, H. F. M., & Syroit, J. E. M. M. (1997). Severity of initiation revisited: Does severity of initiation increase the attractiveness of real groups? *European Journal of Social Psychology, 27*, 275–300.

Lord, C. G. (2004). Attitude variance: Its causes and consequences. In G. Haddock & G. R. Maio (Eds.), *Contemporary perspectives on the psychology of attitudes* (pp. 299–323). London: Psychology Press.

Lord, C. G., Ross, L., & Lepper, M. R. (1979). Biased assimilation and attitude polarization: The effects of prior theories on subsequently considered evidence. *Journal of Personality and Social Psychology, 37*, 2098–2109.

Lore, R. K., & Schultz, L. A. (1993). Control of human aggression: A comparative perspective. *American Psychologist, 48*, 16–25.

Lorenz, K. (1966). *On aggression*. London: Routledge.

Luchies, L. B., Finkel, E. J., McNulty, J. K., & Kumashiro, M. (2010). The doormat effect: When forgiving erodes self-respect and self-concept clarity. *Journal of Personality and Social Psychology, 98*, 734–749.

Lundgren, S. R., & Prislin, R. (1998). Motivated cognitive processing and attitude change. *Personality and Social Psychology Bulletin, 24*, 715–726.

Luo, S., & Klohnen, E. C. (2005). Assortative mating and marital quality in newlyweds: A couple-centered approach. *Journal of Personality and Social Psychology, 88*, 304–326.

Lydon, J. E., Fitzsimons, G. M., & Naidoo, L. (2003). Devaluation versus enhancement of attractive alternatives: A critical test using the calibration paradigm. *Personality and Social Psychology Bulletin, 29*, 349–359.

Lynas, M. (2009, December 22). How do I know China wrecked the Copenhagen deal? I was in the room. *The Guardian*. Retrieved from http://www.guardian.co.uk

Maass, A., & Clark, R. D., III. (1983). Internalization versus compliance: Differential processes underlying minority influence and conformity. *European Journal of Social Psychology, 13*, 197–215.

Maass, A., & Clark, R. D., III. (1984). Hidden impact of minorities: Fifteen years of minority influence research. *Psychological Bulletin, 95*, 428–450.

Maass, A., & Volpato, C. (1994). Theoretical perspectives on minority influence: Conversion versus divergence? In S. Moscovici, A. Mucchi-Faina, & A. Maass (Eds.), *Minority influence* (pp. 135–147). Chicago, IL: Nelson-Hall.

MacBrayer, E. K., Milich, R., & Hundley, M. (2003). Attributional biases in aggressive children and their mothers. *Journal of Abnormal Psychology, 112,* 698–708.

Mackie, D., & Cooper, J. (1984). Attitude polarization: Effects of group membership. *Journal of Personality and Social Psychology, 46,* 575–585.

Mackie, D. M. (1986). Social identification effects in group polarization. *Journal of Personality and Social Psychology, 50,* 720–728.

Mackie, D. M. (1987). Systematic and nonsystematic processing of majority and minority persuasive communications. *Journal of Personality and Social Psychology, 53,* 41–52.

MacNamara, D. E. J. (1991). The victimization of whistle-blowers in the public and private sectors. In R. J. Kelly & D. E. J. MacNamara (Eds.), *Perspectives on deviance: Dominance, degradation, and denigration* (pp. 121–134). Cincinnati, OH: Anderson.

MacNeil, M. K., & Sherif, M. (1976). Norm change over subject generations as a function of arbitrariness of prescribed norms. *Journal of Personality and Social Psychology, 34,* 762–773.

Macrae, C. N., & Bodenhausen, G. V. (2000). Social cognition: Thinking categorically about others. *Annual Review of Psychology, 51,* 93–120.

Macrae, C. N., Bodenhausen, G. V., & Milne, A. B. (1998). Saying no to unwanted thoughts: Self-focus and the regulation of mental life. *Journal of Personality and Social Psychology, 74,* 578–589.

Macrae, C. N., Bodenhausen, G. V., Milne, A. B., & Jetten, J. (1994). Out of mind but back in sight: Stereotypes on the rebound. *Journal of Personality and Social Psychology, 67,* 808–817.

Macrae, C. N., Bodenhausen, G. V., Milne, A. B., Thorn, T. M. J., & Castelli, L. (1997). On the activation of social stereotypes: The moderating role of processing objectives. *Journal of Experimental Social Psychology, 33,* 471–489.

Macrae, C. N., & Johnston, L. (1998). Help, I need somebody: Automatic action and inaction. *Social Cognition, 16,* 400–417.

Macrae, C. N., Milne, A. B., & Bodenhausen, G. V. (1994). Stereotypes as energy-saving devices: A peek inside the cognitive toolbox. *Journal of Personality and Social Psychology, 66,* 37–47.

Macrae, C. N., Moran, J. M., Heatherton, T. F., Banfield, J. F., & Kelley, W. M. (2004). Medial prefrontal activity predicts memory for self. *Cerebral Cortex, 14,* 647–654.

Madey, S. F., Simo, M., Dillworth, D., Kemper, D., Toczynski, A., & Perella, A. (1996). They do get more attractive at closing time, but only when you are not in a relationship. *Basic and Applied Social Psychology, 18,* 387–393.

Maier, N. R. F. (1967). Assets and liabilities in group problem solving: The need for an integrative function. *Psychological Review, 74,* 239–249.

Maio, G. R., Bell, D. W., & Esses, V. M. (1996). Ambivalence and persuasion: The processing of messages about immigrant groups. *Journal of Experimental Social Psychology, 32,* 513–536.

Maio, G. R., & Esses, V. M. (2001). The need for affect: Individual differences in the motivation to approach or avoid emotions. *Journal of Personality, 69,* 583–615.

Maio, G. R., Esses, V. M., Arnold, K., & Olson, J. M. (2004). The function-structure model of attitudes: Incorporating the need for affect. In G. Haddock & G. R. Maio (Eds.), *Contemporary perspectives on the psychology of attitudes* (pp. 9–33). London: Psychology Press.

Maio, G. R., & Haddock, G. (2015). *The psychology of attitudes and attitude change* (2nd ed.). London: Sage.

Maio, G. R., Haddock, G., Manstead, A. S. R., & Spears, R. (2010). Attitudes and intergroup relations. In J. F. Dovidio, M. Hewstone, P. Glick, & V. M. Esses (Eds.), *Handbook of prejudice, stereotyping and discrimination* (pp. 261–275). London: Sage.

Maio, G. R., & Olson, J. M. (Eds.). (2000). *Why we evaluate: Functions of attitudes.* Mahwah, NJ: Erlbaum.

Maio, G. R., Pakizeh, A., Cheung, W., & Rees, K. J. (2009). Changing, priming, and acting on values: Effects via motivational relations in a circular model. *Journal of Personality and Social Psychology, 97,* 699–715.

Maisey, D. S., Vale, E. L. E., Cornelissen, P. L., & Tovée, M. J. (1999). Characteristics of male attractiveness for women. *Lancet, 353,* 1500.

Malle, B. F. (2006). The actor-observer asymmetry in attribution: A (surprising) meta-analysis. *Psychological Bulletin, 132,* 895–919.

Malle, B. F. (2011). Time to give up the dogmas of attribution: An alternative theory of behavior explanation. In J. M. Olson & M. P. Zanna (Eds.), *Advances in experimental social psychology* (Vol. 44, pp. 297–352). San Diego, CA: Academic Press.

Malle, B. F., Knobe, J. M., & Nelson, S. E. (2007). Actor-observer asymmetries in explanations of behavior: New answers to an old question. *Journal of Personality and Social Psychology, 93,* 491–514.

Manning, R., Levine, M., & Collins, A. (2007). The Kitty Genovese murder and the social psychology of helping: The parable of the 38 witnesses. *American Psychologist, 62,* 555–562.

Mantell, D. M. (1971). The potential for violence in Germany. *Journal of Social Issues, 27,* 101–112.

Mantell, D. M., & Panzarella, R. (1976). Obedience and responsibility. *British Journal of Social and Clinical Psychology, 15,* 239–245.

Marcus-Newhall, A., Pedersen, W. C., Carlson, M., & Miller, N. (2000). Displaced aggression is alive and well: A meta-analytic review. *Journal of Personality and Social Psychology, 78,* 670–689.

Markman, H. J. (1981). Prediction of marital distress: A 5-year follow-up. *Journal of Consulting and Clinical Psychology, 49,* 760–762.

Markus, H. (1977). Self-schemata and processing information about the self. *Journal of Personality and Social Psychology, 35*, 63–78.

Markus, H. (1978). The effect of mere presence on social facilitation: An unobtrusive test. *Journal of Experimental Social Psychology, 14*, 389–397.

Markus, H., & Kitayama, S. (1991). Culture and the self: Implications for cognition, emotion, and motivation. *Psychological Review, 98*, 224–253.

Markus, H., & Kitayama, S. (1994). A collective fear of the collective: Implications for selves and theories of selves. *Personality and Social Psychology Bulletin, 20*, 568–579.

Markus, H., & Kunda, Z. (1986). Stability and malleability of the self-concept. *Journal of Personality and Social Psychology, 51*, 858–866.

Markus, H., & Nurius, P. (1986). Possible selves. *American Psychologist, 41*, 954–969.

Marques, J. M., Yzerbyt, V. Y., & Leyens, J.-P. (1988). The 'black sheep effect': Extremity of judgments towards ingroup members as a function of group identification. *European Journal of Social Psychology, 18*, 1–16.

Marrow, A. J. (1969). *The practical theorist: The life and work of Kurt Lewin.* New York: Basic Books.

Marsh, H. W. (1990). A multidimensional, hierarchical model of self-concept: Theoretical and empirical justification. *Educational Psychology Review, 2*, 77–172.

Marshall, G. D., & Zimbardo, P. G. (1979). Affective consequences of inadequately explained physiological arousal. *Journal of Personality and Social Psychology, 37*, 970–988.

Martin, R., & Hewstone, M. (2001a). Afterthoughts on afterimages: A review of the afterimage paradigm in majority and minority influence research. In C. K. W. De Dreu & N. K. De Vries (Eds.), *Group consensus and minority influence: Implications for innovation* (pp. 15–39). Oxford: Blackwell.

Martin, R., & Hewstone, M. (2001b). Conformity and independence in groups: Majorities and minorities. In M. A. Hogg & R. S. Tindale (Eds.), *Blackwell handbook of social psychology: Group processes* (pp. 209–234). Oxford: Blackwell.

Martin, R., & Hewstone, M. (2008). Majority versus minority influence, message processing and attitude change: The source-context-elaboration model. In M. P. Zanna (Ed.), *Advances in experimental social psychology* (Vol. 40, pp. 237–326). San Diego, CA: Academic Press.

Martin, R., & Hewstone, M. (Eds.). (2010). *Minority influence and innovation: Antecedents, processes and consequences.* Hove, UK: Psychology Press.

Martin, R., & Hewstone, M. (2012). Minority influence: Revisiting Moscovici's blue-green afterimage studies. In J. R. Smith & S. A. Haslam (Eds.), *Social psychology: Revisiting the classic studies* (pp. 91–105). London: Sage.

Martin, R., Hewstone, M., & Martin, P. Y. (2003). Resistance to persuasive messages as a function of majority and minority source status. *Journal of Experimental Social Psychology, 39*, 585–593.

Martin, R., Hewstone, M., & Martin, P. Y. (2007). Systematic and heuristic processing of majority- and minority-endorsed messages: The effects of varying outcome relevance and levels of orientation on attitude and message processing. *Personality and Social Psychology Bulletin, 33*, 43–56.

Martin, R., Hewstone, M., & Martin, P. Y. (2008). Majority versus minority influence: The role of message processing in determining resistance to counter-persuasion. *European Journal of Social Psychology, 38*, 16–34.

Martin, R., Martin, P. Y., Smith, J. R., & Hewstone, M. (2007). Majority versus minority influence and prediction of behavioral intentions and behavior. *Journal of Experimental Social Psychology, 43*, 763–771.

Mashek, D. J., & Aron, A. (2004). *Handbook of closeness and intimacy.* Mahwah, NJ: Erlbaum.

Mashek, D. J., Aron, A., & Boncimino, M. (2003). Confusions of self with close others. *Personality and Social Psychology Bulletin, 29*, 382–392.

Maslach, C. (1979). Negative emotional biasing of unexplained arousal. *Journal of Personality and Social Psychology, 37*, 953–969.

Mason, M. F., & Morris, M. W. (2010). Culture, attribution and automaticity: A social cognitive neuroscience view. *Social Cognitive and Affective Neuroscience, 5*, 292–306.

Mason, W., & Suri, S. (2012). Conducting behavioral research on Amazon's Mechanical Turk. *Behavioral Research Methods, 44*, 1–23.

Masuda, T., & Nisbett, R. E. (2001). Attending holistically versus analytically: Comparing the context sensitivity of Japanese and Americans. *Journal of Personality and Social Psychology, 81*, 922–934.

Matsumoto, D., Yoo, S. H., & Fontaine, J. (2008). Mapping expressive differences around the world: The relationship between emotional display rules and individualism versus collectivism. *Journal of Cross-Cultural Psychology, 39*, 55–74.

Mayer, A. (1903). Über Einzel- und Gesamtleistung des Schulkindes [On the single and total performance of the schoolchild]. *Archiv für die Gesamte Psychologie, 1*, 276–416.

Mayer, N. D., & Tormala, Z. L. (2010). 'Think' versus 'feel' framing effects in persuasion. *Personality and Social Psychology Bulletin, 36*, 443–454.

Mayle, P. (1993). *Hotel Pastis.* London: Hamish Hamilton.

McAdams, D. P. (2008a). American identity: The redemptive self. *General Psychologist, 43*, 20–27.

McAdams, D. P. (2008b). Personal narratives and the life story. In O. P. John, R. W. Robins, & L. A. Pervin (Eds.), *Handbook of personality: Theory and research* (pp. 242–262). New York: Guilford.

McArthur, L. A. (1972). The how and what of why: Some determinants and consequences of causal attribution. *Journal of Personality and Social Psychology, 22*, 171–193.

McBurnett, K., Lahey, B. B., Rathouz, P. J., & Loeber, R. (2000). Low salivary cortisol and persistent aggression in boys referred for disruptive behavior. *Archives of General Psychiatry, 57*, 38–43.

McClelland, D. C., & Burnham, D. H. (1976). Power is the great motivator. *Harvard Business Review, 54*, 100–110.

McConahay, J. B., Hardee, B. B., & Batts, V. (1981). Has racism declined? It depends on who is asking and what is asked. *Journal of Conflict Resolution, 25*, 563–579.

McCracken, G. (1986). Culture and consumption: A theoretical account of the structure and movement of cultural meaning of consumer goods. *Journal of Consumer Research, 13*, 71–84.

McCrae, R. R., & Costa, P. T., Jr. (1987). Validation of the five-factor model of personality across instruments and observers. *Journal of Personality and Social Psychology, 52*, 81–90.

McCrea, S. M., Hirt, E. R., & Milner, B. J. (2008). She works hard for the money: Valuing effort underlies gender differences in behavioral self-handicapping. *Journal of Experimental Social Psychology, 44*, 292–311.

McCullough, M. E., Bellah, C. G., Kilpatrick, S. D., & Johnson, J. L. (2001). Vengefulness: Relationships with forgiveness, rumination, well-being, and the Big Five. *Personality and Social Psychology Bulletin, 27*, 601–610.

McCullough, M. E., Rachal, K. C., Sandage, S. J., Worthington, E. L., Jr., Brown, S. W., & Hight, T. L. (1998). Interpersonal forgiving in close relationships: Theoretical elaboration and measurement. *Journal of Personality and Social Psychology, 75*, 1586–1603.

McDougall, W. (1908). *An introduction to social psychology*. London: Methuen.

McElreath, R., & Boyd, R. (2007). *Mathematical models of social evolution: A guide for the perplexed*. Chicago: University of Chicago Press.

McGarty, C., Haslam, S. A., Turner, J. C., & Oakes, P. J. (1993). Illusory correlation as accentuation of actual intercategory difference: Evidence for the effect with minimal stimulus information. *European Journal of Social Psychology, 23*, 391–410.

McGill, A. L. (1989). Context effects in judgments of causation. *Journal of Personality and Social Psychology, 57*, 189–200.

McGrath, J. E. (1984). *Groups: Interaction and performance*. Englewood Cliffs, NJ: Prentice Hall.

McGregor, I., Nail, P. R., Marigold, D. C., & Kang, S. J. (2005). Defensive pride and consensus: Strength in imaginary numbers. *Journal of Personality and Social Psychology, 89*, 978–996.

McGuire, W. J. (1969). The nature of attitudes and attitude change. In G. Lindzey & E. Aronson (Eds.), *Handbook of social psychology* (2nd ed., Vol. 3, pp. 136–314). Reading, MA: Addison-Wesley.

McGuire, W. J. (1985). Attitudes and attitude change. In G. Lindzey & E. Aronson (Eds.), *Handbook of social psychology* (3rd ed., Vol. 2, pp. 233–346). New York: Random House.

McGuire, W. J., & McGuire, C. V. (1988). Content and process in the experience of self. In L. Berkowitz (Ed.), *Advances in experimental social psychology* (Vol. 21, pp. 97–144). San Diego, CA: Academic Press.

McGuire, W. J., McGuire, C. V., & Cheever, J. (1986). The self in society: Effects of social contexts on the sense of self. *British Journal of Social Psychology, 25*, 259–270.

McLean, S. (2010). *Business Communication for Success*. Retrieved from http://catalog.flatworldknowledge.com/catalog/editions/74

Mead, G. H. (1934). *Mind, self, and society*. Chicago: University of Chicago Press.

Meade, R. D. (1985). Experimental studies of authoritarian and democratic leadership in four cultures: American, Indian, Chinese and Chinese-American. *High School Journal, 68*, 293–295.

Meeus, W. H. J., & Raaijmakers, Q. A. W. (1986). Administrative obedience: Carrying out orders to use psychological-administrative violence. *European Journal of Social Psychology, 16*, 311–324.

Meeus, W. H. J., & Raaijmakers, Q. A. W. (1995). Obedience in modern society: The Utrecht studies. *Journal of Social Issues, 51*, 155–175.

Meier, B. P., & Wilkowski, B. M. (2013). Reducing the tendency to aggress: Insights from social and personality psychology. *Social and Personality Psychology Compass, 7*, 343–354.

Mendelson, M. J., & Aboud, F. E. (1999). Measuring friendship quality in late adolescents and young adults: McGill Friendship Questionnaires. *Canadian Journal of Behavioural Science, 31*, 130–132.

Merrin, J., Kinderman, P., & Bentall, R. P. (2007). 'Jumping to conclusions' and attributional style in persecutory delusions. *Cognitive Therapy and Research, 31*, 741–758.

Messé, L. A., Hertel, G., Kerr, N. L., Lount, R. B., Jr., & Park, E. S. (2002). Knowledge of partner's ability as a moderator of group motivation gains: An exploration of the Köhler discrepancy effect. *Journal of Personality and Social Psychology, 82*, 935–946.

Mezulis, A. H., Abramson, L. Y., Hyde, J. S., & Hankin, B. L. (2004). Is there a universal positivity bias in attributions? A meta-analytic review of individual, developmental, and cultural differences in the self-serving attributional bias. *Psychological Bulletin, 130*, 711–747.

Miceli, M. P., Dozier, J. B., & Near, J. P. (1991). Blowing the whistle on data-fudging: A controlled field experiment. *Journal of Applied Social Psychology, 21*, 271–295.

Miceli, M. P., & Near, J. P. (1992). *Blowing the whistle: The organizational and legal implications for companies and employees*. New York: Lexington.

Miceli, M. P., Near, J. P., & Dworkin, T. M. (2008). *Whistle-blowing in organizations*. New York: Routledge.

Michotte, A. (1963). *The perception of causality*. New York: Basic Books.

Miles, D. R., & Carey, G. (1997). Genetic and environmental architecture on human aggression. *Journal of Personality and Social Psychology, 72*, 207–217.

Milgram, S. (1963). Behavioral study of obedience. *Journal of Abnormal and Social Psychology, 67*, 371–378.

Milgram, S. (1965). Some conditions of obedience and disobedience to authority. *Human Relations, 18*, 57–76.

Milgram, S. (1974). *Obedience to authority: An experimental view*. New York: Harper & Row.

Milgram, S., Liberty, H. J., Toledo, R., & Wackenhut, J. (1986). Response to intrusion into waiting lines. *Journal of Personality and Social Psychology, 51*, 683–689.

Miller, A. G. (1986). *The obedience experiments: A case study of controversy in social science*. New York: Praeger.

Miller, A. G. (1995). Obedience. In A. S. R. Manstead & M. Hewstone (Eds.), *Blackwell encyclopedia of social psychology* (pp. 418–423). Oxford: Blackwell.

Miller, A. G. (2004). What can the Milgram obedience experiments tell us about the Holocaust? In A. G. Miller (Ed.), *The social psychology of good and evil* (pp. 193–239). New York: Guilford.

Miller, A. G., Collins, B. E., & Brief, D. E. (1995). Perspectives on obedience to authority: The legacy of the Milgram experiments. *Journal of Social Issues, 51*, 1–19.

Miller, A. G., Gordon, A. K., & Buddie, A. M. (1999). Accounting for evil and cruelty: Is to explain to condone? *Personality and Social Psychology Review, 3*, 254–268.

Miller, D. T., Downs, J. S., & Prentice, D. A. (1998). Minimal conditions for the creation of a unit relationship: The social bond between birthdaymates. *European Journal of Social Psychology, 28*, 475–481.

Miller, D. T., & Morrison, K. R. (2009). Expressing deviant opinions: Believing you are in the majority helps. *Journal of Experimental Social Psychology, 45*, 740–747.

Miller, D. T., & Ross, M. (1975). Self-serving biases in the attribution of causality: Fact or fiction? *Psychological Bulletin, 82*, 213–225.

Miller, G. A., Galanter, E., & Pribram, K. H. (1960). *Plans and the structure of behavior*. New York: Holt, Rinehart & Winston.

Miller, G. E., & Wrosch, C. (2007). You've gotta know when to fold 'em: Goal disengagement and systemic inflammation in adolescence. *Psychological Science, 18*, 773–777.

Miller, J. G. (1984). Culture and the development of everyday social explanation. *Journal of Personality and Social Psychology, 46*, 961–978.

Miller, N., Pedersen, W. C., Earleywine, M., & Pollock, V. E. (2003). A theoretical model of triggered displaced aggression. *Personality and Social Psychology Review, 7*, 75–97.

Miller, N. E. (1941). The frustration-aggression hypothesis. *Psychological Review, 48*, 337–342.

Miller, R. S. (1997). Inattentive and contented: Relationship commitment and attention to alternatives. *Journal of Personality and Social Psychology, 73*, 758–766.

Miller, R. S., & Perlman, D. (2008). *Intimate relationships*. New York: McGraw-Hill.

Miller, T. R., Cohen, M. A., & Rossman, S. B. (1993). Victim costs of violent crime and resulting injuries. *Health Affairs, 12*, 186–197.

Mischel, W. (1977). On the future of personality measurement. *American Psychologist, 32*, 246–254.

Mischel, W., Ayduk, O., Berman, M. G., Casey, B. J., Gotlib, I. H., Jonides, J., ... Shoda, Y. (2011). 'Willpower' over the life span: Decomposing self-regulation. *Social Cognitive and Affective Neuroscience, 6*, 252–256.

Mischel, W., Ebbesen, E. B., & Raskoff Zeiss, A. (1972). Cognitive and attentional mechanisms in delay of gratification. *Journal of Personality and Social Psychology, 21*, 204–18.

Mischel, W., Shoda, Y., & Rodriguez, M. L. (1989). Delay of gratification in children. *Science, 244*, 933–8.

Mitchell, J. P., Banaji, M. R., & Macrae, C. N. (2005). The link between social cognition and self-referential thought in the medial prefrontal cortex. *Journal of Cognitive Neuroscience, 17*, 1306–1315.

Miyamoto, Y., & Kitayama, S. (2002). Cultural variation in correspondence bias: The critical role of attitude diagnosticity of socially constrained behavior. *Journal of Personality and Social Psychology, 83*, 1239–1248.

Mlicki, P. P., & Ellemers, N. (1996). Being different or being better? National stereotypes and identifications of Polish and Dutch students. *European Journal of Social Psychology, 26*, 97–114.

Moede, W. (1920). *Experimentelle Massenpsychologie [Experimental crowd psychology]*. Leipzig, Germany: Hirzel.

Moghaddam, F. M. (2005). The staircase to terrorism: A psychological exploration. *American Psychologist, 60*, 161–169.

Moghaddam, F. M. (2006). *From the terrorists' point of view*. Westport, CT: Praeger.

Mojzisch, A., Grouneva, L., & Schulz-Hardt, S. (2010). Biased evaluation of information during discussion: Disentangling the effects of preference consistency, social validation, and ownership of information. *European Journal of Social Psychology, 40*, 946–956.

Mojzisch, A., & Schulz-Hardt, S. (2010). Knowing others' preferences degrades the quality of group decisions. *Journal of Personality and Social Psychology, 98*, 794–808.

Mojzisch, A., Schulz-Hardt, S., Kerschreiter, R., Brodbeck, F. C., & Frey, D. (2008). Social validation in group decision-making: Differential effects on the decisional impact of preference-consistent and preference-inconsistent information. *Journal of Experimental Social Psychology, 44*, 1477–1490.

Mok, A., Morris, M. W., Benet-Martínez, V., & Karakitapoğlu-Aygün, Z. (2007). Embracing American culture: Structures of social identity and social networks among first-generation biculturals. *Journal of Cross-Cultural Psychology, 38,* 629–635.

Möller, I., & Krahé, B. (2009). Exposure to violent video games and aggression in German adolescents: A longitudinal analysis. *Aggressive Behavior, 35,* 75–89.

Monahan, J. L., Murphy, S. T., & Zajonc, R. B. (2000). Subliminal mere exposure: Specific, general, and diffuse effects. *Psychological Science, 11,* 462–466.

Monin, B., Sawyer, P. J., & Marquez, M. J. (2008). The rejection of moral rebels: Resenting those who do the right thing. *Journal of Personality and Social Psychology, 95,* 76–93.

Monteith, M. J. (1993). Self-regulation of prejudiced responses: Implications for progress in prejudice-reduction efforts. *Journal of Personality and Social Psychology, 65,* 469–485.

Monteith, M. J., & Mark, A. Y. (2005). Changing one's prejudiced ways: Awareness, affect, and self-regulation. In W. Stroebe & M. Hewstone (Eds.), *European review of social psychology* (Vol. 16, pp. 113–154). Hove, UK: Psychology Press.

Monteith, M. J., Sherman, J. W., & Devine, P. G. (1998). Suppression as a stereotype control strategy. *Personality and Social Psychology Review, 2,* 63–82.

Monteith, M. J., Spicer, C. V., & Tooman, G. D. (1998). Consequences of stereotype suppression: Stereotypes on AND not on the rebound. *Journal of Experimental Social Psychology, 34,* 355–377.

Montepare, J. M., & Zebrowitz-McArthur, L. (1988). Impressions of people created by age-related qualities of their gaits. *Journal of Personality and Social Psychology, 55,* 547–556.

Montoya, R. M., Horton, R. S., & Kirchner, J. (2008). Is actual similarity necessary for attraction? A meta-analysis of actual and perceived similarity. *Journal of Social and Personal Relationships, 25,* 889–922.

Moreland, R. L., & Beach, S. R. (1992). Exposure effects in the classroom: The development of affinity among students. *Journal of Experimental Social Psychology, 28,* 255–276.

Moreland, R. L., & Levine, J. M. (1982). Socialization in small groups: Temporal changes in individual-group relations. In L. Berkowitz (Ed.), *Advances in experimental social psychology* (Vol. 15, pp. 137–192). New York: Academic Press.

Moreland, R. L., & Myaskovsky, L. (2000). Exploring the performance benefits of group training: Transactive memory or improved communication? *Organizational Behavior and Human Decision Processes, 82,* 117–133.

Morf, C. C., Horvath, S., & Torchetti, L. (2011). Narcissistic self-enhancement: Tales of (successful?) self-portrayal. In M. D. Alicke & C. Sedikides (Eds.), *Handbook of self-enhancement and self-protection* (pp. 399–424). New York: Guilford.

Morf, C. C., Horvath, S., & Zimmermann, T. D. (2011). *In the mind of a male narcissist: Worthlessness primes aggresion.* Manuscript submitted for publication.

Morf, C. C., & Mischel, W. (2012). The self as a psycho-social dynamic processing system: Toward a converging science of selfhood. In M. R. Leary & J. P. Tangney (Eds.), *Handbook of self and identity* (2nd ed., pp. 21–49). New York: Guilford.

Morf, C. C., & Rhodewalt, F. (1993). Narcissism and self-evaluation maintenance: Explorations in object relations. *Personality and Social Psychology Bulletin, 19,* 668–676.

Morf, C. C., & Rhodewalt, F. (2001). Unraveling the paradoxes of narcissism: A dynamic self-regulatory processing model. *Psychological Inquiry, 12,* 177–196.

Morf, C. C., Torchetti, L., & Schürch, E. (2011). Narcissism from the perspective of the dynamic self-regulatory processing model. In W. K. Campbell & J. D. Miller (Eds.), *Handbook of narcissism and narcissistic personality disorder: Theoretical approaches, empirical findings, and treatments* (pp. 56–70). Hoboken, NJ: Wiley.

Mori, K., & Arai, M. (2010). No need to fake it: Reproduction of the Asch experiment without confederates. *International Journal of Psychology, 45,* 390–397.

Morris, M. W., & Peng, K. (1994). Culture and cause: American and Chinese attributions for social and physical events. *Journal of Personality and Social Psychology, 67,* 949–971.

Morris, M. W., Williams, K. Y., Leung, K., Larrick, R., Mendoza, M. T., Bhatnagar, D., … Hu, J.-C. (1998). Conflict management style: Accounting for cross-national differences. *Journal of International Business Studies, 29,* 729–747.

Morris, P. H., & Lewis, D. (2010). Tackling diving: The perception of deceptive intentions in association football (soccer). *Journal of Nonverbal Behavior, 34,* 1–13.

Morrison, E. W., & Herlihy, J. M. (1992). Becoming the best place to work: Managing diversity at American Express Travel Related Services. In S. E. Jackson (Ed.), *Diversity in the workplace: Human resources initiatives* (pp. 203–226). New York: Guilford.

Morrison, K. R., & Miller, D. T. (2008). Distinguishing between silent and vocal minorities: Not all deviants feel marginal. *Journal of Personality and Social Psychology, 94,* 871–882.

Moscovici, S. (1976). *Social influence and social change.* London: Academic Press.

Moscovici, S. (1980). Toward a theory of conversion behavior. In L. Berkowitz (Ed.), *Advances in experimental social psychology* (Vol. 13, pp. 209–239). New York: Academic Press.

Moscovici, S., Lage, E., & Naffrechoux, M. (1969). Influence of a consistent minority on the responses of a majority in a color perception task. *Sociometry, 32,* 365–380.

Moscovici, S., & Marková, I. (2006). *The making of modern social psychology: The hidden story of how an international social science was created.* Cambridge, UK: Polity.

Moscovici, S., & Personnaz, B. (1980). Studies in social influence: Minority influence and conversion behavior in a perceptual task. *Journal of Experimental Social Psychology, 16,* 270–282.

Moscovici, S., & Zavalloni, M. (1969). The group as a polarizer of attitudes. *Journal of Personality and Social Psychology, 12,* 125–135.

Moskowitz, G. B. (2005). *Social cognition: Understanding self and others.* New York: Guilford.

Moskowitz, G. B., Gollwitzer, P. M., Wasel, W., & Schaal, B. (1999). Preconscious control of stereotype activation through chronic egalitarian goals. *Journal of Personality and Social Psychology, 77,* 167–184.

Moskowitz, G. B., & Ignarri, C. (2009). Implicit volition and stereotype control. In W. Stroebe & M. Hewstone (Eds.), *European review of social psychology* (Vol. 20, pp. 97–145). Hove, UK: Psychology Press.

Moskowitz, G. B., Salomon, A. R., & Taylor, C. M. (2000). Preconsciously controlling stereotyping: Implicitly activated egalitarian goals prevent the activation of stereotypes. *Social Cognition, 18,* 151–177.

Moskowitz, G. B., Stone, J., & Childs, A. (2012). Implicit stereotyping and medical decisions: Unconscious stereotype activation in practitioners' thoughts about African Americans. *American Journal of Public Health, 102,* 996–1001.

Mucchi-Faina, A., Maass, A., & Volpato, C. (1991). Social influence: The role of originality. *European Journal of Social Psychology, 21,* 183–197.

Mueller, C. M., & Dweck, C. S. (1998). Praise for intelligence can undermine children's motivation and performance. *Journal of Personality and Social Psychology, 75,* 33–52.

Mugny, G. (1982). *The power of minorities.* London: Academic Press.

Mugny, G., Butera, F., Sanchez-Mazas, M., & Pérez, J. A. (1995). Judgments in conflict: The conflict elaboration theory of social influence. In B. Boothe, R. Hirsig, A. Helminger, B. Meier, & R. Volkart (Eds.), *Perception, evaluation, interpretation* (pp. 160–168). Göttingen, Germany: Hogrefe and Huber.

Mugny, G., & Pérez, J. A. (1991). *The social psychology of minority influence.* Cambridge, UK: Cambridge University Press.

Mullen, B. (1986). Atrocity as a function of lynch mob composition: A self-attention perspective. *Personality and Social Psychology Bulletin, 12,* 187–197.

Mullen, B., Anthony, T., Salas, E., & Driskell, J. E. (1994). Group cohesiveness and quality of decision making: An integration of tests of the Groupthink hypothesis. *Small Group Research, 25,* 189–204.

Mullen, B., Brown, R., & Smith, C. (1992). Ingroup bias as a function of salience, relevance, and status: An integration. *European Journal of Social Psychology, 22,* 103–122.

Mullen, B., & Copper, C. (1994). The relation between group cohesiveness and performance: An integration. *Psychological Bulletin, 115,* 210–227.

Mullen, B., Johnson, C., & Salas, E. (1991). Productivity loss in brainstorming groups: A meta-analytic integration. *Basic and Applied Social Psychology, 12,* 3–23.

Mullen, B., & Riordan, C. A. (1988). Self-serving attributions for performance in naturalistic settings: A meta-analytic review. *Journal of Applied Social Psychology, 18,* 3–22.

Mummendey, A., Kessler, T., Klink, A., & Mielke, R. (1999). Strategies to cope with negative social identity: Predictions by social identity theory and relative deprivation theory. *Journal of Personality and Social Psychology, 76,* 229–245.

Mummendey, A., & Otten, S. (1998). Positive–negative asymmetry in social discrimination. In W. Stroebe & M. Hewstone (Eds.), *European review of social psychology* (Vol. 9, pp. 107–143). Chichester, UK: Wiley.

Mummendey, A., & Schreiber, H.-J. (1984). 'Different' just means 'better': Some obvious and some hidden pathways to in-group favouritism. *British Journal of Social Psychology, 23,* 363–367.

Mummendey, A., & Wenzel, M. (1999). Social discrimination and tolerance in intergroup relations: Reactions to intergroup difference. *Personality and Social Psychology Review, 3,* 158–174.

Muramoto, Y. (2003). An indirect enhancement in relationship among Japanese. *Journal of Cross-Cultural Psychology, 34,* 552–566.

Muraven, M., & Baumeister, R. F. (2000). Self-regulation and depletion of limited resources: Does self-control resemble a muscle? *Psychological Bulletin, 126,* 247–259.

Muraven, M., Gagné, M., & Rosman, H. (2008). Helpful self-control: Autonomy support, vitality, and depletion. *Journal of Experimental Social Psychology, 44,* 573–585.

Murchison, C. (Ed.). (1935). *Handbook of social psychology.* Worchester, MA: Clark University Press.

Murdoch, D., Pihl, R. O., & Ross, D. (1990). Alcohol and crimes of violence: Present issues. *International Journal of the Addictions, 25,* 1065–1081.

Murphy, S. T., & Zajonc, R. B. (1993). Affect, cognition, and awareness: Affective priming with optimal and suboptimal stimulus exposures. *Journal of Personality and Social Psychology, 64,* 723–739.

Murray, H. A. (1943). *Thematic Apperception Test Manual.* Cambridge, MA: Harvard University Press.

Murray, R. K., & Blessing, T. H. (1983). The presidential performance study: A progress report. *Journal of American History, 70,* 535–555.

Murray, S. L., Holmes, J. G., Bellavia, G., Griffin, D. W., & Dolderman, D. (2002). Kindred spirits? The benefits of egocentrism in close relationships. *Journal of Personality and Social Psychology, 82,* 563–581.

Murray, S. L., Holmes, J. G., & Griffin, D. W. (1996). The benefits of positive illusions: Idealization and the construction of satisfaction in close relationships. *Journal of Personality and Social Psychology, 70,* 79–98.

Mussweiler, T. (2006). Doing is for thinking! Stereotype activation by stereotypic movements. *Psychological Science, 17,* 17–21.

Mussweiler, T., Rüter, K., & Epstude, K. (2006). The why, who, and how of social comparison: A social cognition perspective. In S. Guimond (Ed.), *Social comparison and social psychology: Understanding cognition, intergroup relations and culture* (pp. 33–54). New York: Cambridge University Press.

Myers, D. G. (1978). Polarizing effects of social comparison. *Journal of Experimental Social Psychology, 14,* 554–563.

Myers, D. G., Bach, P. J., & Schreiber, F. B. (1974). Normative and informational effects of group interaction. *Sociometry, 37,* 275–286.

Myers, D. G., & Bishop, G. D. (1970). Discussion effects on racial attitudes. *Science, 169,* 778–779.

Myers, D. G., & Kaplan, M. F. (1976). Group-induced polarization in simulated juries. *Personality and Social Psychology Bulletin, 2,* 63–66.

Myers, D. G., & Lamm, H. (1976). The group polarization phenomenon. *Psychological Bulletin, 83,* 602–627.

Nadler, A. (2002). Inter-group helping relations as power relations: Maintaining or challenging social dominance between groups through helping. *Journal of Social Issues, 58,* 487–502.

Nadler, A., & Fisher, J. D. (1986). The role of threat to self-esteem and perceived control in recipient reaction to help: Theory development and empirical validation. In L. Berkowitz (Ed.), *Advances in experimental social psychology* (Vol. 19, pp. 81–122). Orlando, FL: Academic Press.

Nadler, A., Harpaz-Gorodeisky, G., & Ben-David, Y. (2009). Defensive helping: Threat to group identity, ingroup identification, status stability, and common group identity as determinants of intergroup help-giving. *Journal of Personality and Social Psychology, 97,* 823–834.

Nadler, A., & Saguy, T. (2004). Trust building and reconciliation between adversarial groups: A social psychological perspective. In H. J. Langholtz & C. E. Stout (Eds.), *The psychology of diplomacy* (pp. 29–46). Westport, CT: Praeger.

Naipaul, S. (1980). *Black and white.* London: Hamish Hamilton.

Navarick, D. J. (2012). Historical psychology and the Milgram paradigm: Tests of an experimentally derived model of defiance using accounts of massacres by Nazi Reserve Police Battalion 101. *The Psychological Record, 62,* 133–154.

Neal, D. T., Wood, W., Labrecque, J. S., & Lally, P. (2012). How do habits guide behavior? Perceived and actual triggers of habits in daily life. *Journal of Experimental Social Psychology, 48,* 492–498.

Near, J. P., & Miceli, M. P. (1985). Organizational dissidence: The case of whistle-blowing. *Journal of Business Ethics, 4,* 1–16.

Neely, J. H. (1977). Semantic priming and retrieval from lexical memory: Roles of inhibitionless spreading activation and limited-capacity attention. *Journal of Experimental Psychology: General, 106,* 226–254.

Neff, K. D. (2003). Development and validation of a scale to measure self-compassion. *Self and Identity, 2,* 223–250.

Nemeth, C., Mosier, K., & Chiles, C. (1992). When convergent thought improves performance: Majority versus minority influence. *Personality and Social Psychology Bulletin, 18,* 139–144.

Nemeth, C., Swedlund, M., & Kanki, B. (1974). Patterning of the minority's responses and their influence on the majority. *European Journal of Social Psychology, 4,* 53–64.

Nemeth, C. J. (1986). Differential contributions of majority and minority influence. *Psychological Review, 93,* 23–32.

Nemeth, C. J. (1995). Dissent as driving cognition, attitudes, and judgments. *Social Cognition, 13,* 273–291.

Nemeth, C. J., & Kwan, J. L. (1985). Originality of word associations as a function of majority vs. minority influence. *Social Psychology Quarterly, 48,* 277–282.

Nemeth, C. J., & Wachtler, J. (1983). Creative problem solving as a result of majority vs. minority influence. *European Journal of Social Psychology, 13,* 45–55.

Neuberg, S. L. (1996). Social motives and expectancy-tinged social interactions. In R. M. Sorrentino & E. T. Higgins (Eds.), *Handbook of motivation and cognition: The interpersonal context* (Vol. 3, pp. 225–261). New York: Guilford.

Neuberg, S. L., & Fiske, S. T. (1987). Motivational influences on impression formation: Outcome dependency, accuracy-driven attention, and individuating processes. *Journal of Personality and Social Psychology, 53,* 431–444.

Newcomb, T. M. (1943). *Personality and social change: Attitude formation in a student community.* New York: Dryden.

Newcomb, T. M. (1961). *The acquaintance process.* New York: Holt, Rinehart and Winston.

Newman, L. S., & Erber, R. (Eds.). (2002). *Understanding genocide: The social psychology of the Holocaust.* Oxford: Oxford University Press.

Nicholson, I. (2011). 'Torture at Yale': Experimental subjects, laboratory torment and the 'rehabilitation' of Milgram's 'Obedience to Authority'. *Theory & Psychology, 21,* 737–761.

Nijstad, B. A. (2009). *Group performance.* Hove, UK: Psychology Press.

Nijstad, B. A., Stroebe, W., & Lodewijkx, H. F. M. (2002). Cognitive stimulation and interference in groups: Exposure effects in an idea generation task. *Journal of Experimental Social Psychology, 38,* 535–544.

Nisbett, R. E. (1993). Violence and U.S. regional culture. *American Psychologist, 48,* 441–449.

Nisbett, R. E. (2003). *The geography of thought: How Asians and Westerners think differently … and why.* New York: Free Press.

Nisbett, R. E. (2009). *Intelligence and how to get it: Why schools and cultures count.* New York: Norton.

Nisbett, R. E., Caputo, C., Legant, P., & Marecek, J. (1973). Behavior as seen by the actor and as seen by the observer. *Journal of Personality and Social Psychology, 27,* 154–164.

Nisbett, R. E., & Cohen, D. (1996). *Culture of honor: The psychology of violence in the south*. Boulder, CO: Westview.

Nisbett, R. E., Peng, K., Choi, I., & Norenzayan, A. (2001). Culture and systems of thought: Holistic versus analytic cognition. *Psychological Review, 108*, 291–310.

Nisbett, R. E., & Ross, L. (1980). *Human inference: Strategies and shortcomings of social judgment*. Englewood Cliffs, NJ: Prentice Hall.

Nisbett, R. E., & Wilson, T. D. (1977). Telling more than we can know: Verbal reports on mental processes. *Psychological Review, 84*, 231–259.

Nissani, M. (1990). A cognitive reinterpretation of Stanley Milgram's observations on obedience to authority. *American Psychologist, 45*, 1384–1385.

Nolan, J. M., Schultz, P. W., Cialdini, R. B., Goldstein, N. J., & Griskevicius, V. (2008). Normative social influence is underdetected. *Personality and Social Psychology Bulletin, 34*, 913–923.

Norenzayan, A., Choi, I., & Nisbett, R. E. (2002). Cultural similarities and differences in social inference: Evidence from behavioral predictions and lay theories of behavior. *Personality and Social Psychology Bulletin, 28*, 109–120.

Northcraft, G. B., & Neale, M. A. (1987). Experts, amateurs, and real estate: An anchoring-and-adjustment perspective on property pricing decisions. *Organizational Behavior and Human Decision Processes, 39*, 84–97.

Norton, M. I., Frost, J. H., & Ariely, D. (2007). Less is more: The lure of ambiguity, or why familiarity breeds contempt. *Journal of Personality and Social Psychology, 92*, 97–105.

Nosek, B. A. (2005). Moderators of the relationship between implicit and explicit evaluation. *Journal of Experimental Psychology: General, 134*, 565–584.

Nosek, B. A. (2007). Implicit-explicit relations. *Current Directions in Psychological Science, 16*, 65–69.

Nosek, B. A., Banaji, M. R., & Greenwald, A. G. (2002). E-research: Ethics, security, design, and control in psychological research on the Internet. *Journal of Social Issues, 58*, 161–176.

Nosek, B. A., Greenwald, A. G., & Banaji, M. R. (2005). Understanding and using the Implicit Association Test: II. Method variables and construct validity. *Personality and Social Psychology Bulletin, 31*, 166–180.

Nosek, B. A., Greenwald, A. G., & Banaji, M. R. (2007). The Implicit Association Test at age 7: A methodological and conceptual review. In J. A. Bargh (Ed.), *Social psychology and the unconscious: The automaticity of higher mental processes* (pp. 265–292). New York: Psychology Press.

Novotny, T. E., Romano, R. A., Davis, R. M., & Mills, S. L. (1992). The public health practice of tobacco control: Lessons learned and directions for the States in the 1990s. *Annual Review of Public Health, 13*, 287–318.

Nuttin, J. M., Jr. (1985). Narcissism beyond Gestalt and awareness: The name letter effect. *European Journal of Social Psychology, 15*, 353–361.

Nuttin, J. M., Jr. (1987). Affective consequences of mere ownership: The name letter effect in twelve European languages. *European Journal of Social Psychology, 17*, 381–402.

Nuttin, J. M. (1990). In memoriam: John T. Lanzetta. *European Journal of Social Psychology, 20*, 363–367.

Nuwer, H. (1999). *Wrongs of passage: Fraternities, sororities, hazing, and binge drinking*. Bloomington, IN: Indiana University Press.

Oakes, P. J., Haslam, S. A., & Turner, J. C. (1994). *Stereotyping and social reality*. Oxford: Blackwell.

Oakes, P. J., & Turner, J. C. (1980). Social categorization and intergroup behaviour: Does minimal intergroup discrimination make social identity more positive? *European Journal of Social Psychology, 10*, 295–301.

Ochsner, K. N., Beer, J. S., Robertson, E. R., Cooper, J. C., Gabrieli, J. D. E., Kihlstrom, J. F., & D'Esposito, M. (2005). The neural correlates of direct and reflected self-knowledge. *Neuroimage, 28*, 797–814.

Ochsner, K. N., & Lieberman, M. D. (2001). The emergence of social cognitive neuroscience. *American Psychologist, 56*, 717–734.

Oliner, S. P., & Oliner, P. M. (1992). *The altruistic personality: Rescuers of Jews in Nazi Europe*. New York: Free Press.

Olson, M. A., & Fazio, R. H. (2001). Implicit attitude formation through classical conditioning. *Psychological Science, 12*, 413–417.

Olson, M. A., & Fazio, R. H. (2004). Reducing the influence of extrapersonal associations on the Implicit Association Test: Personalizing the IAT. *Journal of Personality and Social Psychology, 86*, 653–667.

Olweus, D. (1979). Stability of aggressive reaction patterns in males: A review. *Psychological Bulletin, 86*, 852–875.

Olweus, D. (1994). Bullying at school: Long-term outcomes for the victims and an effective school-based intervention program. In L. R. Huesmann (Ed.), *Aggressive behavior: Current perspectives* (pp. 97–130). New York: Plenum.

Omoto, A. M., & Snyder, M. (1993). AIDS volunteers and their motivations: Theoretical issues and practical concerns. *Nonprofit Management and Leadership, 4*, 157–176.

Omoto, A. M., & Snyder, M. (2002). Considerations of community: The context and process of volunteerism. *American Behavioral Scientist, 45*, 846–867.

Omoto, A. M., & Snyder, M. (2010). Influences of psychological sense of community on voluntary helping and prosocial action. In S. Stürmer & M. Snyder (Eds.), *The psychology of prosocial behavior: Group processes, intergroup relations, and helping* (pp. 223–243). Chichester, UK: Wiley-Blackwell.

Omoto, A. M., Snyder, M., & Martino, S. C. (2000). Volunteerism and the life course: Investigating age-related agendas for action. *Basic and Applied Social Psychology, 22*, 181–197.

Oppenheim, A. N. (1992). *Questionnaire design, interviewing and attitude measurement*. London: Pinter.

Ruback, R. B., & Thompson, M. P. (2001). *Social and psychological consequences of violent victimization*. Thousand Oaks, CA: Sage.

Rubin, M., & Hewstone, M. (1998). Social identity theory's self-esteem hypothesis: A review and some suggestions for clarification. *Personality and Social Psychology Review, 2*, 40–62.

Rubin, Z. (1973). *Liking and loving: An invitation to social psychology*. New York: Holt, Rinehart and Winston.

Rude, S. S., Durham-Fowler, J. A., Baum, E. S., Rooney, S. B., & Maestas, K. L. (2010). Self-report and cognitive processing measures of depressive thinking predict subsequent major depressive disorder. *Cognitive Therapy and Research, 34*, 107–115.

Runciman, W. G. (1966). *Relative deprivation and social justice: A study of attitudes towards social inequality in twentieth-century England*. London: Routledge & Kegan Paul.

Rusbult, C. E. (1980). Commitment and satisfaction in romantic associations: A test of the investment model. *Journal of Experimental Social Psychology, 16*, 172–186.

Rusbult, C. E. (1983). A longitudinal test of the investment model: The development (and deterioration) of satisfaction and commitment in heterosexual involvements. *Journal of Personality and Social Psychology, 45*, 101–117.

Rusbult, C. E., & Farrell, D. (1983). A longitudinal test of the investment model: The impact on job satisfaction, job commitment, and turnover of variations in rewards, costs, alternatives, and investments. *Journal of Applied Psychology, 68*, 429–438.

Rusbult, C. E., & Martz, J. M. (1995). Remaining in an abusive relationship: An investment model analysis of nonvoluntary dependence. *Personality and Social Psychology Bulletin, 21*, 558–571.

Rusbult, C. E., & Van Lange, P. A. M. (1996). Interdependence processes. In E. T. Higgins & A. W. Kruglanski (Eds.), *Social psychology: Handbook of basic principles* (pp. 564–596). New York: Guilford.

Rusbult, C. E., Van Lange, P. A. M., Wildschut, T., Yovetich, N. A., & Verette, J. (2000). Perceived superiority in close relationships: Why it exists and persists. *Journal of Personality and Social Psychology, 79*, 521–545.

Rusbult, C. E., Verette, J., Whitney, G. A., Slovik, L. F., & Lipkus, I. (1991). Accommodation processes in close relationships: Theory and preliminary empirical evidence. *Journal of Personality and Social Psychology, 60*, 53–78.

Rushton, J. P. (1989). Genetic similarity, human altruism, and group selection. *Behavioral and Brain Sciences, 12*, 503–559.

Russell, G. W. (2004). Sport riots: A social-psychological review. *Aggression and Violent Behavior, 9*, 353–378.

Russell, N. J. C. (2010). The making of an (in)famous experiment. *The Psychologist, 23*, 780–783.

Ryan, R. M., Bernstein, J. H., & Brown, K. W. (2010). Weekends, work, and well-being: Psychological need satisfactions and day of the week effects on mood, vitality, and physical symptoms. *Journal of Social and Clinical Psychology, 29*, 95–122.

Ryan, R. M., & Deci, E. L. (2008). From ego depletion to vitality: Theory and findings concerning the facilitation of energy available to the self. *Social and Personality Psychology Compass, 2*, 702–717.

Ryen, A. H., & Kahn, A. (1975). Effects of intergroup orientation on group attitudes and proxemic behavior. *Journal of Personality and Social Psychology, 31*, 302–310.

Saguy, T., Tausch, N., Dovidio, J. F., & Pratto, F. (2009). The irony of harmony: Intergroup contact can produce false expectations for equality. *Psychological Science, 20*, 114–121.

Salas, E., & Fiore, S. M. (2004). *Team cognition: Understanding the factors that drive process and performance*. Washington, DC: American Psychological Association.

Salmivalli, C. (2010). Bullying and the peer group: A review. *Aggression and Violent Behavior, 15*, 112–120.

Sam, D. L., & Berry, J. W. (Eds.). (1997). *Cambridge handbook of acculturation psychology*. Cambridge, MA: Cambridge University Press.

Sanbonmatsu, D. M., & Fazio, R. H. (1990). The role of attitudes in memory-based decision making. *Journal of Personality and Social Psychology, 59*, 614–622.

Sanders, G. S. (1981). Driven by distraction: An integrative review of social facilitation theory and research. *Journal of Experimental Social Psychology, 17*, 227–251.

Sanders, G. S., Baron, R. S., & Moore, D. L. (1978). Distraction and social comparison as mediators of social facilitation effects. *Journal of Experimental Social Psychology, 14*, 291–303.

Sandstrom, M. J., & Jordan, R. (2008). Defensive self-esteem and aggression in childhood. *Journal of Research in Personality, 42*, 506–514.

Sanfey, A. G., Rilling, J. K., Aronson, J. A., Nystrom, L. E., & Cohen, J. D. (2003). The neural basis of economic decision-making in the ultimatum game. *Science, 300*, 1755–1758.

Sani, F. (Ed.). (2008). *Individual and collective self-continuity: Psychological perspectives*. Mahwah NJ: Erlbaum.

Sanitioso, R., Kunda, Z., & Fong, G. T. (1990). Motivated recruitment of autobiographical memories. *Journal of Personality and Social Psychology, 59*, 229–241.

Sasfy, J., & Okun, M. (1974). Form of evaluation and audience expertise as joint determinants of audience effects. *Journal of Experimental Social Psychology, 10*, 461–467.

Sassenberg, K., Kessler, T., & Mummendey, A. (2004). *When creative means different: Activating creativity as a strategy to initiate the generation of original ideas*. Unpublished manuscript. Jena, Germany: Friedrich-Schiller University.

Sassenberg, K., & Moskowitz, G. B. (2005). Don't stereotype, think different! Overcoming automatic stereotype activation by mindset priming. *Journal of Experimental Social Psychology, 41*, 506–514.

Saucier, D. A., Miller, C. T., & Doucet, N. (2005). Differences in helping Whites and Blacks: A meta-analysis. *Personality and Social Psychology Review, 9,* 2–16.

Sbarra, D. A., Law, R. W., & Portley, R. M. (2011). Divorce and death: A meta-analysis and research agenda for clinical, social, and health psychology. *Perspectives on Psychological Science, 6,* 454–474.

Schachter, S. (1951). Deviation, rejection, and communication. *Journal of Abnormal and Social Psychology, 46,* 190–207.

Schachter, S. (1964). The interaction of cognitive and physiological determinants of emotional state. In L. Berkowitz (Ed.), *Advances in experimental social psychology* (Vol. 1, pp. 49–80). New York: Academic Press.

Schachter, S. (1994). *Leon Festinger. Biographical memoirs* (Vol. 64). Retrieved October, 2005, from http://www.nap.edu

Schachter, S., Nuttin, J., De Monchaux, C., Maucorps, P. H., Osmer, D., Duijker, H., … Israel, J. (1954). Cross-cultural experiments on threat and rejection. *Human Relations, 7,* 403–439.

Schachter, S., & Singer, J. (1962). Cognitive, social, and physiological determinants of emotional state. *Psychological Review, 69,* 379–399.

Schaefer, C. E., & Mattei, D. (2005). Catharsis: Effectiveness in children's aggression. *International Journal of Play Therapy, 14,* 103–109.

Schaller, M., & Maass, A. (1989). Illusory correlation and social categorization: Toward an integration of motivational and cognitive factors in stereotype formation. *Journal of Personality and Social Psychology, 56,* 709–721.

Schatzel-Murphy, E. A., Harris, D. A., Knight, R. A., & Milburn, M. A. (2009). Sexual coercion in men and women: Similar behaviors, different predictors. *Archives of Sexual Behavior, 38,* 974–986.

Scheepers, D., De Wit, F., Ellemers, N., & Sassenberg, K. (2012). Social power makes the heart work more efficiently: Evidence from cardiovascular markers of challenge and threat. *Journal of Experimental Social Psychology, 48,* 371–374.

Scheepers, D., Spears, R., Doosje, B., & Manstead, A. S. R. (2006a). Diversity in in-group bias: Structural factors, situational features, and social functions. *Journal of Personality and Social Psychology, 90,* 944–960.

Scheepers, D., Spears, R., Doosje, B., & Manstead, A. S. R. (2006b). The social functions of in-group bias: Creating, confirming, or changing social reality. In W. Stroebe & M. Hewstone (Eds.), *European review of social psychology* (Vol. 17, pp. 359–396). Hove, UK: Psychology Press.

Scheepers, D., Spears, R., Manstead, A. S. R., & Doosje, B. (2009). The influence of discrimination and fairness on collective self-esteem. *Personality and Social Psychology Bulletin, 35,* 506–515.

Scherer, K. R., & Scherer, U. (1981). Speech behavior and personality. In J. K. Darby (Ed.), *Speech evaluation in psychiatry* (pp. 115–135). New York: Grune & Stratton.

Schiappa, E., Gregg, P. B., & Hewes, D. E. (2005). The parasocial contact hypothesis. *Communication Monographs, 72,* 92–115.

Schimmack, U., Oishi, S., & Diener, E. (2005). Individualism: A valid and important dimension of cultural differences between nations. *Personality and Social Psychology Review, 9,* 17–31.

Schlenker, B. R. (2012). Self-presentation. In M. R. Leary & J. P. Tangney (Eds.), *Handbook of self and identity* (2nd ed., pp. 542–570). New York: Guilford.

Schlenker, B. R., & Wowra, S. A. (2003). Carryover effects of feeling socially transparent or impenetrable on strategic self-presentation. *Journal of Personality and Social Psychology, 85,* 871–880.

Schmeichel, B. J., & Martens, A. (2005). Self-affirmation and mortality salience: Affirming values reduces worldview defense and death-thought accessibility. *Personality and Social Psychology Bulletin, 31,* 658–667.

Schmeichel, B. J., & Vohs, K. (2009). Self-affirmation and self-control: Affirming core values counteracts ego depletion. *Journal of Personality and Social Psychology, 96,* 770–782.

Schmitt, D. P., & Allik, J. (2005). Simultaneous administration of the Rosenberg Self-Esteem Scale in 53 nations: Exploring the universal and culture-specific features of global self-esteem. *Journal of Personality and Social Psychology, 89,* 623–642.

Scholten, L., van Knippenberg, D., Nijstad, B. A., & De Dreu, C. K. W. (2007). Motivated information processing and group decision making: Effects of process accountability on information processing and decision quality. *Journal of Experimental Social Psychology, 43,* 539–552.

Schreiber, E. (1979). Bystander's intervention in situations of violence. *Psychological Reports, 45,* 243–246.

Schreiber, F., Bohn, C., Aderka, I. M., Stangier, U., & Steil, R. (2012). Discrepancies between implicit and explicit self-esteem among adolescents with social anxiety disorder. *Journal of Behavior Therapy and Experimental Psychiatry, 43,* 1074–1081.

Schuette, R. A., & Fazio, R. H. (1995). Attitude accessibility and motivation as determinants of biased processing: A test of the MODE model. *Personality and Social Psychology Bulletin, 21,* 704–710.

Schultze, T., Faulmüller, N., Schmidt-Hieber, J., & Schulz-Hardt, S. (2013). *Do hidden profiles exist outside the laboratory? An answer based on computational simulation.* Unpublished manuscript, University of Goettingen.

Schulz-Hardt, S., Brodbeck, F. C., Mojzisch, A., Kerschreiter, R., & Frey, D. (2006). Group decision making in hidden profile situations: Dissent as a facilitator for decision quality. *Journal of Personality and Social Psychology, 91,* 1080–1093.

Schulz-Hardt, S., Frey, D., Lüthgens, C., & Moscovici, S. (2000). Biased information search in group decision making. *Journal of Personality and Social Psychology, 78,* 655–669.

Schulz-Hardt, S., Hertel, G., & Brodbeck, F. C. (2007). Gruppenleistung und Leistungsförderung [Group performance and its facilitation]. In H. Schuler & K.-H. Sonntag (Eds.), *Handbuch der Arbeits- und Organisationspsychologie* (pp. 698–706). Göttingen, Germany: Hogrefe.

Schulz-Hardt, S., & Mojzisch, A. (2012). How to achieve synergy in group decision making: Lessons to be learned from the hidden profile paradigm. In W. Stroebe & M. Hewstone (Eds.), *European review of social psychology* (Vol. 23, pp. 305–343). Hove, UK: Psychology Press.

Schumpeter, J. (1908). *Das Wesen und der Hauptinhalt der theoretischen Nationalökonomie [The Nature and Essence of Theoretical Economics].* München und Leipzig: Duncker und Humblot.

Schwartz, S. H. (1992). Universals in the content and structure of values: Theoretical advances and empirical tests in 20 countries. In M. P. Zanna (Ed.), *Advances in experimental social psychology* (Vol. 25, pp. 1–65). San Diego, CA: Academic Press.

Schwartz, S. H. (1994). Beyond individualism and collectivism: New cultural dimensions of values. In U. Kim, H. C. Triandis, Ç. Kağıtçıbaşı, S. C. Choi, & G. Yoon (Eds.), *Individualism and collectivism: Theory, method and applications* (pp. 85–119). Thousand Oaks, CA: Sage.

Schwartz, S. H. (2004). Mapping and interpreting cultural differences around the world. In H. Vinken, J. Soeters, & P. Ester (Eds.), *Comparing cultures: Dimensions of culture in a comparative perspective* (pp. 43–73). Leiden, NL: Brill.

Schwartz, S. H., & Gottlieb, A. (1976). Bystander reactions to a violent theft: Crime in Jerusalem. *Journal of Personality and Social Psychology, 34,* 1188–1199.

Schwartz, S. H., & Sagiv, L. (1995). Identifying culture-specifics in the content and structure of values. *Journal of Cross-Cultural Psychology, 26,* 92–116.

Schwarz, N. (1994). Judgment in a social context: Biases, shortcomings, and the logic of conversation. In M. P. Zanna (Ed.), *Advances in experimental social psychology* (Vol. 26, pp. 123–162). San Diego, CA: Academic Press.

Schwarz, N. (1999). Self-reports: How the questions shape the answers. *American Psychologist, 54,* 93–105.

Schwarz, N., Bless, H., Strack, F., Klumpp, G., Rittenauer-Schatka, H., & Simons, A. (1991). Ease of retrieval as information: Another look at the availability heuristic. *Journal of Personality and Social Psychology, 61,* 195–202.

Schwarz, N., & Clore, G. L. (1983). Mood, misattribution and judgments of well-being: Informative and directive functions of affective states. *Journal of Personality and Social Psychology, 45,* 513–523.

Schwarz, N., Groves, R. M., & Schuman, H. (1998). Survey methods. In D. T. Gilbert, S. T. Fiske, & G. Lindzey (Eds.), *Handbook of social psychology* (4th ed., Vol. 1, pp. 143–179). Boston, MA: McGraw-Hill.

Schwarzwald, J., Raz, M., & Zvibel, M. (1979). The application of the door-in-the-face technique when established behavioral customs exist. *Journal of Applied Social Psychology, 9,* 576–586.

Sears, D. O. (1986). College sophomores in the laboratory: Influences of a narrow data base on social psychology's view of human nature. *Journal of Personality and Social Psychology, 51,* 515–530.

Sears, D. O. (1988). Symbolic racism. In P. A. Katz & D. A. Taylor (Eds.), *Eliminating racism: Profiles in controversy* (pp. 53–84). New York: Plenum.

Sedikides, C. (1993). Assessment, enhancement, and verification determinants of the self-evaluation process. *Journal of Personality and Social Psychology, 65,* 317–338.

Sedikides, C., Campbell, W. K., Reeder, G. D., & Elliot, A. J. (1998). The self-serving bias in relational context. *Journal of Personality and Social Psychology, 74,* 378–386.

Sedikides, C., Gaertner, L., & Toguchi, Y. (2003). Pancultural self-enhancement. *Journal of Personality and Social Psychology, 84,* 60–79.

Sedikides, C., & Green, J. D. (2004). What I don't recall can't hurt me: Information negativity versus information inconsistency as determinants of memorial self-defense. *Social Cognition, 22,* 4–29.

Sedikides, C., Gregg, A. P., & Hart, C. M. (2007). The importance of being modest. In C. Sedikides & S. J. Spencer (Eds.), *The self* (pp. 163–184). New York: Psychology Press.

Sedikides, C., Rudich, E. A., Gregg, A. P., Kumashiro, M., & Rusbult, C. (2004). Are normal narcissists psychologically healthy?: Self-esteem matters. *Journal of Personality and Social Psychology, 87,* 400–416.

Sedikides, C., & Skowronski, J. J. (1997). The symbolic self in evolutionary context. *Personality and Social Psychology Review, 1,* 80–102.

Sedikides, C., & Strube, M. J. (1997). Self-evaluation: To thine own self be good, to thine own self be sure, to thine own self be true, and to thine own self be better. In M. P. Zanna (Ed.), *Advances in experimental social psychology* (Vol. 29, pp. 209–269). San Diego, CA: Academic Press.

See, Y. H. M., Petty, R. E., & Fabrigar, L. R. (2013). Affective-cognitive meta-bases versus structural bases of attitudes predict processing interest versus efficiency. *Personality and Social Psychology Bulletin, 39,* 1111–1123.

Seidel, E.-M., Eickhoff, S. B., Kellermann, T., Schneider, F., Gur, R. C., Habel, U., & Derntl, B. (2010). Who is to blame? Neural correlates of causal attribution in social situations. *Social Neuroscience, 5,* 335–350.

Selfhout, M., Denissen, J., Branje, S. J. T., & Meeus, W. (2009). In the eye of the beholder: Perceived, actual, and peer-rated similarity in personality, communication, and friendship intensity during the acquaintanceship process. *Journal of Personality and Social Psychology, 96,* 1152–1165.

Seligman, M. E. (1975). *Helplessness: On depression, development, and death.* San Francisco, CA: Freeman.

Semin, G. R., & Rubini, M. (1990). Unfolding the concept of person by verbal abuse. *European Journal of Social Psychology, 20,* 463–474.

Sengupta, N. K., & Sibley, C. G. (2013), Perpetuating one's own disadvantage: Intergroup contact enables the ideological legitimation of inequality. *Personality and Social Psychology Bulletin, 39,* 1391–1403.

Shackelford, T. K., Schmitt, D. P., & Buss, D. M. (2005). Universal dimensions of human mate preferences. *Personality and Individual Differences, 39*, 447–458.

Shallice, T. (1988). *From neuropsychology to mental structure.* New York: Cambridge University Press.

Shanab, M. E., & Yahya, K. A. (1978). A cross-cultural study of obedience. *Bulletin of the Psychonomic Society, 11*, 267–269.

Shaver, P. R., & Mikulincer, M. (2009). Attachment styles. In M. R. Leary & R. H. Hoyle (Eds.), *Handbook of individual differences and social behavior* (pp. 62–81). New York: Guilford.

Shavitt, S. (1990). The role of attitude objects in attitude functions. *Journal of Experimental Social Psychology, 26*, 124–148.

Sheeran, P. (2002). Intention-behavior relations: A conceptual and empirical review. In W. Stroebe & M. Hewstone (Eds.), *European review of social psychology* (Vol. 12, pp. 1–36). Hove, UK: Psychology Press.

Sheeran, P., Milne, S., Webb, T. L., & Gollwitzer, P. M. (2005). Implementation intentions and health behaviour. In M. Conner & P. Norman (Eds.), *Predicting health behaviour: Research and practice with social cognition models* (2nd ed., pp. 276–323). Buckingham, UK: Open University Press.

Sheldon, K. M., Ryan, R., & Reis, H. T. (1996). What makes for a good day? Competence and autonomy in the day and in the person. *Personality and Social Psychology Bulletin, 22*, 1270–1279.

Shelton, J. N. (2003). Interpersonal concerns in social encounters between majority and minority group members. *Group Processes & Intergroup Relations, 6*, 171–185.

Shelton, J. N., & Richeson, J. A. (2005). Intergroup contact and pluralistic ignorance. *Journal of Personality and Social Psychology, 88*, 91–107.

Shepard, R. N. (1998). *Carl Iver Hovland: A biographical memoir.* Retrieved from http://www.nap.edu

Shepela, S. T., Cook, J., Horlitz, E., Leal, R., Luciano, S., Lutfy, E., … Worden, E. (1999). Courageous resistance: A special case of altruism. *Theory and Psychology, 9*, 787–805.

Sheridan, C. L., & King, R. G. (1972). Obedience to authority with an authentic victim. *Proceedings of the Annual Convention of the American Psychological Association, 7*, 165–166.

Sherif, M. (1935). A study of some social factors in perception. *Archives of Psychology (Columbia University), 187*, 60.

Sherif, M. (1936). *The psychology of social norms.* New York: Harper & Row.

Sherif, M. (1966). *In common predicament: Social psychology of intergroup conflict and cooperation.* Boston, MA: Houghton Mifflin.

Sherif, M. (1967). *Group conflict and co-operation.* London: Routledge & Kegan Paul.

Sherif, M., Harvey, O. J., White, B. J., Hood, W. R., & Sherif, C. W. (1961). *Intergroup cooperation and competition: The Robbers Cave experiment.* Norman, OK: University of Oklahoma.

Sherif, M., & Sherif, C. W. (1969). *Social psychology.* New York: Harper & Row.

Sherman, J. W. (2010). Social neuroscience and its contribution to social psychological theory: Introduction to the special issue. *Social Cognition, 28*, 663–666.

Shiffrin, R. M., & Schneider, W. (1977). Controlled and automatic information processing: Perceptual learning, automatic attending, and a general theory. *Psychological Review, 84*, 127–190.

Shoal, G. D., Giancola, P. R., & Kirillova, G. P. (2003). Salivary cortisol, personality, and aggressive behavior in adolescent boys: A 5-year longitudinal study. *Journal of the American Academy of Child and Adolescent Psychiatry, 42*, 1101–1107.

Shore, B. (1996). *Culture in mind: Cognition, culture, and the problem of meaning.* New York: Oxford University Press.

Shotland, R. L., & Straw, M. K. (1976). Bystander response to an assault: When a man attacks a woman. *Journal of Personality and Social Psychology, 34*, 990–999.

Shrauger, J. S., & Schoeneman, T. J. (1979). Symbolic interactionist view of self-concept: Through the looking glass darkly. *Psychological Bulletin, 86*, 549–573.

Sidanius, J., & Pratto, F. (1999). *Social dominance: An integrative theory of social hierarchy and oppression.* Cambridge, UK: Cambridge University Press.

Siegel, A. E., & Siegel, S. (1957). Reference groups, membership groups, and attitude change. *Journal of Abnormal and Social Psychology, 55*, 360–364.

Sigman, S. J. (1991). Handling the discontinuous aspects of continuous social relationships: Toward research on the persistence of social forms. *Communication Theory, 1*, 106–127.

Silvia, P. J., & Duval, T. S. (2001). Objective self-awareness theory: Recent progress and enduring problems. *Personality and Social Psychology Review, 5*, 230–241.

Silvia, P. J., & Eichstaedt, J. (2004). A self-novelty manipulation of self-focused attention for Internet and laboratory experiments. *Behavior Research Methods, Instruments, & Computers, 36*, 325–330.

Sim, J. J., Correll, J., & Sadler, M. S. (2013). Understanding police and expert performance: When training attenuates (vs. exacerbates) stereotypic bias in the decision to shoot. *Personality and Social Psychology Bulletin, 39*, 291–304.

Simon, B. (1992). The perception of ingroup and outgroup homogeneity: Reintroducing the intergroup context. In W. Stroebe & M. Hewstone (Eds.), *European review of social psychology* (Vol. 3, pp. 1–30). Chichester, UK: Wiley.

Simon, B., Aufderheide, B., & Kampmeier, C. (2001). The social psychology of minority-majority relations. In R. Brown & S. L. Gaertner (Eds.), *Blackwell handbook of social psychology: Intergroup processes* (pp. 303–323). Oxford: Blackwell.

Simonton, D. K. (1981). The library laboratory: Archival data in personality and social psychology. In L. Wheeler (Ed.), *Review of personality and social psychology* (Vol. 2, pp. 217–243). Beverly Hills, CA: Sage.

Simonton, D. K. (1986). Presidential personality: Biographical use of the Gough Adjective Check List. *Journal of Personality and Social Psychology, 51*, 149–160.

Simpson, J. A., Gangestad, S. W., & Lerma, M. (1990). Perception of physical attractiveness: Mechanisms involved in the maintenance of romantic relationships. *Journal of Personality and Social Psychology, 59*, 1192–1201.

Simpson, J. A., Rholes, W. S., & Nelligan, J. S. (1992). Support seeking and support giving within couples in an anxiety-provoking situation: The role of attachment styles. *Journal of Personality and Social Psychology, 62*, 434–446.

Sinaceur, M., Thomas-Hunt, M. C., Neale, M. A., O'Neill, O. A., & Haag, C. (2010). Accuracy and perceived expert status in group decisions: When minority members make majority members more accurate privately. *Personality and Social Psychology Bulletin, 36*, 423–437.

Sinclair, L., & Kunda, Z. (1999). Reactions to a black professional: Motivated inhibition and activation of conflicting stereotypes. *Journal of Personality and Social Psychology, 77*, 885–904.

Singelis, T. M. (1994). The measurement of independent and interdependent self-construals. *Personality and Social Psychology Bulletin, 20*, 580–591.

Singelis, T. M., Bond, M. H., Sharkey, W. F., & Lai, C. S. Y. (1999). Unpackaging culture's influence on self-esteem and embarrassability: The role of self-construals. *Journal of Cross-Cultural Psychology, 30*, 315–341.

Singer, P. (2009). *The life you can save: Acting now to end world poverty*. New York: Random House.

Singer, T., & Lamm, C. (2009). The social neuroscience of empathy. *Annals of the New York Academy of Sciences, 1156*, 81–96.

Singer, T., Seymour, B., O'Doherty, J. P., Stephan, K. E., Dolan, R. J., & Frith, C. D. (2006). Empathic neural responses are modulated by the perceived fairness of others. *Nature, 439*, 466–469.

Sivasubramaniam, N., Murry, W. D., Avolio, B. J., & Jung, D. I. (2002). A longitudinal model of the effects of team leadership and group potency on group performance. *Group & Organization Management, 27*, 66–96.

Slater, M., Antley, A., Davison, A., Swapp, D., Guger, C., Barker, C., … Sanchez-Vives, M. V. (2006). A virtual reprise of the Stanley Milgram obedience experiments. *PLoS One, 1*, 1–10.

Slater, M., Rovira, A., Southern, R., Swapp, D., Zhang, J. J., Campbell, C., & Levine, M. (2013). Bystander responses to a violent incident in an immersive virtual environment. *PLoS ONE 8*, 1–13.

Slater, P. E. (1955). Role differentiation in small groups. *American Sociological Review, 20*, 300–310.

Slavin, R. E. (1978). Student teams and achievement divisions. *Journal of Research and Development in Education, 12*, 39–49.

Slepian, M. L., Rule, N. O., & Ambady, N. (2012). Proprioception and person perception: Politicians and professors. *Personality and Social Psychology Bulletin, 38*, 1621–1628.

Sloman, S. A. (2005). *Causal models: How people think about the world and its alternatives*. New York: Oxford University Press.

Smith, C. M., & Tindale, R. S. (2010). Direct and indirect minority influence in groups. In R. Martin & M. Hewstone (Eds.), *Minority influence and innovation: Antecedents, processes and consequences* (pp. 263–284). Hove, UK: Psychology Press.

Smith, C. M., Tindale, R. S., & Steiner, L. (1998). Investment decisions by individuals and groups in 'sunk cost' situations: The potential impact of shared representations. *Group Processes & Intergroup Relations, 1*, 175–189.

Smith, E. R. (1991). Illusory correlation in a simulated exemplar-based memory. *Journal of Experimental Social Psychology, 27*, 107–123.

Smith, E. R. (1993). Social identity and social emotions: Toward new conceptualizations of prejudice. In D. M. Mackie & D. L. Hamilton (Eds.), *Affect, cognition, and stereotyping: Interactive processes in group perception* (pp. 297–315). San Diego, CA: Academic Press.

Smith, E. R., & Miller, F. D. (1983). Mediation among attributional inferences and comprehension processes: Initial findings and a general method. *Journal of Personality and Social Psychology, 44*, 492–505.

Smith, H. S., & Cohen, L. H. (1993). Self-complexity and reactions to a relationship breakup. *Journal of Social and Clinical Psychology, 12*, 367–384.

Smith, J., & Haslam, S. A. (Eds.). (2012). *Social psychology: Revisiting the classic studies*. Thousand Oaks, CA: Sage.

Smith, M. B., Bruner, J. S., & White, R. W. (1956). *Opinions and personality*. New York: Wiley.

Smith, P. B. (2004). Acquiescent response bias as an aspect of cultural communication style. *Journal of Cross-Cultural Psychology, 35*, 50–61.

Smith, P. B., & Best, D. L. (Eds.). (2009). *Cross-cultural psychology* (four volumes). London: Sage.

Smith, P. B., & Bond, M. H. (1998). *Social psychology across cultures*. London: Prentice Hall.

Smith, P. B., Bond, M. H., & Kağıtçıbaşı, Ç. (2006). *Understanding social psychology across cultures: Living and working in a changing world*. London: Sage.

Smith, P. B., Fischer, R., Vignoles, V. L., & Bond, M. H. (2013). *Understanding social psychology across cultures: Engaging with others in a changing world* (2nd ed.). London: Sage.

Smith, P. K., Ananiadou, K., & Cowie, H. (2003). Interventions to reduce school bullying. *Canadian Journal of Psychiatry, 48*, 591–599.

Smith, P. K., Morita, Y., Junger-Tas, J., Olweus, D., Catalano, R., & Slee, P. (1999). *The nature of school bullying: A cross-national perspective.* London: Routledge.

Smith, P. K., Singer, M., Hoel, H., & Cooper, C. L. (2003). Victimization in the school and the workplace: Are there any links? *British Journal of Psychology, 94,* 175–188.

Smith, P. M. (1995). Leadership. In A. S. R. Manstead & M. Hewstone (Eds.), *Blackwell encyclopedia of social psychology* (pp. 358–362). Oxford: Blackwell.

Snyder, C. R., & Higgins, R. L. (1988). Excuses: Their effective role in the negotiation of reality. *Psychological Bulletin, 104,* 23–35.

Snyder, M. (1974). Self-monitoring of expressive behavior. *Journal of Personality and Social Psychology, 30,* 526–537.

Snyder, M. (1984). When belief creates reality. In L. Berkowitz (Ed.), *Advances in experimental social psychology* (Vol. 18, pp. 247–305). Orlando, FL: Academic Press.

Snyder, M. (1987). *Public appearances, private realities.* New York: Freeman.

Snyder, M., & Cunningham, M. R. (1975). To comply or not comply: Testing the self-perception explanation of the 'foot-in-the-door' phenomenon. *Journal of Personality and Social Psychology, 31,* 64–67.

Snyder, M., & DeBono, K. G. (1985). Appeals to image and claims about quality: Understanding the psychology of advertising. *Journal of Personality and Social Psychology, 49,* 586–597.

Snyder, M., & Kendzierski, D. (1982). Acting on one's attitudes: Procedures for linking attitude and behavior. *Journal of Experimental Social Psychology, 18,* 165–183.

Snyder, M., Tanke, E. D., & Berscheid, E. (1977). Social perception and interpersonal behavior: On the self-fulfilling nature of social stereotypes. *Journal of Personality and Social Psychology, 35,* 656–666.

Sober, E., & Wilson, D. S. (1998). *Unto others: The evolution and psychology of unselfish behavior.* Cambridge, MA: Harvard University Press.

Solomon, S., Greenberg, J., & Pyszczynski, T. (1991). A terror management theory of social behavior: The psychological functions of self-esteem and cultural worldviews. In M. P. Zanna (Ed.), *Advances in experimental social psychology* (Vol. 24, pp. 93–159). San Diego, CA: Academic Press.

Son Hing, L. S., Bobocel, D. R., Zanna, M. P., & McBride, M. V. (2007). Authoritarian dynamics and unethical decision making: High social dominance orientation leaders and high right-wing authoritarianism followers. *Journal of Personality and Social Psychology, 92,* 67–81.

Son Hing, L. S., & Zanna, M. P. (2010). Individual differences. In J. F. Dovidio, M. Hewstone, P. Glick, & V. M. Esses (Eds.), *Handbook of prejudice, stereotyping and discrimination* (pp. 163–178). London: Sage.

Sparks, G. G., & Sparks, C. W. (2002). Effects of media violence. In J. Bryant & D. Zillmann (Eds.), *Media effects: Advances in theory and research* (2nd ed., pp. 269–285). Mahwah, NJ: Erlbaum.

Spears, R., Jetten, J., Scheepers, D., & Cihangir, S. (2009). Creative distinctiveness: Explaining in-group bias in minimal groups. In S. Otten, K. Sassenberg, & T. Kessler (Eds.), *Intergroup relations: The role of motivation and emotion* (pp. 23–40). New York: Psychology Press.

Spears, R., & Smith, H. J. (2001). Experiments as politics. *Political Psychology, 22,* 309–330.

Spence, J. T., Deaux, K., & Helmreich, R. L. (1985). Sex roles in contemporary American society. In G. Lindzey & E. Aronson (Eds.), *Handbook of social psychology* (3rd ed., Vol. 2, pp. 149–178). New York: Random House.

Spence, K. W. (1956). *Behavior theory and conditioning.* New Haven, CT: Yale University Press.

Spengler, S., Von Cramon, D. Y., & Brass, M. (2009). Was it me or was it you? How the sense of agency originates from ideomotor learning revealed by fMRI. *Neuroimage, 46,* 290–298.

Sperduti, M., Delaveau, P., Fossati, P., & Nadel, J. (2011). Different brain structures related to self- and external agency attribution: A brief review and meta-analysis. *Brain Structure and Function, 216,* 151–157.

Spitzberg, B. H. (1999). An analysis of empirical estimates of sexual aggression victimization and perpetration. *Violence and Victims, 14,* 214–260.

Sriram, N., & Greenwald, A. G. (2009). The Brief Implicit Association Test. *Experimental Psychology, 56,* 283–294.

Srivastava, S. (2012). Other people as a source of self-knowledge. In S. Vazire & T. D. Wilson (Eds.), *Handbook of self-knowledge* (pp. 90–104). New York, NY: Guilford.

Srull, T. K., & Wyer, R. S., Jr. (1980). Category accessibility and social perception: Some implications for the study of person memory and interpersonal judgments. *Journal of Personality and Social Psychology, 38,* 841–856.

Staats, A. W., & Staats, C. K. (1958). Attitudes established by classical conditioning. *Journal of Abnormal and Social Psychology, 57,* 37–40.

Stangor, C., Sechrist, G. B., & Jost, J. T. (2001). Changing racial beliefs by providing consensus information. *Personality and Social Psychology Bulletin, 27,* 486–496.

Starbuck, W. H., & Farjoun, M. (2005). *Organization at the limit: Lessons from the Columbia disaster.* Oxford: Blackwell.

Stasser, G., & Birchmeier, Z. (2003). Group creativity and collective choice. In P. B. Paulus & B. A. Nijstad (Eds.), *Group creativity* (pp. 85–109). New York: Oxford University Press.

Stasser, G., Kerr, N. L., & Bray, R. M. (1982). The social psychology of jury deliberations: Structure, process, and product. In N. L. Kerr & R. M. Bray (Eds.), *The psychology of the courtroom* (pp. 221–256). New York: Academic Press.

Stasser, G., & Titus, W. (1985). Pooling of unshared information in group decision making: Biased information sampling during discussion. *Journal of Personality and Social Psychology, 48*, 1467–1478.

Staub, E. (1989). *The roots of evil: The origins of genocide and other group violence.* Cambridge, MA: Cambridge University Press.

Steblay, N., Hosch, H. M., Culhane, S. E., & McWethy, A. (2006). The impact on juror verdicts of judicial instruction to disregard inadmissible evidence: A meta-analysis. *Law and Human Behavior, 30*, 469–492.

Steele, C. M. (1988). The psychology of self-affirmation: Sustaining the integrity of the self. In L. Berkowitz (Ed.), *Advances in experimental social psychology* (Vol. 21, pp. 261–302). San Diego, CA: Academic Press.

Steiner, I. D. (1972). *Group processes and productivity.* New York: Academic Press.

Stephan, F. F. (1952). The relative rate of communication between members of small groups. *American Sociological Review, 17*, 482–486.

Stephan, W. G. (1987). The contact hypothesis in intergroup relations. In C. Hendrick (Ed.), *Review of personality and social psychology: Group processes and intergroup relations* (Vol. 9, pp. 13–40). Thousand Oaks, CA: Sage.

Stephan, W. G., Diaz-Loving, R., & Duran, A. (2000). Integrated threat theory and intercultural attitudes: Mexico and the United States. *Journal of Cross-Cultural Psychology, 31*, 240–249.

Stephan, W. G., & Finlay, K. (1999). The role of empathy in improving intergroup relations. *Journal of Social Issues, 55*, 729–743.

Stephan, W. G., & Stephan, C. W. (1985). Intergroup anxiety. *Journal of Social Issues, 41*, 157–175.

Sternberg, R. J. (1986). A triangular theory of love. *Psychological Review, 93*, 119–135.

Sternberg, R. J., & Barnes, M. I. (1988). *The psychology of love.* New Haven, CT: Yale University Press.

Stokoe, E., & Edwards, D. (2007). 'Black this, black that': Racial insults and reported speech in neighbour complaints and police interrogations. *Discourse & Society, 18*, 337–372.

Stone, J., & Moskowitz, G. B. (2011). Non-conscious bias in medical decision making: What can be done to reduce it? *Medical Education, 45*, 768–776.

Storms, M. D. (1973). Videotape and the attribution process: Reversing actors' and observers' points of view. *Journal of Personality and Social Psychology, 27*, 165–175.

Storms, M. D., & Nisbett, R. E. (1970). Insomnia and the attribution process. *Journal of Personality and Social Psychology, 16*, 319–328.

Stotland, E. (1969). Exploratory investigations of empathy. In L. Berkowitz (Ed.), *Advances in experimental social psychology* (Vol. 4, pp. 271–314). New York: Academic Press.

Strack, F., & Deutsch, R. (2004). Reflective and impulsive determinants of social behavior. *Personality and Social Psychology Review, 8*, 220–247.

Strauman, T. J. (1992). Self-guides, autobiographical memory, and anxiety and dysphoria: Toward a cognitive model of vulnerability to emotional distress. *Journal of Abnormal Psychology, 101*, 87–95.

Strauman, T. J., & Higgins, E. T. (1988). Self-discrepancies as predictors of vulnerability to distinct syndromes of chronic emotional distress. *Journal of Personality, 56*, 685–707.

Straus, M. A. (1979). Measuring intrafamily conflict and violence: The Conflict Tactics (CT) Scales. *Journal of Marriage and the Family, 41*, 75–88.

Straus, M. A., Hamby, S. L., Boney-McCoy, S., & Sugarman, D. B. (1996). The revised Conflict Tactics Scales (CTS2): Development and preliminary psychometric data. *Journal of Family Issues, 17*, 283–316.

Streeter, S. A., & McBurney, D. H. (2003). Waist-hip ratio and attractiveness: New evidence and a critique of a 'critical' test. *Evolution and Human Behaviour, 24*, 88–98.

Strickland, L. H., Aboud, F. E., & Gergen, K. J. (Eds.). (1976). *Social psychology in transition.* New York: Plenum.

Stroebe, K., Lodewijkx, H. F. M., & Spears, R. (2005). Do unto others as they do unto you: Reciprocity and social identification as determinants of ingroup favoritism. *Personality and Social Psychology Bulletin, 31*, 831–845.

Stroebe, W. (2011). *Social psychology and health* (3rd ed.). Maidenhead, UK: Open University Press.

Stroebe, W. (2012). The truth about Triplett (1898), but nobody seems to care. *Perspectives on Psychological Science, 7*, 54–57.

Stroebe, W. (2013). Firearm possession and violent death: A critical review. *Aggression and Violent Behavior, 18*, 209–721.

Stroebe, W., & Diehl, M. (1981). Conformity and counterattitudinal behavior: The effect of social support on attitude change. *Journal of Personality and Social Psychology, 41*, 876–889.

Stroebe, W., & Diehl, M. (1988). When social support fails: Supporter characteristics in compliance-induced attitude change. *Personality and Social Psychology Bulletin, 14*, 136–144.

Stroebe, W., Diehl, M., & Abakoumkin, G. (1996). Social compensation and the Köhler effect: Toward a theoretical explanation of motivation gains in group productivity. In E. H. Witte & J. H. Davis (Eds.), *Understanding group behaviour: Small group processes and interpersonal relations* (Vol. 2, pp. 37–65). Hillsdale, NJ: Erlbaum.

Stroebe, W., & Keizer, K. E. (in press). The social psychology of consumer behavior. In L. Steg, A. P. Buunk, & T. Keizer (Eds), *Applied social psychology: Understanding and managing social problems.* New York: Cambridge University Press.

Stroebe, W., Nijstad, B. A., & Rietzschel, E. F. (2010). Beyond productivity loss in brainstorming groups: The evolution of a question. In M. Zanna (Ed.), *Advances in experimental social psychology* (Vol. 43, pp. 157–203). Burlington: Academic Press.

Stroebe, W., Postmes, T., & Spears, R. (2012). Scientific misconduct and the myth of self-correction in science. *Perspectives on Psychological Science, 7,* 670–688.

Stroebe, W., Stroebe, M. S., & Domittner, G. (1988). Individual and situational differences in recovery from bereavement: A risk group identified. *Journal of Social Issues, 44,* 143–158.

Strube, M. J. (2005). What did Triplett really find? A contemporary analysis of the first experiment in social psychology. *American Journal of Psychology, 118,* 271–286.

Strube, M. J., Lott, C. L., Lê-Xuân-Hy, G. M., Oxenberg, J., & Deichmann, A. K. (1986). Self-evaluation of abilities: Accurate self-assessment versus biased self-enhancement. *Journal of Personality and Social Psychology, 51,* 16–25.

Strube, M. J., & Roemmele, L. A. (1985). Self-enhancement, self-assessment, and self-evaluative task choice. *Journal of Personality and Social Psychology, 49,* 981–993.

Stryker, S. (1980). *Symbolic interactionism: A social structural version.* Menlo Park, CA: Benjamin Cummings.

Stryker, S., & Vryan, K. D. (2003). The symbolic interactionist frame. In J. Delamater (Ed.), *Handbook of social psychology* (pp. 3–28). New York: Kluwer Academic/Plenum.

Stürmer, S., & Snyder, M. (Eds.). (2010). *The psychology of prosocial behavior: Group processes, intergroup relations, and helping.* Chichester, UK: Wiley-Blackwell.

Stürmer, S., Snyder, M., Kropp, A., & Siem, B. (2006). Empathy-motivated helping: The moderating role of group membership. *Personality and Social Psychology Bulletin, 32,* 943–956.

Stürmer, S., Snyder, M., & Omoto, A. M. (2005). Prosocial emotions and helping: The moderating role of group membership. *Journal of Personality and Social Psychology, 88,* 532–546.

Suls, J., Martin, R., & Wheeler, L. (2002). Social comparison: Why, with whom, and with what effect? *Current Directions in Psychological Science, 11,* 159–163.

Suls, J., & Wheeler, L. (Eds.). (2000). *Handbook of social comparison: Theory and research.* New York: Kluwer Academic/Plenum.

Sumpton, R., & Gregson, M. (1981). The fundamental attribution error: An investigation of sensitivity to role-conferred advantages in self-presentation. *British Journal of Social Psychology, 20,* 7–11.

Sunnafrank, M., & Ramirez, A. J. (2004). At first sight: Persistent relational effects of get-acquainted conversations. *Journal of Social and Personal Relationships, 21,* 361–379.

Sunstein, C. R. (2009). *Going to extremes: How like minds unite and divide.* New York: Oxford University Press.

Swami, V., & Furnham, A. (2008). *The psychology of physical attraction.* New York: Routledge.

Swann, W. B., Jr. (1984). Quest for accuracy in person perception: A matter of pragmatics. *Psychological Review, 91,* 457–477.

Swann, W. B., Jr., & Bosson, J. K. (2008). Identity negotiation: A theory of self and social interaction. In O. P. John, R. W. Robins, & L. A. Pervin (Eds.), *Handbook of personality: Theory and research* (3rd ed., pp. 448–471). New York: Guilford.

Swann, W. B., Jr., & Buhrmester, M. D. (2012). Self-verification: The search for coherence. In M. R. Leary & J. P. Tangney (Eds.), *Handbook of self and identity* (2nd ed., pp. 405–424). New York: Guilford.

Swann, W. B., Jr., Hixon, J. G., Stein-Seroussi, A., & Gilbert, D. T. (1990). The fleeting gleam of praise: Cognitive processes underlying behavioral reactions to self-relevant feedback. *Journal of Personality and Social Psychology, 59,* 17–26.

Swann, W. B., Jr., Johnson, R. E., & Bosson, J. K. (2009). Identity negotiation at work. In B. Staw, & A. Brief (Eds.), *Research in Organizational Behavior* (Vol. 29, pp. 81–109). Amsterdam, The Netherlands: Elsevier.

Swann, W. B., Jr., Stein-Seroussi, A., & Giesler, R. B. (1992). Why people self-verify. *Journal of Personality and Social Psychology, 62,* 392–401.

Swart, H., Hewstone, M., Christ, O., & Voci, A. (2011). Affective mediators of intergroup contact: A three-wave longitudinal study in South Africa. *Journal of Personality and Social Psychology, 101,* 1221–1238.

Swartz, M., & Watkins, S. (2003). *Power failure: The inside story of the collapse of Enron.* New York: Doubleday.

Sy, T., Coté, S., & Saavedra, R. (2005). The contagious leader: Impact of the leader's mood on the mood of group members, group affective tone, and group processes. *Journal of Applied Psychology, 90,* 295–305.

't Hart, P. (1990). *Groupthink in government: A study of small groups and policy failure.* Lisse, NL: Swets & Zeitlinger.

't Hart, P., Stern, E., & Sundelius, B. (1997). *Beyond groupthink.* Ann Arbor, MI: University of Michigan Press.

Tafarodi, R. W., Lo, C., Yamaguchi, S., Lee, W. W.-S., & Katsura, H. (2004). The inner self in three countries. *Journal of Cross-Cultural Psychology, 35,* 97–117.

Tajfel, H. (1969). Cognitive aspects of prejudice. *Journal of Social Issues, 25,* 79–97.

Tajfel, H. (1978a). *Differentiation between social groups: Studies in the social psychology of intergroup relations.* New York: Academic Press.

Tajfel, H. (1978b). Social categorization, social identity and social comparison. In H. Tajfel (Ed.), *Differentiation between social groups* (pp. 61–76). London: Academic Press.

Tajfel, H. (1981). *Human groups and social categories: Studies in social psychology.* Cambridge, MA: Cambridge University Press.

Tajfel, H. (1982a). *Social identity and intergroup identifications.* Cambridge, UK: Cambridge University Press.

Tajfel, H. (1982b). Social psychology of intergroup relations. *Annual Review of Psychology, 33,* 1–39.

Tajfel, H., Billig, M. G., Bundy, R. P., & Flament, C. (1971). Social categorization and intergroup behaviour. *European Journal of Social Psychology, 1*, 149–178.

Tajfel, H., Jaspars, J. M. F., & Fraser, C. (1984). The social dimension in European social psychology. In H. Tajfel (Ed.), *The social dimension: European developments in social psychology* (Vol. 2, pp. 1–5). New York: Cambridge University Press.

Tajfel, H., & Turner, J. C. (1979). An integrative theory of intergroup conflict. In W. G. Austin & S. Worchel (Eds.), *The social psychology of intergroup relations* (pp. 33–47). Monterey, CA: Brooks Cole.

Tajfel, H., & Turner, J. C. (1986). The social identity theory of intergroup behavior. In S. Worchel & W. G. Austin (Eds.), *Psychology of intergroup relations* (pp. 7–24). Chicago, IL: Nelson-Hall.

Tajfel, H., & Turner, J. C. (2004). The social identity theory of intergroup behavior. In J. T. Jost & J. Sidanius (Eds.), *Key readings in social psychology: Political psychology* (pp. 276–293). New York: Psychology Press.

Tajfel, H., & Wilkes, A. L. (1963). Classification and quantitative judgement. *British Journal of Psychology, 54*, 101–114.

Talaska, C. A., Fiske, S. T., & Chaiken, S. (2008). Legitimating racial discrimination: Emotions, not beliefs, best predict discrimination in a meta-analysis. *Social Justice Research, 21*, 263–296.

Tam, T., Hewstone, M., Harwood, J., Voci, A., & Kenworthy, J. (2006). Intergroup contact and grandparent–grandchild communication: The effects of self-disclosure on implicit and explicit biases against older people. *Group Processes & Intergroup Relations, 9*, 413–429.

Tangney, J. P., Baumeister, R. F., & Boone, A. L. (2004). High self-control predicts good adjustment, less pathology, better grades, and interpersonal success. *Journal of Personality, 72*, 271–322.

Taubman Ben-Ari, O. (2000). The effect of reminders of death on reckless driving: A terror management perspective. *Current Directions in Psychological Science, 9*, 196–199.

Taubman Ben-Ari, O., Florian, V., & Mikulincer, M. (1999). The impact of mortality salience on reckless driving: A test of terror management mechanisms. *Journal of Personality and Social Psychology, 76*, 35–45.

Tausch, N., Becker, J. C., Spears, R., Christ, O., Saab, R., Singh, P., & Siddiqui, R. N. (2011). Explaining radical group behavior: Developing emotion and efficacy routes to normative and nonnormative collective action. *Journal of Personality and Social Psychology, 101*, 129–148.

Tausch, N., & Hewstone, M. (2010). Intergroup contact. In J. F. Dovidio, M. Hewstone, P. Glick, & V. M. Esses (Eds.), *Handbook of prejudice, stereotyping and discrimination* (pp. 544–560). London: Sage.

Tausch, N., Hewstone, M., Kenworthy, J. B., Psaltis, C., Schmid, K., Popan, J. R., … Hughes, J. (2010). Secondary transfer effects of intergroup contact: Alternative accounts and underlying processes. *Journal of Personality and Social Psychology, 99*, 282–302.

Taylor, D. A., Gould, R. J., & Brounstein, P. J. (1981). Effects of personalistic self-disclosure. *Personality and Social Psychology Bulletin, 7*, 487–492.

Taylor, S. E., & Brown, J. D. (1988). Illusion and well-being: A social psychological perspective on mental health. *Psychological Bulletin, 103*, 193–210.

Taylor, S. E., & Fiske, S. T. (1978). Salience, attention, and attribution: Top of the head phenomena. In L. Berkowitz (Ed.), *Advances in experimental social psychology* (Vol. 11, pp. 249–288). New York: Academic Press.

Taylor, S. E., Kemeny, M. E., Aspinwall, L. G., Schneider, S. G., Rodriguez, R., & Herbert, M. (1992). Optimism, coping, psychological distress, and high-risk sexual behavior among men at risk for acquired immunodeficiency syndrome (AIDS). *Journal of Personality and Social Psychology, 63*, 460–473.

Taylor, S. E., Kemeny, M. E., Reed, G. M., Bower, J. E., & Gruenewald, T. L. (2000). Psychological resources, positive illusions, and health. *American Psychologist, 55*, 99–109.

Taylor, S. E., Lerner, J. S., Sherman, D. K., Sage, R. M., & McDowell, N. K. (2003). Portrait of the self-enhancer: Well adjusted and well liked or maladjusted and friendless? *Journal of Personality and Social Psychology, 84*, 165–176.

Taylor, S. E., & Lobel, M. (1989). Social comparison activity under threat: Downward evaluation and upward contacts. *Psychological Review, 96*, 569–575.

Taylor, S. E., Wayment, H. A., & Carrillo, M. (1996). Social comparison, self-regulation, and motivation. In R. M. Sorrentino & E. T. Higgins (Eds.), *Handbook of motivation and cognition* (Vol. 3, pp. 3–27). New York: Guilford.

Tellis, G. J. (2004). *Effective advertising: Understanding when, how, and why advertising works.* Thousand Oaks, CA: Sage.

Temkin, J., & Krahé, B. (2008). *Sexual assault and the justice gap: A question of attitude.* Oxford: Hart.

Terry, D. J., & Hogg, M. A. (1996). Group norms and the attitude-behavior relationship: A role for group identification. *Personality and Social Psychology Bulletin, 22*, 776–793.

Terry, M. L., & Leary, M. R. (2011). Self-compassion, self-regulation, and health. *Self and Identity, 10*, 352–362.

Tesser, A. (2000). On the confluence of self-esteem maintenance mechanisms. *Personality and Social Psychology Review, 4*, 290–299.

Tesser, A., Campbell, J., & Mickler, S. (1983). The role of social pressure, attention to the stimulus, and self-doubt in conformity. *European Journal of Social Psychology, 13*, 217–233.

Tetlock, P. E. (1979). Identifying victims of groupthink from public statements of decision makers. *Journal of Personality and Social Psychology, 37*, 1314–1324.

Tetlock, P. E. (1983). Accountability and complexity of thought. *Journal of Personality and Social Psychology, 45*, 74–83.

Tetlock, P. E. (1994). Political psychology or politicized psychology: Is the road to scientific hell paved with good moral intentions? *Political Psychology, 15,* 509–529.

Tetlock, P. E. (1998). Social psychology and world politics. In D. T. Gilbert, S. T. Fiske, & G. Lindzey (Eds.), *Handbook of social psychology* (4th ed., Vol. 2, pp. 868–912). Boston, MA: McGraw-Hill.

Tetlock, P. E. (2002). Social functionalist frameworks for judgment and choice: Intuitive politicians, theologians, and prosecutors. *Psychological Review, 109,* 451–471.

Tetlock, P. E., & Levi, A. (1982). Attribution bias: On the inconclusiveness of the cognition-motivation debate. *Journal of Experimental Social Psychology, 18,* 68–88.

Thibaut, J. W., & Kelley, H. H. (1959). *The social psychology of groups.* New York: Wiley.

Thompson, L. L., Levine, J. M., & Messick, D. M. (1999). *Shared cognition in organizations: The management of knowledge.* Mahwah, NJ: Erlbaum.

Thurstone, L. L. (1928). Attitudes can be measured. *American Journal of Sociology, 33,* 529–554.

Tice, D. M. (1991). Esteem protection or enhancement? Self-handicapping motives and attributions differ by trait self-esteem. *Journal of Personality and Social Psychology, 60,* 711–725.

Tice, D. M. (1992). Self-concept change and self-presentation: The looking glass self is also a magnifying glass. *Journal of Personality and Social Psychology, 63,* 435–451.

Tice, D. M., & Baumeister, R. F. (1990). Self-esteem, self handicapping, and self-presentation: The strategy of inadequate practice. *Journal of Personality, 58,* 443–464.

Tice, D. M., Butler, J. L., Muraven, M. B., & Stillwell, A. M. (1995). When modesty prevails: Differential favorability of self-presentation to friends and strangers. *Journal of Personality and Social Psychology, 69,* 1120–1138.

Tice, D. M., & Wallace, H. M. (2003). The reflected self: Creating yourself as (you think) others see you. In M. R. Leary & J. P. Tangney (Eds.), *Handbook of self and identity* (pp. 91–105). New York: Guilford.

Tiedens, L. Z., & Leach, C. W. (Eds.). (2004). *The social life of emotions.* Cambridge, MA: Cambridge University Press.

Tindale, R. S., & Davis, J. H. (1983). Group decision making and jury verdicts. In H. H. Blumberg, A. P. Hare, V. Kent, & M. F. Davies (Eds.), *Small groups and social interaction* (Vol. 2, pp. 9–38). Chichester, UK: Wiley.

Tindale, R. S., Davis, J. H., Vollrath, D. A., Nagao, D. H., & Hinsz, V. B. (1990). Asymmetrical social influence in freely interacting groups: A test of three models. *Journal of Personality and Social Psychology, 58,* 438–449.

Tindale, R. S., & Kameda, T. (2000). Social sharedness as a unifying theme for information processing in groups. *Group Processes & Intergroup Relations, 3,* 123–140.

Todd, A. R., Molden, D. C., Ham, J., & Vonk, R. (2011). The automatic and co-occurring activation of multiple social inferences. *Journal of Experimental Social Psychology, 47,* 37–49.

Toffler, B. L., & Reingold, J. (2003). *Financial accounting: Ambition, greed, and the fall of Arthur Andersen.* New York: Broadway.

Toma, C. L., Hancock, J. T., & Ellison, N. B. (2008). Separating fact from fiction: An examination of deceptive self-presentation in online dating profiles. *Personality and Social Psychology Bulletin, 34,* 1023–1036.

Tooby, J., & Cosmides, L. (1989). The innate versus the manifest: How universal does universal have to be? *Behavioral and Brain Sciences, 12,* 36–37.

Torrance, E. P. (1954). The behavior of small groups under the stress conditions of 'survival'. *American Sociological Review, 19,* 751–755.

Tovée, M. J., Tasker, K., & Benson, P. J. (2000). Is symmetry a visual cue to attractiveness in the human female body? *Evolution and Human Behavior, 21,* 191–200.

Trafimow, D., Silverman, E. S., Fan, R. M.-T., & Law, J. S. F. (1997). The effects of language and priming on the relative accessibility of the private self and the collective self. *Journal of Cross-Cultural Psychology, 28,* 107–123.

Trafimow, D., Triandis, H. C., & Goto, S. G. (1991). Some tests of the distinction between the private self and the collective self. *Journal of Personality and Social Psychology, 60,* 649–655.

Triandis, H. C. (1972). *The analysis of subjective culture.* New York: Wiley.

Triandis, H. C. (1989). The self and social behavior in differing cultural contexts. *Psychological Review, 96,* 506–520.

Triandis, H. C. (1995). *Individualism and collectivism.* Boulder, CO: Westview.

Triplett, N. D. (1898). The dynamogenic factors in pacemaking and competition. *American Journal of Psychology, 9,* 507–533.

Trivers, R. L. (1971). The evolution of reciprocal altruism. *Quarterly Review of Biology, 46,* 35–57.

Trope, Y. (1980). Self-assessment, self-enhancement, and task preference. *Journal of Experimental Social Psychology, 16,* 116–129.

Trope, Y. (1983). Self-assessment in achievement behavior. In J. M. Suls & A. G. Greenwald (Eds.), *Psychological perspectives on the self* (Vol. 2, pp. 93–121). Hillsdale, NJ: Erlbaum.

Trope, Y. (1986). Self-enhancement and self-assessment in achievement motivation. In R. M. Sorrentino & E. T. Higgins (Eds.), *Handbook of motivation and cognition: Foundations of social behavior* (Vol. 1, pp. 350–378). New York: Guilford.

Trope, Y., & Gaunt, R. (2000). Processing alternative explanations of behavior: Correction or integration? *Journal of Personality and Social Psychology, 79,* 344–354.

Tropp, L. R. (Ed.). (2012). *The Oxford handbook of intergroup conflict*. New York, NY: Oxford University Press.

Tropp, L. R., Hawi, D., Van Laar, C., & Levin, S. (2012). Cross-ethnic friendships, perceived discrimination, and their effects on ethnic activism over time: A longitudinal investigation of three ethnic minority groups. *British Journal of Social Psychology, 51*, 257–272.

Tropp, L. R., & Mallett, R. K. (Eds.). (2011). *Moving beyond prejudice reduction: Pathways to positive intergroup relations*. Washington DC: American Psychological Association.

Tropp, L. R., & Pettigrew, T. F. (2005). Differential relationships between intergroup contact and affective and cognitive dimensions of prejudice. *Personality and Social Psychology Bulletin, 31*, 1145–1158.

Tsapelas, I., Aron, A., & Orbuch, T. (2009). Marital boredom now predicts less satisfaction 9 years later. *Psychological Science, 20*, 543–545.

Tuan, Y. F. (1980). The significance of the artifact. *Geographical Review, 70*, 462–472.

Tucker, J. A., Vuchinich, R. E., & Sobell, M. B. (1981). Alcohol consumption as a self-handicapping strategy. *Journal of Abnormal Psychology, 90*, 220–230.

Tuckman, B. W. (1965). Developmental sequence in small groups. *Psychological Bulletin, 63*, 384–399.

Tuckman, B. W., & Jensen, M. A. (1977). Stages of small-group development revisited. *Group and Organization Studies, 2*, 419–427.

Turner, J. C. (1985). Social categorization and the self-concept: A social cognitive theory of group behavior. In E. J. Lawler (Ed.), *Advances in group processes: Theory and research* (Vol. 2, pp. 77–122). Greenwich, CT: JAI Press.

Turner, J. C. (1991). *Social influence*. Buckingham, UK: Open University Press.

Turner, J. C. (1999). Some current issues in research on social identity and self-categorization theories. In N. Ellemers, R. Spears, & B. Doosje (Eds.), *Social identity: Context, commitment, content* (pp. 6–34). Oxford: Blackwell.

Turner, J. C., Hogg, M. A., Oakes, P. J., Reicher, S. D., & Wetherell, M. S. (1987). *Rediscovering the social group: A self-categorization theory*. Oxford: Blackwell.

Turner, J. C., & Reynolds, K. J. (2011). Self-categorization theory. In P. A. M. Van Lange, A. Kruglanski, & E. T. Higgins (Eds.), *Handbook of theories in social psychology* (Vol. 2, pp. 399–418). London: Sage.

Turner, J. C., & Tajfel, H. (1986). The social identity theory of intergroup behavior. In S. Worchel & W. G. Austin (Eds.), *Psychology of intergroup relations* (pp. 7–24). Chicago: Nelson-Hall.

Turner, J. C., Wetherell, M. S., & Hogg, M. A. (1989). Referent informational influence and group polarization. *British Journal of Social Psychology, 28*, 135–147.

Turner, M. E. (2001). *Groups at work: Theory and research*. Mahwah, NJ: Erlbaum.

Turner, M. E., Pratkanis, A. R., Probasco, P., & Leve, C. (1992). Threat, cohesion, and group effectiveness: Testing a social identity maintenance perspective on groupthink. *Journal of Personality and Social Psychology, 63*, 781–796.

Turner, R. N., Hewstone, M., Voci, A., & Vonofakou, C. (2008). A test of the extended intergroup contact hypothesis: The mediating role of intergroup anxiety, perceived ingroup and outgroup norms, and inclusion of the outgroup in the self. *Journal of Personality and Social Psychology, 95*, 843–860.

Tversky, A., & Kahneman, D. (1973). Availability: A heuristic for judging frequency and probability. *Cognitive Psychology, 5*, 207–232.

Tversky, A., & Kahneman, D. (1974). Judgment under uncertainty: Heuristics and biases. *Science, 185*, 1124–1131.

Twenge, J. M., Baumeister, R. F., DeWall, C. N., Ciarocco, N. J., & Bartels, J. M. (2007). Social exclusion decreases prosocial behavior. *Journal of Personality and Social Psychology, 92*, 56–66.

Twenge, J. M., & Campbell, W. K. (2003). 'Isn't it fun to get the respect that we're going to deserve?' Narcissism, social rejection, and aggression. *Personality and Social Psychology Bulletin, 29*, 261–272.

Twenge, J. M., Catanese, K. R., & Baumeister, R. F. (2003). Social exclusion and the deconstructed state: Time perception, meaninglessness, lethargy, lack of emotion, and self-awareness. *Journal of Personality and Social Psychology, 85*, 409–423.

Tzeng, O. C., & Jackson, J. W. (1991). Common methodological framework for theory construction and evaluation in the social and behavioral sciences. *Genetic, Social, and General Psychology Monographs, 117*, 49–76.

Uleman, J. S., Saribay, S. A., & Gonzalez, C. M. (2008). Spontaneous inferences, implicit impressions, and implicit theories. *Annual Review of Psychology, 59*, 329–360.

USDHEW (US Department of Health Education and Welfare). (1964). *Smoking and health: A report of the Surgeon General*. Washington, DC: US Government Printing Office.

Uskul, A. K., Kitayama, S., & Nisbett, R. E. (2008). Ecocultural basis of cognition: Farmers and fishermen are more holistic than herders. *Proceedings of the National Academy of Science, 105*, 8552–8556.

Valkenburg, P. M., & Peter, J. (2007). Preadolescents' and adolescents' online communication and their closeness to friends. *Developmental Psychology, 43*, 267–277.

Valkenburg, P. M., & Peter, J. (2009). Social consequences of the Internet for adolescents. *Current Directions in Psychological Science, 18*, 1–5.

Vallacher, R. R., & Wegner, D. M. (1987). What do people think they're doing? Action identification and human behavior. *Psychological Review, 94*, 3–15.

Van de Vliert, E. (2009). *Climate, affluence, and culture.* Cambridge, UK: Cambridge University Press.

Van de Vliert, E., Huang, X., & Levine, R. V. (2004). National wealth and thermal climate as predictors of motives for volunteer work. *Journal of Cross-Cultural Psychology, 35,* 62–73.

Van den Bos, K., & Lind, E. A. (2002). Uncertainty management by means of fairness judgments. In M. P. Zanna (Ed.), *Advances in experimental social psychology* (Vol. 34, pp. 1–60). San Diego, CA: Academic Press.

van Dick, R., Tissongton, P. A., & Hertel, G. (2009). Do many hands make light work? How to overcome social loafing and gain motivation in work teams. *European Business Review, 21,* 233–245.

Van Ginkel, W. P., & Van Knippenberg, D. (2008). Group information elaboration and group decision making: The role of shared task representations. *Organizational Behavior and Human Decision Processes, 105,* 82–97.

Van Goozen, S. H. M. (2005). Hormones and the developmental origins of aggression. In R. E. Tremblay, W. W. Hartup, & J. Archer (Eds.), *Developmental origins of aggression* (pp. 281–306). New York: Guilford.

Van Hiel, A., Hautman, L., Cornelis, I., & De Clercq, B. (2007). Football hooliganism: Comparing self-awareness and social identity theory explanations. *Journal of Community and Applied Social Psychology, 17,* 169–186.

Van Horn, K. R., Arnone, A., Nesbitt, K., Desilets, L., Sears, T., Griffin, M., & Brudi, R. (1997). Physical distance and interpersonal characteristics in college students' romantic relationships. *Personal Relationships, 4,* 25–34.

Van Knippenberg, D. (2000). Work motivation and performance: A social identity perspective. *Applied Psychology: An International Review, 49,* 357–371.

Van Knippenberg, D., & Ellemers, N. (2003). Social identity and group performance: Identification as the key to group-oriented efforts. In S. A. Haslam, D. Van Knippenberg, M. J. Platow, & N. Ellemers (Eds.), *Social identity at work: Developing theory for organizational practice* (pp. 29–42). New York: Psychology Press.

Van Knippenberg, D., Lossie, N., & Wilke, H. (1994). In-group prototypicality and persuasion: Determinants of heuristic and systematic message processing. *British Journal of Social Psychology, 33,* 289–300.

Van Laar, C., Levin, S., Sinclair, S., & Sidanius, J. (2005). The effect of university roommate contact on ethnic attitudes and behavior. *Journal of Experimental Social Psychology, 41,* 329–345.

Van Lange, P. A. M., Rusbult, C. E., Drigotas, S. M., Arriaga, X. B., Witcher, B. S., & Cox, C. L. (1997). Willingness to sacrifice in close relationships. *Journal of Personality and Social Psychology, 72,* 1373–1395.

Van Leeuwen, E. (2000). *Unpublished lecture slides.*

Van Oudenhoven, J. P., Groenewoud, J. T., & Hewstone, M. (1996). Cooperation, ethnic salience and generalization of interethnic attitudes. *European Journal of Social Psychology, 26,* 649–661.

Van Oudenhoven, J. P., Prins, K. S., & Buunk, B. P. (1998). Attitudes of minority and majority members towards adaptation of immigrants. *European Journal of Social Psychology, 28,* 995–1013.

Van Overwalle, F. (2009). Social cognition and the brain: A meta-analysis. *Human Brain Mapping, 30,* 829–858.

Van Vugt, M., & Hart, C. M. (2004). Social identity as social glue: The origins of group loyalty. *Journal of Personality and Social Psychology, 86,* 585–598.

Van Yperen, N. W., & Buunk, B. P. (1990). A longitudinal study of equity and satisfaction in intimate relationships. *European Journal of Social Psychology, 20,* 287–309.

Vanberg, V. (1975). *Die zwei Soziologien [The two sociologies].* Tübingen, Germany: Mohr.

Vanman, E. J., Saltz, J. L., Nathan, L. R., & Warren, J. A. (2004). Racial discrimination by low-prejudiced Whites: Facial movements as implicit measures of attitudes related to behavior. *Psychological Science, 15,* 711–714.

Vasquez, E. A., Denson, T. F., Pedersen, W. C., Stenstrom, D. M., & Miller, N. (2005). The moderating effect of trigger intensity on triggered displaced aggression. *Journal of Experimental Social Psychology, 41,* 61–67.

Vasquez, E. A., Lickel, B., & Hennigan, K. (2010). Gangs, displaced, and group-based aggression. *Aggression and Violent Behavior, 15,* 130–140.

Vaughn, R. (1980). How advertising works: A planning model. *Journal of Advertising Research, 26,* 27–33.

Vazire, S. (2010). Who knows what about a person? The Self-Other Knowledge Asymmetry (SOKA) model. *Journal of Personality and Social Psychology, 98,* 281–300.

Veltkamp, M., Aarts, H., & Custers, R. (2009). Unravelling the motivational yarn: A framework for understanding the instigation of implicitly motivated behaviour resulting from deprivation and positive affect. In W. Stroebe & M. Hewstone (Eds.), *European review of social psychology* (Vol. 20, pp. 345–381). Hove, UK: Psychology Press.

Verkuyten, M., & Masson, K. (1996). Culture and gender differences in the perception of friendship by adolescents. *International Journal of Psychology, 31,* 207–217.

Verkuyten, M., & Pouliasi, K. (2002). Biculturalism among older children: Cultural frame switching, attributions, self-identification, and attitudes. *Journal of Cross-Cultural Psychology, 33,* 596–609.

Verona, E., & Sullivan, E. A. (2008). Emotional catharsis and aggression revisited: Heart rate reduction following aggressive responding. *Emotion, 8,* 331–340.

Verplanken, B. (2006). Beyond frequency: Habit as mental construct. *British Journal of Social Psychology, 45,* 639–656.

Verplanken, B., Aarts, H., Van Knippenberg, A., & Moonen, A. (1998). Habit versus planned behaviour: A field experiment. *British Journal of Social Psychology, 37,* 111–128.

Verplanken, B., & Orbell, S. (2003). Reflections on past behavior: A self-report index of habit strength. *Journal of Applied Social Psychology, 33,* 1313–1330.

Verwijmeren, T., Karremans, J. C., Stroebe, W., & Wigboldus, D. H. J. (2011). The working limits of subliminal advertising: The role of habits. *Journal of Consumer Psychology, 21,* 206–213.

Verwijmeren, T., Karremans, J. C., Stroebe, W., Wigboldus, D., & Van Ooijen, I. (2010). *Vicary's victory: Subliminal ads in movies affect brand choice.* Unpublished manuscript, Radboud University of Nijmegen, Netherlands.

Victoroff, J., & Kruglanski, A. W. (Eds.). (2009). *Psychology of terrorism.* New York: Psychology Press.

Vieth, A. Z., Strauman, T. J., Kolden, G. G., Woods, T. E., Michels, J. L., & Klein, M. H. (2003). Self-system therapy (SST): A theory based psychotherapy for depression. *Clinical Psychology: Science and Practice, 10,* 245–268.

Vinokur, A., & Burnstein, E. (1974). Effects of partially shared persuasive arguments on group-induced shifts: A group-problem-solving approach. *Journal of Personality and Social Psychology, 29,* 305–315.

Vinokur, A., & Burnstein, E. (1978). Novel argumentation and attitude change: The case of polarization following group discussion. *European Journal of Social Psychology, 8,* 335–348.

Visser, P. S., Bizer, G., & Krosnick, J. A. (2006). Exploring the latent structure of strength-related attitude attributes. In M. Zanna (Ed.), *Advances in experimental social psychology* (Vol. 38, pp. 1–67). San Diego, CA: Academic Press.

Visser, P. S., & Krosnick, J. A. (1998). Development of attitude strength over the life cycle: Surge and decline. *Journal of Personality and Social Psychology, 75,* 1389–1410.

Visser, P. S., Krosnick, J. A., & Lavrakas, P. (2000). Survey research. In H. T. Reis & C. M. Judd (Eds.), *Handbook of research methods in social psychology* (pp. 223–252). New York: Cambridge University Press.

Vohs, K. D., & Finkel, E. J. (Eds.). (2006). *Self and relationships: Connecting intrapersonal and interpersonal processes.* New York: Guilford.

Vohs, K. D., & Heatherton, T. F. (2000). Self-regulatory failure: A resource-depletion approach. *Psychological Science, 11,* 249–254.

Volz, K. G., Kessler, T., & Von Cramon, D. Y. (2009). In-group as part of the self: In-group favoritism is mediated by medial prefrontal cortex activation. *Social Neuroscience, 4,* 244–260.

Vonofakou, C., Hewstone, M., & Voci, A. (2007). Contact with out-group friends as a predictor of meta-attitudinal strength and accessibility of attitudes toward gay men. *Journal of Personality and Social Psychology, 92,* 804–820.

Vroom, V. H., & Jago, A. G. (1988). *The new leadership.* Englewood Cliffs, NJ: Prentice Hall.

Wageman, R. (2001). How leaders foster self-managing team effectiveness: Design choices versus hands-on coaching. *Organization Science, 12,* 559–577.

Wagner, U., & Zick, A. (1995). The relation of formal education to ethnic prejudice: Its reliability, validity and explanation. *European Journal of Social Psychology, 25,* 41–56.

Waldzus, S., Mummendey, A., Wenzel, M., & Boettcher, F. (2004). Of bikers, teachers and Germans: Groups' diverging views about their prototypicality. *British Journal of Social Psychology, 43,* 385–400.

Walker, A., Flatley, J., Kershaw, C., & Moon, D. (2009). *Crime in England and Wales 2008/09* (Vol. 1). Retrieved February 28, 2012, from http://webarchive.nationalarchives.gov.uk/20110218135832/http://rds.homeoffice.gov.uk/rds/pdfs09/hosb1109vol1.pdf

Wallace, H. M., & Baumeister, R. F. (2002). The performance of narcissists rises and falls with perceived opportunity for glory. *Journal of Personality and Social Psychology, 82,* 819–834.

Waller, B. M., Hope, L., Burrowes, N., & Morrison, E. R. (2011). Twelve (not so) angry men: Managing conversational group size increases perceived contribution by decision makers. *Group Processes & Intergroup Relations, 14,* 835–843.

Waller, J. (2002). *Becoming evil: How ordinary people commit genocide and mass killing.* Oxford: Oxford University Press.

Waller, P. F. (2002). Challenges in motor vehicle safety. *Annual Review of Public Health, 23,* 93–113.

Walster, E., Aronson, V., Abrahams, D., & Rottmann, L. (1966). Importance of physical attractiveness in dating behavior. *Journal of Personality and Social Psychology, 4,* 508–516.

Wan, E. W., & Sternthal, B. (2008). Regulating the effects of depletion through monitoring. *Personality and Social Psychology Bulletin, 34,* 32–46.

Wang, Q., & Conway, M. A. (2004). The stories we keep: Autobiographical memory in American and Chinese middle-aged adults. *Journal of Personality, 72,* 911–938.

Ward, C. A., Bochner, S., & Furnham, A. (2001). *The psychology of culture shock* (2nd ed.). Hove, UK: Routledge.

Waters, H., Hyder, A., Rajkotia, Y., Basu, S., Rehwinkel, J. A., & Butchart, A. (2004). The economic dimensions of interpersonal violence Retrieved October 29, 2010, from http://whqlibdoc.who.int/publications/2004/9241591609.pdf

Weary, G., Harvey, J. H., Schwieger, P., Olson, C. T., Perloff, R., & Pritchard, S. (1982). Self-presentation and the moderation of self-serving attributional biases. *Social Cognition, 1,* 140–159.

Webb, E. J., Campbell, D. T., Schwartz, R. D., & Sechrest, L. (2000). *Unobtrusive measures.* Thousand Oaks, CA: Sage.

Webb, T. L., Sheeran, P., & Luszczynska, A. (2009). Planning to break unwanted habits: Habit strength moderates implementation intention effects on behavior change. *British Journal of Social Psychology, 48*, 507–523.

Weber, R., & Crocker, J. (1983). Cognitive processes in the revision of stereotypic beliefs. *Journal of Personality and Social Psychology, 45*, 961–977.

Webster, D. M., & Kruglanski, A. W. (1994). Individual differences in need for cognitive closure. *Journal of Personality and Social Psychology, 67*, 1049–1062.

Weeden, J., & Sabini, J. (2005). Physical attractiveness and health in Western societies: A review. *Psychological Bulletin, 131*, 635–653.

Wegener, D. T., Petty, R. E., & Smith, S. M. (1995). Positive mood can increase or decrease message scrutiny: The hedonic contingency view of mood and message processing. *Journal of Personality and Social Psychology, 69*, 5–15.

Wegner, D. M. (1987). Transactive memory: A contemporary analysis of the group mind. In B. Mullen & G. R. Goethals (Eds.), *Theories of group behavior* (pp. 185–208). New York: Springer.

Wegner, D. M. (1994). Ironic processes of mental control. *Psychological Review, 101*, 34–52.

Wegner, D. M. (2002). *The illusion of conscious will.* Cambridge, MA: MIT Press.

Weick, K. E. (1985). Systematic observational methods. In G. Lindzey & E. Aronson (Eds.), *Handbook of social psychology* (3rd ed., Vol. 1, pp. 567–634). New York: Random House.

Weigel, R. H., & Newman, L. S. (1976). Increasing attitude-behavior correspondence by broadening the scope of the behavioral measure. *Journal of Personality and Social Psychology, 33*, 793–802.

Weiner, B. (1979). A theory of motivation for some classroom experiences. *Journal of Educational Psychology, 71*, 3–25.

Weiner, B. (1985). An attributional theory of achievement motivation and emotion. *Psychological Review, 92*, 548–573.

Weiner, B. (1986). *An attributional theory of motivation and emotion.* New York: Springer.

Weiner, B. (2006). *Social motivation, justice, and the moral emotions: An attributional approach.* Mahwah, NJ: Erlbaum.

Weisband, S. (2002). Maintaining awareness in distributed team collaboration: Implications for leadership and performance. In P. J. Hinds & S. Kiesler (Eds.), *Distributed work* (pp. 311–333). Cambridge, MA: MIT Press.

Wells, G. L., & Petty, R. E. (1980). The effects of overt head movements on persuasion: Compatibility and incompatibility of responses. *Basic and Applied Social Psychology, 1*, 219–230.

Wells, S., & Graham, K. (1999). Frequency of third-party involvement in incidents of barroom aggression. *Contemporary Drug Problems, 26*, 457–480.

West, S. G., Biesanz, J. C., & Pitts, S. C. (2000). Causal inference and generalization in field settings. In H. Reis & C. M. Judd (Eds.), *Handbook of research methods in social and personality psychology* (pp. 40–84). Cambridge, UK: Cambridge University Press.

Wetherell, M. (1982). Cross-cultural studies of minimal groups: Implications for the social identity theory of intergroup relations. In H. Tajfel (Ed.), *Social identity and intergroup relations* (pp. 207–240). Cambridge, MA: Cambridge University Press.

Wetherell, M., Stiven, H., & Potter, J. (1987). Unequal egalitarianism: A preliminary study of discourses concerning gender and employment opportunities. *British Journal of Social Psychology, 26*, 59–71.

Wheelan, S. A. (1994). *Group process: A developmental perspective.* Boston, MA: Allyn & Bacon.

Wheelan, S. A., Davidson, B., & Tilin, F. (2003). Group development across time: Reality or illusion? *Small Group Research, 34*, 223–245.

White, J. W., Koss, M. P., & Kazdin, A. E. (Eds.). (2011). *Violence against women and children* (Vol. 1: *Mapping the terrain*). Washington, DC: American Psychological Association.

White, M. J., Brockett, D. R., & Overstreet, B. G. (1993). Confirmatory bias in evaluating personality test information: Am I really that kind of person? *Journal of Counseling Psychology, 40*, 120–126.

White, P. A. (1984). A model of the layperson as pragmatist. *Personality and Social Psychology Bulletin, 10*, 333–348.

White, P. A. (1989). A theory of causal processing. *British Journal of Psychology, 80*, 431–454.

White, P. A. (2009). Property transmission: An explanatory account of the role of similarity information in causal inference. *Psychological Bulletin, 135*, 774–793.

White, P. A. (2012). The experience of force: The role of haptic experience of forces in visual perception of object motion and interactions, mental simulation, and motion-related judgments. *Psychological Bulletin, 138*, 589–615.

White, R., & Lippitt, R. (1968). Leader behavior and member reaction in three 'social climates'. In D. Cartwright & A. Zander (Eds.), *Group dynamics: Research and theory* (3rd ed., pp. 318–335). New York: Harper & Row.

Wicker, A. W. (1969). Attitudes versus actions: The relationship of verbal and overt behavioral responses to attitude objects. *Journal of Social Issues, 25*, 41–78.

Wicklund, R. A., & Gollwitzer, P. M. (1982). *Symbolic self-completion.* Hillsdale, NJ: Erlbaum.

Wiederman, M. W. (1993). Evolved gender differences in mate preferences: Evidence from personal advertisements. *Ethology and Sociobiology, 14*, 331–351.

Wienke, C., & Hill, G. J. (2009). Does the 'marriage benefit' extend to partners in gay and lesbian relationships?: Evidence from a random sample of sexually active adults. *Journal of Family Issues, 30*, 259–289.

Wieselquist, J., Rusbult, C. E., Foster, C. A., & Agnew, C. R. (1999). Commitment, pro-relationship behavior, and trust in close relationships. *Journal of Personality and Social Psychology, 77*, 942–966.

Wiesenthal, D. L., Hennessy, D. A., & Totten, B. (2000). The influence of music on driver stress. *Journal of Applied Social Psychology, 30,* 1709–1719.

Wilder, D. A. (1977). Perception of groups, size of opposition, and social influence. *Journal of Experimental Social Psychology, 13,* 253–268.

Wilder, D. A. (1984). Intergroup contact: The typical member and the exception to the rule. *Journal of Experimental Social Psychology, 20,* 177–194.

Wilder, D. A., & Shapiro, P. N. (1989). Role of competition-induced anxiety in limiting the beneficial impact of positive behavior by an out-group member. *Journal of Personality and Social Psychology, 56,* 60–69.

Williams, H. L., Conway, M. A., & Cohen, G. (2008). Autobiographical memory. In G. Cohen & M. A. Conway (Eds.), *Memory in the real world* (pp. 21–90). New York: Psychology Press.

Williams, K. D. (2001). *Ostracism: The power of silence.* New York: Guilford.

Williams, K. D., Cheung, C. K. T., & Choi, W. (2000). Cyberostracism: Effects of being ignored over the Internet. *Journal of Personality and Social Psychology, 79,* 748–762.

Williams, K. D., & Karau, S. J. (1991). Social loafing and social compensation: The effects of expectations of co-worker performance. *Journal of Personality and Social Psychology, 61,* 570–581.

Williams, R. B., Barefoot, J. C., Califf, R, M., Haney, T. L., Saunders, W. B., Pryor, D. B., ... Mark, D. B. (1992). Prognostic importance of social and economic resources among medically treated patients with angiographically documented coronary artery disease. *Journal of the American Medical Association, 267,* 520–524.

Williams, R. M., Jr. (1947). The reduction of intergroup tensions: A survey of research on problems of ethnic, racial, and religious group relations. *Social Science Research Council Bulletin, 57,* 153.

Wilner, D. M., Walkley, R. P., & Cook, S. W. (1955). *Human relations in interracial housing.* Minneapolis, MN: University of Minnesota Press.

Wilson, A. M. (2002). Attitudes towards customer satisfaction measurement in the retail sector. *International Journal of Market Research, 44,* 213–222.

Wilson, J. (2000). Volunteering. *Annual Review of Sociology, 26,* 215–240.

Wilson, T. D. (2002). *Strangers to ourselves: Discovering the adaptive unconscious.* Cambridge, MA: Harvard University Press.

Wilson, T. D., & Brekke, N. (1994). Mental contamination and mental correction: Unwanted influences on judgments and evaluations. *Psychological Bulletin, 116,* 117–142.

Wilson, T. D., & Dunn, E. W. (2004). Self-knowledge: Its limits, value, and potential for improvement. *Annual Reviews of Psychology, 55,* 493–518.

Wilson, T. D., & Gilbert, D. T. (2003). Affective forecasting. In M. P. Zanna (Ed.), *Advances in experimental social psychology* (Vol. 35, pp. 345–411). San Diego, CA: Academic Press.

Wilson, T. D., Lindsey, S., & Schooler, T. Y. (2000). A model of dual attitudes. *Psychological Review, 107,* 101–126.

Wilson, T. D., & Nisbett, R. E. (1978). The accuracy of verbal reports about the effects of stimuli on evaluations and behavior. *Social Psychology, 41,* 118–131.

Winston, J. S., Strange, B. A., O'Doherty, J., & Dolan, R. J. (2002). Automatic and intentional responses during evaluation of trustworthiness of faces. *Nature Neuroscience, 5,* 277–283.

Winter, D. G. (1987). Leader appeal, leader performance, and the motive profiles of leaders and followers: A study of American presidents and elections. *Journal of Personality and Social Psychology, 52,* 196–202.

Winter, D. G., & Stewart, A. J. (1977). Power motive reliability as a function of retest instructions. *Journal of Consulting and Clinical Psychology, 45,* 436–440.

Winter, L., & Uleman, J. S. (1984). When are social judgments made? Evidence for the spontaneousness of trait inferences. *Journal of Personality and Social Psychology, 47,* 237–252.

Wiseman, J. P. (1986). Friendship: Bonds and binds in a voluntary relationship. *Journal of Social and Personal Relationships, 3,* 191–211.

Witte, E. H. (1989). Köhler rediscovered: The anti-Ringelmann effect. *European Journal of Social Psychology, 19,* 147–154.

Witte, E. H., & Davis, J. H. (Eds.). (1996). *Understanding group behavior* (Vol. 1 and 2). Mahwah, NJ: Erlbaum.

Wittenbaum, G. M., Hubbell, A. P., & Zuckerman, C. (1999). Mutual enhancement: Toward an understanding of the collective preference for shared information. *Journal of Personality and Social Psychology, 77,* 967–978.

Wittenbrink, B., Judd, C. M., & Park, B. (1997). Evidence for racial prejudice at the implicit level and its relationship with questionnaire measures. *Journal of Personality and Social Psychology, 72,* 262–274.

Wittenbrink, B., & Schwarz, N. (Eds.). (2007). *Implicit measures of attitudes.* New York: Guilford.

Wofford, J. C., & Liska, L. Z. (1993). Path-goal theories of leadership: A meta-analysis. *Journal of Management, 19,* 857–876.

Wood, J. V. (1989). Theory and research concerning social comparisons of personal attributes. *Psychological Bulletin, 106,* 231–248.

Wood, W. (2000). Attitude change: Persuasion and social influence. *Annual Review of Psychology, 51,* 539–570.

Wood, W., Lundgren, S., Ouellette, J. A., Busceme, S., & Blackstone, T. (1994). Minority influence: A meta-analytic review of social influence processes. *Psychological Bulletin, 115,* 323–345.

Worchel, S., Andreoli, V. A., & Folger, R. (1977). Intergroup cooperation and intergroup attraction: The effect of previous interaction and outcome of combined effort. *Journal of Experimental Social Psychology, 13*, 131–140.

Wright, E. F., Voyer, D., Wright, R. D., & Roney, C. (1995). Supporting audiences and performance under pressure: The home-ice disadvantage in hockey championships. *Journal of Sport Behaviour, 18*, 21–28.

Wright, E. F., & Wells, G. L. (1988). Is the attitude-attribution paradigm suitable for investigating the dispositional bias? *Personality and Social Psychology Bulletin, 14*, 183–190.

Wright, S. C., Aron, A., McLaughlin-Volpe, T., & Ropp, S. A. (1997). The extended contact effect: Knowledge of cross-group friendships and prejudice. *Journal of Personality and Social Psychology, 73*, 73–90.

Wright, S. C., & Lubensky, M. E. (2009). The struggle for social equality: Collective action versus prejudice reduction. In S. Demoulin, J.-P. Leyens, & J. F. Dovidio (Eds.), *Intergroup misunderstandings: Impact of divergent social realities* (pp. 291–310). New York: Psychology Press.

Wright, S. C., Taylor, D. M., & Moghaddam, F. M. (1990). Responding to membership in a disadvantaged group: From acceptance to collective protest. *Journal of Personality and Social Psychology, 58*, 994–1003.

Wrosch, C., & Miller, G. E. (2009). Depressive symptoms can be useful: Self-regulatory and emotional benefits of dysphoric mood in adolescence. *Journal of Personality and Social Psychology, 96*, 1181–1190.

Wundt, W. (1911–1912). *Völkerpsychologie: Eine Untersuchung der Entwicklungsgesetze von Sprache, Mythus und Sitte [Ethnopsychology: An investigation into the laws of development of language, myth, and custom]* (3rd ed. Vol. 2). Leipzig, Germany: Engelmann.

Wyer, N. A. (2007). Motivational influences on compliance with and consequences of instructions to suppress stereotypes. *Journal of Experimental Social Psychology, 43*, 417–424.

Wyer, R. S., Jr., & Frey, D. (1983). The effects of feedback about self and others on the recall and judgments of feedback-relevant information. *Journal of Experimental Social Psychology, 19*, 540–559.

Yamagishi, T., & Kiyonari, T. (2000). The group as the container of generalized reciprocity. *Social Psychology Quarterly, 63*, 116–132.

Yamaguchi, S., Greenwald, A. G., Banaji, M. R., Murakami, F., Chen, D., Shiomura, K., … Krendl, A. (2007). Apparent universality of positive implicit self-esteem. *Psychological Science, 18*, 498–500.

Young, A. W., & Leafhead, K. M. (1996). Betwixt life and death: Case studies of the Cotard delusion. In P. W. Halligan & J. C. Marshall (Eds.), *Method in madness: Case studies in cognitive neuropsychiatry* (pp. 147–171). Hove, UK: Psychology Press.

Yukl, G. A. (2012). *Leadership in organizations* (8th ed.). Upper Saddle River, NJ: Prentice Hall.

Yzerbyt, V., & Kuppens, T. (2009). Group-based emotions: The social heart in the individual head. In S. Otten, K. Sassenberg, & T. Kessler (Eds.), *Intergroup relations: The role of motivation and emotion* (pp. 143–161). Hove, UK: Psychology Press.

Yzerbyt, V., Rocher, S., & Schadron, G. (1997). Stereotypes as explanations: A subjective essentialistic view of group perception. In R. Spears, P. J. Oakes, N. Ellemers, & S. A. Haslam (Eds.), *The social psychology of stereotyping and group life* (pp. 20–50). Oxford: Blackwell.

Zaadstra, B. M., Seidell, J. C., Van Noord, P. A., Te Velde, E. R., Habbema, J. D., Vrieswijk, B., & Karbaat, J. (1993). Fat and female fecundity: Prospective study of effect of body fat distribution on conception rates. *British Medical Journal, 306*, 484–487.

Zaccaro, S. J., Rittman, A. L., & Marks, M. A. (2001). Team leadership. *Leadership Quarterly, 12*, 451–483.

Zajonc, R. B. (1965). Social facilitation. *Science, 149*, 269–274.

Zajonc, R. B. (1968). Attitudinal effects of mere exposure. *Journal of Personality and Social Psychology, 9*, 1–27.

Zajonc, R. B. (1980). Compresence. In P. B. Paulus (Ed.), *Psychology of group influence* (pp. 35–60). Hillsdale, NJ: Erlbaum.

Zajonc, R. B. (1998). Emotions. In D. T. Gilbert, S. T. Fiske, & G. Lindzey (Eds.), *The handbook of social psychology* (4th ed., Vol. 2, pp. 591–632). Boston, MA: McGraw-Hill.

Zajonc, R. B., Heingartner, A., & Herman, E. M. (1969). Social enhancement and impairment of performance in the cockroach. *Journal of Personality and Social Psychology, 13*, 83–92.

Zaki, J., Schirmer, J., & Mitchell, J. P. (2011). Social influence modulates the neural computation of value. *Psychological Science, 22*, 894–900.

Zanna, M. P., & Cooper, J. (1974). Dissonance and the pill: An attribution approach to studying the arousal properties of dissonance. *Journal of Personality and Social Psychology, 29*, 703–709.

Zanna, M. P., & Hamilton, D. L. (1972). Attribute dimensions and patterns of trait inferences. *Psychonomic Science, 27*, 353–354.

Zanna, M. P., Higgins, E. T., & Taves, P. A. (1976). Is dissonance phenomenologically aversive? *Journal of Experimental Social Psychology, 12*, 530–538.

Zanna, M. P., & Rempel, J. K. (1988). Attitudes: A new look at an old concept. In D. Bar-Tal & A. W. Kruglanski (Eds.), *The social psychology of knowledge* (pp. 315–334). Cambridge, UK: Cambridge University Press.

Zebrowitz, L. A. (1990). *Social perception*. Belmont, CA: Brooks.

Zhang, S., & Hunt, J. S. (2008). The stereotype rebound effect: Universal or culturally bounded process? *Journal of Experimental Social Psychology, 44*, 489–500.

Zillmann, D. (1978). Attribution and misattribution of excitatory reactions. In J. H. Harvey, W. J. Ickes, & R. F. Kidd (Eds.), *New directions in attribution theory and research* (Vol. 2, pp. 335–368). Hillsdale, NJ: Erlbaum.

Zillmann, D., & Bryant, J. (1974). Effect of residual excitation on the emotional response to provocation and delayed aggressive behavior. *Journal of Personality and Social Psychology, 30*, 782–791.

Zimbardo, P. G. (1969). The human choice: Individuation, reason, and order versus deindividuation, impulse, and chaos. In W. T. Arnold & D. Levine (Eds.), *Nebraska Symposium on Motivation* (Vol. 17, pp. 237–307). Lincoln, NE: University of Nebraska Press.

Zimbardo, P. G. (2006). On rethinking the psychology of tyranny: The BBC prison study. *British Journal of Social Psychology, 45,* 47–53.

Zimbardo, P. G. (2007). *The Lucifer effect: Understanding how good people turn evil.* New York: Random House.

Zimbardo, P. G., Ebbesen, E. B., & Maslach, C. (1977). *Influencing attitudes and changing behavior* (2nd ed.). Reading, MA: Addison-Wesley.

Zimbardo, P. G., Maslach, C., & Haney, C. (2000). Reflections on the Stanford prison experiment: Genesis, transformations, consequences. In T. Blass (Ed.), *Obedience to authority: Current perspectives on the Milgram paradigm* (pp. 193–237). Mahwah, NJ: Erlbaum.

Zuckerman, M. (1979). Attribution of success and failure revisited, or: The motivational bias is alive and well in attribution theory. *Journal of Personality, 47,* 245–287.

Zuckerman, M., Kieffer, S. C., & Knee, C. R. (1998). Consequences of self-handicapping: Effects on coping, academic performance, and adjustment. *Journal of Personality and Social Psychology, 74,* 1619–1628.

Glossary

accentuation effect when (social) categories are correlated with a continuous dimension (e.g., skin colour, eye shape) there is a judgemental tendency to overestimate *similarities within*, and *differences between* the categories on this dimension.

accessibility the extent to which information is easily located and retrieved.

accountability a processing goal whereby perceivers believe they will have to justify their responses to a third party and be held responsible for their impressions; this typically leads to less stereotypical impressions.

acculturation the process whereby two cultural groups that come into contact with one another cause changes in one or both parties.

acquiescent responding a tendency for a respondent to agree with all items on scales measuring attitudes, beliefs or values, even those that contradict one another.

actor–observer difference proposed general tendency for people to explain their own behaviour in more situational terms, but other people's behaviour in more dispositional terms.

affective component of attitude the feelings or emotions associated with an attitude object.

aggression any form of behaviour intended to harm or injure another living being who is motivated to avoid such treatment.

Aggression Questionnaire (AQ) self report instrument to measure stable individual differences in trait aggressiveness.

aggressive cues situational cues with an aggressive meaning that increase the accessibility of aggressive cognitions.

aggressive scripts cognitive representation of when and how to show aggressive behaviour.

altruism refers to behaviour carried out to benefit others without anticipation of external rewards; it is driven by exclusively empathic motivation.

analysis of non-common effects observers infer intentions behind actions by comparing the consequences of the behavioural options that were open to the actor and identifying distinctive outcomes.

anchoring/adjustment heuristic a cognitive heuristic that makes us place weight upon initial standards/schemas (anchors) and as a result means we may not always adjust sufficiently far from these anchors to provide accurate judgements.

arousal: cost–reward model suggests that observing an emergency creates a sense of arousal in the bystander, which becomes increasingly unpleasant. Bystander responds by considering costs and rewards of helping or not helping.

attachment theory the theory that proposes that the development of secure infant–caregiver attachment in childhood is the basis for the ability to maintain stable and intimate relationships in adulthood.

attitude an overall evaluation of a stimulus object.

attitude functions the psychological needs fulfilled by an attitude.

attitude–behaviour relation the degree to which an attitude predicts behaviour.

attitudinal ambivalence a state that occurs when an individual both likes and dislikes an attitude object.

attribution theories a group of theories about how individuals manage to infer the 'causes' underlying the behaviour of others, or even their own behaviour.

attributional biases systematic distortions in the sampling or processing of information about the causes of behaviour.

audience inhibition the experience of individual bystanders whose behaviour can be seen by other bystanders. In an emergency bystanders may fear embarrassment by their actions, resulting in lower likelihood of them helping.

augmenting principle the assumption that causal factors need to be stronger if an inhibitory influence on an observed effect is present. The converse of the discounting principle.

authoritarian personality personality syndrome characterized by a simplistic cognitive style, a rigid regard for social conventions and submission to authority figures (associated with prejudice towards minority groups and susceptibility to Fascism).

autokinetic effect perceptual illusion, whereby, in the absence of reference points, a stationary light appears to move.

automatic process a process that occurs without intention, effort or awareness and does not interfere with other concurrent cognitive processes.

availability heuristic a cognitive shortcut that allows us to draw upon information about how quickly information comes to mind about a particular event, to deduce the frequency or likelihood of that event.

averaging perceivers compute the (weighted or unweighted) mean value of pieces of information about a person; when other information is strongly positive, additional mildly positive information yields a less positive impression.

back-translation translation of a research questionnaire that has already been translated from one language to a second language back into the original language by a translator who has not seen the original version.

balance theory a cognitive consistency theory that assumes that individuals strive to maintain consistency or balance (objects or persons perceived as belonging together are evaluated similarly) in their social perceptions.

base rate information   information that gives us an idea about how frequent certain categories are in the general population.

behavioural component of attitudes   past behaviours (also present and future anticipated behaviours) associated with an attitude object.

Bennington study   a longitudinal field study of social influence showing how political attitudes of initially conservative female students changed over time towards the liberal attitudes that were predominant on this college campus.

better than average effect   the finding that more than 50 per cent of participants report themselves to be better than average on a variety of criteria.

bicultural identity   seeing oneself as having simultaneous membership of two culturally-distinct groups.

bicultural identity integration   present when a person sees their alternate identities as compatible with one another.

brainstorming   a group technique aimed at enhancing creativity in groups by means of the uninhibited generation of as many ideas as possible concerning a specified topic.

bullying   (also known as *mobbing*) denotes aggressive behaviour directed at victims who cannot easily defend themselves, typically in schools and at the workplace.

bystander effect   refers to the phenomenon whereby the likelihood of any one person helping in an emergency situation decreases as the number of other bystanders increases.

categorization   the tendency to group objects (including people) into discrete groups based upon shared characteristics common to them.

catharsis   release of aggressive tension through symbolic engagement in aggressive behaviour.

causal attribution   the process whereby social perceivers arrive at conclusions about the causes of another person's behaviour.

causal power   an intrinsic property of an object or event that enables it to exert influence on some other object or event.

causal schema   knowledge structure shaping attributions. Causal schemas may be either abstract representations of general causal principles (e.g., multiple necessary and multiple sufficient causes schemas) or domain-specific ideas about cause and effect.

central trait   a dispositional characteristic viewed by social perceivers as integral to the organization of personality.

coefficient of relatedness (r)   between two individuals can be calculated by knowing how many steps removed individuals are from a common ancestor (e.g., coefficients of relatedness between children–parents and grandchildren–grandparents are .5 and .25, respectively).

cognitive component of attitudes   beliefs, thoughts and attributes associated with an attitude object.

cognitive dissonance   a state of imbalance among beliefs, including the beliefs that support a person's attitude.

cognitive dissonance theory   assumes that dissonance is an aversive state which motivates individuals to reduce it (e.g., by

changing beliefs, attitudes or behaviour, and searching for consonant, or avoiding dissonant, information).

cognitive miser   a view of people as being often limited in processing capacity and apt to take shortcuts where possible to make life simple.

cognitive neo-associationist model   explains aggressive behaviour as the results of negative affect that is subjected to cognitive processing and activates a network of aggression-related thoughts and feelings.

cognitive response model   assumes that attitude change is mediated by the thoughts, or 'cognitive responses', which recipients generate as they receive and reflect upon persuasive communications.

cognitive restriction   a capability loss in group tasks that involve idea generation, which occurs when an idea mentioned by another group member makes people focus on the particular category this idea belongs to, at the expense of generating ideas from other categories.

cognitive stimulation   a capability gain in group tasks that involve idea generation, which occurs when an idea mentioned by another group member stimulates a cognitive category one would otherwise not have thought of.

cognitive styles   people with an analytic style focus on the main element within information that they are processing; people with a holistic style focus on the relations between the different elements in information that they are processing.

cohesion   the force that binds members to the group.

collective violence   instrumental use of violence by people who identify themselves as members of a group against another group in order to achieve political, economic or social objectives.

common ingroup identity model   this model seeks to reduce bias between groups by changing the nature of categorization from ingroups versus outgroups to a single, more inclusive identity. The model harnesses the forces of ingroup favouritism to reduce bias and promote helping.

communal relationship   refers to an interpersonal association between individuals who are more concerned with what their partner gets rather than what they themselves receive, or relationships in which people's primary concern is being responsive to the other person's needs.

companionate love   refers to the feelings of intimacy and affection we feel for another person when we care deeply for the person but do not necessarily experience passion or arousal in his or her presence.

compliance   a response whereby the target of influence acquiesces to a request from the influence source (also refers to change in behaviour to match a norm without change on a private level).

confederate   an accomplice or assistant of the experimenter who is ostensibly another participant but who in fact plays a prescribed role in the experiment.

configural model   a holistic approach to impression formation, implying that social perceivers actively construct deeper meanings out of the bits of information that they receive about other people.

Conflict Tactics Scales (CTS)   instrument for measuring intimate partner violence by collecting self-reports of perpetration and/or victimization.

conformity   see *majority influence.*

consensus information   evidence relating to how different actors behave towards the same object.

consistency   a behavioural style indicating that the same position is maintained across time; seen as central to minority influence.

consistency information   evidence relating to how an actor's behaviour towards an object varies across different situations and times.

consistency theories   a group of theories (see balance theory, cognitive dissonance theory) proposing that people prefer congruence or consistency among their various cognitions, especially among their beliefs, values, and attitudes.

construct   an abstract theoretical concept (such as social influence).

construct validity   the validity of the assumption that independent and dependent variables adequately capture the abstract variables (constructs) they are supposed to represent.

contact hypothesis   intergroup contact will reduce prejudice if it (1) has acquaintance potential; (2) takes place under conditions of equal status; (3) involves cooperation towards a common goal; and (4) takes place in a supportive normative climate.

contingency approaches   emphasize situational factors in the study of leadership (e.g., task or follower characteristics) and how these moderate the relationship between leader traits or leadership behaviours and leadership effectiveness.

continuum model of impression formation   views impression formation as a process going from category-based evaluations at one end of the continuum to individuated responses at the other, dependent on the interplay of motivational and attentional factors.

control group   a group of participants who are typically not exposed to the independent variable(s) used in experimental research.

controlled process   a process that is intentional, under the individual's volitional control, effortful and entailing conscious awareness.

convergent validity   established by showing that different measures of the same construct (e.g., self-report, implicit, observation) are significantly associated with each other.

conversion   a change in private response after exposure to influence by others; internalized change; a change in the way one structures an aspect of reality.

coordination losses   describe the diminished performance of a group if it fails to coordinate the contributions of its individual members in an optimal manner.

correspondence bias   the proposed tendency to infer a personal disposition corresponding to observed behaviour even when the behaviour was determined by the situation.

correspondent inference theory   proposes that observers infer correspondent intentions and dispositions for observed intentional behaviour under certain circumstances.

counterattitudinal behaviour   behaviour (usually induced by monetary incentives or threats) which is inconsistent with the actor's attitude or beliefs.

covariation theory   proposes that observers work out the causes of behaviour by collecting data about comparison cases. Causality is attributed to the person, entity or situation depending on which of these factors covaries with the observed effect.

cover story   a false but supposedly plausible explanation of the purpose of an experiment; the intention is to limit the operation of demand characteristics.

crisis in social psychology   a crisis of confidence among social psychologists that started in the late 1960s and was overcome in subsequent decades. During the crisis years, social psychologists questioned the values, the methods and the scientific status of their discipline.

cross-cultural replication   a test of whether the results of a study are the same if it is repeated as exactly as possible in another cultural context.

cultural masculinity–femininity   the extent to which gender roles in a nation are seen as differentiated (masculinity) or similar (femininity).

culture   a social system that is characterized by the shared meanings that are attributed to people and events by its members.

cyberbullying   involves the use of modern technology, such as computers, mobile phones or other electronic devices to inflict intentional harm on others.

debriefing   the practice of explaining to participants the purpose of the experiment in which they have just participated, and answering any questions the participants may have.

decategorization   reducing the salience of intergroup boundaries through highly personalized contact; attention to idiosyncratic rather than category-based information about outgroup members should, over time, reduce the usefulness of the category, and reduce prejudice.

deindividuation   a state in which individuals are deprived of their sense of individual identity, and are more likely to behave in an extreme manner, often antisocially and violating norms.

delay of gratification   the ability to resist the temptation of an immediate reward and wait for a later larger reward.

demand characteristics   cues that are perceived as telling participants how they are expected to behave or respond in a research setting; that is, cues that 'demand' a certain sort of response.

dependent variable   the variable that is expected to change as a function of changes in the independent variable. Measured changes in the dependent variable are seen as 'dependent on' manipulated changes in the independent variable.

depressive realism   the idea that depressed people's interpretations of reality are more accurate than those of non-depressed people.

derogation of alternatives   the tendency of romantically involved individuals, as compared to singles, to give lower attractiveness ratings to attractive opposite-sex others.

descriptive norms Norms that tell us about how others will act in similar situations.

desired selves contain our potential (possible selves), as well as the wishes and aspirations (ideal self), and the duties and obligations (ought self) that we, or significant others, hold for us.

diffusion of responsibility the process by which responsibility is divided between the number of bystanders present; as more people are present in an emergency, responsibility is diffused between them and each individual bystander feels increasingly less responsible than if they were alone.

direct aggression aggressive behaviour directed immediately at the target, such as hitting or shouting abuse.

direct reinforcement experience of positive consequences of aggressive behaviour (e.g., status gain among peers) that increases the probability of future aggressive acts.

disclosure reciprocity people tend to match each other's level of self-disclosure.

discounting principle the presence of a causal factor working towards an observed effect implies that other potential factors are less influential. The converse of the *augmenting principle*.

discourse analysis a family of methods for analysing talk and texts, with the goal of revealing how people make sense of their everyday worlds.

dispensability effect a reduction in group members' task-related effort because their individual contribution seems to have little impact on group performance.

displaced aggression tendency to respond to frustration with an aggressive response directed not at the original source of the frustration but at an unrelated, more easily accessible target.

display rules cultural understandings as to whether emotions should be expressed openly.

dissociation model proposes that two different processes can occur independently, and that one does not inevitably follow from the other (e.g., Devine's proposed dissociation between automatic and controlled processes in stereotyping).

distinctiveness information evidence relating to how an actor responds to different objects (or 'entities') under similar circumstances.

distraction while listening to a persuasive communication, individuals are distracted by having to perform an irrelevant activity or by experiencing sensory stimulation irrelevant to the message.

door-in-the-face technique compliance technique in which the requester begins with an extreme request that is almost always refused, then retreats to a more moderate request, which he or she had in mind all along (also known as a 'reciprocal concessions' procedure).

dual-process theories of persuasion theories of persuasion postulating two modes of information processing, systematic and non-systematic. Modes differ in the extent to which individuals engage in content-relevant thoughts and critical evaluation of the arguments contained in a message.

eco-cultural theory a theory that proposes that different forms of culture have arisen as adaptations to differing environmental challenges to survival.

ego depletion a temporary reduction of one's self-regulatory capacities due to restricted energy resources after sustained self-control efforts.

ego-defensive function when attitudes help to protect our self-esteem.

embeddedness versus autonomy characteristic of a culture in which relations with one's long-term membership groups are prioritized, rather than emotional and intellectual separateness from others.

emotional contagion the transfer of moods and emotions among people in a group.

empathic concern an emotional state consisting of emotions such as compassion, warmth and concern for another person.

empathy the experience of understanding or sharing the emotional state of another person.

encoding the way in which we translate what we see into a digestible format to be stored in the mind.

entitativity the degree to which a collection of people is perceived as being bonded together in a coherent unit.

equity theory a theory that seeks to explain relationship satisfaction in terms of perceptions of fair versus unfair distributions of resources within interpersonal relationships.

ethnocentrism the tendency to judge ingroup attributes as superior to those of the outgroup and, more generally, to judge outgroups from an ingroup perspective.

eureka effect describes the situation when the correct solution to a problem, once it is found, is immediately recognized as being correct by group members.

European Association of Social Psychology (EASP) an association formed by European researchers in 1966 to further social psychology in Europe (originally named the European Association of Experimental Social Psychology (EAESP)).

evaluation apprehension a learned response to the presence of others when performing a task, whereby the performer experiences arousal when anticipating evaluation by these others (can affect social facilitation, and also helping behaviour).

evaluative conditioning changes the liking for a stimulus by repeatedly pairing it with another more polarized positive or negative stimulus.

evolutionary psychology an approach that explains human behaviour and preferences based on their 'reproductive value'; that is, their value in producing offspring.

evolutionary social psychology is an application of evolutionary theory to social psychology.

exchange relationship refers to an interpersonal association between individuals who are concerned with what their partner gets and what they themselves receive to ensure equitable benefits.

excitation transfer theory transfer of neutral physiological arousal onto arousal resulting from frustration, thus augmenting negative affect and enhancing the strength of an aggressive response.

expectation states theory argues that status differences within a group result from different expectations that group members have about each other.

experiment a method in which the researcher deliberately introduces some change into a setting to examine the consequences of that change.

experimental confound when an independent variable incorporates two or more potentially separable components it is a confounded variable. When an independent variable is confounded, the researcher's ability to draw causal inferences is seriously compromised.

experimental group a group of participants allocated to the 'experimental' condition of the experiment.

experimental scenario the 'package' within which an experiment is presented to participants.

experimenter expectancy effect produced unintentionally by the experimenter that increases the likelihood that participants will confirm the experimenter's hypothesis.

explicit measures of attitude measures that directly ask respondents to think about and report an attitude.

extended contact hypothesis mere knowledge that an ingroup member has a close relationship with an outgroup member can improve outgroup attitudes.

external validity refers to the generalizability of research findings to settings and populations other than those involved in the research.

factorial experiment an experiment in which two or more independent variables are manipulated within the same design.

false consensus bias the assumption that other people generally share one's own personal attitudes and opinions.

field experiment a true randomized experiment conducted in a natural setting.

field theory a framework adopted by Kurt Lewin which represented the individual as an element in a larger system of social forces.

foot-in-the-door technique compliance technique in which the requester first asks for a small favour that is almost certain to be granted, then follows this up with a request for a larger, related favour.

forgiveness forgiveness is defined as a prosocial motivational change toward the offender, despite the offender's hurtful behaviour.

frustration–aggression hypothesis assumes that frustration – that is, blockage of a goal-directed activity – increases the likelihood of aggressive behaviour.

General Aggression Model (GAM) integrative framework explaining how personal and situational input variables lead to aggressive behaviour via cognitive appraisal and negative affective arousal.

geographic regions approach method for testing the heat hypothesis by comparing violence rates in cooler and hotter climates.

goal a positively valued behavioural end-state that encompasses the purposeful drive/motivation to engage in a behaviour/action/judgement.

goal dependent where an outcome is conditional upon a specific goal being in place (e.g., goal-dependent automatic stereotype activation).

group a group exists when two or more individuals define themselves as members of a group.

group commitment a psychological bond of a group member with the group and its goals including the desire to maintain group membership.

group composition specifies how certain characteristics are distributed within a group.

group emotions emotions experienced as members of social groups rather than as individuals, reflecting appraisals of events in terms of group level concerns and coping resources.

group identification the degree to which people see themselves in terms of a group membership (group-level self-definition) and the degree of value and emotional attachment to the group (group-level self-investment).

group leadership influencing, motivating or enabling (oneself and) others to contribute towards the effectiveness and viability of work groups.

group learning a generic term for several learning processes that can only occur if several people work interactively on the same task.

group performance management the sum of activities aimed at maximizing (or improving) the group-specific component of group performance.

group polarization tendency to make decisions that are more extreme than the average of group members' initial positions, in the direction already favoured by the group.

group socialization the efforts of the group to assimilate new members to existing group norms and practices.

group synchronization the sum of activities aimed at optimizing the collaborative generation, modification and integration of individual contributions in a group.

group task types group tasks are distinguished depending on whether the task is divisible between group members, whether the quality or quantity of the output is relevant, and how individual contributions are related to the group's performance.

groupthink a syndrome of poor group decision-making in which members of a cohesive ingroup strive for unanimity at the expense of a realistic appraisal of alternative courses of action.

group-to-group transfer a group learning process whereby a *particular* group's capability to perform a group task improves as a result of social interaction between its group members during repeated collective task performance.

group-to-individual transfer a group learning process whereby a group member's ability to perform a task *alone* improves as a result of social interaction between group members during repeated collective task performance.

group-to-individual-in-group transfer a group learning process whereby a group member's ability to perform a task *within groups* improves as a result of social interaction between group members during repeated collective task performance.

habituation process whereby the ability of a stimulus to elicit arousal becomes weaker with each consecutive presentation.

heat hypothesis hypothesis that aggression increases with higher temperatures.

helping behaviour actions that are intended to provide some benefit to or improve the well-being of others.

heuristic a well-used, non-optimal rule of thumb used to arrive at a judgement that is effective in many but not all cases; stereotypes are often said to function as heuristics.

heuristic processing assessing the validity of a communication through reliance on heuristics; that is, simple rules like 'statistics don't lie', 'experts can be trusted', 'consensus implies correctness', rather than through evaluation of arguments.

heuristic-systematic model (HSM) attitude change to persuasive communications is mediated by heuristic and/or systematic processing: when motivation and ability are high, systematic processing is likely; when they are low, individuals rely on heuristic cues.

hidden profile a group decision situation in which information is distributed among group members such that no individual group member can detect the best solution based on his or her own information.

hierarchy versus egalitarianism characteristic of a culture in which inequality is accepted and deference is given to one's seniors, rather than granting equality to all people.

hormones higher levels of testosterone and lower levels of cortisol have been linked to aggression, but they need to be considered in combination with environmental influences.

hostile aggression aggressive behaviour motivated by the desire to express anger and hostile feelings.

hostile attribution bias tendency to attribute hostile intentions to a person who has caused damage when it is unclear whether or not the damage was caused accidentally or on purpose.

hypothesis a prediction derived from a theory concerning the relationship between variables.

identity negotiation a process by which we establish who we are through mutual give-and-take interactions with others.

illusory correlation effect the tendency to perceive a relationship that does not actually exist, or to perceive one that does exist as stronger than it actually is; in group terms the erroneous tendency to associate one group more with one stereotypic or evaluative dimension than another.

implementation intentions 'if–then' plans that specify a behaviour that one will need to perform in order to achieve a goal, and the context in which the behaviour will occur.

implicit egotism nonconscious or automatic positive evaluation of self-associated objects.

implicit goal operation the process whereby a goal that enables people to regulate responses (e.g., to overcome stereotyping) is engaged without conscious awareness.

implicit measures measures of constructs such as attitudes that are unobtrusively assessed (e.g., by reaction time) so that participants are unaware of what is being assessed.

implicit measures of attitude measures that assess spontaneous evaluative associations with an object, without relying on a verbal report.

implicit personality theory an integrated set of ideas held by a social perceiver about how different traits tend to be organized within a person.

implicit self-esteem the positivity of a person's automatic or nonconscious evaluation of him- or herself.

impulsive helping immediate, non-deliberative form of helping that does not appear to involve a conscious decision-making process, and in which the helper does not attend to the presence of other bystanders.

independent variable the variable that an experimenter manipulates or modifies in order to examine the effect on one or more dependent variables.

independent versus interdependent self while the independent self emphasizes autonomy and individualism and defines the self via internal attributes like traits, an interdependent self stresses the connection to others and defines the self in terms of relationships with others.

indirect aggression aggression delivered behind the target person's back by damaging the target's peer relationships, e.g., through spreading rumours.

individual capability gains and losses improvements or impairments in individual group members' ability to successfully perform a task due to social interaction within the group.

individualism–collectivism individualist nations are those in which people describe themselves in ways that emphasize their autonomy from others; collectivist nations are those in which people describe themselves in ways that emphasize their links with others.

individual-to-individual transfer individual learning processes whereby a group member's ability to perform a task on their own improves as a result of repeated individual task performance.

individuating information information about a person's personal characteristics (not normally derived from a particular category membership).

informational influence influence based on accepting the information obtained from others as evidence about reality.

ingroup bias behaviours or evaluations that favour the ingroup over the outgroup; ingroup favouritism treats the ingroup more positively, outgroup derogation treats the outgroup less positively (e.g., in giving fewer rewards) or more negatively (e.g., in giving punishments).

ingroup reappraisal realization that ingroup norms, customs and lifestyles are not inherently superior to those of outgroups; this process is implicated in the generalization of positive contact effects to other outgroups.

initiation the role transition of entry into a group, often accompanied by some ritual.

injunctive norms Norms that specify what behaviour *should* be performed.

innovation see *minority influence*.

instrumental aggression aggressive behaviour performed to reach a particular goal, as a means to an end.

interaction effect a term used when the combination of two (or more) independent variables in a factorial experiment yields an effect that differs from the sum of the main effects.

intergroup aggression aggressive encounters between groups or aggression based on group membership rather than individual characteristics, such as football hooliganism.

intergroup anxiety a negative affective state experienced when anticipating future, or experiencing actual, contact with an outgroup member, stemming from the expectation of negative consequences for oneself during intergroup interactions.

internal validity refers to the validity of the inference that changes in the independent variable result in changes in the dependent variable.

Internet experiment an experiment that is accessed via the Internet; participants access the experiment via the web, receive instructions and questions on their computer screen and provide responses via their keyboard or touch screen.

interpersonal aggression aggressive behaviour between individuals rather than groups.

interpersonal cohesion cohesion based on liking of the group and its members.

intimate partner violence perpetration or threat of an act of physical violence within the context of a dating or marital relationship.

intrinsic motivation behaviour is said to be intrinsically motivated if people perform it because they enjoy it. This enjoyment is sufficient to produce the behaviour and no external reward is required. In fact, external rewards (e.g., financial contributions) are likely to reduce intrinsic motivation.

introspection the process by which one observes and examines one's internal states (mental and emotional) for behaving in a certain way.

investments the level of resources (time, emotional involvement, money, self-disclosure and so on) put into a relationship, which increases the costs of withdrawing from the relationship.

jigsaw classroom a cooperative teaching method designed to reduce prejudice in diverse classrooms.

kin selection (also known as *inclusive fitness theory*) proposes that we have evolved to favour people who are genetically related to us, and are more likely to help close relatives (kin) than strangers.

Köhler effect a motivation gain in groups which involves weaker group members working harder than they would do individually in order to avoid being responsible for a weak group performance.

laboratory experiment a study, conducted in the laboratory, in which the researcher deliberately introduces some change into a setting, while holding all other factors constant, to examine the consequences of that change.

laissez-faire leaders leaders who engage in 'non-leadership'; that is, avoid making decisions, hesitate in taking action and are often absent when needed.

leader traits relatively stable personal characteristics (e.g., personality, intelligence, motivational dispositions) which are thought to predict leader emergence and leadership effectiveness.

leaderless groups groups with no appointed leader but which display effective leadership behaviours which are infused by the group members themselves (shared leadership) and/or by agents external to the group.

leadership behaviour observable acts that are meant to influence, motivate or enable others to contribute towards the effectiveness of a work unit or organization.

leadership effectiveness the impact of leadership on the accomplishment of group and organizational objectives, on the behaviour, perceptions, attitudes, values, motivation or well-being of followers and peers, and on the accomplishments of those who lead.

leadership (in organizations) influencing, motivating or enabling others to contribute towards the effectiveness of work units and organizations.

leadership style a pattern of leadership behaviour which is repeatedly shown and evident across a variety of situations.

learned helplessness theory the proposal that depression results from learning that outcomes are not contingent on one's behaviour.

lexical decision task a cognitive measure of how quickly people classify stimuli as real words or nonsense words that enables researchers to assess if some categories of words are made more accessible as a result of an experimental manipulation/processing goal. Quicker responses to certain word categories indicate increased accessibility.

lowballing technique compliance to an initial attempt is followed by a more costly and less beneficial version of the same request.

main effect a term used to refer to the separate effects of each independent variable in a factorial experiment.

majority influence (conformity) social influence resulting from exposure to the opinions of a majority, or the majority of one's group.

manipulation check a measure of the effectiveness of the independent variable.

mastery versus harmony characteristic of a culture in which achievement is sought and esteemed, rather than harmony with nature.

media violence–aggression link hypothesis that exposure to violent media contents makes media users more aggressive.

mediating variable a variable that mediates the relation between two other variables.

mere exposure effect increase in liking for an object as a result of being repeatedly exposed to it.

meta-analysis a set of techniques for statistically integrating the results of independent studies of a given phenomenon, with a view to establishing whether the findings exhibit a pattern of relationships that is reliable across studies.

methodological individualism the assumption that collective action must be explained by showing how it results from individual decisions and behaviour; collective behaviour is seen as essentially behaviour of the individuals who form the collective.

minimal group paradigm a set of experimental procedures designed to create groups based on essentially arbitrary criteria (with no interaction within or between them, and with no knowledge of who else belongs to each group) whose members show intergroup discrimination.

minority influence (innovation) situation in which either an individual or a group in a numerical minority can influence the majority.

misattribution of arousal people mistakenly attribute part of their arousal to an external stimulus that is not the actual cause of their arousal.

mobbing aggressive behaviour involving a power differential between perpetrators and victims, i.e., directed at victims who cannot easily defend themselves, typically studied in schools and the workplace.

MODE model a model of attitude–behaviour relations in which motivation and opportunity are necessary to make a deliberative consideration of available information.

modelling learning by imitation, observing a model being rewarded or punished for his or her behaviour.

motivation losses and gains decreases or increases in group members' motivation to contribute to group task performance.

multicomponent model of attitude a model of attitude that conceptualizes attitudes as summary evaluations that have cognitive, affective and behavioural antecedents.

mutual differentiation (or *categorization approach to improving intergroup relations*) making group affiliations salient during contact to give members of the respective groups distinct but complimentary roles.

naïve scientist model a metaphor for how social information is processed that likens social perceivers to academic researchers who formulate theories and use data to test hypotheses in order to predict and control behaviour.

nation-level factor analysis an analysis across many nations of data in which the mean response for each survey item for each nation is treated as the unit of analysis.

need for cognition an individual difference variable which differentiates people according to the extent to which they enjoy thinking about arguments contained in a communication.

need for cognitive closure refers to the desire of individuals for a definite answer to a question – any answer, as opposed to uncertainty; the need reflects an individual difference variable, but can also be situationally induced.

need to belong the intrinsic motivation to affiliate with others and be socially accepted.

negative interdependence a situation in which bonds between individuals or groups are characterized by conflicts of interests, often leading to antagonism or *realistic conflict*.

negative-state-relief model this model argues that human beings have an innate drive to reduce their own negative moods; helping behaviour can elevate mood – thus in this model people help for egoistic rather than altruistic reasons.

nominal group a number of individuals who perform a task individually and work independently of each other; nominal groups are used to determine the potential performance of groups.

normative influence influence based on conforming to the positive expectations of others: people avoid behaving in ways that will lead to social punishment or disapproval.

norms belief systems about how (not) to behave, that guide behaviour but without the force of laws, and reflect group members' shared expectations about typical or desirable activities.

obedience to authority complying with orders from a person of higher social status within a defined hierarchy or chain of command.

object appraisal function when attitudes help serve as an energy-saving device.

one-dimensional perspective on attitudes a perspective that perceives positive and negative elements as stored along a single dimension.

one-shot case study a research design in which observations are made on a group after some event has occurred or some manipulation has been introduced.

operationalization the way in which a theoretical construct is turned into a measurable dependent variable or a manipulable independent variable in a particular study.

outcome dependency a motivational objective in which participants believe they will later meet a target and work together on a jointly judged task; shown to lead to less stereotypical target impressions.

outgroup bias a tendency to favour the outgroup over the ingroup in terms of evaluations or reward allocations.

outgroup homogeneity effect a tendency to see the outgroup as more homogeneous than the ingroup.

participant observation a method of observation in which the researcher studies the target group or community from within, making careful records of what he or she observes.

participants people who take part in a psychological study.

passionate love a state of intense longing for union with another individual, usually characterized by intrusive thinking and preoccupation with the partner, idealization of the other and the desire to know the other as well as the desire to be known by the other.

peer nominations method for measuring (aggressive) behaviour by asking other people (e.g., classmates) to rate the aggressiveness of an individual.

perceived behavioural control the notion that behavioural prediction is affected by whether people believe that they can perform the relevant behaviour.

perceived partner responsiveness the perception that a relationship partner is responsive to our needs.

peripheral trait a trait whose perceived presence does not significantly change the overall interpretation of a person's personality.

physical aggression behaviour that is intended to inflict physical harm on the target person.

pluralistic ignorance emergency bystanders look to others in reacting to the event; as each person fails to react, they look at non-reacting bystanders, and interpret the event as not requiring a response.

positive differentiation involves making the group positively different from a comparison outgroup on available dimensions of comparison (e.g., by means of more positive evaluations or reward allocations) (see also *ingroup bias*).

positive interdependence a situation in which there are positive bonds between individuals or groups characterized by cooperation, reciprocity and mutual benefits.

positive–negative asymmetry evidence that people show more ingroup bias when distributing positive rewards than punishment or penalties.

post-experimental enquiry a technique advocated by Orne (1962) for detecting the operation of demand characteristics. The participant is carefully interviewed after participation in an experiment, the object being to assess perceptions of the purpose of the experiment.

post-test only control group design an experimental design in which participants are randomly allocated to one of two groups; one group is exposed to the independent variable, another (the control group) is not.

post-traumatic stress disorder (PTSD) characteristic patterns of symptoms observed in survivors of traumatic experiences such as rape.

potential group performance (group potential) the performance that would have occurred if the members of a group had worked independently of each other and not as a group; a common benchmark to evaluate actual group performance.

power distance the extent to which hierarchy and deference are accepted within a nation.

prejudice an attitude or orientation towards a group (or its members) that devalues it directly *or indirectly*, often to the benefit of the self or own group.

primacy effect the tendency for earlier information to be more influential in social perception and interpretation.

priming activating one stimulus (e.g., bird) facilitates the subsequent processing of another related stimulus (e.g., wing, feather).

principle–implementation gap acceptance of racial equality in principle is accompanied by resistance to specific policies that would bring about such racial equality.

probabilistic contrast comparison of the frequency of an effect in the presence of a potential cause with its frequency in the absence of that cause.

probe reaction task a simple reaction time task that assesses residual attentional capacity, that is, the amount of attention that is left over from performing the primary task. This task does not take away attention from the primary task (it is not a resource depleting task).

production blocking a process loss typical of brainstorming tasks in face-to-face groups; since in a group only one person can speak at a time, the other group members cannot express their own ideas at the same time.

proportion of shared genes refers to the amount of genetic material shared by humans (and animals); humans have an almost identical proportion of shared genes with any randomly selected other human being.

prosocial behaviour refers to behaviour defined by society as beneficial to other people; it excludes behaviour that is motivated by professional obligations, and may be driven by more selfish (egoistic) and/or more selfless (altruistic) motivations.

prosocial personality an enduring tendency to think about the rights and welfare of others, to feel concern and empathy, and to act in a way that benefits them.

public goods game participants are allocated tokens, and can then (secretly) decide how many to keep and how many to contribute to a public pot; contributing nothing is termed *free riding*.

quasi-experiment an experiment in which participants are not randomly allocated to the different experimental conditions (typically because of factors beyond the control of the researcher).

quota sample a sample that fills certain prespecified quotas and thereby reflects certain attributes of the population (such as age and sex) that are thought to be important to the issue being researched.

random allocation (sometimes called *random assignment*) the process of allocating participants to groups (or conditions) in such a way that each participant has an equal chance of being assigned to each group.

reactance theory reactance is an aversive state caused by restriction of an individual's freedom of choice over important behavioural outcomes. Reactance is assumed to motivate the individual to re-establish the restricted freedom.

reactivity a measurement procedure is reactive if it alters the nature of what is being measured.

realistic conflict theory a theory developed by Sherif that holds that conflict and competition between groups over valued resources can create intergroup hostility and prejudice.

rebound effect where suppression attempts fail; used here to demonstrate how a suppressed stereotype returns to have an even greater impact upon one's judgements about a person from a stereotyped group.

recategorization recommends replacing salient ingroup–outgroup distinctions at a subordinate level with a common ingroup identity at a superordinate level that includes both former ingroup and outgroup members.

reciprocal altruism a theory designed to explain altruism towards strangers by proposing that helping non-kin may have evolved if the cost of helping another is offset by the likelihood of the return benefit.

referent informational influence individuals identify with a particular group and conform to a prototypical group position.

reflected appraisals inferences regarding others' appraisals of us that we gain by observing other people's reactions towards us.

relational aggression behaviour that is intended to harm the target person through damaging his or her social relationships, for example negative comments behind the person's back.

relationship commitment an individual's intent to maintain the relationship and to remain psychologically attached to it.

relationship superiority the tendency of romantically involved individuals to perceive their own relationship as better than the average relationship.

relative deprivation a resentful feeling that the self or ingroup is worse off than the other or outgroup.

reliability the degree to which a measure is free from measurement error; a measure is reliable if it yields the same result on more than one occasion or when used by different individuals.

representativeness heuristic a mental shortcut whereby instances are assigned to categories on the basis of how similar they are to the category in general.

Ringelmann effect describes the finding that in physical tasks such as weight pulling, the average performance of individual group members decreases with increasing group size.

role the behaviours expected of a person with a specific position in the group.

role transition a change in the relation between a group member and a group.

salience attention-grabbing property of objects or events depending on perceptual features such as vividness, perceiver sensitivity or some combination of the two.

sampling the process of selecting a subset of members of a population with a view to describing the population from which they are taken.

scapegoat theory a theory that holds that prejudice is due to aggression that is displaced towards members of an outgroup (scapegoats), because the group or set of circumstances that was the source of frustration is not within reach.

schema a cognitive structure or mental representation comprising pre-digested information or knowledge about objects or people from specific categories, our expectancies about objects or groups, and what defines them.

self-assessment motive striving to reach an accurate and objective understanding of the self.

self-awareness a psychological state in which one's attention is directed at the self.

self-categorization theory theory explaining how the process of categorizing oneself as a group member forms social identity and brings about various forms of both group (e.g., group polarization, majority–minority influence) and intergroup (e.g., intergroup discrimination) behaviours.

self-concept the cognitive representation of our self-knowledge consisting of a sum total of all beliefs we have about ourselves. It gives coherence and meaning to one's experience, including one's relations to other people.

self-construals a person's views and knowledge about him- or herself is shaped through an active construal process that plays out in interaction with the social environment. This process is motivated by how one would like to see oneself.

self-determination theory a motivational theory that accounts for people's reasons for self-regulation: if self-regulation is motivated by external pressure it is effortful and can lead to psychological conflict. However, if self-regulation is freely chosen it is much more efficient without being depleting.

self-disclosure verbally revealing information about oneself to another person.

self-efficacy beliefs about one's ability to carry out certain actions required to attain a specific goal (e.g., that one is capable of following a diet, or to help someone).

self-enhancement motivation to enhance the positivity of our self-conceptions, often over what would be objectively warranted. Achieved by various strategies (e.g., self-serving attributions, basking in reflected glory, positive self-presentations).

self-esteem the overall evaluation that we have of ourselves along a positive–negative dimension.

self-esteem hypothesis the prediction that ingroup bias will lead to an increase in group level self-esteem or satisfaction.

self-fulfilling prophecy when an originally false expectation leads to its own confirmation. The social perceiver's initially incorrect beliefs about a target cause that target to act in ways that objectively confirm those beliefs.

self-handicapping the tendency to engage in self-defeating behaviours in order to provide a subsequent excuse for failure and augment ability attributions in the case of success.

self-monitoring an individual difference variable measuring the extent to which people vary their behaviour across social situations (high self-monitors) versus behaving consistently (low self-monitors).

self-perception theory the theory assumes that when inner states are ambiguous, people can infer these states by observing their own behaviour.

self-presentation a range of strategies that we adopt in order to shape what others think of us.

self-reference effect the tendency to process and remember self-related information better than other information.

self-regulation the process of controlling and directing one's behaviour in order to achieve desired thoughts, feelings, and goals.

self-schemas mental structures that help us organize and guide the processing of self-related information.

self-serving attributional biases motivated distortions of attribution that function to maintain or increase self-esteem.

self-verification motivation to affirm firmly held self-beliefs, arising from a desire for stable and coherent self-views.

self-worth contingencies domains – both internal (e.g., virtue) and external (e.g., power) – on which we stake our self-worth.

sexual aggression forcing another person into sexual activities through a range of coercive strategies, such as threat or use of physical force, exploitation of the victim's inability to resist, or verbal pressure.

shared or team leadership responsibility for leadership functions, the exercise of leadership behaviour and perceptions about leadership roles are shared among group members (sometimes including agents external to the team).

similarity–attraction effect we like others who are similar to us; others who are like us.

simple random sample a sample in which each member of the population has an equal chance of being selected and in which the selection of every possible combination of the desired number of members is equally likely.

social adjustment function when attitudes help us identify with liked others.

social cognition a large topic within social psychology concerned with understanding how we think about ourselves and other people and how the processes involved impact upon our judgements and behaviour in social contexts.

social comparison a process of comparing oneself with others in order to evaluate one's own abilities and opinions.

social compensation a motivation gain in groups that occurs if stronger group members increase their effort in order to compensate for weaker members' suboptimal performance.

social competition a motivation gain in groups that occurs if the group members want to outperform each other during group tasks in which the individual contributions are identifiable.

social desirability refers to the fact that research participants are likely to want to be seen in a positive light and may therefore adjust their responses or behaviour in order to avoid being negatively evaluated.

social dominance orientation an individual difference variable that captures a desire for hierarchical group relations.

social facilitation an improvement in the performance of well-learned/easy tasks and a worsening of performance of poorly-learned/difficult tasks due to the presence of members of the same species.

social identity that part of our self-concept corresponding to group memberships, and the value and emotional significance attached to these memberships.

social influence change of attitudes, beliefs, opinions, values, and behaviour, as a result of being exposed to other individuals' attitudes, beliefs, opinions, values, and behaviour.

social loafing a motivation loss in groups that occurs when group members reduce their effort due to the fact that individual contributions to group performance are not identifiable.

social neuroscience an interdisciplinary field devoted to understanding how biological systems implement social processes and behaviour.

social perception the process of collecting and interpreting information about another person's individual characteristics.

social reality constraints evidence that the outgroup is clearly better on a certain dimension can make ingroup bias on that dimension difficult to justify.

social support a partner's responsiveness to another's needs.

socio-emotional behaviours behaviours during group interactions that are directed at interpersonal relations.

sociometer theory a theory that posits that our self-esteem functions as a signal of the degree to which we feel accepted or rejected by other people.

speaking hierarchy hierarchy within a group based on who talks most.

staffing level the degree to which the actual number of group members is similar to the ideal number of group members.

staircase model describes the pathway to terrorism as a succession of steps explaining why out of large numbers of disaffected people in a society only very few end up committing terrorist acts.

status evaluation of a role by the group in which a role is contained or defined.

steam boiler model part of Konrad Lorenz's theory of aggression, assuming that aggressive energy is produced continuously within the organism and will burst out spontaneously unless released by an external stimulus.

stereotype a cognitive structure that contains our knowledge, beliefs and expectancies about some human social group.

stereotype suppression the act of trying to prevent an activated stereotype from impacting upon one's judgements about a person from a stereotyped group.

strong reciprocity a human predisposition to cooperate with others and to punish those who defect, even when this behaviour cannot be justified in terms of self-interest, extended kinship or reciprocal altruism.

subliminal advertising advertising slogans that are presented so briefly (or faintly) that they are below the threshold of awareness.

sucker effect a motivation loss in groups that occurs when group members perceive or anticipate that other group members will lower their effort: to avoid being exploited, they reduce their effort themselves.

summation perceivers add together pieces of information about a person; when other information is strongly positive, additional mildly positive information yields a more positive impression.

superordinate goals goals that can only be achieved by two groups working together cooperatively, to mutual benefit.

survey research a research strategy that involves interviewing (or administering a questionnaire to) a sample of respondents who are selected so as to be representative of the population from which they are drawn.

systematic processing thorough, detailed processing of information (e.g., attention to the arguments contained in a persuasive communication); this kind of processing relies on ability and effort.

task behaviours behaviours during group interactions that are directed at task completion.

task cohesion cohesion based on attraction of group members to the group task.

team awareness understanding of the ongoing activities of others which provides a context for one's own activity.

terror management theory a theory that assumes that people cope with the fear of their own death by constructing worldviews that help to preserve their self-esteem.

terrorism politically motivated violence, intended to spread fear and terror among members of a society in order to influence the decision-making or behaviour of political agents.

theory a set of abstract concepts (i.e., constructs) together with propositions about how those constructs are related to one another.

theory of planned behaviour an extension to the theory of reasoned action that includes the concept of perceived behavioural control.

theory of reasoned action a model in which behaviour is predicted by behavioural intentions, which are determined by attitudes and subjective norms.

thought-listing a measure of cognitive responses; message recipients are asked to list all the thoughts that occurred to them while being exposed to a persuasive message.

time periods approach method for testing the heat hypothesis by comparing violence rates in the same region during cooler and hotter periods.

trait aggressiveness denotes stable differences between individuals in the likelihood and intensity of aggressive behaviour.

transactional leaders leaders who focus on the proper exchange of resources, who give followers something in exchange for something the leaders want.

transactive memory a system of knowledge available to group members with shared awareness of each other's expertise, strengths and weaknesses.

transformational (charismatic) leaders leaders who focus on aligning the group or organizational goals with the followers' needs and aspirations by developing an appealing vision (whereby organizational needs are placed above self-interest).

triangulation the use of multiple methods and measures to research a given issue.

true randomized experiment an experiment in which participants are allocated to the different conditions of the experiment on a random basis.

two-dimensional perspective on attitudes a perspective that perceives positive and negative elements as stored along separate dimensions.

uncertainty avoidance the extent to which a nation is averse to risk and uncertainty.

unobtrusive measures (also called *non-reactive measures*) measures that the participant is not aware of, and which therefore cannot influence his or her behaviour.

utilitarian function when attitudes help us maximize rewards and minimise costs.

validity a measure is valid to the extent that it measures precisely what it is supposed to measure.

value-expressive function when attitudes help express our values.

variable the term used to refer to the measurable representation of a construct.

violence behaviours carried out with intention to cause serious harm that involve the use or threat of physical force.

volunteerism when individuals give time and effort willingly without expecting rewards.

weapons effect finding that individuals who were previously frustrated showed more aggressive behaviour in the presence of weapons than in the presence of neutral objects.

whistle blowing a specific form of disobedience, in which people report corruption or unethical practice within an organization.

willingness to sacrifice the tendency to forego immediate self-interest to promote the well-being of the partner or the relationship.

working self-concept subset of relevant self-knowledge that is activated and guides our behaviour in a given situation.

Name Index

Aaker, J. L.   222, 498
Aarts, H.   107, 197, 367
Abakoumkin, G.   415
Abbey, A.   298
Abbott, A. S.   435
Abelson, R. P.   67, 184
Aberson, C. L.   156, 462
Aboud, F. E.   18, 372
Abrahams, D.   360
Abrams, D.   131, 382, 462, 473
Abramson, L. Y.   70–1, 76, 84
Ackerman, P.   314–15
Adair, W. L.   518
Adams, J. S.   365
Aderka, I. M.   140
Adler, K. K.   159
Adorno, T. W.   443–4
Afifi, T. D.   376
Agnew, C. R.   369, 382
Aguirre-Rodriguez, A.   222
Aharpour, S.   517
Ahearne, M.   399
Aime, F.   257
Ainsworth, M. D. S.   375
Ajzen, I.   19, 175, 191–2, 195, 196
Akhtar, S.   156
Albarracín, D.   177, 196
Alberts, H. J. E. M.   162
Aldag, R. J.   263, 264
Alford, C. F.   269
Alicke, M. D.   83, 84, 127
Allan, S.   130
Allen, J. L.   315–16
Allen, V. L.   249, 250
Allik, J.   138
Alloy, L. B.   72
Allport, Floyd Henry   7, 13, 20, 23,
   235–6, 493
   biography   12
Allport, Gordon W.   6–7, 8, 18, 173, 235,
   443, 449, 472–4, 475, 476, 480
   biography   472
Alonso-Arbiol, I.   255
Altemeyer, B.   444, 445
Altis, N. A.   219

Altman, I.   362, 373
Alvaro, E. M.   252, 256
Alwin, D. F.   14
Amabile, T. M.   77–8, 128–9
Amato, P. R.   376
Ambady, N.   60
Amichai-Hamburger, Y.   482
Amir, Y.   474, 492
Amodio, D. M.   22, 162, 177, 452, 453
Ananiadou, K.   298
Anastasio, P. A.   478
Andersen, S. M.   130
Anderson, Craig A.   277, 278, 285–6,
   289–90, 292
   biography   285
Anderson, K. B.   287
Anderson, N. H.   59
Andreoli. V.A.   473
Andrews, F. M.   49
Anthony, T.   263
Arai, M.   248
Archer, J.   276, 280–1, 288, 297
Arends-Toth, J.   521
Arendt, H.   264
Argyle, M.   317
Ariely, D.   373, 374
Armitage, C. J.   196
Armor, D. A.   127, 147
Arndt, J.   155
Arnold, K.   178, 181
Arnold, M. B.   76
Aron, A.   130–1, 364, 365, 370–1, 482
Aron, A. P.   364
Aron, E. N.   130, 370, 482
Aronson, E.   36, 45, 168, 218, 219, 224,
   388, 474, 475
Aronson, V.   360
Ascani, K.   246
Asch, Solomon E.   7, 8, 57–8, 59, 60,
   88–9, 90, 247–50, 270, 492, 499,
   511, 512
   biography   247
Atkins, C. J.   350
Auerhahn, K.   288
Aufderheide, B.   478

Averill, J. R.   294
Avolio, B. J.   431, 434
Ayduk, O.   166
Aylor, B.   362

Bach, P. J.   261
Bachman, B. A.   478
Back, K.   16, 360–2
Back, M. D.   362
Bacon, P. L.   143
Bailey, J. A.   298
Bakeman, R.   48
Baker, S. M.   252
Baker. W. E.   520
Baldwin, M. W.   130, 176–7
Bales, Robert F.   48, 381, 393, 394, 398
   biography   393
Balluerka, N.   355
Banaji, M. R.   44, 49, 99, 115, 119, 135,
   144, 149, 187, 189, 190, 468
Bandura, A.   160, 196, 268, 284, 294
Banfield, J. F.   144, 456
Banks, C.   240
Banse, R.   113
Barbee, A. P.   359
Barber, J. P.   73
Barch, D. M.   162
Barclay, L. C.   158
Bargh, John A.   5, 6, 7, 50, 90, 98, 99,
   106–7, 110, 112, 115, 120, 133, 149,
   197–8
   biography   107
Barlow, F. K.   481
Barndollar, K.   197
Barnes, P. J.   322
Barnett, O. W.   288
Baron, R.   237
Baron, R. A.   30–1, 275
Baron, R. M.   40, 41, 89
Baron, R. S.   237, 381–2
Baron, S. H.   240
Barry, C. T.   159
Barsade, S. G.   395, 398
Bartholomew, K.   354
Bartholow, B. D.   277, 292

Bartlett, F. C.   20
Barton, R.   73
Bass, B. M.   426, 429, 430, 431
Bassett, R.   246
Bassili, J. N.   190
Bates, J. E.   287
Batson, C. Daniel   32–3, 313–15, 324, 325, 327, 339
  biography   313
Batts, V.   113
Baum, A.   350
Baum, E. S.   71
Baumann, M. R.   414, 421
Baumann, N.   164
Baumeister, Roy F.   138, 147–8, 150, 155, 156, 157, 158–9, 160, 161, 162, 163, 164–5, 305, 352, 382, 454, 466
  biography   162
Baumrind, D.   268
Baxter, L. A.   373
Bazarova, N. N.   258
Beach, S. R.   362–3
Beaman, A. L.   246, 322
Becker, E.   149, 155
Becker, J. C.   470–1, 483
Becquart, E.   449
Beer, J. S.   127, 144
Beggan, J. K.   149
Beilock, S. L.   165
Belk, R. W.   222
Belknap, J.   297
Bell, D. W.   180
Bell, S. M.   375
Bellah, C. G.   367
Bellavia, G.   363
Bem, D. J.   128, 168, 176, 227
Ben-David, Y.   341
Ben-Ze'ev, A.   59
Bendersky, C.   401
Benet-Martínez, V. L.   143, 498, 522, 524–5
Benson, P. J.   359
Bentall, R. P.   72
Bente, G.   60
Berent, M. K.   215, 254
Berger, A.   294
Berger, C. R.   363
Berger, J.   400
Berkman, L. F.   349, 350
Berkowitz, Leonard   270, 281, 282–3
  biography   282
Bermeitinger, C.   219
Berntson, G. G.   22, 177, 179

Berridge, K.   149
Berry, A.   137
Berry, D. S.   59
Berry, John W.   478, 500, 521, 522, 523, 524, 525
  biography   522
Berscheid, Ellen S.   349, 357, 358, 360, 362, 363, 365
  biography   357
Bessière, K.   373
Bettencourt, B. A.   288, 476–7
Betz, A. L.   175
Betzig, L.   366
Bevan, S.   31
Bickman, L.   326
Bieneck, S.   295, 298, 306
Bierhoff, H. W.   312, 323
Bierman, K. L.   373
Biesanz, J. C.   31
Billig, M.   445
Billig, M. G.   3–4, 455, 457–8, 515
Binet, A.   12
Birch, K.   314–15
Birchmeier, Z.   419
Birnbaum, M. H.   44
Biro, S.   61
Birring, S. S.   280–1
Birum, I.   448
Bishop, G. D.   258
Bizer, G.   184
Björkqvist, K.   276
Black, S. L.   31
Blackhart, G. C.   155
Blackwood, N. J.   85
Blair, I. V.   110, 115, 119
Blakemore, S. J.   453
Blaney, P. H.   132, 160
Blank, A.   247
Blankenship, K. L.   180
Blanton, H.   130
Blascovich, J.   138
Blass, T.   265, 268, 270
Blau, P. M.   9
Bless, H.   95
Blessing, T. H.   432
Bobocel, D. R.   445
Bocchiaro, P.   269
Boden, J. M.   158
Bodenhausen, G. V.   4, 90, 96, 97, 99, 110, 115, 118, 127, 159, 451
Boettcher, F.   466
Bohn, C.   140

Bohner, G.   193, 209, 470–1
Bolger, N.   40
Bolsin, S. N.   270
Bonacci, A. M.   159
Bonanno, G. A.   156
Boncimino, M.   131
Bond, C. F.   237
Bond, M. H.   45, 492, 506
Bond, R.   249, 250, 511–12
Bond, R. N.   135
Boneva, B.   373
Boninger, D. S.   215, 254
Bonner, B. L.   414
Bono, J. E.   427
Bornstein, M. H.   375
Bornstein, R. F.   362
Borofsky, G. L.   332
Bos, M. W.   127
Bosch, J. D.   287
Bosnjak, M.   222
Bosson, J. K.   157, 167
Botvinick, M. M.   162
Boudreau, L. A.   89
Boulton, M. J.   299
Bourhis, R. Y.   459
Bourke, J.   268
Bower, G. H.   84
Bower, J. E.   154
Bowers, D. G.   428
Bowlby, John   129, 353, 375, 382
  biography   354
Boyd, R.   337
Bradford, D. L.   434
Brandstätter, V.   197
Brandt, M. J.   468
Branigan, C.   21
Branje, S. J. T.   363, 372
Branscombe, N. R.   27, 131, 465, 470
Brass, M.   145
Brauer, M.   260
Braver, T. S.   162
Bray, R. M.   473
Brédart, S.   449
Brehm, J. W.   226, 228
Brekke, N.   115
Brennan, K. A.   354, 355
Brett, J. M.   518
Brewer, M. B.   36, 41, 96, 97, 101, 110, 459, 460, 466, 470, 476–7
Briceland, L.   270
Brief, A. P.   270

Brief, D. E.   265
Briñol, P.   177, 216, 254
Brock, T. C.   203, 204, 205, 206
Brockett, D. R.   129
Brockner, J.   516–17
Brodbeck, F. C.   426
Brodbeck, Felix C.   257, 419, 422, 423–4, 425, 426
Brotzman, E.   270
Brounstein, P. J.   364
Brown, Christy   97
Brown, J. D.   73, 84, 127, 136, 143, 146, 246
Brown, K. W.   166
Brown, L. L.   365
Brown, R.   81, 110, 114, 132, 143, 146, 147, 302, 444, 452, 459, 463, 473, 476, 478, 481, 517
Browning, C. R   270
Bruder, M.   462
Brunell, A. B.   157
Bruner, J. S.   59, 181
Bruyneel, S.   162
Bryant, J.   283
Buck, P. O.   298
Buckley, T.   314–15
Buddie, A. M.   268
Buhrmester, D.   373, 375
Buhrmester, M.   44
Buhrmester, M. D.   153
Bukowski, M.   110
Bunderson, J. S.   435
Bundy, R. P.   3–4, 455, 457–8, 515
Burger, J. M.   246–7, 268
Burgess, M.   149
Burks, V. S.   287
Burnham, D. H.   432
Burns, J. M.   430
Burnstein, E.   21, 258, 260
Burroughs, J. E.   155
Burrowes, N.   259
Burrows, L.   5, 50, 106, 107
Busath, G. L.   292–3
Bushman, B. J.   138, 156, 159, 277, 288, 290, 292, 293, 305
Buss, A. H.   277, 278, 287, 452
Buss, D. M.   21, 156, 357, 509
Buswell, B. N.   143
Butera, F.   256
Butler, J. L.   150
Buunk, B. P.   18, 130, 147, 244, 366, 369, 422, 521
Byrne, D.   363, 464

Cacioppo, John   22, 39, 51, 177, 178, 179, 235, 246, 252, 349
    biography   179
Cai, H.   143, 151
Cairns, E.   302, 482
Cairns, K. J.   148
Calabrese, R.   363
Call, V. R. A.   333
Callero, P. L.   333
Calvert-Boyanowsky, J.   75
Camerer, C. F.   339
Cameron, J.   128
Cameron, L.   482
Campbell, A.   302
Campbell, C.   331
Campbell, Donald T.   36, 38–9, 41, 48, 49, 50, 240, 383, 454
    biography   36
Campbell, J.   73, 149, 150, 243, 420
Campbell, J. D.   156
Campbell, W. K.   148, 150, 151, 158
Canary, D. J.   373
Cann, A.   246
Cannon, W. B.   73
Capozza, D.   517
Caprariello, P. A.   362
Carey, G.   280
Carlsmith, J. M.   36, 177, 226–7
Carlson, M.   281, 282, 315
Carnot, C. G.   215, 254
Carpenter, M.   61
Carr, T. H.   165
Carré, J. M.   60
Carrell, S. E.   130
Carrick, R.   107, 187
Carrillo, M.   244
Carter, C. S.   162
Cartwright, D.   14, 21
Carvallo, M.   149
Carver, C. S.   120, 128, 160–1
Casey, R. J.   356
Cassidy, C.   326, 328, 329
Castano, E.   461
Catanese, K. R.   161
Cate, R. M.   366
Chaiken, Shelly   148, 204, 207, 208–9, 210–11, 214, 215
    biography   207
Chance, Z.   374
Chang, K.   151
Chanowitz, B.   247
Chaplin, W.   73
Chartrand, T. L.   50, 107, 149

Chatard, A.   165
Chatzisarantis, N. L. D.   162
Cheever, J.   134–5
Chen, J. M.   128
Chen, M.   5, 50, 106, 107
Chen, S.   130, 142–3, 207, 504, 506
Chen, X.   252, 256
Chen, X.-P.   517
Chen, Y.-R.   516–17
Cheng, P. W.   68
Chernyshenko, O. S.   421
Cherry, F. E.   330, 332
Chertkoff, J. M.   341
Chhokar, J. S.   426
Chiao, J. Y.   144
Childs, A.   115
Chiles, C.   254
Chiodo, L. M.   156
Chiu, C.-Y.   70, 143
Choi, H.   224
Choi, H.-S.   388
Choi, I.   80, 142, 500, 501, 502
Choi, Y.   142
Christ, O.   474, 481, 482
Christensen, C.   435
Christy, C. A.   331
Chuang, Y. C.   215, 254
Chung, C. K.   128
Cialdini, R. B.   18, 150, 238, 240, 242, 243, 244, 245–6, 248, 250, 315–16
Cihangir, S.   28, 466
Cini, M. A.   389
Clark, C. L.   354, 355
Clark, M. S.   325, 371, 375
Clark, R. D., III.   252, 312, 325
Claus, J.   219–21
Clauss, A.   416
Claypool, H. M.   212
Clifford, M. M.   356
Clinton, A. M.   298
Clore, G. L.   473, 483
Coan, J. A.   351
Coch, L.   15
Cocking, C.   342, 343
Cohen, A. R.   434
Cohen, B. P.   401
Cohen, D.   517–18
Cohen, E.   473
Cohen, E. G.   473
Cohen, G.   131
Cohen, G. L.   134
Cohen, J. D.   162
Cohen, L. E.   289

Cohen, L. H.   137
Cohen, M. A.   304
Cohen, R. L.   14
Cohen, S.   350
Coie, J. D.   305
Colbert, A. E.   427
Cole, C. M.   246
Coleman, K.   295
Collins, A.   318
Collins, B. E.   265
Collins, M. E.   472, 473, 474
Collins, N. L.   350, 373
Collins, W. A.   375
Comblain, C.   132
Conger, J. A.   430, 431
Conner, M.   196
Conolley, E. S.   248
Converse, P.   14
Converse, P. D.   162, 164
Conway, M. A.   131–2
Cook, K. E.   136
Cook, S. W.   473, 474
Cook, T. D.   38–9, 41
Cooley, C. H.   129
Coon, H. M.   143, 504
Cooper, C. L.   299–300
Cooper, G.   221
Cooper, H. M.   19, 45, 288
Cooper, J.   177, 221, 227, 237, 261, 262
Cooper, J. B.   50
Copper, C.   398
Corcoran, D. M.   325
Corman, M. D.   289
Corneille, O.   247, 449
Cornelis, I.   300
Cornelissen, P. L.   359
Cornell, D. P.   137
Correll, J.   100, 115, 138, 452
Cosmides, L.   138
Costa, P. T., Jr.   428
Coté, S.   398
Cottrell, C. A.   470
Cottrell, N. B.   236–7
Covington, M. V.   128
Cowie, H.   298
Coyne, J. C.   350
Coyne, S. M.   276, 288, 373
Craig, W.   298
Craiger, J. P.   334
Craik, F. I. M.   144
Crandall, C. S.   452
Crane, M.   483
Crano, W. D.   252, 256

Crawford, M. T.   384
Creswell, J. D.   154
Crewe, I.   263
Crick, N. R.   276
Croak, M. R.   476–7
Crocker, J.   137, 139–40, 156, 157, 482
Cross, D.   298
Cross, S. E.   142, 143
Crowley, M.   332
Crowther, S.   329
Crump, M. J. C.   44
Crutchfield, R. S.   248
Cruz, M. G.   435
Cuddy, A. J. C.   470
Culbertson, K. A.   298
Culhane, S. E.   118
Cullen, F. T.   297
Cummins, D. D.   248
Cunningham, J. A.   373
Cunningham, M. R.   246, 359
Cunningham, W. A.   190
Custers, R.   107, 197
Cutrona, C. E.   350
Czellar, S.   189

D'Argembeau, A.   132
Dabbs, J. M.   399
Dahlberg, L. L.   295
Dainton, M.   362
Dalrymple, S.   270
Dambrun, M.   447
Dana, E. R.   160
Darley, John M.   32–3, 267, 317–22, 323,
      324, 325, 327, 328, 330, 336
   biography   319
Das, E. H.   224, 292–3
David, B.   257
Davidov, M.   375
Davidson, A. R.   192
Davidson, B.   257, 261, 394
Davidson, R. J.   351
Davis, D.   376
Davis, J. H.   259
Davis, K. E.   17, 62, 63, 297
Davis, M. H.   481
Dawkins, R.   336, 337, 453
Day, H. R.   474
De Clercq, B.   300
De Dreu, C. K. W.   252–3, 420
De Hoog, N.   224
de Lemus, S.   110
De Longis, A.   350
De Vries, N. K.   162, 252–3, 257

De Wit, F.   50
De Wolff, M. S.   375
Deaux, K.   143
Dechesne, M.   155
DeChurch, L. A.   395
Deci, E. L.   128, 137, 157, 166, 228
Dehle, C.   298
Deichmann, A. K.   146
Dekel, S.   156
Delgado, M. R.   60
Demir, M.   372
DeNeve, K. M.   278
Deng, C.   143
Denissen, J.   363
Dennis, A. R.   418
Denson, T. F.   277, 302
DePaulo, B. M.   129
Deppe, R. K.   152
Derlega, V. J.   312–13
DeRosa, D. M.   418
Deschamps, J.-C.   478
Deshon, R. P.   162, 164, 258, 422
Deutsch, M.   15–16, 209, 243–4, 250,
      260–1, 394, 472, 473, 474
Deutsch, R.   195, 198
Devine, Patricia G.   5, 21, 96, 98, 99, 110,
      113–14, 118, 162, 452, 481
   biography   98
Devos, T.   135
DeWall, C. N.   155
Dewitte, S.   162, 164
Diaz-Loving, R.   464
Dickel, N.   193
Diehl, M.   227, 228, 414, 415
Diener, E.   301, 349, 504
Dierselhuis, J.   385–6
Dijker, A. J. M.   468–9
Dijksterhuis, A.   105, 107, 108, 110, 120,
      127, 138, 197, 216
Dill, K. E.   285, 286, 287
DiMaggio, P.   143
Dindia, K.   373
Dion, K.   175, 357
Dirks, K. T.   425
Dishion, T. J.   372
Dixon, J.   46, 47, 467, 483
Dodge, K. A.   287, 305
Dohmen, T. J.   164
Doise, W.   261
Dolan, R. J.   60, 356
Dolderman, D.   363
Dollard, J.   281
Domittner, G.   31

Doob, L. W.   281
Dooley, J. J.   298
Doosje, B.   27, 470
Doran, L. I.   270
Dorfman, P. W.   426, 512
Dorr, N.   278
Doucet, N.   326
Dovidio, J. F.   110, 175, 193, 312, 315, 316,
        317, 325, 326, 341, 462, 465, 467, 477,
        478, 482, 484–5
Downey, G.   135
Downing, L. L.   301
Downs, A. C.   356
Downs, D. L.   137, 454
Downs, J. S.   149
Dozier, J. B.   269
Dratel, J. L.   270
Driscoll, D. M.   96
Driskell, J. E.   263, 401
Druen, P. B.   359
Drury, J.   342–4
Dryer, D. C.   363
Du Plessis, I.   448
Duarte, S.   447
Duck, S.   373
Duckitt, J.   447–8
Duffy, S. M.   364, 500
Dugatkin, L. A.   337
Dukerich, J. M.   270
Dunbar, R. I. M.   59, 453
Duncan, B. D.   314–15
Duncan, B. L.   99, 100
Duncan, L. A.   461
Dunn, E. W.   127
Dunn, J.   372
Dunning, D.   127, 134, 148
Dunton, B. C.   119, 187, 216
Duran, A.   464
Durham-Fowler, J. A.   71
Durrheim, K.   46, 47, 483
Dutton, D. G.   326, 364
Dutton, K. A.   136
Duval, S.   159–60
Duval, T. S.   159, 160
Dweck, C. S.   69–70
Dworkin, T. M.   269
Dziurawiec, S.   353

Eagly, Alice   9, 45, 173, 177, 185, 190,
        193, 204, 207, 208, 209, 215, 260, 262,
        288, 332
    biography   173
Earing, B.   248

Earleywine, M.   281
Easterlin, R. A.   349
Eastwick, P. W.   360, 362, 373, 374
Eaton, A. A.   184, 192
Eaton, J.   159
Eberhardt, J. S.   22
Edwards, D.   47, 88
Egloff, B.   362
Ehrenberg, K.   113
Ehrlinger, J.   127
Eichstaedt, J.   159
Eidelson, R.   391
Eisenberger, N. I.   352, 391–2
Eisenberger, R.   128
Eisenstadt, D.   159
Ekman, P.   492
Elfenbein, H. A.   403
Elizur, Y.   355
Elkes, R.   246
Ellemers, Naomi   27, 50, 399, 463, 464,
        465–6
    biography   465
Eller, A.   482
Elliot, A. J.   150
Ellis, H.   353
Ellison, N. B.   374
Ellsworth, P. C.   36
Elms, A. C.   268
Elsbach, K. D.   36
Engels, R. C. M. E.   372, 373
Englich, B.   103–4
English, T.   142–3, 504, 506
Ensari, N.   476
Enzle, M. E.   149
Epley, N.   105, 146–7
Epstein, S.   138
Epstude, K.   130
Erdmann, G.   75
Erez, M.   425
Eron, L. D.   277, 292
Ervin, C. R.   363
Eskenazi, J.   219
Esser, J. K.   263
Esses, V. M.   175, 178, 180, 181, 190,
        462, 470
Evans, D.   326, 327–8
Exum, M. L.   288

Fabrigar, L. R.   179
Fahy, R. F.   343
Fairfield, M.   150
Falk, C. F.   515
Falomir-Pichastor, J. M.   256

Falvo, R.   517
Fan, E.   263
Fan, R. M.-T.   143
Fantz, R. L.   89
Farjoun, M.   263
Farnham, S. D.   138
Farquharson, J.   386
Farrell, D.   382
Faulkner, J.   461
Faulmüller, N.   419
Fazio, Russell H.   119, 128, 184, 185,
        187–8, 189, 190, 192–3, 195, 198, 215,
        216, 217, 227, 452
    biography   188
Feeney, B. C.   350, 375
Feeney, J. A.   355
Fehr, B.   73
Fehr, E.   336, 338, 339
Feigenbaum, R.   84
Feinstein, J. A.   213
Fejfar, M. C.   165
Felber, J.   294
Feldman Barrett, L.   375
Feldman, S. I.   135
Felson, M.   289
Fennis, B. M.   222, 246, 247
Ferguson, C. J.   292
Fernyhough, C.   72
Festinger, Leon   16, 19, 47, 130, 177,
        205–6, 225, 226–7, 243, 250, 260–1,
        360–2, 382, 388, 398
    biography   16
Fhanér, G.   225
Fiedler, K.   95, 451
Field, S. C.   96
Fincham, F. D.   367
Fine, G. A.   36
Finkel, E. J.   360, 362, 367, 368, 373, 374
Finkelstein, M. A.   334–5
Finkenauer, Catrin   372, 373, 375, 376
Finlay, K.   481, 483
Fiore, S. M.   395
Fireman, B.   269
Fischer, A. H.   248, 470, 517
Fischer, P.   292, 322
Fish, D.   81
Fishbein, M.   19, 175, 191–2, 195
    biography   195
Fisher, B. S.   297
Fisher, H. E.   365
Fisher, J. D.   340
Fisher, K.   447, 448
Fiske, D. W.   36

Fiske, Susan T.   51, 65, 67, 81, 82, 87, 89, 90, 95, 96, 97, 100, 101, 104, 105, 110–11, 112, 113, 119, 442, 452, 468, 470
  biography   112
Fitzsimons, G. M.   369
Flament, C.   3–4, 455, 457–8, 515
Flanagan, M.   278
Flatley, J.   297
Fletcher, G. J.   375
Fletcher, J. F.   190
Flores, N. M.   465
Florian, V.   155
Flowers, M. L.   263
Floyd, K.   373
Fode, K. L.   18
Folger, R.   473
Fong, G. T.   148
Fontaine, J.   506
Forgas, J. P.   84
Försterling, F.   61, 65
Forsyth, D. R.   238
Foster, C. A.   369
Foster-Fishman, P. G.   420, 435
Foster, J. D.   156
Fraley, R. C.   355
Frank, R. H.   60
Franklin, J.   71
Frankowski, R.   287
Franz, T. M.   435
Fraser, C.   131
Fraser, S. C.   246, 267
Freedman, J. L.   246, 267
Freeman, J. B.   60
Freese, L.   401
Freifeld, T. R.   334
French, J. R. P.   15
Frenkel-Brunswik, E.   443–4
Freud, S.   281
Frey, B. S.   341, 342
Frey, D.   148, 257, 322, 422, 423–4
Frick, P. J.   159
Frieze, I. H.   297, 356
Frijda, N. H.   469
Frith, C. D.   356, 453
Frith, U.   356, 453
Fritsche, I.   298
Fritzsche, B. A.   334–5
Frost, J. H.   374
Fujita, K.   161
Fuller, S. R.   263, 264
Fultz, J.   315–16
Funder, D. C.   85

Furman, W.   373
Furnham, A. F.   67

Gächter, S.   336, 338
Gaertner, L.   84, 151, 154, 454, 455, 459, 505
Gaertner, S. L.   60, 312, 325, 326, 477, 478
Gagné, M.   166
Gagnon, A.   459
Gaillard, A. W. K.   422
Galanter, E.   160
Galinsky, A. D.   483
Gallup, G. G.   144
Gamson, W. A.   269
Gangestad, S. W.   359
Gangi, C. E.   145
Gansberg, M.   318
Garcia-Marques, T.   212
Garcia, S. M.   328
Gardner, W. L.   179
Garolera, J.   498
Gaunt, R.   79, 80
Gawronski, B.   79, 113, 452
Geen, R. G.   293
Gelfand, M. J.   506–7
Gentile, D. A.   293
Gentile, J. R.   293
George, J. M.   395
Gerard, H. B.   209, 243–4, 248, 250, 260, 261, 394
Gergen, K. J.   17–18, 45, 46, 168
Gerhardt, M. W.   427
Gerin, W.   350–1
Geyer, A. L.   250
Geyskens, K.   162
Giancola, P. R.   277, 281, 288–9
Gibbons, F. X.   18, 130, 160, 244
Gibson, D. C.   218
Gibson, J. J.   89
Gibson, S.   267
Giesler, R. B.   153, 154, 244
Gifford, R. K.   450
Gigone, D.   420
Gilbert, Daniel   76, 78–9, 80, 83, 86, 90, 154, 244
  biography   76
Gilbert, P.   130
Gillath, O.   355
Gilovich, T.   103, 105
Gintis, H.   339
Glass, D. C.   237
Glazer, M. P.   269
Glazer, P. M.   269

Glick, P.   442, 468, 470–1
Gliner, M. D.   260
Glover, G. H.   81
Goethals, G. R.   261
Goffman, E.   167
Goldie, J.   270
Goldman, B. M.   137
Goldman, R.   39
Goldstein, A. P.   300
Goldstein, N. J.   238, 247, 248, 250
Gollwitzer, P. M.   109, 150, 197
Gonzales, M. H.   36
Gonzalez, C. M.   79
González, R.   478
Goodhead, G.   403
Gordijn, E.   252, 257, 469
Gordon, A. K.   268
Gordon, L. J.   152
Gosling, S. D.   44
Goto, S. G.   140, 504
Gottlieb, A.   323
Gould, R. J.   364
Govers, P. C. M.   222
Govorun, O.   127, 143
Grafeman, S. J.   159
Graham, K.   330
Grammer, K.   359
Grannemann, B. D.   158
Grant, A. M.   257
Graves, J.   412
Graves, N.   270
Green, J. D.   148
Greenberg, J.   147, 148, 155, 159, 277, 402, 461
Greenberg, K. J.   270
Greene, C. N.   428
Greene, D.   128, 147, 228, 229
Greenland, K.   478, 481
Greenlees, I. A.   361
Greenwald, Anthony   32, 44, 49, 115, 129, 135, 138, 149, 187, 188, 189, 190, 203, 204, 205, 207, 217
  biography   205
Greer, L. L.   401
Gregg, A. P.   148, 157, 159
Gregg, P. B.   482–3
Gregson, M.   78
Greitemeyer, T.   292, 305, 322, 421–2, 424, 425
Grice, H. P.   88
Griffin, D. W.   363, 369
Griffin, R. S.   298
Griskevicius, V.   238

Groenewoud, J. T.   478
Groom, R. W.   290
Gross, A. M.   298
Grotpeter, J. K.   276
Grouneva, L.   421
Grove, T.   260
Groves, R. M.   33
Grube, J. A.   333
Gruenewald, T. L.   154
Grusec, J. E.   375
Grzelak, J.   312–13
Gudykunst, W. B.   509
Guerin, B.   237
Guerra, N. G.   285
Guerreschi, M.   61
Guimond, S.   447
Gupta, V.   426, 512
Gureckis, T. M.   44
Gurtman, M. B.   99, 465
Gutsell, J. N.   162

Haag, V.   257
Haaland, G. A.   206
Haan, B.   373
Hackman, J. R.   411–12
Haddock, Geoffrey   173, 174, 175, 176,
    178–9, 184, 185, 187, 189–90
Hagger, M. S.   162
Haines, H.   12
Halabi, S.   341
Halevy, N.   391
Hall, L.   127
Hall, P. A.   197
Ham, J.   79–80
Hamilton, D. L.   21, 58, 384, 449, 450–1
Hamilton, V. L.   89, 267, 268
Hamilton, W. D.   336–7
Han, H. A.   189
Hancock, J. T.   374
Hane, M.   225
Haney, C.   240–1, 492
Hanges, P. J.   426, 512
Hankin, N. L.   84
Hannon, P. A.   367
Hantula, D. A.   418
Harari, H.   246, 330
Harari, O.   330
Hardee, B. B.   113
Hardin, C. D.   99
Hardy, R.   376
Harker, L.   349–50
Harkins, S.   413–14
Harlow, T.   137

Harmon-Jones, C.   177
Harmon-Jones, E.   162, 177
Harpaz-Gorodeisky, G.   341
Harris, D. A.   298
Harris, L.T.   51, 65
Harris, V. A.   62–3, 76, 88
Hart, C. M.   157, 390
Hart, H.   246
Hartup, W. W.   372
Harvey, R. D.   131
Harwood, J.   481
Harzing, A. W.   497
Haslam, S. A.   29, 35, 50, 241, 263, 268,
    270, 402, 450, 451, 452, 465, 467
Hass, R. G.   159
Hassebrauck, M.   240
Hastie, R.   259, 420, 421
Hatfield, E.   365
Haugtvedt, C. P.   184, 213, 215
Hause, K. S.   373
Hautman, L.   300
Havermans, R. C.   216
Hawi, D.   483
Hawker, D. S. J.   299
Hayes, A. F.   134
Hays, N. A.   401
Hazan, C.   129, 353, 354
Hazlett, S.   150
Healy, M.   156, 462
Heatherton, T. F.   144, 162, 163–4, 165,
    456
Hechter, M.   9
Hedges, L. V.   19, 45
Heerdink, M. W.   248
Heffernan, M.   270
Hehman, E.   60
Heider, Fritz   16–17, 61–2, 85, 86, 89, 90
    biography   62
Hein, G.   339–40
Heine, S. J.   84, 143, 151, 494–5, 505, 515
Heingartner, A.   236
Heinitz, K.   433
Helmreich, R. L.   143
Henchy, T.   237
Henderlong, J.   128
Hendrick, S. S.   373
Hendriks, M.   107
Hennessy, D. A.   306
Hennigan, K.   302
Henningsen, D. D.   435
Henri, V.   12
Henrich, J.   494–5
Henry, R. A.   422

Henton, J. M.   366
Henwood, K. L.   35
Heppner, W. L.   137
Herek, G. M.   182, 263
Herlihy, J. M.   474
Herman, C. P.   163
Herman, E. M.   236
Hermsen, S.   110
Hernandez, A. C. R.   332
Herrera, V. M.   298
Hersh, S. M.   241
Herskovits, M.   521
Hertel, G.   416, 417, 419, 422, 425
Hesson-McInnis, M.   86
Hetherington, E. M.   375
Hewes, D. E.   482–3
Hewstone, Miles   49, 65, 92, 131, 147,
    185, 215, 252–3, 254, 255–6, 257, 302,
    462, 463, 474, 476, 478, 481, 482
Higgins E.T.   98, 133–4, 135, 150, 159,
    165, 177
Higgins, R. L.   150
Hill, G. J.   364
Hilton, D. J.   62, 65, 67, 76, 78, 86, 87, 88
Hilton, J. L.   189, 452
Hinde, R. A.   372
Hinduja, S.   299
Hinkle, S.   459
Hinsz, V. B.   259
Hirt, E. R.   152–3
Hixon, J. G.   153, 154
Hodges, B. H.   250
Hodgkins, S.   197
Hodson, G.   462, 470
Hoeksema-Van Orden, C. Y. D.   422
Hoel, H.   299–300
Hoffman, E. L.   240
Hofling, C. K.   270
Hofstede, Geert   493, 494–6, 497–9, 500,
    503, 504, 506, 511, 521
    biography   494
Hogarth, R. M.   104
Hogg, M. A.   131, 256, 257, 261, 326,
    382, 385–6, 397, 462, 464, 473,
    478, 479–80
Holland, R. W.   107, 193, 194, 215
Hollander, E. P.   395
Hollway, W.   48
Holmes, J. G.   130, 363, 369, 375
Holt, R.   259
Holzberg, A. D.   148
Homan, A. C.   248
Homans, G. C.   9

Hong, Y.-Y. 70, 143
Hood, W. R. 240, 454
Hope, L. 259
Hope, R. O. 474
Hopkins, N. 326
Horcajo, J. 254
Hornsey, M. J. 247, 269, 478, 479–80
Hornstein, H. A. 325
Horowitz, L. M. 363
Horton, R. S. 363
Horvath, S. 156–7, 159
Horwitz, I. B. 513
Horwitz, M. 457
Horwitz, S. K. 513
Hosch, H. M. 118
Hosey, K. 246
Hoshino-Browne, E. 138
Houben, K. 216
House, P. 147
House, Robert J. 426, 429–30, 432, 512
    biography 430
Houston, D. A. 184, 215
Hovland, Carl Iver 14–15, 21, 203, 205
    biography 15
Howard, A. 193
Howard, E. 373
Howard, J. A. 333
Howard, M. L. 463
Hoyle, R. H. 165
Huang, X. 313
Huart, J. 449
Hubbell, A. P. 421
Huesmann, L. Rowell 277, 284–5,
    290–2, 294
    biography 285
Hüffmeier, J. 417, 422
Hull, J. G. 165
Hundley, M. 287–8
Hunt, J. S. 119
Hunter, J. A. 463
Huntsinger, J. R. 189
Huo, Y. J. 465
Hurst, M. H. 373
Huskinson, T. 178–9, 189
Huston, M. 372
Huston, T. L. 312
Huth, P. 263
Huynh, Q. -L. 135
Hyde, J. S. 84, 143

Ignarri, C. 109
Ilies, R. 427, 428
Illic, M. 470–1

Imada, T. 501
Ingham, A. G. 412
Inglehart, R. 520, 521
Insko, C. A. 454, 455, 459
Inzlicht, M. 162
Isenberg, D. J. 262
Ishii, K. 501
Islam, M. R. 83, 478, 481
Itkin, S. M. 473
Ito, T. A. 288
Iyer, A. 446

Jaccard, J. J. 192
Jackman, M. R. 483
Jackson, J. R. 119, 187, 216
Jackson, J. W. 27
Jackson, L. M. 462
Jacobs, R. C. 240
Jacobson, C. K. 270
Jacobson, R. P. 238
Jago, A. G. 435
James, K. 402
James, William 73, 125–6, 139, 145, 167
    biography 125
Janis, I. L. 15, 27–8, 29–30, 203, 262–3
Janke, W. 75
Jarvis, B. 213
Jaspars, J. 67
Jaspars, J. M. F. 131
Javidan, M. 426, 512
Jefferson, A. 60
Jefferson, T. 48
Jeffery, K. M. 483
Jelicic, M. 118
Jemmott, J. B. 78
Jensen, M. A. 392–3, 394
Jentzsch, I. 328
Jetten, J. 4, 90, 110, 127, 247, 446,
    465, 466
Johansson, P. 127
John, O. P. 44, 187
Johnson, A. L. 384
Johnson, B. 193
Johnson, B. T. 45, 196
Johnson, C. 193, 412
Johnson, D. J. 369
Johnson, E. A. 270
Johnson, J. L. 367
Johnson, J. T. 78
Johnson, K. 127
Johnson, M. H. 89, 354
Johnson, M. K. 144
Johnson, M. P. 297

Johnson, R. D. 301
Johnson, R. E. 167
Johnson, R. M. 357
Johnson, T. J. 84
Johnston, L. 107, 120, 482
Joinson, A. N. 59
Jones, E. E. 15, 17, 21, 62–3, 64, 76, 81,
    85, 88, 150, 168, 227, 452
Jones, J. T. 149
Jones, Warren 397
Jordan, C. H. 138, 157, 159
Jordan, R. 159
Jordet, G. 164
Josephs, R. A. 143
Jost, J. T. 468, 473
Jostmann, N. B. 162
Joule, R. V. 246
Jourard, S. M. 372
Judd, Charles M. 31, 40, 49, 100, 115,
    260, 450, 452
    biography 31
Judge, T. A. 157, 427, 428, 431, 432–3
Jung, D. I. 434
Jussim, L. J. 175

Kafetsios, K. 355
Kahn, A. 473
Kahneman, D. 102, 104, 105, 451
Kaiza, P. 295
Kalick, S. M. 357
Kallgren, C. A. 238, 240, 242
Kalven, H. 259
Kameda, T. 395
Kampe, K. K. W. 356
Kampmeier, C. 478
Kamzan, M. 326
Kanagawa, C. 142
Kaney, S. 72
Kang, S. J. 147
Kanki, B. 251
Kanthak, J. 422
Kanungo, R. N. 430, 431
Kao, C. F. 214
Kaplan, M. F. 260, 262
Kaplan, R. M. 350
Karakitapoğlu-Aygün, Z 525
Karasawa, M. 143, 502–3
Karau, S. J. 415, 416
Karpinski, A. 189, 452
Karremans, Johan C. 219–21, 367,
    368, 369
Kashima, E. S. 508
Kashima, Y. 508

Kashy, D. A.   40
Kasser, T.   166, 281
Kassin, S. M.   65, 118
Katz, D.   181
Katz, T.   516–17
Katzenstein, G.   424
Kaukiainen, A.   276
Kawachi, I.   349
Kawakami, K.   110, 119, 175, 193
Kawamura, T.   500
Kazdin, A. E.   277
Keating, C. F.   388, 389
Keenan, J. P.   144
Keizer, K.   240, 242–3
Kelley, Harold   9, 15, 17, 59, 61, 64, 65–8,
     84, 86, 87, 90, 203, 366, 371, 382
   biography   64
Kelley, W. M.   144, 456
Kelling, G. L.   242
Kelly, A. E.   375
Kelly, J. B.   297
Kelly, J. R.   396
Kelman, H. C.   267, 268
Keltner, D.   349–50
Kemeny, M. E.   154
Kemmelmeier, M.   143, 504
Kendrick, D. T.   21
Kenny, David A.   31, 40, 129
   biography   41
Kent, A.   248
Kenworthy, J.   254, 302, 481
Kerkhof, P.   373
Kernberg, O. F.   159
Kernis, M. H.   137, 140, 157, 158
Kerr, Norbert   259, 382, 414, 415, 416
   biography   415
Kerschreiter, R.   257, 419, 421, 422, 423–4
Kershaw, C.   297
Kessler, T.   108, 456, 462
Key, C. W.   292–3
Kieffer, S. C.   150
Kiesler, C. A.   250
Kiesler, S.   373
Kiesler, S. B.   250
Kihlstrom, J. F.   23, 133–4
Kilduff, G. J.   403
Kilpatrick, S. D.   367
Kim, K.   144
Kim, U.   478
Kim, Y.   166
Kimmel, P. R.   519
Kinderman, P.   72
King, A.   263

King, R. G.   268–9
Kirchner, J.   363
Kirillova, G. P.   281
Kirker, W. S.   134
Kirsh, S. J.   290
Kirwil, L.   294
Kitayama, Shinobu   84, 89, 140, 143, 151,
     243, 500–3, 504, 505
   biography   504
Kiyonari, T.   454
Klandermans, B.   10
Klauer, K. C.   113
Klein, C. T. F.   213, 215
Klein, O.   131
Klein, R.   135
Klein, S. B.   133–4, 144, 145
Klein, W. M.   130
Klem, A.   182
Klentz, B.   246, 322
Klinesmith, J.   281
Kling, K. C.   143
Klink, A.   462
Klohnen, E. C.   363
Klomek, A. B.   299
Klucharev, V.   250
Knafo, A.   509
Knee, C. R.   150
Knight, R. A.   298
Knobe, J. M.   81, 86
Knowles, M. L.   155
Kobayashi, C.   81
Koestner, R.   228
Kohl, J.   246
Köhler, O.   15, 416
Koole, Sandler L.   138, 149, 162, 164
Koops, W.   287
Koriat, A.   294
Korte, C.   312
Koss, Mary P.   277, 298
   biography   277
Krägeloh-Mann, I.   61
Krahé, Barbara   277, 290, 293, 294, 295,
     298, 306
Kraus, S. J.   191, 192, 193
Kraut, R.   373
Kravitz, D. A.   12
Krebs, D.   314
Kreiner, D. S.   219
Kropp, A.   329
Krosnick, J. A.   33, 175, 184, 185, 193,
     215, 254
Kross, E.   164, 166
Krueger, J. I.   156

Krug, E. G.   295
Kruger, J.   127
Kruglanski, A. W.   59, 111, 182, 213–14,
     215
Krull, D. S.   78, 79, 80
Kubacka, K. E.   373
Kuiper, N. A.   133–4
Kulik, J.   132
Kumar, S.   86
Kumashiro, M.   159, 367, 368
Kunda, Z.   95, 101, 110, 134, 147, 148
Kundu, P.   248
Kunst-Wilson, W. R.   175
Kurman, J.   506
Kushigian, R. H.   341
Kuyper, H.   130
Kuzmanovic, B.   59, 60
Kwan, J. L.   254
Kwang, T.   44
Kyes, C. B.   420

Labrecque, J.   198
Ladd, D.   422
Lage, E.   251
Lagerspetz, K. M.   276
Lahey, B. B.   281
Lai, A. S. Y.   506
Laird, R. D.   287
Lake, R. A.   326
Lakey, C. E.   137
Lalljee, M.   67
Lally, P.   198
Lalwani, N.   160
Lamb, R.   67
Lamberth, J.   363
Lamm, C.   340
Lamm, H.   258, 261
Landis, D.   474
Landry, S. H.   375
Langer, E. J.   247
Langlois, J. H.   356, 357, 359, 363
LaPiere, R. T.   191
Larsen, J. T.   500
Larson, D. W.   71
Larson, J. H.   366
Larson, J. R., Jr.   420, 435
Latané, Bibb   317–22, 323, 324, 325, 330,
     336, 413–14, 415
   biography   318
Laughlin, P. R.   424
Laurenceau, J.-P.   375
Lavrakas, P.   33
Law, J. S. F.   143

Lax, M. L.   145
Lazarus, R. S.   294
Le, B.   382
Lê-Xuân-Hy, G. M.   146
Leach, C. W.   459, 460, 470
Leafhead, K. M.   72
Leana, C. R.   263
Leary, M. R.   136, 137, 154–5, 157, 382,
    454, 466
LeBon, G.   301
Lee-Chai, A.   197
Lee, F.   524–5
Lee, H.   166
Lee, L.   333
Lefkowitz, M. M.   277
Legrand, D.   145
Lehman, D. R.   151
Leitner, J. B.   60
Lemay, E. P. J.   375
Lenton, A. P.   110
Leonardelli, G. J.   466
LePage, A.   282
LePine, J. A.   157
Lepore, L.   110, 114, 452
Lepper, M. R.   128, 215, 228, 229
Lerma, M.   359
Lerner, J. S.   156
Lesar, T. S.   270
Leslie, A. M.   61
Leu, J.   524–5
Leung, A. K. Y.   517
Leve, C.   263
Levenson, R. W.   165
Leventhal, H.   75
Levi, A.   84–5
Levin, J.   158
Levin, S.   445, 474, 483
Levin-Sagi, M.   161
Levine, John M.   238, 243, 247, 249, 250,
    251, 254, 256, 262, 386–7, 388, 389,
    390, 392, 395
    biography   386
Levine, Mark   318, 326, 327–8, 329, 331, 467
Levine, R. V.   313, 509
Levinger, G.   412
Levinson, D. J.   443–4
Levy, L.   248
Levy, R.   350–1
Lewicki, R. J.   134
Lewin, Kurt   15–16, 17, 21, 23, 381, 433,
    492, 512
    biography   15
Lewinsohn, P. M.   71, 73

Lewis, D.   89
Leyens, J. P.   247, 464, 464–5
Liberman, A.   148
Liberman, N.   161
Liberty, H. J.   238
Lichter, E. L.   298
Lickel, B.   302, 383–4
Lieberman, A.   207
Lieberman, J. D.   277
Lieberman, M. D.   22, 352, 391–2
Liebert, R. M.   30–1
Likert, R.   186
Lind, E. A.   238
Lindenberg, S.   240, 242–3
Linder, D. E.   227
Lindoerfer, J. S.   263
Lindsay, J. J.   285
Lindsey, S.   4, 216
Linville, P. W.   137
Lipkus, I.   367
Lippitt, R.   15, 17, 433, 492, 512
Liska, L. Z.   430
Livingstone, Andrew G.   462
Lloyd, B. B.   288
Lloyd, S. A.   366
Lobel, M.   130
Locher, P.   357
Lodewijkx, H. F. M.   387–8, 417, 455
Loeber, R.   281
Lombardi, W.   98
Lopez, D. F.   130
Lord, C. G.   189, 215, 259
Lore, R. K.   280
Lorenz, K.   280, 305
Lossie, N.   257
Lotan, R. A.   473
Lott, C. L.   146
Lozano, R.   295
Lubensky, M. E.   483
Luchies, L. B.   368
Luhtanen, R. K.   137, 139–40
Lumsdaine, A. A.   14, 203, 205
Lundgren, S.   252
Lundgren, S. R.   245
Luo, S.   363
Lupiáñez, J.   110
Luszczynska, A.   198
Lüthgens, C.   257
Lutzenberger, W.   61
Lydon, J. E.   369
Lynas, M.   519
Lynn, A. R.   175
Lyons, M. P.   356

Ma, J. E.   110
Maass, A.   252, 254, 451
MacBrayer, E. K.   287–8
Maccoby, E. E.   375
Maccoby, N.   205, 206
MacCoun, R. J.   259
MacDonald, G.   136
MacKenzie, S. B.   399
Mackie, D. M.   212
MacNamara, D. E. J.   269
MacNeil, M. K.   240
Macrae, Neil   4–5, 6–7, 90, 97, 110, 112,
    115, 117–18, 120, 127, 144, 152–3, 159,
    160, 451, 456
    biography   118
Madden, T. J.   196
Madey, S. F.   359
Madson, L.   143
Maestas, K. L.   71
Maheswaran, D.   209, 210–11
Maier, N. R. F.   435
Maio, Gregory R.   173, 174, 175, 176,
    178–9, 180, 181, 185, 481
Maisey, D. S.   359
Maitner, A. T.   385–6
Majika, E. A.   184
Malle, B. F.   33, 81, 85, 86, 444
Mallett, R. K.   474
Malmstrom, E. J.   294
Malone, P. S.   76, 78, 80, 83, 86, 90
Maniaci, M. R.   362
Mann, J.   477
Manning, Rachel   318
Manstead, Antony S. R.   175, 462, 465,
    467, 517
Mantell, D. M.   267
Marcus-Newhall, A.   281, 282
Marigold, D. C.   147
Mark, A. Y.   90
Markman, H. J.   376
Marková, I.   20
Marks, M. A.   434
Markus, Hazel R.   84, 89, 133, 134,
    135, 140, 142, 143, 237, 243, 502,
    503–4, 505
    biography   133
Marques, J. M.   464–5
Marrow, A. J.   15
Marsh, H. W.   136
Marshall, G. D.   75
Martijn, C.   162
Martin, B.   12
Martin, P. Y.   215, 255–6

Martin, Robin 130, 215, 252–4, 255–6, 257
Martino, S. C. 333
Martorana, P. 263
Martz, J. M. 368
Mashek, D. J. 131
Maslach, C. 75, 240–1, 492
Mason, M. F. 80
Mason, W. 44
Masson, K. 509
Masuda, T. 500
Matsumoto, D. 506
Mayer, A. 12
Mayer, N. D. 179
Mayle, P. 95
McAdams, D. P. 132
McAndrew, F. T. 281
McArthur, L. A. 65, 67
McArthur, L. Z. 59
McAuslan, P. 298
McBride, M. V. 445
McBurnett, K. 281
McClelland, D. C. 432
McClure, J. 86
McConahay, J. 113, 114
McConnachie, A. 270
McCormick, C. M. 60
McCoslin, M. J. 216
McCracken, G. 222
McCrae, R. R. 428
McCrea, S. M. 152–3
McCullough, M. E. 367
McDaniel, P. 288
McDevitt, J. 158
McDonel, E. C. 128
McDonnell, J. V. 44
McDougall, W. 10
McDowell, N. K. 156
McElreath, R. 337
McElwee, R. O. B. 134
McGarty, C. 451
McGhee, D. E. 115, 187, 216
McGill, A. L. 87
McGrath, Joseph E. 398
  biography 398
McGregor, H. A. 277
McGregor, I. 147
McGrew, W. C. 361
McGuire, C. V. 134–5
McGuire, William J. 134–5, 203, 204, 207
  biography 205
McIntosh, A. 212
McKenna, K. Y. A. 482

McKillop, K. J. 375
McLaughlin-Volpe, T. 482
McLeod, P. L. 258
McNulty, J. K. 368
McQuirk, B. 322
McWethy, A. 118
Mead, G. H. 129
Meade, R. D. 492, 512
Meehan, C. 386
Meek, D. 259
Meeus, W. 363, 372
Meeus, W. H. J. 269, 270
Meier, B. P. 305
Mendelson, M. J. 372
Merckelbach, H. 118
Mercy, J. A. 295
Merrin, J. 72
Mesmer-Magnus, J. R. 395
Messé, L. A. 332, 416, 422
Metalsky, G. I. 72
Meyerowitz, J. A. 148
Mezulis, A. H. 84
Miceli, M. P. 269
Michinov, N. 447
Michotte, A. 61
Mickler, S. 243
Miedema, J. 120
Mielke, R. 462
Mihic, L. 470
Mikulincer, M. 155, 354
Milburn, M. A. 298
Miles, D. R. 280
Milgram, Stanley 9, 17, 36–8, 41, 45, 46, 238, 264–8, 270, 492, 512
  biography 264
Milich, R. 287–8
Miller, A. G. 264, 265, 267, 268, 270
Miller, C. E. 260, 262
Miller, C. T. 326
Miller, D. T. 84, 148, 149, 261
Miller, F. D. 79
Miller, G. A. 160
Miller, G. E. 165
Miller, J. A. 246
Miller, J. G. 45, 80
Miller, L. C. 373
Miller, L. S. 290–2
Miller, Neal E. 281
  biography 281
Miller, Norman 277, 281, 282, 288, 302, 315, 326, 476–7
Miller-Perrin, C. L. 288
Miller, R. S. 369

Miller, T. R. 304
Mills, J. 325, 371, 388
Milne, A. B. 4, 90, 97, 110, 118, 127, 152–3, 159, 451
Milne, S. 197
Milner, B. J. 152–3
Milner, K. R. 422
Minde, T. 478
Miner, A. G. 421
Mintzer, A. 355
Mischel, W. 9, 73, 126, 146, 164, 166
Mitchell, J. P. 144
Mitchell, T. R. 429
Miyamoto, Y. 501
Mlicki, P. P. 465–6
Mochon, D. 373–4
Modigliani, A. 269
Moede, W. 12, 13, 20
Moffitt, G. 385–6
Moghaddam, F. M. 302–3, 304, 467
Mohr, D. 246
Moise-Titus, J. 292
Mojzisch, A. 257, 419, 420, 421, 422, 423–4
Mok, A. 525
Mok, D. 478
Molden, D. C. 79–80
Moll, J. 110
Möller, I. 287, 290, 294, 295, 298
Monahan, J. L. 175, 176
Mondloch, C. J. 60
Monin, B. 270
Monshouwer, H. J. 287
Monteith, M. J. 5, 90, 99, 110, 113, 115, 118–19
Montepare, J. M. 60
Monto, M. A. 332
Montoya, R. M. 363
Moon, D. 297
Moore, D. L. 237
Moreland, R. L. 238, 251, 262, 362–3, 386–7, 388, 390, 392, 395, 396
Morf, Carolyn C. 126, 138, 150, 156–7, 158, 159
Morgan, R. 61
Mori, K. 248
Morling, B. 138
Morris, C. G. 411–12
Morris, K. A. 244
Morris, M. L. 143
Morris, M. W. 80, 524–5
Morris, P. H. 89
Morrison, E. R. 259

Morrison, E. W.   474
Morrison, J.   270
Morrison, K. R.   261
Morry, M.   149
Mortensen, C. R.   238
Morton, J.   89, 353
Mosakowski, E.   512–13
Moscovici, Serge   20, 21, 250–2, 253, 255, 256, 257, 258
  biography   258
Mosier, K.   254
Moskowitz, G. B.   95, 98, 104, 108–9, 110, 115, 119, 209, 328, 483
Mowrer   281
Moya, M.   110
Moylan, S. J.   84
Mucchi-Faina, A.   254
Mueller, C. M.   69
Muellerleile, P. A.   196
Mugny, G.   252, 256
Mullen, B.   147, 148, 263, 278–9, 301, 398, 401, 412, 463
Mummendey, Amélie   108, 460, 462, 464, 465, 466, 478
  biography   464
Muraven, M.   162, 163, 164, 166
Muraven, M. B.   150
Murchison, C.   13
Murdoch, D.   288
Murphy, P.   473
Murphy, S. T.   175
Murray, H. A.   364
Murray, R. K.   432
Murray, S. L.   363, 369
Murrell, A.   477
Murry, W. D.   434
Musselman, L.   359
Mussweiler, T.   49–50, 103–4, 130
Myaskovsky, L.   396
Myers, D. G.   258, 261

Nadler, Arie   313, 340–1
  biography   340
Naffrechoux, M.   251
Nagao, D. H.   259
Naidoo, L.   369
Nail, P. R.   147
Naipaul, S.   397
Nathan, L. R.   452
Navarick, D. J.   270
Neal, D. T.   198

Neale, M. A.   104, 257
Near, J. P.   269
Neely, J. H.   98
Neff, K. D.   157
Nelligan, J. S.   355
Nelson, B. C.   155
Nelson, G.   370, 482
Nelson, S. E.   81, 86, 372
Nemeth, Charlan Jeanne   251, 254, 257
  biography   254
Neuberg, S. L.   57, 90, 96, 97, 101, 110–11, 112–13, 119, 452, 470, 478
Newcomb, M. D.   332
Newcomb, Theodore M.   13, 14, 363
  biography   14
Newman, L. S.   147–8, 192, 270
Newsom, J. T.   18, 246
Newstrom, J. W.   426, 428
Nezlek, J.   248
Nezlek, J. B.   355
Ng, M.   197
Nicholson, I.   268
Nida, S.   322
Niemeyer, G.   416
Nijstad, Bernard A.   417, 418, 420
Nisbett, Richard E.   75, 80, 81, 83, 85, 87, 127, 176, 187, 289, 360, 500–1, 502, 517–18
  biography   75
Nissani, M.   267
Nitz, K.   280
Nolan, J. M.   248
Nordgren, L. F.   127
Norenzayan, A.   80, 494–5, 500, 501, 502, 509
Northcraft, G. B.   104
Norton, M. I.   374
Nosek, B. A.   44, 135, 189, 190
Novick, L. R.   68
Nurius, P.   135
Nuttin, J. M.   20
Nuttin, J. M., Jr.   138, 149
Nuwer, H.   389

O'Doherty, J.   60
O'Neill, O. A.   257
Oakes, M. A.   143
Oakes, P. J.   256, 326, 382, 450, 451, 452, 462, 464
Ochsner, K. N.   22, 144
Oishi, S.   504
Okun, M.   237
Oliner, P. M.   334, 336

Oliner, S. P.   334, 336
Olkin, I.   45
Olson, J. E.   356
Olson, J. M.   127, 147, 148, 181
Olson, M. A.   185, 189, 190, 216, 452
Olsson, A.   127
Olweus, D.   287, 298
Omoto, A. M.   329, 333–4, 362
Opp, K. D.   9
Oppenheim, A. N.   33, 49
Orbell, S.   197
Orbuch, T.   371
Orne, M. T.   18, 42
Orobio de Castro, B.   287
Orpinas, P.   287
Orwell, G.   262
Osborn, A. F.   412
Osgood, C. E.   186
Osswald, S.   305
Osterhouse, R. A.   205, 206
Österman, K.   288
Ostrom, T. M.   21, 203, 204
Otten, S.   460, 465
Ouellette, J. A.   225, 252
Overall, N. C.   375
Overstreet, B. G.   129
Owens, P.   263
Oxenberg, J.   146
Oyserman, D.   143, 504, 521
Özdemir, M.   372

Packer, D. J.   269
Padilla-Walker, L. M.   373
Paek, H. J.   224
Paladino, M. P.   461
Paleari, F. G.   367
Panzarella, R.   267
Paolini, S.   481, 482
Papastamou, S.   250–1
Paris, M.   130
Park, G.   258
Park, H.   502–3
Park, J. H.   461
Park, L. E.   157
Parker, J. H.   474
Parker, K. C.   399
Parker, R. N.   288
Parks, M. R.   373
Parrott, D. J.   277
Pascual-Leone, A.   144
Patchin, J. W.   299
Patil, S. V.   257
Patnoe, S.   474, 475

Paulhus, D. L.   42, 150, 157, 187
Paulson, R. M.   192
Pavlova, M.   61
Payne, B. K.   452
Pearce, C. L.   434
Peckham, V.   412
Pedersen, W. C.   277, 281
Pelham, B. W.   78, 138, 149
Pendry, Louise   96, 107, 111, 112, 115
Peng, K.   500, 501, 523, 524
Pennebaker, J. W.   128, 359
Penner, L. A.   312, 317, 334–6
Pennington, N.   259
Penrod, S.   259
Peplau, L. A.   364
Perdue, C. W.   99, 465
Pérez, J. A.   252, 256
Perie, M.   134
Perrett, D.   61
Perrett, D. I.   359
Perrin, R. D.   288
Perry, M.   277, 278, 287
Perry, R. B.   125
Personnaz, B.   252
Peter, J.   373
Peters, M. J. V.   118
Peterson, C.   154
Peterson, R.   263
Pettigrew, T. F.   78, 446, 474, 477, 478, 481
Pettit, G. S.   287
Petty, Richard E.   177, 178, 179, 184, 203,
    204, 205, 206, 207, 212–13, 214, 215,
    216, 223–4, 235, 246–7, 252, 254
  biography   207
Phelps, E. A.   22, 60, 190
Phil, R. O.   288
Philbrick, K.   509
Phinney, J. S.   522
Piccolo, R. F.   428, 431, 432–3
Pickering, T. G.   350–1
Pickett, C. L.   466
Pieper, C.   350–1
Pierce, C. M.   270
Pierce, J. L.   426, 428
Pietromonaco, P.   98
Pietromonaco, P. R.   375
Piliavin, I. M.   323–4
Piliavin, Jane Allyn   312, 313, 315, 317,
    323–5, 333
  biography   324
Pinquart, M.   372
Pitts, S. C.   31
Plant, E. A.   481

Platow, M. J.   463
Pliner, P.   246
Plomin, R.   280
Podolski, C.-L.   292
Podsakoff, P. M.   399
Poehlman, T. A.   190
Polivy, J.   163
Pollock, D. A.   50
Pollock, V. E.   281, 288
Pollozek, F.   322
Postmes, T.   23, 28, 270, 326, 466
Potter, J.   18, 35, 45, 88
Pouliasi, K.   509, 522
Povey, D.   295
Prager, K.   373, 375
Pratkanis, A. R.   218, 219, 224, 263
Pratto, F.   33
Preacher, K. J.   190
Prentice, D. A.   149
Preston, M.   246
Preuschoff, K.   339
Pribram, K. H.   160
Price, J.   130
Priester   177
Prins, K. S.   521
Prislin, R.   238, 244, 245
Probasco, P.   263
Prosser, A.   326, 327–8
Proulx, G.   343
Puce, A.   61
Pugh, M. D.   401
Pyszczynski, T.   147, 148, 155, 156, 159,
    165, 461
Pyzalski, J.   298

Quiamzade, A.   256

Raaijmakers, Q. A. W.   269, 270
Rabbie, J. M.   454, 455, 457
Rabow, J.   332
Raine, A.   281
Ramaswamy, J.   501
Ramirez, A. J.   363
Randall, P.   298
Rank, S. G.   270
Rankin, R. E.   50
Rapson, R.   365
Rathouz, P. J.   281
Rayner, C.   299
Raz, M.   246
Reber, R.   184
Reed, G. M.   154
Reeder, G. D.   85–6, 150

Regalia, C.   367
Reicher, S.   50, 131, 241, 256, 268, 270,
    326–8, 329, 334, 342–3, 344, 382, 464,
    467, 492
Reid, L. N.   224
Reingen, P. H.   246
Reingold, J.   270
Reips, U.-D.   44
Reis, H. T.   166, 268, 349, 362, 363, 373,
    374, 375
Reisenzein, R.   75
Rennicke, C.   156
Rennison, C. M.   295
Reno, R. R.   238, 240, 242
Reuband, K.-H.   270
Reynolds, K. J.   131, 465
Rhee, S. H.   280
Rhodewalt, F.   138, 150, 156, 158, 168
Rholes, W. S.   355
Rich, B. L.   157
Richards, M.   376
Richardson, D. R.   275
Richeson, J. A.   99, 481
Ridge, R. D.   292–3
Ridgeway, C. L.   400, 401
Riecken, H. W.   47
Rietzschel, E. F.   418
Rindfleisch, A.   155
Rindfuss, R. R.   362
Ring, K.   17
Ringelmann, Max   12, 409, 412, 413
  biography   412
Riordan, C. A.   148
Ritter, J. M.   356, 359
Ritter, S. M.   369
Rittman, A. L.   434
Rivara, F. P.   304
Roberts, A. R.   359
Roberts, J. C.   161
Robertson, L. S.   225
Robins, R. W.   127, 136
Robinson, D. T.   153
Robinson, J. P.   49
Robinson-Staveley, K.   237
Roccas, S.   391
Rochat, F.   269
Rochat, P.   61
Rodriguez Mosquera, P. M.   517
Roe, S.   295
Roemmele, L. A.   146
Roese, N. J.   127, 147, 148
Roets, A.   214, 215
Rogers, C. R.   146

Rogers, T. B.   133–4
Roggman, L. A.   359
Rohner, R. P.   493
Rohrer, J. H.   240
Rokeach, M.   464
Romero, V.   156, 462
Roney, C.   164
Rooney, S. B.   71
Ropp, S. A.   482
Rose, S. M.   362
Roseman, I. J.   470
Rosenberg, M.   139
Rosenholtz, S. J.   400
Rosenthal, A. M.   318
Rosenthal, R.   18, 43
Rosman, H.   166
Rosnow, R. L.   43
Ross, Deborah   288
Ross, Dorothea   284
Ross, E. A.   10
Ross, L.   75, 79, 83, 85, 147, 215
Ross, L. D.   77–8
Ross, M.   84, 132, 148, 504–5
Ross, S. A.   284
Rossman, S. B.   302
Rothman, A. J.   184
Rothman. G.   464
Rottmann, L.   360
Rovine, M. J.   375
Rovira, A.   331
Rowe, D. C.   280
Rowold, J.   433
Ruback, B. R.   399
Rubin, M.   131, 147, 462, 517
Rubin, Z.   372
Rubini, M.   517
Ruby, P.   145
Rude, S.   71
Rudich, E. A.   159
Rule, N. O.   60
Rusbult, Caryl E.   147, 159, 364, 366–7,
   368, 369, 371, 382
   biography   367
Rushton, J. P.   337–8
Russell, G. W.   288
Russell, J.   356
Russin, A.   110
Russo, E.   254
Rüter, K.   130
Rutland, A.   482
Rutt, D. J.   373
Ryan, R.   166
Ryan, R. M.   228

Ryen, A. H.   473
Rytina, S.   269

Saari, D.   246
Saavedra, R.   398
Sacchi, S.   461
Sadler, M. S.   115
Sage, R. M.   156
Sagiv, L.   391, 497
Saguy, T.   340, 467, 483, 484–5
Salaman, L.   384
Salas, E.   263, 395, 412
Salmivalli, C.   298–9
Salomon, A. R.   115
Saltz, J. L.   452
Sam, D. L.   522
Sanbonmatsu, D. M.   198
Sanders, G. S.   237
Sandstrom, M. J.   159
Sanford, R. N.   443–4
Sani, F.   461
Sanitioso, R.   148
Santelli, A. G.   159
Saribay, S. A.   79
Sasfy, J.   237
Sassenberg, K.   50, 108
Saucier, D. A.   326
Savage, D. A.   341
Savitsky, K.   103, 105
Sawin, D. B.   356
Sawyer, P. J.   270
Schachter, Stanley   16, 47, 73–6, 238,
   360–2, 390, 395, 491–2
   biography   74
Schaefer, H. S.   351
Schaller, M.   461
Schatzel-Murphy, E. A.   298
Scheepers, D.   50, 465, 466, 467
Scheier, M. F.   120, 128, 160–1
Scherer, K. R.   59
Scherer, U.   59
Schiappa, E.   482–3
Schimmack, U.   504
Schlenker, B. R.   167, 168
Schmader, T.   302
Schmeichel, B. J.   155, 160, 161
Schmidt-Hieber, J.   419
Schmitt, D. P.   138, 509
Schmitt, M. T.   131
Schmukle, S. C.   362
Schneider, W.   79
Schoeneman, T. J.   129
Scholten, L.   420

Schooler, T. Y.   4, 216
Schoormans, J. P. L.   222
Schot, J. C.   454
Schreiber, E.   330
Schreiber, F.   140
Schreiber, F. B.   261
Schreiber, H.-J.   464, 478
Schroeder, D. A.   312, 316, 317, 325
Schuette, R. A.   198
Schultz, L. A.   280
Schultz, P. W.   248
Schultze, T.   419
Schulz-Hardt, Stefan   257, 419–22, 423–4
Schumpeter, J.   456
Schürch, E.   156, 158
Schütze, S.   298
Schuurman, M.   252
Schwartz, I.   156
Schwartz, J. L. K.   115, 187, 216
Schwartz, L.   270
Schwartz, P.   372
Schwartz, R. D.   48
Schwartz, S.   391
Schwartz, Shalom H.   323, 495–8, 503,
   504, 509, 511, 517
   biography   495
Schwarz, N.   33, 78, 88, 103, 105, 184, 187
Schwarzwald, J.   246
Sears, D. O.   43, 182, 193
Sears, R. R.   281
Seashore, S. E.   428
Sechrest, L.   48
Sechrist, G. B.   473
Sedikides, C.   83, 84, 146, 148, 150–1, 157,
   159, 505
See, Y. H. M.   179
Seidel, E.-M.   85
Selfhout, M.   363
Seligman, M. E.   70–1
Seligman, M. E. P.   154
Selimbegović, L.   165
Semin, G. R.   517
Sengupta, N. K.   483
Sevincer, A. T.   502–3
Shackelford, T. K.   509
Shallice, T.   120
Shanab, M. E.   270
Shapiro, P. N.   481
Sharkey, W. F.   506
Sharon, I.   492
Sharp, M.   49
Shaver, P. R.   129, 353, 354, 355, 373, 374,
   375, 376

Shavitt, S.   183, 223
Sheeran, P.   197, 198
Sheffield, F. D.   14, 203, 205
Sheldon, K. M.   166
Shelton, J. N.   481
Shepela, S. T.   317, 334
Sher, K. J.   165
Sheridan, C. L.   268–9
Sherif, C. W.   454
Sherif, Muzafer   3, 4, 6, 7, 13–14, 20,
    238–40, 243, 245, 247, 300, 381, 454–5,
    457, 462, 473
  biography   454
Sherman, D. K.   156, 385–6
Sherman, J. W.   5, 22, 118
Sherman, S. J.   128, 246, 384
Shiffrin, R. M.   79
Shoal, G. D.   281
Shomrony, A.   159
Shore, B.   143
Shotland, R. L.   332
Showers, C. J.   143
Shrauger, J. S.`   129
Sibley, C. G.   483
Sicoly, F.   132
Sidanius, J.   33
Siegel, A. E.   447
Siegel, S.   447
Siem, B.   329
Sigman, S. J.   373
Sikström, S.   127
Silani, G.   339
Silito, S. D.   414
Silverman, E. S.   143
Silvia, P. J.   159
Sim, J. J.   115
Simmel, M.   61, 62
Simon, B.   450, 478
Simonton, D. K.   29, 30, 432
Simpson, Jeffry A.   355–6, 359, 369, 375
  biography   356
Sims, H. P., Jr.   434
Sinaceur, M.   257
Sinclair, L.   110
Sinclair, S.   474
Singelis, T. M.   504, 505, 506, 517
Singer, J.   73–4, 75, 76, 395
Singer, J. A.   132
Singer, M.   300
Singer, P.   311
Singer, T.   339, 340
Sirgy, M. J.   222
Sivasubramaniam, N.   434

Skowronski, J. J.   159
Slater, M.   269, 331
Slater, P. E.   48, 393
Slavin, R. E.   473
Slepian, M. L.   60
Slovik, L. F.   367
Slugoski, B. R.   62, 67, 76
Smart, L.   158
Smart, S. A.   246
Smith, B. A.   435
Smith, C.   147, 463
Smith, C. L.   418
Smith, C. M.   257, 259, 414
Smith, C. T.   189
Smith, E. R.   79, 451, 469
Smith, H. J.   46
Smith, H. S.   137
Smith, J. R.   10, 215, 254, 268
Smith, K. E.   375
Smith-Lovin, L.   153
Smith, M. B.   181, 182
Smith, P. K.   298, 300
Smith, P. M.   434
Smith, Peter B.   45, 249, 250, 492, 511–12
Smith, S. M.   184, 215
Sniezek, J. A.   421
Snyder, C. R.   150
Snyder, C. R. R.   95, 96
Snyder, M.   9, 60, 183–4, 193, 246, 325,
    329, 333–4, 357, 358, 362
Sobell, M. B.   150
Sociedade, P.   357
Solomon, S.   155, 159, 277, 461
Somech, A.   425
Sommers, S. R.   137, 139–40
Son Hing, L. S.   445
Sörensen, S.   372
Southern, R.   331
Spangenberg, E. R.   219
Spangler, W. D.   432
Sparks, C. W.   292
Sparks, G. G.   292
Spears, Russell   23, 27, 28, 46, 103, 110,
    131, 175, 270, 326, 455, 462, 463, 465,
    466, 467, 470
Spence, J. T.   143
Spence, K. W.   236
Spencer, S. J.   138, 159
Spengler, S.   145
Sperduti, M.   145
Spicer, C. V.   118
Spoor, J. R.   396
Sriram, N.   189

Srivastava, S.   44
Srull, T. K.   99
Staats, A. W.   216
Staats, C. K.   216
Stack, A. D.   305
Stafford, L.   373
Stallworth, L. M.   33
Stangier, U.   140
Stangor, C.   473
Stanley, J. C.   36
Starbuck, W. H.   263
Stasser, G.   259, 419, 420
Staub, E.   158, 268
Staw, B. M.   403
Stayton, D.   375
Steblay, N.   118
Steblay, N. M.   246
Steele, C. M.   146
Steffen, V. J.   288
Steg, L.   240, 242–3
Steil, R.   140
Stein, D. S.   270
Stein-Seroussi, A.   153, 154
Steinberg, L.   375
Steiner, Ivan D.   410
  biography   410
Steiner, L.   414
Steinmetz, J.   71
Steinmetz, J. L.   77–8
Stenstrom, D. M.   302
Stephan, C. W.   478, 481
Stephan, F. F.   398
Stephan, W. G.   464, 474, 478, 481, 483
Stephen, E. H.   362
Sternthal, B.   162
Stevens, N.   372
Stewart, A. J.   432
Stiff, C.   162
Stillwell, A. M.   150
Stiven, H.   35
Stokoe, E.   47
Stollak, G. E.   332
Stone, J.   115
Storms, M. D.   75, 82–3
Story, A. L.   134
Strack, F.   95, 103–4, 195, 198
Strange, B. A.   60
Strassberg, D. S.   373
Strauman, T. J.   135
Straus, M. A.   295
Straw, M. K.   332
Strejc, H.   373
Strickland, L. H.   18

Strickland, O. J. 422
Stringer, M. 463
Stroebe, M. S. 31
Stroebe, Wolfgang 12, 19, 23, 31, 209,
    219–21, 222, 225, 227, 228, 246, 247,
    270, 414, 415, 417, 418, 455, 459
Strube, M. J. 11, 12, 84, 146
Struthers, C. W. 159
Stryker, S. 167, 333
Stürmer, S. 325, 329, 340
Suci, G. J. 186
Sukel, H. 118
Sullivan, E. A. 305
Suls, J. 130
Sumpton, R. 78
Sun, C. R. 137
Sunnafrank, M. 363
Sunstein, C. R. 258
Suri, S. 44
Sutcliffe, K. M. 435
Sutton, R. M. 86
Swander, D. V. 240
Swank, P. R. 375
Swann, William B. Jr. 60, 153–4, 167
  biography 153
Swapp, D. 331
Swart, H. 474, 481
Swartz, M. 270
Swedlund, M. 251
Sweeney, J. D. 424
Sy, T. 398
Syme, S. L. 350
Syroit, J. E. M. M. 387–8

't Hart, P. 263
Tafarodi, R. W. 143
Tagini, A. 132
Tagiuri, R. 59
Tajfel, Henri 3–4, 6–7, 20–1, 131, 254,
    301, 326, 381, 382, 402, 449, 455,
    456–8, 459, 462, 465, 466, 467–8, 515,
    516, 517
  biography 456
Takata, T. 151
Takemura, K. 501, 515
Talaska, C. A. 452
Tam, T. 481
Tambor, E. S. 137, 454
Tanke, E. D. 357, 358
Tannenbaum, P. H. 186
Tasker, K. 359
Taubman Ben-Ari, O. 155
Tausch, Nicole 467, 470, 474, 480, 484–5

Taves, P. A. 177
Taylor, C. M. 115
Taylor, D. A. 362, 364, 373
Taylor, D. M. 467
Taylor, Shelley E. 73, 81, 82, 83, 84, 87,
    89, 95, 100, 101, 104, 105, 127, 130,
    143, 146, 147, 154, 156, 244
  biography 128
Teasdale, J. D. 70–1
Tellis, G. J. 223
Temkin, J. 298
Temple, E. 81
Terdal, S. K. 137, 454
Terry, D. J. 473
Terry, M. L. 157
Tesser, A. 148, 243
Tetlock, P. E. 29, 46, 84–5, 89, 111, 263
Thibaut, John Walter 9, 366, 382
  biography 382
Thomas-Hunt, M. C. 257
Thomas, L. A. 22
Thomson, J. A., Jr. 156
Thornhill, R. 359
Thurstone, L. L. 13
Tice, D. M. 129, 150, 167
Tilin, F. 394
Tindale, R. S. 257, 259, 395, 414
Tissongton, P. A. 425
Titus, L. J. 237
Titus, W. 419
Todd, A. R. 79–80, 99
Todd M. 44
Todorov, A. 65
Toffler, B. L. 270
Toguchi, Y. 84, 151, 505
Toledo, R. 238
Toma, C. L. 374
Tomaka, J. 138
Tooby, J. 338
Tooman, G. D. 118
Torchetti, L. 156, 159
Torgler, B. 341
Tormala, Z. L. 179
Torrance, E. P. 414
Toshima, M. T. 350
Totten, B. 306
Tovée, M. J. 359
Trafimow, D. 86, 140, 143
Tredoux, C. 483
Triandis, Harry C. 140, 151, 507
  biography 507
Triplett, N. D. 10–12, 235–6, 409
Trivers, R. L. 338

Trope, Y. 79, 80, 146, 161, 260
Tropp, L. R. 474, 481, 483
Trost, M. R. 18, 238, 243, 244–5, 246, 250
Trötschel, R. 197
Trzesniewski, K. H. 136
Tsapelas, I. 371
Tuan, Y. F. 222
Tucker, J. A. 150
Tuckman, B. W. 392–3, 394, 395
Tudor, M. 370, 482
Turner, John C. 21, 131, 243, 256, 257,
    261–2, 264, 326, 343, 382, 394, 401,
    402, 403, 451, 452, 456, 459, 462, 464,
    465, 467, 476, 516, 517
  biography 465
Turner, M. E. 263
Turner, R. N. 482
Tversky, A. 102, 104, 105, 451
Twenge, J. M. 155, 158, 161
Tyler, R. B. 465
Tzeng, O. C. 27

Uchida, Y. 143, 151
Udal, A. 212
Uhlmann, E. 190
Uleman, J. S. 79, 107
Unger, R. 357
Uskul, A. K. 501, 502–3

Valacich, J. S. 418
Vale, E. L. E. 359
Valkenburg, P. M. 373
Vallacher, R. R. 161
van Baaren, R. B. 127
Van de Vijver, F. 521
Van de Vliert, E. 249, 313
Van den Bos, K. 238
Van der Eijnden, R. J. J. M. 369
Van der Linden, M. 132
van Dick, R. 425
Van Dijk, M. 159
Van Dyne, L. 257
Van Ginkel, W. P. 395
Van Goozen, S. H. M. 280
Van Hiel, A. 214, 215
Van Horn, K. R. 362
Van Ijzendoorn, M. H. 375
Van Kleef, G. A. 248, 401
Van Knippenberg, A. 107, 138, 193, 194,
    197, 215
Van Knippenberg, Daan 257, 395, 397,
    399, 402, 420
Van Laar, C. 483

Van Lange, P. A. M.   147, 269, 367, 368, 369, 371
Van Leeuwen, E.   457
Van Ooijen, I.   219
Van Oudenhoven, J. P.   478, 521
Van Overwalle, F.   90
Van Schie, H. T.   369
Van Vugt, M.   390
Van Yperen, N. W.   366
Vanberg, V.   9
Vanman, E. J.   452
Vasquez, E. A.   277, 302
Vaughan, G. M.   12
Vaughn, L. S.   359
Vaughn, R.   223
Vazire, S.   44, 129
Vedder, P.   522
Veenvliet, S.   470
Veerman, J. W.   287
Veltkamp, M.   197
Venkatesan, M.   206
Verette, J.   147, 367, 369
Verkuyten, M.   509, 522
Vernon, M. L.   376
Vernon, R. A.   470
Verona, E.   305
Verplanken, B.   193, 194, 197, 215
Verwijmeren, T.   219, 221
Vicary, J.   218, 219, 221
Vinokur, A.   258, 260
Visser, L.   454
Visser, P. S.   33, 184, 193
Voci, A.   185, 481, 482
Vogeley, K.   60
Vohs, K. D.   156, 157, 160, 161, 162, 163–4, 247
Voigt, H.   331
Vollrath, D. A.   259
Volpato, C.   254
Volz, K. G.   456, 458
Von Cramon, D. Y.   145, 456
Vonk, R.   79–80
Vonofakou, C.   482
Voss, C. W.   219
Voyer, D.   164
Vroom, V. H.   435
Vryan, K. D.   167
Vuchinich, R. E.   150

Wachtler, J.   254
Wackenhut, J.   238
Wade, G.   478
Wadsworth, M.   376

Wageman, R.   434
Wagner, C.   448
Wagner, U.   452
Wahl, J.   357
Wahrman, R.   401
Waizenhöfer, E.   298
Walder, L. O.   277
Waldman, I. D.   280
Waldzus, S.   466
Walker, A.   297
Walkley, R. P.   473
Wallace, H. M.   129, 156, 161
Wallace, L. A.   373
Waller, B. M.   259, 260
Waller, J.   267
Waller, N. G.   355
Waller, P. F.   228
Walster, E.   356, 357, 360, 365
Walther, J. B.   258
Wan, E. W.   162
Wang, Q.   132
Wänke, M.   177
Wann, D. L.   465
Warren, J. A.   452
Warren, W. L.   287
Waters, H.   304
Watkins, S.   270
Wayment, H. A.   244
Weary, G.   84
Weaver, K.   328
Webb, E. J.   48
Webb, T. L.   197, 198
Webster, D. M.   182, 213–14, 215
Wegener, D. T.   180
Wegner, D. M.   161
Weiby, M.   84
Weick, K. E.   47
Weigel, R. H.   192
Weiner, Bernard   17, 69, 70
    biography   69
Weisband, S.   436
Weiss, W.   205
Welchans, S.   295
Wells, G. L.   88, 177, 205
Wells, S.   330
Wenzel, M.   466
West, M. A.   257–8
West, S. G.   31
Wetherell, M.   18, 35, 45, 256, 261, 326, 382, 464, 515
Wheelan, S. A.   394
Wheeler, L.   130
Wheeler, M. A.   144

Whitaker, J. L.   305
Whitchurch, E.   146–7
White, B. J.   454
White, J. W.   277
White, M. J.   129
White, P. A.   87, 88, 89
White, R. K.   15, 17, 433, 492, 512
White, R. V.   330
White, R. W.   181
Whitney, G. A.   367
Wicker, A. W.   18, 191
Wicklund, R. A.   150, 159–60
Wiechmann, D.   422
Wiederman, M. W.   361
Wienke, C.   364
Wiers, R. W.   216
Wieselquist, J.   369
Wiesenthal, D. L.   306
Wigboldus, D.   219, 469
Wilder, D. A.   248, 474, 475, 476, 481
Wilhelmy, R. A.   248
Wilke, H.   257
Wilkes, A. L.   449
Wilkowski, B. M.   305
Williams, C. J.   119, 187, 192–3, 216
Williams, H. L.   131
Williams, K. D.   352, 391–2, 413–14, 415, 416
Williams, R. B.   350
Williams, R. M., Jr.   472
Willis, H.   147
Wills, T. A.   350
Wilner, D. M.   473
Wilson, A. M.   317
Wilson, D. S.   453
Wilson, J.   317
Wilson, J. Q.   242
Wilson, T. D.   4, 36, 115, 127, 176, 216, 360
Winkielman, P.   149
Winston, J.   453
Winston, J. S.   60
Winter, D. G.   432
Winter, L.   107
Wiseman, J. P.   372
Witte, E. H.   416
Wittenbaum, G. M.   421
Wittenbrink, B.   100, 115, 452
Wofford, J. C.   430
Wolfe, C. T.   137
Wolpert, I.   326
Wong, N.   155

Wong, T. J. 464
Wood, C. 162
Wood, J. V. 244
Wood, W. 198, 225, 238, 244–5, 250, 252, 257
Worchel, S. 227, 473
Wowra, S. A. 168
Woycke, J. 432
Wright, E. F. 88, 164
Wright, R. D. 164
Wright, S. C. 467, 482, 483
Wrightsman, L. S. 49
Wrosch, C. 165
Wu, C. -H. 359
Wu, F. C. W. 280–1
Wundt, W. 491
Wyer, N. A. 119
Wyer, R. S., Jr. 99, 148, 177

Xenias, D. 481
Xu, J. 470, 471

Yahya, K. A. 270
Yamagishi, T. 454
Yoo, S. H. 506
Yoon, H. J. 224
Yorges, S. L. 422
Young, A. W. 72
Young, R. D. 165
Yovetich, N. A. 147, 369
Yuan, N. P. 298
Yukl, Gary 426, 429, 430
    biography 431
Yzerbyt, V. 451, 461, 464–5, 469, 470

Zaadstra, B. M. 359
Zaccaro, S. J. 434
Zajonc, Robert 107, 130, 149, 175–6, 216, 236, 362
    biography 176
Zanna, Mark P. 58, 138, 159, 174, 175, 177, 190, 197, 227, 261, 445
    biography 174

Zavalloni, M. 258
Zawacki, T. 298
Zebrowitz, L. A. 357
Zebrowitz-McArthur, L. 60
Zehr, C. E. 197
Zeisel, H. 259
Zelditch, M. 400
Zhang, J. J. 331
Zhang, S. 119
Zhou, S. 483
Zick, A. 452
Zillmann, D. 283
Zimbardo, P. G. 75, 240–1, 269, 301, 492
Zimmermann, T. D. 157, 159
Zuckerman, C. 421
Zuckerman, M. 84, 150
Zukova, J. 113
Zvibel, M. 246
Zwi, A. B. 295

Subject Index

Note: Page numbers in **bold** indicate glossary definitions. Page numbers in *italic* refer to illustrations.

abusive relationships   368
accentuation effect   449, **597**
accessibility of information   98–9, **597**
accommodation: relationships   367, 369
accountability, perceiver   111, **597**
acculturation   521–5, **597**
   attitudes to   523
   bicultural identity integration   522–5
achievement
   attributions   69–70
   cultural value   496
   needs   384
   priming goal of   197–8
acquiescent responding   497, 499,
   504, **597**
actor-observer difference   81, 87, **597**
   intentional behaviours   86
   reversing   82–3
actual and potential group
   performance   409–18
actual selves   135, *136*
additive tasks   410, 411
   motivation losses   415
   social compensation   416
   see also brainstorming
adjustment
   heuristic, cognition   104, 105
   marital   376
   migrants   522
   social, attitudes helping   181
advertising
   and affective/cognitive needs   178–9
   brand images and culture   498
   dating adverts   361
   Guardian advertising campaign   100–1
   matching to consumer goals   221–2
   matching message to product   223–4
   and self-monitoring   183–4
   subliminal   217–21
affective component of attitudes
   175–6, **597**
agency, sense of   145
aggression   275–307, **597**

alcohol consumption   288–9
biological approaches   280–1
bullying   275, 298–300
   displaced   281
gender differences   288
high temperature   289–90
individual differences   287–8
information sources   277–9
intergroup   300–4
intimate partner violence   275, 294–7
learning   284, 288, 294
measurement/study of   276–9, 295–7
and media violence   30–1, 277, 290–4
physical   278, 280, 285, 287, 295, 297
prevention and intervention   304–6
psychological approaches   281–6
sexual   277, 297–8
situational influences   288–94
social information processing
   models   284–5
as social problem   294–304
theories of   279–86
see also violence
Aggression Questionnaire (AQ)   277,
   278, **597**
aggressive cues   281–2, 305, **597**
aggressive scripts   285, **597**
alcohol consumption
   and aggression   288–9
   and cognitive dissonance   228
   escaping the self   165
   taxation reducing   225
altruism   312–17, **597**
   evolution and genetics   336–9
   life-threatening emergencies   341–3
altruistic punishment   338–9
ambivalence, attitudinal   180
analysis of non-common effects
   62–3, **597**
analytic versus holistic cognition   500,
   501, 502–3
anchoring/adjustment heuristic   103–4,
   105, **597**

anger
   aggression theories   282–3, 285
   attributions   73, 74, 75
   intergroup emotion   469–70
   measuring using AQ   278
   music reducing   306
   and relationship deterioration   371
   trait aggressiveness   287
anti-smoking campaigns   229
anxiety
   attachment style   354–5, 356
   existential   155
   intergroup   481
archival data, aggression   279
archival research   29–50
   data on aggression   279
argument quality
   advertising messages   223–4
   impact on implicit attitudes   216
   minority-majority influence   252–4
   and systematic message processing
   212, 213, 214
arousal
   aggression theories   283–4, 293,
   294, 305
   misattribution of   73–6, *364*
arousal: cost-reward model   323–4,
   325, **597**
assumptive help   340–1
attachment theory   353–6, **597**
   and perceived responsiveness
   375
   and social appraisal   129
attention conflict, task performance   237
attitude-behaviour relation
   191–9, **597**
attitude change
   implicit attitudes   216–17
   incentive-induced   224–9
   minority influence   255–6
   persuasive communication   203–24
attitude components   174–9
attitude functions   181–4, **597**

attitude measurement 13–14, 185–90, 191–2
attitude strength 185
attitude structure 179–80
attitudes 173–4, **597**
attitudinal ambivalence 180, **597**
attraction, psychological 360
attractiveness 356–7
  contextual influences 359
  features determining 357–9
  self-enhancing illusion 146–7
attribution theories 16–17, 61–2, **597**
  achievement 69–70
  arousal/emotion 73–6
  conversations 88
  correspondence inference 62–3
  covariation 64–8
  depression 70–3
  intentional behaviour 85–6
  naïve scientist model 86–8
attributional biases 76, **597**
  actor-observer difference 81–4, 87
  conversational approach 87–8
  correspondence bias 76–81
  self-serving 81, 83–5, 148, 150
audience inhibition 319, 322–3, **597**
augmenting principle 66, 67, **597**
authoritarian leadership 512
authoritarian personality 3, 8–9, 17, 443–4, **597**
authoritarianism, right-wing 444
  as ideology 445–8
autobiographical memories 131–2
autocratic leadership 15, 17, 433, 435, 512
autokinetic effect 13–14, 238–9, **597**
automatic processes **597**
  dispositional inferences 79–80
  social cognition 96–108
  social perception 90
autonomy/autonomous
  helping style 341
  independent self 140
  individualist nations 494, 496–7
  leadership 512, 513
  self-regulation 166
availability heuristic 103, 105, 451, **597**
averaging 59, **597**
avoidant attachment style 354, 356

back-translation 497, **597**
balance theory 16, **597–8**
base rate information 102–3, **598**
battered women, investment model analysis 368
behavioural component of attitudes 176–7, **598**
belongingness, need for 352–3, **604**
benevolent sexism 442, 470–1
Bennington study, social influence 14, **598**
better than average effect (BAE) 505–6, **598**
bias(es)
  correspondence 63, 76–81, 88, 501, 502–3
  discussion biases, groups 420–1
  due to stereotype activation 100–1, 115
  evaluation, groups 421–2
  false consensus 76
  hostile attribution 287–8
  self-enhancing 83, 147, 151
  self-protective 83, 129
  self-serving 81, 83–5, 150
  see also ingroup bias
Bible text, inciting aggression 292–3
bicultural identity 522, **598**
bicultural identity integration 522, 524–5, **598**
biological approaches
  aggression 280–1
  group formation 382
  see also social neuroscience
Bobo Doll paradigm 284
bogus pipeline procedure 452
bookkeeping model, stereotype change 482
brain mapping/brain activation 22, 65
brainstorming 410, **598**
  consensus information 64–5, 67
  coordination losses 412, 414
  individual capability losses/gains 417–18
  interactive versus nominal 412, 414
brand choice, subliminal priming influencing 220–1
brand images and culture 498
'broken windows theory' of crime 242
bullying 275, **598**
  cyberbullying 298, 299
  link to suicide 299
  school and workplace 298–300

bystander effect 318, **598**
  decision-making model 319, 322–3
  and emergency situations 320–1
  Kitty Genovese case 317–18
  overcoming 322–3
  and social identity 328–9
  see also prosocial behaviour

Capgras Syndrome, attributions 72
categorization 97–9, **598**
  accentuation effects 449
  impression formation 110–13
  judgemental heuristics 101–5
  priming, effects on behaviour 105–8
  schemas 100–1
  self-categorization 131, 256–7, 261–2, 464
  stereotype activation and goals 109
  stereotype suppression 110–20
  varying levels of 476–80
catharsis 304–5, **598**
causal attribution 61–88, **598**
  accuracy of 85
  bias in 76–85
  in conversations 88
  correspondent inference 62–3
  covariation 64–8
  depression 70–3
  emotion/arousal 73–6
  and intentions 85–6
  naive scientist metaphor 86–8
  success and failure 69–70
causal power 68, **598**
causal schemas 66–7, **598**
central trait 58, **598**
charismatic (transformational) leaders 430–1, 432, 512, 513, **608**
charitable donation 311, 328–9, 333, 339
coefficient of relatedness (r) 336–7, **598**
cognitive algebra model 59, **598**
cognitive closure, need for 213–15, **604**
cognitive component of attitude 174–5, **598**
cognitive dissonance 177, **598**
cognitive dissonance theory 18, 225–7, **598**
  and group initiation 388
  and incentives/sanctions 228
  self-perception theory challenging 227–8

cognitive miser   105, 451, **598**

cognitive neo-associationist model   282–3, **598**

cognitive response model, persuasion   204–6, **598**

cognitive restriction   417, **598**

cognitive stimulation   418, **598**

cognitive styles   500–3, **598**

cohesiveness, group   398, 399

   and groupthink   27, 28, 262, 263

collective violence   300, **598**

collectivism/collectivist cultures   494–5

   cognitive style   500–3

   conformity   499, 511–12

   and group honour   517, 517–18

   interdependency   140, 504

   interpersonal relations   509–10

   negotiation   518

   self-enhancement biases   151

   situational attributions   80–1

   social identity theory   515–17

   social loafing study   514–15

commitment

   groups   386–90, 395

   relationships   365, 367, 368–9

common ingroup identity model   326, 477, **598**

   dual categorization   479–80

communal relationships   371–2, **598**

companionate love   365, **598**

comparison with others   243–5

comparison, group polarization   260–1

comparison level, relationships   366

competence versus warmth   51, 470, 472

competition

   'boys camp' study   454

   and intergroup comparison   402, 403

   social   415, 416, 516, 517

   social facilitation effect   10–12, 235–7

   swimming, motivation gains   417

compliance   245–7, **598**

confederate   37, **598**

configural model   59, **599**

conflict

   attention   237

   between injunctive & descriptive norms   242

   during group development   393

   group decision making   423–4

   intergroup   27, 467–8

   intergroup, and social change   484–5

majority-minority influence   251, 251–2, 254

   over resources   462

   realistic conflict theory   3, 454, 462, 464

Conflict Tactics Scales (CTS)   295, 297, **599**

conformity   243, 248–50

   Asch's studies   7–8, 247–9

   cultural differences   499, 511–12

   to group norms   394–5, 464–5

   normative & informational influence   243–4

   reasons for   249–50

   referent informational influence   257

   to social norms and prejudice   446, 448

confound, experimental   41

conjunctive tasks   411, 415, 416, 417, 422

consensus information   64–5, 67, **599**

consistency information   64–5, 67, **599**

consistency, minority influence   251, **599**

consistency theories   16, **599**

construct: defined   27, **599**

construct validity   41, **599**

contact hypothesis   472–6, **599**

   extended version of   482–3

contempt, group-based   470

contingency approaches, leadership   428–30, **599**

continuum model of impression formation   110–11, **599**

control group: defined   39, **599**

controlled processes   95, 97, **599**

   and correspondence bias   79, 80

   dissociation model of stereotyping   113–15

   motivational factors   112, 119

convergent validity   50, **599**

conversion, minority influence   252, **599**

conversion model, stereotype change   482

conversion theory, Moscovici study testing   255–6

coordination losses   412–14, **599**

correspondence bias   63, 76–81, 88, **599**

   cultural differences   501, 502–3

correspondent inference theory   62–3, **599**

cost-reward model: emergency intervention   323–5

Cotard's delusion, attributions   72

counterattitudinal behaviour   225–8, **599**

covariation theory   17, 64–5, **599**

cover story   43, **599**

crime

   alcohol's causal effect   288

   death penalty, attitudes to   198

   heat hypothesis   289, 290

   intimate partner   295

   and norm violation   242–3

   statistics   278, 288, 297

crisis in social psychology   17–19, **599**

cross-cultural replication   491–2, **599**

cultural masculinity-femininity   494, **599**

culture   491–3, **599**

   cognitive styles   500–3

   group processes   511–15

   Hofstede's dimensions   494–5

   intercultural relations   519–25

   intergroup relations   515–19

   interpersonal relations   509–11

   methodological issues   496–9

   nations as cultures   493

   and self-construal   503–8

   values, Schwartz   495–6

Cyberball, social exclusion   352

cyberbullying   298, 299, **599**

cybernetic systems   160

data collection methods   47–51

dating   361, 374

debriefing   38, **599**

decategorization   476, 477, 478, 480, **599**

deception

   in research   6, 38, 268

   self-deception   148–9

decision making

   groups   258–64

   heuristics   101–5

   hidden profile task   419–24

   juries   259–60

defensive helping   341

deindividuation   241, 301, **599**

delay of gratification paradigm   164

demand characteristics   18, 19, 42–3, **599**

democratic leadership   15, 17, 433, 434, 435, 492, 512

dependency-orientated help   341

dependent variable   37–8, **599**

depression

   and attribution   70–3, 84

   and self-regulation   165

depressive realism   73, **599**

derogation of alternatives   369, **600**

descriptive norms   238, 240, 241, 242, **600**
desired selves   126, 135, **600**
dieting
   and ego depletion   162–4
   escaping the self   165
diffusion of responsibility   319, 325, **600**
   bystander intervention in
      emergencies   320–1
direct aggression   276, **600**
direct reinforcement   284, **600**
directive leaders   435
disclosure   372–4
disclosure reciprocity   373, **600**
discounting principle   66–7, **600**
discourse analysis   35–6, **600**
discrimination *see* prejudice
discussion biases, groups   420–1
disease threat and xenophobia   461
disjunctive tasks   410–11, 415, 416
disobedience   269–70
dispensability effect   414, 415, 418, **600**
displaced aggression   281, 302, **600**
display rules, emotional expression   506,
   507, **600**
dispositional attributions   61–2
   actor-observer difference   81–3
   correspondence biases   76–80
   correspondent inference   62–3
   cultural differences   80–1
   intentional behaviour   85–6
dissociation model, stereotyping   113,
   600
dissonance theory *see* cognitive dissonance
   theory
distinctiveness information   64–5,
   67, **600**
distinctiveness theory   134–5
distinctiveness threat, groups   465–6
distraction   206, **600**
divergence: groups   390
domestic violence   288, 289
   bystander intervention   329
   intimate partner violence   294–7
door-in-the-face technique   245, **600**
drive theory   236
dual categorization/identity
   model   478–80
dual process models   451–2
   automaticity and control, Devine
      113–15, 451–2
   'conversion theory', Moscovici   251–2
   persuasion   207–12, **600**
   social attitudes, Duckitt   448

eco-cultural theory   493, 500, 501, **600**
effort withdrawal, women using as
   self-handicap   152–3
egalitarianism   109, 110
   moderating stereotypic activation
      109, 110
   replacing stereotypic thoughts
      with   113–15
   versus hierarchy   496, 497
ego-defensive function   181–2, **600**
ego depletion   162, 163–4, **600**
egoism-altruism debate   313–16
egotism, implicit   149
egotism, narcissistic   158–9
elaboration likelihood model
   (ELM)   39–40, 252–3
embeddedness versus autonomy   496,
   497, **600**
emergency intervention   317
   arousal: cost–reward model   323–5
   decision-making model   319, 322–3
   impact of social identity   326–9
   in life-threatening situations   342–4
   situational determinants   317–19
   violent situations   330–1
emotional contagion   395, 398, **600**
emotional prejudice   469–70
emotional support   343, 350
emotions
   attributions of bodily feelings   73–6
   and helping behaviour   329
   influence on attitudes   175–6
   intergroup   468–71
   love   365, 509–10
   Schacter's two factor theory   74
   and the self   164, 165, 166
   and self-presentation   149, 150
   within groups   393, 395
   see also anger; anxiety; fear
empathic concern   315, 316, 335, **600**
empathy   311, **600**
   brain activation   340
   contact promoting   481
   interventions promoting   483
   leading to helping behaviour   313–16,
      329
   measurement of prosocial
      personality   335
empathy-altruism hypothesis   313,
   315, 316
encoding: defined   100, **600**
entitativity   383, 384, **600**
   group identification   385–6

equality: and positive intergroup
   contact   484–5
equity theory   365–6, **600**
escapist behaviour   165–6
ethical issues
   aggression/violence research
      276, 330
   bystander research   331, 342
   obedience studies   268–9
   research principles/standards   38
   research strategy   31
ethnocentrism   441, **600**
ethological perspective: aggression   280
eureka effect   411, **600**
Europe, development of social
   psychology in   19–21
European Association of Social
   Psychology (EASP)   20, **600**
evaluation apprehension   236–7,
   322, **600**
evaluation bias, groups   421–2
evaluative conditioning   175, **600**
   changing implicit attitudes   216, 217
evaluative priming   187–8
evolutionary (social) psychology   21–2,
   357, **600**
   female body symmetry   359
   group formation   382
   group living   453
   helping behaviour   336–9
   mate preference   361
   need to belong   352–3
   role of attractiveness   357
   xenophobia   461
exchange relationship   371, 372, 382, **600**
excitation transfer theory   283–4, **600–1**
exclusion, social   155, 351–2, 391–2
existential threats, groups   461–2
exit: from a group   390–1
expectancy-value models, attitudes   175,
   195, 217, 225
expectation states theory   400–1, **601**
experimental confound   41, **601**
experimental group   39, **601**
experimental method   13, 30
   criticisms of   18, 45–6
experimental scenario   36–7, **601**
experimenter expectancy effect   18, 19,
   43, **601**
experiments   30–3, **601**
   criticisms of   18, 45–6
   design of   38–41
   features of   36–8

validity threats 41–3
web-based 43–4
explicit measures of attitude 185,
    186–7, **601**
    and attitude change 216–17
    prejudice measures 193, 195, 452
    reliability and validity 189–90
    social desirability concerns 187, 452
explicit self-esteem 138, 140, 143
explicit self-knowledge 135–6
extended contact hypothesis 482–3, **601**
external validity 43, **601**

F-scale (Fascism) 444
facial features
    and personality 59–60
    physical attraction 359
    self-enhancement bias 146–7
facilitation *see* social facilitation
factorial experimental design 39, **601**
failure
    attributions for 69, 84, 148
    cultural differences 505, 506, 516
    effect of closeness 150–1
    group decision-making 27–8, 262
    self-regulatory 163–4
    to solve hidden profiles 419–22
false consensus bias 76, **601**
familiarity: link to liking 362–3
favouritism, ingroup 326, 338, 455–6
    cultural differences 516–17
    and group existence threats 461
    minimal group paradigm 457–8
    national group membership 301–2
    and social reality constraints 463
fear
    appeals, advertising 224
    and attachment style 353, 354, 355
    emotional prejudice 470
    intergroup emotion theory 469
    neuroscience of 22
    of punishment 281
    of subliminal advertising 218
    triggering aggression 282–3
feeling versus thinking goods 222–3
field experiment: defined 6, **601**
field theory 15, **601**
films, embedding brand names in 221
foot-in-the-door technique 246, 267, **601**
forgiveness 367–8, **601**
friendship 372
    cultural differences 497, 509
    extended contact hypothesis 482

functions of 372
link to proximity 360, 362
predictor of reduced prejudice 477
similarity aiding 363–4
frustration-aggression hypothesis 281–2,
    601
'Fukushima 50' volunteers 311–12

gender differences
    attractiveness & status preference 361
    helping behaviour 332
    physical aggression 278, 288, 295–7
    self-esteem 143
    self-handicapping behaviour 152–3
    self-knowledge 140, 143
gender roles
    cultural differences 494
    helping behaviours 332
general aggression model (GAM) 285,
    286, **601**
    explaining high temperature
        effect 289–90
genetic factors
    aggression 279, 280
    helping behaviour 336–8
    need to belong 352–3
geographic regions approach 289, **601**
global warming 290
globalization, effect on values 519–21
goal dependence 110, **601**
goals 107, **601**
    abstract 161
    activation of 107–8
    and competitive behaviour 3–4
    consumer 222
    effect of priming on 107–8
    group 243, 249, 383, 416, 434
    implicit 108, 110
    inferential 80
    and intentions 197–8
    overriding stereotype
        activation 108–10
    path-goal theory, leadership 429–30
    performance 399
    self-regulatory standards 160–1
    superordinate 454, 455
goods, consumer 222–4
group-to-group transfer 425, 436, **601**
group-to-individual-in-group
        transfer 425, 436, **602**
group-to-individual transfer 424–5,
    436, **602**
group cohesiveness 398

and groupthink 27, 28, 262, 263
and performance 399
group commitment 386–7, **601**
    and conformity to norms 395
    and initiation rituals 388–9
    maintenance stage 389–90
group composition 419–22, **601**
group decision making 258–64
    bystander behaviour 319–23
    group polarization 258, 259, 260–3
    hidden profiles 419–24
group design 434
group development 392–4, 435–6
group distinctiveness, threats to 465–6
group emotions 469–70, **601**
group honour 517–18
group identification 458–61, **601**
    dual categorization/identity model
        478–80
    entitative groups 385–6
    impact on social influence 256–7
    measuring 391
    and prejudice 458–61
    and prosocial behaviour 325–6
    and social identity 131, 458–9
group leadership 433–6, **601**
group learning 424–5, **601**
    group leadership supporting 435–6
group loyalty 397, 517
group norms 395, 397, 464–5, 482
    autokinetic studies 13–14, 239, 245
    condoning aggression 301–2
    and helping 326–7
    measuring 391
    polarization 261
group performance
    actual and potential 409–11
    and cohesion 399
    leadership helping to improve
        433–6
    management 418–26, **601**
    process losses versus gains 411–18
group polarization 258, 259, 260–3, **601**
group potential 409–18
group socialization 386–90, **601**
group synchronization 422–4, **601**
    and leadership 434–5
group task types 410–11, **601**
group values, threats to 464–5
groups 381, **601**
    cultural differences 511–15
    group level analysis 392–401
    helping behaviour 325–8

groups (*continued*)
  individual level analysis   386–92
  intergroup analysis   401–4
  phenomenology of   381–6
  and prejudice   453–71
groupthink   262–4, **601**
  archival analyses   29–30
  Janis's theoretical model   27–8

habit formation   225
habits and behavioural prediction   196,
    197, 198
habituation   294, **602**
Hamilton's rule, altruism   336–7
harmony versus mastery   496, 497
hazing (initiation rituals)   389
health
  anti-smoking campaigns   203, 229
  and attractiveness   357
  benefits of social ties   350
  implementation intentions   197
  and self-enhancement   154–5
heat hypothesis   289–90, **602**
helping behaviour   312–13, **602**
  and altruism/empathy   313–16
  bystander research   317–23
  costs and rewards   323–5
  in emergencies   320–1, 341–4
  field experiment   32–3
  and gender   331–2
  genetics and evolution   336–9
  long-term, sustained   332–6
  motivations for   323–9
  negative aspects of   340–1
  neuroscience of   339–40
  and violence   330–1
heuristic   96, **602**
  anchoring/adjustment   104, 105
  availability   103, 105, 451
  representativeness   102–3, 104–5
heuristic processing   208–9, **602**
  biasing systematic processing
    210–11
  and instability of attitude change/
    formation   215
heuristic-systematic model (HSM)
    207–9, **602**
hidden profiles, group decision
    making   419–24, 435, **602**
hierarchy
  and prejudice   444–6, 459, 460
  social/status and discrimination
    466–8, 473

of speaking, groups   398, *400*
  versus egalitarianism, cultures   496,
    497, **602**
historical perspectives   10–19
holistic versus analytic thinking   500, 501,
    502–3
Holocaust   264–5, 326, 328
honour killings   517–18
hormonal link to aggression   280–1, **602**
hormone-markers, beauty features   359
hostile aggression   276, **602**
hostile attribution bias   287–8, **602**
hostility
  and automatic stereotype
    activation   99
  elicited by violent media   293, 294
  intergroup   3, 300, 461, 470, 475
  measure of   278, 287
HSM (heuristic-systematic model)   207–9
Hull–Spence drive theory   236
hypothesis: defined   29, **602**

IAT *see* implicit association test (IAT)
ideal selves   135, *136*
identity negotiation   167, **602**
Identity Theory   333
illusions
  autokinetic effect   13–14, 238–9
  self-enhancing   127, 143, 146–7
illusory correlation effect   450–1, **602**
implementation intentions   197,
    198, **602**
implicit association test (IAT)   188–9
  attitude change   216
  implicit self-esteem   138, 140–1
  prejudice and stereotyping   452
implicit attitudes, changing   216–17
implicit egotism   149, **602**
implicit goal operation   108–10, **602**
implicit measures   49–50, **602**
  attitude change   216–17
  of prejudice   193, 195, 451–3
implicit measures of attitude   185,
    187–9, **602**
  behaviour prediction   193–5
  evaluative priming technique   187–8
  Implicit Association Test (IAT)   188–9
  reliability and validity   189–90
implicit personality theory   59, **602**
implicit self-esteem   138–40, **602**
  and explicit modesty, Asians   151
  low levels of and aggression   159
  measuring with the IAT   141–2

implicit self-knowledge   135–6
impression formation   57–60
  configural model   59
  continuum model   110–11
  individuated   110, 111, 112
  judgemental heuristics   101–2
  motivational factors   111–13
impression management   42
impression motivation   209
impulsive helping   324, **602**
incentive-induced attitude change   225–9
inclusive fitness theory
    (kin selection)   337
independent variable: defined   37, **602**
independent versus interdependent
    self   140, 142–3, **602**
  and friendships   509
  in-group favouritism   516–17
  scale measuring   505
  variation over time   507–8
indifference, in relationships   371
indirect aggression   276, **602**
individual-to-individual transfer   424,
    436, **602**
individual capability gains and
    losses   417–18, **602**
individual differences
  acculturation attitudes   523
  attachment anxiety and avoidance
    scale   355
  attitude strength   185
  identification   391
  intelligence theory   70
  intimate partner aggression   296
  Motivation to Control Prejudiced
    Reactions Scale   119
  need for cognition   214
  need for cognitive closure   215
  personality assessment   428
  prosocial personality   335
  Rosenberg Self-Esteem Scale
    (RSES)   138
  self-construal   505
  self-esteem IAT   141–2
  self-monitoring   183
  social comparison   244
  social desirability   42
  social dominance orientation   446
  trait aggression   278
individual mobility   467, 468
individualism
  ideology of   467
  and the independent self   140

methodological   9–10
post-materialism link   521
individualism-collectivism   494–5, **602**
   and cognitive style   500–3
   conformity   249
   and dispositional attributions   80–1
   negotiation   518–19
   and self-enhancement   151
   social loafing study   514–15
individuating information   110, **602**
inequality   445
   acceptance of   483, 496
   awareness of   484–5
influence
   informational   244
   majority-minority   250–8
   normative   243–4, 260–1, 262, **604**
   referent informational   257
information processing
   and aggression   284–5
   cultural differences   500–1
   persuasion theories   204, 207–16
   and self-schemas   133–4
informational influence   244, **602**
   and group polarization   262
   referent   257
ingroup bias   453–80
   defined   455, **602**
   dual categorization reducing   479–80
   group identification   458–61
   minimal   455–6, 457–8, 466
   neuroscientific evidence   458
   positive differentiation   462
   recategorization reducing   477
   self-esteem hypothesis   462–3
   socio-structural theories   467–8
ingroup inclusion   326, 328
ingroup reappraisal   481, **603**
inhibition
   bystander behaviour   322–3
   social, and task performance   236–7
initiation, group   387–8, **603**
   'hazing' in student societies   389
injunctive norms   238, *241*, 242, **603**
instrumental aggression   276, **603**
instrumental support   350
interaction effect   39–40, **603**
interaction process analysis (IPA)   393,
   398, 399–400
   coding system   393–4
interdependence
   and culture   504, 505, 507–8, 509
   and intergroup relations   515–19

positive and negative   455
social loafing, cultural
   differences   514–15
interdependence, requirement in close
   relationships   371
interdependent self *see* independent versus
   interdependent self
intergroup aggression   300–4, **603**
intergroup anxiety   481, **603**
intergroup comparison   402–3,
   463–4
intergroup conflict   27, 467–8
intergroup contact and prejudice
   reduction   472–6
   extended contact hypothesis   482–3
   models of contact   476–80
   psychological processes   480–1
intergroup emotion theories   468–71
Intergroup Helping as Status Relations
   (IHSR) model   341
intergroup relations, cultural
   differences   515–19
internal validity   41, **603**
Internet experiment   **603**
Internet experiments   44
interpersonal aggression   300, **603**
interpersonal attraction   356–64
interpersonal cohesion   398, **603**
interventions
   aggression prevention/
      reduction   304–6
   prejudice reduction   472–85
intimacy groups   383, 384, 387
intimate partner violence   275,
   294–7, **603**
intimate relationships
   and attachment style   355
   cross-cultural variation   509
   disclosure   373, 375
   perceived partner
      responsiveness   375–6
intrinsic motivation   229, **603**
   versus extrinsic rewards   128–9
introspection   126–8, **603**
intuitive lawyers,
   self-enhancement   147–8
investment model, Rusbult   366–7, 368
investments: defined   366, **603**
ironic processes model of mental
   control   116–17

jigsaw classroom   474, 475, **603**
Jonestown mass suicide   397

judgemental heuristics   102, 104–5
jury decision-making   259–60

kin selection   337–8, **603**
Köhler effect   416, 417, 418, **603**

laboratory experiment: defined   6, **603**
laissez-faire leaders   430, 431, 433, **603**
latent worthlessness   157
leader traits   426–7, **603**
leaderless groups   434, **603**
leadership (in organizations)   426, **603**
leadership behaviour   426, 427–8, **603**
   contingency approaches   428–30
   impact of leadership style   433–4
   Leader Behaviour Description
      Questionnaire (LBDQ)   427–8
leadership effectiveness   426, **603**
   contingency approaches   428–9
   and personality traits   426–7, 428
leadership style   433–4, **603**
   cross-cultural research   512–13
   and group performance   433–6
learned helplessness theory   70–1, 73,
   84, **603**
learning
   of aggression   284
   group   424–5
'legitimizing myths', hierarchical social
   order   445
lexical decision task   99, 117,
   306, **603**
life-threatening situations, intervening
   in   342–4
Likert scales   186
littering studies   240, *241*, 242–3
looking-glass self   129
love   365, 509–10
lowballing technique   246–7, **603**
loyalty: groups   397, 517

main effect: defined   39, **603**
majority influence   247–58, **603**
   Asch paradigm   247–50
   jury decision making   259
   theories of   251–8
manipulation check   37, **603**
maritime disasters: emergency
   response   341, 342, 343
mass panic   341, 342
mass suicide   397
mastery versus harmony, cultural
   dimension   496, 497, **603**

matching marketing messages
  to consumer goals 221–3
  to consumer product 223–4
maximum difference strategy 455–6,
  457–8, 459–60
media violence-aggression link 277,
  287–8, 290–4, **603**
medial prefrontal cortex (MPFC) 144
mediating process 27–8
mediating variable 40, **604**
memory
  autobiographical 131–2
  transactive 395, 396
mere exposure effect 176, 362–3, **604**
  changing implicit attitudes 216
mere presence (of others) and task
  performance 236, 237
meritocracy ideology 445
message repetition and attitude
  change 212
meta-analysis: defined 45, **604**
methodological individualism 9–10, **604**
migrant acculturation 521–3
'mindreading' 85–6
minimal group paradigm 4, 21, 455, 456,
  457–8, 459–60, 462, 466, **604**
minimal ingroup bias 455–6, 457–8, 466
minority influence 247, **604**
  consistent behavioural style 251
  Moscovici's conversion theory 251–2
  resistance to persuasion 255–6
  theories of 251–8
misattribution of arousal 73–6,
  364, **604**
mobbing *see* bullying
MODE model 198, **604**
modelling 288, **604**
  and media violence 287–8, 294
moderation (interaction effect) 40
modesty norms 506
monitoring
  self-monitoring and attitudes
    183–4, 193
  and self-regulation 161–2
mood
  emotional contagion 395, 398
  negative state-relief model 315
moral reasoning, measure of 335
mortality rates and social ties 350
motivation
  altruistic versus egoistic 313–16
  attributions 69
  to control prejudice scale 119

heuristic and systematic
  processing 208–9
ingroup versus outgroup helping 340
intentional behaviour 85–6
intrinsic 128–9, 229
MODE model 198
self-determination theory 166
for self-knowledge 145–57
and self-serving biases 81, 83,
  84–5
for volunteering 333–4
motivation losses and gains 414,
  415–17, **604**
  and group learning 425
  group under-performance 413–14
  in individual capability 417–18
motives *see* goals
multicomponent model of attitude
  174–9, **604**
music and anger/stress reduction 306
music lyrics and aggression 292
mutual differentiation 478, **604**

naïve scientist model 86–7, **604**
narcissism 156–7
  threatened egotism and
    violence 158–9
narratives 132
nation-level factor analysis 494, **604**
need to belong 352–3, **604**
  and group esteem/respect 454, 461
  and group formation 382, 384
need for cognition (NFC) 213, **604**
  persuasion study 178–9
  scale measuring 214
need for cognitive closure 213–15, **604**
  scale measuring 215
negative affect/emotion 148–9
  and aggressive behaviour 281, 282,
    283, 290
  guiding attitudes 175
  self-regulation drawback 165
  and subliminal brand advertising 221
negative interdependence 455, **604**
negative-state-relief model 315–16, **604**
negotiation 518–19
  cultural differences 518–19
  identity negotiation 167
  of roles in groups 389–90
neuroscience *see* social neuroscience
newcomer influence, groups 388
nominal groups 412, 414, **604**
non-common effects, analysis of 62, 63

non-reactive measures *see* unobtrusive
  measures
norm violation, promoting antisocial
  behaviour 240, 242–3
normative influence 243–4, **604**
  conformity 248
  group polarization 260–1, 262
  groupthink 262
norms 237–41, **604**
  and anti-social behaviour 240–1
  cultural differences 506–7, 511
  defined 238
  descriptive and injunctive 240, *241*, 242
  formation and transmission 238–40
  influence on behaviour 240–1
  modesty 151, 506
  political correctness 464
  prejudice and discrimination 464–5, 473
  subjective 195, 196
  violation and spread of disorder 242–3
  see also group norms

obedience to authority 264–70, **604**
  disobedience 269–70
  ethical issues 268–9
  Milgram's paradigm 264–6
  motives underlying 267–8
  situational determinants 266
object appraisal function 181, 182, **604**
observational measures 47–8
one-dimensional perspective,
  attitudes 179–80, **604**
one-shot case study 38–9, **604**
online dating 374
operationalization 37, **604**
ought selves 135, *136*
outcome dependency 111, 112, **604**
outgroup bias: defined 468, **604**
outgroup derogation 302, 459–60,
  469–70
outgroup helping 326, 329
outgroup homogeneity effect 449–50,
  604
outgroup threats: discrimination and
  prejudice 461–6
overstaffing 389

pan-cultural self-enhancement 151
participant: defined 29, **604**
participant observation 47, **604**
partner preferences
  cultural differences 509–10, 511
  evolutionary psychology 357, 359

gender differences 361
speed dating 360
passionate love 365, **605**
passivity: in emergencies 321, 322
path-goal theory of leadership 429–30
peer nominations 277, **605**
perceived behavioural control 196, **605**
perceived partner responsiveness 374–6, **605**
performance *see* group performance; task performance
peripheral trait 58, **605**
persecutory delusions 72
personality
  attitude-behaviour link 193
  authoritarian 3, 8–9, 17, 443–4
  Big Five Personality Test 428
  of brand image 222
  and forgiveness 367–8
  leader traits 426–7
  prosocial 334–6
  psychology 8–9
  social dominance orientation 444–8
  social penetration theory 373, *375*
personalized contact 476–7, 478
perspective taking 335, 483
persuasion 203–24
  advertising as applied 217–24
  and attitude content 178–9
  cognitive response model 204–6
  dual-process theory 207–16
  and group decision making 258–60
  information processing model 204
  majority and minority influence 252, 254
  systematic processing theories 203–7
physical aggression 278, 280, 285, 287, 295, 297, **605**
physiological research methods 50
placebo effect
  empathic emotion 315
  misattribution of arousal 73–5
  self-awareness 165
  self-help tapes 219
planned behaviour theory 195–7, **608**
pluralistic ignorance 319, 322, **605**
polarization: groups 258
population mobility 520
positive differentiation 462, 463–4, 466, **605**
positive interdependence 455, **605**
positive intergroup contact 483–5

positive-negative asymmetry 460, 465, **605**
possible selves 135
post-experimental enquiry 42, **605**
post-materialist values 520–1
post-test only control group design 39, **605**
post-traumatic stress disorder (PTSD) 298, **605**
potential group performance 409–11, **605**
  and process losses & gains 411–18
power distance 494, **605**
prejudice 441–3, **605**
  classic studies of 3–5
  cognitive approach 449–53
  explicit & implicit measures 451–2
  group approaches 258, *260*, 453–71
  implicit and explicit measures of 193, 195
  interventions to reduce 472–85
  motivation to control 119
  personality approaches 443–9
  and social neuroscience 453
  stereotyping research 99–118
  see also stereotypes
presence of others
  effect on task performance 235–7
  see also bystander effect
primacy effect 59, **605**
priming 5, 98–9, **605**
  and bicultural identity integration 522–3, 524–5
  effect on behaviour and goals 105–8
  evaluative 187–8
  implementation intentions 197–8
  and media violence-aggression link 293
  self-construals in response to 507–8
  subliminal 175, 219–21
principle-implementation gap 483, **605**
prison studies
  deindividuation 240–1, 301
  promotion prospects 467
probabilistic contrast 68, **605**
probabilistic sampling 34
probe reaction task 112, **605**
production blocking 414, 418, **605**
proportion of shared genes 337, **605**
prosocial behaviour 311–12, **605**
  altruism and helping 312–17
  bystander intervention 317–23
  cultural variations 509, *510*

evolutionary and genetic explanations 336–9
  neuroscience of 339–40
  real world 340–4
  search issues 330–6
  underlying motivations 323–9
prosocial personality 334–6, **605**
proximity: relationships 360–2
psychological attraction 360
public goods game 338, **605**
public opinion surveys 190
punishment
  for aggression 305
  altruistic 338–9

qualitative approaches 34–6, 328
quality of alternatives: investment model 366–7, *367*, 368
quasi-experiment **605**
quasi-experiments 30–1
questionnaires 48, 49
  back-translation 497
  survey research 33–4
quota sample 34, **605**

racial equality, acceptance of 483
racial prejudice 441, 446, 452, 469, 473
  brain mapping studies 22, 190
  contact reducing 481
  motivation to control 119
  overcoming 475
  scale measuring control of 119
random allocation 30, **605**
reactance theory 228, **605**
reactivity 48, **605**
realistic conflict theory 3, **605**
  prejudice and discrimination 454–6
  threats to resources 462
reasoned action theory 195–7, **608**
rebound effect, stereotype suppression 5, 117–20, **606**
recategorization 111, 477, 478, *479*, **605**
reciprocal altruism 338, **606**
'reciprocal concessions' procedure 245–6
reciprocity
  in altruistic behaviour 338, 339
  disclosure 373, 376
  ingroup 454, 455
referent informational influence 257, 261, **606**
reflected appraisals 129, **606**
reflective-impulsive model (RIM) 198
regulatory (ego) depletion 162, 163–4

rejection
  causal attributions 71
  of offers of heap 340–1
  and self-esteem 139–40
  sensitivity to 135
  social exclusion 351–2
  sociometer theory 154–5
relational aggression 276, **606**
relationship commitment 367, 369, **606**
relationship superiority 369, **606**
relationships
  abusive 368
  attachment theory 353–6
  cultural differences 509–10, 511
  dating 361, 374
  and disclosure 372–4
  effect of rejection 351–2
  ending of 376
  enhancement 367–71
  and need to belong 352–3
  partner responsiveness 374–6
  romantic 364–71
  satisfaction and stability 365–7
  social support 350–1
  types of 371–2
  and wellbeing 349–50
relative deprivation theory 462, 464, **606**
reliability 47, **606**
  attitude measures 190–1
  questionnaires 49
remembrance, groups 387, 392
representativeness heuristic 102–3,
    104–5, **606**
research methodology 3–6, 27–30
  data collection methods 47–51
  experimentation 36–46
  strategies 30–6
responsiveness 374–6
reward allocation strategies,
    groups 457–8
'rewardingness', group membership 387
rewards and costs
  methodological individualism 9–10
  prosocial behaviour 323–6
  relationships 365–6
rewards, intrinsic-extrinsic
    trade-off 128–9
right-wing authoritarianism 444, 445,
    447–8
RIM (reflective-impulsive) model 198
Ringelmann effect 412, **606**
  coordination losses 413–14
  early studies 12

rituals: group initiation 387–8, 389
rivalry, intergroup 403
role 381, **606**
  role schemas 102
  social roles, control and bias 77–8
  and status 398–401
role identities 333
role negotiation 390
role transition 386–7, **605**
romantic relationships 364–71
  couple-serving bias 147
  cultural differences 509–10
  rejection in, possible causes 71

sacrifice: in relationships 366,
    368–9
salience 79, **606**
  group membership 401–2
  mortality 155–6
  subgroup relations 479–80
sampling 34, **606**
  and covariation analysis 64–5
sanctions and attitude change 224–5
  cognitive dissonance theory 225–6
  paradoxical effects of 228–9
satisfaction in relationships 365–7
  and attachment style 355
  and psychological well-being
    349–50
  self-expansion theory 369–71
  and similarity 363
scapegoat theory 3, **606**
schadenfreude, group emotion 470
schema(s) 96, **606**
  activation and behaviour 105–8, 120
  causal 66–7
  and impression formation 101, *102*
  mental models 130
  and self-concept 133–5
  and 'Shooter Bias' 100–1
scientific method 6–7, 27, 35, 45
the self and the social world 125–6
self-assessment motive 146, **606**
self-awareness 159–60, **606**
  and monitoring 161–2
  need to escape 165
self-categorization theory 256–7,
    464, **606**
  group polarization 261–2
  origins in social identity theory 131
self-change 167–8
self-concept 133–6, **606**
self-construals 125, **606**

  cultural differences 503–8
  independent versus interdependent
    140, 142–3
  varying over time 507–8
self-criticism 151
self-determination theory 166, **606**
self-disclosure 372–3, **606**
self-distancing 166, 167
self-efficacy 196, **606**
  of followers 430
  role in helping 323
  and self-focus 160
self-enhancement 143, **606**
  cultural differences 151, 504–6
  implicit 148–9
  information processing 147–8
  items from BIDR scale 42
  motives 146–53
  narcissists' 156–7
  positive illusions of self 146–7
  reasons for 154–6
  and self-presentation 149–51
  and self-verification 153–4
  unconscious processes driving 148–9
self-esteem 136–40, **606**
  contingencies of self-worth 137,
    139–40
  cultural differences 151, 505, 506
  'dark side' of high 158
  effects of social exclusion on 155, 352
  ego-defensive function protecting 181
  gender differences 143
  and group acceptance 454
  implicit and explicit 138, 140
  ingroup bias increasing 462–3
  maintenance of, self-serving bias 84
  measures of 138, 141
  and narcissism 156–7, 158–9
  pros and cons of pursuing 156–7
  reciprocal liking enhancing 364
  and self-compassion 157
  sociometer theory 154–5
  subliminal messages to improve 219
  terror management theory 155
  trait and state 136–7
  unstable, effects of 137, 158
self-esteem hypothesis 462, 466, **606**
self-expansion model 370–1
self-focus 117, 120, 159–60, 162, 164–6
self-fulfilling prophecies 60, **606**
  of depressives 73
  expectation states theory 400, 401
  and social stereotypes 358

self-handicapping 150, **606**
  gender differences 152–3
self-interest and helping 338–9
self-knowledge 126–32
  cultural and gender influences 140–3
  neural correlates 143–5
  see also self-concept
self-monitoring 183–4, **606**
  moderating attitude-behaviour
    relation 193
self-narratives 132
self-other difference 81–4
self-perception theory 128–9, **606**
  and behavioural component of
    attitudes 176–7
  challenging dissonance theory 227–8
  and use of incentives 228
self-presentation 149–50, **606**
  and self-change 167–8
self-reference effect 133–4, **606**
self-reflection 126–7, 132, 159, 166
self-regulation 160, **607**
  autonomous 166
  consequences of 164–5
  depletion 162–4
  monitoring 161–2
  standards 160–1
  strength 162
  see also self-awareness
self-report methods/measures 48–9
  aggression 277, 278, 287
  prejudice control 119
  self-esteem 138
  social desirability questionnaire 42
self-schemas 133, **607**
  active versus stored 134–5
  and information processing 133–4
self-serving attributional biases 81, 83–5,
    148, 150, **607**
self-specificity 145
self stability and change 167–8
self-verification 153–4, **607**
self-worth contingencies 137, **607**
selfishness: life-threatening
    emergencies 341–3
semantic differential scales 186–7
sex differences *see* gender differences
sexual aggression 297–8, **607**
shared cognition, groups 395
shared leadership 434, **607**
similarity
  genetic explanation of aggression 280
  of group members 383, 384

and helping behaviour 337–8
  relationships 363–4
similarity-attraction effect 363–4, **607**
simple random sample 34, **607**
smoking
  campaigns to stop 203, 229
  incentives and sanctions 225, 228, 229
social adjustment function 181, **607**
social appraisal 129
social categories, group types 383–4
social categorization 97–9
  accentuation explanation 459
  approach to majority-minority
    influence 256–7
  decategorization 477
  and intergroup behaviour 457–8
  and prejudice 449, 450
social change
  role of intergroup conflict 484–5
  social identity theory 467
social cognition 95
  categorization 97–9
  controlled versus automatic
    processes 95–6
  defined 21, 95, **607**
  heuristics 101–5
  schema activation and
    behaviour 105–8
  schemas 100–1
  stereotypes, controlling 108–20
social comparison 18, 129–30, 243–5
  defined 130, 237, **607**
  and group membership 382
  and group polarization 260–1
  insecure 467
  measurement of 244
social compensation 415, 416, **607**
social competition 415, 416, 468, 516,
    517, **607**
social coordination, universal need 496
social creativity 463–4, *468*, 516
social desirability 41–2, 452, **607**
social dominance orientation 444–8, **607**
social exchange theory 382
social exclusion
  from groups 391–2
  immediate effects of 351–2
  sociometer theory 155
social facilitation 10–12, 13, 20, **607**
  and task performance 235–7
social hierarchy and
    discrimination 466–8
social identity 131

and bystander effect 328–9
cultural differences 516–17
defined 456, **607**
  group identification and
    prejudice 458–61
  and ingroup bias, neuroscience
    456, 458
  and intergroup aggression 301, 302,
    303–4
  and intergroup behaviour 461–4
  intergroup emotions 469
social identity theory 131, 301–2, 326,
    456, 468
  cross-cultural support for 516–17
  explaining outgroup bias 468
  and positive differentiation 462
  and social change 467
  'social creativity' strategy 463–4
  and status legitimacy 462–3
  versus Identity Theory 333
social influence 235
  compliance, inducing 245–7
  defined 237, **607**
  group decision making 258–64
  normative and informational 241–5
  numerical majorities &
    minorities 247–58
  obedience to authority 264–70
  social facilitation 235–7
  social norms 237–41
social loafing 12, 414, 415, 416, **607**
  cultural differences 512, 514–15
social neuroscience 51, **607**
  attributional processes 90
  brain mapping 22–3
  contact with others relieving
    distress 351
  helping behaviour 339–40
  prejudice 453
  self-knowledge 143–5
social norms *see* norms
'social pain', exclusion as form of 391–2
social penetration theory 373, *375*
social perception 57, **607**
  automatic and controlled 90
  impression formation 57–61
  self-fulfilling prophecy 358
  and social behaviour 120
  and social reality 88–90
social psychology
  characteristics of 6–7
  classic studies 3–6
  in Europe 19–21

social psychology (*continued*)
  history of   10–19
  new perspectives   21–3
  unique perspective   7–10
social reality   88–90
  constraints   463–4, **607**
  and group norms   395
  testing of   243
social responsibility, measure of   335
social support   350–1, **607**
  and conformity   249
socialization, groups   386–90
socio-emotional behaviour   393–4, **607**
socio-structural theories:
    discrimination   467–8
sociobiological perspective, groups   382
sociology   9–10
sociometer theory   154–5, **607**
source status, majority versus
    minority   252–4, 255–6
speaking hierarchy, groups   398, **607**
spontaneous behaviour, MODE
    model   198
staffing level: defined   389, **607**
staircase model   303–4, **607**
standards, self-regulatory   160–1
Stanford prison experiment   240–1,
    301, 467
state self-esteem   137
status
  gain and bullying   298–9
  collectivist cultures   515
  defined   392, **607**
  group, and discrimination   462–4
  group hierarchy   398–401
  and intimate relationships   361, 509–10
  and obedience to authority   264–6
  and offer of help   340–1
  and production blocking   414
  social dominance theory   444–5
  source, majority versus
    minority   252–4
steam boiler model, aggression   280, **607**
stereotypes   4–5, 49–50, 95–6, **607**
  automatic processes   96–108
  changing   482
  cognitive account   450–3
  dissociation of automatic & controlled
    components   113–14
  implicit goals overriding activation
    of   108–10
  impression formation   110–12
  priming studies   105–8

rebound effect   5, 117–20
  replacing with egalitarian
    responses   113–15
  stereotype content model   470–1
  suppression of   6, 115–20, **607**
  'what is beautiful is good'   356–7, 358
strangers: prosocial behaviour
  bystander intervention   331, 332
  cross-cultural variations   509, *510*
  donation of money to   311, 328–9
  reciprocal altruism   338
stress reduction
  role of music   306
  social support   350–1
strong reciprocity   339, **607**
subjective norms   195, 196
subjective validity   243
subliminal advertising   217–21, **607**
subtyping model, stereotypes   482
success attributions   69–70, 84, 87
sucker effect   415, **607**
suicide
  Al Qaida terrorists   461
  cyberbullying   299
  and need to escape self-awareness   165
  'revolutionary', Jonestown   397
summation   59, **607**
superordinate goals   454, 455, **608**
superordinate identity   326, 477–80
support: close relationships   350–1
survey research   33–4, 190, **608**
survival, universal need   496
system justification theory, outgroup
    bias   468
systematic processing   203, **608**
  majority and minority influence   252,
    253, 254
  persuasion   203–16

Tajfel matrices   456, 457–8,
    459–60
task behaviours   393, **608**
task cohesion   398, **608**
task design   434
task groups   *383, 384,* 387
task performance
  group cohesiveness   399
  and group learning   424–5, 436
  minorities leading to creative   254
  motivation losses   414–15
  social facilitation   235–7
team awareness   436, **608**
team leadership   434, **607**

team performance *see* group performance
teams/teamwork
  multicultural   512–13
  social identity   516–17
  social loafing   414, 415, 416, 514
television
  political debates and attitude
    change   204
  violence, long-term effects   291–2
temperature-aggression link   289–90
terror management theory   155–6,
    461, **608**
terrorism   275, **608**
  behaviour in response to   342–3
  staircase model   303–4
terrorist suspect, erroneous shooting
    of   101
theory of planned behaviour   195–8, **608**
theory of reasoned action   195–8, **608**
theory, defined   27, **608**
thinking versus feeling goods   222–3
thought-listing   205, 211, 213, **608**
threat(s)
  to ego, narcissistic violence   158–9
  posed by outgroup   461–6
  social regulation of neural
    response   351
time periods approach   289, **603**
time pressures and helping
    behaviour   32–3
TOTE loop   159, *160*
trait aggressiveness   287, **608**
  questionnaire items   278
trait self-esteem   136
traits, leader   426–7
transactional leaders   430, 431, 433, **608**
transactive memory   395, **608**
  performance benefits of group
    training   396
transformational leaders   430–1,
    432–3, **608**
triangulation   36, **608**
true randomized experiment   30, **608**
two-dimensional perspective on
    attitudes   179–80, **608**

uncertainty and group
    identification   385–6
uncertainty avoidance   494, **608**
unobtrusive measures   43, 48, **608**
  archival research   29–30
  implicit measures   49
  observation   48

utilitarian function   181, **608**
   versus value-expression   182–4
utilitarian perspective
   consumer goods   222–4
   groups   382

validity   41–3, **608**
   attitude measures   190
   construct   41
   convergent   50
   external versus internal   41–3
   question   49
   subjective   243
   threats to   41–3
value-expressive function   182, **608**
   advertising campaign   224
   versus utilitarian attitudes
      182–4
values
   global trends   119–21
   group honour   517–18
   post-materialist   520–1

relating to basic needs   496
   threats to group   464–5
variables   27, **608**
   dependent   37
   independent   37
   mediating   40
violence
   alcohol-related   288
   bystander behaviour   330–1
   defined   276, **608**
   financial costs of   304
   intergroup   300–4
   intimate partner   294–7
   media-violence link   287–8, 290–4
   and narcissism   158–9
   sexual   297–8
   temperature link   289–90
   towards children   331
   see also aggression
virtual reality
   bystander research   331
   obedience research   269

online dating   374
   video games and violence   292, 305
voluntary relationships   372
volunteerism   333–4, **608**
   psychological aspects   329
volunteers in experiments
   bystander behaviour   328–9
   validity issues   43, 44

warmth versus competence   51, 470–1
'we-ness' concept   324–5
weapons effect   282, 283, **608**
web-based experiments   43–4
well-being: and social relationships
   349–50
whistle blowing   269–70, **608**
willingness to sacrifice   368–9, **608**
working self-concept   134–5, **608**
workplace bullying   299–300
World Values Survey   313, 520, 521

xenophobia and disease threat   461

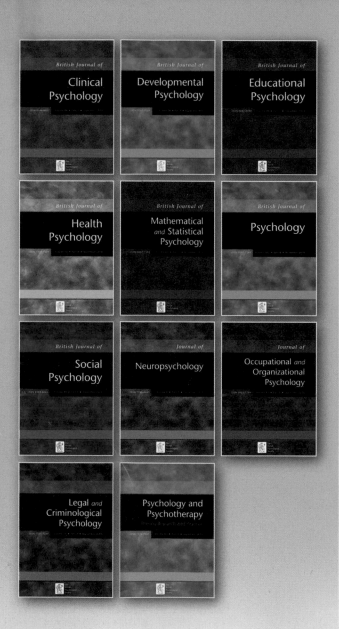